INTERNATIONAL FINANCE

TRANSACTIONS, POLICY, AND
REGULATION

TWELFTH EDITION

By

HAL S. SCOTT
Nomura Professor of International Financial Systems
Harvard Law School

NEW YORK, NEW YORK
FOUNDATION PRESS
2005

© 1995–2004 FOUNDATION PRESS
© 2005 By FOUNDATION PRESS
   395 Hudson Street
   New York, NY 10014
   Phone Toll Free 1–877–888–1330
   Fax (212) 367–6799
   fdpress.com
Printed in the United States of America

ISBN 1–58778–854–3

 *TEXT IS PRINTED ON 10% POST CONSUMER RECYCLED PAPER*

PREFACE

This is the twelfth edition of the textbook on international finance. Several major changes in the field occurred since the eleventh edition was published a year ago.

Capital markets regulation in the U.S. has continued to explode. This last year saw continuing issues in the use of structured financed to manage corporate earnings. It also saw major developments in the adoption of international accounting standards in the EU and the U.S. Further elaboration of the two new European Union Directives on the single financial services market—the Prospectus Directive and the Financial Markets Instruments Directive are discussed in Chapter 4. As the manuscript was being readied for the publisher, Europe was still trying to digest the implications of the no votes in France and the Netherlands on the proposed amendments to the EU Constitution. Chapter 6 on Japan has been substantially updated as the financial system appears headed for recovery.

There was continued debate over the implementation of Basel II, as the U.S. and Europe parted ways on implementation, a matter covered in Chapter 7. The final rules on securitized assets, swaps and project finance are dealt with in Chapters 12, 15 and 17, respectively. Chapter 13 deals with the accelerated development of electronic trading of equity, stock exchange mergers and the SEC's market structure rules. Chapter 16 covers the continued fall out from the mutual fund trading scandals and the use of soft dollars, as well as the new regulation of hedge fund advisers. Chapter 19 deals with the Argentine debt default and bond exchange.

The book is organized into five parts. Part One deals with the international aspects of major domestic markets, Part Two with infrastructure for financial markets, Part Three with instruments and offshore markets, Part Four with emerging markets, and Part Five with the fighting of terrorism.

While the approach of this book is rooted in government policy and regulation, the book introduces the student to basic financial concepts and transactions. Exchange rate regimes, for example, are necessary background for an understanding of the European Monetary Union. Only the most basic financial theory is presented. The conception of the field is original and complements existing texts written for finance or economics courses.

I gratefully acknowledge the dedicated assistance of my editor Melissa Greven who, as in the past, has been invaluable with editing and proofing.

Hal S. Scott
Cambridge, Massachusetts, June 2005

SUMMARY OF CONTENTS

TABLE OF CONTENTS

CHAPTER THREE   **International Aspects of U.S.**
                             Banking Markets 95

CHAPTER FOUR   **The European Union: The Single**
                          Market in Financial Services 133

INTERNATIONAL FINANCE

TRANSACTIONS, POLICY, AND REGULATION

CHAPTER ONE

INTRODUCTION

This chapter begins with a discussion of definitions of international finance, and the national authorities, multilateral organizations, and intergovernmental institutions that regulate them. Second, it describes the major instruments that comprise international finance. Third, it discusses the costs and benefits of internationalization. It concludes with a road map of the rest of the book.

The markets for international finance include a variety of participants. The suppliers of funds are often referred to as savers and may be depositors or investors, depending on the transaction. The users of funds may be borrowers or issuers, depending on the transaction.

Financial intermediaries come between the savers and users. Traditionally, banks intermediate between savers (as depositors) and users (as borrowers) of funds. Banks as principals have continuing obligations to depositors and bear credit risk. Securities companies help savers (investors) and users (issuers) transact business directly. The saver invests in the user by buying its securities. The security company does not normally have to hold bonds or shares very long, and has no continuing obligation to the investor or the issuer. The investor bears the risks of the issuer's performance. In addition, financial intermediaries may be counterparties on financial contracts such as derivatives—a matter we examine in later chapters.

A.   INTERNATIONAL FINANCIAL TRANSACTIONS

1.   DEFINITIONS

Generally, international financial transactions involve some cross-border activity with respect to a payment, credit or investment, or financial contract.[1]

The cross-border aspect of finance can arise from the fact that the activity of the provider and the user of funds may be located in two different countries. A lender can market and transfer funds to a borrower in another

---

[1] G. Dufey and T. Chung, "International Financial Markets: A Survey" in *Library of Investment Banking* (R. Kuhn ed. 1990).

country, or the borrower can seek and attain funds from the lender in the lender's country.

Similarly, an issuer of securities can market and distribute securities to investors in another country, or foreign investors can make investments by coming to the issuer's country, as when a foreign investor buys a U.S. equity on a U.S. stock exchange.

During the 1960s, a new phenomenon in international financial transactions developed, the use of offshore markets. Markets for Dollar-denominated loans, deposits, and securities in jurisdictions other than the United States were able to avoid U.S. banking and securities regulations. This gave birth to the so-called euromarkets. Once having located abroad, particularly in London, these markets survived even when the domestic on-shore regulation that gave rise to them was relaxed.

According to Maughan, financial markets have developed from domestic to domestic-offshore, whereby domestic markets are connected to each other through offshore markets, to global, whereby domestic markets connect directly.[2] The shift to global markets, according to Maughan, results from deregulation and liberalization.

In Table 1A, below, statistics on international lending are presented following Ralph Bryant's definition of "international" as claims:

- on foreign residents in foreign currency,
- on foreign residents in the bank's home currency, or
- on domestic residents in foreign currency.[3]

Table 1A
Assets Reported by Banks Located in Selected Countries
(US$ billions, June 2002)

Banks in	Types of International Lending (by location of bank) (in %)					
	International Total	Claim on Currency	Non-resident Foreign	Non-resident Home	Resident Foreign	Total
			12/31/82			
Japan	11		37	14	49	100
U.S.	17		2	98	—	100
U.K.	72		68	4	28	100
			6/30/02			
Japan			65	27	8	100
U.S.			4	96	—	100
U.K.			69	8	23	100

---

[2] D. Maughan, "Global Capital Markets and the Implications for Financial Institutions" talk given at Harvard Law School (September 20, 1993).
[3] R. Bryant, *International Financial Intermediation* (1987).

Japan and the United States are similar. In 1982, both had a low percentage of international lending. This is because their international business is dwarfed by their large domestic economies. U.S. international business was largely Dollar loans to non-residents (claim on non-resident in the home currency), while Japan had mainly Dollar loans to residents and non-residents.

The U.K. has a very high percentage of international business. It is an offshore banking center, specializing in making foreign currency loans to non-residents, e.g. Dollar loans to Germans. What significant changes in this picture appear in 2002? The only important change is in Japan, where lending to non-residents in Dollars and Yen increased and Dollar loans to residents shrank substantially.

Table 1B, below, shows the total international assets of banks from five countries as an absolute amount and as a percentage of total international assets of banks from all countries. Looking strictly at the location of the bank (the first two columns), banks in Germany have the highest percentage of international assets, followed by Japan, the U.S., the U.K., and France. However, if one takes into account related offices, so that a U.S. branch in the U.K. is counted as U.S. and not U.K., the U.K. appears a lot less international, and the U.S. becomes a close second to Germany.

Table 1B
International Assets of Banks in Selected Countries by
Nationality of Ownership
(US$ billions, end-June 2002)[4]

Banks based in:	Total	as % of total	with related offices	as % of total
France	1,301.0	8.9	409.3	9.2
Germany	2,839.4	19.4	761.0	17.1
Japan	1,560.0	10.7	462.8	10.4
U.K.	1,389.0	9.5	287.7	6.5
U.S.	1,520.2	10.4	687.8	15.5
Total (all countries)	14,594.8	100.0	4,446.2	100.0

Choice of an offshore center is determined by a variety of factors, such as avoiding home country regulation (some offshore centers are more resistant to extraterritorial reach), infrastructure (educated elite, telecommunications, and aviation), and time zones. Becoming an offshore center can be important to a country's economy, as in the case of London. It generates employment and taxes, and becomes a modifying force for domestic financial regulation.

---

[4] Bank for International Settlements, *International Banking and Financial Market Developments*, Tables 2A, 2C, 4A, and 8 (June 2003).

There are different types of centers. Some are functional, like London, whereas others are just booking centers like the Bahamas. Transactions are booked there to minimize taxes and escape regulation. Much of the world's international financial activity goes on in offshore banking centers.

Economic definitions of international transactions would normally exclude cases where foreign citizens resident in a country engaged in a transaction in that country, for example a U.S. citizen resident in Japan buying securities issued in Japan. Nonetheless, such transactions may pose concerns for countries like the U.S. that believe they should protect their citizens abroad by exercising extraterritorial jurisdiction.

More generally, definitions of international transactions almost never include purely domestic activity, e.g. a Japanese citizen borrows from a Japanese bank in Japan. Nonetheless, in a worldwide integrated financial system what happens in one country's economy has substantial impact on other economies. For this reason, this book not only covers how the three major economies, the United States, Japan, and the European Union, regulate their international financial transactions, but also how they generally regulate their domestic financial systems. An understanding of domestic regulation is also important because it is a baseline for international regulation. For example, a Japanese bank entering the U.S. encounters special regulation due to its international activity; but this is over and above its need to comply with Japanese domestic regulation. The European Union is a special case. Its internal regulation is itself international since it establishes rules for transactions between its different Member States.

Researchers at the International Monetary Fund (IMF) compared the assets of banks owned more than 50 percent by foreigners to the assets of all banks in certain countries of Asia (Korea, Malaysia, Thailand), Central Europe (the Czech Republic, Hungary, Poland), and Latin America (Argentina, Brazil, Chile, Colombia, Mexico, Peru, Venezuela). The study reported that foreign control of bank assets was mainly below 10 percent in 1994 but rose substantially by 1999, in most cases to over 40 percent. In almost all countries, the foreign banks' return on equity was significantly higher than that of domestic banks, many of which showed losses.[5]

Notes and Questions

1. According to Dufey and Chung ("International Financial Markets: A Survey," in *Library of Investment Banking* (R. Kuhn ed., 1990)), a banking transaction is international if it involves a foreign resident in the domestic (or national) banking market or involves offshore markets. A loan by a U.S. bank to a foreign resident, or a deposit from a foreign bank to a U.S. bank,

---

[5] D. Mathieson and G. Schinasi, *International Capital Markets: Developments, Prospects, and Key Policy Issues* (September 2000), pp. 153, 166.

both involving cross-border movement of funds, is an international transaction in the U.S. domestic market. Consider the following for Citibank, a U.S. bank with a New York headquarters:

a. Suppose Citibank (New York) made a Deutschmark loan to a U.S. company. Dufey and Chung would presumably classify this as a "Euro-loan" and therefore an international transaction. But their classification is not certain because no foreign resident is involved and the lender and borrower are subject to the regulations of their home country.

b. Suppose Citibank's U.K. branch or U.K. subsidiary made a sterling loan to a resident of the U.K. According to Dufey and Chung, this is not an international transaction. Do you agree with this aspect of their definition?

2. Dufey and Chung define a securities transaction as international according to the same criteria. A sale of securities of a U.S. corporation to a foreign resident, or a sale of the securities of a foreign corporation to a U.S. resident, would be international securities transactions involving the U.S. domestic market. Please consider the following:

a. If a Japanese company issued securities in Tokyo, and they were bought in Tokyo by a U.S. citizen residing in Tokyo, Dufey and Chung would not classify this as an international transaction. Do you agree with this aspect of their definition?

3. Compare Bryant's definition of international banking transaction with the Dufey and Chung definition. Bryant's explicitly includes foreign currency lending to residents. Which do you prefer? Should any factors in addition to currency and residence be included in a comprehensive definition?

2. REGULATION

a. NATIONAL GOVERNMENTS

National governments are the principal regulators of international financial transactions. Often at least two jurisdictions may take an interest in the same transaction. Consider, for example, a case in which a U.S. depositor places funds in a Japanese bank. The U.S. would be concerned with protecting the U.S. depositor from risk, while Japan will be worried about the safety and solvency of its banks. Japan will also have to decide whether to extend deposit insurance to foreign depositors (in fact, it does not). Or suppose a U.S. investor purchases Yen-denominated Japanese securities in the U.K. The U.S. may be concerned with assuring that its investors (even offshore) receive adequate disclosure, Japan may be concerned with the international use of its currency, and the U.K. may be generally concerned with financial transactions occurring in the U.K.

b.   MULTILATERAL INSTITUTIONS

For international finance, the IMF and the World Bank, both established in 1944 and based in Washington, D.C., are quite important. The IMF, a multilateral institution controlled by the U.S. and other industrial countries, was set up to help member countries maintain agreed exchange rates. However, with the abandonment of fixed rates in 1972, its mission has shifted to dealing with the short-term financial needs of developing countries and the promulgation of international standards. It had about $154 billion in assets as of June 2003, funded by contributions of 184 members and borrowings. The World Bank began as the International Bank for Reconstruction and Development (IBRD) to help Europe rebuild after the war. It now is a major international long-term lender to developing countries. It had $230 billion in assets as of June 30, 2003. We will talk more about the IMF when we come to the chapters of the book involving the emerging markets.

The International Finance Corporation (IFC) is an affiliate of the World Bank. It was established in 1956 to promote private sector development. Unlike the World Bank, the IFC can invest in private entities. It has carved out a niche analyzing investment opportunities in developing countries and helping them solve investment problems, whether of information or structure. It has outstanding investments of almost $20 billion in projects, mostly in the form of long-term loans.

The U.S. controls about 17.5 percent of the votes in the two institutions based on its contributions to funding. About 61 percent of the votes are controlled by industrialized countries. It is clear that the developed countries and particularly the U.S. have the major say in what these institutions do.

c.   INTERGOVERNMENTAL GROUPS

There are a number of important inter-governmental groups that coordinate international policy. A brief description of the most important ones follows. The International Monetary and Financial Committee (IMFC) is the key policy group within the IMF.

IMFC

"The IMFC has the responsibility of advising, and reporting to, the Board of Governors on matters relating to the Board of Governors' functions in supervising the management and adaptation of the international monetary and financial system, including the operation of the adjustment process, and in this connection reviewing developments in global liquidity and the transfer of resources to developing countries; considering proposals by the Executive

Board to amend the Articles of Agreement; and dealing with disturbances that might threaten the system."[6]

The IMFC has 24 members, listed below, who are Governors of the IMF (generally ministers of finance or central bank governors). The membership reflects the composition of the IMF's Executive Board: each member country that appoints, and each group of member countries that elects, an Executive Director appoints a member of the IMFC.

IMFC Membership

Governors of the IMF for:

Algeria	France	Netherlands
Angola	Gabon	Russia
Australia	Germany	Saudi Arabia
Belgium	Iceland	Switzerland
Brazil	India	United Arab Emirates
Canada	Italy	United Kingdom
Chile	Japan	United States
China	Malaysia	Venezuela

FSF

The Financial Stability Forum (FSF) was established in 1999 to enhance cooperation in the area of financial market supervision and surveillance among national and international supervisory bodies and international financial institutions. It has 42 members, consisting of 26 senior representatives of national authorities responsible for financial stability in 11 significant international financial centers (in Australia, Canada, France, Germany, Hong Kong, Italy, Japan, the Netherlands, Singapore, the United Kingdom, and the United States); six senior representatives of four international financial institutions (Bank for International Settlements, IMF, Organization for Economic Cooperation and Development, and the World Bank); seven senior representatives of three international regulatory and supervisory bodies (Basel Committee on Banking Supervision, International Organization of Securities Commissions, International Association of Insurance Supervisors); a representative each of two committees of central bank experts (Committee on the Global Financial System and Committee on Payment and Settlement Systems); and the Chairman, currently Roger Ferguson, Jr., the Vice Chairman of the U.S. Federal Reserve Board.

---

[6] IMF, *A Guide to Committees, Groups, and Clubs: A Factsheet* (April 2003).

G7, G8, and G10

The Group of Seven (G7) major industrial countries have held annual economic summits (meetings at the level of head of state or government) since 1975. At the level of finance minister and central bank governor, the G7 superseded the G5 as the main policy coordination group during 1986-87. Since 1987, the G7 finance ministers and central bank governors have met at least semi-annually to monitor developments in the world economy and assess economic policies. The Managing Director of the IMF usually, by invitation, participates in the surveillance discussions of the G7 finance ministers and central bank governors.

G7 Members

Canada	Japan
France	United Kingdom
Germany	United States
Italy	

The G8 (also sometimes know as the Political 8 or P8) was conceived when Russia first participated in part of the 1994 Naples Summit of the G7. Again in 1997, Russia joined the Denver Summit of the Eight, for political discussions.

G8 Members

Canada	Japan
France	Russia
Germany	United Kingdom
Italy	United States

The Group of Ten (G10) refers to the group of countries that have agreed to participate in the General Arrangements to Borrow (GAB). The GAB was established in 1962, when the governments of eight IMF members—Belgium, Canada, France, Italy, Japan, the Netherlands, the United Kingdom, and the United States—and the central banks of two others, Germany and Sweden, agreed to make resources available to the IMF for drawings by participants, and, under certain circumstances, for drawings by nonparticipants. The following international organizations are official observers of the activities of the G10: The Bank for International Settlements (BIS), European Commission, IMF, and Organization for Economic Cooperation and Development (OECD).

G10 Members

Belgium	Netherlands
Canada	Sweden
France	Switzerland
Germany	United Kingdom
Italy	United States
Japan	

d.   FUNCTIONAL REGULATORS

There are a number of international regulatory groups for specific areas of regulation. For example, in banking, intergovernmental groups such as the Banking Supervision Committee at the Bank for International Settlements (BIS) in Basel plays an important role. In many ways, it is the most important financial regulator. In securities, there is the International Organization of Securities Commissioners (IOSCO), and in accounting there is the International Accounting Standards Board (IASB). We will focus on their activities in subsequent chapters.

Notes and Questions

1.   Is there a real need for these various international regulatory bodies? How would you characterize the overall pattern of current international regulation?

B.   THE MAJOR FINANCIAL MARKETS COMPARED

The major international financial markets are foreign exchange, lending and securities (debt and equity), and derivatives. Data is given on the foreign exchange and derivatives markets in Chapters 14 and 15, respectively. Here the focus is on banking and securities markets.

Aggregate data that allow one to compare the evolution of these markets over many decades until the present do not exist. For almost 30 years up to the mid-1990s, the OECD reported statistics for funds raised on international loan and bond markets, changing the series once, after 1982. Table 1C shows that in the early 1980s international loan markets were larger even than bond markets. Both were much larger than equity offers.

Table 1C
Funds Raised by Non-Sovereigns on International Markets, 1967-1996
(in US\$ billions)[7]

INSTRUMENT	1967	1972	1977	1982	1987	1992	1996
Loans	-	8.8	34.2	103.6	122.9	124.6	349.7
Of which:	-						
Syndicated Euro-loans		8.8	34.2	90.8	80.3	116.2	345.2
Bonds	**5.2**	**10.9**	**34.8**	**75.5**	**180.8**	**333.7**	**708.8**
Distribution:							
Euro-bonds	2.2	6.5	18.7	50.3	140.5	276.1	589.8
Foreign bonds	3.0	4.4	16.1	25.2	40.3	57.6	119.0
Type:							
Floating-rate notes	-	-	2.2	15.3	13.0	43.6	165.7
Straight bonds	5.1	9.5	31.1	7.2	121.3	265.4	464.4
Convertibles	-	1.1	1.2	2.6	18.2	5.2	25.6
with equity warrants	-	.1	.1	.5	24.8	15.7	8.8
Equity offers	-	-	-	-	**20.4**	**25.3**	n.a.
Total	**5.2**	**19.7**	**69.0**	**179.1**	**324.1**	**483.6**	

The BIS also collects data about international financial markets, using slightly different terms and grouping the markets in somewhat different ways. For some instruments, the BIS tables give amounts outstanding on a specific date. This is called the stock of funds and is reported in "Stock end-2004" in Table 1D, below. For example, on December 31, 2004, investors held about \$14 trillion in debt instruments. It is interesting to compare the stock of funds raised on international and domestic markets. As of September 2004, the stock of bonds and notes raised on international markets was \$12.1 trillion, or 35.6 percent of the \$34.0 trillion on domestic markets, up from 24.7 percent in 2002.[8]

The BIS data on new issues in Table 1D shows equity significantly trailing debt. For example, in 2004 total equity issued was \$214 billion as compared to \$7 trillion or 3 percent of total debt. However, this is misleading because debt constantly recycles, as issues come to maturity or are refinanced, while equity does not. A better comparison would between international equity and debt outstanding, but we have no complete data on the former. McKinsey's data shows that in 2004 (based on September data) that the total value of equity outstanding was \$33.1 trillion compared to

---

[7] Organization for Economic Cooperation and Development, Table F.T-O.a, "International Capital Markets Statistics" (1996), OECD Financial Market Trends (November 1997), and International Monetary Fund, International Capital Markets: Developments, Prospects, and Policy Issues 189 (August 1995). Time series changes after 1982.
[8] See BIS Quarterly Review, *International Banking and Financial Market Developments* (June 2003 and March 2005), Table 13B.

$31.5 of debt but these totals do not distinguish between international and domestic holdings—they count all.[9]

The BIS data does not include government debt, which is a significant part of the international capital market. For example, as of 2004, government debt securities outstanding were $21.2 trillion as compared with corporate debt of $31.5 trillion.[10]

Table 1D
Funds Raised by Non-Sovereigns on International Markets, 1994-2004
(in US$ billions)[11]

Instruments	Net Issues					Stock-end
	1994	**1998**	**2000**	**2002**	**2004**	**2004**
Money Market	3.2	9.8	122.0	2.3	61.0	663.8
Of which:						
Commercial Paper	0.5	22.2	76.8	19.3	40.4	483.3
Bonds & Notes	168.0	668.7	1016.2	1013.7	1562.8	13,264.3
Of which:						
Floating rate	53.5	173.0	333.2	201.1	644.4	3,668.8
Straight fixed	132.7	479.6	674.5	801.0	924.6	9,225.0
Equity-related	-18.2	16.1	8.4	11.6	-6.2	370.5
	New Issues					
Syndicated credit	250.4	902.2	1460.3	1299.7	1811.8	
Money Market	197.2	551.9	844.8	1198.8	1921.9	
Of which: Commercial Paper	38.4	380.6	625.6	970.4	1468.3	
Bonds & Notes	385.7	1076.2	1767.2	2038.8	3304.9	
Of which:						
Floating rate	78.7	247.8	557.0	597.8	1260.6	
Straight fixed	273.9	796.9	1163.8	1397.4	1987.0	
Equity-related	33.1	31.5	47.0	43.4	57.3	
Equity	—	125.7	313.8	89.3	214.5	
Total	833.3	2656.0	4386.1	4626.8	7253.1	

In the late 1990s, corporate bonds routinely reached jumbo proportions. In 1999, for example, about $1.6 trillion in international bonds were issued. In June 2000, Deutsche Telekom issued eight bonds that totaled $14.6 billion.[12] This was part of a long-term rising trend in corporate debt.

---

[9] D. Farrell, A. Key, and T. Shavers, *Mapping The Global Capital Markets,* The McKinsey Quarterly, Special Edition (2005). (McKinsey)
[10] Id., at 2.
[11] *BIS Quarterly Review, International Banking and Financial Market Developments,* February 1995 - March 2005; 1994, Tables 8, 9, 12; 1996-1997, Tables 8, 11a, 11b; 1998 Tables 10, 13a, 13b, 18; 1999 Tables 10, 13a, 13b, 17; 2000-2005 Tables 10, 13a, 13b, 18.
[12] M. Peterson, "Heyday of the Capital Markets," Euromoney (September 2000), p. 305.

U.S. non-financial firms, for example, had debt that was 28 percent of U.S. gross domestic product in 1960. By 1999, the ratio was 45 percent.[13]

U.S. investors have found international bond markets increasingly important to them, and foreign investors in U.S. securities have grown in importance relative to U.S. GDP. From 1975 to 2004, foreign ownership grew from 20 percent to 44 percent of U.S. treasuries, from 1 percent to 25 percent of U.S. corporate bonds, and from 4 to 12 percent of U.S. equities.[14]

C.   HOW GLOBALIZED ARE FINANCIAL MARKETS?

There are difficulties in defining and measuring the globalization of financial markets. There appear to be four main approaches. First, one can look at the correlation of prices between markets. The higher the correlations in rates of returns on similar assets across countries, arguably the more integrated the markets. One might also look to integration across asset classes internationally as compared to domestically.

A second approach looks at quantity. For example, one can look at portfolio diversification. The evidence here is that investors overweight domestic securities in their portfolios. This so-called "home bias" effect is prevalent to various degrees in all local markets. "For example, in 2001, the portfolio share of foreign equities of U.S. investors was 22 percent of what it would have been had these investors held the world market portfolio, so that the home bias measure was 78 percent. The measure averaged 63 percent in 2001 for a sample of 18 developed countries."[15] There is continued debate as to whether this home bias is due to transactions costs, information availability, or just a preference for what investors are familiar with.[16]

The focus of portfolio diversification is the behavior of investors. To the extent investors' portfolios are not diversified, they are less willing to invest internationally than would otherwise be the case. Quantity approaches may also look at the actual amount of cross-border flows over time. The BIS data presented above indicates that by this measure globalization is increasing. Stultz finds for the United States, that trading by foreign investors in U.S. stocks and bonds increased from 5.76 percent of GDP in 1977, to 344.18 percent of GDP in 2003, or a factor of 60.[17] The U.S. is a major beneficiary of capital flows as investments by foreigners in the U.S. finances the U.S.'s chronic and deep trade deficits. In fact, the U.S. imports an

---

[13] C. Osler and G. Hong, "Rapidly Rising Corporate Debt: Are Firms Now Vulnerable to an Economic Slowdown?" Federal Reserve Bank of New York Current Issues in Economics and Finance (June 2000).

[14] McKinsey, supra note 9, p. 11.

[15] R. Stultz, "The Limits of Financial Globalization" Draft (2005), p. 8.

[16] See e.g. R. Portes and H. Rey, "The Determinants of Cross-Border Equity Flows," 65 Journal of International Economics 269 (2005).

[17] Id., at 7.

astounding 71.9 percent of the capital exported by other countries. Of the capital exporting countries, Japan is the highest, accounting for 20.5 percent of all exports.[18]

A third approach looks at the links between savings and investment levels within countries. Feldstein and Horioka[19] have showed that there is a very tight link between domestic savings and investment levels. However, as investors diversify internationally, these rates should become less closely related to each other. Recent studies have shown these domestic links continue to be strong.

A fourth approach looks at formal barriers to trade in financial assets. This can be done by constructing indexes of openness. Quinn has shown, for example, that out of an index of 1-12, most developed countries have become fully open by 1997.[20] However, these indexes only deal with explicit barriers rather than implicit ones. For example, the U.S. may be fully open to foreign banks, but may calculate their capital adequacy differently, or be fully open to foreign companies listing in the U.S., but require them to reconcile their accounts to U.S. GAAP. Further, implicit barriers may be created just because two countries have different rules. For example, integration of global equity markets are impeded because the U.S. has different rules for distributing securities than do other countries, thus making global offerings more expensive than they would be if all countries have the same rules. In fact, this book largely focuses on the manner in which implicit barriers restrict cross-border financial flows.

D. COSTS AND BENEFITS OF THE INTERNATIONALIZATION OF FINANCE

A debate about whether the internationalization of finance—often referred to as globalization—is good or bad rages worldwide. The potential benefits of international finance are fairly clear. First, access to worldwide capital markets may allow a country to smooth its financial needs, borrowing in bad times and lending in good times. Second, international markets can promote domestic investment and growth by allowing countries to import capital. Third, globalization may enhance macroeconomic discipline—capital flows may police bad government behavior, although this discipline may be modified by sovereign bailouts, a problem we examine in Chapter 19. Fourth, internationalization may discipline regulators. The possibility of financial

---

[18] F. Cave, "IMF Warns Financial Markets Against Complacency," *Financial Times*, April 5, 2005.

[19] M. Feldstein and C. Horioka, "Domestic Savings and International Capital Flows, 90 Economic Journal 314 (1980). See also C. Kearney and B. Lucey, "International Equity Market Integration: Theory, Evidence and Implications," 13 International Review of Financial Analysis 571 (2004).

[20] D. Quinn, "The Correlates of Change in International Financial Regulation," 91 American Political Science Review 531 (1997).

institutions changing the locale of their operations, or investors investing in foreign markets abroad, may constrain excessive domestic regulation. Fifth, internationalization may increase competition, and therefore lead to more efficient banking systems or cheaper securities offerings.

Economists debate the effect of financial integration on growth. A study of 57 countries, using many measures of financial integration, was not able to reject the hypothesis that international financial integration does not accelerate economic growth even when controlling for particular characteristics of the country.[21] On the other hand, it seems clear that domestically better financial systems do increase growth by providing information about possible investments and by allocating capital, by monitoring investments and exerting corporate governance after providing finance, by facilitating the trading, diversification and management of risk, by mobilizing and pooling savings and by easing the exchange of goods and services.[22]

There are also some potential costs of globalization. First, markets are not politically correct, so hostile or poorly performing markets may fail to attract capital, and may experience capital outflows and unemployment. Second, the volatility of capital flows can quickly destabilize an economy, as was the case in the 1997 Korean crisis, where short-term international bank lending quickly dried up. Third, the entry of foreign institutions, while increasing competition and efficiency, can lead to the demise of local financial institutions. Fourth, the integration of the world's financial system can result in quick transmissions of economic shocks between world economies, a phenomenon often referred to as contagion.[23] This book examines many of the costs and benefits.[24]

Notes and Questions

1. Is more globalization inevitable? How does law and regulation affect its pace?

2. A Joint Statement of the Asian, European, Japanese, Latin American and U.S. Shadow Financial Regulatory Committees, "Enhancing International Financial Market Integration," (November 15, 2004) concludes that there are major regulatory obstacles to integration. Countries, including the U.S., restrict the access of foreign firms and securities issues to their

---

[21] H. Edison, R. Levine, L. Ricci, and T. Slok, "International Financial Integration and Economic Growth," 21 Journal of International Money and Finance 749 (2002).

[22] R. Levine, "Finance and Growth," NBER Working Paper 10766 (September 2004).

[23] M. Ehrmann, M. Fratzscher, and R. Rigobon, "Stocks, Bonds, Money Markets and Exchange Rates: Measuring International Financial Transmission," NBER Working Paper 11166 (March 2005).

[24] See P. Agénor, "Benefits and Costs of International Financial Integration: Theory and Facts" (2003) 26 *The World Economy*, pp. 1089-1118. For a recent critique of globalization, see J. Stiglitz, "The Social Costs of Globalization," *Financial Times*, February 25, 2004.

markets, both directly and indirectly. The WTO has made little progress in eliminating these barriers. As discussed in the next chapter, the U.S. regulatory requirements for foreign issues, such as use of U.S. GAAP accounting standards or compliance with Sarbanes-Oxley, can also restrict global integration.

3. An active area of inquiry is the role of legal institutions in explaining financial development. Basically, the literature finds that the Anglo-Saxon countries with stronger protection of property rights have had higher levels of financial development.[25] One study finds that effective legal institutions, particularly those requiring disclosure and enforcing those requirements, also reduce firms' cost of capital. The effects of disclosure requirements are strongest for markets that are the least integrated. Enforcement appears not to matter at all in the most integrated markets. The authors say that these findings are consistent with the notion that, in integrated economies, risk is priced globally.[26] What do you think of these findings?

E.   THE ROAD MAP

The book is organized into five parts. Part I deals with the international aspects of major domestic markets, the U.S., the EU, and Japan. Part II deals with the infrastructure of international finance: capital adequacy, foreign exchange regimes, the payment system, and clearing and settlement. Part III deals with instruments and offshore markets. It covers the euromarkets, asset securitization, stock market competition, derivatives, and offshore mutual funds. Part IV deals with emerging market issues, project finance, privatization, emerging market debt, and banking reforms. Part V covers the attempt to control the financing of terrorism.

This book is a blend of different perspectives on international finance. While concentrating on law and regulation, it also provides information on important transactions and major markets. Finally, it attempts to provide perspective and critical analysis with respect to the current policy issues in the field.

---

[25] R. La Porta, F. Lopez-de-Silanes, A. Shleifer, and R. Vishny, "Law and Finance," 106 J. of Political Economy (1998), pp. 1113-1155.
[26] L. Hail and C. Leuz, "International Differences in Cost of Equity Capital: Do Legal Institutions and Securities Regulation Matter?," (December 2004).

INTERNATIONAL ASPECTS OF MAJOR DOMESTIC MARKETS

Part I presents the international aspects of the world's major domestic financial markets, the United States (Chapters 2 and 3), the European Union (Chapters 4 and 5), and Japan (Chapter 6). We focus on banking and securities markets. The international aspects of these markets involve cross-border transactions. For example, for United States domestic banking markets, this part covers the entry and operation of foreign banks serving U.S. customers. For U.S. securities markets, the international aspects involve foreign issuers selling securities to U.S. investors and U.S. issuers selling securities to investors outside the United States. One important theme is the difficulty of applying a pure national treatment standard to foreign firms.

For the European Union, our primary interest is the operation of the internal market and the rules for the conduct of banking and securities within the Union. The creation of the European Economic and Monetary Union (EMU), and the advent of the Euro, are events of enormous importance to international finance. EMU will likely lead to further integration and expansion of European markets.

For Japan, the theme is the effect of the Big Bang reforms of financial markets and the problem of troubled financial institutions.

CHAPTER TWO

INTERNATIONAL ASPECTS OF U.S. CAPITAL MARKETS

This Chapter begins with some background data on the degree to which the U.S. capital market is internationalized and then examines how the United States regulates: (1) the distribution and trading of securities issued by foreign companies in the United States; and (2) the distribution outside the United States of securities issued by U.S. and foreign companies to U.S. investors. This requires some basic understanding of securities regulation in general.

The traditional goal of securities regulation, investor protection, may have to be tempered in a "global market" by: (1) the desire of U.S. investors to invest and trade in foreign securities; (2) the reality that they may do so outside the United States; and (3) the importance to the United States of maintaining the world's leading domestic capital market, which requires openness to foreign issuers.

Our focus is on the regulation of the securities markets, primary and secondary, rather than on the firms participating in these markets. Institutional regulation, however, will be the major focus for banking. This difference is driven by the nature of the primary regulatory concerns, investor protection in securities markets and safety and soundness of banks.

Much of this Chapter is dominated by the U.S. response to Enron and the other corporate scandals that began at the turn of the century. This response resulted not only in a major legislative initiative, Sarbanes-Oxley, but also a number of market reforms initiated by settlements with the Attorney General of New York, Eliot Spitzer, and the Securities & Exchange Commission. This new regulatory structure has significantly affected the attractiveness of the U.S. market for both foreign investors and issuers— whether it has made the market more or less attractive is a key issue for the future.

A.   INTERNATIONALIZATION OF U.S. SECURITIES MARKETS

1.   THE INFLUENTIAL ROLE OF U.S. SECURITIES MARKETS

The size of the U.S. capital markets, relative effectiveness of market regulators, and financial innovation by market participants have contributed to the substantial influence of U.S. capital markets on other markets, both foreign and international. In general, the U.S. regulatory system has allowed financial innovation to take place—both in the U.S. domestic securities market and in the dollar sector of the Eurobond market.

2.   MARKET SIZE

At the end of 2000, the market capitalization of U.S. equities exceeded $15.1 trillion, about 47 percent of the world's stock market capitalization. This compares with $2.6 trillion or about 43 percent of the world's stock market in 1986. Whereas Japan, the second largest market in 1986, was approximately two-thirds as large as the U.S. market, by 2000 the U.S. market was almost five times as large as that of Japan. The dominant position of the U.S. securities markets can be explained, in part, by the size of the U.S. domestic economy which, with a GDP in excess of $10 trillion in 2001, is by a considerable margin the largest in the world.

3.   MARKET COMPOSITION

Within the United States the pattern of share ownership has changed significantly since the 1980s. The percentage of direct household holdings of all corporate stock has decreased from 68 to 41 percent, whereas indirect household holdings through trusts and estates, life insurance companies, private pension funds and mutual funds, increased from 16 to 28 percent. While the market has become more institutional, direct holdings are still quite significant, and thus protection of individual investors remains an important policy issue.[1]

If one looks at the measures of internationalization (see Table 2A below),[2] the U.S. market has become significantly more internationalized over the last decade. While the percentage of international activity is low, this reflects the extremely large size of the U.S. domestic market.

---

[1] NYSE, Share Ownership 2000 (2000).
[2] NYSE, LSE, and C. Bertaut and W. Griever, "Recent Developments in Cross-Border Investment in Securities," 90 Federal Reserve Board Bulletin 19 (2004).

Table 2A			
Internationalization of U.S. Securities Markets (%)			
	1986	2001	
Foreign Securities/Total Securities Held in U.S.	3.0	9.8	(for equity only)
Foreign Listings NYSE	3.7	16.4	(2004) (460)
Foreign Listings LSE	20.0	12.3	(2004) (350)
Foreign Issues (FI)/Total Issues, Volume NYSE	3.5	9.5	
U.S. Trades FI/Total Trades FI	31.0	17.0	(1999)
U.S. Global Equity Market Cap	28.0	48.0	(1999)

A more internationalized market is important to the U.S. It offers investors more choice at lower cost (as opposed to investing in foreign issuers abroad), supplies more competition in the primary market, increasing investor returns, and deepens the secondary markets, adding to liquidity.

4.   MARKET INNOVATION

The U.S. securities markets and its regulation appear to have influenced the shape of other markets. Many securities innovations or regulatory changes which were first introduced in the U.S. securities market have now been introduced around the world. Examples include the trading of standardized options which began in the U.S. in 1973, the deregulation of brokerage commission rates which occurred in the U.S. in the 1970s and was emulated in the early 1980s in Canada, Australia and the United Kingdom, and the increasing use of U.S. quotation and transaction systems in Japan, the United Kingdom and Singapore. U.S. securities firms maintain a sizable presence in most international financial centers.

5.   FOREIGN STOCK LISTINGS AND INTERNATIONAL STOCK TRADING

Listing on a foreign exchange may broaden an issuer's shareholder base and, in some markets, it is necessary in order for domestic institutions to purchase the company's shares. For example, in France local insurance companies may be prohibited from purchasing shares that are not listed on a French bourse. In addition to greater access to capital and diversification of one's equity base from the home country, there may be additional benefits accompanying a listing on an organized and reputable exchange such as the NYSE. These may include: (1) enhancement of international image from association with a prestigious stock exchange; (2) ability to represent compliance with rigorous U.S. disclosure standards (bonding); (3) increased liquidity from increased trading; (4) potential use of U.S. stock to make acquisitions; and (5) cultivation of investors from a U.S. customer base (relevant to retail firms); and (6) increased analyst following.[3]

J. Siegel has mounted a forceful challenge to the bonding explanation for foreign firms listing in the United States.[4] Siegel shows that the SEC rarely enforces U.S. laws against foreign firms. Further Siegel shows that the difficulty of engaging in discovery of information abroad combined with the requirement that plaintiffs be able to plead scienter (intent) with sufficient specificity to survive a dismissal of a cause of action raises substantial obstacles to private enforcement of U.S. liability rules. Siegel points out that derivative actions, a powerful enforcement weapon, is not available to sue foreign corporations because such actions are based on the law of the company's place of incorporation, which is, of course, abroad for foreign corporations. Siegel shows, in detail, how managers of Mexican firms with ADRs have engaged in significant self-dealing without liability. Siegel's study is an example of the classic point that the law on the books may not be the law in action. Does this research discredit the bonding hypothesis? It is likely that investors believe that foreign firms, in general, that cross-list do signal their voluntary compliance with U.S. law, even if such law is extremely

---

[3] J. Hicks, "The Listing of Daimler-Benz A.G. Securities on the NYSE: Conflicting Interests and Regulatory Policies," (1994) 37 German Yearbook of International Law, pp. 360, 365-368; J. Fanto and R. Karmel, "A Report on the Attitudes of Foreign Companies Regarding a U.S. Listing," NYSE Working Paper 97-01 (March 1997). See also G.A. Karolyi, "What Happens to Stocks that List Shares Abroad? A Survey of the Evidence and its Managerial Implications," NYSE Working Paper 96-04 (September 1996), finding evidence that foreign listings increased overall liquidity, particularly for foreign companies listing on the NYSE. This study also found that "the stock's exposure to domestic market risk is significantly reduced and is associated with only a small increase in global market risk and foreign exchange risk, resulting in a net reduction in the cost of equity capital of 114 basis points on average." (Executive Summary). See also C. Doidge, G.A. Karolyi, and R. Stultz, "Why are Foreign Firms Listed in the U.S. Worth More?," 71 J. of Financial Economics 205 (2004) finding that foreign companies listed in the U.S. have higher valuations, 37 percent more for exchange-listed firms. The authors attribute this to the U.S. regulatory regime which limits the ability of controlling shareholders to extract value from a firm. A leading advocate of the bonding explanation for cross-listings has been John Coffee, Jr., "Race to the Top?: The Impact of Cross-Listings and Stock Market Competition on International Corporate Governance," Columbia University Working Paper (2002). W. Reese and M. Weisbach, "Protection of Minority Shareholder Interests, Cross-listings in the United States and Subsequent Equity Offerings," NBER Working Paper 8164 (March 2001) find that firms from civil law countries (weak minority shareholder protection), after cross-listing in the U.S., place the majority of their subsequent equity issues outside the U.S., whereas firms from common law countries (strong minority shareholder protection) place subsequent issues in the U.S. The authors state "[t]his empirical finding is consistent with a view that firms with strong protection at home tend to cross-list in order to access U.S. investors and/or markets, while firms from countries with weak shareholder protection will cross-list for the purpose of voluntarily bonding themselves to U.S. securities and market regulations, allowing them to raise capital more easily at home and elsewhere outside the U.S.," at p. 26.

[4] "Can Foreign Firms Bond Themselves Effectively by Renting U.S. Securities Laws," MIT Working Paper (November 27, 2002).

difficult to enforce. Siegel wrote his piece before the high profile cases of Parmalat, the Italian dairy firm, and the Dutch supermarket firm, Ahold, both of which the SEC has charged with misstating its profits. This followed an intensive SEC investigation of France's Vivendi Universal SA.[5] The SEC has also recently brought a civil suit against Ricardo Salinas, the Chairman of TV Azteca, and one of Mexico's richest individuals, based on an allegedly false certification of a financial statements—as discussed below such certifications are now required by Sarbanes-Oxley.[6] Based on this new vigilance, Siegel's attack on the bonding hypothesis seems less convincing.

Amir Licht contends that the bonding hypothesis is flawed because foreign firms do not bond to the same rules as U.S. firms.[7] As we shall see, foreign firms are treated differently. However, these differences pale in contrast to the similarities, most importantly liability under 10b-5.

U.S. exchanges have undertaken initiatives to increase the number of foreign listed companies. The American and New York Stock Exchanges in June 1987 received approval from the Commission to revise their listing standards. Some foreign corporations apparently had been reluctant to list on U.S. exchanges due to differences in listing standards in the U.S. and their home country. Now certain listing standards may be waived by the American and New York Stock Exchanges if those standards conflict with the laws and practices found in the home market of a foreign corporation. The rule revisions afford U.S. exchanges a better opportunity to compete on an international basis and may provide U.S. investors with greater access to foreign securities.

It would appear likely that such revisions have contributed to the dramatic increase of foreign listings on U.S. exchanges over the past decade. In 1986 only 59 foreign companies were listed on the NYSE, representing 3.7 percent of all listings. By 1999, 406 foreign corporations were listed on the New York Stock Exchange (NYSE), 13.4 percent of the total listings. In contrast, the London Stock Exchange, although maintaining the largest listing of foreign firms, experienced a decrease in the number of foreign listings over the same period (512 to 448).[8]

Accompanying the increase in the number of cross-listings has been an increase in the volume of trading in foreign shares on many exchanges. Trading in foreign equity issues has increased on the NYSE, from 1.2 billion shares in 1986 to 29.1 billion shares in 2001. This increase has caused holdings of non-U.S. equities to increase to almost 10 percent of total equity

---

[5] M. Schroeder and S. Ascarelli, "New Role for SEC: Policing Companies Beyond U.S. Borders," *The Wall Street Journal*, July 30, 2004.

[6] J. Authers and S. Silver, "SEC Tunes in to Azteca," *Financial Times*, January 20, 2005.

[7] "Cross-listing and Corporate Governance: Bonding or Avoiding," 4 Chicago J. Int'l. Law 141 (2003).

[8] Further, foreign companies were delisting from the Tokyo Stock Exchange in 1990-1998 due to lack of investor interest and the general fall of activity accompanying the plunge of the Nikkei.

holdings by U.S. investors in 1999 from less than 5 percent in 1988.[9] Between 1986 and 2000, total U.S. activity in foreign securities (purchases and sales) increased from a then-record high of $438.5 billion in 1986 to in excess of $3.5 trillion in 2000.[10]

Much of this Chapter will be taken up with a discussion of the Sarbanes-Oxley reforms of corporate governance and the increased level of enforcement of the securities law by both the SEC and state officials. Anecdotal evidence suggests these developments have decreased the interest of foreign firms in listing in the U.S. despite the fact that some accommodation to foreign firms have been made in the application of the Sarbanes-Oxley rules. One commentator believes Sarbanes-Oxley will have a similar effect as the U.S. withholding tax in the 1960s, and drive listing business abroad. On the other hand, some argue that firms will seek out the United States to bond to an even higher level or regulation.[11]

The SEC has taken measures designed to decrease trading in certain securities registered on the Over-the-Counter Bulletin Board (OTCBB). In January 1999, the SEC required that such securities be registered under s. 12 of the 1934 Securities Act, 64 Fed. Reg. 1255 (1999). The number of ADRs listed on OTCBB plummeted from 201 in 1997 to 6 in 1998 and average daily dollar volumes dropped from $92 million to $26 million. The numbers of foreign listings and ADRs have both remained relatively stable since 1998, however average daily trading volumes of foreign securities have increased from $1.6 million in 1998 to $10.8 million in 2000.

Much of the trading volume on the OTCBB was forced into the "Pink Sheets," twice daily quotations of stocks published by the National Quotation Bureau.[12] Stocks traded on the Pink Sheets need not be registered. Some 3,300 stocks are traded on the Pink Sheets, and trading volume amounts to an estimated $75 million per day (January 2003), quite small when contrasted to the $41 billion per day average for the NYSE in December 2002. This is generally a very thin market, and it is highly questionable whether investors should be forced to bear the risk of trading foreign issues in such thin markets. Of course, to allow trading in wider markets would undercut the need for registration.

6.   INTERNATIONALIZATION OF PORTFOLIO INVESTMENT FLOWS

U.S. investors have increased their purchases of foreign stocks since elimination of the interest equalization tax in 1974. In 1986, U.S. purchases of foreign stocks totaled $51.7 billion. In 2000, U.S. investors purchased $1.8

---

[9] "Flow of Funds Accounts," Board of Governors of the Federal Reserve System.
[10] NYSE Fact Book 2001, at p. 63. http://www.nyse.com/pdfs/2001_factbook_07.pdf
[11] J. Plender, "A Modest Gain for Europe at U.S. Expense, Competition for Listings Hots Up," *Financial Times,* March 28, 2005.
[12] Since 1999 the Pink Sheets moved online into real time and market makers publish their bids and offers.

trillion of foreign stocks. Over the same period, U.S. investors have increased their purchases of foreign debt securities from $169.8 billion in 1986 to $959 billion in 2000.[13]

Foreign investors' purchases of US stocks have mirrored the growth of U.S. corporations' presence in overseas markets. In 1986, foreign investors' purchased $148.1 billion of U.S. stocks. In 2000 foreign purchases of U.S. equity totaled $3.6 trillion.[14] Foreign ownership of U.S. debt has also increased dramatically over the past twenty years. Between 1984 and 2000, foreign holdings of U.S. long-term securities increased from $254 billion (6 percent of total U.S. long-term securities held) to $3.4 trillion (11 percent).[15]

The purchase of U.S. government debt by foreigners is particularly important. Foreign investors' share of the U.S. government bond market has grown substantially over the last 20 years, from a 20 percent share in 1980 to 40 percent ($1.3 trillion) in 2000.

Notes and Questions

1. How internationalized are U.S. securities markets? Have the markets become more internationalized since 1986?

2. Why should the United States care whether or not its securities markets are internationalized?

3. What do you think of the bonding hypothesis as an explanation of why foreign companies seek listings in the U.S.? A recent study, D. Wójcik, G. Clark, and R. Bauer, "Corporate Governance and Cross-listing: Evidence from European Companies," (Draft, September 2004), finds that between 2000 and 2003 that the largest European companies cross-listing on U.S. exchanges had higher corporate governance ratings in terms of disclosure and the structure of boards of directors. They also find that this governance advantage traces back to a few years before cross-listing which would seem to suggest that improved corporate governance was not cause by cross-listing but rather that better governed companies cross-list. A recent comprehensive review of the bonding literature is G. Karolyi, "The World of Cross-Listings and Cross-Listings of the World: Challenging the Conventional Wisdom," (Working Paper, August 2004).

---

[13] U.S. Treasury Bulletin (March 2001).

[14] NYSE Fact Book 2001.

[15] Federal Reserve Statistical Release Z.1, Flow of Funds Accounts of the United States; Bureau of Public Debt, Monthly Statement of the Public Debt of the United States. [Table F of original Chapter]

B.   THE BASIC U.S. SECURITIES LAW FRAMEWORK[16]

1.   GENERAL RULES[17]

a.   SECURITIES STATUTES

In general, seven federal statutes govern the distribution of U.S. securities: the Securities Act of 1933, the Securities Exchange Act of 1934, the Public Utility Holding Company Act of 1935, the Trust Indenture Act of 1939, the Investment Advisers Act of 1940, the Investment Company Act of 1940, and the Sarbanes-Oxley Act of 2002. With the exception of the Public Utility Holding Company Act, these statutes are applicable to foreign securities as well. Responsibility for the administration and enforcement of these statutes rests in the Securities and Exchange Commission (SEC), an independent agency empowered to adopt regulations and perform quasi-judicial functions.

b.   SECURITIES ACT REGISTRATION

Under the Securities Act of 1933, an issuer must register with the SEC before making a public offering. Upon filing, the SEC determines, normally within two to five days, whether the registration statement will be reviewed. As a general rule, first-time offerings are reviewed, a process that takes four to six weeks. During that time, securities may be offered orally or through a preliminary prospectus, but may not be sold. This restriction acts to limit the issuer's promotional activity. Upon satisfactory review and upon request by the issuer, the SEC will declare the registration effective and authorize the sale of securities. Even after effectiveness, stringent standards prohibit distribution of materials similar to a prospectus if unaccompanied by a copy of the registered prospectus.

Two types of registrations are generally available: registration of conventional offerings and shelf registration. In a conventional offering, the securities are expected to be offered soon after filing and the filed statement relates directly to this imminent offering. The offering price and other related terms, such as the underwriting syndicate, discounts, and offering commissions can be filed as an amendment at the same time the issuer asks the SEC to declare the registration effective. Alternatively, the registration may be declared effective without the information, as long as the issuer files a later prospectus.

---

[16] International Financial Law Review 62-84 (Supp. July 1990).
[17] The following description relies heavily on G. Palm and D. Walkovik, *United States: A Special Guide to Securities Regulation Around the World.*[17] I have summarized and updated this excellent work.

In contrast, shelf registration provides the issuer with greater flexibility and enables it to respond quickly to market conditions by allowing advance registration of securities expected to be sold within a two-year period. As with registration of conventional offerings, a registration statement and a prospectus is filed with the SEC and after possible review and upon request by the issuer are made effective. Securities can be sold any time within the two-year period following effectiveness but must be accompanied by a supplement prospectus enumerating the specific terms of the offering and noting any developments in the issuer's status. For the non-U.S. issuer, the SEC imposes the additional requirement that updated financial statements, dating not more than six months, be kept on file with the SEC. Though these financial statements need not be audited, the requirement, nevertheless, may cause "black out" periods during which securities may not be offered.

c.   EXCHANGE ACT REGISTRATION AND REPORTING

The Exchange Act of 1934 requires registration under the 1933 Act of securities listed on U.S. stock exchanges or quoted on NASDAQ or the OTCBB and provides ongoing disclosure requirements for all securities registered under the Securities Act of 1933 (suspended for any year where the securities are held by less than 300 U.S. residents).

For non-Canadian, non-U.S. private issuers, the relevant forms are Form 20-F and Form 6-K. Form 20-F contains financial information similar to that disclosed in Form F-1 under the Securities Act and must be filed within six months of the close of the fiscal year of the issuer. Form 6-K requires the issuer to provide the SEC with any information made public by the regulations of its own country, filed with and made public by a non-U.S. stock exchange, or provided to its security holders. Such information is not considered "filed" and thus is not subject to the liability provisions of the Exchange Act for false or misleading documents filed with the SEC. If a foreign company simply cross-lists without issuing new shares (a Level 2 offering), Form 20-F requires only partial reconciliation of the issuer's financial statement with U.S. GAAP (item 17) rather than the full reconciliation requirement for the raising of capital (a Level 3 offering) (item 18).

d.   FORM 20-F REGISTRATION

Many of the items of Form 20-F incorporate by reference provisions of Regulation S-K which contains standard instructions for filing forms under the Securities and Exchange Act of 1934. The requirements of Form 20-F include the following:

(i)   Information regarding the terms of the securities, the terms of the offering, the plan of distribution of the securities and the use of proceeds.

(ii) A description of the business of the issuer, including: (i) a discussion of the general development of the business over the past five years; (ii) principal products produced and services rendered and the principal markets for and methods of distribution of such products and services; (iii) a breakdown of total revenues during the past three years by categories of activity and into geographical markets, with a narrative discussion of material differences between relative contributions to operating profit as compared to relative contributions to revenues; and (iv) special characteristics of the registrant's operations or industry which may have a material impact on future financial performance, and any material country risks unlikely to be known by investors, including dependence upon a few major customers or suppliers, governmental regulation, expiration of material contracts or rights, unusual competitive conditions, cyclicality of the industry and anticipated raw material or energy shortages. Additional disclosures required of electric or gas utilities, companies with oil or gas operations, banks and insurance companies are set out in industry guides adopted by the SEC. Additional information is required of registrants which have not received revenues from operations during each of the three preceding years.

(iii) A brief description of the location and general character of the principal plants, mines and other materially important physical properties of the registrant. In the case of an extractive enterprise, material information as to production, reserves, locations, development and the nature of the registrant's interests is to be given. (Generally, only proven oil or gas reserves and proven or probable other reserves may be disclosed.)

(iv) Selected financial data for each of the last five years, including revenues, income, assets and long-term obligations.

(v) A management discussion of the registrant's financial condition, changes in financial condition and results of operations for each year for which financial statements are presented (three years), including information as to trends, commitments and material events and uncertainties relating to liquidity, capital resources and results of operations.

(vi) Prescribed information as to material pending legal proceedings, control of the registrant by a parent or others and 10 percent shareholders, the nature of any trading market for the securities registered, exchange controls and other governmental, legal or charter limitations affecting non-resident holders of the registrant's securities, withholding or similar taxes to which U.S.

holders would be subject under the laws of the country in which the registrant is organized, the directors and executive officers of the registrant and the aggregate compensation paid to them as a group for services in the last year, outstanding options to purchase from the registrant securities of the class being registered, and information otherwise made public as to the interest of management or controlling shareholders and certain associated persons in material transactions with the registrant.

(vii)   A description of the securities to be registered.

(viii)   Audited balance sheets as of the end of each of the two most recent fiscal years and audited statements of income and changes in financial position for each of the three most recent fiscal years. Financial statements must meet the following requirements:

(a) If the last audited balance sheet is dated more than six months prior to the effective date of the registration statement, interim unaudited financial statements are required. This requirement has had a significant impact on the ability of non-U.S. issuers which publicly release financial statements on a semi-annual basis only. In view of the time required to prepare such financial statements, this requirement has had the effect of creating 'blackout periods' during which the public capital markets in the U.S. have been unavailable to such issuers.

(b) Generally, the statements must be presented in the currency of the registrant's country.

(c) The statements must disclose an informational content substantially similar to statements which comply with U.S. generally accepted accounting principles (GAAP) and Regulation S-X.

(d) The statements may be prepared according to U.S. GAAP or, alternatively, according to an identified comprehensive body of accounting principles together with a discussion and quantification of material variations from U.S. GAAP and Regulation S-X in the accounting principles, practices and methods used in preparing the financial statements.

(e) In contrast to ongoing Exchange Act reporting requirements, the statements and notes are required to include supplementary information required by U.S. GAAP and Regulation S-X, such as business segment and pension information, unless the securities registered are to be offered only upon exercise of rights granted pro rata to all existing security holders of a class, pursuant to a dividend or interest reinvestment plan or upon the conversion of outstanding convertible securities or the exercise of outstanding warrants (all of which are referred to herein as offerings to existing security holders).

Disclosure requirements are relaxed in some important ways for foreign issuers. They can disclose aggregate remuneration and options rather than for individual directors and officers. Nor do they have to disclose details of material transactions with insiders. 20-F only requires foreign issuers to disclose 10 percent owners of voting securities, as compared with a 5 percent for U.S. issuers. In addition, foreign issuers need only disclose aggregate securities owned by insiders, rather than specific holdings of each insider as required for U.S. issuers.

e.   REGISTRATION EXEMPTIONS: PRIVATE PLACEMENTS

In the case of non-public and limited offerings, known as "private placements," s. 4(2) and Regulation D provide exemptions from the registration requirements of the Securities Act of 1933. The exemptions have proved useful to non-U.S. issuers desiring limited U.S. distribution of securities also being offered abroad.

Section 4(2). Section 4(2) exempts from registration "transactions by an issuer not involving any public offering" made in the U.S. or to U.S. nationals. The rationale behind the exemption provision is that purchasers of offerings falling under s. 4(2) do not require the protection provided by the Securities Act registration requirement. To fall under the s. 4(2) exemption, however, the offering must meet the following requirements:

There must be a limited number of offerees and purchasers with a possible exception for large institutional investors.

No general promotion is allowed.

Information provided to or known by offerees and purchasers must be comparable to that provided through the registration process to the extent that they are material to the transaction. U.S. GAAP standards need not be met.

Offerees and purchasers must be able to evaluate the investment.

The transaction must be designed to prevent resale and distribution by purchasers in a way that would have disqualified the initial offering from exemption under s. 4(2). The limitation is not applicable to sales to non-U.S. persons.

When the private placement offering is made in conjunction with a public offering abroad, the transactions must be designed to restrict the U.S. offerings to private placements.

Regulation D. Regulation D acts as a safe harbor rule for all transactions that meet the requirements of Rule 506. To fall under the safe harbor protection of Rule 506, the following requirements must be met:

Issuers must reasonably believe or there must actually be no more than 35 U.S. persons, other than "accredited investors," that are purchasers of the securities. Accredited investors include institutional investors, directors and officers of the issuer, and persons meeting certain minimum net worth standards.

Purchasers who are not accredited investors must be provided with information comparable to that provided in a registration statement, made aware of any additional information provided to accredited investors, furnished with such information upon request, and given an opportunity to verify information provided.

There must be no general promotion.

Issuers must adopt reasonable measures to ensure that purchasers are not buying to resell. Reasonable measures include direct inquiries, written disclosure to the purchaser on the limits to distribution of the security, and placing legends to this effect on the securities.

Although Rule 506 is most often used for investors who are natural persons, the majority of non-public transactions with institutional investors entail s. 4(2).

f.   AUDITOR INDEPENDENCE

The SEC imposes a stringent requirement of independence in the use of accounting firms. No principal of the firm may hold material interests in the issuer's securities or have held any position or performed any service "incompatible with the audit function." These statements must be updated every six months, a requirement that can prove burdensome to some non-U.S. issuers.

g.   LIABILITY

Liabilities for false and misleading information under the Securities Act and Exchange Act are imposed on a wide range of persons. Under s. 11(a) of the Securities Act of 1933, the issuer, any persons who signed the registration statement, and directors, underwriters, accountants, and other experts who prepared or certified the registration statement can incur civil liabilities. With the exception of the issuer, a person will be exempt from liability if that person can show that despite reasonable diligence, it could reasonably believe and did believe that the statement was accurate and that there were no omissions rendering the statement misleading. Sections 11(b) and (c) set the standard of reasonableness as that required by a prudent man in the management of his own property. Recovery for s. 11 violations are, in general, limited to the difference between the price paid for the security and the market value at the time of suit or the price at which the security was sold before the suit. Section 12 provides additional grounds for recovery.

Section 18(a) of the Exchange Act of 1934 similarly holds issuers and related persons liable if the security's purchase or sales price was affected by the purchaser's reliance on a false or misleading statement. Even where the false statement is not misleading, the issuer may be liable through s. 10(b) and Rule 10b-5 thereunder for statements made knowingly and recklessly. A controlling person of any person held liable is jointly and severally liable, unless that controlling person can show that he did not know and did not have reasonable grounds to know of the liable person's alleged acts.

In 2003, it became known that major accounting firms in the U.K. were adding riders to their audit opinions saying that only shareholders, and not third parties, could rely on their work. This was prompted by a U.K. court opinion which suggested that liability of auditors to banks that had lent to their clients could be avoided by such disclaimers. The SEC is looking into whether such disclaimers for U.K. companies listed in the U.S. raises legal or policy issues under U.S. law.

h.   THE "AIRCRAFT CARRIER" PROPOSAL

On November 3, 1998, the SEC proposed a wide range of changes to the rules currently governing the distribution of securities, for example various rules restricting communications with prospective buyers before registration is effective.[18] The revisions generally left disclosure requirements intact. The SEC's proposals were motivated, in part, by attracting a greater volume of transactions to the U.S. public market through registration and thus reducing reliance on use of Rule 144A (discussed below). Generally, the proposal would greatly reduce restrictions on distribution of securities for large seasoned issuers—those reporting to the SEC for one year and having either a public float of $75 million and $1 million U.S. average trading volume (ADTV), or a public float of $250 million.

After 6 years at sea, a new and improved aircraft carrier came back to port in late November 2004 when the SEC made new proposals.[19] This proposal would significantly relax communications during the waiting period for a "well-known seasoned issuer." Such an issuer must have outstanding a minimum of $700 million of common equity market capitalization held by non-affiliates or, solely for the purpose of debt offerings, have issued $1 billion of registered debt securities within the last three years. Some relaxation is also available for other issuers. The proposal would also eliminate various restrictions on shelf offerings and dispense with the need to deliver physical prospectuses to potential investors. Instead a prospectus

---

[18] SEC Release No. 33-7606; 34-40632; IC-23519.
[19] SEC, Securities Offering Reform, 69 Federal Register 67392 (November 17, 2004).

filed with the SEC would constitute delivery to investors on the theory that electronic access (which is presumed) is equivalent to delivery.

i.   SELECTIVE DISCLOSURE

Effective October 23, 2000, the SEC adopted a controversial rule, Regulation FD, preventing selective disclosure by companies of material non-public information.[20] This was designed by the SEC to fill the gap in insider trading law created by the Supreme Court's decision in *Dirks v. Securities and Exchange Commission*,[21] which held that it would not be a breach of fiduciary duty for a company to divulge material non-public information to analysts unless the company received a benefit. Without such benefit, the analyst's tippees would not violate Rule 10b-5 by trading on such information. While lawyers still advised their clients after *Dirks* not to disclose such information since a benefit might be found, the SEC thought more had to be done, hence Regulation FD.

The SEC toned down the Regulation from its proposed form due to a hostile industry reception. As adopted, there is no private liability, e.g. under 10b-5, for violating the Regulation; it is enforced solely by the SEC. It only covers reckless violations and communications by "senior officials." It does not apply to disclosures in connection with registered offerings, and does not prohibit confidential communications. Studies as to the effects of this regulation on information asymmetries and volatility have reached contradictory results.[22] One study has found that analyst coverage has

---

[20] Release No. 33-7881 (August 15, 2000).

[21] 463 US 646 (1983).

[22] There was preliminary evidence that the Regulation was limiting issuer communications with analysts, J. Junewicz, "The SEC Raises the Stakes in Issues-Analyst Communications," 33 Securities and Commodities Regulation 237 (November 2000), and that the information discontinuities it has created had increased volatility in equity markets, J. Chaffin, "Disclosure Rule Attracts Flak," *Financial Times*, April 7, 2001. A survey of the Securities Industry Association showed that 72 percent of the respondents thought the quality of disclosures has been poorer after the adoption of Regulation FD. A. Beard, "New Disclosure Rules Come under Attack," *Financial Times*, May 18, 2001. Two studies have found no increase in volatility: V. Eleswarapu, R. Thompson, and K. Venkataraman, "The Impact of Regulation Fair Disclosure: Trading Costs and Information Asymmetry," Draft (October 2001) and F. Heflin, K.R. Subramanyam, and Y. Zhang, "Regulation FD and the Financial Information Environment," Working Paper (2001). The former study also found no increase in trading costs following the introduction of Regulation FD, suggesting that there was no increase in information asymmetry or the exploitation of inside information. See also S. Sunder, "Investor Access to Conference Call Disclosures: Impact of Regulation Fair Disclosure on Information Asymmetry," Draft (January 2002) for similar findings. However, other studies have found an increase in volatility, see e.g. B. Bushee, D. Matsumoto, and G. Miller, "Managerial and Investor Responses to Disclosure Regulation: The Case of Reg FD and Conference Calls," Working Paper (November 2002); V. Štraser, "Regulation Fair Disclosure and Information Asymmetry" Working Paper (March 2002). Regulation FD may also have particular costs for small firms seeking to disclose complex information, where private one-on-one communication may be more efficient than public communication. A study shows that the cost of capital for these firms increased after the

dropped for small firms as a result of Regulation FD who could not use the same transmission channels, e.g. conference calls, as do large firms. The effect was more pronounced for firms communicating complex information.[23] One unanticipated effect of Regulation FD is to increase the value of rating agencies. Rating agencies are exempted from selective disclosure provisions. As a result, ratings changes now have more impact on the market since they now possess confidential information not available to equity analysts.[24]

Regulation FD, as proposed, would have applied to foreign as well as domestic issuers. The effect would have been for SEC policies to govern how foreign issuers (most of which have foreign listings) made disclosures to analysts in their own markets. Foreign regulators, like many commentators, believed that the proposal could delay the timely release of information to their own markets in order to avoid selective disclosure liability under U.S. law. Some countries, however, like the U.K., have policies requiring issuers to promptly disclose material information even in the absence of insider trading.[25] As adopted, Regulation FD excluded foreign private issuers.[26]

The SEC has begun enforcement of Regulation FD. For example, the SEC found in 2002 that Raytheon had violated Regulation FD by selectively communicating to eleven analysts quarterly and semi-annual earnings guidance. In the case of Siebel, the SEC found that the company intentionally disclosed material non-public information at a technology conference.[27]

j.   REGULATION OF SECURITIES FIRMS

Broker-dealers are regulated by the SEC in various respects, particularly with regard to capital, dealt with in Chapter 7, and trading practices. However, the SEC did not historically regulate holding companies or affiliates of broker dealers. While holding companies including banks are regulated by the Federal Reserve Board, holding companies not involving banks have been effectively unregulated. Under the proposed Conglomerate

---

promulgation of Regulation FD. A. Gomes, G. Gorton, and L. Madureira, "SEC Regulation Fair Disclosure, Information, and the Cost of Capital," Working Paper (March 29, 2004).

[23] A Gomes, G. Gorton, and L. Madureira, "SEC Regulation Fair Disclosure, Information, and the Cost of Capital," NBER Working Paper 10567 (June 2004).

[24] P. Jorion, Z. Liu, and C. Shi, "Informational Effects of Regulation FD: Evidence From Rating Agencies," 76 J. of Financial Economic 309 (2005).

[25] I. Taylor, S. Orton, and S. Parkes, "Selective Disclosure by Companies to Analysts," (2001) Journal of International Financial Markets, p. 174.

[26] See M. Fox, Regulation FD and Foreign Issuers: "Globalization's Strains and Opportunities," (2001) 41 Va. J. Int'l L., p. 653.

[27] S.K. Kang, "Fair Disclosure: What Issuers Can Learn from SEC Actions," (January 2003) International Financial Law Review, p. 23. In 2003, the SEC imposed a $1 million penalty on Schering-Plough for providing negative information to four institutional investors before releasing the information to the market as a whole. These analysts heavily sold as the price dropped by 17.6 percent, accounting for 30 percent of the trading volume, during the period before the general release. F. Norris, "SEC Penalises Schering-Plough over a Fair Disclosure Violation," *The New York Times*, September 10, 2003.

Directive of the European Union, discussed in Chapter 4, the EU would assume authority to regulate unregulated holding companies of investment firms operating in the EU that were not already subject to "equivalent" regulation by another country. This caused the SEC to adopt a new holding company regulation for U.S. securities firms to enable them to avoid EU regulation. A holding company, meeting certain requirements, may voluntarily register with the SEC as a supervised investing bank holding company (SIBHC). SEC regulation of SIBHCs includes requirements for a group-wide internal risk management control system, record keeping, and periodic reporting. These requirements include the reporting of capital consistent with the standards of Basel II (see Chapter 7 for a discussion of these standards) but does not set minimum group-wide capital requirements.[28]

k.   SROs and RESOURCES

The U.S. system of securities regulation relies, in part, on self-regulation of the brokerage industry through the National Association of Securities Dealers (NASD) and the stock exchanges, such as the NYSE and AMEX. NASD has played an increasingly important role in regulation through its jurisdiction over broker-dealers. It was a party to the research analyst settlement and has taken a major initiative in regulating IPO allocations. NASD at present stills owns a significant portion of Nasdaq but recently sold its ownership of the American Stock Exchange. Its intends to divest its remaining ownership in Nasdaq as soon as the SEC approves Nasdaq's status as an exchange (until then it can only be treated like an exchange because it is owned by NASD). NASD has clearly stated its attention to get out of the stock exchange ownership business and function only as a regulator because of the conflict of interest in combining these two roles. NASD has the power to levy fines on broker-dealers. In addition, it has begun to use "timeout" penalties, prohibiting firms from registering additional broker-dealers for a fixed period of time.[29]

Triggered by recent scandals involving alleged abuses by specialists on the NYSE, and trading practice violations on other exchanges, William Donaldson, the SEC Chairman, has indicated that he is rethinking the proper role of self-regulation. The exchanges have tried to forestall radical changes—such as depriving them of SRO status—by reforming their

---

[28] SEC Release No. 34-49831 (Supervised Investment Bank Holding Companies), June 8, 2004. The Commission at the same time adopted a new alternative net capital requirement for broker-dealers, based on Basel II requirements, that are part of consolidated supervised entities—this would include SIBHCs. SEC Release No. 34-49830, June 8, 2004. The Commission's discussion in its SIBHC release seems to argue that such supervision, without the adoption of the alternative capital requirements at the holding company level, should be enough to satisfy the EU's equivalence requirement.

[29] J. Anderson, "Wall Street Turns to the Timeout As Punishment," *The New York Times*, December 8, 2004.

governance in a way to assure more rigorous enforcement of their regulations on their members.

On December 17, 2003, the SEC approved the proposal of the NYSE to eliminate from its Board of Directors all industry members (albeit that former CEOs of industry were proposed as new Board members). This Board directly controls the Audit and Regulatory Oversight and Regulatory Budget Committees.

A separate Board of Executives, appointed by the Board of Directors, drawn from the securities industry, will review exchange performance, membership issues, listed company issues, and public issues related to overall market structure and performance.

A Regulation Enforcement and Listing Standards Committee—not charged with "oversight"—will be composed of members from both Boards, but members of the Board of Directors have a voting majority. This Committee would report to the Regulation Oversight Committee and has jurisdiction over important matters, such as review and advice with respect to the Exchange's market surveillance programs and discipline of member violations.[30]

In November 2004 the SEC proposed a rule aimed at strengthening the role of independent directors in the governance of exchanges.[31] The proposed rule would require exchanges to have a majority independent board and fully independent Nominations, Governance, Audit, Compensation, and Regulatory Oversight Committees. SROs also would be required to effectively separate their regulatory function from their market operations and commercial interests, as the NYSE has already done. Also in late 2004, the SEC put forward a Concept Release Concerning Self-Regulation.[32] This release outlines four possible approaches to SRO reform. First, improved corporate governance—the approach of the November 2004 proposed rule. Another approach would be to increase SRO regulatory independence through mandated SRO internal restructuring, for example by insisting that commercial and regulatory functions be carried on in separate subsidiaries. Another option, for member regulation as opposed to exchange regulation, could consist of the Commission designating a market neutral single self-regulatory organization to regulate all SRO members (currently this task is apportioned between exchanges and NASD). Alternatively, SROs registered with the SEC could compete to regulate members. The final two options would be for a "Universal Non-Industry Regulator," one regulator that would regulate all aspects of the industry, both members and exchanges, or to abolish SROs entirely and turn everything over to the SEC.

---

[30] SEC Release No. 34-48946, NYSE Rulemaking Order Approving Proposed Rule Change Relating to the Amendment and Restatement of the Constitution of the Exchange to Reform the Government and Management Architecture of the Exchange (December 17, 2003).
[31] SEC Release No. 34-50699 (November 18, 2004).
[32] 69 Federal Register 71256 (December 8, 2004).

The ability of the SEC to enforce its rules obviously depends on its resources. From 1991 to 2000, its workload grew by 80 percent while its staff grew by just 20 percent, according to the General Accounting Office, and its salaries were lower than those paid to bank regulators. At the beginning of 2003, substantial increases in appropriations and salaries were being considered.

2.   THE SARBANES-OXLEY ACT

On July 30, 2002, President Bush signed into law the Sarbanes-Oxley Act, a broad but somewhat hasty response to the Enron and other accounting scandals. This is the most important and expansive securities regulation since the enactment of the 1933 and 1934 Acts. Its provisions have been implemented by SEC regulation.

a.   CORPORATE GOVERNANCE

Sarbanes-Oxley is primarily aimed at reforming corporate governance procedures for public companies. It requires various CEO and CFO certifications of financial statements on an annual and quarterly basis. These rules are fully applicable to foreign issuers.[33] In addition, it requires all listed companies to have fully independent audit committees, that is committees composed solely of outside directors. No member of the committee can accept any consulting, advisory or other compensatory fee from the issuer, or be an affiliate of the issuer. It is far from clear that an independent audit committee can prevent accounting fraud; the financial expertise of the audit committee may be much more important. Congress considered but rejected such expertise.[34] Companies must, however, disclose whether or not they have a financial expert on the audit committee and if not, why not.

These audit requirements make a number of exceptions for foreign companies. To accommodate co-determination in Germany, labor representatives who might not be considered "independent," are permitted to serve on the audit committee, and to accommodate two-tier boards, the auditor independence requirements are to apply only to the supervisory or non-management board. In addition, one controlling shareholder or foreign government representative, where the government has a significant shareholding, can sit on the audit committee, assuming they receive no compensation. Finally, where countries provide for auditor oversight through a board of auditors or similar body, separate from the board, such bodies can

---

[33] SEC, Release Nos. 33-8124, 34-46427 (August 29, 2002).
[34] R. Romano, "The Sarbanes-Oxley Act and the Making of Quack Corporate Governance," Yale Law School, Center for Law, Economics, and Public Policy Research Paper 297 (2004).

be substitutes for an independent audit committee, assuming they meet certain requirements, e.g. they contain no executive officers of a company.[35]

The audit committee is required to hire and supervise the outside auditors. Also, companies must disclose whether they have an independent "audit committee financial expert" on the audit committee, and if not why not. An "audit committee financial expert" must himself have certain accounting and auditing skills or have had experience in actively supervising such a person.[36] This rule fully applies to foreign firms.

The Act also created a new Public Company Accounting Oversight Board (PCAOB) under the supervision of the SEC. The Board is responsible for establishing auditing, quality control, attestation and ethics standards for auditors of public companies. Prior to Sarbanes-Oxley, auditors were prohibited from engaging in consulting services. The Act further prohibits auditors from providing specified non–audit services to their audit clients. Such services include legal services. Other countries like France follow a similar approach. Although the findings of many surveys and experimental studies indicate that non-audit services performance affects the perception of an audit firm's independence, empirical evidence on this point is mixed. On the other hand joint provision of services can lead to efficiencies and improved performance as auditors with a broader role learn more about their client. A 2004 model predicts that limiting the scope of non-audit services results in auditors reporting more conservatively (less likely to issue unqualified reports), higher audit fees, less risk taking and lower firm value.[37]

The Act also requires companies to rotate key auditor partners periodically and proscribes a one year cooling off period before certain members of the audit engagement team may accept certain employment positions with the issuer.[38] These rules apply to foreign accounting firms that conduct audits of foreign subsidiaries and affiliates of U.S. issuers, as well as foreign private issuers. Between the proposal of the rules and their final adoption, several of the requirements were modified with foreign firms in mind, e.g. less broad rotation and cooling off periods, but the resulting rules apply equally to domestic and foreign firms. The SEC also made clear that auditors are permitted to provide tax services to audit clients, and this would be equally true for foreign firms even if such services were regarded as legal services by the auditor's home country.

The PCAOB has adopted a paperless registration system for accounting firms that audit U.S.-traded companies, which includes non-U.S.

---

[35] SEC Release No. 33-8220; 34-47654 (April 9, 2003). J. Meyers, L. Myers and Z-V. Palmrose, "Mandatory Auditor Rotation: Evidence from Restatements," Working Paper (July 8, 2003) finds no evidence that auditor rotation decreases the likelihood of financial restatements.
[36] SEC Release Nos. 33-8177, 34-47235 (January 23, 2003).
[37] D. Chan, "The Economic Consequences of Limiting the Joint Provision of Audit and Nonaudit Services," (June 2004).
[38] SEC Release Nos. 33-8183, 34-47265 (January 28, 2003).

as well as U.S. accounting firms. Foreign firms were given until July 2004 to comply. The effect of the registration requirement was to give the PCAOB oversight over foreign audit firms. The EU protested this assertion of jurisdiction and threatened to reciprocate by having each EU country assert jurisdiction over U.S. firms. The EU suggested a mutual recognition approach as an alternative, under which the PCAOB would recognize the adequacy of European regulation. It is unclear whether this was to work on a "block" basis for all EU countries or on a country-by-country basis. In June 2004, PCAOB issued its Final Rules Relating to the Oversight of Non-U.S. Public Accounting Firms.[39] The rules provide that the Board may rely—to the extent it deems appropriate—on foreign inspections under the home country's oversight system. The extent of reliance on the foreign system would be based on the "independence and rigor" of the foreign system, as well as discussions with the foreign regulators. The Board took a similar approach in relying on foreign investigations and sanctions of foreign accounting firms. This approach falls somewhat short of a complete mutual recognition model which contemplates complete deference to foreign authorities.

In February 2005, a new international board, the Public Interest Oversight Board, was created to oversee the setting of auditing standards, in particular it will oversee the standard setting activities of the International Federation of Accountants (IFAC). The Board will not have any enforcement powers—this will be left to national authorities. The new organization was established by IOSCO, the Basel Committee of Bank supervisors, the International Association of Insurance Supervisors, the World Bank and the Financial Stability Forum. It remains to be seen how this organization will relate to national standard setters such as PCAOB.

The Act also prohibits loans to executive officers and directors, and generally increases civil and criminal penalties for violations.

Both the New York Stock Exchange and NASDAQ have adopted new corporate governance listing standards which in some cases go farther than the requirements of Sarbanes-Oxley. Among the requirements of the NYSE are the following: (1) independent directors must comprise a majority of a company's board; (2) boards must convene regular executive sessions in which the non-management directors meet without management; (3) listed companies must have an audit committee, a nominating committee and a compensation committee, each composed solely of independent directors; (4) the chair of the audit committee must have accounting or financial management expertise; and (5) audit committees must have sole responsibility for hiring and firing the company's independent auditors and for approving any significant non-audit work by auditors. For a director to be independent, the board must affirmatively determine that the director has no material relationship with the company. Foreign companies are not required

---

[39] PCAOB Release No. 2004-005, June 9, 2004.

to comply with these rules—except for the requirement for a financial expert on the audit committee—but must disclose any significant ways in which their corporate governance practices differ from those required of domestic companies by the NYSE.[40]

There is no systematic evidence that independent boards will enhance shareholder value. In a comprehensive study before the enactment of Sarbanes-Oxley, Bhagat and Black failed to find any significant correlation between board independence and firm performance.[41] It is conceivable that Sarbanes-Oxley and stock exchange rules made matters worse since it appears to have had the effect of increasing board size by adding independent directors without subtracting executive directors, and some studies show a negative relation between board size and firm value.[42] On a more general level, it is unclear whether better corporate governance in general increases performance. Some studies find such a relationship. A 2003 study by P. Gompers, J. Ishii, and A. Metrick[43] found that firms with strong shareholder rights have future risk-adjusted stock returns that are 8.5 percent per year higher than those of firms with weak shareholder rights, but did not establish causality. The 2003 study also found that poorer corporate governance did not result in underperformance in operating returns, probably a better measure of governance impact.[44] A later study, however, found that while more poorly governed (based on an index) companies have lower stock returns, these returns are not caused by poor governance since analysts predicted the lower returns in advance and that information was impounded into the stock price. It is conceivable that bad businessmen both make poor decisions as to how to govern themselves and how to do business.[45]

On a more theoretical level, there is a substantial question as to whether independent boards with less knowledge, and potentially more conflict and less collegiality than those with insiders, can be as effective. It is

---

[40] NYSE, "Corporate Governance Rule Proposals," submitted to the SEC for approval on August 16, 2002. See SEC, Release No. 34-47021 (December 18, 2002) (extending time to comment until January 17, 2003). On October 9, 2003, the NYSE filed revised proposals with the SEC, further revising proposals filed in April. The main principles outlined in the text are unchanged.

[41] S. Bhagat and B. Black, "The Non-Correlation Between Board Independence and Long Term Firm Performance," 27 J. of Corporation Law 231 (2001). One needs to be careful in evaluating studies of "governance" as to what is meant by the term. For example, H. Daouk, C. Lee, and D. Ng, "Capital Market Governance: How Do Security Laws Affect Market Performance," Draft (February 28, 2005) define governance as strong anti-insider trading laws, better disclosure and lack of restrictions on short-selling, and find firms perform better in countries or markets with such rules. This has nothing to do with the effect of corporate governance rules.

[42] J. Linck, J. Netter, and T. Yang, "Effects and Unintended Consequences of the Sarbanes-Oxley Act on Corporate Boards," (March 2005).

[43] "Corporate Governance and Equity Prices," 118 Quarterly J. Of Economics 107 (2003).

[44] See J. Core, W. Guay, and T. Rusticus, "Does Corporate Governance Cause Weak Stock Returns? An Examination of Firm Operating Performance and Analysts' Expectations," Working Paper (May 2004).

[45] J. Core, W. Guay, and T. Rusticus, "Does Weak Corporate Governance Cause Weak Returns? An Examination of Firm Operating Performance and Analysts' Expectations," (April 2003).

further doubtful whether companies with strong majority shareholders have the same need for independent boards as those with widely dispersed shareholders. Independent boards are not needed to control agency problems in more closely held companies. The case for independent directors in more widely held companies rests on the rationale of minority shareholder protection. Again, there is no systematic evidence that independent directors do a better job at protecting those rights than non-independent directors. In addition, it is not clear that the test for whether a board member is independent will really produce independent directors, or once selected they will remain independent. Take the case of AIG, where reportedly an AIG foundation contributed to the favorite causes of board members.[46] It is worth considering whether the NYSE policy toward foreign companies, requiring a majority of independent directors or an explanation of why there is no independent majority should be adopted for all companies, the approach of the U.K. The U.K. Combined Code and listing standards requires that at least half the board be independent, excluding the chairman, thus permitting a majority of non-independent directors including the chairman. Companies must either follow this policy or explain why they are not doing so.[47]

The Act also addressed the responsibility of attorneys appearing and practicing before the Commission. Such attorneys are required to report evidence of material violations of SEC rules "up-the-ladder" (to their supervisors) within an issuer. In addition, under some circumstances, attorneys are required to effect a "noisy withdrawal"—that is, to withdraw from representing an issuer and notify the Commission of the withdrawal. The Commission is still considering the details of the noisy withdrawal requirement. Evidence of material violations requires "credible evidence, based upon which it would be unreasonable, under the circumstances, for a prudent and competent attorney not to conclude that it is reasonably likely that a material violation has occurred, is ongoing or is about to occur." Foreign attorneys who are not admitted to practice in the United States, and who do not advise clients regarding U.S. law are exempt. Foreign attorneys who do provide legal advice about U.S. law would be covered to the extent they practice before the Commission unless they provide such advice in consultation with U.S. counsel.[48]

b.   CONTINUOUS AND IMPROVED DISCLOSURE

The Act also requires issuers to disclose "on a rapid and current basis" in plain English such information as the SEC may require concerning material changes in their financial condition and operations. The SEC has

---

[46] N. Henderson, "AIG Scandal Could Hurt Official's Chance to Lead Fed," *The Washington Post*, April 12, 2005.
[47] R. Smerdon and L. Hazell, "How Does the New U.K. Combined Code of Corporate Governance Compare with Sarbanes-Oxley," 7 Wall Street Lawyer (October 2003).
[48] SEC Release Nos. 33-8185, 34-47276 (January 29, 2003).

implemented this requirement by accelerating the filing requirements for domestic companies with a public float of at least $75 million, which have been reporting for at least 12 months, have previously filed one annual report and do not qualify for exemptions for small issuers. Over three years, the lag in filing the annual report will decrease from 90 to 60 days, and for the quarterly report from 45 to 35 days. These requirements do not apply to foreign companies.

Prior to the enactment of Sarbanes-Oxley, the SEC had proposed expanding 8-K requirements, which require prompt disclosure of certain material events, to include additional areas of information and to require that 8-Ks be filed within two business days from the triggering event, as opposed to the current requirement of five business or 15 calendar days depending on the nature of the event. The proposal noted that foreign companies are not currently required to file an 8-K, but rather file a 6-K that contains information required to be made public under its home country law, with a stock exchange that the exchange makes public or that is distributed to its security holders.[49] The Commission adopted this proposal in March 2004, requiring that the expanded 8-K reports be filed within four business days from the triggering event (thus providing more time for a considered judgment as to whether disclosure is required), and providing a safe harbor from 10b-5 liability for such filings.[50] There was no mention of changes in 6-K.[51]

Sarbanes-Oxley mandates additional disclosures regarding off-balance sheet transactions, mandated GAAP reconciliation of pro forma financial information, like EBITDA (earnings before interest, tax, depreciation, and amortization), internal controls, and a code of ethics for senior financial officers. These provisions apply to both domestic and foreign issuers. The SEC has also implemented the off-balance sheet disclosure requirement and made it fully applicable to foreign issuers.[52]

The SEC implemented the requirement of reconciliation of *pro forma* information for non-SEC filings in Regulation G.[53] Regulation G does not prohibit use of non-GAAP financial measures but requires that these measures be reconciled to the nearest comparable GAAP measure. This can be costly and complicated and risks having companies abandon the use of such measures which have proven beneficial. The upside is that potentially misleading measures would be controlled.

---

[49] SEC Release Nos. 33-8106, 34-46084 (June 17, 2002).

[50] The SEC estimated that the increased cost for additional 8-K filings could be $44 million per year, while others have estimated it could be ten times as much. D. Bernstein, "Cost of 8-K Rules Could Surpass Sarbanes-Oxley," 23 International Financial Law Review 20 (May 2004).

[51] SEC, Final Rule, Additional From 8-K Disclosure Requirements and Acceleration of Filing Date, Release Nos. 33-8400, 34-49424 (March 16, 2004).

[52] SEC Release Nos. 33-8182, 34-47264 (January 28, 2003).

[53] SEC Release 2003-6, January 15, 2003.

Regulation G does not apply to a non-U.S. company if: (1) the company is listed or quoted outside the U.S.; (2) the non-GAAP measure is not derived from GAAP; and (3) the disclosure is not targeted at the U.S. and is released in the U.S. after it is released abroad.

c.   INTERNAL CONTROLS

Section 404 of Sarbanes-Oxley imposes a requirement that management annually report their internal controls of financial reporting. The internal control report must include a statement of management's responsibility for establishing and maintaining adequate internal control over financial reporting of the company and a management assessment of the effectiveness of such controls. In addition, a registered public accounting firm must verify these statements. These requirements have been implemented in an SEC rule on Management's Report on Internal Control Over Financial Reporting and Certification of Disclosure in Exchange Act Periodic Reports.[54]

The direct cost to companies of implementing Sarbanes-Oxley has been substantial, and compliance with Section 404, particularly the cost for the outside audit, has turned out to be the most significant area of cost. Korn/Ferry, an executive recruitment firm, estimates that the average cost for a Fortune 1000 company is $5.1 million, or $5 billion overall for those companies.[55] The Financial Executives International, surveyed 217 firms with an average of $5 billion in revenues and found that the first-year 404 costs averaged $4.36 million per firm.[56] Some have argued that the cost burden for smaller companies are even more significant since costs are not generally proportionate to size.[57] In response to these concerns, the SEC has created an advisory committee to examine the impact of the legislation on smaller public companies.[58] These are only measures of direct cost. Additional and probably more important costs may arise from the fact that the prospect of such costs may deter companies from going public, or foreign companies from listing in the U.S. There is another side to costs, however—the potential costs to a company outside the U.S. that does *not* comply with Sarbanes-Oxley corporate governance rules. Moody's, the credit rating agency, said it would reassess the credit rating of companies that did not full audit internal controls.[59]

After intense lobbying by the European Union and small companies, in March 2005 the SEC extended the compliance dates for these firms from

---

[54] SEC Release Nos. 33-8238 and 34-47986 (June 5, 2003).
[55] D. Roberts, "Sarbanes-Oxley Compliance Costs Average $5m," *Financial Times*, November 12, 2004.
[56] http://www.fei.org/404_survey_3_21_05.cfm
[57] M. Morgenstern and P. Nealis, "The Impact of Sarbanes-Oxley on Mid-Cap Issuers," (2004).
[58] SEC Release No. 2004-174, December 16, 2004.
[59] Global Risk Regulator, "Capital Cost of Ducking Sarbanes-Oxley," (December 2004), p. 20.

July 15, 2005 to July 15, 2006.[60] The SEC was obviously concerned with the impact the prospect of large costs could have on foreign firms listing or continue to list in the U.S. and of small firms going public. In addition, in May 2005, the Commission issued a statement urging accounting firms to focus their energies (and fees) on controls that could have major risks rather than a check the box approach and to take a different approach for smaller companies.[61] It remains to be seen whether such guidance will have a substantial impact on cost reduction given the potential liability of management, boards and outside auditors for what prove in hindsight to be inadequate controls. Some groups, such as the Business Roundtable, believe the solution to the problem must involve limits on auditor liability.

Table 2B, below, looks at the applicability of the Sarbanes-Oxley and stock exchange rules to foreign issuers:

Table 2B	
Sarbanes-Oxley and Stock Exchange Treatment of Foreign Issuers	
CEO and CFO certifications of financial statements	Fully Applicable
Independent audit committee	Limited Exemptions
Outside auditor independence	Less stringent overall
Stock Exchange requirements	Exemption with disclosure of differences
Attorney Obligations	Fully Applicable
Continuous and Improved Disclosure	Fully Applicable
Auditor Registration	Selective recognition of foreign regimes

What explains this pattern? The SEC rules start with the premise of national treatment, but then take foreign problems into account by adjusting the overall standard where there might not be significant impact, and/or the statute does not permit differentiation, e.g. the level of audit partner rotations, or granting exemptions where there is a true conflict with foreign law, e.g. permitting labor representatives on the audit committee.

One interesting feature of the application of Sarbanes-Oxley to firms currently listed in the U.S. is the general difficulty foreign firms have in delisting to avoid the requirements. There is no general right to delist. The NYSE requires foreign firms to obtain the approval of the Board of Directors, publish a press release announcing the delisting and notifying at least its

---

[60] SEC Release No. 33-8545, 34-51923, March 2, 2005.
[61] SEC Release No. 2005-74, May 16, 2005.

largest 35 U.S. shareholders of the delisting. However, even if these conditions can be satisfied, the foreign firm would still be subject to the 1934 Act and Sarbanes-Oxley as long as its shares were held by more than 300 U.S. shareholders (500 for companies with less than $10 million in assets). As a practical matter, foreign firms would have to repurchase most of their U.S. shares.[62] This aspect of the regulatory regime has been attacked by European business leaders. A number of European companies have claimed they would withdraw from the U.S. if it were feasible. The European business leaders have proposed to the SEC that they exempt a company from U.S. reporting requirements, including Sarbanes-Oxley, if U.S. trading in its securities was less than 5 percent of global volume during a company's fiscal year. A second proposal would be to increase the minimum number of shareholders needed to trigger reporting from 300 to 3000. The third proposal would be to base the minimum number on a percentage of worldwide investors rather than an absolute figure.[63]

d.   U.S.-EU REGULATORY DIALOGUE

The impact of Sarbanes-Oxley on foreign firms created tensions with foreign countries, particularly Europe whose firms were most affected. Europe, an economy roughly the size of the U.S., has been the source of a significant demand for U.S. capital through the entry of its firms into U.S. public markets. Firms that had already entered were required to comply and could not easily withdraw from the public markets as just discussed, and firms that had considered entering U.S. markets now faced new and significant costs. In response to these problems, the United States and the European Union created a forum for discussion, called the U.S.-EU Regulatory Dialogue. On the U.S. side, the Treasury has taken the lead with the Federal Reserve and the SEC also participating. The EU Commission is the sole interlocutor for the EU. The dialogue process contributed to some of the SEC compromises on the application of Sarbanes-Oxley to foreign firms, e.g. allowing German firms to have labor representatives on its audit committee. The Dialogue had no formal role in this process—it was the SEC which had the authority to deal with the implementation of Sarbanes-Oxley. However, the Treasury's broad perspective on the U.S.-EU relationship and its deep concern with the health and efficiency of U.S. capital markets, may have contributed to the willingness of the SEC to react sympathetically to EU concerns. The major Sarbanes-Oxley issue still before the Dialogue is to ease the deregistration process for foreign firms seeking to exit the U.S. public markets.

There are other important issues on the Dialogue agenda including international accounting standards (examined below), the impact of the EU

---

[62] M. Perino, "American Corporate Reform Abroad: Sarbanes-Oxley and the Foreign Private Issuer," Working Paper, http://papers.ssrn.com/sol3/papers.cfm?abstract_id=439501.

[63] T. Tassell, "European Business Steps up SEC Battle," *Financial Times*, December 10, 2004.

Conglomerates Directive (examined in Chapter 4), and the implementation of the Basel II capital accord (examined in Chapter 7). In addition, the Dialogue may soon be moving to take a more proactive role—to eliminate barriers to the creation of a Trans-Atlantic capital market (TACM). TACM consists of the cross-border operations of securities firms (including banks in the securities business) and cross-border provision of securities products, like equity, debt and derivatives, sold by corporate and sovereign issuers. This could entail more attention on eliminating de facto barriers arising from different rules in the two markets on the offering, distribution, and trading of securities, as well as the enforcement of these rules, that impede further integration of the two markets.[64] This can be accomplished by aligning rules within the territory of both markets or by easing restrictions on engaging in offshore transactions as proposed at the end of this Chapter.

A major concern about the Dialogue is whether U.S.-EU financial issues can be resolved in isolation from greater differences between the two sides, over matters like Iraq and trade. One critical issue on the economic front is whether the U.S. and EU will seek to compete or collaborate. For example, the EU might respond to increasing U.S. regulation by providing a less regulated alternative, rather than pursuing efforts to relax U.S. regulation and further the integration of the two markets.

3.   INVESTMENT BANKING PRACTICES

a.   INDEPENDENT RESEARCH

Following the fall of Enron, questions arose in early 2002 as to why research analysts had not discovered the types of off-balance sheet transactions Enron was engaging in and disclosed this to their clients. This inquiry led to a more general inquiry into the independence of sell-side analysts, analysts of issues being underwritten by the banks. When the SEC was slow to act, during a period when its Chairman Harvey Pitt was under political attack, the lead in the investigation was taken by Eliot Spitzer, the New York Attorney General. The poster child of abuse was Jack Grubman, an analyst for Salomon Smith Barney, the investment banking arm of Citigroup, who had achieved fame and fortune in touting telecommunications issues underwritten by Salomon.[65]

In May 2002, NASD and the NYSE adopted rules to address analyst conflicts. The rules included requirements that prohibit analysts from: (1)

---

[64] See Statement of K. Dam and H. Scott, "The U.S.-E.U. Financial Markets Dialogue," Before the Committee on Financial Services, U.S. House of Representatives, June 17, 2004. See also Shadow Financial Regulatory Committee, "Toward a Single Transatlantic Market in Financial Services," Statement No. 203 (February 9, 2004).

[65] For a good summary of the history, see S. Hilgers, "Under the Influence: Analyzing Wall Street Research Analyst Conflicts of Interest and the Responses Designed to Induce Impartiality," 31 Securities Regulation L. J. 427 (2003).

offering or threatening to withhold a favorable research rating to induce investment banking business; (2) being supervised by the investment banking department; (3) trading in stocks prior to an IPO if the company is in the business sector that the analyst covers, and trading in any stock for some period after the release of a research report; and (4) sharing drafts of research reports with target companies other than to check facts with the approval of the firm's legal/compliance department (to avoid clients from influencing changes). In addition, firms cannot tie analyst compensation to investment banking business, must disclose investment banking business in research reports, and analysts must disclose any financial interest in excess of 1 percent of a company for which they issue a report. These proposals were approved by the SEC in May 2002.[66]

Spitzer and the SEC and NASD were not content to rest here. Instead, in October 2002, these regulators, together with the North American Securities Administrators Association (NASAA) and the NYSE, proposed to settle their claims with various securities firms by requiring them to fund a new independent research organization. This proposal was widely opposed by industry, including NASD, as monopolistic and overly expensive. On December 20, 2002, Spitzer, the SEC, NASD, the North American Securities Administrators, and the NYSE announced a new global settlement of all claims (the Agreement). The terms of the agreement include the severing of links between research analysts and investment banking, including compensation by investment banking for research and the practice of analysts accompanying bankers on road shows. The Agreement also banned spinning, the practice of allocating lucrative IPO shares to corporate executives and directors who are in the position to greatly influence decisions about procuring investment banking services. In addition, for a five-year period, the firms involved will have to contract with at least three independent research firms to provide research to the brokerage firm's customers. On April 28, 2003 the final terms of enforcement actions against ten investment firms and some high profile analysts like Jack Grubman, were announced. These firms were required to pay a total of $875 million in fines. $387.5 million consisted of disgorgement requirements, fund to be returned to investors who lost money as a result of the biased research. In addition, the firms agreed to fund $432.5 million in independent research and $80 million in investor education. Salomon Smith Barney led the way with total payments of $400 million. Finally, each firm must make publicly available its ratings and price target forecasts.

Subsequently in April 2003, the SEC adopted Regulation AC which requires that research reports contain certifications by analysts that their reports represent their own views and disclosures of any payments received in connection with specific recommendations.[67] This rule exempted from its

---

[66] SEC Release 2002-63.
[67] SEC Release No. 33-8193; 34-47384 (February 20, 2003).

application foreign persons located outside the U.S. not associated with a registered broker-dealer that provides research on foreign securities to major U.S. institutions. In addition, for research analysts employed by foreign persons outside the U.S., records of certification of independence made in connection with public appearances apply only to such appearances in the U.S. The SEC dropped the proposal that analysts make certain disclosures during public appearances, instead analysts must keep records of certification in connection with public appearances. And in April 2003, NASD and NYSE dropped its proposal that would have required newspapers and magazines to disclose analysts' stock ownership and other relationships with the companies they cover whenever analysts are interviewed by publications. Analysts would have been required to keep tabs on media compliance and decline further interviews by non-compliers. This spurred objections from the press.

While fines for misbehavior are clearly justified, it is unclear whether regulation of analysts is really needed. Recent research has shown that forecasts made by independent analysts are no more accurate or less biased than forecasts of analysts who face potential conflicts of interest. This result holds even for technology stocks in the late 1990s.[68] It also appears that analyst bias may be stronger for pure brokerage firms than investment banks that do both brokerage and underwriting, suggesting that the real problem is with the conflict between independent judgment and trading rather than underwriting.[69] In addition, one could argue that institutional investors can fend for themselves; they know sell-side analysts may be biased, and track and rate analysts' accuracy. As for retail investors, it is questionable whether regulators should be promoting so-called "independent" research; it would be better to use the money to educate these investors as to why they should *not* be purchasing individual stocks.[70] In addition, it has proved difficult for investors in lawsuits before arbitrators to prove that they lost money as a result of biased research rather than because of a downward turn of the market, further calling into question the extent to which the allegedly biased

---

[68] A. Agrawal and M. Chen, "Do Analyst Conflicts Matter? Evidence from Stock Recommendations," Working Paper (January 2005). See also, P. Bajari and J. Krainer, "An Empirical Model of Stock Analysts' Recommendations: Market Fundamentals, Conflicts of Interest, and Peer Effects," Working Paper (July 21, 2004). Also, A. Ljungqvist, F. Marston, L. Starks, and K. Wei, "Conflicts of Interest in Sell-side Research and the Moderating Role of Institutional Investors," Working Paper (January 18, 2005), find that potential bias is less likely in stocks followed by institutional investors because such firms rate analysts and pay for the research implicitly through soft dollars, e.g. higher trading commissions. Along the same lines, see A. Jackson, "Trade Generation, Reputation, and Sell-Side Analysts," LX The Journal of Finance 673 (April 2005), finding that both analysts with high reputations and those that are optimistic generate more trade for their brokerage firms, and suggesting that analyst optimism to generate trading revenue will persist after the split between research and investment banking.

[69] A. Cowen, B. Groysberg, and P. Healy, "Which Types of Analyst Firms Make More Optimistic Forecasts?," Harvard Business School Working Paper 04-009 (April 14, 2004).

[70] See Statement No. 192, Shadow Financial Regulatory Committee (May 5, 2003).

research caused harm.[71] The only reported case of liability so far is a $1 million arbitral award by a NASD arbitration panel.[72] In *Lentell v. Merrill Lynch & Co.*, 396 F.3d 161 (2nd Cir. 2005), the court dismissed a suit by investors claiming that Merrill's investment banking group had issued biased research reports on internet stocks. The court held that the investors failed to prove causation—that is, any connection between the alleged biased research and their losses. Later in 2005, the Supreme Court decided *Dura Pharmaceuticals v. Broudo,* Slip Opinion No. 03-932, April 19, 2005, making clear that investors must prove that any alleged misrepresentations actually caused their losses. It will be difficult for investors to show that biased research, as opposed to other factors, caused stocks to fall during the burst of the internet bubble.

Apart from whether the split between research and investment banking is necessary to reduce bias or will reduce bias, there is the additional concern of the cost of such regulation. Without investment bank funding, it may no longer be profitable to conduct research on smaller companies. In this regard, it appears that analyst coverage has significantly fallen since the global settlement.[73] It was also possible that, absent research competition, the biggest investment banks may garner a higher percentage of the IPO market. As in many other areas of capital market regulation, Europe has not followed the U.S. approach—it has not required the separation of research and investment banking. However, there may be other problems for analysts in those markets. For example, a French court held Morgan Stanley, which had Gucci as a client, liable for $38 million for defaming LVMH (a Gucci rival) in a critical research report

b.   AIDING AND ABETTING LIABILITY

An area of significant concern for the investment banking industry is possible liability for having aided companies to engage in questionable transactions, like those in Enron.

In March 2003, the SEC filed civil charges against Merrill Lynch for aiding and abetting Enron's securities fraud. Merrill settled for $80 million. Similar allegations were settled by JPMorgan Chase ($135 million) and Citigroup ($120 million). Merrill also faced U.S. criminal charges but agreed to adopt widespread internal reforms in exchange for the Department of Justice forgoing prosecution.[74] Four former Merrill bankers, including the

---

[71] S. Craig, "Despite Pact Over Research, Goal is Elusive," *The New York Times*, January 17, 2005.

[72] J. Anderson, "Merrill to Pay Florida Couple $1 Million," *The New York Times*, March 1, 2005.

[73] R. Wolff, "Security Analysis and Investor Relations: A New Partnership," reporting results of Zach's Investment Research that analysts fell from 6,072 in 1999 to 4,499 in 2003. http://search.netscape.com/ns/search?query=null

[74] C. Groofey, "Enron Accusations Force Banking Rethink," (November 2003) International Financial Law Review, pp. 26-29.

head of investment banking, have been criminally convicted for their role in aiding and abetting fraudulent Enron transactions. SEC charges are often followed by class action litigation in which the potential liability may be even more serious. In May 2004, Citigroup agreed to a $2.65 billion settlement of a suit brought by WorldCom investors. JPMorgan Chase followed by setting aside an additional $3.7 billion in reserves for its lawsuits. Another example of aiding and abetting liability is the case of the SEC against AIG, charging that the insurance company sold Brightpoint Inc., a mobile-phone distributor, a backdated insurance policy to cover up losses. AIG settled for a $10 million fine.[75]

Bankers may be exposed to aiding and abetting liability from not only regulators, but from other litigants, including trustees in bankruptcy or special masters of failed firms. Parmalat demonstrates that suits of this type may be filed by foreign trustees seeking to offset claims by creditors with liability claims against them. In Parmalat, for example, Citigroup claimed it was owed about $685 million (€536 million) but Enrico Bondi, the Italian government appointed administrator, sued Citigroup in New Jersey state court in 2004 for $10 billion in losses allegedly caused to Parmalat by Citigroup's attempts to aid Parmalat in disguising the true level of its debt.[76] Bondi has brought similar suits against a number of other banks.

Many of the aiding and abetting cases, such as Enron, have involved claims that investment banks, through the use of derivatives or other forms of structured finance, have helped corporations misstate their earnings. This has raised the troublesome question as to the line between good and bad practices. For example, it should be rather clear that a bank entering into a foreign exchange swap that enables its counterparty to hedge foreign exchange risk, and therefore to avoid losses if exchange rates move against it, has done nothing wrong. On the other hand, it should also be relatively clear that a bank that paid a client $100 for a loan worth $50, and received a commission of $10, with the right to resell the loan to the client at face value some time in the future, was enabling the client to misstate its net worth. But there is a lot of room in the middle of these two extreme examples. As we shall see in Chapters 12, 14, and 15, derivatives play an important role in the modern financial system in reducing risk. In trying to prevent misrepresentation, we must be careful not to go to far or we will increase risk for corporations and their shareholders.

In 2004, the SEC, along with other financial institution regulators, attempted to bring some clarity to this area by issuing a proposed Policy Statement describing the procedures financial institutions should follow with

---

[75] R. Smith and T. Francis, "AIG is Charged by SEC with Fraud," *The Wall Street Journal*, September 12, 2003.
[76] D. Reilly and A. Galloni, "Parmalat Overseer Files Suit in U.S. Against Citigroup," *The Wall Street Journal*, July 30, 2004.

respect to structured finance products.[77] The Statement also sets forth the types of transactions that should be scrutinized carefully for legal and reputational risk, including "transactions with questionable economic substance or business purpose or designed primarily to exploit accounting, regulatory or tax guidelines, particularly when executed at year end or at the end of a reporting period." In order to make such a judgment, the financial institution would have to understand how its client was going to use a particular product. The proposed Statement also would require the financial institution to inquire as to the client's accounting and disclosure of the transaction. Such disclosures and accounting treatment of the transaction as a whole may not be clear, however, at the time that the financial institution sells the structured product. Comments on the Proposed Statement were due by June 18, 2004. Yet, as of this writing, the regulators have not issued the Statement in final form, indicating that it has raised many difficult issues.[78]

Bankers are not the only ones being held responsible for corporate scandals. In a significant new development, outside directors of WorldCom who, like directors of other companies, were covered by corporate insurance and indemnities) have been required to put $25 million of their own money up to settle their portion of a class action lawsuit, representing about 20 percent of their combined personal net worth.[79]

c.   STATE AND/OR FEDERAL ENFORCEMENT

A continuing issue of concern has been the heavy involvement of state authorities, like Eliot Spitzer, the New York Attorney General, in the enforcement of securities laws. The question is whether state authorities have the necessary expertise (probably yes in the case of New York) or proper incentives. While the SEC balances enforcement against the needs and importance of well-functioning capital markets, state authorities may not. On the other hand, one would think that New York authorities would be aware of the big role the securities industry plays in its economy.

Interestingly, due to preemption under the National Bank Act, the states have little power over national banks. The Office of Comptroller of the

---

[77] Department of the Treasury, Office of Thrift Supervision, Federal Reserve System, Federal Deposit Insurance Corporation, SEC, Policy Statement: Interagency Statement on Sound Practices Concerning Structured Finance Activities, May 13, 2004.

[78] See e.g. Comment by Covington & Burling, SEC File No. S7-22-04, July 19

[79] J. Weil, "WorldCom's Ex-Directors Pony Up," *The Wall Street Journal*, January 6, 2005. While this settlement was temporarily invalidated when the judge overseeing the case ruled that the settlement was unfair to the remaining investment bank defendants because it prevented them from reducing their own liability by the amount of losses the jury might attribute to the responsibility of the directors. The last remaining investment bank defendant JPMorgan settled its portion of the case on March 17, 2005 for $2 billion and the settlement by the other remaining corporate defendant Arthur Andersen in April 2005, appeared to revive the settlement of the WorldCom directors. R. Sidel, "JPMorgan to Pay $2 Billion as Street's Bill for Bubble Soars," *The Wall Street Journal,* March 17, 2005.

Currency has the power under the National Bank Act to preempt state regulation, and national banks are shielded from state enforcement actions by the fact that "visitorial powers" reside exclusively in the federal domain.[80] This might be a more appropriate model for securities regulation than the current overlapping state and federal regime. Our capital markets are if anything more national and global than our banking markets, and thus should not be regulated by the states. Spitzer has played an important role in uncovering wrongdoing. He should bring his information to the SEC or if necessary the Congress or the people, rather than becoming an enforcer himself. Enforcement often takes the form of settlements, as in the analyst case, and such enforcement should weigh heavily the national concerns over the effectiveness of the capital markets that will not be uppermost in the minds of state officials. Federal regulation is also preferable because regulation is the purview of independent agencies like the SEC or Federal Reserve Board that are properly insulated from the political process. An elected New York attorney general is necessarily political. There is deep suspicion that elected officials may be partisan in enforcing the law. Recently the Chamber of Commerce and others have begun to openly question Spitzer's actions and motives.[81] Spitzer is currently running for Governor of New York and soliciting campaign contributions from businesses that could be the target of his investigations or prosecution. This creates a real perception of conflict of interest and risks being seen as extortion.[82]

Business, however, also thinks the enforcement effort has gone too far, in general. They have questioned whether SEC enforcement, which has greatly increased as a result of Spitzer's presence (the SEC has been attacked for not pursuing cases Spitzer has brought), has also gone too far. The Business Roundtable, which represents the chief executives of the nation's largest firms, says aggressive enforcement could be thwarting legitimate risk-taking.[83]

Some progress on conflict between state and federal regulations has been reported. A working group of 12 SEC and NASAA officials has been created.[84] However, this has limited utility if Spitzer and other state Attorneys General are not included. Spitzer, who announced his candidacy

---

[80] Office of the Comptroller of the Currency, Bank Activities and Operations; Real Estate Lending and Appraisals, Final rule, January 6, 2004 (regulations); Bank Activities and Operations, January 6, 2004 (visitorial powers).

[81] D. Wighton, "Spitzer Critics Determined To Turn Tables on NY Bogeyman," *Financial Times*, April 25, 2005.

[82] See the following articles: Daniel Gross, "Eliot Spitzer: How New York's Attorney General Became the Most Powerful Man on Wall Street," Slate.com, October 21, 2004; Mark Lasswell, "Spitzer's Blitz," Management Today, January 19, 2005; William J. Holstein, "The Candidate," *The Wall Street Journal*, April 19, 2005.

[83] A. Parker, "Backlash Against the Enforcer," *Financial Times*, March 17, 2005. Spitzer replied to his critics in an editorial in *The Wall Street Journal*, "Strong Law Enforcement is Good for the Economy," April 5, 2005.

[84] *The Wall Street Journal*, September 15, 2002.

for Governor of New York on December 7, 2004, was reported by *The New York Times* and *Financial Times* on December 25 to have said that "he believed the era of state attorneys general crusading against misdeeds on Wall Street was ending. He said he was concerned that 50 different investigations would balkanize regulations, and added that once-lax federal agencies had become more aggressive about rooting out fraud and wrongdoing."[85] Spitzer immediately issued a press release indicating that the lead line in *The New York Times* story that he would "cede investigations to federal authorities" was wrong. His release said that since federal enforcement had become more active it would be "less likely that states would have to take the lead or act alone in confronting new problems. He noted this as a positive development." He went on to say he would not withdraw from any area in which he was then involved or turn cases over to federal authorities.[86] Any way you read this, Spitzer envisions less of a role for the states in the future.

Another aspect of the enforcement debate is the appropriateness of using criminal prosecution against firms. As the case of Arthur Andersen shows (a federal prosecution) such actions can be a death sentence. This could have particular untoward effects in the case of financial firms whose failure could trigger a chain reaction of failures of other firms, nationally and abroad. The recent overthrow by the Supreme Court of the criminal conviction of Andersen, on the grounds that the jury was improperly instructed as to the requirement that Andersen "knowingly" engaged in a crime (destruction of documents) is a bitter irony—obviously the impact of this conviction to Andersen cannot be undone.[87]

It is a separate matter whether corporations should be the objective of civil fines. While such fines are ultimately usually borne by innocent shareholders, one SEC Commissioner, Roel Campos, has argued this is a cost that we must bear to deter corporate wrongdoing. On the other hand, two Republican Commissioners, Paul Atkins and Cynthia Glassman, voted against fines imposed against some corporations, in late 2004. Overall SEC fines have soared, rising 17 percent to $3 billion in fiscal year 2004, as compared with $1.39 billion in fiscal year 2003.[88]

One wonders whether fines and criminal actions against individuals would not be sufficient to achieve this end.[89] It is, however, likely that actions against key officials of corporations will also impose losses on shareholders.

---

[85] *The New York Times*, Section 1, Column 5.
[86] Press Release, Statement by the Office of New York Attorney General Spitzer, December 25, 2004.
[87] Arthur Andersen LLP v. United States, Slip Opinion No. 04-368, May 31, 2005.
[88] D. Solomon, "As Corporate Fines Grow, SEC Debates How Much Good They Do," *Financial Times*, November 12, 2004.
[89] R. Campos, "Regulators Must Not Abandon Corporate Penalties," *Financial Times*, April 13, 2005.

Also, the real losses to shareholders may result from the damage to the reputation of a company and its management from the public attention of charges of any kind. Marsh & McLennen reportedly lost $50 billion in value, 42 percent of its value in the month following Spitzer's announcement of his investigation on October 14, 2004, as compared to the $850 million fine it paid the State of New York. The possibility to inflict such staggering losses on investors counsels caution in going public with charges before the facts are fully vetted. Federal regulators or law enforcement officials are more likely to take such care than state politicians.

A key element in enforcement of securities laws against foreign issuers or financial firms is the ability to get cooperation from foreign enforcement officials. Key parts of the enforcement system are Memoranda of Understanding (MOUs) and Mutual Legal Assistance Treaties (MLATs) entered into between the United States and other countries. These agreements authorize foreign assistance in the investigation and prosecution of securities fraud.[90]

d.   RESTRICTIONS ON IPO ALLOCATIONS

As discussed above, the research analyst settlement of 2002 banned spinning, the practice of allocating lucrative IPO shares to corporate directors and directors. In 2003, the SEC fined Robertson Stephens $33 million for allocating IPOs in exchange for excessive commissions and markdowns from customers, practices that had been apparently prohibited by prior SEC and NASD rules.[91] These cases were followed by others in which civil charges were brought against underwriters for sharing profits with customers. In October 2003, a jury deadlocked in the criminal trial of Frank Quattrone, the former star technology banker at Credit Suisse First Boston. Quattrone had been charged with destroying evidence in connection with an SEC investigation of IPO allocations. Quattrone was convicted in a retrial in May 2004 and received a sentence of 18 months in prison. These cases were followed by new regulations.

In 1999, before the Voluntary Initiative and Report of the Advisory Committee (discussed below), NASD had proposed to the SEC to tighten its Rule 2790 by prohibiting NASD members from selling any "new issues" (not just "hot issues") to any account in which a "restricted person" (most broker-dealers, their affiliates, or other securities industry participants and related persons) has a beneficial interest. The premise for such a rule is the widely observed underpricing of IPOs, with the result that being allocated shares in

---

[90] See "International Securities Law Enforcement: Recent Advances in Assistance and Cooperation," (1994) 27 Vanderbilt Journal of Transnational Law, p. 635.
[91] The violation was illegal profit sharing that violated SEC Rule 15c1-2(b) and NASD Rule 2110 requiring "just and equitable principles of trade," an obviously capacious standard. See R. Levy, "The Law and Economics of IPO Favoritism and Regulatory Spin," December 2003.

an IPO has been of significant value. The Rule was approved by the SEC in October 2003.[92]

In 2003, attention continued to focus on IPO allocations.[93] Under the so-called "Voluntary Initiative" of the SEC, firms agreed to observe certain practices in allocations of "hot" IPOs, those that trade at a premium in the initial secondary market.[94] In addition, a NYSE/NASD IPO Advisory Committee, convened at the request of the SEC, issued a Report and Recommendations, May 2003 (Advisory Committee). These documents suggest that a prohibition be placed on the following types of IPO allocations to:

1. Officers/directors of existing investment banking clients, including family and friends;

2. Officers/directors of a U.S. public company in a "hot" IPO, "spinning";

3. Prospective investment banking clients;

4. Particular individuals selected by the underwriters;

5. Those agreeing to purchase more in the aftermarket, "laddering."

In addition, others have suggested prohibitions on allocations to other institutional customers, e.g. brokerage clients, large institutional buyers of the IPO, or those based on commitments to hold for given period of time.

The Advisory Committee also proposed a prohibition on discriminatory "flipping penalties," e.g. imposing penalties against individuals but not institutions that trade quickly after purchase.

What is the problem with the first four allocations listed above? Is there a diversion of corporate opportunities from the IPO issuer—giving away something of value that should go to the issuer? This should be curable by getting the issuer's consent. In fact, the issuer may choose to compensate the underwriter in soft dollars through this method. A 2004 study found that a significant determinant of IPO allocations to mutual funds was whether such funds directed significant brokerage to the underwriters. The study found that for every Dollar a mutual fund family paid for trade execution it earned back $1.17 through returns on underpriced IPOs in 1996-1998 and $5.14 in 1999, when first day returns on IPOs averaged 73 percent.[95] The author concludes that a substantial benefit from underpriced IPOs went to mutual funds; presumably the underwriters got back this value in brokerage

---

[92] SEC Release No. 34-48701.

[93] For a good survey of the economic literature on IPO allocations, see J. Ritter and I. Welsh, "A Review of IPO Activities, Pricing, and Allocations," NBER Working Paper 8805 (February 2002).

[94] SEC, "Voluntary Initiative Regarding Allocations of Securities in 'Hot' Initial Public Offerings to Corporate Executives and Directors," (September 5, 2003).

[95] J. Reuter, "Are IPO Allocations for Sale? Evidence from Mutual Funds," Working Paper (May 2004).

fees, although it does look like they overpaid. Are we to assume that the issuers were unaware that someone, whether underwriters or those to whom they allocated shares, was benefiting from the underpricing of shares? If so, this problem could be addressed by a disclosure requirement to issuers rather than restrictions on IPO allocations. On the other hand, there is some evidence that by the time pricing and allocation decisions are made by the underwriter the issuers have very little say in the process.[96] This may just be sour grapes on behalf of issuers who think their firms are worth more than they are. One would think that underwriters that take advantage of issuers at the last minute would incur substantial costs to their reputations even though the issuers are usually not themselves repeat players.

Some have argued that issuers permit the underpricing of securities because the managers of the issuers may be "bribed" through the promise of future rewards from the underwriters, e.g. giving the managers of the issuers future allocations of hot IPOs.[97] This would be a diversion of a corporate opportunity by the managers and would constitute a breach of their fiduciary duty to their companies; as such it would be illegal and already expose these managers to liability. Restrictions on allocations of IPOs have ranged far beyond prohibitions on allocating IPO shares to managers of issuers that previously engaged in IPOs. One must also consider the possibility that the issuers do not object to the managers receiving cheap IPO shares in the future—it is a soft way for the issuers to compensate their managers.

Interestingly, other markets have not pursued the U.S. approach to prohibiting particular IPO allocation practices. The EU has been entirely silent on the matter. The U.K regards IPO quid-pro-quo allocations as a questionable practice but focuses on disclosure to and consent by the issuer to allocations.[98]

In December 2004, the NYSE and NASD proposed to adopt rules restricting IPOs.[99] Their proposals provide, as to quid pro quo allocations, that underwriters may not offer or threaten to withhold shares on the basis of compensation that is excessive in relation to the services provided by the underwriter, e.g. an underwriter could not allocate shares to a mutual fund in exchange for excessive commissions on trades. As to spinning, the proposal provides that no underwriter may allocate IPO shares to an executive officer or a company if the underwriter has or expect to receive compensation for investment banking business from the person or firm to whom the shares are allocates. As to flipping, no underwriter may get a commission on shares

---

[96] M. Malone, Going Public 197-98 (1991).

[97] S. Griffith, "Spinning and Underpricing: A Legal and Economic Analysis of the Preferential Allocation of Shares in Initial Public Offerings," 69 Brooklyn L. Rev. 583, 616 (2004).

[98] Wilmer, Cutler & Pickering, EU Financial Services Briefing, "The FSA's Proposed Response to Conflicts of Interests in Relation to Investment Research and Issues of Securities," February 20, 2003.

[99] SEC, Release No. 34-50896, December 20, 2004.

flipped (bought and then sold) by a customer unless the underwriter has assessed a penalty bid against the flipper. In addition, the lead managing underwriter must provide the issuer with a regular report of indications of interest, including the names of interested institutional investors and the number of shares indicated by each, as well as a report of aggregate demand from retail investors. After the settlement, a report has to be made to the issuer about the allocations. Again the question is why the disclosure provisions do not suffice.

Also, in December 2004, the SEC proposed to amend Regulation M, which provides for anti-manipulation rules concerning securities offerings, to deal with laddering.[100] This proposal would lengthen the "restricted period," the period during which an underwriter cannot attempt to induce investors to make aftermarket bids or purchases. Currently, that period is generally 5 days before IPO pricing until the completion of the distribution. The Commission notes, however, that in its enforcement action against JPMorgan Securities, the attempts to induce after-market purchase occurred earlier in the underwriting process. As a result, the Commission proposes to restrict such attempts as soon as an issuer reaches an understanding that a broker-dealer is to act as its underwriter or at such time that the broker-dealer becomes a participant in the distribution. The Commission's proposal would also address allocations by prohibiting conditioning or "tying" an allocation of shares on an agreement by the customer to buy shares in another less desirable ("cold") offering, or to pay excessive trading commissions on unrelated securities transactions—these proposals overlap with the NYSE and NASD proposals.

There is a substantial literature showing that the allocations of shares in an IPO is an important part of bookbuilding, the process in what shares are allocated in exchange for information about investor demand.[101] While this practice cannot explain some of the allocations, one must be careful in reforming the IPO process not to prevent what has proved to be a very efficient pricing system.

One way to avoid IPO allocation problems is for the issuer to auction its shares. Google, the search engine company, used a "Dutch" auction in its IPO. In a pure Dutch auction, bids are accepted starting with the highest and moving down until all shares are sold. The price is the clearing price, the highest price that insures all offered shares are sold. The Google auction received mix reviews. Some said it was a failure because the $85 price was 37

---

[100] SEC Release Nos. 33-8511; 34-50831, December 9, 2004.

[101] F. Cornelli and David Goldreich, "Bookbuilding and Strategic Allocation," 56 J. of Finance 2337, 2340 (2001). But see F. Degeorge, F. Derrien, and K. Womack, "Quid Pro Quo in IPOs: Why Bookbuilding is Dominating Auctions," European Corporate Governance Institute Finance Research Paper 65/2005 (November 2004) (book-built issues are more likely to be followed and recommended by analysts and supported in the aftermarket, but there are no valuation or return differentials to suggest these types of promotion produce value for issuers).

percent lower than the top of the range it had declared to the SEC the previous month and only 19.6 million shares were sold rather than the expected 25.7 million–presumably more shares could only be sold at a lower clearing price. It is unclear whether these difficulties resulted from the nature of the auction or a poor IPO market for tech stocks.[102] This risks overpayment by retail investors, with subsequent recrimination and lawsuits. Retail investors were deterred in part by the difficulty in mastering the procedures for participating in the auction. Ironically, one commentator gloated that the IPO was a success because the stock traded close to its $85 auction price the day after the offering—no money was left on the table, he said.[103] Two days later, however, the stock was trading at $108.31, up 27 percent from its offering price.

4.   SPECIAL RULES FOR FOREIGN PRIVATE ISSUERS (APART FROM SARBANES-OXLEY)

Accommodation to foreign issuers started early in the SEC's history when foreign issuers were exempted in 1935 from the proxy rules (§14) and the short-swing profits rules (§16) of the 1934 Act. The proxy rules give shareholders rights in the governance of the issuer, while the short-swing profit rules prevent insiders or 10 percent shareholders from selling stock within six months of a purchase or purchasing within six months of a sale.

The SEC currently makes other important regulatory accommodations for "foreign private issuers." A foreign private issuer is defined in Rule 3b-4 of the Exchange Act of 1934 and Rule 405 of the Securities Act of 1933 to include all foreign issuers other than: (1) foreign governments; and (2) foreign issuers that have more than 50 percent of their outstanding voting securities held of record by U.S. residents and that also have: (a) U.S. citizens or residents making up a majority of their executive officers and directors; and (b) more than 50 percent of their assets located in the United States or have their business administered principally in the United States.[104]

a.   THE RULE 12G3-2(b) EXEMPTION

The Rule 12g3-2(b) exemption establishes special rules for continuous reporting by foreign issuers. Companies with total assets over $5 million and a class of equity held by at least 500 shareholders, of whom 300 reside in the United States, are subject to the reporting requirements of the Exchange Act of 1934. Rule 12g3-2(b) of the 1934 Act, first adopted in 1967, exempted non-

---

[102] K. Delaney and R. Sidel, "Engine Trouble: How Miscalculations and Hubris Hobbled Celebrated Google IPO," *The Wall Street Journal*, August 19, 2004.

[103] J. Surowiecki, "Comment: Ignore Wall St's Whining: Google's IPO Worked," *Financial Times*, August 20, 2004.

[104] See S. Kinsey, "Foreign Private Issuers," Securities and Commodities Regulation 79 (April 25, 2001).

U.S. companies from the reporting requirements of the Exchange Act so long as they did not make public offerings in the United States or list their shares on a U.S. securities exchange (including the NYSE and NASDAQ), provided that the companies furnished the SEC with copies of material information made public in their local jurisdictions or sent to foreign investors in their securities (home country reports). The SEC described the reason for this exemption as follows:

> "[A] distinction is made between foreign issuers that voluntarily enter the United States securities markets and those companies whose securities are traded in the United States without any significant voluntary acts or encouragement by the issuer. Currently, this distinction is accomplished by deeming all foreign companies having either securities listed on a United States exchange or having made a public offering of securities registered under the Securities Act as having voluntarily entered the United States market. Other foreign companies whose securities are traded in the United States through no direct acts of the issuers are deemed not to have taken any voluntary acts to enter the United States markets."[105]

There may be three additional reasons for the adoption of the Rule: (1) that the SEC was relatively satisfied in 1967 with the level of information being disclosed by non-U.S. companies in their home markets; (2) there was no reason to believe a significant U.S. shareholder base would develop for issuers relying on the rule; and (3) the world's capital markets were not nearly as integrated as they are today.[106]

The Rule originally discriminated between the trading of foreign securities on organised stock markets like NYSE where securities must be registered and are fully subject to the 1934 Act reporting requirements, and stock traded through other means, as through NASDAQ, OTCBB and the Pink Sheets, where the Rule 12g3-2(b) exemption applied. In 1983, the SEC revised the Rule by terminating the exemption for foreign issuers quoted on NASDAQ; however, the SEC grandfathered indefinitely securities of foreign issuers who were in compliance with the terms of the exemption and listed on NASDAQ as of October 6, 1983.[107]

In March 1997, the SEC required that securities traded on OTCBB be registered under §12 of the '34 Act, as of April 1, 1998. While the Commission acknowledged the transparency benefits (dissemination of price information) of trading foreign issues on OTCBB, as compared with the Pink Sheets,

---

[105] "Integrated Disclosure System for Foreign Private Issuers, Securities Act Release No. 6360" (November 20, 1981) [1981-1982 Transfer Binder] Fed. Sec. L. Rep. (CCH) & 83,054, at pp. 84,643.

[106] E. Greene, D. Braverman, and S. Sperber, "Hegemony or Deference: U.S. Disclosure Requirements in the International Capital Markets," (1995) 50 Business Lawyer, pp. 413, 426-429.

[107] Exchange Act Release No. 20264, 48 Federal Register 46,736 (October 6, 1983).

which only provide for non-firm quotations updated twice daily, it believed transparent trading in unregistered stock was inconsistent with the full disclosure rationale of the securities laws.[108]

The March 1997 SEC policies forced over 3500 firms that were not registered to either become registered or move to the Pink Sheets. 75 percent of these firms moved to the Pink Sheets, where they were not subject to disclosure requirements. This movement had a negative impact on the stock prices of these firms and resulted in permanent decreases in liquidity.[109]

Some have argued that the exemption should be repealed entirely, with the effect that all foreign issues trading in the U.S. would be subject to registration and reporting requirements, but this would force such securities to be traded abroad where there would well be fewer protections for U.S. investors.

b.   MORE ONEROUS RULES FOR FOREIGN ISSUERS

On May 8, 2001, outgoing Acting SEC Chairman Laura Unger sent a letter to Frank Wolf, Chairman of the U.S. House Appropriations Sub-committee that regulates the SEC, indicating that the SEC will require overseas companies to disclose if they are doing business in any countries where U.S. sanctions apply, e.g. Iran, Sudan, and Libya. Unger wrote: "[o]ur aim is to make available to investors additional information about situations in which the material proceeds of an offering could—however indirectly—benefit countries, governments, or entities that, as a matter of U.S. foreign policy, are off-limits to U.S. companies."[110] Wolf was apparently furious that PetroChina, a Chinese national oil company, was able to get a New York listing in 2000 when it was selling oil to Sudan. This requirement would be one of the few cases in which special requirements are imposed on foreign issuers.

c.   THE RELAXATION OF OTHER RULES

In January 1997, the SEC adopted a new Regulation M which significantly eased restrictions on trading new foreign issues during their distribution.[111] Actively traded equities, those with an average daily trading volume of $1 million or more and a public float of at least $150 million, were exempted from any restrictions. It has been argued that this "would effectively result in the worldwide implementation of pricing and stabilizing activities conducted on the basis of home-country regulation and practice subject to the general anti-fraud requirements of the U.S. securities laws

---

[108] SEC Release No. 34-38456 (March 31, 1997).
[109] B. Bushee and C. Leuz, "Economic Consequences of SEC Disclosure Regulation: Evidence from the OTC Bulletin Board," 39 J. of Accounting and Economics (forthcoming 2005).
[110] E. Alden, "SEC Seeks Closer Watch on Overseas Groups," *Financial Times*, May 11, 2001.
[111] 62 Federal Register 520 (January 3, 1997).

[which remain applicable]."[112] It appears that these domestic reforms were in part motivated to bring U.S. rules more into line with those in other major markets, thereby facilitating "global" offerings.

On October 19, 1999, the SEC adopted a number of exemptions to tender offer rules and registration requirements which made it easier for foreign issuers and bidders to engage in transactions with U.S. security holders of non-U.S. companies.[113]

The NYSE has proposed exempting "world class" foreign companies, defined as those with revenue of $5 billion, and market capitalization of $2 billion, or average weekly trading volume outside the United States of at least $1 million or 200,000 shares from GAAP reconciliation, permitting them instead to submit their independently home audited financial statements, as long as they included a written explanation of any material differences between home country and U.S. accounting practices.[114] Under s. 105 of the National Securities Market Improvement Act of 1996, the SEC now has explicit authority to exempt securities of large companies from normal registration requirements.

Notes and Questions

1.   What are the major problems encountered by foreign companies in issuing securities in the U.S. market through a public offering?

2.   Sarbanes-Oxley covers a wide range of corporate governance and disclosure issues. Foreign firms have been subject to some but not all of these new requirements. Is there any consistent pattern in the exemption policies? How should one decide this question? Do you expect that these new rules will increase the reluctance of foreign firms to list in the United States?

3.   What do you think of the PCAOB's selective recognition approach?

4.   Should Regulation FD be applied to foreign issuers?

5.   Should foreign firms be given national treatment, or better or worse than national treatment?

6.   Do you think enforcement of securities and fraud laws against securities firms has gone too far? Secretary of Treasury Snow questioned this in December 2004, suggesting that criminalizing mistakes could have extraordinary negative long-term consequences.[115] How would you evaluate

---

[112] D. Brandon and G. Reiter, "Regulators Move to Harmonise Capital Markets Rules," *International Financial Law Review*, pp. 53-54 (June 1996).

[113] Release No. 33-7759 (October 22, 1999).

[114] J. Cochrane, "Are U.S. Regulatory Requirements for Foreign Firms Appropriate," (1994) 17 *Fordham International Law Journal*, p. 558.

[115] J. Calmes and D. Solomon, "Snow Says 'Balance' Is Need in Enforcing Sarbanes-Oxley Law," *The Wall Street Journal*, December 17, 2004.

the costs and benefits of the explosion in capital markets regulation post-Enron?

7. While the issue of who should enforce, with respect to capital markets regulation, has focused on federal versus state enforcement, and government versus SRO enforcement, there is also the question of who should enforce at the federal level. Currently, federal regulation is fragmented for financial firms—various agencies, e.g. the Federal Reserve and the Office of the Comptroller of the Currency, regulate banks, while the SEC regulates securities firms. To some extent the jurisdiction of these regulators overlaps, as when the SEC seeks to regulate securities activities within banks, as opposed to in banking affiliates, or when the Federal Reserve regulates bank holding companies which include securities firms. Periodic proposals have been put forward to consolidate these regulators, much as the United Kingdom has done when it created the Financial Services Agency. Such reforms have foundered on the desire of agencies and their client firms to maintain separate identities.[116] One reason for considering consolidation that has not been given much attention is that the existing structure focuses primary attention on the issues with respect to the particular firms or markets within the jurisdiction of various regulators without enough consideration on how the activities of the various agencies impact the capital markets or the financial system as a whole.[117]

8. A key rationale for many of the capital market reforms post-Enron is the problem of conflicts of interest. This concern is uppermost in the corporate governance reforms of Sarbanes-Oxley (agents (managers) have different incentives than their owners (shareholders)), the research analyst settlement (the analyst has a conflict between his role as an analyst and his support of the investment bankers), and controls on IPO allocations (the underwriter has a conflict between what is best for his firm and his duty to his client), and aiding an abetting cases (bankers have conflict between role as lender and role as financial adviser; auditors have conflict between role as auditor and role as consultant). Are these real conflicts of interest? If so, should/can they be controlled by regulation in the form of prohibitions–the basic approach post-Enron—or by market discipline, requiring disclosure of the conflicts and relying on the market to police and penalize it?[118]

---

[116] For the latest comprehensive review of the regulatory structure, see U.S. Government Accountability Office, Financial Regulation: Industry Changes Prompt Need to Reconsider Regulatory Structure (October 2004).

[117] Id., at 113.

[118] I. Walter, "Conflicts of Interest and Market Discipline," in C. Borio, W. Hunter, G. Kaufman and K. Tsatsaronis, eds., *Market Discipline Across Countries* 175 (2004).

C.   International Disclosure Standards

In September 1998, the International Organization of Securities Commissioners (IOSCO) issued a consultation document for comment entitled *International Disclosure Standards for Cross-Border Offerings and Initial Listings by Foreign Issuers*. IOSCO formulated a common prospectus that would be used for cross-border offerings and initial listings. The proposal does not include financial statements; work in this area is left to the International Accounting Standards project. IOSCO sought harmonization for international securities transactions. The proposal is organized in two parts. Part I contains information that would be disclosed in a standardized way in all jurisdictions; it includes information that any jurisdiction would already require, e.g. business overview, risk factors, etc., and describes such information in general terms. Part II deals with "disclosure issues outside the scope of the standards," such as materiality, projections and forward looking information, indemnification of directors and officers, and derivatives and market risk. This Part formulates no harmonized standards; instead, it discusses differences among countries on the issues. On September 28, 1999, the SEC adopted a complete revision of Form 20-F which contains the basic disclosure requirements applicable to foreign private issuers based on the IOSCO proposals.[119] This change effects no real relaxation in standards for foreign issuers since the IOSCO proposals basically mimicked existing U.S. requirements.[120]

Countries have taken different approaches to implementing IOSCO rules. Whereas the U.S. and Switzerland apply the rules only to foreign issuers-they are optional, foreign issuers can use U.S. or IOSCO rules-Singapore and Mexico have adopted the rules for both foreign and domestic issuers.[121]

D.   U.S. GAAP and International Accounting Standards

1.   GAAP Reconciliation

In addition to the stringent disclosure requirements of U.S. securities laws, the need to reconcile financial statements with U.S. generally accepted accounting principles (GAAP) has been a major obstacle to foreign companies listing on U.S. exchanges. Reconciliation can be not only time consuming and

---

[119] Release Nos. 33-7745 (September 28, 1999).

[120] See M. Joseph, "How to Meet the SEC's New Form 20-F Rules," (February 2001) International Financial Law Review, p. 14.

[121] S. Wolff, "Implementation of International Disclosure Standards," (2001) 22 University of Pennsylvania Journal of International Economic Law, p. 91.

costly, but conceptually difficult as well. Fundamental categories or concepts in GAAP may not have obvious counterparts in the foreign system.[122]

To avoid these difficulties, a number of German companies attempted to get the SEC to waive the GAAP reconciliation requirements during the early 1990s. In rejecting the proposal, the SEC cited a number of fundamental incompatibilities between the German accounting system and the GAAP, such as German treatment of hidden reserves which allowed German companies to moderate differences in reported income during lean and prosperous years.

Ultimately, Daimler-Benz (one of the companies seeking the original waiver) was successful in negotiating an agreement with the SEC. As part of the compromise, Daimler-Benz agreed to disclose all hidden reserves.[123] A number of other German firms, including Deutsche Telekom and Veba, have followed Daimler-Benz in entering the U.S. capital market. Nonetheless, the general reluctance of German and Swiss firms to seek a listing indicates a concern with GAAP reconciliation even as somewhat relaxed by the SEC.

In April 2004, Credit Suisse, a major Swiss Bank, suffered a severe downward restatement of its 2003 profits after its first-time adoption of U.S. GAAP. Net profits sank to SFr 770 million ($593 million) from SFr 5 billion reported under Swiss accounting standards. Credit Suisse is the only European bank to move to full-scale U.S. GAAP other than Deutsche Bank. Other listed banks reconcile to but do not state their accounts in U.S. GAAP.[124]

German officials have been very critical of the United States position on the necessity for U.S. GAAP reconciliation to obtain a listing. Herbert Biener, Ministerialrat at the German Justice Ministry and the senior civil servant for accounting has stated:

> "In 1991 in Germany, 578 foreign enterprises were listed on stock exchanges. Although they publish only their original financial

---

[122] The requirement for U.S. GAAP reconciliation is based largely on the asserted need for U.S. investors to be able to compare the performance of foreign and U.S. firms. Some finance researchers believe national accounting results can be compared through a "universal translator," a valuation model under which accounting numbers produced under alternative national systems could be translated into consistent measures of firm value. R. Frankel and C. Lee, "Accounting Diversity and International Valuation," NYSE Working Paper 96-01 (1996).

[123] J. Hicks, "The Listing of Daimler-Benz A.G. Securities on the NYSE: Conflicting Interests and Regulatory Policies," (1994) 37 German Yearbook of International Law, pp. 360, 369. See also L. Radebaugh, G. Gebhardt and S. Gray, "Foreign Stock Exchange Listings: A Case Study of Daimler-Benz," (1995) 6 Journal of International Financial Management, p. 2. In addition to the problems Daimler-Benz had in complying with SEC rules, banks had even more problems. For example, Deutsche Bank that owned a substantial portion of many German companies, including 12 percent of DaimlerChrysler, would have to incorporate the financial statements (under GAAP rules) of many of those companies into its own. Perhaps to resolve such difficulties, Deutsche Bank announced plans to move $28.3 billion of its stakes in German companies into newly formed fund management subsidiaries.

[124] H. Simonian, "Credit Suisse Suffers Impact of U.S. Rules," *Financial Times*, April 28, 2004.

statements without reconciliation to German accounting standards, damages to investors have not been reported. A deficiency of comparability of financial statements is therefore no reason for denying mutual recognition. There is no doubt that improved comparability is helpful but, in a market economy, this issue can be solved by competition. If investors prefer enterprises to give comparable information, competitors will consider whether in this case additional information should be used to influence the market price of their securities."[125]

It seems that choice of accounting rules can indeed influence the price of a stock. C. Leuz and R. Verrecchia have found that German firms, which switch from German to U.S. GAAP or International Accounting Standards, have lower bid-asked spreads and higher trading volume, indicating investors believe that the switch has reduced information asymmetry.[126]

2. INTERNATIONAL ACCOUNTING STANDARDS

In April 1994, the SEC eased the GAAP reconciliation requirements for foreign issuers by permitting foreign issuers to file a cash flow statement prepared in accordance with International Accounting Standard (IAS) No. 7 without reconciliation to U.S. GAAP. First-time foreign issuers were only required to reconcile their past two years financial statements (reduced from five years). Some other more minor reconciliation changes were also made. The Commission also accepted further use of IAS standards in lieu of GAAP reconciliation with respect to hyperinflationary accounting[127] and certain business combinations.[128]

In July 1995, the International Organization of Securities Commissions (IOSCO) and the International Accounting Standards Committee (IASC) announced a program to develop a set of accounting standards for companies seeking a listing in global markets and for the raising of cross-border capital. This project resulted in the formulation of 12 standards and was completed in December 1998. They are already accepted by the London Stock Exchange and almost all other European exchanges. IOSCO endorsed these standards in May 2000, but envisioned that regions like the EU or individual countries could require reconciliations to local standards or additional disclosures.[129]

---

[125] H. Biener, "What Is the Future of Mutual Recognition of Financial Statements and Is Comparability Really Necessary," (1994) 3 The European Accounting Review, pp. 335, 341.

[126] C. Leuz and R. Verrecchia, "The Economic Consequences of Increased Disclosure," (2001) 38 J. of Accounting Research, p. 91.

[127] P. Meller, "International Auditing Rules Urged on U.S.," *The New York Times*, February 22, 2002.

[128] 59 Federal Register 65637 (1994).

[129] BNA World Securities Law Report (June 2000).

In its endorsement of the IASC standards, IOSCO stated that national regulators should be able to supplement the IOSCO standards: "Those supplemental treatments are: reconciliation: requiring reconciliation of certain items to show the effect of applying a different accounting method, in contrast with the method applied under IASC standards; disclosure: requiring additional disclosures, either in the presentation of the financial statements or in the footnotes; and interpretation: specifying use of a particular alternative provided in an IASC standard, or a particular interpretation in cases where the IASC standard is unclear or silent. In addition, as part of national or regional specific requirements, waivers may be envisaged of particular aspects of an IASC standard, without requiring that the effect of the accounting method used be reconciled to the effect of applying the IASC method. The use of waivers should be restricted to exceptional circumstances such as issues identified by a domestic regulator when a specific IASC standard is contrary to domestic or regional regulation."[130]

a.   THE SEC POSITION

The SEC has generally encouraged this development while reserving judgment as to whether it will allow such standards to be used in lieu of U.S. GAAP. The primary concern has been that IASC have a mechanism to provide ongoing interpretations of the type available in the United States through the Financial Accounting Standards Board (FASB). Another is that the standards measure up to U.S. standards. A FASB study found 255 variations between U.S. accepted accounting practices and international standards, many of which were significant.[131] Finally, both the SEC and FASB have insisted that IASC be structured in such a way as to be independent from political and industry pressure.

On February 16, 2000, the SEC issued a Concept Release on International Accounting Standards.[132] which sought to determine under what conditions it should accept financial statements of foreign private issuers using IAS. The IAS Release continued to call attention to significant differences between U.S. GAAP and IAS, as well as the fact that IASC standards were more general and less detailed than U.S. rules. The Release expressed concern that IAS rules could be implemented differently in different jurisdictions and sought ways to reduce the development of diverging interpretations of IASC standards.

The SEC Release envisioned three ways in which IAS might be implemented in the U.S. First, the U.S. might implement selected IASC standards, and then follow up with others based on review of the effect of the

---

[130] IASC Standards Assessment Report: Report of the Technical Committee of the International Organisation of Securities Commissions (May 2000).
[131] FASB, The IASC-US Comparison Project (1997).
[132] Release Nos. 33-7801, 34-42430 (IAS Release).

initial step. Second, it could rely on IASC standards for recognition and measurement principles but require U.S. GAAP and SEC supplemental disclosure requirements for footnote disclosures and the level of detail in line items in financial statements. Or third it could accept IASC entirely.[133]

IASC seemed to have successfully addressed its governance issues.[134] But the favorable environment to U.S. allowance of IAS standards in some form was significantly altered by the Enron-Andersen scandal of 2001-2002. This led to the prospect of more rather than less U.S. control over accounting standards for companies with significant U.S. investors. Those favoring U.S. allowance of IAS have tried to turn Enron to their advantage. For example, Sir David Tweedie and Paul Volcker have stressed the independence of the IASC Board from industry pressure as compared with FASB.[135] And Frederik Bolkestein, the former European Union Commissioner in charge of financial services and tax issues, has touted the virtues of IAS in light of the failure of U.S. GAAP to stop Enron's off-books transactions. Bolkestein claims the more general rules of IAS compared to the detailed approach of U.S. GAAP is less likely to be circumvented.[136]

A major breakthrough in the SEC's acceptance of IAS standards occurred in April 2005 after a meeting with officials from the European Union. The SEC indicated that it had developed a "roadmap" with the goal of accepting IAS for foreign companies by 2009. This acceptance would depend on "a detailed analysis of the faithfulness and consistency of the application and interpretation of IFRS in financial statements across companies and jurisdictions" as well as continued progress in the IASB-FASB convergence project discussed below.[137] A key part of the process will be SEC review of reconciliations between IFRS and U.S. GAAP. This will begin in 2006 as European companies that have adopted IFRS for their 2005 financial statements—see discussion below—file reconciliation statements in 2006.

---

[133] SEC Concept Release on International Accounting Standards, Release Nos. 33-7801, 34-42430 (February 16, 2000).

[134] Outgoing SEC Chairman Levitt headed a nominating Committee to select 19 Trustees who, in turn, appoint Members of the IASC Board, the Standing Interpretations Committee, and a new Standards Advisory Council. The Trustees have now been chosen, and the chairman is former Federal Reserve Board Chairman Paul Volcker, the world's most respected person in international finance, and the other trustees are extremely distinguished. A respected European, Sir David Tweedie, has been selected as the Chairman of the IASC Board.

[135] M. Peel, "Volcker Urges Global Body for Accounts," *Financial Times*, February 14, 2002.

[136] P. Meller, "International Auditing Rules Urged on U.S.," *The New York Times*, February 22, 2002.

[137] SEC Release No. 2005-62 (April 21, 2005). Interestingly, the EU press release announcing the same development described an "agreement" on a roadmap and anticipates acceptance in 2007 but no later than 2009. The 2007 date and the term "agreement" are conspicuously absent from the SEC release. See EU Commission Delegation in Washington, D.C., April 21, 2005, www.eurunion.org. The details of the roadmap were oddly released in the form of a forthcoming law review article by the SEC's Chief Accountant. See D. Nicolaisen, "Statement by SEC Staff: A Securities Regulator Looks at Convergence," 25 Northwestern University Journal of International Law and Business Vol. 25 No. 3 (April 2005).

b.   Viability of Multiple Accounting Standards

Even if the U.S. were to allow IAS standards (also known as International Financial Reporting Standards, or IFRS), it would seem unlikely that they would be required for all companies, foreign and domestic. Given the general preference of regulators for U.S. standards and the difficulties of a massive conversion it is much more likely that IAS standards will only be optional for foreign companies. If the option were to be only given to foreign firms, there would be issues concerning the competitive effects of such a system, i.e. domestic firms might be at a competitive disadvantage. Who would enforce such IAS standards would also be an issue. It seems likely that the SEC would insist on a major enforcement role for securities sold to U.S. investors under IAS standards. If national bodies generally enforced IAS rules, particularly given their generality, this could result in uneven application of such rules.[138]

On the other hand, Leuz found in his study of the German "New Market" (a market for small and medium high tech companies launched in 1997 and which collapsed in 2003), where firms had the choice to use U.S. GAAP or IFRS, that bid-ask spreads were unaffected by such choice. This suggests that there might not be much difference in the informational content of these two standards.[139]

There is a significant question whether convergence toward one rule is desirable. Accounting rules reflect, to a significant extent, real differences between countries. Thus, for example, rules requiring defined benefit pension plans to mark assets to market, and thus reveal funding gaps, might have more impact in countries with defined benefit as opposed to defined contribution plans where assets are always equal to liabilities. Also, the U.S. rule-based rather than principle-based approach may be responsive to the more intense legal liability environment in the U.S. Principles may offer less solace to companies looking for certain rules to follow in order to avoid liability. On the other hand, it could be argued that the U.S. "bright line" rules have not resulted in less liability for U.S. accounting firms because plaintiff lawyers can still claim the bright lines do not apply or that the case is governed by one bright line rather than another. There is also the question of whether one standard would preclude useful experimentation and the development of valid alternative models. Finally, there is the practical question as to whether convergence can occur when both sets of rules are constantly changing independently.

---

[138] See R. Dye and S. Sunder, "Why Not Allow FASB and IASB Standards to Compete in the U.S.?," (September 2001) 15 Accounting Horizons, p. 257.

[139] C. Leuz, "IAS versus U.S. GAAP, Information Asymmetry—Based Evidence from Germany's 'New Market,'" 41 Journal of Accounting Research 445 (2003).

c.   CONVERGENCE

In September 2002, IASB and FASB announced a short-term convergence project with the objective of reducing the differences between IAS and U.S. GAAP. It appears that at best, in the short-term, this will produce convergence of principles rather than detailed rules. In October 2003, IASB and FASB reached tentative agreements on some common standards for accounting for business combinations, specifically whether and when liabilities, like "golden parachutes," of the acquired company should be passed onto the balance sheet of the merged entity.[140] In another example of convergence, IASB has adopted the FASB approach to some issues about stock options. These two organizations actively continue to work on convergence.[141]

d.   EUROPEAN ADOPTION OF IAS AND THE PROBLEM OF ACCOUNTING FOR FINANCIAL INSTRUMENTS

Europe has adopted IFRS for European listed companies as of January 1, 2005,[142] and more than 90 other countries will do the same. The EU has also required that its member states set up appropriate enforcement bodies. The United States is the principal holdout. The European Commission approved these standards in October 2004, subject to changes in the most controversial part of IAS, IAS 39 dealing with accounting for financial instruments, including derivatives.[143] Some background on IAS 39 follows.

IAS 39 as proposed in a June 2002 Exposure Draft, as further refined in a December 2003 standard, permitted entities to designate assets or liabilities that could be irrevocably be designated to be measured at fair value with the effect that gains or losses on these items would be recognized in profit or loss. Fair value was defined as "the amount for which an asset could be exchanged, or a liability settled, between knowledgeable, willing parties in an arm' length transaction. Fair value would be established by market prices, or in the absence of such prices by a valuation technique. The reason for providing this option is that the prior proposal could have resulted in a mismatch between assets and liabilities, with one measured at fair value and the other at historical amortized cost. Such mismatches could increase earnings volatility. Hedge accounting rules partially addressed this issue, but only when the position qualified as a hedge. Due to IAS 39's restrictions on hedge accounting, there appeared to be the possibility of many such cases.

This proposal received a great deal of criticism. First, there was concern with the concept of fair value itself—using a value that could not

---

[140] 81 BNA Banking Report 621 (October 27, 2003).
[141] See FASB, Project Updates, Short-Term International Convergence, March 10, 2005.
[142] Regulation (EC) no. 1606/2002 of the European Parliament and the Council, July 19, 2002.
[143] See Commission Regulation (EC) No. 2086/2004 of November 19, 2004, O.J. L363/1, December 9, 2004.

really be verifiable. There was further concern that use of the option might increase rather than decrease volatility if an entity applied the option to only one part of the matched position. Finally, if the option were applied to financial liabilities, it might result in the entity recognizing gains or losses due to changes in its own creditworthiness. Most perversely, according to bank regulators, a reduction in the creditworthiness of a bank could increase its profit by decreasing the value of its liabilities.[144] Others also noted that the Board had introduced the fair value option despite there not being an equivalent option in U.S. GAAP.

In April 2004, IASB made a new proposal. First, it restricted using the fair value option to cases where the fair value was verifiable. For financial institutions, it was envisioned that guidance on the application of this standard could come from supervisors. Secondly, if one used fair value for one side of a matched position, one would be required to use if for the other side as well.

IASB made no changes during this period in its basic approach of requiring derivatives to be marked-to-market where market prices were available. To the extent that such derivative positions are not hedged (which might not be the case, particularly given the restrictions on hedge accounting) or cannot be offset by the fair value option (now narrowed in the revision), the overall effect of IAS 39 would be to increase earnings volatility. It was this effect that engendered opposition from European financial institutions and regulators, and led to the Commission not adopting the part of IAS 39 dealing with hedge accounting. Instead, the Commission said companies had the choice of whether or not to use such accounting. In addition, regulators were concerned that financial institutions would abuse the fair value option and misstate their true condition. This led the Commission to exclude entirely the use of the fair value option.

As a result of the Commission's action, there is now the EU version of IAS 39 and the IASB version which could interfere with comparability. IASB continues to try to devise an acceptable solution that could garner everyone's support. IASB continues to try to come up with a solution that is acceptable to the Commission and bank regulators. Its latest fair value proposal of March 2005 may be successful in resolving the fair value dispute. The essential idea is to set down conditions for using fair value and require disclosure about the validity of these conditions that will limit opportunism. As currently envisioned, there would be three conditions (principles) required for use of the option: (1) elimination of a mismatch that would otherwise arise from measuring items on a different basis; (2) when a group of financial assets and/or financial liabilities is managed and its performance is evaluated on a fair value basis; and (3) instruments with embedded

---

[144] Basel Committee on Banking Supervision, Comments on the IAS 39 Fair Value Option Proposal (July 30, 2004).

derivatives are involved. In connection with the first two conditions, narrative descriptions would be required to clarify how the conditions are satisfied. The revisions also acknowledged the need of regulators of financial firms, in setting capital requirements, to understand the reasons institutions have chosen the fair value option and indicated this need would be satisfied by the additional disclosure requirements.[145]

There is substantial concern that IAS (and for that matter FASB) has introduced too much volatility in earnings. Theoretical literature suggests that more volatile cash flows increase the need and the costs of capital. While accounting rules do not on their own change underlying cash flow volatility, they do change the volatility of accounting earnings. Volatility of earnings may lead to less analyst following due to more forecasting difficulty and the consequential reduction in share prices due to less demand.[146] It is widely observed that companies try to smooth their earnings—indeed, many of the targets of Eliot Spitzer are companies that have allegedly violated accounting rules in an effort to do so.

In addition to general concern with earnings volatility, financial institutions and regulators remain particularly concerned with the volatility effects of accounting rules that require certain positions to be marked-to-market. The EU has not adopted these rules mainly out of a concern with their impact on the volatility of earnings and capital of financial institutions. One study has found that mark-to-market accounting in general injects "artificial" volatility that is misleading, particularly for claims that are long lived, illiquid and senior, the typical claims of banks and insurance companies.[147] The concerns of regulators could be dealt with by having financial institutions subject to regulatory accounting as opposed to financial reporting accounting for purposes of capital requirements and other required ratios. While this would not protect financial institutions from the market effects of volatility it would allow regulators to design accounting rules for their own purposes. This is done already in the U.S. where banking and securities regulators can and have used their own accounting rules for regulatory purposes.

One very practical impact of a change in accounting rules is the possibility that some companies could be in breach of financial covenants. Covenants in loan agreements set financial ratios such as the total amount of debt or debt as a percentage of capital and can restrict additional borrowings or disposals of assets. Many companies have avoided this problem by putting into place a so-called "frozen GAAP" provision that allows them to continue to

---

[145] IASB, Amendments to IAS 39: The Fair Value Option, for meeting of February 16, 2005.

[146] J. Day, P. Omrod, and P. Taylor, "The Adoption of International Financial Reporting Standards: Implications for Volatility and Uncertainty in Relation to Accounting Earnings and Valuation," 20 J. of International Banking Law and Regulation 120 (March 2005).

[147] G. Plantin, H. Sapra, and H. Shin, "Marking-to-Market: Panacea or Pandora's Box," December 2004.

use their old accounting standards in testing the applicability of the covenants—in the longer term the covenants will have to be restated in accord with the new accounting rules.[148] The new accounting standards will significant effects on corporate earnings. For example, the expensing of options led to a 21 percent decrease in the earnings of Alcatel.

The EU has recently called into question the governance of IASB in terms of the influence of the United States on the Board of Trustees (calling for the replacement on one North American with one European) and the Board of Executives and the appropriateness of fund raising from private industry. The number of trustees is due to expand to 22 from 19 with six each from Europe, North America and Asia, and four further places from no particular region. The U.S. representation on the Board is a problem for the EU particularly when the EU and not the U.S. has adopted the IAS standards.

e.   EU COMMISSION ACCEPTANCE OF U.S. GAAP AND SEC ACCEPTANCE
       OF IFRS

The EU will require foreign companies to state their accounts in IFRS as of 2006. This is of direct concern to U.S. companies that currently issue their securities in the EU under U.S. GAAP. U.S. and other non-E.U. companies will only be able to use U.S. GAAP if the EU Commission determines that such standards are "equivalent" to IFRS. The Commission asked the Committee of European Securities Regulators (CESR) to assess this equivalence by June 2005. CESR issued a Consultation Paper on the equivalence issue seeking comment on what approach should be followed.[149] This paper was released in April 2005.[150] CESR concluded that U.S. GAAP was on the whole equivalent to IFRS subject to some conditions: (1) that companies that have special purpose entities (SPEs) which are not consolidated under U.S. GAAP, but are under IFRS, consolidate these entities on U.S. GAAP pro-forma balance sheet and income statements; (2) that the U.S. adopt expensing of stock options which is required under IFRS; and (3) that there be additional disclosures of sometimes a descriptive and sometimes a quantitative nature with respect to some other areas. While these additions are not reconciliation they may result in significant added

---

[148] C. Batchelor, "IFRS Could Cause Breach of Covenants," *Financial Times*, December 23, 2004. See also, J. Day, P. Ormrod and P. Taylor, "Implications for Lending Decisions and Debt Contracting of the Adoption of International Financial Reporting Standards," Journal of International Banking Law Review 475 (2004).

[149] CESR, "Concept Paper on Equivalence of Certain Third Country GAAP and on Description of Certain Third Countries Mechanisms of Enforcement of Financial Information," Consultation Paper (October 2004).

[150] CESR, "Draft Technical Advice on Equivalence of Third Country GAAP and on Description of Certain Third Countries Mechanisms of Enforcement of Financial Information," (April 2005). It was probably no coincidence that this report was issued days after the SEC announced its roadmap on April 21, 2005. Indeed, the CESR advice refers to this meeting in paragraph 8. CESR also accepted the equivalence of Japanese GAAP subject to similar conditions.

expense.[151] The U.S. has adopted option expensing under FASB Accounting Standard No. 123 (revised 2004), Share-Based Payment, but on April 14, the SEC permitted companies to implement the requirement at the beginning of their next fiscal year (the first quarter of 2006 for a calendar-end reporting company) rather than in their next reporting period, which would have been after June 2005 (smaller companies were given more time).[152] The SEC attributed the delay to the need of companies to have more time to implement changes but many found it alarming and unusual that the SEC would override FASB's implementation date.[153] The SEC's action was perhaps related to the political challenge to options expensing being mounted in the U.S. Congress. CESR's position undercuts that challenge insofar as it might result in U.S. companies not being able to use U.S. GAAP accounting in the EU.

CESR's recommendation may or may not be accepted by the Commission or ultimately the Council of Ministers or Parliament. A major problem for U.S. companies is whether the EU will ultimately say U.S. GAAP is equivalent to IFRS when the SEC has not said so—there is only a roadmap that may or not lead to this result. If the EU Commission were to propose to allow U.S. companies freely into the EU under U.S. accounting standards when the SEC has not yet reciprocated, there could well be political opposition in Europe. There is a risk that an accounting trade war could result. One solution for the SEC would have been to allow foreign companies to use IFRS in the U.S. as supplemented by critical provision of U.S. GAAP where the SEC found IFRS materially deficient.[154] This is, in effect, what the approach of CESR has been. It is possible that the SEC may still take this approach.

A major problem in permitting IAS in the U.S. would be enforcement. If the SEC were to enforce IAS, then there could be the U.S. and non-U.S. versions of IAS, since U.S. enforcement would likely be much stronger than enforcement abroad.[155]

Notes and Questions

1. How significant are the IOSCO disclosure standards?

---

[151] B. Jopson, "Japan Set to Challenge CESR Analysis," *Financial Times*, May 17, 2005.

[152] SEC Release, No. 2005-57 (April 14, 2005).

[153] BNA Banking Report, "SEC Overrides FASB, Delays Implementation of New Rules Requiring Expensing of Options," April 18, 2005.

[154] See Shadow Financial Regulatory Committee, Statement 209 on International Accounting Standards, September 20, 2004.

[155] M. Glaum and D. Street, "Compliance with the Disclosure Requirements of Germany's New Market: IAS Versus U.S. GAAP," Journal of International Financial Management and Accounting (2003) found that the average compliance level of companies with IAS or U.S. GAAP on the New Market was low, suggesting that German enforcement of non-German standards, either U.S. GAAP or IAS, was not high.

2. Should the U.S. adopt international accounting standards, with or without more convergence of these standards to U.S. GAAP? If the U.S. does adopt them, should they apply to U.S. as well as foreign firms?

3. Should the EU allow U.S. firms to list in the EU under U.S. GAAP if the U.S. persists in precluding foreign firms from listing under IFRS?

E.   OPENING UP U.S. SECURITIES MARKETS

In recent years, the SEC has taken some important initiatives to make it easier for foreign companies to issue securities in the U.S. market. Rule 144A has liberalized private placement rules. The Multijurisdictional Disclosure System rules (MJDS) have made it easier for Canadian companies to issue publicly traded securities in the U.S., and the ADR system has facilitated issuance and trading in foreign securities. We now turn to each of these developments.

1.   RULE 144A AND PRIVATE PLACEMENTS

a.   THE NEED FOR RULE 144A

In April of 1990, the SEC adopted Rule 144A which made resales of securities that were not fungible with securities trading in public markets and that were sold only to Qualified Institutional Buyers (QIB) exempt from the registration requirements of the 1933 Act. While applicable to both domestic and foreign issuers, its adoption was driven by the concerns of foreign issuers.

The reluctance of foreign issuers to enter the U.S. market was due in part to the stringent registration requirements of U.S. securities laws. The Securities Act of 1933 requires the registration of any securities to be issued under a public offering. An exemption exists, under section 4(2) of the 1933 Act, for private offerings. The exemption, however, is limited to those private placements intended for investment rather than resale and requires a two year holding period. This illiquidity requires users to pay a premium to investors that generally can be avoided by issuing in markets other than the U.S. It is far from clear that key institutional investors like insurance companies want to sacrifice yield for legality. There is continuous evidence that the Rule 144A market lacks liquidity and provides higher yields than public markets.

Rule 144A attempts to remedy the situation by extending the private placement exemption to the resale of securities, thereby increasing liquidity and decreasing the premium. Under Rule 144A, the issuer need only provide, at the purchaser's request, some minimal level of financial information, an obligation considerably less burdensome than the disclosure requirements of registration. Unlike registered offerings where liability for failure to disclose or misstatements is quite strict—under Sections 11 and 12(a)(2) of the '33 Act—Rule 144A disclosure standards are only subject to Rule 10b-5 where the plaintiff must prove intent or recklessness. Even this minimal level of disclosure is waived where the issuer already files reports under the Exchange Act or, as a foreign issuer, files home country reports under Rule 12g3-2(b). Moreover, the information need not comply with GAAP accounting standards. Nonetheless, Rule 144A documentation is often extensive, to avoid 10b-5 liability. Liability standards may be tested in suits regarding the failure of Parmalat, the Italian dairy firm, as it made Rule 144A offerings in 1998 and 2002. Lawsuits in the U.S. have been filed by both Italian and U.S. investors.[156]

Besides its lenient registration and disclosure requirements, the Rule 144A market offers other advantages such as speed and efficiency. While a public offering takes 8-15 weeks to consummate, a Rule 144A offering can be completed in 6–8 weeks. Preparations for a Rule 144A offering are so quick that "overnight" deals have become possible.

b.   REQUIREMENTS OF RULE 144A

Resale. The main requirements under Rule 144A are that resales within the U.S. must be of a non-fungible security to qualified institutional buyers (QIBs). Any resales of securities on an offshore market qualify.

Fungibility. To meet the non-fungibility requirements of Rule 144A, the security must not be exchangeable with the same class of stock as that listed on an exchange or on the NASDAQ. The requirement insures that Rule 144A issued stock does not compete with stock offered through the normal public offering process. In determining whether securities are of the same class, the following guidelines apply:

Common equity securities are of the same class if the terms, rights, and privileges are largely similar.

Preferred equity securities are of the same class if the terms covering dividends, accumulation, voting rights, liquidation preference, participation, convertibility, call, and redemption are largely similar.

Debt securities are of the same class if terms covering interest rate, maturity, redemption, subordination, call, and convertibility are largely similar. However, because fungibility is determined at the time of issuance, issuers are able to by-pass this limitation on convertibility. By listing the securities on the exchanges or on NASDAQ *after* the Rule 144A offering, issuers are able to offer

---

[156] E. Backus and F. Kapner, "Parmalat Plaintiffs Put Hope in U.S. Justice," *Financial Times*, March 11, 2004. Actions against Parmalat officials and U.S. underwriters and accounting firms have also been brought in Italy by Italian prosecutors.

convertible stock that nevertheless meets the fungibility requirement at the time of issuance.

Qualified Institutional Buyer. The requirement that the purchaser be a QIB insures that only those with the most sophisticated knowledge of the securities market are not under the protection of the Securities Act registration and disclosure requirements. To qualify as a QIB, the firm must own and invest a minimum of $100 million in securities or must be owned by firms or individuals all of whom qualify as QIBs. The minimum investment for broker-dealers is $10 million, but less if it acts as an agent for QIBS on a non-discretionary basis. If the firm is a bank or a thrift, it must have a net worth of $25 million. A QIB can only make purchases for itself or for another QIB. Amendments to Rule 144A include as QIBs both insurance company separate accounts (if the insurance company is a QIB) and bank collective and master trusts for pension and other employee benefit plans. The ultimate purchaser must qualify, where sales are made to an adviser or other fiduciary, on behalf of another account.

The seller's responsibility in meeting the QIB requirement is fulfilled if the seller upon reasonable reliance determines that the purchaser is a QIB. Reliance is reasonable where the seller uses information available in publicly disclosed financial statements, documents filed with the SEC or other U.S. or foreign regulatory agency, "recognized security manuals," or a certification document from the executive officer of the purchasing company.

Notice. Rule 144A requires that the purchaser be given notice of the seller's reliance on Rule 144A. The seller has met its requirement if it has taken "reasonable steps" to give notice.

No Solicitation. Rule 144A significantly limits the means that can be used to solicit investors.

c.   IMPACT ON FOREIGN ISSUERS AND PRIVATE PLACEMENT

Although Rule 144A is equally applicable to the securities of domestic and foreign firms, its greatest impact has been in the market for foreign securities. Within one year of Rule 144A's adoption, foreign firms were responsible for one-third of the $16.7 billion in issuance of Rule 144A stock. Their representation in Rule 144A stock issuance was substantially greater than in either the traditional private or public bond markets where they comprised only 16 percent and 7 percent of the offerings respectively. By 1997, 30 percent of all foreign transactions were Rule 144A deals. For many foreign firms hoping to eventually make a full public offering in the U.S., Rule 144A is an ideal way to ease into the U.S. market.

The effect of Rule 144A on the private placements market has been tremendous. In 1997, the private placements market grew by approximately 74 percent with Rule 144A issuance constituting 74 percent of total private placements. At the same time, the traditional private placement market has remained distinct from the Rule 144A market. Insurance companies, which constitute 98 percent of private placement buyers, are not interested in greater liquidity for their securities and are unwilling to forego higher yields for that liquidity. The very reason traditional buyers like insurance companies have purchased private placement securities has been to hold rather than sell.[157]

As one might expect, the yields on Rule 144A debt issues are higher than on public debt issues. This results from the fact that the issuers on the whole are less creditworthy than public issuers. A study based on issuance from 1991-1997 finds that for investment-grade debt, issue costs in the 144A market average 30 basis points greater than in the public market. The study further finds that the Rule 144A market is increasingly the market of choice for international high-yield debt issuers. The Rule 144A market grew from 11 percent of total debt issued by international firms in the U.S. in 1991 to 65 percent in 1997.[158]

The SEC has exempted Rule 144A securities issued by foreigners from the anti-manipulation rules, Rules 10b-6, 10b-7, and 10b-8, which are designed to prevent issuers, underwriters, and other participants in a securities offering in the United States, from supporting the price of the securities.[159]

d.   PORTAL

Rule 144A's success, however, has not come by the anticipated route. The architects of Rule 144A had envisioned the creation of a liquid secondary market through the PORTAL (Private Offering, Resale and Trading Through Automated Linkages) exchange system. Its computer network would post quotations, accessible by personal computers or at designated PORTAL stations by firms previously qualified as QIBs. Clearance and settlement of trade transactions would be handled by PORTAL depositories such as The Depository Trust Company for U.S. securities and CEDEL for non-U.S. securities.

Though PORTAL had the backing of both NASD and the SEC, it has not been fully utilized, due in part to burdensome trading restrictions. A complete overhaul in 1993[160] did little to increase use of the system.

---

[157] Investment companies, e.g. mutual funds, which have a 10 percent statutory restriction on investing in illiquid securities, generally regard 144A securities as illiquid—they do, however, have the legal discretion to classify them as liquid. Many Rule 144A offerings are two part transactions where a foreign issuer both issues shares on a foreign public market and through the U.S. private placement market. This suggests that the investor may get liquidity on the foreign market.

[158] S. Chaplinsky and L. Ramchand, "The Impact of SEC Rule 144A on Corporate Debt Issues by International Firms," 77 J. of Business 1073 (2004).

[159] SEC, Securities Releases Nos. 33-7028, 34-33138, 58 Federal Register 60326 (1993).

[160] Since its inception a number of changes, approved by the SEC, have been made in the PORTAL system. Participants (brokers, dealers and investors) can qualify a prospective investor

Investment banks making markets in Rule 144A securities have been the preferred substitute.

e.   QUASI-PUBLIC OR PRIVATE PLACEMENT

Rule 144A private placements have increasingly come to resemble public offerings, with non-negotiable, public-style covenants, prospectus-like documentation, and a public rating system. The SEC fears that the circumvention of the PORTAL system is creating a quasi-public market with much of the benefits of the public market without the burdens and checks of registration and disclosure.

Some have proposed lowering the QIB requirements, relaxing non-fungibility, and eliminating any information requirement. These reforms would be difficult to achieve given the SEC's quasi-public market concern.

Notes and Questions

1.   Does the availability of Rule 144A make the issue of changes in public offering rules for foreign issuers relatively unimportant?

2.   What changes in Rule 144A would make it more attractive?

2.   THE MJDS APPROACH

We now turn to another technique to open up the U.S. market—generally permitting foreign issuers to use their home country disclosure rules subject to the requirement that accounts be reconciled to U.S. GAAP.

a.   BASIC APPROACH

The SEC adopted the multi-jurisdictional disclosure system (MJDS) in 1991 for qualified securities transactions by Canadian issuers.[161] The large number of Canadian firms issuing registered securities in the United States and the similarities between U.S. and Canadian securities regulation made Canada an obvious choice. The Commission has chosen, however, not to extend this approach to other countries.

MJDS differs significantly from Rule 144A, as Table 2C, below, illustrates.

---

as a QIB rather than having the determination made by NASD. Sales of securities can be made to any investor as long as the sale is in compliance with some exemption, not restricted to Rule 144A. Use of PORTAL's automatic clearance and settlement facilities is no longer compulsory, and may be made through depositories other than the Depository Trust Company (clearance and settlement issues are dealt with in Chapter 13). The quotation system has also become more flexible. "State Street Boston Corporation," (November 1994) 6 The Global Navigator, at p. 4.

[161] 58 Federal Register 30036 (1991).

Table 2C Rule 144A and MJDS Compared		
	144A	MJDS
Investors	QIBs	Public
Market	Secondary	Primary
Issuers	All	Canadian
Regulatory Principle	National Treatment	Home Country Rules

Registration. The MJDS is designed to facilitate securities offerings in multiple markets by subjecting the issuer to the regulations of only one jurisdiction. Specifically, qualified Canadian issuers may use disclosure documents filed with the appropriate Canadian agency in registering with the SEC and in meeting the periodic disclosure requirements. As originally adopted MJDS filings did not require financial statements to be reconciled with U.S. GAAP standards, as long as they met Canada's equivalent but that approach was changed in 1993—reconciliation is now required.[162] Except for rights offerings, compliance with U.S. independent auditing standards apply for audits beginning with the first year the issuer files under MJDS. For prior periods, compliance with Canadian independence standards is sufficient. Moreover, the filed documents are usually not reviewed by the Commission in reliance on the Canadian review process and are made effective immediately. If a simultaneous offering is not being made in Canada, registration does not become effective in the United States until the completion of review by the Canadian authorities.

Prospectus. The MJDS issuer generally uses the same prospectus with its U.S. investors as used with its home jurisdiction Canadian investors. The prospectus, however, must specifically warn its investors of the possibility of tax consequences and the potential need to pursue legal remedies in the issuer's home jurisdiction. Any information that needs to be disclosed in the U.S. but not in its home jurisdiction can be filed with the Commission and disclosed only by reference in the prospectus or registration. Conversely, information that needs to be disclosed in the home jurisdiction but not in the U.S. can be filed with the Commission rather than directly included in the prospectus or registration. The information, however, must be available upon request by the shareholder.

---

[162] 58 Fed. Reg. 35367 (1993). This change was based, in part, on the result of a study of the effect of different accounting rules on the statement of income and equity between the U.S. GAAP and foreign GAAP of several countries including Canada. For Canada, the survey found that while the vast majority of registrants reported income variances of less than 10 percent from that obtained under GAAP, much larger variances did exist in some cases. SEC Division of Corporate Finance, "Survey of Financial Statement Reconciliations by Foreign Registrants" (1993).

Liability. Liability under U.S. civil law and antifraud statutes apply to securities issued under the MJDS. A registration, however, will not be considered misleading or fraudulent simply because it does not contain information required for traditional registrations, because the registration requirements of Canada substitute for U.S. requirements. As long as the issuer complies with Canadian standards, as construed by Canadian authorities, the issuer is in compliance with U.S. regulations as well and suffers no liability for undisclosed information not required to be disclosed under Canadian law.

b.   ADDITIONAL REQUIREMENTS

Securities Act. To take advantage of MJDS exemptions, Canadian firms must have a minimum history of three years filing with a Canadian securities agency and have a specified minimum market value and/or public float. Issuers must be "substantial" as defined by the Commission. For convertible investment grade securities, the value of an issuer's equity must be at least $180 million and the value of their public float at least $75 million to meet the "substantial" requirement. To be considered an investment grade security, it must be rated within the top four ratings of a nationally recognized statistical rating organization (NRSRO). For all other securities, the minimum value for equity shares is $360 million and the minimum public float is $75 million.

The issuer must be a "foreign private issuer," as defined by the Commission[163] or a Canadian crown corporation owned directly or indirectly by the Canadian government. While technically a company with all of its business operations and most of its shareholders in Nigeria could qualify to use MJDS if it were incorporated in Canada and was otherwise a private issuer, in practice this would not be allowed. Only "real" Canadian companies can use MJDS.

While registration under the MJDS allows Canadian issuers to use disclosure documents prepared in accordance to Canadian regulations and renders inapplicable U.S. standards on the preparation of prospectuses, other U.S. requirements relating to the distribution of securities remain intact. For example, U.S. requirements on the delivery of the prospectus, safe harbor provisions on advertisements, and rules on the publication of opinions and recommendations still apply. Also, because Canadian law does not require disclosure of indemnification provisions regarding directors, officers, and controlling persons, MJDS issuers must supplement their registration with such information.

---

[163] A foreign private issuer must have more than 50 percent of its shares owned by non-U.S. shareholders *and* have more than 50 percent of non-U.S. directors and officers and non-U.S. assets *or* have its business principally administered outside the U.S.

Exchange Act. Section 15(d) of the Exchange Act of 1934 requires periodic reporting by issuers registered under the Securities Act that meet certain threshold requirements in terms of assets and number of U.S. resident shareholders. It also requires periodic reporting by issuers whose securities are listed on a stock exchange or on the NASDAQ. In both situations, Canadian issuers using the MJDS can generally satisfy continuous reporting requirements by filing home country reports under Rule 12g3-2(b).

c.   STATE SECURITIES REGISTRATION

The North American Securities Administrators Association (NASAA), encompassing U.S., as well as Canadian and Mexican securities regulators, has attempted to reconcile state law with the MJDS system. After endorsing the MJDS in 1989 and completing a survey of various state laws, NASAA proposed a four point amendment to the Uniform Securities Act (1956). First, it called for the reconciliation of state review periods with Canada's seven day review system. It also asked states to accept the MJDS Form F-7 as a substitute for state forms exempting registration for rights offerings. Third, it called for the acceptance of Canadian accounting standards for financial statements as allowed under the MJDS. Lastly, it asked states to exempt secondary sales of securities for which a registration was effective with the Commission through Forms F-8, F-9, or F-10 from additional registration. Many states have adopted these recommendations.

d.   IMPACT ON CANADIAN ISSUERS

Some of the reasons for the relatively low use of MJDS seem to be: (1) issuers prefer to use the Regulation S exemption in combination with Rule 144A (this technique is discussed at the end of the Chapter); (2) the need for GAAP reconciliation; (3) the fear of prospective 10b-5 liability; (4) the inability, as in Canada, to have U.S. investors pay for securities by installment sale, due to U.S. margin rules preventing the extension of credit in excess of 50 percent in the public offering of securities; and (5) the necessity to comply with state blue sky laws.

e.   REPEAL OF MJDS

There have been reports that the SEC is contemplating abolishing MJDS. The official justifications are: (1) that this represents an anomalous bilateral arrangement given the new thrust to develop harmonized international standards represented by SEC endorsement of IOSCO disclosure rules and the possible endorsement of IAS; and (2) that it has proven unfeasible to extend MJDS to other countries like the U.K. Some feel the real reason is the SEC's lack of confidence in Canadian enforcement of its rules.

f.   EXPANSION OF MJDS

An alternative suggestion would expand the MJDS approach and allow foreign issuers to rely on home country disclosure when foreign markets were "efficient." "Efficiency would be a reflection of certain characteristics of both the company and its home market. The main criteria could be the following: (i) minimum disclosure requirements; (ii) minimum periodic reporting requirements; (iii) satisfactory rules aimed at preventing market manipulation and ensuring market transparency; and (iv) minimum market capitalization and trading volume requirements. It is thought that a company meeting minimum capitalization and trading volume requirements implies a significant following of the company's stock by analysts."[164] However, any such extension would naturally raise fairness questions for domestic companies not given the flexibility of choosing standards granted to foreign competitors.

Still another approach would be to further liberalize MJDS and extend it to other countries. In favor of this approach might be the fact that the London Stock Exchange (and the U.K.), which competes with U.S. stock exchanges for listings, will accept either compliance with international accounting standards, or with U.K. or U.S. GAAP standards.

Most securities offered in Europe use U.K. disclosure standards. If the U.S. were to accept U.K. disclosure standards, including U.K. or IASC accounting standards, as an alternative to U.S. standards, it would greatly reduce the barriers to foreign issuers of distributing securities in the United States. U.K. standards are generally quite close to U.S. standards.[165] Of course, it wouldn't go very far to extend this right only to U.K. companies the way the current MJDS extends only to Canadian companies; one would want to allow any foreign issuer to use U.K. disclosure standards.

Even more ambitious extension has been contemplated by academics. S. Choi and A. Guzman have recommended the adoption of "portable reciprocity," a regime under which a firm would be able to choose the law of any country under which it issued its securities and under which the securities traded. There would be no territorial constraints, so that a U.S., German, or Japanese firm could issue securities in the U.S. under Japanese law, or any other law. The authors contend that investors would apply appropriate discounts to the legal regime, e.g. more discounts for regimes with less disclosure, and issuers could trade off less disclosure for lower prices.[166] It remains doubtful, however, that the SEC would allow individuals

---

[164] E. Greene, D. Braverman, and S. Sperber, "Hegemony or Deference: U.S. Disclosure Requirements in the International Capital Markets," (1995) 50 Business Lawyer, pp. 413, 438.

[165] M. Fallone, "Comparing Disclosure Requirements in the United States with those Found in the United Kingdom," Third Year Paper at Harvard Law School (1999).

[166] "Portable Reciprocity: Rethinking The International Reach of Securities Regulation," (1998) 71 Southern California Law Review, p. 903. For a very similar proposal, see R. Romano, "Empowering Investors: A Market Approach to Securities Regulation," (1998) 107 Yale Law

to buy securities distributed under the law of a country with a low level of required disclosure.

Notes and Questions

1. Do you think that the deference to home-country rules represented by MJDS is a good idea? In what respects does MJDS fail to give such deference? Is such lack of deference justified?

2. What do you think of the Choi and Guzman proposal?

3. Some Europeans have proposed that the U.S. adopt an "equivalence" approach to regulation of foreign firms, exempting firms from U.S. rules if such firms are subject to equivalent regulation.[167] This equivalence test has been used by the E.U. in the case of exempting foreign firms from complying with local (IAS) accounting principles, and in granting exemptions from their regulation of Conglomerates, a matter we examine in Chapter 4. It has also been used by PCAOB in exempting foreign audit firms from U.S. regulation. Equivalence must be defined in a particular case but even then it is hard to define. One commentator has advocated in the context of Section 302 Sarbanes-Oxley certification rules, that an equivalence determination be based on three major considerations: (1) overlapping requirements; (2) the nature and character of conflicting requirements; and (3) the extent of burden on the foreign firm.[168]

3.   THE USE OF ADRS

a.   OVERVIEW OF ADR

American Depository Receipts (ADRs) are the primary method by which U.S. investors hold foreign securities other than Canadian securities. The depository, usually a bank or a trust company, holds the actual stock certificate of the foreign security, and investors hold a negotiable instrument representing their interests. ADRs arc priced in Dollars even though the underlying securities are priced in foreign currencies. They also provide for the payment of dividends in Dollars and the reporting by the depositary in English of significant corporate actions. In addition, ADRs are cleared and settled through the U.S. clearing and settlement process. The depositary charges a fee for these services.

Journal, p. 2359, and R. Romano, "The Need for Competition in International Securities Regulation," Yale ICF Working Paper 00-49 (June 30, 2001).

[167] Alexander Schaub, "Divergence of Rules in the Global Context: A New Challenge for Regulators," in Symposium on Building the Financial System of the 21ˢᵗ Century: An Agenda for Europe and the United States, Harvard Law School Program on International Financial Systems Symposium Report (November 2003), at 73.

[168] M. Benov, "The Equivalence Test and Sarbanes-Oxley: Accommodating Foreign Private Issuers and Maintaining the Validity of U.S. Markets," 16 The Transnational Lawyer 439 (2003).

There are various reasons for foreign companies establishing ADR programs, including: (1) foreign companies can increase their share value if the U.S. puts a higher price/earnings ratio on their stock than their home markets; and (2) U.S. investors can buy the shares more cheaply and conveniently in the U.S. than abroad. In connection with the second point, ADRs can avoid foreign custody fees (a global custodian holding the stock abroad could charge 10-40 basis points per year), provide better foreign exchange rates on dividends (the depositary converts to Dollars in bulk), permit holders to get corporate action reports in English, and avoid inefficient foreign clearing and settlement systems.[169]

It is far from clear, however, that ADRs are attractive to securities dealers and institutional investors, who may think the services provided by the depositary are too expensive. These professionals may themselves be able to more cheaply convert foreign currency dividends into dollars and to keep track of corporate actions. And foreign clearing and settlement systems in some major markets may be even more efficient than systems in the U.S. These professionals might well prefer a mechanism to trade the exact same underlying security in different markets.[170]

b.   ESTABLISHING AN ADR FACILITY

An ADR facility can be established in one of two forms—as a sponsored or as an unsponsored facility.

A **sponsored facility** is one created jointly by the issuer and the depositary through the execution of a deposit agreement and a Form F-6 registration statement. The facility is maintained through income generated from dividend payment fees paid by the issuer, and deposit and withdrawal fees paid by the investors. As part of the deposit agreement, the depositary notifies investors of shareholder meetings and disseminates information provided by the issuer.

An **unsponsored facility** is one that is established independent of the issuer, though issuers are normally solicited for letters of non-objection. Market interest for the issuer's securities serves as the impetus and the depositary usually serves as the sponsor of a new facility. While issuer participation is not necessary in establishing an unsponsored facility, its cooperation may be necessary. If the issuer is not exempt from reporting under the Exchange Act of 1934, the issuer must apply for the 12g3-2(b) exemption. Only then can the depositary file a Form F-6 for the ADR. The facility is maintained through income generated from deposit and withdrawal fees, conversion fees, and other payments by investors. Because the issuer

---

[169] J. Velli, "American Depositary Receipts: An Overview," (1994) 17 Fordham International Law Journal, S38.
[170] The NYSE has considered the creation of a facility for trading the shares of non-U.S. companies in their local currencies under U.S. clearing and settlement rules on the theory that the "repackaging" advantages of ADRs are not worth the fees charged to investors.

does not financially support the facility's maintenance, there is no obligation on the part of the depositary to report corporate actions.

While both sponsored and unsponsored facilities are in existence, there is increasing pressure for ADR facilities to be sponsored by the issuer. The NYSE and the Amex, for example, will not list ADRs that are unsponsored and the NASDAQ highly recommends the same. Over-the-counter markets such as the Pink Sheets and the Bulletin Board continue to accept unsponsored ADRs.

c.   SECURITIES ACT AND EXCHANGE ACT

Securities Act of 1933. The registration requirement of the Securities Act of 1933 is applicable to both the deposited security itself and the ADRs that evidence the security. When an issuer makes a public offering of its securities, both the ADRs and the deposited securities must be registered with the Commission. It is also possible to have a transaction in which the deposited security need not be registered but the issued ADR must be. Foreign securities purchased in the secondary markets may be deposited in an ADR facility without incurring an obligation to register them. When ADRs are issued to the public for those deposited shares, however, the ADRs must be registered as they constitute a public offering.

To register an ADR with the Commission, the depositary signs Form F-6 in place of the issuer. For sponsored facilities, the issuer, a majority of it board, its principal officer, and U.S. representative must also sign. In order to qualify for use of Form F-6 in registered ADRs, the issuer must be registered under the Securities Act or exempt from such. The issuer must also be or be in the process of becoming a reporting issuer under the Exchange Act. An issuer is exempt from the reporting requirements through Rule 12g3-2(b) if information it files abroad meets certain requirements. Lastly, to qualify for use of Form F-6, investors must be able to freely exchange their ADRs for the deposited securities.

Once an issuer meets the requirements for use of Form F-6, it must comply with a limited number of disclosure requirements as mandated by Form F-6. The disclosure requirement includes a prospectus describing the ADRs registered, a notice that information on the issuer is available, and an outline of the fees imposed on the ADRs. Most of this disclosure is provided directly on the ADR certificate.

Exchange Act of 1934. The establishment of an ADR facility will not in and of itself subject the issuer to reporting requirements under the Exchange Act. However, if the ADRs are listed on an exchange or the NASDAQ, they become subject to the Exchange Act and must file Form 20-F and other documents required by laws of the issuer's home jurisdiction. ADRs traded in OTC markets need not provide periodic reports if the issuers maintain a Rule 12g3-2(b) exemption.

Sponsored ADRs are often referred to as being Level I, II, or III. Level I refers to ADRs traded in the OTC; most ADRs are traded in this form. Level II refers to ADRs listed on an exchange that do not, like Level III, involve a new issue of shares to raise capital. ADRs may also be used for private placements as under Rule 144A.

d.   IMPACT OF ADRs

New ADR issues in the U.S. have flattened out during the 1990s despite an unprecedented bull market. In 1998, the volume of new ADRs coming to market fell to $10 billion, a 40 percent drop from 1997, largely as a result of U.S. investor interest in the booming U.S. equity market to the exclusion of foreign issues.[171] But the value of ADR issuance rebounded to over $21.2 billion in 1999, a new record.[172]

H. Jackson & E. Pan[173] observe that there is a declining importance of the ADR market in the United States for foreign issuers with active home markets, in particular European issuers. They show that for the 10 ADR non-European issues in 1995, ADR shares at the end of that year were 123 percent, indicating that home shares flowed into the United States after the issue. From 1995-1999, shares of these issues continued to flow in. In comparison, for the 6 European issues in 1998, only 59 percent of the shares issued remained in ADR form at the end of the year; these shares moved back to the home market. And in 1999, these shares continued to flow out of the United States. The authors posit that institutional investors do not want to trade shares in ADR form in the U.S. but prefer to trade on the more active and deeper home market. For shares from countries with less active home markets, however, such as those from Latin America, trading in ADR form in the United States is preferred. Thus, the overall growth in ADR trading previously observed is due largely to shares from these relatively less active home markets.

In the Argentine financial crisis of 2001, ADRs were used to avoid Argentine capital controls. Argentine investors purchased stocks in Argentina with pesos and then converted the stocks into ADRs and resold them for Dollars in New York. The local peso price of stocks with foreign ADRs was about 40 cents on the Dollar, reflecting the fact that Argentines were willing to pay a substantial price—in fact, a price close to the anticipated devaluation of the Peso—to move funds into Dollars through ADR

---

[171] "Mixed Results for ADRs as Issuance Slows Down," *Financial Times*, March 23, 1999.

[172] Business Wire (December 16, 1999) reporting on Citibank's Year-End Review. As of May 2001, 970 ADRs traded on the Pink Sheets as compared with 540 ADRs on the NYSE or NASDAQ. The Pink Sheet companies include Nestlé, Nintendo, and Volkswagen, large foreign companies that have not listed here. ADRs account for only 5 percent of the companies on the Pink Sheets but they represent half of the dollar volume.

[173] "Regulatory Competition in International Securities Markets: Evidence from Europe in 1999—Part II," (May 2001) Business Lawyer.

conversions. Argentina subsequently imposed controls that made conversions more difficult but they continued to occur.[174]

e.   GDRs AND GDSs

GDRs. Another type of depositary receipt, global depositary receipts or global depositary shares (GDRs or GDSs) have emerged since 1990. These are depositary receipts issued in connection with non-U.S. offerings of foreign securities which are often listed on a foreign stock exchange. When GDRs are issued in combined offerings, both abroad and in the U.S., the U.S. receipts are referred to as either ADRs or GDRs.

GRSs. After the 1998 Daimler-Benz merger with Chrysler, the new DaimlerChrysler stock (DCX) traded in the U.S. in ordinary common stock form rather than as ADRs (the form in which Daimler-Benz had previously traded). Indeed, DCX now trades on 22 exchanges around the world with the same instrument, albeit in different currencies. It is referred to as a global registered share (GRS). Most notably, DCX trades on the NYSE in Dollars and on the Frankfurt Stock Exchange in Euros. Dividends will be paid once a year in Dollars to U.S. registered shareholders and in Euros to German-registered shareholders. Trades are cleared through a bilateral link between the U.S. and German clearing systems. As of January 2003, only three more companies, Celanese AG, also a German company, UBS, a Swiss bank, and Deutsche Bank have obtained a GRS listing on the NYSE.

What explains so little interest in GRSs? Brumm, discusses some obstacles.[175] First, the GRS does require a clearing link between the U.S. and the issuer's home country but many such bilateral links exist. Second, it requires that the shares be issued in registered form (since the U.S. demands this) rather than in bearer form. In many jurisdictions, shares are accustomed to trade in bearer form.[176] Brumm suggests this can be dealt with by converting from bearer to registered form when shares are sold by German investors on the NYSE and back again when sold by U.S. investors on the Frankfurt Exchange, but this would add some cost. Third, a major problem seems to be countries like England which prohibit the transfer of shares on a share registry maintained outside of the issuer's home jurisdiction. Such a requirement is imposed in order to assure stamp taxes are collected on share transfers. Apparently, the ADR form may also be more flexible in some cases.

---

[174] S. Auguste, K. Dominguez, H. Kamil, and L. Tesar, "Cross-Border Trading as a Mechanism for Capital Flight: ADRs and the Argentine Crisis," NBER Working Paper 9343 (November 2002).

[175] See N. Brumm, "Daimler Chrysler Paves the way for New Listing Structure, International Financial Law Review," (December 1999) U.S. Capital Markets Report, p. 62 and G. Karyoli, "DaimlerChrysler AG, The First Truly Global Share," Working Paper (September 1999).

[176] Given the fact that most German companies issue shares in bearer form, and that NYSE listings required registered shares, German companies seeking to list shares rather than ADRs must convert their share from bearer to registered form, a complex process. It is examined in depth by M. Gruson, "Global Shares of German Corporations and Their Dual Listings on the Frankfurt and New York Stock Exchanges," (2001) 22 U. Pa. J. of Int'l Economic Law, p. 185.

One of the reasons Novartis opted for ADR form was because Swiss stock exchange rules prevent its splitting its share price to a level comparable to its U.S. peers. With an ADR, it can obtain a split in the U.S. by merely adjusting the ratio of conversion of ADRs to shares.[177]

In 2003, the Bank of New York proposed issuing unsponsored ADRs on behalf of Celanese due to lack of US interest in its GRSs. The SEC is apparently concerned about the dual trading of GRSs and ADRs. In September, the SEC proposed amending Form F-6 to permanently prohibit the practice. The concern seems to be with possible investor confusion over the two types of securities.[178]

F.   ISSUING SECURITIES ABROAD

The SEC has developed Regulation S, 55 Federal Register 18306 (1990), to deal with the issuance of securities abroad. The SEC takes the position that sales of securities to public U.S. investors, in the U.S. or abroad, require registration, unless exempted.

1.   REGULATION S FRAMEWORK

a.   POLICY

Regulation S purports to embrace the notion that the intent of the registration requirements of the Securities Act is to protect investors in U.S. capital markets, rather than to protect U.S. investors who choose to invest overseas. As the Commission stated, this territorial approach "recognizes the primacy of the laws in which a market is located. As investors choose their markets, they choose the laws and regulations applicable in such markets."[179] In fact, Regulation S has quite a substantial extraterritorial reach.

b.   PRINCIPLES

Regulation S comprises four rules: Rules 901, 902, 903, and 904. Rule 901 contains a general statement of the SEC's territorial approach. Rule 901(a) provides that where the offer and sale of securities occurs "outside the United States," the registration provisions of s. 5 are not applicable. If the offer or sale occurs within the United States, the registration provisions, absent of an exemption, are applicable.

Determining whether an offer and sale have occurred outside the United States is not always an easy matter. The SEC provides that whether

---

[177] W. Hall, "Global Shares Face a Long Uphill Battle," *Financial Times*, May 31, 2000. The costs of establishing a GRS program are quite high compared to ADRs. A. Beard, "Global Shares a Letdown for DaimlerChrysler," *Financial Times*, April 30, 2001.

[178] SEC Release No. 33–8287 (September 11, 2003).

[179] SEC Release No. 33-6863, 34-27942 (April 24, 1990).

an offer and sale are made outside the United States is to be determined on an ad hoc basis. This determination is clarified somewhat by the safe-harbor provisions of Rule 903 and 904. If the offer and sale satisfy the conditions of either of these non-exclusive safe harbor provisions, the transaction will be deemed to have occurred outside the United States.

c.   SAFE HARBOR PROVISIONS: GENERAL CONDITIONS

Regulation S comprises two safe-harbor provisions: (1) an issuer safe harbor (Rule 903); and (2) a safe harbor for resales (Rule 904). Only the former will be discussed here. All offers and sales, whether made in reliance on the issuer or the resale safe harbor, must satisfy two general conditions.

Offshore Transactions. The first general condition for an offer and sale to be considered outside the United States is that the offer or sale is made in an "offshore transaction." To engage in an offshore transaction there: (1) can be no offer or sale to a person in the United States; *and, either* (2a) the buyer is outside the United States, or the seller reasonably believes that the buyer is outside of the United Sates, at the time the buy order is originated; *or* (2b) the transaction is executed on a designated offshore securities market, provided that the seller or its agent does not know that the transaction has been prearranged with a buyer in the United States. The (2b) alternative is hardly ever used because primary distributions are not made through exchanges.

Directed Selling. The second general condition for an offer and sale to be considered outside the United States is that there be not directed selling efforts in the United States. Directed selling efforts are defined as any activity that could reasonably be expected to have the effect of conditioning the market in the United States for any of the securities being offered in reliance on Regulation S. Television and radio advertisements reaching the United States, mailings to U.S. investors, and promotional seminars in the United States are considered directed selling efforts. Certain types of advertising are, however, excluded from the definition of direct selling efforts under Rule 902(b).

In October 1997, the SEC adopted a new rule establishing safe harbors to facilitate U.S. press access to offshore press activities. The safe harbors would clarify the conditions under which journalists may be provided with access to offshore press conferences, offshore meetings, and press materials released offshore, without an issuer losing the Regulation S exemption from registration requirements due to engaging in "directed selling efforts."[180] Congress had directed the SEC to address this issue in s. 109 of the National Securities Markets Improvements Act of 1996.

---

[180] 62 Federal Register 53948 (October 17, 1997).

The use of the internet creates interesting problems for the issue of "directed selling efforts" under Regulation S. The SEC has taken the position that an offering by a foreign firm on its Internet home page, directed at the foreign market, but accessed by a U.S. investor would not violate registration requirements if the website on which the securities are offered includes a prominent disclaimer making it clear that the offer is directed only to countries other than the United States and the website offeror implements procedures that are reasonably designed to guard against sales to U.S. persons in the offshore offering, e.g. by ascertaining the purchaser's residence.[181]

The SEC has taken a more restrictive approach where the offshore offering is made by a U.S. issuer. This flows from its more general concern with the abuse of Regulation S by U.S. offerors. In this case, the SEC not only requires the general precautions for foreign issuers described above but also requires that the U.S. issuer implement "password-type" procedures that are reasonably designed to ensure that only non-U.S. persons can obtain access to the offer. This would require that prospective purchasers demonstrate that they are not U.S. persons before obtaining the password to the site.

d.   ISSUER SAFE HARBOR PROVISION (RULE 903)

Assuming that the general conditions are satisfied, issuers must also satisfy the safe harbor provisions of Rule 903. The issuer safe harbor is applicable to the issuer, its distributors, its respective affiliates, and persons acting on behalf of the foregoing.

For purposes of Regulation S, the SEC separates securities into three categories: Category I, Category II, and Category III, based on the relative likelihood of the securities flowing back to the United States.

Category I securities have the lowest likelihood of flow-back, and, accordingly, the least regulatory restraint. In this Category are securities of "foreign issuers" for which there is no "substantial U.S. market interest," securities offered and sold in "overseas directed offerings," securities backed by the full faith and credit of a "foreign government," and securities sold pursuant to certain employee benefit plans. To satisfy the issuer safe harbor, these securities need only satisfy the general conditions. It is fair to say that for these kind of securities, there is no extraterritorialism of U.S. registration requirements.

Offerings falling within the second issuer safe harbor, Category II, are those by foreign and U.S. companies that are subject to the Exchange Act's reporting requirements as well as offerings of debt securities by nonreporting foreign issuers. To qualify for the Category II issuer safe

---

[181] Statement of the Commission Regarding Use of Internet Web Sites to Offer Securities, Solicit Securities Transactions, or Advertise Investment Services Offshore, III. B, Release Nos. 33-7516, 34-39779 (March 23, 1998).

harbor, the issuer must satisfy not only the general conditions, but must also comply with certain selling restrictions.

Two types of selling restrictions apply to offerings of securities falling within Category II: (1) "transactional restrictions"; and (2) "offering restrictions." The transactional restrictions prohibit offers and sales of such securities in the United States or to a "U.S. person" during a restricted period lasting forty days. The offering restrictions (required to meet both the Category II and Category III issuer safe harbors) are basically procedural in nature. Generally the procedures require that all distributors agree in writing that all offers and sales during the applicable restricted period be made only in accordance with a Regulation S safe harbor or pursuant to registration under the Securities Act of 1933 or an exemption therefrom. Furthermore, the issuer, distributors, and their respective affiliates must include statements in all offering materials that the securities have not been registered under the S1933 Act and may not be offered or sold in the United States or to U.S. persons unless the securities are registered or an exemption from registration is perfected. U.S. law is extraterritorial with respect to these securities. Even though they are offered offshore, as required by the general conditions, they are still subject to restrictions.

The final safe-harbor category, Category III, applies to all securities not within Categories I or II. This category includes offerings of nonreporting U.S. issuers and equity securities of non-reporting foreign issuers when there is a substantial U.S. market interest in such securities. The SEC imposes the most rigorous restrictions on offerings falling within this category due to the Commission's position that these securities have the highest probability of flowing back to the United States.

Category III securities are subject to all of the offering restrictions applicable to Category II securities, as described above. However, the transactional restrictions applicable to Category III offerings are more demanding than those required under Category II.

Debt securities offered pursuant to Category III are subject to a 40-day restricted period. During this period the securities may not be sold to U.S. persons or for the account (or benefit) of U.S. persons. The debt securities must be represented by a temporary global security, which is not exchangeable for definitive securities until the forty-day restricted period has expired. When the global security is exchanged for the definitive security, certification must be effected that a non-U.S. person owns the security or that a U.S. person purchased securities in a transaction that was exempt from the registration requirements of the Securities Act of 1933. If a distributor or other person receiving a selling concession sells prior to the expiration of the 40-day restricted period, it must send a "confirmation or other notice" to the purchaser stating that the purchaser is subject to the same restrictions on offers and sales that apply to the distributor.

The transactional restrictions applicable to Category III equity offerings are even more demanding than the restrictions applicable to debt securities in the same category. Rule 903(c)(3)(iii) prohibits equity securities offered under Category III from being sold to a U.S. person or for the account (or benefit) of a U.S. person for a period of one year. Furthermore, the purchaser of the security must certify that it is not a U.S. person and is not acquiring the securities for the account (or benefit) of any U.S. person. In addition, the purchaser must agree to resell only if it adheres to one of three conditions, namely, that such resale is made in accordance with Regulation S, pursuant to a registration statement, or under an exemption from registration. If a U.S. issuer is utilizing the Category III safe harbor, it must place a legend on the securities offered stating that all transfers are prohibited except as set forth above. Finally, the issuer is required, either by contract or pursuant to a provision in its bylaws, articles, or charter, to refuse to register any transfer not in accordance with the foregoing.

2.   REGULATION S REFORMS FOR U.S. COMPANIES ISSUING SECURITIES ABROAD

The SEC has been concerned with possible abuses of the Regulation S exemption particularly in cases where U.S. issuers seek to escape registration by sham offerings to foreign investors abroad (where the economic investment risk never shifts to the foreign owners) followed by flowback into the U.S. after the expiration of the restrictive period, if any.[182] The SEC has also been concerned about "short selling and other hedging transactions such as option writing, equity swaps, or other type of derivative transactions where purchasers transfer the benefits and burdens of ownership back to the United States market during the restricted period."[183] These concerns suggest that it may be futile, or at best extremely difficult, in the modern financial world to erect barriers between markets.

In 1996, the SEC adopted rules about "Periodic Reporting of Unregistered Equity Sales," to address some of the concerns described above.[184] U.S. companies issuing shares to foreign investors under Regulation S must now report this activity to the SEC (and, thereby, the public) within 15 days. This insures that the market will know about such distributions before the expiration of the normal 40 day restriction on flowback. Such reporting, it is hoped, will reduce the possibility of selling such issues abroad at a steep discount from the U.S. price (due to the avoidance of registration costs and the absence of knowledge on the part of existing investors that their shares are being diluted through the offshore offering). Foreign investors purchasing at a discount should now expect the U.S. price to fall before they

---

[182] SEC, Problematic Practices Under Regulation S, Interpretive Release No. 33-7190 (June 27, 1995).

[183] Id., at 5.

[184] 61 Federal Register (October 18, 1996).

can resell their shares in the U.S. market.[185] The SEC also relaxed domestic disclosure rules regarding reporting requirements concerning financial statements of acquired and to be acquired businesses in order to reduce the incentive of using Regulation S offerings to escape such reporting.[186]

The SEC, however, remained concerned with abuses of Regulation S to distribute unregistered U.S. equity securities abroad. On February 25, 1998, it adopted modifications to Regulation S providing that such securities will be classified as "restricted securities" within the meaning of Rule 144, and their restricted holding periods increased from 40 days to one year. In addition, certain certification and legending requirements are imposed on the sales of restricted equity securities by reporting as well as non-reporting issuers. In effect, the treatment of offshore sales for the covered issuers has been aligned with that for domestic private placements.[187]

The new modifications apply to issuance by U.S. issuers abroad even where there is no substantial U.S. market interest in the securities. The SEC originally proposed that the new rules would also apply to foreign equity securities whose primary market is the U.S., e.g. equity securities mainly traded in the United States, which may then flowback into the United States but did not include this proposal in its final Rule.[188]

Is the application of U.S. law on an extraterritorial basis justified by the need to protect U.S. investors abroad, or in the United States (given the possibilities of flowback)? Note that European countries do not generally at present restrict offshore purchases of their residents, but this may change with the implementation of new prospectus proposals.

3.   REGULATION S - RULE 144A OFFERINGS

Regulation S can be used in conjunction with Rule 144A to sell foreign securities in the United States. Securities issued to the public abroad, subject to Regulation S resale restrictions (Categories II and III), can be sold immediately to U.S. qualifying investors under Rule 144A, typically in ADR form.

The SEC has been concerned that the parallel offerings would risk improper "leakage" of the restricted ADRs traded by sophisticated investors to U.S. public investors when the securities were traded in foreign public markets. To minimize leakage, the SEC issued an interpretive letter in April 1993 requiring that: (1) the unrestricted depositary receipts be distinguished by separate names (e.g. GDR as opposed to ADR) and different CUSIP numbers; (2) that deposits into and withdrawal from the restricted depositary

---

[185] M. Hendrickson, "SEC Adopts Reporting Rules in Attempt to Curb Reg. S Abuses," *Securities Industry News,* October 28, 1996.
[186] 61 Federal Register 54509 (October 18, 1996).
[187] 63 Federal Register 9632 (February 25, 1998).
[188] 62 Federal Register 9258 (February 28, 1997).

facility, e.g. PORTAL, require the owner to agree to specified restrictions on transfer; and (3) that depositors into the unrestricted facility, e.g. DTC, certify that they are not an affiliate or acting on behalf of the issuer of the underlying securities.

A second issue arises under Regulation S, as to whether disclosure of the offshore offering to the U.S. investors would violate the prohibition on directed selling efforts. The SEC, as part of its April 1994 reforms, adopted a new Rule 135(c) safe harbor permitting the issuer to publicly announce certain information concerning the securities offered outside the U.S., but not the name of the underwriters or placement agents. The safe harbor is only available to issuers filing periodic reports under the '34 Act or, in the case of foreign issuers, enjoying a Rule 12g3-2(b) exemption.[189]

4.   PRIMARY OFFSHORE MARKETS - A REFORM PROPOSAL

In "Internationalization of Primary Public Securities Markets,"[190] H. Scott posits that it would be desirable for issuers in public primary securities markets to be able to issue securities to investors worldwide using one set of optimal distribution procedures and disclosure documents, and one set of liability standards and enforcement remedies. The article points out that this state of affairs is currently not possible because the U.S. conditions public issuance in its territory—and to some significant extent to U.S. investors outside its territory—on compliance with its unique set of distribution procedures, disclosure requirements, and enforcement rules.

Harmonization of world rules is not the answer to this problem. There is no reason to assume that the world would choose an optimal level of disclosure, particularly because the U.S. will push for world rules that are closely equivalent to its own. Moreover, there is substantial doubt as to whether worldwide agreement can be reached on the issue of disclosure, let alone distribution and enforcement rules. Nor is mutual recognition the answer. The approach creates basic inequities for domestic issuers and has not worked well in the European Union, which has the advantage of supranational institutions, despite much fanfare about the single passport. Broader versions of mutual recognition, such as portable reciprocity, under which issuers could issue securities anywhere under any law, founder on problems of enforcement.

The Article proposes instead the establishment of an offshore free zone. This would require that the United States, like other countries, permit its investors to participate in the offshore market for primary distributions of foreign issuers free of restrictions other than minimum disclosure requirements. Regulation S, at least for foreign issuers, would be substantially repealed. In addition, foreign issues could be directly advertised

---

[189] 59 Federal Register 21644 (1994).
[190] 63 J. of Law and Contemporary Problems 71 (2000).

in the U.S. on the theory that investors are entitled to know about offshore opportunities. One major benefit of this approach is that it would permit the use of common distribution procedures.[191]

5.   SECONDARY MARKETS - A REFORM PROPOSAL

Benn Steil[192] has suggested a related type reform for secondary markets involving the EU and the United States. He would remove restrictions on EU exchanges having trading screens in brokerage houses in the United States. Screens are only permitted for registered foreign exchanges and the regulatory cost of such registration has deterred foreign exchanges. Steil claims that U.S. investors now incur both U.S. and foreign brokerage costs in trading stocks, although it would seem that an investor could avoid such costs if he/she went directly to a foreign broker (many of which are affiliates of U.S. firms). Easier trading of foreign listed stocks, he claims would eliminate the need of foreign firms to list in the United States, although this may not be the case if U.S. listings are sought as a method of bonding to U.S. rules. Steil would also require the EU to provide the same market access for U.S. exchanges. The proposal would also make companies listed on foreign exchanges whose stocks were traded through U.S. screens immune from U.S. civil and criminal fraud rules. This issue is on the agenda of the U.S.-EU Regulatory Dialogue discussed above.

A mid-term step in this direction would eliminate the legal uncertainty surrounding the ability of investors to place electronic orders through brokers (whether U.S. registered or not) on foreign exchanges. Such investors do not need screens from exchanges—they already get the same information from third-party vendors like Reuters. Currently, some foreign exchanges believe acceptance of such orders could expose them to operating illegally in the U.S. The SEC has cultivated this uncertainty in its Concept Release on Alternative Market Structures, May 23, 1997, and apparently in opinions given to access providers. It should allow such access. There is no reason to distinguish between telephonic and electronic orders.[193]

Notes and Questions

1.   Should the U.S. abolish Regulation S or accept the Scott proposal?

2.   Should the U.S. adopt the Steil proposal?

---

[191] For some refinements of this proposal, see H. Scott, "Internationalisation of Primary Public Securities Markets Revisited" in *Capital Markets in the Age of the Euro: Cross-Border Transactions, Listed Companies and Regulation*, (K. Hopt, E. Wymeersch, and G. Ferrarini eds., 2002).

[192] "Building a Transatlantic Securities Market, International Securities Market Association," (2002).

[193] See Statement 190, Shadow Financial Regulatory Committee (May 5, 2003).

CONCLUSIONS

This has been one of the hottest areas in international financial regulation in the last few years. One of the most important questions for the future is whether and to what extent the U.S. will accept international standards or home country rules for foreign issuers in the U.S. market. With respect to international rules, that the U.S. has a major (but not exclusive) role in shaping, there has been some progress. While the U.S. has accepted IOSCO's financial disclosure rules, it only did so when they were basically identical to existing U.S. rules. While the U.S. has been unwilling to accept international accounting standards, as long as they deviate significantly from U.S. rules, the SEC has now indicated there is a "roadmap" for accepting IFRS. One way to further acceptability of foreign rules is to harmonize, making U.S. and foreign rules more similar to each other. This is what the IOSCO effort IASB-FASB convergence project are about.

A second question is whether and to what extent U.S. rules (or perhaps those of other countries) should be extraterritorial, as is the case for Regulation S, insider trading prohibitions, and a major portion of the Sarbanes-Oxley reforms (those parts that did not conflict directly with home-country rules). This assertion of extraterritorial effect has caused major problems with Europe. Europe, in turn, has taken its own turn at extraterritoriality in the EU Conglomerates Directive.

A third question is the extent to which U.S. capital markets policy will continue to be the trend setter in the rest of the world. One has the sense that Sarbanes-Oxley has traction internationally not just because it must be complied with to enter U.S. public capital markets, but also because the corporate governance reforms it has formulated have appeal in other major markets which have or will have their own Enrons. On the other hand, many of these innovations have yet to be adopted in Europe or Japan.

All three of these issues greatly affect the extent of integration of world capital markets. As long as the U.S. goes its own way, and the rest of the world refuses to adopt that way, the objective of being able to distribute securities to investors worldwide, using one set of optimal-distribution procedures, disclosure documents, and liability rules and enforcement standards, will not be achieved.

CHAPTER THREE

INTERNATIONAL ASPECTS OF U.S. BANKING MARKETS

This Chapter deals with the international aspects of U.S. banking regulation. It begins with some background on the importance of foreign banks in the United States, and the basic features of U.S. regulation of all banks. Major changes have been made in these features by the enactment in November 1999 of the Gramm-Leach-Bliley Act (GLB) which liberalized restrictions on banking activities. The material concentrates on key issues in regulation: systemic risk, safety and soundness, deposit insurance and permissible activities. The Chapter concludes with a discussion of the main provisions of the financial services agreement under the General Agreement on Trade in Services (GATS).

A. THE IMPORTANCE OF FOREIGN BANKS

Foreign banks go to the United States, and abroad generally, for many reasons, but the principal one is to follow their clients. In addition, banks go abroad generally to countries with the highest profit opportunities, in particular where economic growth is higher, the local banking system is on average less efficient and less concentrates, and where regulatory restrictions are less stringent. The degree of economic integration between countries is relatively less important.[1] While it is clear that foreign expansion increases size, it has not been shown to impact significantly on profits—the evidence on profitability is ambiguous.[2]

Foreign banks operate in the United States in various ways. They may operate without a U.S. office, on strictly a *cross-border* basis. Thus, the foreign bank may take deposits of U.S. depositors at an office outside the

---

[1] D. Focarelli and A Pozzolo, "Where Do Banks Expand Abroad?," 79 J. of Business (forthcoming, January 2006).
[2] B. Williams, "The Defensive Expansion Approach to Multinational Banking: Evidence to Date," 11 Financial Markets, Institutions, and Instruments 127 (2002).

United States, or make loans from its foreign office to U.S. borrowers. A foreign bank may establish a presence in the United States by four means.

1.   METHODS OF OPERATION IN THE UNITED STATES

First, foreign banks can operate through *branches* by establishing a domestic office of the foreign bank in the United States. The office can be chartered by the federal government through the Office of the Comptroller of the Currency (OCC), an agency within the Department of the Treasury, or by a state. Branch offices are part and parcel of the foreign bank. A branch is entitled to do normal banking, including taking deposits and making loans. Its powers are generally any banking business permitted to a state or federal bank. Section 1(a) of the IBA (12 U.S.C. §3101(3)) defines a branch as an office which receives deposits. However, as indicated below, offices receiving deposits from non-U.S. citizens or non-residents are treated as agencies.

Secondly, foreign banks may operate through *subsidiaries*. The foreign bank may own a subsidiary bank (de novo or through acquisition) in the United States. The U.S. bank subsidiary may be chartered by the OCC or a state. Typically, the U.S. bank is a subsidiary of a foreign bank, rather than a subsidiary of a separate bank holding company (BHC) which owns both the foreign and U.S. bank. Many foreign countries do not have the BHC form.

Third, the foreign bank may operate through *agencies*. These are U.S. offices of the foreign bank that can make loans and receive foreign deposits or maintain credit balances. As with branches and subsidiaries, agencies may be federal or state chartered. New York permits its agencies to take domestic deposits over $100,000. While treated as agencies under New York law, they are treated as branches under federal law because they take domestic deposits.

Fourth, foreign banks can establish *representative offices*, federal or state-chartered, that do not actually do business in the United States, in the sense that they do not make loans or take deposits. They drum up business for their foreign offices that make the loans and take the deposits. They function as international loan production offices (LPOs).

This Chapter concentrates on branches and subsidiaries, as these are the most important form of operation of foreign banks. As of December 2004, foreign banks maintained 231 U.S. branch offices and 67 U.S. bank subsidiaries. This compared to a total of 7,769 U.S. commercial banks, or about 3.8 percent. All entities of foreign banks held $1.55 trillion in assets, approximately 22 percent of total U.S. banking assets ($7 trillion), and $198.5 billion in business loans, approximately 27.4 percent of the U.S. total. At year-end 2004, 180 of the total 231 branches of foreign banks were state chartered and held about 91 percent of all the assets of branches of foreign banks.

2.   RELATIVE IMPORTANCE

How important are foreign banks to the U.S. economy? Their 24.8 percent market share of business loans would seem to indicate that they are very important. However, it is worth noting that most of their lending is financed by U.S. borrowing. For example, if one looks at U.S. branches and agencies of Japanese banks in 1992, their $61.1 billion of lending ($21.1 billion to U.S. non-banks and $41.1 billion to banks) was mainly financed by borrowings from U.S. banks, $51.6 billion.

Of the largest 10 banking organizations in the world, as of December 31, 2004. July 2002, only one was American, Citigroup, ranking second. Mizuho Holdings of Japan was the biggest bank in the world with $1.3 trillion in total assets.[3]

There may be significant limitations to overall globalization of international banking. Some banking services—such as relationship lending to informationally opaque small businesses—may always be provided by small local banks headquartered in the nation in which the services are demanded.[4]

B.   BASIC FEATURES OF U.S. REGULATORY SYSTEM

The U.S. bank regulatory system, like securities regulation, is quite complicated and is an entire field of study by itself. There follows a brief description of the major features of this system.

Safety and soundness regulation. This type of regulation is intended to prevent banks from failing through controlling risks and ensuring adequate capital. Prevention of failure avoids deposit insurance pay-outs and systemic risk (chain reaction of bank failures through interbank deposit linkage, payment settlement systems, or imitative runs).

Deposit Insurance. The U.S. insures deposits of up to $100,000. This may minimize bank runs and be a form of creditor protection, but it raises a moral hazard issue: since creditors are insured, they do not police bank risk. The bank insurance fund (BIF) is normally funded by bank paid premiums, but in the 1980s this funding was insufficient due to the large extent of thrift and banking failures, and had to be greatly subsidized (over $200 billion) by federal government expenditures. There is now a system of so-called risk-based insurance premiums in which premiums are determined by capital adequacy and supervisory ratings.

---

[3] www.americanbanker.com/rankings.html?rankingchart=/BTHC/Assets/111204BCAssets.htm
[4] A. Berger, et al., "To What Extent Will the Banking Industry be Globalized? A Study of Bank Nationality and Reach in 20 European Countries," 27 Journal of Banking and Finance (March 2003), p. 383. Similar considerations support the continued existence of small local banks within the United States.

Dual Banking System. Banks are chartered by both states, and the federal government through the Office of the Comptroller of the Currency (OCC). National bank powers are regulated by OCC, while state bank powers are regulated by the states, subject to federal limits. National banks are regulated for safety and soundness by OCC, insured state banks by states and their "primary" federal regulator (the Federal Reserve Board (FRB) if the bank is a Fed member and the Federal Deposit Insurance Corporation (FDIC) if it is not). Uninsured state chartered banks are only regulated by the states, but there are very few of these. The dual system comes out of a federalist tradition: unwillingness to concentrate too much power in the national government. The multiplicity of federal regulators has largely resulted from historical factors no longer present, and is retained due to bureaucratic turf protection and distrust of centralized power.

One new significant reason that banks may want to be nationally chartered is that the National Bank Act preempts state law. Such preemption can be extremely valuable to banks wishing to avoid regulation or actions by state supervisory, or law enforcement, officials. Due to this preemption doctrine, national banks, unlike SEC chartered securities firms, have more protection from Elliot Spitzer and other attorneys general. Such preemption extends to so-called "visitorial powers" an old English term for the power to inspect banks or issues subpoenas to them for information. The Office of the Comptroller of the Currency has been extremely vigorous in defending federal preemption from state consumer regulation, and Spitzer has objected publicly and in testimony in Congress.[5] Significantly, two large New York state-chartered banks switched to national charters in 2004, JPMorgan Chase and the New York subsidiary of Hong Kong Shanghai Bank Company.

Activities Regulation. All large banking organizations operate through bank holding company (BHC) form; public shareholders own the BHC, not the bank. This is principally because some activities can be performed through BHCs that cannot be performed through banks or bank subsidiaries. BHCs are regulated by the FRB. BHCs can do activities "closely related to banking," under s. (4)(c)(8) of the Bank Holding Company Act (BHCA). Prior to GLB, while BHC powers were more expansive than "banking," neither BHCs nor banks could generally engage in life insurance, commercial activities, or certain securities activities. With respect to securities, a so-called s. 20 subsidiary (named for s. 20 of the Glass Steagall Act) of the BHC could engage in securities activities to the extent it was not "engaged principally," defined by the Fed as more than 25 percent of gross revenue.

The theory underlying the more restrictive regime for bank (as compared with BHC) activities was that there was less risk to the bank when activities were done through the BHC (in the BHC itself or in a non-bank

---

[5] See T. Davenport, "What Spitzer Might Target at Banks," *American Banker*, November 3, 2004.

subsidiary of the BHC) since BHC losses do not directly impact bank capital. Parallel with BHC power limitations, insurance, commercial and securities firms could not own banks. In the view of the Fed, BHCs were supposed to serve as a "source of strength" for banks—to be ready to inject capital if bank subsidiaries needed it. Thus, they had to be adequately capitalized. All formations of BHCs or acquisitions of banks by BHCs were reviewed by the FRB. GLB significantly changed the regime for the regulation of activities.

Under s. 4(k) of the BHCA, GLB permits a BHC, all of whose subsidiary banks are "well-capitalized" and "well-managed," to become a financial service holding company (FHC) through which it can engage in a full range of financial activities, including insurance, securities and merchant banking (investment in companies, including purely commercial companies, for resale). In statutory terms a FHC is permitted to engage in activities which are "financial in nature." Certain of these financial activities, such as a full range of securities activities, are defined in the statute. FHCs can also engage in additional financial activities, activities "incidental to such financial activities," or "complementary to a financial activity," as determined by the Fed with the agreement of the Secretary of the Treasury. Further, GLB allows a 10-year to 15-year grandfathering for the nonfinancial activities of predominantly financial companies (85 percent of whose gross revenue is financial) that become FHCs by acquiring banks.

GLB also expands the power of well-capitalized and well-managed national banks to engage in financial activities through bank subsidiaries. These are the same financial activities permitted for FHCs with three exclusions: (1) certain underwriting of insurance and annuities; (2) real estate investment or development; and (3) merchant banking (this can be permitted in 2004 if the Fed and Treasury so agree). In the case of banks, activities beyond those specified in the statute (which are the same as for FHCs) are determined by the Treasury with the agreement of the Fed. The total investment of a national bank in all financial subsidiaries is limited to the lesser of 45 percent of the bank's total assets or $50 billion (which is adjusted periodically by an index). As of October 2000, the Office of the Comptroller of the Currency had approved 60 financial subsidiaries pursuant to GLB. Certain non-banking activities can continue to be performed in the bank itself. This is a real turf battle since activities within a bank will be regulated by bank regulators while activities in affiliates will be regulated by "functional" regulators like the SEC. Bank regulators and the SEC have still not decided, five years after the enactment of GLB, as to what securities activities can be performed in the bank.[6]

---

[6] D. Paletta, "Latest SEC Spat Renews Old One over 'Push-Outs'," *American Banker*, October 18, 2004. The controversy has been over the terms of Regulation B as proposed by the SEC, SEC Release No. 34-49879, 69 Federal Register 39682 (June 30, 2004). For the criticisms of the banking agencies see Board of Governors of the Federal Reserve System, Federal Deposit

As of April 2003, 639 FHCs had been formed, including approximately 20 by foreign banking organizations. Only a small number of large FHCs have purchased securities firms since enactment of GLB; rather FHCs have mainly been used to free holding companies from restrictions placed on existing securities affiliates, i.e. limits on underwriting and dealing to 25 percent of the securities affiliate's revenue. No FHC has acquired a large insurance company since the Citi-Travellers merger prior to enactment of GLB.

This liberalization of activities restrictions brings the U.S. in line with other countries. A 1997 study indicated that of the 15 EU countries, Canada, Japan, Switzerland and the United States, only Japan and the United States limited the financial activities of banking organizations.[7] However, other countries still provide more unlimited choice to banking organizations about whether to engage in financial activities in the holding company or bank.

Limited Interstate Banking. Until the passage of the Interstate Banking and Branching Efficiency Act of 1994 (IBBEA), under the Douglas Amendment to the BHCA, BHCs could not acquire a bank outside their home state (the state in which they took the most deposits) unless the state in which the target bank was located permitted the acquisition. By 1994, most states, and all large states, permitted such acquisitions under various conditions. Under the IBBEA, interstate acquisitions, as of September 29, 1995, no longer require state authorization. However, states may require that the acquired bank be in existence for some minimum time not to exceed five years, and may also require the acquirer to comply with various state antitrust and community reinvestment laws (CRA). The federal law also imposes concentration limits. An acquiring company cannot control more than 10 percent of total U.S. deposits or 30 percent of deposits in a particular state without the state's approval. The state may, however, set even more stringent anti-concentration requirements as long as they do not discriminate against out-of-state acquisitions.

The IBBEA repealed the blanket federal restrictions on interstate branching that existed under the 1927 McFadden Act. As of June 1, 1997, interstate branching through mergers is permitted between states unless the states "opt out," and interstate branching through de novo branching is prohibited unless the states "opt in." Only two states, Montana and Texas, opted out of the merger provisions and as of March 2002, 17 had opted-in to the de novo provisions. Many of the host states have opted-in on a reciprocal basis—only allowing banks to branch in that are located in states which

---

Insurance Corporation and Office of the Comptroller of the Currency, Comment letter to the SEC, October 8, 2004.

[7] J. Barth, D. Nolle, and T. Rice, "Commercial Banking Structure, Regulation and Performance: An International Comparison," Office of the Comptroller of the Currency Economics Working Paper 97-6 (February 1997).

permit banks from the host state to branch in. States may impose conditions on interstate branching arising through interstate mergers (the acquired bank's branches become interstate branches of the acquirer) similar to those for acquisitions, e.g. five-year ageing and antitrust and community reinvestment laws. Concentration ratio requirements similar to those for acquisitions also apply.

The Community Reinvestment Act. The Community Reinvestment Act (CRA) of 1977 requires federal banking agencies to encourage banks to meet the credit needs of their local communities (including low and moderate income neighborhoods) consistent with safety and soundness considerations. Communities are defined as the areas contiguous to bank offices.

CRA performance is taken into account by banking regulators whenever a banking organization applies for permission to open a new branch or make an acquisition. Interest groups have used this requirement to file extensive protests against applications based on banks' alleged shortcomings in fulfilling their CRA obligations under the general assessment factors. These protests can lead to hearings and significant costly delays in approving applications.

C.   REGULATION OF FOREIGN BANKS

The following material deals with some key areas of regulation of foreign banks: systemic risk, safety and soundness, deposit insurance, and permissible activities for financial holding companies and banks. Problems of regulation differ depending on whether one is considering branches or subsidiaries.

1.   SYSTEMIC RISK

Avoidance of systemic risk is usually cited as the major objective of bank regulation. Within the international system, it is principally the concern of the host country, although the collapse of a banking system in one country can spill over to other countries as well. The concern with systemic risk, of course, only arises when a bank fails, but this can occur even with the best supervisory control system. We next explore the nature of systemic risk and how it works with respect to subsidiaries and branches of foreign banks. Systemic risk has two distinct meanings. First, it refers to a financial shock that has simultaneous impact on a number of financial institutions. Second, it refers to the chain reaction problem, the possibility that the failure of one bank will affect other banks. To some extent these two versions are interrelated: a major shock can trigger a chain reaction. The focus here is on the chain reaction problem, as that has been the principal justification of bank regulation. The fact that the U.S. economy, not just financial institutions, may suffer from economic shocks has not been thought to justify pervasive regulation of all economic firms.

a.   The Chain Reaction Problem

Systemic risk involves a chain reaction of bank failures that can occur for three principal reasons. First, it can result from the linkage of interbank deposits. This was a major concern when Continental Illinois Bank, a Chicago bank, almost failed in the mid-1980s. Continental held sizable deposits of other banks; in many cases the amount of the deposits substantially exceeded the capital of the depositor banks. These banks generally held such sizable deposits because they cleared payments, for example, checks or wire transfers, through Continental. If Continental had failed, those banks would have failed as well. Section 308 of the FDIC Improvement Act of 1991 gives the Federal Reserve Board powers to deal with this problem. It permits the Board to limit the credit extended by an insured depository institution to another depository institution. This may be feasible with respect to placements by one bank with another since the amount of credit extended is fixed for a given term. Indeed, it appears that the chain-reaction risk arising from bilateral credit exposures from overnight fed funds transactions are quite low—losses would not exceed 1 percent of total commercial banking assets when loss rates are kept to historically observed levels.[8]

It is more difficult to identify and control exposures with respect to interbank clearing accounts where the amount of credit extended is a function of payments traffic. For example, Bank *A* may be credited by its correspondent Bank *B* for an incoming wire transfer of $10 million. Bank *A* is thus a creditor of Bank *B* for this amount. If Bank *B* were to fail, Bank *A* is seriously exposed. It would be quite difficult, without serious changes in the payment system (for example, forcing banks to make and receive all payments through Federal Reserve rather than correspondent accounts), to limit these types of exposures.

Second, a chain reaction of bank failures can occur through payment system linkage. If one bank fails to settle its position in a net settlement system for large value payments, for example, the Clearing House Interbank Payments System (CHIPS) in the United States, other banks which do not get paid may in turn fail. This risk has been substantially eliminated by CHIPS's new net settlement procedures. This problem is explored at length in Chapter 9.

---

[8] C. Furfine, "Interbank Exposures: Quantifying the Risk of Contagion," 35 J. of Money, Credit, and Banking (2003), p. 111. See also, S. Wells, "Financial Interlinkages in the United Kingdom's Interbank Market and the Risk of Contagion," Bank of England Working Paper 230 (2004) looking at exposures in the U.K. interbank market, finding that while a single bank failure is rarely sufficient to cause other banks to fail, it does have the potential to substantially weaken their capital.

Finally, a chain reaction of bank failures can occur through imitative runs. When one bank fails, depositors in other banks, particularly those that are uninsured, may assume that their banks may also fail and so withdraw their funds, exposing these banks to a liquidity crisis and ultimately to failure. This is largely a result of lack of information in the market about the specific causes of the failure of the first bank. This is the typical situation in which the Fed plays the role of lender of last resort.

A recent study argues that the chain reaction of bank failure might be unrelated to linkages between banks.[9] The authors assert that significant bank failures could cause liquidity shortages. The contraction in the common pool of liquidity could then lead to other bank failures. They further argue that bailing out failed banks will not solve the liquidity contraction problem. The study is not clear as to how large failed banks must be as a percentage of the total market to cause a liquidity shortage.

Another recent study[10] attempts to estimate systemic risk in the international financial system. Its key methodological approach is to assess the impact of various financial crises on banks not directly exposed to a particular crisis. The idea is that abnormal returns experienced by these banks must occur through transmission mechanisms, e.g. the payment system, and thus denote the presence of systemic risk. Three different measurement techniques were used: measuring the stock prices, estimates of default extracted from stock prices and estimates of default extracted from equity option prices. The authors find very low levels of systemic risk. The stock price measurement finds that the maximum probability of a systemic failure is 5-29 percent across different crises. Default probabilities only increase at maximum 4 percent (in the 1998 Russian crisis). One weakness of the study is that it ignores off-balance sheet exposures from derivatives which for large banks may be as important as on-balance sheet exposures. One might conclude that studies finding low systemic risk undercut the need for such widespread bank regulation, but others contend that these results show the effectiveness of such regulation. However, some believe that bank regulation itself increases systemic risk by creating moral hazard through government guarantees and bailouts.[11]

b.   SUBSIDIARIES

When a foreign bank operates in a host country through a subsidiary, the host country can protect itself against systemic risk by subjecting the subsidiary to the same rules as other domestic banks. For example, the host

[9] D. Diamond and R. Rajan, "Liquidity Shortages and Banking Crises," NBER Working Paper 8937 (May 2002).

[10] S. Bartram, G. Brown, and J. Hund, "Estimating Systemic Risk in the International Financial System," Working Paper (August 16, 2004).

[11] G. Kaufman and K. Scott, "Does Bank Regulation Retard or Contribute to Systemic Risk," Stanford Law School, Olin Program in Law and Economics Working Paper 211 (December 2000).

country can control the level of deposits the subsidiary takes from other banks or limit the positions it incurs in net settlement payment systems in the same way that it does for domestic banks. Imitative runs could be a major concern to a host country since the failure of any domestic bank, even one that is foreign owned, could cause imitative runs on other domestic banks. Thus, there were reportedly imitative runs on other foreign banks in Hong Kong when Bank of Credit and Commerce International's (BCCI's) subsidiary in that country was closed in 1991 in connection with the worldwide collapse of BCCI. It is much less likely that the failure of the foreign parent will cause a run on host-country banks. While there is some evidence that there was a deposit loss at First American (a U.S. bank subsidiary of BCCI) after the failure of BCCI, it is unclear whether this was caused by the BCCI failure or an independent problem of bad loans. In any event, there were no runs on First American or other non-BCCI domestic banks.

If the failure of a foreign-owned bank would likely cause a chain reaction of bank failures, the host country could use its lender-of-last-resort power to keep the bank afloat. The host-country central bank would be lending to a domestic bank in its own currency—the fact of foreign ownership should not be a major obstacle to central bank support.

c.   BRANCHES

When a foreign bank operates in a host country through a branch, it is more difficult for the host country to deal with the systemic risk problem, particularly as it may manifest itself in the payment system. Branches of foreign banks may be less able than domestic banks to fund settlement obligations quickly in host-country money markets, and their home-country markets could be closed. On the other hand, linkage of interbank deposits should not be a significant problem since domestic banks generally will not clear local currency payments through branches of foreign banks. In addition, imitative runs on domestic banks are less likely to be caused by the failure of a foreign bank; depositors in domestic banks are unlikely to believe their own banks are in trouble just because a foreign bank has failed. The major concern is the payment system.

Unlike the case of the failure of a foreign-owned subsidiary, the failure of the foreign bank itself (along with its host-country branch offices) raises significant lender-of-last-resort issues for the United States. The foreign bank may have to be kept afloat by its own central bank through loans in the home-country currency. But the United States will have no assurance that the home-country central bank will do so. While the Federal Reserve could, in principle, itself extend credit in dollars to the foreign bank, it will be reluctant to do so. Such lending might expose it, and ultimately U.S. taxpayers, to losses. This will be hard to justify when support could have come instead from the home-country central bank.

The host country is likely to take measures to avoid becoming a lender-of-last-resort to a foreign bank. First, it may limit the participation of branches of foreign banks in host-country payment systems. Second, the host country may specially limit the settlement positions of branches of foreign banks in their payment systems or require that these positions be fully collateralized.

It appears that the BCCI banks in Luxembourg and the Cayman Islands and their branches, subsidiaries, and agencies (including the U.S. agencies) cleared a significant amount of their dollar payments through Bank of America, but there is no indication that this resulted in any settlement problems for Bank of America or other CHIPS participants. Perhaps this is partly explained by the fact that the Federal Reserve had advance information of the timing of the closure of the BCCI banks. This information was apparently used to help insure that Bank of America and other U.S. banks were not left exposed when the BCCI banks were closed. For example, Bank of America could have managed BCCI payments in a manner that would assure that outgoing payments never exceeded incoming payments by an amount greater than the collected balances of the BCCI banks. A system for insuring advance warning might be an important way of controlling systemic risk.[12]

Notes and Questions

1. Is systemic risk a major problem for the U.S. banking system? To what extent do the U.S. operations of foreign banks contribute to this problem?

2. Who should be the lender of last resort to foreign banks operating in the U.S. through branches or subsidiaries? The Fed or home-country central bank?

2.   SAFETY AND SOUNDNESS

Maintaining safety and soundness is a key policy objective of host countries which affects their supervision of foreign banks. This type of regulation is designed to avoid bank failures, which cause deposit insurance pay-outs and systemic risk. Deposit insurance payouts could require the injection of public funds when the insurance funds are depleted, as was the case in the 1980s U.S. thrift crisis. Host countries generally have less concern with maintaining the safety and soundness of foreign banks operating through subsidiaries rather than branches because they regulate subsidiaries more fully. Branches, on the other hand, which are part and parcel of the foreign bank, are mainly regulated by home countries.

---

[12] See H. Scott, "Supervision of International Banking Post-BCCI," 8 Georgia State University Law Review (1992), p. 487.

a.   DETERMINATION OF THE "HOME COUNTRY"

Since the adequacy of home-country supervision may be an issue for a host country with respect to subsidiaries, and is clearly an issue in the case of branches, identifying the home country for this purpose is essential. This can be done without much difficulty if two conditions hold: (1) there is one foreign bank parent located in one foreign country; and (2) the principal operations of the bank are carried on in that same country. For example, Deutsche Bank, the ultimate parent of all Deutsche Bank foreign subsidiaries, is located in Germany, and the principal operations of Deutsche Bank, as measured by total assets, are in Germany as well. However, neither of these conditions was met in the case of BCCI, with somewhat disastrous results.

b.   BCCI

BCCI was organized as follows. BCCI Holdings, a Luxembourg holding company, was at the top of the corporate pyramid. This entity, in turn, owned two principal banks, BCCI S.A., incorporated in Luxembourg, and BCCI Overseas, incorporated in the Cayman Islands. These banks had subsidiaries, branches, and agencies in over 69 countries; for example, the Luxembourg bank had over 20 branches in the United Kingdom and a subsidiary in Canada. There were two foreign bank parents rather than one, and neither bank's principal operations were in the countries of incorporation, namely Luxembourg and the Cayman Islands.

Why did this cause problems? The fact that there were two foreign bank parents meant that two countries rather than one were responsible for the safety and soundness of the banking organization as a whole; thus, there was no overall consolidated supervision of the banking organization. In principle, this problem might have been cured if Luxembourg had authority to regulate the entire operations of the bank holding company, BCCI Holdings, but this was not the case. The problem might also have been cured if there had been an international agreement that there could only be one ultimate bank parent, that is, that one of the banks had to become a subsidiary of the other, but this was also not the case.

Where two home countries are responsible, neither country is in the position to determine the safety and soundness of the entire operation, and matters can easily fall between the cracks. Affiliated banks can use intra-affiliate transactions to disguise bad loans. Where multiple regulators are responsible for the safety and soundness of a bank, no one is really accountable. Further, since the principal operations of the banking organization were in neither country, the supervisors in these countries had a limited ability to make judgments about the safety and soundness of their two banks. Perhaps in such cases the home country should be the country of principal operations, which would probably have been the United Kingdom in the case of BCCI. The problem was further compounded by the fact that supervision in the Cayman Islands, and to a lesser extent in Luxembourg, was rather weak. On the other hand, given the fact that multilateral bank operations are by definition spread out over many countries, even one overall regulator needs the active cooperation of foreign supervisors.

c.   SUBSIDIARIES

When a foreign bank operates through a subsidiary, the subsidiary is fully subject to the safety and soundness regime of the host country. The host country can ensure the safety and soundness of the foreign subsidiary through the same techniques it applies to domestic banks, such as capital requirements, examinations or audits, and loan limits. The host country will not necessarily be concerned with the safety and soundness of the foreign parent of the host-country subsidiary. The bankruptcy of the parent may result in a transfer of the ownership of the subsidiary, but it will not necessarily affect the safety and soundness of the subsidiary. The subsidiary can continue to operate even though its parent is bankrupt. This was true in the BCCI case where subsidiary U.S. banks, like the First American banks, continued to operate even though the BCCI bank owners were in insolvency proceedings.

But some countries, most notably the United States, are concerned with the safety and soundness of the foreign parents of host-country subsidiaries. This concern is based on the source of strength doctrine. Under this doctrine, the host country looks to the foreign parent to supply capital to the subsidiary if the subsidiary becomes weak. The basic idea is that the strength of the parent determines whether it will be able to save its subsidiary from difficulty by injecting additional capital. In addition, the host country may be concerned that a weak foreign parent may try to loot a local subsidiary through nonmarket value affiliate transactions, for example, purchasing its assets at below market prices.[13]

The safety and soundness of the foreign parent is not, however, within the regulatory control of the host country. Thus, for example, the safety and soundness of a U.K. banking parent of a U.S. bank is largely determined by the United Kingdom, not the United States. The United Kingdom determines the capital requirements, auditing and examination standards, and loan limits of its banks. And if one of its banks gets into trouble, the United Kingdom determines whether and how to rescue it. And if the foreign parent is not a bank, it may be entirely unregulated by the home country.

---

[13] The Hong Kong subsidiary of BCCI was closed on July 8, 1991, shortly after its parent holding company, BCCI Holdings (Luxembourg) SA, was declared insolvent. The Hong Kong subsidiary's insolvency had been largely caused by the discovery of over $268 million in unrecorded liabilities, some of which were due to other failed BCCI entities. Lending subsidiaries, in turn, may also have been imperiled by loans made to failed affiliates.

d.   BRANCHES

When a foreign bank operates abroad through a branch, the host country is more at the mercy of the home country. The branch is but an office of a bank located in another country. If the foreign bank fails, so do its branches abroad. The viability of the branches is largely determined by the efficacy of supervision by the bank's home country.

It may be tempting to conclude that host countries would be better off if they forced foreign banks to operate in their countries through subsidiaries rather than branches, but this would be incorrect, principally for two reasons. First, many host countries would prefer that local deposits be backed by the entire capital of the bank, which is the case with branch deposits, rather than the capital of the local subsidiary, which is the case with subsidiary deposits. Although the host country may have less control over the capital adequacy of the entire bank than it does over the subsidiary, the amount of capital is likely to be much larger. Also, many host countries (particularly smaller or less developed ones) may prefer to rely on home-country supervision rather than their own. Second branches of foreign banks are more competitive than their subsidiaries in host-country markets. This is largely because the loan capacity of the branch in the host country is a function of the bank's worldwide capital; that capacity would be much less if it were a function of the capital of a host-country subsidiary.

e.   THE BASEL CONCORDAT

The BCCI case raised major issues about the allocation of regulation authority among various jurisdictions. This has been partially dealt with through an international agreement, the Basel Concordat of the Bank for International Settlements (BIS). The BIS, created in 1930 to manage German reparations, is a bank whose depositors are limited to central banks. A significant portion of the world's foreign exchange reserves are held on deposit with the BIS. The BIS serves as a forum for cooperation among central banks and bank supervisors. The Board of Directors are all drawn from the Group of Ten countries (Belgium, Canada, France, Germany, Italy, Japan, the Netherlands, Sweden, Switzerland, the United Kingdom, and the United States). The Basel Committee on Banking Supervision is the key forum within BIS for international banking regulation. This Committee has formulated four minimum standards for the supervision of foreign banks, through promulgation of a Concordat.[14]

(1)   All international banking groups and international banks should be supervised by a home-country authority that capably performs consolidated supervision;

---

[14] Basel Committee on Banking Supervision, *Minimum Standards for the Supervision of International Banking Groups and their Cross-Border Establishments* (July 1992).

(2)   The creation of a cross-border banking establishment should receive the prior consent of both the host-country supervisory authority and the bank's and, if different, banking group's home-country supervisory authority;

(3)   Supervisory authorities should possess the right to gather information from the cross-border banking establishments of the banks or banking groups for which they are the home-country supervisor; and

(4)   If a host-country authority determines that any one of the foregoing minimum standards is not met to its satisfaction, that authority could impose restrictive measures necessary to satisfy its prudential concerns consistent with these minimum standards, including the prohibition of the creation of banking establishments.

f.   U.S. LEGISLATION

In 1991, in the wake of the BCCI scandal, Congress passed legislation greatly strengthening U.S. Government scrutiny of and power over foreign banks. Title II of the legislation contains the Foreign Bank Supervision Enhancement Act of 1991 (FBSEA), designed to strengthen federal supervision, regulation, and examination of foreign bank operations in the United States.

With FBSEA, the U.S. attempted to upgrade the quality and transparency of international banking supervision by retaining its own regulatory power in the event that overseas home country supervision or information available on a particular foreign bank was deemed inadequate.

FBSEA prohibits a foreign bank from establishing a branch, an agency, or acquiring ownership or control of a commercial lending company without the prior consent of the Federal Reserve, regardless of whether the branch or agency is chartered under state or federal law. This means that a foreign bank can no longer avoid U.S. Government scrutiny by obtaining a state charter for its branch or agency, which is what most foreign banks had done prior to FBSEA.

Furthermore, the Fed cannot approve a foreign branch, agency, or acquisition of a lending company unless the foreign bank is "subject to comprehensive supervision and regulation on a consolidated basis" by its home country authorities. The foreign bank must provide the Fed with information necessary to assess the application.[15]

---

[15] The Federal Reserve Board has generally applied the effective consolidated supervision requirement to representative offices of foreign banks even though they do not take deposits, although such a standard is not mandated by IBA. However, the first case of an application by a bank from the Russian Federation to establish a representative office, the Fed did not apply the standard. Promstroybank of Russia, "Federal Reserve System Order Approving Establishment of

Additionally, FBSEA amended the Bank Holding Company Act of 1956 (BHCA) to allow the Fed to consider the "managerial resources"—the competence, experience, and integrity of the officers, directors, and shareholders—and "financial resources" of the foreign bank when deciding whether to approve a foreign bank's application to form a U.S. subsidiary. In many bank failures (including BCCI), the lack of quality and integrity of bank management and the insufficiency of bank financial resources are significant contributing causes.

FBSEA also established additional discretionary standards that the Fed may take into account when assessing an application. These include the consent of the home country supervisor, the nature of the cooperative relationship between the Fed and the home country regulator as to sharing of material information, various assurances of the foreign bank, compliance with U.S. laws, the needs of the community, and the relative size of the bank in its home country. The Fed may impose additional conditions on its approval as it deems necessary (for example, cessation or restriction of certain activities).

FBSEA places the ultimate regulatory sanction of an organizational "death sentence" (termination) in the hands of the Fed. After notice and opportunity for a hearing, the Fed may order a foreign bank operating a state branch, or agency, or commercial lending company to cease operations. In order for the Fed to take such action, the foreign bank must not be subject to "comprehensive supervision or regulation on a consolidated basis" by its home country authorities. In addition, there must be reason to believe that the foreign bank has violated the law or engages in "unsafe or unsound banking practice." Furthermore, the Fed may recommend to the OCC that the license of any federal branch or federal agency be revoked if the Fed has reason to believe that such foreign bank or any affiliate has engaged in conduct for which the activities of any state branch or agency may be terminated as set forth above.

FBSEA effectively eliminated current competitive advantages that may have been available to state branches and agencies by imposing new limitations on their activities. For example, a foreign bank state branch may not conduct business that a federal branch is prohibited from conducting unless the activity is within "sound banking practice." If the foreign bank branch is insured, it cannot engage in any activity that poses "significant risk" to the FDIC fund. Also, state branches and agencies are subject to the same limitations that are applicable to federal branches and federal agencies under the IBA with respect to loans made to a single borrower.

Under FBSEA, the Fed was given authority to examine all U.S. branches of foreign banks (without pre-empting the examination authority of

---

a Representative Office" (April 8, 1996). Does this indicate that banks from different countries may be subject to different standards depending on the political importance of the country?

the other federal and state regulators). The Fed is required to examine each branch or agency of a foreign bank, each commercial lending company or bank controlled by one or more foreign banks or one or more foreign companies that control a foreign bank, and any other office or affiliate of a foreign bank conducting business in any state. Each branch or agency of a foreign bank must be subject to an on-site examination at least once during each 12-month period. The Fed, the OCC, and the FDIC are mandated to coordinate their examinations with each other and with appropriate state regulators, to the extent that such coordination is possible.

Under the GLB Act, the Federal Reserve Board has become the umbrella regulator responsible for the overall safety and soundness of bank holding companies and the new financial service holding companies. The Federal Reserve assesses the holding company on a consolidated or group-wide basis with the objective of ensuring that the "holding company does not threaten the viability of the depository institution subsidiaries."[16] Holding company regulation has mainly been justified on the grounds that the holding company should serve as a source of strength for the banks, i.e. be able to inject capital if needed. The Fed has emphasized that it does not intend to apply bank-like supervision to the non-banking entities of holding companies, or to replace supervision by primary bank regulators.[17] This has relieved concerns of foreign banks and their regulators that the Fed might be intruding into their own supervision of foreign banks and their holding companies.

Financial institution regulation in the United States is highly fragmented among multiple regulators. There are separate regimes for banking, insurance and securities, and dual regulation at the federal and state level for banking and securities. Within banking, there are numerous federal regulators, e.g. Federal Reserve Board, Office of the Comptroller of the Currency, and Federal Deposit Insurance Corporation. In the U.K. and other European countries, financial services regulation has been consolidated into a single regulator. One cost of fragmented federal regulation is regulatory arbitrage, where activities more highly regulated by one regulator move to a different entity regulated by another regulator. Where conglomerates are involved (one company offering multiple financial services, such as Citigroup) there may be significant coordination problems among regulators.

g.   The Daiwa Case: Safety and Soundness Controls Applied

Mr. Toshihide Iguchi, a trader at the New York state-chartered branch of Daiwa Bank (as of 1995 one of the 10 largest Japanese banks and

---

[16] Letter from Richard Spillenkothen, "Framework for Financial Holding Company Supervision" (August 15, 2000), p. 2.
[17] Id., at 3.

the 19th largest bank in the world) lost $1.1 billion from trading U.S. treasuries at its principal New York branch between 1984 and 1995, and he apparently concealed the losses from management until July 1995. Daiwa operated two state-chartered branches in New York City and 12 other branches and agencies in the United States. In addition, Daiwa owned a New York state-chartered bank, Daiwa Trust Company.

Daiwa's losses were not reflected in the books and records of the bank or in its financial statements, and were concealed through liquidations of securities held in the bank's custody accounts and falsification of its custody records. When management discovered the losses in July 1995, they did not promptly report them to U.S. bank regulators (Federal Reserve and New York State Banking Department). These regulators only learned of the losses on September 18, 1995. In addition, it appears that in 1992 and 1993 Daiwa management falsely assured Federal Reserve Board examiners that trading and custody had been split (this reduces the possibility of concealed losses), whereas they had in fact both remained under the control of Mr. Iguchi. These assurances were given as a result of Fed examinations that were mandated under FBSEA. It also appears that the Japanese Ministry of Finance (MOF) knew of the branch losses in August 1995 and did not immediately inform the U.S. regulators (ironically, when the Fed learned of the losses it waited four days before reporting them to New York officials). Daiwa further announced in October 1995 losses of approximately $97 million in its insured bank subsidiary, a trust company, due to trading activities. At least some of these trading activities between 1984-1987 were unauthorized. These losses were concealed by transferring them to offshore facilities. Daiwa had more than a sufficient amount of capital to absorb all of these losses without any threat to its solvency.

As a result, Daiwa's branch license and other U.S. banking operations were terminated by consent orders effective February 2, 1996.[18] Daiwa also faced U.S. criminal charges, brought on November 2, 1996, for defrauding regulators and obstructing justice. If convicted, it might have had to pay up to $1.3 billion in fines. On February 28, 1996, Daiwa entered into a plea bargain under which it pled guilty and was fined $340 million. Daiwa stated that its decision to conceal the losses resulted from the advice of MOF that was concerned about the effect a disclosure would have on the already fragile Japanese financial system.[19]

Criminal charges were also filed against Mr. Iguchi and Mr. Tsuda, the branch manager, and both pled guilty. Iguchi received a four year prison sentence and a $2.6 million fine. Tsuda was sentenced to two months in

---

[18] Board of Governors of the Federal Reserve System, Federal Deposit Insurance Corporation, and New York State Banking Department, Joint Statement (November 1995).
[19] "Daiwa Bank Pleads Guilty to Conspiring to Hide Loss," *The Wall Street Journal*, February 29, 1996.

prison, one year of supervised release to be served in Japan, and a $100,000 fine.

On January 29, 1996, Daiwa announced that it had sold $3 billion in U.S. assets to Sumitomo Bank Ltd., and transferred $1 billion of its remaining assets to its head office in Japan. In addition, Daiwa sold Sumitomo the rights to its U.S. operations for $65 million. In October 1998, Daiwa announced it was closing all of its foreign branches and would liquidate its overseas subsidiaries due to its inability to meet international capital standards.

Daiwa also faced problems in Japan. In September 2000, a Japanese court ordered the executives and former executives of Daiwa to pay $775 million to the bank for the losses caused by the New York branch management. This was then the highest damage award in the history of Japan.[20]

Before Daiwa, the Japanese neither examined nor required audits of the foreign branches of their banks. MOF announced in December 1995 that overseas branches of Japanese banks would be encouraged to obtain external audits and that the Bank of Japan would inspect branches in New York and London. This was in accord with Federal Reserve Board policy announced in November 1996 requiring foreign bank branches with poor management ratings to hire independent accountants to perform audits.

One can legitimately ask whether the Federal Reserve Board and the U.S. government overreacted to Daiwa. No U.S. depositor lost any money because Daiwa honored all of its debts—it was not insolvent. Whereas the bank did violate U.S. law, this might have been with the subtle encouragement of Japanese regulators and may not have justified the draconian measures taken. U.S. measures should be compared with much lighter measures taken by Japanese regulators, e.g. temporary suspension of business against U.S. investment banks such as Credit Suisse First Boston, which assisted Japanese banks in covering up bad Japanese loans. These actions arguably resulted in much larger losses that were paid for by the Japanese taxpayers.

In December 2003, France agreed "in principle" to settle the Executive Life case, a U.S. criminal prosecution that involved Crédit Lyonnais' (a state-owned bank) secret 1991 takeover of Executive Life, an insolvent California insurer. France agreed to pay $475 million, with other defendants, including Crédit Agricole (the current owner of Crédit Lyonnais), contributing an additional $285 million. Most of the funds will go to compensate policyholders of Executive Life for losses resulting from the insurer's collapse.[21] France added another $225 million to the settlement fund in February 2005. Also, in a civil suit, France settled in February 2005 with

---

[20] BNA Banking Report (October 2, 2000).
[21] J. Tagliabue, "Agreement in French Bank Case," *The New York Times*, December 12, 2003.

California's insurance regulator for $600 million. Actions are still pending against François Pinault, a French billionaire who invested in the acquisition of Executive Life.[22]

The latest regulatory action against a foreign bank involves UBS, United Bank of Switzerland, Europe's biggest bank by assets. The Fed fined UBS $100 million for supplying Dollar currency to countries, like Cuba, that are subject to U.S. trade sanctions.[23]

Notes and Questions

1.   What did BCCI teach us about the problems of insuring the safety and soundness of foreign bank owners of U.S. banks?

2.   Is the adequacy of foreign safety and soundness regulation more or less important with respect to branches or subsidiaries of foreign banks?

3.   What problems are there in using the principle of "effective consolidated supervision" as a means of determining whether foreign banks should be allowed to operate in the U.S.? Consider the fact that the 2003 billion dollar losses of Parmalat, the Italian food company, resulted in large part from $5 billion that Bonlat, a Parmalat subsidiary in the Cayman Islands, wrongly claimed it had in a Cayman bank account.

4.   Do you think the U.S. response to Daiwa, or the subsequent cases, was appropriate? Should host country regulators be involved in insuring the safety and soundness of branches of foreign banks?

3.   Federal Deposit Insurance and Bankruptcy Procedures

a.   Deposit Insurance

1.   Prior History

Prior to the adoption of the IBA in 1978, the deposits of foreign bank branches could not be insured by the FDIC. IBA completely reversed course. Section 6(a) of IBA prohibited a foreign bank from establishing a Federal branch that receives "deposits" of less than $100,000 unless the branch obtained FDIC insurance or the Comptroller determined by order or regulation that the branch was not engaged in "domestic retail deposit activities." With regard to state branches, s. 6(b) of the Act provided that no foreign bank could establish, and after September 17, 1979 no foreign bank could operate, a state branch in any state in which the deposits of a state

---

[22] J. Carreyrou and G. Simpson, "How Insurance Spat Further Frayed U.S.-French Ties," *The Wall Street Journal*, April 16, 2004.

[23] J. McKinnon and M. Walker, "Fed Fines UBS $100 Million for Money Transfer Violations," *The Wall Street Journal*, May 11, 2004.

bank would be required to be insured unless: (i) the branch does not accept deposits of less than $100,000; (ii) the branch has obtained FDIC insurance; or (iii) the FDIC determines by order or regulation that the branch is not engaged in "domestic retail deposit activities."

Foreign banks with insured branches were required to pledge assets equal to 10 percent of the average of the insured branch's liabilities. Qualifying assets consisted of a variety of interest-bearing obligations issued by banks, corporations, governmental entities and certain international organizations. In addition, the FDIC imposed an asset maintenance test on insured branches requiring insured branches to maintain eligible assets (generally safe and liquid) payable in United States dollars in an amount at least equal in book value to the amount of the branch's liabilities.[24]

All but a very few branches of foreign banks remained uninsured after the enactment of IBA by limiting their deposits to over $100,000. If foreign banks had chosen the insurance option for their banks, they would have had to pay for the insurance by contributions to the FDIC fund, a cost that would largely be passed on to depositors in the form of lower interest. Large depositors were more interested in having higher interest rates than having the first $100,000 of their deposits insured.

2. CURRENT PROVISIONS

The deposit insurance rules were significantly changed in 1991 with the enactment of the FDIC Improvement Act (FDICIA) when the basic rules were established that we have today. Foreign banks can no longer take insured deposits (deposits under $100,000) through branches; they must now do so through subsidiaries. Existing insured branches, of which there were only 52 in 1991, were grandfathered.

This approach deprives depositors and their insurers of the backing of the worldwide capital of strong foreign banks. These creditors can now only look to the capital of U.S. subsidiaries. Also, this approach limits the competitiveness of foreign banks in U.S. markets. Foreign banks with retail deposit funding will have less lending capacity since they are forced to lend off the capital of subsidiaries rather than worldwide capital. This is not in the interest of potential U.S. borrowers.

An important issue involves the extent to which the home office of a bank might be responsible for paying off local deposits of a foreign branch. This issue can arise where foreign branch deposits are confiscated, e.g. as in

---

[24] New York requires branches of foreign banks licensed by New York to put assets equivalent to 5 percent of their U.S. liabilities in pledge to protect depositors against bankruptcy. This currently amounts in total to $35 billion. New York has now reduced its requirement by capping pledges for individual banks at $400 million, which may reduce the overall pledged amount by about 80 percent. The move by New York may prompt the Comptroller of the Currency to consider relaxing similar requirements for U.S. licensed branches.

the case of Vietnam which confiscated assets of branches of U.S. banks, or frozen. In *Wells-Fargo-Asia Limited v. Citibank, N.A.*,[25] it was decided that, absent an agreement of the parties, under New York law, the head office is liable for a foreign branch's deposits in the case of a freeze. The case of expropriation might be different. In a freeze, the branch has not yet discharged its liabilities to local depositors, whereas in an expropriation it has discharged the depositors' liabilities by paying the expropriating state. Recently, the Congress of Argentina passed a law requiring foreign banks to disclose whether their home offices would honor local deposits.[26]

Section 6 of IBA was further amended in 1994 to deal with policies of the regulatory agencies allowing uninsured branches, in certain instances, to take initial deposits of under $100,000. Under previous FDIC regulation, 12 C.F.R. §346.4 (1995), there were five categories of deposits under $100,000 that could be accepted: business, U.S. government, international organizations, funds received from certain instruments (e.g. cashier's checks issued by the branch) and deposits of non-citizens who are not U.S. residents at the time of deposit. In addition, there was a de minimis exemption for 5 percent of branch deposits (for deposits that could not benefit from a specified exemption). The de minimis exemption was cut to 1 percent and s. 6(b)(2) of the IBA suggests some "Specific Factors" that should inform the formulation of more narrow specified exemptions.

Under the Federal Depositor Preference Law amending the Federal Deposit Insurance Act, 12 U.S.C. s.1821(d)(11), depositors' claims against failed banks are given preferential treatment. This allows the FDIC (as subrogee of insured deposits as well as uninsured deposits), to be paid before other creditors. Deposits in foreign branches of U.S. banks (i.e. deposits only payable abroad) are not given such a preference. The rationale for this exclusion is that such deposits are not generally insured; on the other hand, uninsured deposits in U.S. banks of over $100,000 *are* preferred. However, such large uninsured depositors in U.S. banks do bear part of the cost of deposit insurance as passed on by banks. Of course, inclusion of foreign deposits in foreign branches in the preference would decrease the recovery of the FDIC on behalf of U.S. depositors.

One might have taken another approach to the deposit insurance problem: deposits in a branch of a foreign bank could be covered under the deposit protection scheme of its home country, and the home country could be given jurisdiction over the worldwide assets of any failed bank. This would have the advantage of having the insuring country bear the risk for its own supervisory shortcomings and preserve the unity of the bankruptcy of the bank. But this approach raises problems of its own.

---

[25] 936 F.2d 723 (2d Cir. 1991), *cert. denied* 505 U.S. 1204 (1992) *on remand from* 495 U.S. 660 (1990).
[26] BNA 80 Banking Report (May 19, 2003), pp. 834-35.

First and foremost, there is the issue of consumer confusion. Imagine a potential depositor winding his way through Wall Street, or perhaps even Atlanta, past the offices of various banks, including those of branches of foreign banks. A deposit in each domestic bank would be insured similarly under the United States deposit insurance scheme, but a deposit at each of the branches of foreign banks would be insured differently, according to the various schemes in place in the home countries of these banks.

3.   FUTURE CHANGES

The U.S. is currently considering some basic reforms of its deposit insurance system, including indexation of insurance coverage levels to rates of inflation, fuller authority to charge risk-based premiums, and new ways of calculating target levels of Fund reserves. There has also been an extended debate as to whether the current $100,000 limits on insurance per account should be increased. Those favoring an increase point to the lowering of the effective rate over time due to inflation, while those opposing it point to the moral hazard problem, i.e. that bank depositors will not monitor banks if their deposits are insured, with the result that the banks will be more risky than desirable. The FDIC is also considering whether to reinsure some of its risk in the private insurance market. This would not only reduce FDIC risk, but also the pricing of the reinsurance would perhaps permit the FDIC to more accurately price its own insurance premiums. The issue would, however, then become the safety and soundness of the private insurers.

b.   BANKRUPTCY PROCEDURES: THE CASE OF BCCI[27]

1.   BRANCHES

One way for the host country to limit insurance fund or depositor losses is to require branches of foreign banks to pledge readily marketable assets and to maintain the value of assets at a certain level in excess of liabilities, a "quasi-capital" requirement. These requirements could help to insure that if the foreign bank failed, sufficient branch assets would be available to the host-country authorities to cover losses. As discussed, federally-licensed and many state-licensed branches of foreign banks are subject to such requirements in the United States.

This approach is based on an important but questionable assumption—that the host-country authorities have or should have the legal power to seize branch assets and to control their disposition in the event of

---

[27] When an insolvent foreign bank has no branches or agencies in the U.S.—not the case with BCCI—the bank's bankruptcy is dealt with under the Bankruptcy Code. The usual procedure under §304 of the Code is to establish an ancillary proceeding. Under which the court has the discretion to turn over U.S. assets to the home country liquidator. S. Schwarcz, "The Confused U.S. Framework for Foreign Bank Insolvency: An Open Research Agenda," 1 Review of Law and Economics 81 (2005).

the failure of the foreign bank. If the home-country receiver asserts a claim to the assets of the entire bank, including the assets of foreign branches, the host country may not be able to dispose of the assets of the branch, at least not without causing conflict with the home-country receiver. This kind of problem has arisen in the BCCI litigation in the United States and abroad.

When BCCI failed, its U.S. agencies (the only offices it had in the U.S.) failed with it. While BCCI agencies in New York and California were legally prohibited from taking deposits from individual U.S. citizens or residents, it appears that the BCCI agencies did so anyway. The U.S. assets of the failed BCCI banks, estimated at $550 million, consisted only in minor part of the agencies' assets. Far more important were their alleged stockholdings in several U.S. banks, including First American, and clearing accounts at the Bank of America and other banks. Claims against U.S. assets included less than $20 million owed by the agencies to third parties (non-BCCI entities), as well as a $200 million fine which the Federal Reserve Board sought to levy against BCCI for illegally acquiring certain U.S. banks. There was also the prospect of additional fines as a result of criminal prosecutions by federal and state authorities.

On August 2, 1991, in a bankruptcy proceeding in the U.S. District Court, Southern District of New York, which was dealing with BCCI's United States assets, the liquidators of the Luxembourg holding company and the two subsidiary banks obtained a temporary restraining order (TRO) against any claims to BCCI's U.S. assets, including the assets of the agencies. The TRO was based on s. 304 of the U.S. Bankruptcy Code which permits a court to enjoin the pursuit of claims against the U.S. assets of a bankrupt entity on the theory that the claims should be brought as part of a foreign proceeding (in this case, the insolvency proceedings in Luxembourg and the Cayman Islands).

On October 15, 1991, the foreign liquidators agreed to a consent order entered by the bankruptcy court that permitted the California and New York state regulators of the BCCI agencies to remove the agency assets from the bankruptcy court and to take control of them pursuant to ongoing state liquidation proceedings. The consent order further provided that the foreign liquidators would assert no claims against the agency assets in the state proceedings and that any surplus remaining after the liquidation of the assets and satisfaction of estimated claims against the agencies would be remitted to the bankruptcy court.

On December 19, 1991, the BCCI liquidators agreed to plead guilty to various federal and state criminal charges brought against the BCCI banks. These charges included a federal indictment alleging that BCCI secretly acquired control of several U.S. banks. Under the settlement, $275 million in U.S. assets was used to pay off U.S. creditors of the agencies, to pay part of the outstanding fines, and to increase the capital of U.S. banks illegally owned by BCCI. The $275 million balance of the $550 million in U.S. assets was turned over to the consolidated bankruptcy proceedings in Luxembourg and the Caymans.

The net effect of the United States proceedings was that $275 million in U.S. assets was not consolidated with the worldwide receivership assets of the BCCI banks in the Luxembourg and Caymans proceedings and thus was not available to creditors of those banks. It appeared that the U.S. creditors of the BCCI agencies received full payment of their claims.

Certain observations can be made about these proceedings. As a threshold matter, it is unclear whether assets of agencies or branches of foreign banks are subject to the jurisdiction of the U.S. bankruptcy court at all; assets of failed U.S. banks clearly are not—they are subject to special FDIC procedures. This uncertainty might partially account for the willingness of the BCCI liquidators to have agreed to the bankruptcy consent order of October 15, 1991. They might have done worse with the FDIC. In addition, it appears that U.S. assets of failed foreign banks can be cut off from claims by foreign liquidators through the use of host-country criminal prosecutions.

If U.S. or other country assets of failed foreign banks are not fully consolidated in home-country foreign insolvency proceedings—in what is called the "ring fence" approach—and such assets are substantial, the ability of a foreign receiver to reorganize a failed bank will be severely limited. While this was not a practical alternative in the BCCI case—earlier efforts to reorganize the bank with an infusion of capital from Abu Dhabi had foundered—it could be a problem in future bankruptcies of multinational banks. Indeed, the possible need to reorganize a failed company is a significant rationale for the U.S. Bankruptcy Code's section 304 proceeding. In fact, it was this concern that was behind the decision of U.S. authorities to assert jurisdiction over the London branch assets of Franklin National Bank when that bank was in danger of failing in 1974. The fact that the U.S. authorities had control over all of Franklin's assets was an important factor in their ability to sell the troubled bank to European American Bank.

The failure to consolidate may also result in the inability of non-U.S. creditors to obtain the same pro rata share of all of the bank's assets that they would have obtained if the assets were consolidated. While the creditors of BCCI's U.S. agencies were fully paid off, creditors in the foreign insolvency procedures were not. This was a somewhat arbitrary and discriminatory result.

Apart from the difficulties of preferring some creditors of a bank at the expense of others, the assets of an agency or branch of a foreign bank may have little to do with their actual business activities. It appears that the BCCI banks shifted assets among branches to avoid detection of insolvency. The difficulty of sorting out assets between various offices of a bank illustrates the need for a consolidated bankruptcy proceeding. A further complication arises insofar as the host country asserts jurisdiction over assets of a failed foreign bank that are within its jurisdiction but are not assets of the entities (an agency or branch) operating in its country. For example, part of the U.S. assets of the BCCI banks reportedly consisted of $85 million of deposits of the Tokyo branch of BCCI Luxembourg in U.S. banks. There is no clear rationale for using these assets to satisfy claims of U.S. creditors of U.S. agencies or to make capital infusions into U.S. banks allegedly owned by BCCI, rather than using them to satisfy the claims of Japanese creditors against the Tokyo branch or the claims of worldwide creditors against the Luxembourg bank.

The strongest argument for the host country to preserve the assets of a branch or agency of a failed foreign bank for local creditors is that the host country is at risk for the supervisory failures of the home country. This rationale is much stronger when the host country insures local depositors than when it merely seeks to protect their interests, as in the case of the U.S. agencies of BCCI. And under present law, as discussed above, the U.S. does not insure the branches of foreign banks. Banks seeking to take retail deposits must organize as subsidiaries.

A 2004 article whose authors include the general counsel of the Federal Reserve Bank of New York, Thomas Baxter Jr., sets forth the virtues of territoriality (ring-fencing) under New York law and concludes that the burden is on advocates of universality (unity) to change it.[28] This is lawyers speak for a position that favors territoriality. They argue that a territoriality approach leads to earlier initiation of proceedings by host supervisors seeking to preserve assets. Of course, local supervisors could commence the bankruptcy without having the power to ring-fence assets. The also argue that territoriality will produce better overall supervision and less supervisory moral hazard (if local supervisors can liquidate branches, the home supervisor must cooperate with them). However, it would seem that the home supervisors insuring worldwide depositors (outside the U.S.) have more to lose from failure than host countries. They also contend that local supervisors are in a better position to observe the adequacy of internal controls. This is undoubtedly true but this bears on allocation of supervisory responsibility not bankruptcy territoriality. Finally, they argue that territoriality maximizes asset recovery since local supervisors are in a better position to pursue local wrongdoers. This is also true, but why should the local supervisors keep the fruits of their pursuit solely for the benefit of local creditors? One might cynically suggest that local officials will not expend resources if the fruits of their efforts have to be shared with foreign creditors. This is undoubtedly true and is the best argument for territoriality.

---

[28] T. Baxter Jr., J. Hansen, and J. Sommer, "Two Cheers for Territoriality: An Essay on International Bank Insolvency Law," 78 American Bankruptcy Law Journal 57 (2004).

2.   SUBSIDIARIES

Subsidiaries raise no major problems with respect to depositor protection. Subsidiaries are supervised and insured by the host country, and the host country has jurisdiction over the bankruptcy of its own domestic banks whether or not they are owned by foreign banks. As in the BCCI case, various claims may be asserted against the failed bank's interest in its foreign subsidiaries. For example, there were claims against BCCI's interests in various United States banks allegedly owned by BCCI, but these claims only concerned ownership of the banks, not their supervision or solvency.

3.   BCCI SETTLEMENT

On December 20, 1995, the Luxembourg court in charge of the BCCI bankruptcy reached a worldwide settlement for creditors. The debts of the bank, originally estimated at $14 billion, were reduced to $10 billion through lengthy negotiations. Assets initially estimated at somewhat over $1 billion stood at $3.3 billion (as of April 1996), as a result of a contribution of $1.8 billion from the government of Abu Dhabi (the principal shareholder) $243 million received from the United States, and more than $400 million from Sheikh Khalid bin Mahfouz of Saudi Arabia (a settlement of claims against him by the liquidators). Assets were further increased in 1998 by a settlement with BCCI's accounting firms for $125 million and an additional $70 million contribution from Abu Dhabi. The case was finally settled in September 1998 for around 60 percent of claims. Additional recoveries may come from actions filed by liquidators. In March 2001, the House of Lords decided that the liquidators could bring a $1 billion claim against the Bank of England for negligent supervision.[29] The case still drags on.

Notes and Questions

1.   How was deposit insurance dealt with prior to 1978, by IBA after 1978, and by the amendments to IBA in 1991? Which of the three approaches is preferable? Some countries like Germany insure worldwide deposits. Should the U.S. allow retail or wholesale branches to operate in the U.S. covered by foreign insurance schemes?

2.   What do you think of the U.S. ring-fencing approach?

3.   Should bank regulators be held responsible for the failure to close a bank in a timely manner?

4.   PERMISSIBLE ACTIVITIES

Under s. 8(a) of the IBA, a foreign bank with a branch, agency or commercial lending company in the United States is subject to the BHCA.

---

[29] *Three Rivers District Council v. Governor and Company of the Bank of England* (2001) UKHL/16.

Therefore, absent grandfathering or exemption it must restrict its activities to those "closely related" to banking under s. 4(c)(8) of the BHCA. The definition of foreign bank is very broad and includes the foreign subsidiaries and affiliates of a foreign bank. The IBA's restrictions on the activities of a foreign bank can be far-reaching, applying to the domestic and foreign activities of both its non-banking and banking affiliates.

At the time Congress passed the IBA, many foreign financial institutions owned more than 5 percent of the voting shares of nonbanking companies or were engaging, either directly or through their affiliates, in nonbanking activities in the United States. In order to avoid imposing an undue burden on those institutions, the IBA grandfathered certain investments and activities.

a.   GRANDFATHERING

Section 8(c) of the IBA permits a foreign bank or company to continue, after December 31, 1985, to engage in those nonbanking activities in the United States in which it was lawfully engaged either directly or through an affiliate on July 26, 1978, and to engage directly or through an affiliate in nonbanking activities in the United States which were covered by an application filed on or before July 26, 1978. However, the Federal Reserve Board can terminate the authority to continue such nonbanking activities after December 31, 1985 if it determines that such action is necessary to prevent undue concentration of resources, decreased or unfair competition, conflicts of interest, or unsound banking practices in the United States.

In addition, a foreign bank or company may retain ownership or control of any voting shares (and where necessary to prevent dilution of its voting interest, may acquire additional voting shares) of a nonbanking company provided that: (i) the foreign bank or company owns, controls or holds with power to vote more than 5 percent of the voting shares of the nonbanking company; (ii) the activities engaged in by the nonbanking company are securities activities; (iii) the majority of the voting shares of the nonbanking company have been owned since July 26, 1978 by a company or group of companies organized under the laws of the United States or any state; and (iv) no foreign bank or group of banks owns or controls, directly or indirectly, 45 percent or more of the voting shares of the nonbanking company.

b.   EXEMPTIONS

Section 2(h)(2) of the BHCA, originally enacted as part of the IBA and then later amended, exempts from the activity restrictions of the BHCA investments by foreign bank holding companies in certain foreign corporations principally engaged in banking business outside the United States (the 2(h) exemption). It provides:

"(2) Except as provided in paragraph (3) the prohibitions of section 4 of this Chapter [on nonbanking activities and direct or indirect ownership or control of the voting shares of nonbanking companies] shall not apply to shares of any company organized under the laws of a foreign country (or to shares held by such company in any company engaged in the same general line of business as the investor company or in a business related to the business of the investor company) that is principally engaged in business outside the United States if such shares are held or acquired by a bank holding company organized under the laws of a foreign country that is principally engaged in the banking business outside the United States. For the purpose of this subsection, the term "section 2(h)(2) company" means any company whose shares are held pursuant to this paragraph.

(3) Nothing in paragraph (2) authorizes a section 2(h)(2) company to engage in (or acquire or hold more than 5 percent of the outstanding shares of any class or voting securities of a company engaged in) any banking, securities, insurance, or other financial activities, as defined by the Board in the United States. This paragraph does not prohibit a section 2(h)(2) company from holding shares that were lawfully acquired before August 10, 1987 ..."

The 2(h)(2) exemption is required because foreign banking organizations commonly engage in a wide range of financial, and even commercial activities. If the BHCA were fully applicable to foreign banks with subsidiaries in the U.S., the foreign bank parent, or its affiliates, could only engage in activities that were "closely related to banking," in or *outside* the U.S. This would effectively preclude foreign banks from doing banking in the United States [*emphasis added*].

The statutory 2(h)(2) exemption is fleshed out by Regulation K[30] which provides that a "qualified foreign banking organization" (QFBO), an organization that does mostly banking and does so outside the US, can engage in virtually any activity outside the U.S. A QFBO must have more than half of its worldwide business in banking, disregarding its U.S. banking, and have most of its banking assets and revenues outside the United States. A subsidiary of a QFBO can engage in any activity in the United States that it engages in abroad except for certain financial activities, including insurance and securities. These financial activities can only be engaged in with Board approval, which will not be given if domestic bank holding companies cannot engage in the same activity.

The Federal Reserve Board originally proposed in 1997 to:

"... eliminate from the first prong of the QFBO test (i.e. that more than half its worldwide business be banking), the requirement that all banking activities be conducted within the bank ownership chain. Thus, a

---

[30] 12 C.F.R. §211.23(f).

FBO that had substantial life insurance activities outside of the banking chain would have been able to count such activities as "banking" in calculating whether the majority of its worldwide activities are banking, but not when calculating whether the majority of its banking business is outside of the United States."

The Final Rule did not adopt the 1997 Proposal. The Fed believes that, in light of GLB, elimination of the banking chain requirement would permit a foreign insurance group that owned a foreign bank and qualified as a financial holding company (FHC) to make commercial and industrial investments in the United States beyond those permissible under either the insurance or merchant banking authority, even though a domestic insurance company with FHC status could not make such investments. Therefore, the existing QFBO test was maintained.

The Final Rule added a new provision to the existing QFBO test, however, that would permit FBOs that meet the QFBO test, if banking activities outside the bank ownership chain are counted (limited QFBO), to be eligible for the exemptions afforded a QFBO other than the exemption that permits certain foreign companies in which the limited QFBO has an interest to engage in activities in the United States. In order to be considered a limited QFBO, the organization must include a foreign bank that itself could meet the current QFBO test.

There is a second exemption from the activities exemption in s. 4(c)(9) of the BHCA. This section provides that the Federal Reserve Board may exempt a foreign company from the BHCA activities restrictions if the Fed determines this to be in the public interest. This exemption has rarely been used.

c.   PROVISIONS FOR FINANCIAL HOLDING COMPANIES

The need for grandfathering and exemptions from activities restrictions has been substantially alleviated by GLB which allows foreign banks, like U.S. bank holding companies, to become FHCs with a wider range of permissible activities. GLB permits a well-capitalized and well-managed U.S. BHC to become a financial service holding company (FHC) through which it can engage in a full range of "financial activities," including insurance, securities and merchant banking.[31]

---

[31] If a foreign bank becomes a FHC, grandfather rights for IBA activities are terminated. If a foreign bank is unable to qualify as a FHC, it may not engage in the expanded set of new financial activities, but all of its previously authorized activities are grandfathered. However, giving due regard to the principles of national treatment and competitive equality, the Fed may impose the same prudential restrictions on such grandfathered activities as apply to those activities when engaged in by FHCs. Grandfathering includes s. 20 activities but the Fed has made clear that any underwriting through U.S. offices, whether or not securities are distributed abroad or in the U.S., counts as underwriting subject to the BHCA restrictions. Board of Governors of the Federal Reserve System, Interpretation (February 7, 2003).

Under GLB, the statutory definition of financial activity includes any activity that the Federal Reserve Board has determined under Regulation K to be usual in connection with the transaction of banking or other financial operations abroad.[32] This list includes, in s. 211.10(a) (10), "data processing" without qualification. Currently, under Regulation Y U.S. bank holding companies are only able to engage in data processing for third parties in the U.S. to the extent of 30 percent of total data processing revenues.[33] GLB was widely reported to have removed the barriers between banking and finance but to have preserved the barriers between finance and commerce. Indeed, many of the key players, such as Congressman Leach, the ex-Chairman of the House Banking Committee, publicly supported the reforms on the basis that commerce and finance would be kept separate. The Federal Reserve also actively opposed the combination. Indeed, the proposed banking reforms of President George Bush,[34] which explicitly allowed commercial firms to own bank holding companies, were rejected by many for the very reason that they allowed commerce to be combined with banking. Reform efforts since that time have avoided such a combination.

Under GLB, if a foreign bank is a BHC in the United States because it owns a subsidiary bank in the United States, its subsidiaries must comply with the same "well capitalized" and "well managed" requirements applicable to the subsidiaries of U.S. based BHCs. If, however, the foreign bank operates in the U.S. through branches and wishes to become a FHC, GLB requires that "the Board shall apply comparable capital and management standards ... giving due regard to the principle of national treatment and competitive opportunity." Section 4(l)(3) of the BHCA, as amended. Rigid application of the "well-capitalized" standard to foreign banks could prevent them from becoming FHCs. A well-capitalized bank must maintain leverage capital (capital/total assets) of 5 percent, Tier I risk-based capital of at least 6 percent, and total risk-based capital of at least 10 percent. These standards are substantially higher than international capital standards.

On January 25, 2000, the Federal Reserve Board adopted an interim rule applying the 6 percent Tier I and 10 percent total risk-based standards to foreign banks from countries whose home-country supervisors have adopted the Basel capital standards.[35] However, the proposed leverage ratio (capital over total assets unadjusted for risk) was 3 percent rather than the normal 5 percent. Banks from countries that had not adopted Basel standards were required to obtain a determination from the Board that their capital was comparable to the capital that would be required of a U.S. bank.

The European Commission complained about the leverage requirement, pointing to the fact that it went beyond agreed international

---

[32] See 12 C.F.R. §221.4(b).

[33] 12 C.F.R. §225.28(b)(14).

[34] Embodied in H.R. 1505, 102nd Cong. (1991).

[35] 65 Federal Register 3785, as amended on March 21, 2000, 65 Federal Register 15053.

capital standards. The Fed argued that U.S. banks were subject to a higher leverage requirement (5 percent as compared with 3 percent) and that foreign banks below 3 percent could still qualify as FHCs if they could show "comparable" capital strength to a well-capitalized U.S. bank.

In adopting its Final Rule, the Fed dropped the leverage requirement entirely, bending to the pressure from foreign banks (as well as many in Congress). Instead, a bank's leverage ratio has been added to the list of factors that the Board may look at in determining whether a foreign bank has adequate capital. In addition, the Board changed its approach on the application of the "well managed" standards. The interim rule had required each U.S. branch of the foreign bank to be well managed, while the Final Rule looks at such branches in the aggregate.

d.   GLB AND MERCHANT BANKING

GLB permits FHCs to engage in merchant banking (which can involve the ownership of purely commercial companies). In principle, merchant banking only involves holding shares for investment and resale and does not involve operational control over companies in which the FHC has an investment. But it is very hard to draw lines in this area. Thus GLB, under new BHCA s. 4(k)(4)(H), allows ownership of shares that are "held for a period of time to enable the sale or disposition thereof on a reasonable basis consistent with the financial viability of the activities" and provides that the FHC "not routinely manage or operate" companies in which it has invested "except as may be necessary to obtain a reasonable return on investment upon resale or disposition."

The Federal Reserve Board and the Secretary of the Treasury issued a final rule fleshing out the GLB merchant banking authority.[36] The Rule defines a "merchant banking investment" as an investment by a FHC in a nonfinancial entity. Before a FHC may engage in merchant banking, it must be affiliated with either a securities firm, or an insurance firm and an investment adviser that advises the insurance company. Merchant banking investments must be made through a subsidiary other than a depository institution, but a foreign bank is not a depository for this purpose. However, a U.S. branch of a foreign bank is a depository.

Three mechanisms can be used for merchant banking investments: portfolio investment, a private equity fund controlled by the FHC, or a private equity fund not controlled by the FHC. A FHC may routinely operate and manage its portfolio companies in private equity funds not controlled by the FHC, but not otherwise. The merchant banking Rule further provides that in most cases merchant banking investments may be held for only 10 years, or 15 years if the investment is made through a qualifying private

---

[36] 66 Federal Register 8466 (January 31, 2001).

equity fund. A FHC may not cross-market products or services between a portfolio company and a depository institution.

The Fed has also issued a rule on merchant banking capital.[37] It provides for deductions from capital for certain merchant banking investments. The proposal applies to banks and their holding companies. It would apply to equity investments made under the new GLB merchant banking authority and to equity in non-financial companies under most other authorities. However, investments by an SBIC (small business investment corporation) are exempt and subject to standard capital rules. Many existing private equity investments are organized as SBICs. The rule imposes a capital charge that increases in steps as the level of concentration in equity investments increases, ranging from an 8 percent of Tier I capital deduction for investments up to 15 percent of an organization's Tier I capital, to a 25 percent charge for investments over 25 percent of Tier I capital.

The U.S. Congress in 2003 was considering whether to cut back on GLB in light of concerns that conflicts of interest existed between the banking and securities business of FHCs. In particular, there was a concern that banks were tying loans to underwriting. However such tying would already be prohibited by the anti-tying provisions of existing law, at least where there was market power. Also there are benefits to customers from banks being able to jointly offer services; indeed, these benefits were largely responsible for the GLB. No action was, however, taken.

e.   SARBANES-OXLEY

Section 402 of the Sarbanes-Oxley Act amended Section 13 of the Securities Exchange Act of 1934 to prohibit domestic and foreign issuers from making or arranging loans to their directors and executive officers unless the loans fall within specified exemptions.

One exemption permits insider lending by banks and other depository institutions insured by the FDIC if the loan is subject to insider lending restrictions under the Federal Reserve Act, which are implemented by the Federal Reserve Board's Regulation O. Foreign banks complained that this exemption gives domestic banks an advantage since foreign banks are not subject to such restrictions. As a result, the SEC has proposed to allow a foreign bank or its parent company to make loans to its insiders or the insiders of its parent as long as the bank meets specified criteria, which are generally comparable to those required for domestic banks: (1) the laws of the foreign bank's home jurisdiction require deposit insurance, or the foreign bank's home jurisdiction supervisor provides comprehensive supervision or regulation on a consolidated basis over the bank as determined by the Federal Reserve Board; (2) the laws of the foreign bank's home jurisdiction restrict the foreign bank from making loans to its insiders or those of its

---

[37] 67 Federal Register 3784 (January 25, 2002).

parent company unless certain insider lending restrictions are met; and (3) the foreign bank's board of directors approves any loan that, when aggregated with the amount of all other outstanding loans to the particular insider, exceeds $500,000, and the recipient of the loan has not participated in the vote regarding the loan.[38]

Notes and Questions

1.   Some countries have foreign banks that can engage in almost any activity (universal banks) and other countries permit non-bank affiliates of the bank to engage in these activities. How does IBA and Regulation K handle the problem of the non-U.S. activities of foreign bank holding companies? How does it handle activities within the U.S.? To what extent can a simple national treatment standard be applied to activities of foreign banks?

2.   What do you think of the proposal, prior to GLB, that would have required foreign banks to mimic the structure of U.S. banks by organizing their U.S. banking and securities activities in separate subsidiaries of a U.S. bank holding company. That is, it would have prohibited foreign banks seeking to take advantage of the new securities powers from engaging in banking through direct branches of the foreign bank.

3.   Does it make sense to require foreign banks which operate in the United States only through branches and not subsidiaries to be "well-capitalized" and "well-managed" before they can own securities, insurance or merchant banking affiliates in the United States? Under GLB, a U.S. bank holding company which is not "well-capitalized" or "well-managed" can become a FHC as long as its subsidiary banks are "well-capitalized" and "well-managed."

D.   CONCERN WITH THE OPERATIONS OF U.S. BANKS ABROAD

This Chapter does not generally deal with the regulation of the foreign operations of U.S. banks. Regulation K of the Federal Reserve Board establishes the permissible investments of banking organizations abroad, 12 C.F.R. §211.8, and the primary bank regulators also specify the powers that U.S. banks may exercise through foreign branches. For example, the Federal Reserve specifies the powers of state member banks in §211.3 of Regulation K. Generally, U.S. banks are given wide latitude.

In 2004-2005, Citigroup encountered a number of regulatory problems abroad. Their private banking license in Japan was suspended,

---

[38] K. Blackman, "SEC to Exempt Foreign Banks from Insider Lending Ban," International Financial Law Review (October 2003), p. 19.

they were investigated in Europe for manipulation of sovereign bond markets, and allegations by Italian prosecutors that they violated securities laws in their dealings with the failed agricultural firm, Parmalat. In addition, Citigroup was involved in various domestic regulatory matters, as well. These regulatory exposures translate into financial exposure, through regulatory fines and shareholder lawsuits. As a result, the Federal Reserve Board has indicated that it would not look favorably on any further expansion by Citigroup until it gets its control system in order. The Fed made this statement in the course of approving an acquisition of a small Texas bank in March 2005. The Fed has jurisdiction over any acquisitions by bank holding companies.

E. THE GATS

This Chapter has discussed U.S. attempts to regulate foreign banks doing business in the United States through its power to condition access to its markets. This power has been affected by the GATS.

The 1994 General Agreement on Trade in Services (GATS) resulted from the Uruguay Round of trade negotiations that closed in December 1993. The Uruguay Round produced a new structure, the World Trade Organization (WTO), as well as the agreement on services. Special provisions of GATS apply to financial services. The core principle of GATS, expressed in Article II, is unconditional most-favored-nation (MFN) treatment: each service or service supplier from a member country must be treated no less favorably than any other foreign service or service supplier.

1. STRUCTURE OF THE GATS

The GATS has two major components. The first consists of a so-called framework agreement, which establishes overall rules for trade in services, together with various annexes, including one dealing with issues specific to financial services. The second consists of each country's schedule for specific commitments and a list of MFN exemptions for that country. For financial services, there is a unique additional element, namely, the Understanding on Commitments in Financial Services. Commitments scheduled under the Understanding are extended to all members of the WTO.

2. GENERAL OBLIGATIONS: MFN AND TRANSPARENCY

Two major "general obligations" of the GATS are the MFN principle and "transparency." A country is required to honor a general obligation for *all* services sectors regardless of whether it has included a particular sector in its schedule of commitments. However, subject to certain conditions, the GATS allows a country to take exemptions from the general MFN obligation. The

United States initially took a broad MFN exemption for financial services. No exemptions are permitted from the transparency requirement.

3.   SPECIFIC COMMITMENTS: MARKET ACCESS AND NATIONAL TREATMENT

In the GATS, market access and national treatment are "specific commitments" as opposed to general obligations. As a result, national treatment and market access do not apply across-the-board to all services sectors; instead, they apply only to sectors, subsectors, or activities that are listed in a country's schedule of commitments.

4.   SPECIAL PROVISION FOR FINANCIAL SERVICES: UNDERSTANDING ON COMMITMENTS IN FINANCIAL SERVICES

The Annex on Financial Services and the Understanding on Commitments in Financial Services contain provisions specific to financial services. Countries that choose to schedule commitments in accordance with the Understanding undertake commitments to market access and national treatment for all financial services subsectors and use a negative list approach to scheduling—that is, everything is included unless excepted. The Understanding also contains a standstill provision that limits exceptions to existing nonconforming measures.

5.   ANNEX ON FINANCIAL SERVICES

Prudential Carve-Out. The prudential carve-out for domestic regulation permits a country to take prudential measures "for the protection of investors, depositors, policy holders or persons to whom a fiduciary duty is owed," or "to ensure the integrity and stability of the financial system" regardless of any other provisions of the GATS.

Disagreement over whether a particular national measure falls within the prudential carve-out is subject to WTO dispute settlement procedures and thus, if necessary, to a determination by a dispute settlement panel. However, most regulators do not appear to be particularly concerned about this possibility. For one thing, if a country is concerned that a particular measure might not be generally accepted as prudential in the future, it could list the measure as an exception in its initial schedule of commitments.

Dispute Settlement. Ensuring financial services expertise in the handling of disputes involving financial services was another issue of particular concern to financial services regulators. The concerns of financial officials were addressed by inserting a requirement in the Annex that dispute settlement panels on prudential issues and other financial matters must have the expertise necessary to deal with the specific financial service under dispute.

In December 1997, a final agreement on financial services was reached and the United States joined in, removing the broad most-favored nation exemption it had previously taken. The Asian financial crisis contributed to this result, since many of the countries (such as South Korea) that had resisted market opening now had less choice to do so if they wanted IMF assistance. Reaching an agreement does not, of course, mean that markets are truly "open." It only means that the 148 countries involved in the WTO (as of October 2004) have all made commitments of various kinds. The 1997 agreement "was probably notable more for its airing of issues and the consequent increased transparency concerning the sector than for its concrete achievements in terms of market opening. Many countries' commitments simply specified rules already in place ... and in some cases less than this. ..."[39]

6.   THE DOHA ROUND

In November 2001, the WTO members authorized a new round of trade negotiations, the so-called Doha round, which will once again include financial services. The Committee on Trade in Financial Services has engaged in a broad set of discussions including the impact of liberalizing financial services on capital accounts, the pace and sequencing of financial liberalization, and the links between prudential regulation, transparency rules, and financial services liberalization. These are also discussions as to whether there should be notification requirements or restrictions on the unilateral use of prudential carve-outs. This Committee, and the WTO more generally, could become a big player in international banking regulation in the future.

Nonetheless, the current results of Doha are disappointing. The existing offers for a new set of financial service commitments are limited in scope and scale. Also, WTO does not presently have the mandate to deal with the more difficult questions of indirect barriers to trade such as U.S. requirements prohibiting use of IFRS or EU country restrictions on acquisitions of local banks. There are a variety of these problems, which are prevalent at least as much or even more in developed as compared to less-developed countries.[40]

---

[39] A. Cornford, "The WTO Negotiations on Financial Services: Current Issues and Future Directions," United Nations Conference on Trade and Development, Working Paper 172 (June 2004), p. 6.

[40] Joint Statement of the Asian, European, Japanese, Latin American and the U.S. Shadow Financial Regulatory Committees, Enhancing International Financial Market Integration, November 15, 2004.

CONCLUSIONS

International regulatory issues seem fairly settled in banking. The dispute between the U.S. and EU over the EU's assertion of jurisdiction over conglomerates, seems to be coming to an end as the EU accepts the equivalence of new SEC holding company regulation.

It is interesting that the home-country principle for regulation is firmly accepted in U.S. banking regulation, in contrast to securities regulation. This largely flows from the difference in the purposes of regulation in the two regimes. Banking regulation is mainly concerned with safety and soundness of institutions, while securities regulation is mainly concerned with investor protection. This results from the fact that bank "investors" (depositors) are largely protected by deposit insurance, whereas investors in securities are at risk. Of course, U.S. uninsured depositors, as well as U.S. safety net providers, are at risk from the failure of a bank. However, this has not prevented the U.S. from principally relying on the effectiveness of foreign supervision to avoid this result. There is no other practical alternative; one could hardly require a bank located abroad to be regulated by the U.S.

In terms of possible issues for the future, the biggest will probably be the proper mix between regulation and market discipline. Further relaxation of restrictions on U.S. banking organizations' activities, i.e. commercial activities, may be an important topic in future years. In addition, there is the ongoing issue of consolidation of regulators. As many of the chain reaction problems have been solved, the case for regulation based on systemic risk concerns seems to be weakening.

In banking, in contrast to securities, stronger institutional arrangements have been forged to deal with international problems, most notably those housed at the Bank for International Settlements. It is conceivable that these arrangements could become more formalized, and that a truly international banking regulator might emerge.

CHAPTER FOUR

THE EUROPEAN UNION: THE SINGLE MARKET IN FINANCIAL SERVICES

This Chapter examines the operation of the European Union's (EU) internal market in financial services. The EU market is equivalent to that of the United States. The following comparisons based on 2004 numbers are instructive. U.S. and EU GDP was $11 trillion and $12 trillion respectively. GDP per capita growth in 2004 was 1.8 percent in the U.S. and 1.9 percent in the EU 403 of the 500 largest companies in the world were headquartered in Europe or North America, 247 in North America and 156 in Europe. EU transactions in U.S. securities were projected to be $14.2 trillion in 2005, while U.S. transactions in EU securities would reach $3.7 trillion. One quarter of all U.S. exports and two-thirds of all U.S. foreign direct investment ($87 billion) went to Europe in 2003. The flow of trade and investment between the two markets exceeds $1 trillion annually. U.S. firms employ 3.3 million people in Europe and EU firms employ 3.7 million in the U.S. By any measure these are the two most important economies in the international financial system.

This Chapter details much progress in the integration of EU financial markets. In June 2005, both the French and Dutch soundly rejected amendments to the EU Constitution (55 percent no in France, 61.6 percent no in the Netherlands). This raised significant concern over the future of the EU, and some even speculated that the continuation of the Euro or the adoption of Basel II's changes in capital rules (see Chapter 7) could be affected. This would seem highly unlikely. However, the steam behind further economic integration could wane.

This Chapter begins with some background material on the European Union and its general program to create an internal market free of trading barriers. It then focuses more specifically on securities and banking markets. A key principle underlying the market reforms is mutual recognition.

A.   INTRODUCTION[1]

The treaty that established the European Economic Community (EEC), which is one of three European Communities established under three separate treaties, is generally known as the Treaty of Rome. The other treaties established The European Coal and Steel Community and the European Atomic Energy Community. The term European Community (EC) or European Union (EU) is commonly used to refer to all three European Communities; the EU institutions are common to all three Communities. The 12 original Member States of the European Union were Belgium, Denmark, France, Germany, Greece, Ireland, Italy, Luxembourg, the Netherlands, Portugal, Spain, and the United Kingdom. Austria, Finland and Sweden joined in 1995 bringing the total member countries to 15.

The treaties establishing the European Communities have been revised several times through the Single European Act (1987), the Treaty on European Union, the so-called Maastricht Treaty (1992), and the Treaty of Amsterdam (1997).

Let us look briefly at the key EU institutions. The Commission is the executive branch of the European Community and has responsibility for proposing legislation and for ensuring implementation of EU law by the Member States. Commissioners are appointed by agreement among the governments of the Member States for four-year terms.

The Council of Ministers, which consists of ministers responsible for matters under discussion, is the decision making body and enacts legislation proposed by the Commission. The presidency of the Council rotates among Member States every six months. The "European Council" consists of the heads of state or government and meets semi-annually.

Under the Single European Act, which became effective in July 1987, the requirement of unanimous voting by the Council was replaced with "qualified majority voting" for the Council's adoption of most measures necessary to achieve the internal market. Under qualified majority voting, the number of votes that each Member State exercises in the Council is weighted roughly according to its population. Fifty-four votes (out of a total of 76) are required to adopt legislation.

The European Parliament (EP) is elected directly by the citizens of the Member States every five years. Originally, the Treaty of Rome gave the EP a consultative role only; subsequent treaties have expanded its role. The EP is now empowered to amend and even adopt legislation. Thus, the power of decision in a number of areas is now shared by the Council and the EP. For

---

[1] This section relies heavily on S. Key, "Mutual Recognition: Integration of the Financial Sector in the European Community," 75 Federal Reserve Bulletin (1989) 591. See also J. Mogg, "Regulating Financial Services in Europe: A New Approach," 26 Fordham J. of International Law (2002) 58.

the internal market, including financial services, EU decision-making is defined by a "co-decision" procedure that gives the Council and EP equal power. If the two institutions disagree, a conciliation committee is convened to seek a compromise.

Legislative instruments in the area of financial services are usually directives, and sometimes regulations. A directive is binding on Member States but leaves implementation to the States themselves. A regulation, on the other hand, is directly binding on and directly applicable to the Member States; it is self-implementing. Each form of legislation may confer certain implementing powers on the Commission. A committee always assists the Commission in the exercise of any such implementing powers. The so-called "Comitology Decision" provides certain criteria for the choice of committee procedures.

The European Court of Justice consists of 13 judges appointed by agreement among the governments of the Member States for six-year terms. In general, the Court has original jurisdiction in cases in which the Commission or another Community institution is a party. Other actions are brought in national courts but are referred to the European Court of Justice for preliminary rulings on matters of EC law; such rulings are binding on the national courts. An EC Court of First Instance was created in 1988 to hear actions brought against Community institutions by EC staff or by private parties in certain technical areas; the European Court of Justice has appellate jurisdiction in such cases.

A fundamental objective of the European Union is to create a single internal market. This requires the removal of obstacles to the free movement of goods, persons, services, and capital among Member States. The EU market currently comprises 370 million consumers that could expand to 500 million upon enlargement.

At first, the EU sought to achieve this goal in a number of areas, including financial markets, by harmonizing the rules of each country. The EU Commission's 1985 White Paper, *Completing the Internal Market,* identified 300 pieces of legislation that the Community would have to enact to remove restrictions or to harmonize laws of Member States. This process would have taken too long, if it could have been done at all.

The White Paper announced a new strategy under which the harmonization of *essential* standards would provide the basis for *mutual recognition* by the Member States of the equivalence and validity of each other's laws, regulations, and administrative practices that have not been harmonized at the EC level. Under a policy of mutual recognition, some Member States in effect agree to offer treatment that is more favorable than national treatment to firms from other Member States. But such recognition is premised on minimum harmonization—an agreed level of commonality is necessary for Member States to tolerate differences. This mutual recognition approach is still being refined in many initiatives in the financial services area.

A corollary of mutual recognition is home-country control. If national laws, regulations, and supervisory practices that have not been harmonized at the EU level are to be accorded mutual recognition, home-country rules and supervisory practices must be accepted as controlling the operations of host-country branches and the cross-border provision of services by financial institutions. However, the principle of home-country control adopted by the Community is not absolute. In accordance with judgments of the European Court of Justice and with EC directives, the host country retains the right to regulate branches or the cross-border provision of services to the extent that doing so is necessary to protect the public interest. This system also leads to convergence in rules as institutions headquartered in the state in which the services are provided (host-country state) demand to be treated at least as well as institutions located in other Member States (home-country states).

In December 2002, effective May 1, 2004, the EU summit agreed to admit 10 new members from Eastern Europe: Cyprus, Czech Republic, Estonia, Hungary, Latvia, Lithuania, Malta, Poland, Slovakia, and Slovenia. In addition, Bulgaria and Romania will join in 2007. The admission of Turkey has yet to be decided.

This Chapter focuses on two areas of financial regulation in the European Union—securities and banking.

B.   SECURITIES MARKETS

The EU has focused its efforts in securities markets on facilitating the distribution and trading of securities on a Union-wide basis, rather than having twelve separate markets. This has led to Union-wide disclosure standards and the removal of prohibitions on the Union-wide operation of securities firms. EU equity markets are quite vibrant. During the first quarter of 2005, issuance of equity securities in Europe outstripped issuance in the United States. European equity capital accounted for 41 percent of the total global equity issued, $54.8 billion, as compared with the U.S. with 33 percent, $34.1 billion.[2]

1.   DISCLOSURE: THE OLD REGIME

The EU approach to securities regulation is one of minimum disclosure standards and mutual recognition—a host country recognizes the legitimacy of home country rules.

---

[2] L. Saigol, "European Equity Issuance at Five-year High," *Financial Times*, April 20, 2005.

a.   THE LISTING PARTICULARS DIRECTIVE

"The Listing Particulars Directive, adopted in 1980, is designed to provide equivalent protection for investors throughout the common market, to facilitate cross-border exchange listings, and to promote greater interpenetration of national securities markets within the EU. The Listing Particulars Directive requires that an information sheet, termed 'listing particulars,' in compliance with the Directive's disclosure requirements and a prescribed format, be filed and approved in connection with the admission of securities to listing on any securities exchange in the EU. According to the Directive, in its implementing legislation, each Member State must designate a 'competent authority' to scrutinize listing particulars to determine whether they satisfy the common disclosure standards imposed by it. Subsequent to approval, the listing particulars must be published for the benefit of investors.

1.   THE DISCLOSURE SCHEME

The layout and detailed disclosure requirements of the Listing Particulars Directive are set forth in Schedule A, for equity securities and Schedule B, for debt securities. The areas of disclosure include, inter alia, information concerning: (1) those parties responsible for preparing the listing particulars and for auditing the financial statements; (2) the securities and the listing application; (3) the capitalization of the issuer; (4) the issuer's principal business activities, including a breakdown of net turnover by category of activity and geographical markets for the previous three years, its material contracts, patents, licenses, legal proceedings, employees, and investment policies; (5) the issuer's assets and liabilities, financial position, and profits and losses; (6) the issuer's administration management and supervision, including remuneration, unusual transactions, and equity interests; and (7) recent developments and prospects of the issuer, including recent trends in production, sales, orders, inventories, costs, and selling prices, as well as prospects for the current year. The information is to be presented in an 'easily analyzable and comprehensible' form. Competent authorities are permitted to exempt certain required information if it is deemed to be of 'minor importance' or if disclosure would be 'contrary to the public interest' or 'seriously detrimental to the issuer.' Significantly, the issuer must also include all other information, based on the particular nature of the issuer and the securities, which 'is necessary to enable investors and their investment advisers to make an informed assessment of the assets and liabilities, financial position, profits and losses, and prospects of the issuer and of the rights attaching to such securities.'

The listing particulars, following their review and approval by the competent authority of the Member State, must be published in a widely-distributed newspaper in the Member State or in the form of a free brochure made available to the public. Publication must be made within a reasonable period before the effective date on which the securities are officially listed. This Directive does not require the delivery of the listing particulars to investors either prior to, at the time of, or subsequent to, their purchase of securities. On the other hand, the Public Offering Prospectus Directive (POP) requires publication of a prospectus prior to as public offering of securities. Civil and criminal sanctions for compliance failures under either directive, however, are left to the discretion of the individual Member States."[3]

2.   Mutual Recognition[4]

Member states retain considerable flexibility in adopting additional disclosure requirements but cannot impose these requirements on issues from other EU countries, under the Mutual Recognition Directive of 1987. Such a Member State finds itself in the position of imposing more disclosure requirements and greater regulatory costs on its own domestic issuers, which may pose less of an investment risk than foreign issuers from less-regulated Member States. The domestic pressure to reduce this regulatory disequilibrium is likely to result in lowering the stricter state's disclosure regimen to the common denominator established by the Directive.

The Mutual Recognition Directive does undertake to reduce opportunities for forum shopping. It provides that where an issuer seeks to list its securities simultaneously or within a short interval in two or more Member States, including the Member State where its registered office is located, then the issuer must first secure approval of its home state's competent authority pursuant to its home state's laws.

The Mutual Recognition Directive has greater authority than merely extending mutual recognition to listing particulars. The Directive also extends mutual recognition to public offer prospectuses used in the sale of listed securities in other Member States.

b.   The Public Offer Prospectus Directive

The POP Directive was adopted by the Council of Ministers in 1989. The Directive undertakes to harmonize the disclosure standards of the Member States for public offerings of securities, regardless of whether the securities are to be listed on an exchange. By imposing prospectus requirements similar to those required of listing particulars, this Directive eliminates disclosure disparities that may have been a disincentive to listing on an exchange. It also further develops the EC's integrated disclosure system in which prospectuses and listing particulars ultimately may be used almost interchangeably throughout the common market.

---

[3] M. Warren, "Regulatory Harmony in the European Communities: The Common Market Prospectus," 26 Brooklyn Journal International Law (1990), pp. 19-53.
[4] This section relies heavily on M. Warren, "Regulatory Harmony in the European Communities: The Common Market Prospectus," 26 Brooklyn Journal International Law (1990), pp. 19-53.

1.   THE DISCLOSURE SCHEME

The POP Directive establishes a prospectus regime for the public offering of securities that will not be listed on an EC exchange. Although the disclosure requirements are less detailed in this instance, they reflect the same basic standards set forth in the Listing Particulars Directive.

2.   THE EXCLUSIONS FROM COVERAGE

There are significant coverage exclusions in POP, for private placements, small offerings, minimum purchase offerings, exchange offers, employee offerings, and Eurosecurities. The Eurosecurities exemptions were procured largely by the lobbying efforts of the International Primary Market Association (IPMA), finding its strongest ally in United Kingdom regulators fearful of losing the market that its members control.

[Eurosecurities] shall mean transferable securities which:

— are to be underwritten and distributed by a syndicate at least two of the members of which have their registered offices in different [s]tates, and

— are offered on a significant scale in one or more [s]tates other than that of the issuer's registered office, and

— may be subscribed for or initially acquired only through a credit institution or other financial institution.

Once the threshold definitional criteria are satisfied, the second step in determination of the exemption must be made. The Directive excludes Eurosecurities unless "a generalized campaign of advertising or canvassing was employed."

The "Eurosecurities" exemption has been implemented in different form in different Member States. For example, Germany has said that the "canvassing" prohibition only applies to door-to-door sales, and not apparently to calls to clients. The Netherlands has said that a retail investor may be approached by a financial institution as long as this is not done systematically by way of a general campaign. Neither Germany nor the Netherlands has limited the "Eurosecurities" exemption to particular types of securities, whereas Belgium has limited it to Eurobonds.[5]

The most important limitation in the POP Directive's mutual recognition provision is the contemporaneity requirement. Public offerings must be conducted either simultaneously or within a short interval of each other. Member states must be given advance notice and may impose translation requirements. Lastly, Member States may require additional information specific to its particular market and relating to income tax

---

[5] N.R. van de Vijver, "Euro-securities: Regulatory Aspects, Securities and Capital Markets Law Report," (May 1994), p. 15.

consequences, paying agents, and notices to investors to be included in the prospectus.

The home country system could theoretically lead to less disclosure for investors when securities were offered by companies in countries with low disclosure requirements. This does not seem to have happened because issuers have complied with standards familiar to international investors. Thus, in the case of a Danish public offering in the U.K., the issuer would comply with the higher U.K. disclosure requirements since the lower level of Danish disclosure would not be acceptable.[6] Similarly, French issues abroad follow "international" rather than lower French standards.[7]

If you are a French company can you list first on the Luxembourg Exchange and then the French to take advantage of the less rigorous Luxembourg disclosure rules? POP provides that you must list first in the country of your registered office if you are listing there at all. Could you forum shop by locating your registered office in whatever jurisdiction you want? Until quite recently, the answer to this question was clearly no because countries required firms to have their registered office in the country where the "direction" of the company came from, usually corporate headquarters. But these country requirements were invalidated to some degree in *Centros Ltd v Erhvervs-og Selskabsstyrelsen*.[8] In November 2002, the Court of Justice decided another case, along the same lines, holding that a German law refusing to recognize a Dutch company that had moved its center of administration to Germany, and therefore had no legal capacity and could not sue in court as a Dutch company, were invalid under the Rome Treaty's provision of freedom of establishment.[9]

Notes and Questions

1. What factors allow mutual recognition to work in the EU, as compared to internationally?

2. Why does the EU seek to limit forum shopping within the EU?

2.   DISCLOSURE: THE NEW REGIME

Problems of the Old Regime

The mutual recognition system has not worked particularly well. A 1998 report of the U.K. Treasury, "Public Offers of Securities", finds that

---

[6] C. Rovinescu and G. Thieffry, Cross-Border Marketing," in *The Future for the Global Securities Market–Legal and Regulatory Aspects* (F. Oditah ed., 1996), p. 31.
[7] *ibid.*; see also W. Smith, "The French View of Cross-Border Securities Offerings," in *The Future for the Global Securities Market—Legal and Regulatory Aspects* (F. Oditah ed., 1996), p. 199.
[8] [Danish Companies Board], Case C-212/97, ECJ (March 9, 1999).
[9] *Überseering BV and Nordic Constriction Company Baumanagement (NCC)*, Case 208/00, November 2002. See E. Wymeersch, "The Transfer of the Company's Seat in European Company Law," European Corporate Governance Institute Working Paper 08/2003 (March 2003).

there have been very few cross-border securities offers in the EU despite the promise of the Directives. Indeed, it appears that the 1999 Deutsche Telekom distribution was the first and last European-wide public offering. The obstacles to such offers are the need to make translations of the prospectus, and the need to include information specific to a country, such as paying agents, the income tax system, and the method of notification of investors (together with the cost of the legal advice to determine this). And with listed securities, host states impose additional requirements despite the provisions of the Listing Directive. This spurred initiatives to change the system.[10]

The U.K. Treasury also averts to another possible cause of the low usage of the Directives, even in connection with initial public offers: that large companies list their securities on one exchange in a Member State and let investors come to the exchange. The very premise of the mutual recognition regime, that public offers need to be distributed in several territories, may be wrong. As long as investors (or their representatives) can buy the issue somewhere within the EU, there may be no need to offer the security in multiple territories. A single market could be achieved by simply insuring that Member States not apply their rules to their own investors extraterritorially (as does the United States). In the EU, Member States have generally not applied securities laws extraterritorially, so this has never been a problem.[11]

One additional reason for the low usage of the cross-border directives may be the wide scope for private placements within the EU and the relative ease of the resale of privately distributed securities to public investors. Many countries have broad exemptions from disclosure requirements for sales to sophisticated investors or market professionals, in addition to the "Eurosecurities" exemption.

Economists have tried to measure the degree of financial market integration in the EU. One measurement is the average correlation of real interest rates between the Member States. One study that looked at integration of Euro adopters, found a correlation of .67 as compared with a .57 correlation between countries outside the EU. This is higher, but not as high, as one might expect using the .57 correlation as a benchmark. It is conceivable if non-Euro adopters like the U.K. were included, that the EU correlation might be higher, but it is more likely to be lower given that interest rates are managed within Euroland by the European Central Bank. A second measure is average correlations of stock market returns. Here Euro adopters have a .59 correlation as compared with the rest of the world of .52, again higher but not much.[12]

---

[10] *Financial Services: Implementing the Framework for Financial Markets: Action Plan* (1999).
[11] See also H. Scott, "Internationalization of Primary Public Securities Markets," 63 Law and Contemporary Problems (2000), pp. 71, 82.
[12] H. Askari and J. Chatterjee, "The Euro and Financial Market Integration," 43 Journal of Common Market Studies 1 (2005).

Lamfalussy Proposals

In July 2000, the European Union's Economic and Finance Ministers (ECOFIN) requested that the so-called Wise Men Committee, chaired by Alexandre Lamfalussy, recommend regulatory changes that could improve the functioning of European securities markets. This resulted in the "Final Report of The Committee of Wise Men on The Regulation of European Securities Markets" (February 15, 2001). The Report's basic recommendation was that two new regulatory bodies be created, the European Securities Regulators Committee (CESR) and the European Securities Committee (ESC), to regulate securities markets on an EU wide basis. The ESC acts both in an advisory and regulatory capacity. It has the key power of implementing Commission directives. This achieves a key objective of the Lamfalussy Committee, to create a more flexible law-making process. The CESR advises the Commission and ESC on preparing implementing measures. It supplants the Forum of European Securities Commissions (FESCO) which has formulated proposals for reforms in the past.[13] It is not altogether clear how these two new bodies will divide responsibilities. The European Parliament approved this new procedure in February 2002 subject to various "democratic safeguards." The Commission has agreed with Parliament to accept "sunset clauses" in financial legislation that will enable the Parliament to review the new procedure after four years, and all draft implementing measures, including regulations, will be subject to a three month period in which Parliament can review the proposals.

The new structure of decision-making on EU financial services is set out in Figure 4.1 below:[14]

---

[13] See G. Wittich, "Implementing the Lamfalussy Report: The Contribution of Europe's Securities Regulators," Journal of International Financial Markets (2001), p. 209.
[14] A. Grünbichler and P. Darlap, "Integration of EU Financial Markets Supervision: Harmonization or Unification?," 12 J. of Financial Regulation and Compliance (2004), p. 41.

Figure 4.1
The Lamfalussy/Comitology Architecture

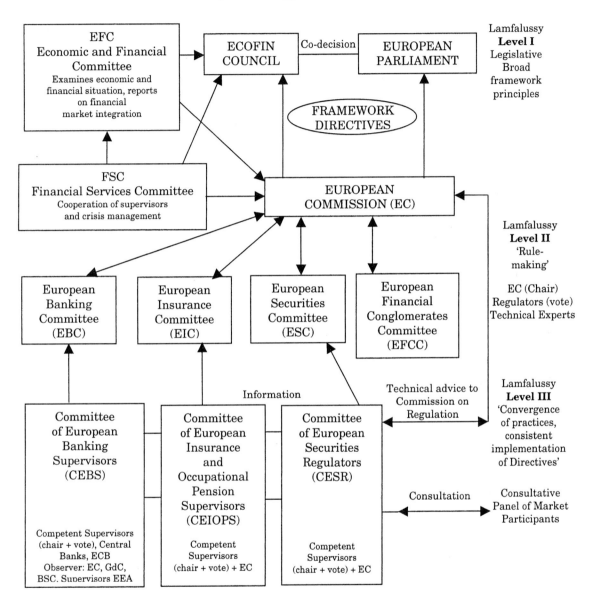

In terms of substantive measures, the Lamfalussy Committee said the following priority issues needed to be addressed by no later than the end of 2003: (1) a single prospectus for issuers, with a mandatory shelf registration system; (2) modernization of listing requirements and introduction of a clear distinction between admission to listing and trading; (3) generalization of the home country principal for wholesale markets; (4) modernization and expansion of investment rules for investment funds and pension funds; (5) adoption of International Accounting Standards; and (6) a single passport for a recognized stock market on the basis of the home country principle.

New Prospectus Directive

The first proposal envisioned a significant change in the existing disclosure regime and has resulted in an important new proposed directive. On May 30, 2001, the European Commission issued a proposal for a new Directive on a common prospectus to be required when securities are offered to the public in primary markets or admitted for trading in secondary markets.[15] This proposal was subsequently amended after consideration by the Parliament.[16] Europe's Finance Ministers agreed to the proposal in November 2002, and a Directive was issued in November 2003.[17] The Committee of European Securities Regulators (CESR) has issued three consultation procedures discussing detailed and technical implementation of the proposed directive, CESR's Advice on possible Level 2 Implementing Measures for the Proposed Prospectus Directive.[18]

The disclosure requirements were to be in accordance with the information requirements set out by IOSCO in Part I of their International Disclosure Standards for cross-border offerings and initial listings. Based on CESR recommendations, the Commission issued a Regulation in April 2004, Regulation 809/2004, setting forth disclosure requirements for different types of issuers. This then resulted in further CESR action designed to insure effective implementation at the national level, in accord with Level 3.

Enforcement of the EU rules will generally be left to the home country (Art. 23). When the host country finds irregularities in an offer, it must refer the matter to the home country. The host country is, however, entitled to act, after informing the home country, if measures taken by the home country prove inadequate or violations of laws and regulations persist.

This Directive requires a common prospectus for any primary public offering or for any securities listed on a "regulated market" (Art. 3(1)). The definition of a "regulated market" is discussed below in connection with the

---

[15] COM(2001) 280 final.
[16] COM(2002) 460 final, August 9, 2002 (Common Prospectus Proposal or CPP).
[17] Directive 2003/71/EC of the European Parliament and of the Council, November 4, 2003.
[18] CESR/02.185b, October 2002 and Addendum to the Consultation Paper, CESR/02-286, December 2002; CESR/03-300, September 2003; CESR/03-399, December 2003.

Directive on Markets in Financial Instruments. Public offering is defined as "a communication to persons in any form and by any means, presenting sufficient information on the terms of the offer and the securities to be offered, so as to enable an investor to decide to purchase or subscribe to these securities. This definition shall also be applicable to the placing of securities through financial intermediaries." Public offering does not include sales to qualified investors such as financial institutions, professionals, or investors who buy at least 50,000 Euros of securities. Persons may also be qualified investors if they are securities professionals, have carried out multiple significant transactions in securities, or have a portfolio in excess of €0.5 million (Art. 2(3)).

The prospectus cannot be published until approved by the home country (Art. 13(1)) of the issuer. Thus, if a Greek company were making a public offering only in London, the offering would have to be approved by Greece rather than the U.K. Once approved by the home country the same prospectus can be used throughout the EU, a continuation of the single passport approach. While most equity issues are distributed in the home state, the same is not true for bonds. In reviewing the proposed Directive, the Finance Ministers have permitted issuers to avoid any regulation for securities with minimum denominations of over €50,000; however, most offshore bond issues have smaller minimum denominations.[19]

Article 15 of the Directive contains rules on advertising. Article 15(1) originally provided (Art. 13(1) of the May 2001 proposal): "Advertisements, notices, posters shall be communicated in advance to the competent authority of the home Member State which shall check them before publication against the principles contained in this Article [that advertisements be fair, accurate and consistent with that contained in the prospectus]. The documents shall state that a prospectus will be published and indicate where investors will be able to obtain it." The requirement for presubmission has now been dropped; however, a competent authority must have the power to monitor such advertising.

The prospectus makes significant changes in the ability to sell unregistered securities to retail investors through banks. Under the current EU securities regulation regime, a multiple state bank syndicate, including Deutsche Bank and Barclays, could sell the securities of a German issuer to various banks in London and Germany, who might purchase them for, or immediately resell them to, retail investors throughout the EU, as long as the retail investors were not procured by a generalized advertising or canvassing campaign, the latter requirement being subject to the interpretation of host states (where the investors are). Such securities would, however, be subject to national laws. But these laws generally provide for disclosure exemptions for offers to sophisticated investors like financial institutions, and, unlike U.S.

---

[19] "Spoilt Choice," The Economist, November 9, 2002.

law, would not generally integrate financial institution resales to investors into the initial offering.

As discussed above, under the current EU regime, so-called "Eurosecurities," not subject to "a generalized campaign of advertising or canvassing," are exempt from any EU disclosure requirements. What is advertising and canvassing is left to various host state requirements. For example, Germany provides that the "canvassing" prohibition only applies to door-to-door sales, and not apparently calls to clients, while the Netherlands provides that an investor may be approached by a financial institution as long as this is not done systematically by way of a general campaign.

Under the Directive, sales to financial institutions would be outside the scope of the proposal since these sales would be to qualified investors (Art.3(a); Art.2(e)(i)). In a sense the "Eurosecurities" exemption has been widened by dropping the requirements for multiple state underwriters and distribution outside the state of the issuer. Under Article 15, only advertising of a public offer would be monitored by the home Member State and be subject to a prospectus requirement. Issuers would continue to be free to sell securities under their own "international style" disclosure documents in London to financial institutions.

In the past, these financial institutions could pass on these securities or resell them to retail customers, but no advertising of such offerings could be made. German retail investors could participate in London offerings through a financial institution, and could apparently receive general advertising about impending offers. The Directive appears to change this practice dramatically. While sales to financial intermediaries are exempt, resales are not unless they separately qualify for an exemption, e.g. are only to qualified investors (Art.3(2),(3)). This means that any sales or resales of securities to the general public, whether in the issuer's own country or offshore (within the EU, including London), will be subject to EU disclosure requirements.

The Directive also contains a private offering exemption. Under the Directive, issuers are not required to comply with disclosure rules for offers to qualified investors plus another 100 investors in each member state who are not qualified investors, or to offers in minimum denomination of €50,000, or to an offer involving some combination of these factors. Unlike in the U.S., anyone can be solicited for such investments—the restrictions apply to investors not offerees.[20]

Unlike in the U.S., the EU will not restrict advertising or reports by underwriters or others during the offering process. Nor will the EU have

---

[20] J. Bartos, "Offering Rules: What the U.S. and Europe Can Teach Each Other," 16 International Financial Law Review (October 2003). (Bartos)

prospectus delivery requirements. The prospectus must be filed and approved but need not be delivered.[21]

The Directive, Arts. 11-12, also incorporates a concept of shelf registration for seasoned issuers and expedited registration for new issuers, based on prior work by FESCO.[22] As in the United States, only new information about newly offered securities would have to be disclosed. Unlike the U.S. system, however, no universal shelf registration statement describing various securities that might be issued and different distribution procedures that might be employed, would be required.

The Directive addresses another issue that has hampered the development of a single internal securities market, the language problem. Currently, cross-border disclosure documents must be distributed in the local language, thus requiring significant translation costs and potential liabilities due to discrepancies in meaning between various language versions. Article 19(1) of the Directive provides that the prospectus shall "be drawn up in a language accepted by the competent authority in the home Member State." Article 19(2) then states: "[w]here an offer to the public is made ... in one or more Member State excluding the home Member State, the prospectus shall be drawn up in a language accepted by the ... [host state] or in a language customary in the sphere of international finance, at the choice of the issuer. ..." The host state may only require that the summary note be translated into its domestic language. Where an issue is made both in the home Member State and other states, then the language must either be that of the home state and in a language acceptable to the host states or one customary in international finance.

The EU proposal raises some interpretative questions. If a French company prepares a prospectus in French, must the U.K. accept it or can it require that the entire prospectus be translated into English? This would seem to turn on whether French is a language "customary in the sphere of international finance." In practice, English is the only customary language in the sphere of international finance, but will the French accept that? There may be significant political pressure for local authorities to insist that prospectuses, and not just summaries, be available in the local language.

Problems are raised by a system in which the summary and the full prospectus are in different languages. The summary is required to contain a warning that "it should be read as an introduction to the prospectus and any decision to invest in the securities should be based on consideration of the prospectus as a whole by the investor." As a commenter has noted, "this is impossible if the investor cannot read the rest of the prospectus."[23] The

---

[21] Bartos, supra note 20, p. 17.

[22] A "European Passport" for Issuers, A Report for the EU Commission (December 2000).

[23] J. Bartos and M. Leppert, "Why Europe's New Prospectus Regime May Fail," 18 International Financial Law Review (August 2003).

Directive deals with this problem by limiting liability—no civil liability can attach solely on the basis of the summary; potential criminal liability does remain, however.[24]

An important issue is how the Directive applies to a non-EU issuer. The Directive requires that a single national EU regulator have authority to approve all public offers and admissions to trading of equity and debt in denominations of less than €1000 (or equivalent in another currency). For non-EU issuers this will be the competent authority of the Member State in which the issuer first makes an offer of such securities to the public after the date of entry into force of the directive. For all other kinds of issues, e.g. debt in denominations of €1000 or more, the non-EU issuer can select the Home Member State on an issue-by-issue basis.[25] Of potentially great importance, Art. 20(1) opens up the possibility of non-EU issuers issuing securities within the E.U. under their own disclosure regime, provided that such prospectuses are in conformity with IOSCO standards and that the information requirements are equivalent to the requirements under the Directive. Currently, U.S. companies distribute securities within the EU using U.S. disclosure requirements. U.S. disclosure requirements meet and go further than IOSCO requirement whereas EU. disclosure requirements appear basically co-extensive with those of IOSCO. Under these circumstances, it is quite unlikely that the EU would not find the U.S. standards equivalent to their own. This is different than the accounting issues discussed in Chapter 2, as there was and continues to be significant differences between IFRS and U.S. GAAP. Nonetheless, one can imagine that at some point, the EU will raise the issue as to why U.S. disclosure requirements are adequate in the EU and EU standards are not adequate in the U.S.

As discussed, the Directive envisions a shelf registration permitting the incorporation by reference of previously filed reports. This creates the possibility that a prospectus in one language will incorporate reports in another, further putting a strain on investor comprehension. Hopefully, the analyst community will address the language issues through their reports.

U.S. issuers will face two particular problems. Incorporation by reference authority only applies to documents filed in a "home member state," thus excluding documents filed in the U.S. In addition, it is unclear whether U.S. issuers will have to state their accounts under IAS standards (which are to come into force in 2005), or whether the EU will accept U.S. GAAP as an alternative.[26]

---

[24] Art.6(2).

[25] See Art 2.1(m)(iii). See also Cleary Gottlieb, "The EU Prospectus Directive—Implications for Non-EU Issuers," November 20, 2003 (London).

[26] Id., at 20.

Notes and Questions

1. How will the offshore (Eurosecurities) market be affected by the implementation of the Prospectus Directive?

2. Will the Prospectus Directive create a single market for the distribution of securities within the EU?

Transparency Directive

In December 2004, the European Parliament and the Council adopted a Directive (MiFID) to increase investor protection and transparency in the form of ongoing reporting obligations for all companies listed on an exchange, a protean 1934 U.S. Act initiative.[27] The Directive requires that companies must file an audited annual financial report and a management report, Art. 4, a half-yearly condensed financial report, Art. 5. Originally, there would also have been a requirement for first and third quarterly reports with financial data but not qualitative information. These requirements were hotly debated. In November 2003, the EU Finance Ministers pared back the requirements, providing that companies will only have to provide quarterly information on "material events," mergers, closures, debt, and equity.[28] In the final Directive, this requirement is even furthered watered down. Art. 6 requires interim management reports during the first and last 6 months of every year describing material transactions that have taken place and a general description of the financial position and performance of the issuer. The Prospectus Directive separately provides that any stock traded on a regulated market update information every year (Art. 10(1)). Like information in the prospectus, it could be provided in English (a language customary in the sphere of international finance), but unlike the prospectus, no translation of summaries into local languages would be required. There is no provision in the Directive for continuous disclosure, as was envisioned in prior consultation documents.

Perhaps this is because such a provision would be thought to be duplicative of Article 6(1) of the Market Abuse Directive (see discussion below), which provides that "Member States shall ensure that issuers of financial instruments inform the public as soon as possible of inside information which directly concerns the said issuers." Art. 6(2) provides that "An issuer may under his own responsibility delay the public disclosure of insider information as referred to in paragraph 1, such as not to prejudice his legitimate interests provided that such omission would not be likely to mislead the public and provided the issuer is able to secure the confidentiality of that information. Member States may require that an

---

[27] Directive 2004/109/EC.

[28] D. Dombey, "EU Drops Plans for 'Required' Quarterly Profit and Loss Data," *Financial Times*, November 26, 2003. For a trenchant critique of the quarterly reporting proposal, see K. Lannoo and A. Khachaturyan, "Disclosure Regulation in the EU: The Emerging Framework," CEPS Task Force Report No. 48 (October 2003).

issuer shall without delay inform the competent authority of the decision to delay the public disclosure of inside information." Inside information is defined in the Directive as information that would have a significant impact on prices.

The Commission proposal was modified by Parliament in March 2004 with respect to the adoption of international accounting standards by the EU in 2005. Generally, firms outside the EU can use national accounting standards if they are found "equivalent" to international accounting standards (see the discussion in Chapter 2). The Directive has also been amended to provide that firms outside the EU with debt securities issued in the EU prior to 2005 need not use IAS reports if their statements give a "true and fair view."

Liability for on-going reporting, as well as under the Prospectus Directive, remains the province of the Member States.

Other Initiatives

Directive 2003/6/EC of the European Parliament and the Council, January 28, 2003, due to be implemented by October 2004, deals with insider dealing and market manipulation (market abuse). Inside information, defined as "information of a precise nature which has not been made public relating to one or more issuers of financial instruments ... which if it were made public, would be likely to have a significant effect on the prices of those financial instruments. ..."[29] Enforcement of measures to prohibit the exploitation of inside information is left to individual Member States. In addition, the Commission continues to implement a takeover regulation, an effort it began in 1995. Its latest proposal, Common Position of the Council of 19 June 2000 on the proposed 13th Directive concerning takeover bids,[30] was rejected by the Parliament, largely under the urging of Germany, in July 2001 on an extraordinary 273-273 vote.[31] For the substance of parliamentary concerns, see Legislative Resolution of the European Parliament, Takeover Bids.[32] The major issues are whether there should be a mandatory bid for minority shares and the extent to which a target board can adopt defensive measures.

3.   PROVISION OF SERVICES: THE OLD REGIME

The EU disclosure requirements deal with securities sold within the EU. Another important element of the single market program is the

---

[29] Art. 1(1) "Information shall be deemed to be of a precise nature if it indicates a set of circumstances which exists or may reasonably be expected to come into existence or an event which has occurred or may reasonably be expected to do so and if it is specific enough to enable a conclusion to be drawn as to the possible effect of that set of circumstances or event on the prices of financial instruments. ..." Commission Directive 2003/124/EC, December 22, 2003, Art.1(1).

[30] [2001] O.J. E.C. C23/1-14, January 24, 2001.

[31] BNA World Securities Law Report 3 (July 2001).

[32] Minutes of December 13, 2000.

institutions providing securities services. The Investment Services Directive (ISD) aims at facilitating the operation of such institutions throughout the Union.

The ISD was adopted in 1993. Its primary purposes are to adopt common minimum authorization (licensing) requirements among the Member States and mutual recognition of the license granted in the "home state" by all other Member States (or "host states").

In addition, the Directive seeks to establish conditions for direct access to domestic stock exchanges for foreign EU investment firms and banks. The ISD requires firms seeking to engage in cross-border services to notify home and host authorities. This raises the issue as to when such services are actually being provided cross-border or only in the home country. For example, if investors from another country invest in securities issued in the home country by a firm from that country, is the service cross-border?[33]

There is also a related provision in Article 15(4) which provides that states (home and host) must allow out-of-state investment firms to obtain electronic access (screens) to regulated markets, i.e. French brokers must be given the opportunity to conduct trades on SEAQ.

Off-Market vs. On-Market Trading

The Club Med countries (France, Italy, Spain, Portugal, Greece, and Belgium) insisted that the Directive embody the notion of "concentration," which in its French conception means that shares in French companies held by French residents must be traded in the French stock market. The United Kingdom refused to buy this and, with the backing of the North Sea group, accepted only a watered-down version.

The ISD permits a Member State to require that securities transactions be carried out on a "regulated market," assuming four conditions are met: (1) the investor must be a resident of that Member State; (2) the investor must not have exercised the right granted by the Directive to opt for an off-exchange market ('explicit authorization' may be required by the host state); (3) the transaction is carried out by the investment firm through its main office or a branch (or under its freedom to provide services) in that Member State; and (4) the securities traded are actually listed on a "regulated market" in that Member State.

The ISD defines a 'regulated market' as: (1) a regularly functioning securities market that is; (2) formally designated by its home state and in compliance with home state regulations; (3) with traded securities satisfying

---

[33] See C. Abrams, "The Investment Services Directive-Who Should Be the Principal Regulator of Cross-Border Services?," European Financial Services Law (1995).

certain listing requirements; and (4) a market that requires compliance with the Directive's reporting and transparency requirements."[34]

This would prevent France from requiring a French investor to conduct trading on the Paris Bourse rather than on an exchange in London if the U.K. designated the London exchange as a regulated market or the investor opted to trade in London.

Transparency

"Related to the concentration notion is the Directive's creation of minimum transparency rules for the regulated exchange markets of the Member States.

The Directive requires: (1) publication at the market opening of the weighted average price, the high and low prices, and the volume during the preceding trading day; and (2) after a two-hour calculation period, publication of the weighted average price and the high and low price (not volume) after a one-hour delay, to be updated every 20 minutes to the close. Assuming a 9:00 a.m. opening, the weighted average traded price, plus the high and low prices, for the period 9:00 a.m. to 11:00 a.m. would be published at 12:00 p.m., and updated every 20 minutes thereafter to cover a two-hour period on a one-hour delayed basis.

However, the Directive permits Member States to except large blocks and illiquid securities."[35]

4.   PROVISION OF SERVICES: THE NEW REGIME

On November 19, 2002, the Commission put forward a proposal for a directive on Investment Services and Regulated Markets (PISD) to substantially revise the existing ISD.[36] This proposal was adopted in modified form by the European Parliament and the Council on April 21, 2004 as the Directive on Markets in Financial Instruments (MFI).[37] 2006 is envisioned as the implementation date. While preserving the single passport for cross-border provision of investment services in Chapter III, Arts. 31 and 32, the MFI adds new regulation in two main areas, trading and investor protection. In particular, the MFI deals with: (1) principles for regulated markets; (2) new provisions relating to "Multilateral Trading Facilities" (MTFs); and (3) trade execution by investment firms.

Regulated Markets

The regulated market provisions apply to a multilateral system, operated by a market operator, which brings together multiple third-party

---

[34] M. Warren, "The Investment Services Directive: The 'North Sea Alliance' Victory over 'Club Med,'" 6 International Securities Regulation Report (1993), p. 6-7.
[35] ibid.
[36] COM(2002) 625 final, Commission Proposal.
[37] Directive 2004/39/EC.

buying and selling interests in financial instruments—in the system and in accordance with non-discretionary rules—in a way that results in a contract, with respect to the financial instruments admitted to trading under its rules and systems, and which is authorized and functions regularly and in accordance with the provisions of Title III [applicable to regulated markets], Art. 4(14).

The MFI abolishes the existing "concentration rule" under which Member States can require that retail orders be executed only on a "regulated market." The Commission points out that there is no evidence that existing use of such a rule, as in France and Italy, improves market efficiency,[38] and that investor protection can be assured through other parts of its proposal.

An MTF is "a multilateral system which brings together multiple third party buying and selling interests in financial instruments—in the system and in accord with non-discretionary rules—in a way that results in a contract." Art. 4(15). These are often referred to as alternative trading systems (ATS). PISD states that the "common feature of these systems is that they support autonomous trading decisions by the system users, without there being any intercession of the system operator to facilitate trades or participate itself (against a proprietary book) in transactions with system users."[39] In short, these are matching systems. The Directive permits an MTF to operate cross-border, through installation of screens, subject to home-country rules, Art. 29. The key difference between MTFs and regulated markets is that only the latter lists shares, and as a result is more highly regulated.

The MFI also requirements for pre-trade and post-trade transparency for internalizing investment firms, MTFs, and regulated markets. An investment firm that operates as "systematic internalizer" (SI)—one that on an organized, frequent, and systematic basis, on its own account, executes client orders outside a "regulated market or an MTF." Art. 4(7). The pre-trade transparency rule for SIs requires that SIs must publish firm quotes in those shares traded on a regulated market for which there is a liquid market, up to a "standard market size." Art. 27(1). Thus, there is no need to publish larges block quotes.

MTFs and regulated markets must make public current bid and offer prices and the depth of trading interests at these prices which are advertised through their systems for shares listed on regulated markets. Art. 29(1). This obligation may be waived depending on the market model, or type or size or order, handled by the MTF.

Investment firms, MTFs, and regulated markets are all subject to post-trade transparency rules requiring them to make public the volume and

---

[38] PISD, p. 9.
[39] PISD, p. 17.

price of transactions as close to real time as possible. Arts. 28, 30, and 45. Deferred reporting is permitted for large blocks.

In the case of both pre- and post-reporting, data is to be published on a "reasonable commercial basis." It is unclear whether this will lead to control over prices charged for data.

Trade Execution

The MFI imposes best execution requirements on investment firms. Firms must take all reasonable steps to get "the best results for their clients taking account price, costs, speed, likelihood of execution and settlement size, nature or any other consideration relevant to the execution of the order." Art.21.

Article 18 requires broker-dealers to identify, prevent, and manage conflicts of interest between the brokerage and dealing business of the firm and to avoid prejudicing execution of client orders in favor of proprietary interests. Article 22 establishes client order-handling rules requiring that orders be handled expeditiously and according to objective rules of precedence and priority.

MFI changes the ISD approach to conduct of business rules to avoid the "common good" problems that exist under the current regime. The MFI calls for the adoption of common business rules through comitology, with different rules applicable to treatment of professional and non-professional clients (Annex II). In the case of branch operations these rules will be enforced by host-states.

MFI also establishes a new regime for dealing with investment advisers. These advisers would enjoy the single passport and be subject to conflict of interest rules. Firms only supplying investment advice could replace capital requirements with professional indemnity insurance.

Notes and Questions

1. What do you think of the fact that liability rules and enforcement of those rules are left entirely to the Member States? Is it a concern that EU Member States do not generally permit class actions as tools of private enforcement. This may change. In Germany, the courts are now facing 15,000 separate claims by shareholders of Deutsche Telekom claiming their $17 billion share sale in 2000 was at an inflated price. Since the offering, the price has substantially declined. The pressure of so many suits may lead Germany and other states to permit some form of class actions.[40]

---

[40] "Deutsche Telekom's 8-Ton Filing Shows 'Americanized' Lawsuits," Bloomberg, November 3, 2004.

5.   UCITS

The UCITS ("undertakings for collective investments in transferable securities" or mutual funds as referred to in the United States)[41] harmonizes national rules on the authorization, supervision, structure, activities, and disclosure obligations of mutual funds. A single license granted by the UCITS' home state permits the UCITS to be marketed throughout the EU. In most cases the home state is responsible for compliance, however, host state marketing rules apply.[42]

The UCITS Directive came into force in most Member States in 1989. A Bank of England survey of 25 firms reported that the Directive had a limited impact on facilitating cross-border funds within the EU.[43] This is the same conclusion reached in a study of Lipper Analytical Services; a U.S. based mutual fund group. It found that only 38 percent of the 5,436 UCITS are marketed outside the country of domicile of their promoters. The rest are "round-trippers," incorporated in a low tax jurisdiction such as Dublin or Luxembourg and then marketed exclusively in the domicile of the promoters.[44] The Directive was amended in 2001 to remove barriers to the cross-border marketing of the funds by widening the range of assets in which funds can invest to include money market instruments, financial derivatives or "fund of funds." In addition, it allowed fund management companies to operate throughout the EU under a single passport and widen the range of activities in which they can engage.[45]

6.   THE STRUCTURE OF EU SECURITIES REGULATION

Should there be a European or EU Securities Commission or a European or EU Financial Service regulator responsible for both securities and banking? In considering this question, note that some countries in the EU, such as Denmark, Germany, Norway, Sweden and the United Kingdom, already have single financial regulators. On the other hand, the U.S. has multiple federal regulators, e.g. Federal Reserve, FDIC, and SEC. Will the call of the Wise Men for a European Securities regulator lead to such a system?

---

[41] Directive 85/611 of December 20, 1985 ([1985] O.J. L375), as amended by Directive 88/220 of March 22, 1988 ([1988] O.J. L100).
[42] L. Garzanti, "Single Market-Making: EC Regulation of Securities Markets," 14 Company Lawyer (1992), p. 43.
[43] "The Developing Single Market in Financial Services," 34 Bank of England Quarterly Bulletin (1994), pp. 341, 345.
[44] N. Cohen, "EU Collective Investment Scheme Laws 'A Failure,'" *Financial Times*, October 28, 1994.
[45] Directive 2001/108 (2002), O.J. L41/35; Directive 2001/107 (2002), O.J. L41/20. See D. Rouch and K. Smith, "The UCITS Directive and the Single European Funds Market: A Case Review," Journal of International Banking Law Review 251 (2005).

If we are talking about a new EU SEC, it is conceivable that CESR could evolve into this role. If CESR were given regulatory authority (as opposed to a interactive consultative role with the Commission), particularly the power to enact immediately binding regulation throughout the 25 Member States, the law-making process would become much more efficient. On the other hand, this would further erode the sovereignty of the Member States and perhaps add the democracy deficit in the EU. A 2005 paper by Philippe Billot lays out an interesting justification blueprint for what he calls ESEC.[46]

There is a serious question whether the legal authority exists under the Rome Treaty to create either a EU securities or financial services regulator. One author claims that there might be authority under Article 308 which provides that the Council acting unanimously on a proposal from the Commission, after consultation with the European Parliament, can take actions which "prove necessary" to "obtain one of the objectives of the Community" where the Treaty has not provided such powers. However, under case law interpreting Article 308, it is quite unclear that Article 308 would support such a move.[47]

Notes and Questions

1.   Should there be an EU Securities Commission?

2.   At present, there is no EU corporate governance code, and it appears governance matters will continue to be left to national law.[48] On the other hand, the Commission has made proposals[49] to revise its regulation of auditing, as reflected in its Eighth Council Directive of 1984, 84/253/EEC, April 10, 1984. The Commission's proposal would strengthen auditor independence and increase public oversight. In one respect it goes beyond Sarbanes-Oxley in requiring the rotation of auditing firms and senior partners. It does not require an independent audit committee, but does require that there be one independent member of the audit committee with accounting and/or auditing expertise.

C.   BANKING MARKETS

In the banking area, the EU approach focuses on facilitating the Union-wide operation of banks while at the same time protecting depositors.

---

[46] "A Plea for an ESEC ... and Soon," prepared for the Third Annual U.S.-E.U. Symposium on the Financial System of the 21st Century, Eltville, Germany, April 2005.

[47] See Giles Thieffry, "Toward a European Securities Commission," International Financial Law Review (October 1999), p. 14.

[48] T. Buck and S. Tucker, "Commissioner Dismisses Need for EU-wide Code," *Financial Times*, January 21, 2005.

[49] Proposal for a Directive of the European Parliament and of the Council COM(2004) 177 final, March 16, 2004.

Europe is still more banking dominated than the United States. Bank loans to Euro area countries (Austria, Belgium, Finland, France, Germany, Ireland, Italy, Luxembourg, the Netherlands, Portugal, and Spain in the Paper) are 100 percent of GDP, twice the ratio in the United States and about the same as Japan. Germany has by far the biggest number of credit institutions, 3,000 as compared with the next largest country, France, with half that many. Consolidation in banking has accelerated rapidly. More than half of the 30 biggest Euro-area banks are the result of recent mergers and the average size of the top five banks as of 1999 (Deutsche Bank, BNP Paribas, ABN-AMRO, HypoVereinsbank, and Crédit Agricole) has doubled since 1995. Loan markets are fairly concentrated in some countries like Belgium where the top 5 banks make 98 percent of the loans or France where they make 77 percent. By any measure, Germany has the least concentrated markets.[50]

Foreign banks' market share in the Euro area is 12.7 percent. It is 4.3 percent in Germany and 9.8 percent in France. The banking system of the U.K. is fairly concentrated and highly international.

1.   THE SECOND BANKING DIRECTIVE

a.   OVERVIEW

"The Second Council Directive on the Co-ordination of Laws, Regulations and Administrative Provisions Relating to the Taking-up and Pursuit of the Business of Credit Institutions and Amending Directive 77/780/EEC (the Second Directive) obliges the Member States of the Community to implement its provisions into their national banking regimes by means of conforming their national banking laws and practices."[51]

As a formal matter, the SBD has been superseded by Directive 2000/12/ EC of the European Parliament and the Council, March 20, 2000, which codifies the SBD along with other legislation relating to banking, e.g. the Capital Adequacy Directive. The substance of the SBD was not changed.

Institutional Coverage

"The Second Directive applies to credit institutions. A credit institution is defined as an 'undertaking whose business is to receive deposits or other repayable funds from the public and to grant credits for its own account.' According to the Second Directive, credit institutions that are authorized and supervised as credit institutions by the competent authorities of their Home Member States (where licensed) will benefit from mutual—i.e. Community-wide—recognition of their banking licenses with respect to the

---

[50] See A. Belaisch, L. Kodres, J. Levy, and A. Ubide, "Euro-Area Banking at the Crossroads," IMF Working Paper WP/01/28 (March 2001).
[51] M. Gruson and W. Feuring, "A European Community Banking Law," in *The Second Banking and Related Directives in the Single Market and the Law of Banking* (R. Cranston ed., 1991).

activities enumerated in the Annex to the Second Directive (the Annex) and for which they are licensed in the Home Member State.

Subsidiaries established in the Community countries by non-Community persons under a license for credit institutions are credit institutions benefiting from the principle of mutual recognition. In other words, non-Community ownership or control of a credit institution does not destroy the mutual recognition of the license of the credit institution.

The License

Credit institutions authorized in the Home Member State will be entitled in each of the other Member States: (i) to establish branches; and (ii) to offer their services freely to individuals and businesses, in each case without the need for any further authorization by the Host Member State. Community credit institutions will be entitled to operate in this way under their Home Member State licenses, which will be a Community-wide 'single banking license.'

The recognition of the Home Member license required by the Second Directive is limited to certain specified banking activities or powers: the Home Member State license is valid in other Member States only with respect to those specified banking activities that are enumerated in the Annex to the Second Directive.

The banking powers permitted by the banking license of a Member State may fall short of the powers enumerated in the Annex. In that case, credit institutions from other Member States may provide services in that Host Member State that credit institutions licensed in that particular Host Member State are not permitted to provide. A probable consequence of the Second Directive is that the powers permitted to banks in all Member States will soon include all the powers set forth in the Annex. The Second Directive brings about an indirect harmonization of law, if only by virtue of self-interest of the Member States.

The Annex to the Second Directive sets forth the activities "integral to banking" that currently, in the opinion of the Commission, constitute the core of the traditional banking services in the Community:

"1.   acceptance of deposits and other repayable funds from the public;

2.   lending, including, *inter alia,* consumer and mortgage credit, factoring with or without recourse, and financing of commercial transactions including forfeiting;

3.   financial leasing;

4.   money transmission services;

5.   issuing and administering means of payment (e.g. credit cards, travelers' checks and bankers' drafts);

6.   guarantees and commitments;

7.   trading for own account or for account of customers in

    (a) money market instruments (checks, bills, CDS, etc.),

    (b) foreign exchange,

    (c) financial futures and options,

    (d) exchange and interest rate instruments,

    (e) transferable securities;

8.   participation in share issues and the provision of services related to such issues;

9.   advice to undertakings on capital structure, industrial strategy and related questions, and advice and services relating to mergers and the purchase of undertakings;

10.   money broking;

11.   portfolio management and advice;

12.   safekeeping and administration of securities;

13.   credit reference services;

14.   safe custody services."[52]

Branch establishment

What if a Greek bank could not do financial leasing in Greece but wanted to do so in Germany even though German banks could not offer the service in Germany? Could it establish a subsidiary in France—which permitted financial leasing—and then branch into Germany? The 8th "whereas" clause in SBD provides an unclear answer:

> "Whereas the principles of mutual recognition and of home Member State control require the competent authorities of each Member State not to grant authorization or to withdraw it where factors such as the activities programme, the geographical distribution or the activities actually carried on make it quite clear that a credit institution has opted for the legal system of one Member State for the purpose of evading the stricter standards in force in another Member State in which it intends to carry on or carries on the greater part of its activities; whereas, for the purposes of this Directive, a credit institution shall be deemed to be situated in the Member State in which it has its registered office; whereas the Member States must require that the head office be situated in the same Member State as the registered office;"

In July 1993, the Commission proposed that the SBD be amended to provide that "the head office of a financial undertaking must be in the same Member State as its registered office and that in which the authorization

---

[52] *ibid.*

[license] is being required."[53] When the European Parliament considered this proposal in March 1994, the Parliament suggested replacing the term "head office" with "central administration, where the most important decision making bodies are established." The Commission supported the idea, but the Council of Ministers rejected it. On its second reading in October 1994, the Parliament supported another alternative to "head office": "where the undertaking's governing bodies are established." This was ultimately resolved by returning to the Commission's 1993 proposals.[54] Article 3 of the SBD has been amended to provide that:

> Each Member State shall require that:
>
> — any credit institution which is a legal person and which, under its national law has a registered office, have its head office in the same Member State as its registered office,
>
> — any other credit institution have its head office in the Member State which issued its authorization and in which it actually carries on its business.

The term "head office" is additionally important because it determines the "home country" for purposes of supervision, as well as for permissible activities (subject to the agreed list). Thus, in the above example, the French subsidiary of the Greek bank's activities would be restricted to those permitted by Greece.

There is a concern that the single market in banking may be partially undermined by government policies preventing cross-border acquisitions. In June 1999, the Portuguese government vetoed a link-up between Spain's Banco Santander Central Hispano (BSCH) and Mundial Confiança (MC), Portugal's third largest financial group. The Commission challenged the Portuguese action on the grounds that it constituted a violation of freedom of establishment as guaranteed by the Treaty of Rome having found that the veto could not be justified on prudential grounds. Portugal then backed down to some extent, allowing BSCH to gain control of two of the MC's subsidiary banks but requiring BSCH to transfer a third bank to Caixa Geral de Depositos (CGD), a state-owned bank.[55] A signal that protectionism may be waning is the acquisition in April 2000 of the French bank Crédit Commercial de France by the U.K. based HSBC.

Allocation of supervision

The Second Directive is based on the principle of "home country control," under which each credit institution will generally be supervised by the authorities of its Home Member State, even in regard to activities carried

---

[53] COM(93) 363 final-SYN 468 ([1993] O.J. C229/10) (1993 Proposals).
[54] European Parliament and Council Directive 95/26/EC ([1995] L168/7, July 18, 1995).
[55] "Portuguese Banking Plays the End Game," Retail Banker International, January 28, 2000.

out across the borders of, or through a branch located in, another Member State. There are only a few exceptions to that rule.

b.   NOTIFICATION

The SBD allows banks to provide cross-border banking services, as well as branch services, as determined by the home state (subject to the agreed list). Article 20 requires that "any credit institution wishing to exercise the freedom to provide services by carrying on its activities within the territory of another Member State for the first time shall notify the competent authorities of the host Member State of the activities on the list in the Annex which it intends to carry on." Banks must also notify their home country authorities of their intention to offer cross-border services and receive approval to do so from the home country.

The notification requirement has raised difficult issues of interpretation with respect to what is a cross-border service. Provision of safe custody services, i.e. the renting of a safe deposit box, is on the Annex list. Would a German bank renting such deposit boxes for a yearly fee to citizens of all EC states have to notify each state of this service? Suppose it had offered the same service in the past for a monthly fee? Suppose the German bank's local EC branches solicit customers for the service, must the German bank still provide a notice?[56] There appears to be a very uneven practice among banks in different countries in supplying notifications. In 1993–94, U.K. and German authorities respectively received 123 and 116 notifications from their own institutions compared with Italy and Spain which respectively received five and three notifications. And in the same period, Belgium received 144 notifications from foreign institutions as compared with the U.K. and Germany that respectively received 59 and 49 notifications.[57] It would seem difficult to attribute this data to actual patterns of services. For example, it seems doubtful that Spanish banks are only offering cross-border services at 2.6 percent the rate of German banks.

The Commission has issued an Interpretative Communication (Communication) covering when notification of a cross-border service is required.[58] It provides that notification will not be required unless "the place of provision of what may be termed the 'characteristic performance' of the service" is carried out in the territory of another Member State. Temporarily visiting another state to carry on an activity preceding the supply of a service, e.g. a survey of property prior to granting a loan, or to conclude a contract for the service would not involve "characteristic performance," and

---

[56] See D. George, "Cross-Border Banking Business and the Second Banking Directive: Legal Uncertainty Resulting from the Notification Requirement," International Banking and Financial Law (September 1994), p. 373.

[57] K. Lannoo, "The Single Market in Banking: A First Assessment," Butterworths Journal of International Banking and Financial Law (November 1995), pp. 485, 487.

[58] No. C209/04 ([1997] O.J., 10.71.97) (1997 Communication).

thus would not require a notice. Nor would engaging in cross-border advertising, whether general or targeted require a notice.

A further issue is raised as to whether a given service is being offered on a cross-border basis or through a branch. Some host states take the view that there is a branch establishment whenever services are provided on a regular basis in their territory. A branch (unlike a cross-border service provider) has the duty to provide statistical information and to pay levies in the host country, and will also be subject to EU deposit insurance requirements.

c.   THE GENERAL GOOD

In 1992, France prohibited a French subsidiary of Barclays from transferring interest on unit trust accounts (mutual funds) to a demand deposit account as an evasion of the French prohibition on paying interest on demand deposit accounts. According to the then-Finance Minister Sapin, remunerated checking accounts would increase the cost of credit and force banks to charge for checking. According to Sapin, checking charges would have the biggest impact on poorer customers for whom checking services were free. Barclays offered this service in the U.K. and "acceptance of deposits and other repayable funds from the public" was on the agreed list of services.

Host states can adopt measures "in the interest of the general good." These measures must be equally applicable to domestic and foreign entities. Such a "safeguard" clause has been common in various EU directives based on mutual recognition. The European Court of Justice, in its landmark decision in *Cassis de Dijon*,[59] held that such clauses did not allow host states to set their own technical or qualitative standards for imported goods where the home states (Member States of origin) had already set essential minimum standards. But EU case law may be departing from this approach by allowing host state "general good" requirements that apply *de jure* and *de facto* to domestic as well as foreign firms.[60]

Mortgage loans have been a focal point for "general good" issues. U.K. building societies offer variable rate mortgages that are not acceptable in Belgium, since Belgium regulates mortgage rates strictly. German banks offer long-term mortgages that prohibit early repayment; this restriction violates consumer protection laws in France and Belgium.

The Commission's 1997 Communication points to six criteria, based in case law, for determining the general good: (1) the measure must not be discriminatory; (2) the measure must not impose higher requirements than those of a Harmonization Directive covering the subject; (3) the measure must have a general good objective; (4) the general good objective must not

---

[59] Case 120/78, 1979 E.C.R. 649.

[60] See G. Hertig, "Imperfect Mutual Recognition for EC Financial Services," 14 International Review of Law and Economics (1994), p. 177.

already be safeguarded in the country of origin; (5) the measure must be capable of guaranteeing that the objective will be met; and (6) the measure does not go beyond what is necessary to achieve the objective pursued. The last criterion, "proportionality," may often be the hardest to satisfy.

In October 2004, the European Court of Justice held in *Caixa-Bank France v. Ministére de l'économie* that France was required to allow its banks to pay interest on current accounts despite arguments by France that such measures protected consumers against higher cost accounts and encouraged long-term savings. The Court held that prohibitions on interest payments were a serious obstacle to foreign banks seeking to do business in the French market and that consumers could be protected by being offered a choice between higher cost accounts with interest and lower ones without. The court also stated that longer-term savings could be encouraged in other ways.[61]

d.   CROSS-BORDER SUPERVISION

The SBD leaves supervision to home countries. The home country must supervise banking groups, and a 1992 Council Directive[62] established the principle of consolidated supervision of the various entities within a banking group. EU banks are subject to common supervisory standards, such as capital requirements, single exposure limits, limitations on investments in non-financial institutions, etc. And EU supervisors are in close touch through various supervisors' committees. The Banking Advisory Committee (BAC) is attached to the European Commission and comprises high level representatives of Member States' supervisory authorities, finance ministries and central banks. The BAC's primary role is to assist the Commission in formulating legislation and to give advice on regulation and supervision.

There are other groups as well. In October 1998, the Banking Supervision Committee (BSC) of the European System of Central Banks was set up to assist the European Central Bank (ECB) in formulating macro-economic policy. The oldest group is the Groupe de Contact (GDC) which is not formally attached to any institution. It is composed of mid-management banking supervisors from EU countries who are involved in the day-to-day supervision of banks. Group members are in regular contact and exchange confidential information on individual cases relevant to banking supervision.[63] In addition, countries have entered into bilateral Memoranda of Understanding (MOU) establishing cooperative procedures, see e.g. the French-German MOU.

The Commission has adopted a new Directive, that had been pending consideration since 1985, providing that when a credit institution with

---

[61] Case C-442/02, Judgment of the Court, October 5, 2004.
[62] 92/30/EEC ([1992] O.J. L110/52, April 28, 1992).
[63] European Commission, Internal Market Directorate General, Institutional Arrangements for the Regulation and Supervision of the Financial Sector (January 2000).

branches in other Member States fails, the insolvency (winding up) process will be subject to a single bankruptcy proceeding in the home state of the failed institution. This is consistent with the home country supervision principle.[64]

The actual conduct of banking supervision in the Member States is done by different institutions. In some countries, it is done by the central bank, e.g. the Banca d'Italia in Italy, in other countries by a banking supervisory agency, e.g. Bundesaufsichtsamt für das Kreditwesen in Germany, the Ministry of Finance, e.g. Austria, or a consolidated supervisory agency with responsibility for all financial institutions, e.g. the Financial Supervisory Authority (FSA) in the United Kingdom.

France has a very fragmented system. It splits banking regulation among several entities, including the Banking Commission which supervises credit institutions and investment firms, the Banque de France (central bank), and the Banking and Financial Regulatory Committee, which promulgates regulation. The Minister for Economic Affairs, Finance, and Industry appoints the members of the regulatory entities, except for the Banque de France. Regulation of securities is entrusted to still another entity, the Commission des Opérations des Bourses (COB), appointed by the Government.[65]

The FSA in the U.K. was created in May 1997, when the new Labor government in the U.K. announced a total restructuring of the regulatory regime for financial services, the most radical feature of which was to transfer banking supervision to the FSA. The plan was implemented in 1998. Banking supervision had previously been conducted by the Bank of England. Another major part of the reform was to fold existing self-regulatory organizations (SROs) into the FSA. The rationale for the change is the existence of universal banking under which financial firms engage in both securities and banking activities.[66] The FSA has a MOU with the Bank of England, entered into in 1997, which makes it clear that the Bank is responsible for the overall stability of the financial system, including monetary policy, whereas the FSA is responsible for the authorization, supervision and regulation of financial institutions. Other countries are beginning to follow this model. Germany adopted a similar plan on the heels of the announcement that Allianz, a leading German insurer, was to acquire Dresdner bank. The German plan, unlike the FSA, did not eliminate the existing separate regulators of banking, securities, and insurance, but would combine them within one central body.

---

[64] 2335 Council-ECOFIN, Press Release (March 12, 2001).
[65] E. Cervellati, "Financial Regulation and Supervision in EU Countries," Faculty of Economics, University of Bologna, 2002.
[66] See "Financial Regulatory Reform in the U.K.," 16 International Banking and Financial Law (1997), p. 47.

A long-standing debate has gone on about whether the central bank should have supervisory power on a EU wide basis because of the possible connection between supervision and monetary policy or whether some other supervisory body should be created. Not surprisingly, the European Central Bank has taken the position that it should be entrusted with this role.[67] Preservation of a supervisory role for the central bank is seemingly inconsistent with consolidation of supervision along the lines of the FSA model because of the unlikelihood that the central bank would become the supervisor of non-banking firms. This issue is further discussed in Chapter 5.

The Treaty entrusts the ESCB with contributing "to the smooth conduct of policies pursued by the competent authorities relating to prudential supervision of credit institutions and the stability of the financial system, Article 105(5) EC Treaty and Article 3.3 ESCB Statute. Further, the ECOFIN Council may entrust the ECB with "specific tasks concerning policies relating to the prudential supervision of credit institutions. ..." Could this be the basis of ECB becoming the EU banking supervisor?

Sir Howard Davies, the former head of the U.K.'s FSA, opposes giving supervisory authority to the ECB. He contends that "concentrating banking supervision in the ECB, or indeed anywhere else, would almost certainly be quite the wrong way to go, at a time when the boundaries between banking and other regulation are becoming blurred."[68]

In April, 2002 the United Kingdom and Germany proposed that banking supervision in the EU be handled by a forum of Member State finance authorities, including the ECB and central banks, but the ECB continues to argue for a central role.[69] In November 2003, the EU Commission extended the "Lamfalussy" approach for securities regulation to banking regulation. A new European Banking Committee (EBC) was created. Like the European Securities Committee (ESC), it assists the Commission in adopting and implementing measures for EU Directives (it replaces the existing Banking Advisory Committee (BAC)). In addition, a new Committee of European Bank Supervisors (CEBS) was created, the counterpart of CESR for securities. It would aim to flesh out implementing technical applications of the Directives.[70] If no overall FSA regulatory structure emerges in the EU, consideration would have to be given for establishing one overall banking supervisor. This is highly preferred by large multinational banks, and would reduce the present high supervisory costs within the EU. One study estimates that there would be a 15 percent institutional cost saving from

---

[67] European Central Bank, *The Role of Central Banks in Prudential Supervision* (March 22, 2001).

[68] H. Davies, "Euro-regulation," 1 The Journal of International Banking Regulation (1999), pp. 113, 116.

[69] See M. Schüler, "How Do Banking Supervisors Deal with Europe-wide Systemic Risk," Centre for European Economic Research Discussion Paper 03-03 (2003).

[70] European Commission, 2004/5/EC (November 5, 2003).

integrated banking supervision.[71] In the meantime, the EU is exploring a lead supervisor approach that might but would not necessarily be the home country supervisor.[72] As we saw in the case of BCCI, it might make more sense to give the supervisory lead to the country where a bank's most important operations were located.

Notes and Questions

1. What do you think of the way the EU deals with the "common good" problem?

2. CONGLOMERATES

In April 2001, the European Commission proposed a new Directive to deal with financial conglomerates.[73] The Council and Parliament agreed to this proposal in 2002.[74] The proposal seeks to eliminate some inconsistencies in existing Directives applicable to what the Commission calls homogeneous financial groups, e.g. banking or insurance groups. In addition, it seeks to insure that regulation of different sectors, e.g. banking, is not undermined by financial conglomerates. Specifically, it seeks to insure that the same capital is not used to support different regulated institutions. It does not seek to regulate capital at the holding company level (as in the United States). The proposal also seeks to address supervisory concerns about intra-group transactions and risk exposures built on three pillars: effective internal management systems, reporting requirements to supervisors, and effective enforcement. It does not seek to impose quantitative limits on such transactions (as in the United States). In addition, it envisions new mechanisms of cooperation among existing supervisors. It would appear that this approach is somewhat at odds with the consolidation approach of the FSA within the U.K. The Commission seeks to preserve and coordinate separate sectoral regulation, whereas the FSA seeks to consolidate regulation in one supervisor. This proposal has caused significant problems in the U.S. since the EU applies the Directive to unregulated subsidiaries of U.S. holding companies. While all subsidiaries of a FSHC or BHC are regulated, the same is not true for firms engaging in insurance or banking that do not own banks. Chapters 2 and 7 discuss how the SEC has responded to this problem.

In October 2003, the FSA issued rules for implementing the Conglomerates Directive. The FSA's approach is particularly important to U.S. firms since most U.S. securities firms with "unregulated" holding

---

[71] M. Schüler and F. Heinemann, "The Costs of Supervisory Fragmentation in Europe," Centre for European Economic Research Discussion Paper 05-01 (2005).

[72] "Lead Supervisor for Big Banks Possible for 2009," 3 Global Risk Regulator, March 2005.

[73] COM(2001) 213 final, April 24, 2001.

[74] Directive 2002/87/EC of the European Parliament and of the Council, December 16, 2002. For a general review of the Directive, see M. Gruson, "Supervision of Financial Conglomerates in the European Union," Journal of International Banking Law Review 363 (2004)

companies have their European operations headquartered in London. It is up to the U.K., under the Conglomerate Directive, as to how to supervise and regulate these firms.

If the FSA decides that these U.S. firms are subject to effective consolidated supervision under the SEC's proposed regulation, discussed in Chapter 2, that would be the end of the matter. If the FSA decides that is not the case, it has indicated it could: (1) itself undertake worldwide supervision, or (2) "look to the group to organize itself in such a way that the objectives of group-wide supervision can be achieved by other means, such as establishment of a European holding company and restrictions of exposures between the European sub-group and the worldwide group ('ring fencing')."[75]

In 2005, the U.K. was working with the SEC to determine whether the new SEC rules were equivalent to those of the EU.[76] Its equivalence review was broken down into two parts, capital adequacy and information exchange. With respect to capital, discussed in Chapter 7, the remaining issue appears to be whether the SEC's net capital rules for broker-dealers satisfy the equivalence test, given that EU securities firms are subject to Basel capital rules. The EU seems wholly satisfied with the SEC approach at the investment bank group level. The more difficult issue seemed to be the extent to which European regulators would have access to SEC information about the entities regulated in the United States.

Notes and Questions

1.   To what extent does the Conglomerates Directive seek to exercise extraterritorial reach?

2.   What accounts for the fact that the EU and the U.S. apparently differ (at least before the new SEC proposal) over the need to regulate the holding companies of securities firms?

3.   Do the EU and the U.S. have similar objectives in regulating financial institutions?

3.   STATE SUBSIDIES AND MERGER RESTRICTIONS

A significant issue for the single market in banking concerns subsidies for state-owned banks that could give such banks competitive advantages. EU competition rules come into play in trying to control such subsidies. For example, when France in July 1995 injected $9.37 billion into Crédit Lyonnais to rescue it from failing, the Commission extracted some promises from France to limit future aid and to reduce by 35 percent the

---

[75] Financial Services Authority, Financial Groups (October 2003), p. 4.
[76] Speech by H. Sants, Managing Director, Wholesale and Institutional Markets, FSA, Keynote Address, February 24, 2005.

presence of the bank outside France, including a sale of a substantial part of its 900 office banking network.

In 1999, the state aid focus was on the German Landesbanks (banks owned by various regional governments). In July, the Commission forced the Westdeutsche Landesbank (WestLB) to repay its owner, the regional government of North-Rhine Westphalia, $834 million, representing the value of a state housing agency that the government had transferred to the bank in 1992 at no cost. The Landesbanks, which do more than a third of Germany's banking business, generally receive guarantees of their assets from their government owners allowing them to obtain AAA credit ratings, thus putting them at a competitive advantage. When WestLB failed to devise a satisfactory plan for repayment, the Commission referred the case to the European Court of Justice. In February 2001, WestLB proposed setting up a subsidiary that would take over competitive activities such as corporate lending and investment banking. WestLB proposed giving its subsidiary a "comfort letter" that looks like a guarantee. The Commission has said this is a step in the right direction but not enough.

Government ownership of banks is pervasive. R. La Porta, F. Lopez-de-Silanes, and A. Shleifer[77] found that average ownership by governments of their 10 largest banks was 41.74 percent. While the U.K. was at zero, France, Germany, and Italy were respectively at 17.26, 36.36 and 35.95 percent. The authors found that government ownership of banks is associated with slower subsequent financial development, lower subsequent growth of per capital income, and with lower productivity.

Despite Commission policies opposing cross-border restrictions on mergers and despite the desire of banks to engage in more cross-border mergers, based on their belief that size increases within Europe are important to making European banks more competitive internationally, some national authorities like Italy continue to put obstacles in the way of such mergers.[78] In 2005, ABN Amro, the large Dutch bank sought to acquire Italy's ninth largest bank by assets, Banca Antoniana Popolare Veneta (Antonveneta). At first, the Bank of Italy, the regulator of Italian banks, appeared to oppose the bid on the grounds of preventing foreign banks from acquiring Italian banks. This resulted in a remonstrance from the EU Commission. The Bank of Italy then seemed to support a counter-bid by Italy's tenth largest bank, Banca Poplare de Lodi (BPL) even though the Italian bank was in a weak financial position. The Bank of Italy appeared to permit BPL to build a large stake in Antonveneta so as to block the merger.[79]

---

[77] "Government Ownership of Banks," NBER Working Paper 7620 (March 2000).
[78] L Crawford and I. Bickerton, "Groups Call on Italy to Ease Rules on Banks," *Financial Times*, October 6, 2004; T. Barber, "Rome Moves to Block Foreign Takeovers of Banks," *Financial Times*, January 17, 2005.
[79] "Machiavellian Manoeuvres," The Economist, May 5, 2005; "Italy Defends Restrictions Over Allowing Foreign Banks Control over Italian Banks," BNA Banking Report, February 28, 2005.

The Bank of Italy has also intervened in another potential takeover—the takeover of Italy's sixth largest bank, Banca Nazionale del Lavoro (BNL) by Spain's Banco Bilbao Vizcaya Argentaria (BBVA). The Italian regulator ruled that it would only allow the takeover if BBVA acquired more than 50 percent of BNL's shares, even though effective control would require less.[80]

While Italy wrestled with acquisitions of Italian banks by other European banks, there were reports of a possible deal in which Unicredito Italiano, Italy's largest bank, would acquire Germany's HVB Group, Germany's second largest bank after Deutsche Bank, for about $20 billion.[81] This would be the biggest pan-European banking merger and, if successful, could well signal more consolidation in the future. It will be interesting to see if Italy's interest in the cross-border acquisition by its largest bank will moderate its opposition to the cross-border acquisition of its smaller banks.

4.   IMPACT OF BANKING POLICY

Although the SBD had entered into force in a majority of Member States, by 1994, the Bank of England reported, based on a survey of 25 firms, that the SBD has had limited impact. Most increased competition was either from existing players in the domestic market or non-banks. Banks have not used the single passport to establish de novo branches in other EU states; future expansion was rather by acquisition. The major use of the directive has been for banks to convert existing subsidiaries into branches to permit a more efficient allocation of capital.[82] These findings differ somewhat from those of a 1997 study of the European Commission.[83] This study found that from 1992-1995, cross-border branches increased by 179, 32 of which represented conversion of existing subsidiaries.[84] One would assume that 179 is a rather small number considering the total number of branches (domestic plus cross-border) in the EU. The study concludes that there was more significant activity from cross-border mergers and acquisitions.[85] However, it also indicated that overall cross-border financial activity increased by a small amount from 1992-1997.[86]

A 2005 study basically confirms the Bank of England finding, 10 years later. The study finds more banking consolidation in Europe than the rest of the world. In the period of 1998-2003, Europe accounted for 62.4

---

[80] T. Buck and L. Crawford, "Brussels to Put Heat on Bank of Italy," *Financial Times*, May 23, 2005.

[81] J. Singer, E. Taylor, and G. Kahn, "Two EU Banks Discuss Merger Worth $20 Billion," *The Wall Street Journal,* May 27, 2005.

[82] "The Developing Single Market in Financial Services," 34 Bank of England Quarterly Bulletin (1994), pp. 341, 344.

[83] Impact on Services, Credit Institutions and Banking, The Single Market Review, Subseries II: Volume 3 (1997).

[84] Id., Table 4.15, p. 55.

[85] Id., at 64.

[86] Id., at 51.

percent of worldwide merger and acquisition activity compared to 19.1 percent in the Americas. However, in the period of 1988-1993, before the single market efforts took effect, Europe accounted for a slightly higher percentage, 63.6 percent.[87] It will be interesting to see whether the expansion of the EU by 10 Member States will increase cross-border mergers and acquisitions within the broader EU.

Notes and Questions

1.   How do you explain the relative lack of cross-border bank mergers in the EU?

2.   Is there a need for a single EU bank regulator? If so, should it be the ECB?

5.   RECIPROCITY

The European Economic Community (EC) adopted its Second Banking Directive on 15 December 1989. Article 9 of this Directive incorporates a reciprocity requirement requiring other countries to give certain specified treatment to EC banks as a condition for banks from these countries taking advantage of the Directive's liberal rules for providing banking services within the EU.

Article 9(3) provides that if the Commission determines "that a third country is not granting Community credit institutions effective market access comparable to that granted by the Community to credit institutions from that third country," the Council may authorize the Commission to open up negotiations to obtain such "comparable competitive opportunities" for EU credit institutions.

Article 9(4) provides that negotiations may also be opened by the Commission on its own, without Council authorization, whenever it appears to the Commission "that Community credit institutions in a third country do not receive national treatment offering the same competitive opportunities as are available to domestic credit institutions and that the conditions of effective market access are not fulfilled." Furthermore, such a determination may also lead to Member States being required to close their markets to "acquisition of holdings by direct or indirect parent undertakings governed by the laws of the third country in question."

Article 9(4) also provides that such acquisition bans cannot apply to acquisitions that have already been made or to future acquisitions of entities already authorized to operate in the EC. Existing authorized institutions from third countries are thus grandfathered, and are treated on a par with EC institutions.

---

[87] F. Allen and W. Song, "Financial Integration and the EMU," 11 European Financial Management 7 (2005).

In short, lack of effective market access for EU institutions can lead to negotiations, whereas lack of national treatment and effective market access can lead to either negotiations or prospective entry bans. There is considerable ambiguity about the use of the word "and." If the "and" is conjunctive, then two findings would be required for an entry ban: lack of national treatment, and effective market access. This holds out the possibility that EU institutions might have effective market access in a country even where there was a lack of national treatment. On the other hand, if the "and" is disjunctive, the EU could impose an entry ban where there was national treatment but no effective market access.

The EU Schedule of Commitments under the GATS, entered into in 1997, precludes use of the SBD reciprocity requirements against countries that tabled their own MFN Commitments (which now includes the U.S.). Once the GATS is actually adopted by such countries (through their treaty approval processes), the reciprocity requirement will be "history."

6.   DEPOSIT INSURANCE

The Council of the European Union issued a Common Position on the Proposal for a Directive on Deposit-Guarantee Schemes on October 25, 1993 which went into effect on January 1, 1995.[88] It provides that there be a minimum insurance of €20,000. Also, a bank from a home country with limits below the host's country can top up by joining the host country's scheme. Certain deposits are excluded from the scheme, for example deposits of other banks or large corporations.

The ceilings for some key countries as of 2000 were:[89]

Deposit Guarantee Ceilings, Selected Countries (Euros)[1]

Country	Ceiling
Germany	Virtually unlimited[2]
Italy	103,291[3]
Japan	60,853
United States	85,708
France	60,980
U.K.	22,222[4]
Spain	20,000

Notes:
1. As of end-1998
2. 30 percent of a private bank's equity capital
3. 100 percent of first Lit 200mm
4. 90 percent of protected deposits, maximum Euro equivalent of £20,000

---

[88] Directive 94/19/EC of the European Parliament and of the Council, [1994] O.J. L135/5, May 30, 1994.
[89] Bank for International Settlements, *70th Annual Report*, June 5, 2000, Table VII.6.

In its May 13, 1997 judgment in C-233/94, Federal Republic of Germany v. European Parliament and the Council of the European Union, ECR 1997, I-2405, the European Court of Justice rejected a German challenge to the Deposit-Guarantee Directive. The Germans brought the case because the Directive prevented Germany until the end of 1999 from providing unlimited insurance to its foreign branches.[90]

Germany was also concerned about having to give unlimited topping up to branches of banks from other EU countries. As a result, it only has "public" insurance at the EU minimum, but permits banks (domestic and other EU) to buy a virtually unlimited private insurance supplement.

In the United States, until 1991, depositors in U.S. branches of foreign banks that took retail deposits had to be insured by the United States. After 1991, retail deposit branches are prospectively prohibited— foreign banks must take retail deposits through subsidiaries. The United States abolished retail insured branches of foreign banks largely out of concern that it—the host state—might have to pay for the supervisory failures of a foreign country. The EU might have followed the same approach but it resisted treating domestic and non-domestic EU branches of EU banks in the same Member State differently.

Notes and Questions

1. The EU scheme prevents home states from providing insurance above the level of host states—the "no export" clause. Do you agree that such a limitation is necessary for an even playing field? The EU scheme permits branches of out-of-state EU banks, whose insurance is below the level of a host state, to join the host state deposit scheme in order to "top-up" their insurance to the level of the host state. Germany has had unlimited insurance coverage for deposits. How do you think it would feel about the no export and top-up provisions? Will out-of-state banks from low insurance countries want to top-up?

CONCLUSIONS

Developments in the EU are important to international financial regulation in three ways. First, the EU is a huge market (expanding in size due to enlargement), one comparable in size to the U.S. Given global financial integration, whatever happens in the EU is important to the rest of the world. Second, the EU is building its domestic market for Europe, a matter of obvious importance to its own citizens. Finally, the EU is a laboratory for international regulation. Its internal system of mutual recognition and

---

[90] See A. Landsmeer and M. Van Empel, "The Directive on Deposit-guarantee Schemes and the Directive on Investor Compensation Schemes in View of Case C-233/94," European Financial Services Law (July/August 1998), p. 143.

minimum harmonization offers a possible blueprint for the international system at large.

A major issue for the EU is how to organize regulation internally. This has many aspects. Most fundamental is the allocation of power between the EU and its Member States. The EU has observed the principle of subsidiarity under which much power is left to the States. One wonders if the current implementation of this model is viable, particularly where enforcement only occurs at the Member State level. In addition, the national implementation of Directives is cumbersome and takes a very long time to accomplish. Charles McCreevy, who became the internal markets commissioner in 2004, has stated that the 25 member states of the EU persistently fail to implement Directives.[91] A second aspect of regulation is how it operates at the EU level. The Lamfalussy process, first adopted for securities regulation and now proposed for banking, seeks to speed-up the Directive process both in the formative and implementing stages. Whether this "comitology" will work is open to serious question. A third aspect of regulation is the degree of harmonization versus mutual recognition. While the "mantra" is mutual recognition, the recent prospectus directive together with the new comitology seems to be evolving more towards harmonization. The Prospectus Directive envisions a common prospectus throughout the EU, not a passport for different home country prospectuses.

There is also the question of convergence. Is European regulation, in content, converging with regulation in the United States? To a great extent, the answer is yes. There is no question that after the implementation of the Prospectus and Transparency Directives, regulation of securities within the EU will be more like that in the United States. These are the EU's '33 and '34 Acts. And the IASB (mainly European) is converging its standards with FASB (the U.S.). To the extent EU regulation of securities is more like that of the U.S., efficiency and ease of business should be increased. On the other hand, there are significant improvements in the European approach to securities regulation not yet adopted by the U.S.—more modern rules for electronic prospectus delivery, lack of restriction on market communications during offerings, and lack of prohibition on solicitations for private offerings.

In the banking area, mutual recognition is the norm—less harmonization is needed in this area and more convergence has already occurred between Member States. Here the EU approach is already largely consistent with the international mutual recognition system.

It remains to be determined whether the failure of the constitutional referendums in France and the Netherlands will slow down or push back the reforms of the internal financial markets.

---

[91] T. Buck, "Members 'Persistently' Ignoring EU Market Laws," *Financial Times*, January 28, 2005.

CHAPTER FIVE

EUROPE'S ECONOMIC AND MONETARY UNION

The creation of the Economic and Monetary Union (EMU) in Europe is one of the major events in international finance in the last quarter century. Its potential impact radiates from foreign exchange markets to markets for banking, bonds, equity, and derivatives.

This chapter first describes the original plan for the organization of EMU and the stages to achieve union by January 1, 1999, as set out in the Maastricht Treaty (the Treaty). It then presents evaluations of the costs and benefits of monetary union in Europe. It then turns to the steps countries took toward convergence, to bring their economies to roughly similar levels of performance and align certain economic policies, laws, and institutions. Finally, the chapter discusses how the union worked after January 1, 1999. The new Euro coins and notes were introduced on schedule in the first two months of 2002, and the changes to the Euro were quite smooth. After initial concern with the strength of the Euro, it has greatly increased in value against the Dollar. The major issues for the future are the possible entry of the U.K. and the "new" Europe, as well as the functioning of the Stability Pact, the agreement on coordination of fiscal policy. It also remains to be seen if the rejection of the constitutional referendum will have an impact on the Euro.

A.   THE DESIGN OF THE EUROPEAN MONETARY UNION

On January 1, 1999, 11 countries in the European Union began the third stage of the Economic and Monetary Union. They were Austria, Belgium, Germany, Finland, France, Ireland, Italy, Luxembourg, Netherlands, Portugal, and Spain. Two other countries—Denmark and the U.K.—had also qualified but decided not to join at that time. In October 2000, the Danish voters rejected entry into EMU and the U.K. has yet to decide to join. In early 2000, the EU decided that Greece was ready to join, which it did in January 2001. Sweden initially had a problem with the required degree of central bank independence—a condition for joining—but later, after surmounting this, did not join. It held a referendum on adopting the Euro in September 2003. The voters soundly rejected the Euro and kept the Krona.

In December 2002, the EU summit approved 10 new members for entry in 2004. Unlike existing EU members like Denmark and the U.K., none of the new members can opt out of EMU. They will be required to adopt the Euro as soon as they are deemed ready, e.g. meet fiscal entry requirements. Some see entry of these new members as early as 2006.

The following section describes the ground rules set by treaty to achieve monetary union in Europe and the key stages in the transition to union.

1.   THE MAASTRICHT TREATY

EC member governments meeting in December 1992 in Maastricht, the Netherlands, agreed to a treaty that would carry them to economic and monetary union in seven years. Their decision grew from recommendations made in 1989 by the Delors Committee. The plan included locking the currencies of each country permanently, following a single monetary policy, and using a single currency managed by the European Central Bank (ECB) in what was originally called the European System of Central Banks (ESCB) but is now referred to as the Eurosystem.

The treaty envisioned an evolution toward monetary union through three stages. In the first, through 1993, EU governments would try to coordinate their economic policies so that their economies could begin to converge, complete the Single Market (see Chapter 4), and adopt a stronger common competition policy. In Stage 2, from 1994 through 1998, EU countries would push their economies to converge toward common inflation rates, long-term interest rates, government deficits, and currency fluctuations within the European Exchange Rate Mechanism. The Treaty set numeric goals for each of these and provided that countries that met the targets would qualify for membership in Stage 3. The Treaty created the European Monetary Institute as a precursor to the European Central Bank, which was to be set up in mid-1998.

"Stage 3 started with the irrevocable locking of exchange rates between participating currencies and with the assumption by the ECB and Eurosystem of their responsibility for issuing and managing the single currency—the Euro—that would replace national currencies.

The primary objectives and basic tasks of the Eurosystem and ECB are laid down in Article 105 of the Treaty and Chapter 2 of the ESCB Statute; and the System's structure, operations, governance, and accountability in Articles 106-8 and 109a and b of the Treaty and Chapters III-VI of the Statute. Their primary objective is to maintain price stability.

The Eurosystem's main tasks are the formulation and execution of the single monetary policy, the holding and management of participating member states' official foreign exchange reserves, promotion of the smooth operation of payments systems (a matter dealt with in Chapter 9), and contribution to 'the smooth conduct of policies pursued by the competent authorities relating to the prudential supervision of credit institutions and the stability of the financial system.' This mandate requires pooling of national responsibility for monetary policy through participation in the Governing Council of the ECB. National central bank governors from participating states are members of that Council, along with a full time Executive Board appointed by the Heads of State or Government of member states. Members of the Executive Board will have non-renewable eight-year terms. The term of office of national central bank governors is at least five years.

No specific *operational* role in prudential supervision is given to the ECB, but the ECOFIN Council (Ministers of Finances from participating member countries) has the power to confer specific tasks relating to policies on prudential supervision on the ECB in due course. This requires a proposal from the Commission, and would require the assent of the European Parliament, and unanimity of all member states in the ECOFIN Council. Furthermore, the ECB and national central banks are empowered to provide clearing and payments facilities, and the ECB is able to issue regulations on those activities within the Community and with third countries.[1]

Accountability to governments is to be secured through the ECOFIN Council, whose President can participate (but not vote) in meetings of the ECB's Governing Council and submit motions for its consideration; and which may invite the President of the ECB to discuss with it matters relating to ECB tasks and objectives. Responsibility for exchange rates remains essentially with the ECOFIN Council (Art. 109 para. 1).

The Treaty contains a number of provisions that strengthen the process of fiscal surveillance begun in Stage 1 and introduce constraints in the size of fiscal deficits and their financing. There was agreement on the three basic fiscal principles of 'no excessive fiscal deficits,' 'no monetary financing,' and 'no bailouts.' Agreement was reached on provisions that prohibit the ECB or national central banks from providing credit facilities to government or to Community institutions or other public sector bodies, and from purchasing debt instruments *directly* from them (Art. 104). There are also provisions that will prevent the Community and governments of member states assuming the financial commitments of other governments or public authorities in the Community (Art. 104b), as a necessary condition for the exercise of effective market discipline on national fiscal policy; and to set up more formal procedures of surveillance over fiscal policy, including numerical triggers designed to prompt a Commission investigation into the fiscal policy of member states (Art. 104c). In extreme cases, if the ECOFIN Council concludes that policy is grossly in error, there is provision for sanctions on member states failing to correct excessive deficits (Art. 104c, para. 11),

---

[1] ESCB Statute Art. 22.

including the imposition of fines."[2] This was implemented in the Stability Pact that is treated at more length below.

Figure 5.1, below, sets forth the structure of the Eurosystem:

Figure 5.1

EMU: The Eurosystem

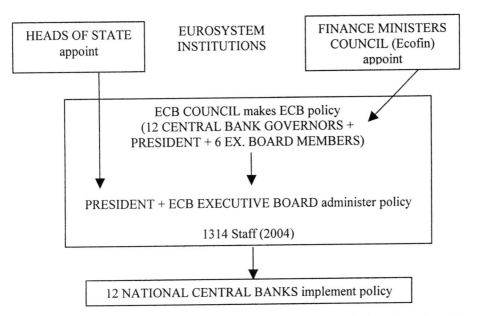

As the new 10 members join the Euro, the size of the Council could get unwieldy, as 10 new central bank governors could be added. Further, there is the issue as to whether small and large countries should be weighted equally in voting on the Council, as they are at present. Equal voting can bias monetary policy in favor of the smaller more numerous countries.[3] In 2004, the EU changed the voting rules of the Council to provide that the number of national central bank governors with votes cannot exceed 15 (currently it is 12). If the number of central bank governors exceeds 15, then voting rights will be rotated according to pre-established rules.[4]

---

[2] "The Maastricht Agreement on Economic and Monetary Union," 32 Bank of England Quarterly Bulletin (1992), p. 64.

[3] H. Berger and T. Mueller, "How Should Large and Small Countries Be Represented in a Currency Union," CESifo Working Paper 1344 (November 2004).

[4] European Central Bank, Annual Report 2004, at p. 164.

2.   THE PROS AND CONS OF MONETARY UNION

As an overall matter, monetary union, especially with a single currency, provides benefits by eliminating transaction costs and the uncertainty associated with exchange rate variability. On the other hand, if labor and capital cannot move freely among the regions of the union, adjustment to some kinds of economic shocks, without changes in the nominal exchange rates of the regions, will lead to unemployment and lost output.

On this basis, the overall cost-benefit balance of EMU may be uncertain because labor mobility in the Community is limited and is bound to remain limited at least for a time. Compared with the U.S. economy, the EU member states show significantly lower labor mobility; have experienced to a greater degree economic shocks that have affected the constituent regions asymmetrically; and, as a result, have relied far more on adjustment of real exchange rates across regions.[5]

Cost and Benefits: The Commission's View

The Commission of the European Communities completed an analysis of the main benefits and costs of forming EMU in advance of the Euro's adoption. The following statement, which is quoted from that study, groups the benefits and costs under five headings.

(i) *Efficiency and Growth.* Elimination of exchange rate uncertainty and transaction costs, and further refinements to the single market are sure to yield gains in efficiency. Through improving the risk-adjusted rate of return on capital and the business climate more generally EMU can strengthen the trend of investment and growth.

(ii) *Price Stability.* This is a generally accepted objective, and beneficial economically in its own right. The problem is that of attaining price stability at the least cost, and then maintaining it. The Community has the opportunity of being able to build its monetary union on the basis of the reputation for monetary stability of its least inflationary Member States. Given the paramount importance of credibility and expectations in winning the fight against inflation at the least cost, this is a great advantage.

(iii) *Public Finance.* A new framework of incentives and constraints will condition national budgetary policies, for which the key-words will be autonomy (to respond to country-specific problems), discipline (to avoid excessive deficits), and coordination (to assure an appropriate overall policy-mix in the Community). EMU will also bring valuable gains for many countries' national budgets through reductions in interest rates, as inflation and exchange risk premiums are eliminated. These benefits will very

---

[5] H. Carré and K. Johnson, "Progress toward a European Monetary Union," Federal Reserve Bulletin (October 1991), pp. 769-76.

probably outweigh the loss of seigniorage revenue to be experienced by some countries (see below).

(iv) *Adjusting to Economic Shocks.* The main potential cost of EMU is that represented by the loss of monetary and exchange rate policy as an instrument of economic adjustment at the national level. This loss should not be exaggerated since exchange rate changes by the Community in relation to the rest of the world will remain possible, whereas within the EMS the nominal exchange rate instrument is already largely abandoned, and EMU will reduce the incidence of country-specific shocks. Relative real labor costs will still be able to change; budgetary policies at national and Community levels will also absorb shocks and aid adjustment, and the external current account constraint will disappear.

Moreover, model simulations suggest that with EMU, compared to other regimes, the Community would have been able to absorb the major economic shocks of the last two decades with less disturbance in terms of the rate of inflation and, to some extent also, the level of real activity.

(v) *The International System.* With the Euro becoming a major international currency, there will be advantages for the Community as banks and enterprises conduct more of their international business in their own currency; moreover, the monetary authorities will be able to economize in external reserves and achieve some international seigniorage gains. EMU will also mean that the Community will be better placed, through its unity, to secure its interests in international coordination processes and negotiate for a balanced multipolar system.

Critique of the Euro

Martin Feldstein, a Harvard economics professor who chaired President Reagan's Council of Economic Advisers, challenged the idea that EMU was a worthwhile goal.[6] I summarize Feldstein's argument in the following points:

First, the benefits do not outweigh the costs under EMU. "A move to a single currency is economically justified if the gains (lower transactions costs and an expanded financial market) ... outweigh the losses (the loss of domestic interest rates and the nominal exchange rate as policy tools)."

Second, a common currency will not enhance trade within the EU and may actually diminish it. Eliminating currency fluctuations within Europe is not necessary to facilitate trade because trading companies can hedge in increasingly efficient markets with low transactions costs. The U.S. and Japan have seen their trade grow in periods of high currency variability.

Third, member countries will no longer be able to use monetary policy to manage domestic interest rates and the exchange rates. So a U.K. exporter (assuming the U.K. had joined EMU) to France competing with a U.S.

---

[6] "The Case Against EMU," The Economist, June 13, 1992, p. 19.

exporter could no longer benefit from a devaluation of Sterling against the Dollar when British costs, but not EMU-wide costs, would have justified a devaluation. The only way for the U.K. to adjust is by lowering wages and prices. Big differences among member countries will persist because their economies differ a lot (in products and imports) and big cultural differences reduce the mobility of labor, which would be a useful safety valve if a member country or region's economy was weak.

Fourth, the big U.S. market and its common currency, the Dollar, do not make a good model because the U.S. also has a common fiscal policy. When a U.S. region's economy turns down, its residents pay less tax and receive more transfers from the federal government. This helps the region recover. Europe's taxes are local and national, not EU-wide.

Fifth, EMU does not guarantee an EU-wide anti-inflationary policy. The Bundesbank forces that policy on many of its neighbors already. The institutional arrangements for the central bank allow politics to play an important role in decision-making, and many people see the European central bank as a device to reduce the power of the Bundesbank by making it share its power with other EMU members.

Sixth, while EMU's economic costs exceed its benefits, it sends a very important signal that political union is underway. This political function would justify EMU in a way that its economic effect does not.

Defense of the Euro

Countering Feldstein was a group of European economists, who argued that "EMU is full of calculated risk. But so is the status quo. ..."[7] They said the transaction costs of hedging are big for smaller firms, devaluation is often ineffective and inflationary, and countries' economies would converge over time. The U.S. has to have a federal tax because labor is so mobile that workers would move to escape taxes applied only at the state level, but Europe's national tax systems are more effective than any for the entire EU because labor mobility is low in Europe. They believed that the European central bank would be even more independent than the Bundesbank because the ECB's powers could only be changed by treaty, while the Bundesbank's powers could be changed by a majority vote in the German legislature. Finally, writing in mid-1992, they pointed to the success of the ERM and the convergence of many EU economies.

The loss of national control over monetary and foreign exchange policy may not be serious. Labor mobility is probably less of an issue than Feldstein suggested, according to some. Mobility should increase as economies integrate and English becomes more widespread, but the speed of these changes cannot be predicted now.[8]

---

[7] See P. De Grauwe, et al., "In Reply to Feldstein," The Economist, July 4, 1992, p. 67.
[8] B. Eichengreen, "European Monetary Unification: A Tour d'Horizon, (1998) 14:3 Oxford Review of Economic Policy, pp. 24, 26-7. (Eichengreen)

"The *singleness* of monetary policy, administered centrally by the ECB, and the *multiplicity* of fiscal policies, run separately for each participant ... could create ... problems," according to Charles Taylor in 1997. Both fiscal and monetary policy can affect aggregate demand in the economy and inflation. The ECB is obliged to maintain price stability, but fiscal policy in which one or more member countries ran large deficits could destabilize prices. If one member country pursued such an expansionary policy, that could have an expansionary effect on other members. Greater integration would bring greater spillover. If the ECB responded by raising real interest rates, the entire union would be hit, hurting investment and long run growth.[9] On the other hand, automatic transfer from a federal (EU) budget to a country with high unemployment could create moral hazard if strong conditions did not accompany the transfer.[10]

The different financial structures of member countries would augment the differential impact of ECB monetary policy. "A given change in the short-term interest rates ... is likely to have a larger effect on lending rates and credit conditions in an economy with a liberalized banking system and much lending at variable rates, as in the U.K., than in one where banks are still relatively cartelized and lending is typically at fixed rates, as in Germany."[11]

As the Euro becomes a reserve currency, it would displace the U.S. Dollar and, to some extent, the Yen. The Euro area would benefit at the expense of the U.S. Indeed, as much as 20 percent of the stock of Dollar assets held by non-residents of the U.S. could be converted into Euro holdings, forcing the Dollar to depreciate.[12]

One problem with EMU is that there is no lender of last resort to the banking system. The ECB is prohibited from bailing out banks. Of course, this could be a plus insofar as it reduces moral hazard. This is more thoroughly discussed below.

In the big picture, the case for EMU is probably political insofar as it binds more closely those EU states that participate. For some, EMU is a key step in creating a Europe that may someday rival the U.S. for wealth and influence.

Due to the adoption of the Euro, national central banks will lose their ability to earn seigniorage. This is the profit a central bank makes by issuing currency, on which it pays no interest, in exchange for bank deposits that it

---

[9] C. Taylor, "The Separation of Monetary and Fiscal Policy in Stage Three of EMU," in *European Economic and Monetary Union: The Institutional Framework* (M. Andenas, C. Hadjiemmanuil, and I. Harden eds., 1997), p. 171. (Taylor)

[10] Eichengreen, supra note 8, p. 30.

[11] Taylor, supra note 9, p. 176.

[12] See R. Portes and H. Rey, "The Emergence of the Euro as an International Currency," NBER Working Paper 6424 (1998).

can invest to make interest. Member states will share seigniorage earnings of the ECB, but only based on their share of ECB capital, which is determined by a country's share in EU population and GDP, an index that does not track foregone seigniorage. Germany was a big loser on seigniorage (due to the strong demand for DM currency), losing €41.1 billion, while France gained €23.5 billion.[13] It is also interesting to note that there will be an additional seigniorage windfall of about $15 billion, as it is estimated that this amount of legacy currencies will not be traded in for Euros. The new EU members will also benefit from seigniorage. For the poorer countries, Bulgaria and Romania, the gains could be quite substantial, .50 to one percent GDP per year.[14]

Notes and Questions

1.   What do you see as the major costs and benefits of the European monetary union?

2.   Feldstein, and others, see the political goals of monetary union in Europe as much more compelling than the economic goals. What are the political goals?

3.   R. Glick and A. Rose, "Does a Currency Union Affect Trade? The Time-Series Evidence," 46 European Economic Review 1125 (2002) find that dissolutions of and exits from currency unions are common. From 1948-1997, there were 130 switches out of but only 16 switches into currency unions.

B.   THE TRANSITION: GETTING TO STAGE 3

The Treaty came into force on November 1, 1993, despite opposition and even court challenges in several countries. Many called this creative accounting.

1.   CONVERGENCE

In 1992, few EU countries met the convergence criteria for inflation, deficits, debt, exchange rates, and long-term interest rates.

The EU settled several outstanding issues in mid-1997. In June, EU leaders agreed on a stability and growth pact, promising to coordinate economic policy but committing little new money to support employment. Gradually, for eleven countries the key indicators converged, so that even by mid-1997 it appeared that all but Greece would qualify. The EMI confirmed this in March 1998, and during a meeting May 1-3, 1998, the heads of state

---

[13] H. Feist, "The Enlargement of the European Union and the Redistribution of Seigniorage Wealth," CESifo Working Paper 408 (January 2001).

[14] D. Gros, "Profiting from the Euro? Seigniorage Gains fro Euro Area Accession," 42 Journal of Common Market Studies 795 (2004).

officially set the membership in Stage 3 even though several countries barely qualified by some criteria.

2.   THE SHIFT FROM MULTIPLE CURRENCIES TO ONE

To shift to the Euro from the currencies of Stage 3, members made three decisions. Decision 1 was that the value of the Euro against the Dollar (and therefore other non-Stage 3 currencies) would equal the Dollar value of the ECU on December 31, 1998 and be set by foreign exchange markets after that. This was decided by Article 1091(4) of the treaty as interpreted by the European Council.

Decision 2 was the value of the currencies of the countries in Stage 3 against each other (cross-rates) and was officially announced on May 2, 1998 by the European Council of the EU in the *Joint Communiqué on the Determination of the Irrevocable Conversion Rates for the Euro*. A cross rate is the rate of one currency against another, e.g. the DM against the French Franc. Cross rates were important in Stage 3 because the rates affected the terms of trade among the members. If one national currency unit of the DM was the equivalent in Euro of three French Francs, then French goods would be less costly to buyers in Germany than if the DM was the equivalent of only two Francs. The one-to-three cross rate would promote the sale of French goods to Germany and undercut the sale of German goods in France. It would take a long time for costs in the two countries to adjust to this imbalance.

The cross rates had to be in place on January 1, 1999 when the currencies acquired irrevocable rates (called conversion factors) against the Euro and therefore against each other.

Decision 3, on December 31, 1998, fixed the conversion factor of each old currency against the Euro when it came into existence on January 1, 1999. That is, from 1999 on, the DM should have a fixed conversion factor of DM1.95583 to a Euro (see Table 5A below).

Table 5A Irrevocable Rates of Each Stage 3[15] Currency against the Euro set December 31, 1998	
Stage 3 Member and Currency	**Rate against one Euro**
GERMANY (DEM)	1.95583
BELGIUM/LUXEMB. (BEF/LUF)	40.3399
SPAIN (ESP)	166.386
FRANCE (FRF)	6.55957
IRELAND (IEP)	0.787564
ITALY (ITL)	1,936.27
NETHERL. (NLG)	2.20371
AUSTRIA (ATS)	13.7603
PORTUGAL (PTE)	200.482
FINLAND (IM}	5.94573

On December 31, 1998 the ECB calculated the final value of the ECU, in Dollars, using the Dollar market rates of each currency against the ECU that day. Since 1 ECU equaled 1 Euro, this final ECU/$ rate became the official Euro/$ rate. Also from that day on, the cross-rates for all currencies of countries entering Stage 3 were their official bilateral cross rates, described above. The ECB also calculated the irrevocable rates of each stage 3 currency against the Euro (see Table 5A above).

---

[15] Council Regulation (EC) No. 2866/98 of 31 December 1998, Official Journal of the European Communities 31 December 1998, L359/1.

Figure 5.2
Euro/$ Exchange Rate: January 1, 1999 – June 13, 2005

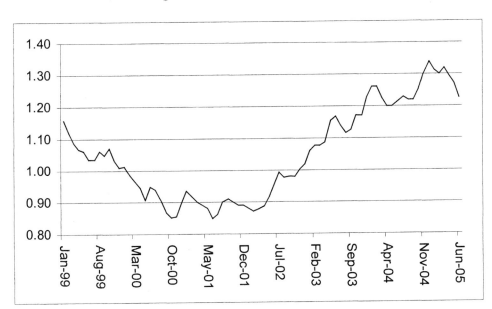

When markets opened on January 4, 1999, the market set the rate of one Euro to $1.17. By the "Big Mac test," the Euro was 13 percent overvalued.[16] In any case, the Euro fell against the Dollar to below $0.90 in May 2000. In part, this was due to weak economic performance by Germany and concern about the government's direct involvement in the economy. In part, market sentiment soured on the Euro. By September 2000, the Euro had fallen to less than $0.90 and the ECB raised interest rates by 0.25 percentage point with little impact on the Euro's value, and the Euro reached a low of $0.82 by October. In 2003, however, the Euro made a strong comeback. By May 1, 2004, the Euro had risen to over $1.17, its initial value, and by January 2005, the Euro was at $1.30. By the end of May 2005, the Euro had fallen to 1.25, and then fell further after France and the Netherlands rejected the amendments to the EU Constitution in June.

There has been much debate over whether the Euro can ever challenge the Dollar for currency supremacy. Benjamin Cohen[17] thinks not. He cites four factors: (1) inertia of monetary behavior; (2) cost of doing business in Euros is higher than the Dollar; (3) anti-growth bias built into

---

[16] A Big Mac hamburger cost an average of $2.98 in the 11 European countries in early January, compared to only $2.63 in the U.S., according to "Food for Thought," The Economist, January 9, 1999, p. 68.
[17] "Global Currency Rivalry: Can the Euro Ever Challenge the Dollar?," 41 J. of Common Market Studies (2003), p. 576.

EMU limiting the return on Euro-denominated assets; and (4) ambiguous government structure, particularly with regard to the ECB.

The Euro continued to gain market share, increasing 15 percent in 2002 in loan and deposit markets, and in 2003 constituted 36 percent of all claims, compared to 45 percent for the Dollar.[18] On the other hand, the growth of the Euro as a reserve currency has been slower. The IMF estimated that around 13 percent of the official foreign exchange reserves of its member countries was denominated in Euro at the end of 2001, as compared with 60 percent for the Dollar, with no change since 1999.[19] In 2002-2003, the Dollar slightly increased its market share to 63 percent while the Euro grew to 19 percent. The question in 2005 was whether the depreciation of the Dollar, due to the continuing U.S. current account deficit, $600 billion and 6 percent of GDP in 2004, and projected higher in 2005, would lead central banks to diversify their currency holdings more into Euro. This concern seemed somewhat alleviated as the Dollar increased in value from March to May 2005. It remains to be seen whether the constitutional crisis in the EU will lead to further weakening of the Euro and its attraction as a reserve currency.

Notes and Questions

1. What are the costs and benefits to the EU of the rise of the Euro against the Dollar?

C. EURO TRANSITION

Stage 3 was itself transitional, and EMI set a schedule for its further evolution into 2002.

1. FROM 1999 TO 2002: EMI'S SCHEDULE

The transition from national currencies to the Euro was gradual. In May 1995, the EMI published the *Green Paper on the Practical Arrangements for the Introduction of the Single Currency* (the Green Paper), and in November 1995, after discussing the Green Paper with many affected groups in the public and private sector, the EMI published *The Changeover to the Single Currency* (The Changeover). The Changeover identified several key periods:

At the starting date of Stage 3 (January 1, 1999), the Euro started to be used in scriptural, non-cash form but national banknotes remained the only banknotes with legal tender status. The Eurosystem started conducting its single monetary policy in the European currency. Financial markets

---

[18] BIS Quarterly Review (June 2003) pp. 14-15.

[19] Bank of England, *Practical Issues Arising from the Euro* (November 2002). (Bank of England)

largely changed over to the Euro on January 1, 1999 or soon after. However, most private individuals and most enterprises continue to operate in the national monetary units.

At the latest three years after the start of Stage 3 (January 1, 2002), the ESCB was to start issuing Euro banknotes and start exchanging the national banknotes and coins against the Euro. At the end of the period, all economic agents, including the public sector, had to complete the changeover to the Euro.

The introduction of Euro notes and cash was on schedule, and took place in the first two months of 2002. Table 5B below[20] sets out the dates until which commercial and national central banks will replace legacy notes and coins for Euros:

Table 5B			
Time limits for exchanging legacy coins			
State	**Commercial banks**	**National central banks**	
	Notes/coins	**Notes**	**Coins**
Austria	*	unlimited	unlimited
Belgium	12/31/2002	unlimited	end of 2004
Finland	*	10 years	10 years
France	6/30/2002	10 years	3 years
Germany	*	unlimited	unlimited
Greece	*	10 years	2 years
Italy	*	10 years	10 years
Ireland	*	unlimited	unlimited
Luxembourg	6/30/2002	unlimited	end of 2004
Netherlands	12/31/2002	1/1/2032	1/1/2007
Portugal	6/30/2002	20 years	end of 2002
Spain	6/30/2002	unlimited	unlimited
* At least until March 1, 2002, afterwards to be decided individually by banks.			

Six months after the first day of introduction of the European banknotes and coins (July 1, 2002), the changeover to the Euro was to have been completed for all operations and all agents. National banknotes and coins, which were to gradually disappear from circulation, would lose their legal tender status when the Euro ones become the only banknotes and coins to have the status of legal tender within the European currency area. The distribution process was completed in early 2002.

The official reason that it would take up to three and one-half years for cash transactions to change to the Euro was logistical. Old banknotes and coins had to be replaced by the new ones. The EMI estimated that at the end

---

[20] From G. Yeowart, "How to Get Ready for the Euro," *International Financial Law Review* (December 2001), p. 17.

of 1994 more than 12 billion banknotes and 70 billion coins, with a weight of more than 300,000 tons, were in circulation in the EU Member States. Retooling automated teller machines, teller assist systems, and coin-operated machines would take time. The public had to be educated.

Since EMU would not initially include all EU or EMS members, a new exchange rate mechanism (ERM) was set up on January 1, 1999 to replace the EMS. Membership was voluntary. Denmark and Greece chose to join, while Sweden and the U.K. stayed out. The ECB and central banks of non-Euro EU countries defined the operating procedures. The EU prescribed a mechanism based on central rates with the Euro and with fluctuations of 15 percent above or below that rate. So the Euro would form the core currency, around which currencies of the non-Stage 3 members of EMS could fluctuate. After Greece joined EMU in 2001, Denmark was the only participant until Estonia, Lithuania an Slovenia joined in 2004 and Latvia joined in 2005.

D.   THE EURO TODAY

The Euro today seems largely successful but there are still some significant issues regarding its functioning.

1.   LENDER OF LAST RESORT

It is not clear how the lender-of-last-resort function will be discharged under EMU. The powers of the ECB are dealt with in Article 18 of the Statute of the ECB, which provides:

> "18.1 In order to achieve the objectives of the ESCB and to carry out its tasks, the ECB and the national central banks may ... conduct credit operations with credit institutions and other market participants, with lending being based on adequate collateral.
>
> 18.2 The ECB shall establish general principles for ... credit operations carried out by itself or the national central banks, including for the announcement of conditions under which they stand ready to enter into such transactions."

A banking and financial crisis could demand more from the EMU institutions than they are able to deliver. They would have to provide liquidity quickly and lead organized workouts. It is not clear how this could be done given that only the ECB could provide such liquidity and it is prohibited from doing so.

Article 21 of the Statute of the ECB provides that "Overdrafts or any other type of credit facility with the ECB or with the national central banks in favour of ... central governments ... shall be prohibited." Moreover, as provided in Article 18.1, the ECB when it loans must obtain adequate collateral. An insolvent bank cannot give good collateral because it has no capital, so it cannot receive a loan from the ECB. Because bank supervision is separated from the ECB and dispersed across the eleven member countries, the ECB will lack systematic information about troubled banks. The ECB must rely on the bank's national central bank (NCB) to determine if collateral is good and, more broadly, if the bank is merely illiquid. The NCB can shift the cost of a bailout to the ECB (and so to all Stage 3 countries) by deciding that questionable assets are in fact good. Of course, the ECB is aware of this. If it is unable to evaluate assets offered as collateral, it may be unable to provide liquidity quickly at the crucial time. So the ECB cannot be counted on to act as lender of last resort in a way the Bundesbank would have done earlier.

Nonetheless, the debt instruments of different countries trade at very small yield spreads from each other despite significant differences in country credit ratings. For example, Italy and Finland had debt-to-GDP ratios of 106 and 45 percent respectively in 2004 with a meager yield spread on two year government bonds of 11 basis points.[21] How can this be? Is it clear that Articles 18 and 21 actually prevent the ECB from buying government debt? Would it be possible for countries to buy each other's debt? Do yield spreads misprice government debt because a high proportion of such debt is held within the countries by institutions controlled by the governments or because of the artificial trading rules of MTS, the trading platform on which government bonds trade (see discussion below)?

One explanation of the small differences in yield spreads (risk premia) on the euro-denominated debt of Eurosystem members is that the ECB treats the debt of Eurozone national governments as equivalent for the purposes of collateral in repurchase agreements. It is argued that while this should only suppress differences in default risk for the relatively short durations of the repurchase agreements—commonly two weeks and generally less than three months—these policies may be viewed as long-term and thus effect the convergence of longer term interest rates. A proposal in 2005 argues that the ECB should assign market prices to collateral.[22] However, there is a chicken and egg problem of obtaining a market price when current ECB policy treats all collateral alike.

Notes and Questions

1. How would NCBs and the ECB react to a major banking crisis in the EU?

---

[21] W. Munchau, "Eurozone Cannot Rely on Bonds Bail-out," *Financial Times*, July 12, 2004.
[22] W. Buiter and A. Sibert, "How Open-Market Operations by the ECB Weaken Financial Market Discipline, and What to Do About it?," Draft (May 28, 2005).

2.   IMPACT ON FINANCIAL MARKETS

Stage 3 immediately affected the cost and pricing of goods and services. Not all businesses could pass their conversion costs on to customers. Banks were not allowed to levy fees when converting accounts to EMU. Retailers could pass most of their costs on to customers. Both national governments and the EU picked up some of the costs of training and public education. The consulting firm BCG estimated that banks would lose $5 billion in revenues each year after EMU was in place because FX business associated with the national currencies would disappear. So it came as no surprise when the Bank of England found overall FX turnover in London did fall 5-10 percent in 1999 and turnover in other EU foreign exchange markets fell 15-30 percent.[23]

There is much speculation about whether EMU will lead to more integration among the financial than has previously been achieved by the Single Market initiatives, e.g. the Second Banking Directive and the Investment Services Directive. We touched on this subject in Chapter 4. While there is some conflicting evidence, the study by Askari and Chatterjee[24] shows that since the adoption of the Euro, interest rate correlations among Euro non-adopters has increased more than it has for adopters—adopters up from .35 to .41, compared to an increase from .66 to .67 for adopters. The story is similar for stock market index returns—non-adopters increased from .33 to .62, compared to adopters that increased from .35 to .69. While correlations are higher for adopters, this is hard to attribute to the advent of the Euro.

In government bond markets, all instruments redenominated to Euro immediately. The markets, however, continued to vary by country, since the risk of each issue varies according to the risk associated with each country's government. Thus a German government bond may be of lower risk than one issued by the Italian government (but see our later discussion of lender of last resort). It does appear, however, that EMU has resulted in less yield spread between government bonds in different countries. In addition, and perhaps related to yield convergence, all government bonds have become more liquid.[25] Although each government continues to have the authority to tax, it cannot create money to repay its debt. In this way, the government's debt in Euro is like debt in a foreign currency, which is usually rated lower than debt in the home currency. Some private issuers of Euro securities could even receive higher credit ratings than their governments.

---

[23] Bank of England, supra note 19, p. 33.

[24] H. Askari and J. Chatterjee, "The Euro and Financial Market Integration," 43 Journal of Common Market Studies 1 (2005).

[25] M Pagano and E. von Thadden, "The European Bond Markets under EMU," Working Paper (November 2004) (Pagano and Thadden); see also K. Bernoth, J. von Hagen and L. Schuknecht, "Sovereign Risk in the European Government Bond Market," European Central Bank Working Paper 369 (June 2004).

Government bond markets were shaken in 2004 by a huge Citigroup trade. Most government bonds trade over MTS, a quote-driven electronic trading platform. A key rule for trading the most liquid bonds is the commitment of dealers to quote continuously two-way firm prices with a maximum spread. On August 2, 2004, Citigroup sold almost €12 billion across more than 200 bonds within seconds, pushing down prices by about 15 cents, and then bought back € 4 billion and earned an estimated € 15 million at the expense of other market makers. Citigroup was able to earn this profit because of its informational advantage—it alone knew it was going to make such a sizeable trade and because of the obligation of dealers to keep bid-ask spreads within certain parameters.[26] Its trading strategy also employed exploiting price differences between the prices in the futures and cash markets. The episode calls into question the overall liquidity of a market in which one trade, albeit very large, can drive down prices to such an extent. MTS, was a trading system created by the Italian Treasury which had an interest in minimizing bid-ask spreads on Italian bonds even though they were more risky than bonds of many other EMU participants.[27] This event spurned many investigations of the propriety and legality of the Citigroup trade throughout the EU, which are still ongoing. In Germany, BaFin brought civil charges relating to manipulation of the Eurex government bond futures Frankfurt prosecutors did not bring criminal charges. In France, the Treasury lowered Citigroup's ranking in its league table of primary-debt dealers, which has affected its participation in the French bond market.

Corporate bond markets in 1999, as expected, became broader and deeper as institutional investors sought greater diversity and many companies began to issue in Euro. Euro area currencies accounted for $273 billion in net private issues in 1998, but more than doubled to $657 billion in 1999, after the introduction of the Euro.[28] Much of the growth has been fuelled by increased holding of Euro denominated bonds by Euroland rather than foreign investors.[29]

Pricing mechanisms were needed for instruments in the new currency. For medium and long-term instruments, normally a security would be priced off a reference rate provided by an instrument that was very low risk and traded in a liquid market. In the U.S., Treasury securities serve as benchmarks. The benchmark for Euro issues is still being established.

In the interbank market for Euro deposits, a mechanism was needed to set a short-term rate for banks in all member countries. Bank trade associations designed an interbank offer rate for the Euro, to be called EURIBOR. The European Banking Federation announced plans to calculate

---

[26] Pagano and Thadden, supra note 25, pp. 15-16.
[27] J. Gapper, "The Market's True Manipulators," *Financial Times*, February 10, 2005.
[28] Pagano and Thadden, supra note 25, p. 8.
[29] C. Detken and P. Hartmann, "The Euro and International Capital Markets," 3 International Finance (2000) 54.

this rate from quotes given daily by a large panel of banks in each Euro member country. The Federation published "a new Euro area-wide overnight effective rate" using "actual rates at which trades take place in the money market, weighted by volume. ..."[30]

At a technical level major changes took place in the conventions in these markets. Each national financial market had many conventions to resolve practical issues for trading and settling transactions in foreign exchange, securities, and money. The topics included the number of days in a year (360 or 365), the number of days to settle a trade, the expression of prices in decimals or fractions, and coupon frequency (annual or semi-annual). New standards were needed because, when the Euro replaced each national currency, it became impossible to know from a security denominated in Euro which nation's conventions applied. Many international security associations cooperated to design new conventions.

3.   FISCAL AND MONETARY POLICY AND THE STABILITY PACT

The architects of EMU recognized that there was a danger in constructing a monetary union, with a single monetary policy conducted by the ECB, along side separate fiscal policies conducted by individual Member States. Part of the concern was that irresponsible fiscal policies in particular Member States might create inflationary pressures that would lead the ECB to raise interest rates. Responsible fiscal states would then be forced to bear the higher interest rate costs created by the profligate states. This concern led the architects to impose deficit limitations on countries entering into EMU, and to impose ongoing deficit constraints under the Stability and Growth Pact of 1996 (the Pact).[31] A recent study finds that a large inflation differential between currency union members is consistently associated with a high likelihood of currency union dissolution.[32]

At the Dublin summit in December 1996, EU leaders agreed to a "Stability Pact." Any EMU country that ran a fiscal deficit greater than 3 percent of GDP for longer than 10 months would have to make a non-interest bearing deposit with the EC and, if it did not remedy the problem within two years, would have to pay a fine (if voted by two-thirds of the EMU members of the European Council) of 0.2 percent of GDP, plus 0.1 percent of GDP for each year the deficit exceeded 3 percent, up to a total of 0.5 percent in fines. Less severe sanctions would require the country to publish more information

---

[30] See Bank of England, supra note 19, p. 100.

[31] It was widely reported that countries had employed a number of questionable accounting conventions to meet the fiscal requirements for entry, and it came to light in 2004 that Greece had provided inaccurate data, understating its budget deficit by 2.1 percentage points per year since 1997 before joining the euro zone in 2001. P. Meller, "Europe to Sue Over Data Greece Gave on Economy," *Financial Times*, December 2, 2004.

[32] Volker Nitsch, "Have a Break, Have a ... National Currency: When Do Monetary Unions Fall Apart?," CESifo Working Paper 113 (January 2004).

before issuing government securities or reduce loans to the country by the European Investment Bank. A country can exceed the 3 percent limit if the excess is exceptional (unusual events outside of control of the Member State or a severe economic downturn), temporary (if Commission budget forecasts indicate the deficit will fall below 3 percent once the "exceptional" situation passes), or limited in size (undefined). A country with a decline in GDP of over 2 percent within the past four quarters could be exempted from penalties by the Council of Ministers.[33] The Pact also provides that overall national debt should not be greater than 60 percent of GDP, but the deficit limitation has attracted the most discussion.

Economists criticized this pact as so inflexible that it could create serious damage in a major recession. Rarely during the last 30 years had a country reported a 2 percent decline in GDP over four quarters, and so rarely could a country expect to receive an exemption. Countries would be too limited when using deficit financing as a tool of fiscal policy to restore economic growth. During the 1993 recession, member government deficits had averaged 6 percent and were high in countries like France (5.8 percent), Belgium (6.6 percent), and the U.K. (7.7 percent). If countries anticipated the ceiling, they would hold the deficit much lower than 3 percent to give themselves flexibility in a recession. This could keep their fiscal policy too tight and impede economic growth. On the other hand, many countries had barely met the 3 percent limit to qualify for EMU membership. They would probably hover near the 3 percent limit for some time, leaving them no room for further deficit if the economy went into recession. If the 3 percent limit prevented effective macroeconomic responses, the political reaction, critics feared, would undermine EMU. These same concerns provoked Romano Prodi, the President of the European Commission, to call the Stability Pact "stupid" in late 2002.

The problem with proposed solutions was that they could introduce too much flexibility. This had been a concern for some time. In 1995, former President of France, Valery Giscard d'Estaing, said the rules on budget deficits should be flexible enough to adjust for recessionary fiscal policy. Officials in the EU, Germany, and France immediately denounced his suggestion.

During 1999, the ECB warned that several member countries were adopting policies that would push their deficits to the 3 percent ceiling. In 2002, Germany exceeded the 3 percent limit and the EU Commission forecasts a 3.4 percent deficit in 2003. Germany succeeded in avoiding a warning in 2002 from the Council in exchange for new commitments to bring its budget into line. France appeared unwilling in 2003 to correct the

---

[33] See Resolution of the European Council, June 17, 1997; Council Regulation on Speeding Up and Clarifying the Implementation of the Excessive Deficit Procedure," 1467/97 (July 7, 1997); Council Regulation on the Strengthening of the Surveillance and Coordination of Economic Polices, 1466/97 (July 7, 1977).

problem. Indeed, the French cabinet approved a budget for 2004 with a deficit equivalent to 3.6 percent of GDP, well above the 3 percent ceiling. The EU stated it was considering an enforcement action but then granted France another year to rein in its deficit.[34] During the summer of 2003, the fiscal situation worsened in France and Germany; the Commission projected a general government deficit for 2003 of 4.0 percent of GDP for France and 4.2 percent of GDP for Germany. In November 2003, the EU Council Ministers, at the urging of France and Germany, voted to suspend the enforcement of the Pact over the objection of the Commission. The Commission had proposed to give the two countries a formal notice under Articles 104(8) and (9) of the EC Treaty that the two countries had not taken effective measures in response to earlier Council recommendations. This formal notice required that the States correct the problem or face formal sanctions. The vote of the Council, which passed by a narrow majority, 7 states for and 4 against, did not include the non-Euroland countries, e.g. the U.K., which raised an arguable procedural issue. There was also the more general question as to the legality of the entire suspension procedure. The EU Commission and the ECB voiced their deep concern. The Dutch Finance Minister said that all 12 members of the Euro would now pay the price of French and German fiscal incontinence. In July 2004, the European Court of Justice ruled that the finance ministers had illegally suspended the Pact, but also stated that it was up to Ecofin as to whether to impose sanctions—which it was unlikely to do given the positions of France and Germany.

The deficit issue also affects the speed at which the 10 new member states can join the EMU, since new entrants must meet convergence criteria, including a 3 percent deficit limit. It appears several of them do not. The President of the ECB, Jean-Claude Trichet, recently stated that it was "absolutely obvious" that a lack of fiscal discipline among the current 12 members of the Euro area set a bad example for the 10 countries who joined the EU in May.

As Figure 5.3 below shows, in 2003,[35] 4 of the 12 EMU member states went beyond the deficit threshold and seven surpassed the debt limit. In 2004, six members were on course to exceed the 3 percent deficit bound—for France and Germany it is the third straight year.

---

[34] R. Graham, J. Johnson, and G. Parker, "Breach of EU Pact Defended by Chirac," *Financial Times*, September 26, 2003; G. Parker and J. Johnson, "France Given More Time to Pull Back Budget Deficit," *Financial Times*, October 21, 2003.
[35] D. Clement, "Ties That Bind," The Region (Federal Reserve Bank of Minneapolis, December 2004).

Figure 5.3
The Stability and Growth Pact[36]

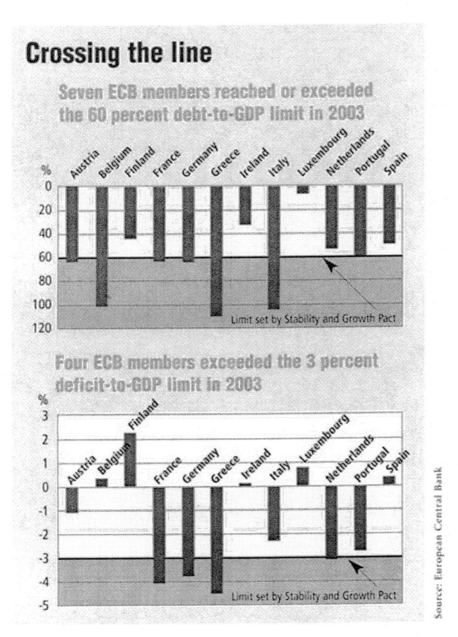

[36] The Region, Federal Reserve Bank of Minneapolis (December 2004).

Academic proposals to reduce the problems posed by the Stability Pact included structural change and a new instrument. One idea was to create one European agency that would issue debt for the governments of all 11 member countries. The governments would no longer do so.[37] The other idea was for the EU to set an overall ceiling for the deficit of all EMU members, issue permits to each member to incur a share of that deficit, and then allow members to trade the permits. Countries that needed to incur a larger deficit than permitted would buy some portion of the permit given to another member country.[38] There were also more moderate calls for more "flexibility" in applying the existing rules. For example, some called for shaping the rules to the particular circumstances of a case in which experts rather than policy-makers would determine the rules for a particular country. Increased flexibility was to be accompanied by more certain enforcement in the truly bad cases. Better enforcement would require more transparency about national budgetary processes.[39]

In September 2004, the Commission proposed a rather vague relaxation of the deficit limitations. The basic idea seemed to be that a breach of the 3 percent limit would not trigger automatic sanctions, but rather the need for a country plan to remedy the deficit. The pace of adjustment could differ across countries, and there would be an increased focus on debt levels rather than deficits. Further, the definition of "exceptional" circumstances could be broadened. There was considerable disagreement over the right approach among policy makers. Within Germany, the Bundesbank opposed any relaxation of the Pact, while Chancellor Schroeder thought more flexibility was needed than permitted by the Commission proposal.[40]

In March 2005, the European Union Finance Ministers announced a plan to substantially reform the Pact.[41] The main anchors of the Pact, the deficit limit of 3 percent of GDP and the maximum debt-to-GDP ratio of 60 percent were to remain. In addition, a medium-term budgetary objective of "close to balance or in surplus," and the commitment to cut deficit and debt in good times was added.[42] The Commission would issue policy advice and then warnings to countries that failed to consolidate in upswings. However, many exceptions to the rules were granted. A country could claim it was a victim of a severe economic downturn, to be newly defined as a "negative growth rate" or "an accumulated loss of output during a protracted period of very low

---

[37] V. Boland and E. Tucker, "De Silguy Proposal May Confound Skeptics," *Financial Times*, August 4, 1999.

[38] See A. Casella, "Tradable Deficit Permits: Efficient Implementation of the Stability Pact in the European Monetary Union," NBER Working Paper 7278 (August 1999).

[39] R. Beetsma and X. Debrun, "Implementing The Stability and Growth Pact: Enforcement and Procedural Flexibility," European Central Bank Working Paper 433 (January 2005).

[40] G. Schroeder, "A Framework for a Stable Europe," *Financial Times*, January 17, 2005.

[41] Council of the European Union, Presidency Conclusions, 7619/05, Annex II, March 23, 2005.

[42] This was suggested by C. Marinheiro, "Has the Stability and Growth Pact Stabilised," CESifo Working Paper 1411 (February 2005).

growth relative to potential growth," rather than negative 2 percent growth, as presently. A country could also claim—if the breach of the rules is small and temporary—that other factors justified a breach, such as spending on development aid or European policy goals such as research, European unification, i.e. German reunification, or pension reform. In addition, the Council specified that as a rule the deadline for correcting an excessive deficit (as newly determined) would be the second year after its occurrence but that a longer period could be granted. Sanctions presumably remain as a last resort but are not mentioned in the Council plan. It is now up to the Commission to draft amendments to existing regulations to reflect the plan.

At this point, there appears no real restraint on individual country deficits.[43] Fiscal integration is not a medium term possibility. This then raises the question as to whether a monetary union can function without any real fiscal constraints on members.

Notes and Questions

1.   What do you think of the March 2005 reform of the Stability Pact?

4.   CONTINUITY OF CONTRACT

Within the EU

When the Euro was substituted for national currencies, the issue arose as to whether a development of such magnitude might allow existing contracts denominated in national currencies to be voided on the grounds of frustration or force majeure. Under U.K. law, the doctrine of frustration applies where performance of the contract has become physically or legally impossible (i.e. the subject-matter of the contract no longer exists, or performance has become illegal), or where performance will no longer achieve the commercial object of the contract and will instead result in a "radically different" outcome. Generally, if the event which allegedly frustrates a contract is foreseeable, a court will not find a contract frustrated. However, where an event was foreseeable, but both parties assumed it would not transpire, and had no intent that their contract continue if it did, a court might still apply the doctrine.[44]

Article 3 of the 235 Regulation[45] provides for the continuity of contracts under EMU:

"The introduction of the Euro shall not have the effect of altering any term of a legal instrument or of discharging or excusing performance under any legal instrument, nor give a party the right unilaterally to

---

[43] M. Feldstein, "The Euro and the Stability Pact," NBER Working Paper 11248 (March 30, 2005).

[44] Financial Law Panel, "Economic and Monetary Union: Continuity of Contracts in English Law" (1998).

[45] Council Regulation (EC) No. 1103/97, O.J. No. L 162, 19/06/1997.

alter or terminate such an instrument. This provision is subject to anything which parties may have agreed."

Trade associations designed solutions to problems that their members could encounter. Over 1,100 securities firms signed the International Securities and Derivatives Association (ISDA) *EMU Protocol* of May 6, 1998. It provided that "an event associated with economic and monetary union ... will not have the effect of altering any term of, or discharging or excusing performance" or "give a party the right unilaterally to alter or terminate" an agreement or transaction. Parties could override this provision in writing by expressly referring to the protocol or EMU. A major problem was the disappearance of price sources on January 1, 1999. For example, a Franc floating rate loan outstanding in 1998 would use PIBOR (Paris Interbank Offering Rate) as the reference rate and rely on a Reuters screen for PIBOR. But PIBOR would disappear with Stage 3. The *Protocol* specified what would happen if such a price source disappeared. If no successor rate appeared, several other possible sources were given, including the use of EURIBOR.

In Non-EU Jurisdictions

One of the concerns most troubling to EU bankers was whether contracts governed by the law of non-EU states would recognize that the changeover was not an event permitting termination. When the law of a non-EU state (such as New York) governs a contract, said one legal commentator, one must establish: (1) whether the single currency will be recognized by the law of the non-member state as replacing the existing national currency of the relevant member state; (2) whether the contract will be treated under that law as non-revocable following the introduction of the single currency; and (3) whether there are any grounds on which it might be claimed under that law that a money obligation ought to be revalued or devalued to allow for any depreciation or appreciation in the purchasing power of the money in which the debt was originally denominated.[46]

Bankers urged the EU Commission to coordinate with other major governments and to establish a commission to review such contracts. On July 29, 1997, New York enacted a law that closely parallels the EU regulations on frustration, so as to protect contracts governed by New York law against frustration claims. New York General Obligations Law, §5-1602 (1)(a) provides:

> "If a subject or medium of payment of a contract, security or instruments is a currency that has been substituted or replaced by the Euro, the Euro will be a commercially reasonable substitute and substantial equivalent that may be either: (i) used in determining the value of such currency; or (ii) tendered, in each case of the conversion

---

[46] See G. Yeowart, "Legal Repercussions of a Single European Currency," International Financial Law Review (December 1995).

rate specified in, and otherwise calculated in accordance with, the regulations adopted by the council of the European Union."

Section 5-1602(2) of the New York law further provides:

"None of: (a) the introduction of the Euro; (b) the tendering of Euros in connection with any obligation in compliance with paragraph (a) or (b) [dealing with the ECU] of subdivision one of this section; (c) the determining of the value of any obligation in compliance with paragraph (a) or (b) of subdivision one of this section; or (d) the calculating or determining of the subject of the medium of payment of a contract, security or instrument with reference to interest rate or other basis that has been substituted or replaced due to the introduction of the Euro and that is a commercially reasonable substitute and substantial equivalent, shall either have the effect of discharging or excusing performance under any contract, security or instrument, or give a party the right to unilaterally alter or terminate any contract, security or instrument."

Notes and Questions

1. Suppose there is a floating rate loan in French Francs that is redenominated in Euros. The loan calls for interest at PIBOR (Paris Interbank Offering Rate) which, after redenomination, is interpreted by the lender as referring to PIBOR for Euro. Will this new interest rate stand up under New York law? Is it clear that the rate would always be a "commercially reasonable substitute and substantial equivalent?"

2. How would this issue be dealt with under Article 3 of the 235 Regulation?[47]

5. U.K. ENTRY INTO EMU

Currently, the United Kingdom is not an EMU member, although debate over its entry has been intense. Reasons for opposition are varied. The U.K. economy has prospered outside EMU, and there is a fear of losing economic and political independence. Gordon Brown, the Chancellor of the Exchequer proposed five economic issues in 1997 that had to be resolved before entry: (1) whether there can be sustainable convergence between the U.K. and the other EMU economies; (2) whether there will be sufficient flexibility to cope with economic problems; (3) the effects on foreign investment; (4) the impact on London's role in the financial services markets; and (5) whether entry would promote higher economic growth, stability and a

---

[47] See M. Gruson, "The Introduction of the Euro and Its Implications for Obligations Denominated in Currencies Replaced by the Euro," 21 Fordham International Law Journal 65, 100-107 (1997).

lasting increase in employment.[48] Many studies have been done on these issues with no conclusive result. The U.K.'s position seems to be that it is committed in principle to adopting the Euro but is as yet unable to do so in practice because of the economic tests.[49]

Some have argued that U.K. entry into EMU would undercut the ability of London to remain a relatively unregulated financial center as compared to continental Europe, but this misses the point that London is already subject to EU financial regulation as a member state in the European Union and that the U.K. has adopted a decidedly more pro-regulatory stance under the Labor government of Prime Minister Blair and as a result of the creation of the Financial Services Agency.

E.   WILL THE EURO SURVIVE?[50]

A key question is whether a member that wants to withdraw from the monetary union could do so without serious damage to itself or the other members. This depends on the scenario for withdrawal. The question is important because the Treaty does not contemplate failure.

The Treaty has left in place many institutions, such as national central banks and national payments systems whose continued existence might facilitate breakup. But there would be two fundamental problems that would greatly impede it.

The breakup of the Euro would not merely return countries and markets to the status quo ante prior to the adoption of the Euro. Two key new problems would have to be faced: the difficulty re-establishing a national currency and legal uncertainty attending the re-denomination of existing contracts in a new currency.

1.   RE-ESTABLISHING NATIONAL CURRENCIES

If the Euro falls apart, countries will want to replace the Euro with their own national currencies. The difficulties of the replacement process will depend on whether the Euro survives for some countries or whether it dissolves entirely.

Assume that Italy leaves EMU and desires to re-establish the Lira while the other EMU countries continue to use the Euro. Italy could well experience substantial difficulties in re-establishing the Lira as the national currency.

---

[48] See Statement on Economic and Monetary Union by the Chancellor of the Exchequer, October 27, 1997.

[49] I. Ivanov, "The EMU and the Euro: Why the City of London is Saying 'No,'" paper written for International Trade, Investment and Finance, University of Chicago (August 7, 2004).

[50] This section relies heavily on H. Scott, "When the Euro Falls Apart," (1998) 1 International Finance, p. 207.

Italy could try to force exchanges of existing Euro cash or bank accounts in Italy for Italian Lira, but such forced exchanges would seem extremely problematic. What would be the rationale for forcing Italians to give up Euros for new Lira, as compared to dollars for new Lira? Both Dollars and Euro would remain as major international currencies. How would such forced exchanges be accomplished?

As for cash, Italy could seal its borders for some short period and order that all Euros in Italy be surrendered for new Lira (a typical measure where monetary unions suffer total breakup), or in the short term require all Euros held by Italian citizens (or even foreigners in Italy) to be stamped with a new Lira symbol. But people would hold Euro cash back and take it out of Italy as soon as the borders were reopened. Further, the moment the borders were reopened the preferred Euro currency would come flowing back into Italy.

As for bank accounts, Italy could order all Euro bank accounts of Italian citizens to be re-denominated into the new Lira, but what would this accomplish? It would not ensure that such accounts remained in new Lira. Depositors would take their losses and get into some other currency outside Italy as soon as possible. This result could only be forestalled by imposition of foreign-exchange controls for some substantial period of time, isolating Italy financially and economically from the rest of Europe.

Once the Euro becomes the currency of Italy, it may prove very difficult for Italy to re-establish the Lira and thereby get control of its own monetary policy. Italy may become "Euroized" in the same way that countries in Latin America have become dollarized. Transactors will want to hold Euros because they are likely to be more valuable than Lira, and dual pricing of Euros and the new Lira will allow transactors to contract and pay in Euros.

Complete breakup makes it easier for the withdrawing countries, even those whose new currencies would be perceived as "weak," to re-establish national currencies. However attractive the common currency might be compared to the new national currencies, it will disappear. This is not to say that such a process will be easy. If national currencies are replaced over a period of time, some of the problems of partial breakup could well exist for those countries going first. The experience with the Austro-Hungarian breakup demonstrates that countries must generally close their borders for some period of time to stamp old currencies or swap old currencies for new ones and that such border closings will not be totally effective.

In a complete breakup, each country will set a conversion rate for Euros into new national currencies. If, based on the new conversion rates, the Euro will have more real value (in terms of purchasing power) in one country rather than another, transactors will try to exchange the Euro in those countries where it will have more value. This will lead to hold backs from exchange in countries where new currencies will be relatively less valuable and movement of currencies to countries with better value. For example, if an Italian thought he could get more real value by exchanging Euros in Germany, he would hold back from exchanging Euros in Italy. If the last country to make a conversion, say Germany, has a strong new currency, it may find that a large portion of outstanding Euros will be held back from exchanges in other countries for later exchange in Germany. This could result in inflationary pressures as the last converting country is forced to expand the currency money supply. These problems, however, are temporary, and can be greatly minimized by a degree of coordinated action.

After the rejection of the constitutional referendum by France and the Netherlands in June 2005, the Italian welfare minister, Roberto Maroni, reportedly urged a temporary reintroduction of the lira.[51] While talk of temporary currency changes is completely foolish, the statement shows that the possibility of the Euro falling apart and the difficulty of reestablishing legacy currencies is not an entirely theoretical matter.

2. CONTINUITY OF CONTRACT

The second significant breakup problem concerns the enforceability of re-denominated contracts between debtors of withdrawing countries and their creditors, particularly foreign creditors. We have already seen that EU legislation provides for continuity of contract for adoption of the Euro; but no such legislation assures continuity upon breakup.

If Italy, or any other EMU member, were to withdraw from EMU and redenominate Euro-denominated contracts, such as government bonds, loans or commercial contracts, with the new Lira or other new national currency, the courts of the re-denominating country would almost certainly enforce that re-denomination—they would be bound to do so by the laws providing for the re-denomination. The issue would be much more complicated if the re-denomination were put at issue in a foreign court.

Foreign courts would normally determine whether the re-denomination was effective by reference to *lex monetae*, the law of the currency issuer. Thus, when Germany replaced the mark with the Reichsmark in the 1920s, courts of other countries enforced re-denominated contracts because they resolved the matter under German law, the *lex monetae*. However, this default principle is not easily applied to national currency re-denomination of Euro contracts. What is the *lex monetae*? If Italy re-denominated Euro contracts, Italy is the issuer of the replacement currency, the new Lira, but may not be regarded as the issuer of the replaced currency, the Euro. Where a monetary union is involved, all of the participating countries are joint issuers of a currency under a common legal arrangement and EU law could be regarded as the *lex monetae*. Note that if

---

[51] G. Parker, "Air of Crisis Hangs Over Meeting of Ministers," *Financial Times*, June 7, 2005.

reference was made to EU law as lex monetae, the Italian re-denomination would be ineffective. Whatever Italy did, EU law would continue to provide that all contracts issued in Italy, once denominated in Euros, would continue to be denominated in Euros.

It can be argued that in such a case, courts should apply the proper law of the contract, that is apply the law specified in the contract. For many obligations, for example Italian government bonds, this would be Italian law. Under Italian law, government bonds issued in Italy are "titoli del debito publico"—public debt securities which are assumed to be governed by Italian law. On the other hand, Italian government bonds issued outside of Italy can provide for Italian or foreign law.[52] In practice, however, all present issues of Italian debt are subject to Italian law. This means that under the proper law of the contract approach, courts would uphold the re-denomination of Italian bonds. However, with respect to other obligations, such as private debt, foreign law might apply if it were specified in the contract. If no explicit choice of law is made in the contract, the foreign court would apply its own conflict of law rules—the rules the foreign court uses to decide what law applies to a contract where no explicit choice has been made in the contract itself. This could lead the court to the law of Italy or a foreign law.

Would foreign law, if applicable, such as the law of the United States or Germany, enforce the re-denomination or provide instead that the contracts must be honored in Euros or are breached if not honored in Euros? This is far from clear given the lack of precedents. There are no court cases involving the withdrawal of a country from a surviving monetary union. If foreign law would apply to a substantial number of outstanding contracts, there could be severe economic disruption attending a partial withdrawal as parties seek to resolve the legal uncertainties.

If EMU broke up entirely, the legal problems would also be severe. Although the *lex monetae* could no longer be that of the EU, given the end of the Euro, it would be unclear whether the *lex monetae* was the law of one or the other of the exiting states. All of the EMU countries would be re-denominating contracts, and conflicts could easily arise among the terms of their re-denomination laws. For example, suppose Germany provided that any debt obligations of a German creditor, e.g. loans by German banks, were to be re-denominated in new Deutschmarks, while Italy provided that all loans of Italian debtors, including loans from German banks, were to be re-denominated in new Lira. Similar problems were experienced when Germany was divided into two states in 1948. Again, the solution could only be to decide the proper law of the contract, with the attendant uncertainties of that determination.

---

[52] This is provided for in Article 9 on "Issuance of Government Bonds in Foreign Currency" of Decree Law No. 149 of 20 May 1993.

Notes and Questions

1. Why do neither the Maastricht Treaty nor the implementing laws and regulations set up a process to permit an orderly dismantling of the union?

2. Will the Euro fall apart?

3. You are advising a potential investor in new bonds to be issued by a company in one of the Euroland countries. Assume the investor believes there is a significant chance that the Euro would fall apart. What provisions, if any, would you recommend be included in the bond?

4. If the Euro does fall apart, can the EU go back to the situation that preceded it, including the single market and ERM, or will the break up of EMU mean the break up of the EU?

CONCLUSIONS

The conversion to the Euro is a fait accompli. It is now a strong currency, having risen significantly above the value of the Dollar from its former lows. Two main issues remain. First, there is the question of additional accessions, most critically that of the U.K. Without the inclusion of the U.K., the center of the EU financial market is offshore (at least with respect to the Euro currency area). There is also the issue of the long-term survival of the Euro. If the Stability Pact has effectively been abolished, and there is no centralization of fiscal policy, all countries will pay for the incontinence of some. It is ironic that the main backer of the Pact, Germany, now opposes its enforcement. Dealing with fiscal constraint is the challenge that remains. A further blow to the Euro may have been struck by the rejection of the constitutional referendum by France and the Netherlands in June 2005—but that remains to be seen.

It appears that the Euro has strengthened the integration of the EU financial markets. Its success could be a long-term key factor in the EU's competitiveness, both economically and politically, with the U.S. Its demise would be a serious if not fatal blow to the entire EU enterprise.

CHAPTER SIX

JAPANESE FINANCIAL MARKETS

Japan still has the world's second largest economy. However, for over a decade, its economic growth has been low, with GDP around 2 percent, its stock market has plunged, the Nikkei fell from ¥40,000 in 1989 to as lows as ¥8,000 in 2003 (¥11,553 as of February 11, 2005), land values fell from a value of ¥2,000 trillion in 1991 to ¥1,000 trillion in 2004. The financial system has been in crisis, with a cost to taxpayers of around 20 percent of Japan's GDP.[1] The situation began to improve in 2004. Japan's long financial crisis has many facets. This Chapter focuses on the institutional elements, including regulation, while acknowledging that such factors as fiscal and economic policy have also been important. It seems clear, however, that macroeconomic policy has been significantly impeded by the weakness of the financial system.

This Chapter is divided into two parts. Part A deals with banking and Part B with capital markets. With respect to banking, the Chapter begins with a description of the structure of the Japanese banking system, and how foreign banks are regulated. It then turns to an examination of the non-performing loan problem. The other major topics are capital adequacy, corporate restructuring, deposit insurance, restructuring of bankrupt debtors and Japanese banks, the role of the postal savings system, and the effectiveness of the Financial Services Agency, which supervises financial firms and is trying to resolve the bad debt problem.

Japanese capital markets are still underdeveloped despite major reforms in the regulation of those markets. One intriguing question is why.

---

[1] T. Hoshi and A. Kashyap, "Japan's Financial Crisis and Economic Stagnation," 18 J. of Economic Perspectives 3 (2004) (Hoshi and Kashyap)

A.   BANKING MARKETS

1.   STRUCTURE OF JAPANESE BANKING TODAY

Big Bang, instituted in 1996, rejected the system in place since the Second World War under which Japan had mobilized savings to fuel the country's remarkable economic recovery and then miracle growth. Financial firms, in a cartel-like system, guided by the Ministry of Finance (MOF) and the Bank of Japan (BOJ), its central bank, had channeled funds at low rates to high value-added manufacturers, whose exports contributed to the country's ever stronger trade balance.

a.   DOMESTIC FINANCIAL INSTITUTIONS

Japan's City banks are based in major cities, ranked among the world's largest by assets. Through a series of government-mandated mergers, their numbers have fallen from 12 to 4—the Mizuho group, Sumitomo Mitsui, Bank of Tokyo Mitsubishi, and UFJ—plus a fifth, Resona, that was bankrupt in mid-2003. Once the largest in the world, the first 4 ranked in the bottom half of the world's top 20 banks.[2] A complete picture of the Japanese financial system is set forth in Table 6A below:

---

[2] "Analysis of the World's Capital and Money Markets," Euromoney (June 2003).

Table 6A
An Overview of the Japanese Financial Systems[3]

	Number of			Total assets		Deposits outstanding	Loans and discounts outstanding
	Institutions	Branches[f]	Employees[f]	Trillion ¥ (%-total)	% of GDP	Trillion ¥ (%-total)	Trillion ¥ (%-total)[g]
Banks							
City banks (consolidated)[a]	7	2,853	104,847	410 (20.9)	81.9	260 (23.5)	238 (27.6)
Others[b]	227	12,221	238,760	436 (22.3)	87.2	289 (26.2)	259 (30.1)
Cooperative financial institutions[c]	2,444	11,197	173,709	394 (20.1)	78.8	317 (28.7)	154 (17.9)
Non-depository financial institutions							
Life insurance	43	15,807	380,864	184 (9.4)	36.7	— (—)	47 (5.5)
Other insurance	59	4,869	87,501	33 (1.7)	6.6	— (—)	4 (0.5)
Remaining[d]	293	2,256	94,898	95 (4.8)	19.0	— (—)	— (—)
Public financial institutions							
Postal savings	1	24,773	62,422	242 (12.3)	48.3	239 (21.6)	0.7 (0.1)
Government financial institutions[e]	8	311	11,250	166 (8.5)	33.2	— (—)	159 (18.5)
Total financial system (excluding the Bank of Japan)	3,082	74,287	1,154,251	1,960 (100)	391.7	1,105 (100)	861.7 (100)

Source: International Monetary Fund (2003b).
[a] The city bank figures include their 141 foreign branches that have 21.4 percent of their assets, 12.3 percent of their deposits and 11.4 percent of their loans.
[b] Includes three long-term credit banks, 39 trust banks, 64 regional banks, 53 regional II banks, 73 foreign banks and 5 other bridge and Internet banks.
[c] Includes 349 Shinkin banks and the Shinkin Central Bank, 204 credit cooperatives and the National Federation of Credit cooperatives, 21 labor credit associations and the Rokinren bank, 1227 agricultural cooperatives and credit federations, 638 fishery cooperatives and credit federations, the Shoko Chukin Bank and the Norinchukin Bank.
[d] Includes 290 Securities companies and three money market dealers.
[e] Includes the development bank of Japan, Japan Bank for International Cooperation, and six financial corporations.
[f] The data on branches and employment are not available for the agricultural and credit cooperative, and the fishery and credit cooperatives.
[g] Column total does not sum to 100 because of rounding.

Japanese banks have been in deep trouble. In 2002, the average income of the top two fell 500 percent and return on equity dropped by 15 percent. In comparison, all but one of the other top 20 international banks

---

[3] Hoshi and Kashyap, supra note 1.

reported positive return on equity, for example, 13 percent for the top 5 U.S. banks. In international markets, Japanese financial institutions have become increasingly marginal, as their foreign business has contracted with the slowing of growth at home.

In addition to the City banks, there are 27 trust banks, which are mainly engaged in asset management, while also providing commercial banking services. Two long-term credit banks, Aozora and Shinsei, are successors to their failed predecessors. These banks were remnants of the post-Second World War era of financial segmentation, when long-term credit banks dominated long-term lending because of their legislated monopoly on obtaining long-term funds. Today, these banks have the same basic power as the City banks. 105 regional banks serve smaller local and regional companies, and have a relatively much larger retail deposit base than the City banks. Five hybrids, like eBANK Corporation, the Japan Net Bank Ltd., and Sony Bank Inc., engage in electronic banking.

Japanese banks are permitted to engage in a full range of securities and insurance activities through subsidiaries. Japanese holding companies have been permitted, but only a few banking organizations have established them. The activities that bank and non-bank bank holding companies can engage in are the same.[4]

Foreign banks are not a big factor in Japan in terms of lending. In December 2004, they had about 4 trillion yen in loans outstanding as compared to Japanese banks with 500 trillion, or less than 1 percent. with branches in Japan are, of course, primarily supervised by their home countries. While foreign banks were never much of a factor, they shrunk their lending by about 32 percent in 2004. Foreign banks with branches in Japan are, of course, primarily supervised by their home country. Article 49 of the Banking Law, does, however, impose an obligation on foreign banks to notify their supervisor, the Financial Supervisory Agency (FSA), whenever there is a change in circumstances at the head office of an important branch, e.g. change in amount of capital or merger. This is further detailed by Cabinet Office Ordinance.

b.   CROSS-BORDER OPERATIONS

The Japanese Banking Law defines a "foreign bank" as an entity conducting banking business under the legislation of a foreign country.

As of 2003, there were 73 foreign banks in Japan. Korea and the U.S. each had 9 banks. Most of the others were from Asia, and a few major countries in Europe. For decades, foreign bank market share has been quite small.

---

[4] See S. Kawai and K. Muraoka, "Banking Regulation in Japan and the Treatment of Foreign Banks," in *Regulation of Foreign Banks* (M. Gruson and R. Reisner eds., Supp. 2003).

Foreign banks operate in Japan through subsidiaries, branches, and representative offices.

Subsidiaries

The application criteria and capital and other requirements for the Japanese banking subsidiary of a foreign bank are essentially the same as those required for establishment of a domestic bank. However, where the level of shareholding in a Japanese banking subsidiary by foreign bank shareholders exceeds a certain threshold percentage as specified by Cabinet Office Ordinance, the FSA will examine whether the foreign country in which the principal office of the foreign bank parent is located extends reciprocity, i.e. whether the subsidiary of a Japanese bank would be permitted to conduct a banking business in the foreign country.

Branches

A foreign bank intending to make an application for a banking license with respect to its branch in Japan must submit an application to the FSA. As with establishment of a new bank, it is typical for there to be a period of preliminary consultation with the FSA before the application is officially filed. The application will be examined based on almost the same criteria as for a new Japanese bank.

Representative Offices

A foreign bank interested in the Japanese financial market, even if it does not intend to open a subsidiary or branch in Japan, may establish a representative office (*chuzaiin-jimusho*), which may engage in various banking related functions incidental to the business of banking such as the collection of data and providing an informational function as to the available services of the home office. A representative office is not permitted to engage in the business of banking or act as agent for the parent bank. In practice, establishment of a representative office is usually a preliminary step for a foreign bank to obtain a banking license through a subsidiary or branch.

Supervision of Foreign Banks

Unlike the U.S., Japanese Banking Law does not require that all foreign banks operating in Japan be subject to effective consolidated supervision by their home countries. Japan examines branches of foreign banks in Japan and foreign branches of Japanese banks outside Japan. However, it is doubtful if Japanese examination of foreign branches of Japanese banks outside Japan is effective.

2.   NON-PERFORMING LOANS

The major preoccupation of the Japanese banking system in the last decade has been non-performing loans (NPLs). The Chapter now turns to the causes, including failure of macroeconomic policies, the size of the problem, and the efforts of the government to deal with it.

a.   CAUSES OF THE PROBLEM

The initial cause of the bad loan problem was the collapse of stock and real property values in 1990. Banks had substantial investment in both equities and real estate. The ensuing recession pushed borrowers into bankruptcy; the value of bankruptcies in both 1991 and 1992 was eight times the 1989 value. Other causes could include the inability of banks to engage in capital markets activities (until the reform of the Japanese version of the Glass-Steagall Act from 1993-1997), the decision of large Japanese companies to use international capital markets for funding rather than to borrow from Japanese banks, and competition from government financial institutions like Japan Post.[5]

NPLs, however, continued to grow in the 1990s. One reason was that bad loan reporting became more accurate. More fundamentally, as the economy soured, the borrowers' condition progressively worsened.[6]

Japan's weak economy impeded efforts to reduce the NPLs or their impact on the banks. With no growth, borrowers could not earn enough to service loans that became relatively more costly because of deflation. Even with low interest rates of 0.001 percent, the real cost of credit was positive to borrowers, but the spread was too low for banks to meet even their administrative costs. Japan's vaunted high private savings rate fell to 6.9 percent in 2001, from 14 percent in 1990 and over 30 percent in the early 1970s. By 2002, the economy was in its fourth recession in 10 years.

The government's macroeconomic options were limited. Lowering interest rates would not induce growth because interest rates were already almost negative. BOJ's rediscount rate was below 1 percent for much of the late 1990s and early 2000s. In March 2001, as consumer prices dropped for the second year in a row, and as imports rose and exports fell, BOJ accepted a zero-rate policy. At least one observer urged the government to go further, arguing that the central bank should simply create money with which to buy the banks' bad loans.[7]

New fiscal stimulus was limited by the very large existing government debt, brought on by earlier stimulus policies. For example, in August 1998, the government cut taxes by the equivalent of $41 billion and raised spending by $69 billion. Then in early 1999, the government decided to issue an extra $1.2 trillion in Japanese Government Bonds over five years. A substantial amount would fund the government's support to ailing banks. These bond issues increased the government's debt by 60 percent and gave Japan the highest ratio of government debt to GNP in the industrial world.

---

[5] Hoshi and Kashyap, supra note 1.
[6] Japanese Financial Services Agency, *Transition of Non-Performing Loans (NPLs) Based on the Financial Reconstruction Law*, February 7, 2003.
[7] J. Sachs, "Danger in Flogging Japan," *Financial Times*, April 24, 1998; K. Belson, "Japan Moves to Aid Economy and Ease Investor Fears," *The New York Times*, May 21, 2003.

Government debt was 140 percent of GDP in 2002. One long projection put it from 260 percent to 380 percent of GDP in 2030. Hugh Patrick, however, thinks the debt problem is overstated:[8]

> "Japanese government debt is a major long-run problem, but it is much less of a problem today than is commonly perceived. While government gross debt is 151 percent of GDP, more than half of that involves double accounting since it is held by government institutions and the central bank. Using a unified public sector budget measure, Japanese net debt as of March 31, 2003, is 64 percent of GDP. The U.S. level is 44 percent."

The full extent of the bad debt revealed itself slowly since 1990, in part because neither the banks nor the government announced it for many years, as described in the next section. The process itself contributed to public dissatisfaction with the way the crises were handled. Further delays in reviving the banks risked prolonging the credit drought.

b.   SIZE OF THE PROBLEM

Over the 1990s, *reported* NPLs continued to grow. In just seven years, from 1993 to 2000, non-performing loans grew from less than 1 percent of total bank loans to almost 15 percent. As of February 2004, NPLs were reported to be ¥30 trillion ($285 billion), about seven per cent of GDP ($4.1 trillion).

The size of NPLs was probably much higher according to many observers who believed that the FSA had a policy of letting the banks not report the full extent of their NPLs. Both the government and banks revised the bad debt numbers upward so regularly that they destroyed confidence in any set of figures. One interesting aspect of the banking crisis is the possibility that Mitsubishi Tokyo Financial Group (MTFG), formed through the merger of Mitsubishi and Bank of Tokyo in 1996, may have done better than its peers. This may due to the fact that it was the one Japanese bank listed on the New York Stock Exchange (in 1989) and thus subject to U.S. disclosure requirements about loan loss reserves. In addition, it had major operations in California (UnionBanCal) that was a source of technological and management input to the bank.[9]

At first, the LDP (Liberal Democratic Party) Government took steps to disguise the extent of the problem at individual banks and for banks as a group. It allowed banks not to classify as NPLs any loans which they had

---

[8] "Whither the Japanese Economy," in Symposium on Building the Financial System of the 21st Century: An Agenda for Japan and the United States, Harvard Law School Program on International Financial Systems and the International House of Japan, Briefing Book (October 2003), at 19. (Patrick)
[9] Kyota Omori (MTFG), presentation to the Seminar on the Japanese Financial System, Princeton University, April 2005.

"restructured" by substantially reducing the interest rate. Banks could deduct from taxes the lost interest. Trust banks, previously obliged to report only interest actually received, were allowed to book as received unpaid interest not more than six months overdue.[10]

There was also an issue as to whether bad loans were properly classified. For example, the FSA reported at the end of March 2001 "bad" loans of ¥33 trillion ($264 billion), but did not include in this number "doubtful" loans of ¥117 trillion ($936 billion). The FSA said that only about ¥14 trillion ($112 billion) of the doubtful or "carefully monitored" loans were bad.

The issue was widely debated. The opposition party to the LDP argued that the two categories should be combined because Japanese banks' finances were much less transparent than U.S. banks and the economic downturn argued against hoping that recovery would improve the banks' balance sheets. Combining the two would have suggested bad loans of ¥150 trillion ($1.2 trillion) in 2001, about 25 percent of GDP.[11]

The government delayed dealing with the NPL problem because of the social cost that would follow from the corporate bankruptcies associated with loan write-offs. Japan hoped that its economy would turn around. As growth resumed, the corporate debtors would return to profitability and become able to repay their debts. Indeed, one major cause of the growth of NPLs was new bad loans to old bad borrowers.

Foreign bank "creative" techniques helped to disguise the extent of NPLs. Most notable was the case of Credit Suisse First Boston (CSFB) whose banking license was suspended for helping Japanese banks make complex transactions to disguise losses and evade inspection. In 1994, CSFB had offered a service to Japanese banks by touting a document entitled "Restructuring an Investment Portfolio." In formal financial language, it explained exactly how Credit Suisse could offer its Japanese clients ways to conceal losses on their balance sheet. CSFB offered "dozens of plans." "A Japanese bank holding a bad loan, for example, could 'sell' the loan to a subsidiary at its face value, record the 'profit,' and then lend money to the same subsidiary to cover up the subsidiary's actual loss. Since there was no consolidated accounting, any losses went unrecorded."[12] The FSA reinstated CSFB's license at the end of December 2000, then barely two months later a Tokyo district court convicted Credit Suisse Financial Products of violating the securities law and obstructing an FSA investigation by trying to hide

---

[10] R. Thomson, "Japan's Banks Under Heavy Pressure," *Financial Times*, March 24, 1993 and R. Thomson, "Japanese Banks Put Off Facing Up to Bad Loans," *Financial Times*, May 14, 1993.
[11] G. Tett, "Opposition Party Puts Japan's Bad Loans at $1,200bn," *Financial Times*, April 20, 2001.
[12] G. Tett and N. Nakamae, "Tokyo Turns Against Its 'Friendly' Foreign Banks," *Financial Times*, May 21, 1999.

relevant documents. The court fined CSFB about $333,000 and sentenced its former branch manager, Shinji Yamada, to four months in jail.[13]

Other foreign and Japanese banks have had similar problems. Lehman Brothers was investigated, Deutsche Bank was reprimanded and banned from trading OTC derivatives for six months, and Citibank (with Merrill Lynch) was implicated in a scandal. Foreign bankers argued that the services were tacitly approved by the government at the time and that they were being made "scapegoats for the government's mismanagement." Other foreign bankers said they had chosen not to provide these types of services because it was not ethical.

In 2002, the FSA adopted a policy requiring NPLs to be reduced to 4 percent of total bank loans by March 2005. In September 2004, FSA reported that NPLs were 23.8 trillion down 2.8 percent from March 2004, representing 4.5 percent of bank loans. Despite the decrease overall (due to dispositions and improvements through workouts), new bad loans grew by 23.3 trillion over the same period. FSA expected the banks to meet the 4 percent target on time. The reductions in bad loans had the effect of shrinking bank balance sheets in about half from March 2002 to September 2004.

In 2004, bank shares increased in value, and some banks, like SMFG, began reporting profits.[14] Nonetheless, in June 2004, the FSA ordered UFJ Bank, the fourth largest bank in assets, to fix internal controls and said they might consider criminal charges against the bank for allegedly hiding documents and computer records to understate their bad loans.[15] Such prosecutions were brought against three former executives in December 2004, together with actions for fines against both UFJ and the executives. The three officials received suspended prison sentences in April 2005.

In May 2005, Tatsya Ito, the FSA Minister, announced that the bad loan crisis was over, as banks had halved their non-performing loans from 2002 levels in accord with government policy. The FSA stated that the combined bad-loan ratio of the top seven banks stood at 2.93 percent in March 2005 as compared with 8.42 percent in March 2002. While MTFG, Mizuho and Resona reported profits, MTFG and UFJ reported losses. There is still concern however whether the NPL problem is really behind the banking system. Banks continue to generate what will likely become new bad loans through new loans to zombie borrowers.

---

[13] P. Abrahams, N. Nakamae, and D. Ibison, "Japan Moves on Credit Suisse in U.K.," *Financial Times*, December 9, 1999; M. Tanikawa, "Japanese Court Convicts a Bank," *The New York Times*, March 9, 2001.

[14] D. Ibison, "Bad Loan Problem Starting to Ease," *Financial Times*, April 29, 2004.

[15] M. Fackler, "Tokyo Accuses UFJ Bank of Covering Up Bad Loans," *The Wall Street Journal*, June 21, 2004.

c.   GOVERNMENT ATTEMPTS TO REDUCE NPLS

The Finance Ministers of Japan and the U.S. in a press release dated June 17, 1998 described measures Japan would adopt to deal with NPLs:

1.   Dispose of bad assets more aggressively. The accumulated bad assets need to be removed from the books of financial institutions and to be liquidated to restore confidence and lending activity. The Japanese Government will ensure that Japanese banks sell off bad assets and will put in place the legal and institutional measures necessary to sell the collateral underlying bad loans.

2.   Rapidly restructure financial institutions. The "convoy" system will be abandoned. We will take aggressive measures to restructure the financial system and institutions in accordance with the market mechanism. The use of public funds to financial institutions to avoid systemic risks will be conditioned stringently so as to induce restructuring.

3.   Improve transparency and disclosure. Recognizing the importance of transparency and disclosure in improving capital market efficiency and reducing uncertainty, Japanese banks will be required to disclose the full extent of nonperforming loans on a consolidated basis, based on world-class accounting and disclosure standards by end of March 1999.

4.   Strengthen banking supervision and prudential standards. Government oversight and supervision of the financial sector will be improved to ensure that prudent standards are being met and to thereby promote confidence in the system. The new Financial Supervisory Agency will receive appropriate enforcement powers and more examiners.

These points represent the core of any serious effort to address the bad debt problems. The problem was that they have been only partially implemented.

1.   THE COOPERATIVE CREDIT PURCHASING COMPANY (CCPC) APPROACH

The government encouraged banks to transfer bad loans to a special entity, the CPCC, so that the banks could get a tax break without removing the loans completely from their books. Banks could not fully deduct provisions for their bad loans from income for tax purposes, but they could deduct the losses incurred in the sale.

The CCPC was established by joint action of Japanese banks in 1992, with a ten year life. A bank would sell the CCPC bad loans, along with the collateral, usually worth no more than 70 percent of the loan principal when the loan was made. CCPC valued the collateral and paid the bank that value, financed by a loan from the bank. The bank continued to manage the loan and the collateral. If the collateral was sold for less than its transfer price to CCPC, the bank made up the difference. Contrasted with the amount of bad loans, these transfers were modest. By January 1995, the CCPC had bought NPLs with a par value of ¥7.3 trillion, paying ¥3.3 trillion ($36.2 billion). The problem was that the bank continued to be responsible for the loans; it only recognized losses for tax purposes.

2.   CURRENT APPROACH

A major way to deal with the NPLs of banks was for the government to buy them from the banks. This would inject needed capital into the banks and allow bank management to focus on the future. Management of the existing bad loans could then be separately attended to by the government. But such purchases require substantial public funds.

In December 1995, the government appropriated ¥685 billion to deal with the problem of failing Jusen, housing loan companies. In February 1998, ¥30 trillion in additional funds were appropriated, ¥17 trillion in an account of the Depositor Insurance Corporation (DIC) for the full protection of depositors in failed banks and ¥13 trillion for DIC to inject in failing banks to enhance their capital. This was not enough. In October of the same year another ¥60 trillion was appropriated, allocated as follows: ¥18 trillion to purchase bad loans of banks under "temporary public control"; ¥25 trillion to invest (probably as preferred shares) in viable banks with capital ratios over 8 percent; ¥17 trillion to deal with the disposal of bankrupt banks. This added up to about ¥91 trillion, or $840 billion at June 2005 exchange rates. Japanese GDP in 2004 was about $3.7 trillion, so total public funds were about 22 percent in current terms.

In terms of capital injections, apart from the ¥685 billion bailout of the Jusens, capital injections were made in a number of banks: ¥1.8 trillion in March 1998, ¥7.5 trillion in March 1999 into 15 major banks (75 percent took the form of convertible preferred shares, 17 percent subordinated debt, and 8 percent nonconvertible preferred shares (or two City banks only), and ¥1.96 trillion in Resona in May 2003, for a total of about ¥12 trillion, a truly massive bailout.[16]

Notes and Questions

1.   If you were dealing with the NPL problem in Japan what would you do differently than what the Japanese did?

2.   Why did Japan have such difficulty in resolving the NPL problem?

3.   CAPITAL ADEQUACY

Japan subscribes to the Basel Accord's 8 percent capital requirement for internationally active banks. Other banks have a 4 percent capital

---

[16] The data on appropriations and capital injections is from Nobuchika Mori, Deputy Consul General, Consulate General of Japan in New York and Minister, Embassy of Japan to the U.S., presentation to the Seminar on the Japanese Financial System, Princeton University, February 23, 2005

requirement. Both types of banks must also have adequate capital on a consolidated basis. If you do not know the size of a bank's NPLs, you cannot say its capital is adequate. The private sector consensus by mid-2002 was that Japanese banks were bankrupt "by a significant amount." The size of the shortfall depended on the size of the losses from NPLs.

Japanese bank capital was significantly impacted by the stock market since they held a significant amount of their assets in equities. If the Nikkei dropped to under 7,000, simulations by Daiwa Research Institute put bank capital at 8.4 percent of risk-weighted assets, assuming the NPL data were not understated. However, simulations by Bank of America put capital under 8 percent if the Nikkei fell below 8,000. The Nikkei crossed 8,000 on March 10, 2003, 20 years after it last crossed it, going up.[17]

Banks have been ordered by FSA to reduce their shareholding, from the current 140-150 percent of capital level to 100 percent.

a.   BANK MEASURES TO INCREASE CAPITAL

The devices banks used to improve their capital were questionable. The very low prices of bank stock in Japan had eliminated domestic equity markets as a source for recapitalization. Some banks issued new capital in the form of privately placed preferred shares to companies or insurers to which they were closely related. This raised the issue of the permanence of such capital if the affiliates asked for repayment. This practice was not new. Banks had issued subordinated debt that one study found funded about half of their capital losses from 1990-1995. The main buyers then were the banks' affiliated financial and non-financial firms.[18]

Many Japanese banks were only able to meet or exceed the 8 percent minimum capital ratio because they include deferred tax assets (DTAs) in capital. Since the banks are not allowed to set off most of their loan loss provisions against taxable income, they book about half the provisions as deferred tax assets that will reduce tax payments due later when the losses are actually incurred. An LDP task force calculated that on September 30, 2002, the effect of excluding deferred tax assets from capital would reduce the reported 10.6 percent Tier 1 and 2 capital ratios to 5.5 percent for the 13 largest Japanese banks. These tax credits expire after 5 years, so the banks need sufficient income during that period against which to use them, a questionable outcome.

If sufficient profits were not generated (and it was highly doubtful that they could be), banks could not use tax deferred assets as capital. Minister Takenaka originally proposed changing the tax law to allow banks to deduct almost all loan provisions from income, but the LDP rejected this.

---

[17] "Banks Can Keep Capital Ratios Above 8%," Nikkei Weekly, March 11, 2003.
[18] See A. Horiuchi and K. Shimizu, *The Deterioration of Banks' Balance Sheets in Japan: Risk-Taking and Recapitalization* (1996).

In April 2003, however, the government reconsidered expanding the tax exemption and allowing long carry forwards and carry backs.[19]

After the failure of Resona in 2003, discussed below, which had 77 percent of its capital in DTAs, other banks substantially reduced their DTAs. Nonetheless, DTAs continued to be important. UFJ, for example, in September 2004 claimed a capital ration of 9.92 percent, but without DTAs their ratio would have been only 7.1 percent. The government has considered imposing a 10 percent of capital limit on DTAs, the approach of the U.S., but has not done so.

b.   GOVERNMENT MEASURES

1.   MIXED SIGNALS

Mixed signals from the government about capital adequacy have undercut reforms. For example, responding to a wave of recapitalizations (e.g. Mizuho Bank doubled its capital by issuing preferred shares of ¥2,100 billion), the FSA issued new rules in early 2003, to prevent bank from selling new shares to shaky companies. But the rules were vague, critics found.[20]

Mizuho also tried to increase capital relative to assets by reducing loans to companies. The FSA reprimanded the bank and ordered it to improve this lending, particularly to small and medium sized firms.[21] Throughout the crisis, the government has vacillated between seriously addressing the NPL problem and cutting off insolvent borrowers from additional funding.

2.   MARK-TO MARKET REQUIREMENTS AND MARKET SUPPORT

Banks were required, starting in early 2002, to mark their securities to market at mid- and end-year. Given stock market losses, this would further deplete bank capital. Remarkably, the Nikkei 225 index started to rise in early February 2002 and closed 20 percent higher at the end of March, the end of the fiscal year. This was largely because the government suddenly banned short sales of stock. Short sellers had to buy shares to cover their positions, raising demand. Critics found the move a flagrant intervention to manipulate the market at the end of the fiscal year, with short-lived benefits.

---

[19] A. Kashyap, "Sorting Out Japan's Financial Crisis," NBER Working Paper 9384 (December 2002). (Kashyap); "Banks Rely on Deferred Tax Assets To Achieve Key 8 percent Capital Ratio," Nikkei Weekly, March 3, 2003.

[20] "Rules Vague On Banks' Share Allotments," Nikkei Weekly, February 21, 2003.

[21] D. Ibison, "Mizuho Reprimanded for Cutting Corp Lending," *Financial Times*, January 31, 2003.

3. SHARE BUY-BACKS

BOJ announced in September 2002 that it would buy shares held by banks. It set aside ¥2 trillion ($16.3 billion) to use over the next 12 months, half by March 2003. It stated that it would buy actively traded stocks rated at least BBB- from banks whose stock holdings exceeded its Tier 1 capital but not more than ¥500 billion ($4 billion) from any one bank. BOJ would hold the shares in trust and sell them between 2007 and 2017 depending on the market impact.[22] BOJ's announcement stunned markets. Critics questioned whether banks would want to sell shares to BOJ on which the banks would be forced to realize losses and whether it was desirable for BOJ to become a shareholder in Japanese companies.

While the amounts were modest, as measured against the size of the banks' balance sheets, in March 2003, as the Nikkei descended through 7,800, BOJ raised the limit on stock purchases to ¥3 trillion. As of March, BOJ had bought ¥1.1 trillion worth of stock.[23] In addition, the government had created the Bank Shareholdings Purchase Corp in January 2002, funded by banks, to stabilize the market by buying shares as the banks unwound their cross-shareholdings.

4. CONSTRAINTS ON BANK LENDING

There has been much debate in Japan as to whether the poor capital position of Japanese banks has been responsible for lack of lending during the "lost decade." Some argue that lack of lending was due to the general slowdown of the economy and lack of demand, particularly as the best borrowers moved into world capital markets. Surveys were done during the period in attempts to show that Japanese medium sized businesses were able to get funds when needed. Nonetheless, lending declined significantly. In January 2005, lending declined by 2.7 percent, the 85th straight month of such declines.

4. CORPORATE RESTRUCTURING

Corporate restructuring was essential for Japan to remedy its economic problems. Lack of restructuring may be as serious as not dealing with NPLs because it leaves potentially productive assets in unproductive use.

Hugh Patrick[24] states:

"Some 1408 of a comprehensive sample of 2972 non-financial listed companies have a liabilities to operating cash flow ratio in excess of 10. Among these, 171 are larger companies (assets of more than ¥300

---

[22] Bank of Japan, *Stock Purchase Guidelines*, October 11, 2002.
[23] Bank of Japan, Annual Review 2003, p. 41.
[24] Patrick, supra note 8, p. 17.

billion, \$2.5 billion). They employ more than 3.6 million. Of these, 33 companies are in extraordinary distress, with an average liabilities to cash flow ratio of 30.9 and a debt to equity ratio of 29.9; and another 42 are deeply distressed, with an average liabilities to cash flow ratio of 27.0 and a debt to equity ratio of 6.8. Authors of another study estimate that of the total 3362 listed non-financial companies, 938 (27.9 percent) would not be able to cover interest costs out of operating profits if their borrowing rate was increased by only 0.5 percent, everything else equal."

The existing mechanisms of corporate restructuring have not been successful. Banks have not yet done much to structure required workouts, although this may be changing. RCC engineered restructurings have not proved significant; indeed, until 2003 RCC, could not incur losses on the bad loans they acquired from the banks. Court-administered bankruptcies have been severely obstructed by a system that gives major power to shareholders and employees.

The Koizumi government set up, in May 2003, a publicly financed entity called the Industrial Revitalization Corporation of Japan (IRCJ). Its job is "to overhaul major debtor companies. ..." The IRCJ has about ¥10 trillion (\$84 billion) in funds to invest, 75 percent of which it can use to buy bad loans from the banks. This was about 25 percent of the official figure for banks' bad debt.[25] The IRCJ was given no power to impose restructurings on banks and their debtors—the troubled company and its main bank had to jointly apply to IRCJ for assistance.[26]

In principle, IRCJ was supposed to give support to companies classified as "borrowers requiring attention" (including "special attention" and "doubtful" debtors considered capable of rehabilitation). The IRCJ was empowered to purchase the loan obligations from the debtor's banks and draw up a reorganization plan in cooperation with the main bank and the debtor company if the IRCJ determined that more loans can be collected by reorganizing the company than by liquidating it and the reorganization plan agreed on by the main bank and the debtor company was considered feasible.[27]

It is questionable as to how well this has worked. Initially banks only came to the IRCJ with six restructurings of medium-sized businesses. One

---

[25] K. Belson, "Japan's Fiscal Year Winds Down, with Less Anxiety," *The New York Times*, February 20, 2003.

[26] The discussion of IRCJ has been greatly informed by A. Saito (President and CEO of IRCJ), "Business Restructuring in Japan and the Role of IRCJ," presentation to the Seminar on the Japanese Financial System, Princeton University, April 6, 2005.

[27] Shinjiro Takagi, "Inauguration of the Industrial Revitalization Corporation of Japan: One of the Last Resorts to Recover Japan's Economical Prosperity," in Symposium on Building the Financial System of the 21ˢᵗ Century: An Agenda for Japan and the United States, Harvard Law School Program on International Financial Systems and the International House of Japan, Briefing Book (October 2003).

reason for this low level of activity was that IRCJ valued the bank loans lower than the banks, and by implication lower than the FSA. Moreover, banks had converted much of their bad debt into equity and IRCJ challenged the banks to write off this equity. Thus, banks using IRCJ restructuring would face additional write-offs. In addition, there were the general difficulties of restructuring. In Japan, this was complicated by the difficulties in creditor coordination between the debtor's main bank and the rest of the creditors. The number of creditor banks per debtor in Japan is generally greater than in the U.S. or U.K. Further, the smaller banks want the main bank to have more responsibility for losses—on the theory that they relied on the main bank's credit judgment in lending to the debtor

As of March 2005, IRCJ had picked 41 companies for bailout and had completed its resolution of 7. The companies include retail giant Daiei Inc., cosmetics maker Kanebo Ltd., home builder Misawa Homes Holdings Inc., Mitsui Mining Co. and two condominium builders—Daikyo Inc. and Dia Kensetsu Co. One reason for the increased activity was pressure on the banks to resolve their NPLS by FSA. In the case of Daiei, UFJ was the main bank, and due to its failure to dispose of NPLs, and the hiding of the size of NPLs, it received a business improvement order from FSA, requiring it to move more expeditiously to resolve its NPLs.[28] IRCJ has finished picking candidates for bailout. It must dispose of the loans within three years of acquisition. IRCJ has claimed that its importance should not be judged only on its own restructurings—claiming that it has shown how restructurings can be done effectively and thus stimulated banks to do their own restructurings without the assistance of IRCJ.

A major development in 2003 and thereafter was the sale of bad debt by Japanese banks to foreign banks who were prepared to impose harsh measures on borrowers. For example, in early 2003, Merrill Lynch bought $843 million in bad loans from UBJ, Japan's then fourth largest bank.

5.   RESTRUCTURING JAPANESE BANKS[*]

Japan's government has been willing to a limited extent to restructure Japanese banks by taking control of clearly insolvent banks and reorganizing them, by merging existing large apparently viable banks to create larger ones in the belief that this would reduce inefficiency and excess banking services in the system, and by selling banks to foreign investors.

---

[28] T. Kotaro, "Daiei's Rehabilitation—IRCJ's Support Must be Based on Strict Assessment and Markey Mechanisms," Rieti, October 26, 2004.
[*] I would like to thank Mimi Sasaki-Smith, a research fellow with the Program on International Financial Systems, for helping me to update this material.

a.   CONSOLIDATION

The government consolidated the big banks. The Tokyo-Mitsubishi Bank had already formed by 1998. After further mergers with other Mitsubishi entities, the Mitsubishi-Tokyo Financial Group (MTFG) was formed in 2001. Dai-Ichi Kangyo Bank, Industrial Bank of Japan (IBJ), and Fuji Bank formed as Mizuho Bank in September 2000 and became the largest in the world, measured by assets and capital. Sumitomo Bank and Sakura Bank merged in April 2001 into the Sumitomo Mitsui Banking Corp. (SMBC), and then was further reorganized as part of the Sumitomo Fitsui Financial Group (SMFG), creating the second largest bank in the world at the time. Sanwa, Tokai, and Toyo Trust and Banking merged in January 2002 to become UFJ Holding Inc (UFJH). Resona was the product of a forced merger of Daiwa Bank and Asahi Bank—both among the world's largest banks.

While the banks reorganized, simplifying business lines and shedding assets, the impediments to success were great. For example, the old management persisted after the mergers. The formal opening of a unified Mizuho Bank on April 1, 2002 was followed by weeks of paralysis when computer systems failed to integrate. Payments disappeared, ATMs across the country failed to work, the web site displayed customers' accounts and pin numbers, and many accounts had double deductions. Technical snags are understandable, but the more serious problems were the inability to integrate staffs and systems of the merged banks. Bigger was not necessarily better.

In 2004-2005, the saga of UFJ's merger with MTFG unfolded. UFJ was pressured into some form of merger by its weak condition and need for capital. It reported ¥402.8 billion of losses in FY 2003. Senior management had resigned when its profits had fallen more than 30 percent below its stated goal for three consecutive year—such resignations were required by FSA as a result of UFJ taking public funds. In May 2004, UFJH announced the sale of UFJ Trust Bank to the Sumitomo Trust & Banking Corp. (STBC), a subsidiary of SMFG, but then cancelled the sale after UFJH and MTFG entered into talks about a merger of all their operations in July 2004. SMFG then sued UFJ over the cancellation of the trust bank merger, trying to enjoin the UFJH and MTFG merger, and made a hostile tender offer, a one-for-one stock swap for the shares of UFJ. UFJ rebuffed the offer and accepted a capital injection for preferred shares from MTFG for ¥700 billion in September 2004. The Supreme Court had held in August that merger talks between UFJ and MTFG could proceed—leaving SMFG with a damage claim against UFJ for breach of contract. The UFJH-MTFG is expected to be completed by September 2005.

The UFJ saga was unprecedented. There had never been a hostile tender offer for a Japanese bank and hostile tender offers are extremely rare in general. This may represent the dawn of a more active form of capitalism, in open fights for corporate control. The question remains, however, whether ever bigger banks are the solution to Japan's banking sector problem—whether size will translate into more or less profitability.

In February 2005, SMFG and Daiwa Securities, Japan's second largest securities firm, announced merger talks. If successful, this would represent the creation of Japan's first full-fledged financial conglomerate. SMFG and Daiwa had previously set up in 1999 a brokerage firm to cater to corporate customers, and all of the other big banks have midsize brokerage firms but none the size of Daiwa.

b.   CLOSURE AND NATIONALIZATION

Nine months after the Finance Minister announced in February 1997 that the government would support the 20 largest banks "if they faced difficulties in disposing of non-performing loans," the government closed the 10th largest, Hokkaido Takushoku Bank, and transferred its assets to a regional bank. The traditional search for a merger partner failed.[29]

Under Article 102 of the Deposit Insurance Company Law, the Prime Minister may take the measures listed below. The decision has to be taken after a deliberation of a Council for Financial Crisis that consists of the Prime Minister, the Chief Cabinet Secretary, the Minister for Financial Stability, the Commissioner of the FSA, the Minister of Finance, and the Governor of the BOJ:

Type I Measure: for insolvent financial institutions	DIC invests in shares; can reduce stated capital
Type II Measure: for insolvent or failed institutions	DIC provides aid to protect creditors; institution controlled by financial receiver
Type III Measure: for failed insolvent institutions where the Type II measure is insufficient	Nationalization of the financial institution without compensation to existing shareholders[30]

The two big cases came back to back—Long Term Credit Bank (LTCB), the 10th largest, in October 1998, and Nippon Credit Bank in December. The Deposit Insurance Corporation (DIC) took over ownership of both. The DIC guaranteed the banks' liabilities, including not only deposits but also very substantial bond obligations and derivatives. About 850 of LTCB's borrowers, who were expected to go bankrupt, saw their loans transferred to RCC. BOJ loaned LTCB over $20 billion.

---

[29] G. Robinson, "Reassurance for Japanese Banks," *Financial Times*, February 11, 1997. See S. Strom, "Bailing Out of the Bailout Game," *The New York Times*, November 18, 1997.

[30] M. Fukao, "Weakening Market and Regulatory Discipline in the Japanese Financial System," Preliminary Paper for the Chicago Fed-BIS Conference, Market Discipline: The Evidence across Countries and Industries, October 30-November 1, 2003.

DIC dismembered the banks, selling viable units to other domestic and foreign banks or nonbanks, such as GE Capital. In September 1999, a group of U.S. investors, including Citigroup, under the leadership of Ripplewood, a U.S. private equity fund, acquired the rest of LTCB, renamed Shinsei, for about $1 billion. The government removed ¥5 trillion in bad loans, and added loan loss reserves. Ripplewood acquired a put for remaining bad loans. The government committed to inject up to ¥450 billion and buy collateral backing LTCB loans if the value of the loans value fell over 20 percent in 3 years. This arrangement generated some disputes between Shinsei and DIC.[31] The terms of the DIC indemnity continued to be at issue when Shinsei made a $2.4 billion international public offering in February 2003. Although the DIC issue was resolved, there is some continuing resentment over Shinsei's success, making it appear that the Japanese government did not negotiate a good deal. In 2005, Japan enacted tax changes that imposed a 20 percent tax on the returns of private equity investors—some referred to the this as the Shinsei Tax. Some interpreted the tax as payback for the high returns achieved by these firms.

Nationalizations abated until Resona Bank, then the fifth largest, with assets of $360 billion, failed on May 17, 2003, after its Tier 1 capital fell to barely 2 percent on March 31, 2003. The government stepped in quickly, promising to provide liquidity and injecting ¥2 trillion ($17 billion) in new capital, raising regulatory capital to about 10 percent. Former shareholders were diluted but not eliminated, a result which triggered criticism. While the government claimed the bank was not insolvent at the time of capital injection—thus precluding a takeover of ownership—this claim has been actively contested.[32]

Just before Resona failed, 77 percent of its Tier 1 capital consisted of deferred tax assets. Its failure was triggered when Resona's auditor, Tomatsu, refused to let it recognize DTAs more than three months into the future because of its uncertain earnings prospects. Further fears were raised about Resona's longer-term prospects when it announced huge losses ($16.2 billion) for the first half of 2003. These numbers made it relatively clear that Resona was insolvent when it was bailed out.[33]

In September 2003, a major regional bank, Ashikaga Bank, was nationalized after reporting negative net worth of minus 3.7 percent. All equity was eliminated, unlike the case with Resona. The bank continued its normal operations while FSA sought to transfer its business to another bank;

---

[31] N. Nakamae and P. Abrahams, "U.S. Group Set to Buy LTCB," *Financial Times*, September 28, 1999.

[32] D. Ibison, "Japan's Opposition Raises Stakes in Resona Row," *Financial Times*, October 30, 2003

[33] D. Ibison, Resona, "Loss Raises New Fears," *Financial Times*, October 11/12, 2003.

the BOJ provided it with liquidity. Ashikaga's failure could have significant political impact; it accounts for nearly half of Tochigi prefecture's loans.[34]

As a result of the various government injections into the banking system, a very high percentage of bank capital is held by the government. Fukao estimated that in March 2003 that the Japanese banking system had ¥8.8 trillion in adjusted capital (book value + 60 percent of unrealized capital gains—DTA—estimated under reserving) of which the government held about 83 percent.[35]

c.   GOVERNMENT'S PREFERRED SHARES

When DIC injected funds into banks that continued to operate, it received preferred shares that it could convert into common stock. If the price of common fell, the government would receive more common stock and have greater voting power than if the common price rose. The ¥7 trillion ($59 billion) injected in 1998-99 would, if the preferred shares were converted, give the government control over the banks.[36] In 2003, the government announced that it would not convert its preferred shares into common for at least two more years. It further stated that if a bank's profits remained below a target return for two years after April 1, 2003, the government would first order remedial action and then consider conversion.[37]

d.   NEW PRIVATE OWNERSHIP

1.   NON-TRADITIONAL JAPANESE OWNERS

Some nationalized banks were sold to non-banking firms. Japan's Softbank Corporation, an investor in internet businesses, led the group that bought Nippon Credit Bank, taking 48.8 percent of the shares of the new bank, called Aozora, with Orix, a leasing company, and Tokio Fire and Marine, an insurer, as its main partners. Small portions were held by foreign groups.[38]

2.   FOREIGN OWNERS

Japan has sensibly begun to allow foreign owners of Japanese banks. A major challenge for Japan's banks is to change business strategy and management techniques. A foreign owner can bring expertise, systems, and technology. The Koizumi government said it will, despite domestic

---

[34] M. Nakamoto, "Japan Faces up to Banking Reality," *Financial Times*, December 1, 2003.

[35] Hoshi and Kashyap, supra note 1, based on M. Fukao, "Weakening Market and Regulatory Discipline in Japanese Financial System," Mimeo, Keio University (2003).

[36] A. Adelson, "Putting a Braver Face on Japan's Bad Loans," *The New York Times*, May 2, 1999.

[37] D. Pilling, "Japan Gives Banks More Time with New Rules on Nationalization," *Financial Times*, April 4, 2003.

[38] A. Harney, "Bank Chief's Suicide Shatters Aozora's Credibility," *Financial Times*, September 22, 2000.

controversy, continue to let foreign investors buy stakes in Japanese banks. To some extent, this is related to its trade agreement with the U.S.

After struggling for years for a larger share of Japan's banking market, foreign banks received a lift from the Financial Services Agreement signed on February 12, 1995 by the U.S. Secretary of the Treasury and the Ambassador of Japan to the United States. Major elements included:

(a) Japan would publish standards for licensing, explain adverse licensing decisions to applicants, make compliance with administrative guidance voluntary, put oral administrative guidance in writing upon request, and publicize items of guidance that are common to "a multiple number of persons"

(b) The Japanese government will "strongly request" local groups advising it about financial services to allow foreign participation. Foreign financial service suppliers can join relevant Japanese trade associations and be treated in the same manner as Japanese members.

(c) Foreigners will receive "meaningful and fair opportunities to be informed of, comment on, and exchange views with officials" about measures concerning financial services in Japan.

This Agreement is discussed at greater length below. Despite the easing of entry restrictions, some foreign commercial banks have concluded that Japan's banking markets are unattractive and have withdrawn. As of the end of December 2002, there were 9 U.S. banks operating 31 branches in Japan, followed by 9 Korean banks with 12 branches, 7 German banks with 7 branches; 5 French banks with 6 branches; and 5 Taiwanese banks with 6 branches.[39]

Some foreign financial institutions and non-bank investors, however, have concluded that investment in Japanese banks provide an attractive business opportunity. The Fleet Financial Group, the ninth largest U.S. bank, negotiated the purchase of a lending unit from Sanwa Bank in 1998. Prudential Insurance (U.S.) and Mitsui Trust & Banking set up an asset management joint venture in July 1998. As previously mentioned, GE Capital bought a securities unit from the failed Long Term Credit Bank. Foreign banking groups, including Chase Manhattan Bank, UBS of Switzerland, and Cerberus (a private equity investor), acquired a minority position in Aozora Bank, controlled by Softbank. The controlling role of Ripplewood, Citigroup, and other foreign investors in Shinsei Bank, the successor to LTCB, was described above. In 2003, Cerberus acquired a controlling stake in Aozora by increasing its minority stake through acquisition of Softbank's 49 percent share. They appointed an American to

---

[39] T. Aritake, "Japan Banks Shut 61 Overseas Branches in Three Years, Reflecting Weak Condition," BNA Banking Report, March 3, 2003.

run the bank, making more visible the foreign presence. In late 2003, Shinsei appointed an American investment banker as its vice chairman who became Chairman in 2005.

The government called for an even greater foreign influx. Foreign investment banks, particularly from the U.S., have responded. They invested large stakes in City banks during 2002-03. Sumitomo Mitsui sold ¥495 billion in stock to foreigners, one-third going to Goldman Sachs. UFJ received ¥120 billion from Merrill Lynch.[40] Mizuho has formed alliances with a number of foreign banks.

Some investors in Japanese banks have already made money. Wilbur Ross, the American corporate turnaround artist, is selling a regional bank and a credit card company for $410 million, twice what he paid in 2001. Under the deal, Bank of Kansai Ltd., owned by the Sumitomo Mitsui Financial Group, is to pay 80 percent in cash and 20 percent in stock on July 1 to buy Kansai Sawayaka Bank Ltd. from Nippon Investment Partners, which Mr. Ross controls.[41]

Foreign banks are not a factor in Japanese retail markets, but this is not unique to Japan—this is traditionally the most difficult market for a foreign bank to penetrate due to national loyalties and the need for an extensive branch network. These hurdles can only be overcome by acquiring Japanese banks with a retail business, which has not yet happened in Japan. However, overall foreign banks are a presence in the Japanese overall lending markets, accounting for 13.7 percent of total loans and discounts. Foreign banks dominate foreign exchange trading in Japan, accounting for over 70 percent of the average trading value in that market. These figures come from the Bank of Japan. In addition, foreign banks play the major role in the market for NPLs.

e.   DIRECTOR LIABILITY

In Chapter 3, we discussed the Daiwa scandal where the failure of the bank to report trading losses to the New York Federal Reserve Bank resulted in the termination of its U.S. banking license. There were also repercussions in Japan. In 2000, the Osaka District Court in a shareholders derivative action ordered 11 current and former directors of Daiwa to pay $775 million in damages, finding the directors responsible for the lack of internal controls and concentration of losses. Hopefully, the prospect of such liability, for the directors as well as management, will be an ex-ante deterrent to cover-ups of losses.[42]

---

[40] D. Ibison, "Japan's Bank Malaise Infects Whole Economy," *Financial Times*, March 15, 2003.

[41] J. Brooke, "Turnarounds are Drawing Prospectors to Japan," *The New York Times*, June 4, 2003.

[42] See B. Aronson, "Reconsidering the Importance of Law in Japanese Corporate Governance: Evidence from the Daiwa Bank Shareholder Derivative Case," 36 Cornell International L.J. (2003), p. 11.

Notes and Questions

1. Should Japan sell more of its banks and NPLs to foreigners?

2. Do you think the Resona bank problem was handled correctly?

6.   DEPOSIT INSURANCE

Big Bang had called for an end to a guarantee for all depositors and was to substitute protection by the Deposit Insurance Corporation (DIC) of retail deposits, up to ceiling amount. Deposits in branches of foreign banks are not covered by deposit insurance.

The government, however, delayed implementing this goal. Unlimited deposit insurance on time deposits ended only in April 1, 2002, a year after the date originally set. Time deposits became insured only up to ¥10 million (about $75,000) per person per bank. A year later—April 2003—demand deposits were to have the same limit, but in October 2002, the government announced that it would continue to guarantee demand deposits, ordinary deposits, and certain other deposits without limitation until April 2005.[43] Supporters of this delay foresaw the possibility of a run on banks, particularly smaller ones, given the uncertainty about the banks' solvency. Depositors might shift deposits abroad or to the Postal Savings System. Others feared that this delay removed an incentive to encourage savers to distinguish between sound and weak banks, thus decreasing the potential for market discipline.

Notes and Questions

1. Would you put a ceiling on demand deposit insurance in 2005?

7.   POSTAL SAVINGS SYSTEM

The Postal Savings System is the largest financial institution in Japan, with $2.3 trillion in deposits as of 2003. The total deposits in the System, ¥239 trillion in 2003, compared to ¥260 trillion in the City banks. It takes deposits, purchases government bonds, and finances government entities through the Fiscal and Investment Loan Program (FILP). It holds about 30 percent of savings accounts. It is the world's largest financial institution.

The Postal Savings System has long been an important part of the Japanese financial system. The system rose to prominence around 1980 when it attracted 20 percent of personal deposits, in response to its offering anonymous ten-year, high-yielding, fixed-interest deposits free of withholding tax, guaranteed by the government. For some period it paid higher rates of interest, but that advantage has ended.

---

[43] "LDP Panels Back Bill to Delay Adoption of Refund Cap," Nikkei Internet, October 21, 2002; FSA, *New Deposit Insurance System*, December 12, 2002.

The existence of the Postal Savings System distorts competition with the private sector (because of its government guaranteed deposits, its zero cost of capital, its non-taxed income and its exemption from funding the deposit insurance system) and could itself become a mega bad bank due to losses on FILPs. One continuing issue is that the System is regulated by the Ministry of Public Management, Home Affairs, Posts and Telecommunications, rather than the FSA. One study has found that at least 68 percent of the FILP loans are bad, meaning that the public corporations and agencies that have borrowed from Postal Savings to funds these loans are technically bankrupt.[44] Of course, this does not mean that the central government will not make good on these loans, if necessary. Despite its shortcomings, during the "lost decade" the System served as a safe haven for depositors. In April 2003, the government transformed the system into Japan Post, a public corporation, but the Postal Savings System remains largely unchanged.[45]

In 2004, Prime Minister Koizumi announced his intention to privatize the Japan Post, including Postal Savings over 10 years. Under the plan, four areas of service will become separate businesses in 2007—mail delivery, management of the 25,000 post offices, savings deposits and life insurance. Thus, Postal Savings will become one of four subsidiaries of a holding company owned by the government. At this time, employees would lose their civil service status and branches would be tasked with operating to achieve returns rather than provide subsidies to the government. In addition, the FSA would take over the regulatory role. Privatization of each subsidiary would then occur over the next decade. When privatization occurs, government guarantees of deposits will be removed.

Privatization raises a number of important issues. First, a privatized Postal Savings System will remain a mammoth financial institution. This will make it a formidable competitor with the rest of the private sector, perhaps a dominant competitor. Second, the size of the System, will raise serious too-big-to-fail problems even if the formal government guarantee is removed. Third, it is questionable whether this organization has the expertise to find alternative investments to its now mandated investments in JGBs and FILP loans, thus increasing the probability of insolvency. Fourth, the impact on the JGB market itself could be significant once this assured source of demand is removed. Fifth, the new System will have to restructure its bad FILP assets and raise a sizeable amount of capital. Some have advocated going much further, advocating that postal savings be broken up into a number of smaller banks or that caps be placed on the amount of

---

[44] T. Doi and T. Hoshi, "FILP: How Much Has Been Lost? How Much More Will be Lost?," Working Paper (February 26, 2002).
[45] K. Belson "Japan Puts Deregulation to Big Test," *The New York Times*, March 28, 2003; "Leviathan Unbound," The Economist, March 29, 2003.

deposits similar to proposals made about Fannie Mae and Freddie Mac, the government sponsored mortgage institutions in the United States.

8.   THE REGULATORS

A number of reorganizations of the regulatory system took place in the 1990s.

a.   BOJ INDEPENDENCE

The Bank of Japan's independence was enhanced on April 1, 1998. Monetary policy is now set by a board consisting of three representatives from BOJ and six outsiders. The board elects the Chairman, who is expected to be the BOJ governor. MOF is no longer able to remove BOJ officials or force delays in implementing BOJ policy, but BOJ is required to coordinate policy with MOF and MOF is able to approve the central bank's budget.[46] It is generally thought that BOJ has weak regulatory powers as compared to FSA. BOJ, like FSA, examines banks. In addition, its role as lender to banks, which has expanded significantly as part of expansionary monetary policy, gives it an important power as creditor of banks. More fundamentally, its role as lender of last resort in a financial crisis, means that its views must be respected.

b.   REFORMS CREATING THE FSA

The historic power of MOF over the financial system ended in the 1990s, mainly as a result of the blame it received for the failure of the financial system. Its power was first limited with the enactment of Administrative Procedure Law No. 88 of 1993 (APL), the first general statute governing administrative procedure in Japan. The APL specifically addressed administrative guidance, a pervasive and opaque way to exert bureaucratic power. The APL instructed regulators not to exceed the scope of their duties as set by the relevant law and to rely on voluntary compliance, not threats. Regulators should make the rules clear to the concerned party and, if requested, give their directions in writing unless to do so would be very inconvenient. When more than one person was concerned, the regulator was to apply standard rules and to publicize them in most cases.

Proposals to reform MOF grew in the mid-1990s. In February 1996, the Prime Minister launched a study of proposals to break up MOF. In March 1997, the cabinet approved a proposal to create a new supervisory agency, the Financial Supervisory Agency (FSA), independent of MOF and reporting directly to the Prime Minister, to license financial firms, close insolvent ones,

---

[46] W. Dawkins and R. Lambert, "Bank of Japan Set to Win Greater Self-rule," *Financial Times*, February 6, 1997.

and control the deposit insurance corporation. MOF would draft legislation and advise about insolvent banks.[47]

MOF's efforts to preserve its domain were weakened by scandals. In late 1997 and early 1998, leading banks were accused of bribing MOF and officials, with lavish entertainment and gifts. Former senior MOF officials were arraigned. Two committed suicide just before their hearings. In the wake of these scandals, the finance minister and his political aides resigned in January 1998. This allowed the appointment of a new minister from outside MOF; indeed, he had earlier been a prosecutor in Tokyo. The governor of the BOJ resigned when the central bank was also tarred by scandal.[48]

The new FSA created in 2001 amalgamated its two transitional predecessors, the Financial Supervisory Agency and the Commission for Financial Reconstruction, which controlled government funds injected into the banks. Now the FSA licenses, inspects, and supervises banks, securities companies, and insurance companies, as well as managing and resolving financial crises and overseeing the Deposit Insurance Corporation (DIC). MOF continues to make policy and draft financial legislation.

The DIC resources grew as premiums increased five times and the government injected funds. DIC gained power to collect and investigate abuses, in anticipation of more failures.

The FSA is a powerful agency which, like the FSA in the United Kingdom, regulates all financial institutions—banks, insurance companies and securities firms. As we discuss in the next section, the Securities and Exchange Surveillance Committee (SESC) is part of FSA. There is a question whether this consolidation of power is a good idea, particularly in a country that has suffered from bureaucratic excess in the past. Some countervailing weight does come from BOJ, but it is limited. MOF continues to have important powers through their control of budget and tax policy. Further, most of the senior officials of FSA have come from MOF. Whether this is merely a transitional phenomenon remains to be seen.

The FSA approach to regulation is different than the approach MOF used in the past. First, it is much more at arms length from the banks. This has resulted from the lessons of the past where close relationships led to forebearance. Second, FSA is much more transparent in its approach, adopting written rules and regulations rather than relying on informal administrative guidance.

---

[47] See W. Dawkins, "Independent Agency to Police Japanese Financial Sector," *Financial Times*, February 27, 1997.
[48] See S. WuDunn, "Japan Names Outsider as Finance Minister," *The New York Times*, January 31, 1998.

c.   THE CHANGING LEADERSHIP

In October 2002, the government revitalized its financial team with a new, aggressive leader. Heizo Takenaka became Minister for Economics, and the head of the FSA. He immediately warned that no bank was too big to fail and that the government would clean up the NPLs even if bankruptcies and unemployment rose. He said that banks had to write off much of their NPLs quickly.

But fierce opposition from banks and other LDP leaders prevented Takenaka from even releasing the details of his plan. Koizumi's support weakened and the government only announced in late October that, with help from the Bank of Japan, it planned to cut NPLs in half by March 2005. It would consider providing banks with more capital and force banks to raise provisions through tighter credit assessment. Takenaka, who had described a banking "crisis" a month earlier, said he meant a "critical situation" and that "the banks are basically healthy."

After letting some time pass, Takenaka returned to pressing for a faster resolution. He required banks to use discounted cash flows to value their loans, which forced another $3.5 billion in write-offs for the period ending April 2003.

Notes and Questions

1.   How would you compare the banking regulatory structure in the U.S., U.K. and Japan?

B.   CAPITAL MARKETS

Japan's financial system has been traditionally dominated by banks and bank lending. Financing through the capital markets was a minor part of financial activity. This was partially due to the fact that banks were prohibited from engaging in securities activities until 1997. Securities markets also suffered from very restrictive regulation, lack of transparency, and tight limits on foreign firms. Japan has made many efforts to stimulate its capital markets in recent years, as discussed below. But these measures have had limited effects. In Japan, securities (stock, bonds or mutual funds) constituted, as of March 2004, about 13.6 percent of financial assets as compared with 53.9 percent in the United States. On the other hand, Japanese assets held in deposits or cash were 55.2 percent as compared with 13 percent in the United States. As you read this material on the capital markets, ask yourself why Japanese investors are so reluctant to invest in securities.

In 1996 the Hashimoto government enacted sweeping capital market reforms under the rubric of "Big Bang," a term used to describe similar 1986 U.K. reforms of its financial market. The key components of the reform were free, fair, and global. Big Bang reforms were the product of two financial causes.

First, there was the depressed state of banking, as detailed in Part A. There was hope that revived capital markets, which were also depressed, could take up some of the slack. There was a widespread lack of confidence in capital markets, reinforced by the failure in 1997 of Yamaichi Securities, the smallest of the big four securities firms. This was then the largest business failure ever in Japan. This failure also undermined confidence in the supervision of securities firms: it appeared that MOF had known since 1991 that Yamaichi hid significant losses.

Revelations about ties of securities firms to gangsters further eroded confidence. In early 1997, Nomura Securities admitted having made illegal payments to compensate gangsters for investment losses. MOF fined Nomura and prohibited certain lucrative activities as a penalty. The police arrested the former president, Ryuataro Sakamaki, after he admitted having met with one of the gangsters. Later Nomura was excluded for some time from underwriting certain government bond issues, a penalty that was estimated to lower the firm's profits by about 15 percent.

Second, there was increasing pressure from other countries, principally the United States, for Japan to open up to foreign firms. This was reflected in Japan's Financial Services Agreement of 1995 with the U.S. discussed in Section B below.

1.   THE BIG BANG IN CAPITAL MARKETS

Big Bang included the following sweeping reforms:

1.   ending fixed commissions and deregulating other fees (starting in April 1998 for large issues and freeing completely within the following 12 months);

2.   ending product restrictions;

3.   liberalizing asset management regulation (e.g. register rather than license suppliers and disclose better);

4.   easier entry and exit, including by non-securities firms as discount brokers;

5.   ending restrictions on a variety of instruments (e.g. asset-backed securities or stock options), exchange, and OTC operations;

6.   the own-risk principle;

7.   ending government price-keeping operations, which propped up prices by asking state-owned enterprises and private firms to buy shares in down markets;

8.   permitting electronically-processed data filing and disclosure;

9.   thorough and substantial disclosure;

10. transparent regulation;

11. active punishment for violation of rules;

12. a legal system to support financial innovation, including derivatives;

13. ending the 20 percent ceiling on pension fund investments in equities and requiring them to disclose the market values of their positions;

14. promoting mutual funds by, for example, allowing banks and others to distribute them and letting mutual funds as well as pension funds to invest in unlisted securities;

15. ending the Foreign Exchange Law in April 1998, replacing the need for permission with simplified reporting after the fact, and allowing securities firms and others to do foreign exchange business, investors to order from foreign securities firms directly, and individuals and corporations to open bank accounts and hold assets abroad, and generally ending constraints on domestic and cross-border FX operations;

16. harmonizing Japanese accounting with international standards; and

17. reviewing, in order to rationalize, all tax rules for fairness, neutrality, and simplicity, which included ending the tax on securities transactions, double taxation of dividends, and withholding taxes on JGBs and other public sector bonds.

Another important reform was to allow banks into the securities business by eliminating the Japanese version of the Glass-Steagall Act. In the 1993-1997 period banks were allowed to establish trust and securities subsidiaries and securities firms could own banks and trust companies. In 1998, the structure of a financial holding company was introduced (holding companies had been prohibited since World War II as a result of the fear of industrial concentration, termed Zaibatsu).

In 1998, the government passed more implementing legislation. It clarified banks' powers to provide equity based derivatives. Fixed commissions were ended on transactions over ¥50 million ($435,000) and brokers began to offer clients discounts up to 50 percent. Notice of securitization to individual debtors was to be replaced by public notice, making securitization much easier. The ¥10 million minimum investment for commodity futures was abolished. Markets responded positively at this point. New issues in the corporate bond market were 56 percent more in 1997 than 1996.[49]

---

[49] G. Tett, "Japan's Brokers Hint At Price War After Big Bang," *Financial Times*, March 27, 1998; G. Tett, "Japanese Corporate Bonds Boom as Banks Cut Lending," *Financial Times*, June 1, 1998.

In 1999, securities firms were allowed to engage in most activities by simply registering with MOF, whose discretion in granting a license was limited to high risk activities like OTC derivative trading. All restrictions on issuance of corporate bonds and commercial paper by non-bank financial institutions ended. Securities firms could offer asset management services and banks could sell OTC investment trust funds. Mutual funds, rather than simply contractual investment trusts, could be offered and offers could be private as well as public. Loopholes to escape consolidated accounting were closed. Financial holding companies were encouraged. Withholding tax ended for payments to foreign holders of JGBs.[50]

More reforms were called for in 2002. The Financial System Council, which advised Koizumi, proposed expanding the number and type of brokers by reducing their minimum capital and easing licensing rules. Companies should also disclose more about possible law suits and executive compensation. The supervisory powers and resources of the Securities and Exchange Surveillance Commission should be enhanced without necessarily creating a powerful independent agency like the U.S. Securities and Exchange Commission, as some critics urged.[51]

2.   LICENSING REQUIREMENTS FOR FOREIGN SECURITIES FIRMS

A foreign securities firm must register to conduct a securities business in Japan through its Japanese branch, under the Foreign Securities Firms Law of Japan (the FSF Law). All applicants must certify that the same kind of businesses that they are applying for have been conducted by the applicants continuously for three years or longer. The amount of the applicant's paid-in capital cannot be less than the amount equivalent to ¥100 million and the applicant's net worth must not be less than the same amount. An applicant must show that all of the other business conducted by it at any of its branches is a securities-related business as permitted under the FSF Law.

A Foreign Securities firm must obtain a license from the Commissioner of the Financial Services Agency in order to conduct any of the following businesses:

> (a) over-the-counter securities derivative transactions, such as over-the-counter securities options transactions (the minimum paid-in-capital requirement for this type of business is the equivalent of ¥1 billion)

---

[50] Analytica Japan, *Japan's Big Bang* (December 12, 1997), p. 30.

[51] "Govt Panel to Propose Beefing up SESC's Oversight Power," Nikkei Interactive Net, December 2, 2002; "Proposals to Aid Stock Market Focus on Investor Confidence," Nikkei Weekly, December 23, 2002. A detailed compilation of measures taken can be found in Mineko Sasaki-Smith, "The Japanese Financial System: Why Has the Big Bang Reform or the Capital Markets Not Worked Better?," presentation to the Seminar on the Japanese Financial System, Princeton University, March 28, 2005.

(b) principal (as against "sub") underwriting of securities (the minimum paid-in-capital requirement for this type of business is the equivalent of ¥3 billion, or the equivalent of ¥500 million, depending on the type of underwriting); and

(c) dealing or brokering of securities through an electronic information processing system vis-à-vis a number of persons using the following method to determine sale prices (the minimum capital requirement for this type of business is the equivalent of ¥300 million):

   (i) the prices on a stock exchange, with respect to listed securities;

   (ii) the prices published by the relevant securities dealers association, with respect to over-the-counter securities;

   (iii) negotiated prices between customers; and

   (iv) other methods prescribed by the subordinate ordinances.

When the license is granted, the Commissioner may impose certain conditions on the license. Such conditions must be the minimum conditions necessary for the public interest and investor protection.

Japan branches of a registered foreign securities company must maintain a capital adequacy ratio of 120 percent or more. The details of the formula for calculating the capital adequacy ration are prescribed by subordinate ordinances.

A registered foreign securities company must report to the Commissioner the capital adequacy ratio as of the end of each month and whenever the capital adequacy ratio falls below, or increases to, 140 percent.

In principle, the formula for calculating such capital adequacy ratio is as follows:

$$\text{Capital Adequacy Ratio} = \frac{A - B}{C}$$

Where A is the amount of paid-in capital and certain reserves as prescribed by the subordinate ordinances; B is the amount of certain fixed assets and other items as prescribed by the subordinate ordinances; and C is the amount of certain risk assets (such as certain securities held by the company) as prescribed by the subordinate ordinances.

3.   THE FINANCIAL SERVICES AGREEMENT (FSA) OF 1995:
     LIBERALIZATION OF CROSS-BORDER CAPITAL FLOWS

a.   THE FSA AGREEMENT

Japan's cross-border transactions were also traditionally restricted, largely through foreign exchange controls. This changed, beginning in 1995, with the conclusion of a Financial Services Agreement with the United States. Pursuant to Article V of the FSA, rules governing offshore securities activities changed in the mid-1990s. MOF introduced a comprehensive system of notification for the offshore issuance of securities by residents and yen securities by non-residents. It confirmed that it would not restrict the maturity structure or set financial criteria for corporate bonds issued by residents offshore. MOF reduced the 90-day seasoning requirement for resident issuers' Euroyen bonds to 40 days.

In Article V, the government of Japan agreed to introduce a new advance approval system allowing manufacturing firms in Japan to deposit funds abroad for portfolio investments of at least ¥100 million equivalent offshore and report only afterwards. Non-financial corporations and individuals could "directly invest, without solicitation," in securities derivatives listed on overseas exchanges. Corporate investors meeting certain standards could invest for their own accounts in financial futures and options listed abroad, without separate approval or notice. Securities companies, insurance companies, and investment trust companies would no longer be required to get advance approval to trade for their own account in currency spot options listed abroad.

The two governments stated that restriction of securities activities should be minimal and for prudential purposes only. Japan confirmed that for this purpose "any instrument will constitute a security to the extent that it satisfies the definition of a 'security' ... in Article 2 of the Securities Exchange Law (SEL)" and that no one needed the government's acknowledgment, before issue, that an instrument was a security. If asked, however, the government would respond expeditiously. The government confirmed that certain new instruments were within the definition, including certain types of asset backed securities, foreign closed-end funds, and bonds with debt warrants, though it did not mention equity derivatives.

b.   IMPACT ON FOREIGN FIRMS

Over the 1990s, partially as a result of the FSA Agreement and Big Bang, foreign securities firms came to dominate Japanese capital markets. As of 2003, most of the 45 securities companies came from abroad. Their dominance was substantially aided by the financial difficulties of the Big Four Japanese firms. As already discussed, Yamaichi had become bankrupt in 1997. Nomura, the largest, was hampered by a series of scandals. And

Citigroup acquired 25 percent of Nikko Securities Company in 1998, after which Nikko formed a joint venture with Salomon Smith Barney, a Citigroup subsidiary. The alliances between the Japanese City banks and foreign investment banks further threatened the Japanese securities firms.

Based on figures from the Tokyo Stock Exchange, foreigner's share in brokerage trading in 2004 was about 40 percent. In an equity league table looking at equity deals (IPOs, equity and equity-related issues), foreign firms had 22 percent of the market and a foreign firm in partnership with a Japanese firm, Nikko Citigroup, had another 14.9 percent of the market. Nomura and Daiwa still led the way with a total market share of 45.7 percent. Foreign firms were less prominent in M&A deals with Japanese involvement completed in 2004. This is based on data from Thomason Financial.

Despite the relative success of some foreign securities firms, many withdrew from Japan or scaled back, particularly in the retail area. Merrill Lynch closed 75 percent of its retail offices, Morgan Stanley closed all, and Charles Schwab, a leading U.S. discount broker, closed a venture.[52] Most foreign firms, like most Japanese investment houses, were losing money. In 2003, 18 of 21 foreign brokers had no profit. This was not surprising, since Tokyo Stock Exchange commissions fell 22 percent in fiscal 2003. Many foreign investment companies were shifting to less costly financial centers in Asia.[53]

Foreign firms were also affected by crackdowns of the FSA. Some of the crackdown was related to schemes to assist Japanese banks to avoid detection or resolution of NPL problems. In addition, the U.K. firm Schroders failed to report certain obligations in its asset management business for five years; BNP Paribas Securities made improper trades; and WestLB Securities Pacific also broke the law.[54]

The most significant crackdown against a foreign financial institution came in 2004 when FSA ordered Citibank to close its private-banking operations in Japan. This is the harshest penalty since the actions against CSFB in 1999. The regulators accused Citibank of failing to prevent transactions that may have been linked to money laundering or stock manipulation, and for failing to make adequate disclosure of the risk of investments. FSA also accused Citibank officials of trying to obstruct its

---

[52] K. Belson, "Morgan Stanley Ends Small-Investor Push in Japan," *The New York Times*, November 14, 2001; K. Belson, "Charles Schwab Will Close Its Online Venture in Japan," *The New York Times*, December 8, 2001.
[53] D. Ibison, "Allure of Tokyo Exchange Fades as Almost All Brokers Lose Money," *Financial Times*, May 28, 2003.
[54] E. Terazono, "Japanese Regulators Fine BNP Paribas Securities," *Financial Times*, June 10/11, 2000; D. Ibison, "FSA Investigates NSSB in Japan," *Financial Times*, January 19, 2001. Times, May 28, 2003.

investigations.[55] In April 2005, the FSA ordered Cititrust Banking Corp., the Japanese trust unit of Citigroup, to suspend indefinitely all new business operations effective May 2, after Cititrust's failure to comply with Japanese mutual fund registration requirements.

4.   RULES FOR ISSUANCE OF FOREIGN SECURITIES IN JAPAN

Foreign issues sold in Japan to public investors may use financial statements based on GAAPs of the home countries, if the FSA accepts that those GAAPs are sufficiently protective of Japanese investors and the public interest. Thus, U.S. GAAP, U.K. GAAP, German GAAP, French GAAP, and other major country's GAAP are acceptable alternatives to Japanese GAAP in Japan. Audit by certified accountants by their home countries are also acceptable if they are admitted as comparable to Japanese CPAs. Therefore, 73 U.S. companies used their financial statements based on U.S. GAAP audited by U.S. CPAs when they sold their securities in Japan during the period from July 2002 through June 2003. IAS is acceptable only when it is accepted as GAAP in the issuer's home country, for instance in Germany.

Japanese accounting standards have undergone substantial change in the 1990s. The Japanese have argued that they are equivalent to IFRS in asking the EU Commission to accept Japanese GAAP as equivalent to U.S. GAAP. As discussed in Chapter 2, the EU will require foreign public firms to state their accounts in IFRS, as adopted by the EU, unless the Commission determines that another standard, such as U.S. or Japanese GAAP is equivalent.[56]

For all public issues in Japan, domestic or foreign, annual reports and mid-year reports are required under the Securities and Exchange Law. But the Tokyo Stock Exchange is going to start to require listing companies to provide quarterly reports, and the government is considering amending the Securities Exchange Law to require quarterly reports. Immediate reports are required, if there is any new material information between mandated reports.

Public companies in Japan are subject to proxy rules under the Securities Exchange Law or the Commercial Code. They must choose one of these two proxy rules. The contents of these rules are very similar. Most public companies have chosen the proxy rules under the Commercial Code. Issues of foreign companies are not exempted from such provisions, as in the U.S.

---

[55] FSA, Administrative Actions on Citibank, N.A. Japan Branch, September 17, 2004; SESC, Recommendation Based on the Inspection Result of Citibank, N.A., September 14, 2004. Citigroup, Inc., Citibank, N.A. Branch Statement Regarding FSA Announcement, September 17, 2004.

[56] Letter of December 21, 2004 from Toru Shikibu, Deputy Commissioner for International Affairs, FSA, to Fabrice Demarigny, Secretary General, Committee of European Securities Regulators. See also, M. Mizuno, "The Impact of New Accounting Standards on Japanese Companies," 9 Pacific Economic Review 357 (2004).

Japan does not permit foreign issues traded in Japan—even OTC—to file home country reports in lieu of required Japanese reports.

Japan has not adopted IOSCO's disclosure rules for public issues but they are very similar to Japan's.

Japan has a similar procedure to U.S. Rule 144.[57]

5.   STOCK EXCHANGES AND THE BOND MARKETS

This section concentrates on the bond market. We will look at the role and functioning of Japanese stock exchanges in Chapter 13. However, certain recent changes in Japanese regulation of foreign participation in stock exchanges may be noted here. The international competitiveness of Japanese stock exchanges and opportunities for formal alliances with overseas stock exchanges to date have been limited, due principally to a prohibition on the holding by any person or entity, including an overseas stock exchange, of more than 5 percent of the voting rights of a stock exchange in Japan. Under recent amendments to the Securities Exchange Law (Amendments), this 5 percent limitation was abolished, and as a general rule a single shareholder will now be able to hold up to 50 percent of the voting rights in a stock exchange.

As Figure 6.1 shows, government debt in Japan dominates the bond market, and has become more predominant during the 1990s as government debt substantially increased, both to prime the pump, and to finance public injection of funds into failing or failed banks. In 2002, the government bond market was at the ¥500 trillion level, as compared with the ¥125 trillion level of the corporate market. Figure 6.1 also shows that the corporate bond market did increase in absolute size in the 1996-1998 period of Big Bang reform, but has shrunk again with the downturn of the early 2000s. There is little evidence that one of the aspirations of Big Bang, to have the bond market compensate for the weakness of the banking market, was achieved.

---

[57] This information has been helpfully supplied by Professor Shinsaku Iwahara, a leading Japanese banking specialist on the Law Faculty of Tokyo University, based on information he received from the FSA.

Figure 6.1
Japan's Bond Markets: Public and Corporate Bonds 1988-2002[58]

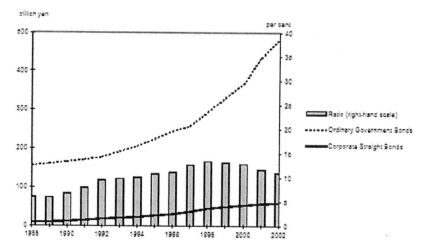

Japan's economic and financial problems also took their toll on Japanese issues abroad. Moody's downgraded JGBs in November 1998. The economic and financial recovery did not go far enough, according to Moody's. It put Japanese Yen debt under review in early 2000. Moody's did not say that it expected Japan to default on Yen debt. Rather, it was concerned that the relative growth of debt in Japan might undermine the country's economic recovery, which would in turn make it hard for the government to reduce the debt. In September 2000, Moody's downgraded JGBs to AA2, two steps below the top rating, then downgraded them again to AA3, and then to A2, below Botswana, in 2002. Standard & Poor's and Fitch followed suit. With the prospect of government debt equaling 149 percent of GDP in late 2003 and over 200 percent by 2010, rating agencies saw the risk of inflation and default.[59]

6.   GOVERNMENT INTERVENTION IN CAPITAL MARKETS

Government interventions to stimulate the stock market undermined Big Bang and the relaxing of capital controls of the Financial Services Agreement. In the early 1990s, government price keeping operations (PKO) and moratoria on new equity underwriting for listed shares were a form of direct intervention in the markets which was contrary to the spirit of "free" markets contemplated by Big Bang. But the interventions continued

---

[58] Amounts outstanding at the end of the year. Bank of Japan, Japan Securities Dealers Association.
[59] M. Williams, P. Dvorak, and G. Zuckerman, "S&P Lowers Japan's Domestic and Foreign Credit Rating," *The Wall Street Journal*, February 23, 2001; M. Wolf, "How to Avert a Ratings Disaster," *Financial Times*, March 27, 2002.

afterward in various forms. As reports that speculators were short selling in anticipation that share prices would fall, the government restricted short sales effective October 1998. Hedge funds could no longer easily short the Japanese market, previously a popular pastime.[60]

The constant threat of market intervention, even if not always implemented, overhung the market. Proposals became common for government spending to support the stock market, such as having the government buy stock itself or guarantee a fund that would buy stock.

The tax system was revamped to support prices. To encourage investors to trade, the government, replaced the 1.05 percent tax on stock sales with a 10 percent withholding tax on capital gains.

In March 2003, the FSA announced a six-point plan to stabilize the stock market. The major goal was to discourage speculative selling. The FSA capped proprietary short selling by securities firms. It urged insurers and pension funds to limit the shares they lent to foreign funds, which used the shares to sell short. It urged firms to sell less in down markets or, if they were banks, to sell to the Banks' Shareholding Purchase Corp. This would discourage banks from selling proprietary shares when the market fell.

The FSA also urged the securities industry to pass rules that prevented brokers from placing large orders to sell just before the market close. To encourage corporations to buy back their stock, the FSA for three months eased the rules that limit the timing and volume of share buybacks. The limits existed to prevent market manipulation. The FSA allowed companies to buy in the last 30 minutes of trading and quadrupled the amount they could buy. Finally, the FSA directed the Securities and Exchange Surveillance Commission and stock exchanges to "rigorously monitor the market."[61]

The government did, however, reject a proposal to suspend fair value accounting temporarily when Economics and FSA Minister Takenaka opposed it.[62]

We have already discussed the Bank of Japan plan of purchasing equities from banks. As of March 10, 2003, BOJ had bought ¥906 billion.

7.   DISCLOSURE PRACTICES

There is substantial doubt as to the accuracy of disclosures by Japanese companies. In December 2004, the FSA found that one in 10 listed

---

[60] J. Martinson, "Hedge Funds Unnerved by Short-Selling," *Financial Times*, October 23, 1998; G. Tett, "Anger over Japan's New Curbs on 'Short-Selling,'" *Financial Times*, October 23, 1998.

[61] "FSA Coalition Draw Up Plans to Stabilize Market," *Nikkei Weekly*, March 17, 2003.

[62] "Emergency Proposal Calls for Expanding BOJ Asset Purchases," Nikkei Interactive Net, March 14, 2003.

Japanese companies deceived investors in financial statements.[63] These findings help explain why there is not more activity in Japanese capital markets. In late 2004, FSA announced plans to improve disclosure by prompting issuers to engage in more accurate disclosure through "voluntary reviews" of their statements, the establishment of staff within SESC to monitor compliance with disclosure requirements, and to promote electronic filing of information. In addition, and more importantly, FSA has imposed a Section 404 type Sarbanes-Oxley requirement for audited internal controls, will introduce a civil money penalty system for breaches of continuous disclosure requirements as of April 2005, and will require disclosure of new items. It will also strengthen the powers of the CPAAOB for auditor oversight, created in 2004 on the model of the U.S. PCAOB.[64]

8. CORPORATE GOVERNANCE AND CORPORATE CONTROL

Another important factor in the development of a capital market is investor confidence in the governance of corporations. Japanese corporations have traditionally not been oriented towards maximizing general shareholder wealth. More important has been the welfare of various stakeholders, principally affiliated investors (Keiretsu) and employees. From 1993-2002, there has been massive reform in corporate governance.[65] These reforms can broadly be characterized as enhancing management flexibility, for example streamlined merger and divestiture procedures and facilitation of the issuance of stock options, and enhancing the monitoring capabilities of boards and auditors.[66]

A key part of the traditional Japanese governance structure has been the statutory auditor, a weak cousin of the German supervisory board. The statutory auditor monitors board compliance with law and reviews the financial statements. Effective 2005, at least half of the board of audit must be comprised of outside auditors.

In 2002 a major reform was adopted. Large firms (most publicly listed firms) were allowed to abolish their boards of audit and replace them with a U.S. style committee system, which were to include audit, nomination and compensation committees, each of which were to have at least three members, a majority of whom were "outside" directors. However, the definition of "outside" was broad enough to include employees of a parent

---

[63] D, Ibison and B. Jopson, "Deceit Revealed in Japanese Companies," *Financial Times*, December 21, 2004.

[64] FSA, Further Measures for Ensuring Confidence in the Disclosure System, December 24, 2005.

[65] C. Milhaupt, "A Lost Decade for Corporate Reform in Japan?: What's Changed, What Hasn't, and Why," Columbia Law School, Center for Law and Economic Studies Working Paper 234 (2003).

[66] R. Gilson and C. Milhaupt, "Choice as Regulatory Reform: The Case of Japanese Corporate Governance," Columbia University Law School, Center for Law and Economic Studies Working Paper 251 (2004).

company and of sister companies. Through March 31, 2004, only 71 firms, less than 3 percent of eligible firms, has adopted the new structure. A recent appraisal of this reform believes it may create a powerful new technique for managerial entrenchment and "stakeholder tunneling"—the diversion of resources away from shareholders toward employees, banks and other constituencies.[67] If the study is correct, shareholders may find investment in the Japanese capital markets even less attractive than they have in the past.

An important device in insuring managerial accountability to shareholders is the ability of one company to acquire another through a hostile tender offer. This technique has had an important role in the United States. Hostile takeovers are extremely rare in Japan. In 2005, the Japanese corporate world was stunned when Livedoor, an internet service provider, owned by a 32 year-old entrepreneur, Takafumi Horie, made a hostile bid for Nippon Broadcasting System. In response to the hostile bid, Nippon sought to merge with Fuji TV—Nippon owned 22.5 percent of Fuji's stock. By March 2005, Livedoor had obtained enough shares to control 45 percent of Nippon and Fuji had acquired 37 percent. Livedoor's bid was financed in large part by a ¥80 billion loan from Lehman Brothers, a U.S. investment bank. Livedoor had used the after-hours market to acquire a significant portion of its shares in Nippon to avoid normal public notice requirements for takeover bids.

In March 2005, the High Court of Japan upheld a District Court ruling preventing Nippon from issuing more shares to Fuji. The takeover battle ended in April 2005 when Fuji agreed to pay Livedoor about ¥147.4 billion which resulted in a substantial profit for Livedoor on its investment in Nippon. Since the Livedoor bid, many companies have adopted takeover defenses.

It is unclear whether Livedoor will trigger further hostile takeovers or result in takeover proof tactics, perhaps facilitated by changes in corporate law. Thus, the possibility that a virtuous circle could be created, in which the capital markets strengthen corporate governance, which in turn strengthens investor interest in the capital market, remains to be seen.

9.   REGULATORS

There are two regulatory schemes used in regulating the securities markets and securities industry: public regulation and self-regulation (self-regulation is a regulatory scheme that is unique to the securities markets, and is regulation conducted by the stock exchanges and the Japanese Securities Dealer Association (JSDA), acting as a legally-recognized self-regulatory organizations).

---

[67] *ibid.*

Formerly, the Securities Bureau of Ministry of Finance was the entity responsible for public regulation in Japan. A new regulatory body called the Securities and Exchange Surveillance Committee (SESC) was established (under the Law to Ensure Fair Transactions) as an external bureau attached to the Ministry of Finance under the Securities Exchange Law amendments in May 1992. The SESC began operating in July of the same year.

Thereafter, the SESC became a part of the Financial Supervisory Agency (FSA), when the FSA was created in June 1997. However, after the creation of the Financial Reconstruction Commission (FRC), accompanying the worsening of the financial crisis, both the FSA and the SESC were reorganized under the FRC. The SESC is currently part of the FSA after the FRC was abolished pursuant to the reorganization of the Japanese central government that took place in January 2001.

The SESC has enforcement and audit powers. It also has on-site inspection powers to monitor compliance by securities firms and self-regulatory organizations with transactional rules, and can recommend that the Prime Minister, Commissioner of the Financial Services Agency, or the Minister of Finance impose an administrative disposition.

Furthermore, the SESC is delegated the authority to conduct investigations of banks and other financial institutions that engage in securities functions concerning their compliance with regulations designed to ensure the fairness of transactions (e.g. regulations concerning firewalls between banks and their securities subsidiaries).

10. JURISDICTION OF THE SECURITIES AND EXCHANGE LAW (SEL)

The Financial Law Board, an influential group of experts, issued in 2002 their Interim Report Concerning Application of Finance-Related Laws and Regulations to Cross-Border Activity, and Particularly Issues Under the Securities and Exchange Law (Law Board). This Report primarily examines the application of the SEL to financial activity outside Japan. This section summarizes that Report.

a.   BUSINESS REGULATIONS

The SEL requires a person who wishes to engage in the "securities business" to register (SEL Article 28). The SEL stipulates that the conduct of any of the acts set forth in Article 2(8) thereof as a business, e.g. trading in securities, or intermediating, brokering or agency, etc., constitutes engaging in the securities business. The SEL prescribes stringent regulations on securities companies that have registered, including restrictions on their scope of business, imposition of a duty to submit various reports and filings, restrictions on methods of transactions, capitalization restrictions, and a requirement for inspections and reports.

Registration as a securities company under the SEL assumes that the company is a Japanese stock company. Foreign companies which intend to engage in the securities business in Japan through a Japanese branch must register pursuant to Article 3(1) of the Law Concerning Foreign Securities Firms (or in the case of certain business activities obtain a permit as prescribed in Article 7(1) thereof).

This regulatory system presents the question of whether an act of engaging in the securities business, as a business, is limited to cases in which the entity engages in acts within Japan, or whether under certain circumstances this would also cover acts committed outside of Japan.

The Financial Services Agency published an administrative guideline in December 1999 which stated that "acts by a foreign securities firm such as presenting ... advertisements or offering information in connection with securities transactions ... on a website, etc., in principle constitute *soliciting*" which would require a foreign securities firms to register.

The Law Concerning Foreign Securities Firms allows a "foreign securities firm" outside of Japan to conduct certain of the acts of securities trading from abroad and directed toward persons within Japan without registering, if the other parties are financial institutions, or the like, or if acts of soliciting are not performed.

b.   TRADING REGULATIONS

The various regulations under the SEL include insider trading regulations, a prohibition against market manipulation and other regulations in the form of direct restriction against unfair trading and similar acts. The Law Board, at p. 9, states:

> "These regulations are more concerned with protecting the legal interests in fair trading on markets in which securities trading is conducted and the mechanism of fair price formation rather than protecting the interests of particular investors, and from this perspective there is good reason to take the position that Japan's SEL can be applied to the extent necessary to achieve these objectives even if the "acts" are not committed within Japan."

c.   INCIDENTAL REGULATIONS

Incidental regulations under the SEL include those for disclosure of information (issue disclosure) at the time of issuing securities, ongoing disclosure (distribution disclosure), the system for disclosure of block holdings, and disclosure in connection with public tender offers. The Board states, at 12:

> "These disclosure regulations each differ somewhat in their intent, but their basic objective is to have the necessary information provided for the purpose of protecting investors in connection with securities

trades. When studying the application of these regulations it would seem that the appropriate course would be to impose a duty of disclosure, etc., within a reasonable range to the extent useful from the perspective of the purposes of disclosure."

This is a rather vague conclusion. It generally supports the idea of requiring reports on block holdings or trade offers involving Japanese listed companies even if the transactions occurred abroad.

It states, however, that current application of the regulation requiring block holding reports does not impose a duty to report if a party outside of Japan acquires shares in a foreign country through a transaction that takes place outside of Japan, but in all other cases a reporting requirement is held to exist.[68]

d.   NO-ACTION LETTERS

The institution in 2003 of a no action letter system may greatly aid in resolving legal uncertainty in this and other areas of Japanese law.

Under this new system, foreign and domestic financial institutions can submit questions for governmental ruling and then know in advance whether or not they are properly complying with current regulations. An institution begins the process by submitting a questionnaire to the FSA. The FSA is responsible for responding in writing with the appropriate answer, its answer in principle to be given within 30 days. Given its very limited resources, the FSA may utilize outside experts when asked to issue a no-action letter. The FSA has only approximately 1,000 employees.

Notes and Questions

1.   Why have foreign securities firms been so successful in Japan, as compared to foreign banks?

2.   Why have the Japanese capital markets played such a secondary role to banks, given the sustained banking crisis of the 1990s? A major reason may be general lack of confidence of investors in the capital market. Such confidence was undermined by the losses investors suffered in the markets after the burst of the bubble, various scandals involving Japanese securities firms, the potential for stock manipulation by the government or companies whose public float is small compared to holdings of affiliates as a result of cross-holding, poor corporate governance of Japanese companies, and lack of accurate disclosure. In addition, there is the general malaise of the economy. Given the continued poor performance of Japanese stocks, the capital market is not attractive to Japanese investors. Interestingly, Japanese investors have not sought out investments in foreign markets as an alternative. Foreign securities in December 2004 were only 0.5 percent of financial assets

---

[68] Law Board, note 24, p. 13.

of households. Another factor, on the supply side of the bond market is that borrowers prefer to deal with their main banks in a non-transparent way. This may be just a home bias phenomenon, or may represent Japanese fear of devaluation of foreign currencies as against the Yen. Japan is reportedly thinking of adopting something like a Sarbanes-Oxley Act. Would this be a good idea? Do you think the impending merger of SMFG and Daiwa securities might change the situation?

CONCLUSIONS

Japan, like the EU, is a major player in the international financial system. Until its economic downturn in the 1990s, it seemed to be pursuing a different path than the West with respect to its financial system and its economy in general. Its approach involved substantial management of competition by MOF and cartel behavior by its banks. The financial system was dominated by banking, and development of the capital markets suffered. There was little participation by foreign financial institutions.

As this Chapter indicates, this has substantially changed. The Japanese financial system is now much closer to that of the U.S. and Europe, MOF is no longer managing competition, and foreign financial institutions now dominate capital market activity and are beginning to be a factor in banking. Japan like the U.S. has been reluctant, however, to import international standards; e.g. like the US it has resisted IAS standards. On the other hand, it has permitted foreign GAAP from certain countries. Further, it seems less willing than the U.S. to relax its rules, or to allow home country rules, in recognition of foreign differences.

Japan's international presence has contracted, in terms of the importance of Japanese financial institutions abroad, as a result of the domestic crisis. Solving this crisis remains the central issue in Japan. While there seems to be some economic upturn, smaller banks continue to fail, and the resolution of the NPL problem, is still ongoing despite substantial progress.

PART II

INFRASTRUCTURE OF FINANCIAL MARKETS

This Part covers the backbone and back office of financial markets.

It begins with Chapter 7 on Capital Adequacy. This is the most important and fundamental form of regulation of financial activity, and applies to both banks and securities firms. It is the cornerstone of international banking regulation, as capital standards for banks are formulated by the Basel Committee on Banking Supervision.

Chapter 8 deals with foreign exchange regimes. While foreign exchange issues are mainly one for economists rather than lawyers, risks of foreign exchange must be taken into account in most international financial transactions.

Chapter 9 deals with the payment system, focusing on U.S. Dollar payments. The U.S. Dollar payment system is important worldwide given the substantial number of international transactions that are denominated in U.S. Dollars. The Chapter covers the operations and the regulation of the system. Chapter 10 covers the clearance and settlement of securities trading both in the U.S. and internationally. Like the payment system, the clearance and settlement system is fundamental to the operation of international financial markets.

CHAPTER SEVEN

CAPITAL ADEQUACY

As we have seen, banking regulation is premised on a concern with systemic risk and losses to the public safety net designed to avoid such risks. The central feature of this regulation is capital adequacy. Major banks operate on a cross-border basis and host countries depend on the supervisory efforts of foreign regulators. This situation led to efforts to establish international standards for capital adequacy through the Basel Committee on Banking Supervision (the Basel Committee). The Basel Accord efforts have become the crown jewel of international banking regulation.

After reviewing the background of the Accord, this Chapter discusses the definition of capital and then turns to the determination of the amount of capital required for the three risks covered by the Basel Accord: credit, market, and operational risk.

The implementation of the revisions of the Basel Accord, Basel II adopted in June 2004, has caused a major split between the United States and the rest of the world, as the U.S. is only implementing the changes applicable to its most sophisticated banks whereas the EU and other countries plan to apply the Accord to all banks. The technical difficulty of the revisions has raised questions about the ability and advisability of bank supervisors mandating such rules for the banking industry.

A. BACKGROUND OF THE BASEL ACCORD

In 1976 the Bank for International Settlements (BIS), concerned about the need to coordinate banking supervision in member countries, set up the Committee on Banking Regulations and Supervisory Practices as a standing committee of the central bank governors of the Group of Ten (G10) countries. Eventually called the Basel Committee on Banking Supervision, its members include Belgium, Canada, France, Germany, Italy, Japan, Luxembourg, the Netherlands, Spain, Sweden, Switzerland, the United Kingdom, and the United States. Each has a representative of its central bank (and bank supervisor, if different) on the Committee.[1]

The initial activities of the Basel Committee coordinated procedures, not substantive rules. In 1976, its Basel Concordat allocated responsibility

---

[1] Much of the history is drawn from P. Cooke, *Bank Capital Adequacy* (1991).

among home and host supervisors of banks with offices in more than one country and/or doing cross-border business. It modified the Concordat in 1983 to ensure that every international bank would be subject to consolidated supervision by one regulator—that is, one supervisor would have an overview of all the bank's activities, anywhere in the world.

The rules on capital convergence marked the entry of the Basel Committee into the arena of substantive rules. Given the wide variation between the G10 countries' rules about capital and the fact that this variation affected competition among banks in international markets, any attempt to align the rules could affect banks' profits and operations.

U.K. and U.S. regulators led the way with an initiative in 1986 to relate capital requirements to the riskiness of assets. This departed from the previous practice of relying exclusively on a leverage ratio, under which capital was a fixed percentage of the value of the assets regardless of its risk. Regulators of other industrial countries then joined the effort. In July 1988, the Basel Committee accepted an 8 percent minimum capital rule with the following elements (this regime is now known as Basel I):

THE KEY ELEMENTS OF THE BASEL CAPITAL ACCORD

Definition of Capital

1. Capital is split between Tier I (equity and disclosed reserves) and Tier II or supplementary elements (undisclosed reserves, asset revaluation reserves, general provisions, hybrid debt/equity instruments and subordinated term debt). The inclusion of the individual Tier II elements is at national discretion.

2. Deductions from capital cover goodwill, investments in unconsolidated financial subsidiaries and, at national discretion, holdings of other banks' capital.

3. Tier II elements are only eligible up to 100 percent of Tier I; subordinated debt must not exceed 50 percent of Tier I; and general provisions are limited to 1.25 percent of risk assets.

Risk Weighting of Assets

1. For on-balance sheet assets five basic buckets of risk weightings are applied (0 percent, 10 percent, 20 percent, 50 percent and 100 percent). The main buckets are central governments, public sector entities, banks and non-bank corporates.

2. For off-balance sheet items, a system of credit conversion factors is used. These include such categories as commitments and contingencies. The conversion factors are applied to the nominal principal amount of exposure in order to produce a credit equivalent amount, which in turn is weighted according to the category of the counterparty. Interest rate and foreign exchange rate contracts are treated similarly, but take into account adjustments based on their particular nature.

Required Ratios

1. Banks should hold a minimum of 8 percent capital by the end of 1992.

These Basel I rules applied to banks with significant international operations—"internationally active banks"—but countries could choose to apply them to all banks. Both the U.S. and the EU applied the rules to all of their banks. The EU did so in two directives, one on Own Funds (89/299/EEC) and the other on Solvency (89/647/EEC). These laws were incorporated into a new directive on the Taking Up and Pursuit of the Business of Credit Institutions (2000/12/EEC). The U.S. also applied the rules at the bank holding company level. It was up to national supervisors to enforce the capital rules, but as we saw in Chapter 3, some countries (like the U.S.) would not allow banks to operate in their countries if their capital fell below the Basel requirements.

The level of capital can also be used to trigger regulatory interventions. In the United States, the prompt corrective action regime is built on capital adequacy as determined under the Basel Accord. The Federal Deposit Insurance Corporation Improvement Act of 1991 (FDICIA) designates five levels of capital. "Well capitalized" banks have 10 percent or more risk-weighted capital, 5 percent in Tier I, and are minimally supervised. "Adequately capitalized" banks have 8-10 percent risk-weighted capital, 4-5 percent in Tier I, and are monitored more often. "Undercapitalized" banks, with 3-6 percent risk-weighted capital and 3-4 percent in Tier I, are required to develop a recovery plan and limit growth. Significantly undercapitalized banks, with less than 3 percent risk-weighted capital, are required to recapitalize and to restrict their transactions with affiliates and payments on deposits. Finally, "critically undercapitalized" banks, with a book value net worth (minus goodwill) of below 2 percent of assets, are to be sold or closed quickly. Apart from supervisory intervention, regulatory permissions (such as in the U.S. for establishing a financial service holding company) can also depend on the level of capital. Banks that are not well-capitalized pay higher insurance premiums. In July 2004, JPMorgan Chase's capital temporarily fell below 10 percent, to 9.79 percent, costing them $31.5 million in additional deposit insurance premiums because they were no longer well-capitalized. 60 U.S. banks are in the well capitalized category.[2]

Banks from about 120 countries have adopted the Basel I rules. They were motivated to do so by a number of considerations. To some extent observance of Basel standards has become a mark of respectability for many developing countries. In addition, the IMF has prodded banking systems to adopt the Basel standards and monitors them for compliance. For developed countries outside of the G10, observance of Basel standards is a virtual necessity since many countries, most notably the U.S., require compliance with Basel as a condition for foreign banks to do business. In other words, the U.S. requires foreign banks with U.S. branches to comply with Basel standards. The Basel Accord is not a treaty and is thus not formally binding on the subscribing countries. In most cases, however, the agreement did not require legislative approval since central banks and supervisors had existing authority to implement the Basel Accord through regulation.

The Basel Committee was quite explicit that the rules applied only to credit risk. After completing these rules, the Basel Committee turned its attention to setting capital standards for market and operational risk, which are examined in Part D of the Chapter.

Banks can adapt to capital requirements in a number of ways. As they approach the minimum 8 percent ratio under the Basel Accord, they may increase retained earnings by cutting dividends, issue new capital instruments (which may be expensive), reduce assets (i.e. by lending less or

---

[2] B. Rehm, "A Costly Capital Dip for Chase," *American Banker*, August 31, 2004.

securitizing) or shift assets to categories requiring less capital (i.e. engage in regulatory arbitrage).

B.   GENERAL ELEMENTS AND THE DEFINITION OF CAPITAL

Countries implemented what could count as capital somewhat differently. The U.S. adopted the following approach under Basel I:

Table 7A
Summary Definition of Qualifying Capital[3]

Components	Minimum Requirements
Core Capital (Tier I)	Must equal or exceed 4 percent of weighted risk assets
Common stockholders' equity	No limit
Qualifying non-cumulative perpetual preferred stock	No limit; banks should avoid undue reliance on preferred stock in Tier I
Minority interest in equity accounts of consolidated subsidiaries	Banks should avoid using minority interests to introduce elements not otherwise qualifying for Tier I capital
Less: Goodwill and other intangible assets	
Supplementary Capital (Tier II)	
Allowance for loan and lease losses	Limited to 1.25 percent of weighted risk assets
Perpetual preferred stock	No limit within Tier II
Hybrid capital instruments and equity contract notes	No limit within Tier II
Subordinated debt and intermediate-term preferred stock (original weighted average maturity of 5 years or more)	Subordinated debt and intermediate-term preferred stock are limited to 50 percent of Tier I; amortized for capital purposes as they approach maturity
Revaluation reserves (equity and building)	Included in 1998, when up to 45 percent of pre-tax net unrealized holding gains on available for sale equity securities (measured as the excess of fair value over historical cost) was allowed in Tier II capital
	On a case-by-case basis as a matter of policy after formal rulemaking
Deductions (from sum of Tier I and Tier II)	
Investments in unconsolidated subsidiaries	As a general rule, one-half of the aggregate investments will be deducted from Tier I capital and one-half from Tier II capital
Reciprocal holdings of banking organizations' capital securities	
Other deductions (such as other subsidiaries or joint ventures) as determined by supervisory authority	
Total Capital (Tier I + Tier II − Deductions)	Must equal or exceed 8 percent of weighted risk assets

---

[3] Federal Reserve System, Risk-Based Capital Guidelines (2004) 12 C.F.R. 208, App. A.

These requirements are for state-member banks, and apply at the bank level. The Fed also has capital guidelines for bank holding companies.[4] For major banking organizations, the rules concerning what counts as a capital instrument are mainly relevant only at the holding company level because it is the holding company and not the bank that issues these instruments. Since capital requirements for holding companies are not currently determined by Basel, the Fed is not bound by these requirements in determining what qualifies as capital. In fact, the Fed's capital requirements for holding companies are more liberal. For example, the Fed permits cumulative perpetual preferred stock to count as Tier I capital (up to 25 percent of total Tier I capital) for holding companies, while excluding these instruments entirely (in accord with Basel) from capital for banks.

Tier I capital is primarily composed of equity, which is basically the value of assets minus the value of liabilities. If assets are overvalued (a common occurrence with bad loans of banks) the actual amount of equity may not equal the book value of equity. Such a situation is hard to avoid in the case of banks due to the lack of a market or fair valuation technique for most loans. Tier I capital includes earnings calculated on an ongoing basis. The present value of the earnings' stream (or market values of equity, which are often used to value companies) is not, however, used in defining capital.

Holders of qualifying non-cumulative perpetual preferred stock have no right to missed dividends, despite their priority over common stock holders. This type of stock is almost equivalent to equity insofar as it is a permanent (non-withdrawable) form of capital that is subordinated to creditors.

Goodwill, which some countries include in the definition and/or calculation of capital, is deducted from Tier I capital because it is hard to value and may be valueless in a crisis.

Tier II capital is less residual than Tier I. The inclusion of loan loss reserves in Tier II capital was the subject of a major debate among the countries. Although all of the countries eventually agreed to cap the loan loss reserves that could be treated as capital, some governments decided—and were permitted—to accept a higher limit than that adopted by the U.S. Loan loss reserves are supposed to be held to cover future unknown losses, not present losses. Present losses should be reflected in write-offs of assets or lower values of assets; the 1.25 percent figure for this type of loss was based on historical experience of loan losses.

Revaluation reserves also attracted great debate among the countries. The Accord permitted regulators to allow as Tier II capital up to 45 percent of unrealized appreciation of a bank's equities and real estate. Some governments, including Japan, did so from the start. The U.S. prohibited the

---

[4] Federal Reserve System, Capital Adequacy Guidelines for Bank Holding Companies, 12 C.F.R. §225, App. A (2004).

use of such reserves until 1998, when it permitted certain unrealized gains on equity securities to be calculated as Tier II capital. The importance of revaluation reserves depends on one's accounting system. When the Japanese allowed the 45 percent reserve, equities were mainly accounted for at historical cost, so capital could not include the value of the appreciation of the equities. While equities were generally prohibited to U.S. banks under the Glass-Steagall Act, under U.S. accounting rules equities that were actively traded were marked-to-market, thus giving U.S. banks the benefit of 100 percent of the appreciation as part of capital.

The fact that the Japanese were able to use revaluation reserves as part of capital, given their significant holdings of equities, resulted in devastating losses for these banks in the post-1990 period, when the Nikkei plunged in value.

Bank holding companies have searched for hybrid instruments that are sufficiently similar to equity to qualify as Tier I capital but at the same time sufficiently like bonds to let the issuer deduct for tax purposes payments made to investors as interest (note that dividends are not deductible).

In October 1996, the Fed classified as Tier I capital for bank holding companies (BHCs) new instruments with these features, called trust-preferred securities. Since that time approximately 820 BHCs have issued over $77 billion of these securities. Trust preferred are perpetual cumulative preferred securities issued out of a special purpose entity (SPE), usually in the form of a trust, in which the BHC owns all of the common stock. The Basel Committee agreed in October 1998 to a common definition for acceptable new capital instruments of this sort and limited them to 15 percent of Tier I capital. Recent revisions in the FASB rules for consolidation, Interpretation No. 46 (discussed in Chapters 12 and 15), could *prevent* the consolidation of the trust entity with the bank, thus putting in danger reliance on this form of capital. Accounting firms and their banks have taken different views in their 10-Qs of the effect of the Interpretation.[5] The Federal Reserve Board has recently adopted a rule that allows consolidation of trust preferred securities for capital requirements, whatever the FASB accounting treatment, with stricter quantitative limits and clearer qualitative standards.[6] The Board, however, will only apply the 15 percent Basel limitation to internationally active banks, not to banks that opt into advanced IRB. The latter would be subject to a 25 percent of Tier I capital limitation (this point will be better understood after reading the material below on implementation of Basel II by the United States).

---

[5] T. Davenport, "Split Decision: No 10-Q Trust-Preferred Consensus," *American Banker*, November 17, 2003.
[6] Federal Reserve System, "Final Rule, Risk-Based Capital Standards: Trust Preferred Securities and the Definition of Capital," March 4, 2005.

In addition to the risk-weight capital rules, U.S. bank regulators apply a simple rule that Tier I capital must equal 3 percent of assets for the highest-rated banks and of 4 percent of assets for all other banks.[7]

Special rules for U.S. branches of foreign banks required them to hold 5 percent of their liabilities in capital equivalency deposits. In 2002, U.S. regulators changed the rule to set the branches' capital using risk weights and reduced minimum capital from $3 million to $2 million. This reduced the capital burden for 52 banks' U.S. branches, by approximately $1.6 billion.[8]

Notes and Questions

1. Consider the components of Tier I capital. What do they have in common? Why are they included in Tier I rather than Tier II?

2. The 4 percent + 4 percent = 8 percent ratios were based on a 1987 "calibration" study that found that most banks could meet those requirements. Is this the best way to decide on the appropriate level of capital? By 1996, some regulators were wondering if the ratios were too low.

3. While the Basel Accord specifies that it applies only to international banks, many countries including the U.S. decided to apply the standards to all banks. Is this appropriate?

C. CREDIT RISK

1. RISK-WEIGHTING

As already discussed, the credit risk rules of Basel I require the risk-weighting of assets. This was implemented in the U.S. by the Federal Reserve Board as follows.

Table 7B
Summary of Risk Weights and Risk Categories

"Category 1: Zero percent

1. Cash (domestic and foreign) held in the bank or in transit

2. Balances due from Federal Reserve Banks (including Federal Reserve Bank stock) and central banks in other OECD countries

3. Direct claims on, and the portions of claims that are unconditionally guaranteed by, the U.S. Treasury and U.S. Government agencies and the central governments of other OECD countries, and local currency claims on, and the portions of local currency claims that are unconditionally guaranteed by, the central governments of non-OECD countries (including the central banks of

---

[7] 62 Federal Register 55692 (1997).
[8] 67 Federal Register 41619 (2002).

non-OECD countries), to the extent that the bank has liabilities booked in that currency

4. Gold bullion held in the bank's vaults or in another's vaults on an allocated basis, to the extent offset by gold bullion liabilities

5. Claims collateralized by cash on deposit in the bank or by securities issued or guaranteed by OECD central governments or U.S. government agencies for which a positive margin of collateral is maintained on a daily basis, fully taking into account any change in the bank's exposure to the obligor or counterparty under a claim in relation to the market value of the collateral held in support of that claim

Category 2: 20 percent

1. Cash items in the process of collection

2. All claims (long- or short-term) on, and the portions of claims (long- or short-term) that are guaranteed by, U.S. depository institutions and OECD banks

3. Short-term claims (remaining maturity of one year or less) on, and the portions of short-term claims that are guaranteed by, non-OECD banks

4. The portions of claims that are conditionally guaranteed by the central governments of OECD countries and U.S. government agencies, and the portions of local currency claims that are conditionally guaranteed by the central governments of non-OECD countries, to the extent that the bank has liabilities booked in that currency

5. Claims on, and the portions of claims that are guaranteed by U.S. government-sponsored agencies

6. General obligation claims on, and the portions of claims that are guaranteed by the full faith and credit of, local governments and political subdivisions of the U.S. and other OECD local governments

7. Claims on, and the portions of claims that are guaranteed by, official multilateral lending institutions or regional development banks

8. The portions of claims that are collateralized by cash on deposit in the bank or by securities issued or guaranteed by the U.S. Treasury, the central governments of other OECD countries, and U.S. government agencies that do not qualify for the zero percent risk-weight category, or that are collateralized by securities issued or guaranteed by U.S. government sponsored agencies.

9. The portions of claims that are collateralized by securities issued by official multilateral lending institutions or regional development banks

10.   Certain privately-issued securities representing indirect ownership of mortgage-backed U.S. government agency or U.S. government-sponsored agency securities

11.   Investments in shares of a fund whose portfolio is permitted to hold only securities that would qualify for the zero or 20 percent risk categories

Category 3: 50 percent

1. Loans fully secured by first liens on one- to four-family residential properties on multi-family residential properties that have been made in accordance with prudent underwriting standards, that are performing in accordance with their original terms, that are not past due or in nonaccrual status, and that meet other qualifying criteria, and certain privately-issued mortgage-backed securities representing indirect ownership of such loans. (Loans made for speculative purposes are excluded.)

2. Revenue bonds or similar claims that are obligations of U.S. state or local governments, or other OECD local governments, but for which the government entity is committed to repay the debt only out of revenues from the facilities financed

3. Credit equivalent amounts of interest rate and foreign exchange rate related contracts, except for those assigned to a lower risk category

Category 4: 100 percent

1. All other claims on private obligors.

2. Claims on, or guaranteed by, non-OECD foreign banks with a remaining maturity exceeding one year

3. Claims on, or guaranteed by, non-OECD central governments that are not included in item 3 of Category 1 or item 4 of Category 2; all claims on non-OECD state or local governments

4. Obligations issued by U.S. state or local governments, or other OECD local governments (including industrial development authorities and similar entities), repayable solely by a private party or enterprise

5. Premises, plant, and equipment; other fixed assets; and other real estate owned

6. Investments in any unconsolidated subsidiaries, joint ventures, or associated companies—if not deducted from capital

7. Instruments issued by other banking organizations that qualify as capital—if not deducted from capital

8. Claims on commercial firms owned by a government.

9. All other assets, including any intangible assets that are not deducted from capital."

The basic idea of risk weighting assets is that less risky assets require less capital to protect against loss than do riskier assets.

Note that the members of the OECD are Australia, Austria, Belgium, Canada, the Czech Republic, Denmark, Finland, France, Germany, Greece, Hungary, Iceland, Ireland, Italy, Japan, Korea, Luxembourg, Mexico, the Netherlands, New Zealand, Norway, Poland, Portugal, Spain, Sweden, Switzerland, Turkey, the United Kingdom, and the United States. It is obviously a great over-simplification to regard all of these countries, or their banks, as having the same credit risk.

There is also an element of credit allocation in the ratings, as reflected in the 50 percent risk-weight for residential mortgages. The U.S. reportedly insisted on this break given the importance of these loans to the banking system. Completely secured commercial loans carry a 100 percent risk-weight.

All private credits are risk-weighted the same, 100 percent. This is a major distortion of reality as these credits cover a wide range of risks, as reflected in credit ratings of public companies.

In April 1998, the Basel Committee changed the risk weight for loans to OECD securities firms. If the securities firms were subject to capital adequacy rules "comparable to" those in Basel for banks, then banks lending to those securities firms could weight the loan at 20 percent rather than 100 percent.[9]

A later amendment addressed the original rule's provision that allowed OECD supervisors to permit domestic banks lending to a domestic public sector entity (other than the central bank) to assign a risk weight from 0 percent to 10 percent, whereas foreign banks lending to the same entities would have to hold capital for a 20 percent risk-weight because the borrower was a public entity in another country. In September 2001, the Basel Committee announced that if an OECD supervisor allows a 0-10 percent risk weight for domestic public sector entities, foreign supervisors may let their banks use the same 0-10 percent weight when lending to those entities. This would level the playing field.[10]

During the mid-1990s, dissatisfaction with the Basel Accord's credit risk standards mounted. A study by the Federal Reserve Bank of Boston said

---

[9] See Basel Committee on Banking Supervision, Amendment to the Capital Accord, April 1998.
[10] Basel Committee Newsletter No. 2 (September 2001).

that capital ratios did not help regulators identify problem banks. By late 1996, the Chairman and Vice Chairman of the Federal Reserve System were both suggesting that the credit risk standards were too simplistic, and that banks were engaging in "regulatory capital arbitrage." Two simple examples were the incentive to hold investments in U.S. government debt with 0 percent risk-weight rather than loans to private sector firms with a 100 percent risk-weight, and to lend to riskier borrowers at a 100 percent risk-weight rather than to less risky borrowers with the same risk-weight.

Notes and Questions

1.   The basic idea of risk weighting assets is that less risky assets require less capital to protect against loss than do riskier assets. How could one do this better than the drafters?

2.   To what extent should national regulators add stricter capital requirements? Banks with subprime lending programs needed to set aside much more capital than would otherwise be required, according to U.S. supervisors in 2001. Subprime borrowers "have weakened credit histories that include payment delinquencies, and possibly more severe problems such as charge-offs, judgments, and bankruptcies." The higher risk inherent in these programs meant that an institutions should hold capital 1.5 to 3 times higher than that required for similar assets that were not subprime. This guidance applies to pools of such assets, not isolated loans. It would not apply if the loans are well secured and the borrowers only slightly below prime. On the other hand, the supervisors recognized that in some cases the capital might have to reach even 100 percent of the loans outstanding. The extent of additional capital would be up to the bank examiner.[11]

2.   OFF-BALANCE SHEET (OBS) ITEMS

Before the Basel Accord, capital adequacy referred to the level of capital relative to loans and other assets carried on a bank's balance sheet. During the early 1980s, however, commercial banks sought more business for which they could charge fees without generating liabilities or assets. The Basel I rules required that capital be held against these OBS items. The Federal Reserve Board implemented these requirements as follows.

---

[11] OCC, Board of Governors of the Federal Reserve System, FDIC, and Office of Thrift Supervision, *Expanded Guidance for Subprime Lending Programs,* January 31, 2001.

Table 7C
Credit-Conversion Factors for Off–Balance Sheet Items
for State Member Banks

100 percent Conversion Factor

1. Direct credit substitutes. (These include general guarantees of indebtedness and all guarantee-type instruments, including standby letters of credit backing the financial obligations of other parties.)

2. Risk participations in bankers' acceptances and direct credit substitutes, such as standby letters of credit.

3. Sale and repurchase agreements and assets sold with recourse that are not included on the balance sheet.

4. Forward agreements to purchase assets, including financing facilities, on which drawdown is certain.

5. Securities lent for which the bank is at risk.

50 percent Conversion Factor

1. Transaction-related contingencies. (These include bid bonds, performance bonds, warranties, and standby letters of credit backing the nonfinancial performance of other parties.)

2. Unused portions of commitments with an original maturity exceeding one year, including underwriting commitments and commercial credit lines.

3. Revolving underwriting facilities (RUFs), note issuance facilities (NIFs), and similar arrangements.

20 percent Conversion Factor

Short-term, self-liquidating trade-related contingencies, including commercial letters of credit.

Zero percent Conversion Factor

Unused portions of commitments with an original maturity of one year or less, or which are unconditionally cancelable at any time, provided a separate credit decision is made before each drawing.

Conversion works as follows. Assume a bank has a stand-by trade letter of credit of 100. This may be converted to the balance sheet at 50 percent, producing an asset of 50. This asset would be risk-weighted according to the risk weight of the obligor, i.e. 100 percent for a private company, or 0 percent for an OECD government.

The basic idea behind each conversion factor is that the more an item is likely to be called and the greater the risk that the counterparty will be unable to pay, the closer it is to an asset and the higher the conversion factor should be.

3.   THE EFFECT OF THE CREDIT RISK RULES

a.   THE ACCORD AND THE CREDIT CRUNCH

As the Basel Accord became final in 1992, a slowdown in bank lending seemed to be creating or intensifying a recession in the U.S. and other industrial countries. According to critics, the Accord contributed to the slowdown.

The major problem in this regard was that the Accord encouraged banks to invest in government bonds (with zero risk weight and therefore no capital cost) rather than lend to commercial and consumer borrowers subject to as much as 8 percent capital. One study found that between 1989 and 1992, regulators "scrutinized lending standards and loan holdings more rigorously causing banks to ration credit ... [which] resulted in banks reducing their holdings of loans and increasing their holdings of government securities."[12]

However, many studies of the capital rules and credit crunch have not found a simple causal relationship.[13] One study concluded that banks not subject to formal action by their regulator do not quickly shrink their assets to satisfy capital requirements and that when they do reduce assets it is through the sale of existing assets rather than by cutting off existing customers.[14]

b.   TOWARD A MORE LEVEL INTERNATIONAL PLAYING FIELD

An important goal of the Accord was to level the playing field so that no government could give its banks a competitive advantage over other countries' banks by setting low capital adequacy rules. It is highly doubtful that the Accord has accomplished this objective.

1.   LIMITS OF THE ACCORD: THE U.S. AND JAPAN

Analysis of the competitive effect of the Accord across many countries is thwarted by the many factors that shape international competition. A comparison of Japan and the United States by H. Scott and S. Iwahara revealed the power of these factors.[15] They argue that comparative advantage,

---

[12] J Wagster, "The Basel Accord of 1988 and the International Credit Crunch of 1989-1992," Journal of Financial Services Research (1999), pp. 123–93.

[13] See S. Sharpe, "Bank Capitalization, Regulation, and the Credit Crunch: A Critical Review of the Research Findings," Federal Reserve Board Finance and Economics Discussion Series 95-20 (1995).

[14] See J. Peek and E. Rosengren, "Bank Regulation and the Credit Crunch," 19 Journal of Banking and Finance (1995), p. 679.

[15] H. Scott and S. Iwahara, "In Search of a Level Playing Field: The Implementation of the Basel Capital Accord in Japan and the United States" 1-11 Group of Thirty Occasional Paper 46 (1994) (Scott-Iwahara)

accounting, tax and legal rules, and government safety nets have a much greater effect on competitive advantage among banks than did capital ratios.

Scott and Iwahara found that the stronger Japanese safety net had a substantial impact on capital ratios. They found that the capital on the books of the 10 largest Japanese banks in 1993 was substantially lower than that of the top 10 U.S. banks: 9.67 percent and 13.60 percent of assets for Japanese and U.S. banks, respectively. Japanese banks could hold lower levels of capital than U.S. banks because they enjoyed a more ironclad safety net.[16]

2.   THE EFFECT OF THE JAPANESE BANKING CRISIS

Since the early 1990s, Japan's banks and the Japanese financial system generally have faced a deepening crisis. From late 1997, observers argued that many big Japanese banks probably held negative capital. Yet Japanese banks continued to report capital in excess of the 8 percent minimum requirement. They could do so because the regulators allowed them to include as capital deferred tax assets (potential tax credits over the next five years which might never be used if the banks do not generate future profits) and public funds (preferred shares held by the government that the banks are expected to repay later). Big Japanese banks hold over 50 percent Tier I capital in deferred tax assets alone. U.S. and European banks, in comparison, hold just 10 percent in both types of assets.

3.   THE NEW BASEL ACCORD—BASEL II

The Basel Committee has sought since early 1999 to amend the original Accord. After a lengthy process, full of much debate, the Basel Committee adopted the new rules in June 2004.[17] The standardized and foundation IRB approaches will be implemented from year-end 2006, but the advanced approaches (apparently including those for operational risk, discussed below) will be implemented a year later. The Basel Committee did not preclude further changes in the advanced version as a result of the year delay. It appears that Basel II may be more like Basel 2.0 (in software language) to be continuously updated by later "releases."

Under Basel II, the Committee adopted three pillars of bank capital regulation. The first pillar is the minimum regulatory capital charge. Pillar 2 is supervisory review, which encourages supervisors to assess banks' internal approaches to capital allocation, internal assessments of capital adequacy,

---

[16] See also V. Acharya, "Is the International Convergence of Capital Adequacy Regulation Desirable?" (2003) LVIII J. of Finance, pp. 2745-2781. ("The lack of complementary variation between minimum bank capital requirements and regulatory forbearance leads to a spillover from more forbearing to less forbearing economies and reduces the competitive advantage of banks in less forbearing economies." p. 2745)

[17] Basel Committee on Banking Supervision, International Convergence of Capital Measurement and Capital Standards (June 2004). The U.K. has been pushing to put implementation off until the end of 2007. Global Risk Regulator, Breaking News Service, October 8, 2004.

and (subject to national discretion) provides an opportunity for the supervisor to indicate where such approaches do not appear sufficient.

The third pillar recognizes that market discipline has the potential to reinforce capital regulation and other supervisory efforts to ensure the safety and soundness of the banking system. Thus, the Committee has adopted a wide range of disclosure initiatives designed to make the risk and capital positions of a bank more transparent. The new requirements are to apply to bank holding companies (which is already the case in the U.S.) as well as banks.

Pillar 1 is the major focus of this Chapter. It consists of three different approaches to determine capital for credit risk, with increasing levels of required sophistication: the standardized approach; the foundation Internal Ratings-Based Approach (F-IRB); and the advanced Internal Ratings-Based Approach (A-IRB).

a.   THE STANDARDIZED APPROACH

The Committee replaced the four Basel I risk weight categories with a more complex set, in what it calls the *standardized approach*. This approach would allow banks to use external credit assessments by rating agencies in order to weight the risk of loans to borrowers in certain classes. The Committee used Standard & Poor's classifications as an example and said that other rating agencies could also be used if their standards met such criteria as objectivity, independence, and transparency. The Committee recognized that the rating agencies had a mixed track record identifying high risk companies and were slow to change ratings.

For sovereigns and central banks, only the highest rated (AAA to AA-) would be given a zero risk weight. The Committee adopted a 20 percent risk weight for sovereigns rated A+ to A-, 50 percent for those rated BBB+ to BBB-, 100 percent for those rated BB+ to B-, and 150 percent for those below B-. The Committee devised special rules for claims on non-central government public sector entities and multilateral development banks.

For loans to banks, the Committee adopted two options. One was to give the bank a risk weight that was (in most cases) one category less favorable than that of the sovereign of the bank's home country (i.e. if the sovereign was weighted 20 percent, the bank would be weighted 50 percent). The risk weight for the loan to the bank would be 20 percent (if the sovereign's rating were AAA to AA-), 50 percent (A+ to A-), 100 percent (BBB+ to BBB- and BB+ to B-), and 150 percent (below B-). The second option uses ratings issued by a qualifying rating agency. Most banks would be weighted 50 percent, but AAA to AA- banks would be weighted 20 percent, BB+ to B- would be weighted 100 percent, and below B- weighted 150 percent. For credits of 3 months or less, the rates would be reduced by one rating category, subject to a floor of 20 percent and a ceiling of 150 percent (below B-).

Claims on securities firms receive the same treatment as banks if the firms were comparably regulated and subject to the new Basel Rules, i.e. like EU securities firms. Otherwise, they would be treated as corporates.

For loans to corporate borrowers, those borrowers rated AAA to AA- are weighted at 20 percent, A+ to A- at 50 percent, BBB+ to BB- at 100 percent, and below BB- at 150 percent.

Unrated borrowers are weighted at 100 percent, with the exception that the weight would be 50 percent for the second option in loans to banks. This result has the perverse effect of giving an incentive to some borrowers to remain unrated, in order to get a 100 percent (rather than 150 percent) risk weight.

Past-due unsecured loans with provisions less than 20 percent of their value are assigned a 150 percent risk weight.

Retail exposures receive special treatment under Basel II. The risk weight for residential mortgages dropped to 35 percent, although loans secured by commercial real estate kept their 100 percent weight. Other retail exposures in diversified portfolios have risk weights below unrated corporate exposures. Loans to small and medium-sized businesses can also receive retail weights.

Off-balance sheet items were assigned credit conversion factors similar to those applicable under Basel I.

The Committee has devised a complex set of rules to assess the impact on capital requirements of credit risk mitigants, such as collateral (including most types of financial instruments), derivatives, guarantees (by all firms meeting a threshold credit rating), and netting. For collateral, capital mitigation first depends on legal certainty about the right of the bank to realize on the collateral. There is a simple and comprehensive approach for collateral. Under the simple approach, banks would substitute the risk-weighting of eligible collateral for the risk-weighting of the counterparty (generally subject to a 20 percent floor). Alternatively, banks can use the comprehensive approach which allows a fuller offset of eligible collateral against exposures by effectively reducing the exposure amount by the value ascribed to the collateral. This requires the banks to follow various guidelines for calculating the value of the exposure and the value of the collateral. Basic guidelines are set forth for other credit risk mitigants, but national supervisors are granted discretion within such guidelines.

Under the present Basel Accord and Basel II, there is substantial concern about whether the standardized methodology gets things right.

Several studies have suggested that Basel requires too much capital for good risks and too little for poor ones.[18]

b.   THE INTERNAL RATINGS-BASED APPROACH

An alternative to the standardized approach for sophisticated banks is the internal ratings-based (IRB) approach. There are two variations of the IRB, the foundation IRB (F-IRB) and the advanced IRB (A-IRB). A-IRB is intended to be used only by the most sophisticated banks; the bank supervisor would assess the breadth and quality of the bank's system for rating credit risk of individual loans before permitting use of this approach. Bank supervisors would need to check the number of gradations of risk, the link between the rating scale and measurable loss (i.e. does the bank's internal rating scale take recovery rates into account), the range of risk factors, the clarity of the bank's criteria, and the usefulness of historical data.

The "foundation" IRB approach requires few direct inputs by banks. Banks must estimate the probability of default (PD) for each grade of asset, but otherwise use the supervisory parameters for the other key inputs. Generally under A-IRB, the banks can use their own internal assessment for all inputs in calculating their regulatory capital requirements.

There are four inputs that are needed under both the foundation and advanced IRB approaches. These inputs are different for wholesale and retail exposures. The first input is the probability of default (PD) of a borrower. Under A-IRB, for wholesale exposures the general minimum PD (except for sovereigns and similar entities) is three basis points, with an adjustment for asset correlation. The second input is the estimated loss severity for each exposure (LGD), defined as the amount that the bank will lose if there is a default. This input factor takes into account collateral and guarantees. The final two elements are the exposure at default (EAD), defined as how much of the loan is still outstanding, and its remaining maturity (M). LGD, EAD and M are provided by supervisors in the foundation IRB approach, but in the advanced IRB approach banks are expected to provide LGD and EAD, and must provide M (subject to supervisory review and validation). For each exposure, the risk weight is a function of PD, LGD, and M.

The retail exposure category encompasses the majority of credit exposures to individuals. There are three categories: (1) residential mortgages; (2) qualifying revolving exposures, i.e. credit lines; and (3) other exposures, i.e. auto loans. Unlike wholesale exposures, retail exposures are risk-weighted in pools rather than on an individual basis. As with wholesale exposures, for retail exposures there would be a 3 basis point minimum for PD under A-IRB and a 10 percent LGD minimum for most residential

---

[18] See M. Crouhy, D. Galai, and R. Mark, "The Use of Internal Models: Comparison of the New Basel Credit Accord with Available Internal Models for Credit Risk," in H. Scott ed., *Capital Adequacy Beyond Basel: Banking, Securities, and Insurance* (2004). (Scott-Capital)

mortgages. Under the A-IRB approach, capital is based on an evaluation of possible losses over a one-year time horizon, with a confidence level of 99.9 percent.

After the bank determines the PDs and LGDs for all applicable exposures, those inputs can be mapped onto regulatory risk weights through a complicated formula. The risk weights are calibrated to include coverage for both expected and unexpected losses. Unexpected loss is a probability-based assessment of the losses that would occur under severe stress conditions. The risk weights are expressed as a continuous function, which provides maximum risk sensitivity and flexibility in accommodating diverse bank risk rating systems.

If a bank has a high degree of single-borrower or single-group credit risk concentrations (a "non-granular" portfolio) within its non-retail credit portfolios, the bank would be required to increase its regulatory capital minimum by a specified granularity adjustment. The adjustment would result in a reduction in capital for a bank with a relatively low degree of single-borrower risk.

The IRB Approaches sets special rules for credit risk mitigants and loan loss provisions. The use of collateral, guarantees, and other credit risk mitigants is reflected in the LGD values set forth by the Committee for IRB banks. This makes sense since these safeguards should affect loss given default. Basel defines eligible collateral (i.e. that which is allowed in the Standardized Approach, plus receivables, specified real estate, and other types of collateral that meet listed criteria), specifies the methodology to recognize it, and describes some exceptions. IRB banks may apply the credit risk mitigants to their calculation of either LGD or PD. Credit derivatives with payouts not triggered by restructuring may still mitigate risk if the bank has full control over restructuring the underlying obligation.

The allowance for loan and lease losses that cannot be included in Tier II capital (for which the limit is 1.25 percent of assets), can be used to offset expected loss under the A-IRB approach. Basel II would also permit favorable treatment of partial charge-offs potentially requiring no capital against the remaining portion of the exposure; however, the U.S. would impose a charge.

The IRB approach produces a statistical measurement of both the unexpected losses and expected losses that banks face in relation to their credit risk. Contrary to its initial proposals, the Basel Committee, as a result of U.S. objections, only requires capital against the unexpected losses. However, the Committee also has provided that any shortfalls between expected losses and actual reserves will result in deductions from capital, with 50 percent coming from both Tier I and Tier II. Excess provisions would be eligible as capital, up to 20 percent of Tier II capital. This requirement directly affects the definition of capital, a matter which the Basel Committee has otherwise avoided in Basel II.[19]

c.   IMPACT OF BASEL II ON BANK CAPITAL RATIOS

Throughout the Basel II process, the question lurking in the background was what the impact of the new rules would be on the overall capital ratios of banks. The Committee tried to gauge the impact of their rules on international banks in a 2003 Quantitative Impact Study (QIS3), based on data from 186 banks from G10 countries and 177 banks from 30 other countries. All EU countries were represented. The Committee divided the banks into large international (Group 1) and smaller more specialized (Group 2). The overall finding of QIS3 was that, compared to the capital rules applied of Basel I, Basel II would substantially reduce the capital required for retail assets of most banks, because Basel II lowered the risk weights for retail assets. Basel II's new charge for operational risk (discussed later), however, would more than offset this reduction for banks applying the standardized approach (but not the other approaches). Banks whose required capital would rise most under Basel II were the large banks in G10 countries; according to QIS3 capital would rise an average of 11 percent for those using the standardized approach and 3 percent for those using the F-IRB Approach. Retail is a relatively smaller business for these banks; hence they do not benefit as much from retail exposures' reduced risk weights. However, the large retail G-10 banks are likely to use the A-IRB Approach; when this approach was applied to them, their overall capital charge fell an average of 2 percent.

The methodology of QIS3 was widely criticized. For example, Andrew Kuritzkes, a leading consultant on these issues, said that applying the Basel II standards to the asset mix of typical large U.S. banks would reduce these banks' required capital by an average of 10 percent to 15 percent below the 8 percent now required under Basel I.[20] A 2003 FDIC study showed that Basel II would produce substantial reductions in capital for U.S. banks. Whereas QIS3 showed a 17 percent reduction in credit risk at U.S. banks, FDIC believed the reduction to be much greater if historical credit losses were used rather than the credit loss assumptions used by banks in submitting QIS3 data. Indeed, the FDIC believed some banks' capital could be so low as to trigger regulatory intervention under prompt corrective action. This view was disputed by other U.S. federal agencies.

As a result of the continuing controversy, U.S. banking agencies, as did the U.K. Financial Services Authority (FSA), conducted a fourth

---

[19] Basel Committee, Press Release, October 11, 2003, Attachment. These proposals were further elaborated in Basel Committee, Modifications to the Treatment for Expected and Unexpected Loss in the New Basel Accord, January 30, 2004.
[20] R. Garver, "Basel Rules Seen Lowering Requirements up to 15 Percent," *American Banker*, May 6, 2003.

quantitative impact study, QIS4. The U.S. study was conducted on the largest banks that would be subject to advanced IRB, as these were the only U.S. banks that would be subject to Basel II (see discussion below on U.S. implementation). QIS4, completed in 2005, showed that capital levels at some banks would rise by 50 percent and drop at others by 50 percent. At half the banks, capital levels would drop 26 percent.[21] These results resulted in Congressional hearings and calls for delay in implementing Basel II (scheduled for 2008 in the U.S.). It did result in a delay by the federal agencies in issuing their guidelines to U.S. banks for implementing Basel II while they looked into why Basel II would have the impact found in QIS4. As of this writing, the results of QIS4 have not been released publicly.

d.   HOLDING COMPANY CAPITAL

Basel II also requires that its rules be applied at the holding company level on a consolidated basis. This requirement has been controversial for a number of reasons.

Holding companies include insurance and securities affiliates to whom it may not be appropriate to apply the Basel bank-concentric capital rules. Basel recognizes this in part by not consolidating insurance; instead, it requires the holding company to deduct its entire insurance-related investment. This approach wrongfully assumes that the investment has no value—even where an insurance company may have an ascertainable market value. The deduction approach implicitly risk-weights the insurance subsidiary's assets at 1250 percent, which is often a highly indefensible position.[22]

In theory it would make sense to apply capital requirements *only* at the holding company level, based on different methodologies for different businesses. This is what financial institutions' own economic models do. However, from a regulatory perspective, this would require cross-guarantees among all holding company units (i.e. treating the entire enterprise as one unit). Bank regulators are very unlikely to agree to that.

e.   IMPLEMENTATION OF BASEL II

Regulators have responded to Basel II with different degrees of enthusiasm. The EU has indicated that it will apply Basel II to all of its banks. The U.S., however, made a major change in policy. The Fed announced that it would only require the top 10 banks—those with over $250 billion or more of commercial banking assets or a total on-balance sheet foreign exposure of $10 billion or more—to use A-IRB, and expected that another 10 banks would voluntarily seek to use A-IRB. Combined, these

---

[21] D. Paletta, "Whither Basel II? Regulators Spar; Lawmakers Fume," *American* Banker, May 12, 2005.

[22] See H. Scott, "Introduction: Looking Beyond Basel," in Scott-Capital, supra note 18.

banks accounted for two-thirds of the international activity of U.S. banks and were generally the ones with which banks from other countries would compete in world markets. All other U.S. banks (approximately 8,000 in total) would continue to adhere to Basel I, unless they chose to use Basel II's A-IRB, and qualified for it (an unlikely event).[23] Thus, while the EU would apply the standardized or F-IRB approach to most of its banks, these two "command-style" regulations would apply to no U.S. banks. The U.S. position was set out in a notice of advanced rule-making (ANPR) by the U.S. regulatory agencies on July 3, 2003. As discussed above, as of May 2005, these rules had not yet been issued while regulators contemplated the results of QIS4.

One study found that Basel I banks would be at a competitive disadvantage to Basel II banks with respect to loans to small-to-medium enterprises (SME loan).[24] Another study, by former Fed economists, predicts that residential mortgage portfolio capital levels will drop so significantly at the 20 or so banks that adopt Basel II that they will hold a major competitive advantage over the other 7000 banks and thrifts that do not adopt Basel II. They predicted that non-adopting banks would lose $1 billion per year in net income due to a reduction of their share of the market and the reduced price they earn on such investments.[25] Mainly as a result of the concerns of smaller banks, U.S. regulators now contemplate some major revisions in Basel I. Since these will not be Basel II, perhaps they will be called Basel IA.[26]

It is expected that more than 100 countries (including India and China), prompted by similar reasons for adopting Basel I, will adopt Basel II. This compares with the 120 that adopted Basel I. It is difficult to assess what this means, given that the U.S. believed that the standardized rules of Basel II—which would be appropriate for most banks in the world—were deemed too complicated for U.S. banks. Competitive effects in Europe have led many

---

[23] R. Ferguson Jr., Vice Chairman of the Federal Reserve Board, "Concerns and Considerations for the Practical Implementation of the New Basel Accord," remarks at ICBI Risk Management 2003 Conference, December 2, 2003. (Ferguson)

[24] A. Berger, "Potential Competitive Effects of Basel II on Banks in SME Credit Markets in the United States," Federal Reserve Board Finance and Economics Discussion Series Working Paper 2004-12 (February 2004).

[25] P. Calem and J. Follain, "An Examination of How the Proposed Bifurcated Implementation of Basel II in the U.S. May Affect Competition Among Banking Organizations for Residential Mortgages," paper presented at the 2005 AREUEA Meetings, January 14, 2005. This has been disputed, however, by several Federal Reserve Board economists in a report issued on April 11, 2005. In their view, large banks would gain at the expense of the GSEs not smaller banks. D. Hancock, A. Lehnert, W. Passmore, and S. Sherlund, "An Analysis of the Potential Competitive Impacts of Basel II Capital Standards on U.S. Mortgage Rates and Mortgage Securitization" (April 2005). These findings have been refuted by the former Fed economists, P. Calem and J. Follain, "The Potential Competitive Impacts of Basel II in the U.S. Market for Residential Mortgages," statement before the U.S. House of Representatives Subcommittees on Financial Institutions and Consumer Credit and on Domestic and International Monetary Policy (May 11, 2005).

[26] Global Risk Regulator, "U.S. Plans to Offset Basel II Effects on Small Banks," March 11, 2005.

banks to apply for Advanced IRB; for example, 47 in Germany alone. It is doubtful, however, whether all of these banks are actually qualified, in terms of technology and technical expertise. Since Europe is applying Basel II to all banks, any differential competitive impact of the three levels of Basel II will be difficult to address.

Many banks have criticized the rules as getting risk wrong for particular transactions and being too complicated.[27] Standard & Poor's has articulated an additional concern; it is worried that Basel is placing too much reliance on banks' internal ratings under the IRB approach and has stated that it may downgrade banks that stringently follow Basel II.[28]

f.   TRADING BOOK PROPOSALS

Even after the final Basel II rules were issued in June 2004, the Basel Committee continued work on some technical issues that could have major impact on bank capital. In April 2005, the Committee issued a new Consultative Document dealing with these issues, "The Application of Basel II to Trading Activities and the Treatment of Double Default Effects." Two of the proposed rules related mainly to derivatives—how to deal with capital requirements for counterparty risk and credit default swaps (the double default problem)—and they are discussed in Chapter 15. Another proposal deals with capital requirements for unsettled and failed trades—and it is discussed in Chapter 10. Also, a proposal was issued to define what constituted the "trading book" rather than the "banking book" given that different capital requirements applied to assets carried on these two books. This issue is discussed below under Market Risk.

g.   CRITICISM OF BASEL II

Consultative Paper 2 (CP2), which preceded Consultative Paper 3 (CP3), the last proposal before the adoption of Basel II, incorporated most of the basic principles in Basel II. CP2 was the focal point for debate over these principles. The general complaint among bankers and scholars was that CP2 imposed increasingly complicated layers of rules on very different players in highly diverse markets.

One of the most comprehensive responses to CP2 came from the Shadow Financial Regulatory Committee (SFRC), which consists of U.S.-based scholars in law, finance, and economics (including this author). The SFRC argued that, given the weak state of knowledge and practice, no single formula could "provide a credible and robust measure of capital adequacy."[29]

---

[27] See i.e. C. Pretzlik, "Proposed Bank Rules Raise Fears for Capital Markets," *Financial Times*, August 11, 2003.

[28] See i.e. C. Pretzlik, "S&P Threatens Downgrades on Basel II Rules," *Financial Times*, August 27, 2003.

[29] SFRC, Statement No. 169, "The Basel Committee's Revised Capital Accord Proposal" February 26, 2001, p. 1.

Rather than creating a level playing field with common rules, the Basel II could make things worse. Applying the four methodologies—Basel I rules, the standardized approach, F-IRB, and A-IRB—together would generate great confusion and leaves supervisors with much more discretion than Basel I, risking serious non-uniform application of the rules. By applying the rules only to banks (as Basel does) and not to securities firms, Basel II adds to the competitive inequality between the two groups.

1.   STANDARDIZED APPROACH

Critics of the standardized approach pointed out that the CP2 still relied on risk weights that were arbitrary and failed to differentiate enough among types of credit quality. For example, one analyst calculated a range of "appropriate" capital given the performance of differently rated issuers and found a low of 1.4 percent for AAA issuers up to a high of 17 percent for those rated below B-. This contrasts with the range of 1.6 percent to 12 percent for the standardized approach.[30] These risks weights were also inconsistent. For example, borrowers with the same external ratings may receive different risk weights from Basel II depending on whether they are corporations, foreign governments, or agencies, and whether the credit is a loan or securitized.[31]

In addition the standardized approach ignores the impact of diversification, treating one $100 million loan to a single borrower the same as 100 $1 million loans. It may also rely too much on private rating agencies. Even in the U.S., most banks hold portfolios in which only a small portion of loans is rated by agencies, and rating agencies played an even smaller role in the public markets of many other industrial countries. In addition, a conflict of interest exists because the issuers (borrowers) pay the rating agencies' fees.

2.   IRB APPROACH

Wrong parameters

The IRB approach has also attracted criticism on many counts. First, critics have said that the concept of loss is narrow. B. Hirtle, M. Levonian, M. Saidenberg, S. Walter, and D. Wright[32] identify two approaches to defining loss. One approach used by Basel, is to define loss as default. A second approach, now used by banks and much more nuanced, is to define loss as either default or a reduction in credit quality, as when a loan becomes riskier and must be shifted to a lower credit category that would require a higher

---

[30] See H. Jackson, "The Role of Credit Rating Agencies in the Establishment of Capital Standards for Financial Institutions in a Global Economy," in *The Challenges Facing Financial Regulation 311* (E. Ferran & C. Goodhart, eds, 2001).

[31] "Bankers Snub Changes to Basel Accord, Particularly Use of External Rating Systems," 74 Banking Report (April 10, 2000).

[32] "Using Credit Risk Models for Regulatory Capital: Issues and Options," Federal Reserve Bank of New York Economic Policy Review (March 2001), p. 19.

return. A bank that cannot receive that return has a loss. However, by using a simple default/no default concept of loss for each credit classification, Basel II does not take into account losses that arise as credits migrate from one category to another.

Second, the time horizon for loss is short. Hirtle et al.[33] identify three approaches to setting an appropriate time horizon. First, one may look at a single year as the period in which to estimate the risk of loss. This is the industry practice, according to Hirtle, and is used by Basel II. Second, other periods, usually longer, could be set. Third, a bank might set the time horizon as the remaining life of each loan. This would most accurately reflect the length of exposure for most commercial banks.

A final criticism of Basel II is that the parameters are general, not tailored to the needs of different jurisdictions. Any set of rules that is proposed for adoption by many countries must take into account the way differences in local law and financial practice would affect the implementation of the proposed rules. Of particular concern is the fact that the Basel II does not take account of the relation between internal ratings and laws dealing with bankruptcy and accounting.

Weak implementation by banks and regulators

The Committee leaves national regulators much more discretion than under Basel I. Of particular concern is the fact that regulators can decide whether banks in their countries qualify for either of the IRB approaches.

Political decisions and credit allocation

The Basel Committee's approach is a product of political compromises. When the German government warned that it would oppose earlier proposals because they would limit lending to small and medium sized businesses that depend largely on banks for funds, the Basel Committee made special rules reducing capital for such loans.[34]

Micromanagement

Overall the Basel Committee micromanaged the scope and application of the IRB Approach. This is particularly true for the F-IRB Approach, which at least in the early years would apply to most if not all banks. For almost every problem it considers, Basel II sets out how a bank is to implement the rule. It decides the categories banks must use to group credits in their portfolio (sovereign, corporate, etc.). It sets a one year probability of default for each borrower grade, then sets a 0.03 percent floor (excepting sovereign credits). When estimating LGD, a bank using the F-IRB approach is mandated specific rates that it must use. For example, under F-IRB, a bank would have to assume a 50 percent LGD for senior corporate

---

[33] *ibid.*
[34] H. Simonian, P. Ehrlich, and J. Willman, "Germans Warn over Banking Capital Rules," *Financial Times*, November 1, 2001.

claims lacking collateral. When collateral exists, the Committee specifies the methodologies to calculate LGD.

h.   INTERNAL CREDIT MODELS

Basel II does not permit banks to employ their own internal credit models. Basel's IRB Approach rejects analysis of the credit risk of the portfolio as a whole, which is key to the internal models for credit risk that banks use today. The idea is that risks of credits in the portfolio are correlated to different degrees, i.e. that a diversified portfolio would have less risk than a less diversified one.

Banks employ different methods—or credit risk models—to estimate the probability that actual loan losses will exceed loan loss provisions. The top-down method is often used for consumer and small business loans. This method relies on the historical volatility of charge-offs for the type of loan in question rather than on the individual loans. For example, banks have data for many years showing the default rate on portfolios of consumer loans through all phases of the economic cycle. This experience allows the bank to determine the probability of default for its own portfolio. The bottom-up method, which is generally used for large corporate credit, quantifies credit risk for each loan and, adjusting for correlations among them, aggregates the credit risk of each loan to measure the credit risk of the entire portfolio.[35]

Regulators reject the internal models approach for credit risk on the basis of difficulties that allegedly now exist in model construction, data availability, and model validation procedures. The Fed reached this conclusion after a study of industry practice with internal credit models. In addition, it believes that models would make it difficult to "ensure board comparability of regulatory capital across banks."[36] It is unclear why this is necessary and seems inconsistent with the acceptance of models for market and operational risk.

The limits of existing techniques were severe, according to the Fed. The definition of credit loss provides one example. Most banks used a simple default/no-default definition that failed to capture the extent of actual LGD. Bank models often treated as equal the loss rate and volatility for very different types of loans. At the same time, for identical types of credit, one bank would estimate risk at ten times the rate of another bank simply because of modeling assumptions. Banks' modeling assumptions were often inconsistent. For example, some assumed that the draw-down rates of committed credit lines were independent of changes in the customer's credit quality, even though experience showed that customers draw increasingly on their credit lines as their creditworthiness worsen. The planning horizon was

---

[35] See W. Treacy and M. Carey, "Credit Risk Rating Systems at Large U.S. Banks," Journal of Banking & Finance (2000), p. 167.
[36] Ferguson, supra, note 23, p. 3.

generally much too short. Most banks applied a time horizon of only one year in the belief that the bank could "mitigate its credit exposure" within that time. Some regulators thought this process would often take more than a year.

Limited data about credit risks were a major problem. Model building relied on many assumptions and general estimates because data were not available to estimate precise parameters for "the joint probability distribution of the relevant risk factors." Most loans were not marked to market. Default events were infrequent. Given these limitations, analysts used simplifying assumptions and proxy data. Model validation was hindered by the lack of data that would allow a bank to compare the losses on loans in its portfolio with those in portfolios outside the bank's sample (a procedure known as "back-testing").

Later Fed studies of large banks confirmed these conclusions. A Fed study of 45 large U.S. banks' credit-risk models concluded that "the great majority of the 50 largest holding company rating systems are not really well-prepared to support the most advanced credit-risk modeling techniques."[37] The Basel Committee reached the same conclusions in its report, *Credit Risk Modeling: Current Practices and Applications*, in April 1999. However, even with all of the bank credit model problems, one must query whether there is reason to assume that these models are worse than the "Basel Model." In essence, the Basel Committee subjects bank credit models to a vigorous test that it is unwilling to apply to its own methodology.

A comparison of the capital required by the New Accord's IRB and Standardized approaches with two popular internal models revealed that the Standardized Approach required three to eight times more capital for the highest rated assets than the others, while the IRB Approach set capital at approximately the same level as the model. On the other hand, the Standardized Approach called for significantly less capital than the bank models for a sub-investment grade portfolio: 9.7 percent under the standardized approach, as compared to 26.2 percent and 30.9 percent for two internal models. IRB also required less capital for sub-investment grade debt, 18.3 percent. This means that the Standardized Approach's crude analysis perversely encourages investment in higher risk instruments, as does IRB, while it discourages investment in the less risky instruments.[38]

i.   ACCOUNTING RULES AND CAPITAL

As Scott-Iwahara argue, the impact of capital rules is highly dependent on accounting rules. Thus Basel I by definition had different impact in different countries with different accounting rules. This basic fact

---

[37] J. Seiberg, "Fed Study: Bank Risk Models Too Weak for Setting Capital," *American Banker*, November 18, 1998.
[38] Scott-Capital, supra note 18.

has gone largely ignored in the Basel II process, perhaps because of the possibility that the adoption of international accounting standards might make this moot. This is unlikely given the U.S. resistance to such adoption. Even if the SEC were to permit foreign listed companies, including foreign banks, to use IFRS, there is little or no possibility that such an option would be available for domestic companies, including U.S. banks (even those within a foreign-controlled holding company). Furthermore, as we have seen in Chapter 2, there will be two flavors of IFRS for banks and other holders of financial instruments, one with a full-blown IAS 39 as promulgated by IASB, and another with carve-outs of the fair-value option as adopted by the EU, and perhaps other countries.

In the past banking regulators in some countries, including the U.S., defined regulatory capital differently than accounting capital. Since Basel I adopted common definitions of capital, this can now only be done within the Basel guidelines. The U.S., for example, is free not to count revaluation reserves within the Basel guidelines, but it would not be free to count as capital an item not permitted by Basel. Bank regulators have been concerned with the impact of IAS 39 on bank capital. While this problem has been solved, at least temporarily in the EU, by its refusal to incorporate certain features of IAS 39 into its adoption of IFRS, another approach could have been to have adopted IAS in full, but to redefine the calculation of Basel capital for banks to exclude the objectionable features of IAS 39. This was not a practical approach, however, given the exclusion of the redefinition of capital from the Basel II project, and the timetable for the adoption of Basel II. Perhaps we will see something along these lines in the future.

Notes and Questions

1. What will the impact be on the goal of attaining a level playing field of the U.S. only applying the IRB approach to the top 10 U.S. banks and 10 others who choose it, leaving the other U.S. banks subject to Basel I, while the E.U. applies Basel II to all banks? U.S. officials say that because the biggest U.S. banks account for almost all U.S. international banking operations, the competitive effect will be negligible. Do you agree?

2. Given that the U.S. may only apply Basel II to 20 banks, and that the U.S. continues to have problems with the more "advanced" methodology, would it make more sense for the U.S. to adopt its own national rules and scrap Basel II entirely?

3. Is the standardized approach of Basel II an improvement over Basel I?

4. Is reliance on bank credit models preferable to reliance on Basel II's IRB approach?

5. The Basel II rules for securitization will be discussed in Chapter 11, while the rules for credit default swaps and project finance will be discussed, respectively, in Chapters 15 and 17.

4.   MARKET DISCIPLINE ALTERNATIVE

An entirely different approach to capital adequacy would let the market make judgments about capital adequacy. It would also permit regulators to make intervention decisions based on markets judgments. Market discipline would give banks incentive to hold adequate capital. While market discipline is part of Basel II, the guidelines generally deal with disclosure[39] rather than mechanisms for insuring market judgments can be made given disclosure.

The SFRC has offered a proposal that would apply explicit market discipline to banks by having investors in subordinated debt police the banks that issued it. The idea behind this is that subordinated debt is at risk for problem banks, unlike other debt, like deposits, that is protected by the safety net. Through its yield subordinated debt might provide signals for market participants and regulators.

The SFRC believes that subordinated debt must be limited in several ways if it is to serve a useful role as capital. First, to ensure that it is subordinate to all other liabilities, it cannot receive any benefit from an FDIC rescue of the bank. Second, it must have a minimum remaining maturity of one year to ensure that capital is available when needed. Third, the subordinated debt can only be redeemed by issuing more subordinated debt to ensure that it does not disappear as a bank encounters troubles, and redemption would require regulatory approval if the bank is undercapitalized. Fourth, it should be sold in denominations exceeding $100,000 to ensure that investors are sophisticated and understand that the debt is not insured. Finally, the regulator must be able to instruct the bank to stop paying principal and interest on the subordinated debt if the bank's capital falls below designated levels.

The SFRC would require that large banks issue subordinated debt equal to at least 2 percent of their assets and off-balance sheet liabilities links. Formal guidelines would link market price signals to existing requirements that regulators strictly supervise (and even close) banks as their capital weakens. For example, when the yields on a bank's subordinated debt reach junk levels (BBB or lower) and remain there for three months, the regulators would have to examine the bank, raise the cost of deposit

---

[39] The level of disclosure required for effective market discipline may need to be significantly improved, see The Joint Forum, Financial Disclosure in the Banking and Insurance Sectors: Issues and Analysis (May 2004), but if the subordinated debt alternative described herein were adopted, lack of disclosure might itself be a cause for high yields on such debt, thereby forcing institutions to improve disclosure if they were to avoid tighter supervisory control.

insurance, require a recovery strategy, and limit payments to depositors and investors (as well as the growth of the bank's assets).

Reaction to the SFRC proposal has been mixed. One quantitative study concluded that while regulators have no clear informational advantage over bond markets, the market signals would only be useful if they supplemented regulators' data or reduced their cost.[40] A theoretical analysis led to the conclusion that this would not happen. Subordinated debt was found to have few advantages over equity and was sometimes inferior to it, since equity prices conveyed at least the same information as sub-debt.[41]

According to the U.S. Treasury and the Federal Reserve, mandatory subordinated debt could encourage market discipline but additional evidence is needed to answer practical questions for implementation of such a scheme. *The Feasibility and Desirability of Mandatory Subordinated Debt* (December 2000) study reviewed the existing market and evaluated many proposals to use subordinated debt, including that of the SFRC. One question was whether the subordinated debt market is big enough, in terms of the number of instruments, issuers, and investors, to enable it to play a disciplinary role. Illiquidity in normal times, let alone in crisis, could undermine its signaling effect. The study did find a deep corporate bond market, with over $1 trillion in issues a year. But banks and BHCs issued only about $9 billion in subordinated debt each year from 1995-1999. The 50 largest BHCs issued about four times each year. The 20 largest issuers averaged issues of $200 million each. Consequently the subordinated debt market is not deep and liquid compared to the market for all commercial bonds; absent a liquid market, issuance of sub debt could be difficult and costly.

A 2005 study published in the Journal of Finance is highly skeptical of the utility of sub debt. The usefulness of sub debt depends on the market and regulators being able to get signals of bank solvency from credit-spreads of sub debt from a benchmark like U.S. treasury securities. The study found, however, that credit-spread changes are influenced by market variables to such an extent that one would be unable to find any consistent dominant relationship between changes in credit-spreads and changes in firm risk variables. The study also concluded that firm-specific risks were unaffected by the issue of sub debt, thus calling into question the preventive rationale for requiring the issuance of sub debt. The study did find, however, that credit-spreads do reflect more firm-specific risk factors for firms that regularly issue sub debt, a requirement of the SFRC proposal.[42]

---

[40] R. Deyoung, M. Flannery, W. Lang, and S. Sorescu, "The Information Content of Bank Exam Ratings and Subordinate Debt Prices," 33 Journal of Money, Credit, and Banking (2001), p. 900.

[41] M. Levonian, "Subordinated Debt and the Quality of Market Discipline in Banking," Research and Supervision: A Workshop on Applied Banking Research Oslo, Norway, June 12-13, 2001 at the Norges Bank.

[42] C. Krishnan, P. Ritchken and J. Thomson, "Monitoring and Controlling Bank Risk: Does Risky Debt Help?," LX Journal of Finance 343 (2005).

Another problem, perhaps related to the findings of this study, is that market discipline can only work if banks disclose sufficient information for the market to gage their riskiness. Regulators can be concerned that bad information about banks could cause a liquidity crisis. There is a particular concern that release of information about regulatory appraisals of bank solvency could impede frank disclosures by banks to regulators. Rating agencies may be beneficiaries of these policies since banks do commonly give information to these agencies that they do not give to the public. Interestingly, rating agencies enjoy an exemption from the application of Regulation FD, discussed in Chapter 2, that prevents public companies from giving information to selected analysts.

In contrast to the situation in the U.S., subordinated debt markets are remarkably active in Europe. Over the 1990-2001 period, 5,600 subordinated debt issues took place in ten EU countries, and the banks that issued subordinated debt represented more than 50 percent of banking assets in those countries. Indeed, the U.S. subordinated debt market is no larger than that of Germany. However, in Europe, there is low frequency of issuance and a long-term maturity (i.e. no rapid turnover) that would be inconsistent with the SFRC's recommendation that requires regular access to these markets; major banks, however, are more regular users.[43]

It is also possible that equity prices can reflect bank default risk, and thus also be a source of market discipline. Equity is even less likely to be rescued in a bailout than subordinated debt. In principle, option theory permits the extraction of a default risk from an equity price, although this may be difficult to do in practice due to distortion from safety nets. There is evidence that share prices can partially predict future changes in a bank's condition.[44] Unlike subordinated debt markets, equity markets do not generate regular issuance, so the discipline would come from price signals on outstanding equity rather than from market acceptance of new issues.

Notes and Questions

1. As between Basel II, more reliance on bank credit models, and the SFRC's recommendation, which is the better approach to regulation of bank capital?

---

[43] Basel Committee on Banking Supervision, "Markets for Bank Subordinated Debt and Equity in Basel Committee Market Countries," Working Paper 12 (August 2003).

[44] M. Flannery and S. Nikolova, "Market Discipline of U.S. Financial Firms: Recent Evidence and Research Issues," Chicago Fed-BIS Conference on Market Discipline: The Evidence Across Countries and Industries, October 30-November 1, 2003. See also J. Kranier and J. Lopez, "How Might Financial Market Information Be Used for Supervisory Purposes" 29 Federal Reserve Board of San Francisco Economic Review (2003). Another study suggests that interest rates on loans charged by banks could also be a valuable source of information about bank risk. D. Morgan and A. Ashcraft, "Using Loan Rates to Measure and Regulate Bank Risk: Findings and an Immodest Proposal," 24 J. or Financial Services Research 181 (2003).

D. MARKET RISK

This part of the Chapter examines capital adequacy for market risk, which is the risk that there might be an adverse change in the price of an asset. While the Basel Committee sets market risk standards for banks, which in some countries (such as the U.S.) have been applied to bank holding companies, the Basel Committee does not set such standards for securities companies. The EU, however, applies the Basel standards directly to securities firms through its Capital Adequacy Directive (CAD). Other countries, like the U.S. and Japan, apply standards set by securities regulators (i.e. the SEC) to securities firms. The International Organization of Securities Commissions (IOSCO) tried to issue common capital standards for its members but the effort collapsed in late 1992. As part of the latest Consultative Papers, the Basel Committee has not proposed to change its market risk standards.

One important difference between the Basel market risk and credit risk standards is that the market risk standards accept bank models, including models regarding the effects of portfolio diversification, albeit with restrictive parameters.

This section sketches the range of risks faced by securities operations and then describes the building block approach of the Basel Committee (and the CAD) and the comprehensive approach, used by the SEC in the United States, in setting capital requirements.

1. RISKS ASSOCIATED WITH SECURITIES OPERATIONS

Securities activities are subject to a variety of risks. The type and amount of risk depends on the nature and extent of the activities of securities firms and banks. The most important of these risks are market risk and counterparty risk.

Market risk, also called "position risk," is the risk of an adverse movement in a security's price. For example, the market value of a security purchased by a firm may fall before it can be resold. In the case of an equity security (i.e. stock), concerns about the financial performance of the corporate issuer may lead to a decline in the price of the security. In the case of a debt security (i.e. bond), the non-payment of principal or interest by the issuer, or a change in interest rates, may lead to a decline in the value of the security.

Counterparty risk, also called "settlement risk," is the risk that a firm's trading partner will be either unwilling or unable to meet its contractual obligation. For example, a buyer may contract to purchase a security from a second-party seller and then commit to selling the security to a third party. The original buyer would then be exposed to the risk that the original seller may default and not deliver the security.

There is also a concern with systemic risk. Systemic risk is the risk that a failure of one firm could severely impair the workings of the financial system and, at an extreme, cause a complete breakdown of the system as a whole. Generally the concern about systemic risk is less for securities companies than for banks, given that securities firms do not issue government insured liabilities or demand deposits. This makes the accuracy of capital or level of compliance with such standards less important for securities firms than for banks. In many countries (including the U.S.) the primary objective of regulation of the capital of securities firms is to provide sufficient liquid assets to meet liabilities, including customer liabilities, and to foster confidence in the securities industry and the financial system in general.

Differing country capital standards may also have competitive effects, both within a country where securities firms and banks compete for the same securities business, as well as between countries. For example, if banks have more stringent capital standards than those imposed on competing securities firms within the same country, then the banks may be at a competitive disadvantage relative to the securities companies, due to the costs associated with holding the higher capital amounts.

2.   THE BASEL COMMITTEE APPROACH

The Basel Committee designated two approaches to capital adequacy for market risk, the "building block" standardized approach and the "internal model" approach for large financial firms. The Basel Standard was presented as a proposal at the end of April 1993, elaborated in April 1995 and issued as an amendment to the 1988 Accord in January 1996.

a.   THE STANDARDIZED APPROACH

The Basel Standard sets formulas to compute capital for a bank's trading book against whose current market value the capital is charged. The trading book includes a bank's proprietary positions in financial instruments held to benefit in the short term from actual or expected differences between their buying and selling prices, to hedge other trading book items, for short-term sale, or to execute a trade with a customer. Non-trading book items remain subject only to the credit risk rules. The lines between the trading book and the banking book are not always clear.

The April 2005 proposals on Basel II try to clarify the lines.[45] The proposal reflects the concern that banks may be too aggressively placing credit-risk products, like credit default swaps or tranches of collateralized debt obligations (see Chapter 15), in the trading book to get better (lower) capital treatment, given that short-term traded assets generally require less

---

[45] Basel Committee on Banking Supervision, Consultative Document, The Application of Basel II to Trading Activities and the Treatment of Double Default Effects (April 2005).

capital than assets held for longer periods. The proposal provides that an exposure other than for short-term or that constitutes a hedge of a banking nook exposure should not be included in the trading book.

The "building blocks" for calculating capital for market risk are the separate calculations of general and specific position risk. The distinction between specific and general risk is basic in finance theory and practice. Specific risk refers to the risks associated with the issuer itself. General risks are those not associated with an issuer, such as changes in the market or economy. For equity position risk, the standard applies to long and short positions in all instruments. Long and short positions in the same issue may be reported on a net basis.

The capital charge for specific risk is 8 percent of the gross position in all stocks (i.e. the sum of longs and shorts), unless the portfolio is both liquid and well-diversified, in which case the capital charge is 4 percent. Given the different characteristics of national markets in terms of marketability and concentration, national authorities have discretion to determine the criteria for liquid and diversified portfolios. The general market risk charge is 8 percent of the net portion of all stocks, and all longs and shorts are netted.

Basel permits countries to use a "comprehensive approach" similar to that of the SEC (see below) if they demonstrate that the effect of such approach is at least as stringent as that of the Basel Standard.

Table 7D, below, illustrates how the system described above would work for a range of hypothetical equity portfolios, assuming a capital charge of 4 percent for the gross positions and 8 percent for the net positions.

Table 7D

Case	Sum of Long positions	Sum of Short positions	Gross position (sum of cols 1 & 2)	Specific risk: 4 percent of gross	Net position (difference between cols 1 & 2)	General risk: 8 percent of net	Capital required (gross + net)
1	100	0	100	4	100	8	12
2	100	25	125	5	75	6	11
3	25	100	125	5	75	6	11
4	0	100	100	4	100	8	12

The EU's Capital Adequacy Directive (CAD) approach, which is based on the Basel Standard, is essentially the same as the Basel approach. The major differences are that CAD's specific risk requirements are 4 percent for undiversified portfolios, and 2 percent for diversified liquid portfolios, rather than the 8 percent and 4 percent requirements of Basel.

The Basel Standard and CAD provide that, in addition to other forms of capital, firms may also hold what is called Tier III capital for market risk, up to 250 percent of a bank's Tier I capital that is required to support market risks. The main component of Tier III capital is subordinated debt that does not meet the Tier II requirements. The notion is that this shorter-term instrument is acceptable as capital for short-term position risk, while longer-term instruments are needed as capital for credit risk. The Basel Standard requires that subordinated loan capital have an initial maturity of at least two years, be fully paid and, unless national regulators approve, subject to no early repayment arrangements other than that the debtor is being wound up. No servicing of principal or interest is permitted if to do so would put the firm's capital below other required levels.

Notes and Questions

1. How does Basel calculate general risk for equity? Suppose a bank's assets consist of $100 in long equity positions and $85 in short equity positions and its liabilities are $140. What is its required capital?

a. The first step in the calculation is to net the long and short positions in each security, then add all securities that are net long and all that are net short. Long means the investor holds the stock now. The risk is that the value of the stock will decline. Short means the investor must deliver stock at a set price on a future date but the investor does not own the stock at the time of the sale. The investor must buy the stock to deliver it. The risk is that the price of the stock will rise. For example, a short investor sells 100 IBM shares on January 1 at $100/share and promises to deliver them on April 1, when he will receive $100/share for them. He does not own those shares now. When he buys, if the price has fallen (e.g. to $75/share), he makes $25 a share. If it rises above $100, he loses. This is a short position. One could also sell short for delivery at settlement (3 days after the trade in the U.S.).

b. The general risk rule requires capital equal to 8 percent of the net position in the market. With these facts, the overall net position is the larger net position ($100) less the smaller net position ($85), or $15. Eight percent of $15 is $1.2 capital for general risk.

　　1. Why allow a net short position to offset a net long position?

　　2. Why require 8 percent capital?

　　3. Why is $15 the general or market risk?

c. How does Basel calculate the capital needed for specific risk for equity? The rule for specific risk is that the bank must hold capital equal to 8 percent of the overall gross position or only 4 percent if the portfolio is highly liquid and diversified. To get the overall gross position, one adds the net long position ($100) and the net short position ($85), giving $185. Four percent of $185 is $7.4.

1. Why add net long and net short positions?

2. Why distinguish between highly liquid and other positions?

3. What would account for the divergence in the specific risk ratios of the CAD (4 percent generally and 2 percent for highly liquid and diversified) and the Basel approach (8 percent and 4 percent)?

b.   INTERNAL MODELS-BASED REGULATION OF CAPITAL

The inadequacies of the standardized methods led the Basel Committee to permit a different approach, one relying on the financial institution's own system of risk analysis to set the appropriate level of capital. Regulators acknowledged that the inadequacies of the Basel standard included: (1) the treatment of each part of the portfolio separately rather than taking diversification into account; and (2) the lack of recognition that some markets can be more or less volatile than others.

1.   TYPES OF INTERNAL MODELS USED BY BANKS

Bank models are based on value-at-risk (VaR) methodology. VaR is the amount of potential one-day profit and loss, due to general market movements that can occur with a 99 percent (or at least 95 percent) probability. Banks use two kinds of internal tests to determine this: covariance analysis and historical simulation.

Covariance analysis uses summary statistics, calculated from historic data on price volatilities and correlations within and between markets. Price changes are assumed to be normally distributed.

Historical simulation uses the bank's trading book over the past one or two years to calculate the changes in the value of the book that would have been experienced had the book been held throughout the period. The bank calculates the 99 percent confidence interval without assuming that the price changes are normally distributed, by computing the loss that was not exceeded on 99 percent of occasions.

2.   THE BASEL COMMITTEE'S RULES FOR INTERNAL MODELS

The Basel Committee set minimum standards for the use of internal models. To qualify, a bank must have: (1) an active independent risk control unit; (2) actively involved directors and senior managers; (3) a model closely integrated in daily risk management; (4) regular stress tests for exceptional plausible conditions; (5) thorough compliance procedures; and (6) regular internal review by the bank's internal audit unit.

If a bank qualifies, the internal model used by the bank must include prescribed parameters. The following are required for equity positions (note that those for other positions are similar):

(1) compute VaR daily;

(2) use risk factors corresponding at least to each equity market in which the bank has a significant position, and even better to market sectors (i.e. by industry), and ideally also to individual stocks in which the bank's positions are concentrated;

(3) use a 99th percentile confidence interval;

(4) use a one year historical observation period;

(5) calculate VaR assuming a minimum instantaneous price shock equivalent to a 10-trading-day move in prices (what is called the "holding period");

(6) recognize empirical correlations within and across broad risk categories (note that the supervisor must be satisfied with the system and it must be adjusted if market prices change materially); and

(7) set the capital charge as the higher of: (i) the previous day's VaR; or (ii) three times the average of the daily VaR of the preceding sixty business days.

The resulting capital is then multiplied by a factor of no less than three because, according to the Basel Committee, models for one day not only do not capture the impact of cumulative charges over more extended periods of time, but also oversimplify and miss intra-day trading risk and exceptional circumstances.

The bank's internal model must be back-tested regularly and is subject to a "plus factor" if the test reveals weaknesses. Back-testing compares the model's risk measure (looking forward in time) with the actual daily changes in portfolio value (after they occur). The bank counts the number of times the model was wrong in order to determine whether the capital required by the model, at the 99 percent confidence level, actually covered 99 percent of the trading results.

The basic problem with back-testing is that when a model fails in a test, there is no way to know if the model or the test was faulty. The portfolio used by the model to predict likely loss over the next day is never the actual portfolio throughout the day. Trading during the day changes the portfolio and commissions earned change the income on the actual portfolio from what is in the model's portfolio.

The Basel Committee decided that when back-testing of 250 trading days (12 months) revealed:

- 10 or more exceptions (the red zone), the supervisor would assume the bank's model had a problem, investigate the problem, and raise the "plus factor" by one (i.e. from 3 to 4).

- 5-9 exceptions (the yellow zone), the bank would have to prove to the supervisor that the model is sound (i.e. that low probability events occurred) and the supervisor would have the discretion to raise the plus factor by a fraction of one.

- 4 or fewer exceptions (the green zone) would require no action by the supervisor.

The "plus factor" means that instead of multiplying the VaR by three, the bank would have to multiply it by three plus some additional amount. An additional factor of one makes the multiple four.

An analysis of model risk found that the basic three times multiplier was more than twice what it should be.[46] On the other hand, the Long Term Capital Management (LTCM) hedge fund collapsed in August 1998 in part because the long historical parallel movement of rates on public and private bonds ended unexpectedly. LTCM's sophisticated models did not recognize this change and LTCM bet, incorrectly that the rates would converge. Many commentators have noted that the big problems for investors follow basic discontinuities in historical relationships.

3.   THE PRE-COMMITMENT APPROACH

An alternative to the Basel internal models approach is found in P. Kupiec and J. O'Brien, *A Pre-Commitment Approach to Capital Requirements for Market Risk*.[47] The authors argue that a bank should commit in advance to a "maximum loss exposure" over a set future period and allocate capital to meet that exposure. The regulators then apply penalties, such as fines, if the actual losses exceed the commitment.

In 1997, the New York Clearing House Association reported that 10 banks had tested the precommittment method over the period of one quarter and found that each set aside enough capital using it. This led them to conclude that the pre-commitment approach is a viable alternative to internal models.[48]

Fixing the penalty was identified as the main problem of the pre-commitment approach. Banks argued that requiring disclosure that the model failed was a sufficient penalty. Regulators were concerned that a "one-size-fits-all" penalty would not be adequate, compelling them to tailor penalties to each bank.

---

[46] J. Kerkhof, B. Melenberg, and H. Schumacher, "Model Risk and Regulatory Capital" (February 22, 2002).

[47] Federal Reserve Board Finance and Economics Discussion Series No. 95-36 (1996).

[48] See J. Considine, "Pilot Exercise—Pre-Commitment Approach to Market Risk," 4 Federal Reserve Bank of New York Economic Policy Review (1998), p. 131.

A critic of the pre-commitment approach, a member of the Managing Board of Germany's central bank, argued that supervisors cannot and should not rely on banks to assess their own risks. Moreover, the pre-commitment approach applies after the bank has shown it failed to maintain adequate capital; in other words, fining a bankrupt bank is too late.[49]

Notes and Questions

1. The premise of the Basel internal models approach is that individual banks are much more capable and motivated than regulators to manage the risk of their trading books. Does this premise make sense?

2 Does the Basel approach provide sufficient regulatory safeguards to protect against the uncertainties of internal models? For example, the multiplication factor of three for the capital charge, and the "plus factor" if back testing reveals problems with the model, are designed to address the short-term perspective of the models. Do they accomplish their goal efficiently?

3. The Long Term Capital Management (LTCM) hedge fund collapsed in August 1998 partly because the long-standing historical parallel movement of rates on public and private bonds ended. LTCM's sophisticated models did not recognize this change and LTCM bet, incorrectly, that the rates would converge. Many commentators note that big problems for investors follow basic discontinuities in historical relationships. Does this problem mean regulators should not permit reliance on internal models?

3.   THE COMPREHENSIVE APPROACH TO POSITION RISK: THE SEC

The SEC sets net capital requirements for brokers and dealers.[50] The main element of the SEC rules is its emphasis on customer protection over avoiding bankruptcy. To this end, it requires enough liquid capital to meet customer liabilities.

Net capital is total capital reduced by various charges and "haircuts" that measure trading risk. A firm may choose either the basic or the alternative requirement.

Basic Method

The basic requirement is set out below:[51]

---

[49] K. Engelen, "The Basel Capital Accord," The International Economy (March/ April 1998), p. 33.

[50] 17 C.F.R. §240.15c3-1 (2003).

[51] G. Haberman, "Capital Requirements of Commercial and Investment Banks: Contrasts in Regulation," Federal Reserve Bank of New York Quarterly Review (Autumn 1987).

	Table 7E
	SEC Net Capital Computation
Total capital:	Equity
	Allowable subordinated debt
	Allowable credits
Less deductions:	(Illiquid assets)
	(Unsecured receivables)
	(Charges for aged credit exposure)
	(Market risk haircuts)
Net capital requirement:	6 2/3 percent aggregate indebtedness, or
	2 percent aggregate debit items

Total capital consists of net worth plus subordinated liabilities, augmented by allowable credits. To be counted as capital, subordinated debt must have a minimum term of one year and may not be prepayable without the prior written approval of the broker-dealer's examining authority (New York Stock Exchange or NASD).

Broker-dealers are prohibited from distributing equity capital through dividends or unsecured loans to owners if doing so would reduce the firm's net capital below to 120 percent of the basic requirement.

Total capital is reduced by nonallowable assets and various special charges. An asset is considered nonallowable if it cannot be immediately or quickly converted into cash.

Haircuts are based on the fact that the prices of marketable assets and liabilities may move adversely during liquidation, thereby reducing net capital. The deduction for price risk in the firm's proprietary positions (i.e. haircuts) represent percentages of the market value of the security and the forward positions held by the broker-dealer. Haircuts for equity are a deduction of: (1) 15 percent of the market value of the greater of the long or short positions; and (2) to the extent that the market value of the lesser of the long or short positions exceeds 25 percent of the market value of the greater of the long or short positions, the percentage deduction on such excess is 15 percent of the market value of such excess. Some believe this haircut rule tries to discourage short positions.

The basic method requires that net capital exceed 6 2/3 percent of aggregate indebtedness, which includes all liabilities less those specifically exempted. In essence, aggregate indebtedness is any liability not adequately collateralized, secured, or otherwise directly offset by an asset of the broker-dealer. Aggregate indebtedness also includes contingent, off-balance sheet obligations.

Alternative Method

The alternative method, which is used by most large security firms, requires that net capital exceed 2 percent of aggregate debit items, which are liabilities to customers such as free credit balances on monies payable against securities loaned.[52]

In December 1997, the SEC proposed to adopt a standard similar to the BIS building block method to calculate capital for market risk on interest bearing instruments. The firm would be required to determine the general risk and specific risk of its portfolio.[53] This proposal was not, however, adopted.

In June 2004, the Commission adopted a new voluntary Alternative Net Capital Requirement for broker-dealers that are part of "consolidated supervised entities."[54] These requirements are based on Basel II. This permits broker-dealers that are part of a bank holding company, which is already subject to Basel II, to calculate its capital consistent with the approach of the overall holding company. Prior to this rule, Citigroup was required to calculate its holding company capital under Basel rules but to calculate its investment banking subsidiary capital under the quite different SEC rules. This new alternative gives Citigroup the option to eliminate this problem. In addition, it permits independent investment banks that would not otherwise be subject to Basel, because they are not part of a bank holding company, e.g. Morgan Stanley, to use Basel rules (subject to some SEC modifications). Investment banks may chose to use the new alternative if it would reduce their capital, and perhaps as an added insurance that the EU will find that they are subject to "equivalent" regulation under its new proposed Conglomerates Directive (see Chapter 2).

Notes and Questions

1.   How would you describe the difference between the SEC's and Basel's approach to market risk?

2.   Does the difference between banks and securities firms suggest that we should have different capital rules for the two types of firms even when they take on identical market risks? Note the EU applies the same market risk rules to banks and securities firms, while the U.S. has not done so—albeit under the new SEC alternative, securities firms are permitted to use Basel rules.

---

[52] 17 C.F.R. §240.15c3-3a Exhibit A.

[53] See SEC Proposed Net Capital Rule, 17 CFR Part 240 (Release No. 34-39455).

[54] SEC Release No. 34-49830, June 8, 2004. If a broker-dealer without a holding company regulator, e.g. either the SEC or Federal Reserve Board, seeks to adopt this new alternative, its holding company must make certain undertakings, including reporting its capital based on Basel standards, much like a holding company that is supervised by the SEC. If a broker-dealer is regulated by the Fed at the holding company level, it will not be regulated or subject to SEC capital requirements at the holding company level.

E.   OPERATIONAL RISK

The Basel II rules require that banks hold 12 percent of their minimum regulatory capital for operational risk. Operational risk is defined as "the risk of loss resulting from inadequate or failed internal processes, people and systems or from external events. This definition includes legal risk, but excludes strategic and reputational risk." It does not include the risk of adverse business conditions, such as low demand, that many people associate with operations. Operational risk charges are formally included in Pillar 1, but the rules also require strong supervisory control (Pillar 2) and disclosure (Pillar 3).

The Committee has adopted three ways to calculate operational risk capital. In order of increasing sophistication and risk, they are the Basic Indicator Approach, the Standardized Approach, and the Advanced Management Approach. A bank may use different approaches for different parts of its operations, but needs regulatory approval to revert to a lower level after being approved for a higher one.

The Basic Approach applies a 15 percent capital charge to average annual gross income over the past 3 years. The Standardized Approach applies to more sophisticated banks. Standardized loss factors are applied to standardized indicators of risk in eight business lines (i.e. asset management) into which a bank allocates its gross income. The loss factors, or betas, vary by business line from 12 percent to 18 percent. For example, a bank would multiply gross income from corporate finance by 18 percent, from commercial banking by 15 percent, and from retail banking by 12 percent. The total capital is the sum of the eight charges.

The Advanced Management Approach (AMA) allows banks to use internal models to calculate capital for operational risk. To qualify, banks' internal operational risk measurement systems must meet two sets of criteria. First, qualitative criteria include a requirement that an independent function to manage operational risk that is closely integrated with day-to-day risk management and well documented with regular reporting up to the board. Internal or external auditors must review it regularly, while external auditors and supervisors must be able to validate the system. Second, quantitative criteria require a demonstrated ability to handle severe low probability, high loss events at a 99.9 percent confidence level. AMA allows banks to mitigate risk with insurance, but only up to 20 percent of the total operational risk charge. It sets rules for eligible insurers, policy cancellation or non-renewal, maturity, and the methodology to recognize insurance.

In line with its decision to apply only the Basel II A-IRB credit risk to the most advanced banks, the U.S. will apply only the AMA operational risk rules to these banks. Other U.S. banks will have no operational risk charges. The U.S. approach could cause significant international problems.

"Operational risk is generally measured on a consolidated basis, often by business line. That diversification benefits exist on a consolidated basis suggests that operational risk estimated from the bottom-up—by, say, legal entity—would not only be more difficult but might well add up to more than the total from the top down."[55]

Basel may misdefine operational risk. One can think of operational risk as all risk remaining after one removes financial risk (i.e. credit risk, position risk, and foreign exchange risk). This non-financial risk has two components. One is business risk, that for some reason a firm's revenues will fall short of costs. Basel ignores this risk, which is very important for most firms, perhaps in the range of 17 percent of all risk. The other is non-business or event risk, that something unanticipated will happen. External event risk can be dealt with by insurance better than by capital, which is one reason the CP3's arbitrary 20 percent ceiling on insurance is a mistake. Internal event risk is better dealt with by management controls than by capital.[56]

It is somewhat ironic that Basel II permits full use of models in AMA, where operational risk models are completely untested, compared to the restrictive use of models for credit risk (not taking full account of portfolio diversification). Perhaps, this is understandable in the sense that the regulators did not have a standardized methodology (their own models) to offer up in the place of bank models. Operational risk is an extremely complicated set of different risks, ranging from computer malfunctions to legal risk. Bank regulators have focused on the need for banks to have a credible data base of past loss-event data, but it is far from clear that this data base will be a sufficient basis from which to make predictions of the future.

F.   HOME-HOST PROBLEMS

Increasing attention is being given to a problem arising out of the fact that different banks within the same holding company may apply different approaches to Basel and that banks using the AMA approach for operational risk on a holding company wide basis may leave particular banks within the holding company with too little capital from the perspective of bank regulators.[57]

It is quite conceivable that different banks within a holding company may apply different versions of Basel II. For example, a U.S. subsidiary of a bank holding company might qualify for A-IRB but its affiliate in India may

---

[55] Ferguson, supra note 23, p. 7.

[56] A. Kuritzkes and H. Scott, "Sizing Operational Risk and the Effect of Insurance: Implications for the Basel II Capital Accord" in Scott-Capital, supra note 18.

[57] B. Bernanke, Governor of the Federal Reserve System, "The Implementation of Basel II: Some Issues for Cross-Border Banking," Remarks at the Institute of International Bankers' Annual Breakfast Dialogue, October 4, 2004.

use the standardized approach. For U.S. banks, this difference is certain to exist because of the U.S. decision not to adopt any but the most advanced form of Basel II. Foreign banks operating under the standardized or foundation approach abroad will not be able to do so in the United States. Difficulties may arise within a banking organization in coordinating different capital requirements in different countries.

For U.S. banks using A-IRB, their foreign competitors may get a short term advantage—assuming that Basel II reduces capital—since A-IRB will not be implemented until the end of 2007 while the foundation and standardized approaches will be implemented by the end of 2006.

Within the EU, as discussed in Chapter 4, there are difficulties in determining the lead supervisor for purpose of validating models for A-IRB banks. This problem exists as well internationally, e.g. a bank holding company with two A-IRB banks, one in the U.S. and one in the E.U.

More difficult problems arise with respect to operational risk. Basel II's AMA allows the consolidated and individual bank units to benefit from group-wide risk diversification. However, regulators of particular subsidiaries will be concerned about the capital supporting their particular bank, rather than the holding company as a whole. This follows from the fact that an individual bank within a holding company that fails will not necessarily have a claim on consolidated capital or the capital of other affiliates. The Basel Committee has proposed[58] that "significant" subsidiaries will have to calculate stand-alone operational risk capital requirements while other subsidiaries can use an allocated portion of the group-wide requirements—but supervisors of less "significant" subsidiaries may not accept this.

This problem highlights the difficulty of moving to group-wide models for credit and market risk. The benefits of calculating capital on a group-wide basis—the method most banks use for business operations—may not be achievable without fundamental reform of country-by-country bank regulation, or changes in how bank insolvencies are handled. For example, the home-host problem could be solved by giving a failed bank a claim on the consolidated capital of the holding company. This approach has been explored in the past within the United States.

Notes and Questions

1. Can operational risk be meaningfully defined so as to permit setting capital requirements?

---

[58] Basel Committee on Banking Supervision, Principles for the Home-host Recognition of AMA Operational Risk Capital (January 2004).

2. Why wouldn't provisions for anticipated losses or insurance be sufficient to handle non-business risk—the type of risk for which Basel requires capital?

3. Legal risk is a component of operational risk, e.g. litigation risk. Is this likely to be the same in different jurisdictions? If not, to what extent does Basel take jurisdictional differences into account?

4. Can operational risk requirements be meaningfully applied at the individual bank level, as opposed to the holding company level? How should the home-host problem of Basel II's approach to operational risk be resolved?

CONCLUSIONS

Regulation of the capital of financial institutions has become the centerpiece of financial regulation, and the work of the Basel Committee has made the regulation of bank capital the most internationalized area of financial regulation. International co-operation has been premised on the impact of national capital requirements on international competition and the potential spillover effects of the failure of a bank (or the failure of the home country regulator to do its job) on other countries.

The current difficulties of Basel II have called into question whether international co-operation can continue to be successful. While Basel II will continue to be applied to internationally active banks, the U.S. has decided that these banks must adopt the most advanced form of the system, leaving the vast amount of work done on the standardized and F-IRB approach irrelevant to the U.S. While all U.S. banks did comply with Basel I, this will no longer be the case with Basel II, raising significant issues of competitive equity within the U.S. While Basel I found wide international acceptance beyond the G-10 members of the Basel Committee, the prospect for widespread adoption of Basel II, particularly in the developing world, is not good. This will erode the key role of Basel in formulating international banking standards for the world as a whole.

At the heart of the difficulty is the question as to the right mix of market discipline, bank models, and command and control regulation. Surely in the long term, and perhaps much sooner, one would expect models and the market to displace positive rules. Obviously, as regulation itself decreases, so will international regulation. While bank capital requirements have led the way in international efforts, they may have to move aside for areas in which mandatory international rules are more necessary, e.g. for accounting standards.

CHAPTER EIGHT

FOREIGN EXCHANGE REGIMES

Foreign exchange rates affect virtually all international economic activity, especially finance. Indeed for many economists foreign exchange issues *are* international finance. This Chapter examines the interplay between exchange rate regimes, government policy, and foreign exchange markets. We present the basics of fixed and floating exchange rate systems, and consider the way spot and forward exchange markets work. In general, foreign exchange rates today present fewer legal or regulatory issues than they did when we had a "system" of fixed rates with rules administered by the IMF.

A.   BASIC TYPES OF EXCHANGE RATE SYSTEMS

An exchange rate gives the prices at which two currencies are sold for each other. Different systems determine these prices. Four types of systems during the last century tended toward either flexible rates set by supply and demand or rates fixed by governments. The first, the gold standard, existed for decades until it ended with the First World War. The second was called the gold exchange standard. It operated from the mid-1920s to the early 1930s. The third foreign exchange regime followed the Second World War and was known as the Bretton Woods system. It was based on the U.S. Dollar and gold and lasted to 1973. Today we have a mixture of floating rates. Before discussing the individual regimes, this Chapter briefly analyzes the concept of a country's balance of payments, a recurring topic throughout.

The balance of payments of a nation is simply an accounting statement of its transactions with the rest of the world. A country's exchange rate affects its balance of payments and its balance of payments affects the currency's strength against other currencies. As the statement measures flows, it reflects only changes in assets and liabilities, not absolute levels of these elements. Payment inflows, from non-residents, are recorded as a "plus." Outflows, to non-residents, are expressed as a "minus." For example, exports are registered as a plus because they reflect payments flowing into the country from the sale of goods.

The balance of payments consists of three accounts: the current account, the capital account, and the official reserves. The current account measures trade in goods, services, and gifts between nations. It primarily includes exports and imports of goods, measuring the "balance of trade." This trade balance is in surplus when exports exceed imports and in deficit when imports exceed exports. For 1997, the United States had a current account balance deficit of $418 billion, owing to a substantial trade imbalance.[1] A surplus in the current account is associated with a strengthening of a country's exchange rate and a deficit with a falling exchange rate. For example, exports from the U.S. are largely denominated in Dollars. Payment for them means that a foreigner must buy Dollars and sell the foreign currency. This tends to strengthen the Dollar in certain exchange regimes. When imports exceed exports, however, the process is reversed and the Dollar weakens, all other things being equal.

The capital account records international movements of financial assets and liabilities, such as loans and equity investments. In recent years, this account has helped offset the current account deficit in the U.S. balance of payments, as capital inflows into the U.S. grew relative to outflows. Any difference between the current account and capital account is made up by the official reserves that are the country's official holdings of gold and hard currencies (other than its own). These holdings increase if the current and capital accounts together are in surplus and decrease if the accounts are in deficit. Management of the official reserves is a key consideration in the way some countries manipulate their exchange rates. For example when a government supports its currency, it sells its holdings of official reserves to pay for the cost of "propping up the currency."

1.   FIXED RATE SYSTEMS: THE GOLD STANDARD

The gold standard that existed around the world prior to the First World War was heavily dependent on the British Pound. However, the effect of the war upon Britain caused it to abandon the gold standard temporarily. Since the Pound had financed most of the world payments, Britain's wartime decision seriously reduced confidence in the gold standard. The gold exchange standard which emerged from the First World War differed from its predecessor. The Dollar and the Franc emerged as dominant reserve assets.

The basic mechanics underlying the gold standard nevertheless merit consideration in light of periodic efforts to return to this type of regime. "Under a gold standard each country stands ready to convert its paper or fiat money into gold at a fixed price. This fixing of the price of gold fixes exchange rates between paper monies. For example, if the U.S. Federal Reserve (the Fed) agrees to buy and sell gold at $40 per ounce, and the Bank of England agrees to £20 per ounce, the exchange rate between the Pound and Dollar in

---

[1] U.S. Commerce Department, "International Trade in Goods and Services" (April 2003).

the form of paper currency or commercial bank deposits will be $2/£."[2] If the exchange rate is not $2/£, for example if it were $1.60/£, the rate would be forced back to $2/£ since it is cheaper to buy gold from the Bank of England for £1, ship the gold to the U.S., and sell it to the Federal Reserve for $2.

"The price-level adjustment mechanism under the gold standard is known as the price-specie adjustment mechanism, where "specie" is just another word for precious metal. Assume that Britain has a balance-of-payments deficit with the U.S. With Britain buying more from the U.S. than the U.S. is buying from Britain, there is an excess supply of Pounds."[3] With flexible exchange rates this will reduce the value of the Pound below $2/£, but with a gold standard this will not happen. As illustrated above, "as soon as the Pound dips even slightly below $2, people will sell pounds to the Bank of England in return for gold, ship the gold to the U.S., and sell the gold to the Federal Reserve for Dollars. This gives people $2 for each Pound. Therefore, the result of the British balance-of-payments deficit is the movement of gold from the Bank of England to the U.S. Federal Reserve.

The movement of gold from Britain, the deficit country, to the U.S., the surplus country, has effects on both countries' money supplies. This is because in standing ready to exchange gold for paper money at a fixed price, central banks have to make sure they have sufficient gold on hand for those occasions when many people wish to return paper money for gold. Prudent banking requires that a minimum ratio of gold reserves to paper money be held, and indeed, this used to be mandated in many countries, including the U.S., which required that the Dollar be backed by at least 25 percent in gold reserves. The maintenance of a minimum reserve ratio means that as the Bank of England loses gold, it is forced to reduce the amount of its paper money in circulation. At the same time, the increase in the Federal Reserve gold reserves allows it to put more paper money into circulation.

Under classical economic analysis, the fall in the money supply in the deficit country would cause a general fall in prices. At the same time, the increase in the money supply in the surplus country (in the world we are describing, one country's deficit in the other country's surplus) would cause a general increase in prices. With prices falling in the deficit country, Britain, and increasing in the surplus country, the U.S., there is a decline in British prices versus U.S. prices. This makes British exports more competitive in the U.S., helping them increase. At the same time, U.S. goods in Britain become less competitive than Britain's own import substitutes, so that British imports decline. With British exports increasing and imports decreasing, Britain's deficit declines. Indeed, until the deficit has been completely eliminated there will be an excess supply of Pounds, the sale of Pounds to the Bank of England, the shipment of gold to the U.S., a decrease in the British

---

[2] M. Levi, *International Finance* (2d ed. 1990), pp. 476–80.
[3] *ibid.*

money supply, an increase in the U.S. money supply, increasing competitiveness of British products at home and abroad, and a continued reduction in the British deficit."[4]

Practice was often different than theory. To avoid adjustment, governments often abandoned the required reserve ratio between gold and paper money when the maintenance of that ratio ran counter to other objectives, such as full employment, that might follow from the contraction of money in the deficit country, Great Britain in the example.[5]

The policy of not allowing a change in reserves to change the supply of money is known as sterilization or neutralization policy.

Nonetheless, a number of twentieth-century economists and politicians have favored a return to the gold standard. What appeals to the adherents of this view is the discipline that the gold standard placed on the expansion of the money supply and the resulting check this placed on inflation.

2.   FIXED RATE SYSTEMS: THE BRETTON WOODS DOLLAR STANDARD

As the Second World War was ending, financial leaders from many Allied countries met in Bretton Woods, New Hampshire, where they agreed in 1944 to a new regime embodied in a treaty, eventually signed by most nations. The U.S. Dollar, then the world's strongest currency, would be fixed to gold. The U.S. government promised to give any holder of Dollars gold at the rate of $35 for an ounce of gold. Other countries tied their exchange rates to the U.S. Dollar at agreed rates that could fluctuate around it in a narrow band. To maintain these par values, the countries agreed to sell their currency if it approached the upper limit or to buy their currency at the lower limit with their foreign exchange reserves (mainly gold and Dollars at first).

The International Monetary Fund, which was established at Bretton Woods, could make funds available to a deficit country if the country adopted agreed policies to improve their economic situation. Devaluation was discouraged but not outlawed. The new system of fixed rates was embodied in the 1944 IMF treaty. The U.S. was not obligated to maintain a one-to-one ratio of Dollars to gold. However, it held reserves at a level that gave people confidence it could meet any demand for gold. Since the Dollar was used for international transactions and since governments held Dollars as reserves, demand for gold in exchange for Dollars was relatively low. But by the time the system broke down in the early 1970s, U.S. reserves were so low that confidence had evaporated.

---

[4] *ibid.*
[5] See K. Dam, *The Rules of the Game* (1982).

The fixed-rate Dollar standard assumes a price adjustment mechanism. Assume that Germany has a balance of payments surplus with the U.K. The increase of German exports will generate increased demand for the Deutschmark (DM, pre-Euro), as U.K. importers must obtain DM to pay for DM denominated imports. The Bank of England will supply more DM to U.K. importers, which will decrease its reserves. Or if it holds reserves in Dollars, it will sell the Dollars to obtain DM and then supply the DM to the importers, similarly decreasing reserves. A decrease in reserves will contract domestic money (under the gold standard type rule of the system), setting in motion domestic adjustment. However, this can be avoided if a country experiencing deficits and declining reserves can borrow additional reserves from other countries or the IMF. Countries that are facing a deficit and losing reserves will be forced into a devaluation because their reserves and ability to borrow will eventually be gone. On the other hand, the countries enjoying surpluses will be under no pressure to revalue their currencies and may instead allow reserves to keep growing. This represents one of the major problems with the gold and Dollar standards, namely that the responsibility for adjustment, whether via a change in the exchange rate or an automatic change in money supply and prices, falls on deficit countries more heavily than on surplus countries.

Notes and Questions

1. Why would a country adopt a fixed rate exchange rate system, given that it deprives the country of an independent monetary policy—i.e. the need to maintain exchange rates determines the expansion/contraction of money?

2. Why would a country seek to avoid making the adjustments necessary to maintain fixed exchange rates?

3.   FLOATING RATE REGIMES—AN OVERVIEW

The Bretton Woods regime expired in 1973 when major industrial countries said they would let foreign exchange markets determine the value of their currencies. The U.S. government said it would no longer support the Dollar's value. The EC decided to float members' currencies together against the Dollar.

Supply and demand for currencies were supposed to set currency prices, although each country could intervene in the market for its own currency to maintain orderly adjustment of rates. If, for example, Germany enjoyed a balance of payments surplus with the U.K., the price of DM (again pre-Euro) against the U.K.£ would increase, e.g. the DM would revalue and the £ devalue. This in turn would increase the price of German goods versus U.K. goods, making U.K. exports more competitive and eventually correcting the payments imbalance. This system, unlike fixed rate systems, allowed domestic monetary policy to operate independently of exchange rates. This removed the "discipline" of fixed rates, but such discipline was often lacking in practice.

Governments, however, often resisted changes in exchange rates. Governments intervened in markets to weaken the rate of their currencies so as to promote exports. Such interventions will only work as long as official reserves (owned or borrowed) are sufficient. An alternative is to raise domestic interest rates in order to make it more attractive to hold one's currency. But such increases in domestic interest rates can slow internal growth. Yet another alternative is to adopt trade or capital controls, attacking the demand and/or supply of currencies. During the early Reagan years, the U.S. remained passive while Japan and Europe set targets on the value of their currencies. By the mid-1980s, the U.S. had decided to intervene in markets so as to devalue the Dollar against other currencies, notably the Yen. The willingness to manage the float has persisted since then.

Notes and Questions

1.   Why would countries adopt floating exchange rates, given that the lack of commitment to maintain exchange rates removes controls on the tendency to engage in inflationary monetary policy?

2.   How would one know what the real exchange rate policy of a country is? Is there a difference between de jure and de facto policies?

3.   How would countries adjust if their trade is not in balance? Suppose that Germany exports more to Britain than it imports from Britain and that there are no other offsetting flows. What happens next? How does this compare with adjustment in the fixed rate regime?

4.   What are the rules for the floating rate regimes described? Is there an appropriate role for government intervention if market forces are supposed to dominate?

B.   TYPES OF EXISTING EXCHANGE RATE SYSTEMS

The IMF classifies exchange rate systems in a way designed to take account of the variation and complexity that now characterize regimes around the globe. It classifies countries on the basis of their actual (rather than officially announced) exchange rate regime, ranked by the degree of exchange rate flexibility and the government's power to manage monetary policy.[6] It is, however, quite difficult to classify systems de facto due to imperfect knowledge about what regimes countries actually follow.

---

[6] See B. Johnson, et al., International Monetary Fund, "Exchange Rate Arrangements and Currency Convertibility: Developments and Issues" 36-37 (1999).

1.   EXCHANGE ARRANGEMENTS WITH NO SEPARATE LEGAL TENDER

There are some regimes in which the currency of another country circulates as the sole legal tender or in which a country belongs to a monetary or currency union where the same legal tender is shared by members of the union (as with the Euro). Adopting such regimes leaves no scope for national monetary authorities to conduct independent monetary policy.

As of the end of 1997, the IMF identified 26 countries in this group. Of these, 14 were members of the CFA franc zone, which used a common currency, and another 6 were in a similar zone in the Caribbean. Of the remainder, Kiribati used the Australian Dollar, San Marino used the Italian Lira, and four used the U.S. Dollar. Of these six, Panama had the largest economy. Now, of course, all of the Euro countries belong to such a regime.

Dollarization, in which the U.S. Dollar serves as the substitute, is a common form of this practice. Several Latin American countries have moved to accept the Dollar. Ecuador and El Salvador adopted it in 2000, joining Panama, which used the Dollar for decades. In Argentina, which used the Dollar as a second currency for many years, the central bank suggested in January 1999 that the U.S. Dollar become the sole currency of the country but that has not occurred. Mexico has debated whether to adopt the Dollar as its national currency. Note that a partial, informal dollarization was common in former Socialist countries, which allowed the Dollar to serve as a second currency. Vietnam, for example, permitted the use of the Dollar for domestic transactions until 2000.

The effect of dollarization is to forego all monetary independence. The reason is to ensure that local politics do not lead to inflationary monetary policies. According to one study, "neither theory nor evidence suggests that removing all scope for an independent monetary policy will necessarily accelerate the pace of reform."[7] In a study of Panama's use of the Dollar, the authors concluded that dollarization does not guarantee fiscal discipline, does not help eliminate currency risk, slows GDP growth, and might slightly increase its volatility. On the other hand, however, dollarized economies tend to do very well against inflation and may even reduce the impact of external confidence shocks, although not external real shocks.[8]

A country that issues currency receives income from doing so because it pays the holder of cash no interest. A person who takes cash from a bank gives the bank a deposit in exchange. The bank gets the cash from the central bank and pays for the cash through a debit to its account at the central bank.

---

[7] B. Eichengreen, "When to Dollarize," 34 Journal of Money, Credit, and Banking (February 2002), p. 1.

[8] See M. Klein, "Dollarization and Trade," NBER Working Paper 8879 (April 2002). S. Edwards, "Dollarization and Economic Performance: An Empirical Investigation," NBER Working Paper 8274 (May 2001).

The central bank then has a liability in cash. It may, in the future, have to redeem the cash but until that time it can use the proceeds to invest in interest earning assets. The income generated is known as seigniorage. Under dollarization, the government loses the benefits of seigniorage. If Argentina were to use the U.S. Dollar, the seigniorage would go to the government of the U.S., not Argentina. Recent legislation proposed in the U.S. would share increased U.S. seigniorage with dollarizing countries, but this has been opposed by the U.S. Treasury.

A dollarized Argentina would become completely exposed to U.S. monetary policy, over which it would have no control. In addition, it could not act as a lender of last resort to its own banks, because their accounts would be in U.S. Dollars. Furthermore, the local populace could react in a hostile manner to the loss of the local currency as a national symbol.

Notes and Questions

1.   Are there any countries that you would recommend should dollarize?

2.   How does dollarization affect the U.S.?

2.   CURRENCY BOARD ARRANGEMENTS

A currency board is a monetary regime based on a commitment to exchange domestic currency for a specified foreign currency at a fixed exchange rate, combined with restrictions on the issuing authority to ensure the fulfillment of its legal obligation. This implies that domestic currency be issued only against foreign exchange and that new issues of domestic currency be fully backed by foreign assets. This eliminates traditional central bank functions such as monetary control and the lender of last resort.

The IMF identified eight countries in 2000 that used currency boards: Djibouti (since 1949), Brunei (1967), Hong Kong (1983), Argentina (1991), Estonia (1992), Lithuania (1994), Bulgaria (1997), and Bosnia (1997).[9]

By its nature, a currency board with ample reserves should not be subject to speculative attacks. Yet Hong Kong's board came under attack in October 1997. One explanation was that the board was not unambiguously seen as willing to carry out its promise to redeem or provide currency at the given rate. To counter the market perceptions, the board accepted liability for losses Hong Kong banks might suffer on their substantial dollar assets if the rate changed. Its credibility as a passive implementer was restored.[10] Argentina abandoned its 1:1 peg of the Peso to the U.S. Dollar in 2001, as the country's economy collapsed and the government defaulted on its debt.

---

[9] M. Mussa, P. Masson, A. Swoboda, E. Jadresic, P. Mauro, and A. Berg, "Exchange Rate Regimes in an Increasingly Integrated World Economy," IMF Occasional Paper 193 (2000).
[10] K. Kasa, "Why Attack a Currency Board," FRBSF Economic Letter 99-36, November 26, 1999.

Advocates of currency boards accused the government of failing to implement the rules.

3.   CONVENTIONAL FIXED PEG ARRANGEMENTS

Under conventional fixed pegs, a country pegs its currency (formally or de facto) at a fixed rate to a major currency or a basket of currencies. The basket is used to determine a weighted composite based on the geographical distribution of trade, services, or capital flows from currencies within the basket. In a conventional fixed pegged arrangement, the exchange rate fluctuates within a narrow margin of at most +/-1 percent around a central rate and the monetary authority stands ready to maintain the fixed parity through intervention, limiting the degree of monetary policy discretion.

The IMF identified, as of the end of 1997, 38 countries pegged to a single currency (of which the largest were Egypt and Nigeria) and another 16 pegged to a composite of other currencies (Kuwait and Pakistan were the largest economies in this subset). As of 2005, this category also included China.

Many smaller or non-industrial countries fix or peg their exchange rates against the currency of one or more major trading partners, then adjust as their costs change relative to the partners' costs. Pakistan, for example, might fix the Rupee against a basket of other currencies, dominated by the U.S. Dollar and the Japanese Yen. If inflation in Pakistan outstrips that in its partner countries, the Government might devalue by announcing a lower fixed rate of exchange for the Rupee. The central bank would intervene in financial markets to maintain the new rates or use direct rules. Other countries that peg only against a single currency, such as the Dollar, include The Bahamas, Egypt, Iran, and pre-2003 war Iraq.

4.   PEGGED EXCHANGE RATES WITHIN BANDS

Under this system, the value of the currency is maintained within margins of fluctuations around a formal or de facto fixed peg that are wider than the +/-1 percent. This includes the arrangements of the countries in the exchange rate mechanism of the European Monetary System (EMS) (replaced with ERM-II on January 1, 1999). The degree of monetary policy discretion depends on the degree of band width.

At the end of 1997, in addition to the cooperative arrangement of the European Monetary System described below, 14 other countries were in this group. They included several of the larger developing countries, such as Brazil, China, Ukraine, and Vietnam.

The European Monetary System

The best example of this type of exchange rate regime is the European Monetary System (EMS), which was called the snake when it began in 1972. It can be used to illustrate the mechanics and problems of such a system.

The purpose of the EMS was to keep the exchange rates of the countries in the European common market within a narrow band of each other in order to promote trade and speed economic integration. The EMS was built around a basket of currencies, each with a fixed amount that gave it a weight in a basket called the European Currency Unit (ECU). The fixed amount of each member currency was set by agreement roughly in line with the relative size of the member's economy in the EU. Every five years the amounts were reviewed and could be changed to reflect changes in the underlying economy. The members could also, by unanimous action, agree to change the amount at other times, such as when the U.K. joined the EMS in 1990. At that time, the amounts of each currency were those set out in Table 8A.

Table 8A[11]
Composition of the ECU

Currency	Amount	Weight[a]
Belgian Franc	3.431	8.1
French Franc	1.332	19.3
Lira	151.8	9.8
Dutch Guilder	0.2198	9.4
Deutschmark	0.6242	30.2
Danish Krone	0.1976	2.5
Irish Punt	0.008552	1.1
Peseta	6.885	5.3
Drachma	1.44	0.7
Sterling	0.08784	12.8
Escudo	1.04741	0.8
		100.0

[a] Weights based on exchange rates on 12 October 1990.

The weight of each currency in the ECU was determined by multiplying its rate in the market against the Dollar by its amount in the ECU. For example, 0.6242 Deutschmark had a weight of 30.2 percent of the ECU. The Dollar value of the ECU was determined by summarizing the Dollar value of all component currencies in the ECU.

Countries were to maintain the stability of their currencies against the ECU. When the amounts of each currency in the ECU basket were fixed by agreement, their central rates against the ECU were also fixed. When the U.K. joined in 1990, for example, the central rates of each currency were

---

[11] Table B from 30 Bank of England Quarterly Bulletin 479 (1990).

those given in Table 8B. From these central rates against the ECU, one could determine the central cross-rates of each currency against all other currencies in the ECU basket.

Table 8B[12]
Central rates of EMS currencies against the ECU since
October 8, 1990
Units of national currency per ECU

Belgian/Luxembourg Franc	42.4032
Danish Krone	7.84195
French Franc	6.89509
Deutschmark	2.05586
Irish Punt	0.767417
Lira	1538.24
Dutch Guilder	2.31643
Peseta	133.631
Sterling	0.696904
Drachma	205.311
Escudo	178.735

The Exchange Rate Mechanism allowed each currency to float within an agreed range around its central cross-rate with each of the other currencies. When the U.K. joined, each long-term member had to keep its currency within a band 2 1/4 percent above and below each other currency. Each newcomer—the U.K., Spain, and Portugal—had to keep its currency within a 6 percent band above and below the central cross-rates. For example, on October 8, 1990, the cross-rates between Sterling and the Deutschmark were as follows:[13]

Table 8C
£ and DM Cross-Rates in the Exchange Rate Mechanism: Upper
Limit, Central Rate, and Lower Limit on October 8, 1990

	DM 100 = £	£1 = DM
Upper limit	35.997	3.132
Central Rate	33.8984	2.95
Lower limit	31.928	2.778

When a currency gets to the edge of the band with another currency, the governments are supposed to intervene. For example, if the Pound rises to DM 3.132, then the German and U.K. governments both sell Pounds and buy DM. If the Pound falls to DM 2.778, both the German and U.K. governments buy Pounds and sell DM.

---

[12] Table C from 30 Bank of England Quarterly Bulletin 479 (1990).
[13] Table A from 30 Bank of England Quarterly Bulletin 479 (1990).

Governments may intervene other than by buying and selling currency. They may change interest rates, in order to attract or discourage cross-border flows of funds that affect the exchange rates. They may use monetary or even fiscal policy to affect the rates. They may also seek to change their currency's cross-rate, but this is seen as a last resort.

Britain withdrew from the EMS on September 16, 1992, the victim of a market whose participants believed, despite repeated assertions of commitment by the British government, that the U.K. could do nothing to prevent an inevitable devaluation of the Pound. Others argued that the pound had been the victim of speculative attacks. The withdrawal demonstrated the fragility of the EMS.

Those who argue that the markets overwhelmed the ERM central banks recount the events in the currency market in the months before the U.K. withdrew. In June, Danish voters had rejected a referendum to ratify the Maastricht treaty for economic and monetary union of EC members. The treaty, which was eventually signed December 1992, set a timetable and criteria for economic convergence that would permit monetary union. The Danish vote cast doubt on Europe's commitment to convergence and hence even the ERM.

Speculation against the Lira led Italy to devalue 7 percent on September 12, 1992, despite massive intervention by European central banks to support the Lira. Foreign exchange traders decided "the emperor had no clothes,"[14] meaning that the central banks supporting the ERM lacked the power to make it hold.

After September 12, the U.K. was the next target. The Pound Sterling was very near the bottom of the band against the DM. The new prime minister, John Major, facing an election the next spring, had incurred a large fiscal deficit and allowed interest rates to fall in order to stimulate the recession-ridden economy. Raising interest rates or devaluing the pound were not politically acceptable.

On September 16, a tidal wave of position-taking against Sterling swept the markets. Companies and institutional investors with Sterling assets tried to hedge in the foreign exchange markets. Thousands of speculators bet on devaluation. The Bank of England, armed with reserves of $40 billion, and the central banks of Germany and France, bought Sterling and sold DM, but Sterling hit the lower ERM limit mid-morning. The Bank of England raised short-term interest rates from 10 percent to 12 percent at 11:00 a.m., then to 15 percent at 2:00 p.m. At 4:00 p.m., having spent $15 billion of its reserves, the Bank of England stopped buying Sterling and at 7:45 p.m. took it out of the ERM and let it devalue.

---

[14] See S. Hansell, "Taming the Trillion-Dollar Monster," Institutional Investor International (December 1992), p. 47 and International Monetary Fund, "World Economic Outlook Interim Assessment" 1-6 (1993).

In this story, huge powerful markets react convulsively to events and swamp any efforts by governments to support a currency. Another view is that the governments' policies failed because they were crippled by flaws in fundamental economics. By implication, the policies would not have failed if economic fundamentals were strong.

There is evidence of problems with fundamentals. Inflation rates in countries like the U.K., Italy, Spain, and Portugal were persistently higher than in Germany, Belgium, and the Netherlands over several years. The ERM prevented the currencies from adjusting enough to reflect the different inflation rates. Given inflation from 1987 to 1992, for example, the Italian Lira should have devalued 18 percent against the DM, but had not. The Pound should have, but had not, devalued 10 percent against the DM since the U.K. joined the ERM in 1990. Conditions in the countries in 1992 suggested the divergence would widen.

Testing the two explanations of the crisis was difficult but important. If the speculative attacks themselves created the imbalances, then one could conclude that the EMS and probably the convergence required for monetary union were doomed because of their vulnerability. In a statistical analysis of all speculative attacks on OECD countries since 1969, Eichengreen, Rose, and Wyplosz identified prior macroeconomic problems preceding speculative attacks on currencies not in the ERM, but failed to identify them in the attacks on the ERM. While the authors did not conclude that the speculators created the ERM crises, their study suggests that effect.[15]

5.   CRAWLING PEGS

Under this system, a currency is adjusted periodically in small amounts at a fixed, preannounced rate or in response to changes in selective quantitative indicators (past inflation differentials vis-à-vis major trading partners, differentials between the target inflation and expected inflation in major trading partners, and so forth). The rate of crawl can be set to generate inflation adjusted changes in the currency's value ("backward looking") or at a preannounced fixed rate below the projected inflation differentials ("forward looking"). Maintaining a credible crawling peg imposes constraints on monetary policy in a similar manner as a fixed peg system.

At the end of 1997, only seven countries were in this group, including three smaller Latin American countries and Turkey.

---

[15] B. Eichengreen, A. Rose, and C. Wyplosz, "Speculative Attacks on Pegged Exchange Rates: An Empirical Exploration with Special Reference to the European Monetary System," NBER Working Paper 4898 (October 1994).

6.   EXCHANGE RATES WITHIN CRAWLING BANDS

Under this system, a currency is maintained within certain fluctuation margins around a central rate that is adjusted periodically at a fixed pre-announced rate or in response to changes in selective quantitative indicators. The degree of flexibility of the exchange rate is a function of the width of the band, with bands chosen to be either symmetric around a crawling central parity or to widen gradually with an asymmetric choice of the crawl of upper and lower bands (in the latter case, there is no preannouncement of a central rate). The commitment to maintain the exchange rate within the band continues to impose constraints on monetary policy, with the degree of policy independence being a function of the band width.

This group included 11 countries in 1997, such as Russia, Israel, and several countries in Eastern Europe and South America.

Notes and Questions

1.   Many economists believe that any version of fixed rates other than dollarization or currency boards (so-called corner solutions) are bad for emerging markets. Why might that be? Can you see any virtue in such systems?

7.   MANAGED FLOATING WITH NO PREANNOUNCED PATH FOR THE EXCHANGE RATE

Under this system, a monetary authority influences the movements of the exchange rate through active intervention in the foreign exchange market without specifying or precommitting to a preannounced path for the exchange rate. Indicators for managing the rate are broadly judgmental, including for example, the balance of payments position, international reserves, parallel market developments, and the adjustments may not be automatic.

The IMF identified 23 countries in this group, including many from Eastern Europe and the former Soviet Union, a few African countries, and Singapore.

8.   INDEPENDENT FLOATING

Under this system, the exchange rate is market determined, with any foreign exchange intervention aimed at moderating the rate of change and preventing undue fluctuations in the exchange rate, rather than at establishing a level for it. In these regimes, monetary policy is in principle independent of exchange rate policy.

As many as 44 countries are in this category. Most OECD countries like the U.S. that are not part of EMU float independently. In addition, many countries float in Africa and Asia, particularly those that are English speaking (e.g. Ghana and India, respectively), as do a few countries in Latin America, such as Peru. Whether a country is engaged in managed floats or independent floats is very difficult to determine.

9.   OVERALL TRENDS

The major trend in exchange rate regimes has been to flexible arrangements. Between 1976 and 1996, the use of flexible arrangements grew substantially while pegs declined, according to an IMF study.[16] Independently floating regimes grew from 1 country in 1976 to 36 in 1996, while other floating arrangements grew from 10 to 29. Pegs to the U.S. Dollar fell from 42 to 19, pegs to the French Franc held steady at 13, pegs to other single currencies fell from 7 to 5, and pegs to composite currencies fell from 24 to 20. Part of the growth occurred as IMF membership grew with the collapse of the Soviet Union. Part, however, was by choice, as member countries opted for more liberal regimes. The cost of managing a pegged rate became too high with the external shocks and higher variability of currencies in major economies.[17] The dramatic changes included a big shift by industrial countries from pegged or managed floating regimes to those with more flexibility, and by developing and emerging countries from pegged to managed floating.

10.   THE DEBATE ABOUT THE NON-SYSTEM

a.   EXCHANGE RATE REGIME FOR MAJOR COUNTRIES

People referred to the international monetary "non-system" by the late 1980s. They observed that no agreement existed among the world's nations about how to share responsibilities to correct significant balance of payments disequilibria. Although the Dollar still served as the reserve currency, its strength eroded against currencies like the Yen and the Deutschmark/Euro.

Proponents of new systems abound. One proposal built on the European Monetary System. It would define zones in which currencies could fluctuate without government intervention, specify government's duties when a currency reached the edge of a band, and provide rules for realignment.[18] Another proposal would set target rates to reflect economic fundamentals, realign the targets continuously as the fundamentals shifted, allow relatively broad bands (say ten percent above or below the target rate), and even allow currencies to move outside those bands temporarily. A more ambitious version would have the G-7 follow a blueprint for economic policy

---

[16] See IMF *World Economic Outlook* (October 1997), at 79.
[17] See IMF *Survey*, November 17, 1997, at 357.
[18] See P. Kenen, "Ways to Reform Exchange-Rate Arrangements," in *Bretton Woods: Looking to the Future* (Bretton Woods Commission ed., July 1994).

coordination to meet agreed current account targets, assisted by a permanent secretariat (possibly in the IMF).[19]

The problem for these proposals was that many people believed the "non-system" was not particularly bad. In their view, exchange rates had been relatively stable from 1987. Changing fundamentals justified the decline in the dollar after that time.[20] One leading scholar argued that it was a mistake to see countries as being forced to choose between fixed rates or a completely floating system. In his view, different regimes are appropriate for different countries or for the same country at different times. Very large countries may find floating best because it gives them some control over their monetary policy, while small open countries or those with a history of hyperinflation may prefer fixed regimes since they lack effective control over monetary policy. Many countries could, however, prefer the middle ground of some partial float. Examples include those trying to end high inflation, with an overvalued peg, or with a large neighbor with which they are tightly linked.[21]

b.   THE DOLLAR EXCHANGE RATE

In 2004, the current account deficit was $694 billion and it was projected to be even higher in 2005. The U.S. budget deficit of $412 billion was also substantial. These persistent twin deficits have contributed to the decline of the Dollar. From 2002 to December 2004 the Dollar was in decline by over 30 percent against the Euro and Sterling. But the trade-weighted decline against all currencies is much less, 15 percent.[22]

The sharp depreciation of the Dollar can have some important effects on the U.S. economy. While exports should increase, more expensive imports can cause inflation thereby resulting in higher interest rates as the Fed attempts to counter the effects of inflation, and a resulting contraction in GDP. However, the connection between the falling Dollar and rising prices of imports is a complicated one. During the period of the 30 percent fall in the value of the dollar, the prices of imported manufacturing goods from the European Union rose only by 9 percent, indicating that the principal impact of decline were lower profit margins rather than higher prices. This means that the lower price of the Dollar has not had a significant impact on U.S. inflation. The increase in domestic rates by the Fed appears more related to

---

[19] See C. Bergsten and J. Williamson, "Is the Time Ripe for Target Zones or the Blueprint?," in *Bretton Woods: Looking to the Future* (Bretton Woods Commission ed., July 1994).

[20] See M. Wolff, "In Praise of the International Monetary Non-System," *Financial Times*, March 28 1994.

[21] J. Frankel, "No Single Currency Regime is Right for All Countries or At All Times," NBER Working Paper 7338 (September 1999).

[22] M. Dooley, D. Folkerts-Landau, P. Garber, "The Revived Bretton Woods System: Alive and Well," Deutsche Bank, Global Markets Research (December 2004) (Bretton Woods Two)

domestic inflation caused by high deficit spending.[23] Some have argued that the Dollar would have to fall by at least another 20 percent to eliminate the trade deficit.[24]

Financing for the twin deficits comes from abroad through the sale of Treasury securities. A major concern is whether foreign financing of these deficits will continue at its current levels without a substantial increase in interest rates to attract investors, the majority of which are foreign central banks. Substantial increases in interest rates would risk causing recession and loss of jobs. Some argue that there will be no fall off in the demand for Treasuries even as the Dollar might depreciate further. This might be because foreign investors will find a cheaper Dollar even more attractive (with its growth potential).[25] Or it may be because foreign central banks, like that of China, will continue to accumulate Dollars through currency interventions (to keep the Dollar-Yuan peg in place) and will then invest those Dollars in U.S. treasuries. Indeed, ironically, if the Chinese were to float the Yuan, as demanded by the U.S., there would be less accumulation of Dollars by central banks (China is the second leading holder of U.S. Treasuries) and possibly less deficit financing available (this assumes central banks may be more willing to hold U.S. treasuries than investors in general). Ben Bernanke, the newly appointed Chairman of the U.S. Council of Economic Advisers, contends that a "global savings glut" created by growth in emerging economies will, in any event, keep the demand for the Dollar strong.[26] Much of this analysis assumes the Dollar might depreciate further, but between March and June 2005 it was appreciating. This is also evidence that there is no significant sell-off of Dollars by central banks.

There is one bright side to a weaker Dollar—an increase in U.S. wealth. Exchange rate movements change the relative value of assets in countries. An example is the size of net U.S. financial claims on residents of other countries, in the form of bonds, stock held in portfolios, and direct investment. By the end of 2001, U.S. residents held claims on foreign residents of $9.2 trillion (these are assets for U.S. residents). Non-residents held claims on U.S. residents of $6.9 trillion. These are U.S. liabilities. Net U.S. liabilities exceeded U.S. assets by $2.3 trillion. The net figure had doubled from the end of 1999. Over 30 percent of this increase was due to the strong Dollar. The rising Dollar lowered the Dollar value of assets and liabilities held in other currencies. It does not affect the Dollar value of assets and liabilities held in Dollars, of course. But securities in foreign currencies are a larger share of total U.S. liabilities than of U.S. assets, so the impact of

---

[23] Remarks by A. Greenspan, "Current Account," at Advancing Enterprise 2005 Conference (February 4, 2005).
[24] M. Obstfeld and K. Rogoff, "The Unsustainable Current Account Position Revisited," NBER Working Paper 10869 (October 2004).
[25] Bretton Woods Two, supra note 22.
[26] The Economist, "Wide Gap, Wide Yawn," March 17, 2005.

Dollar appreciation was greater on liabilities than assets.[27] This means that a falling Dollar can actually serve to offset the current account deficit by increasing U.S. net worth. One study calculates that from 2002-2004, as the Dollar fell in value, that its foreign asset position grew by 5.5 percent.[28]

In 2004, the Bush Administration articulated three types of economic policies to address the current account deficit: U.S. savings via tax incentives for households and a lower budget deficit; structural reforms to fuel growth in the rest of the world (increased consumption and investment in the rest of the world could reduce the trade deficit by increasing U.S. exports and offset the recessionary impact of higher U.S. interest rates) and the adjustment of U.S. exchange rates.[29] What would you do if you were in charge?

C.   CAPITAL CONTROLS AND FOREIGN EXCHANGE REGIMES

One way governments tried to counter the financial and economic impact of foreign exchange markets was to control the movement of capital into and out of their country. In the period after the Second World War, many countries—industrial, developing, and socialist—turned to capital controls. They hoped that these controls would give freer rein to domestic monetary policy, prevent the inflationary effects of financial inflows, prevent domestic savers and financial intermediaries from misreading foreign exchange risk (assuming that the exchange rate was managed rather than set by the market) or speculating against the currency, and repress the domestic financial system to keep the cost of funds low for the government and domestic firms. The goal was to segregate domestic and international financial markets.[30]

The two main types of capital controls are direct controls, relying on administrative action, and indirect controls, relying on the market. Direct controls generally set quantitative limits on the cross-border movement of funds and rely on banks to enforce them. Anyone who wants to import or export capital can only do so with permission from the exchange authorities working through the banks. Indirect controls distinguish among types of foreign exchange transactions, applying differential taxes, multiple exchange rates, or compulsory deposits to those transactions that are favored or not.[31]

---

[27] C. Tille, "The Impact of Exchange Rate Movements on U.S. Foreign Debt," 9 Federal Reserve Bank of New York Current Issues in Economics and Finance (January 2003), p. 1.

[28] P. Lane and G. Milesi-Ferretti, "Financial Globalization and Exchange Rates," IMF Working Paper 05/03, January 2005 (Table 7).

[29] J. Taylor, Keynote Address, American Enterprise Institute Conference on Policy Challenges of Global Payment Imbalances, (November 4, 2004).

[30] See A. Ariyoshi, K. Habermeier, B. Laurens, I. Otker-Robe, J. Canales-Kriljenko, and A. Kirilenko, "Capital Control: Country Experiences with Their Use and Liberalization," IMF Occasional Paper 190 (2000). (Ariyoshi-IMF)

[31] Id., at 7.

The controls may be used in conjunction with the managed foreign exchange regimes described above. Countries that peg their currency, for example, may rely on capital controls. On the other hand, floating rate regimes are not compatible with capital controls, nor are regimes tied to another currency, such as dollarization or currency boards.

The effectiveness of capital controls seems to vary over the short- and long-run. Controls seem to moderate the impact of short-term capital inflows initially, but are hard to maintain for very long, particularly when the country has a sophisticated financial system, as in Brazil or Chile. When capital outflows grow, controls may delay domestic adjustments. Controls imposed on outflows during a financial crisis receive mixed reviews. Malaysia seemed to have benefited from focused capital controls that allowed the domestic economy some breathing space to recover from the 1997 financial crisis described in Chapter 19. Extensive capital controls imposed in Romania, Russia, and Venezuela, however, reduced access to foreign capital. Long-standing capital controls in India and China may have helped reduce their vulnerability to regional crises in the late 1990s, but so did other domestic economic policies. A study of 160 currency crises in 69 developing countries from 1975-97, controlling for "macroeconomic, political, and institutional characteristics," concluded that capital controls do not insulate economies from currency problems; rather they appear to increase the vulnerability of economies to speculative attack."[32] A big debate about the transition from capital controls is whether it should be rapid or deliberate. Despite speedy decontrols in some countries, many observers seem countries should decontrol gradually while they build their domestic financial systems.[33]

One of the major arguments the Chinese have advanced for not adjusting their exchange rates—a matter more fully discussed below is the fear that such flexibility would require the removal of capital controls, which in turn could lead to an outflow of bank deposits abroad, further weakening the already fragile Chinese banking system. This contention can be questioned. First, it is far from clear bank deposits would leave the country if capital controls were weakened. In Japan, which has no capital controls, deposits remained in a bankrupt banking system for close to a decade. Second, it is far from clear that more flexible exchange rates require a weakening of outward capital controls. An IMF paper contends that an exchange rate can still fluctuate on the basis of supply and demand in the presence of capital controls.[34] Third, it is far from clear that capital controls

---

[32] R. Glick and M. Hutchison, "Capital Controls and Exchange Rate Instability in Developing Economies," Federal Reserve Bank of San Francisco Pacific Basin Working Paper (December 2000).

[33] See Ariyoshi-IMF, supra note 31.

[34] E. Prasad, T. Rumbaugh, and Q. Wang, "Putting the Cart Before the Horse? Capital Account Liberalization and Exchange Rate Flexibility in China," IMF Policy Discussion Paper 05/01, January 2005.

are truly binding, given the potential for evasion through manipulated trade transactions or the use of bribes (see Chapter 19). Finally, the Yuan could be adjusted by a revaluation rather than through floating, making the issue of need to adjust capital controls moot.

b.   EXCHANGE RATE REGIMES FOR EMERGING MARKETS

Common wisdom today based on the Asian crisis is that exchange rate systems should be bipolar, either a "hard-peg" or freely floating.[35]

It may not matter whether a small economy uses a fixed or floating regime. A study of five small open economies (Czech Republic, Greece, Hungary, Israel, Poland) "found no empirical evidence that the pressures on exchange rates, interest rates and stock markets were primarily influenced by the exchange rate regime in place."[36] Another study, this one of East Asian economies, concluded that "average differences in macroeconomic performance under pegging and floating in the region were relatively modest."[37]

In 2005, one of the most hotly debated exchange rate issues concerned the Dollar/Yuan (Chinese) exchange rate. The Chinese have pegged their currency to the Dollar at around 8.28 to 1 for about a decade. As the Dollar has depreciated substantially since 2002, this has had the effect of creating a highly undervalued Yuan, given the sizeable Chinese trade surplus and importation of foreign capital. This has caused a political stir in the U.S., as the Congress fears (or perhaps more importantly their constituents) the loss of foreign jobs abroad as a result of undervalued Chinese imports displacing more expensive domestic goods. Until recently the U.S. Treasury resisted Congressional calls to put more pressure on the Chinese. This could have been for a variety of reasons, ranging from the technical readiness of the Chinese to float their currency without removing their system of capital controls to an unwillingness to alienate the Chinese whose help we were actively seeking in dealing with the North Korean nuclear threat. In May 2005, however, the policy of the United States shifted to calling for an immediate 10 percent revaluation of the Yuan (many believe the Yuan is undervalued by as much as 25-40 percent). The "shadow" Yuan, traded offshore via so-called non-deliverable forward contracts, hit 7.8 to the Dollar in January, about 6 percent higher than the pegged rate.[38] There has been a substantial influx of Dollars into China in 2005 in anticipation of a revaluation, putting pressure on the pegged rate, prompting China to impose

---

[35] S. Fischer, "Exchange Rate Regimes: Is the Bipolar View Correct?," 15 Journal of Economic Perspectives (2001), p. 3.

[36] Z. Darvas and G. Szapary, "Financial Contagion in Five Small Open Economies: Does the Exchange Rate Regime Really Matter?," International Finance (April 2000).

[37] R. Moreno, "Pegging and Macroeconomic Performance in East Asia," Federal Reserve Bank of San Francisco Pacific Basin Working Paper (December 2000).

[38] The Economist, "What's it Worth?," May 19, 2005.

capital controls on some inward flows and to relax controls on outward investment.[39]

U.S. policy seems largely for political consumption since most experts believe that such a revaluation will actually have little impact on U.S. trade deficits or job loss.[40] Nonetheless, the Administration threatened in testimony before Congress to cite the Chinese for "currency manipulation" under U.S. trade law unless change was forthcoming.[41] Title 22 U.S.C. §5304 requires the Secretary of Treasury to analyze on an annual basis whether countries manipulate the rate of exchange between their currency and the Dollar for purposes of preventing effective balance of payments adjustment or gaining unfair competitive advantage in international trade. The Treasury has taken the position that a country could be said to manipulate its exchange rate if it intentionally acts "to set its exchange rate at levels such that for a protracted period the exchange rate differs significantly from the rate that would have prevailed in the absence of action by the authorities."[42]

Notes and Questions

1. What exchange rate system would you recommend for emerging market countries?

2. What exchange rate system would you recommend for developed countries? What exchange rate system would you recommend for emerging market countries?

Notes and Questions

1. How would capital controls affect cross-border and offshore financial transactions and activities? For example, would Citibank's bank subsidiary in Bombay, India be likely to want India to remove its exchange controls? How would capital controls in South Africa be likely to affect the development of the Johannesburg Stock Exchange and the exchanges of neighboring countries? Would Swiss banks, on balance, want all countries to abolish their capital controls?

2. Developing countries with large economies, such as China and India, have apparently used capital controls to insulate themselves from the vagaries of international capital flows. Why would a country like Indonesia, with a population of almost 200 million and a diversifying economy, reject capital controls as ineffective?

---

[39] B. Perrett, "China Moves Again to Ease Upward Pressure on Yuan," Reuters, May 22, 2005.

[40] A. Balls, "China Told by U.S. to Revalue Renminbi by 10%," *Financial Times*, May 24, 2005. On the other hand, the Chinese have claimed that export growth in China could slow significantly if the Yuan were to appreciate—perhaps not to the U.S.

[41] Testimony of Treasury Secretary John W. Snow, before the Senate Committee on Banking, Housing and Urban Affairs on the Treasury's "Report to Congress on International Economic and Exchange Rate Policies (Exchange Rate Report)," May 26, 2005., p. 4.

[42] Department of the Treasury, Report to the Committee on Appropriations on Clarification of Statutory Provisions Addressing Currency Manipulation (March 11, 2005), p. 2.

3.   Do you agree with the editors of The Economist, who announced in May 2003, that they favor carefully designed capital controls? Trade in capital is different from trade in goods because, they said, unlike trade markets "international markets in capital are prone to error" and "punishment for big financial mistakes can be draconian, and tends to hurt innocent bystanders. ..." This was, they said, a major change in their free-trade philosophy. They recognized that governments often abused capital controls. Developed economies should do without controls because they have the markets and institutions to handle the flows, and developing countries should aim in that direction for the longer-term, not just yet. The editors cited approvingly Chile's simple and transparent tax on short-term inflows; the tax fell as maturities lengthened. Outflows should be free, to encourage investment. Their view implied an immediate change in policy. Through bilateral trade agreements and the WTO, the U.S. was requiring emerging markets to open their financial markets completely, and often soon. These "new free-trade arrangements" to assure "complete capital-account liberalization" were "a mistake." For treaty purposes, the U.S. should see such a tax as a prudential rule.[43]

D.   FOREIGN EXCHANGE MARKETS

Foreign exchange markets include cash, spot, forward, swap, futures, and options. Here we focus on the spot and forward markets. Elsewhere in the book we treat derivatives markets. The cash market transfers bank notes at both a retail level, or users such as travelers, and a wholesale level among banks. It is relatively small.

Daily worldwide foreign exchange turnover in traditional markets (spot, forward and forex swaps) grew from $590 billion in 1989 to $1.5 trillion, then fell to $1.2 trillion in 2001 with the introduction of the Euro and on-line trading, described below. The rate of growth measured in nominal Dollars was already slowing: 26 percent in 1995-98, compared to 48 percent from 1992-95 and 42 percent from 1989-92. Part of the slowdown reflected the increased strength of the Dollar against other currencies. Transactions increasingly took place in two locations: London (26 percent of all activity in 1989 and 31 percent in 2001) and New York (16 percent in 1989 and 2001). The shares of other centers by 2001 were: Tokyo - 9 percent (down from 15 percent in 1989), Singapore - 6 percent, Hong Kong 4 percent, Zurich - 4 percent, and Frankfurt - 5 percent. Most transactions – by 2001, 90 percent – involved the U.S. Dollar, though trading of "exotic" currencies, such as those of emerging markets, increased. In most countries, the spot market dominated, but its share of all FX trading had declined worldwide from about

---

[43] "A Place for Capital Controls and Where Capital Controls Make Sense," The Economist, May 1, 2003.

60 percent in 1989 to 32 percent in 2001; in the remainder, the share of forex swaps was five times larger than forwards in 2001.

In addition to the traditional markets, daily turnover in currency derivatives (mainly options) was $60 billion and OTC interest rate derivatives (mainly swaps) was $489 billion by 2001.[44]

1.   THE SPOT FOREIGN EXCHANGE MARKET[45]

The spot foreign exchange market is where currency can be bought or sold for immediate delivery, usually two days following the transaction. The price at which the currency is quoted is known as the "spot rate."

The foreign exchange market is the largest financial market in the world. It is an informal organization of the larger commercial banks and a number of foreign exchange brokers for buying and selling foreign currencies. The spot markets are extremely efficient. Spreads between buying and selling prices can be smaller than a tenth of a percent of the value of a contract. This is about one-fortieth of the spread international travelers pay to exchange currency notes.

This efficiency is also seen in the tremendous speed with which exchange rates respond to the continuous flow of information on the market. The participants are linked together by telephone, Telex, and a satellite communications network called the Society for Worldwide International Financial Telecommunications (SWIFT). Owing to the speed of communications, significant events have almost immediate impact everywhere in the world despite the huge distances separating market participants. In fact, some of the major foreign exchange players in London, New York, and Tokyo maintain 24-hour operations. This is why the foreign exchange market is as efficient as a conventional stock or commodity market housed under a common roof.

The banks and foreign exchange brokers, in all countries, collectively establish exchange rates. Each dealer gets a sense of where the market is headed and takes positions to buy or sell on the basis of these assumptions and corresponding to orders received from customers. The feel for the market in each currency as well as the goal of trying to balance the books, is what determines the position the banker is willing to take. If it is determined that the bank's exposure in Euros should be balanced and, further, customers wish to sell Euros, the bank will enter the market to sell Euros.

Once the amount of buying or selling of a currency has been decided, the banker will contact other foreign exchange dealers to "ask for the market." The banker does not reveal whether he wants to buy or sell, but

---

[44] See Bank for International Settlements, "Triennial Central Bank Survey of Foreign Exchange and Derivatives Markets Activity in 2001," (October 19, 1998), and "Turnover on Foreign Exchange Markets Tumbles," *Financial Times*, May 13, 2001.
[45] See M. Levi, *International Finance* (2d ed. 1990), pp. 29-37.

rather might inquire, "What's your market in Euros?" This means he is asking for the price at which the other party is willing to buy and sell Euros for U.S. Dollars. The reason for the veil of secrecy is that the stakes are incredibly high. A mere difference in quotation of the fourth decimal place of a price can mean thousands of Dollars on a large order.

If the banker who has been called wants to sell Euros, he will quote on the side that is felt to be cheap for Euros, given this banker's sense of the market. For example, if the banker believes that other banks are selling Euros at $1.1328/Euro he or she might quote $1.1326/Euro as the selling price to attract business. The banker actually quotes both the buying and selling price. Having considered the two-way price, the caller will state whether he desires to buy or sell Euros and the amount. Once the rate has been quoted, custom requires that it must be honored regardless of the decision of the caller and the amount that is involved. The caller has about one minute to decide and it is permissible to change the rate after this time. While it is only exchange rates between banks that are settled in the spot market, exchange rates paid by banks' clients are based on these interbank rates. Banks charge their customers slightly more than the going selling or ask rate, and pay their customers slightly less than the buying or bid rate.

The method for conducting business with brokers is different from that of banks dealing with each other. A bank calls a broker and states how much foreign currency it wants to buy or sell and the rate at which it is willing to transact. This means that it will not ask for a two-way market but will offer to buy or sell at a set rate for a certain amount. The broker will announce to other banks what rates and amounts are available, always showing the best quotes to the potential counterparties. If the two sides of the market are equivalent so that a bank will meet the exchange rate demanded by another bank, a trade will be struck. Until an agreement has been met, neither of the two parties are aware of the identity of the other. Once the contract is created, the broker provides the names of the two banks and receives a fee from each of them. This fee makes dealing through brokers more costly than direct exchange, encouraging larger institutions to try to make a market between themselves before turning to a broker.

In 1992, electronic foreign exchange brokerage services were introduced. Within the next two years, at least four competing services appeared. Two leading providers were Reuters and Electronic Broking System. Electronic broking allowed banks' dealers, particularly in smaller banks, to by-pass the brokers and offer, buy, or sell orders directly to other banks' dealers. Trades are anonymous and prices transparent, unlike trades with brokers. By 1996, electronic broking accounted for over 33 percent of all spot transactions and over 50 percent of Yen-Dollar spot transactions in Tokyo.[46]

---

[46] See T. Ito and D. Folkerts-Landau, *International Capital Markets* (IMF, 1996), pp. 126-9.

Leading international banks, handling 30 percent of FX business, established a central clearing bank linking national systems to provide instantaneous settlement. CLS Bank International began operations in September 2002, two to three years behind schedule. This system is dealt with in some detail in Chapter 9.

2.   THE FORWARD MARKET

In the forward market, the parties contract to deliver currency at a specified date in the future, at a price agreed upon today. Forward exchange quotations are common in the most heavily traded currencies. Banks will give each other quotations only for rather short periods, such as 30 days, 90 days, and 180 days. Banks tailor contract periods for their customers from two days to several years. The longer contracts carry greater spreads between the buy and sell prices because as maturity increases the market thins, making it more difficult for banks to offset their positions.

Forward contracts may also be written as part of a swap arrangement, the simplest form of which matches an exchange of one currency for another on the current spot value date and a reverse exchange on a forward basis. Since the two foreign exchange transactions are made at preset exchange rates, there is no exchange risk in this transaction, but considerable counterparty risk can be involved as one transaction is not made until the contract matures.

3.   THE 1997 INTERNATIONAL FOREIGN EXCHANGE MASTER AGREEMENT (IFEMA)

The British Bankers Association and the Foreign Exchange Committee, as advisory committee sponsored by the Federal Reserve Bank of New York, made up of participants in the foreign exchange market, have formulated rules affecting certain aspects of spot and forward exchange transactions. These rules were most recently revised in 1997. The rules are intended to reflect "best practice" in the market.

As a Master Agreement, its provisions can readily be incorporated into particular foreign exchange contracts.

The rules govern such matters as close-out netting, force majeure, and events of default.

The provisions of this Master Agreement were at issue in a case brought by Kuok Oil & Grains PTE Ltd. against foreign banks including Deutsche Bank (DB) over the terms of the "close-out" netting of certain of its foreign exchange contracts following the imposition of Malaysian exchange controls in September 1998. The case eventually was settled. The following is an excerpt from the expert report of Professor Scott in that case.

Background Information On Financial Markets

The spot foreign exchange market is one in which a currency can be bought or sold for immediate delivery, usually two days following the transaction. The amount of the currencies are usually delivered by payments made through the payment systems of the countries whose currencies are involved. For example, suppose a deal is struck for Party A to deliver to Party B 1000 US Dollars (USD) in exchange for Malaysian Ringgit (RM) at a spot rate of 1 USD = 4 RM. Within two days, Party A would transfer USD 1000 to Party B through the U.S. payment system, and Party B would transfer 4000 RM to Party A through the Malaysian payment system. Daily worldwide foreign exchange turnover in traditional markets (spot, forward and swaps) was estimated to be USD 1.5 trillion in 1998, 40% of which were spot transactions.

In the forward foreign exchange market, parties contract today to deliver currency at a specified date in the future, at a price agreed upon today. Forward exchange contracts often come in maturities of one month, three months and six months. For example, suppose a three month forward exchange contract in which Party A sells Party B USD 1000 at a forward exchange rate of 1 USD = 4.2 RM. In three months, Party A has to deliver 1000 USD to Party B and Party B has to deliver 4200 RM to Party A, again through the U.S. and Malaysian payment systems. Assuming the spot rate was 1 USD = 4RM at the time the forward exchange contract was struck, the USD would be at a forward exchange premium against the RM, that is the market expects the USD to appreciate against the RM in three months....

Parties often use forward exchange and swap transactions, as well as futures and options contracts, to hedge foreign exchange exposures in their business. For example, suppose Company A is buying a commodity in Malaysia from Company B in RM and selling it to Company C in Singapore in USD. Further suppose the current exchange rate is USD 1 = 4 RM, that the commodity will be purchased today at the price of 4000 RM payable in two months, and has been sold for delivery in two months at the price of USD 1000 plus a profit. If in two months the RM appreciates against the Dollar, so that USD 1 = 3.8 RM, Company A's profit may be adversely affected. It will need USD 1052.63 to buy 4000 RM (4000/3.8) to pay for the commodity, and will only receive USD 1000 from the resale of the commodity, thus losing USD 52.63.

Company A can protect itself through hedging its foreign exchange exposure through the use of a forward exchange contract. If Company A enters into a USD 1000 forward exchange contract with a two month maturity at the rate of USD 1 = 4 RM, so that the forward exchange contract matures on the date payment is due to Company B, it will be protected against changes in the USD/RM exchange rate. If the rate in two months moves to USD 1 = 3.8 RM, Company A will still lose USD 52.63 on the commodity trade. But it will make an offsetting gain on the forward exchange contract. It will obtain 4000 RM for its 1000 USD on the forward exchange, and be able to resell the 4000 RM in the spot market for USD 1052.63. Alternatively, Company A can simply use the 4000 RM proceeds from the forward exchange contract to make the required 4000 RM payment on its supply contract. Without the ability to hedge, commodity dealers would have to have higher profit margins to compensate them for increased currency risk which means lower prices for suppliers and higher prices for purchasers.

If Company A entered into the same 1000 USD forward exchange contract at USD 1 = 4 RM, without having any underlying commodity transaction, its forward exchange contract would be speculative rather than a hedge. If the RM appreciated in two months in the spot market to USD 1 = 3.8 RM, Company A would make a profit of USD 52.63 on the exchange transaction with no offsetting loss on the commodity transaction. It would pay USD 1000 to obtain 4000 RM under the forward exchange contract, and turn around and sell the 4000 RM in the spot market for USD 1052.63. On the other hand, if the RM depreciated, so that spot price in two months was USD 1 = 4.2 RM, Company A would lose money. It would again purchase 4000 RM for USD 1000 under the forward exchange contract, but the RM would now only be worth USD 952.38 (4000/4.2) in the spot market. . . .

The Exchange Control Malaysia Measures (ECM)

As understood by the financial community, the ECM measures imposed by the Malaysian Government on September 1, 1998 were intended to prevent further depreciation of the RM against the USD and other major currencies by combating speculation against the RM.

Based on the press accounts, as well as my conversations with bankers and economists, it was generally perceived in world financial markets that the purpose of the ECM measures was to control speculation against the RM, not to interfere in foreign trade transactions or legitimate hedging transactions related to foreign trade.

Based on the materials supplied to me involving this matter and my meetings with KUOK in Singapore from May 10-12, 2000, I conclude that the KUOK forward exchange transactions were not speculative transactions in RM of the type which the ECM measures were designed to combat. They were engaged in the international trading of edible oils and grains, and purchased some of their commodities from Malaysian suppliers. They entered into forward exchange contracts as a hedge, to protect themselves against the fluctuation of the RM against the USD. All of the transactions entered into by KUOK involved purchases of the RM which had the effect of strengthening rather than weakening its value against the USD.

It is my understanding that KUOK had, before the imposition of the ECM Measures, regularly instructed Deutsche Bank to use the proceeds of its forward exchange contracts to pay KUOK's suppliers and that, in fact, KUOK held no RM account with DB.

Based on the underlying purpose of the ECM Measures, a reasonable banker would expect that the KUOK forward exchange transactions would be approved by Malaysian authorities.

The Close Out By DB Of Kuok's Foreign Exchange Contracts

In foreign exchange contracts, parties have the obligation to deliver the currencies they promise to deliver unless otherwise agreed. Thus, on the KUOK forward exchange contracts with DB, DB had the obligation to deliver RM.

As of September 1998, provisions of certain banking industry standard form contracts provided for the closing out of foreign exchange contracts if either party to the contract were prevented from performing by reason of force majeure, act of state, illegality or impossibility. See for example, paragraphs 5.1, 6.1, and 6.2 of The 1997 International Foreign Exchange Master Agreement (IFEMA) promulgated by the Foreign Exchange Committee (FEC) in association with The British Bankers' Association, the Canadian Foreign Exchange Committee and the Tokyo Foreign Exchange Committee.

Such terms did not apply, however, to the KUOK foreign exchange contracts with DB since they were not specifically incorporated into these contracts. Industry practice requires that counterparties agree to be bound by the terms of Master Agreements; they are not automatically incorporated into contracts.

The FEC is made up of institutions representing commercial banks, U.S. and foreign (including DB), investment banks, and other foreign exchange dealers and brokers. It is coordinated through the Federal Reserve Bank of New York which serves as an ex officio member of the Committee. On September 2, 1998, FEC issued a press release recommending close out of RM positions. It urged the parties to RM transactions to "contact each other to facilitate speedy agreement" as to how this should be done. It did not recommend that the banks in Singapore impose a unilaterally determined solution.

It is my understanding that the close out procedures adopted by the Singapore Foreign Exchange Market Committee of the Singapore Association of Banks, which included the USD/RM rate of 4.00, were adopted without consultation with or the agreement of KUOK, a party to a substantial number of RM transactions with DB.

If IFEMA had applied to the KUOK foreign exchange contracts with DB, DB would have been required under Section 5.1(b)(I)(A)(3) to use a close out rate of USD 1 = 3.8 RM because this was the rate at which RM could be bought for USD. Moreover, under Section 6.1, the applicable calculation would have been made by KUOK and not DB. As stated in the 1997 IFEMA Guide, p. 11, if the Non-Defaulting Party [KUOK] determines not to enter into replacement transactions, the settlement amount would be based on market prices, as reflected in quotations from brokers or dealers or reports or other evidence of actual trades."

KUOK entered into a number of forward exchange contracts with DB at the average contracted forward exchange rate of USD 1 = 4.2 RM. After the imposition of exchange controls by the Malaysian Government on September 1, 1998, DB closed out KUOK outstanding forward exchange contracts on September 8 using an exchange rate of USD 1 = 4.0 RM.

It is my understanding that DB closed out the contracts as follows. Suppose KUOK had sold USD 1,000,000 for RM under a forward exchange contract entered into on June 29, 1998 with a maturity date of November 2, 1998 (approximately a four month forward exchange contract) at a rate of USD 1 = 4.2700 RM. Under the contract, KUOK was required to deliver USD 1,000,000 to DB on November 2, 1998 in exchange for 4,270,000 RM.

Since DB was closing out the contract on September 8, about two months in advance, it calculated the present value of the RM. It used RM zero coupon interest rates to discount RM, e.g. the rate used for two month maturities was 26.8454. Using a standard present value formula, 4,270,000 RM in two months would be worth about 4,104,076 RM,[47] or USD 1,026,016 at the USD/RM exchange rate of 4.0. It used the USD SIBOR rate, e.g. 5.625%, to discount the Dollar side of the contract. Using a standard present value formula, USD 1,000,000 in two months would be worth about USD 990,920.[48] Thus, KUOK would receive USD 35,096 from DB (USD 1,026,016 - USD 990,920).

---

[47] Present Value = $\dfrac{\text{RM } 4,270,000}{(1+ 26.8454\%)^{(2/12)}}$

[48] Present Value = $\dfrac{\text{USD} 1,000,000}{(1+ 5.625\%)^{(2/12)}}$

I reiterate my view that DB was not entitled to close out its forward exchange contracts with KUOK. Assuming arguendo that these contracts were to be closed out, DB should have the burden of establishing that the rate of exchange and rate of discount used to arrive at a close out amount were appropriate and fair.

Assuming arguendo that these contracts were to be closed out, it was unreasonable for DB to use a rate of 4.0 for converting RM to USD. The close out should have been at the rate of 3.8, since this would be the rate KUOK would then get in the market when it purchased RM for USD. This was KUOK's replacement cost. The rate of 4.0 was arbitrary even though it was recommended by the Singapore Foreign Exchange Market Committee of the Association of Banks in Singapore. The appropriate rate had to be determined by reference to the actual market rate not by a an arbitrary determination of any single organization. The only market rate after the imposition of the ECM Measures was 3.8. The fact that this rate was fixed by government authorities does not mean that this was not the market rate, as 3.8 was the rate at which RM was actually exchanged for the USD in the market.

Again assuming arguendo that these contracts were to be closed out, and further assuming the discount rate used for RM in calculating the close out amount was 26.8454%, I conclude that this discount rate was unrealistic. This conclusion is based on my understanding that RM could no longer be invested at that rate after the imposition of ECM on September 1, 1999. The 26.8454% rate was previously available in the offshore market for RM borrowings before the imposition of ECM but that offshore market ceased to function after the imposition of ECM.

Conclusions

The KUOK forward exchange transactions were not speculative transactions in RM of the type which the ECM measures were designed to combat.

A reasonable banker would have expected that the KUOK settlement of forward exchange transactions would be approved by Malaysian authorities.

Assuming arguendo that the KUOK forward exchange contracts with DB were to be closed out, DB should have the burden of establishing that the rate of exchange and rate of discount used to arrive at a close out amount were appropriate and fair.

Assuming arguendo that the KUOK forward exchange contracts with DB were to be closed out, the close out should have been at the rate of 3.8, since this would be the rate KUOK would get in the market when it purchased RM for USD.

Again assuming arguendo that these contracts were to be closed out, the use of a discount rate of 26.8454% would be unrealistic since this rate was no longer available in the market.

The provisions of the Master Agreement referred to in Scott's Report read as follows.

Section 5. Close-Out And Liquidation

5.1   Manner of Close-Out and Liquidation.

(a) Close-Out. If an Event of Default has occurred and is continuing, then the Non-Defaulting Party shall have the right to close out all, but not less than all, outstanding Currency Obligations (including any Currency Obligation which has not been performed and in respect of which the Value Date is on or precedes the Close-Out Date) except to the extent that in the good faith opinion of the Non-Defaulting Party certain of such Currency Obligations may not be closed out under applicable law. Such close-out shall be effective upon receipt by the Defaulting Party of notice that the Non-Defaulting Party is terminating such Currency Obligations. Notwithstanding the foregoing, unless otherwise agreed by the Parties in Part X of the Schedule, in the case of an Event of Default in clause (ii), (iii) or (iv) of the definition thereof with respect to a Party and, if agreed by the Parties in Part IX of the Schedule, in the case of any other Event of Default specified and so agreed in Part IX with respect to a Party, close-out shall be automatic as to all outstanding Currency Obligations, as of the time immediately preceding the institution of the relevant Insolvency Proceeding or action. The Non-Defaulting Party shall have the right to liquidate such closed-out Currency Obligations as provided below.

(b) Liquidation. Liquidation of Currency Obligations terminated by close-out shall be effected as follows:

(i) Calculating Closing Gain or Loss. The Non-Defaulting Party shall calculate in good faith, with respect to each such terminated Currency Obligation, except to the extent that in the good faith opinion of the Non-Defaulting Party certain of such Currency Obligations may not be liquidated as provided herein under applicable law, as of the Close-Out Date or as soon thereafter as reasonably practicable, the Closing Gain, or, as appropriate, the Closing Loss, as follows:

(A) for each Currency Obligation calculate a "Close-Out Amount" as follows:

(1) in the case of a Currency Obligation whose Value Date is the same as or is later than the Close-Out Date, the amount of such Currency Obligation; or

(2) in the case of a Currency Obligation whose Value Date precedes the Close-Out Date, the amount of such Currency Obligation increased, to the extent permitted by applicable law, by adding interest thereto from and including the Value Date to but excluding the Close-Out Date at overnight LIBOR; and

(3) for each such amount in a Currency other than the Non-Defaulting Party's Base Currency, convert such amount into the Non-Defaulting Party's Base Currency at the rate of exchange at which, at the time of the calculation, the Non-Defaulting Party can buy such Base Currency with or against the Currency of the relevant Currency Obligation for delivery (x) if the Value Date of such Currency Obligation is on or after the Spot Date as of such time of calculation for the Base Currency, on the Value Date of that Currency Obligation or (y) if such Value Date precedes such Spot Date, for delivery on such Spot Date (or, in either case, if such rate of exchange is not available, conversion shall be accomplished by the Non-Defaulting Party using any commercially reasonable method); and

(B) determine in relation to each Value Date: (1) the sum of all Close-Out Amounts relating to Currency Obligations under which the Non-Defaulting Party would otherwise have been entitled to receive the relevant amount on that Value Date; and (2) the sum of all Close-Out Amounts relating to Currency Obligations under which the Non-Defaulting Party would otherwise have been obliged to deliver the relevant amount to the Defaulting Party on that Value Date; and

(C) if the sum determined under (B)(1) is greater than the sum determined under (B)(2), the difference shall be the Closing Gain for such Value Date; if the sum determined under (B)(1) is less than the sum determined under (B)(2), the difference shall be the Closing Loss for such Value Date.

(ii) Determining Present Value. To the extent permitted by applicable law, the Non- Defaulting Party shall adjust the Closing Gain or Closing Loss for each Value Date falling after the Close-Out Date to present value by discounting the Closing Gain or Closing Loss from and including the Value Date to but excluding the Close-Out Date, at LIBOR with respect to the Non-Defaulting Party's Base Currency as at the Close-Out Date or at such other rate as may be prescribed by applicable law.

(iii) Netting. The Non-Defaulting Party shall aggregate the following amounts so that all such amounts are netted into a single liquidated amount payable to or by the Non-Defaulting Party: (x) the sum of the Closing Gains for all Value Dates (discounted to present value, where appropriate, in accordance with the provisions of Section 5.1(b)(ii)) (which for the purposes of the aggregation shall be a positive figure); and (y) the sum of the Closing Losses for all Value Dates (discounted to present value, where appropriate, in accordance with the provisions of Section 5.1(b)(ii)) (which for the purposes of the aggregation shall be a negative figure).

(iv) Settlement Payment. If the resulting net amount is positive, it shall be payable by the Defaulting Party to the Non-Defaulting Party, and if it is negative, then the absolute value of such amount shall be payable by the Non-Defaulting Party to the Defaulting Party....

Section 6. Force Majeure, Act Of State, Illegality And Impossibility

6.1 Force Majeure, Act of State, Illegality and Impossibility.

If either Party is prevented from or hindered or delayed by reason of force majeure or act of state in the delivery or receipt of any Currency in respect of a Currency Obligation or if it becomes or, in the good faith judgment of one of the Parties, may become unlawful or impossible for either Party to make or receive any payment in respect of a Currency Obligation, then the Party for whom such performance has been prevented, hindered or delayed or has become illegal or impossible shall promptly give notice thereof to the other Party and either Party may, by notice to the other Party, require the close-out and liquidation of each affected Currency Obligation in accordance with the provisions of Section 5.1 and, for such purposes, the Party unaffected by such force majeure, act of state, illegality or impossibility (or, if both Parties are so affected, whichever Party gave the relevant notice) shall perform the calculation required under Section 5.1 as if it were the Non-Defaulting Party. Nothing in this Section 6.1 shall be taken as indicating that the Party treated as the Defaulting Party for the purpose of calculations required by Section 5.1 has committed any breach or default.

6.2 Transfer to Avoid Force Majeure, Act of State, Illegality or Impossibility.

If Section 6.1 becomes applicable, unless prohibited by law, the Party which has been prevented, hindered or delayed from performing shall, as a condition to its right to designate a close-out and liquidation of any affected Currency Obligation, use all reasonable efforts (which will not require such Party to incur a loss, excluding immaterial, incidental expenses) to transfer as soon as practicable, and in any event before twenty (20) days after it gives notice under Section 6.1, all its rights and obligations under the Agreement in respect of the affected Currency Obligations to another of its Designated Offices so that such force majeure, act of state, illegality or impossibility ceases to exist. Any such transfer will be subject to the prior written consent of the other Party, which consent will not be withheld if such other Party's policies in effect at such time would permit it to enter into transactions with the transferee Designated Office on the terms proposed, unless such transfer would cause the other Party to incur a material tax or other cost.

Notes and Questions

1. If you were representing the banks, how would you argue against Scott's position?

CONCLUSIONS

The study of foreign exchange regimes and the decision as to which regimes are preferable is essentially a matter of economics rather than law or regulation. Indeed, the area of foreign exchange has traditionally been what economists mean by international finance. Foreign exchange arrangements are a key part of the infrastructure of the international financial system.

It is clear that the choice of a foreign exchange regime can have a huge impact on a country's economy, as we have seen from the failure of various versions of fixed rates in recent financial crises.

CHAPTER NINE

THE PAYMENT SYSTEM

Broadly speaking, the payment system is comprised of the institutions and technologies used for one party to transfer value to another. In modern economies, value is transferred by cash or through claims on banks. Claims on banks may be transferred by a variety of devices, including checks, credit cards, and wire transfers. Our focus in this Chapter is on large value transfers through wire transfers, as these are the most important payments in international financial transactions. Each major country has its own large value systems, but the Dollar systems have a significant international as well as domestic importance, due to the importance of the use of the Dollar as a reserve and transaction currency, and the size of the Eurodollar market. Thus, the U.S. large value transfer systems play a key role in international financial transactions.

This Chapter first examines the operation of the U.S. large value transfer systems, Fedwire and CHIPS, in terms of how they operate, the risks they pose, and current efforts to control those risks. The Chapter then turns to "Herstatt risk" and some aspects of cross-border and offshore payment systems.

A. THE USE OF THE U.S. PAYMENT SYSTEM FOR INTERNATIONAL TRANSACTIONS[1]

There are numerous methods of making Dollar payments in the United States, such as by cash, credit card, paper (check or draft), or electronic means (wire transfer). Payments by "wire transfer" are transmitted through banks or other depository institutions. "Wire transfer" is a generic term to describe a transaction in which the drawer, which may be an individual, a corporation, or a bank, instructs his bank (by telephone, computer, or written instruction) to debit his account and transfer funds to the account of a payee. The payee receives payment in the form of a credit to his account.

There are three means by which wire transfers can be made in the United States: (1) in-house or correspondent transfer; (2) Fedwire; or (3)

---

[1] This section relies heavily on H. Scott, "Where are the Dollars?—Offshore Funds Transfers," 3 Banking and Finance Law Review (1989), pp. 243, 252-263.

CHIPS. This section discusses the use of these methods for purely domestic transactions, and then shows how they may be used to transfer Dollars from and to parties holding accounts with banks located outside the United States.

Figure 9.1

IN-HOUSE WIRE TRANSFER

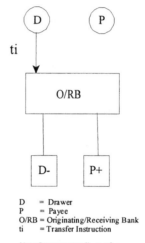

D   = Drawer
P   = Payee
O/RB = Originating/Receiving Bank
ti   = Transfer Instruction

Note: Payees generally receive advices from their banks of credits entered on transfer instructions.

1.   IN-HOUSE AND CORRESPONDENT TRANSFERS

If the drawer (the party originating the transfer) and the payee (the beneficiary of the transfer) hold accounts at the same bank, the bank of account merely makes a book transfer by debiting the account of the drawer and crediting the account of the payee. The entire transaction is handled on the books of one bank and is therefore referred to as an in-house transfer.

If the accounts of the parties are with different banks, correspondent transfers may be used to effect the payment and settle accounts between the originating bank (the bank holding the drawer's account) and the receiving bank (the bank holding the payee's account).

Figure 9.2

CORRESPONDENT WIRE
TRANSFER - I

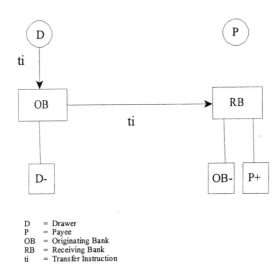

D   = Drawer
P   = Payee
OB = Originating Bank
RB = Receiving Bank
ti   = Transfer Instruction

The originating bank, having debited the drawer's account on a payment instruction, may use a communication system, such as the internet, to instruct the receiving bank to credit the account of the payee. Settlement between the banks can be effected by the receiving bank charging the correspondent account of the originating bank held at the receiving bank. This requires the originating bank to hold a balance or have credit sufficient to cover the payment with the receiving bank.

Alternatively, the receiving bank (RB) may hold an account with the originating bank (OB). In that event, as shown below, a rolling settlement takes place. OB debits its customer and credits the RB account, a type of in-house transfer. RB, in turn, credits its customer's account. No balances need to be maintained by RB with OB.

Figure 9.3

CORRESPONDENT WIRE
TRANSFER II

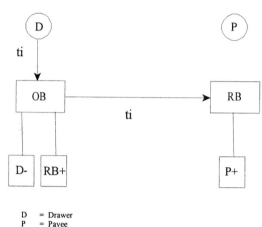

D   = Drawer
P   = Payee
OB = Originating Bank
RB = Receiving Bank
ti   = Transfer Instruction

In the event that OB and RB do not hold accounts with each other, OB may make use of a correspondent to transfer the funds to RB. One possibility is to use an intermediary bank (IB) which holds an account of both OB and RB. In this case, OB debits the drawer's account, IB debits the OB account and credits the RB account, and RB, having been notified by IB of its credit for the benefit of the payee, credits the payee's account. This transaction would require OB to hold a sufficient balance or credit at IB to cover the payment.

Figure 9.4

CORRESPONDENT WIRE TRANSFER - III
W/INTERMEDIARY

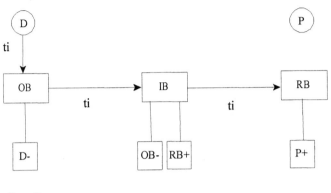

```
D    = Drawer
P    = Payee
OB   = Originating Bank
RB   = Receiving Bank
IB   = Intermediary Bank
ti   = Transfer Instruction
```

There are many variations on the theme of correspondent transfers. Another possibility is that IB-X holds an account with OB and also holds the account of RB. In that event, a rolling settlement can take place through account entries. OB debits the drawer and credits IB-X, IB-X credits RB, and RB credits the payee. In this case, there is no need for banks to maintain balances with each other.

Figure 9.5

CORRESPONDENT WIRE TRANSFER - IV
W/INTERMEDIARY

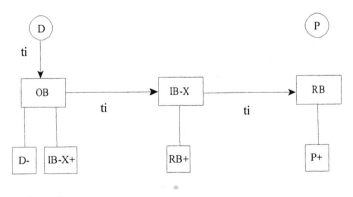

```
D     = Drawer
P     = Payee
OB    = Originating Bank
RB    = Receiving Bank
IB-X  = Intermediary Bank
ti    = Transfer Instruction
```

In-house and correspondent transfers in the United States may be used by foreigners to transfer Dollars to United States or foreign payees. Suppose a London drawer (LD) wants to transfer Dollars from his London bank (LOB) to a payee (NYP) which holds an account at a New York bank (NYRB). If LOB and NYRB both hold Dollar accounts at the same New York bank (NYIB), LOB debits LD, NYIB debits LOB and credits NYRB, and NYRB credits NYP. This is an in-house transfer at NYIB, which is a correspondent of both LOB and NYRB.

Now suppose LD wants to transfer dollars from its LOB account to a London payee (LP) who banks with another London bank (LRB). If LOB and LRB both hold Dollar accounts with NYIB, the transaction is the same as above, except that LRB, after receiving the credit from NYIB, credits LP on its books in London. Again, there may be many variations on this theme, but as long as interlinked accounts exist between LOB and LRB, provided by correspondents, a correspondent transfer may be used. No data are collected on the overall use of in-house or correspondent transfers in the United States payment system, but the Dollar amounts and the number of transactions are substantial.

2.   FEDWIRE

Fedwire is a communication and settlement system owned by the twelve United States Federal Reserve Banks. Fedwire is used as follows. Having debited the drawer on the payment instruction, the originating bank instructs its Federal Reserve Bank (FRB) to transfer the funds to the account of the payee at the receiving bank. If FRB holds the accounts of both the originating and receiving banks, it debits the former and credits the latter, and notifies the receiving bank of the credit. The receiving bank then credits the account of the payee.

Figure 9.6

FEDWIRE TRANSFER

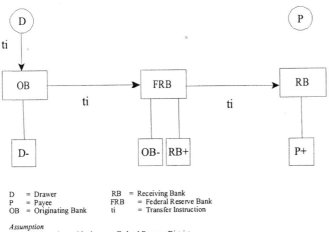

D	= Drawer	RB	= Receiving Bank
P	= Payee	FRB	= Federal Reserve Bank
OB	= Originating Bank	ti	= Transfer Instruction

Assumption
OB and RB are located in the same Federal Reserve District

If the receiving bank holds its account with a different Reserve Bank, FRB-R (the receiving bank's Reserve Bank), FRB-O (the originating bank's Reserve Bank) debits the originating bank and communicates the instruction to FRB-R. FRB-R credits the account of the receiving bank and notifies the receiving bank of the credit. The receiving bank then credits the account of the payee. The two Reserve Banks settle their own accounts through correspondent accounts.

Fedwires are often more convenient than correspondent transfers because a large number of United States banks maintain Federal Reserve accounts. The Federal Reserve Banks (Fed), taken together, serve the IB role. Since in most cases the Fed will hold both the OB and RB accounts, there is no need to look for private intermediaries in each transaction. Fedwire can be used in connection with correspondent transfers. If the receiving bank does not hold a Fedwire account, the originating bank can send a Fedwire to the receiving bank's correspondent that holds a Fed account, for further credit to the receiving bank and its customer.

Fedwire can also be used for transactions involving overseas customers. If LD (a party in London) wants to transfer funds from LOB (his London bank) to NYP (a payee in New York) at NYRB (the payee's bank), and LOB holds an account with its New York correspondent bank (NYCB1), LOB debits LD, NYCB1 debits LOB and sends a Fedwire to NYRB for NYP.

Fedwire is a real time gross payment system. There is no netting; each transaction settles separately on the Fed's books. In 2003, Fedwire transferred about $1.7 trillion per day (U.S. GNP was $11.3 trillion in 2003), with the average size of a transaction about $3.5 million. All depository institutions (not securities firms) may have access, including branches of foreign banks. Over 9000 depository institutions used Fedwire in 2002.

Banks sending Fedwires commonly overdraft their accounts (daylight overdrafts). The total of all banks' peak daylight overdrafts per day was about $130 billion in 1993, while average overdrafts were $70 billion.[2] In 2002, peak overdrafts ranged between $70 to $91 billion, while average overdrafts ranged between $22 to $30 billion. If a bank fails with an overdraft outstanding, the Fed has a loss. The Fed does not take money back from the banks that received payments from the failed bank. The principal reason is that Fedwires are final when sent; they are "good funds." Receiving banks need to know that the funds are good so they can allow the receivers to use them. Finality supports the high velocity of money in the economy, particularly in the financial system.

Could the Fed just prohibit overdrafts? This would risk a slowdown in the economy and possible gridlock. For example, Citibank wouldn't be able to send funds to JPMorgan Chase until BankAmerica sent them to Citibank, but BankAmerica can't send to Citibank until it get funds from JPMorgan Chase, but JPMorgan Chase can't send funds to BankAmerica until it gets them from Citibank.

Overdrafts of Fed accounts can occur as a result of a variety of different transactions, including transfers of book-entry securities. When book-entry securities are bought by a dealer, such as Morgan Stanley, they are delivered electronically to its clearing bank's (CB) account with the Fed. CB's securities account is credited and its funds account is debited. CB then makes corresponding entries on its own books to the funds and securities accounts of Morgan Stanley. Deliveries of book-entry securities during the day are substantial, and cause very substantial overdrafts on the accounts of the clearing banks (there are only a handful with any volume). In 1993, of the total peak daylight overdrafts of about $130 billion, securities were close to $100 billion. The overdrafts are extinguished at the end of the day when the dealer sells out or finances (for example, by repo transactions in which securities are exchanged for cash for a defined period) its position.

---

[2] The peak daylight overdraft for a given day is the greatest value reached by the sum of daylight overdrafts in Federal Reserve accounts for all depository institutions at the end of each minute during the day. Another measure of overdrafts is average overdrafts. This is the sum of average per-minute daylight overdrafts for all institutions. H. Richards, "Daylight Overdraft Fees and the Federal Reserve's Payment System Risk Policy," (1995) 81 Federal Reserve Bulletin 1065, p. 1069, n.7 (Richards); D. Hancock and J. Wilcox, "Intraday Management of Bank Reserves: The Effect of Caps and Fees on Daylight Overdrafts," 28 J. Money, Credit and Banking (1996), pp. 870, 873 (Figure 2).

3.   CHIPS

The Clearing House Interbank Payments System (CHIPS or CHIP Co.) is a division of The Clearing House Payments Company. It is owned by the following banks or their U.S. banking affiliates: ABN AMRO Bank, The Bank of New York, Bank of America, Bank of Tokyo-Mitsubishi, Bank of California, BB&T, Citibank, Scotland's Citizens Bank, Comerica Bank, Deutsche Bank, HSBC Bank, JPMorgan Chase Bank, KeyBank, M&T, National City Bank, PNC Bank, SunTrust, U.S. Bank, Wachovia Bank and Wells Fargo Bank. This new corporate structure replaced the New York Clearing House in 2004.

As of 2005, there were 53 CHIPS participants, the majority of which were foreign banks from 22 countries. CHIPS transfers were about $1.3 trillion per day, and the average transfer was about $5 million.

CHIPS is a communications and net settlement system for payments by and to two classes of participant banks located in New York City: "settling" and "non-settling" participants. All participants can send payment instructions during the day to each other through a central CHIPS switch linked to their own terminals and computers.

a.   CHIPS BEFORE 2001

An example of a CHIPS transfer is as follows. Bank OB, a CHIPS participant, sends a payment instruction, on behalf of Customer D, through the CHIPS computer and switching system to Bank RSB (a "settling" receiving bank). The instruction tells Bank RSB to credit the account of Customer P.

Figure 9.7

CHIPS

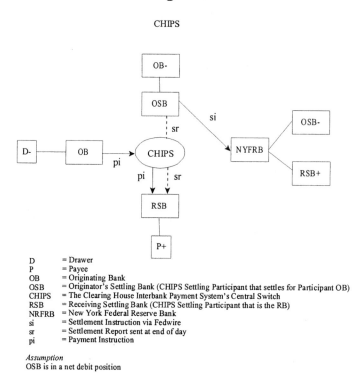

D	= Drawer
P	= Payee
OB	= Originating Bank
OSB	= Originator's Settling Bank (CHIPS Settling Participant that settles for Participant OB)
CHIPS	= The Clearing House Interbank Payment System's Central Switch
RSB	= Receiving Settling Bank (CHIPS Settling Participant that is the RB)
NRFRB	= New York Federal Reserve Bank
si	= Settlement Instruction via Fedwire
sr	= Settlement Report sent at end of day
pi	= Payment Instruction

Assumption
OSB is in a net debit position

CHIPS is regularly used for transactions involving foreign banks. Rather than using Fedwire, LOB's (London Bank's) New York correspondent NYCB1 can send a CHIPS transfer to NYRB (New York receiving bank) for NYP (New York payee) or to the New York correspondent of LRB (London receiving bank), NYCB2, for credit to LRB, and ultimately LP (London Payee).

CHIPS reportedly has a 95 percent share of international large-value payments but only about 5 percent of domestic large-value ones. The latter go over Fedwire. A significant portion of CHIPS volume is the Dollar settlement of foreign exchange transactions but this may change with the advent of new clearing arrangements for these transactions, as discussed below.

CHIPS is often used in connection with correspondent transfers to effect payments, particularly where foreign banks are involved. An originating bank may instruct its correspondent to transfer funds to a payee at a receiving bank. The originating bank and its correspondent will settle through a debit to the account of the originating bank with the correspondent. But the correspondent then uses CHIPS to transfer funds to the payee at the receiving bank.

Before 2001, all CHIPS transfers were settled on a net basis at the end of the day. A stylized net settlement is depicted in Figure 9.8 below.

Figure 9.8

2. Transactions among Four Participants in a Funds Transfer Clearinghouse

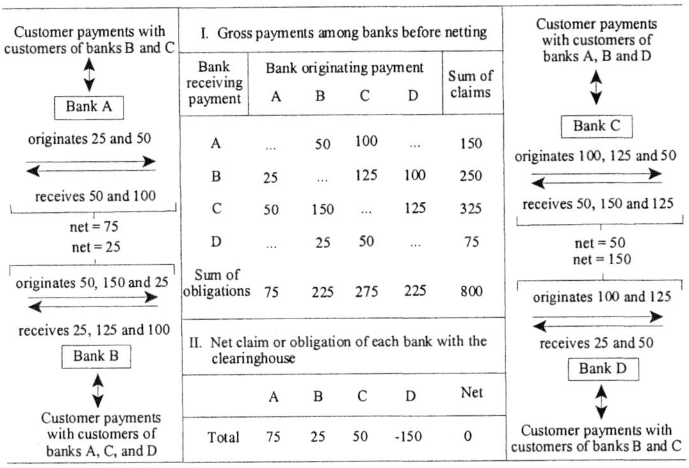

I. Gross payments among banks before netting

Bank receiving payment	Bank originating payment A	B	C	D	Sum of claims
A	...	50	100	...	150
B	25	...	125	100	250
C	50	150	...	125	325
D	...	25	50	...	75
Sum of obligations	75	225	275	225	800

II. Net claim or obligation of each bank with the clearinghouse

	A	B	C	D	Net
Total	75	25	50	-150	0

Source: G. Juncker, B. Summers and F. Young, A Primer on the Settlement of Payments in the United States, 77 Federal Reserve Bulletin 847 (1991).

The vertical part of the diagram shows the transfers that have been originated, while the horizontal shows the transfers received. Thus, Bank A's position is as follows. It has originated (sends) of 25 to B and 50 to C = 75, which it owes, and has funds owed to it (receives) of 50 from B and 100 from C = 150. On net, it has a claim (is a creditor) for 75 (150 receives - 75 sends). What happens if D fails? Under CHIPS Rule 13, a delete and unwind procedure would be applied. All transactions would be deleted and the settlement positions of all banks would be recalculated:

Table 9A

	A	B	C	D	Net
Pre-Failure	75	25	50	-150	0
Post-Failure	75	-50	-25	xx	0

Is A unaffected? A was owed 75 before and is still owed 75. The problem is whether B and C are going to be able to come up with the 75. B is suffering a 75 loss: unpaid receives from D (100) - unpaid sends to D (25). C is also out 75, 125 receives - 50 sends.

What could A do if B and C do not come up with the 75? A has a right to take funds back from its customers under normal contracts, but there is a question of whether it can get the funds. If not, it will fail. We are looking at the essence of systemic risk, a chain reaction of bank failures triggered through the payment system.

What would the Fed do? The Fed would not allow a chain reaction of bank failures; it will almost certainly have to cover D's 150 obligation and absorb D's credit risk—in a sense the Fed is liable for the net debit positions of the CHIPS banks. No matter how many times the Fed said it is not responsible (so that banks would limit risks) everyone knew it would bail out the system.

Before 2001, CHIPS used an end-of-day net settlement procedure. Immediately after the system closed for the day at 4:30 p.m. Eastern Time, participants were notified of their final net settlement obligations. The settlement payments for the settling banks that settled directly for themselves and the other participants were made over Fedwire into the special settlement account at the Federal Reserve Bank of New York. This is illustrated in Figure 9.7 above by the debit to OSB and credit to RSB at the NYFRB.

b.   CHIPS TODAY

In 2001, there was a fundamental change in the operation of the CHIPS system. CHIPS changed from an end-of-day multilateral net payment system to one that supplies intraday finality, and arguably eliminates most risk from a settlement failure. Two essential changes have been made. CHIPS has adopted a system of prefunded balances maintained in a "prefunded balance account" on the books of the Federal Reserve Bank of New York (FRBNY). These balances are roughly equivalent to the $3 billion of Treasury collateral that had previously protected against settlement failures. CHIPS uses a computer program, "the balance release algorithm," to control the release of the payments to and from participants. Payments are only released against actual balances and are settled when made.

Each participant is required to deposit its initial prefunded balance requirement to the prefunded balance account at FRBNY no later than 9 a.m. Normally this would be done by Fedwire. The amount of the balance will be determined by the Clearing House based on a participant's past activity. As originally designed, participants could not make any additional deposits to or withdrawals from the prefunded balance account between the time they have paid their initial prefunded balance and the final end of day clearing. The prohibition on additional prefunding was subsequently changed. Now participants can increase their prefunding during the day. In addition, a participant can designate messages as priority payments, which will give them priority in the sequencing. These changes eliminated some delays in processing. Concerns still exist about delays in processing very large payments, and as a result they may be sent over Fedwire.

"The balance in a participant's account during the day will vary based upon the release and receipt of payment messages to other participants. In no case, however, can a balance go below zero or rise to more than two times the initial prefunded balance. This latter limit prevents any one participant from absorbing system liquidity by building an excessive balance. Payment messages will ordinarily be released in batches, involving two or several participants (bilateral or multilateral netting). The balance release algorithm is designed to ensure that these debits and credits do not cause any participant's balance to fall below zero or exceed the maximum. The netting and the posting of the debits and credits constitute final settlement of all payment messages in each batch. CHIPS payment messages are no longer subject to final settlement at the end of the day. They will be finally settled upon receipt."[3]

CHIPS closes at 5:00 p.m. "At that time, CHIPS runs an 'initial closing netting and release.' In this procedure, CHIPS removes the maximum available balance restraint and runs the balance release algorithm one more time. This should cause the release of additional payments. It is estimated that after this procedure, 99.6 percent of all CHIPS messages comprising 97.5 percent of all value will have been released and settled. Only about $30 billion in payments will remain.

CHIPS then calculates a net balance for each participant without releasing any of the remaining payments. This net balance is then reduced by any remaining balance available to the participant, to establish a 'final prefunded balance requirement.'"[4] Participants then have 30 minutes to fund this amount. There is no longer a special class of settling participants. In the event that one or more participants do not send in final prefunded balances, CHIPS will run the balance release algorithm one final time, and release all payments that can be netted with the balances available. Any payment messages still unreleased will expire and CHIPS will so notify the senders.

In the event of a participant's failure to pay its final prefunded balance requirement, there would be a delete and unwind procedure, as under the old system, but the effect would be negligible. The simulations show that if the two participants with the largest final prefunded balance requirements did not pay these amounts, unreleased Dollars would be around $2-2.8 billion. This settlement failure would not trigger a chain reaction of bank failure. In effect, systemic risk has been purged from the CHIPS system. These effects are in contrast to what would have occurred in the past

---

[3] Payments Risk Committee (of the Federal Reserve Bank of New York), Intraday Liquidity Management in the Evolving Payment System: A Study of the Impact of the Euro, CLS Bank and CHIPS Finality (April 2000). See also CHIPS Rules and Administrative Procedures, November 2003.
[4] *ibid.*

if a participant were not to pay its net debit balance. "Each of the remaining participants would have had to take a piece of the participant's net debit balance (the remaining participant's additional settlement obligation, or ASO). If a remaining participant defaulted on its ASO, its collateral would be sold to meet its obligation. If more than two major participants failed to settle, the loss-sharing arrangement might not apportion all of the failed participants' settlement obligations among the remaining participants and the resulting delete and unwind could have resulted in the collapse of CHIPS."[5]

B.   FEDWIRE AND CHIPS: RISK REDUCTION MEASURES

1.   FEDWIRE

The Fed has adopted a two-pronged strategy to control daylight overdrafts on Fedwire, ceilings on and pricing of overdrafts.

a.   CEILINGS

The policy on ceilings is set out at Board of Governors of the Federal Reserve System, *Federal Reserve Policy Statement on Payment System Risk*.[6]

To limit the aggregate amount of daylight credit extended by Reserve Banks, each institution that incurs daylight overdrafts in its Federal Reserve account must adopt a net debit cap, i.e. a ceiling on the aggregate net debit position that it can incur during a given interval.

Cap categories and associated cap levels, set as multiples of capital, are:

Table 9B
Net Debit Cap Multiples

Cap Category	Two-Week Avg.	Single Day
High	1.50	2.25
Above Average	1.125	1.875
Average	0.75	1.125
De Minimis	0.20	0.20
	$10 million	$10 million
Exempt-from-filing	(0.20)	(0.20)
Zero	0.0	0.0

[5] *ibid.*
[6] 57 Federal Register 40455, 40457 (1992); Board of Governors of the Federal Reserve System, "Proposals to Modify the Payments System Risk Reduction Program; Self-Assessment Procedures, Caps for U.S. Branches and Agencies and Agencies of Foreign Banks" (1993) 58 Federal Register, 44677.

The purpose of the higher single-day cap is to limit excessive daylight overdrafts on any day and to assure that institutions develop internal controls that focus on the exposures each day, as well as over time.

The two-week average cap is measured against the average, over a two-week reserve maintenance period, of an institution's daily maximum net debit positions in its Federal Reserve account. In calculating the two-week average, individual days on which an institution is in an aggregate net credit position throughout the day are treated as if the institution was in a net position of zero. The number of days used in calculating the average is the number of business days the institution's Reserve Bank is open during the reserve maintenance period.

An institution that wishes to establish a net debit cap category of high, above average, or average must perform a self-assessment of its own creditworthiness, credit policies, operational controls, policies and procedures, and operating controls.

Since the inception of the self-assessment process for establishing net debit caps, concerns were raised regarding the administrative burden raised by the self-assessment procedures. In an attempt to reduce burden on institutions electing to complete a self-assessment, the Board developed a matrix that combines an institution's supervisory rating and Prompt Corrective Action capital category into a creditworthiness rating. This "Creditworthiness Matrix" is shown below.

Table 9C Creditworthiness Matrix			
	Supervisory composite rating		
Capital level	Strong	Satisfactory	Fair
Well Capitalized Adequately Capitalized Undercapitalized	Excellent Very Good Full Assessment	Very Good Very Good Full Assessment	Adequate Adequate Below Standard
Note: Institutions with a capital level or supervisory rating not shown in the matrix would receive a creditworthiness of "below standard."			

In 2002, the Federal Reserve Board considered but rejected lowering self-assessed net debit caps and eliminating two-week average caps. The Board determined that 96 percent of depository institutions use less than 50 percent of their daylight overdraft capacity for their average peak overdrafts. As for the larger banks which are more intensive users of their daylight overdraft capacity, the Board decided to wait to assess the impact of the new Continuous Linked Settlement (CLS) system for settling foreign exchange transactions, discussed later on in this Chapter. The Board also determined not to adopt a policy of automatically rejecting payments that exceeded caps in order to preserve the flexibility in the existing system.[7]

Prior to 2002, for U.S. agencies and branches of foreign banks, net debit caps on daylight overdrafts in Federal Reserve accounts were calculated by applying the cap multiples for each cap category to consolidated "U.S. capital equivalency."[8]

For a foreign bank whose home-country supervisor adhered to the Basel Capital Accord, U.S. capital equivalency was equal to the greater of 10 percent of worldwide capital or 5 percent of the total liabilities of each agency or branch, including acceptances, but excluding accrued expenses and amounts due and other liabilities to offices, branches, and subsidiaries of the foreign bank. In the absence of contrary information, the Reserve Banks presumed that all banks chartered in G-10 countries met the acceptable prudential capital and supervisory standards and considered any bank chartered in any other nation that adopted the Basel Capital Accord (or that requires capital at least as great and in the same form as called for by the Accord) eligible for the Reserve Banks' review of whether they met acceptable prudential capital and supervisory standards.

For all other foreign banks, U.S. capital equivalency was measured as the greater of: (1) the sum of the amount of capital (but not surplus) that would be required of a national bank being organized at each agency or branch location; or (2) the sum of 5 percent of the total liabilities of each agency or branch, including acceptances, but excluding accrued expenses and amounts due and other liabilities to offices, branches, and subsidiaries of the foreign bank.

In addition, any foreign bank could incur daylight overdrafts above its net debit cap up to a maximum of 10 percent of its worldwide capital, provided that any overdrafts above its net debit cap were collateralized.

These limits were the subject of criticism, particularly by the EU. While U.S. banks could get daylight overdraft capacity based on worldwide capital, foreign banks could not. This led to changes in the approach.

The policy with respect to capital for foreign bank offices (FBOs) was changed effective February 2002.[9] For U.S. branches and agencies of foreign banks, net debit caps on daylight overdrafts will be calculated by applying the cap multiples for each cap category to the FBO's U.S. capital equivalency measure, which is equal to the following: (1) 35 percent of capital for FBOs that are FHCs (financial service holding companies); (2) 25 percent of capital

---

[7] 67 Federal Register 54,424 (August 22, 2002).

[8] The term "U.S. capital equivalency" is used in this context to refer to the particular capital measure used to calculate daylight overdraft net debit caps, and does not necessarily represent an appropriate capital measure for supervisory or other purposes.

[9] Board of Governors of the Federal Reserve System, Policy Statement, 66 Federal Register 64419 (December 13, 2001).

for FBOs that are not FHCs and have a strength of support assessment ranking (SOSA) of 1; (3) 10 percent of capital for FBOs that are not FHCs and are ranked a SOSA 2; and (4) 5 percent of the liability "net due to related depository institutions" for FBOs that are not FHCs and are ranked a SOSA 3.

The SOSA ranking is composed of four factors, including the FBO's financial condition, the supervisory system in the FBO's home country, the record of the home country's government in support of the banking system, and the ability of the FBO to access and transmit U.S. Dollars.

The collateral provisions of the old policy became unnecessary due to the new authority for all banks to use collateral, as discussed below.

b.   PRICING

Daylight overdrafts have been priced since April 1994.[10] The overdraft fee is 36 basis points (annual rate), quoted on the basis of a 24-hour day, as applied to daily average overdrafts. To obtain the daily overdraft fee (annual rate) for the standard Fedwire operating day, the quoted 60 basis point fee is multiplied by the fraction of a 24-hour day during which Fedwire is scheduled to operate. Under the current 18-hour Fedwire operating day, the overdraft fee is 27 basis points (36 x 18/24). The Board permits a bank to deduct 10 percent of its capital from daily average overdrafts.

Is the 36 basis point fee high or low? How could that be determined? Originally, the Fed contemplated a fee of 60 basis points. Since the inception of pricing, daylight overdrafts have dropped by 40 percent. Peak overdrafts fell from nearly $125 billion per day, on average, during the six months preceding April 14, 1994 (the inception of pricing) to about $70 billion in the six months following April 14, and currently are around $100 billion. While the absolute amounts of daylight overdrafts have now risen substantially from 1994 post-pricing, the ratio of the average value of funds-related overdrafts to funds transferred has remained relatively constant at 1.5 percent.[11] Pricing also seems to have affected the concentration of overdrafts. In the six months preceding the implementation of fees, ten institutions with the largest overdrafts accounted for 80 percent of total average overdrafts; post-pricing they accounted for only 70 percent.[12]

Since the Federal Reserve began pricing daylight overdrafts, an average of only about 350 depository institutions have paid fees in a given year, and most of these institutions pay less than $1000 per year. In 2002,

---

[10] This policy is set out at Federal Reserve Policy Statement on Payment System Risk, as amended effective December 18, 2001, pp. 4-5.

[11] S. Coleman, "The Evolution of the Federal Reserve's Intraday Credit Policies," Federal Reserve Bulletin (February 2002), pp. 68, 77. (Coleman)

[12] Richards, supra note 2.

total fees paid were only about $24 million. A few banks account for most of these fees.

An important consideration in price increases was the fear that volume would switch to netting systems (like CHIPS), thus increasing systemic risk in the Fed's view.[13] Figure 9.9, below,[14] indicates the change in Dollar value on Fedwire and CHIPS from 1990 to early 1995. The spike in CHIPS volume immediately preceding pricing seems to indicate that banks cannot simply pass on to customers the costs of their daylight overdrafts, given that competitors may not incur such fees at all.

Figure 9.9

Change in dollar values of Fedwire and CHIPS funds transfers, 1990-95

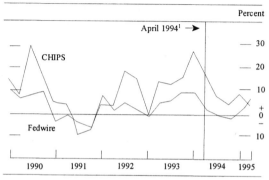

Note: Four-quarter change of quarterly averages of daily values.
1. 10 basis point daylight overdraft fee implemented.

The most intense controversy over pricing of daylight overdrafts had to do with the measurement of daylight overdrafts. There are many transactions other than the sending or receiving of Fedwires that can affect the level of balances in Fed accounts, for example check debits and credits. The Fed has adopted a complicated measurement system.[15] The system was changed somewhat in 1996.[16]

Any real time gross settlement system like Fedwire requires users to have a certain amount of liquidity—Fed balances—to support payments during the day. While the allowance of daylight overdrafts reduces what would otherwise be the liquidity requirement, it does not eliminate the

---

[13] (1995) 60 Federal Register 12559.

[14] Richards, supra note 2, p. 1076.

[15] See Board of Governors of the Federal Reserve System, "Modification of the Payments System Risk Reduction Program; Measurement of Daylight Overdrafts" (1992) 57 Federal Register 47093.

[16] (November 18, 1996) 61 Federal Register 58691.

liquidity requirement given overdraft ceilings, and these ceilings come at a cost given pricing. One way banks seek to reduce their liquidity costs on Fedwire is to concentrate payments at peak times, and then synchronize them with other banks to avoid gridlock. Outgoing payments during peak times can be funded by synchronized incoming payments thus reducing what would other be the Fed balance requirement, given that outgoing payments in non-peak times would have to be funded by the bank's own Fed balances. This peak time payment activity is concentrated around 4:00 p.m.[17] In effect, Fedwire may be converging with CHIPS.

Under the Monetary Central Act of 1980, the Federal Reserve is required to recover its costs (direct and indirect) through its prices, thus eliminating any public "subsidy" or competitive advantage over the private sector, e.g. CHIPS.[18] In addition, the prices must include a private sector adjustment factor (PSAF) to cover imputed costs—costs that would have been incurred had Fedwire services been provided by a private firm(s). These imputed costs make an adjustment for cost of capital and an estimated allowance for taxes. It is unclear whether the daylight overdraft prices charged by the Fed are sufficient to cover the Fed's cost of supplying daylight overdrafts.

c.   COLLATERAL

In December 2001, the Board took an important new step by allowing depositary institutions to obtain additional daylight credit by pledging collateral. This was intended to address the liquidity needs of the few institutions that might be actually constrained by their net debit caps.[19] Banks were permitted to use existing collateral pledged to support discount window loans when that collateral was not being used for that purpose. The Board expected that very few banks would use the new facility since 97 percent of all Fedwire users use less than 50 percent of their net debit caps for their average peak overdrafts. The Board is considering adopting a two-tiered pricing system for daylight overdrafts, with lower fees on collateralized overdrafts.[20]

Under the new 2002 policy, collateral is an option not a requirement. One can still incur daylight overdrafts under one's cap without any collateral. Should the next step be to make collateralization of all overdrafts mandatory and to abandon pricing? This is the approach taken in some foreign systems.

---

[17] J. McAndrews and S. Rajan, "The Timing and Funding of Fedwire Transfers," 6 Federal Reserve Board of New York Economic Review (2000), p. 17. See also, M. Bech and K. Soramäki, "Gridlock Resolution in Interbank Payment System," Bank of Finland Discussion Paper 9 (June 13, 2001).

[18] 12 U.S.C. §248a.

[19] Board of Governors of the Federal Reserve System, Policy Statement (December 13, 2001) 66 Federal Register 64419.

[20] 67 Federal Register 54,424 (August 22, 2002).

Notes and Questions

1.   Assume a U.S. bank has $10 billion in capital and $6 billion in daily average overdrafts over the current 10 hour Fedwire operating day (8:30 a.m. to 6:30 p.m.). How much will the bank pay in daylight overdraft fees to the Fed, assuming pricing has been fully phased-in, that is after April 11, 1996, and there are no further changes to the pricing methodology? Consider that the Fed allows a bank to deduct 10 percent of its capital from daily average overdrafts.

2.   Is the 60 basis point fee high or low? How could that be determined?

3.   Can banks simply pass on to customers the costs of their daylight overdrafts?

4.   Under the new 2002 policy, collateral is an option not a requirement. One can still incur daylight overdrafts under one's cap without any consequences, i.e. without fees or collateral. Should the next step be to make collateralization of all overdrafts mandatory and to abandon pricing? This is the approach taken in some foreign systems.

2.   CHIPS

In the CHIPS system, three principal devices (apart from membership admission requirements) were employed to minimize the probability and impact of a settlement failure: (1) ceilings in the form of bilateral and net debit caps; (2) collateralized "Additional Settlement Obligations" (ASOs); and (3) ensuring the validity of netting in bankruptcy. With the change in 2001, ceilings and ASOs have been dropped. Netting validity remains important.

The whole CHIPS system is built on multilateral netting. In the United States, bank bankruptcies are not dealt with under the Bankruptcy Code; instead, almost all bank bankruptcies are handled under banking law rules of the FDIC, as a receiver.

A major issue of concern would be whether the FDIC as receiver would respect the CHIPS netting. Suppose the failed bank (FB) had sent out transfers of $12 billion, and received transfers of $11 billion (the difference being the prefunded balance).

The FDIC might ignore the CHIPS netting and take the position that FB has not been paid for the $11 billion in funds it received, and make claims against the CHIPS participants that sent these funds to FB. This would remit the CHIPS banks to making unsecured claims for the $12 billion they received from FB against the FDIC. Under the netting arrangements, the maximum loss (assuming FB's assets were worth zero) of the banks would be $0. Under a FDIC gross approach, disaggregating transfers sent from those received, the maximum loss of the banks would be $23 billion. They would pay for the $12 billion in transfers sent to FB and get nothing for the $11 billion in transfers received.

The Payments System Risk Reduction provisions of the Federal Deposit Insurance Corporation Improvement Act of 1991[21] deal with this problem. They insure that netting will be effective. The key provision affecting CHIPS (12 USC Section 4404) provides:

Section 4404. Clearing organization netting

(a) General netting rule

Notwithstanding any other provision of law, the covered contractual payment obligations and covered contractual payment entitlements of a member of a clearing organization to and from all other members of a clearing organization shall be netted in accordance with and subject to the conditions of any applicable netting contract.

(b) Limitation of obligation to make payment

The only obligation, if any, of a member of a clearing organization to make payment with respect to covered contractual payment obligations arising under a single netting contract to any other member of a clearing organization shall be equal to its net obligation arising under that netting contract, and no such obligation shall exist if there is no net obligation.

(c) Limitation on right to receive payment

The only right, if any, of a member of a clearing organization to receive payment with respect to a covered contractual payment entitlement arising under a single netting contract from other members of a clearing organization shall be equal to its net entitlement arising under that netting contract, and no such right shall exist if there is no net entitlement.

(d) Entitlement of failed member

The net entitlement, if any, of any failed member of a clearing organization shall be paid to the failed member in accordance with, and subject to the conditions of, the applicable netting contract.

(e) Obligations of failed members

The net obligation, if any, of any failed member of a clearing organization shall be determined in accordance with, and subject to the conditions of, the applicable netting contract.

(f) Limitation on claims for entitlement

A failed member of a clearing organization shall have no recognizable claim against any member of a clearing organization for

---

[21] 12 USC. s. 4401 *et seq.*

any amount based on such covered contractual payment entitlements other than its net entitlement.

(g) Effectiveness notwithstanding status as member

This section shall be given effect notwithstanding that a member is a failed member.

This statute only goes so far. CHIPS participants include substantial numbers of branches of foreign banks whose bankruptcy would be handled abroad, and foreign countries may not have clear rules establishing the validity of netting in bankruptcy.

The major industrialized countries' central banks have promulgated minimum standards for "Netting Schemes" which includes the requirement that "[n]etting schemes should have a well founded legal basis under all relevant jurisdictions."[22] The New York Fed has received letters from counsel to CHIPS participants stating that their home countries would respect the netting. But these are only opinions; in many cases the law is unclear. Furthermore, it is clear that in some major countries netting might not be respected. In Italy and the Netherlands, bank liquidators employing the so-called "zero-hour" rule were able to revoke all payments of a failed bank on the day it becomes bankrupt so that the situation of the bank is restored to that prevailing at the end of the previous day (literally midnight or the "zero-hour").[23]

The problem of the uncertainty of foreign laws may not be that serious, however, for U.S. banks. As the BCCI bankruptcy demonstrated, any foreign bank that fails will have substantial Dollar balances held with U.S. banks, and U.S. authorities are likely to use these assets for the benefit of U.S. creditors, including U.S. banks.[24]

The Lamfalussy Minimum Standards for Netting, in addition to the requirement for a sound legal basis (standard 1), are:

"2. Netting system participants should have a clear understanding of the impact of the particular system on each of the financial risks affected by the netting process.

3. Multilateral netting systems should have clearly-defined procedures for the management of credit risks and liquidity risks which specify the respective responsibilities of the netting provider and the participants. These procedures should also ensure that all parties have both the incentives and the capabilities to manage and

---

[22] Bank for International Settlements, "Report of the Committee on Interbank Netting Schemes of the Central Banks of the Group of Ten Countries," 5 (1990). (Lamfalussy Report)

[23] Working Group on EC Payments Systems, Report to The Committee of Governors of The Central Banks of The Member States of the European Economic Community on Minimum Common Features for Domestic Payment Systems 27 (1993).

[24] See H. Scott, "Multinational Bank Insolvencies: The United States and BCCI," in *Comparative Commercial Insolvency Law* (J. Ziegel ed., 1994).

contain each of the risks they bear and that limits are placed on the maximum level of credit exposure that can be produced by each participant.

4.   Multilateral netting systems should, at a minimum, be capable of ensuring the timely completion of daily settlements in the event of an inability to settle by the participant with the largest single net debit position.

5.   Multilateral netting systems should have objective and publicly-disclosed criteria for admission, which permit fair and open access.

6.   All netting systems should ensure the operational reliability of technical systems and the availability of backup facilities capable of completing daily processing requirements."

The Federal Reserve Board implemented these requirements in December 1994.[25]

Notes and Questions

1.   Has CHIPS eliminated systemic risk? If so, what are the consequences for bank regulation?

2.   Suppose Bank F, a CHIPS participant, fails at the end of the day. Further suppose that Bank A has sent $7 billion to Bank F during the day and received $6 billion. The difference was funded by A's pre-funded balance. If netting were respected by F's bankruptcy trustee, what claims, if any, would the banks have against each other? What claims would they have if the bankruptcy trustee did not respect netting?

3.   GROSS VERSUS NET SETTLEMENT

The United Kingdom had a version of the pre-2001 CHIPS net settlement system called CHAPS but had no equivalent to Fedwire. CHAPS was converted into a Fedwire, real-time gross settlement system in 1995. The main idea was there was less systemic risk in a Fedwire type gross system. Central banks have argued that net settlement systems are undesirable, particularly since the central banks will effectively be forced to assume that risk.[26]

However, there is a much higher cost for banks in a gross system—they must hold balances sufficient to support payments (on a gross basis). While such burden is ameliorated by daylight overdrafts, these overdrafts are limited and priced.

A key issue is whether RTGS should supplement or substitute netting systems. And a related issue is whether substitution would be the natural

---

[25] (1994) 59 Federal Register 67534 (Fed Netting Policy).
[26] See P. Allsopp, "Payments Systems and Risk," Banking World (May 1993), pp. 22-24.

outcome of market developments (i.e. the ascendancy of a superior technology) or the effect of central bank regulations imposing gross settlement for certain classes of payments.

D. Schoenmaker[27] has compared the total costs of Fedwire and CHIPS (before CHIPS changed its mode of operation in 2001).

Table 9D

Total costs of net and gross settlement (in $ mln).

	Repayment ratio m		
NET SETTLEMENT	m = 0	m = 0.4	m = 0.8
Cost of settlement failure	37.4	22.5	7.5
Cost of pledging collateral	6.1	6.1	6.1
Cost of settlement delay	26.8	26.8	26.8
Total costs	70.3	55.4	40.4
GROSS SETTLEMENT	Turnover ratio V = 27.8		
Cost of pledging collateral	65.1		
Cost of settlement delay	48.9		
Total costs	114.0		

The cost of settlement failure is the maximum level of intraday overdrafts multiplied by the probability of bank failure. Overdrafts on CHIPS are the sum of the net debit positions to be settled at the end of the day. The bank failure rate, 0.16 percent, is based on data from 1960-1990 on U.S. bank failures. The study considered repayment rates of the failed bank of 0, 40, and 80 percent. The turnover ratio is total payments divided by total overdrafts. The cost of pledging collateral in CHIPS (a requirement before 2001) is based on the amount of collateral pledged and an opportunity cost of 25 basis points on an annual basis. The cost of pledging collateral in Fedwire, where there is actually no such pledge, is the fees paid under pricing for overdrafts. The cost of settlement delay was derived from a complicated calculation as to the costs banks would incur in trying to reduce collateral costs in CHIPS or pricing costs in Fedwire.

The study concludes that gross settlement systems are more expensive. "The result is intuitive. To make the payment system failure-proof, banks have to cover their payments with collateral or reserves [or pay pricing fees]. The cost of maintaining sufficient collateral or reserves is considerable under gross settlement. In contrast, the cost of improving the risk management of netting schemes is found to be moderate."[28]

---

[27] "A Comparison of Alternative Interbank Settlement Systems," London School of Economics Financial Markets Group Discussion Paper 204 (1995), p. 26.
[28] Id., at 29.

Kahn et al. conclude that there is less settlement risk in net settlement systems than in RTGS systems: gridlock cannot occur, trading delays are minimal, and less collateral may be needed. The authors further contend that net settlement offers a better way of enforcing creditors priority: "[b]y substituting each party's original payment obligation with an obligation to a centralized counterparty, a net settlement system can allow for offsets that could not occur under a decentralized (i.e. gross) settlement system. In other words, netting in effect replaces a difficult-to-enforce debt obligation with another, inherently more enforceable one."[29] A cynic might ask whether the fact that central banks own and operate RTGS systems has accounted for the efforts of central banks to discourage such systems.

Notes and Questions

1. How would you compare Fedwire and CHIPS in terms of risk and efficiency?

2. Should a country have both an RTGS and net settlement system, only an RTGS, or only a net settlement system?

3. Should RTGS systems be operated by central banks or the private sector?

C.   HERSTATT RISK

An important risk in the payment system is the settlement risk on foreign exchange transactions. This is often called Herstatt risk after a German bank that failed in 1974. Reduction of this risk is a top priority for central bankers.[30]

On June 26, 1974, the Bundesaufsichtsamt für das Kreditwesen withdrew the banking license of Bankhaus Herstatt, a small bank in Cologne active in the FX market, and ordered it into liquidation during the banking day but after the close of the interbank payments system in Germany. Prior to the announcement of Herstatt's closure, several of its counterparties had, through their branches or correspondents, irrevocably paid Deutschmarks to Herstatt on that day through the German payments system against anticipated receipts of U.S. Dollars later the same day in New York in respect of maturing spot and forward transactions.

---

[29] C. Kahn, J. McAndrews, and W. Roberds, "Settlement Risk under Gross and Net Settlement," 35 J. of Money, Credit, and Banking 591, 604 (2003). G. Selgin, "Wholesale Payments: Questioning the Market-Failure Hypothesis," 24 International Review of Law and Economics 333 (2004) also questions the replacement of net settlement with real time gross settlement systems.

[30] See Bank for International Settlements, *Settlement Risk in Foreign Exchange Transactions* (1996), pp. 5-9, 15-17, 22-24, 36-38.

Upon the termination of Herstatt's business at 10:30 a.m. New York time on June 26, (3:30 p.m. in Frankfurt), Herstatt's New York correspondent bank suspended outgoing U.S. Dollar payments from Herstatt's account. This action left Herstatt's counterparty banks exposed for the full value of the Deutschmark deliveries made (credit risk and liquidity risk). Moreover, banks which had entered into forward trades with Herstatt, not yet due for settlement, lost money in replacing the contracts in the market (replacement risk), and others had deposits with Herstatt (traditional counterparty credit risk). Another version of the problem is illustrated in Figure 9.10 below:

Figure 9.10

HERSTATT RISK

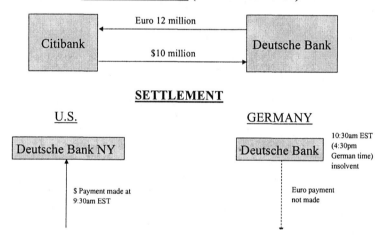

3-13-01 FX Contract (Settlement 3-15-01)

In this case, Citibank will be out $10 million, due to the use of the different payment systems in different time zones.

To contain the systemic risk inherent in current arrangements for settling foreign exchange transactions, it is first necessary to develop a workable definition of foreign exchange settlement exposure. BIS uses the following one:

> "A bank's actual exposure—the amount at risk—when settling a foreign exchange trade equals the full amount of the currency purchased and lasts from the time a payment instruction for the currency sold can no longer be cancelled unilaterally until the time the currency purchased is received with finality."

Although settling a trade involves numerous steps, from a settlement risk perspective a trade's status can be classified according to five broad categories:

Status R: *Revocable.* The bank's payment instruction for the sold currency either has not been issued or may be unilaterally cancelled without the consent of the bank's counterparty or any other intermediary. The bank faces no current settlement exposure for this trade.

Status I: *Irrevocable.* The bank's payment instruction for the sold currency can no longer be cancelled unilaterally either because it has been finally processed by the relevant payments system or because some other factor (e.g. internal procedures, correspondent banking arrangements, local payments system rules, laws) makes cancellation dependent upon the consent of the counterparty or another intermediary; the final receipt of the bought currency is not yet due. In this case, the bought amount is clearly at risk.

Status U: *Uncertain.* The bank's payment instruction for the sold currency can no longer be cancelled unilaterally; receipt of the bought currency is due, but the bank does not yet know whether it has received these funds with finality. In normal circumstances, the bank expects to have received the funds on time. However, since it is possible that the bought currency was not received when due (e.g. owing to an error or to a technical or financial failure of the counterparty or some other intermediary), the bought amount might, in fact, still be at risk.

Status F: *Fail.* The bank has established that it did not receive the bought currency from its counterparty. In this case the bought amount is overdue and remains clearly at risk.

Status S: *Settled.* The bank knows that it has received the bought currency with finality. From a settlement risk perspective the trade is considered settled and the bought amount is no longer at risk.

A major reason why FX settlement risk is interday as well as intraday is that banks may originate settlements in advance of their value date (the date on which they are due) and not be able to cancel them upon discovery that their counterparty cannot settle. What might be done to make it easier to cancel payments in advance of their value date? Note that under Article 4A of the United States Uniform Commercial Code, 4A-211, governing wire transfers, payments can, in principle, be cancelled up to the time they are credited to the beneficiary, if intervening banks cooperate. However, CHIPS Rule 2 prevents cancellation of any order received by CHIPS, whether or not the order has been passed on to the beneficiary.

CLS Bank

CLS Services, Ltd. has established a new system called Continuous Linked Settlement (CLS) to deal with Herstatt risk, which went operational in September 2002 after years of planning. Seventy of the world's largest banks, as well as all of the world's main central banks, participate. In principle, CLS permits simultaneous transfers of both legs of a foreign exchange transaction through existing national payment systems. IBM has developed the system and Swift provides the network communications system.[31]

The CLS Bank, which is chartered as a U.S. Edge Corporation (a limited purpose bank), settles currency transactions whose underlying obligations are either netted or gross. The Bank settles the payments for the transactions on a real-time not netted basis, transferring funds on both currency legs of the transaction at the same time by postings to the accounts of its members, a so-called payment versus payment system. The CLS Bank is the counterparty to both sides of the payment. CLS members pay the CLS Bank and receive payments from the CLS Bank. Members hold multicurrency accounts at the Bank. Currently, 15 currencies are eligible for CLS settlement: the Australian Dollar, the Canadian Dollar, Danish Krone, Euro, Japanese Yen, Pound Sterling, Norwegian Krone, Singapore Dollar, Swedish Krona, Swiss Franc, and the United States Dollar. Four currencies were added at the end of 2004: the New Zealand Dollar, Hong Kong Dollar, Korean Won and South African Rand.

The Bank pools member balances in each currency, and, provided members have a sufficient overall net balance, will settle transactions in any currency. Like in the new CHIPS system, an algorithm is employed to make maximum settlement use of a CLS member's balances. CLS Bank holds its own accounts at the central banks of the currencies involved. Members are able to pay in funds and receive settlement proceeds through the national payment systems.

Each member is required to pay in balances at CLS Bank to cover currency short positions within certain limits. Prior to each day's settlement period, which lasts for the five hours (three hours in Asia Pacific) that the RTGS payment systems in all time zones overlap, CLS commences the settlement of queued instructions. During the settlement cycle, new funds are taken in, transactions are settled, and funds are paid out. Banks can incur overdrafts up to a set ceiling in individual currencies but must have positive balances overall, taking account of fluctuations in exchange rates. CLS Bank

---

[31] J. Sandman, "CLS Settlement System Set for October Launch," *Securities Industry News*, March 26, 2001.

holds lines of credit with "liquidity providers" (the actual members themselves) to cover individual currency overdrafts.[32]

Below is a stylized version of two CLS transactions involving two banks:

Figure 9.11
CLS
Current Exchange Rates   (100¥ = $1; 1.5€ = $1)

BANK A (US) Accounts		BANK B (GERMANY) Accounts	
Actual Currency	$ Equivalent	Actual Currency	$ Equivalent
¥10,000,000,000	$100,000,000	¥5,000,000,000	$50,000,000
€50,000,000	$33,333,333	€25,000,000	$16,666,666
$100,000,000	$100,000,000	$50,000,000	$50,000,000
	$233,333,333		$116,666,666

FX TRANSACTIONS

¥10 billion
1. A ←————————→ B   Will settle
$100 million

¥20 billion
2. A ←————————→ B   Will not settle
$200 million

The first transaction will settle. Although B does not have $100,000,000 (only $50,000,000), B could convert other currencies to Dollars. They would convert at then current exchange rates. The second transaction will not settle because B does not have enough funds—B's total Dollars are $116 million. This transaction will be put into queue until B has enough funds.

On October 29, 2002, CLS Bank settled 15,200 transactions, totaling $395 billion, which required only $17 billion of payments between member banks, a 95 percent reduction. This is a strong indication of the substantial reduction of Herstatt risk effected by CLS. Nonethless, it appears that less than 50 percent of foreign exchange deals settle through CLS, $0.7 trillion out of $1.9 trillion in daily turnover, in the third quarter of 2004. This is not due to the failure to include more currencies—the 15 currencies presently

---

[32] See C. Khan and W. Roberds, "The CLS Bank: A Solution to the Risks of International Payments Settlement?," (2001) Carnegie-Rochester Conference Series on Public Policy 54, pp. 191-226; W. Mundt, "The Case for Continuous Linked Settlement, Payment Systems Worldwide," PRC Report (Winter 1997-98), pp. 63-64. For an earlier version of the same idea developed in connection with the Euro, see H. Scott, "A Payment System Role for a European System of Central Banks," in *Committee for the Monetary Union of Europe, For a Common Currency,* (1990) pp. 77-106 and "The Role of the European System of Central Banks in the Payment System," in *Committee for the Monetary Union of Europe, The Economic and Monetary Union: The Political Dimension* (1991), pp. 101-115.

eligible constitute about 95 percent of the foreign exchange market. It is rather due to the limited use of CLS by non-bank financial institutions and non-financial companies.[33]

Banks are seeking more active cooperation of central banks so that a bank could collateralize with its own central bank borrowing from another central bank, e.g. a Japanese bank could post collateral with the Bank of Japan to borrow Dollars from the Federal Reserve Bank of New York. Alternatively, CLS may be able to create its own internal collateral pool.

Notes and Questions

1.   Will CLS completely eliminate Herstatt risk?

2.   Could the CLS concept be extended to cover transactions other than those in foreign exchange? Would this be desirable?

D.   SOME ASPECTS OF THE INTERNATIONAL PAYMENT SYSTEM

1.   OFF-SHORE DOLLAR PAYMENT SYSTEMS

One aspect of the international payment system is offshore settlement. For example, there are various methods by which banks can clear dollar payments outside the United States through formal clearing systems. For example, there are the London Dollar Clearing Scheme (LDC) and the Tokyo Dollar Clearing System.

LDC clears United States Dollar checks and banker's drafts and payments (LDC items). Direct access to the clearing, administered by the Association for Payment Clearing Services (APACS), was limited in 1987 to seven major English banks (Settlement Banks), but other banks (Agency Banks) have indirect access to the clearing through correspondent accounts with the banks that have direct access.

LDC is a net settlement system. On the basis of a day's clearing activities in London, each Settlement Bank has a net position. A Settlement Bank's net positions are settled through New York on the same business day that they arise in London. Positions are determined by 4:30 p.m. London time or 11:30 a.m. New York time. Instructions to New York correspondents must be sent out by 12:00 p.m. New York time, leaving ample time during the same business day in New York to complete the settlement.

A net debtor Settlement Bank would instruct its New York correspondent to transfer funds to the New York correspondent account of the

---

[33] D. Sawyer, "Continuous Linked Settlement and Foreign Exchange Settlement Risk," 15 Payments System Worldwide 4 (Winter 2004-2005).

Settlement Agent (each Settlement Bank acts in this capacity on a rotating basis). This transfer could go through CHIPS or be a book transfer on the books of a New York bank that is the correspondent for both the Settlement Agent and the net debtor Settlement Bank. Conversely, the Settlement Agent transfers funds to the New York correspondent of a net creditor Settlement Bank.

In addition to the LDC net settlement among Settlement Banks, bilateral settlements must take place between LDC Settlement Banks, e.g. Lloyd's Bank, and their Agency Banks, e.g. Bankers Trust's London branch (BTL). Thus, for a day's LDC clearing, (BTL) may be in a net credit or net debit position with Lloyd's. If BTL is in a net credit position, Lloyd's would transfer funds, through its correspondent in New York, via CHIPS, to Banker Trust's New York head office (BTNY) for the account of BTL. If BTL were in a net debit position, BTL would transfer funds, through BTNY, via CHIPS, to Lloyd's New York correspondent, the settlement could take place by book-entries on the books of BTNY to the accounts of BTL and Lloyd's.

The Tokyo Dollar Clearing (TDC), which has existed since the occupation of Japan after World War II, is presently a clearing of all types of electronic dollar transfers among participant banks and branches in Tokyo, operated by JPMorgan Chase Manhattan's Tokyo branch (Chase-Tokyo).

Participating banks send electronic transfers to each other during the Tokyo day that may represent payments for any transactions between participants, e.g. the Dollar payment on a foreign exchange transaction or payments by a customer of one participant in favor of a customer of another participant. Customers receiving payments get credit on the books of their banks in Tokyo. All payments are routed through the computer system of Chase-Tokyo.

At the end of the day's clearing (3:00 p.m. Tokyo time), Chase calculates the net debit and net credit positions of participants, and communicates this information to the participants and to Chase New York. Chase New York then transfers credits to net creditors, on its books, through CHIPS, or by Fedwire, by 10:00 a.m. New York time (midnight same day in Tokyo). Net debtors must transfer credits to Chase in New York by the end of the CHIPS day. Net credit transfers by Chase are conditional on the net debtors settling with Chase by the end of the day.

As with LDC, TDC settlement takes place entirely in New York. But, also like LDC, the actual payments that underlie the TDC net calculation are made in Tokyo. There are other offshore Dollar payment systems, e.g. Hong Kong particularly in highly dollarized countries, e.g. Argentina.

2. EUROPEAN UNION

The European Union has taken three important initiatives with respect to large value payment systems within the EU: (a) formulation of minimum common standards; (b) improving the efficiency of cross-border retail transfers; and (c) preparation for EMU.

a.   MINIMUM COMMON STANDARDS

In November 1993, the Committee of Governors of the EU central banks issued a report on "Minimum Common Features for Domestic Payment Systems." This report established ten principles for EU Interbank Funds Transfer Services (EU IFTS) covering six areas: access conditions, risk management policies, legal issues, standards and infrastructures, pricing policies, and operating hours. Three of the most important principles relate to access, the need for RTGS systems, and the requirements for multilateral netting systems.

One of the access principles provides that "[n]o discrimination can be made between home-based credit institutions and credit institutions licensed in other EC countries which ask to participate in local interbank funds transfer systems, either through their local branches or directly from another member state. The applicants, however, may be required to establish that they can meet the relevant legal provisions of the host country. They also have to comply with the necessary technical requirements of the system; these requirements, however, should not be discriminatory." This policy seems directly related to the goal of establishing a single market for banking services represented by the Second Banking Directive. In 1995, there were 162 branches of foreign banks participating in EU IFTS of which 104 were from other EU countries.[34]

Remote access to payment systems (directly from the home country rather than through a local branch) has not yet been generally accepted due to various problems. For example, physical presence may be needed under back-up procedures requiring physical exchanges of data if electronic transmission is down. Having a settlement account with an overdraft facility at the local central bank is a condition for direct membership in most EU IFTS. Remote access raises the issue of whether and how the remote central bank can insure liquidity and perform the function of lender of last resort for the local system.[35]

Another important principle requires "[a]s soon as feasible, every Member State should have a real-time gross settlement system into which as many large-value payments as possible should be channeled. Such systems should settle across accounts at the central bank and have sound legal, technical, and prudential features which are compatible across member states." By the end of 1996, RTGS systems are expected to be in operation in

---

[34] Working Group on EU Payments Systems, Report to the Council of the European Monetary Institute, Developments in EU Payment Systems in 1994 (1995), p. 4
[35] Id., at 6-7.

all EU countries with the exception of Austria and Luxembourg.[36] This principle, as elaborated below, is important for the implementation of EMU since EMU uses the linked RTGS systems of the participants to make Euro transfers.

A third principle states: "[p]rovided that they settle at the central bank, large-value net settlement systems may continue to operate in parallel to real-time gross settlement systems but, in the near future, they should: (a) settle on the same-day as the exchange of the payment instruments; and (b) meet the Lamfalussy standards in full." The allowance of net settlement systems is significant given the general debate on the relative merits of RTGS and net settlement systems. However, the RTGS principle, requiring channeling into that system, seems to favor RTGS.

In May 1998, the European Parliament and Council adopted a Directive on Settlement Finality to insure the validity of payment netting. This is accomplished by providing for the legal enforceability of netting arrangements, the irrevocability of payment orders and the determination of which insolvency law is applicable in the event a payment system participant becomes insolvent. In addition, it recognizes the validity of collateral arrangements furnished in connection with payment systems.[37]

b.   EFFICIENT RETAIL CROSS-BORDER TRANSFERS

On December 4, 1995, the Council of Ministers adopted a Common Position with respect to certain retail (less than ECU 30,000) cross-border credit transfers.[38] Each cross-border transfer of currency requires the cross-border processing of information and often requires a foreign exchange transaction, e.g. X with a French Franc account in Paris wishes to pay Sterling to a London account. Articles 3 and 4 of the new Directive requires that credit institutions explain clearly to clients (originators and beneficiaries) the terms and conditions under which a payment will be made.

Article 6 of the Directive sets an upper limit of five business days (absent agreement) that a credit institution can take to execute an originator's transfer instruction. If the originator's credit institution fails to meet its obligation, it must compensate the beneficiary's institution with interest from the end of five days (or any earlier agreed date) to the date the funds are credited; this interest is, in turn, passed on to the beneficiary. If the reason for delay is due to the action of an intermediary bank, the originating bank can look to it for indemnity.

Article 7 of the Directive obliges the originator's bank to execute a transfer for the full amount (without the deduction of fees) unless the originator has otherwise specified. It anticipates, however, that the

---

[36] Id., at 9.
[37] [1998] O.J. L166, Directive 98/26/EC.
[38] [1995] O.J. C353/52, December 30, 1995.

beneficiary's bank can deduct fees from the beneficiary. The Commission hopes to avoid the situation where, due to the deduction of fees by the originating bank, the beneficiary would look back to the originator for additional compensation.

Finally, Article 8 provides that if a transfer is not complete within five business days, the originator has the option of asking for his money back, up to ECU 10,000, plus interest. The originating bank, and each intermediary institution in turn, generally have the right to recover the recredited funds, plus related costs and interest, from its transferee.

In December 2001, the European Parliament and the Council issued Regulation No. 2560/2001 on cross-border payments in Euro.[39] It provides that charges for cross-border payments in Euro of up to 50,000 will have to be aligned with domestic transaction charges within the home state of the executing bank. This prescription takes place for cash machines and bankcards of up to 12,500 Euro in July 1, 2002 and for credit transfers of up to the same amount by July 1, 2003. The rules will be extended to transactions of up to 50,000 by January 1, 2006. According to some studies, cross-border charges can be up to 20 times those for domestic transactions. Is this just price-gouging or are they more costly to make?

c.   EUROPEAN MONETARY UNION

EMU requires a large value transfer system for Euro. The existence of such a system is especially important for the conduct of monetary policy that requires a reliable method for the European System of Central Banks (ESCB) to pay for and receive payment for Euro-denominated bonds. EMI and its successor, the European Central Bank (ECB), created a RTGS payment system called TARGET to fulfill this function. TARGET establishes a linkage, provided by SWIFT, between national RTGS systems. Only payments related to the implementation of the single monetary policy have to be processed through TARGET. Use of TARGET for other cross-border payments is optional. Banks access TARGET through a national RTGS system, which need not be their own. For example, Lloyds Bank in London can access TARGET through the Banque de France, if the Banque de France were to decide to allow such access.

TARGET is not itself a RTGS system because, unlike national RTGS systems, it provides no facility for the settlement of payments. TARGET transfers from Italian to German banks, for example, will be settled by correspondent accounts between Banca d'Italia and the Bundesbank.

There are two principal reasons the linkage approach was adopted, rather than the building of a new EU system. First, the countries participating in EMU were not known enough in advance to build a new

---

[39] [2001] O.J. L344/13, December 28, 2001.

system. Secondly, the EU principle of subsidiarity—not doing centrally what can be done locally—argues for keeping in existence, rather than replacing, national systems.

Unlimited but fully collateralized intraday credit is provided to RTGS participants fulfilling the general counterparty eligibility of the European Central Bank (ECB). In July 1998, the ECB decided to grant access to TARGET to national central banks (NCBs) and participants in RTGS systems operating in Euro but located in non-Euro area countries of the EU. The ECB will only provide intraday credit to a non-Euro area NCB and its RTGS participants, if the non-Euro ECB is in an overall credit position vis-à-vis the other NCBs participating in or connected to TARGET taken together. Non-Euro area NCBs may provide collateralized intraday credit in Euro to participants subject to certain conditions set by the ECB.[40]

In 2002, TARGET processed payments amounting to an average of €1.5 trillion per month consisting of an average of 253,000 transactions per month. Domestic traffic represented 68 percent in value and 78 percent in volume.

3.   INTERNATIONAL STANDARDS

The Basel Committee on Payment and Settlement Systems has developed international standards for important payment systems.[41] The principles are as follows:

"Core Principles for systemically important payment systems

I.   The system should have a well founded legal basis under all relevant jurisdictions.

II. The system's rules and procedures should enable participants to have a clear understanding of the system's impact on each of the financial risks they incur through participation in it.

III. The system should have clearly defined procedures for the management of credit risks and liquidity risks, which specify the respective responsibilities of the system operator and the participants and which provide appropriate incentives to manage and contain those risks.

IV.*   The system should provide prompt final settlement on the day of value, preferably during the day and at a minimum at the end of the day.

V.* A system in which multilateral netting takes place should, at a minimum, be capable of ensuring the timely completion of daily

---

[40] European Central Bank, "Third Progress Report on the Target Project" (November 1998), pp. ii-iii.

[41] *Core Principles for Systematically Important Payment Systems* (January 2001).

settlements in the event of an inability to settle by the participant with the largest single settlement obligation.

VI. Assets used for settlement should preferably be a claim on the central bank; where other assets are used, they should carry little or no credit risk and little or no liquidity risk.

VII.   The system should ensure a high degree of security and operational reliability and should have contingency arrangements for timely completion of daily processing.

VIII.   The system should provide a means of making payments that is practical for its users and efficient for the economy.

IX. The system should have objective and publicly disclosed criteria for participation, which permit fair and open access.

X. The system's governance arrangements should be effective, accountable and transparent.

    * Systems should seek to exceed the minima included in these two Core Principles.

Responsibilities of the central bank in applying the Core Principles

A. The central bank should define clearly its payment system objectives and should disclose publicly its role and major policies with respect to systemically important payment systems.

B. The central bank should ensure that the systems it operates comply with the Core Principles.

C. The central bank should oversee compliance with the Core Principles by systems it does not operate and it should have the ability to carry out this oversight.

D. The central bank, in promoting payment system safety and efficiency through the Core Principles, should cooperate with other central banks and with any other relevant domestic or foreign authorities."

As we shall see in Chapter 20, these core principles along with many others, are subject to IMF monitoring and probably will be subject to some kind of enforcement in the future. They apply, in principle, to all countries. Systemically important payment systems are those where, "if the system were insufficiently protected against risk, disruption within it could trigger or transmit further disruptions among participants or systemic disruptions in the financial area more widely."[42]

The first core principle requires a well founded legal basis under all relevant jurisdictions. This requires a clear law of contracts, rules to

---

[42] Id, at 7.

establish when the system achieves final settlement, and bankruptcy laws that insure the finality of payments made before a bank fails, including netting arrangements. It further requires clear laws regarding collateral since many systems depend on such collateral.

CONCLUSIONS

The payment system is another key part of the infrastructure of the international financial system, particularly the dollar payment system which must be generally used in Dollar transactions, whether such transactions occur in the U.S. or abroad.

The most important development in these systems is the significant reduction in risk. Net settlement systems like CHIPS have used algorithms to sequence payment processing so as to reduce the impact of the failure to settle to quite manageable proportions. Indeed, it could be argued that real time gross settlement systems like Fedwire are no longer superior from a risk reduction point of view. The one major concern for net settlement systems is the validity of netting in cases of bank insolvency.

Herstatt risk, the risk arising from the settlement of foreign exchange transactions, has been greatly reduced by better risk management by banks and the advent of the CLS Bank.

CHAPTER TEN

CLEARANCE AND SETTLEMENT

This Chapter examines the clearance and settlement of securities. Efficient and reliable systems are a necessity for domestic and cross-border portfolio investment. This chapter begins by looking at the basic elements and mechanics of the clearing and settlement process, with emphasis on the clearing and settlement of U.S. equities through the Depository Trust and Clearing Corporation (DTCC).

Second, it explores the risks, systemic and nonsystemic, of clearing and settlement, and the Group of 30 recommendations to reduce them.

Third, it explains the mechanisms through which securities traded in one country can be cleared and settled in another. The focus there will be on inter-market linkages and international systems such as Euroclear.

Finally, it looks at how clearing and settlement systems may evolve in the future.

A. THE BASIC ELEMENTS

1. OVERVIEW

This section begins with an overview of how clearance and settlement works, and then turns to the risks its involves.

"Clearing and settlement is what happens after the trade. 'Clearing' confirms the identity and quantity of the financial instrument or contract being bought and sold, the transaction price and date, and the identity of the buyer and seller. It also sometimes includes the netting of trades, or the offsetting of buy orders and sell orders. 'Settlement' means payment to the seller and delivery of the stock certificate or transferring its ownership to the buyer.

Many markets have 'clearing houses' that handle both the clearing process and some of the settlement process. This is the most common system in the United States for exchange-traded financial products. Many markets, including the U.S. markets, have 'depositories,' that hold stocks and bonds for safekeeping on behalf of their owners. Depositories may transfer ownership of stocks and bonds by 'book entry' (a computer entry in the depository's record books) instead of physical delivery of certificates to the buyer, which saves time and money.

a.   THE GOALS OF CLEARING AND SETTLEMENT

The chief aims of clearing and settlement are efficiency and safety. The faster and more accurately a trade can be processed, the sooner the same capital can be reinvested, and at less cost and risk to investors.

The soundness of clearing and settlement systems in one nation can also impact other nations. The failure of a clearing member at a foreign clearing house could affect a U.S. clearing house through the impact on a common clearing member. To reduce the risk of such an occurrence, different countries' clearing and settlement systems are coordinated with each other, for example, by sharing risk information and harmonizing trade settlement dates.

b.   CLEARING

A key role of a clearing house is to assist in the comparison of trades and sometimes, as in the United States, also to remove counterparty risk from the settlement process. Clearing houses can provide the buyer with a guarantee that he will receive the securities—or other interest—he purchased, and provide the seller with a guarantee that the payment will be received.

A trade in the United States (as well as in Japan, Canada, and some other countries) cannot settle through the central systems until it has been matched, i.e. buyers' and sellers' records of the trade are compared and reconciled. A clearing house has an interface with a market in which trades are executed and from which the clearing house receives information on the trades. The clearing house may receive previously "locked-in" trades (trades which have already been matched), or it may match the trades itself. Close to 99 percent of equity trades in the U.S. are locked in at the time of trade execution in the local market, e.g. at the NYSE.

A clearing member delivers trade information to the clearing house and may hold positions both for itself (proprietary positions) and on behalf of its customers. Other traders in a market, who are not clearing members, must clear their trades through a member of a clearing house for that market. A clearing house controls the risks of the clearing and settlement process through its relationships with its clearing members. For example, it may have minimum capital requirements for clearing members, use margins or mark-to-market procedures, and require that its clearing members place collateral in a guarantee fund as protection against default by other clearing members. In the event of the failure of a clearing member, the clearing house may also have the ability to assess all other clearing members.

The depository records and arranges the legal transfer of ownership of securities, and holds securities for safekeeping. The clearing house instructs the depository on how the transaction is to be settled. There is an important relationship between the banks and the depository. When a bank acts in a custodial role, e.g. delivering securities and receiving payments on behalf of its customers, instructions on payment and title transfer are sent to the bank by the customer. The depository, in turn, as an accounting system for immobilized or dematerialized instruments, and/or as a central vault for the physical instruments themselves, interfaces with the banks as custodian."[1]

c.   SETTLEMENT

Settlement has two sides, the delivery of securities and the transfer of funds. These are usually not done in the same system, as funds transfers are usually made through the general payment system, rather than through a system dedicated to payments for securities. However, there are some systems that are dedicated, such as the Fed's book entry system for government securities. In addition, we shall see that international clearers, such as Euroclear, provide both sides of settlement.

Note that settlement occurs at two levels: between the parties to the trade, e.g. two broker-dealers (b/d), and between the b/ds and their customers. The timing between these two levels may be important. If a b/d must settle with another b/d before settlement occurs between the b/d and his customer, the b/d may have risk, e.g. b/d purchases the security, it goes down in value and the customer does not pay.

It is quite important whether or not the delivery of securities and the payments occur relatively simultaneously. If securities are delivered before funds, the party that has delivered the securities is out the cash, and is at risk for a failure to pay. Conversely, if funds are paid out before securities are received, the party that has paid the funds is at risk for the failure to deliver the securities.

2.   CLEARANCE AND SETTLEMENT IN THE UNITED STATES: THE DTCC

Clearance of equities in the United States is done principally by the National Securities Clearing Corporation (NSCC). After NSCC's merger with the Depository Trust Company (DTC) in 1999, the combined NSCC-DTC became DTCC. The DTCC holding company now owns both NSCC and DTC.

---

[1] Office of Technology Assessment, U.S. Congress, *Trading around the Clock* (1990), Ch. 5, "International Clearing and Settlement: What Happens After the Trade."

NSCC has over 400 direct clearing participants, and a total of direct and indirect participants of 1800 (indirect participants trade through direct participants). NSCC effects clearing and settlement of 95 percent of all equity trades in the United States, and also clears corporate bonds, as well as some other securities, e.g. municipal bonds. In 2002, NSCC processed about $81 trillion in 4.1 billion securities transactions.

DTC is a New York limited purpose trust company, a quasi-bank, which is the world's largest securities depository. It has 600 bank and securities firm participants. DTC holds securities (individual or global certificates) and accounts for the ownership interests of its participants in the form of book-entries. It also has funds accounts in connection with institutional settlement. In 2002, it had about $21 trillion worth of securities in custody.

NSCC's clearance and settlement process normally requires three business days. Trade information is received either in the form of locked-in trades already matched by the computer systems of the exchange or market; or, as buy and sell data reported by market participants. The latter still must be compared and buy and sell orders matched. Locked-in trades are entered directly in the NSCC computer system on the same day as the trade. This sharply reduces the need for the matching of buy and sell orders at the clearing house level.

Table 10A
NSCC Clearance and Settlement Process for Depository
Equity Shares[2]

T+3 day	Clearance and Settlement
T (trade date)	Trade occurs and trade information is sent to NSCC, mostly on a "locked-in" basis.
T+1	Results of trade comparison and matching are sent to direct participants.
T+2	NSCC determines participants' net settlement positions.
T+3	Settlement date—securities are delivered and payment is made.

Table 10A, above, describes in a simplified manner the T+3 trading, clearance, and settlement of an equity trade that is not netted with other trades. Figure 10.1, below, describes the entire process.

---

[2] NSCC.

Figure 10.1
T+3 Clearance and Settlement of Depository-Eligible Equity Shares

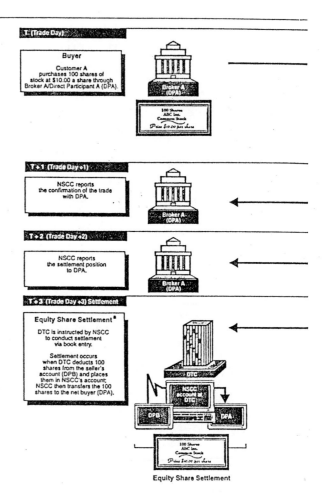

Figure 2.1: T+3 Clearance and Settlement of Depository-Eligible Equity Shares

T: (Trade Day)

Buyer

Customer A purchases 100 shares of stock at $10.00 a share through Broker A/Direct Participant A (DPA).

Broker A (DPA)

100 Shares ABC Inc. Common Stock Price $10.00 per share

T+1 (Trade Day +1)

NSCC reports the confirmation of the trade with DPA.

Broker A (DPA)

T+2 (Trade Day +2)

NSCC reports the settlement position to DPA.

Broker A (DPA)

T+3 (Trade Day +3) Settlement

Equity Share Settlement [a]

DTC is instructed by NSCC to conduct settlement via book entry.

Settlement occurs when DTC deducts 100 shares from the seller's account (DPB) and places them in NSCC's account; NSCC then transfers the 100 shares to the net buyer (DPA).

DTC

NSCC account at DTC

DPB   DPA

100 Shares ABC Inc. Common Stock Price $10.00 per share

Equity Share Settlement

(Figure 10.1 continued)

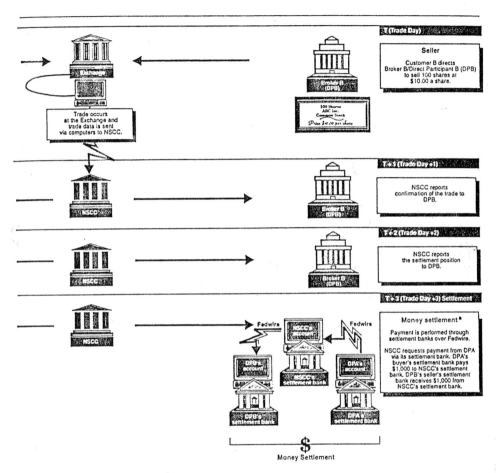

*Equity share and money settlement is normally done on a net basis such that the single purchase of 100 shares would be combined with DPA's and DPB's other trades to produce one net equity share settlement and money settlement.

Source: GAO analysis of NSCC data.

Equity share settlement. The settlement of equities has two parts—share and money settlement. The movement of the shares takes place through DTC accounts. NSCC instructs DTC to move shares from the accounts of net sellers to NSCC's account and then from NSCC's account to the accounts of net buyers. If the amount of shares is insufficient to satisfy all delivery obligations, NSCC uses a random allocation algorithm to determine to whom securities should be delivered.

Money settlement. The other phase of settlement is the money settlement. The net money settlement is determined on T+3 and can be settled with a single payment between NSCC and participants through settlement banks. Every trading day, NSCC generates a settlement statement. This statement tells each participant what its net money obligation is, based upon the Dollar value of the participant's equity shares delivered and the Dollar value of its payment obligation. Each participant has a settlement bank that has guaranteed that it will pay or receive the money settlement on the participant's behalf. Settlement banks are required to make payment before Fedwire closes.

Ownership of shares is handled through a tiered system of book-entries. Corporate registrars have a limited role in accounting for changes in ownership since most shares on registers are held in the name of Cede & Co., the nominee name of DTC. So when investor A sells to investor B, no change is made on the books of the registrar when the issue is held at DTC. DTC accounts on its books for the ownership interests of its members, broker-dealers and custodian banks, and the broker-dealers and custodians then account for the ultimate ownership of customers on their books.

DTC, apart from accounting for the ownership of securities and funds, also performs other functions, e.g. it collects and distributes dividends and interest.

a.   THE NSCC FAIL PROCESS

In 2003, the fail rate—the percentage of trades that did not settle on the settlement date—was 5 percent of the total net Dollar value of cash and securities due on the settlement date. Since DTCC takes the counterparty position and guarantees the settlement of all matched trades, DTCC is exposed to various credit, market, and non-market risks. The ways in which clearing houses protect themselves against such risks are critically important.

When trades are matched, NSCC becomes the counterparty to the trades. This now occurs at midnight of T+1 at the latest. Suppose A sells B 100 IBM at $100 per share, and the trade is locked-in at T+1. What is the risk for NSCC? First, there is the risk that B may fail to pay NSCC. If this occurs, NSCC must still pay A $10K on the settlement date, T+3. If the price of IBM has gone down, the IBM shares NSCC gets from A may be worth less than $10K. If they were worth only $5K, because they are now selling at $50 per share, NSCC has a $5K loss.

It is also possible that A may not deliver the shares to NSCC on T+3, even though NSCC must deliver the shares to B. If the price of IBM shares has gone up, NSCC must buy the shares at a higher price than $10K, the funds it gets from B. If the shares were worth $15K, because they are now selling at $150 per share, NSCC has a $5K loss.

How does NSCC protect itself against these risks? There are two periods of concern, the interim period (between the trade and settlement), T to T+3, and the period after settlement, T+3 and after. Securities' settlement is actually supposed to take place before 3:00 p.m. on T+3. Money settlement occurs between 4:00–5:00 p.m.

In the interim period, the clearing fund for each member is supposed to cover potential losses, based on a 20-day rolling average of a participants' portfolio value away from the stock price. Participants pay in on sells where the stock rises, and on buys where the stock falls. But the 20-day average measures positions and market risk in the past; this could have already changed as of today, and could further change in the future. Normally, the money due is only actually collected once a month, but it can be collected as often and as quickly as needed.

After the interim period, if the party does not settle a trade on T+3, NSCC must perform as counterparty. Failures to pay can result in NSCC closing out the position of the failing party. Failures to deliver usually result in a mark-to-market procedure. These procedures are further elaborated below.

Failure to Pay

Failure to pay usually means insolvency. However, there can be unusual situations, floods, riots, etc. Payment settlements are now all by Fedwire. Late payments must include interest.

In case of insolvency, NSCC closes out the failing broker's (FB) positions on T+3. It will pay for/deliver securities according to FB's contracts. NSCC has a three-day market risk on FB's positions. It loses on price decreases on long positions (NSCC must pay the delivering broker the contract price in exchange for securities worth less than the contract price) and price increases on short positions (NSCC must pay for securities at the T+3 price and only gets back the lower contract price).

Failure to Deliver

(a) The routine case

A failure to deliver occurs routinely when the delivering broker (DB) does not have the required securities. DB may not, for example, have received them from the customer and is unwilling to borrow them.

If DB fails to deliver on T+3, it must pay NSCC any positive difference between the T+2 price (the last closing market price) and contract price. Thus, if the trade was at $100 and the price at T+2 was $150, DB must pay NSCC $50 on T+3. The $50 is passed on to the receiving broker (RB) on the same date. NSCC has no loss, because it has taken no position in the stock. DB has paid over its $50 loss, as of T+2, to RB, which had a corresponding $50 gain.

If DB delivers on T+4, RB would pay the T+2 closing price, $150 to NSCC (the mark-to-market price), and NSCC would pay DB $150. In effect, the deal is still done at the $100 contract price. RB has paid $150 on T+4, but had previously received the $50 mark payment on T+3; net payments are $100. DB gets $100 net, $150 from NSCC minus its previous mark payment of $50.

(b) Insolvency

Tables 10B and 10C below deal with what happens when DB declares insolvency on either T+3 or T+4. Table 10B, below, shows how the mark-to-market system works, assuming the market prices in the left column.

Table 10B NSCC's Mark-to-Market System			
Day	Closing price of stock	Mark-to-market price	Mark
T (day of trade)	100 (trade price)	N.A.	N.A.
T + 2	150	N.A.	N.A.
T + 3	190	150	50
T + 4	220	190	40
T + 5	250	220	30
Note: T = day of trade. NSCC becomes counterparty at midnight on T+1.			

The mark-to-market price is the price RB pays for the delivery of stock and the mark is the amount the DB must pay if delivery is not made on the indicated date.

Table 10C, below, shows NSCC's exposure on T+3 and T+4 depending on whether or not NSCC can purchase the stock on the date of insolvency before the market closes, and whether or not DB has paid the mark due on the date of insolvency.

Table 10C NSCC's Exposure when Broker Fails to Deliver and Becomes Insolvent				
	Timing of insolvency on the day insolvency occurs:			
	after market close		before market close	
	before mark payment	after mark payment	before mark payment	after mark payment
T + 3	P_{T+4} - K (1)	P_{T+4} - C_{T+2} (2)	P_{T+3} - K (3)	P_{T+3} - C_{T+2} (4)
T + 4	P_{T+5} - C_{T+2} (5)	P_{T+5} - C_{T+3} (6)	P_{T+4} - C_{T+2} (7)	P_{T+4} - C_{T+3} (8)
Note:	K = contract price (established on day T) P_x = market price of stock on day X C_x = closing price of stock on day X Numbers in parentheses correspond to the various cases described below.			

Let us go through each of the cases represented in Table 10C. For purposes of this discussion, we shall use the prices given in Table 10B, and we shall assume for simplicity that the market price at which NSCC can acquire the stock on a given day is equal to that day's closing price.

Case 1

NSCC must purchase the stock at the T+4 price, P_{T+4}, because DB became insolvent after the market closed on T+3. NSCC receives the contract price, K, from RB. NSCC thus loses up to P_{T+4} - K (there would be no loss if P_{T+4} turned out to be less than K). Assuming the prices given in Table 10B, NSCC loses 220 - 100 = 120.

Case 2

NSCC must again purchase the stock for P_{T+4}. Since the position has been marked to market, and RB has already received a mark payment of 50, RB pays NSCC the T+3 mark-to-market price, C_{T+2}, that is 150. NSCC thus loses 220 - 150 = 70.

Case 3

NSCC can purchase the stock at T+3 since the insolvency occurs before the market closes and will pay RB the contract price, K. NSCC thus loses 190 - 100 = 90.

Case 4

NSCC can purchase the stock at T+3, but here RB has received the 50 mark, and the position is marked-to-market on T+3 to the T+2 closing price, 150. NSCC loses 190 - 150 = 40.

Case 5

NSCC purchases the stock for P_{T+5}. We assume no T+4 mark has been paid, so that the position has not been marked-to-market on T+4. RB pays the T+2 closing price, i.e., the T+3 mark-to-market price. Note that RB's payment is equal to the contract price of 100 plus the T+3 mark of 50. NSCC loses 250 - 150 = 100.

Case 6

NSCC again purchases the stock for P_{T+5}. RB has received two marks, 50 on T+3 and 40 on T+4, and pays 190, the T+4 mark-to-market price (which is the T+3 closing price). DB has paid the contract price plus the two marks. NSCC loses 250 - 190 = 60.

Case 7

NSCC purchases the stock before the market closes for P_{T+4}. Since no T+4 mark has been paid, and the position has not yet been marked-to-market, at T+4 DB pays 150, the T+3 mark-to-market price (which is the same as the T+2 closing price). NSCC loses 220 - 150 = 70.

Case 8

NSCC again purchases the stock for P_{T+4}. As in Case 6, RB pays 190, the T+3 closing price (i.e. the T+4 mark-to-market price). NSCC loses 220 - 190 = 30.

3.   MULTILATERAL NETTING

A key aspect of clearance and settlement is multilateral netting. Multilateral netting is achieved in several ways. In some cases, the clearing house acts as a central counterparty, e.g. as with NSCC in the United States. Participants enter into a transaction bilaterally. The clearing house subsequently is substituted as the buyer to the seller and the seller to the buyer, and any obligations between the participants pursuant to the original transaction are discharged. The clearing house keeps a running record of its net position vis-à-vis each participant for each security and each settlement date. For a given set of transactions, this process leaves each participant with net obligations to deliver to, or receive from, the clearing house amounts of securities equal to its multilateral net position vis-à-vis other participants in the clearing house. For each settlement date, each participant's payment obligations are settled by a single payment to, or from, the clearing house.

In other multilateral netting schemes, the clearing house guarantees completion of all matched, unsettled transactions among its participants. In still other arrangements, the clearing house calculates a multilateral net position for each participant vis-à-vis other participants but neither substitutes itself as central counterparty nor guarantees completion of transactions. The latter arrangements are often called "position netting"; obligations are routinely settled by delivery and payment of the net amounts, but in the event of a default, the multilateral net positions are not legally binding on participants.

Legally binding multilateral netting has the potential to reduce both principal risk and replacement-cost risk. Principal risk can be reduced because the value of the securities that must be delivered to settle a given value of trades typically is far smaller than the gross value of the securities traded. Replacement-cost risk can be reduced because potential losses from replacing some trades are offset by gains from replacing other trades. The magnitude of potential risk reductions depends on trading patterns. Principal risks can be reduced dramatically when participants both buy and sell substantial amounts of the same securities. Assuming that securities prices are positively correlated, smaller but still significant reductions in replacement-cost risk can be achieved if participants are buyers of some securities and sellers of others.

Regardless of the pattern of trading, multilateral netting by a clearing house can reduce replacement-cost risk by facilitating prompt closeout and replacement of unsettled transactions. Because a single counterparty or guarantor replaces multiple counterparties, there is no need for multiple negotiations to close out unsettled transactions. Also, multilateral netting arrangements generally specify procedures for determining the value of unsettled positions and for allocating losses to surviving participants.

Netting arrangements also are designed to reduce liquidity risk. In a multilateral netting system, all of a participant's obligations to deliver or receive a *particular* security on a specific settlement day are discharged through making or receiving a single delivery. In addition, *all* of a participant's obligations to make or receive payment on settlement day are discharged through making or receiving a single payment. If a security is to be received, the amount to be received is no larger, and generally is considerably smaller, than the sum of the amounts that would be delivered in the absence of netting. Likewise, if a cash payment is to be received, the amount to be received is reduced by netting. Consequently, the liquidity pressures arising from unanticipated failures to receive securities or payments can be greatly diminished by legally binding multilateral netting. Clearing houses in the United States typically report that multilateral netting reduces the value of deliveries by 70 percent to 90 percent, implying potential reductions of that magnitude in both principal and liquidity risks.

Notes and Questions

1. Assume there is a multilateral netting system. A buys 100 IBM from B at $1, B buys 50 IBM from C at $3, and C buys 40 IBM from A at $2. Calculate the net securities and cash positions of the three parties.

2. How can DTCC protect itself from the failure of a participant to deliver securities or pay for them?

4.   GROUP OF THIRTY STANDARDS

Many of the changes in clearance and settlement in the 1990s have been spurred on by the Group of Thirty's proposed standards. The Group of Thirty is a think tank sponsored by major financial institutions that formulated its proposals in *Special Report, Clearance and Settlement in the World's Securities Markets* (1988). Other industry groups like the International Securities Services Association (ISSA)[3] have helped implement the Group of Thirty proposal. In addition, the Bank for International Settlements has hosted a joint effort between its Committee on Payment and Settlement Systems and IOSCO to formulate recommendations for clearance and settlement systems worldwide.[4]

a.   THE STANDARDS

1.   By 1990, all comparisons of trades between direct market participants (i.e. brokers, dealers, and other exchange members) should be compared within 1 day after a trade is executed, or T+1.

2.   Indirect market participants—institutional investors, or any trading counterparties which are not broker/dealers—should be members of a trade comparison system which achieves positive affirmation of trade details.

3.   Each country should have an effective and fully developed central securities depository, organized and managed to encourage the broadest possible industry participation.

4.   Each country should study its market volumes and participation to determine whether a trade netting system would be beneficial in terms of reducing risk and promoting efficiency.

5.   Delivery versus payment should be the method for settling all securities transactions.

6.   Payments associated with the settlement of securities transactions and the servicing of securities portfolios should be made consistent across all instruments and markets by adopting the "same day" convention.

7.   A "rolling settlement" system should be adopted by all markets. Final settlement should occur on T+3 by 1992.

8.   Securities lending and borrowing should be encouraged as a method of expediting the settlement of securities transactions. Existing regulatory

---

[3] Recommendations 2000.
[4] *Report of the CPSS-IOSCO Joint Task Force on Securities Settlement Systems, Consultative Report* (January 2001).

and taxation barriers that inhibit the practice of lending securities should be removed by 1990.

9.   Each country should adopt the technical standard for securities messages developed by the International Organization for Standardization (ISO Standards 7775 and 6166).

Table 10D, below, gives the status at year-end 1999 of implementation of those proposals in major countries. There are three categories for DvP (delivery versus payment): (1) complete, where there is a simultaneous and irrevocable exchange of securities (on the delivery side) and cash value (on the payment side); (2) qualified, where there is no simultaneous exchange of cash and securities but where there are "conditions or safeguards providing conditions close to those" found in a "complete" system; or (3) non-DvP. Note that France (the Paris Bourse) had a monthly settlement cycle. This is now T+3.

Table 10D
Group of Thirty: Current Status of International Settlement Recommendations-Equities[5]

Recommendation No.	1	2	3	4	5	6	7	8	9
Country:	Institutional Comparison	T+2 Affirmation	Securities Depository	Securities Netting	DVP	Same-Day Funds	Rolling Settlement on T+3	Securities Lending	ISO/ISIN
Australia	Yes	Yes	Yes	Yes	Complete	Yes	T+3	Yes	Yes
Austria	Yes	No	Yes	Yes	Complete	Yes	T+3	Yes	Yes
Belgium	Yes	Partial	Yes	Yes	Qualified	Yes	Bi-weekly	No	Yes
Canada	Yes	Yes	Yes	Partial	Qualified	Yes	T+3	Yes	No
France	Yes	Yes	Yes	Yes	Qualified	Yes	Monthly	Yes	Yes
Germany	Yes	Yes	Yes	Yes	Qualified	Yes	T+2	Yes	Yes
Hong Kong	Yes	Yes	Yes	Yes	Qualified	Yes	T+2	Yes	Yes
Italy	Yes	Yes	Yes	Yes	Qualified	Yes	T+3	Yes	Yes
Japan	Yes	No	Yes	Yes	Qualified	Partial	T+3	Yes	Yes
Singapore	Yes	Yes	Yes	Yes	Qualified	Partial	T+5	No	Yes
Spain	Yes	Yes	Yes	Yes	Qualified	Yes	T+3	Yes	Yes
Switzerland	Yes	No	Yes	No	Complete	Yes	T+3	Yes	Yes
United Kingdom	Yes	Partial	Yes	No	Qualified	Yes	T+5	Yes	Yes
United States	Yes	Partial	Yes	Yes	Qualified	Yes	T+3	Yes	CUSIP

These proposals were important in standardizing clearing and settlement systems. This generally reduced risk, made it easier for firms to use multiple systems, and increased transactional efficiency. Sometimes standardization can hinder innovation, but here there seemed to be institutional convergence around the Group of Thirty proposals.

---

[5] State Street Bank and Trust Co., *The Guide to Custody in World Markets* (1997, 2000).

b.   T+3

One of the key standards, T+3, was widely resisted. It is important to note that the SEC adopted a new Rule 15c6-1 on October 6, 1993, which required T+3 settlement by June 1, 1995, 58 Federal Register 52891 (1993); the industry did not do so voluntarily. In line with the SEC change, the Federal Reserve Board amended Regulation T (Credit by Brokers and Dealers) by shortening by two days the time for customers to meet initial margin calls or make full cash payment to broker-dealers. Under the new rule, customers have two business days after the completion of the standard settlement cycle.[6]

The SEC has permitted another important change, allowing customers to have certificateless direct registration of certificates; the customer's name can appear directly on the books of the issuer and the customer receives a statement of ownership from the issuer rather than a certificate. Before customers could only avoid holding certificates by holding them in street name through their brokers. Or put another way, customers seeking to hold securities directly had to do so by keeping the paper themselves.[7]

There is no stopping with T+3. Already some countries, like Germany and Hong Kong, have T+2, and Hong Kong has debated going to T+0.[8] Both the Fed and the SEC have urged that the U.S. go to T+1. It now appears that this cannot be done before 2004. The system cost of moving to T+1 in the United States is estimated to be $8 billion but this will be recouped by lower costs in the future. Importantly, movement to T+1 would reduce daily settlement exposure by $750 billion daily and as a consequence reduce by one-third the size of the required clearing fund to guarantee trades.[9] A T+1 settlement date for cross-border trades would create significant difficulty because under current arrangements the foreign exchange trade needed to provide the settlement currency would not be completed until T+2. In July 2002, the Securities Industry Association (SIA) put off a decision to move to T+1 until 2004.

The objective of decreasing settlement time from T+3 is often linked to the desirability of achieving straight-through-processing (STP), which means that "once a determination is made to buy or sell securities, the order can be routed to the appropriate market, executed, reported back to the trading parties and then settled—all with no manual intervention."[10] In the last few years, the industry has decoupled these objectives, and focused more

---

[6] That cycle is T+3 as of June 1995 (1994) 59 Federal Register 53565.
[7] (1997) 62 Federal Register 64034.
[8] C. Kentouris, "Hong Kong Custodians Balk at T+0," *Securities Industry News*, July 19, 1999.
[9] C. Kentouris, "SIA Report: Shorter Settlement Feasible No Earlier than 2004," *Securities Industry News*, July 31, 2000.
[10] DTCC, "Paving the Way to Straight-through Processing: A White Paper to the Industry on T+1," (July 2000), p. 4.

on STP. Movement from T+3 to T+2 would require more automated payment, elimination of physical certificates, and faster data entry. T+2 settlement is also difficult because foreign exchange settlement for cross-border transactions are processed on a T+2 cycle.[11] One would need to accelerate this in order to have funds by T+2.

5.   THE SECOND GENERATION GROUP OF THIRTY STANDARDS

The Group of Thirty has recently formulated a second generation of standards that are much more encompassing than the first. There are 20 recommendations under three broad headings, as follows:

Creating a Strengthened, Interoperable Global Network

1. Eliminate paper and automate communication, data capture, and enrichment.
2. Harmonize messaging standards and communication protocols.
3. Develop and implement reference data standards.
4. Synchronize timing between different clearing and settlement systems and associated payment and foreign-exchange systems.
5. Automate and standardize institutional trade matching.
6. Expand the use of central counterparties.
7. Permit securities lending and borrowing to expedite settlement.
8. Automate and standardize asset servicing processes, including corporate actions, tax relief arrangements, and restrictions on foreign ownership.

Mitigating Risk

9. Ensure the financial integrity of providers of clearing and settlement services.
10. Reinforce the risk management practices of users of clearing and settlement service providers.
11. Ensure final, simultaneous transfer and availability of assets.
12. Ensure effective business continuity and disaster recovery planning.
13. Address the possibility of failure of a systemically important institution.
14. Strengthen assessment of the enforceability of contracts.
15. Advance legal certainty over rights to securities, cash, or collateral.

---

[11] C. Kentouris, "Next Day? Not Today," *Securities Industry News*, March 22, 2004.

16. Recognize and support improved valuation and closeout netting arrangements.

Improving Governance

17. Ensure appointment of appropriately experienced and senior board members.

18. Promote fair access to securities clearing and settlement networks.

19. Ensure equitable and effective attention to stakeholder interests.

20. Encourage consistent regulation and oversight of securities clearing and settlement service providers.

Recommendation 15 is the key legal recommendation. It envisions improvements in certainty in four areas: (1) choice-of-law rules, e.g. implementation of the new PRIMA Convention discussed later in this Chapter; (2) protection against intermediary insolvency, making sure persons holding securities have senior status in the intermediary's bankruptcy; (3) effectiveness of pledging arrangements; and (4) finality, rules providing when securities transfers are final.

6.   SEC CONCEPT RELEASE

In March 2004, the SEC published a Concept Release on further improvements in the clearance and settlement process.[12] The release seeks comment on whether the completion of the confirmation and affirmation process should be completed on the trade date (T+0). The Commission is also seeking comment on shortening the settlement cycle to a shorter period than T+3, and reducing reliance on the use of physical securities.

Notes and Questions

1.   Are common clearing and settlement standards necessary or desirable? Why have they been formulated by a private think tank?

2.   What are the costs and benefits of accelerating T+?

B.   THE UNITED KINGDOM: A DIFFERENT MODEL

Until 1994, the United Kingdom had a fortnightly settlement (once every two weeks). They also had a paper based settlement system with no central depository. This changed with the advent of CREST.

CREST began operations in July 1996 and was fully operational by the end of 1997, with 69 shareholders subscribing to £12 million in capital of

---

[12] SEC Concept Release, Securities Transactions Settlement, Release Nos. 33-8398, 34-49405, IC 26384, March 11, 2004.

CRESTCo., the operating company. The Bank of England led the effort to develop the service.[13] In 2002, CRESTCo. merged with Euroclear, the international clearer, discussed below.

Basic Process

CREST is only used for London Stock Exchange (LSE) trades. As of 2001, it adopted T+3 settlement. There is no paper to transfer or evidence legal title. Electronic messages effecting register entries replaced stock transfer forms (paper) for U.K. equity trades between CREST participants. The only written part of the transfer process is the register entries—book-entry transfers or BETs—which will remain prima facie evidence of legal title to the corresponding shares.

Netting

Until February 2001, CREST had no netting and settled trades on a trade-by-trade basis on both the securities and cash side. The lack of netting made many of the Group of Thirty standards irrelevant to CREST and called into question the Group of Thirty convergence paradigm.

In February 2001, LSE, CREST, and the London Clearing House (LCH) commenced operations for a central counterparty (CCP) facility for trades on the LSE's SETS electronic order book system. This permits optional bilateral netting. 50 percent of SETS trades on LSE were netted in 2002. As of yet, however, there is no multilateral netting. In October 2003, LSE was considering switching its clearing business to Eurex Clearing owned by Deutsche Börse. This in turn had put on hold merger talks between LCH and Clearnet, the Paris-based clearer owned by Euronext.[14]

Settlement

Payment operates through two tiers of accounts. Both the purchaser and seller of shares has an account with a settlement bank (tier one) and each settlement bank in turn has one with the CREST system's bank, the Bank of England (Bank) (tier two). To enable trade-by-trade settlement, the purchaser's settlement bank has to have sufficient funds in its account with the Bank for the Bank to be able to transfer the purchase price to the seller's settlement bank's account with the Bank at the settlement time. It is up to the purchaser's settlement bank whether it requires funds from the purchaser or gives it credit.

Share Ownership

There is no central nominee shareholder as in DTC. A central nominee shareholder would be the nominee on registers for all CREST participants' CREST shares, and, as such, the sole legal owner of them, as SEPON is now for all LSE market makers' U.K. shares.

---

[13] "The CREST Project," 35 Bank of England Quarterly Bulletin (1995), p. 60.
[14] A. Skorecki, "LSE Doubts Hold up LCH Link with Clearnet," *Financial Times*, October 30, 2003.

Each U.K. company has one register for each class of its shares. Indeed, the preservation of the share registration system, which benefits banks serving as registrars, had a significant impact in shaping the CREST system.

Stock Lending

In the past, there have been problems with stock lending in the United Kingdom. The availability of stock lending is important in avoiding failures to deliver. If a party does not have the security, and has sold it (has shorted the stock), it can borrow it from another party. This has raised tax problems for the Inland Revenue. Prior to July 1, 1991, a 15 percent withholding tax was imposed on the lender on dividends paid on shares that were part of a borrowing arrangement. The concern was that "stock lending" might be used as a device by which domestic "borrowers" that really bought the stock would escape the withholding tax. The lender recovered the tax from a charge to the borrower, thus raising the cost of stock borrowing. Many of these lenders were foreign institutions, who would normally not have a withholding tax imposed on dividends under various U.K. tax treaties. After July 1, no withholding tax was to be imposed on qualified "pool" foreign lenders.

C.   INTERNATIONAL DIMENSIONS

We now turn to some international aspects of clearing and settlement. As Figure 10.2, below, indicates,[15] there are various alternative channels through which a non-resident of the country of issue of a security could effect settlement of a cross-border trade: (1) through direct access to (membership in) the Central Securities Depository (CSD) in the country of issue, e.g. DTC in the United States; (2) through a local agent (a local bank that is a member of the CSD in the country of issue); (3) through a global custodian that employs a local agent as sub-custodian; (4) through a CSD in the non-resident's own country that has established a link (usually direct) to the CSD in the country of issue; or (5) through an International Central Securities Depository (ICSD), e.g. Euroclear or Clearstream, that has established a direct or indirect (though a local agent) link to the CSD in the country of issue.

Direct access is often not a real alternative since CSDs typically prohibit foreign residents from becoming participants, with the exception of foreign CSDs and ICSDs. Moreover, certain functions would be difficult to perform without a local presence, e.g. matching of settlement instructions. Use of a local agent in the country of issue is probably the most common

---

[15] Bank for International Settlements, *Report of the Committee on Payment and Settlement Systems, Cross-Border Securities Settlements* (1995), p. 13.

method for settling cross-border trades. Foreign residents may contract with local agents directly or use global custodians to do so. "A global custodian provides its customers with access to settlement and custody services in multiple markets through a single gateway by integrating services performed by a network of sub-custodians, including the global custodian's own local branches and other local agents."[16]

Figure 10.2

Alternative channels for settling cross-border securities trades

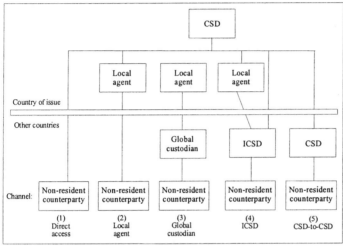

Source: Bank for International Settlements.

1.   LINKAGES

Numerous CSD-CSD links have been established which are used primarily to settle trades of stocks listed in two countries. What is the purpose of such links? Investors typically hold securities in custody in the home country of the traded security. This is because this is where most of the trades with respect to that security occur. Without the linkage, the selling party's custodian, in Figure 10.3, below, would physically have to move the security to Japan where it would be received by the buyer. The buyer, in turn, even if Japanese, might want to move the security back to the U.S. Securities would then constantly be moved in and out of the trading country with the attendant expense. If there were no physical security to move, e.g. no certificates were issued, interaction would be simpler but still expensive, as book transfers in and out of each country's system would constantly have to be made.

---

[16] Id., at 15.

Figure 10.3

Cross Border Linkage–Cross Exchange Trade

U.S. buyer (S) buys 100 IBM shares cross-listed on Tokyo Stock Exchange (TSE) from Japanese seller. How would this transaction be settled?

Securities Settlement

DTC (DTC Rules)		JSCC
S's Custodian	JSCC (link)	Buyer
-100	+100	+100

Cash Settlement

Buyer pays Seller Yen through Japanese payment system

Investors typically hold securities in custody in the home country of the traded security, the U.S. (NYSE) in the IBM example. This is because this is where most of the trades with respect to that security occur.

Figure 10.4 depicts a cross-border trade, where an investor outside the market country trades the stock.

Figure 10.4

Cross Border Linkage–Cross Border Trade

U.S. investor sells 100 Mitsubishi Chemical, listed on TSE to Japanese buyer.

Securities Settlement

JSCC (JSCC Rules)

Seller's Custodian Bank (link)	Buyer
-100	+100

Cash Settlement

Japanese buyer pays Seller's custodian bank through Japanese payment system

---

This trade is not handled through bilateral links between Central Securities Depositories (CSDs) like DTC and JSCC, because this is a trade of a Japanese stock on TSE—the previous cross-listed example, on the other hand, was a U.S. stock traded on both the U.S. and Japanese exchanges. Here, the U.S. seller goes through its global custodian who holds Japanese stock at JSCC through its local Japanese entity or an independent sub-custodian. The custodian's participation in the Japanese system is the link.

2.   ICSDs

The ICSDs, Euroclear, and Cedel (now Clearstream) were originally set up to provide settlement and custody services for Eurobonds. Euroclear was founded in 1968 by the Brussels office of Morgan Guaranty Trust Company of New York (MGT). In September 1999, J.P. Morgan announced it was bowing out of Euroclear. Euroclear's European users were uncomfortable that a principal U.S. banking organization was the operator of their clearing system, reportedly earning $235 million in 1998. In contrast, Clearstream was more European. The Euroclear System (Euroclear) is now operated by

Euroclear Banks S.A./N.V., a Belgian bank established in 2002 (Euroclear Bank). Euroclear is owned by 119 large financial institutions. It owns a number of national clearers, such as CRESTCo. in the U.K., and Sicovam, the French Clearing Organization, now Euroclear France. Euroclear is a major player. In 2002, its turnover was about $24 trillion and the value of securities it held was $10.6 trillion. This compares with 2002 turnover of DTCC of $81 trillion and custody of $20.5 trillion.[17]

a.   THE EUROCLEAR SYSTEM

Participants in the Euroclear System are able to make use of four basic services through a single point of entry at the Euroclear Operations Center (EOC) in Brussels: multi-currency securities clearance and settlement, securities lending and borrowing, custody, and money transfer.

Securities Clearance and Settlement

Participants provide Euroclear with instructions to receive securities if they are purchasers, or to deliver securities if they are sellers. Euroclear attempts to match a participant's valid receipt instruction with a counterparty participant's delivery instruction to ensure that the terms of the trade are identical. The matching process takes place continuously throughout the day.

Processing takes place both in real-time during the day and in batches overnight. Real-time processing allows trades to be settled on T+0, thus greatly reducing risk. Transactions may be settled against payment in more than 43 settlement currencies. Delivery versus payment is ensured because settlement cannot occur unless the seller has securities and the buyer has cash available to exchange.

The System operates through simultaneous book-entry movement of cash and securities through a transaction-by-transaction algorithm that recycles cash and securities received during the securities settlement processing in order to enable participants to settle as many matched transactions as possible with all available resources. Participants may link instructions and/or specify the priority that controls the sequence in which their instructions are processed.

Securities Lending and Borrowing

The Euroclear securities lending and borrowing program is designed to improve the efficiency of securities settlement and increase market liquidity. The service allows participants with buy and hold portfolios of securities to earn lending fees thereby increasing overall portfolio yield (without loss of ownership benefits) by lending securities to other participants who seek to avoid fails because of lack of securities.

---

[17] The legal framework for Eurobank's operation is Belgian Royal Decree No. 62, November 10, 1967.

The benefit of integrating securities lending and borrowing into the securities settlement processing is that borrowings correspond exactly to participants' needs, thereby eliminating the risk of over- and under-borrowing. Settlement efficiency has been further enhanced by the inclusion of equities in the borrowing program.

To protect against concentrated borrowings, aggregate borrowings in an issue and borrowing by a single participant are each limited to specified percentages of the outstanding issue.

Custody

Securities are immobilized in the Euroclear depositary network, which includes major depositary banks, national clearing systems, and central banks in more than 25 countries around the world. For example, securities listed on the NYSE, deposited with Euroclear, are held through a U.S. bank in New York. These securities are in turn held by that bank at DTCC.

Central management of the network, including effecting and monitoring of external receipts and deliveries of securities, is carried out by Euroclear Bank.

Each issue of securities accepted into the Euroclear System is assigned to and held by one depositary, usually the most conveniently located of the Euroclear depositaries (specialized depositary). Once deposited into the System, all securities are held on a fungible basis.

If a depositary accepts the deposit of a physical security for which it is not the specialized depositary, its ability to authenticate that security may be limited. For that reason, the particular security is "frozen" until it is authenticated by the specialized depositary. In addition, the number of entry points where particular types of securities can be accepted is limited. This helps determine clear responsibility for deposited securities and, by enhancing controls, both the system and its participants are protected.

Money Transfer

In order to facilitate the transaction settlement processing, participants open a cash account with Euroclear Bank. This cash account is divided into sub-accounts, one for each currency accepted in the Euroclear System.

The cash accounts are used primarily for settlement of securities transactions. In addition, money transfer transactions can be executed through the participants' cash accounts: book transfers of funds between participants, wire transfers by debit of a cash account for payment outside the System, preadvices of funds to be received, foreign exchange conversions, and crediting of funds by a correspondent.

Participants can manage their cash accounts on the basis of daily cash reports, which give details of pending and processed cash movements and balances.

Participants are able to use EUCLID, SWIFT, telex, or mail to send money transfer instructions.

DvP

DvP is an important requirement for a settlement system. How does Euroclear achieve this? When a trade is between two Euroclear participants, and processed overnight, trade is final during the overnight cycle so that in the morning sellers get final credits. However, since most of the markets are closed when the processing cycle is finished, Euroclear Bank cannot be sure that its cash correspondents have received funds from buyers. Thus, Euroclear Bank assumes a credit risk. Similarly, it may have to assume risk for settling a trade between a Euroclear participant and a party who has elected to settle in a local CSD. For example, it may give out the cash proceeds to a participant seller before receiving cash through the local CSD.[18] This is much less of a problem in real-time processing that is much more the case presently. These exposures may raise concerns for the Belgian regulation of Euroclear Bank.

International Clearing of U.S. Equities

In principle, Euroclear could clear and settle a trade in IBM on the NYSE, and thus be a competitor of DTCC. Section 17A of the 1934 Securities Act requires "clearing agencies" clearing U.S. securities to be registered with the SEC. Neither Euroclear nor Clearstream, the other major international clearer, have registered, so as to avoid U.S. regulation. However, Clearstream and Euroclear have obtained SEC exemptions from the requirement to clear and settle U.S. Treasury securities and equities with foreign counterparties.

Cedel's (the predecessor of Clearstream) argument for the exemption for the clearance of government securities was based on its development of the Global Credit Support Service, a real-time system for posting and receiving collateral among swaps counterparties which could substantially reduce swaps credit risk (more on this in Chapter 15). Euroclear sought approval to bolster its securities lending and repo capabilities. The permission to the two clearers were conditioned upon a volume limit of 5 percent of the total average daily dollar value of the aggregate volume of U.S. entities in treasuries, and agreement to notify the SEC of any changes in the organizations' operational rules. It is not altogether clear why Clearstream or Euroclear should be required to register with the SEC in order to clear U.S. securities. The argument would be the U.S. interest in the well-functioning of its markets.

---

[18] M. Dine, "Delivery Versus Payment In A Cross-Border Environment," 7 Payment Systems Worldwide (1996), p. 29.

In granting the exemption to Cedel, the SEC detailed the various standards for clearing agency registration and the means by which Cedel addressed the standard. These standards relate to the organization and processing capacity and financial strength of the applicant, as well as principles of corporate governance, and access. The SEC side-stepped an access issue of some import. Cedel Bank limited participation to commercial banks, investment banks, and broker-dealers, excluding investment companies from direct participation. Investment companies held securities at Cedel through bank custody accounts. Section 17A(b)(3) says investment companies must have access to clearers, but the SEC concluded that Cedel's practice was acceptable. The SEC also ignored the s. 17A requirement that the clearing agency be able to enforce compliance with its rules.[19] In February 1998, the SEC granted the same exemption to Euroclear for government securities.[20]

Both Cedel and Euroclear were given approval later in 1998 to clear U.S. equity trades involving foreign counterparties. This enabled Euroclear to settle trades of the handful of U.S. securities listed on EASDAQ for which Euroclear generally acts as settlement agent. Euroclear's role in settling U.S. equities was further extended in April 1999 when it began generally settling U.S. equities for non-U.S. Euroclear participants.

Euroclear and other international clearing mechanisms may rightly be seen as competing with domestic arrangements. These international mechanisms may eventually make domestic systems obsolete. They offer greater market liquidity, more efficient use of member collateral to back borrowings, and potential economies of scale. One might question the need to improve these domestic systems, with the attendant expense, when an international alternative exists. This also calls into question the entire effort of the Group of Thirty.

The market share of international clearance and settlement services (ICSDs), like Euroclear and Clearstream, is quite high with respect to cross-border debt such as Eurobonds, and they have a significant share of national debt instruments, but their share of equities is quite small. This has been attributed to lack of harmonization among national markets with respect to certain practices. I. Giddy, A. Saunders, and I. Walter[21] argue that differences in settlement cycles impede ICSD settlement. For example, they point out that an investor selling U.K. stocks (T+5 settlement) and buying German stocks (T+2) would have to borrow money for three days to bridge the settlement date differences. Other examples cited by the authors are

---

[19] See K. Tyson-Quah and S. Weinberger, "Cedel Wins SEC Exemption to Clear T-bills," *International Financial Law Review* (May 1997); E. Luce, "Euroclear to Settle U.S. Treasuries," *Financial Times*, June 19, 1997.

[20] Release No. 34-39643.

[21] "European Financial Market Integration: Clearance and Settlement Issues," 38 New York University Salomon Centre Working Paper S-95-19 (1995).

differences in paper versus book-entry securities, bearer versus registered shares, taxation of cross-border transactions, and multiple currencies.[22] One might add potential choice and conflict of law problems—at least two countries' laws are potentially applicable.

Notes and Questions

1. Assuming Euroclear registered in the U.S., could it effectively compete with DTCC?

2. How would you compare DvP under DTCC and Euroclear?

3. Are cross-border links an alternative to Euroclear?

b.   EUROPEAN CLEARING

Many users of Euroclear and Clearstream would like to see one European clearing and settlement system. Currently there are over 20 clearing organizations and existing networks are expensive. There is much debate about how expensive this is. Some have estimated that clearing and settlement costs in Europe are 7-10 times those of the United States but this is disputed.[23] Users would also like to see one CCP, whereas today various organizations such as the LCH (London Clearing House), Clearnet (Paris Bourse), and Eurex Clearing (Deutsche Börse) now compete. Some estimate that one CCP would reduce costs by $950 million per year.[24]

Competition among clearing systems is beginning to bring down fees. Deutsche Börse cut clearing and settlement fees eight percent in 2003, and Euroclear France is cut them by 40 percent, compared with 2001.[25]

The Wise Men Report in 2001, on needed improvements in securities regulation in the EU (see Chapter 4) urged the consolidation of clearing and settlement systems. Since then, the Commission has launched an investigation into whether anti-competitive practices are responsible for the lack of consolidation. The focus is on so-called "vertical silos" which refers to the arrangements under which trades on certain exchanges must be cleared through particular agents. Thus, trades on Deutsche Börse must be cleared through Clearstream, which is owned by Deutsche Börse (DB), and trades on Euronext, the combined Paris-Amsterdam-Brussels exchange, must be cleared through Euroclear. In March 2004, DB made a dramatic announcement that trades on Deutsche Börse would no longer have to be cleared through Clearstream. For this to have a real effect another entity would have to be authorized by Germany to clear such trades.[26]

---

[22] Id., at 20-30.
[23] See K. Lannoo and M. Levin, *The Securities Settlement Industry in the EU: Structure, Costs and the Way Forward,* CEPS Research Report (December 2001).
[24] "European Share Trading, Nothing Settled," The Economist, January 20, 2001.
[25] A. Skorecki, "European Exchanges Slash Fees," *Financial Times,* October 1, 2003.
[26] A. Skorecki, "Deutsche Börse Softens Its Stance," *Financial Times,* March 3, 2004.

When DB and the London Stock Exchange (LSE) contemplated merging in 2000, the plan was for DB to retain Clearstream as a separate company which would continue to settle DB trades, and LSE would continue to maintain its own clearing and settlement arrangements. One analyst believes this would have been inefficient since economies can be achieved by using a common clearing and settlement agent. One problem for the merger partners in coming to this result, it is argued, is that both sides have private information about the costs of clearing and settlement that cannot be verified by the other side. This seems implausible given the usual due diligence that accompanies mergers—why is information about clearance and settlement more opaque than information about the costs of trading? The actual problem in the proposed merger was that the parties wanted a merger of equals which could not occur if Clearstream was in included in the deal on the side of DB. This merger is also discussed in Chapter 13.

Vertical silos contrast with the situation in the United States where one user-owned organization, DTCC, clears and settles trades for all exchanges. The vertical approach permits the integration of clearance and settlement with trading but inhibits the integration of clearance and settlement across different exchanges. Japan has adopted the U.S. approach.[27] In December 2003, the heads of 17 leading banks and insurance companies urged the European Commission to regulate clearing and settlement as it were a public utility, forcing consolidation into one system, following the DTCC model in the U.S. Euroclear said it supported consolidation but not new regulation.[28] It was reported in April 2003, that Clearstream faced a fine from the Commission due to its discriminatory treatment in supplying clearing services to Euroclear—the two systems interconnect through a "bridge" due to inter-system of transactions of common customers.[29]

Another part of the consolidation problem is that some countries, e.g. Italy and Spain, provide that only one organization can hold electronic shares in their country. This makes it difficult for international clearers to compete with the locally authorized depository.

In April 2004, the EU Commission issued a paper setting forth its plan for dealing with clearance and settlement issues within the EU.[30] The Commission envisions the following measures. First, the creation of a new Advisory and Monitoring Group to assist in implementing new measures.

---

[27] C. Kentouris, "Japan's JASDEC Picks Horizontal Structure," *Securities Industry News*, April 15, 2002.

[28] P. Norman and A. Skorecki, "Brussels Urged to Regulate Trade Clearing," *Financial Times*, December 22, 2003.

[29] *Financial Times*, April 1, 2003.

[30] Commission of the European Communities, Communication from the Commission to the Council and the European Parliament, *Clearing and Settlement in the European Union–The Way Forward*, COM(2004) 312 final, April 28, 2004.

Second, a new Directive on clearing and settlement which would provide for rights of "access and choice." This would permit:

"investment firms and banks: the right to access Securities Clearing and Settlement Systems located in other Member States;

Central Counterparties: the right of access to Central Counterparties and Securities Settlement Systems located in other Member States;

Securities Settlement Systems: the right of access to Securities Settlement Systems located in other Member States; and

Regulated markets and Multilateral Trading Facilities: the right to enter into appropriate arrangements with Central Counterparties and Securities Settlement Systems located in other Member States."[31]

The Directive would also establish a common EU-wide regulatory and supervisory framework, including capital adequacy requirements and high level principles on risk management and investor protection, and certain principles of corporate governance. Third, it would minimize legal and tax obstacles to cross-border clearance and settlement. The current EU legal framework already addresses some problems. The Directive on Settlement Finality[32] and Financial Collateral Arrangements[33] insure the validity of netting and adopt the PRIMA approach (discussed below) to conflicts of law. The Commission indicates it will push for adoption by the EU and Member States of PRIMA and establish a new EU-wide framework for the treatment of interests in securities held with an intermediary (also see discussion below of general problem). Finally, the Commission highlights competition policy, but proposes no new initiatives in that sphere.

DTCC has an initiative to become a global CCP. In discussing the possibilities of consolidation, DTCC states: "[d]ifferences in law, which impact the perfection of legal rights that a CCP may have to exercise in the event of a participant's failure, may be difficult to reconcile. And regulators may legitimately oppose cross-jurisdictional mergers since it is they who must protect information; ensure fair access to services, and safe and sound operations; and intervene if the CCP itself fails."[34]

Notes and Questions

1.   What should the EU do about clearing and settlement?

c.   RIGHTS IN DEMATERIALIZED SECURITIES

ICSD arrangements involve the indirect holding of investments. The investor holds his securities through a facility such as Euroclear that

---

[31] Id., at 16.

[32] Directive 02/47 of 6 June 2002, OJ 2002 L168/43

[33] Directive 98/26 of 19 May 1998, OJ 1998 L166/45

[34] DTCC, *Central Counterparties: Development, Cooperation and Consolidation* (October 2000).

delegates the holding to a national depositary. This raises some important legal issues as to the investors' rights in the securities.

Chain of entitlements and the multi-tiering of intermediaries and security entitlements

"The relationships between the various parties engaged in the trade of an international issue can be viewed from a chain: from the issuer through the various tiers of intermediary to the ultimate investor.

In the case of a new debt issue, participants may pay for their participation through their account with their ICSD, which transfers funds to the underwriter against delivery of the global note. The ICSDs are the sole holders of record in the books of the issuer and the investor has no direct relationship with the issuer. The global note which represents the underlying security is permanently immobilized, and customers of the ICSD cannot normally acquire definitive notes or procure physical delivery; their interest takes the form of a securities entitlement against the ICSD, with associated rights to dividends, interest, redemption payments, etc. It is not an entitlement to a specific security from the issuer but a right to share pro rata in the pool of fungible rights in the issue held by the ICSD."[35] And down the line a customer of the participant in the ICSD has a claim for the value of its securities. So if a broker for Customer A holds 100 IBM at Euroclear, Customer A has a claim against the broker for 100 IBM.

Fungibility

"A securities account in the name of an investor may be fungible or non-fungible. Property is fungible when any unit of it is considered interchangeable with any other unit for the purpose of delivery or transfer obligations. Whether property is fungible depends not on its physical characteristics but on the nature of the obligation owed with respect to it. If the depositee is not obliged to return the deposited property *in specie* but has the right to deliver its equivalent in type and number or amount, the asset is fungible.

Although securities are fungible inter-se, they are different from deposits. Whereas the depositor of money has a purely contractual claim, there being no obligation on a bank to segregate deposited funds for customers either individually or collectively, the custodian of securities in a fungible account will typically be required by the deposit agreement or by law to hold the pool of securities of that type for all interested depositors collectively, whether by way of trust (as in England) or under some other legal regime which confers on depositors co-ownership rights (as in Belgium and Luxembourg). The distinction is of great importance in the event of insolvency of the custodian, for the depositor of money will be a mere

---

[35] R. Goode, "The Nature and Transfer of Rights in Dematerialized and Immobilized Securities," in *The Future For The Global Securities Market: Legal and Regulatory Aspects* (F. Oditah ed., 1996), pp. 114-124.

unsecured creditor (though in some legal systems having priority rights), whereas the depositor of securities will have co-ownership rights and the securities will not form part of the custodian's assets available for distribution among its creditors."[36]

An indirect holder of securities in an ICSD carries a triple risk: the inability to enforce rights directly against the issuer where the custodian is the holder of record and is unable or unwilling to do so on his behalf; the insolvency of the custodian, to the extent of any deficiency in the pool of securities available to account holders; and the loss of securities held by the custodian in circumstances where it is able to disclaim responsibility for the loss.

As regards permanent global notes, the right of direct enforcement, so far as not given by the applicable law, can be taken care of in various ways: by provisions in the trust deed (where there is one) executed by the issuer; by an irrevocable deed of covenant executed by the issuer at the time of issue of the global note by which, in the event of the permanent global note becoming void, account-holders acquire direct rights against the issuer; and by provisions in the global note itself entitling the custodian to exchange it for definitive certificates in stated events, such as an event of default. In the absence of such an event, the account-holder relies on the contractual duties assumed by the custodian to perform services on his behalf, such as collecting and crediting dividends, interest and redemption moneys, exercising voting rights, and the like.

For protection against insolvency of the custodian, the account-holder (investor or secured creditor) needs assurance that the law will recognize the priority of his entitlement over the claims of the custodian's general creditors. Specifically the investor or secured creditor needs to know that securities in the hands of the custodian for his account will not be available to the custodian's own creditors but will be held for him to the extent of his interest or, if securities or moneys have been lost, proportionate to his interest.

Governing Law

One of the terms of competition between Clearstream and Euroclear is the legal framework protecting investors holding securities in the two systems. The rights in Clearstream are governed by Luxembourg law and the rights in Euroclear by Belgian law. In 1998, E. Bettelheim wrote an article concluding that Luxembourg law was preferable since: (1) Belgian law does not "deem" all securities credited to accounts with the Euroclear Operator as being located in Belgium (and, therefore, might not be governed by Belgian law under conflicts of law analysis); (2) Belgian law does not provide for the transfer of title by book entry or for the enforceability of transfer of title clauses in collateral transactions; (3) there is no broad statutory provision in

---

[36] *ibid.*

Belgian law for netting on insolvency; and (4) Belgian law does not provide a firewall against the insolvency of a clearing agency like the Euroclear Operator.[37]

Consider the following hypothetical devised by Professor Roy Goode. Assume that a German corporation issues debt securities represented by a single global certificate immobilized at the DTC and registered in the books of the issuer in the name of Cede & Co., DTC's nominee, with part of the initial distribution being made to U.S. investors and part of it being made to non-U.S. investors. An English broker purchases an interest in the securities and takes delivery of the interest by book-entry to its account with Morgan Guaranty Trust Company, Brussels office, as the former operator of Euroclear. The Euroclear operator holds a position in the securities for the benefit of Euroclear participants through an account with a New York bank participant of DTC. Under Article 8 of the Uniform Commercial Code, interests in securities held through accounts with the New York bank and DTC would be defined as "security entitlements." Interests in securities held through the Euroclear operator are defined by Belgian Royal Decree No. 62 as non-traceable co-proprietary rights or a "universalité" represented solely by an account in Belgium (i.e. a package of rights very similar to a security entitlement). Suppose that the English broker sells the securities to a French broker by book-entries on the records of the Euroclear operator. It would be far from clear which law governs the validity of the transfer from the English broker to the French broker?

a. New York law because the global certificate is located in New York?

b. German law because the issuer is organized under the laws of Germany?

c. English law because the English broker/transferor is an English company?

d. French law because the French broker/transferee is organized under the laws of France?

e. Belgian law because the Euroclear accounts are located in Belgium? (This would be the result under Section 8-110 of Article 8 of the UCC and under Belgian law).

The system of entitlements can have some unforeseen consequences. In *Fidelity Partners, Inc. v. First Trust Company of New York*,[38] Fidelity Partners, an assignee of a judgment creditor of the Philippine Export and Foreign Loan Guarantee Corporation (PG) brought an action in the United

---

[37] "Collateral Held in Euroclear and Cedel: A Legal Comparison," 8 Journal of International Banking and Financial Law (1998), p. 363. This was the subject of a rebuttal in an article by Euroclear lawyers, L. De Ghenghi and B. Servaes, "Collateral Held in the Euroclear System: A Legal Overview," 9 Journal of International Banking and Financial Law (1999), p. 83.

[38] 1997 U.S. Dist. LEXIS 19287 (S.D.N.Y.).

States to recover PG's $1.75 million interest in certain bonds issued by the Philippine government. Under the Foreign Sovereign Immunities Act (FSIA), 28 USC. §1610, it could only levy on property in the United States (and not abroad) since PG is a Philippine government agency. PG's interest in the bonds was held through ING Bank of Manila (ING) located in the Philippines. ING held its interest in the bonds on the books of Euroclear, through Morgan Guaranty's Brussels branch. Morgan Guaranty's London office was the sub-custodian of the bonds since it was the only recorded owner of the global bond of which PG's interest comprises a part. The court denied Fidelity's attempt to levy on various accounts in the U.S., holding that Fidelity could only garnish the ING account, since this was the only the account on which PG's interest was recorded. A levy on that account, located in the Philippines, was barred by the FSIA.

Harmonization

On December 13, 2002, the 62 member states of the Hague Conference on Private International Law, adopted the Hague Convention on the Law Applicable to Certain Rights in respect of Securities Held with an Intermediary (PRIMA Convention). The approach adopted is to look to the law of the location of the intermediary maintaining the account to which the securities are credited—the place of the relevant intermediary approach or PRIMA. The important question of perfection of security interests will be determined by that jurisdiction. The major question that was addressed by the Convention was how to determine where the relevant intermediary is located. The first step, under Article 4, is to look to the law expressly agreed between the account holder and its direct intermediary, provided that the intermediary has an office in the chosen state that regularly maintains securities accounts. If the previous rule does not apply, Article 5(1) provides that the law will be that of the location of the office of the intermediary which a written agreement specifically states was the office through which the intermediary entered into the agreement. If this second possibility does not apply, then under Article 5(2) and (3), the law of the place of incorporation of the relevant intermediary applies. The principal reporters for the Convention were Sir Roy Goode of England and Hideki Kanda of Japan.

The EU has adopted a Directive on Financial Collateral to address another problem in cross-border securities activities, the validity of netting.[39] This Directive built on the 1998 Settlement Finality Directive 1998/26/EC. The Finality Directive insures that payment orders and securities transfers, in particular those involved in multilateral netting, are final, and cannot be cherry picked by trustees in bankruptcy. This problem was explored in Chapter 9.

The importance of netting for securities settlement is underscored by its inclusion in the Group of Thirty standards. The 2002 Collateral Directive

---

[39] Directive 2002/47/EC on Financial Collateral Arrangements.

is aimed at putting collateral arrangements outside the reach of the bankruptcy trustee by adopting uniform rules on the perfection of security interests. Rules about perfecting security interests in collateral now differ among EU member states, as do rules about their validity in bankruptcy. This 2002 Directive also includes a provision recognizing the validity of close-out netting, Article 7, thus reinforcing the Settlement Finality Directive.

Currently, a new effort is underway to specify property rights in dematerialized securities.[40] This effort would harmonize the laws in this area, rather than relying on the conflicts of law solutions of the PRIMA Convention. This Convention has yet to be ratified by the EU.

Notes and Questions

1.   How would you answer Professor Goode's hypothetical?

2.   Does the PRIMA Convention help answer the hypothetical?

D.   FUTURE ARRANGEMENTS

An influential report of Morgan Guaranty Trust Co., the former operator of Euroclear, sets forth some possible infrastructure models for the future.[41] It includes three models: (1) Worldclear; (2) Global Hub; and (3) Bilateral Links.

The Report identified three costs associated with the then current arrangements–these costs are still present today. First, there are friction costs. These are costs associated with cross-border securities clearance, settlement, and custody. These can be explicit (e.g. fees) or implicit (e.g. risks). They can arise in connection with a securities transaction or over the life of a security (e.g. settlement or custody fees).

Second, there are pipeline liquidity risks. These are risks associated with delays in a settlement pipeline arising primarily from gaps in time between the processing cycles of various CSDs and between the processing cycles of CSDs and national payment systems.

Finally, there is legal risk of the kind we have already examined. The Report then discusses how various models of clearance and settlement handle these risks.

Multiple-Access Model

The multiple-access model consists of one or more CSDs in each country, local custodians, ICSDs, global custodians, and market participants.

---

[40] See European Financial Markets Lawyers Group, *Harmonization of the Legal Framework for Rights Evidenced by Book-Entries in Respect of Certain Financial Instruments in the European Union* (June 2003).

[41] Morgan Guaranty Trust Company of New York, Brussels Office as Operator of Euroclear, *Cross-border Clearance, Settlement and Custody: Beyond the G30 Recommendations* (1993).

The multiple-access model enables market participants to settle transactions in domestic, foreign, or international securities through a variety of channels. This is the system we have today.

Figure 10.5, below, from the Report shows *some* of the possibilities; many more channels exist.

Figure 10.5
Multiple Access Model

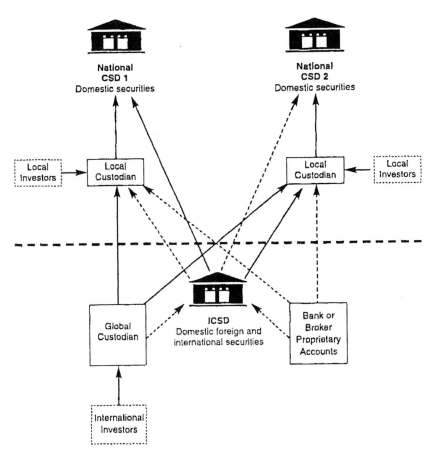

➤   Signifies the access option selected for cost or efficiency reasons by each player (bank, broker, custodian or ICSD).

--➤   Signifies an alternative option that might be selected on the basis of competitive analysis.

Various alternative models are suggested. The two most important are Worldclear and Global Hub. First, one could have Worldclear.

Worldclear

The Worldclear model is the most radical model for restructuring the cross-border settlement infrastructure. It assumes the establishment of a single, global CSD to perform the safekeeping, clearance, and settlement functions for all securities—domestic, foreign, and international (see Figure 10.6 below).

Figure 10.6
Worldclear Model

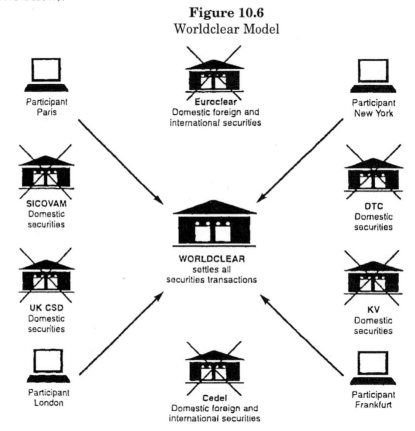

→ Each partcipant has a securities account with Worldclear for all securities

Worldclear would replace national and international CSDs with a single, centralized, global CSD. All participants of existing CSDs would become participants of Worldclear. It would maintain the cash and securities accounts for all wholesale market participants, and effect all transfers in its own electronic files. Worldclear nevertheless assumes that multiple national currencies and payment systems continue to exist.

Worldclear would raise substantial monopoly problems and would concentrate all risks from clearance and settlement in one system. These two negatives would outweigh the substantial reduction of the costs it could effectuate.

Global Hub

The global hub model assumes the establishment of a single, global CSD with both "home-market securities" and "other-market securities" links with each national and international CSD for settling cross-market transactions in all securities. A "home-market securities link" is a bilateral link in which the global hub essentially acts as a participant of a national or international CSD. It would permit transactions to be settled between the global hub and any of the participants of the CSD with respect to securities held by such CSD ("home-market securities"). An "other-market securities link" is a bilateral link in which a CSD acts as a participant of the global hub. It would permit transactions to be settled between any pair of CSDs with respect to securities that are not held by either CSD ("other-market securities") (see Figure 10.7 below).

Each CSD would continue to perform the safekeeping function for all home-market securities. Its securities accounts would reflect the positions both of its participants and of the global hub in its home-market securities. Its securities accounts would also reflect the positions of its participants in all other securities. It would perform the clearance and settlement function for all transactions in its home-market securities when at least one of the counterparties is a participant in its system. It would perform the same function for transactions between two of its participants in all other securities.

The global hub would perform all clearance and settlement functions for all transactions between the various CSDs and ICSDs. It would maintain cash and securities accounts for each CSD (but not their participants), and effect transfers in all securities through its own electronic records.

In contrast to an ICSD, the global hub would not have any participants except for other CSDs.

Figure 10.7
Global Hub Model

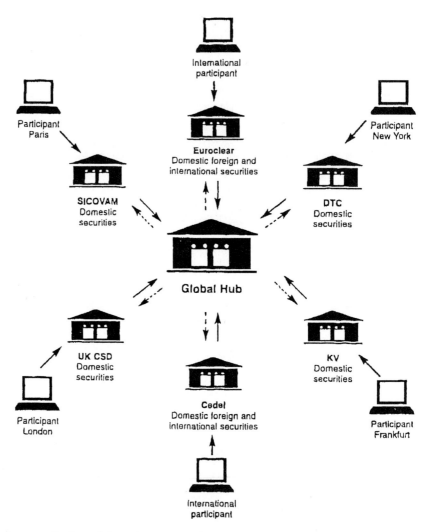

→ Each participant has a securities acccount with its home CSD for all home-market securities accessible through the Global Hub.

--→ Home-market Link: Global Hub has securities accounts with the home CSD reflecting its positions in home-market securities held for other CSDs. This allows the Global Hub to settle yransactions between participants of the home CSD and other CSDs.

→ Other-market Link: home CSD has a securities accounts with the Global hub reflecting its positions in other-market securities. This allows its participants to settle transactions with participants of all other CSDs.

In May 1999, Euroclear made a new proposal, *The Hub and Spokes Clearance and Settlement Model,* to establish a pan-European settlement system. Under this proposal, Euroclear, the Hub, would continue to directly serve its global clients. National depositories, the Spokes, would no longer need to establish bilateral links, under the bilateral model proposed by the European Central Depositories Association, but would link to Euroclear, as under the Global Hub model discussed above, for cross-border trades. Euroclear as Hub to the Spokes, given its holding of cash accounts, would be able to provide DvP settlement that many securities depositories cannot do given that securities and cash transfers occur in two separate systems.

Notes and Questions

1.   Some in Europe want a version of Worldclear, at least in the EU. Would that be a good idea, if it were privately owned?

E.   CAPITAL REQUIREMENTS

In April 2005, the Basel Committee proposed that special rules apply to capital requirements for unsettled or failed trades.[42] Currently the Basel Accord provides no rules for these trades and countries have developed different approaches. The EU generally allows a 5 business day graced period for failed DvP transactions before requiring capital at which point they are subject to charges on the exposures. These charges increase to 100 percent after 46 days, subject to a flat 8 percent risk weight. For non-DvP, the charge starts immediately, with a one day grace period for cross-border transactions. The U.S. applies a standard risk weight of usually 100 percent but in some cases 20 percent to the full notional amount of trades that fail to settle. Five days after the settlement date, the current exposure of the failed trade is deducted from capital and capital is required against the position.[43]

Generally under the proposal, standard (T+5) DvP transactions would not have any capital charges for up to 4 business days after the settlement date. After that time, the positive current exposure would be deducted from capital. DvP transactions with settlement lags longer than T+5 would be treated like forward contracts and subject to more demanding capital requirements. For non-DvP transactions, with a T+5 settlement lag, there is no capital requirement up to the first contractual payment or delivery leg. From the first contractual or payment delivery leg up to one day after the second leg, the transaction is treated as a loan. Thereafter, the bank that has paid but not received securities, will deduct the entire payment from capital,

---

[42] Basel Committee on Banking Supervision, Consultative Document, The Application of Basel II to Trading Activities and the Treatment of Double Default Effects, April 2005.

[43] Id., at paragraph 319. This description of the U.S. approach by the Basel Committee is confusing insofar as it says that the fail is treated as a loss, and thus subtracted from capital, but at the same time capital is required against the position.

plus replacement cost, if any, on the securities. This treatment will apply until the second leg is completed, if ever. For non DvP transactions with a settlement lag of longer than T+5, the treatment is the same, except up to the time at which the first contractual leg is to be performed, both parties will treat their exposure as a forward contract.

It appears from the proposal that this approach will apply regardless of whether a bank is generally using the standardized or IRB approaches. It is unclear how the U.S. will implement this proposal for banks not using advanced IRB—generally the only part of Basel II the U.S. is adopting.

CONCLUSIONS

Clearance and settlement is the back office of the securities markets, and thus another important part of the infrastructure of the international financial system. One notable aspect of this area of activity is that many of the important rules have been harmonized through the work of a private think tank, the G-30, composed mainly of financial institutions. Private efforts have probably succeeded because overall public investor protection issues are not significant. Where they do exist, as in the movement from T+1 to T+3, and now to T+1, public authorities like the SEC have become involved. Harmonization has been demanded because of the economies of scale achievable from using common systems worldwide and because of the high cross-border level of transactions. In this area, home or host country rules do not appear acceptable.

While common rules have been largely achieved, significant structural issues remain. Within Europe, the demand for consolidation of providers is impeded by the "silo" problem of exchanges owning clearers. While this is not the case in the U.S., the fact that stock exchanges feed data directly to DTCC appears to put them at a competitive advantage as against international systems like Euroclear. Euroclear's ability to compete in the U.S. may also be affected by the difficulty in meeting U.S. registration requirements. The inability to centralize international clearing through a few international providers results in the need for multiple linkages among national systems, with attendant expense.

On the purely legal front, the validity of netting, as in the payment system, remains a problem. Solving the problem is not merely a technical one, because netting validity involves priorities for counterparties (often large financial firms) at the expense of unsecured creditors. In addition, more work needs to be done in providing legal certainty for dematerialized securities.

INSTRUMENTS AND OFFSHORE MARKETS

Part III deals with instruments and offshore markets. These subjects are linked because many of the instruments of interest are offered offshore. In offshore markets, the transactors, as well as the currencies transacted in, are usually foreign to the local market. For example, London and Hong Kong are centers for transactions in Dollars between many non-British or non-Hong Kong institutions. These markets exist largely because of restrictions in domestic markets, as well as time zone and expertise advantages in offshore markets such as London.

This part begins with the traditional banking "Euromarkets" for deposits and loans (Chapter 11), and for bonds. This Chapter also discusses how global securities, involving coordinated use of several major domestic markets, may displace offshore markets.

Newer types of financial instruments are offered in both domestic and offshore markets, such as securitized debt (Chapter 12) and derivatives. The materials on derivatives focus on futures and options traded on exchanges around the world (Chapter 14), and swaps which are entered into off exchanges, often in offshore markets (Chapter 15). Derivatives have had tremendous growth in recent years, and the Barings crisis shows why regulation of instruments traded on exchanges is important.

For equity worldwide, the primary focus is on competition among the world's stock exchanges (Chapter 13). This Chapter poses the question as to whether there is convergence in trading systems and whether this portends an era of consolidation of the world's stock exchanges. The market for offshore mutual funds is profoundly segmented by tax and regulation as between the United States and the rest of the world (Chapter 16) and includes hedge funds, now a major player in the world's financial markets.

CHAPTER ELEVEN

EUROMARKETS

Mystery shrouds the origins of the Eurocurrency markets, the major part of the offshore markets. One story, set in the period immediately after the Second World War, has Soviet firms holding Dollars in banks outside the U.S. to avoid the risk that the U.S. might confiscate its funds.

The Euromarkets have played a significant part in international finance. This Chapter begins with an explanation of what a Eurodollar and, by extension any Eurocurrency, is. We then turn to the Eurodollar loan and bond markets.

A. INTRODUCTION TO THE EUROCURRENCY MARKET

Eurodollars are "deposit liabilities, denominated in Dollars, of banks outside the United States.

The location of the banks is important primarily because it affects the regulations under which the banks operate and hence the way that they can do business."[1] For example, U.K. banks with Eurodollar deposits are not subject to U.S. reserve requirement regulations, and in the past have avoided U.S. interest rate ceilings (these have now been repealed). They are also free from the long-arm of U.S. asset freezes or seizures, as detailed in Chapter 21. The fact that foreign banks issuing deposit liabilities are free from U.S. reserve requirements allow them to pay higher rates of interest for their deposits.

"Eurodollar deposits are in principle obligations to pay literal dollars—i.e. currency (or coin), government-issued fiat. Eurodollar banks are called on to discharge a negligible part in this form. Deposit obligations are, however, typically discharged by providing a credit or deposit at another bank—as when you draw a check on your bank which the recipient "deposits" in his.

To meet their obligations to pay cash, banks keep a 'reserve' of cash on hand. To meet their obligations to provide a credit at another bank, banks keep deposits at other banks (including the Central Bank). Like cash, deposits at other banks need be only a small fraction of assets.

---

[1] M. Friedman, "The Eurodollar Market: Some First Principles," The Morgan Guaranty Survey (October 1969), pp. 4-14.

Eurodollar banks are not subject to legal reserve requirements, but they must keep a prudential reserve in order to be prepared to meet withdrawals of deposits when they are demanded or when they mature. An individual bank will regard as a prudential reserve readily realizable funds both in the Eurodollar market itself (e.g. Eurodollar call money) and in the U.S. But for the Eurodollar system as a whole, Eurodollar funds cancel, and the prudential reserves available to meet demands for U.S. Dollars consist entirely of deposits at banks in New York or other cities in the U.S., and U.S. money market assets that can be liquidated promptly without loss. Prudential reserves of Eurodollar institutions are a small fraction of total Dollar-denominated obligations.

The ultimate increase in the amount of Eurodollars from an initial transfer of deposits from other banks to Eurodollar banks depends on the amount of their Dollar assets Eurodollar banks choose to hold in the form of cash assets in the U.S., and the "leakages" from the system—i.e. the final disposition of the funds borrowed from Eurodollar banks (or acquired by the sale of bonds or other investments to them). The larger the fraction of such funds held as Eurodollar deposits, the larger the increase in Eurodollars in total."[2]

This description of Eurodollars can be extended to other currencies, e.g. Euro Yen or even "Euro" Euro. All are deposits held in banks outside the country (or countries) of the currency issuer. So, a deposit of Euros in a U.K. bank would be a "Euro" Euro.

On the asset side, a Eurodollar loan is a loan in Dollars by a bank outside the United States. These loans are generally funded by Eurodollar liabilities. Many Eurodollar loans are syndicated, i.e. made by a group of banks put together by a lead manager.

Various countries have established special arrangements that allow banks to accept domestic deposits from foreigners without making them subject to at least some domestic banking regulations. The U.S. permits U.S. banks to operate international banking facilities (IBFs) that are not subject to reserve requirements on deposits from foreigners. The goal was to allow banks in the U.S. to compete with offshore financial centers. In fact, however, the IBFs have not seriously challenged offshore financial centers like London or Singapore. This seems to be because IBFs are not the exact duplicates of foreign deposits—for example, they are still subject to U.S. freezes and seizures and FDIC insurance premiums—and because transactional expertise has built up in offshore markets which operate when U.S. markets are asleep. Also, the U.S. feared that domestic funds might move to the IBFs, so it imposed complex rules to prevent such a shift.

---

[2] *ibid.*

In the first decades of the Euromarkets' existence, national governments were very concerned about their existence and rapid growth largely out of fear that they would lose control of monetary policy. These fears were quelled when central banks found that they could still use open market operations to control money supply. If governments were concerned about the domestic impact of offshore markets, they could close them down through capital controls and prohibitions on domestic financial institutions operating in such markets. This would, of course, have a devastating effect on the use of their currencies for reserves and transactions.

Notes and Questions

1. Be sure you understand the definition of a eurodollar. How is a eurodollar different from a domestic Dollar?

2. Consider the relation between interest rates in the eurocurrency and domestic deposit markets. The following chart compares the two rates in on deposits in U.S. Dollars and Deutschmarks from 1982 to 1996.

Deutschmark Rates

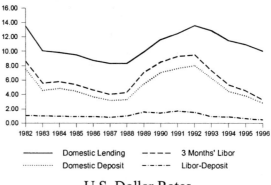

U.S. Dollar Rates

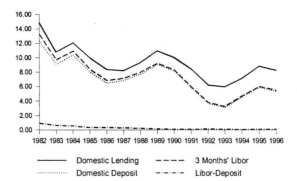

a. What relation would you expect to see between the London Interbank Deposit Rate (LIBOR) and domestic deposit rates. What accounts for this relationship?

b. Since the Eurocurrency markets are unregulated, why are not the interest rates on the various Eurocurrencies closely correlated?

B. SYNDICATED EURODOLLAR LOANS: AN OVERVIEW

The market for syndicated Eurocurrency loans grew dramatically from 1991 to 1995, leveled in 1996, became a borrowers' market, and then, when Russia defaulted on its debt in mid-1998, became a lenders' market. The Table at the end of this section describe the growth into 1997, after which point the time series ends. After this time, Eurocurrency loans were reported as part of all international loans. International loans include all loans across borders, so they would include a Dollar-denominated loan to a French borrower from either a U.S. bank or a U.K. bank. Only the latter would be a Eurodollar loan. In the mid-1990s, much of the growth refinanced outstanding loans or financed acquisitions, infrastructure projects, or the restructuring of national industries, such as telecommunications. By 1999 and through 2000, jumbo loans to fund mergers and acquisitions dominated the market, squeezing out the ordinary corporate loans and accounting for most new lending. In 2000, a syndicated loan of $30 billion, the largest ever, supported the hostile takeover of Mannesmann A.G. by Vodaphone. M&A financings brought the syndicated loan market together with the Eurobond market. Banks could easily raise large amounts in the loan market relatively short term as they hurried to finance the M&A transaction, then refinance longer term in the Eurobond market.[3] The Vodaphone funding did just this. Borrowers were generally based in countries of the OECD.[4]

Eurocurrency loans are made by a syndicate of banks. The lead manager deals with the borrower and other participants about the terms. It elicits the participation of other banks and may assume an underwriting risk, i.e. commit to lend a fixed amount whether or not other participants can be obtained. By 1999, ten banks lead managed 80 percent of the syndicated loans in Europe.[5] Other managing banks may share responsibilities with the lead manager. They may have regional responsibilities in a large international loan. "Participants" are simply the banks that provide funds. The agent bank deals with the ongoing administration of the loan, communicating between the borrower and the participants. It coordinates the disbursements to the borrower, the calculation of interest due, and the distribution of the payments from the borrower to the participants.

---

[3] R. Bream, "Surge in M&A Comes to the Rescue," *Financial Times*, May 19, 2000.
[4] "Loan Market in the 1980s" 30 Bank of England Quarterly Bulletin (1990), p. 71.
[5] J. Dyson, "Big Banks Learn to Flex their Muscles," Euromoney (July 1999), p. 140.

As well as earning a margin over the London Interbank Offering Rate (LIBOR), the interbank deposit market, or any other benchmark when the loan is drawn, banks in the syndicate will receive various fees. The lead manager and other banks in the lead management team, who may be responsible for various aspects of documentation, will generally receive some form of front-end management fee. Other participants will usually expect to receive a participation fee for agreeing to join the facility; the actual size of the fee will vary with the size of the commitment. Once the credit is established, members of the syndicate will often receive an annual facility or commitment fee, again proportional to their commitments. Loan documents may sometimes incorporate a penalty clause, whereby the borrower agrees to pay a fee or give some consideration to the lenders in the event that it pre-pays its debts prior to the specified term.

Increasingly Eurocredit participations can be traded in the secondary market.

There are three main methods by which loan participations may be transferred: novation, assignment, and subparticipation. Novation involves the replacement of one legal agreement with another, thus extinguishing the contractual relationship between the original creditor and the debtor; assignment and subparticipation are non-recourse funding arrangements which do not normally involve the debtor as they assume the preservation rather than the cancellation of the original loan.

In December 1996, leading banks formed the Loan Market Association (LMA), whose purpose was to encourage corporate and governmental borrowers, particularly in developing and transition countries, to let their paper trade in secondary markets. The LMA would draft legal language and design methods to settle the transactions. It argued that the increased liquidity would lower the cost of funds for the borrowers.[6] Some of the growing liquidity in the secondary market during the 1990s might have been due to special conditions. For example, liquidity in 1998 might have occurred, in part, because the Japanese banks were unloading their portfolios to fund problem loans at home.[7] By 2000, the LMA estimated a secondary market of $30 billion in Europe and over $150 billion in the U.S. Institutional investors were a small but growing source of demand in Europe, perhaps less than 5 percent, but accounted for over 40 percent of all investors in the US secondary market.[8]

There are some important features of the Eurocredit market. First, the loans tend to be in very large amounts—they include very large loans to sovereign borrowers. The loans can be organized quickly through the well-

---

[6] See G. Gapper, "Banks Seek to Set Up Secondary Market for Debt," *Financial Times*, December 17, 1996.

[7] J. Dyson, "Big Banks Learn to Flex their Muscles," Euromoney (July 1999), p. 142.

[8] B. Beasley-Murray, "Reality Hits Mad Merger Pricing," Euromoney (July 2000), p. 122; R. Bream, "Institutions Move in on Leveraged Loans," *Financial Times*, November 17, 2000.

established network of banks, principally in London. Lenders can easily fund these loans in the interbank Eurocurrency deposit market. The loans can be drawn down in tranches. While the Dollar is the predominant currency, usually over 60 percent of all loans, other major currencies are also used. Later in the Chapter, the Eurobond market is discussed. To some extent these two markets compete with each other, but many borrowers do not have the reputation or credit rating to make the bond market a practical alternative.

It appears that the spreads on syndicated loans in the European markets (most of which are in the Euromarket (offshore with respect to its currency)) are much narrower than U.S. loans to the same kinds of borrowers. This finding indicates a lack of global integration of syndicated loan markets which may be accounted for by a "home bias"— the tendency of lender and borrowers to stay home—or perhaps by regulatory or tax factors. Euromarkets may be more competitive because when borrowers and lenders do business outside their home countries, they do so in the Euromarkets.

Table 11A, below, gives an idea of the borrowers.

Table 11A

Medium-term international bank loans by borrowing country[9]
($ billion)

Borrowers	1991	1993	1994	1995	1996	1-9 1997
OECD area	87.8	116.4	212.5	329.4	311.8	245.2
Non-OECD	27.6	20.0	23.4	40.8	33.4	43.7
International development institutions	0.6	0.3	0.3	-	-	0.1
Total	**116.0**	**136.7**	**236.2**	**370.2**	**345.2**	**289.0**

Notes and Questions

1. What is a syndicated Eurocurrency loan (Eurocredit)?

2. Who are the parties to a Eurocredit?

3. Compared to a standard bank loan, what are the special features of a Eurocredit?

---

[9] Covers the aggregate of foreign and Euro medium-term bank loans, excluding loan renegotiations. OECD, *Financial Market Trends* (October 1994, p. 69, November 1996, p. 141, and November 1997, p. 121.

C.   THE ALLOCATION OF RISK AMONG THE PARTIES TO A EUROCREDIT BASED ON SAMPLE AGREEMENT

The standard contract for a eurocredit describes who will bear various risks. Some clauses are common to many types of loans. Others, more peculiar to a eurocredit, are the subject of this section. The following clauses come from a sample Revolving Credit Agreement put together by Anthony Gooch and Linda Klein.[10] Assume that in mid-1996, a government-owned Korean firm negotiates a $250 million 5-year Eurocredit with the terms described in this sample agreement: advances of 1, 3, or 6 months and a 1 percent margin or spread. Lenders include banks from Europe, Japan, and the U.S. A major U.S. bank lead manages.

This is a multi-option revolving credit facility. Within the $250 million limit, the borrower can draw funds priced either as a Eurocurrency loan based on LIBOR or as a "swing-line" loan based on the U.S. prime rate, which is the rate the banks charge their best customers. The swing-line option was a common alternative in Eurodollar facilities. They can be faster; LIBOR-based advances generally require at least three business days' advance notice so that the lenders can make their funding arrangements in the London interbank market. The swing-line option also serves as a stopgap if the lenders cannot fund a desired advance in the London market. The discussion of the documentation below omits complications introduced by the swing-line alternative.

For these services, the borrower agrees to pay interest described below and several fees. A 1 percent commitment fee is paid annually on the unused part of each commitment. A 1/4 percent facility fee is paid annually on the full commitment, used or not. The management fee, paid at signing, is 1 percent of the total commitments (in this case, $250 million). Each year both the agents receive $10,000. All payments are made either by or to the Eurodollar agent or the swing-line agent, as appropriate.

Sovereign immunity is waived. New York law governs this agreement, although many Eurocredits are governed by U.K. law.

We concentrate here on key clauses. Some concern the relation between the borrowers and the lenders, others the relation between managers, agents, and the participating banks.

1.   THE BASIC TERMS OF THE LOAN

a.   ADVANCES AND REPAYMENT

The clauses below are rather straightforward.

---

[10] *Loan Documentation* (2nd ed., 1991).

Advance means any Eurodollar Advance or Swing-Line Advance.

Commitment, with respect to any Bank at any time means the amount designated as such and set forth opposite the name of that Bank on the signature pages hereof, subject to reduction as provided herein.

2.1. *Commitment to Lend.* (a) On the terms and subject to the conditions set forth herein, each Bank shall make Advances hereunder through its Lending Branch to the Borrower from time to time in an aggregate principal amount at any one time outstanding not exceeding that Bank's Commitment. Failure by any Bank to make an Advance to the Borrower shall not relieve any other Bank of its obligations hereunder. No Bank shall have any responsibility for any failure by any other Bank to fulfill its obligations hereunder.

2.2. *Term.* The "Term" of each Advance shall mean the period beginning with the applicable Disbursement Date and, (i) in the case of a Eurodollar Advance, ending on the day numerically corresponding to that Disbursement Date in the first, third or sixth month thereafter. ...

2.3. *Notice of Intention and Commitment to Borrow.* (a) The Borrower may request Eurodollar Advances hereunder by delivering to the Eurodollar Agent a notice substantially in the form set forth in Exhibit D [not included] ... not later than 1:00 p.m. (London time) on the third Banking Day before the day on which the Borrower wishes to make the borrowing. ...

The aggregate principal amount of Eurodollar Advances to be made on a Disbursement Date must be $50,000,000 or a higher integral multiple of $5,000,000. The aggregate principal amount of all Advances to be made on a Disbursement Date shall be an amount which, when taken together with all other Advances outstanding on that Disbursement Date (excluding any Advances to be repaid from the proceeds of Advances to be made on that date), does not exceed the Total Commitment.

2.4. *Disbursements.* (a) The Eurodollar Agent shall promptly advise each Bank by telex or facsimile transmission of the contents of each request for Eurodollar Advances hereunder, and the amount of the Eurodollar Advance to be made by that Bank on that date, which shall be that Bank's Pro Rata Share of the aggregate principal amount of all the Eurodollar Advances to be made on that date determined on the basis of the respective Commitments of the Banks, subject to such rounding as the Eurodollar Agent may determine. Except as otherwise expressly provided in Subsection 2.4(b), by 10:00 a.m. (New York City time) on each Disbursement Date, each Bank shall, subject to the conditions set forth herein, make available to the

Eurodollar Agent the amount so specified, in funds settled through the New York Clearing House Interbank Payments System or such other same-day funds as the Eurodollar Agent may at the time determine to be customary for the settlement in New York City of international banking transactions denominated in Dollars, by deposit to the Eurodollar Agent's account specified in or pursuant to Section 7.1. Subject to the conditions set forth herein, and except as otherwise expressly provided in Subsection 2.4(b), the Eurodollar Agent shall, on that Disbursement Date, credit the funds so received to the account specified by the Borrower pursuant to Subsection 2.3(d).

(b) Any Bank that is obligated to make a new Advance hereunder on a day on which the Borrower is obligated to repay an outstanding Advance of that Bank shall apply the proceeds of its new Advance to make the repayment, and only an amount equal to the excess (if any) of the amount being so borrowed from that Bank over the amount being so repaid to that Bank shall be made available by that Bank to the relevant Agent and remitted by that Agent to the Borrower. ...

3.1.   *Repayment.* Except as otherwise expressly provided herein, the Borrower shall repay each Advance on the last day of its Term.

3.2.   *No Prepayment of Eurodollar Advances.* Except as provided in Section 3.4 and Section 3.5 [omitted], the Borrower may not prepay Eurodollar Advances.

16.3.   *Currency.* (a) If any expense required to be reimbursed pursuant to Article 15 is originally incurred in a currency other than Dollars, the Borrower shall nonetheless make reimbursement of that expense in Dollars, in an amount equal to the amount in Dollars that would have been required for the person that incurred that expense to have purchased, in accordance with normal banking procedures, the sum paid in that other currency (after any premium and costs of exchange) on the day that expense was originally incurred. ...

(b) Each reference in this Agreement to Dollars is of the essence. The obligation of the Borrower in respect of any amount due under this Agreement or the Notes shall, notwithstanding any payment in any other currency (whether pursuant to a judgment or otherwise), be discharged only to the extent of the amount in Dollars that the person entitled to receive that payment may, in accordance with normal banking procedures, purchase with the sum paid in the other currency (after any premium and costs of exchange) on the Banking Day immediately following the day on which that person receives that payment. If the amount in Dollars that may be so purchased for any reason falls short of the amount originally due, the Borrower shall pay such additional amount, in Dollars, as is necessary to compensate for the shortfall. Any obligation of the Borrower not discharged by that payment shall, to the fullest extent permitted by applicable law, be due as a separate and independent obligation and until discharged as provided herein, shall continue in full force and effect.

Clause 3.1 prohibits prepayment. Some agreements permit prepayment but add a "broken funding indemnity clause" that obligates the borrower to pay lenders for any losses they incur due to early payment. The problem is that the banks would "need to liquidate or redeploy the deposits they took to fund the loan for the interest period concerned."[11] If interest rates fell after the period began, the bank would not earn as much on the new investment and might even lose money. The indemnity clause assumes that banks match their floating rate loans with deposits to fund them.

b.   INTEREST RATE DETERMINATION

Eurocurrency loans are at floating rates. As documented below, at 4.1, "interest shall accrue on each Advance during its Term ... at a rate per annum equal ... to the sum of the Margin (or spread) and LIBOR for that Advance. ..." So, suppose Advance 1 was at 5 ¼ percent (LIBOR at that time). The interest rate would be 5 ¼ + 1 (the spread) or 6 ¼ percent on an annualized basis.

LIBOR is the bank rate and represents the cost of funds to the lending banks. LIBOR changes over the life of the loan; here it would change every one, three, or six months depending on the option selected by the borrower. Obviously, longer repricing periods carry higher rates of interest. The margin reflects the fixed costs of the bank over the life of the loan, including risk, plus a profit. The borrower can try to limit its upside interest rate risk over the entire life of the loan by capping interest rates or stretching out repricing periods.

> "'LIBOR,' with respect to any Eurodollar Advance, means the rate of interest (expressed as an annual rate) determined by the Eurodollar Agent to be the arithmetic mean (rounded up to the nearest one sixteenth of one percent (1/16 percent)) of the respective rates of interest communicated to the Eurodollar Agent by the several Reference Banks as the rates at which each of them would offer a deposit in Dollars for a period coextensive with the Term of the Advance in the amount of $5,000,000 (or, if that amount is not representative of the normal amount for a single deposit transaction in that currency in that market at the time, such other amount as is representative thereof), to major banks in the London interbank market at approximately 11:00 a.m. (London time) on the second London Banking Day before the commencement of the Term of that

---

[11] See L. Buchheit, "How to Negotiate the Broken Funding Indemnity Clause," International Financial Law Review (April 1994), p. 20.

Advance; *provided, however,* that if any of the Reference Banks fails so to communicate a rate, LIBOR shall be determined on the basis of the rate or rates communicated to the Eurodollar Agent by the remaining Reference Bank or Reference Banks.

'Reference Bank' means each of the respective principal London offices of Biggest Bank, N.A., Average Quoter Bank Plc and Small & Obscure Banking Company, and *'Reference Banks'* means those offices collectively.

4.1. *Basic Rate.* (a) Except as otherwise expressly provided in Section 4.2 [omitted], interest shall accrue on each Advance during its Term, from and including the first day of that Term, to but excluding the last day thereof, at a rate per annum equal, (i) in the case of Eurodollar Advances, to the sum of the Margin and LIBOR for that Advance. ..."

The move to the European Monetary Union and the Euro created a problem for banks: how would they determine the benchmark interbank offer rate? EURIBOR would replace national interbank rates, like FIBOR (Frankfurt) in Germany. But EURIBOR's benchmark banks would include banks from other countries than Germany, some of which would presumably have lower credit ratings than the German banks and therefore raise the benchmark above what it would have been if only German banks contributed to it. In December 1997, the European Banking Federation issued rules. A panel of 64 qualified banks would include 4 from countries outside EMU and 60 from inside it. Banks were to meet strict size standards. Each country would have a maximum number of banks that could participate on the panel; if any country had more banks qualified to be panelists than its quota, the banks would rotate membership.[12]

Notes and Questions

1. Eurodollar loans have variable rates of interest over the life of the loans based on movement of LIBOR. Why do they have a fixed margin?

2. How could a borrower protect itself against a large rise in LIBOR over the life of the loan?

3. The "broken funding indemnity clause" assumes banks match floating rate loans with floating rate deposits. Should the clause be dependent on evidence that this is the case? If rates move up instead of down, should the bank pay the borrower in case of prepayment?

---

[12] See G. Graham, "Banks Settle Dispute on EURIBOR Rate," *Financial Times,* December 16, 1997.

c.   EVENTS OF DEFAULT: THE CROSS DEFAULT CLAUSE

One of the key remedies of lenders in a syndicated Eurocurrency loan is the cross-default clause. In the loan documentation it provides:

> "12.1   If ... the Borrower ... fails to pay any ... indebtedness when it becomes payable ... and any ... party [to that debt] has the right to accelerate the maturity of any amount owing [the Agreement also provides for such acceleration] ... [then]

> 12.2   ... the Eurodollar agent shall, upon the request of Majority Banks [those with a majority of the value of the loans outstanding] ... declare the obligations of each Bank ... terminated ... and ... all amounts payable ... immediately."

The logic of the clause is that it prevents the bank on whose loan the Borrower has defaulted from getting repaid in advance of other banks, because it enables these banks to declare default and therein ensure they get repaid at the same time. Equal repayment would be assured by another clause, the pari passu clause, which provides that all loans in default must be paid pro-rata. Thus, if there were two loans, one for $100 and the other for $300, the second would get three-quarters of all repayments.

The problem with the cross-default is that it can put all loans into default and thus make it impossible to repay any. Majority action requirements provide some safeguard against this.

d.   ADVERSE CHANGE

The Adverse change clauses permit the lenders to modify their obligations in certain circumstances. Two of the most important clauses relate to increased costs and illegality.

The increased costs clause makes the borrower liable for the increased costs of the lender. Obviously, the extent of this obligation, and how increased costs would be determined, could be an important subject of negotiation.

> "15.4. *Increased Costs.* The Borrower shall reimburse each Bank in Dollars on demand for all costs ... as determined by that Bank, that are attributable to that Bank's Advances or the performance by that Bank of its obligations ... and that occur by reason of the promulgation of any law, regulation or treaty ... including, without limitation, any such cost or reduction resulting from: (i) the imposition or amendment of any tax other than (A) any tax measured by the net income of that Bank or its Lending Branch and imposed by the jurisdiction in which that Bank's principal office or Lending Branch is situated and (B) any Taxes [separately defined] (any such cost or reduction occurring by reason of the imposition or amendment of any tax referred to in clauses (A) and (B) of this Section being

expressly excluded from the coverage of this Section); (ii) the imposition or amendment of any reserve, special deposit or similar requirement against assets of, liabilities of, deposits with or for the account of, or loans by, that Bank; or (iii) the imposition or amendment of any capital requirements or provisions relating to capital adequacy that have the effect of reducing the rate of return on such Bank's or the relevant Lending Branch's capital as a consequence of its Advances or its obligations hereunder to a level below that which it could have achieved but for such adoption, change or compliance. If a Bank has sold one or more participations in its Advances, costs incurred and reductions in amounts receivable by the participants shall be deemed to be attributable to the relevant Advances for purposes of this Section; *provided, however,* that the Borrower shall not be required to reimburse any Bank for an amount greater than the amount that would have been due if that Bank had not sold participations in its Advances."

The motive for the illegality clause, set forth below, was to protect banks if their home governments closed the entire Eurocurrency market by regulation. While this has never happened, it still could. Asset freezes or other controls may prohibit Eurodollar lenders from fulfilling commitments.

"3.5.   *Illegality.* If any Bank determines at any time that any law, regulation or treaty or any change therein or in the interpretation or application thereof makes or will make it unlawful for the Bank to fulfill its commitment in accordance with Section 2.1, to maintain an Advance or to claim or receive any amount payable to it hereunder, the Bank shall give notice of that determination to the Borrower, with copies to the Agents, whereupon the obligations of that Bank hereunder shall terminate and the Bank's Commitment shall be reduced to zero. The Borrower shall repay the Advances of that Bank in full at the end of their respective Terms; *provided, however,* that, if the affected Bank certifies to the Borrower that earlier repayment is necessary in order to enable that Bank to comply with the relevant law, regulation or treaty and specifies an earlier date for repayment, the Borrower shall make repayment on the earlier date so specified. Repayment pursuant to this Section shall be made without premium but together with interest accrued on the Advances being repaid to the date of repayment and all other amounts then payable to the relevant Bank by the Borrower hereunder."

Notes and Questions

1.   Suppose in 1997, a Japanese bank lender has to increase its bad loan provisions due to a new MOF policy. Must the Korean borrower compensate the Japanese bank, or terminate and payoff the loan?

2.   ALLOCATION OF RISK AMONG MANAGERS, AGENTS, AND PARTICIPATING BANKS

Since many banks lend but only a few deal directly with the borrower, an information asymmetry exists in most cases between the managers and other participating banks. This creates an agency problem, in that a lead bank may withhold information about the borrower to the detriment of other participants. K. Panyagometh and G. Roberts found that as the credit ratings of borrowers become more available, syndicated loans to that borrower become more likely. They also found that the manager's reputation (measured by the number of deals it does each year) increases the likelihood that a loan will be syndicated.[13] So participants are alert to the agency problem.

A key legal issue is the extent of lead manager's duty to the other lenders. A typical exculpatory clause would be:

"14.2. *Exculpation.* The Agents and the Managers and their respective directors, officers, employees and agents shall have no responsibility for: (i) the truth of any representation or warranty made by the Borrower or the Guarantor in this Agreement or any other document delivered in connection with this Agreement; (ii) the validity or enforceability of this Agreement or any such document; (iii) any failure of the Borrower or the Guarantor to fulfill any of its respective obligations under this Agreement or any such document; or (iv) any action taken or omitted to be taken in connection with this Agreement or the Notes, absent gross negligence or willful misconduct. Each Agent shall be entitled to rely in good faith on any communication or document believed by it to be genuine and to have been sent or signed by the proper person or persons and on the opinions and statements of any legal counsel or other professional advisors selected by it and shall not be liable to any other person for any consequence of any such reliance."

What is or is not "gross" negligence or willful misconduct can be an important matter of interpretation. Moreover, contractual limitations on liability can be overridden by fiduciary duties imposed by statutes or common law. This possibility makes choice of law clauses quite important.

S. Sequeira[14] reports about a case in which "the relationship between the arranger and the syndicate banks was a 'classic example' of a situation where a duty of care did arise." The facts giving rise to this statement were that the arranger of a syndicate had told prospective participants that it would inform them of the terms of a crucial insurance policy guaranteeing

---

[13] K. Panyagometh and G. Roberts, "Private Information, Agency Problems and Determinants of Loan Syndications: Evidence from 1987-1999," Working Paper (April 25, 2002).

[14] "Syndicated Loans-Let the Arranger Beware," Butterworths Journal of International Banking and Financial Law (March 1997), p. 117.

part of the loan. The syndicate members alleged that the arranging bank failed to disclose the terms and they sustained losses when the insurance was not adequate to meet the defaulted amount. The court found a duty of care in tort and that the contractual limitations on the arranger's liability were not enough to exclude this liability for acts before the contract was made. The author concluded that "although loan documents will continue to contain clauses [exonerating] ... the arranger and agent from liability, ... the arranger [must] ... exercise sufficient care [preparing] ... the information memorandum. ..."[15]

This result can be questioned, given that sophisticated parties had agreed to an exculpatory clause, and that the bank participants could have, if they had been concerned, inquired about the adequacy of insurance coverage.

When is the majority constrained if it wants to change the terms of a loan? In *Redwood Master Fund Ltd v. TD Bank Europe Ltd*,[16] the judge said that while the court might protect a minority of participants if the majority discriminated against them in bad faith, on the facts of that case the discrimination was commercially justified and benefited all lenders. The participants originally held in the same proportion two of the three tranches of the loan, one short-term and the other medium-term. Some participants had sold their medium-term loans, and only held the short loans. At the borrower's request to reduce the overall loan, the majority voted to allow the borrower to draw on the short-term tranche to pay the medium-term tranche. The exposure of the lenders still holding equal proportions of both tranches was unaffected. The exposure of the minority of lenders holding only the short-term tranche rose, and they sued.[17]

The extent of fiduciary obligations of participating banks to the borrower arose in the U.K. in 2000. Deutsche Bank (DB) initially took a small participation (8 percent) in a syndicated loan to United Pan-Europe Holdings NV (UPC) in 1997, and then with an affiliate took over 50 percent of each of two syndicated loans to UPC in 1998. As a participant, Deutsche Bank received confidential financial and business information from UPC that described the borrower's strategy and capabilities. In 1999, UPC sought to acquire a German company in its industry, telecommunications. Deutsche Bank at first seemed to offer to finance the acquisition, but ultimately also bid on the target and won. UPC sued in the U.K., arguing that Deutsche Bank broke its contractual obligation to treat confidentially the information it received as a syndicated lender and that the bank also breached its fiduciary duty to the borrower. UPC asked the court to enjoin the bank from selling the company and, instead, to transfer the company to UPC, upon payment of the purchase price on the theory that Deutsche Bank held the

---

[15] Id., at 118.

[16] Unreported, December 1, 2002.

[17] E. Cheyney, "Syndicated Loans-Position of Minority Lenders," Butterworths Journal of International Banking and Financial Law (March 2003), p. 88.

company under a constructive trust. The lower court declined, but was reversed on appeal. The appellate court first found a possible contractual obligation: there was "at least an arguable case that ... the value of the [confidential] information was not restricted to what UPC's bid might be but extended to ... wider considerations" such as the way UPC's business strategy would affect its approach to the bid. The appellate court also found that Deutsche Bank "was under some fiduciary duty to UPC, the scope of which could only be determined at the trial." A fiduciary, said the court, "has undertaken to act for or on behalf of another in a particular matter in circumstances which give rise to a relationship of trust and confidence." The duty of loyalty would arise "from the key banking relationship ... between UPC and DB, the mutual trust and confidence without which it could not properly operate and the requirement ... that UPC pass to DB confidential information ... on a regular basis."[18] In a challenge to this decision, Alan Berg argued that "a bank which participates in a syndicated loan cannot sensibly be said to have undertaken 'to act for or on behalf' of the borrower." The lender's interests differ from the borrower's. "Deutsche Bank was contractually entitled to use the information in its own interest and contrary to those of UPC."[19]

Notes and Questions

1. Suppose Citibank was the lead manager for our hypothetical loan to the Korean borrower. Further assume that Citi knew, but did not tell, small regional U.S. participants that the Korean economy was highly leveraged (debt/GNP), the won was greatly overvalued, the borrower was corrupt, with many bad loans, the borrower had other outstanding loans from Citi, and the loan circular was inaccurate. The borrower defaulted 12 months later. Would the other banks have recourse against Citi?

D.   EUROBONDS

1.   THE MARKET

Eurobonds are traditionally defined as bonds which are issued, and largely sold, outside the domestic market of the currency in which they are denominated. Thus, bonds issued in Dollars in London would be Eurobonds. It would not include another type of international bond, a bond issued by a foreign company in Dollars in the U.S., so-called "Yankee" bonds. Eurobonds are typically underwritten by an international syndicate of banks, are exempt

---

[18] *United Pan-Europe Communications N.V. v Deutsche Bank AG*, 2000 WL 699349 (CA), [2000] 2 B.C.L.C. 461, paras 35 and 37.
[19] A. Berg, "UK Court Ruling Imposes Fiduciary Duties on Capital Markets," International Financial Law Review (July 2000), pp. 25, 27.

from any withholding taxes (i.e. taxes on coupon payments deducted at source), and are bearer in nature (i.e. no register of ownership is maintained). Originally, investors were attracted in particular by (and thus prepared to pay a premium for) the bearer status of Eurobonds and their freedom from liability to withholding tax.

In the early 1960s, the U.S. imposed an interest equalization tax (initially 15 percent) on interest paid by foreign debt issuers to investors in the United States. The tax was intended to decrease U.S. investment in these securities because such transactions were putting downward pressure on the Dollar. Investments in foreign bonds denominated in Dollars resulted in the issuer exchanging the Dollar proceeds for local currency. Since there were fixed exchange rates at this time, the U.S. had to offset market pressure by buying Dollars with its reserves. The tax discouraged the investments because it increased the cost of borrowing in the U.S. market by 1 percent, since the issuer had to compensate investors for the tax.

So foreigners issued their Dollar-denominated bonds to U.S. and other investors outside the United States. Thus originally, the Eurodollar bond replaced Yankee bonds, bonds issued by foreigners to U.S. investors in the United States.

The Eurobond market prospered even after the tax was abolished in 1974. Total Eurobonds issued in 1993 were $400 billion.

Eurobond market investors have typically been "name-conscious," so most issuers have been highly-rated borrowers from OECD countries. Between 1985 and 1990, issues by non-OECD countries averaged only 3.7 percent of total Eurobond issuance. Continental European investors—traditionally "name-conscious" and placing a premium on bearer instruments and freedom from withholding tax—have been a major source of demand for Eurobonds.

As a general rule, only highly rated companies issue in the market. For example, one triple-A rated issuer with an excellent name, and that is close at hand, Harvard University, had a $100 million Eurobond issue in January 1996. Average seven-year Eurobond spreads over government bonds for triple-A rated borrowers are in the low 20s (basis points), rising to close to 50 basis points for single-A borrowers, and jumping to 450 basis points for borrowers with speculative grade ratings.[20] In 1998, given generally low interest rates in the world's most developed economies, investors looked for higher yield in the Euromarkets, with the result that some Euro junk bonds (bonds with a sub-investment grade rating) have been issued.[21]

Given the importance of credit ratings to access to bond markets, there has been an increased focus on the credit rating process. The essential

---

[20] "Investors Resume Search for Yield," *Financial Times*, July 17, 1995.
[21] E. Luce and S. Davies, "World Loan and Bond Market Double Act Falls Victim to Crisis," *Financial Times*, February 16, 1998.

problem is that rating agencies are paid by the companies they rate. This concern has led to consideration by the EU and the U.S. as to whether these agencies should be regulated.[22] The rating agencies have argued that all that is needed is additional transparency. Others believe more is needed—a code of conduct based on principles established by IOSCO.[23]

Issuance of Eurobonds by the U.S. private sector, the largest national group of issuers in the early 1980s, more than halved in the 1990s for a variety of reasons: for example, the use of shelf registration in the United States accelerated the process of domestic bond issuance and reduced one of the competitive advantages enjoyed by the Eurobond market. The abolition of withholding tax in the U.S. domestic market also contributed to a decline in the attractiveness of the Eurobond market to U.S. borrowers.

Secondary market

Investors' desire for liquidity (e.g. the ability to buy or sell bonds in sizable amounts before they mature without much influencing the price) has led to the development of a sizable secondary market in Eurobonds.

The secondary market is primarily an over-the-counter market, even though most Eurobonds are listed on the London or Luxembourg Stock Exchanges. Listings are normally obtained because some institutional investors are not allowed to purchase unquoted securities.

There has been a growing integration—in terms of increased substitutability and interactions—between the Euro, domestic, and foreign bond markets.

Integration

The two major differences of form which distinguished Eurobonds from domestic and foreign bonds have gradually been eroded. Fiscal reforms have led to the dismantling of withholding tax regimes in a number of major OECD countries (e.g. in the United States in 1984, Germany in 1989, and France—for foreign investors only—in 1989). Also, the bearer status of Eurobonds is not unique, bearer bonds were, and are, issued in a number of domestic markets e.g. Germany, Switzerland, and Luxembourg. The increasing role of institutions as Eurobond investors means that the anonymity associated with bearer status is less valued.

The Eurobond market is no longer the only bond market which is genuinely international in character. Over the years the traditional domestic bond markets have attracted increasing international investor interest as

---

[22] SEC, Concept Release, Rating Agencies and the Use of Credit Ratings under the Federal Securities Laws, Release Nos. 33-8236; 34-47972 June 4, 2003; I. Simensen, "Bond Market Participants Seek Changes," *Financial Times*, September 7, 2004.
[23] IOSCO Statement of Principles Regarding the Activities of Credit Rating Agencies, A Statement of the Technical Committee of IOSCO, September 25, 2003.

investors have sought portfolio diversification. Moreover, as discussed at the end of this Chapter, the Global Bond market has also developed.

2.   THE EFFECT OF REGULATION

There is a significant relationship between national regulation and the growth or contraction of the Eurocurrency bond markets. National regulation initially prevented German companies from issuing in the markets. In 1992, these restrictions were relaxed. The new rules permitted listing on foreign exchanges, issuance under foreign rather than German law and clearance of bonds through Cedel or Euroclear in addition to (or instead of) the *Kassenverein,* the German bond-clearing system. The Bundesbank also removed the minimum two-year maturity for foreign issues, which boosted the Euro-DM medium-term and commercial paper markets. Once German issuers had the option of using the Euromarkets, their demand for such issuance was significantly influenced by the level of German regulation of domestic issues—as restrictions in the domestic German market eased, the comparative attraction of Euro issuance decreased. This story has been repeated for a number of countries. Indeed, the possibility of Euro issuance—once accepted—becomes a source of pressure for domestic deregulation.

Trade associations, like the International Primary Market Association (IPMA) and the Bond Market Association, play an important role in the creation of standardized terms, like calculation of interest. For example, they have proposed to change the method of calculating interest from assuming there are 360 days in a year, with 12 months of 30 days, to using 365 days and the actual days in any month to calculate interest.[24]

London has been the major home of the Euromarkets. While London remains offshore to continental Europe with respect to its currency—since it has not adopted the Euro—it remains subject to EU regulation. As we saw in Chapter 5 on the European single financial market, London has tried to protect its position in the "Eurocurrency Market" from the effect of EU regulation. The London Stock Exchange (LSE) is the major player in the Eurobond listing market, with 60 percent of all new Eurobond issues and 70 percent of the secondary market. However, under new EU accounting rules, issuers in the U.K. (and Luxembourg) have to use IFRS standards in 2005 unless their home GAAP rules are found equivalent. Furthermore, listed bonds may be subject to the stricter disclosure rule of the EU Properties Directive, effective July 1. The LSE plans to create an "alternative" market for Eurobonds that would apparently not be subject to the new rules since this new market would not be "regulated." London has already created an alternative investment market in equities (AIM) to escape these new listing requirements. This plan was stimulated by the announcement of Switzerland's SWX exchange that Eurobonds could trade on its exchange

---

[24] *Financial Times,* May 30, 1997.

under home GAAP accounting rules and the light disclosure rules under the Prospectus Directive for trading wholesale securities. A major problem with this approach is the requirement of many countries that institutions, like mutual funds and insurance companies, trade in securities listed on a regulated market.[25] Nonetheless, in March 2005, Switzerland's exchange had its first listing of a eurobond, one issued by a Brazilian bank.

Notes and Questions

1.   What accounts for the continued growth of the Eurobond market?

2.   Will there be a Euro Eurobond market? Will the euromarkets ever wither away?

3.   ISSUING PROCEDURES

a.   REGISTRATION

Eurobonds do not generally have to be registered when sold in European countries. Issuers can take advantage of exemptions in local law for bonds distributed to institutional buyers; banks are the initial buyers. This issue is discussed in Chapter 4.

The fact that Eurobonds are usually exempt from registration requirements does not mean that there are no disclosures made about the issuer. If the bonds are listed in London or Luxembourg, they are subject to the exchanges' disclosure requirements and the minimum standards of the Listings Directive. In addition, since many Eurobonds are sold in London, their distribution will be subject to the disclosure requirements of the IPMA, a London-based membership group for euro-issuers. Such disclosure requires a degree of due diligence—checking up on material facts—by the issuer and, to some extent, the lead manager. Investors may be less concerned because: (a) they are generally better credits; and (b) lead managers, in order to preserve their reputation with institutional investors, may be prepared to compensate investors.[26]

Eurobonds can be issued through so-called MTN (medium term note programs). These programs set up general documentation that permits multiple issues over time without new prospectuses. Despite the name, the actual maturities are the same as for Eurobonds.

Why do issuers seek to avoid registration? Naturally, they seek to avoid the costs and potential liabilities. But perhaps most importantly, absent registration, bonds can be brought promptly to market based on market conditions. There is no need to wait for approval or clearance of a

---

[25] M. Evans, "Swiss Make Play for Eurobond Market," International Financial Law Review 15 (December 2004).

[26] R. Foster, "Due Diligence: An Accident Waiting to Happen," International Financial Law Review (March 1996), p. 23.

registration statement. Lack of registration may make it difficult for lower credit rated companies to sell Eurobonds—institutional investors would want more disclosure on no name companies. Eurodollar issuers have higher credit ratings than issuers in the U.S. domestic market, 47 percent of SP ratings in Eurobonds are AAA, compared to 2 percent in U.S. bonds.

Can U.S. investors buy (or can issuers sell to them) Eurobonds that have not been registered in the United States? This depends on the treatment of the issue under Regulation S, examined in Chapter 2. If there is high "substantial U.S. market interest," (SUSMI), which would certainly be the case if the bond issuer was a U.S. "reporting" company (had public issues in U.S. market), the issuer would have to comply with the Regulation S restrictions. Regulation S provides that in such case, U.S. investors cannot buy the bonds for 40 days after the initial distribution. During this period, no bearer bonds can be issued because bearer bonds could be easily bought by U.S. investors. So, a temporary global note is used for the first 40 days, requiring investors to register. During this period investors can buy or sell interests in the note.

b. UNDERWRITING

Two underwriting techniques are used in the Euromarket, so-called bookbuilding and bought deals.

1. BOOKBUILDING—"OPEN PRICED"—AND "BOUGHT" DEALS

In "open priced" underwriting the bond issue is launched on tentative terms (i.e. coupon and issue price) in order to test market demand and, based upon market response, final pricing terms are then agreed with the issuer. Only then are legally binding underwriting commitments entered into. In this method the issuer takes a risk that during the period in which the market is sounded out (the "offering period"), market rates move against the rate it would prefer to pay on its bonds.

Negotiated or "bookbuilding" deals, which originated in the United States, have now become a standard practice in the Euromarket. In these deals, the issuer retains an underwriter, who structures the terms of offering. The price of the issue is set after the prospectus is circulated to an underwriting group without a price and preliminary indications of interest are obtained; then the issue is priced. During this period, the registration can become effective, i.e. cleared by the SEC—which might take up to three weeks.

The underwriter fixes a price, usually in terms of a discount from par, to make a spread on the transaction that compensates for the service, e.g. the issuer receives 99 for a bond that the underwriter knows it can sell for 100. The service is structuring the deal, a corporate finance function, as well as delivering the agreed proceeds to the issuer.

During the early 1980s, the speed with which an issue was brought to the market had to increase due to rapid currency and interest rate fluctuations and, as a consequence, since that time a new method of underwriting known as the "bought deal" (or "pre-priced deal") has been used in the overwhelming majority of new Euro market issues of bonds.

In a "bought deal" the underwriter buys bonds (or equities) from the issuer at a fixed price, meaning with a fixed coupon and with an agreed amount of proceeds going to the issuer. Standard documentation is set by a dealers association (ISMA).

Under this technique one or more lead managers jointly and severally agree with the issuer before and regardless of syndication to firmly underwrite the entire issue at a fixed issue price and a specific coupon, so that the issuer has certainty as to its cost of funds. Only after the issuer has agreed these fundamental terms with the lead manager does the lead manager launch the issue and invite other managers to underwrite a portion of the issue at the terms already agreed.

How do bookbuilding and fixed pricing affect IPO pricing relative to the true value of the security? A major difference in approach between the two is whether price discovery takes place in the premarket through roadshows and meetings (book building) or the aftermarket (fixed price). W. Busaba and C. Chang[27] say that, contrary to others' analysis, informed investors will be able to force the issuer to underprice in either case.

Fixed pricing: When fixed pricing is used, informed investors will only buy underpriced securities, crowding out uninformed investors who are left with higher priced issues. To counter this, the issuer may keep informed investors out of the IPO by selling only to retail investors. But the informed investors can use their knowledge to buy the securities in the aftermarket from the uninformed investors in the IPO. Uninformed investors know they are vulnerable to what is called the winner's curse and this weakens demand for the IPO. The issuer counters by underpricing the issue.

Bookbuilding: As the issuer builds the book, it wants informed investors to reveal their view of the true value of the security. This is valuable information because it allows the issuer to minimize underpricing. The informed investor has an incentive to misrepresent its interest in the security before issue so the issuer will misprice it and the investor can take its profit in the aftermarket. The issuer tries to allocate securities to investors with strong interest and a history (known to the investment banker) of loyalty, recognizing that it must underprice to get them at all. The winner's curse is absent because price discovery takes place before issue.

In both cases, aftermarket trading forces more underpricing. The impact is greater in bookbuilding. The authors show that "misrepresenting

---

[27] In *Bookbuilding vs Fixed Price Revisited: The Effect of Aftermarket Trading* (June 2002).

information during bookbuilding and then trading in the aftermarket generates a higher profit on average for the informed investors than aftermarket trading in fixed-price offerings."

Europe has yet to regulate IPO research or allocation practices. It appears that investment banking sponsored research, which increased issuer following, contributed to the choice of bookbuilding in France in the 1990s, where at the beginning of the period bookbuilding and auctions had about the same market share. It also appears that bookbuilding did not result in valuation or return differentials as compared with auctions.[28] Two studies conflict as to whether bookbuilding allocations are given to investors providing more information or for other reason, e.g. quid pro quos on future transactions or willingness to hold onto the issue rather than "flip" it in the after market.[29] The lack of IPO allocation regulation in Europe raises the possibility of that market moving out of the U.S. to Europe.

2.   FIXED-PRICE REOFFER

Under a fixed-price reoffer, the underwriting participants are supposed to offer and reoffer shares at the fixed-price of the offering. Once the lead manager is satisfied that most of the bonds have been placed with end investors the bond issue is allowed to find a free market price. Until that time, borrowers may expect the lead manager and other underwriters to support the bond price at the fixed-price reoffer level; however, other participants in the deal may not do so.[30] Members of syndicates who cannot sell their bonds sometimes sell them back anonymously to the lead manager via a broker, contrary to the syndicate rules, and still pocket their underwriting fees.[31] One solution to this problem is to allocate bonds from a new issue only to houses that have actual demand. Alternatively the lead manager can set up a selling group of non-underwriters who only earn a fee on the bonds they sell.

Notes and Questions

1.   In a "bought deal" the underwriter buys bonds (or equities) from the issuer at a fixed price, meaning with a fixed coupon and with an agreed amount of proceeds going to the issuer. Standard documentation is set by a dealers association (ISMA). Suppose the underwriter agrees to give the issuer $10 million in proceeds at a coupon rate of 8.25 percent. Further assume that

---

[28] T. Jenkinson and H. Jones, "Bids and Allocations in European Bookbuilding," 59 J. of Finance 2309 (2004) (not provided on basis of information); F. Cornelli and D. Goldreich, "Bookbuilding and Strategic Allocation," 56 J. of Finance 2337 (2001) (provided on basis of information).

[29] F. Degeorge, F. Derrien and K. Womack, "Quid Pro Quo in IPOs: Why Bookbuilding is Dominating Auctions," CEPR Discussion Paper 4462 (June 2004).

[30] S. Webb, "Bond-dumping Rears its Head," *Financial Times*, April 11, 1994.

[31] A. Sharpe, "Eurobond Market Shows Signs of Wear and Tear," *Financial Times*, April 26, 1995.

each bond is $100 (there are 100,000 bonds). How does the underwriter make money? How might the underwriter lose money?

2. Will the underwriter seek to have a higher or lower coupon rate than the market demands? How can the issuer control the underwriter setting the premium too high?

4.   TAXATION

The possibility of withholding taxes imposed at source represents a key problem for the viability of the Eurobond market.

U.S. Withholding Taxes

Until 1984, the United States imposed a withholding tax on interest paid by U.S. issuers on bonds issued to foreigners. The tax was not only aimed at the foreign investors, but also domestic investors who might invest through a foreign entity.

Let us take an example. Suppose there is a $100 interest payment due on a bond payable to a person or entity outside the United States. Given a withholding tax of 25 percent, the foreign interest recipient would only get $75. While the foreigner could get a refund if he or she owed less than a 25 percent tax to the U.S., this would be time consuming and costly.

Such taxes make investment in U.S. bonds unattractive to foreigners and mechanisms were sought to avoid the payment of the taxes. Figure 11.1, below, diagrams a common technique that was used:

Figure 11.1

Tax Treaties to Avoid Withholding Taxes

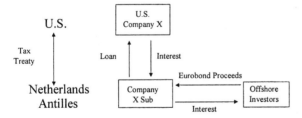

The issuer finds a "tax haven" jurisdiction, in the example, the Netherlands Antilles, that itself imposes no taxes and has a tax treaty with the U.S. providing for no withholding taxes. The U.S. company seeking to issue Eurobonds, U.S. company X, forms a subsidiary (company X sub) in the tax haven. The subsidiary then issues Eurobonds to foreign investors. The proceeds from the bond issue are upstreamed as a loan to the parent that pays the subsidiary interest, which the subsidiary uses to service the Eurobonds.

While this structure does avoid withholding taxes, there is a risk that the tax haven will itself impose taxes in the future or that the U.S. will terminate its tax treaty with the tax haven. To cover that risk, the bonds provide for gross-up to insure the bondholder always gets the full amount of interest.

Again, an example. Assume a $100 interest payment is due (pretax) and that a 25 percent withholding tax is now imposed. The gross-up provision would require the issuer to pay $133.33—the tax would be $33.33, the investor would still receive $100. Since this would be extremely expensive for issuers, the bonds have call provisions that allow the issuers to call the bonds (redeem them). The call price is often specified to be par, which would not be attractive to investors who hold bonds that paid higher rates than currently available in the market since these bonds would have an actual value in excess of par.

In 1984, the U.S. repealed its withholding taxes and concentrated on stopping tax avoidance through use of bearer bonds—the form in which most Eurobonds were issued.

In order to issue bearer securities that are free of withholding taxes, U.S. issuers must now comply with three separate, but interrelated, sets of tax rules, that are under three separate statutes: the Tax Equity and Fiscal Responsibility Act of 1982 (TEFRA); the Tax Reform Act 1984 (the TRA); and the Interest and Dividend Tax Compliance Act of 1983 (IDTCA).

The U.S. now imposes a tax on bearer bonds issued by U.S. companies of 1 percent of the face value of the bonds x number of years to maturity unless the following conditions are met: (1) the interest is payable outside the U.S.; (2) a legend on the bond indicates that interest paid on the bonds is subject to U.S. tax; and (3) the bonds are sold under an "arrangement reasonably designed" to ensure the securities are not sold or distributed to U.S. persons. Tax treaties with tax havens cannot be used to avoid bearer bond restrictions since there are no exemptions in those treaties for the bearer bond tax.

Obviously these reforms have abandoned the objective of making sure foreigners do not escape interest payments. This policy must be pursued through other means.

Notes and Questions

1.   Is it true that gross-up would put an investor in the same position as before the imposition of a withholding tax? Assume a French investor has become subject to a Swiss withholding tax of 25 percent, and that a $100 interest payment is grossed up to $133.33. Further assume that France taxes

all income at 50 percent. Finally, posit that France may or may not give French taxpayers a tax credit for Swiss taxes paid.

The EU Withholding Tax

The European Union agreed on June 20, 2000, after years of acrimonious debate, to a framework for tax on the payment of income on savings (deposits) or investments (bonds). The idea was to tackle widespread tax evasion that was facilitated by the use of bearer bonds. At the time, 11 of the 15 member states of the EU did not tax interest on the savings or investments of individuals based in other member states, some say to attract capital. The agreement adopted two tools to deal with this problem. A Member State could require that a minimum tax on European savings or investment could be imposed by paying agents (banks paying out interest for issuers) at source in the form of a 20 percent withholding tax on cross-border payments to individuals within the EU. Alternatively, a Member State could provide that paying agents provide information about the income to their own fiscal authorities, which would pass it on to the tax authorities of the state in which the beneficial owner resided for tax purposes.[32]

The problem for the EU was that the use of either tool could harm some member's financial market. A withholding tax might cause the center of activity for the Eurobond market to move from the U.K to Switzerland or at least pose heavy administrative costs on issuers which could ultimately fall on investors.[33] An exchange of information might end the appeal of a country with strong bank secrecy laws like Luxembourg, where non-residents held 90 percent of all savings accounts. Even if all EU members used these tools, other countries might not and so gain a competitive advantage in financial markets.

The June 2000 agreement addressed these problems by giving authority to the European Commission to negotiate with Switzerland, the U.S., and other key countries acceptance of measures equivalent to information exchange.

The EU gave some consideration to exempting Eurobonds from the proposal. ISMA has noted, however, that Eurobonds are exceedingly difficult to define. They note that "no *universally accepted*, legal definition exists for the term 'Eurobond' itself. Even the markets most basic understanding that a Eurobond is a bond issued outside the home market of its currency has been thrown into question with the introduction of the Euro. ..."[34]

---

[32] J. Kirwin, "EU States Agree to Long-Term Framework for Cross-Border Tax on Savings Income," BNA Banking Report (June 26, 2000), p. 1173.
[33] R. Baron, *Serious Damage: The Impact of the Withholding Tax on the City of London* (Centre for Policy Studies, 1999). ISMA, *The May 1998 Proposal for the Taxation of Cross-border Interest Payments,* Circular No. 3 (1999).
[34] Id., at 12.

In November 2000, the EU grandfathered all Eurobonds in circulation before March 1, 2001, exempting them from the 20 percent tax that could be imposed in 2003. It was not clear, however, if the exemption applied to bonds circulating before the cut-off date but later increased by the issuer. Sovereign borrowers often increase outstanding bonds rather than issue new ones in order to take advantage of the liquidity of the existing security.[35]

The EU found it very difficult to reach an accommodation with the Swiss. After a long stand-off, on January 21, 2003, the EU finance ministers announced the principles for an arrangement that the Swiss approved. The twelve EU members without bank secrecy laws would share information automatically with each other about each other's citizen's deposits in their country. The three EU members with bank secrecy laws—Austria, Belgium, and Luxembourg—could keep their laws as long as Switzerland had its bank secrecy laws. The three would, however, levy a 15 percent withholding tax on the interest due residents of other EU countries. For these three, the tax would rise to 20 percent in 2007 and 35 percent from 2011. These three countries would transfer 75 percent of the tax withheld to the home governments of the account holders, and keep the remainder.[36] This was formalized in a Council Directive of June 3, 2003.[37]

Switzerland said it would do the same as the three EU countries. It would assess withholding tax on interest due to individual residents of EU countries, at first 15 percent, then 20 percent in 2007, and 35 percent from 2001. Banks and brokers as paying agents, rather than account holders, would collect and pay the tax to the Swiss government. Switzerland would transfer 75 percent of these receipts to the appropriate EU governments, the same ratios as the three Member States. It would not share revenues from withholding tax on domestic interest or dividends. It would share information only on request bilaterally, as before.[38]

The outcome was second best. Information sharing was a more effective way to stymie tax evasion than sharing withholding tax but the compromise allowed Austria, Belgium, and Luxembourg a veto over whether to share information down the road, even if Switzerland, other European tax havens, and the U.S. were all sharing information on request. The major practical problem was that other tax havens, such as Hong Kong, the Bahamas, or Panama, were not included in the arrangement. Funds could simply shift to them. But if other countries do agree with the 12 to share

---

[35] P. Norman and V. Boland, "EU Finance Ministers Reach Deal on Savings Tax," *Financial Times*, November 28, 2000, and A. Ostrovsky, "Sovereigns Wrong-Footed by Withholding Tax Change," *Financial Times*, March 2, 2001.

[36] P. Meller, "Europe Acts on Secrecy in Banking," *The New York Times*, January 22, 2003.

[37] 2003/48/EC.

[38] "EU Officials Target Non-Resident Savings," Swissinfo, January 24, 2003; Swiss Federal Department of Finance, Taxation of Savings, www.efd.admin.ch, June 5, 2003.

information automatically, the compromise will be seen as a valid first step.[39] The agreement between the EU and Switzerland becomes effective on July 1, 2005.

Notes and Questions

1.   What do you think of the EU approach to withholding taxes? It appears the EU-Swiss Agreement does not cover derivatives. Can deposit and bond transactions be restructured as derivatives to avoid the tax?

5.   GLOBAL BONDS

A study by D. Miller and J. Puthenpurackal has collected some useful information about the use and cost of issuing Global bonds.[40] Global bonds are debt instruments that are sold in large offerings simultaneously in multiple markets at the same offer price unlike the typical Eurobond issue that is sold only in London. The first Global bond was issued by the World Bank in 1989 and the first U.S. Global bond was issued by Walt Disney in 1996. They are often offered in multiple tranches of differing size and maturity. Since part of the issue is placed in the U.S., Global bonds must be registered with the SEC. They are the counterpart to Global Depositary Shares discussed in Chapter 2. Unlike the shares, however, the bonds have significant use.

Each Global bond is deposited with the Depositary Trust Company (DTC) and DTC is the only registered owner. Purchasers of bonds in the U.S. must go through DTC while purchasers abroad can go through international clearers like Euroclear or Clearstream that in turn hold the bond through their DTC depositaries. Global bonds trade and settle like home market instruments from the perspective of investors. So Euromarket investors trade and settle Global bonds just like Eurobonds and U.S. investors trade and settle them just like U.S. bonds. A Euromarket investor wishing to trade a U.S. bond would have to open an account with a new broker/dealer that had an account at DTC, whereas such an investor in Global bonds does not incur this additional transaction cost.

Cross-market trades in Global bonds, a U.S. investor trading with a Euromarket investor occur as follows. the U.S. investor would conduct the transaction through DTC while the Euromarket investor would use the DTC depositary of Euroclear or Clearstream. This integrated settlement process also lowers transaction costs.

Using a sample of 230 Global bond issues of 94 companies from the U.S. and abroad from 1996 to 2003, a study found that firms were able to lower their cost of debt capital by about 20 basis points by issuing these

---

[39] D. Spencer, "EU Agrees at Last on Savings" Journal of International Taxation (May 2003), p. 6.
[40] "Security Fungibility and the Cost of Capital: Evidence From Global Bonds," European Bank Working Paper Series 426 (January 2005).

securities. The benefit arises out of increased liquidity from a large offering of fungible securities and lower issuing costs.

CONCLUSIONS

The Eurodollar markets in deposits, loans and bonds, serve an important function in the international financial system, permitting transactions to take place, under a more liberal legal and regulatory regime, than might occur in the home countries of the transactors. This is not only important to the transactors themselves, but the existence of the market serves to constrain local authorities who wish to compete with the Euromarkets.

While these markets have obvious benefits, there are also significant costs. First, they may be used to evade taxes. Here the concern is more with offshore booking centers like the Grand Caymans than offshore transactional markets like London. The EU has tried to deal with this problem within the EU, and between the EU and Switzerland, but other offshore alternatives remain. In addition, these markets (particularly the booking centers) may be used for other criminal activity such as money laundering and the financing of terrorism, subjects taken up in Chapter 21.

CHAPTER TWELVE

ASSET SECURITIZATION

A. INTRODUCTION

This Chapter examines the securitization of loans. Traditional securitization occurs when a pool of loans, whether mortgage loans or credit card receivables, is created and then securities representing interests in this pool are sold. This activity differs from other forms of securitization, such as substituting securities for loans, as when a borrower shifts from bank credit to commercial paper (CP), or decomposing a large standard bank loan into loan participations.[1]

The purchase of these pooled assets is funded, according to Morrison,[2] by issuing investment grade securities that are:

> "primarily serviced by the cash flows of a discrete pool of receivables or other financial assets, either fixed or revolving, that by their terms convert into cash within a finite time period plus any rights or other assets designed to assure the servicing or timely distribution of proceeds to the security holders."

The U.S. Federal Reserve Board Handbook on Compliance, Section 4030.1—Asset Securitization states:

> "While the objectives of securitization may vary from institution to institution, there are essentially five benefits that can be derived from securitized transactions. First, the sale of assets may reduce regulatory costs. The removal of an asset from an institution's books reduces capital requirements and reserve requirements on the deposits funding the asset. Second, securitization provides originators with an additional source of funding or liquidity. The process of securitization basically converts an illiquid asset into a security with greater marketability. Securitized issues often require a credit enhancement, which results in a higher credit rating than what would normally be obtainable by the institution itself. Consequently, these issues may provide the institution with a cheaper form of funding. Third, securitization may be used to reduce interest-rate risk

---

[1] See T. Frankel, *Securitisation* 6 (1991) and *International Securitisation* 5 (H. Morrissey, ed, 1992).

[2] In "Securitisation International Guide," International Financial Law Review (Supp. August 1993), p. 3.

by improving the institution's asset-liability mix. This is especially true if the institution has a large investment in fixed-rate, low-yield assets. Fourth, by removing assets, the institution enhances its return on equity and assets. Finally, the ability to sell these securities worldwide diversifies the institution's funding base, which reduces the bank's dependence on local economies."

The financial industry distinguishes between mortgage-backed securities (MBS) and asset-backed securities (ABS). MBS are securities representing a share in a pool of mortgages. MBS markets are big in the U.S., with amounts outstanding above $1 trillion. Mortgages in the U.S. are mainly single family mortgages, with the remainder split between retail and office mortgages.

ABS, the subject of this Chapter, are securities representing shares in a variety of assets other than mortgages, such as automobile loans, credit card receivables, trade receivables, home equity loans, leases of real property or equipment like airplanes, education loans, junk bonds, boat loans, and even oil or gas reserves. In the U.S., publicly placed ABS issues are estimated to be $225 billion in 2005. Auto and credit card assets will back about 58 percent of all ABS.[3] Very few small business loans were securitized. ABS now appear increasingly in Europe and Japan. The assets employed in ABS transactions are often less standardized than mortgages and therefore may introduce additional complexity.

This Chapter describes cross-border asset securitization in general, including the reasons a firm securitizes and the elements of a securitized transaction. It uses as an example the securitization of the loan receivables of an Australian firm, Broken Hill Proprietary Ltd. (BHP). It presents for comparison the development of the ABS markets in Germany. The Chapter also addresses legal problems common to cross-border ABS. Finally, it summarizes the Basel II rules on capital requirements for ABS.

B.   KEY ISSUES IN STRUCTURING AN OFFERING

Some years ago, the Australian firm BHP securitized loan receivables it held in a cross-border transaction arranged by Deutsche Bank—Germany's largest bank. Based in Melbourne, BHP was Australia's largest publicly-owned company and one of the biggest natural resources companies in the world. While almost 70 percent of its assets were in Australia, BHP had sizable overseas operations in North America, the United Kingdom, South America, and in the Pacific/Oceania region.

BHP had made interest-free loans with a maximum maturity of 20 years to its employees to help them buy BHP stock and options when the

---

[3] JPMorgan, ABS Monitor, June 1, 2005.

company was threatened with an external takeover. Subsequently, the company wanted to remove the loans from its balance sheet in order to replace them with profitable assets and reduce its large U.S. Dollar debt. BHP accomplished this by securitizing these loans. The loans, in Australian dollars, were sold to the Australian unit of a trust in Jersey. A sister unit of the Jersey trust issued Euro-CP to fund the purchase, mainly in Deutschmark (DM) and Dollars, to investors in Europe and Asia. Deutsche Bank supplied many supporting services. The BHP deal was apparently the first of its kind worldwide to securitize loans made to help employees buy company shares. The Euro-CP was backed by BHP employee loans. The schematic illustration in Figure 12.1 below shows the elements of an ABS transaction.

As shown in Figure 12.1, the Corporation originates the assets for the ABS by selling receivables, e.g. from loans, credit cards, or other assets. In the BHP case, BHP sold its employee (Debtors) loan assets. The assets were sold to a Special Purpose Vehicle (SPV), which is a trust or corporation created for the transaction by the originator or a third party, such as a bank. The SPV in the BHP case was Rhein-Main Securitization No. 4 Ltd. (RMS No. 4), an entity based in Australia and part of a group established by Deutsche Bank in the offshore financial center of Jersey.

In a traditional securitization, the SPV pays the originator with funds it receives by issuing securities backed by the cash flow from the assets. In the case of BHP, Rhein-Main Securitization Ltd., a sister unit of RMS No. 4, issued Euro-CP to investors mainly from the Mid-East and Europe and backed by the employee loans. Thus, the first SPV (RMS No. 4) transferred the assets to the second SPV, RMS Ltd., which actually issued the securities to investors. The originator usually services the receivables for a fee, collects principal and interest payments from the debtors, and transfers them to the SPV for the investors. BHP did this. Third parties, usually banks, guarantee the credit and liquidity of the SPV so the securities issued are given a top rating from private credit rating agencies like Standard and Poor's. Deutsche Bank, which had the highest rating available, guaranteed the BHP SPV. Third parties may also provide other services, such as arranging the transaction, underwriting and dealing in the securities where appropriate, acting as trustee, serving as issuer and paying agent, and administering the SPV's activities. Deutsche Bank provided all of these services.

Figure 12.1

Simplified Structure of an ABS Transaction

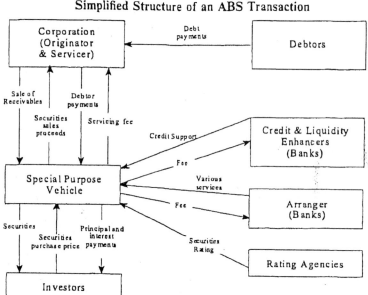

The following sections present the types of assets, or receivables, that are securitized, the characteristics of SPVs, their forms, and the ways in which they and their assets are protected from various claimants such as creditors in bankruptcy and tax collectors. The types of investors and securities are described along with the process for rating the instruments. The BHP securitization illustrates each factor. It is, of course, only one of many types of securitization.

1.   SECURITIZABLE ASSETS

Securitizations often have the following features:

1. Large pool: Scale makes an ABS issue feasible, and permits diversification.

2. Low default rate: High asset quality and small credit risk reduce the financing costs for the ABS.

3. Insensitivity to interest rate changes: The debtors' payments should not be altered by changes in interest rates.

4. Limited prepayment risk: The debtor should not be able to repay the loan prematurely. Prepayment can reduce the interest earned on the receivable for the originator and the SPV and exposes

them to reinvestment risk of the liquidated receivables, which can be particularly damaging if interest rates are falling.

5.   Short maturity: Shorter maturities of the receivables ease management of the interest rate risk.

6.   Relatively homogeneous pools: Similar credit quality, maturity and interest rate profile help to reduce the uncertainty of financial flows.

Not all assets have the above features, so not all are equally amenable to securitization. Mortgages most readily fit the criteria. Indeed, securitization began with mortgages and now over one-third of all mortgages in the U.S. are securitized. Consumer loan receivables, in particular automobile loans and credit card balances, were the first types of assets used for ABS because they meet a number of the requirements. Increasingly, non-consumer receivables are being securitized, particularly trade receivables, leases, and commercial mortgages.

2.   THE SPECIAL PURPOSE VEHICLE

The SPV must have a legal form, own the receivables, manage the cash flows, and be bankruptcy-remote in order to effectuate a successful securitization. This requires a true sale. Its assets cannot be subject to claims of parties other than the investors, e.g. creditors of the originator of the assets. If ownership of assets held by the SPV is not fully transferred to the SPV, then claimants on a bankrupt seller-originator could have a claim on the assets that are supposed to be off the originator's balance sheet and solely securing the funds of the investors in the SPV.

The SPV for BHP's loans was designed by Deutsche Bank for European corporations wishing to securitize assets and for European investors in ABS. The bank set up the Rhein-Main Securitization Group (RMS Group) in Jersey. RMS Group had three characteristics: (1) it was a "multi-seller" vehicle; (2) it issued Euro-CP; and (3) it dealt in multiple currencies. It was a multi-seller because it could simultaneously hold different kinds of assets (receivables) from a variety of corporate originators. These receivables backed the securities issued by the SPV.

The SPV must also be free of tax. The costs of securitization rise if the flow of funds is taxed as it passes through the originator and the SPV before reaching the investor.

In the BHP case, BHP guaranteed that none of the transferred loan receivables were in default and that no legal risks existed with regard to the validity and enforceability of the loan agreement between BHP and the loan debtors.

As part of its acquisition of the loans, RMS No. 4 (and ultimately Deutsche Bank) received the right of recourse to the debtor's employee's BHP stock if the loan debtor defaulted on the repayments. BHP accepted a number of covenants specifying performance indicators for the loans. Historically the employee loans had very high quality, as BHP employees had almost never defaulted. The continuous increase in the value of BHP's stock over the previous 5 years meant that it had outperformed the benchmark Australian All Ordinaries Index by more than 50 percent. In addition, BHP retained the dividends on the employees' shares and credited them to the employees' outstanding loan balance. BHP had a record of over 50 consecutive years of stable or increasing dividend payments.

If BHP broke any covenant, a two-step process would be triggered. During a grace period of three days to one week, BHP would be required to provide updated information to RMS No. 4 and correct the situation. If the problem was not corrected, RMS No. 4 could take a number of steps, the most drastic of which would be to stop buying BHP loans as required by the liquidity and credit enhancement contracts. The portion of the BHP loan portfolio owned by RMS No. 4 would be liquidated, and issuance of CP backed by BHP receivables would stop.

3.   THE FORM OF THE SPV

The SPV can take the legal form of a trust or a corporation. The trust is common in Anglo-American jurisdictions. In civil law countries that lack the trust concept, a separate corporation must be established.

Deutsche Bank set up the RMS Group but held no ownership interest in any of its affiliates. No personnel interlock existed between Deutsche Bank staff and directors and officers of the Rhein-Main Group.

A separate limited liability subsidiary of RMS Group Holding Company was used for each originator, e.g. RMS No. 4 for BHP. Marketing and tax considerations rather than law, accounting rules, or rating agencies prompted this approach. Originators in Europe preferred to separate their asset pool in this way to avoid commingling with other asset pools. Deutsche Bank found that administrative procedures and accounting were easier under this scheme, rather than if multiple pools were held by one company (particularly with pools in different currencies).

However, Deutsche Bank decided not to have each securitization company issue securities itself. Rather, the single issuer, Rhein-Main Securitization Ltd. (RMS Ltd.), was a limited liability company set up under Jersey law. It was managed by a board of directors appointed by its sole shareholder, Rhein-Main Securitization Holding Ltd. It sold securities backed by the assets in all of the separate SPVs. The structure of the overall securitization scheme is set out in the chart below.

Figure 12.2

BHP Securitization

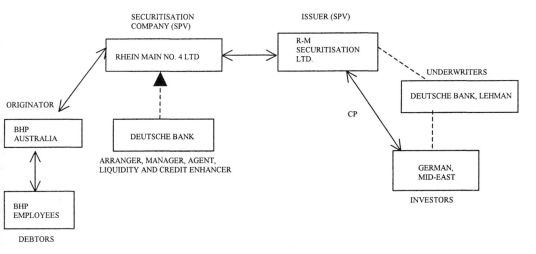

Three basic SPV structures exist:

• *Pass through*: The SPV sells the investor a share or participation representing an undivided pro-rata interest in the pooled assets and a right to a pro-rata share of cash flows. In the U.S., the SPV must take the form of a passive self-liquidating trust that passes the payments directly to the investor without reconfiguring them, if the trust is to escape tax. The investor has a property interest in the assets of the SPV, and its receipts vary with the performance of the SPV.

• *Pay through*: The SPV sells the investor securities that reconfigure the cash flows from the assets, often creating two or more classes of securities. Each class is entitled to payments from the single pool's cash flow, but some classes have seniority (e.g. with rights to the immediate maturities or fixed payments) and other classes are junior (e.g. with rights to the longer maturities or a residual interest). The junior securities act as buffers for the senior security against prepayment and other fluctuations or losses in the cash flows. The senior security is debt, and the junior securities are more like equity. Risk is allocated this way in order to tap investors with different preferences for risk. Sophisticated investors, often institutions, are more able to evaluate the risk of junior securities. In contrast, less sophisticated investors are more likely to take the senior securities. The SPV may offer floating rates or divide interest and principal revenue streams into IOs (interest only) and POs (principal only). The investor's interest is only in the securities issued by the SPV, not the underlying assets, although the investor may take a security interest in those assets as further protection.

• *Collateralized debt*: An originator/issuer sells the investor debt which gives the right to receive a stated interest and principal, independent of the assets' cash flow (but generated by it) and secured by assets that remain on the originator's books.

The RMS/BHP SPVs combined elements of the pass-through and pay-through structures.

4.   BANKRUPTCY REMOTENESS

A critical function of the SPV is to protect the investor from the bankruptcy risk of the originator. The SPV must also be protected from its own bankruptcy. Protection against bankruptcy is accomplished by contractual arrangements, limitations in the SPV's charter, making sure there is a true sale, support by the originator, and credit and liquidity enhancement by third parties.

Contractual and charter protection. An SPV's corporate charter and its contractual arrangements severely limit the activities in which it may engage. Typically, the SPV may incur no debt other than issuing the ABS. In the BHP case, RMS No. 4 was a separate special purpose company that could not incur any material debt other than that relating to the purchase of receivables from the originator. RMS Ltd., the issuer, was a special purpose company that could only incur the debt of the CP it issued (backed by the flow from the receivables). Every party to a contract with the issuer or securitization company had to sign a "no petition" agreement not to file for the issuer's or securitization companies' bankruptcy until one year and one day after all sums outstanding and owing under the latest maturing CP had been paid.

A true sale. In the securitization context, a true sale requires the transfer of all risks and benefits to the purchaser. It must be irrevocable and without recourse. U.S. courts will generally examine the transfer, its documentation, accounting, timing and price to determine whether a true sale occurred. A true sale from the originator to the SPV (and the resulting "corporate separateness" of the SPV) should preclude a court dealing with an originator's bankruptcy from piercing the corporate veil and reclaiming assets transferred to the SPV as a fraudulent conveyance.

In Germany, there were uncertainties concerning true sale treatment so this transaction was structured to use a non-German SPV.

5.   ACCOUNTING TREATMENT

Accounting rules govern whether a transfer of assets to an SPV will be treated as a sale, with the consequence that the transferor (BHP) does not have to account for the transferred assets on its books (i.e. to consolidate the SPV's assets with its own). In the U.S., accounting treatment is governed by the Statement of Financial Accounting Standards No. 140 (FAS 140), issued in September 2000. FAS 140 provides that the transferor has surrendered control over transferred assets if all of the following conditions are met:

a. The transferred assets have been isolated from the transferor—put presumptively beyond the reach of the transferor and its creditors, even in bankruptcy or other receivership.

b. Each transferee (or, if the transferee is a qualifying special-purpose entity (SPE), each holder of its beneficial interests) has the right to pledge or exchange the assets (or beneficial interests) it received, and no condition both constrains the transferee (or holder) from taking advantage of its right to pledge or exchange and provides more than a trivial benefit to the transferor.

c. The transferor does not maintain effective control over the transferred assets through either: (1) an agreement that both entitles and obligates the transferor to repurchase or redeem them before their maturity; or (2) the ability to unilaterally cause the holder to return specific assets, other than through a cleanup call (an option that permits an originating bank or a servicing bank to call the securitization exposures).

As discussed in Chapter 2, in January 2003, in response to Enron, the Financial Accounting Standards Board (FASB) issued Interpretation No. 46 formulating new rules regarding when so-called variable interest entities (VIEs) must be consolidated with another entity. It requires that a company must consolidate a VIE if the company "absorbs a majority of the entity's expected losses, receives a majority of its expected residual returns, or both, as a result of holding variable interests, which are the ownership, contractual or other pecuniary interests in an equity."[4] FASB Interpretation No. 46 specifically excluded from its scope the kinds of securitizations covered by FAS 140, ¶4c. However, the basis for this exclusion was unclear.

In June 2003, FASB issued an Exposure Draft to amend Statement 140 to make it more consistent with its VIE rule under Interpretation No. 46. It is still considering these revisions as of May 2005. Specifically, FASB proposed to prohibit an entity from being a qualifying SPE—and thus to force the consolidation of its assets with those of the transferor if—

> "it enters into an agreement that obligates a transferor, its affiliates, or its agents to deliver additional cash or other assets to fulfill the SPE's obligations to beneficial interest holders (except certain servicing advances and forward contracts to transfer additional financial assets). For example, a qualifying SPE would not be

---

[4] FASB Summary, FASB Interpretation No. 46.

permitted to enter into the following arrangements with a transferor, its affiliates, or its agents:

a. A liquidity commitment, financial guarantee, or other commitment to deliver additional cash or other assets to the SPE or its beneficial interest holders to fulfill the SPE's obligations to its beneficial interest holders.

b. A total return swap, other derivative instrument, or other arrangement requiring delivery of assets to a qualifying SPE."

In addition, this proposed FASB Statement would prohibit a qualifying SPE that can reissue beneficial interests [securities] from holding liquidity commitments, financial guarantees, or other commitments that entitle it to receive assets in addition to the original transfer if necessary to fulfill obligations to beneficial interest holders unless:

a. No party (including affiliates or agents) provides a commitment with a fair value that is more than half the aggregate fair value of all such commitments.

b. No party (including affiliates or agents) that makes decisions about reissuing beneficial interests provides such a commitment.

c. No party (including affiliates or agents) that holds beneficial interests that are not the most senior in priority provides such a commitment.

The International Accounting Standard's Board's (IASB) rules are less complicated than those of FASB, reflecting IASB's more "principle" based approach. IAS 27 requires a company (a parent) to consolidate the statements of all enterprises "controlled" by the parent. Control is presumed when the parent has more than one-half the voting power of an enterprise. But even if there is less than one-half of the voting power, control will exist, ¶12, when the parent maintains:

(a) power over more than one half of the voting rights by virtue of an agreement with other investors;

(b) power to govern the financial and operating policies of the enterprise under a statute or an agreement;

(c) power to appoint or remove the majority of the members of the board of directors or equivalent governing body; or

(d) power to cast the majority of votes at meetings of the board of directors or equivalent governing body.

IAS 27 is supplemented by SIC-12 (Standing Interpretations Committee), applicable to an SPE, which is defined as "an entity ... created to accomplish a narrow or well-defined objective. ..." SIC-12 provides that an SPE should be consolidated when "the substance of the relationship between an enterprise and the SPE indicates that the SPE is controlled." The following circumstances are identified, ¶10, which may indicate control:

(a) in substance, the activities of the SPE are being conducted on behalf of the enterprise according to its specific business needs so that the enterprise obtains benefits from the SPE's operation;

(b) in substance, the enterprise has the decision-making powers to obtain the majority of the benefits of the activities of the SPE or, by setting up an "autopilot" mechanism, the enterprise has delegated these decision making powers;

(c) in substance, the enterprise has rights to obtain the majority of the benefits of the SPE and therefore may be exposed to risks incident to the activities of the SPE; or

(d) in substance, the enterprise retains the majority of the residual or ownership risks related to the SPE or its assets in order to obtain benefits from its activities.

6.   TAXATION

International asset securitizations are structured to minimize taxation of the receivables transfer and the cash flows between the debtor, SPV, and investors. The tax applicable to each party depends on the jurisdiction in which each is located for tax purposes.

The receivables transfer may generate a sales tax or force the originator or SPV to recognize a gain or loss. Some countries levy a registration or stamp duty on the originator's sale. When the purchase price exceeds the face value of the asset, gain may be taxed as income to the originator, and a loss would also be recognizable. Some countries, including the U.K., use the fair market value of the receivables rather than their face value to determine gains and losses.

Australia taxes the transfer of interest-bearing securities whenever the sale is to a non-resident. This is a form of sales tax. Returning to the BHP case, in order to avoid this unfavorable Australian tax treatment, the Jersey-based RMS Group incorporated its subsidiary RMS No. 4 in Australia. This entity was established with the sole purpose to buy the BHP employee loans. Australian law governed the contract between RMS No. 4 and BHP, including the transfer of the loan receivables. Selling to an Australian entity avoided the Australian transfer tax.

Some countries withhold tax on interest payments in general or if the payments leave the country, but many countries do not. The ABS transaction would be structured to avoid withholding tax on interest paid either by the debtors to the SPV or by the SPV to the investors. Cross-border payments often find relief in double tax treaties between the affected countries.

To avoid double taxation, the SPV must be designed to avoid treatment as a corporate entity for tax purposes. The U.S., U.K., and France permit tax-exempt trusts or trust-like SPVs. Otherwise, a tax haven like the Cayman Islands serves the purpose, although some havens lack double taxation treaties. Competition among tax havens leads them to strengthen the infrastructure for securitizations. The Cayman Islands, for example, launched a stock exchange in January 1998 that lists many structured debt securities, such as collateralized bond or loan obligations.[5] Concern about possible abuse led the U.S. Internal Revenue Service to propose rules that would restrict the activities and arrangements of Financial Asset Securitization Investment Trusts.[6]

7. CREDIT, LIQUIDITY, AND OTHER ENHANCEMENTS

Investors usually demand very high investment grade securities in an ABS. The assets themselves do not earn this grade without enhancements that reduce risks of credit, liquidity, currency, and prepayment.

Credit enhancement reduces the risk of default by the debtors on the underlying assets. It is based on the historical performance of the receivables and usually covers between 5 percent and 20 percent of the outstanding receivables. It may be provided internally, by extra collateral or by third party guarantors. Over-collateralization sets the nominal amount of the receivables above the nominal value of the ABS issued, in order to provide a buffer against debtor default. A spread account accumulates differences in the interest rates on the receivables and the lower rate on the ABS in a reserve to offset debtor defaults. A senior/subordinated debt structure protects the senior securities. In many securitizations, the underwriters or dealers of the security agree to buy the complete subordinated tranche. Third parties, usually banks or insurers, provide unconditional guarantees, such as irrevocable standby letters of credit, on which the SPV can draw if debtors default.

In the BHP case, the RMS credit enhancement applied to non-performing receivables. It consisted of a standby letter of credit provided by Deutsche Bank in the amount of 5 percent of the pool of outstanding receivables in the BHP securitization.

Liquidity enhancement reduces the risk that a failure by the servicer to transfer the debtors' payment to the SPV on time might prevent ABS investors from being paid. Liquidity may be enhanced by the same internal techniques as credit enhancement (over-collateralization, spread account, etc.) or by third party guarantees. These techniques bridge the

---

[5] See A. Nealon, "Cayman Rules for Listing Structured Bonds," 17 International Financial Law Review (December 1998), pp. 52-54.
[6] C. Adelman, "FASITs Pose New Challenges in U.S. Structured Finance," 19 International Financial Law Review (May 2000), pp. 12-16.

timing differences between the due dates of the ABS and the receipt of payments from the debtors.

In the BHP case, RMS No. 4 had a liquidity facility to ensure that payments were made in full to the investors when they fell due as long as the assets met the quality standards. A syndicate of banks led by Deutsche Bank covered fully any shortfalls in the payment stream due to timing differences.

The liquidity facility for RMS No. 4 supported only performing receivables; such receivables could not be in default or more than a certain number of days past due. The liquidity banks would pay, in the same currency as the receivables, advances due to RMS No. 4, which would then transfer the funds to the SPV securities issuer. The liquidity facility addressed three other risks:

1. Commingling: As it serviced the receivables, the originator received the payments by the debtors and usually deposited these payments in the same bank accounts used for receipts from non-securitized receivables. In the originator's bankruptcy, it could be extremely difficult to separate these funds. The liquidity banks would fund the amounts due until the payments on receivables were credited to the securitization company's bank account.

2. Dilution: even if the originator's debtors claimed set-off, trade discount, or other reductions in their payments due, the originator was obliged to pay the securitization company the full amount owed, but the liquidity banks would pay if the originator failed to do so.

3. Invalid assignment: if the transfer of the receivables to the securitization company was invalid or contested, the liquidity banks would provide the funds.

Currency risk hedging in international asset securitizations shields the investors from exchange rate movements against the currency of the receivables and the ABS. Third parties, usually banks, provide foreign exchange or currency swap agreements.

In the BHP case, RMS No. 4 had to hedge fully the currency risk in a cross-currency securitization by entering into short-term foreign exchange agreements or long-term currency swaps with highly rated counterparties such as Deutsche Bank. These transactions hedged the effect of a mismatch between the currencies of the outstanding CP and those of the receivables in the securitized pool.

An adverse change in interest rates had the same consequences as the exchange rate movement by increasing the effective interest rate on future CP issues, and therefore the cost of funding, over RMS No. 4's projection at the time of purchase. Unless there was a sufficient reserve to cover all interest due on the outstanding CP, the stop-issuance mechanism prevented the issuance of a new tranche of securities.

Other enhancements. Receivables with a longer maturity, such as mortgages or automobile loans, usually carry a prepayment risk. Many investors look for a predictable cash flow. They seek payment at a known date because they need funds specifically at that time. Institutional investors, such as pension funds or insurers, forecast their funding requirements and gear the maturity of their assets to these needs. For such investors, one risk is that the debtors may fully repay their debt before the end of the contracted period. In a falling interest rate environment, premature liquidation of the receivables exposes the SPV to reinvestment risk, i.e. the repaid funds can only be reinvested at lower rates of return. Enhancements may protect against these risks.

8.   INVESTORS AND THE TYPES OF ASSET BACKED SECURITIES (ABSs)

The size and characteristics of the targeted investor group largely determine the form of the ABS. Investors in ABSs tend to be institutions, particularly in the Euromarkets. These investors are primarily interested in the price, yield, and maturity of the ABS. Rates can be fixed or variable and maturities do not have to correlate with those of the underlying receivables, because the ABSs are in different classes designed to have various maturities and interest rates.

Market liquidity is important to ABS investors. Rather than hold longer-term bonds to maturity, ABS investors usually require an active and liquid secondary market. CP is attractive to this type of investor because its maturities of less than one year reduce funding and credit risk. This allows the investor to accept a lower return, which makes CP attractive to issuers. Investors usually hold CP to term. Since CP are privately placed and do not require a secondary market, the minimum needed for an issue is considerably less; issues of $20 million or even less are feasible.

The Commercial Paper. In the BHP case, the RMS CP were privately placed at a discount and redeemed at par mainly with institutional investors in Germany (40 percent), elsewhere in Europe (25 percent), and in the Middle and Far East. Most of the CP had been in Deutschmark and Eurodollars, but it also included the European currency unit (ECU), Swiss Francs, Canadian Dollars, and Dutch Guilders. The maturity of the CP ranged between seven days and one year, but the bulk of the paper matured in one to three months, and a small percentage matured in six months. While there was no legal requirement to receive a rating in the Euromarket, the CP had a top rating, A-1+/P-1.

RMS Ltd. continuously issued CP backed by the securitization companies' receivables and enhancements. Investors were informed that receivables funded the CP. They did not know all the originators or which pool of receivables backed their CP, though RMS kept track of this information through internal accounting. Overcollateralization of one pool could be used to pay investors in CP issued for another pool. If one pool encountered problems, the credit enhancement contracts with Deutsche Bank allowed the investors the protection of all the bank's letters of credit. CP gave the SPV more flexibility to pool receivables from different originators. Most Eurobond issues created a new issuing company for each pool of receivables.

Regulatory issues affect the form of security. Many jurisdictions require registration and reporting for publicly offered and traded securities. Some securities, like CP and Eurobonds, may be exempt from registration requirements. Institutional investors including insurance companies and pension funds may be limited (by law or their corporate statutes) in the amount or type of a particular class of securities they may buy.

In the BHP case, German law was important to RMS because it placed much of its CP with German investors. The Bundesbank regulated Germany's money market, and it prohibited banks from issuing debt securities with a maturity of less than two years (this included Euro-DM CP). The rule did not extend to non-banks, however, and RMS Ltd. was not considered a bank.[7]

German securities law generally required disclosure of detailed information in a prospectus. The obligation did not apply to CP with a maturity of less than one year or to securities offered only to institutional investors, however. For Eurosecurities, no prospectus was required if the minimum tranche sold to an individual investor was more than DM 80,000.[8] Since the Rhein-Main CP would qualify for an exemption, it had no obligation to publish a prospectus.

Deutsche Bank obtained the informal approval of the other central banks in whose currencies it planned to issue CP. Several selling restrictions applied. In the U.K. and Australia, the CP could be advertised and sold only to institutional investors. In Switzerland, the dealers agreed to comply with any laws, regulations, and guidelines of the Swiss National Bank regarding the offer and sale of the CP. And finally, the CP could not be offered or sold to persons residing in Jersey, as this might affect the income-tax exempt status of the issuer, RMS Ltd.

SEC Regulation AB. In December 2004, the SEC adopted Regulation AB that enacted major changes to the disclosure regime for the

---

[7] This conclusion was reached by analogy to factoring companies whose operations did not fall within the scope of the definition of "banking business" of the German Banking Law (Kreditwesengesetz).

[8] See §2 Law Regarding Securities Prospectuses (Gesetz uber Wertpapier-Verkaufsprospekte vom 13.12.1990).

offer of ABS on the U.S. public market, effective in 2006.[9] AB offerings are quite different from those of corporate securities as they constitute a pool of underlying assets in which the investor has an interest. The investor needs information about the characteristics of the pool as well as the legal structure involved, e.g. the use of SPVs. In the past, the SEC addressed the differences through a patchwork of special rules, no action letters and informal guidance.

The SEC's ABS rules begin by supplying a definition of ABS to which the rules apply: "a security that is primarily serviced by the cash flows of a discreet pool of receivables or other financial assets, either fixed or revolving, that by their terms convert into cash within a finite period of time, plus any rights or other assets designed to assure the servicing or timely distribution of proceeds to the security holders. ..."[10] The SEC disclosure requirements relate to the background, experience, performance and role of the parties, as well as to historical performance data about the asset pools. No special rules exist for foreign issuers.

With respect to the portfolio, the historical data required is referred to as "static pool data," and this was an area that was heavily commented on by industry in the proposal stage. This information has typically been viewed as confidential and only supplied to ratings agencies. Such data can be provided via and Internet website

9.   RATINGS

Investors require the SPV to get independent ratings of its securities. As a separate legal entity without deep pockets, the SPV lacks the reputation of a large corporation and typically cannot rely on its name. The complex technical detail in an asset securitization means that rating agencies offer a quick professional estimate about the quality of the issuer at significant savings to potential investors.

A rating is an opinion about the ability and obligation of the SPV to make full and timely payments on the security. Standards vary for short-term (less than one year) and long-term securities. Rating agencies, which are paid by the SPV, generally examine five types of risk: debtors' credit risk; operational risks of payments among all parties; legal and tax risks for the receivables and securities; risk that any party will not perform; and sovereign risk.

Notes and Questions

1.   Why securitize? What are the costs and benefits of securitization to the originator?

2.   Concerning bankruptcy remoteness:

---

[9] Release Nos. 33-8518; 34-5095, December 22, 2004.
[10] 17 C.F.R. §229.1101(c)(1).

a.   Why is it important to rely on asset quality rather than the originator's creditworthiness?

b.   How would relying on asset quality facilitate international transactions in ABS?

c.   How important would the originator's home country be in asset securitization? Would it matter if the country was Australia or Zambia?

d.   When a bank originates assets, it is important to the investors that the SPV be remote from the bank. What reasons would the bank have to be sure the SPV was remote?

e.   Under what circumstances should a court recharacterize a sale of assets? Suppose the seller guarantees the collection of all the receivables. Canadian courts take the view "that the retention of significant risk by the seller ... should not compromise a lawyer's ability to provide a clean true sale opinion. ... Where the parties' intention to sell assets is clearly evidenced ..., the courts will not recharacterize the transaction. ..."[11]

3.   Why are credit, liquidity, and other enhancements necessary if the quality of the assets is kept so high? Who benefits from the use of enhancements?

4.   How important are rating agencies for securitization? Why? Could securitization take place in countries that lack rating agencies? What are the alternatives to ratings?

C.   THE DEVELOPMENT OF NATIONAL ABS MARKETS IN GERMANY AND EUROPE

This section focuses on the development of securitization in Germany and Europe. The U.S. led the way in the development of a securitization industry. Germany lagged, then pushed through reforms in the late 1990s and addressed problems posed by, among other things, its code law system.

ABS markets in Europe are smaller than those in the U.S.; they grew more slowly until the mid-1990s, at which point their development surged. From less than 10 percent of the size of the U.S. market in 1995, the

---

[11] M. Fingerhut, "Securitization Takes Off in Canada," International Financial Law Review (November 2000), p. 39.

European ABS markets grew to 40 percent by 1999.[12] Asset backed bond issues grew 29 percent in 2002 to reach $370 billion.[13]

National ABS markets in Europe grew at varying speeds. From the late 1980s, the U.K. dominated in Europe though its share fell to about 50 percent of all structured issues in 2000. In the mid-1990s, France ranked second and Italy third. Germany rose from a trivial 0.1 percent of all ABS issues to second place by the end of the decade, accounting for 13 percent in mid-2000, and then retreated to fifth place in 2002. Anticipating the Euro, several countries streamlined their markets, including France, Italy, and Spain. Germany followed a bit later.

1.   PFANDBRIEFE

In Germany, a debt security called the Pfandbriefe, in existence since 1769, has been a major financing tool for mortgage banks which are governed by a special mortgage banking law. Many of the mortgage banks are owned by the big German universal banks. The Pfandbriefe allows the mortgage bank to refinance long-term mortgage loans by selling interests in a pool of such loans on the bank's books to investors. Pfandbriefe are collateralized by the bank's pool of mortgages, but no specific mortgages back particular Pfandbriefe. Strict loan-to-value limits and tight regulatory supervision minimize the risk of these securities, and they bear no prepayment risk. The law required the volume and interest rate of the mortgage loans on the bank's books to be at least as high as those of the Pfandbriefe, to protect the investors. If the mortgage bank defaulted, the Pfandbriefe investors might have recourse to the bank's other assets. Institutional investors like insurance companies were subject to no ceiling on their holdings of Pfandbriefe, which counted toward the insurers' mandated coverage ratios. Big German universal banks were major investors in Pfandbriefe. Thus they could be on both sides of the transaction.

German Pfandbriefe became increasingly popular among foreign investors in the mid-1990s. They were issued in various currencies, including French Francs, U.S. Dollars, and Euros. By early 1999 when jumbos were redenominated in Euros, outstanding Pfandbriefe equaled $1.1 trillion. From 2001, however, the market softened.[14]

---

[12] A. Sharma and H. Paris, "Securitisation in Emerging Markets: A Development Opportunity," International Finance Corporation Development Paper (February 2001), p. 6.

[13] A. van Duyn and J. Chaffin, "Asset-Backed Bonds Set for Year of Growth," *Financial Times*, January 26, 2001; A. van Duyn, "Securitised Market Grows in Europe," *Financial Times*, January 21, 2003.

[14] See U. Harnischfeger, "Pfandbriefe Success Encourages Imitators," *Financial Times*, April 15, 1999; "German Pfandbriefe: Rising to the Challenge," Guide to European Mortgage Bonds Euromoney (June 2002), p. 6.

2.   OTHER TYPES OF SECURITIZATIONS

Other types of securitization in Germany include auto loans, credit card and other consumer loans, and public sector receivables. None of these were securitized in Germany until mid-1998.

a.   HISTORICAL LIMITS

Captive finance companies of car manufacturers supply many of the auto loans in Germany. The spreads on auto loans are very narrow, since financing is an important marketing tool.

Credit cards were introduced in Germany in the mid-1980s, but were only modestly used at first. Consumer loans were plentiful. Most purchases they funded were subject to guaranty and warranty periods of at least 6 months for the goods purchased. If the goods were inadequate, the consumer could refuse to pay the loan, exchange the goods, or lower the purchase price. This made it difficult to securitize the loan.

The large infrastructure projects in East Germany after reunification in 1990 and the ensuing budget crisis prompted debate about public finance. One suggestion was to securitize public sector receivables from infrastructure projects like interstate highways and sewage treatment. Most Germans were skeptical about this proposal.

German receivables could be securitized through SPVs abroad. Some domestic car manufacturers in Germany securitized their North American receivables through ABS-programs in the U.S. For example, Daimler Benz of North America issued two public ABS totaling $1.2 billion, and Volkswagen and BMW securitized through U.S. issues. German corporations were reluctant to sell their receivables, as doing so still carries the stigma of a last resort financing effort by companies in financial distress.

German banks comfortably exceeded the minimum capital ratios prescribed by the capital adequacy rules. Until 1997, the Federal Banking Supervisory Office, which regulates banks, opposed the securitization of bank loans, citing residual legal or moral recourse risk which would not be reflected in the bank's balance sheets undertaking securitization transactions. The only publicly known transaction of this sort in Germany, a securitization of consumer loans by Citibank's German subsidiary KKB Bank via an SPV in the Cayman Islands in 1990, was apparently not prohibited only because the regulators learned about it too late to stop it. While no formal opinion, law, or regulation prohibited banks from securitizing their loans, the bank regulators repeatedly stated their serious concerns about such transactions.

b.   MORE RECENT INITIATIVES

A basic shift in government policy in Germany preceded the take-off of the country's ABS market in the late 1990s. In May 1997, Germany's

Banking Supervisory Office issued the "Circular Regarding the Sale of Customer Receivables of Credit Institutions in Connection with ABS Transactions." Advisory rather than with the binding force of law, the circular explained how lenders could remove receivables from their balance sheet (for purposes of determining required capital) and how bank secrecy rules could be respected when receivables were transferred as part of an ABS. The circular required a true sale, no recourse, no substitution of receivables, and limited repurchase of receivables. It limited the originator's ability to finance the SPV as well as its moral obligation for the receivables. In September 1997, the Supervisory Office issued another circular which permitted banks to repackage sovereign and quasi-sovereign loans for OECD countries and, to a limited extent, other countries. A new German Insolvency Code, which took effect at the start of 1999, clarified the rights in bankruptcy of the liquidator against assigned assets, but excluded true sales used to create ABS.[15] In 2003 SPVs were exempted from trade tax obligations.[16] In November 2004, the problems seem solved as the first ABS transaction with a German SPV was used. It was, in fact, called a true sale securitzation and has spawned a true sale securitization market in Germany.[17]

A year after the governmental initiative to promote ABS started, German banks began to issue MBS and to use their own commercial loans as receivables. In April 1998, Dresdner Bank issued a DM2 billion ABS using CP and medium-term notes. Dresdner was allowed to provide liquidity to the SPV. Deutsche Bank issued a DM1.4 billion ($800 million) MBS one month later and an ABS three months later. The MBS broke new ground in Europe with an unrated tranche and interest-only tranches. The ABS attracted investors by offering a way for them to take positions in German corporations, since Germany's bond market was undeveloped. One estimate put the potential German MBS market at over $10 billion annually if banks merely securitized 5 percent of outstanding mortgages each year. Even the mortgage banks that offer Pfandbriefe securitized as well. Their governing law limits their use of mortgages to back their *Pfandbriefe* to 60 percent of their total mortgages.

Germany also turned to securitization in bank-government partnerships to strengthen the financial sector. Five large German banks working with the government set up a securitization vehicle in 2003 to receive up to $50 billion of their good loans, largely made to small and medium-sized enterprises (SMEs), and to issue bonds. The state-owned Kreditanstalt für Wiederaufbau (KfW) would run the pool. KfW's triple A rating and tax-free operation would reduce costs. Banks with high funding costs would get access to new funds. The government also hoped this would

---

[15] E. Reudelhuber, "The Issuance of Asset-Backed Securities by Credit Institutions in Germany, Part 2," Butterworths Journal of International Banking and Financial Law (March 1998), p. 98.
[16] A. van Duyn, "German Banks Kick-Start ABS," *Financial Times*, May 6, 2003.
[17] Joint Press Release of ABN-AMRO and Volkswagen Bank GMBH, November 15, 2004.

free bank capital for more lending to SMEs, which were short on credit, as the economy slowed. This would also promote the market's development.[18]

The different laws governing securitization among European countries hindered the market's development. Major banks set up the European Securitization Forum, which published *A Framework for European Securitization* (May 2002) to help their countries work towards a common legal approach needed for a Continental market. Although it stopped short of proposing changes for law in individual countries, nevertheless the Framework set guidelines that countries could follow in many areas, including: origination; sale; transfer and isolation of assets; ownership; data protection and banking secrecy; vehicles; bankruptcy; enhancement; tax; accounting; regulatory treatment; listing and reporting; and investors' rights.

Notes and Questions

1.   What explains the late development of the German markets for MBS and ABS?

2.   How close a substitute for an MBS is the Pfandbriefe? Are they identical? If not, are the differences important?

3.   German banks are universal banks supplying most corporate finance in the form of commercial loans. German capital markets have been traditionally weak compared to those of the U.S. or U.K. How would this affect the development of the German ABS market?

D.   LEGAL ISSUES FOR CROSS-BORDER ABS

An ABS may involve a cross-border transaction in various ways. For example, the originator may be in one country and those receiving the proceeds may be in another. The SPV company or trust may be in a different country than the assets, or the assets may be in one currency, while payments to investors are made in another.

Cross-border securitization brings several benefits to the parties to the transaction and to their economies, according to Tamar Frankel.[19] By disaggregating functions across countries, Frankel says, the parties can structure the transaction so that each stage can be performed in the country where it can be done most efficiently or most cheaply. Of course, she adds, a country must manage the downside, meaning that cross-border securitization also may facilitate avoidance of regulation, taxes, and exchange restrictions.

---

[18] M. Landler, "5 Big Banks in Germany in Loan Pool," *The New York Times*, April 13, 2003; A. van Duyn, "German Banks Kick-Start ABS," *Financial Times*, May 6, 2003.

[19] "Cross-Border Securitisation: Without Law, But Not Lawless," 8 Duke Journal of Comparative & International Law (1998), pp. 255, 265.

Some complex issues involving the applicable law arise in cross-border ABS transactions. The issues are relatively straightforward for matters involving the contractual relations between the investors and the SPV that issues the securities to them, as the security itself can usually designate the applicable law. More difficult matters arise, however, which involve the investors' and the SPV's ownership rights in the assets. For example, a major potential trap for the SPV, the investors, and the trustee occurs when the originator continues to manage most assets. In this scenario, the receivables' obligors continue to pay the originator, not the SPV directly, and the originator could convey multiple interests in the same asset.

The problems for proprietary interests arise at two levels in the ABS transaction. First, at the Originator/SPV level, the SPV's interests in the assets provided by the originator must be fully protected from claims by others with a possible interest in them. Second, at the SPV/investor level, the investors' interests in the assets taken by the SPV must be protected as well.

It can be difficult to identify which jurisdiction's law applies at either level. Suppose, for example, that a covenant against liens is in a loan agreement governed by English law but the originator is located in Mexico, whose own law may govern the lien. What law should govern? Should it be the law where the receivable is located, the law of the contract creating the receivable, the law where the assignor is located, or the law where the obligor is located? The challenge is magnified when receivables or obligors are located in many jurisdictions.[20]

E.   CAPITAL ADEQUACY RULES FOR ABS

In June 2004, the Basel Committee issued its new capital rules, including requirements for ABS.[21] These rules, in general, are discussed in Chapter 7. The ABS rules apply to both traditional and synthetic securitizations. Traditional securitizations are discussed in this Chapter, while synthetic securitizations, such as credit derivatives, are discussed in Chapter 15 on swaps.

Basel II lays out the criteria, called "operational requirements," needed to transfer assets effectively from the originating bank's books so that the originating bank does not need to hold capital against them. These operational requirements apply to both the standardized and IRB approaches.

---

[20] See S. Bazinas, "An International Legal Regime for Receivables Financing: UNCITRAL's Contribution," 8 Duke Journal of Comparative & International Law (1998), p. 315.

[21] Basel Committee on Banking Supervision, *International Convergence of Capital Measurement and Capital Standards*: A Revised Framework (June 2004).

1.   OPERATIONAL REQUIREMENTS

Basel II, ¶554, sets out the following operational requirements:

(a) Significant credit risk associated with the securitized exposures has been transferred to third parties.

(b) The transferor does not maintain effective or indirect control over the transferred exposures. The assets are legally isolated from the transferor in such a way (e.g. through the sale of assets or through subparticipation) that the exposures are put beyond the reach of the transferor and its creditors, even in bankruptcy or receivership. These conditions must be supported by an opinion provided by qualified legal counsel.

The transferor is deemed to have maintained effective control over the transferred credit risk exposures if it: (i) is able to repurchase from the transferee the previously transferred exposures in order to realize their benefits; or (ii) is obligated to retain the risk of the transferred exposures. The transferor's retention of servicing rights to the exposures will not necessarily constitute indirect control of the exposures.

(c) The securities issued are not obligations of the transferor. Thus, investors purchasing the securities only have a claim to the underlying pool of exposures.

(d) The transferee is an SPE and the holders of the beneficial interests in that entity have the right to pledge or exchange them without restriction.

(e) Clean-up calls (an option that permits an originating bank or a servicing bank to call the securitization exposures (e.g. ABS) before all of the underlying exposures have been repaid) must satisfy [certain conditions].

(f) The securitization does not contain clauses that (i) require the originating bank to alter systematically the underlying exposures such that the pool's weighted average credit quality is improved unless this is achieved by selling assets to independent and unaffiliated third parties at market prices; (ii) allow for increases in a retained first loss position or credit enhancement provided by the originating bank after the transaction's inception; or (iii) increase the yield payable to parties other than the originating bank, such as investors and third-party providers of credit enhancements, in response to a deterioration in the credit quality of the underlying pool.

2.   STANDARDIZED APPROACH[22]

Banks using the standardized approach for the underlying exposures must use the standardized approach for securitization exposures.

In general, originators that provide credit enhancement at the outset of securitization must hold the same amount of capital as if the assets were held on the balance sheet.

When banks invest in securitized assets, the standardized approach determines capital by risk weights for securities issued by the SPV based on external ratings. Banks must use this standardized approach if they apply the standardized approach to the credit risk of the underlying, or securitized, asset. The risk weights vary with maturity and quality of the credit rating. For long-term exposures, weights are 20 percent (for securitization exposures rated AAA to AA-), 50 percent (A+ to A-), 100 percent (BBB+ to BBB-), 350 percent (BB+ to BB-), and B+ and below or unrated, a deduction of the amount of the asset from capital (generally 50 percent from Tier I and 50 percent from Tier II.

For short-term exposures, weights are 20 percent (A-1/P-1), 50 percent (A-2/P-2), 100 percent (A-3/P-3). All other ratings (including unrated) must be deducted from capital.

Although the value of unrated assets is normally deducted from regulatory capital, an exception is made for the most senior tranche. For this tranche, the bank can use the average risk weight of the underlying asset, if it is known to the bank (this is also known as the look through approach). If the bank cannot determine the risk weights of the underlying assets, the unrated position must be deducted.

The standardized approach also sets more detailed rules for liquidity facilities, instruments mitigating credit risk such as collateral, guarantees, and credit derivatives. These often use the same approach as that provided for non-securitized assets.

3.   IRB APPROACH

Banks using the IRB approach for the underlying exposures must use the IRB approach for securitization exposures.

The maximum capital requirement under IRB is the maximum capital requirement that would have been assessed against the underlying exposures had they not been securitized. Two approaches are provided for

---

[22] As discussed in Chapter 7, U.S. banks will not use the Basel II standardized approach. It is unclear what this means for securitization, given that Basel I contained no provisions on this matter.

IRB, an external ratings-based approach (RBA) if ratings exist or can be implied, or, if not, a supervisory formula (SF).[23]

RBA uses external ratings of the securitized exposure weighted according to the composition of the pool. Each of eleven categories of rating receive three possible risk weights that vary depending on the tranche's seniority and diversification (referred to as granularity) measured by the number of underlying exposures in the asset pool. Weights also vary by maturity. A long-term AAA-rated securitization exposure, for example, has risk weights of 7 percent (senior), 12 percent, or 20 percent (non-diversified).

SF sets capital charge based on supervisory formulas that use inputs the bank supplies, including KIRB (the ratio of the IRB capital requirement on the underlying assets to the exposure amount of the pool), L the credit enhancement level of the tranche (the ratio of (a) all securitization exposures subordinate to the tranche in question to (b) the amount of exposures in the pool), T the "thickness" of exposure (the ratio of the nominal size of a tranche to the notional amount of exposures in the pool), and N, the effective number of exposures in the pool. The SF specifies loss-given default (LGD) and determines how to take account of credit enhancement.

CONCLUSIONS

International asset securitization is an important aspect of the world's international financial system. It permits lenders to manage credit risk by transferring the risk to a wide pool of investors, and it allows the investors to add credit risk to their portfolios. Credit derivatives, examined in Chapter 15, accomplish similar objectives.

Securitization requires an extensive legal and accounting framework. Crucial in this respect is the ability to remove assets from the balance sheet through a transfer to a SPV. Current accounting reforms, in light of Enron, to define true sale have struggled with drawing the line between valid securitization, that can result in deconsolidation, and other forms of transfer that should require consolidation.

Securitization by originating and investing banks will be significantly impacted by the revisions of Basel II. Capital rules, like accounting rules, require a determination of true sale. Reduced capital for securitization will only be provided if the transaction removes risk from the balance sheet of the originating bank. In addition, Basel's methodology for determining the amount of capital for different securitized positions has been subject to significant debate.

---

[23] Another approach, the Internal Assessment Approach, is provided for asset backed commercial paper.

CHAPTER THIRTEEN

STOCK MARKET COMPETITION

One important feature of the world's financial system is increased competition between stock markets (including electronic networks) both within and among countries. Stock markets compete over trading volume in securities. Trading increases the commissions or fees for firms that are members of the market. An important element of trading volume is listings. Listings also produce revenue in their own right; listings can cost as much as $500,000 and $75,000 per year, respectively, on the NYSE and NASDAQ, plus charges for initial listings. The amount of listing revenue reduces transaction fees charged to firms and thus increases their net profit per trade.

Within countries such competition is usually zero-sum, in that issuers are unlikely to list on more than one exchange—although that may be changing. On an international level the issue is more complicated. If an issuer lists on only one exchange, for most companies in the U.S. and Japan that exchange is likely to be in the home country. For European issuers, however, given the variety of exchange choices in a single time zone and the adoption of the Euro, there is active competition for single listings among countries.

Increasingly, major issuers cross-list securities—that is, they list securities on foreign as well as their domestic exchanges. We have already examined the reasons for cross-listing in Chapter 2, but we can add here some further observations. Multiple listings may change the risk characteristics of the securities, e.g. market covariance or beta, making such securities more generally attractive.[1] Cross-listings on either the NYSE or the London Stock Exchange (LSE) seem to be associated with a considerable increase in firm visibility. In effect, cross-listing is a form of advertising.[2]

Cross-listings may also provide increased access to capital when local markets cannot provide enough capital, provide access to a currency (foreign

---

[1] K. Smith and G. Sofianos, "The Impact of an NYSE Listing on the Global Trading of Non-U.S. Stocks," NYSE Working Paper 97-02 (June 1997).
[2] H. Baker, J. Nofsinger, and D. Weaver, "International Cross-Listing and Visibility," NYSE Working Paper 99-01 (January 1999).

stock) for stock-based takeovers, and serve as a means of compensating and motivating executives (e.g. U.S. executives of a foreign firm may find U.S. market stock options attractive). Several studies have found that non-U.S. firms benefit from a U.S. listing by decreasing their cost of capital.[3] Cross-listings may also reflect the desire of issuers to "bond" themselves to more strict disclosure rules and enforcement so as to win the trust of investors.[4]

In some cases, cross-listing results in losses of trading volume in the home country; while in others it increases home country volume as the cross-listing expands the total volume of trading. Cross-listing has triggered competition among exchanges for cross-listings, e.g. the NYSE and the LSE may compete for the foreign listing of a German company, and for the share of volume in cross-listed stocks.

Competition among exchanges may force needed changes in the home country rules and systems. As will be shown later in this Chapter, this has been the story in Europe, where competition between London and the continent has caused dramatic changes in the way the exchanges are operated. Stock market liquidity, which often accompanies growth, is positively correlated with economic growth, capital accumulation and productivity improvements.[5] Thus, countries may have a great interest in the results of stock market competition.

A foreign company that cross-lists in the U.S. may reduce its cost of capital. As discussed in Chapter 2, this may result from the fact that investors have more protection when companies are subject to U.S. rules, for example minority shareholders in takeovers. This assumes that the cross-listing company's home country offers less protection for shareholders than the U.S. This same reasoning underlies the paper of A. Ahearne, W. Griever, and F. Warnock, *Information Costs and Home Bias: An Analysis of U.S. Holdings of Foreign Equities*.[6] They find that the home country bias of U.S. investors to underweight foreign equities in their portfolios—U.S. investors hold an average 12 percent, whereas foreign equities account for about 50 percent of the value of equities worldwide—is significantly due to inadequate disclosure rules in many foreign countries. They show that countries with a greater share of firms that have public U.S. listings, either debt or equity, tend to be less severely underweighted in U.S. equity portfolios.

On the other hand, Chapter 2 details the possible effect of Sarbanes-Oxley in deterring foreign companies from listing in the U.S. and the desire

[3] K. Lins, D. Strickland, and M. Zenner, "Do Non-U.S. Firms Issue Stock on U.S. Equity Markets to Relax Capital Constraints?," Working Paper (November 1999).
[4] See J. Coffee, Jr., "Competition Among Securities Markets: A Path Dependent Perspective," Columbia Law and Economics Working Paper 192 (March 25, 2002).
[5] R. Levine and S. Zervos, "Stock Markets, Banks and Economic Growth," 3 The American Economic Review (1998), p. 537.
[6] Board of Governors of the Federal Reserve System International Finance Paper 691 (December 2000).

of some foreign companies already listed to drop their listings and deregister their securities. This suggests that excessive regulation by a country can so increased a company's cost of capital to make listing on a market in that country unattractive. The decision of the SEC to defer the application of Section 404 of Sarbanes-Oxley to foreign companies reflects the concern of the U.S. about continuing to attract foreign companies to the U.S. market.

A. Licht[7] looks at the case of Israeli companies which list only in the United States and not in Israel. He argues that this may result from managerial opportunism since some disclosure requirements, in particular conflict of interest disclosures, are higher in Israel than for foreign companies listing in the U.S. This is due to the less demanding disclosure standards under SEC Form 20-F for foreign issuers than for domestic issuers with respect to matters of aggregate remuneration and options. As discussed in Chapter 2, these lower standards for foreign issuers were probably adopted on the assumption that such disclosures were not required in the home country, and that requiring them in the U.S. would unduly deter foreign issuers from entering into the U.S. public capital markets. This assumption may not always be the case. Licht does not explain why the market would not penalize Israeli companies through lower stock prices for trying to avoid disclosure of potentially negative information.

When stocks are cross-listed, the question arises as to the relative contribution of trading on each exchange to price discovery. C. Eun and S. Sabherwal[8] find that most price discovery occurs on the exchange where there is higher total trading and medium-sized trades, and is inversely related to the size of the bid-ask spreads. While this study only looked at Canada, one would expect similar results for most stocks cross-listed from Europe, given the high proportion of trades in the home market.

A 1999 study by M. Pulatkonak and G. Sofianos[9] identifies various factors that explain the share of trading of the NYSE and home exchanges in cross-listed stocks. The most important factor is the time zone effect, which explains 40 percent of the variation in U.S. market share. The closer the home exchange is to New York, the greater the NYSE share. Another important factor is whether the stock is from a developed or emerging market. Competing with a developed home market lowers the U.S. market share by 30 percentage points. R. Portes and H. Rey[10] find that market size, efficiency, and geographic proximity are the most important determinants of

---

[7] "Managerial Opportunism and Foreign Listing: Some Direct Evidence," Draft (January 10, 2001).

[8] "Cross-Border Listings and Price Discovery: Evidence from U.S.-Listed Canadian Stocks," LVIII Journal of Finance (2003), p. 549.

[9] "The Distribution of Global Trading in NYSE-Listed and Non-U.S. Stocks," NYSE Working Paper 99-03 (March 1999).

[10] "The Determinants of Cross-Border Equity Flows: The Geography of Information," Working Paper (January 2000).

cross-border purchases and sales of equity. Regulation may also play an important role. U. Bhattacharya and H. Daouk[11] found that of the 103 countries that have stock markets, 87 had insider trading laws, but only 38 had ever enforced them through a prosecution. While the cost of equity in a country did not change after the introduction of insider trading laws, it decreased significantly after the first prosecution.

This Chapter examines the terms and consequences of this competition. It begins by looking at competition in the U.S. market and then turns to a comparison of other major markets.

A.   U.S. MARKET

We begin with a description of the U.S. securities markets. We then turn to competition between the NYSE and NASDAQ, issues of market structure generally, and the effect of circuit breakers.

1.   OVERVIEW OF THE U.S. MARKET

a.   THE USERS OF THE MARKETS

The predominant trend of the past 20 years has been the growth in size and diversity of users of the equity markets. In 1975, institutions owned 30 percent of U.S. equities, but by 1992 they owned slightly more than 50 percent. A joint study of the Investment Company Institute and the Securities Industry Association, Equity Ownership in America (2002), indicates that in 2002 there were 84.3 million individual investors in equities. Many of these individuals appeared to hold equities either in the form of individual stocks inside employer-sponsored retirement funds, 12.3 million, or in the form of stock mutual funds, 70.5 million. Only 31.5 million individuals owned individual stock outside an employer-sponsored retirement plan. The median age of these individual stock holders was 48 with a median household income of $75,000 and median household financial assets of $200,000. These individual investors did not have all of their money in individual stocks—26 percent had funds in employer-sponsored retirement plans and 81 percent had funds in stock mutual funds. The median value of individual stock holdings outside employer plans was $25,000, while the mean was $157,000. Using the mean of $25,000, the 31.5 million individuals had $787.5 billion invested in individual stocks. Many of these individuals had professional advice in selecting their stocks—13 percent used financial planning firms and 47 percent used full service brokers.

The absolute amount of retail investor activity is greater than in years past, but the *percentage* of market activity attributable to direct

---

[11] "The World Price of Insider Trading," Working Paper (2000).

individual investor participation in the market has declined. By 1992, block trades (which are effected almost exclusively by institutions) accounted for 50 percent of NYSE volume (an increase from 16 percent in 1975), and program trades (negligible in 1975) accounted for another 11 percent of NYSE volume in 1992.[12]

b.   STRUCTURE OF THE EQUITY MARKETS

1.   PRIMARY EXCHANGES: THE NYSE

There are seven stock exchanges in the United States registered under Section 6 of the Securities Act of 1934. The two primary exchanges—the NYSE and the Amex—list most of the stocks traded on an exchange. The five U.S. regional stock exchanges include: the Boston Stock Exchange (BSE), the Philadelphia Stock Exchange (Phlx), the Cincinnati Stock Exchange (CSE), the Chicago Stock Exchange (CHX), and the Pacific Stock Exchange (PSE). These exchanges primarily trade securities that also are listed on the primary markets.

The NYSE is the largest U.S. market, with a $19.7 trillion market capitalization, of which $12.6 trillion represented domestic listed companies. This compares to NASDAQ with a $3.5 trillion market capitalization for domestic companies. It is owned by 1366 seat holders. The last seat sale in 2005 before the announcement of the merger described below was for $975 thousand, down $500,000 from the price in the previous year, and a $2.65 million price 4½ years ago.

This section describes the current operation of the NYSE. Its mode of operations, particularly the balance between floor and electronic trading is likely to change soon, given the merger of the NYSE with the publicly traded electronic exchange Archipelago, announced in April 2005. The merger would actually be structured as a reverse merger in which the larger NYSE would be subsumed into Archipelago thereby making NYSE Group (the new name of the combined entity) a publicly traded company. Under the proposed transaction, existing NYSE seat holder will receive $400 million in cash and 70 percent of the shares in the new merged company, NYSE Group Inc. Archipelago shareholders would have the remaining 30 percent stake in the new company. The deal was initially valued at $3.5 billion, but had risen to over $4.5 billion by June 2005, due to a steep rise in the price of Archipelago, implying a value to each seat holder of close to $3 million (a substantial premium over the last sale price before the merger was announced). The seat price on June 3, 2005 was $2.38 million.

The NYSE is principally an order market in which brokers bring customer orders to a central point to be matched. On the NYSE this matching

---

[12] See SEC, *Market 2000: An Examination of Current Equity Market Developments* (January 1994).

is not automatic; rather it is done through the specialist. Stock exchange specialists act as both brokers and dealers. As brokers, specialists buy and sell for the public, by executing limit orders that are brought to them by floor brokers on behalf of customers. They also execute market orders that reach them through the automated order routing system, SuperDOT. A limit order specifies the price at which an investor is willing to buy or sell. Limit orders are put in the specialist's "book" until they can be executed at the designated price or a better price. A market order is an order to buy or sell immediately at the prevailing price. Specialists are prohibited by law from handling customer orders other than limit orders. The specialist's book is, for most NYSE stocks, a computer screen. With some exceptions, the specialist is not required to show this screen to other traders, exchange members, or the public, although he must disclose aggregate price information. However, since 2001, the NYSE has sold access to the specialist's limit order book through its OpenBook service for which it charges data vendors $5000 per month. The data feed has a 5 second delay (it began with a 10 second delay), which can be an eternity in trading, so in real time specialists still have an informational advantage.[13] Nonetheless OpenBook did increase pre-trade transparency and one study finds that OpenBook reduced the price impact of trades, i.e. increased liquidity, and shifted trading from the floor to limit orders.[14] In 2004, the NYSE applied to the SEC for the ability to sell OpenBook in real time but the proposal engendered opposition from industry about the proposed charges and has not yet been approved by the SEC.

As dealers, specialists buy and sell for their own account. They have an "affirmative obligation" to do so when it is necessary to provide liquidity. Specialists provide liquidity by buying or selling when there are no other bidders or offerers at or near the market price. The specialist tries to keep prices from making big jumps, by making a bid or offer that acts as a bridge when there is a wide gap between bids and offers. The specialist also has a "negative obligation" *not* to trade for his own account when there are already customers wanting to trade at or near the market price. In 2004, 80 percent of the trading on NYSE is done through this floor auction system.

In 2000, the NYSE introduced a process in 2000 for the more automatic trading of small orders through a new system called NYSE Direct+™. This system allows member firms (and permits member firms to allow their customers) to specify limit orders of 1,099 shares or less as "Auto ex" orders.[15] These orders receive automatic electronic execution against the NYSE quotation to the extent that a matching bid or offer is available at the time the Auto ex order is received. Clients are only permitted to use the

---

[13] NYSE Rulemaking, SEC Release No. 34-45138, December 7, 2001.
[14] E. Boehmer, G. Saar, and L. Yu, "Lifting the Veil: An Analysis of Pre-trade Transparency at the NYSE," LX J. of Finance 783 (2005).
[15] NYSE Special Committee on Market Structure, Governance and Ownership, Market Structure Report (March 23, 2000), pp. 35-36.

system for one trade every 30 seconds. Currently, about 6 percent of trading on the NYSE is electronic. This initiative was part of a more general plan of the NYSE to give customers the choice as to how they want to trade, whether though the floor auction process or through automatic matching; they call this Network NYSE. In January 2004, in response to increased competition from electronic communications networks (ECNs)—the NYSE now only has 80 percent of the market in the trading of its own stock, much less than even five years ago—and in response to the new SEC NMS proposal discussed below (where qualifying as a "fast" market could produce more trading volume), the NYSE has proposed changing the size and 30 second limitation, thus promising to greatly increase the proportion of electronic trading on the exchange. However, under the proposal, auto-execution would still only be able to occur if the size of the bid/offer is greater than 100 shares, which could "freeze" NYSE Direct where there are best bid/offer small orders.

In 2003, the NYSE had net income of $49.6 million on revenues of $1.07 billion. Listings accounted for 27.6 percent of revenue in 2003. This was significantly less than the 41 percent figure in 1999. The decrease was due to the slowdown in market activity. Data processing and market data fees were 21 percent and 16.1 percent, respectively. Trading fees were 14.7 percent.

The number of specialists has shrunk rapidly in recent years. There are now only five specialist firms, and all but one are affiliated with large financial service firms (like Goldman Sachs who acquired Speer Leeds in 2000). Indeed, the top five firms do 80 percent of the business. Specialists acquire the right to make the market in a stock by applying to an Allocation Committee, which is formally not part of the NYSE; absent misbehavior there is rarely a switch from one specialist to another, so most of the competition relates to new listings. Should this specialist concentration be of concern to the NYSE? A recent study is somewhat inconclusive, finding no improvement or deterioration in the trading performance of stocks as a result of specialist consolidations.[16]

In April 2003, it came to light that the NYSE had launched an investigation into its specialist firms in response to allegations that specialists were engaging in "front-running." This occurs when a specialist uses its knowledge of customers' orders to trade in advance for its own profit. This triggered renewed debate about the role of specialists and the possible fairness advantage of more pure electronic matching systems. What is and what is not front running is not easily determined. If the specialist steps in front of a potential buyer to improve the price offered to the seller, this is permissible. But it may be that the specialist does so in the expectation that the buyer he pre-empted will bid again at a higher price. It is unclear whether this should be considered a violation.

---

[16] B. Hatch and S. Johnson, "The Impact of Specialist Firm Acquisitions on Market Quality," 66 Journal of Financial Economics (2002), p. 139.

A key issue in judging whether violations have occurred is the time period for which trades are examined. The idea is that the longer it takes to complete a trade, the higher the possibility that the specialist may step in front of the market. The SEC insisted that this period be moved from 60 to 14 seconds, despite the claims of specialists that some trades cannot be completed that quickly.[17]

In February 2004, the NYSE, the SEC, and the specialist firms reached a settlement under which the firms would disgorge $155 million to investors and pay an additional $85 million in fines. This action reinforced concerns about whether the NYSE or other exchanges could be relied upon to discharge their SRO obligations.[18] Charges against the NYSE itself, for failure to police the specialists, remain a possibility. In April 2005, fifteen individual NYSE specialists were criminally indicted by federal prosecutors and were charged civilly by the SEC for front-running. In addition, the NYSE settled civil charges with the SEC for failure to adequately supervise the specialists. The NYSE agreed to set aside $20 million to improve its regulation.[19]

A key question about the specialist system is whether it results in unfair advantages to traders on the floor. Some institutions like Fidelity have accused the specialists and floor traders of running a trading system that benefits themselves rather than external order flow providers.[20] A 2004 article gives some support to this view finding that the specialists' limit order book is informative about future price movements and that specialists use this information in ways that favor them and sometimes the floor brokers over limit orders.[21] This study was, however, based on data from 1990-1991 before the advent of many changes in the market and regulation at the NYSE. Furthermore, the study admits that the cost of the specialist advantages must be weighed against the benefits of their obligation to provide liquidity, which the study has not done.

Questions have also been raised about whether Richard Grasso, the former Chairman of the NYSE, exerted improper influence on specialists to more actively trade shares of certain firms (e.g. AIG, whose CEO Maurice Greenberg formerly served on the Board of the NYSE). In addition, attention continued to focus on the $140 million retirement package Grasso got when he left the NYSE.

---

[17] S. Craig, K. Kelley, and I. Dugan, "Tense Times for Big Board Specialists," *The Wall Street Journal*, October 20, 2003.

[18] D. Solomon and S. Craig, "SEC Blasts Big Board Oversight of 'Specialist' Trading Firms," *The Wall Street Journal*, November 3, 2003.

[19] A. Lucchetti and K. Scannell, "Fifteen Indicted in NYSE Case," *The Wall Street Journal*, April 13, 2005.

[20] Greg Farrell, "Critics say Human Frailties Taint NYSE," USA Today, October 14, 2003.

[21] L. Harris and V. Panchapagesan, "The Information Content of the Limit Order Book: Evidence from NYSE Specialist Trading Decisions," 8 J. of Financial Markets 25 (2005).

The various problems with specialists have called into question the very existence of the trading system that gives specialists a central role. This has prompted some, such as Fidelity, to claim that the scandals show the superiority of electronic matching systems; Goldman Sachs has called for the elimination of specialists and pure electronic handling for the most liquid stocks.[22]

The NYSE still plays an important price discovery function. Most securities markets set prices equal to or based on the primary market prices. For example, the regional exchanges and third market makers usually base their quotations on the primary market quote, and many of them simply autoquote the primary markets.

The NYSE also serves as the market of last resort during times of market stress. During volatile market conditions, when normal liquidity is unavailable in the index-derivatives markets, market participants channel their stock orders to the NYSE, particularly to the floor where discretionary trading takes place. This was partially demonstrated in the market crash of 1987 where participants withdrew electronic limit orders and vastly increased floor trading.[23]

As a result of 1975 amendments to the Securities Acts and implementing rules of the SEC, the NYSE participates with the seven regional exchanges and the National Association of Securities Dealers (NASD) in three plans to distribute market data: (1) the Consolidated Tape Association Plan (CTA Plan) which consolidates and reports trade data from all participating markets; (2) the Consolidated Quotation Plan (CQ Plan) which consolidates and reports quotation data from all participating markets; and (3) the Intermarket Trading System (ITS) Plan which permits participants to route orders among the participating markets to execute trades with the best-priced quotes. Subscribers pay for CTA Plan and CQ Plan data. The revenue from the NYSE data, provided to the Plans through so-called Network A was about $125.2 million after expenses in 1998, of which the NYSE only captured $93.2 million or 74 percent; the balance was distributed to NASD and the regional exchanges.

In an attempt to compete with NASDAQ, the NYSE has changed its listing standards in 2003 for the first time in 30 years to attract fast growing foreign firms. Before the change, foreign firms needed to have overall earnings of $100 million for the three previous years and at least $25 million in each of those years. The overall three year $100 million requirement was retained, but now a firm can have lost money in the first year. The changes

---

[22] J. Hechinger, "Fidelity Urges NYSE to Revamp Trading Operation," *The Wall Street Journal*, October 14, 2003; V. Boland, G. Silverman, and D. Wells, "Goldman Sachs Wants NYSE Reform," *Financial Times*, November 21, 2003.

[23] M. Goldstein and K. Kavajecz, "Trading Strategies during Circuit Breakers and Extreme Market Movements," 7 J. of Financial Markets 301 (2004). (Extreme Market Movements)

are designed to lure precisely those companies that have heretofore been attracted to the NASDAQ market.

Notes and Questions

1. What is the value of a specialist?

2. Should the SEC be concerned about listing standards? Suppose it could be shown that lower listing standards on NASDAQ in the late 1990s—permitting firms to list based on market capitalization rather than profitability—resulted in the listing of firms that lost more value during the burst of the bubble than those listed on the basis of profitability.[24]

2. NASDAQ

NASDAQ is an interdealer quotation system which is registered as a national securities association under §15A of the Securities Exchange Act of 1934 (Exchange Act). NASDAQ consists of competing market makers for each security. Customer orders are not normally reflected in the market makers' quotes. Unlike the exchange market, limit orders are handled individually by each market maker.

Initially, NASDAQ was considered primarily an "incubator" market. When its companies matured financially, they usually became listed on exchange markets. NASDAQ now is a major market in its own right. Based on volume, it is the second largest securities market in the world after the NYSE.

At the time of the Securities Acts Amendments of 1975, Congress and the Commission found it unnecessary to regulate NASDAQ as an exchange. Although certain trading characteristics of NASDAQ are functionally similar to those of the traditional exchanges, the Commission believed that these similarities did not transform NASDAQ into an exchange. Nevertheless, the NASD is subject to regulation under §15A of the Exchange Act that is substantively similar to the regulation for national securities exchanges under §6 of the Exchange Act.

In a quote market, like NASDAQ, dealers quote bid and offer prices to other dealers. For example, a dealer may quote a bid of 95 (the price at which she will buy) and an offer of 98 (the price at which she will sell). The bid-offer spread compensates the dealer for the risk of taking positions in a stock (which decreases as the trading depth and volume increases). On NASDAQ, many dealers make markets in the same stock. Their inventory consists of their own positions and those of their customers.

The NASDAQ market came under attack in 1994 for colluding to maintain wide spreads on its quotes. W. Christie and P. Schultz, two

---

[24] A. Klein and P. Mohanram, "Why Did So Many Poor-Performing Firms Come to Market in the Late 1990s?: Nasdaq Listing Standards and the Bubble," April 2005.

economists, found that NASDAQ's dealers' quotes rarely ended in odd-eighth amounts, i.e. 5 1/8, 5 3/8, instead moving in even-eighths, i.e. 5 2/8, 5 4/8 (quarter-dollars).[25] The study suggested that this resulted from collusion and that collusion might also explain NASDAQ's relatively high bid-offer spreads. This study triggered a wide scale investigation in October of that year by the U.S. Department of Justice.

In August 1996, the SEC promulgated rules that took effect in 1997 designed to protect investors trading on NASDAQ. The rules force NASDAQ dealers to publicly display all investor limit orders that are between 100-10,000 shares, to notify the public of the absolute best prices at which they are willing to trade any stock (this includes quotes supplied in "private" markets such as Instinet), and to expand the size of any offered block of stock at the best market-wide price to include a customer's limit order at the same price (for example, a dealer's offer to sell 500 shares of stock would have to be expanded to 700 if a customer delivered a 200 share offer at the same price). Some recent studies suggest that the trading costs of NASDAQ securities have fallen in the presence of the new rules.

H. Bessembinder[26] found that after the implementation of these reforms, NASDAQ's trade execution costs were still larger than those of the NYSE, though the differential was smaller than that documented in earlier years. The average of quoted spreads was 0.78 percent of the share price on the NYSE as compared to 1.03 percent on NASDAQ. Differences in commissions between the two exchanges did not appear to account for the difference, at least for retail customers.

NASDAQ also agreed to settle its dispute with the SEC over collusion by spending $100 million to improve its surveillance of the market.[27] In addition, in November 1996 NASDAQ significantly raised its listing standards.

NASD, the parent association that owned NASDAQ, sold off a significant portion of its shares to the public in 2001 as part of its plan to be just an SRO, a regulator of broker-dealers and markets, perceiving that ownership of exchanges posed a direct conflict with its regulatory role. In December 2004, it also sold off its entire interest in the American Stock Exchange to the seat holders. At the same time NASD sold off part of its interest in NASDAQ, NASDAQ applied to the SEC to become an exchange.[28] Until it is granted this status it must remain affiliated with NASD. NASDAQ's right to list and to charge for data fees depends on its being either

---

[25] "Why do NASDAQ Market Makers Avoid Odd-Eighth Quotes?," 49 J. of Finance (1994), p. 1813.

[26] "Trade Execution Costs on NASDAQ and the NYSE: A Post-Reform Comparison," NYSE Working Paper 98-03 (August 1998).

[27] J. Taylor, "NASD Will Spend $100 Million to Fulfill Settlement with SEC," *The Wall Street Journal*, August 7, 1996.

[28] Release No. 34-44396, June 7, 2001.

owned by NASDAQ or becoming an exchange.[29] The SEC has yet to approve NASDAQ's exchange application, apparently for the reason that the SEC has insisted that an exchange have a central limit order book (CLOB), where all orders received by traders are posted. Currently NASD retains ownership of 54.7 percent of NASDAQ and has voting control as well.[30]

NASDAQ has gone part of the way toward establishing a CLOB. In January 2001, the SEC approved a new quotation system for NASDAQ, SuperMontage.[31] By centralizing and displaying more of the market's stock quotes, the system makes NASDAQ more of a conventional stock exchange and less a network of market makers. New trading screens display the three best bids and offers for every stock, as well as each market maker or ATS's (alternative trading system or electronic communication network, ECN) single best bid and offer. Previously, NASDAQ only showed each market maker or ATS's best price. Large institutions can post bids or offers anonymously, which is an important right in facilitating the trading of large blocks. The system enables investors to direct orders to the ATS or market maker of their choice. NASDAQ dealers profit from the spread, while ATSs charge an access fee of as much as 1.5 cents per share. Orders may only be preferenced on the basis of best bids or offers; the SEC rejected preferencing options based on size and price (which would have allowed big blocks to trade ahead of smaller ones).[32] The problem for NASDAQ's exchange status, is that market makers do not post all their limit orders—some of them they execute themselves, thus "internalizing" some orders.

The implementation of SuperMontage has helped NASDAQ repatriate some of its market share from ATSs but the overall story is still bad. As of January 2003, NASDAQ's share of trading in its own stocks had risen modestly to 19.8 percent. This is still extremely low as compared with the NYSE that reportedly captures close to 80 percent of the trading in its listed stocks. Also, NASDAQ began in 2004 to cross-list shares that are listed on the NYSE, engaging in direct competition for the trading of NYSE stocks.

On April 22, 2005, 2 days after the NYSE announced its deal with Archipelago, NASDAQ announced a merger with Instinet, acquiring the firm for $$934.5 million. This marked a combination with one of NASDAQ's principal competitors in the trading of NASDAQ listed stocks.

3.   TRADING VOLUMES AND COSTS: NYSE V. NASDAQ

With regard to its share of U.S. equity trading volume, NASDAQ has caught up and surpassed the NYSE. In 1992, NASDAQ average Dollar daily

---

[29] J. Labate, "NASDAQ Files for Exchange Status," *Financial Times*, December 11, 2000.
[30] NASD, 2004 Annual Report.
[31] SEC Release No. 34-43863, January 19, 2001.
[32] M. Schroeder and G. Ip, "Plan to Upgrade NASDAQ Gains Approval from the SEC," *The Wall Street Journal,* January 11, 2001; M. Hendrickson, "Concessions Lead to SuperMontage OK," *Securities Industry News,* January 15, 2001.

trading volume was approximately $3.5 billion as compared with approximately $7 billion on the NYSE. This can be compared to 1982, when trading on NASDAQ was approximately $.3 billion compared with the NYSE's approximately $2 billion. By year-end 1999, NASDAQ had surpassed the NYSE, having $41.5 billion compared with $35.4 billion for the NYSE.

In 2002, NASDAQ as a whole traded 441.6 billion shares compared to 363.1 billion at NYSE. However, the total dollar volume traded at NASDAQ for 2002 was $7.2 billion compared to $10.3 trillion at the NYSE. In 2004, the average daily Dollar value of NASDAQ was $34.8 billion compared to $46.1 billion at NYSE. The comparison of trading volumes on NASDAQ and NYSE is fraught with difficulty because trading is measured differently on the two exchanges. NASDAQ dealers generally participate on one side of every trade, counting the buy and sell as two separate transactions, whereas NYSE specialists that match orders count them as a single transaction.[33] Trends are, however, more reliable.

There is considerable debate and disagreement about whether the costs of trading are lower on the NYSE or NASDAQ. Several studies have found that the costs of trading on exchanges like the NYSE are lower than NASDAQ, as measured by the impact of the trading on prices and the total bid-ask spread.[34] On small market orders of 100-499 shares, NASDAQ is faster but NYSE spreads are narrower. On medium orders of 500-1999 shares, the NYSE has a small advantage on both speed and spreads, and on very large orders of 2000-4999 shares, the NYSE has a pronounced advantage on both speed and spreads. However, one study has found that there is no NYSE cost advantage when the non-NYSE market's quotes are competitive with those of the NYSE.[35]

L. Chan and J. Lakonishok[36] investigated the comparative execution costs of trading on NASDAQ and the NYSE, as measured by commissions and market impact for institutional investors (the investors most sensitive to cost differences). The authors found that NASDAQ had a comparative advantage for stocks with a 1991 market capitalization below $1.2 billion, which accounted for 88 percent of the NASDAQ trading programs. The

---

[33] NYSE, "Markets Still Count Volume Differently," 9 The Exchange (April 2002), p. 1.

[34] See J. Affleck-Graves, S. Hedge and R. Miller, "Trading Mechanisms and the Components of the Bid-Ask Spread," 49 Journal of Finance (1994), pp. 1471-1472. A 1996 study found lower costs for large, medium and small capitalization stocks. H. Bessembinder and H. Kaufman, "A Comparison of Trade Execution Costs for NYSE and NASDAQ-Listed Stocks," Working Paper (November 1996). See also, R. Huang and H. Stoll, "Dealer versus Auction Markets: A Paired Comparison of Execution Costs on NASDAQ and the NYSE," Journal of Financial Economics (1996), p. 41 (NYSE costs lower in study of high capitalization stocks). A 2001 SEC Study reaches the same result. "Report on the Comparison of Order Executions Across Equity Market Structures," (January 8, 2001).

[35] H. Bessembinder, "Quote-based Competition and Trade Execution Costs in NYSE-listed Stocks," 70 J. of Financial Economics 385 (2003).

[36] "A Cross-Market Comparison of Institutional Equity Trading Costs," NBER Working Paper 5374 (1995).

NYSE, on the other hand, had a distinct advantage in trading the largest stocks (with market capitalization over $4.5 billion), which constituted 32 percent of the NYSE trading programs, or 51 percent of the value. A recent SEC Study of the Office of Economic Analysis, based on data from January-June 2004, comparing 113 closely matched pairs of firms, finds just the opposite—NYSE with lower effective spreads for small and medium sized orders and NASDAQ with lower spreads on larger orders. The study also found that NASDAQ order execution was faster although NASDAQ "fill rates," the rate that orders are actually executed, were significantly lower on NASDAQ.[37]

Fidelity's research shows that executions of market orders up to 10,000 shares for NYSE stocks have better (lower) effective spreads on electronic markets (Nasdaq and ECNs) than executions of market orders received by the NYSE specialists. The share-weighted effective spread was 2.17 cents for electronic market executions versus 3.06 cents for the NYSE.[38]

Price competition between NASDAQ and the NYSE seems to have improved by decimalization, the quotation of stocks in cents rather than 16ths (6.25 cents). Decimalization has had the general effect of lowering spreads on all markets. The NYSE converted to decimalization in February 2001, and NASDAQ fully converted by April 2001. A preliminary analysis of conversion indicates a tightening of bid-ask spreads by 37 percent on NYSE-listed stocks and 50 percent on NASDAQ traded stocks. Both quoted and effective spreads of NASDAQ stocks remained wider than comparable stocks traded on the NYSE.[39]

Notes and Questions

1. What is the difference between an order and a quote market?

2. What is the difference between a floor-based and an electronic market?

3. What are the key terms of competition between stock exchanges?

4. ALTERNATIVE TRADING SYSTEMS (ATSS)

Several types of ATSs offer institutions and broker-dealers the opportunity to trade off the exchanges and NASDAQ. These are normally screen-based automated trading systems typically sponsored by broker-dealers. The most prominent of the ECNs are INET, part of the Instinet Group, which has announced a merger with NASDAQ, Madoff Investment

---

[37] SEC, Office of Economic Analysis, "Comparative Analysis of Execution Quality on NYSE and NASDAQ Based on a Matched Sample of Stocks," December 15, 2004.

[38] G. Meng and A. Chitaley, "Comparison of Effective Spreads for the NYSE Trades versus Electronic Markets in the NYSE Stocks," version 1.1, November 7, 2004.

[39] K. Chung, B. Van Ness, and R. Van Ness, "Are NASDAQ Stocks More Costly to Trade than NYSE Stocks? Evidence after Decimalization," Working Paper (July 2001).

Securities, the National Stock Exchange, POSIT (The Portfolio System for International Trading) and ArcaEx, part of Archipelago, which has announced a merger with NYSE. Many of the ECNs, like INET, charge access fees to customers seeking to hit limit orders posted on the system, e.g. .0030 cents, and give a liquidity rebate to customers providing limit orders, e.g. .0020 cents. POSIT is an electronic crossing system that matches market orders 15 times per day at the midpoint of the National Best Bid and Offer prices (NBBO), thus allowing buyers and sellers to interact without affecting the market price. ArcaEx is actually an electronic stock exchange produced by the merger of the ECN Archipelago with the Pacific Stock Exchange. It went public in 2004. INET and ArcaEx have together about half of the trading volume in NASDAQ listed stocks, and there were rumors in early 2005 that ArcaEx would buy INET. This would make it an even more formidable competitor of the traditional exchanges.

Advancements in telecommunications and trading technology over the past decade have fostered the growth of ATS. They have been used by institutional investors to reduce execution costs, avoid market maker spreads, and trade in volume without incurring the market impact costs that could result if orders were handled on the organized markets.

On December 8, 1998, the Securities and Exchange Commission adopted a new regulatory scheme for ATS. The new scheme requires an ATS either to register as a national securities exchange or as a broker dealer and to comply with new requirements under Regulation ATS.[40]

Regulation ATS

Rule 3b-16 expands the concept of an exchange to mean any "organization, association, or group of persons that:

(1) Brings together the orders for securities of multiple buyers and sellers; and

(2) Uses established, non-discretionary methods (whether by providing a trading facility or by setting rules) under which such orders interact with each other, and the buyers and sellers entering such orders agree to the terms of a trade."

The new interpretation is intended to capture systems that centralize orders, either by the display or the processing and execution of orders. Orders include "any firm indication of a willingness to buy or sell a security, as either principal or agent, including any bid or offer quotation, market order, limit order, or other priced order," and are executable without further meaningful negotiation.

An exchange-run system must deal with multiple buyers and sellers in contrast to systems operated by a single dealer who acts as a counterparty to all trades. Similarly, systems that do not provide for order interaction,

---

[40] See S. Miller and L. Mullen, "Alternative Trading Systems," Traders Magazine, March 1, 1999.

such as those that route orders to order-execution facilities, will not qualify as exchanges. In addition, exchanges must use "established, non-discretionary methods" for order interaction.

An ATS includes any system that qualifies as an exchange and does not exercise self-regulatory functions. Regulation ATS applies to any ATS that chooses broker-dealer registration over exchange registration, although certain systems are not required to comply with Regulation ATS. Exempted entities include, among others, those registered (or exempt from registration) as national securities exchanges, and systems operated by national securities associations.

An ATS with five percent or more of the trading volume in any listed or NASDAQ National Market or Small-Cap security that displays orders for those securities to more than one subscriber or other user must link with a self-regulatory organization (SRO), like the NYSE, NASD or AMEX, to display the ATS's best bids and offers for those securities on the SRO. The ATS must also provide the SRO's members with access to those bids and offers on equal terms to other bids and offers on the SRO.

An ATS with 20 percent or more of the trading volume for most equity securities and certain categories of debt securities must also provide fair access to membership in the ATS. The ATS must also maintain adequate systems capacity, integrity and security standards.

Broker dealers operating ATSs must weigh exchange registration against broker-dealer registration that comes with additional requirements.

Exchange status would permit self-regulation as well as revenue from the distribution of price and trade information. On the other hand, membership in an exchange is limited to broker dealers, which means that institutional and retail customers would no longer be able to directly subscribe to a system that chooses to register as an exchange.

Some commentators have criticized the SEC's new rules regarding ATSs. The criticism stems from the fact that the new regulation does not allow the ATSs to be grouped and regulated along "functional" lines. Rather, the new rules call for an ATS to fit into two different regulatory moulds little different from those employed by the original Securities Exchange Act; i.e. national securities exchanges or broker dealers. The critics contend that only by creating flexible regulatory regimes that adapt as the technology changes will the U.S. be able to ensure its competitiveness.[41]

One major complaint of both NASDAQ and NYSE with respect to ATSs is that they do not bear the same kind of regulatory costs as exchanges. In 2002, NASDAQ spent approximately $80 million, or more than 10 percent of its budget, on regulation. One issue, however, is whether the more

---

[41] See J. Macey and M. O'Hara, "Regulating Exchanges and Alternative Trading Systems: A Law and Economics Perspective," 28 Journal of Legal Studies (1999), p. 17.

automated ATSs need the same level of regulation as trading venues with more human intervention.[42]

In September 2002, the SEC required Island to join the National Market System (NMS) for the three major exchange-traded funds (traded index funds) in which they had obtained a major market share. Island competed with the American Stock Exchange for the trading of these funds. This was pursuant to Regulation ATS's requirement that any ATS handling more than 5 percent of the volume in any security must provide that security's quotes to a national securities exchange or association. This requirement would prevent internal-crossing in Island and expose Island quotes to orders outside the system.[43]

The NYSE has been concerned that some broker-dealers and ATSs are using the current arrangements to free-ride on NYSE market information in order to internalize trades and to use the NYSE liquidity to lay-off their proprietary positions, and are vastly underpaying for the services. As a result, the NYSE has proposed to withdraw from the CTA and CQ Plans, subject to SEC approval, which has yet to be forthcoming.[44] Additionally the NYSE has stated that it sees no need for a mandated ITS, since broker-dealers have developed their own technology to perform the same functions more efficiently.[45] On the other hand, some brokers (like Charles Schwab) are complaining that existing fees are discriminating against on-line brokers.[46]

An SEC Advisory Committee issued its report on *Market Information: A Blueprint for Responsible Change* (Seligman Report).[47] The Report recommended no changes in how the SEC reviews existing fees for market data. Instead, it focused on how consolidated market data is distributed. It recommended that the SEC should permit a new system of competing consolidators rather than having the CTA as the sole consolidator. Some commentators have urged that the exchanges and ATSs be free to sell their data in whatever way they want at any price they can get. This raises the question of whether the exchanges have an effective monopoly in supplying their own data which would prevent market forces from setting data prices. On the other hand, if any one exchange tried to charge too high prices, it might lose its business to other exchanges or ATSs.

Competition among exchanges has also led to after-hour trading on ATS systems. Volatility in traded stocks is quite substantial. For example, on February 24, 2000, Wal-Mart's price rose 8 percent on volume of just 400 shares, and its next day price came down to approximately that of the regular

---

[42] See I. Clary, "NASDAQ Seeks Uniform Rules," *Securities Industry News*, May 5, 2003.
[43] I. Clary, "Island Faces Deadline to Join NMS," *Securities Industry News*, September 23, 2002.
[44] NYSE Letter to the SEC commenting on the Concept Release (April 10, 2000).
[45] NYSE, Press Release (April 6, 2000).
[46] M. Hendrickson, "Data Panel Unlikely to Reach Consensus," *Securities Industry News*, April 23, 2001.
[47] September 14, 2001.

closing on the previous day. The NYSE has criticized such trading but at the same time has a self-interest in doing so, since less after-hour off-exchange trading might mean more regular hour on-exchange trading.[48]

5.   FRAGMENTATION

NYSE Rule 390 was designed to "encourage order flow concentration and to discourage member firms from matching orders internally without exposing them to the auction process. Until recently, Rule 390 prohibited, with certain exemptions, member firms from effecting proprietary trades and in-house agency crosses in NYSE-listed securities off an organized exchange. In 1976, the SEC limited the scope of Rule 390 by exempting agency transactions, provided the same member firm does not represent both sides of the trade (in-house agency crosses): in other words, *member firms could effect one-sided agency trades anywhere, anytime.*"[49] In-house (two-sided) agency crosses remained subject to Rule 390. "In addition, SEC Rule 19c-3 exempts from Rule 390 securities *initially* listed on a U.S. exchange after April 26, 1979. At any time member firms may trade NYSE-listed securities on any organized domestic exchange where the securities are cross-listed or have unlisted trading privileges as well as on organized foreign exchanges. Outside of Exchange business hours, member firms may also trade NYSE-listed securities in *foreign* over-the-counter markets. Broker-dealers that are not members of the NYSE are not subject to Rule 390."[50]

On December 10, 1999, the NYSE filed with the SEC a proposal to rescind Rule 390, which the Commission approved on May 5, 2000.[51] The rescission of Rule 390 allows NYSE members to act as over-the-counter market makers or dealers in all NYSE-listed securities. The SEC had previously approved a change to the ITS Plan, favored by NASD, that allows NASD members unrestricted access to ITS. This permits them to trade all of the NYSE securities.[52]

When the SEC published the proposed Rule 390 change for comment,[53] it expressed concern that as a consequence of the change, a significant amount of order flow that currently is routed to the NYSE may be divided among a number of different dealers in the over-the-counter market where there may be a reduced opportunity for order interaction, thus reducing quote competition and the opportunity of transactors to obtain the best price. In reality, the Commission is concerned with two sources of

---

[48] See S. Pulliam, "Grasso Says After-hours Trade Can Cause Volatility in Market," *The Wall Street Journal*, June 2, 2000.

[49] J. Hasbrouck, G. Sofianos, and D. Sosebee, "New York Stock Exchange Systems and Trading Procedures," NYSE Working Paper 93-01 (1993), p. 18.

[50] *ibid.*

[51] Release No. 34-42758

[52] Release No. 34-42212 (December 9, 1999).

[53] Release No. 34-42450 (February 23, 2000).

fragmentation: internalization, which occurs when a broker-dealer matches buy and sell orders internally without exposing them to competing orders in other trading locations, and payment for order flow, which occurs when a broker or dealer receives compensation to route an order to a particular market, regardless of whether that market will produce the best price for the customer. The issue of market fragmentation appears to be a major issue for the future. Some of the problems of fragmentation are illustrated by Figure 13.1, below.[54]

Figure 13.1

How Market Structure Affects Orders

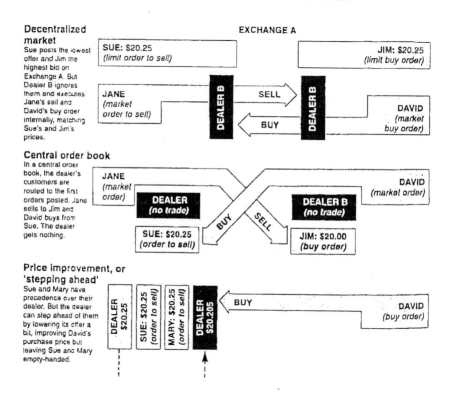

The SEC outlined six options for dealing with fragmentation: (1) markets and brokers improve the disclosure of the details of trade execution and order routing so that investors have more complete information on which to base their decisions; (2) brokers and dealers make internally crossed trades only at a price better than the National Best Bid or Offer (NBBO) then

---

[54] M. Schroeder and R. Smith, "Firms Propose Sweeping Change to Structure of the Stock Market," *The Wall Street Journal*, February 29, 2000.

outstanding (this is the NYSE's proposal); (3) all market centers would be required to expose their market and marketable limit orders in an acceptable way to price competition (for example, a market maker would be required to expose certain orders to the market before executing trades as principal); (4) markets would be required to satisfy the first order or quote that improved on NBBO before executing other trades at that price; (5) intermarket trading priorities would grant time priority to the first limit order or dealer quotation that improved the NBBO for a security; and (6) a national market linkage system that would provide price/time priority, i.e. a centralized limit order book (CLOB).

The CLOB alternative has been advocated by a group of Wall Street's largest firms, self-styled the "Working Group." They agree with the NYSE that the ITS system should be eliminated and propose to replace it with a "Super National Market System." The new market would be built around a central order book with price-time priority, so that orders to buy a stock at a particular price would be executed across different markets in the order received, no matter which trading system they are placed on. This would prevent firms such as Schwab from matching customer orders internally or through selected brokers on a pay for order basis, when better or earlier orders are available from other markets.[55]

The NYSE has opposed CLOB for several reasons. First, since CLOB would not likely apply to large orders (since firms would not want to expose their position on block orders), the market would be fragmented between large and small orders. Second, the proposal would favor some players at the expense of others (e.g. large-firm CLOB proponents will be able to use CLOB retail prices to price large orders off of CLOB). Third, most CLOB models would eliminate the liquidity supplied by specialists, which would be particularly troublesome in a steeply declining market and would generally result in wider bid-ask spreads. Fourth, CLOB will be a marketplace mandated by regulation and will eliminate competition between markets.[56] This last point has also been made by Federal Reserve Board Chairman Greenspan in testimony before the U.S. Senate Committee on Banking, Housing, and Urban Affairs on April 13, 2000.

Another NYSE rule that some claimed restricted competition was Rule 500 which requires that companies can delist only after obtaining a two-thirds majority shareholder vote with no more than 10 percent objecting. The requirement for shareholder removal was eliminated in 1999. In 2003, the NYSE eliminated the remaining requirements, the need for approval of the audit committee and notification to a company's 35 largest shareholders.[57]

---

[55] *ibid.*
[56] NYSE Market Structure Report, pp. 27-33.
[57] SEC, Exchange Act Release No. 41634 (July 21, 1999); Release No. 34-48697 (October 24, 2003).

The SEC has adopted Rules 11Ac1-5 and 11Ac1-6 to require markets and broker-dealers to make available to the public reports that include uniform statistical measures of execution quality on a stock-by-stock basis. The measurements include price improvement and disimprovement, speed of execution, limit order fill rates and the "realized spread"—the spreads actually paid by investors (i.e. not just quoted spreads). The rules are preceded by a preliminary note stating that the rules do "not create a reliable basis to address whether any particular broker failed to obtain the most favorable terms reasonably available under the circumstances for customer orders." Broker-dealers will have to disclose the existence of any payment-for-order flow or internalization arrangement they engage in.

Notes and Questions

1.   How do ECNs compete with exchanges?

2.   What, if anything, should be done about market fragmentation?

6.   THE SEC'S 2004 NATIONAL MARKET SYSTEM PROPOSAL

On February 26, 2004, the SEC made significant proposals affecting the future market structure in the U.S.[58] Some estimate that implementation could cost over $1 billion in the first two years.[59] The proposal would modify the so-called trade-through rule, which presently requires a market receiving an order for a NYSE stock to transfer it to another market which is quoting the best price on the order (the NBBO) unless the receiving market executes the order at the NBBO. The trade-through rule does not currently apply to NASDAQ listed stocks.

A major problem with the trade-through rule is that it ignores the value of speedy execution. The receiving market, typically an ECN or a "fast" market, may be able to execute the order faster than a slower market, e.g. the NYSE, even if the slower market is quoting a better price. Initially, the SEC proposal would have allowed markets to ignore a superior price in another market as long as the receiving market's price was within one to five cents of the better price, if the receiving market was "fast" and the superior price market was "slow." Fast markets are generally electronic markets and slow markets are floor-based auction markets like the NYSE. Fast markets would, however, have had to transfer orders to others fast markets quoting superior prices. This system would have hurt slower, and arguably better priced markets like the NYSE , who could have lost market share. This was a major reason why NYSE sought to automate a bigger percentage of its trades through Direct+. The Commission's proposal also envisioned that persons placing orders could opt-out of trade-through protection on an order-by-order

---

[58] SEC, Proposed Rule NMS, Release No. 34-49325.
[59] I. Clary, "$1B Trade-through Reform," *Securities Industry News*, March 8, 2004.

basis. The NYSE has opposed this change, as investors might seek execution in a faster-changing market.

In May 2004, after holding hearing on its proposal, the SEC indicated that it was considering using a fast and slow quote approach in place of its fast and slow market proposal.[60] Under this system, receiving markets could not trade through fast quotes on other markets—that is quotes that would be executed immediately upon receipt. On December 15, 2004, the SEC once again revised its trade-through proposal (the Reproposal).[61]

Under the Reproposal, the SEC made clear that trade-through would only protect quotations that were immediately accessible through automatic execution. Under those circumstances it found no reason for continuing to provide an opt-out. Instead it proposed specific exceptions to the trade-through where it though there might be a good reason for opting-out. The Commission offered two alternatives with respect to the scope of the quotations to be protected by the trade-through rule. The first alternative (Market BBO Alternative) would protect only the best bids and offers—this is the current scope of protection. Under the second alternative (Depth of Book Alternative or DOB), not only would the best BBOs be protected, but any market could voluntarily secure protection for all of the quotes on its book below the best bid and offer. Suppose Market A is displaying an order for 2000 at 10 (the NBBO) and for 3000 at 10.01 If Market B receives an order for 5000 shares, under the Market BBO, Market B would only have to send a 2000 share order to Market A—Market B could execute the remaining 3000 shares on its own market (subject to general best execution requirements), whereas under DOB, Market B would have to send the entire 5000 order to Market A. Many commentators, including John Thain of the NYSE, have criticized the DOB as an attempt to implement a CLOB, which would preclude market innovation and create a government utility. While the proposal is "voluntary" many believe that market centers will be forced to display DOB as a result of competition., and of course the proposal is mandatory with respect to seeking out the best DOB prices that are displayed.[62] Thain believed that the DOB would effectively preclude floor based auctions and the resulting price improvement. He also believes that the proposal could drive large trades upstairs or overseas.

Some commentators believe there is no need for any trade-through rule. In their view, market forces and the general obligation of best execution can insure that investors get the best price. In addition, those commentators believe that investors should be free to opt out of the rule if they so desire. Fidelity, in particular, has objected to the impact of the trade-through rule on

---

[60] SEC, Proposed Rule, Release No. 34-49749, May 20, 2004.
[61] SEC, Proposed Rule, Release No. 34-50870, December 15,2004.
[62] See John A. Thain, "The Quest for the Right Balance," Wall Street Journal, December 21, 2004; Y. Amihud and H. Mendelson, Comment on Regulation NMS—"Trade-Through Rule," filed with the SEC on January 25, 2005.

its ability to do block trades (which account for almost one-third o NYSE trading volume)—the rule would require them to parcel out the block to get the best prices rather than doing the whole block at a negotiated price.[63]

In addition to changes in the trade-through rule, the Reproposal would regulate access charges and rules for various trading systems. Access fees would be capped at $0.003 per share. It would also ban sub-penny pricing in stocks over $1.00 and establish new rules prohibiting repeated or continual locking or crossing of markets—as a result of bid and offer quotes being entered at the same price.

The proposal would also change the current system for the dissemination and pricing of market data. Market data generated $424 million in fees in 2003, $386 million of which was divided among the exchanges and NASDAQ.[64] In 2002, the Cincinnati Stock Exchange, now the National Stock Exchange, lured Island ECN away from executing trades on NASDAQ by sharing its market data revenue. Currently revenues from supplying market data are allocated to SROs based solely on share volume. This has given rise to schemes to increase artificially such volume, e.g. by wash sales or phony sales. In general, the proposed new formula in the Reproposal would divide market data revenues equally between trading and quoting activity—thus rewarding markets with superior quotes. The SEC rejected the "competing consolidation" model of the Seligman Report due to the confusion it might cause to investors.[65]

On April 7, 2005, after a contentious open meeting and a 3-2 vote (Chairman Donaldson joining the two Democrats, Roel Campos and Harvey Goldschmid) the SEC adopted Regulation NMS as proposed, with the Market BBO Alternative for the trade-through rule and no opt-out. As of June 3, 2005 this Regulation has not been published by the SEC. There is at least a possibility that there may be further developments, given the resignation of Chairman Donaldson effective June 30, 2005. The issue is further confused by the proposed merger of the NYSE with Archipelago, an electronic exchange. While the NYSE supported the adoption of the trade-through rule, Archipelago did not.

7.   THE SEC'S 2004 GOVERNANCE PROPOSAL AND SRO CONCEPT RELEASE

Within the United States, regulation of trading venues is entrusted to a system of self-regulation supervised by the SEC. Thus, the NYSE is a SRO with respect to its own operations. In response to the trading scandals discussed above, it revamped its governance to provide for both a Board of Directors and a Board of Executives. The Board of Directors appoints the

---

[63] Eric Roiter, Comment on NMS, filed with the SEC on January 26, 2005. See also, Princeton University, Policy Task Force Report of Woodrow Wilson School Students, Comment filed with the SEC on January 14, 2005.
[64] I. Clary, "Data Battle Brewing," *Securities Industry News*, April 26, 2004.
[65] I. Clary, "Market Data Missive," *Securities Industry News*, March 22, 2004.

Board of Executives. The Board of Directors is composed of nine independent directors, a non-executive independent Chairman, and the CEO. The Board of Executives is 22 members representing the various constituencies of the NYSE plus the NYSE Chairman and CEO. One of the Committees of the Board is the Regulatory Committee, which is composed of independent members, and has full responsibility for supervising the SRO function of the exchange, together with the Chief Regulatory Officer.

NASD is the SRO for NASDAQ and has assumed, through an outsourcing contract, most of the SRO functions for the AMEX (although the AMEX remains the SRO). NASD is also the SRO for ECNs in the sense of assuring the integrity of its trading through monitoring of its tapes—its role in regulating ECNs is much reduced from what it is for an exchange given the electronic nature of the operation and the lack of listing. NASD has sold part of NASDAQ (and seeks to sell the rest once NASDAQ's status as an exchange is approved) and its interest in AMEX in order to remove its inherent conflict in both owning and regulating an exchange—which remains a problem at NYSE despite its independent board and regulatory committee structure.

The SEC issued another important proposal in 2004 concerning the governance of the exchanges.[66] The proposal would require a majority of the directors of SROs (the exchanges and NASD) to be independent, and directors of key committees, like audit and regulation, to be entirely independent. It would also enhance the reporting and disclosure of the SROs.

The SRO Concept Release raises fundamental issues about the role of SROs in the future.[67] The SEC is concerned that added competition in trading markets may result in less effective regulation—as traders search for venues with less regulation. These pressures could erode regulation particularly given the inherent conflict of interest in venues regulating and disciplining themselves. In addition, the SEC is also concerned with whether publicly owned for profit trading venues can be as effective regulators as those owned by members, with the failures of SROs to enforce their rules (see the NYSE specialist scandal), and how SROs will generate revenues to support regulation.

The Commission envisioned the following alternative regulatory approaches: (1) particular enhancements to the existing system, e.g. more disclosure and better governance as proposed in the SEC governance rule making; (2) making the regulatory function independent of the exchange, through the creation of independent subsidiaries—this would go beyond the NYSE model which has the chief enforcement officer report to a committee of

---

[66] SEC, Fair Administration and Governance of Self-Regulatory Organizations, Release No. 34-50699, 69 Federal Register 71126 (December 8, 2004).
[67] SEC, Concept Release Concerning Self-Regulation, Release No. 34-50700, 69 Federal Register 71256 (December 8, 2004).l

independent directors; (3) the creation of one SRO to regulate all SRO members leaving regulation of operations to individual SROs—NASD currently allows SROs like the NYSE to regulate its own members; (4) have multiple competing SROs to regulate members; (5) create one SRO to regulate members and market operations; or (6) abolish SROs in favor of complete regulation by a new agency or by the SEC.[68]

An important reason for the existence of SROs, particularly with respect to regulation of market operations, is that it is very difficult for an off-site governmental agency to regulate trading on exchanges that use floor-based auctions. People have to be around to monitor people. If exchanges become completely electronic, this rationale will disappear. Today, NASD can monitor ECNs through analysis of their computer data. Even given floor-based systems, remote regulators could have an on-going presence at exchanges. In 2004, the American Stock Exchange largely outsourced its regulatory function to NASD under an arrangement where AMEX regulatory personnel became employees of NASD. A key consideration preventing the SEC from taking on this role is lack of revenue. The SEC would have to be given the power by Congress to impose fees to support this activity. The SEC, unlike the Federal Reserve Board, is currently not self-funded.

Major exchanges in Europe, such as the Deutsche Börse, LSE, and Euronext have already demutualized. The NYSE is using its merger with Archipelago to do the same. One issue about public ownership in the U.S. is whether it is consistent with a continuing SRO role for the new exchange—an issue the SEC will have to address in its SRO rulemaking. The NYSE has proposed to handle this issue by having the new NYSE Group's regulatory activities conducted by a nonpublic, not for profit entity governed by a wholly independent board of directors.[69] Whether this will satisfy the SEC remains to be seen.

As discussed above, NASDAQ has itself gone partially public as a result of NASD divested a significant portion of its shares and is regulated by its prior owner (which still retains sizeable share ownership).

Notes and Questions

1. What do you think of the SEC's NMS proposal? The EU's Financial Markets Instruments Directive, reviewed in Chapter 4, has no trade-through rule, or regulation of access, pricing or data fees. Instead, it relies on requiring trading venues to disclose their quotes and trades and imposes a general obligation of best execution. What accounts for the different approach in Europe

---

[68] See the thoughtful piece by J. Seligman, "Cautious Evolution or Perennial Irresolution: Stock Market Self-Regulation During the First Seventy Years of the Securities and Exchange Commission," 59 Business Lawyer 1347 (2004), exploring these options.

[69] BNA Banking Report, "On NYSE-Archipelago Deal, Donaldson Says SEC Keen to Protect Publicly Owned Markets," April 25, 2005.

2. Will differences in market structure regulation between the E.U. and U.S. impede further integration of these markets or the creation of a Transatlantic capital market? Should the U.S. take account of prices in the London market or other foreign markets where U.S. stocks trade in designing a trade-through rule?

9.   CIRCUIT BREAKERS

Following the market break of 1987, the NYSE adopted certain circuit breakers to halt trading when there was a steep fall in the market. Starting on October 19, 1988, if the Dow Jones Industrial Average were to decline by 250 points from the previous day's close, then trading in all stocks would be halted for one hour. Additionally it was decided that if the Dow were to plummet by 400 points from the previous day's close, then trading in all stocks would be halted for two hours.[70]

When the rule went into effect in 1988, a 250 point move represented 12 percent and a 400 point move represented 19 percent of the Dow Jones Industrial Average (DJIA or Dow). Given the rise of the Dow since that time, by March 13, 1996 a 250 point move represented only 4.5 percent of the average. It was widely perceived that the "devaluation" was a problem, but there was debate about how it should be fixed. Some argued that the circuit breakers should be expressed in terms of percentages of market averages. Others contended that a well known and certain circuit breaker, i.e. 250 points, would have a stronger ex-ante effect in restraining breaks since the amount of a triggering price break, expressed as a percentage of the DJIA, would constantly change with changes in the average. Finally, others suggested doing a split of the Dow much as highflying stocks are split.

In February 1997, the SEC approved changing the 250 point-1 hour circuit breaker to a 350 point-30 minute rule and the 400 point-2 hour breaker to a 550 point-1 hour rule. The 350 point rule required a drop of about 5 percent of the Dow when adopted. The Commodity Futures Trading Commission also approved changes in the futures rules. Trading of futures on the S&P 500 stock index will stop when the index is down 45 points, and again when down 75 points; the previous limits were 30 and 50 index points.[71]

The 350/550 circuit breakers were triggered for the first time on October 27, 1997. The 350 point level, which represented a 4.5 percent decline in the Dow, was reached at 2:36 p.m. When trading resumed at 3:06 p.m., the Dow declined an additional 200 points, and the second circuit breaker was triggered at 3:30 p.m. which had the effect of closing the market (the normal closing time is 4:00 p.m.). The market had declined 554 points for the day, the largest single-day point drop in Dow history, but this only represented a total decline of 7.2 percent, making it the 12th highest

---

[70] "Systems and Trading Procedures," NYSE Circuit Breakers (March 31, 1993).
[71] *The Wall Street Journal*, February 3, 1997.

percentage fall and representing only one-third of the Dow's 22.7 percent decline on October 19, 1987.[72]

This experience set off another round of debate on circuit breakers. Apart from the renewal of the argument over absolute numbers versus percentages, there was additional concern over whether the market should be closed as a result of the triggering of a circuit breaker. This made it impossible for investors to effectively place "market on close" orders, orders instructing brokers to buy/sell at the closing price. Normally, closing sell order imbalances are published at 3:50 p.m. to attract buyer interest. Such buy orders may play a key role in bringing the market into balance without large price movements. Some believed that selling pressure was accelerated on October 27 by investors who believed that the circuit breakers would preclude this procedure.

M. Goldstein and K. Kavajecz conducted a study of the 1997 market break. They found that upon the first execution of the circuit breaker (2:36 p.m.), little liquidity was provided to the market (i.e. there was a lack of order submission, cancellation or change in the limit order book). But more dramatically, on Tuesday, October 28, 1997 there was a liquidity drain, as the limit order book was uncharacteristically thin and empty; it was left to floor members and specialists to supply liquidity. It appears that the uncertainty of when and whether circuit breakers will be imposed may be worse than the certainty of prices falling.[73] A 2005 study summed up the main conclusion of studies of trading halts—that they do not reduce volatility or liquidity in stock markets; instead volume and volatility increase after the halt.[74]

A new revision of the circuit breakers went into effect in April 1998. It operates as follows: (1) a 10 percent drop halts trading for 1 hour if it occurs before 2:00 p.m., and for 30 minutes if it occurs between 2:00 p.m. and 2:30 p.m., but does not halt trading at all after 2:30 p.m.; (2) a 20 percent drop occurring before 1:00 p.m. halts trading for 2 hours, and between 1:00 p.m. and 2:00 p.m. for 1 hour, and closes the market for the day after 2:00 p.m.; and (3) a 30 percent drop closes the market for the day no matter when it occurs. These percentages are actually expressed as absolute numbers, calculated on a quarterly basis.

Notes and Questions

1.   Are circuit breakers, in general, a good idea? If so, what do you think of the latest round of revisions? Will the adoption of circuit breakers in

---

[72] J. Cochrane, "Trading Halts and Program Trading Restrictions," Testimony before the Subcommittee on Securities of the U.S. Senate Committee on Banking, Housing and Urban Affairs (January 29, 1998).

[73] Extreme Market Movements, supra note 23.

[74] Y. Kim and J. Yang, "What Makes Circuit Breakers Attractive to Financial Markets," 13 Financial Markets, Institutions and Instruments 109 (August 2004).

the U.S. market influence the competition between U.S. and foreign markets for listings?

2.   Assuming a foreign company trades on both a U.S. and foreign exchange in the same or an overlapping time zone, what will be the effect of a U.S. circuit breaker on trading in the foreign market, assuming trading in the company is not suspended in the foreign market in coordination with the U.S. suspension?

10.   BLOCK TRADES

The Market 2000 study indicates that most blocks in NYSE stocks are negotiated off the exchange ("upstairs"), but are executed on the exchange ("downstairs"). A later study of Dow Jones stocks found that 83 percent of trading value in orders of 10,000 shares or more are directly executed downstairs without upstairs intervention. However, the mean size of the downstairs sample was smaller (19,520 shares) compared with the mean of the upstairs sample (38,600 shares). The study found that the downstairs market accommodated large-block trades with minimal price movements and observed that the downstairs market offered immediacy and less potential for information leakage. The study also suggests that these benefits may be less important in upstairs markets, where traders can credibly signal that their trades are not motivated by superior information. It concludes that the primary benefit of the upstairs market may not be to the initiator but rather to the counterparties who are reluctant to submit large limit orders and thus offer free options to the market. Upstairs markets "allow these traders to selectively participate in trades screened by block brokers who avoid trades that may originate from traders with private information. Thus the upstairs market's major role may be to enable transactions that would not otherwise occur in the downstairs market."[75]

A general problem for a block trader is that traders on the other side may believe that the block trader has an informational advantage and thus only agree to trade the block at unfavorable prices to the block trader. This can happen both on the floor of a physical exchange, NYSE, where floor brokers or the specialist price the trade or in limit order trading where limit order traders offer unfavorable pricing to a displayed block. In addition, in a floor setting, the block trader may be particularly sensitive to the possibility of front running. As a result, it appears that the upstairs market, consisting of negotiated deals between traders serves an important function. Traders who know each other can certify trades as uninformed. In addition, there may be generally more liquidity upstairs than downstairs. A 2005 study finds that actual execution costs upstairs are on average only 20 percent as they

---

[75] A. Madhavan and M. Cheng, "In Search of Liquidity: Block Trades in the Upstairs and Downstairs Markets," 10 Review of Financial Studies (1997), pp. 175, 201.

would be if block trades were executed in the downstairs limit order book.[76] Another possible was for block orders to be handled is through internalization—brokers can match large block orders against each other on an anonymous basis but this gives an informational advantage about market movements to the internalizer. This problem can be eliminated through an ECN designed for block trades such as Posit and Liquidnet in the United States. Liquidnet matches blocks by size and then allows the parties anonymously to negotiate a price.[77]

Consider this example of off-exchange trading of blocks. In May 1997, Carl Icahn sold his 19.9 million-share stake in RJR Nabisco Holdings Corp. to Goldman Sachs & Co. for more than $730 million. Goldman bought the stock outside the U.S. after markets there closed and resold it before the markets opened up the next day. Neither the purchase or resale hit the NYSE tape although they were reported to the Exchange. Icahn knew he might have taken a discount, since he did not get a "market" price for his stock, but was concerned that a sale on the exchange would prompt short selling, and Icahn wanted to get the deal done quickly.[78]

B.   FOREIGN MARKETS

We turn now to the characteristics of two important foreign exchanges, London's SEAQ International and the Tokyo Stock Exchange (TSE).

London Stock Exchange

The trading system of the LSE is a competing dealer market in which dealers display quotes over computer terminals. The system is very similar to NASDAQ. The heart of the London market is the SEAQ system, which allows registered market-makers to change quotes and report transactions.

Studies have found the spreads on LSE comparable to the spread on NASDAQ.[79] Spreads range from 1.16 percent (for the 10 percent of most actively traded stocks) to 6.87 percent (for the 10 percent of least actively traded stocks).

One of the most controversial accommodations to market-makers was the LSE ruling in February 1989 permitting the delayed publication of the transaction size and price until the following day for transactions exceeding

---

[76] H. Bessembinder and K. Venkataraman, "Does an Electronic Stock Exchange Need an Upstairs Market," 73 J. of Financial Economics 3 (2004).

[77] http://www.liquidnet.com/company/about.jsp

[78] G. Ip, "More Large Stock Sales are Handled 'Off Board,'" *The Wall Street Journal*, April 9, 1997.

[79] H. Stoll reports spreads for 820 NASDAQ/NMS stocks in December 1984. "Inferring Components of the Bid Ask Spread: Theory and Empirical Tests," 44 Journal of Finance (1989), pp. 115-134.

100,000 pounds. The argument for such delay was that market-makers disclosing such a large trade would cause prices to move against them and make it difficult to unwind their position. The Elwes Committee accepted this argument and recommended a smaller delay of up to 90 minutes (now implemented) in the publication of price information for large transactions, those more than three times the normal market size (then £750,000).

The LSE made a fundamental change in the way its stocks are traded by adopting a new trading system, SETS, in October 1997. SETS has a two-tiered system where smaller orders may be crossed on brokers' own books or may be pooled into bigger orders that qualify for matching. Very large "block trades" may be matched or done through a registered principal trader. Unlike the old market makers, registered principal traders are only obliged to deal in particular shares when there are no offers to buy or sell from other traders on the electronic book. This is quite close to the NYSE specialist system. Proponents of the change pointed to the comparative efficiency of competitor home-country order-driven systems like the Paris Bourse. The implementation of the Investment Services Directive allows stocks on Paris and other European exchanges to be traded on screens in London and vice-versa.

By mid-1998 SETS had roughly 125 companies, yet had been beset by problems of low usage and volatile prices. Complaints from company executives about the dramatic swings of their stock prices on SETS, especially during the beginning and end of the trade day, prompted the LSE to institute a number of reforms designed to increase liquidity. The LSE delayed its opening time to make it more difficult for traders to manipulate the market in the early-opening hours. Additionally, the LSE introduced a system to correct the erratic swings in its prices.[80] LSE reports that over 50 percent of all trades are now conducted through SETS.

The original primary purpose of SETS was to reduce trading costs for small investors. In a study after the implementation of SETS, N. Naik and P. Yadav[81] found that public investors trading through limit orders (liquidity suppliers) benefited from the change because they earned the spread. For example, an investor could place a limit buy order at 2 and a limit sell order at 2.5; if both orders were fulfilled, that investor would earn the 0.5 spread. When investors trade with dealers, who have superior information and no longer have to make two way quotes, they lose part of this spread. This is reflected in increased dealer positioning revenue after the change. The

---

[80] See C. Kentouris, "With Usage Low, LSE Modifies SETS Order Book," *Securities Industry News,* June 1, 1998; G. Graham, "London Stock Exchange Opens Later for Trading," *Financial Times,* July 20, 1998; P. John, "London Stock Exchange Sets out Its Revamped Trading Stall," *Financial Times,* December 14, 1998.

[81] "The Effects of Market Reform or Trading Costs of Public Investors: Evidence from the London Stock Exchange," London Business School, Institute of Finance and Accounting Working Paper 296 (June 1999).

researchers were unable to determine whether public investors were better off as a result of the change because they had no data as to how investors would fare without limit orders, but it seems reasonable to assume that the possibility of capturing spread may make public investors better off. On the other hand, dealers may be worse off; although they capture some of the spread on limit orders, they also face more competition from public investors placing limit orders.

The LSE demutualized in 2000 and raised over an additional $2 billion by a share offering in 2001.

Tokyo Stock Exchange

Structurally, in terms of a trading mechanism, the Tokyo market is characterized by three major elements: a continuous auction market based on order-book system, a high degree of automation, and integration of cash and derivative markets.[82]

The Tokyo market is a continuous public auction market based on an order-book system and is entirely computerized. There is no trading floor.

An order-book system is preferred to a board or open-outcry system chiefly because of fairness considerations. The TSE believes that an open order-book permits the fairest treatment of all orders, large and small, by matching them in strict compliance with the auction principle and making the matching process visible to all concerned.

Historically, Japan has had no tradition of dealers' quoting asks and bids to make markets for brokers and public investors. More essentially, as a matter of capital market policy, Japan emphasizes the importance of concentrating all orders into a single market in order to provide best prices to investors. Given this policy, public limit orders, which are generally not allowed to compete with market maker bids and asks under a quote-driven system, must be fully provided for. If not, there will be an incentive for brokerage firms handling public orders to create in-house limit-order books and order matching systems or to act as dealers, resulting in fragmentation of market to the detriment of investors' interests.

The absence of market makers or specialists raises the issue of stability. The TSE claims that the widespread participation of different types of investors and the cross-shareholding system act to stabilize the market.

There are two TSE procedures to limit volatility. First, when there is a major order imbalance, special quotes are publicly disseminated. If counter orders come in, the orders will be matched at the special quote and the original quote will be withdrawn. If no orders come in at the quote, the quotes are adjusted up or down within certain parameters. Second, the TSE sets

---

[82] See M. Sato, "The Tokyo Equity Market: Its Structure and Policies," in *Capital Markets and Financial Services in Japan* (Japan Securities Research Institute, 1992).

daily price limits (including special quotes) in absolute yen amounts for individual stocks.

Limit orders on the TSE are purely matched. After the opening (which uses a special procedure called *itayose*), market orders are "matched" under the *zaraba* (continuous trading) method as follows.

1.   Assume the last trade was at ¥100 and assume there is a limit buy order at ¥100. A market sell order is fulfilled at the price of the last trade and matched against the limit buy order.

2.   Assume the last trade was at ¥100 and assume the best limit buy order is ¥99. A market sell order is fulfilled at ¥99 and matched with the best limit buy order.

3.   Assume the last trade was at ¥100 and there is no limit order. A market sell order is matched against a market buy order at ¥100.

4.   Assume the last trade was at ¥100 and there is a limit buy order at ¥101. A market sell order is matched against the limit buy order at ¥100. This gives price improvement to the buy order.

5.   Assume the last trade was at ¥100 and there is a limit buy order at ¥101 but there is no market order. After a warning, the next market sell order is matched at ¥101 with the limit buy order.

Listing costs that include but are not restricted to fees vary significantly among exchanges. A Tokyo listing is reported to cost three to four times as much as other leading markets, mainly for translating reports for Japanese permits and observing regulations. The poor performance and the low trading volume of the TSE have caused a significant number of foreign companies to delist. As of September 1997 36 foreign companies were listed, as compared to 127 in 1991. There has been a steady fall in listings over the 1991-1997 period despite the fact that listing fees were lowered in December 1994. They are currently at a maximum of about $235,000 (the actual fees depend on total number of shares issued and the number of Japanese shareholders). In 1997, the TSE lowered other listing requirements. Minimum shareholder equity is now reduced to $8.4 million from the old level of $84 million and minimum profits required for the three years before listing have been reduced to about $1.68 million from $16.8 million.[83] The TSE has explored possible cross-listing arrangements with the Shanghai Exchange in order to revitalize its international position.[84]

A new market, NASDAQ Japan, which operated as a section of the Osaka Securities Exchange, was launched in June 2000 to trade growth

---

[83]   G. Robinson, "Tokyo Exchange to Relax Rules," *Financial Times*, September 18, 1997; "Relaxation of Listing Requirements for Foreign Companies," Securities & Capital Markets Law Report (February 1995).

[84]   D. Ibison and R. McGregor, "TSE in Talks on Alliance with Shanghai," *Financial Times*, August 23, 2002.

companies. It was a joint venture between NASDAQ and Softbank, a leading Japanese company. One commentator stated that this initiative did not address one of the main obstacles to new listings, a Japanese Commercial Code requirement that the par value of shares be at least ¥50,000 ($473) which limits the number of shares issued and encourages volatility.[85] The Tokyo Stock Exchange launched its own market for venture companies, "Mothers," in December 1999. As of June 2001, NASDAQ Japan had only 56 listings with no high profile names. Mothers listed only 29 stocks. NASDAQ pulled out of its Japanese venture in August 2002, citing low levels of market activity, lack of support from the Japanese financial industry, and opposition to its trading platform.[86]

Notes and Questions

1. How would you compare the trading and price reporting systems of SEAQ and TSE to the NYSE and NASDAQ?

2. Japan has taken a similar "lite" approach to market structure regulation as has the EU. Like the EU it imposes a best execution obligation on brokers. These brokers then into contracts with customers defining exactly what this obligation requires. There is no government regulation of data provision or prices.

C. LONDON V. CONTINENTAL EXCHANGES

Competition among Europe's complex web of markets began historically with different national exchanges separated by different market structures and nationalist sympathies. It evolved by showing a steady trend toward convergence of the different structures.

In Chapter 4, when we looked at the Club Med countries' position on the Investment Services Directive, it appeared that their competitive strategy was protectionism, i.e. keep other exchanges like SEAQ from trading Club Med country securities. We saw that strategy failed. France, one of the leaders of Club Med, has now shifted its strategy to one of forceful competition with SEAQ. The Paris Bourse (CAC) is also promoting the virtues of its order-driven system (similar to TSE) over SEAQ's market-maker system (which SEAQ, in turn, has changed). Paris also has adopted new rules for trading large blocks.

All trades on the Paris Bourse (CAC trades) were traditionally required to be made at a single price regardless of the size of the order; all supply and demand was matched centrally at a single price. Under the new rules, block trades can be separately negotiated at a price within a weighted

---

[85] B. Rahman, "NASDAQ Japan Passes Early Test," *Financial Times*, June 27, 2000.
[86] V. Boland, "NASDAQ Draws Back from Plan for 24-hour Marketplace," *Financial Times*, August 8, 2002.

average price spread for standard block sizes determined by the Council des Bourses de Valeur (CBV, the governing board of the Bourse). The weighted average price spread for a particular share offering is calculated from the outstanding sale and purchase order for a standard block size registered in the market. The standard block size is set for each quarter based on the volumes of transactions and quantities of shares normally marketed in the previous quarter. So-called "structuring" blocks, in excess of a fixed amount or 10 percent of a company's capital, have greater leeway. There has been no compromise with prompt reporting; once these off-market block trades have been completed, they must be promptly reported.

Another competitive move by CAC in 1996 was to deploy a communications system in London that allows traders in London to trade CAC stocks from screens in their London offices in real time. This takes advantage of the Investment Services Directive to offer cross-border services. CAC has also set up its Eurocac system for dealers to trade in the stocks of European blue chips regardless of where they are listed. As of 1997, Eurocac had 60 stocks, 30 of which were Italian and 10 German.[87] Finally, it is important to note that the French stock trade transaction tax was eliminated in 1993.

It appears that CAC and other continental exchanges have made inroads into SEAQ's market share in the trading of their securities. While SEAQ initially may have traded 25 percent of the volume in French equities, and perhaps even 50 percent in French blue chips, according to Paris Bourse officials in 1995 trading in blue chips on SEAQ was only 25 percent of total volume.[88] M. Pagano[89] finds that the Italian, German and French markets repatriated a substantial portion of trading from SEAQ. He offers three reasons for this: (1) the increase in liquidity, immediacy and transparency of Continental markets; (2) the declining willingness of London dealers to commit substantial capital to market making in Continental stocks following significant losses on such stocks in the early 1990s; and (3) a preference of institutional investors for the Continental trading systems.

Paris has also been a pioneer in selling its trading technology to other exchanges. In 1997 it made major sales of its technology to the Sao Paulo stock exchange and the Chicago Mercantile Exchange. Technology sales could be an increasingly important revenue source and basis for competition among exchanges in the future.

Some studies have found that one advantage of trading on SEAQ (a dealer market) over CAC (an order market) is that trading on SEAQ need not be anonymous. This permits the disciplining of traders exploiting

---

[87] M. Anslow, "Selling SuperCAC," *Securities Industry News*, May 19, 1997.
[88] A. Benos and M. Crouhy, "Changes in the Structure and Dynamics of European Securities Markets," 4 HEC School of Management Discussion Paper (July 1995).
[89] "The Changing Microstructure of European Equity Markets," paper presented at the University of Genoa Conference on European Investment Markets (September 1996).

informational advantages, which as we have seen is a major justification of the NYSE's specialist system.[90]

Germany has also made some strides in becoming more competitive. Germany's equity market has not been traditionally important due to the predominance of bank financing. Equity investment in Germany has been estimated at between 5.5 and 11 percent of total investment, as compared with 18 percent in the U.K. and 21 percent in the U.S.[91] However, the privatization of East German companies, the general advantages of capital market financing, and the desire of the country to become a major player in international capital markets, are producing change. About 12.33 million people (19.3 percent of the population) owned shares at the end of 2000, which is about double the level of 1997; and investors in mutual funds increased by 10 percent over the same period.[92]

Germany's regulatory system has been greatly strengthened through the creation of the Federal Supervisory Office for Securities Trading and the adoption of prohibitions on insider trading. Germany (similar to the United States) has eight regional exchanges. These exchanges use an open-outcry trading method under which public orders and market-makers compete for exposed individual orders in a system somewhat like the NYSE. The Frankfurt exchange has 75 percent of German exchange trading.[93]

Stock market competition in Europe occurs in the context of competition between London and Frankfurt for supremacy as a financial center. London outstrips Frankfurt by most measures, including assets under management, ($4.132 billion versus $1.456 billion), number of foreign banking institutions (478 versus 320), cross-border bank lending share (31 percent versus 5.4 percent), foreign equity turnover share (52 percent versus 5.8 percent), and OTC derivatives trading share (36 percent versus 12.7 percent). However, Frankfurt is well positioned with respect to the increasing importance of the Euro and as the home of the European Central Bank.[94]

There have been significant efforts to establish Pan-European stock markets for second-tier firms. The EU Commission has promoted this idea.

---

[90] L. Glosten, "Is the Electronic Open Limit Order Book Inevitable?," 49 Journal of Finance (1994), pp. 1152-1153. See also G. Franke and D. Hess, "Anonymous Electronic Trading Versus Floor Trading," 32-33 Internationalisierung der Wirtschaft, Sonderforschungsbereich 178, Series II, No. 285 (1985).

[91] R. Butler, "Last Call for Germany's Equity Market: Deutsche Telekom's Privatisation Launches Government Effort to Spur Retail Investment in Economy," *Institutional Investor*, November 1996.

[92] R. Benoit, "Big Rise in Number of Germans Owning Shares," *Financial Times*, January 10, 2001.

[93] For a comprehensive review of changes in Germany, see J. Freis Jr., "An Outsider's Look into the Regulation of Insider Trading in Germany: A Guide to Securities, Banking, and Market Reform in Finantzplatz Deutschland," 19 Boston College International and Comparative Law Review (1996), p. 11.

[94] C. Batchelor, E. Crooks and T. Major, "Deutsche Bank Plans London 'Leaning Tower,'" *Financial Times*, February 8, 2002.

The EASDAQ (European Association of Securities Dealers Automated Quotation) began operations in September 1996, using the NASDAQ market-maker quote based system to establish a market for fast-growing companies. It has had somewhat of a slow start. As of January 31, 2001, it only had 60 companies and a small market capitalization. In April 2001 NASDAQ announced its acquisition of a 58 percent stake in EASDAQ, which will now be called NASDAQ Europe. NSCC, the clearing arm of the U.S.'s DTCC, will help manage clearing and settlement services.

EASDAQ has competition from another venture, Euro NM, to trade smaller capitalized companies. Euro NM has linked four new national systems trading small companies, the French Nouveau Marché, the German Neuer Markt (part of the Frankfurt Stock Exchange), the Belgian Nouveau Marché, and the Dutch NMAX. By June 1998 Euro NM had 101 listings and a market capitalization of over $20 billion. In December 1998 Euro NM announced plans for Sweden, Denmark, and Switzerland to join, giving Euro NM a clear edge in its battle with EASDAQ.

The German Neuer Markt had grown to be by far the biggest member of Euro NM; as of May 2000, it had 60 percent of the listings and more than 80 percent of the market capitalization, and 20 percent of its listings were foreign issuers. Due to the dot.com crash, it had a 90 percent downturn between January 2000 and July 2001, resulting in calls for stricter regulation and listing standards. Many came to refer to it as the Suckermarkt. It announced closure in September 2002, another victim of the burst of the bubble.[95]

EASDAQ requires companies applying for admission to trading to publish a prospectus, and public offerings of EASDAQ listed securities are subject to the European Union POP Directive examined in Chapter 4. EASDAQ securities can be traded through screens placed in a number of EU countries.

Finally, one should not ignore the competition from ATSs, like the U.K.'s Tradepoint, to the traditional European exchanges. In October 2000, Tradepoint announced a merger with the Swiss Stock Exchange (SWX) which formed a combined trading system, Virt-x, that opened for trading in June 2001. Trading in all Swiss blue chip shares and Tradepoint's pan-European trading were to be based in London and governed by U.K. regulatory standards.[96] The ambition of Virt-x to become a European trading platform did not succeed. It failed to win more than 10 percent of the trading in European blue chips, and most of its trading was in Swiss stocks. In 2003, Virt-x was taken over by SWX.

---

[95] S. Ascarelli and G. Sims, "German Neuer Markt Exchange Will Be Shut down Amid Scandals," *The Wall Street Journal*, September 27, 2002.

[96] V. Boland, "Tradepoint and SWX Seal Virt-x Merger," *Financial Times*, October 24, 2000.

A key question is how the Euro will affect the development of stock markets in Europe. This issue was examined in Chapter 4. It is likely that it will continue to promote further integration of national markets but the evidence on this is not clear.[97]

A study based on 2001 data shows low concentration of market shares on European exchanges. The three firm concentration ratio was 68.2 percent, and the five firm ratio 82.4 percent. London, Euronext, and Deutsche Börse led the way with respective market shares of 28.9, 24. 8, and 14.4 percent.[98]

D.   ALLIANCES AND MERGERS

Until 2005, mergers were not a factor in the U.S., but that year saw the announcement of two significant mergers, the NYSE with Archipelago and NASDAQ with Instinet. Europe has also been the scene of merger activity, some successful and some not.

In July 1998 the London and Frankfurt Stock Exchanges announced the formation of a strategic alliance, apparently ending an acrimonious struggle between the two exchanges over supremacy in the quickly converging European market. The alliance was to feature the top 300 companies in the European Union. Members of the two exchanges were to have reciprocal membership with each other. As such, the London Stock Exchange would no longer deal in German stocks and vice-versa. Instead, members of the London exchange that wanted to deal in German equities would do so as regular remote members of the German exchange and the same would be the case for German traders wishing to deal in London equities. In addition, the two exchanges were to have a common index, the listing criteria were to be the same, and the hours between the two markets were to be harmonized.

This was to be the first step in the creation of a pan-European exchange. After London and Frankfurt took the lead, the Paris, Madrid, Milan, Amsterdam, Brussels, and Zurich exchanges joined the alliance. However, the exchanges were unable to solve some basic problems, most importantly the adoption of common trading systems (which would have required significant technology changes with high attendant costs) and common clearing and settlement systems (Chapter 10 elaborates on these problems). As a result, the participating bourses adopted a "virtual" solution

---

[97] Compare J. Yang, I. Min and Q. Li, "European Stock Market Integration: Does EMU Matter," 30 J. of Business Finance and Accounting 1253 (2004) (EMU increases integration) with H. Askari and J. Chatterjee, "The Euro and Financial Market Integration," 43 Journal of Common Market Studies 1 (2005) (EMU has not increased integration).

[98] A. Anderson, "Competition between European Stock Exchanges," Working Paper (May 27, 2003).

that would allow users of each exchange access to stocks listed on the other using existing technology.[99]

1.   EURONEXT

The idea of one pan-European exchange came to a halt—at least temporarily in March 2000 when the Paris Bourse merged with the Brussels and Amsterdam exchanges under the name of Euronext, with a combined market capitalization of $1.7 trillion. It appears that this was a pre-emptive move by Paris after its discussions for a merger with the London Stock Exchange broke down.[100] Each exchange remains intact as a subsidiary of a Euronext, N.V. a Dutch-based holding company, and each exchange continues to have its own listings, trading system, and separate regulator. Euronext claims to have a "single trading platform," but this only means that members on one exchange can trade in the same capacity on all three exchanges.[101] In 2001, Euronext became a more formidable competitor when it outbid LSE and acquired Liffe, the London International Financial Futures and Options Exchange. In 2004, Euronext raised the competition ante against the London exchange by announcing it planned to offer trading in the FTSE 100, London's most widely traded stocks.[102]

2.   iX: THE FAILURE OF THE LONDON-FRANKFURT MERGER

The Paris-led merger was followed by the announcement of a merger of the London and Frankfurt stock exchanges on May 3, 2000, under the new name of iX for International Exchange. This plan was abandoned on September 13 of the same year but it is interesting to review the proposed structure and why the merger failed.

Each exchange was to own 50 percent of iX. Since the big German banks were the major owners of the Frankfurt exchange, while LSE ownership was diffused among 290 members, the German banks would have been the biggest shareholders of the new combined entity. Deutsche Bank, for example, would have owned 8.5 percent of the new exchange.

As of March 2000, the LSE had a market capitalization of about $2.8 trillion and the Deutsche Börse had $1.5 trillion; the LSE had average daily dollar volume of $468 billion, as compared with $365 billion for Deutsche Börse. The combined market capitalization of $4.3 trillion made iX the 4th largest stock market in the world, after the NYSE ($11.2 trillion), NASDAQ ($6.2 trillion) and Tokyo ($4.5 trillion). While London was bigger at the time of the proposed merger, the growth rate and profitability of Frankfurt was higher.

---

[99] V. Boland, "Plan for Single Europe Bourse Shelved," *Financial Times*, September 24, 1999.
[100] V. Boland, "Paris Exchange Seeks to Woo New Partners," *Financial Times*, April 26, 2000.
[101] S. Hirsch and V. Marquette, "EURONEXT: The First Pan-European Exchange, An Overview from Creation to Completion," Journal of International Financial Markets (2001), p. 105.
[102] N. Cohen, "Euronext Plans for U.K. Trades," *Financial Times*, March 22, 2004.

iX was to have been headquartered in London under the leadership of the former CEO of the Frankfurt exchange, Werner Siefert. Blue-chip stocks were to be traded in London under U.K. regulation and technology stocks were to be traded in Frankfurt under German regulation. iX had agreed to have a central counterparty to trades but it was unclear exactly how that was to be arranged. Several other issues, including the currency in which stocks would trade in London (Euro, Sterling or both) and the integration of trading and clearing and settlement systems, remained to be resolved. Deutsche Börse's 50 percent ownership of Clearstream (formerly Cedel) was left outside of the deal (see Chapter 15 for more information on Clearstream). This was apparently done because Deutsche Börse would have been the dominant partner in a merger if its Clearstream ownership were to be included.

iX was to have a link with NASDAQ. NASDAQ planned to trade the technology stocks centered in Frankfurt when Frankfurt was closed. This fit into NASDAQ's general strategy to be the centerpiece of 24-hour global trading.

It is not clear exactly why the iX merger failed, but four factors seemed to have played important roles. First, the division between the blue chip trading in London and the technology trading in Frankfurt was not altogether clear. Second, there was criticism from the brokerage community of the failure to create a common clearing and settlement system for stocks traded on the two exchanges. Third, there were significant regulatory issues arising out of the differences in regulation in the two countries. Foremost of these was transparency, or price reporting. In London, a five day delay was permitted for the reporting of block trades unless the block trade had been 90 percent unwound in which case the trade must be reported immediately; in Frankfurt, traders had to report trades by the end of the day unless they were executed off the exchange (representing 30 percent of all trades) in which case they were not reported at all.[103] Deutsche Börse announced, however, that it was in favor of using the London rules for the price reporting of all issues. The German and British regulatory authorities, the Federal Securities Trading Supervisory Office (BAWe) and the Financial Services Authority, respectively, issued a joint statement on August 21, 2000 describing six task forces that had been set up to review regulatory issues.[104]

There were also problems of corporate structure and governance that would have made a complete merger difficult. Under German law the exchange would have had to remain a separate body, as it was a quasi-public corporation. Reportedly, there were also problems as to how the disclosure regimes in the two countries were to work together. While there were differences in how listing standards, periodic disclosure and ad hoc disclosure

---

[103] NYSE Research (April 24, 2001) (communication to author).

[104] The work of these task forces is elaborated on in S. Bergstrasser, "Regulatory Implications of an Exchange Merger," in *Capital Markets in the Age of the Euro: Cross-border Transactions, Listed Companies & Regulation* (G. Ferrarini, K. Hopt, E. Wymeersch, eds., 2002), p. 289.

were dealt with by the two exchanges, it is unclear why these differences would have prevented the merger. The shares in Frankfurt could have traded under Frankfurt rules, and the shares in London under London rules. There were also issues about how the two different regimes for insider trading and market manipulation would have been handled. Again, it is not clear why these differences could not have been allowed, particularly in cases that there were no dual listings, since all trading in a given stock would take place under the rules of one country.

The final factor that may have accounted for the merger failure was the hostile bid for the LSE launched in September 2000 by the OM Group, a technology group that ran the Stockholm stock exchange. Although, the hostile bid was eventually rejected on November 11 (after the friendly merger fell through), the OM bid may have raised issues about the pricing of the friendly merger, in particular whether the iX's 50-50 approach undervalued London.[105]

3.   LSE AND DEUTSCHE BÖRSE: ROUND TWO AND THE SAME RESULT

In December 2004, Deutsche Börse (DB) made a takeover bid for LSE but LSE rejected a proposed offer of $2.6 billion. Since the earlier talks in 2000, DB has acquired 100 percent of Clearstream,, which clears and settles all of DB's trades, while LSE contracts with LCH/Clearnet for such services. Clearstream contributes about 33 percent of DB's total revenue.[106] DB's market capitalization in December 2004 was about £4.5 billion as compared to LSE at £1.5 billion, while LSE's share of European share trading was 36 percent compared to 13 percent of DB (based on 2003).[107] Unlike the 2000 proposal, there would be no reallocation of share trading between the two exchanges—the current national listing structures would remain in place.

One key issue in the merger, discussed in Chapter 10, was how clearing and settlement would be handled. LSE owner/customers were concerned that they would have to use Clearstream rather than seeking the most efficient clearer. Another key factor was how the shareholders of the two exchanges, concentrated in several institutions, would view such a merger. Also, the ownership of DB had become 93% foreign. The owners are also users of the exchange so that their prime consideration was the impact of a merger on the price of transaction services. Shareholders of DB also expressed concerns about the 50 percent premium that was being offered for LSE shares.

Regulation continued to be a matter of concern. In February, Callum McCarthy the head of the FSA, warned that U.K. companies and shareholders might lose the higher degree of protection they now enjoy if LSE

---

[105] "Shocking Times in Throgmorton Street," The Economist, September 2, 2000.

[106] N. Cohen and P. Jenkins, "Shaping Up for a Perfect Fit," *Financial Times*, December 15, 2004.

[107] P. Davies, "LSE Rejects £1.3bn Deutsche Börse Bid," *Financial Times*, January 28, 2005.

were sold to a foreign buyer. He said one way to avoid this would be for the holding company of the two exchanges to be in the U.K. This in turn could trigger concerns in Frankfurt. There were also possible antitrust issues.

While DB and LSE continued to pursue talks after LSE's rejection of the initial bid, eventually institutional foreign shareholders of DB, such as hedge funds, Fidelity and Merrill Lynch, scuttled further pursuit of the merger in March 2005 and then forced both the CEO, Werner Siefert, and the Chairman, Rolf Breuer (also the Chairman of Deutsche Bank) out of their roles at the exchange. After the bid, DB's shares rose by a third reflecting the fact that the market believed the deal was a bad one for DB.[108]

Euronext is also pursuing LSE, and reportedly is prepared to offer a higher price. The details of any proposal have not become public as of June 2005.

Notes and Questions

1.   Is Euronext a pan-European exchange? If not, will there be one in the future?

2.   Are there significant regulatory obstacles to cross-border exchange mergers?

E.   WORLDWIDE COMPETITION

I. Domowitz, J. Glen and A. Madhavan[109] measure trading costs across 42 countries for the 1996-1998 period. Total costs are composed of explicit costs including commissions, taxes and fees (but not clearing and settlement). Implicit cost refers to the market impact of a trade as measured by comparing the price of a trade with a benchmark price (the mean of the day's open, close, high and low prices). Some of the country results are shown in Table 13A below.

---

[108] P. Jenkins, "The Eclectic Survivor," *Financial Times*, May 14, 2005; D. Reilly and E. Taylor, "Deutsche Boerse Ends Bid To Purchase LSE," *The Wall Street Journal*, March 7, 2005.
[109] "Liquidity, Volatility and Equity Trading Costs Across Countries Over Time," 4 International Finance (2001), p. 221.

Table 13A			
	Total Costs	Explicit Costs	Implicit Costs
Argentina	76.9	47.3	29.6
Brazil	58.0	36.7	21.4
Canada	52.4	25.3	27.1
France	29.5	22.8	6.7
Germany	37.7	24.3	13.4
Japan	41.3	31.7	9.5
U.K.	54.5	39.3	15.2
U.S.	38.1	8.3	29.8

The study finds that implicit costs are inversely related to market capitalization and positively related to volatility. The study also finds that automated systems, as in Japan and France, significantly reduce implicit costs.

M. Pagano, A. Röell and J. Zechner[110] show that between 1986 and 1997, the number of European companies cross-listing their shares increased considerably, but most of the increase occurred on U.S. exchanges (half to NYSE). At the same time, the number of U.S. firms cross-listing in Europe fell by one-third. The authors found that this was part of a bigger picture which included the inability of European exchanges (with the exception of Frankfurt and to some extent London) to attract any new listings. The companies most likely to cross-list in the United States are high tech companies and/or companies that have rapidly expanded through leverage and are in need of capital. According to the authors, the European exchanges have lost out to the U.S. because they have the higher trading costs—with the exception of the U.K., and lower accounting standards and shareholder protection. In addition, U.S. markets have a better analyst following for high tech companies, are more liquid and larger. These advantages may decrease as European capital markets integrate in the post-Euro period.

Worldwide cross-listings should generally increase as regulatory differences among countries decrease. As we saw in Chapter 2, high U.S. disclosure standards and the present requirement for U.S. GAAP reconciliation have deterred many foreign companies from listing in the U.S. If foreign countries were to move closer to U.S. disclosure standards and if the U.S. were to accept IAS accounting standards, cross-listings in the U.S. should increase. A similar point was made in a recent study of N. Yamori and T. Baba,[111] where the authors predicted that cross-listing of Japanese companies should increase as a result of the "Big Bang" since Japanese

---

[110] "The Geography of Equity Listing: Why do European Companies List Abroad," 57 Journal of Finance (2002), p. 2651.
[111] "Japanese Management Views on Overseas Exchange Listings: Survey Results," Federal Reserve Bank of San Francisco Pacific Basin Working Paper PB99-05 (October 1999).

companies will be required to adopt international disclosure and accounting standards. As we also saw in Chapter 2, U.S. adoption of Sarbanes-Oxley, particularly Section 404 requiring internal controls, may also be deterring foreign companies from listing in the United States.

European-based systems may try to come to the U.S. to compete with U.S. exchanges. Consider Tradepoint's approval to operate in the United States without being required to register as an exchange. Such approval permits investment fund managers to trade LSE stocks in the U.S. without using a broker as an intermediary—since all traders on registered exchanges must be registered broker-dealers. This move by Tradepoint is part of the growing picture of cross-continental competition by which exchanges on one continent expand into others through the use of computer technology.

The SEC's grant of an exemption to Tradepoint from stock exchange registration is conditional on low volume. Tradepoint's average daily volume involving a U.S. member cannot exceed $40 million, and its worldwide average daily volume cannot exceed 10 percent of the average daily volume of the LSE. This indicates that the SEC could well have a different approach for exchanges with more appeal.

Indeed, foreign exchanges would like the same automatic access to the U.S. that EU exchanges have to EU countries under the Investment Services Directive.[112] Chapter 2 discussed Benn Steil's proposal on behalf of the Council of Foreign Relations to this effect.

One of the most important areas in worldwide competition is for the listing of Asian companies, particularly Chinese companies. The main competitors are LSE and the NYSE and Nasdaq. In 2005, South Korea's Kumho Tire opted to list in the U.K. and Seoul rather than on the NYSE, and a month later China Air chose London and Hong Kong rather than New York. NYSE and NASDAQ have both applied to Chinese regulators to establish offices in China to attract investors.

CONCLUSIONS

This Chapter focuses on competition between trading venues, principally exchanges. Countries play a key role in this system. On the one hand, countries erect cross-border obstacles to competition between domestic and foreign exchanges, usually in the name of investor protection (U.S. exchange registration requirements), the need for local control (Japan in the past), or the need for single country control in the case of mergers (Germany in the case of iX). On the other hand, countries shape their regulatory systems, e.g. corporate governance standards, insider trading prohibitions, or disclosure rules, to attract foreign listings. This is the bonding hypothesis.

---

[112] J. Clarke, "European Invasion," *Securities Industry News*, June 18, 2001.

In addition to regulatory obstacles, the exchanges themselves, often with the blessing of their regulators, have erected their own barriers, domestic and international, to competition. This seems to be on the way out, however, as is demonstrated by the NYSE's abolition of Rule 390. Nonetheless, in Europe, the use by exchanges of silos for clearing and settlement, has limited cross-border competition.

A key area for future concern is the structure of competition between ATSs (ECNs) and traditional stock exchanges. This issue has many complicated dimensions ranging from fairness (more regulatory obligations of "SRO" exchanges compared to ATSs), to free or cheap riders (use by ATSs of exchange data), to the concern with trading fragmentation.

The ATS issue may ultimately be resolved by technology and liability. ATS technology is evolving beyond mere matching to the possibility of electronic recreation of the floor-based auction system (perhaps even with specialists). Exchanges and ATSs may converge on technology as exchanges seek increasingly to use electronic systems and ATSs seek to build in auction features. This is certainly one of the messages of the merger between the NYSE and Archipelago. The liability issue may be even more important for resolving the issue. Human intervention carries with it the possibility of misbehavior, and attendant liability, as the specialist scandal at the NYSE shows. This misbehavior can be eliminated in large part by using more controllable machines and programs.

CHAPTER FOURTEEN

FUTURES AND OPTIONS

A. INTRODUCTION

Derivatives are financial instruments whose value is based on or derived from other assets or variables. Futures and options are among the best known. A futures contract is an agreement to buy or sell an asset at a set time in the future for a set price. No cash is paid at the time the contract is entered into. Two types of options exist. A call option gives the holder the right to buy an asset by or at a set date for a set price. A put option gives the holder the right to sell an asset by or at a set date for a set price.

Today, financial futures and options markets span the globe. The underlying asset may be a deposit in a major currency, a bond issued by a major government, equity in a firm, or an index of a leading stock market. This chapter examines derivatives traded on exchanges. Chapter 15 examines derivatives traded on exchanges.

These markets have a long pedigree. Futures markets began hundreds of years ago, giving farmers and traders firm prices for crops well before harvest. U.S. futures exchanges opened in the mid-1800s. Options markets appeared in Europe and America in the 1700s, but not until the early 1900s was an exchange-like association set up. The Chicago Board of Exchange opened the first options exchange in 1973.

This Chapter examines the international financial futures and options markets. It begins with an introduction to futures and options, concentrating on their underlying theories, the mechanics of their trading, and the reasons behind their use. The second part of the Chapter links this descriptive foundation to a case study involving the collapse of Barings Bank, an event that led to significant changes in regulation.

B. FUTURES, OPTIONS, AND MARKETS: AN INTRODUCTION

1. FUTURES

Futures exist for many different types of assets. For example, there are futures contracts on wheat, on Treasury Bills, stock indices, like the S&P 500 or FTSE 100, shares of individual companies, and even other derivatives. Hedgers and speculators are the two basic types of investors in futures.

Hedgers are people who use futures contracts to offset their risks with regard to a particular asset. Speculators, on the other hand, buy and sell futures contracts with the sole goal of earning a profit. They usually base their decisions on their perceived sense of the price movement of the underlying asset in the contract.

The Chicago Mercantile Exchange has produced an account of some of the different kinds of interest rate futures available to investors:[1]

> The 13-week U.S. Treasury bill futures contract is an agreement to buy or sell, at a given time in the future, a U.S. Treasury bill with 13 weeks to maturity and a face value of $1,000,000. The three-month Eurodollar Time Deposit futures contract implies an agreement to place a deposit (lend) or to take a deposit (borrow), at a given time in the future, of $1,000,000 in Eurodollars for three months in the London Interbank Market. The One-Month LIBOR futures contract implies an agreement to place a deposit or to take a deposit of $3,000,000 in Eurodollars for one month in the London Interbank Market.
>
> The CME's three-month Euro Deutschmark (also known as Euromark) futures and options are the Exchange's first non-Dollar denominated short-term interest rate contracts. The Euromark futures contract calls for a 3-month deposit of Deutschmarks. The contract size is DM1,000,000. With the addition of Euromark contracts, the CME's interest rate complex offers investors a way to utilize short-term interest rate markets on both sides of the Atlantic.

All of these contracts are traded using a price index, which is derived by subtracting the interest rate from 100. For instance, an interest rate of 10 percent translates to an index price of 90. If interest rates move higher, the price of the contract falls; if rates move lower, the contract price rises.

The futures price is directly related to the cash price of the *deliverable* security (for example, an already-issued 1-year or 6-month T-bill that will mature 91 days after the T-bill futures' first delivery day). On the futures' delivery date, the futures contract becomes a cash position, so that the two prices are the same at that point. Prior to contract delivery, the futures price (yield) reflects the market price (yield) of the deliverable security, as well as the financing rate associated with holding the deliverable security until the contract delivery date.

If the short date financing rate is higher than the yield on the deliverable security, there is a cost of carrying the deliverable; and the yield implied by the futures price would tend to be lower than the deliverable's yield. Conversely, if the financing rate is lower than the deliverable's yield,

---

[1] Chicago Mercantile Exchange, *Using Interest Rate Futures and Options* (1993).

there is a profit from carrying the deliverable, and the futures yield will have to be higher.

2.   OPTIONS[2]

As stated above, a call option confers the right to buy an asset at an agreed exercise or strike price by or at a set time in the future. A put option confers the right to sell at the strike price by or at a set time in the future. Option positions and investment strategies can become quite complex. For simplicity, we draw on examples of stock options (i.e. which are not complicated by interest payments). American options can be exercised at any point before the expiration date. European options cannot be exercised before the expiration date.

Hull describes profit and loss opportunities available to parties to option contracts as follows: "On one side is the investor who has taken the long position (i.e. has bought the option). On the other side is the investor who has taken a short position (i.e. has sold or written the option). The writer of an option receives cash up front but has potential liabilities later. His or her profit/loss is the reverse of that for the purchaser of the option." The following figures show the profit and loss to buyers (Figures 14.1 and 14.2) and writers (Figures 14.3 and 14.4) of a call and put option.

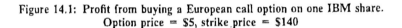

Figure 14.1: Profit from buying a European call option on one IBM share.
Option price = $5, strike price = $140

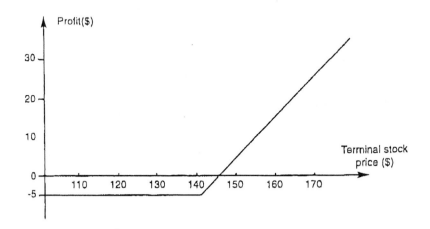

---

[2] This section relies heavily on J. Hull, *Introduction to Futures and Options Markets* (1991), pp. 213-220.

Figure 14.2: Profit from buying a European put option on one Exxon share.
Option price = $7, strike price = $90

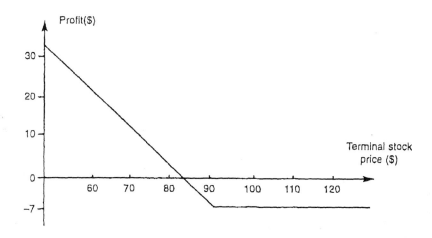

Figure 14.3: Profit from writing a European call option on one IBM share.
Option price = $5, strike price = $140

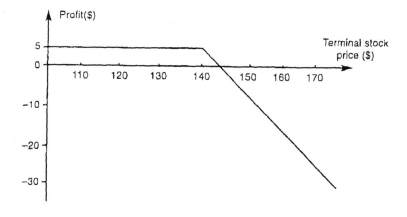

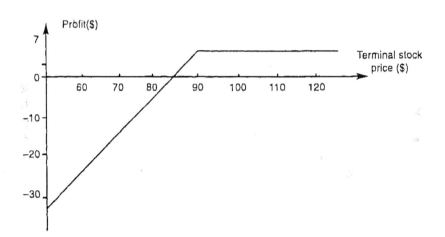

Figure 14.4: Profit from writing a European put option on one Exxon share. Option price = $7, strike price = $90

There are a number of different trading strategies involving a single option on a stock and the stock itself. The profits from these are illustrated in Figure 14.5. In this figure the dashed line shows the relationship between profit and stock price for the individual securities constituting the portfolio, while the solid line shows the relationship between profit and stock price for the whole portfolio.

In Figure 14.5a the portfolio consists of a long position (purchase) in a stock plus a short position in a call option (writing an option). The investment strategy represented by this portfolio is known as *writing a covered call*. This is because the long stock position "covers" or protects the investor from the possibility of a sharp rise in the stock price. In Figure 14.5b a short position in a stock is combined with a long position in a call option. This is the reverse of writing a covered call, also known as writing a naked call. In Figure 14.5c the investment strategy involves buying a put option on a stock and the stock itself. This is sometimes referred to as a *protective put strategy*. In Figure 14.5d a short position in a put option is combined with a short position in the stock. This is the reverse of a protective put.

Figure 14.5: Profit from buying (a) a long position in a stock combined with a short position in a call, (b) a short position in a stock combined with a long position in a call, (c) a long position in a put combined with a long position in a stock, (d) a short position in a put combined with a short position in a stock

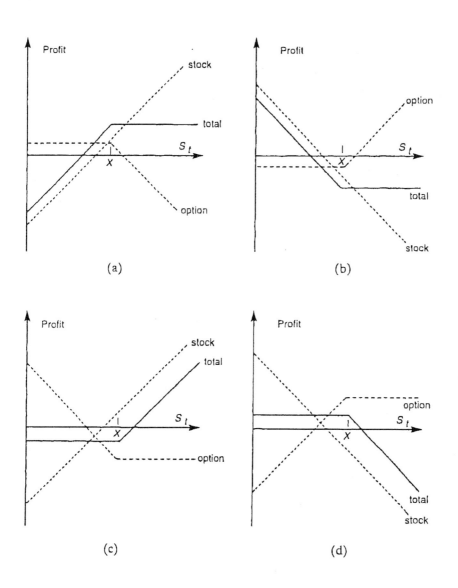

Put-call parity holds that the current value of a call on a stock equals the current value of an associated put plus the current market price of the stock, less the present value of the strike price. The relationship is most easily demonstrated with a European put and call on a stock that does not pay dividends, and ignores transactions costs, margins, and taxes. The idea is that if put and call prices are not in put-call parity, arbitrage is possible. One "could make a certain profit on zero investment by selling the relatively overpriced option and using the proceeds to buy the relatively underpriced option, together with an appropriate position in the stock and borrowing or lending. ... The portfolio would require no cash outflow (or inflow) on the expiration date of the options."[3]

An example may help to illustrate this potential for arbitrage. Suppose you create two investment portfolios. For the first, you purchase a share of IBM for $50 and a put on IBM stock with a strike price of $50 (i.e. the protective put strategy discussed above). At the same time, you create a second portfolio by buying a call option on a share of IBM with an exercise price of $50. Additionally, you invest the present value of $50 in a savings account (so that on the exercise date you will have exactly $50).

Based on the above facts, two outcomes on the exercise date are possible. IBM might be selling for more than $50. In the case of the first portfolio, you could sell your share for profit and discard the put. Likewise, in the second portfolio, you could take the $50 out of the bank account, exercise the call, and simultaneously sell the share back on the open market. In both cases, you will reap precisely the same profit. On the other hand, IBM might be selling for less than $50. In the first portfolio, you will exercise your put and retain the $50. In the second portfolio, you will throw away the call, and hold onto the $50 from the savings account.

Under both outcomes, these portfolios have the same payoffs. Consequently, they should, theoretically, have the same price. Investors who engage in arbitrage look for differences among baskets of assets that should be priced equally. Thus, arbitrage is merely a way to make a profit by exploiting differences in the price of two portfolios that should have equivalent prices.

3.   THE MARKETS

There are many venues for trading options and futures. The Chicago Mercantile Exchange (CME) is one of over 55 futures and options exchanges around the world. CME formed in 1919 to trade futures, emerging from an exchange for agricultural commodities founded in 1874. It set up the International Monetary Market (IMM) in 1972 to trade foreign currency futures. Today, chicken and live hog futures and options trade alongside

---

[3] J.C. Cox and M. Rubenstein, *Options Markets* (1985), pp. 39-44.

those denominated in Yen and Swiss Francs, London's FTSE 100 share index, Japan's Nikkei Stock average, and the S&P 500 index, among others.

In the U.K. the leading exchange until 2002 was the London International Financial Futures Exchange (LIFFE). It merged with Euronext, which includes exchanges formerly based in Belgium, France and the Netherlands. Eurex, which by many measures is now the world's largest derivatives exchange, combines the Swiss exchange (SOFFEX) and the Deutsche Terminborse (DTB). In Japan there is the Tokyo International Financial Futures Exchange (TIFFE).

Most exchanges have been traditionally owned by their members, but this is changing. The trend toward public membership started abroad when in 2000 LIFFE opened investment to non-members and was later taken over by Euronext. The Singapore International Futures Exchange Ltd. (SIMEX) merged with Singapore's Stock Exchange as the first step to selling shares to the public. CME went public in 2002, the International Stock Exchange (ISE) in 2005 (its price soaring 70 percent after the IPO), and the Chicago Board of Trade (CBOT) plans to do so in 2005.

Large U.S. exchanges such as CME and CBOT still use open-outcry pits for trading, but they are moving to electronic trading. This is a similar trend as we saw for equity markets in Chapter 13. About 75 percent of CBOT's financial futures, which account for most of its business, are now traded electronically.[4] About 57 percent of the trading volume on CME is also electronic.[5] More recent electronic-based system startups, the Chicago Board of Options Exchange (CBOE) founded in 1973, and the International Securities Exchange (ISE) founded in May 2000, have obtained significant market share. As of 2003, ISE had become the third largest options exchange (32 percent volume) and the largest equity options exchange. An important future development may be the development of one-stop shopping. The American Stock Exchange (AMEX) combines trading in equities, options and Exchange-traded funds (ETFs), and the CBOT, traditionally an options exchange, began trading a futures contract on the S&P stock index.

Clearing mechanisms raise several important issues for the markets. Does a clearing house have the authority to impose and monitor margin and collection rules on all participants? This is addressed in the discussion of Barings. Should futures and securities exchanges have shared or independent clearing houses? Advantages of a shared clearing house include scale economies that reduce cost, better information about the entire market, and easier monitoring by the regulators. On the other hand, keeping clearing houses separate limits the bad effect of inadequate control by one clearing house.

---

[4] J. Grant, "Chicago Takes A Wild Ride," *Financial Times*, March 16, 2005.
[5] Annual Report 2004.

Clearing mechanisms vary across countries. In Japan and France, for example, clearing occurs within the exchange. Most British exchanges use a separate entity, such as the London Clearing House Limited. In the U.S., futures clearing is closely associated with the exchange, either as a separate clearing house (until 2003, for example, CBOT owned the Board of Trade Clearing Corporation) or a department of the exchange (such as the case of the CME). The clearing house monitors all transactions during the day to determine the net position of each member broker. Non-member brokers do business through members.

In the U.S., the Options Clearing Corporation (OCC) issues and clears publicly offered options traded on the exchanges. The OCC is owned by five exchanges, including the New York Stock Exchange and the Chicago Board of Options Exchange.

Notional principal amounts outstanding are huge, as shown in Table 14A below.

Table 14A
Markets for selected derivative instruments[6]

Instruments	Notional principal outstanding, in billions of U.S. dollars						
	1988	1993	1997	1998	1999	2000	9/2002
Exchange-traded instruments	1,306.0	7,839.3	12,202.2	13,549.3	13,521.7	14,156.0	28,617.7
Interest rate:							
Futures	895.4	4,960.4	7,489.2	7,702.2	7,913.9	7,827.3	10,326.8
Options[1]	279.2	2,362.4	3,639.9	4,602.8	3,755.5	4,719.2	16,142.0
Currency:							
Futures	11.6	29.8	51.9	38.1	36.7	40.0	37.6
Options[1]	48.0	81.1	33.2	18.7	22.4	20.4	30.9
Stock market index							
Futures	27.8	119.2	211.5	321.0	334.3	366.5	323.3
Options[1]	44.0	286.4	776.5	866.5	1,458.9	1,182.5	1,757.1

[1] Calls and puts.

Actual exposures are far less than the notional amounts. Some estimate that the amount at risk through counterparty default represents between 2 percent and 4 percent of the contract's notional value on average.[7]

Since 2000, the SEC has been trying to implement a national market system for options, much like the one for equities discussed in Chapter 13. In November 2000, in order to reduce intermarket trade-throughs (making a

[6] Table based on data from Futures Industry Association, various futures and options exchanges, ISDA and BIS calculations, from Bank for International Settlements, 64th Annual Report 112 (1994); Bank for International Settlements, International Banking and Financial Market Developments (February 1997 and December 2002).
[7] 32 Bank of England Quarterly Bulletin (1992), p. 402.

trade on an option on an exchange despite the fact that a better bid/offer is available elsewhere), the Commission promulgated the Trade-through Disclosure Rule, Rule, 11Ac1-7 under the Exchange Act. This requires a broker-dealer to disclose to its customers when an order has been executed at an inferior price to a publicized quote—however, an exchange which participated in a Commission-approved linkage plan was exempt.[8] This requirement—and the exemption—prompted the options Exchanges to propose a linkage system which the SEC approved in July 2000.[9] Amendments to this system were subsequently approved in May 2002,[10] triggering the ultimate repeal of the Disclosure Rule, since the Linkage Plan largely prevents trading through a better price. It appears that spreads have considerably narrowed with linkage.[11] In February 2004, the SEC issued a concept release addressing numerous issues about the market structure of the options market; it is the counterpart to the NMS concept release for equities markets.[12]

4. PROTECTING THE EXCHANGE: MARGIN RULES

The major tool used by exchanges to protect themselves from defaults by members on contract obligations are margin rules. The exchanges do so by setting margin rules between the broker and the customer. In addition clearing houses set margin rules for the brokers themselves, since the clearing houses that become parties to (or guarantors of) the trades—which is the main function of clearing houses—are directly at risk from the failure of brokers.

The focus here is on margin rules on futures and options to reduce risk; however, note also that central banks may also use margin rules for equities as part of monetary policy. For example, suppose someone buys equity on the New York Stock Exchange. The Federal Reserve Board sets initial margin requirements. Assume that the buyer pays for part of the stock and gets a loan from the broker for the remainder of the cost until full payment is made. The broker holds the stock as security for the loan. The initial margin rules determine the amount of the loan by requiring a down payment as a percent of the stock's current market value. In this regard, one should note that the Fed limits margin lending on foreign as well as domestic stocks. Pursuant to Regulation T, the Fed lists foreign stocks that are eligible for margin lending by U.S. brokers and dealers in the same way as domestic stocks.[13]

---

[8] SEC, Exchange Act Release No. 43591 (November 17, 2000).
[9] SEC, Exchange Act Release No. 43085 (July 28, 2000).
[10] SEC, Exchange Act Release No. 46001 (May 30, 2002). This was implemented in 2003 in two phases.
[11] R. Battalio, B. Hatch, and R. Jennings, "Toward a National Market System for U.S. Exchange-Listed Equity Options," LIX J. of Finance 933 (April 2004).
[12] SEC, Exchange Act Release 34-49175 (February 3, 2004).
[13] See 12 CFR 224.1-2.

Margin rules for customers' futures contracts. For customers' futures contracts, long and short positions are subject to margin rules. In the U.S., exchanges require that a customer buying a position pay at the time of purchase an initial margin that is a share of the current price of the future's contract. The amount is usually a small percentage (e.g. five percent) and varies depending on whether the position is a hedge or speculative and on the contract's variability. The customer may satisfy the margin requirement by putting up cash or securities.

The maintenance margin is set daily against the current market value of the contract, which is marked-to-market daily.

Any loss in value is deducted entirely from the margin account and any gain is added. This is called the variation. The broker passes the variation to the exchange, which in turn passes it to the broker on the other side of such a transaction. The customer, who also has a margin account, can withdraw any amount above the initial margin; consequently, any shift raises one margin account and lowers the other. Whenever a customer's margin account falls below the minimum maintenance level, the broker makes a margin call and the customer must return the margin deposit to its initial level. If the customer cannot meet a margin call and its margin account is insufficient to offset the decline in the contract's market value, the broker is obliged to pay the exchange any shortfall.

For example, suppose there is a contract for $5,000 and the interest margin is 5 percent, or $250. Further suppose the maintenance level is 75 percent of the initial margin, or $188. If on the following day the current market value of the contract is $4900, the margin account of the Long Customer is only $150 ($250 minus the $100 loss), which is below the maintenance level of $188. The broker gives a margin call for $100 to return the margin to its initial $250 level. This is illustrated in Table 14B below:

Table 14B		
Margins for Futures Contracts: Long Party		
	Day 1	Day 2
a. Contract current market value (CMV)	$5,000	$4,900
b. Initial margin required (5 percent)	250	-
c. Buyer's margin a/c	250	250
d. Deduct CMV decline	-	100
e. Adjusted a/c balance	-	150
f. Required maintenance margin (75 percent of b)	-	188
g. Margin call	-	100
h. Margin a/c after call	-	250

The margin account of a Short Customer is increased by $100, since the Short Customer benefits by the fall in price. If the current market value had fallen only $50, the margin account of the Long Customer would be reduced by that $50 but there would be no maintenance margin call. The exchange is not exposed; the debit to the Long Customer's account funds the credit to the Short Customer's account.

Margin rules for brokers' futures contracts. A member broker (or clearing member) has many customer accounts as well as its own proprietary accounts. Futures exchange clearing houses set margins for all member brokers' futures contracts. The clearing house usually calculates gains or losses on each broker's total long positions and on its total short positions in each contract at the end of the trading day. Some clearing houses net the sums (offsetting gains in shorts (or longs) against losses in longs (or shorts)), While others gross them (adding both). The clearing house then adjusts the broker's clearing margin account for each contract by the gain or loss, and the broker tops up or withdraws funds as appropriate. U.S. futures clearing houses use simulation analysis and pricing theory to measure the potential risk of one-day price moves to a specified level at a given probability.

Clearing houses make "super" margin calls if a customer or proprietary position could endanger a member's capital, and the member must post the required margin payment within one hour. Members are required to use settlement banks to make margin payments; if the settlement banks cannot advance the payment needed, the member will fall back on prearranged credit from other banks. Therefore, banks do their own credit check on members.

Rules governing the margin requirements of a broker's proprietary accounts and its customers' accounts vary. Most exchanges require the broker to differentiate between them and require higher margins for customer accounts. In the case of Barings (discussed below), SIMEX required separation of accounts while OSE combined the accounts. LIFFE requires differentiation if the broker itself segregates the customers. Germany's DTB requires differentiation. If the broker defaults, LIFFE prohibits set-off between proprietary and customer accounts, while DTB merges all accounts.

Margin rules for options. Purchasers of call and put options have no margin requirements because the options are required to be paid in full. An option writer, however, is required to maintain funds in a margin account. This is because there is the risk that the option writer could default if the option is exercised. The size of the margin required depends on the nature of the option. There are initial and maintenance margins when the option is naked (that is, the option position is not combined with an offsetting position in the underlying stock). Maintenance margins increase for options "in the money"—ones that purchasers will exercise—and decrease for options "out of the money."

Cross margining. Cross margining programs permit the clearers of options and futures to calculate and collect a single clearing system margin requirement based upon each participating member's total portfolio of offsetting options, futures, and options on futures.

Cross margining may also take place between cash and futures markets. The idea is that someone trading the same underlying asset in both markets should not be forced to duplicate margin requirements if the two positions offset one another. Cross margining agreements, made since 2000, now link the Government Securities Clearing Corporation (GSCC) on the cash side and, for various futures, the Board of Trade Clearing Corporation (BOTCC), the New York Clearing Corporation, the CME, and the BrokerTec Clearing Company. The benefits of cross margining are increased liquidity, improved information sharing, and risk management.[14]

Margin rules based on forecast price movements. A more sophisticated approach to margining uses portfolio analysis to estimate the risk of the investor's full range of securities. One of the systems used by many large exchanges is called SPAN. LIFFE used SPAN, and when LIFFE and the London Traded Options Market merged in March 1992, the LIFFE margining rules extended to options. SIMEX also uses SPAN.

Intraday or end-of-day margining. Margins may be imposed on an intraday basis. LIFFE, through the London Clearing House, CBOT, and CME make at least one intra-day assessment. SIMEX had the authority to do so but rarely used it with Baring Futures (Singapore), as we shall see below.

Single stock futures. In mid-2002, U.S. regulators set margin rules for single stock futures, which until that time had been prohibited. The general rule requires a margin for each long or short position of 20 percent of its current market value.[15]

Notes and Questions

1. Overall, what is the purpose of the margin rules for futures contracts?

2. For margin rules for customers' futures contracts:

    (a) Work through the example on p. 11.

    (b) How do margin rules for futures differ from the margin rules for someone who buys stock long? Does the initial margin have the same function? What would explain why the maintenance margins are treated differently?

3. For margin rules for brokers' futures contracts:

---

[14] J. Ingber and N. Poulos, "A Coming Together of Marketplaces: The Advent of Cross-Margining Between the Cash and Futures Markets," Journal of International Financial Markets (2002), p. 148.

[15] CFTC "Customer Accounts and Margin Requirements," 17 Code of Federal Regulations Part 41, §41.45 (amended July 31, 2002) and SEC "Required Margins" §242.403(b) (amended August 1, 2002).

(a) Which is more important to mitigate systemic risk, individual customer margins with the broker or member margins with the exchange? As long as a member can meet its margin calls, is the exchange protected?

(b) Is it good policy to calculate positions and margin requirements at the end of the day?

4. How are the many different types of margin rules that one finds on exchanges likely to affect competition and cooperative ventures among exchanges?

C. FUTURES AND OPTIONS EXCHANGES: COMPETITION AND REGULATION

Futures and options exchanges compete to be the first to design popular new contracts. To succeed, the contract requires "a large cash market, volatility, an active dealer community, the absence of a good cross-hedging vehicle, multiple applications for its use and a careful specification. ..."[16]

Exchanges often compete in the same contracts. CME and CBOT, for example, each offer competing contracts on at least one of five underlying securities. LIFFE, which introduced futures and options on the German government security (the bund), continued to dominate trading in them until 1997, when Eurex won out. In 1999, more than 33 percent of the Eurex trading volume was futures on the German bund.

Futures exchanges in Europe competed to offer the first contracts in the Euro. MATIF, the French exchange, and LIFFE designed interest rate futures based on EURIBOR, the Euro interbank rate. Many interest rate contracts in the pre-Euro currencies were displaced by the Euro: LIFFE offered contracts for DM (so did DTB), FF (so did MATIF), Eurolira, and ECU. MATIF depended on the FF contract for 50 percent of its trading volume, while LIFFE depended on two DM interest contracts, and a U.K. interest contract for over 50 percent of its trading volume.

Exchanges have different strategies. When LIFFE found it difficult to introduce new contracts, its growth strategy was to win new users (pension funds and retail buyers), to trade two more hours in order to overlap with the Chicago market, and to link with other exchanges. Other European exchanges compete by offering electronic trading; LIFFE had only floor trading until late 1998. In 2000, LIFFE introduced futures on individual stocks, leading its competitors and pushing the U.S. exchanges to press for legislative changes that would allow them to do the same.

---

[16] J. Raybould, "London's Futures Exchanges," City Research Project of London Business School (September 1994).

Competition is increasingly international. CBOT allied with Eurex, jointly owned by Deutsche Börse and the Swiss Stock Exchange, in mid-2000. When CBOT decided in 2003 to switch its alliance to Euronext instead, Eurex announced its plans to compete directly with U.S. exchanges by creating contracts on leading U.S. stocks, bonds, and indexes for trading in a new derivatives exchange that Eurex would set up in the U.S. and did so in February 2004. While its U.S. volume has been minimal, under 5 percent, its U.S. presence has expanded its global business, as U.S. investors access its European trading platforms through the U.S. The regulatory obstacles at CFTC for futures exchanges to enter the U.S. are much lower than those applicable to securities exchanges that were examined in Chapter 2.

Eurex has a clearing link with its EU products that enable U.S. participants in The Clearing Corporation (CC) to clear EU products through their existing clearing arrangements. This allows these participants to consolidate portfolios for the purpose of margining and providing collateral. It is currently applying to the CFTC to enhance the link. The enhancement would allow a trader executing on the U.S. exchange to have its positions carried by Eurex Clearing in the EU rather than by CC. This would be facilitated by Eurex Clearing becoming a "special clearing member" of CC and holding an account with Eurex Clearing to hold trades and effect daily margin settlements and deliveries. These kinds of links for equities were discussed in Chapter 10. Critics of the arrangement have contended that this may create more risk for customer funds if CC is not adequately regulated. This has led to talks between CESR, the Committee of European Securities Regulators (see Chapter 4) and the CFTC, and spurred wider talks about what could be done by the two regulators to encourage a Transatlantic derivatives market. This has also become a topic for the U.S.-EU Regulatory dialogue. Facilitation of a Transatlantic derivatives market is much easier than in the case of equities, where accounting and disclosure differences pose serious obstacles. The regulatory obstacles at CFTC for futures exchanges to enter the U.S. are much lower than those applicable to securities exchanges that were examined in Chapter 2.

International cooperation will not be easy as domestic firms seek to protect themselves from international competition. It is important to note that the two Chicago exchanges, CBOT and CME, sought to block Eurex's entry. First, they tried to use financial inducements (reported at $100 million) to get the small traders that owned 85 percent of CC to refuse to allow CC to offer clearing services to Eurex. Eurex responded by filing an antitrust suit against CBOT and CME. In October 2003, the shareholders of CC accepted Eurex's planned investment. Second, the Chicago exchanges tried to put political pressure on the CFTC to delay or deny Eurex's application to open the new exchange. This in turn triggered talks between U.S. Treasury Secretary Snow and Germany's Finance Minister, Hans

Eichel.[17] These two blocking efforts failed. Eurex has filed a lawsuit seeking damages from CBOT's and CME's alleged anti-competitive behavior. When CBOT and CME lowered fees in response to the Eurex entry, Eurex considered expanding its suit.[18] Third, the two Chicago exchanges began more active collaboration. In November 2003, CME began clearing CBOT trades.

As U.S. exchanges' share of the volume on world derivatives exchanges has declined, the U.S. exchanges have pressed their regulators to reduce the impact of domestic regulation. The Commodity Futures Trading Commission (CFTC), an independent federal agency founded in 1974, regulates exchanges for futures on all commodities. The Commodity Futures Modernization Act (H.R. 5660) (CFMA), passed December 15, 2000, streamlines the role of the CFTC and reduces its regulation of certain types of exchanges to help them compete more effectively against OTC markets. Among other major changes, the CFMA allows certain electronic trading facilities for sophisticated commercial entities to trade financial futures (other than securities or indexes) free of regulation.[19]

The CFMA also repealed the ban on futures on single stocks, attempted to clarify that swaps are excluded from CFTC and SEC regulation, and gave foreign brokers easier access to U.S. investors.

Competition among exchanges often involves home governments. For example SIMEX locked horns with several of its neighbors over instruments it introduced on their securities. In mid-1996, SIMEX announced that as of January 1997 it would offer a futures contract on the Taiwan stock index compiled by Morgan Stanley Capital International. CME proposed a similar contract. Taiwan securities regulators initially opposed these initiatives because they wanted such a contract introduced in Taiwan. They threatened to stop sharing data with Morgan but ultimately backed down. Japanese regulators have also been concerned about offshore trading in options on Japanese stocks traded on the Nikkei due to a fear that such activity could drive down the Japanese market.

The impact of trading in derivatives markets on volatility in the underlying market is a major issue of academic research. A review of the literature in 1995 reported that most studies found interest rate futures or options markets either improve stability or have no effect on the cash market. Exchange rate futures, however, tend to increase the volatility of the underlying market.[20] However, another study found that when options were

---

[17] J. Grant and D. Sevastopulo, "Chicago Exchanges Call for Freezing of Eurex's U.S. Bid," *Financial Times*, November 7, 2003.

[18] E. Rigby, "Eurex Considers CBOT Fees Lawsuit," *Financial Times*, April 16, 2004.

[19] See the discussion in Chapter 15. Commodity Futures Trading Commission, "A New Regulatory Framework for Trading Facilities, Intermediaries and Clearing Organizations," 66 Federal Register(2001), p. 14262.

[20] See A. Chatrath, S. Ramchander, and F. Song, "The Role of Futures Trading Activity in Exchange Rate Volatility," Journal of Futures Markets (1996).

not well regulated in the U.S., from 1973-80, they temporarily increased underlying stock prices (possibly due to market manipulation). After federal regulations took effect in 1980, options had a negative effect, dampening the price of the underlying stock for at least four years.[21] Two later studies found that European options reduced fundamental volatility and that in Japan, while Nikkei stock options traded on the Osaka exchange increased Nikkei volatility, similar options traded on SIMEX did not. For Korea during the 1997 crisis, the futures market appeared to destabilize the stock market. Index futures volumes rose dramatically starting 3 months before the crisis began, then reverted to normal. Foreign investors in the futures markets played a significant role in the Korean crisis; during the crisis, sales in the futures market undercut prices in the cash market, which was an unknown phenomenon in Korea before that time.[22]

Speculators attacking a country's currency sometimes also attack the country's equity market in what is called a "double play." Hong Kong faced a double play situation in August 1998. First, speculators sell stock short, either in the cash or futures market. Since they profit if the stock prices fall, the next step is to help that happen. Rising interest rates may weaken stock prices. One way to make this happen is to make big spot sales of the currency, which increases the supply of money and forces the central bank or monetary authority to tighten liquidity and drive up interest rates. A second way to force up interest rates is to borrow big in the interbank market or other money markets (for example, to finance short sales of equity). One analysis concluded that the government can "never simultaneously reduce speculation in the equity and the money markets."[23]

Notes and Questions

1. How does regulation affect competition between Eurex and the Chicago exchanges?

D.   CROSS-BORDER ELECTRONIC ACCESS TO FUTURES EXCHANGES

A major issue for regulators of futures exchanges is how to treat foreign exchanges that want to provide screens in the host country for trading by brokers and/or customers.

---

[21] See S. Sorescu, "The Effect of Options on Stock Prices," 55 Journal of Finance (March 1997), p. 487-514.

[22] E. Chang, J. Cheng, and J. Pinegar, "Does Futures Trading Increase Stock Market Volatility? The Case for the Nikkei Stock Index Futures Market," 24 Journal of Banking & Finance (2000), p. 727; E. Ghysels and J. Seon, "The Asian Financial Crisis: The Role of Derivative Securities Trading and Foreign Investors," (March 5, 2000).

[23] S. Chakravorti and S. Lall, "The Double Play: Simultaneous Speculative Attacks on Currency and Equity Markets," Federal Reserve Bank of Chicago Working Paper (December 2000).

The CFTC adopted Rule 30.12 in August 2000 to allow exchanges operating primarily outside the U.S. to have electronic access to traders in the U.S. without requiring the foreign exchanges to be designated as U.S. "contract markets," which involves a lengthy registration process and compliance with U.S. trading rules. The rule allows foreign brokers, either affiliated with a U.S. futures commission merchant (FCM) (i.e. a U.S. commodities broker) or regulated by the U.S. to accept orders from certain sophisticated U.S. customers known as "authorized customers," provided that the U.S. FCM carrying the authorized customer's account satisfies certain procedural safeguards and remains well-capitalized. The CFTC set the following standards in this regard:

> "1. the petitioner is an established board of trade that wishes to place within the United States an automated trading system permitting access to its products but whose activities are otherwise primarily located in a particular foreign country that has taken responsibility for regulation of the petitioner;
>
> 2. the petitioner's home country has established a regulatory scheme that is "generally comparable" to that in the U.S. and provides basic protections for customers trading on markets and for the integrity of the markets themselves;
>
> 3. except for certain incidental contacts within the U.S., the petitioner is present in the U.S. only by virtue of being accessible from within the U.S. via its automated trading system;
>
> 4. the petitioner is willing to submit itself to the jurisdiction of the Commission and the U.S. courts in connection with its activities conducted under an exemptive order;
>
> 5. the petitioner's automated trading system has been approved by the petitioner's home country regulator following a review of the system that applied the standards set forth in the 1990 International Organization of Securities Commissions (IOSCO) report on screen-based trading systems or substantially similar standards; and
>
> 6. satisfactory information sharing arrangements are in effect between the Commission and the petitioner and petitioner's regulatory authority;
>
> 7. the petitioner could offer only products that could lawfully be offered in the U.S."

The CFTC decided that it would consider the volume of U.S. trades to decide if a petitioner's U.S. contacts were so extensive that the petitioner required designation as a contract market in the U.S. But the CFTC did not fix a volume amount (or a ceiling for the U.S. share of total trading by the petitioning exchange) that would serve as a ceiling for an exemption.

To determine if a home country regulatory system is "generally comparable" to that in the U.S., the CFTC considers the following factors:

"1. prohibition of fraud, abuse and market manipulation relating to trading on the petitioner's markets;

2. recordkeeping and reporting by the petitioner and its members;

3. fitness standards for intermediaries operating on petitioner's markets, members or others;

4. financial standards for the petitioner's members;

5. protection of customer funds, including procedures in the event of a clearing member's default or insolvency;

6. trade practice standards;

7. rule review or general review of board of trade [exchange] operations by its regulatory authority;

8. surveillance, compliance, and enforcement mechanisms employed by the board of trade and its regulatory authority to ensure compliance with their rules and regulations; and

9. regulatory oversight of clearing facilities."

In the securities market, as the discussion of transatlantic markets, in Chapter 2 shows, the SEC does not presently permit similar cross-border activities for foreign stock exchanges. Why is opening transatlantic access for securities more difficult than for futures? Possibly because the instruments differ. Securities raise more disclosure issues. Commodities and financial instruments are derivatives that require less disclosure. Of course, single stock futures on foreign stocks would pose more problems, due to concern about disclosure regarding the underlying company.

In one view, the regulatory structure in place for futures today is not equipped for electronic exchanges. The existing system assumes that members of the exchanges play a central role in all aspects of the exchange's activities and that the exchanges have the capacity to enforce their regulations against members. But in the new electronic market, the firms that used to be exchange members will become mere subscribers, for whom any single exchange will be much less important than in the past. The exchange will cease to be an SRO because it will have no "self" to regulate and its only power over subscribers will be to deny them access to the exchange.[24]

Notes and Questions

1. Should electronic exchanges be regulated differently than floor-based exchanges?

---

[24] P. McBridge Johnson, "Getting to Grips with Self-Regulation in the New e-Markets," *International Financial Law Review* (June 2000), p. 41.

E.   A CASE STUDY IN THE REGULATION OF FUTURES AND OPTIONS MARKETS: THE BARINGS CASE

The oldest British merchant bank, Baring Brothers, collapsed over the weekend of February 25-26, 1995. A 28-year old employee, Nicholas Leeson, based in Singapore, and trading futures and options contracts, had amassed losses exceeding £860 million. Barings' capital was £540 million. A rescue effort by the Bank of England that weekend failed; other banks would not lend to Barings because, with the derivatives contracts still open, the full extent of Barings' losses could not be fixed.

On March 5, the Dutch bank Internationals Nederlanden Groep NV (ING Bank) won the bid to acquire Barings' securities, asset management, and investment banking operations for £1 (one Pound). It then invested £660 million and assumed most of Barings' debts. On March 8, the acquisition was approved by the U.K. High Court and by the court in the Cayman Islands, where Barings was incorporated.

The Barings crisis raises important issues concerning the regulation of futures and options markets. To what extent is the reliance on margin rules sufficient to protect exchanges and the financial system? Are other safeguards needed? How significant is it that the exchanges and regulators missed what seem to have been major flaws in Barings' management of its futures and options operations? Is greater co-ordination among exchanges and their regulators needed? What are the implications of Barings' activities for deposit-taking institutions? What are the implications of the Bank of England's resolution of the crisis?

In this section we begin with a brief introduction to the Barings Group and then proceed to chronicle the activities that ultimately led to its collapse. Following this, we begin to analyze the performance of the key regulatory bodies that supervised Barings from 1992 until the time of the disaster.

The sources for most of this account are two official accounts: Bank of England, Report of the Board of Banking Supervision Inquiry into the Circumstances of the Collapse of Barings (1995) (BoE Report); and Inspectors appointed by the Minister for Finance, Baring Futures (Singapore) Pte. Ltd. (1995) (Singapore Report).

1.   THE BARINGS GROUP

Barings was a 230-year-old financial group based in London. Barings PLC, the holding company, had over 100 subsidiaries in scores of countries and consisted of five divisions: banking, equity brokering and trading, corporate finance, international finance, and operations. Its activities included merchant banking (wholesale deposit-taking, trading, corporate finance, mergers and acquisitions, and venture capital), investment advice, fund and asset management and advice, unit and investment trust (similar to mutual funds) creation and management, stock registry, real estate investment, financing vehicles, and securities dealing and brokering. Supervision of the key Barings units was scattered among several countries' regulators.

The important units of Barings Group (the Group), and their supervisors, included:

1.   Baring Brothers & Co., Ltd. (BB&Co.), the deposit-taking merchant bank incorporated in the U.K., had specialized in corporate finance and debt trading. The Bank of England was the lead supervisor of BB&Co. in the U.K., but the U.K. Securities and Future Authority (SFA) supervised its U.K. securities operations.

2.   Baring Securities Ltd. (BSL), a subsidiary of BB&Co., was formed from a stock brokering firm acquired by BB&Co. in 1984 that had a strong Asian network. It was BB&Co.'s first important venture into equity securities. Incorporated in the Cayman Islands and headquartered in London, BSL's U.K. operations were supervised by the SFA there. From 1993, BSL handled clients' securities as a broker and a subsidiary, Barings Securities (London) Ltd. (BSLL) made the proprietary investments. BSL owned the following three firms, among many others;

a.   Baring Securities (Japan) Ltd. (BSJ), incorporated in the Cayman Islands, was a broker-dealer in Japan and supervised by the Ministry of Finance there.

b.   Baring Securities (Singapore) Pte. Ltd. (BSS) was incorporated in Singapore to carry out Baring's securities business there. It was a member of the Singapore Stock Exchange and regulated by the Monetary Authority of Singapore.

c.   Baring Futures (Singapore) Ltd. (BFS) carried out Barings' derivatives business in Singapore was incorporated there, and became a non-clearing member of SIMEX in September 1986 and a clearing member on July 1, 1992. With one-third of the staff of BSS and much less senior management attention than BSS, BFS was the unit that Nicholas Leeson managed when the entire Group collapsed. BFS was supervised by SIMEX.

The Group managed its banking business (through BB&Co.) and its securities business (through BSL) separately until 1992, when it started a long process of combining them into what was to become the Barings Investment Bank in late 1994. This slow amalgamation of two very different businesses and cultures contributed to serious confusion in the Group's management. Functions and lines for reporting were vague, overlapping, and often changed. For example, Leeson nominally reported to senior Barings personnel in Singapore, London, and Tokyo.

2.   THE SCAM

a.   THE LEGITIMATE POSITIONS

Nicholas Leeson was employed by BFS. After he was denied a broker's license in the U.K. because of fraud in his application, in March 1992 Barings sent him to Singapore without revealing the U.K. denial when he applied for his license in Singapore. Originally he was responsible only for settlement and he continued to manage BFS's settlement functions (the back office) throughout his tenure. He had no experience trading futures, but began executing trades soon after BFS became a SIMEX clearing member in July 1992.

BFS had four clients; three of them were other Barings companies, and the fourth was the Tokyo office of Banque Nationale de Paris (BNP). BFS mainly executed trades for these customers, since it had no authority to take proprietary positions on its own behalf in 1993 and its authority (from 1994) to take intraday proprietary positions was quite limited. BSL, BFS' largest client, acted as agent for BFS' customers, and BSLL and BSJ used BFS to execute their proprietary trades. In late 1992, BSJ's traders had begun to conduct arbitrage of the cash market. Baskets of stocks on the Tokyo Stock Exchange (TSE), were simultaneously bought and sold (and vice versa) against Nikkei Index futures on the Osaka Stock Exchange (OSE).

The Nikkei 225 Stock Price Average is an index calculated by Nihon Keizai Shinbun, the leading financial news service in Japan. The index was based on a portfolio of 225 stocks listed on the First Section of the TSE. These 225 shares represented about 20 percent of all shares listed on the First Section. Each of the 225 shares had equal weight. Their value was averaged regularly and divided by a constant to adjust for rights issues and other non-market factors. As the total price of the 225 stocks changed, the index changed proportionately. The index itself was not traded on an exchange, though an investor could easily create it by buying individual stocks, as the BSJ traders did. A Nikkei Index future, the Nikkei 225, is a futures contract on the Nikkei Index.

The Nikkei 225 (N225) is also traded on SIMEX, with a lower margin requirement. A SIMEX contract at the time was valued at 500 times the index, and an OSE contract was valued at 1,000 times the index. In other words, if the index was at ¥19,000 the value of a single OSE contract was ¥19 million and the value of a SIMEX contract was half that.

Leeson was involved in two kinds of arbitrage transactions. The first, the "SIMEX/OSE switching business," arose when BSJ discovered it could make money arbitraging price differences between the Nikkei futures indexes on SIMEX and OSE. BSJ would buy a contract on one exchange and sell an offsetting contract on the other exchange, making money on small spreads by investing large amounts. Price differences occurred because demand and supply differed; OSE had most of the Japanese demand, while SIMEX had offshore and local traders' demand. OSE (with an electronic exchange) was slower than SIMEX (with floor trading). From early 1994, Barings allowed Leeson to make proprietary trades up to an intraday limit of 200 Nikkei futures contracts. This represented a normal exposure of about $20 million. If the Nikkei index was ¥20,000, each contract was ¥10 million (500 times the index) or about $100,000. With a 200 contract limit, the exposure would be 200 x $100,000 or $20 million. The amount at risk—determined by the likely movement of the Nikkei over the life of the contract—would be much less, around 5 percent, or $1 million. Barings, however, regarded Leeson as principally executing customer trades; Leeson was not subject to limits on agency trading.

When Leeson traded for Barings, he took the positions on SIMEX and instructed BSJ to take the offsetting positions on the OSE. BSJ could itself trade by taking a position in Japan and instructing Leeson to take the offsetting position on SIMEX.

"Cash/Futures" was the second type of arbitrage in which Leeson engaged. Barings could compare the price of the N225 index futures contract (on OSE or SIMEX) to the prices of the 225 shares traded on the TSE that made up the index (weighting those shares the same as they were weighted in the N225 index). If the prices of the index and underlying shares differed, Barings could buy the cheaper and sell the dearer of the contracts.

Gradually Leeson became known as a successful trader of Nikkei 225 index futures and options. Barings was in an advantageous position to arbitrage because it was one of a few brokers that had seats on both the OSE and SIMEX. As a member, it would see the order flow on both and know before non-members how prices would move. Acting quickly, it could use this knowledge to invest in the stock index futures and options with little risk. Leeson managed this SIMEX/OSE "switching business" and generated profits and losses that were booked to BSL, BSLL, and BSJ.

b.   THE SECRET POSITIONS

On July 3, 1992, two days after BFS started trading on SIMEX, Leeson opened Account 88888, telling SIMEX that it was a house (or BFS) account for BSL. He then instructed a member of his staff to remove the computer-based link between the account and BSL (in London). Indeed, most people in other Barings companies asserted they had never heard of the account. Over the next two and one-half years, Leeson's consistent practice was to book trades initially in a BSJ or BSL account, since they were his "clients," and then transfer trading losses to Account 88888 in a way that allowed him to show large profits for the BSJ and BSL accounts. Leeson's "game" was to appear to make a lot of money for Barings; he was not an embezzler. Such "profits" would increase Leeson's bonus and corporate advancement. Barings awarded Leeson a bonus of £115,000 for 1993 and planned, before his actions destroyed the Bank, to give him £450,000 for 1994.

Leeson used BFS to engage in many activities beyond his authority including: unhedged Nikkei futures (whose number rose from 189 long futures in August 1992 to 61,039 by February 24, 1995); unhedged JGB futures (from 2,120 contracts traded in October 1993 to 54,325 contracts traded in November 1994); and an unhedged combination of options called a short (or top) straddle.

The top straddle became a major source of loss. Leeson created it by writing a put and a call on the Nikkei 225 futures index at the same strike price. He would profit only when the market price stayed close to the strike price. The call writer profits until the market price rises slightly above the strike price. The put writer profits until the market price falls slightly below the strike price. When the put and call are combined, the writer loses money when the index moves beyond either point—slightly above or below the strike price.

Leeson also booked fictitious trades, not executed on the SIMEX floor, to enlarge the BSJ, BSLL and BSL profits even more, while 88888 would take the fictitious loss. These fictitious trades resulted in BFS under-reporting its actual positions to SIMEX. Leeson could do so because SIMEX relied on members' accounting systems to process transactions and report accurately. SIMEX would only uncover fraud in an audit. Table 14C below reports the losses:

Table 14C

Cumulative Losses on Account 88888

End of Period	Amount (S$)
30 September 1992	(8.8 million)
31 October 1993	(12.9 million)
30 November 1993	(65.7 million)
31 December 1994	(373.9 million)
After collapse	(2.2 billion)

The losses grew because Leeson regularly bet incorrectly in the unauthorized and unhedged proprietary positions he took.

c.   FUNDING THE LOSSES IN ACCOUNT 88888

Funding for BFS's operations came almost entirely from its clients in the Barings group. Funding for the S$2.2 billion in ultimate losses on account 88888 was from creditor banks (S$100 million) and other Baring Group companies. BFS would instruct clients to send to BFS funds to meet the cost of trades and margins incurred on their behalf. According to the Singapore Report, as BFS called for ever-increasing funds, BSL found it more and more difficult to reconcile these amounts with the trades for which the funds were being requested. The unreconciled amount rose to approximately £100 million (S$230 million) in 1994 and £320 million (S$736 million) in February 1995. Barings' headquarters referred to its payments to meet these unreconciled balances as "topping up."

Leeson told Barings' Group Treasury that he needed short-term funds to meet intraday advance margin calls by SIMEX and to fund the positions of BSJ which, he said, took longer to raise funds for than BSL. No one in the Group Treasury questioned this. According to the Singapore Report:

> "The Barings Group's risk positions, trading limits and trading performance and the allocation of funding were monitored each day by a high-level Asset & Liability Committee (ALCO). ... ALCO discussed the issue of funding BFS on at least six occasions in January and February 1995. By this time Mr. Leeson's reported trading activities had assumed very large proportions, causing the Baring Group to almost miss a SIMEX margin call on 24 January 1995. However the preoccupation of these meeting was to arrange adequate funding lines to meet Mr. Leeson's large requirements, rather than to investigate the causes underlying these requirements. At some stage, ALCO did decide that Mr. Leeson should be asked to reduce his positions, but this decision was never effectively implemented.
>
> On 20 February 1995, just days before the collapse of the Baring Group, the need to reduce Mr. Leeson's position was again raised at ALCO. Mr. Norris, the Chief Executive Officer of the Baring Group, informed ALCO that he had discussed this issue with Mr. Leeson when they met in Singapore the previous week. Mr. Norris informed ALCO that Mr. Leeson had suggested that his positions should not be reduced and Mr. Norris concurred with this. Mr. Norris denied having had such a discussion with Mr. Leeson or having briefed ALCO in this way, but both facts were corroborated by independent witnesses."

The Barings companies funding BFS in turn raised much of their money from banks. At the time of collapse, BSJ owed Japanese banks over £375 million, of which £50 million was borrowed securities.

d.   THE FAILURE OF EXTERNAL AUDITORS

The work of Coopers & Lybrand, Barings' external auditor, was inadequate. They relied on Leeson and failed to check his explanations or purported transactions with the other parties he named. They accepted photocopies rather than originals; this was important because after Leeson left Singapore, falsified documents were found in his desk, along with paste, scissors, and sources with holes cut in them. He had used them to prove the existence and support of "clients" to explain large trades. The auditors also failed to notice that a confirmation supposedly sent directly to them from a "client" actually had "From Nick & Lisa" at the top of both pages, indicating that its source was Leeson's home fax machine. The Bank of England Report noted that Coopers & Lybrand (Singapore) concluded that BFS's internal controls were adequate in November 1994, even though back- and front-office responsibilities were combined in Leeson.

e.   THE FAILURE OF MANAGEMENT

Senior Barings managers did not catch Leeson. Until December 1994 this was probably because they did not understand derivatives, and corporate responsibility for Leeson was unclear. There was administrative confusion as BB&Co. and BSL (acquired in 1995) tried to integrate. Furthermore, there was a "culture clash" between the corporate finance culture of BB&Co. (the bank) and the wheeler-dealer culture of BSL. After January 1995, it was hard to discipline the big profit maker, and management continued to believe Leeson could not get into trouble because his activities were purportedly so simple.

Notes and Questions

1.   Why did Leeson get away with his scam for so long?

3.   THE REGULATORY ROLE OF SIMEX

To protect itself from risk, SIMEX supervises member (e.g. BFS) compliance with its exchange rules by members, of which BFS was one. SIMEX is the self-regulatory organization for financial futures in Singapore and subject to the oversight of the Monetary Authority of Singapore. SIMEX carried out general surveillance of BFS activities on the exchange and made on-site inspections. BFS had to submit quarterly and annual financial statements certified by an external auditor and daily position reports. SIMEX inspected BFS in April 1993, and fined it S$23,000 for several violations. It inspected BFS again in September 1994, looking only at the segregation of client funds and client margins. SIMEX considered disciplinary action on five counts, notifying BFS on January 16, 1995. BFS replied on January 30 and February 13 that the problems were clerical errors. SIMEX'S Audit and Review Department assessed BFS' liquidity in December 1994 and wrote to BFS on January 27, 1995 that its liquidity was low given the large positions on December 30, 1994. BFS replied on February 10, 1995 and assured SIMEX that there was no problem. The failure occurred shortly thereafter.

SIMEX (in its role as a clearinghouse) was a counterpart to Barings' proprietary and customer contracts. If Barings defaulted, SIMEX had to perform. This put SIMEX and its members at risk. By January 1995, just before the Barings collapse, Barings was a major player at SIMEX, accounting for 13 percent of all trades and 40 percent of all trades in N225 contracts—overall it had a long position.

a.   SIMEX'S MARGIN RULES

The primary method that SIMEX employed to protect itself was margin rules. There were three aspects of these rules that caused difficulty regarding Leeson's activities. First, margins were higher on unhedged portions. The idea was simple; there was more risk that a counterparty might default on unhedged portions. However, Leeson over-reported hedged portions, and neither SIMEX, the bank lenders or Barings detected this. Second, there could be no netting of customer and proprietary positions. This made sense, since counterparties were liable to customers independently of their own positions. Leeson netted those positions, however, and this too escaped detection. Third, there were higher margin requirements for customers than for proprietary positions because customers posed higher risks. Leeson misreported customer as proprietary positions.

These rules could have been changed, e.g. to have the same margin requirements for all positions whether or not they were hedged, and whether or not the account was customer or proprietary. But these changes would have made SIMEX less competitive. SIMEX's margins overall were less onerous than OSE's. SIMEX's effective rate could be as much as one-third below that of OSE, depending on the portfolio. One study found that "unreasonable competition" between SIMEX and OSE "allowed for wildly loose limits on traders in an effort to build exchange volume to attain pre-eminence."[25]

Although margin payments to and from SIMEX took place on T+1 for U.S. Dollar transactions, SIMEX allowed payment on T+2 for Yen-denominated transactions and it allowed initial margins for the Yen transactions to be posted in U.S. Dollars. It also allowed an exception for margins "forthcoming in a reasonable time," which it defined as three days. This increased SIMEX's risk.

b.   SIMEX'S LOSSES

SIMEX eventually uncovered the problems with Account 88888. According to the Singapore Report, Leeson had BFS's settlement clerks regularly reduce the monthly closing balances on 88888 to almost zero at the end of each month by false accounting entries, and then reverse the entries the next morning. But on December 28, 1994, SIMEX noticed a S$100 million discrepancy.

Barings collapsed in late February. After SIMEX discovered the S$100million discrepancy, it closed out the Barings positions. It took nine

---

[25] T. Sanders, "Derivative Ruination in the 1990s: Les Apparences Sont Trompeuses," 43 Thunderbird International Business Review (2001), p. 3.

days to do so during which time the N225 went up. In fact, SIMEX was able to return $33.6 million to Barings after the closeout. Some believed that the Singapore Monetary Authority, which had huge resources, bought contracts in the futures market or in the Japanese cash market (stocks) to prop up the market and avert losses and damage to SIMEX's and Singapore's reputation. In the end, SIMEX luckily escaped from a dangerous situation that was brought on in part by inadequate margins and poor enforcement of its rules.

c.   THE BARINGS COLLAPSE AND ING ACQUISITION

The Bank of England took over BB&Co. on February 27, 1995. Having decided that Barings posed no systemic risk, the Bank of England was prepared to let it fail but preferred to find a buyer. Several foreign banks were interested. The Bank of England accepted ING Bank's offer.

ING Bank did not acquire Barings PLC, the group's holding company, or its subsidiaries other than BSL. It also refused to accept liability for $300 million in notes issued by an offshore financing vehicle of BB&Co. ING Bank offered to pay 7.5 percent of the face value of £100 million in subordinated perpetual bonds that Barings PLC had issued in 1994. Large U.K. insurers were major investors and considered law suits against Barings' directors and Ernst & Young, the administrator, for ignoring the bondholders in the acquisition.

ING Bank acquired Barings' securities, asset management, and merchant banking operations (which particular subsidiaries were included in the purchase is not clear). For this, it paid £1 and promised the Bank of England to invest £660 million more to pay the debts of those operations.

It was not initially clear that ING Bank would acquire Barings' operations in Japan because of their large debt, but ING did so eventually on March 9, 1995. The extent of Barings' Japanese subsidiaries' losses was also not clear; since ING Bank eventually agreed to invest ¥10 billion in the subsidiaries, losses were probably of that magnitude. The losses would have included borrowing to finance its margin calls, overdrafts, and guarantees (most of which were without collateral). The major creditors were 15 Japanese banks. The timing of this acquisition suggests that it was not integral to ING's agreement with the Bank of England.

The ripple beyond Barings was minor. No playing out of systemic risk was discernible in the Barings failure.

Notes and Questions

1.   What danger did Leeson's fraud pose to SIMEX? Were SIMEX's rules to protect itself adequate? One could conclude that existing safeguards on SIMEX, and the Japanese exchanges, are adequate since neither exchange had to draw on more than the margins from Barings. Do you agree with this?

2.   Why did SIMEX not react more quickly after discovering BFS's failure to comply with various rules?

3.   How could Leeson's exposure have gone undiscovered by the exchange for so long?

4.   THE ROLE OF THE BANK OF ENGLAND AS LEAD REGULATOR

Among the financial regulators of U.K. institutions, BoE was the "lead regulator" of the U.K. "College of Regulators" of the Barings Group. It held this status by memoranda of understanding with the other U.K. regulators (such as the Securities and Futures Authority (SFA)) rather than by statute. As lead regulator, BoE received and analyzed data for consolidated (group-wide) capital ratios and consolidated large exposures, and BoE assessed the risks to BB&Co. from the Barings' non-bank units of the Barings Group. BoE did not supervise the non-bank units. The College regulated by exception, which meant that members focused only on institutions that a member specifically identified as of concern. At no meeting of the College was Barings ever identified as such a concern. The regulatory fragmentation in the U.K. arguably contributed to BoE's failure to adequately supervise Barings.

BoE was also the "lead regulator" for purposes of the Basel Concordat. The Basel Committee, which included Japan and the U.K., met quarterly. At no meeting was Barings identified as a concern. Furthermore, Singapore participated in the Offshore Group of Banking Supervision represented by its Monetary Authority. The Committee and the Offshore Group agreed to principles that would help banking supervisors in member countries collaborate. One principle stated that host authorities suspecting or discovering a material problem should communicate immediately with the parent authority. Another specified that host authorities should give parent authority adequate data, particularly about large exposures. Neither regulators in Singapore or Japan informed BoE of concerns over large exposures for Barings.

The BoE had a rule imposing a lending limit of 25 percent of capital, which applied to loans to outsiders or closely related persons. The lending limit required notice to BoE before exceeding the 25 percent ceiling. BoE was apparently aware that BB&Co. was exceeding these limits on its loans to BSL but excused it on the theory of "solo consolidation" (i.e. the idea that BB&Co. and BSL were in reality one company since they were in the process of integrating). These lending exposures ultimately brought down BB&Co. when BSL was unable to repay its loans. This mistake was compounded by the fact that BSL passed the loans onto its subsidiaries, including BSS in Singapore, so that BB&Co. was in fact at risk for the Singapore operation to a high extent of its capital.

The large exposure limit also applied to margins put up with exchanges, on the theory that the margining institution was at risk if the exchange collapsed and was unable to return the margin amounts. Margins were put up by various entities of BB&Co., and BoE failed to aggregate these loans for purposes of assessing exposure limits.

The BoE Report concluded that the "informal concession" which permitted BB&Co. to exceed its large exposure limits to OSE and SIMEX without any limits on the size of the concession was "an error of judgment." Had Barings been held to the 25 percent limit for OSE, Leeson might not have been able to raise funds so readily in late January and February 1995.

The Treasury Committee of the House of Commons published a report in December 1996 which criticized BoE for poor supervision when evaluating banks' internal controls, communicating among its own staff, and applying its own rules. The Barings fiasco served as important background to this conclusion. The Report suggested a conflict of interest, since BoE both supervised and promoted London as a financial center. In July 1998, all financial sector supervisory activities were consolidated within the new Financial Supervisory Agency, and the banking supervisors were transferred from the BoE to the new agency. In June 2000 the U.K. passed the Financial Services and Markets Act, which formally replaced the decentralized supervision that characterized U.K. regulation during the Barings crisis with a "super-regulator."

Notes and Questions

1. Could the BoE have done a better job as lead regulator to prevent the Barings crisis?

2. What was the risk to the U.K. of the Barings scam?

5.   INTERNATIONAL EFFORTS TO AVOID ANOTHER BARINGS CRISIS

When the Barings crisis broke, the regulators of many futures and options markets in East and Southeast Asia, Europe, and North America quickly became involved. Mary Schapiro, then Chairman of the CFTC, played a leading role co-ordinating a regulatory response.

a.   THE WINDSOR DECLARATION

At a meeting on May 16-17, 1995 in Windsor, U.K., representatives of financial futures and options regulators from 16 countries agreed to certain steps they hoped would strengthen international supervision. They formalized these steps in the Windsor Declaration, which is presented below.

The authorities formulated the following goals:

1. support, subject to appropriate confidentiality protections, mechanisms to improve prompt communication of information relevant to material exposures and other regulatory concerns" among market regulators and authorities.

2. review the adequacy of existing arrangements to minimize the risk of loss through insolvency or misappropriation and enhance such arrangements as appropriate" in order to protect customers and reduce systemic risk.

3. promote, in the context of national insolvency regimes, national provisions and market procedures that facilitate the prompt liquidation and/or transfer of positions, funds and assets, from failing members of futures exchanges.

4. the authorities recognized the importance of effective margining systems [to] mitigate the risk of losses arising from the inability of solvent participants to close out or manage their exposures to a failing market member.

5. to support measures to enhance emergency procedures at financial intermediaries, market members and markets and to improve existing mechanisms for international co-operation and communication among market authorities and regulators.

These goals led the authorities to agree to promote the following activities.

"A. active surveillance within each jurisdiction of large exposures by market authorities and/or regulators as appropriate.

B. development of mechanisms to ensure that customer positions, funds and assets can be separately identified and held safe to the maximum extent possible and in accordance with national law.

C. enhanced disclosure by the markets of the different types and levels of protection of customer funds and assets that may prevail, particularly when they are transferred to different jurisdictions, including through omnibus accounts.

D. record-keeping systems at exchanges and clearinghouses and/or market members which ensure that positions, funds and assets to be treated as belonging to customers can be satisfactorily distinguished from other positions, funds and assets.

E. enhanced disclosure by markets to participants of the rules and procedures governing what constitutes a default and the treatment of positions, funds and assets of member firms and their clients in the event of such a default.

F. the immediate designation by each regulator of a contact point for receiving information or providing other assistance to other regulators and/or market authorities, and the means to assure twenty-four hour availability of contact personnel in the event of disruption occurring at a financial intermediary, market member or market.

G. review of existing lists and assuring maintenance by IOSCO of an international regulatory contacts list.

H. the development by financial intermediaries, market members or markets and regulatory authorities of contingency arrangements, or a review of the adequacy of existing arrangements, and enhancement as appropriate."

b. MARCH 1996 DECLARATION FOR INFORMATION SHARING

Almost a year after the Windsor Declaration, futures and options regulators pushed further in their effort to open lines of communication and information sharing. Many supervisory authorities signed the Declaration on Co-operation and Supervision of International Futures Markets and Clearing Organizations in March 1996. The idea behind this agreement was that the authorities (both regulators and some self-regulatory organizations) would share specific types of information in carefully defined circumstances. Key to this was the agreement to assure confidentiality.

The authorities defined events that would permit one to request information from another, e.g. a large decrease in owner's equity in any six month period.

The request could "only be for information ... relevant to the event that actually gave rise to the Request, and may relate only to information which the Requested Authority either maintains or has access to under relevant Laws, Rules and Regulations." It could go to any authority "that regulates a Party to which: (A) the affected Member; (B) an Affiliate of the Member; or (C) a firm with a substantial commercial relationship with the Member belongs."

An authority that receives a request agreed to "use reasonable efforts to obtain information from: (A) its records; (B) any other Authority in the jurisdiction of the Requested Authority which has access to relevant records; or (C) any other source in the jurisdiction of the Requested Authority from which such information might appropriately be sought." If cost becomes an issue, the requesting and requested authorities will consult. If local law interferes with the response, the requested authority will "use its best efforts to facilitate the delivery of information to the requesting Party or to its Authority."

The authority receiving information agrees to use it only to carry out its supervisory responsibilities and never "contrary to conditions relating to the use of that information imposed by the Requested Authority to give effect to Laws, Rules or Regulations in force in the Requested Authority's jurisdiction." Finally, no information may "be used for competitive advantage."

Notes and Questions

1. Does the Windsor Declaration provide for enough cooperation among supervisors to protect against more problems like Barings? If not, what further cooperation would you recommend?

F.   NATIONAL REGULATORY RESPONSES

Some exchanges responded to the concerns raised by Barings. The London Clearing House announced that its members would provide up to £150 million if a party trading through the exchange defaulted on its obligations.[26]

In the U.S., clearing members of the CME, CBOT, and Board of Trade Clearing Corporation became subject to risk-based capital rules effective January 1, 1998. The new rules required members to hold capital in excess of the greater of: (1) minimum Dollar balances set by the clearing organizations; (2) 10 percent of customer and 4 percent of noncustomer risk maintenance margin/performance bond requirements, based on the portfolio's price and volatility for all futures and options on futures; or (3) minimum capital requirements set by the SEC or CFTC.

The CFTC refined its Large-Trader Reporting System. For each clearing member exchanges were to report long and short positions of the member and each customer, as well as buy and sell orders above specified amounts (e.g. 25 to 1000 open contracts). The CFTC's surveillance staff aggregates related accounts across members and exchanges. The staff may contact traders for more information. The CFTC has acknowledged the fact that many customers trade through intermediaries as a major problem.[27]

Singapore integrated its legal regime for securities and derivatives in the Securities and Futures Act of 2001. The Act streamlined licensing, increased disclosure, tightened insider trading rules, and enhanced the Monetary Authority's enforcement powers. Specifically, these enhanced enforcement powers grant extraterritorial reach to "conduct within Singapore in relation to securities or futures contracts listed and traded overseas, and conduct outside Singapore in relation to securities and futures contracts listed or traded in Singapore."

---

[26] See P. John, "LCH Provides Crisis Cover for Derivatives," *Financial Times,* August 6, 1996.
[27] See CFTC, *Backgrounder*, No. 1-01 (October 2001).

CONCLUSIONS

The trading of futures and options presents many of the same issues as were raised in Chapter 13 with respect to the stock exchanges. International regulatory competition is a significant factor, particularly with respect to margin rules, but takes on a rather different cast than for stock exchanges.

As seen in the Barings case, there is a more significant problem of race to the bottom in the regulation of futures and options exchanges. This may arise as a result of the differences in the trading constituency for futures and options. It is more wholesale, and there is no "issuer" seeking to raise capital through "bonding" to certain requirements. This problem is partly responsible for the advent of international co-operation through the Windsor Declaration. No comparable framework exists for stock exchanges. On the other hand, it is questionable whether the failure of a major securities firm—that might result from lax regulation—is a concern of public policy given the relative unimportance of systemic risk from such failure.

This difference in trading constituency may also explain the more relaxed view in the U.S. toward allowing cross-border screens for foreign futures and options exchanges than for foreign stock exchanges.

As in the case of securities, trading on exchanges faces competition from off-exchange alternatives, e.g. swaps, a matter discussed in Chapter 15.

CHAPTER FIFTEEN

SWAPS

In this Chapter, we look at the most important OTC derivative, swaps. Unlike futures and options, this market is not based on a formal exchange. Instead, like the foreign exchange market, it consists of specific contracts negotiated and settled by individual parties (counterparties), albeit with highly standardized documentation.

The Chapter begins with a description of the two most widely used swaps, interest rate and currency swaps, an examination of why parties use them, and some characteristics of the overall market. Next we examine the risk of swaps, with particular attention to newer forms of swaps like credit derivatives. A key question is whether swap risks are different and greater than risks involved in traditional banking activity, deposit-taking and lending. Our examination concentrates on credit and market risk. This sets the scene for a discussion of important regulatory issues, disclosure standards, capital requirements, dealer liability, and netting.[1] We also look at the new Basel rules for swaps.

A.   SWAP TRANSACTIONS AND MARKETS

1.   SWAP TRANSACTIONS: THE BASICS

"Regardless of form, the underlying principle of a swap is the agreement of each of two parties to provide the other with a series of cash flows, based on fixed or floating interest rates and in the same or different currencies. At the outset, the parties view the respective values of the two streams as equal. In other words, when the agreement is formed, the present values of the respective cash flows at the current prevailing interest rates and, if applicable, exchange rates are equal."[2]

A typical interest rate swap obligates the first party to pay an amount equal to the interest which would accrue on an agreed amount during a given period at one type of interest rate and obligates the second party to pay an amount equal to the interest which would accrue on that

---

[1] For a comprehensive survey of issues regarding swap transactions, see S. Henderson, *Henderson on Derivatives* (2003).

[2] S. Henderson, "Swap Credit Risk: A Multi-Perspective Analysis," in *International Banking and Corporate Financial Operations* (K. Lian, H. Kee, C. Cheong, and B. Ong. eds., 1989), pp. 41-47.

agreed amount during the period at another type of interest rate. Often, one rate is fixed and the other is floating. To the extent that payment dates are simultaneous, the parties typically would net the payments, with the party owing the larger amount paying the difference to the other party. Figure 15.1 below is an example of an interest rate swap.

Figure 15.1
Interest Rate Swaps

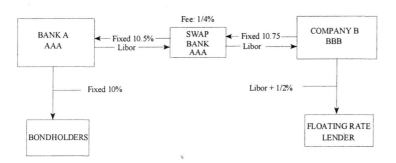

In this example, Bank A, with an AAA credit rating, agrees to pay Swap Bank (a dealer), with a credit rating of AAA, LIBOR in exchange for a 10.5 percent fixed rate, and Company B, with a BBB credit rating, agrees to pay Swap Bank a fixed rate of 10.75 percent in exchange for LIBOR. These agreements to swap interest payments can be in reference to any individual amounts, e.g. $100 million.

The Swap Bank gets a fee of ¼ percent, the spread between the fixed rate it pays out to Bank A and the fixed rate it receives from Company B. There are actually two independent swaps and the obligations on each are completely independent. That is, swap bank must honor its obligations, e.g. its swap with Bank A, even if Company B defaults on its swap.

This diagram also shows some underlying transactions, e.g. Bank A's issuance of fixed rate bonds, and Company B's obligation on a floating rate loan. These obligations are independent from the swaps.

Business firms are termed "end-users," as compared with dealers whose business it is to arrange swaps. These dealers, who are usually AAA rated, are desirable swap partners due to their low credit risk. Bank A might well prefer an AAA counterparty to Company B, with a BBB rating. Dealers, as in this example, often hedge their positions with two offsetting swaps.

The other major swap is a currency swap combined with an interest rate swap. An example is set out below in Figure 15.2.

Figure 15.2
Currency Swaps

5 year
Spot FX rate: US $1.00 = ¥125

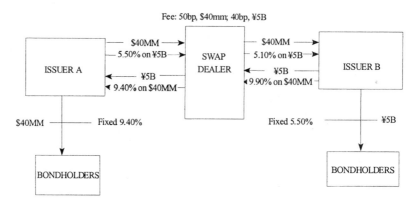

In this example, Issuer A has raised $40mm by issuing bonds paying 9.40 percent and swapped the Dollars with Swap Dealer for 5 years for ¥5 billion, at the current spot FX rate (¥5 billion = $40 million x 125), paying 5.50 percent interest on the Yen and receiving 9.40 percent on the Dollars. At the end of the term, Issuer A must return the ¥5 billion for $40 million. Issuer B has done the reverse, raised Yen from Bondholders and swapped into Dollars. Swaps usually provide for termination upon payment of a fee representing the current value of the swap. So, in our example of interest rate swaps (Figure 15.1 above), if rates increased from the inception of the swap and Swap Bank sought to terminate its swap with Bank A, Bank A would pay a fee to Swap Bank since LIBOR had increased. Termination fees allow dealers to manage their positions, i.e. to cash out of particular swaps.

2. WHY DO END-USERS USE SWAPS[3]

There are three major reasons that end-users enter into swaps: hedging, speculation, and to reduce funding costs. Hedging with foreign currency derivatives, swaps, or exchange traded instruments increases firm value on average by 4.87 percent.[4]

Hedging is a critical function of derivatives, swaps as well as futures and options. Hedging permits parties to significantly reduce their risks. For example, assume in Figure 15.1, our interest rate swap, that Bank A was

---

[3] An important study dealing with this subject is *Group of Thirty, Derivatives: Practices and Principles* (July 1993).

[4] G. Allayanis and J. Eston, "The Use of Foreign Currency Derivatives and Firm Market Value," 14 Review of Financial Studies (2001), p. 244. See also E. Brewer III, W. Jackson III, and J. Moser, "The Value of Using Interest Rate Derivatives to Manage Risk at U.S. Banking Organizations," Federal Reserve Bank of Chicago Economic Perspectives (2001), p. 49.

fully hedged before issuing the fixed-rate bonds. Further, assume that the bank has used its fixed rate bond funding to make floating rate LIBOR loans to customers. If rates decrease, the bank is at risk. By swapping its LIBOR revenues for fixed rates, it hedges its exposure on its bonds. Studies show that that use of derivatives can significantly reduce the stock return volatility of firms, interest rate risk exposure and foreign exchange exposure.[5] Overall, it appears that use of derivatives increases firm value, by some estimates from 4 to 12 percent.[6]

The use of swaps and other derivatives as part of "structured finance" has been questioned since the Enron scandal where derivatives were used to disguise the risk of Enron's business. The line between risk-reduction and deception or window-dressing may be difficult to draw. The liability of financial institutions for aiding and abetting financial misstatements was discussed in Chapter 2. One way to handle this problem would be to make the provider of structured finance responsible for reviewing the customer's proposed accounting treatment and disclosures related to the transaction. This has been approved in an Interagency Policy Statement on Sound Practices Concerning Complex Structured Finance Activities, circulated for comment in May 2004, but as yet not adopted.[7]

A second reason for engaging in derivatives transaction is speculation. Speculation may be the dark-side of derivatives, but speculators are crucial to the market. They are the risk-takers that permit hedgers to lower their risks. As we shall see, it is not altogether clear.

Reduction of funding costs is a major reason for entering into swaps. This can be seen in an analysis of Bank A's funding costs in the interest rate swap, Figure 15.1 above. Table 15A below shows those savings.

---

[5] W. Guay, "The Impact of Derivatives on Firm Risk: An Empirical Examination of New Derivative Users," 26 J. of Accounting and Economics 319 (1999).
[6] R. Stultz, "Should We Fear Derivatives," NBER Working Paper 10574 (June 2004).
[7] The Statement was proposed by the Department of the Treasury, Office of Thrift Supervision, the Federal Reserve System and the SEC. See SEC Release No. 34-49695, May 13, 2004.

Table 15A

Reduction of Funding Costs for Bank A

Assume that Bank A's market cost of floating rate funding is LIBOR

Analysis of Bank A's Savings

1. Direct Cost (to bondholders)	(10)
2. Swap Cost (to Swap Bank)	(LIBOR)
3. Swap Revenue (from Swap Bank)	10 ½
4. Net Cost:	LIBOR – ½
5. Cost Savings:	LIBOR – (LIBOR – ½) = ½

This example shows that if Bank A wanted to fund at floating rates, it would have had to pay LIBOR, but now it pays LIBOR -½ as a result of the swap. Many swaps are driven by cost savings achievable on underlying funding transactions. There is no complete free lunch, however. Bank A has also acquired the risk, albeit small, that Swap Bank might default on its swap. Bank A would not have had this risk if it had gone directly to the market for LIBOR funding.

Most versions of the comparative funding cost advantage theory of swaps are based on the idea that the higher credit rated party has a bigger advantage in borrowing at fixed rates. Empirical studies have confirmed this. Floating rate payers have a higher mean S&P bond rating than fixed rate payers.[8]

While the credit ratings of swap users like Company B may be lower than their bank counterparties, they are considerably higher than firms in general. A Federal Reserve Board study found that the credit rating of firms reporting OTC derivatives that have a senior debt rating is significantly better than all firms with senior debt ratings. Indeed, the ratio of expected default rates for the typical derivative user to the typical firm representing all the firms in the sample was almost exactly one-half. Note that the maximum credit risk-weighting for derivative contracts under the Basel Accord is 50 percent as compared with 100 percent for other credit obligations of private obligors.[9] This may also give a boost to swaps.

One further reason for swaps is to avoid regulation. Consider the currency swaps in Figure 15.2 above. Perhaps issuer A is a U.S. company that needs Yen funding but is unable to issue Yen bonds in Japan because Japanese regulators will not allow an issuer with A's relatively low credit rating to issue bonds, and its rating is not high enough to attract interest in

[8] L. Wall and J. Pringle, "Alternative Explanations of Interest Rate Swaps: A Theoretical and Empirical Analysis," 18 Financial Management (1989), pp. 59-73.
[9] V. Bhasin, "On the Credit Risk of OTC Derivative Users," Federal Reserve Board Finance and Economics Discussion Series 95-50 (1995).

the Euroyen market. Thus, issuer A raises Dollars in the U.S. market and swaps them for Yen.

Consider another example. "A case of tax and regulatory arbitrage through swaps occurred in 1984, when Japan still treated interest 'income' on zero-coupon bonds as nontaxable capital gain, whereas accruing interest 'payments' on zeros were tax deductible by U.S. borrowers. Financing packages utilizing swaps were devised in the market to exploit the discrepancy, enabling a number of U.S. borrowers to procure cheap Dollar funding, effectively at the expense of the Japanese taxpayer."[10] U.S. borrowers could issue zero-coupon Yen-denominated bonds to Japanese investors and swap the proceeds for Dollars.

Swaps may also be used to minimize other taxes. Consider equity swaps, for example. In a simple "total return" equity swap, a foreign party (F) would enter into a swap with a U.S. party (D) under which F pays D annually X percent (the interest on a Treasury bill) and an amount equal to any depreciation in the value of 100 shares of USCo., a U.S. issuer. D pays F an amount equal to the dividends paid on USCo. and any appreciation in its value. F gets the X percent to pay D by investing in a U.S. Treasury bond (paying D the interest on the bond compensates him for his carrying cost on buying the stock), while D hedges its risk by acquiring USCo. stock. F has, in effect, invested in USCo. and a Treasury bond but pays no U.S. withholding taxes. If F had invested directly in stock and the Treasury bond, he would have been subject to withholding payments on dividends; interest payments on the bond are exempt.[11]

It appears that use of derivatives by non-financial institutions is modest. If the median non-financial firm were to simultaneously experience a three standard deviation change in interest rates, exchange rates, and commodity prices, it would collect only $15 million from its entire derivatives portfolio, a quite modest amount compared to firm size and cash flows.[12]

Studies have also highlighted the significant use of derivatives by sovereigns.[13] While use of derivatives may just be another tool for sovereigns to reduce their cost of borrowing, it can also be used to window dress public accounts, thereby decreasing apparent deficits. This may be done to achieve better credit ratings (if use is not transparent) or to meet deficit limits, as under the EU Stability Pact.

---

[10] JPMorgan, "Swaps: Versatility at Controlled Risk," World Financial Markets (April 1991), p. 17.

[11] R. Avi-Yonah and L. Schwartz, "Virtual Taxation—Source-Based Taxation in the Age of Derivatives," Derivatives 247 (May/June 1997).

[12] W. Guay and S. Kothari, "How Much do Firms Hedge with Derivatives?," 70:3 Journal of Financial Economics (2003), pp. 423-461.

[13] G. Piga, "Do Governments Use Financial Derivatives Appropriately? Evidence from Sovereign Borrowers in Developed Economies," 4 International Finance (2001), p. 189.

One important question is why parties would use swaps rather than futures and options. Swaps by definition can be customized and are generally for longer maturities. Also, they allow parties to manage their appetite for credit risk through a choice of counterparty; the exchange or a clearinghouse is almost always the counterparty on futures and options.

The on-off exchange distinction is breaking down. In 2002, the Chicago Board of Trade began trading a 10-year interest rate swap and will soon trade a 5-year contract. So far, the volume is modest; through April 2002, yearly volume was about 123,000 contracts.[14] This compares with 17.3 million futures contracts on U.S. Treasury bonds. The trading unit for the CBOT swaps is the notional price of the fixed-rate side of a plain vanilla swap. In this context "plain vanilla" denotes a swap that has a principal equal to $100,000 and that exchanges semiannual interest payments at a fixed 6 percent per annum for floating interest rate payment based on 3-month LIBOR.[15] In a related development, LIFFE launched a Swapnote in March 2001, a future on Euro interest-rate swaps.[16] In 2002, it appears that for the first time on-exchange trading of derivatives grew faster than off-exchange trading.[17]

Notes and Questions

1.   In the interest rate swap in Figure 15.1, is Bank A's obligation to Swap Bank conditional on its bondholders paying it? Is Swap Bank's obligation to Company B conditional on Bank A paying the Swap Bank?

2.   Calculate Company B's cost savings from entering into the interest rate swap in Figure 15.1. Assume Company B's fixed rate funding would be 11-3/4 percent. Which party, A or B, has greater savings?

3.   Has Company B, in the interest rate swap, hedged its risks?

4.   Consider the FX risk on the currency swap described in Figure 15.2. Assume that the dollar-yen rate changes to $1 = ¥100 during the life of the swap. What is the FX risk for A and B?

3.   OVERALL MARKETS

The estimates of swaps outstanding vary widely. According to BIS, as of June 2004, there were $220.1 trillion in notional amounts outstanding, 74.5 percent of which were interest rate contracts and 12 percent of which were foreign exchange contracts.[18] Swaps activity is highly concentrated. As of June 30, 2000, the two largest dealers, JPMorgan Chase and Deutsche

---

[14] Chicago Board of Trade, *Monthly Statistics* (April 2002).
[15] Chicago Board of Trade, *Interest Rate Swap Complex, 5-Year and 10-year* (2002).
[16] N. Tait, "CBOT to Launch Swaps Futures," *Financial Times*, July 19, 2001.
[17] A. Skorecki, "Bigger Share of Derivatives for Exchanges," *Financial Times*, October 2, 2002.
[18] BIS Quarterly Review, December 2004, Table 19.

Bank, controlled 23 percent and 11 percent respectively of the notional value of interest rate swap contracts outstanding.[19]

B. CREDIT AND MARKET RISKS

1. THE NATURE OF THE RISKS

The risk incurred by a party entering into a swap can be analyzed as consisting of two parts: the rate risk and the credit risk of the counterparty. The rate risk (including currency risk, if applicable, as well as interest rate risk) is that, based on movement of rates in the future, the party will be the net payor under the swap. When rates move against a party, the party is said to be out of the money. When rates move in favor of a party, the party is said to be in the money. A party that is in the money has a credit risk that its counterparty will not perform.

The value of a swap, referred to as its mark-to-market value, can be calculated as the present value of the net payments the holder expects to receive over the life of the contract. An alternative expression of the same value is replacement cost, the cost of obtaining a replacement swap on the same terms and for the time remaining on the initial swap should the counterparty default.

As an example, consider the interest rate swap in Figure 15.1, above. Assume that at the end of the third year of the swap, the market rate for the five-year swap is 12.75 percent fixed for LIBOR. This means the swap is in the money (a good deal) for Company B, since it would now cost Company B 12.75 percent rather than 10.75 percent to get LIBOR. The replacement cost is the present discounted value of this 2 percent differential (multiplied by the notional amount of the swap) over the remaining 2-year life of the swap. Company B would have to pay $2,000,000 ($100,000,000 x .02) more in each interest period to obtain LIBOR. Using the current 2 year swap rate (12.75) as the discount rate, the replacement cost would be $2,000,000/1.1275 + 2,000,000/(1.1275)^2 = $3,347,081$. This cost would only be incurred if Company B's counterparty, Swap Bank, defaulted.

Consider the position of Company A under the same scenario of a 2 percent rise in interest rates. It is out of the money; it has made a bad deal. In the market, it could get 12.75 percent for LIBOR, while under its contract it is only getting 10.50 percent. The loss in the value of its contract is the present discounted value of the 2.25 percent differential in fixed rates (12.75 - 10.50) over the remaining 2-year life of the swap. Company A will be receiving $2,250,000 ($100,000,000 x .0225) less than the market would pay in each interest period. Using the current two year swap rate of 12.75 as the

---

[19] Swaps Monitor, *Data on the Global Derivatives Market* (2000).

discount rate, the loss would be $2{,}250{,}000/1.1275 + 2{,}250{,}000/(1.1275)^2 =$ $\$3{,}765{,}468$. This is a market loss for Company A, assuming A's fixed rate exposure is not hedged.

Finally, consider the position of Swap Bank. It is in the money on its contract with Company A (it would have to pay more now to get LIBOR) and out of the money on its contract with Company B (it could now get more for LIBOR in the market). Swap Bank does have a credit risk on its contract with Company A, but absent default, its market loss on its contract with B is offset by its market gain on its contract with A.

This analysis of risk looks at gains or losses on the contract at a fixed point in time, two years into the contract. Suppose we want to predict the risk of the contract over the life of the swap. Let us go back to credit risk and Company B's position. We know that Company B stands to lose about $3.3 million if Swap Bank were to default at the end of two years. This is referred to as current exposure. But B might stand to lose even more money if interest rates further increased and Swap Bank then defaulted. This is referred to as future or potential exposure.

a.   RISK REDUCTION FOR DEALERS

How can a Swap Dealer deal with market risk? One possibility, as in our paradigm interest rate swap, is to enter into a matched swap with another counterparty. In practice, however, it is very difficult to run a swaps portfolio that is entirely matched. One way to deal with this is to use non-swap interest rate contracts, futures, forwards, or options to hedge swap exposure. However, these hedges are "dynamic" since they need to be adjusted over time due to the fact that non-swap interest rate contracts have a shorter maturity than swaps. Indeed, a major problem in estimating the market risk to a particular institution from swaps is deciding to what extent swap risks are offset or hedged by positions in other instruments. It should be noted that dealers mark-to-market their derivatives portfolio daily in order to assess their value.

Parties, particularly dealers, may have several swaps with the same counterparty. Under the International Swaps and Derivatives Association (ISDA) master agreements, all swaps are regarded as parts of a single agreement. This being the case, if Party X defaults generally or just on one swap, the agreement provides that the counterparty may terminate all (but not less than all) swaps with Party X. The measure of damages, the counterparty's gain or loss, is calculated with respect to all the swaps on a net basis.

Most swappers insist on double A or better credit ratings for counterparties. So to counter the advantage of triple-A banks, investment banks created "credit-enhanced" derivatives subsidiaries. The first triple-A sub, Merrill Lynch Derivative Products, was separately capitalized upon its debut in November 1991 so that it would survive even if parent Merrill Lynch were to go bankrupt.

U.S. bank regulators did not initially allow banks (Citibank and Continental Illinois were denied permission in 1992) to set up AAA subsidiaries. This changed for the first time in May 1996 when the Office of the Comptroller of the Currency permitted NationsBank to do so, stating: "This allows domestic banks to remain competitive with US investment banks and foreign banks in the area of derivative dealing."[20] In 1996, Dai-Ichi Kangyo (DKB), a large Japanese bank, reached an agreement that would allow it to funnel its derivatives business through Merrill Lynch Capital Services' triple-A rated derivatives conduit. Due to concern over the creditworthiness of the bank, DKB thought it desirable to use a triple-A entity, and found it cheaper to use Merrill Lynch's existing entity, which had excess capital, than to spend $300 million to capitalize its own.

A May 1996 study of the Federal Reserve Bank of New York generally questions the efficacy of the use of AAA companies, given their substantial capital investment. These entities have garnered a relatively small percentage of the swaps market. Another problem with these companies is that their risk may not be entirely segregated from that of their parents since AAAs typically hedge customer transactions with mirror transactions with parents. If parents were to default on the mirror transactions, or have an increased risk of defaulting, the AAA would itself be at increased risk and its AAA rating might be jeopardized.

The low market share of triple AAA credits may suggest that pricing in the swaps market does not materially take counterparty creditworthiness into account. Why would that be? R. Litzenberger[21] gives three reasons: first, assuming that bankruptcy probabilities are independent of interest rate levels, gains from the default of a counterparty are just as likely as losses. If you are a fixed-rate payer, you gain from your counterparty's bankruptcy if rates go down, but lose if rates go up. If, however, low interest rates are associated in general with more bankruptcies, and fixed rate payers are generally more risky than floating rate payers, floating rate payers are more likely to lose if rates go down, i.e. when fixed rate payers default. Second, under the one-way payment rules, the solvent party may not have to pay the defaulting party. Third, there is protection against credit risk. Deterioration in credit ratings may terminate swaps, or there may be collateral.

While many dealers report that they do not quote different rates for counterparties of different credit quality, dealers do require their counterparties to establish credit lines, and lower quality credits get smaller credit lines than those with higher credit. One study has stated: "Suppose

[20] O. de Sennerpont Domis, "NationsBank Gets OCC Nod on Derivatives," *American Banker*, May 20, 1996.
[21] "Swaps: Plain and Fanciful," 47 Journal of Finance (1992), pp. 831, 836-838.

that traders of one firm do not offer different prices to different credit risk counterparties but ration them depending on their credit quality. A low rating company will reach the maximum of its credit line faster than a high rating company. It will have to obtain a quote from a globally less favorable dealer [a dealer uniformly charging higher rates, ed.]. At equilibrium, in the market, participants may obtain different rates from different dealers even though no dealers give different quotes to different companies."[22]

In March 1999, the CFTC approved an application of the London Clearing House (LCH), which clears and settles trades on London financial exchanges, for an exemption from regulation that would permit it to clear and settle OTC derivatives, beginning with plain vanilla interest rate swaps and forward exchange rate agreements. The name of the service is SwapClear. Two parties in a swap deal convert their bilateral agreement into separate agreements with the LCH. The plan envisioned that contracts with the LCH as counterparty would require less capital than would otherwise be the case. This may result from the advantages of netting with one rather than several counterparties.[23] SwapClear imposes both initial and variation margin requirements based on daily marking-to-market of the value of the swap.

b.   OVERALL SWAP RISK

A principal methodology used to estimate potential exposure over the remaining life of a swap is the Monte Carlo simulation. The remaining life of the swap is analyzed on the basis of simulations which model movements in swap rates based on different assumptions of interest rate volatility.

A study by K. Simons[24] performed a Monte Carlo simulation for interest rate swaps of various maturities. The study used matched pairs of swaps to control for market risk, i.e. gain on one swap would be exactly offset by loss on the other. This approach allows for isolation of credit risk. Interest rate predictions were based on two scenarios. The first assumed that interest rates follow a random walk in accordance with historical volatility and further assumes that changes are lognormally distributed around a mean corresponding to historical volatility. The second used the forward interest rates implied by the shape of the swap yield curve (maturity on horizontal axis, percentage yields on vertical axis) as a forecast of expected future swap interest rates. The results were as follows:

---

[22] D. Cossin and H. Pirotte, "Swap Credit Risk: An Empirical Investigation on Transaction Data," Journal of Banking & Finance (1997), p. 1351. The study, in fact found, that credit ratings affected swap prices in the aggregate by 3.8 basis points with the biggest impact for non-rated companies.
[23] N. Tait and E. Luce, "Clearing Services Proposal for OTC Derivatives," *Financial Times*, June 17, 1998.
[24] "Interest Rate Structure and the Credit Risk of Swaps," New England Economic Review (July/August 1993), p. 23.

Table 15B
Exposure on a Matched Pair of Swaps as a Percentage of Notional Principal

Swap Maturity	10-Year Flat Rate	10-Year Rising Rate	7-Year Flat Rate	7-Year Rising Rate	5-Year Flat Rate	5-Year Rising Rate	3-Year Flat Rate	3-Year Rising Rate	1-Year Flat Rate	1-Year Rising Rate
Confidence Interval										
99 percent	11.22	13.07	7.78	9.49	5.12	6.44	2.25	2.79	.34	.36
95 percent	8.28	9.24	5.67	6.79	3.59	4.64	1.63	2.02	.24	.25
90 percent	6.93	7.57	4.71	5.54	3.06	3.75	1.37	1.66	.20	.21
75 percent	5.12	5.33	3.37	3.75	2.22	2.54	.98	1.13	.14	.14
Mean Expected Lifetime Exposure	4.03	4.27	2.68	2.97	1.74	2.00	.77	.87	.10	.10

The values in Table 15B indicate the expected replacement costs over the lifetime of the swap. The "flat rate" is based on the random walk methodology, while the "rising rate" is based on the shape of the swap yield curve. The results are interpreted as follows. For a swap with a remaining life of 10 years, the flat rate exposure will be no more than 8.28 and the rising rate exposure will be no more than 9.24 percent of the notional amount in 95 percent of the cases, while the mean expected lifetime exposure is 4.03 and 4.27 percent under the two respective methodologies. The mean expected lifetime exposure is calculated by averaging the expected exposure for each period. The lower mean expected lifetime exposures take into account the fact that the risk reduces as the swap approaches maturity since fewer periods remain in which the difference between the initial and the current rate can accumulate.

One overall point from this study is that the actual risk on a swap may be significant, but for most swaps it is a rather low percentage of the national amount.

Notes and Questions

1. Can a party have both market and credit risk on a swap? At the same time?

2. The G-30 Derivatives Study, supra, note 3, gave the following estimates for the gross replacement costs of the derivatives portfolio of the 50 largest U.S. bank holding companies.

Table 15C

Derivatives Exposure by Lead Banks of 50 Largest U.S. Bank Holding Companies
(Year-End 1990-1992)

Gross Replacement Costs

	Interest Rate Contracts		Currency Contracts		Combined Exposure
Year	$ Billion	Percent of Notional Principal	$ Billion	Percent of Notional Principal	$ Billion
1990	26.2	1.15	76.3	2.82	102.5
1991	47.8	1.61	99.4	3.70	147.2
1992	49.7	1.61	94.3	2.98	144.0

The gross replacement cost is the mark-to-market value for OTC derivatives contracts with positive replacement cost, including swaps, forwards, purchased options, when-issued securities, and forward deposits accepted. Exchange-traded contracts and foreign exchange contracts with less than 14 days maturity are excluded.

Source: Consolidated Reports of Condition and Income.

Can these results for interest rate contracts (which include futures/options and swaps) be squared with the Simons study? Why would exposure on currency contracts be higher than on interest rate contracts?

3. Do you agree with Litzenberger's analysis?

2. DOCUMENTATION

The International Swaps and Derivatives Association (ISDA) was formed to expedite documentation through the development of standard terms. The first step was publication of ISDA's 1985 and 1986 Editions of the Code of Standard Wording, Assumptions and Provisions for Swaps (Swaps Code).

In 1987, the ISDA published two master agreements, presented on printed forms. The first master, the Rate Swap Master, was for U.S. Dollar interest rate swaps only and was governed by New York law. The second, the Rate and Currency Swap Master, was for rate swaps in any currency as well as currency swaps. It was governed by either New York or English law. The provisions in the two agreements are nearly identical in substance.

Each of the agreements consists of two parts, the first of which sets forth the basic terms of the master and the second of which is a Schedule on which some of those terms may be completed, supplemented, or varied.

Existence of the ISDA agreements increases market liquidity, since quotes can be made on standardized contractual assumptions. It does, however, discourage customization—at least beyond the basic choices provided.

The ISDA master agreements were revised in 1992 and again in 2002.[25] The most significant change in 2002 was the introduction of the "close-out amount" as the single valuation measure to apply when a swap is terminated. Close-out amount involves a calculation of how much it would cost a "determining party"—the party entitled to make the calculation under the agreement, the designation of which depends on the cause of termination—to close out the agreement. This requires a determination of how much a determining party would be paid to replace, or provide the economic equivalent of: (1) the material terms of the terminated transaction(s); and (2) the option rights of the parties in respect of the terminated transaction(s). The determining party must exercise good faith and use commercially reasonable procedures in making a determination.

The definition does not mandate a particular way to make the determination but rather lists a number of factors that should be considered, such as market quotations for replacement transactions supplied by third parties, and market data in the form, for example, of rates, prices, yield curves, or volatilities. The definition generally provides that the determining party must "consider" market quotations and data unless such information is not available or would produce a result that would not satisfy the commercially reasonable or good faith standards. The definition explicitly permits the determining party to make use of its own internal valuation models in calculating the close-out amount. It also provides that the Determining Party may consider losses related to terminating, liquidating, or reestablishing a hedge related to the terminated transaction.

The other most significant change relates to force majeure, events which make performance impossible or impractical. The Master Agreement provides that there is no immediate right to terminate in the event of force majeure since the obstacle to performance may only be temporary. ISDA provides for a waiting period of 8 local business days. In the case of illegality, a shorter period of 3 business days is provided on the theory that illegality is not likely to be short-lived, and that only a short period of time is necessary to determine whether performance would actually be illegal.

The European Banking Federation published a 2004 version of its European Master Agreement (EMA). EMA, together with its product annexes covering repurchase transactions, securities lending transactions, foreign exchange transactions and derivatives transactions, is the first multi-product master agreement to include derivatives. One of the principal advantages of such an approach is to permit cross-product netting, e.g. a counterparty's position is netted across all of the covered products.[26]

---

[25] J. Berry, "ISDA Sets New Standards for Derivatives" International Financial Law Review (February 2003) contains an excellent discussion of the 2002 changes.

[26] P. Lastenouse, "The European Master Agreement and Its Derivative Annex," Butterworths Journal of International Banking and Financial Law (June 2004).

C.   CREDIT DERIVATIVES

A fast growing area of swaps is credit derivatives. The total global credit derivatives market in 2004 was about $5 trillion, according to the British Bankers Association, up from about $2 trillion in 2002. This compares with total international bank credit outstanding in June 2004 of $19.9 trillion.[27] Insurance companies have about a 25 percent market share.[28] While the major financial institutions and insurance companies are the major players in terms of dollar volume, a high percentage of their positions are hedged. It appears that on a net basis, insurance and financial guaranty companies, e.g. bond insurers, hold the major positive net positions.[29] Recent data indicate that hedge funds are also major players, only 15 percent of the seller of protection market and 16 percent of the buyer of protection market.[30] There is anecdotal evidence that a variety of institutional investors have significant net positions as well. On the whole there is a net outflow of credit risks from banks to other sectors. However, some banks seeking higher yields, such as the German state-guaranteed Landesbanks have increased their credit risks through participation in this market.[31]

In 2005, there was concern about the risk and liquidity in this market. This was partly due to concerns about the possibility of large defaults, e.g. GM, on which substantial credit derivatives were written, and the general high rate of growth in the market. In 2005, demand soared in the "trading" of credit derivatives as people sought to unwind their positions by taking offsetting positions, e.g. a seller of protection on GM seeking to buy offsetting protection for itself. Or if investors had bought tradeable securities like CDOs (securitized credit derivatives), they could sell their positions in such securities. Regulators, like Tim Geithner, the President of the N.Y. Federal Reserve Bank, expressed increased concern about the risks in these markets.[32] Geithner appeared to be worried by the growth (spurred by hedge funds), concentration and possibly increased risk. The concern was whether the system could absorb a shock without severe consequences to the financial system as a whole. There was also concern that investors might not adequately understand the risks of some of the more complicated credit derivatives.

---

[27] BIS Quarterly Review, March 2003.

[28] Committee on the Global Financial System, Bank for International Settlements, *Credit Risk Transfer* (January 2003), p. 10. (BIS CT Study). Financial Services Authority, *Cross-sector Risk Transfers* (May 2002), p. 3.

[29] Fitch Ratings, *Global Credit Derivatives: Risk Management or Risk* (March 10, 2003), p. 5.

[30] British Bankers Association 2004.

[31] Id., at 9.

[32] G. Tett, "Geithner Reassures Market over Credit Risk," *Financial Times*, May 12, 2005. See also the IMF, Global Financial Stability Report, April 2005, p. 3.

Credit derivatives work in an opposite direction from securitization. Banks have used securitization techniques to get risky loans off their balance sheets. Credit derivatives allow the banks to keep loans on their balance sheets but transfer the default risk to counterparties. This has the potential of reversing the long-term trend of the growth of the capital markets at the expense of the banking markets.

1. TYPES OF TRANSACTIONS

a. CREDIT DEFAULT SWAPS

The major type of credit derivative, a credit default swap, allows a counterparty (usually a financial institution) to buy protection against default of an asset, a loan or bond or receivable, by paying a derivatives dealer, the seller of protection, e.g. a periodic fee, expressed as a percentage of the notional amount of an asset. The seller of protection is required to acquire credit-impaired assets at a given price (physical settlement) or to pay the difference between that price and the current value of reference assets (cash settlement) in the case of a "credit event." An example of cash settlement would be as follows: "[t]hirty days after a company defaults (e.g. it fails to make a bond coupon payment), its bonds are valued at 30 cents on the dollar. If the notional amount of a cash-settled credit default swap referencing that entity's bonds is $10 million, the protection 'seller' would be required to make a payment of $7 million to the protection 'buyer.'"[33] In this example, if the fee were 40 basis points, the protection buyer would pay $10,000 every quarter to the protection seller.

The contingent payment amount made by the seller of protection is often determined by the percentage decline in a "reference obligation" whose value would be correlated with the asset that deteriorated. For example, where the protected asset was a bank loan to Company X, the reference security might be Company X's publicly issued bonds. The payoff would depend on the decline in the value of the reference obligation.

The seller of protection need not hold the assets for which it purchases credit protection. A bank which does not hold certain debt obligations may wish to assume credit risk on such assets without acquiring them. This is the case with the Landesbanks mentioned above. A party may also choose to "short" a reference entity by buying credit protection for obligations it does not hold. It then profits from the default of the reference entity. Another possibility is for a borrower from a bank to sell credit protection on its own debt, a so-called self-referenced credit-default swap. The company thus obtains fee income for not defaulting on its debt.

---

[33] Moody's Investor Service, *Structured Finance, Special Report, Understanding the Risks in Credit Default Swaps* (March 16, 2001). (Moody's)

Credit default swaps may be written on baskets of referenced entities as well as single ones. The simplest form of such derivatives is called a basket swap. A common example is a first-to-default basket. In such a contract, the payment by the protection seller is triggered by a default event by any of the reference entities included in the portfolio. Or the portfolio can be triggered only if there are two or three defaults, so-called second and third to default baskets. Alternatively, payoffs can depend on the size of defaults in an overall portfolio. For example, in a first-loss tranche of 10 percent, first-loss protection sellers are exposed to any defaults in a portfolio that exceed 10 percent.

Definitions of importance to credit derivatives are now covered in an ISDA master agreement issued in January 1998, revised in 1999 and again in 2003. The standard credit events for a corporate swap issuer include bankruptcy, payment default, merger, "cross acceleration," "cross default," credit downgrade, repudiation, and restructuring, although the inclusion of restructuring is under significant debate.

A credit default swap could be linked to an interest rate swap. For example, if Bank A had a 10-year interest rate swap exposure to Company and it wanted to hedge the risk of the company, it could enter into a swap with a third party (TP) under which it would make periodic payments to TP, and TP would pay Bank A in the event Company defaulted on the interest rate swap. The amount of the default payment would be linked to Company A bonds with similar maturities to the swap.

Credit default swaps have become so prominent, that their prices provide an alternative to traditional credit rating services such as S&P and Moody's. The credit spreads on credit default swaps are a market alternative to the expert ratings provided by the agencies.[34]

b.   TOTAL RETURN SWAPS

Another type of credit derivative is the total return swap in which the buyer of protection pays to the seller of protection the total return on an asset, such as a loan or bond, in return for a given payment. For example, Bank B which owns XYZ bond, would agree to pay all positive returns on the bond to dealer (all bond cash flows plus positive mark-to-market movements) in exchange for a fee, e.g. LIBOR plus specified basis points, and loss protection on the bond (negative mark-to-market movements).[35] For another example, an equity investor who thinks the German DAX index (a stock market index) will fall over the next six months might enter into a swap on

---

[34] C. Batchelor, "CDS Market Tilts at Rating Agencies," *Financial Times*, June 16, 2004.
[35] See Bank of England, "Developing a Supervisory Approach to Credit Derivatives," Discussion Paper (November 1996).

which he pays the DAX return every month in exchange for receiving one-month DM LIBOR plus a spread.[36]

c.   TAX RATE SWAPS

Still another innovation is a tax rate swap that allows a specific hedge against a change in tax rates. A company (A) had entered into a large leasing transaction providing tax benefits and, therefore, increased profits that would be lost if corporate tax rates fell. Many companies (B), of course, have higher profits if tax rates decrease. The swap involved approximately $30 million, the profits sought to be protected. Morgan Grenfell arranged a swap by which A made payments to B if tax rates increased and B made payments to A if tax rates decreased. The pricing of the swap presumably involved estimates of the probabilities of tax rate changes.[37]

d.   CLNs AND CDOs

Credit derivative swaps can also be securitized. A Special Purpose Vehicle (SPV), as a seller of protection, would enter into a credit default swap with a financial institution. The SPV would receive a fee for the protection from the financial institution and if a credit default occurred on the referenced credits, e.g. bonds or loans held by the financial institution, the SPV would make payments to the financial institution. The SPV would then transfer its risk to the capital market. Through synthetic collateralized debt obligations (CDOs) or credit-linked notes (CLNs), investors would become sellers of protection to the SPV. The investors would receive a return on their notes, by the SPV passing on to them the fees it receives on its credit default swap, together with a return on their cash investments, and receive back their investment at term absent a credit event. If a credit event occurred, the SPV would make payments to the financial institution, which would be funded by the investors who would thus experience losses of principal.

CDOs can be more complex than just securitizing credit default swaps. The underlying obligations can be a combination of various obligations, including bonds, loans, credit default swaps or other synthetic portfolios. The latter are known as Russian dolls as a way of emphasizing their complexity. The CDOs are typically sliced into tranches representing different credit risks. Typically in a synthetic CDO, the financial institution retains the first loss piece, while the mezzanine tranches are securitized and sold to investors. Most significant CDOs get credit ratings; some are even actively managed.[38]

---

[36] See H. Kat, "Financial Engineering, Credit Derivatives: A New Addition to the Derivatives Toolbox," *Derivatives* (November/December 1997).
[37] T. Corrigan, "Tax Rate Swap Deal opens a Fresh Vista," *Financial Times*, August 18, 1994.
[38] "Russian Doll," The Economist, September 23, 2004.

In a self-referenced CLN, the investor is the corporation whose debt is referenced in the credit default swap. By purchasing an investment with a rate of return linked to its own credit risk, the investor can exploit its informational advantage about its own credit risk. This advantage is presumably known to the sellers of the investment, however, and should be compensated for in the pricing. Further, if the underlying corporation defaults, its losses are compounded by its losses on its investments in itself.[39]

A Hypothetical CDO

A recent report of the Joint Forum largely focuses on CDOs,[40] as the area most needing attention and analysis, as other forms of credit derivatives like default swaps are passing into the standardized, plain-vanilla category. CDOs issued have grown from about $200 billion in 2002 to $445 billion anticipated in 2005.[41] The Report gives a useful analysis of a hypothetical funded CDO based on Table 15D below:

Table 15D[42]
A stylised hypothetical CDO
(Dollar amounts in millions)

Tranche	Attachment points	Notional amount	Credit rating	Spread (basis points)
Equity	0-3%	30	Not rated	1200
Mezzanine	3-10%	70	A	200
Senior	10-100%	900	AAA	10
MEMO				
Entire portfolio	0-100%	1,000	A	60

This is a hypothetical example of a $1 billion synthetic CDO with three tranches. The fact that the CDO is synthetic means the issuer does not actually own the underlying assets—they are merely referenced with respect to their economic characteristics. Such a synthetic CDO could be issued by a commercial bank seeking to hedge loans on its balance sheet.

The unrated equity tranche bears the first $30 million of losses, the single-A-rated mezzanine tranche bears the next $70 million, and the AAA-rated senior tranche bears any losses above the first two tranches, $900 million. In this example, the reference portfolio consists of 100 single-name credit default swaps of $10 million each with an average spread of 60 basis points over LIBOR and an average credit rating of single-A. Attachment

---

[39] P. Ali, "The Conundrum of Self-Referenced Credit-Linked Notes," Journal of International Banking Law Review 326 (2004).

[40] The Joint Forum (the Basel Committee, IOSCO, and IAIS, the International Association of Insurance Supervisors), Credit Risk Transfer (March 2005). See particularly Annex 1, pp. 44-46. (Joint Forum March 2005)

[41] G. Tett, Clouds Sighted off CDO Asset Pool," *Financial Times,* April 18, 2005.

[42] Joint Forum March 2005, supra note 40, p. 45.

points are another way of referring to the interval of losses. In the example, equity has risk on $30 million, or an interval from 0-3 percent of $1billion, and mezzanine bears the next interval of loss, from 3-10 percent, or up to $70 billion (.07 x $1 billion).

The three tranches are typically sold to different investors. For example, the equity tranche in the example, paying LIBOR + 12 percent, may be sold to a hedge fund, while the senior tranche, paying LIBOR + 10 percent, may be sold to a reinsurer or another conservative investor. CDOs can be funded or unfounded. In a funded CDO, as in the example, investors pay in the principal amount of their tranches and defaults cause a writedown of principal. Principal is put into a collateral account and invested in government securities or AAA debt on which investors receive a return in addition to the return from the portfolio. In an unfunded CDO, tranches are structured as swaps with no up-front payments. Investors only receive spread payments. Unfunded payments create counterparty risk for the SPV issuer.

Suppose in the first three months (the hypothetical payment period) no defaults occur on the reference. On the quarterly interest rate payment date, the CDO (the SPV issuer) receives quarterly payments on the reference portfolio's credit default swaps (for example, from a counterparty bank buying protection on its loans)) as well as interest on the collateral account. It distributes the interest received according to a "windfall" of payments, paying first the senior tranche, and then down the line.

Suppose in the fourth month, one of the names in the reference portfolio defaults. If the recovery rate on the name was 40 percent, the CDO will take a loss of $6 million on the $10 million credit. The CDO will write down the value of its portfolio by $6 million, which will be absorbed by the equity tranche, which is responsible for the first $30 million of losses. CDOs can be more complicated. Some investors have bought securities called CDO_2, a CDO which invests in other CDOs (like a fund-of-funds discussed in the next Chapter).

Clearly, credit derivatives are closely related to insurance. An easy way to conceptualize the transaction is that the buyer of protection is buying insurance against credit risk from the seller of protection. The documentation and writing about these transactions seeks to avoid talking about the transactions in these terms largely because of regulatory concerns. If the contracts were regarded as insurance they might be subject to regulation by insurance regulators (posing the threat of control over terms) or become ultra vires for institutions that could not provide insurance, e.g. banks in some countries.[43]

---

[43] See D. Nirenberg and R. Hoffman, "Are Credit Default Swaps Insurance?," Derivatives Report 7 (December 2001).

e.   LIQUIDITY AND TRADING FACILITIES

Inter-dealer brokers, who arrange swaps for dealers, have started to trade credit indicies online. The iTraxx family of CDS indices compile credit default swaps for different companies. As an example, the iTraxx Europe index is based on a portfolio of CDSs on 125 investment grade companies. In 2005, "fixings" began on these indices. Fixings represent a way to establish the value of the indices. Prices are submitted by traders over a two-minute period, and a bid, offer and mid price are calculated electronically at the end of that time. Before "fixings" investors had to rely on the dealing price of a particular bank. These fixings will not only make the indices more attractive but will permit the development of other products based on such indices. Brokers also make markets in options on the index.[44]

In addition, there are now several on-line trading platforms, like those provided by DTCC and SwapsWire, and interdealer systems like Swapstream, that permit electronic "trading" in swaps, including credit derivatives and indices—or more precisely, the on-line completion of transactions. This has developed in response to the expanding demand for such transactions.[45]

Another development designed to provide more liquidity to the market is the regular termination of swap positions by participating banks that agree to net off their positions against each other and settle the differences. This cuts down their exposures and frees up capital for new positions. For example, TriReduce uses an algorithm to match swap positions between participants. The process of termination then takes place on a triangular bias, where three banks are identified that have each have an outstanding position with the next. This service started with interest rate swaps and is now expanding into credit derivatives.[46]

Notes and Questions

1. Why would insurance companies be such major sellers of protection on credit derivatives?

2.   THE RESTRUCTURING ISSUE

Two important issues are how settlement occurs when there is a restructuring and what a restructuring is.

---

[44] D. Duffie, "Irresistible Reasons for Better Credit Models of Credit Risk," *Financial Times*, April 16, 2004.

[45] C. Kentouris, "Credit Derivatives: Making a Market," *Securities Industry News*, December 20, 2004.

[46] A. Skorecki, "CDS Market Could Shrink," *Financial Times*, December 17, 2004.

a.   DELIVERABLE OBLIGATIONS

Conseco, Inc., a U.S. consumer finance company restructured its maturing bank loans in response to an impending liquidity crisis. The consensus was that this was a Credit Event since it resulted from a deteriorating financial condition, although the situation was not entirely clear. Given that a Credit Event occurred, the buyer of the protection was entitled to receive a payment from the seller of protection in return for the physical delivery of assets. Certain buyers delivered bonds, a type of Conseco debt that had deteriorated more than the loans that were the subject of the restructuring.

The delivery of the cheap bonds was made possible by the fact that the underlying ISDA documentation allowed the parties to adopt a broad range of Deliverable Obligations. In a particular swap, the Deliverable Obligation can be so broad as to include both bonds or loans, although the parties are free to define the Deliverable Obligation much more narrowly, e.g. to particular kinds of loans. Some have suggested that when restructurings of the type in Conseco occur, that only short-dated bonds should be deliverable, maturing reasonably close to the maturity date of the swap (these bonds would lose less value than those with longer maturities).

In *Nomura International Plc v Credit Suisse First Boston International*,[47] Nomura had bought credit protection from CSFB with reference to the default of Railtrack. Under the contract, Nomura was entitled to deliver to CSFB certain Railtrack bonds upon a Railtrack default and receive the amount of its protection. Nomura delivered two kinds of bonds, some of which were convertible, at the option of the holder, into equity, and some that were not. The 1999 ISDA definitions provided that deliverable obligations could not be "contingent," and CSFB refused to accept the convertible bonds on the basis that they were contingent. The court held that bonds convertible at the option of the holder, unlike bonds convertible at the option of the issuer, were not contingent. The court stated that the purpose of the requirement of "Not Contingent" was to secure a right of payment of the principal amount that could not be affected in amount by extraneous factors over which the seller of credit, as holder, has no control." In the 2003 ISDA definitions, an extensive definition of "Not Contingent" was supplied. Any obligation is "Not Contingent" if the "obligation may not be reduced as a result of the occurrence or nonoccurrence of an event or circumstance (other than payment)." But all convertible bonds, whether convertible at the option of the issuer or holder, are "Not Contingent." This amendment suggests that ISDA believed that the court reached the right result but for the wrong reason.

The 2003 ISDA definitions give parties a way to limit risks arising out of physical delivery. Under paragraph 3 of the long-form confirmation,

---

[47] [2003] EWHC 160 (Comm).

the parties may specify the particular deliverable obligation categories that are acceptable, e.g. reference obligations only or bonds and/or loans. The parties may also choose a "Modified Restructuring Maturity Limitation." Under §2.33(c) of the definitions, this is "the date that is the later of: (x) the Scheduled Termination Date; and (y) 60 months following the Restructuring Date in the case of a Restructured Bond or Loan, or 30 months following the Restructuring Date in the case of all other Deliverable Obligations." The Restructuring Date is the date on which the Restructuring is legally effective: §2.33(d).

In 2005, ISDA issued a new procedure for cash settlement of credit default swap index trades (an index of CDSs on a basket of companies). Until ISDA's latest move, an index constituent's default would trigger a partial settlement of obligation involving the physical delivery of bonds. But index trading volumes far outstripped the availability of deliverables when Collins & Aikman, the car parts supplier, defaulted in May 2005, that was part of a widely traded CDS index. The ISDA procedure sets up an auction for reference obligations like the Collins & Aikman bonds and a method for outstanding ISDA documents requiring physical settlement without engaging in negotiations with counterparties. Parties can do so by adhering to a new Index Protocol.[48]

b.   WHAT IS A RESTRUCTURING?

The question of what is a restructuring that should constitute an event of default has been hotly contested by market participants. The objective is to define restructuring in a way that is equivalent to a default. Many corporate debt restructurings have nothing to do with credit problems but rather reflect a way to reduce debt costs. For example, a company may wish to shift its borrowings from loans to bonds, or from shorter to longer-term debt maturities. It has been difficult to define a default related restructuring.

Under Section 4.7 of the 1999 ISDA Credit Derivative definitions, restructurings constituting credit events had to fulfill two general conditions. These restructurings must: (1) not have been provided for in the original terms of the obligation, e.g. a planned refinancing; and (2) be a result of a deterioration in the obligor's creditworthiness. It may very difficult to judge whether the second condition is satisfied. A restructuring must also constitute one of the following five cases: (1) a reduction in interest payment amounts; (2) a reduction in principal payment amounts; (3) a postponement or deferral of interest or principal payments; (4) a change in an obligation's priority, e.g. becoming subordinated to new debt; or (5) any change in the currency or composition of any payment of interest or principal.

---

[48] ISDA, 2005 CDS Index Protocol, published on May 26, 2005.

Moody's has criticized this definition since it is not consistent with its own definition of a "distressed exchange" default. Moody's looks to three factors with respect to such exchanges: (1) the extent to which the restructured obligation is a "diminished financial obligation,"—i.e. the degree of monetary impairment suffered by investors; (2) the extent to which the restructuring was involuntary for all investors; and (3) the extent to which the restructuring was done to avoid an imminent payment default. Moody's is concerned about the discrepancy because it gives credit ratings to securitized credit default swaps like credit-linked notes. If ISDA's definition of restructuring is broader than Moody's, investors providing credit protection may be more at risk than would be indicated by application of Moody's usual definitions. Moody's has also argued that the ISDA definition of restructuring was wrong because it permitted restructurings that were completely voluntary and resulted in no financial loss to the investor.[49]

The 1999 ISDA definition of restructuring is basically unchanged by the 2003 definitions. The change in currency provision has been modified to provide that it only applies when the currency is changed to a "non-permitted" currency. A permitted currency is a G-7 currency or the currency of an OECD member with a high sovereign debt rating. It also requires that the default be for a specified minimum amount unless otherwise agreed, i.e. $10 million.

Another change in the definitions was related to ongoing litigation. In *Eternity Global Master Fund Limited v. Morgan Guaranty Trust Company of New York and JPMorgan Chase Bank (Eternity I)*,[50] Eternity, a credit protection buyer, sued Morgan, the credit protection seller, with respect to Eternity's protection on three credit default swaps with reference to certain Argentine bonds. On November 1, 2001, the Argentine government announced its intention to exchange these bonds for loan instruments with lower yields and longer maturities in a "voluntary exchange." Tendered debt would be held in trust, and new secured debt obligations would be issued to tendering debtholders. By December 2001, investors had tendered over $40 billion in debt. On November 2, 2001, Eternity demanded payment on its credit default swaps but Morgan refused. On December 24, 2001, Argentina suspended payment on all of its outstanding debt. Morgan then honored two of the credit derivatives but not the third. This is because the scheduled termination date of the third swap fell on December 17, before the actual suspension of debt on the 24th. The termination date on the other two swaps was after the 24th. With respect to this third swap, the issue was whether a default occurred in November.

Morgan argued that Eternity's breach of contract claim should be dismissed on the ground that there was no event of default. Morgan

---

[49] Moody's, supra note 33, pp. 7-9.
[50] 2002 U.S. Dist. LEXIS 20706 (S.D.N.Y. October 2002).

contended that the 1999 ISDA definitions referred to an "Obligation Exchange" as a restructuring, and then limited "Obligation Exchange" to a mandatory transfer. After first having ruled in favor of Eternity on the breach of contract claim in *Eternity* I, the court reversed itself in *Eternity* II.[51] The court dismissed the contract claim on the ground that the exchange involved "an agreed-upon indefinite deferral of interest and/or principal payments under the Obligations [the tendered bonds]. ..."

The Second Circuit reversed in *Eternity III*.[52] The court questioned whether an exchange on the terms specified could truly have been voluntary—in fact, bondholders only tendered because they thought they would be even worse off without the exchange since Argentina would have to default entirely. It further questioned whether the effect of the suspension was to extend the termination date beyond December 17th. It found the contract ambiguous and thus remanded the case back to the district court for further proceedings, presumably for a trial to determine the intention of the parties. The 2003 ISDA definitions seek to avoid the issue in the *Eternity* litigation by deleting any reference to "Obligation Exchange," thus leaving the issue of whether there has been a default to the five specific requirements of the restructuring definition.

A major consideration in the debate over restructuring is the impact on a bank's capital requirements of having a credit derivative without protection for restructuring. Under Basel II, with respect to the standardized approach, loans covered by credit derivatives will generally be assigned the risk-weight of the seller of protection (unless higher than that of the obligor on the loan.[53] Generally, restructuring involving forgiveness or postponement of interest or principal, must be included as a credit event for capital relief.[54] When restructuring is not covered, then a maximum of 60 percent of the amount of the derivative will be eligible for the risk-weight of the seller of protection. Under the IRB approach, no such limit applies. Given that the United States has indicated it will only apply Basel II in its most advanced form to a limited number of the most sophisticated banks, U.S. banks may not be troubled by the exclusion of restructuring as an event of default—they will still get capital reduction based on their own models of LGD. All EU banks will have to adopt Basel II under the Capital Adequacy Directive, and those who use the standardized approach may not get any capital relief. This has resulted in European banks favoring the inclusion of restructuring. One could argue that ISDA documentation should permit banks to have a choice on the issue, but U.S. banks argue that the legal uncertainty created by the

---

[51] 2003 U.S. Dist. LEXIS 12351 (S.D.N.Y. February 2003)

[52] 375 F.3d 168 (2004).

[53] Basel Committee on Banking Supervision, *International Convergence of Capital Measurement and Capital Standards: A Revised Framework* (Basel II), June 2004, ¶ 96.

[54] Id., at ¶191(a).

inclusion—see the discussion of litigation above—is hurting the overall credit derivatives market.

c.   INCENTIVES

A general concern that arises from the use of credit derivatives is their impact on incentives. The bank which transfers its entire risk on a loan to a credit protection seller will no longer have an incentive to monitor the performance of its borrower. Although the protection seller will have the incentive to do so, it may be less well positioned to do so, as it will possess no contractual rights under the loan covenants. Thus, the cost-adjusted risk of the protection seller may exceed that of the bank, the protection buyer. While the credit protection seller's risk will be reflected in its fee, such arrangements if widely used, could result in higher credit costs. This effect can be minimized if the protection buyer does not transfer all of its risk, but retains an initial tranche of exposure, much like a deductible under an insurance policy. A related issue is whether the absence of credit exposure on behalf of a lender will lead to higher prices for public issued debt since investors cannot depend on banks to monitor risks.[55]

Another concern is that the protection buyer may take action to trigger a default just because of the protection. This might be the case where the market value of the underlying asset whose credit risk it has transferred is less than the value of a credit-default payoff. The ability of credit protection buyers to do so depends on the terms of their credit default documentation. For example, assume that a credit protection buyer is protected against bankruptcy but not restructuring. In such case, the buyer would reject restructuring options in order to accelerate the bankruptcy. This may not be welfare-optimizing behavior if restructuring was the more optimal outcome. A related concern is connected with the possibility of physical delivery. It has been alleged that credit protection buyers in the case of Conseco triggered a credit event in order to profit from its option of delivering bonds worth less than the losses experienced on the Conseco assets held by such buyers.[56]

"In the past, banks often preferred to extend the maturity of their loans and take security in the hope of a successful recovery knowing that they would benefit, relatively speaking, from their security if there was a default in the future. This bet-hedging approach does not fit with the approach of the credit derivatives market which looks for a clear insolvency-

---

[55] A Morrison, "Credit Derivatives, Disintermediation and Investment Decisions," Oxford Financial Research Centre Financial Economics Working Paper 2001-FE-01 (May 2001). See also, E. Pollack, "Assessing the Usage and Effect of Credit Derivatives," International Finance Seminar, Harvard Law School, April 2003; see also Fitch Ratings Global Credit Derivatives: Risk Management or Risk (March 10, 2003).

[56] BIS CT Study, supra note 28, pp. 16-23.

linked credit event and encourages a binary approach to credit management."[57]

Credit derivatives written on sovereign debt pose particular problems. When Argentina failed to timely meet its debt payments, hedge funds submitted substantial claims to dealers. As discussed, the issue arose as to whether there had actually been a default within the meaning of the derivatives contract. Indeed, the interest of bondholders and derivatives counterparties could diverge, with bondholders ready to agree to a restructuring that was not a "default" and with buyers of protection preferring a default.

Notes and Questions

1. Why would a bank buy protection? Why would a bank sell protection?

2. How should ISDA deal with the definition of restructuring?

3. Is the incentives effect a serious problem? If so, what can be done about it?

D.   SYSTEMIC RISK AND PRUDENTIAL REGULATION

1.   THE EXTENT OF SYSTEMIC RISK

The G30 Derivatives Study[58] concluded that there should not be a lot of concern over the systemic risk that might arise from derivatives activity (including swaps). In particular, it noted that the notional amounts of derivatives overstate the size of the market (only replacement value should be relevant), that the participants understand the complexities, that the markets are not highly concentrated (questionable), and that credit risks are less in derivatives than traditional lending (because swap counterparties are generally more creditworthy). Nonetheless, there has been an outcry for more regulation by congressional committees and some regulators. Should we be worried about the risks of swaps? A 1992 ISDA Default Survey, which surveyed swap dealers accounting for over 70 percent of the market, found that the cumulative losses over the history of the involvement of these firms with swaps was $358.36 million, or about .011 percent of the notional amount of swaps outstanding as of December 31, 1991. This also appears to be consistent with the studies of the Long Term Capital Management failure in 1998 examined in Chapter 16.

---

[57] N. Frome and C. Brown, "Lessons from the Marconi Restructuring," International Financial Law Review (September 2003), pp. 19, 21-22.

[58] See Group of Thirty, *Derivatives: Practices and Principles* (July 1993), pp. 60–64.

A 1995 central bank survey of the over-the-counter derivatives markets concludes that these markets have successfully withstood several interest rate cycles and episodes of large changes in exchange rates, and that the price shocks will have less impact than price changes in the debt securities markets. It generally sees derivatives as decreasing rather than increasing systemic risk due to their widespread use in hedging.[59]

The studies cited above do not focus on losses to non-bank counterparties, such as the $102 million loss in the case of Proctor & Gamble. Other substantial user losses have also been reported. A large investment fund of Wisconsin public money reported a $95 million loss due to leveraged swaps based on Mexican and European interest rates.[60] The most noteworthy loss on OTC derivatives was in the case of the Orange County Fund where losses were estimated at $2.5 billion. But these losses were not due to swaps, but mostly to inverse floating rate derivatives which generated less interest, and thus losses, when interest rates increased in 1994.[61]

2. PRUDENTIAL STANDARDS

A key development in 1994 was the formulation by various regulators of prudential guidelines for the derivative operations of banks, largely motivated by concern with systemic risk. The formulation of these standards reflected continued unease about the adequacy of banks' risk management systems. This concern was reflected in the results obtained from a survey of some major swap dealers by the BIS Committee on Banking Supervision. Bankers were asked to compute their exposure on a swap portfolio under certain specified parameters such as a 10-day holding period and a 99 percent confidence level. Exposure calculations varied at the extreme ends by a factor of eight. This could mean (actual numbers are not available) from $30 to $240 million.[62] On the other hand, the Group of Thirty has reported, on the basis of a survey of 300 dealers and 600 end-users, that derivative risks are now well managed by banks, although end-users (including non-dealer banks) lag substantially behind.[63]

The BIS Committee on Banking Supervision has set forth three basic principles of risk management: (1) appropriate oversight by boards of directors and senior management; (2) adequate risk management process

---

[59] J. Kambhu, F. Keane, and C. Benadon, "Price Risk Intermediation in the Over-the-Counter Derivatives Markets: Interpretation of a Global Survey," *Federal Reserve Bank of New York Economic Policy Review* (1996), p. 1.

[60] G. Knecht, "Wisconsin Fund Records a Loss on Derivatives," *The Wall Street Journal*, March 24, 1995.

[61] L. Jereski, "Orange County Fund Losses Put at 2.5 Billion," *The Wall Street Journal*, December 12, 1994. Merrill Lynch, the major defendant in the Orange County case, settled its suit in 1998, L. Wayne and A. Pollack, "Merrill Makes Strategic Move in Ending Suit," *The New York Times*, June 4, 1998.

[62] "Danger—Kids at Play," *Euromoney* (March 1995), p. 43.

[63] *Derivatives: Practices and Principles: Follow-up Surveys of Industry Practice* (December 1994).

that integrates prudent risk limits, sound measurement procedures and information systems, continuous risk monitoring and frequent management reporting; and (3) comprehensive internal controls and audit procedures.[64] Similar standards have been formulated by IOSCO.[65] Both reports discuss the question of how specific regulators should be about management calculation of risk exposure. In May 1995, BIS and IOSCO issued a joint report, *Framework for Supervisory Information about the Derivatives Activities of Banks and Securities Firms*. This is a very detailed statement and represented a breakthrough for collaboration between bank and security regulators at the international level.

In 1998, the BIS Committee on Payment and Settlement Systems and the Euro-currency Standing Committee, issued a report on the ways in which firms seek to control their risks in swap transactions.[66]

As a formal matter, the derivatives activities of banks in the United States are highly regulated by bank supervisors. This regulation involves detailed examination of their activities as well as the capital requirements discussed below. The Office of the Comptroller of the Currency in the United States has been very active in this area.[67] However, there is no regulatory framework for supervision of the derivatives activities of securities firms by the SEC or Commodity Futures Trading Corporation (CFTC). Securities firms are not generally regulated for safety and soundness except through capital requirements, and unregistered affiliates of such firms dealing in swaps have not even been subject to capital requirements, until the SEC's proposal in 2003 in response to the EU's Conglomerates Directive.

Perhaps in an attempt to head off more formal regulation, in March 1995, six major securities firms,[68] in cooperation with the SEC and CFTC, agreed to adopt a *Framework for Voluntary Oversight* (Voluntary Framework) under which the firms would undertake to have certain management controls, submit quantitative reports covering credit risk exposures, evaluate risk relative to capital, and adopt guidelines for dealing with non-professional counterparties to derivatives contracts.

Should securities firms generally be submitted to the same regulatory framework for their derivatives activities as are banks? This was the basic proposal put forward by James Leach, the Chairman of the House Banking Committee, in H.R. 20, introduced on January 4, 1995. It would have created

---

[64] Risk Management Guidelines for Derivatives, July 1994.

[65] Operational and Financial Risk Management Control Mechanisms for Over-the Counter Derivative Activities of Regulated Securities Firms, July 1994.

[66] OTC Derivatives: Settlement Procedures and Counterparty Risk Management, September 1998.

[67] See OCC Banking Circular (BC) 277, October 27, 1993; and OCC, Bulletin No. 94-32, Questions and Answers About BC 277, May 10, 1994.

[68] Credit Suisse First Boston, Goldman Sachs, Morgan Stanley, Merrill Lynch, Salomon Brothers, and Lehman Brothers.

a Federal Derivatives Commission to among other things set principles and standards for federal supervision of all financial institutions. The SEC would have enforced the standards with respect to securities firms. Nothing came of this proposal, however.

One way to reduce the risk on swaps is to require collateral. Increasingly, swaps require the losing side to post collateral. This is, of course, similar to variation margins on futures contracts. Some have advocated moving swaps trading to exchanges with margin requirements and guaranteed settlement typical of futures exchanges.[69] As we saw, this is now beginning to happen, through Swaps Clear.

3. THE ROLE OF THE CFTC AND "LEGAL CERTAINTY"[70]

During the 1990s, there was considerable doubt in the U.S. as to whether the CFTC had jurisdiction over swap transactions. This issue was not merely theoretical since if the CFTC had jurisdiction, absent an exemption from the Commodity Exchange Act (CEA) granted by the CFTC, swap contracts would be possibly invalid and unenforceable.

On December 21, 2000, the Congress passed the Commodity Futures Modernization Act (CFMA) that attempted to resolve these issues. Section 103 of the Act, entitled "Legal Certainty for Excluded Derivative Transactions," defines the conditions under which swaps and other OTC derivatives will be excluded from CEA jurisdiction. It sets forth two routes for exclusion.

a. ROUTE 1 EXCLUSION

Under the first route, the transaction must be between "eligible contract participants (ECPs)" and the transaction must not be executed on a "trading facility."

An ECP includes a list of qualifying persons acting for their own account: (1) regulated financial institutions (including banks, insurance companies, investment companies, broker-dealers, futures commission merchants) or arrangements (commodity pools); (2) corporations or other entities with total assets of at least $10 million, obligations backed by a letter of credit, or a net worth of $1,000,000 and enter into the transaction "in connection with the conduct of the entity's business or to manage the risk associated with an asset or liability owned or incurred or reasonably likely to be owned or incurred by the entity in the conduct of the entity's business"; (3) certain employee benefit plans; (4) various national and international

---

[69] See D. Folkerts-Landau and A. Steinherr, "The Wild Beast of Derivatives: to Be Chained up, Fenced in or Tamed?," in *Finance and the International Economy: The Amex Bank Review* (1994).
[70] This section is based largely on the testimony Professor Scott gave before the U.S. House Committee on Banking and Financial Services on July 19, 2000, on an earlier version of the new legislation.

governmental entities; and (5) a natural person with assets exceeding $10 million or $5 million where the person enters into the transaction "in order to manage the risk associated with an asset owned or liability incurred, or reasonably likely to be owned or incurred by the individual," e.g. for hedging. In addition, the same ECPs (except for investment companies or a natural person) can act as brokers or agents for other ECPs. The CFTC may add to the list of ECPs acting either for their own account or as agents, fiduciaries, or investment managers.

The first route to exclusion prohibits use of a "trading facility" which is defined in s. 3(33) of CFMA as a physical or electronic trading facility in which "multiple participants have the ability to execute or trade agreements ... by accepting bids and offers made by other participants that are open to multiple participants" in the facility. However, the same definition provides that the term "trading facility" does not include an electronic system "to negotiate the terms of and enter into bilateral transactions as a result of communications exchanged by the parties and not from interaction of multiple orders within a predetermined, nondiscretionary automated trade matching algorithm."

b.   ROUTE 2 EXCLUSION: ELECTRONIC TRADING FACILITY (ETF)

Sub-section 103(2) establishes three conditions for exclusion: (1) the transactions must be entered into on a "principal-to-principal basis" by parties trading for their own account or as agents to the extent permitted under the ECP definition; (2) the parties must be "eligible contract participants"; and (3) the transaction must be executed on an electronic trading facility. The sub-§103(2) route does not allow (without specific Commission approval) any agency transactions.

In addition to these exclusions, §407 of CFMA provides that "covered swap agreements" of banks are exempt from the CEA. A covered swap agreement is essentially any swap that would be excluded from the CEA under either of the two routes described above. While some thought the legislation might exclude any swap offered by banks, regardless of whether it was excluded under either of the two routes, this did not come to pass.

Finally, §120 of CFMA provides that no transactions between ECPs shall be unenforceable "based solely on the failure of the agreement, contract, or transaction to comply with the terms and conditions of an exemption or exclusion from any provision of this Act or regulations of the Commission."

There are a number of problems with this approach.

Section 103 continues to give the CFTC substantial discretionary authority over whether certain swap transactions are excluded from CEA coverage. Under both routes to exclusion, one must generally be an ECP to participate in swap transactions excluded from the CEA. While the proposed legislation does determine that certain parties are ECPs, e.g. banks, it leaves to the CFTC the option of adding to the list. Qualification as an ECP is particularly important given that §22 only insures contract enforceability for ECPs.

Of equal importance, the CFMA creates many new terms. The major problem with these terms is that they will create legal uncertainty, as detailed below. The CFTC will acquire substantial power over the conditions of the exclusion of OTC derivatives through its power to issue interpretations or regulations clarifying these terms.

c.   CREATION OF NEW LEGAL UNCERTAINTY

Section 103 together with the relevant definitions in §101, are replete with new terms and concepts that will create significant uncertainty as to whether a given OTC transaction is excluded from the CEA. Some examples follow:

1.   Under the ECP definition, corporations with a net worth of at least $1 million can engage in excluded transactions if the transactions are "in connection with the conduct of the entity's business or to manage the risk associated with an asset or liability owned or incurred or reasonably likely to be incurred by the entity in the conduct of the entity's business." This type of subjective purpose test is inherently uncertain since the purpose of a particular transaction will not be clear on its face.

2.   Under the sub-§103(2) route to exclusion, trading on an electronic facility can be done on a "principal-to-principal" basis but not on an agency basis. Whether or not a particular party is acting as agent or principal may be difficult to determine in particular cases—it will call into play the general law of agency. Furthermore, a party will not easily be able to determine whether his counterparty is acting in such a capacity.

3.   The sub-s§103(1) route to exclusion prohibits use of a "trading facility." Such a facility includes a system where the acceptance of bids and offers are open to multiple participants and where there is an "interaction of multiple orders within a predetermined, nondiscretionary automated trade matching and execution algorithm," but does not include a system "to negotiate the terms of and enter into bilateral transactions as a result of communications exchanged by the parties." Suppose a system is open to multiple participants, who post bids and offers, and results in bilateral transactions. Whether or not it will be excluded or covered by the CEA results from a determination as to whether there was an interaction of the orders in a "nondiscretionary automated trade matching and execution algorithm." Whether or not a system has such an algorithm and whether or not it is nondiscretionary will create uncertainty.

4.   OTC derivatives that are electronically traded under sub-§103(2) are restricted to "principal-to-principal" transactions whereas non-traded OTC transactions under sub-§103(1) can be engaged in on an agency basis. It

will be difficult to determine whether a particular system for entering into transactions does or does not involve trading.

d.   UNDERLYING POLICIES

Many of the new legal uncertainty problems have been created out of a desire to limit which parties can participate in OTC derivative transactions. For example, individuals with a net worth of under $10 million, or corporations with a net worth of less than $1 million, cannot participate in these transactions directly as principals, nor can they participate through financial firms acting as their agents. These same parties are free, however, to trade in risky exchange-traded derivatives, penny stock markets, and other types of risky investments. There is no documented abuse of such investors in OTC derivative markets; indeed the participation of retail investors in such markets is currently minuscule. However, this may be in the process of changing as retail investors participate indirectly in derivatives markets though securitizations such as CDOs. In that case, however, the SEC would have jurisdiction. Since securitized interests sold to the public are securities.

e.   A PREFERABLE APPROACH

A preferable approach would be that derivatives based on non-agricultural products, including all financial derivatives, would be outside the CEA, unless a trading facility for such transactions has specifically requested to be covered and regulated under CEA. Under this approach, transactors would have the choice of trading any financial derivative, whether a future, option, or swap, either over-the-counter or an exchange. This would remove the CFTC from any regulatory role, unless the parties to transactions consent to its jurisdiction. Further, it provides complete legal certainty. If the parties have not consented to CFTC jurisdiction, a transaction would not be subject to CEA. This alternative recognizes that OTC derivatives contracts have become more functionally equivalent over time to exchange-traded derivatives, and that it is arbitrary to force some to be regulated by the CEA while excluding others. The exchanges would be free to set up trading facilities unregulated by the CEA just the way any other transactors could. Indeed, the CFMA moves in this direction by subjecting certain wholesale exchange-traded derivatives to less regulation.

The result would not necessarily mean that all financial derivatives would be traded outside the CEA and the jurisdiction of the CFTC. If transactors and investors believed that these rules were necessary, because they provided needed regulation, they would choose to become subject to the CEA. This would be similar to the choice investors make internationally in trading on a more highly regulated exchange where stocks have dual listings, or the choice securities markets make in issuing stock under the laws of jurisdictions requiring significant disclosure.

This approach would abandon the rearguard action of CFMA in trying to protect the organized exchanges from competition from the OTC market by forcing retail investors or certain type of trading arrangements under the jurisdiction of the CFTC. The organized exchanges currently have less than a 14 percent market share in financial derivatives and their share is falling. If the CFTC wants to reverse this trend, it will adopt regulations that investors and transactors find attractive and necessary. It is undesirable to force retail investors to participate in less efficient markets, and it is undesirable to hamper the development of efficient trading systems outside the CEA.

In the spring of 2002, the Congress began reconsidering whether it had made the right decision in removing swaps from CFTC regulation. This was prompted, in large part, by the use of commodity OTC derivatives by Enron which some believe may have affected energy prices in California. Nothing came of that inquiry.

E. DISCLOSURE REQUIREMENTS

There are several different types of disclosure requirements for swaps: accounting rules, public disclosure of information for purposes of financial reporting, and disclosure of information to market participants or regulators.

1. ACCOUNTING

Until June 1998, U.S. GAAP did not directly address income and balance sheet accounting for swaps. Industry practice was to record as income the net difference in interest payments on interest rate swaps. Neither the notional amount nor the market value of swaps entered into for hedging purposes were recorded on the balance sheet. However, dealers in swaps marked their positions to market on the balance sheet, and recorded changes in value to these positions on the income statement.[71]

Taking hedges into account created two accounting problems. When an entity has two perfectly offsetting positions that are measured using different valuation techniques—one at cost (typically the hedged item) and one at market (the hedging item)—the picture presented may not reflect the true financial situation. If changes in value are only recognized in the hedging item, the picture may be distorted. If hedging items were marked-to-market, there would be an artificial timing mismatch in the realization of gains and losses on the two items. Hedge accounting basically allows deferral of gains and losses on the hedging item until they are realized on the hedged

---

[71] GAO Report, p. 96.

item. This is done by incorporating the gain or loss on the hedging item into the carrying amount of the hedged item.

This approach depends on knowing when one position is hedging another one and when it is not. *Accounting for Futures Contracts*[72] defines a hedge as follows:

"The contract [the hedge] reduces that exposure [on the hedged item] and is designated as a hedge. At the inception of the hedge and throughout the hedge period, high correlation of changes in (1) the market value of the futures [hedge] contract(s) and (2) the fair value of, or interest income or expense associated with the hedged item(s) shall be probably so that the results of the futures contract(s) will substantially offset the effects of price or interest rate changes on the exposed item(s). ..."

The difficulties of identifying a hedge—for example, what is a "high correlation"—led the Financial Accounting Standards Board (FASB), a private professional organization that sets accounting standards, to attempt to formulate a new approach.

In November 1994, FASB proposed eliminating deferral accounting for hedges altogether. All derivatives, including swaps, would be marked-to-market on the balance sheet. However, gains and losses would only be reflected in income for derivatives entered into for trading purposes. For non-trading derivatives, gains and losses resulting from market changes would only be reflected in an equity account; they would only be reflected in earnings when realized. Adoption of this approach would avoid the hedge accounting model of the past that required a one-to-one accounting linkage between the hedging and hedged items.[73]

This approach was opposed by industry groups because it would deprive them of the value of hedging; there would be timing differences between recognition of income on swaps which were marked-to-market and other assets like loans that could not be marked-to-market. It also would not have permitted hedge accounting for "anticipated transactions," where a position is taken on a derivative in anticipation of taking a position on another asset, e.g. X enters into an interest rate swap under which X pays floating for fixed in anticipation of acquiring a floating rate liability.[74]

The accounting issue has been one of the most contentious ever faced by FASB. Indeed, some industry groups sought to set up an organization to

---

[72] Statement of Financial Accounting Standard 80, p. 4.

[73] J. Adams, "Simplifying Accounting for Derivative Instruments, Including Those Used for Hedging" in *Highlights of Financial Reporting Issues* (Financial Accounting Standards Board ed., 1995).

[74] See G. Benston and S. Mian, "Financial Reporting of Derivatives: An Analysis of the Issues, Evaluation of Proposals, and a Suggested Solution," 4 Journal of Financial Engineering (1996), pp. 217, 230-231.

"oversee" FASB, but the SEC came strongly to FASB's defense indicating it would oppose any initiative by any group that sought to undermine FASB's independence.

FASB's subsequent proposal, in the form of an Exposure Draft[75] continued to require that all derivatives be marked-to-market but also permitted using gains or losses in the value of underlying assets to offset the value of derivatives used in certain hedging transactions. Unlike the hedge deferral model in which gains/losses on derivatives are deferred until the time gains/losses are recognized on the hedged items, this proposal accelerated the gains/losses on the hedged items. This would only be possible, however, where the hedged item had a market value, e.g. traded debt or equity. Unlike its earlier proposal, the full change in value of the hedged item would not be realized—only the amount of the change of the derivative. This means a bank with a derivative that gained $10 would only have to report a $10 swing in the price of the hedged item, even if that hedged item actually lost $15.[76] Under a deferral approach, no gain/loss would be realized on the derivative until gain/loss was recognized on the hedged item.

On August 29, 1997, FASB issued a new draft statement, subsequently revised on September 12, 1997.[77] This continued the basic approach in the 1996 draft with two major changes. First, only the portion of the gain or loss on a hedged asset or liability attributable to the risk being hedged would be eligible for accelerated earnings recognition. The 1996 Exposure Draft had proposed that the entire gain or loss on a hedged item (incorporating all risk components) be eligible for accelerated earnings recognition. Suppose that a bank was hedging a fixed rate bond asset with an interest rate swap paying fixed and receiving floating. Any change in the value of the bond due to changes of interest rates would be recognized on an accelerated basis; however, changes in the value of the bond due to changes in the credit rating of the issuer (a risk not hedged) would not. Measurement of which gain or loss to count will be difficult.

Second, all gain and loss on the hedged item could be recognized in current earnings even if it is not fully offset by the gain and loss on the hedging item (this assumes that the gain or loss is attributable to the nature of the risk being hedged).

The financial industry continued to attack the FASB proposals and brought the matter to the U.S. Congress. S. 1560, introduced by Senator Faircloth in November 1997, would have prevented banks from having to implement the FASB proposals unless the standards were approved by bank

---

[75] *Accounting for Derivative and Similar Financial Instruments and for Hedging Activities* (June 20, 1996).
[76] See D. Schiela, "FASB Closes in on Standard on Accounting for Derivatives and Hedging," Derivatives 33 (September/October 1996).
[77] Statement of Financial Accounting Standards No. 13X, Accounting for Derivative Instruments and for Hedging Activities.

regulators (who opposed them), and H.R. 3165 introduced by Rep. Baker in February 1998 effectively shifted standards setting in accounting from FASB to the SEC (although the SEC favored the FASB proposals), and gave companies the right to mount a legal challenge to accounting standards. Chairman Greenspan of the Federal Reserve Board urged FASB to eliminate its proposals and require only large companies to disclose the fair market value of their derivatives in supplements to their financial statements.[78] Despite the political attacks and criticism from the industry, FASB issued its *Accounting for Derivative Instruments and Hedging Activities*[79] which was originally to be effective for fiscal years beginning after June 15, 1999. For calendar year companies, this would be January 1, 2000. In May 1999, FASB delayed the effective date for a year due to difficulties companies were experiencing in implementing the change. Statement 133 basically followed the previous proposal.

On June 15, 2000, FASB issued Statement 138, amending Statement 133 in certain technical respects. This was part of the work of the FAS 133 Derivatives Implementation Group (DIG) to help resolve particular implementation issues.

As previously discussed in Chapter 2, IASB has formulated a number of new accounting standards, in connection both with European adoption of IAS standards by 2005 and the convergence project with FASB. One of the most contentious areas is the accounting for derivatives. IASB is moving even more in the direction of mark-to-market in IAS 39 than FASB's 133, being open to so-called "fair value" accounting which would require institutions to mark-to-market even where there was no reliable third party market quote. This would be done on the basis of various data like yield curves and historical volatility. This has engendered substantial opposition from European banks and some European regulators. Indeed, as described in Chapter 2, when the EU adopted the IAS standards in November 2004 it decided not to adopt certain parts of IAS 39 dealing with fair value.

Another area of accounting for derivatives relates to fall out from Enron. Enron used special-purpose entities, SPEs, to avoid showing the value of certain derivative positions on its balance sheet. This was done under the FASB rules that did not require on book treatment if a third party owned at least 3 percent of the equity of the SPE and Enron did not have formal control of the entity. In fact, Enron exercised effective control of the SPEs. FASB has revised its rules to make consolidation turn on effective control rather than compliance with formal bright line rules.[80] FASB now refers to the SPEs in question as variable interest entities, VIEs (this excludes SPEs used for securitizations, as discussed in Chapter 12). A company must

---

[78] E. McDonald and S. Frank, "FASB Rejects Fed Chairman's Request to Soften Proposed Rule on Derivatives," *The Wall Street Journal*, August 12, 1997.

[79] Statement of Financial Accounting Standards No. 133 on June 1, 1998.

[80] FASB Interpretation No. 46, January 2003.

consolidate a VIE if the company "absorbs a majority of the entity's expected losses, receives a majority of its expected residual returns, or both, as a result of holding variable interests, which are the ownership, contractual or other pecuniary interests in an entity."[81] If these criteria are satisfied, the company is required to consolidate the VIE even if it has no formal voting control over it. Enron had its financial officer take positions in VIEs to avoid consolidation. FASB 46 addresses this problem by stating: "[a]n enterprise with a variable interest in a variable interest entity must consider variable interests of related parties and de facto agents as its own in determining whether" to consolidate.

2. FINANCIAL REPORTING

The SEC has formulated disclosure requirements for public companies, and the Basel Committee and IOSCO have issued guidelines for financial institutions.

a. ACCOUNTING STANDARDS

Accounting standards provide a baseline for financial disclosure. SFAS 119 *Disclosure about Derivative Financial Instruments and Fair Value of Financial Instruments* (October 1994),[82] requires the disclosure of the following information either in the body of the financial statements or in the accompanying footnotes:

- the amounts, nature, and terms of each class of derivatives, including differentiation between instruments held or issued for purposes of trading and purposes other than trading;

- the average, maximum, and minimum aggregate fair values during the reporting period of each class of derivatives held or issued for trading purposes, with differentiation between assets and liabilities;

- the net gains or losses arising from derivatives trading activities during the reporting period and where those net gains or losses are reported in the income statement;

- a description of the entity's objective for each class of derivatives held or issued for purposes other than trading and how these instruments are reported in financial statements; and

- a description of anticipated transactions for which the risks are hedged with derivatives, including the expected time frame for

---

[81] FASB Summary.
[82] Some of the requirements of SFAS 119 already applied to swaps under two prior statements, FASB Statement No. 105, Disclosure of Information about Financial Instruments with Off-Balance Sheet Risk and Financial Instruments with Concentrations of Credit Risk, March 1990, and FASB Statement No. 107, Disclosures about Fair Value of Financial Instruments, December 1991.

the transactions, the amount of related hedging gains and losses that are explicitly deferred, and the transactions or other events that result in recognition of the deferred gains and losses.

The SFAS encourages but does not require disclosure of quantitative information about interest rate risk or other market risks of derivatives that is consistent with the way the entity manages those risks. It also encourages such disclosures about other assets and liabilities.

b.   THE SEC RULES

In February 1997, the SEC adopted its own disclosure rule.[83]

The Commission[84] requires disclosure of: (1) each method used to account for derivatives; (2) types of derivatives accounted for under each method; (3) the criteria required to be met for each accounting method used (e.g. the manner in which the risk reduction, correlation, designation and/or effectiveness tests are applied for hedge accounting); (4) the accounting method used if the specified criteria are not met; (5) the accounting for the termination of derivatives designated as hedges or used to affect directly or indirectly the terms, fair values, or cash flows of a designated item; (6) the accounting for derivatives if the designated item matures, or is sold, extinguished, terminated, or, if related to an anticipated transaction, is no longer likely to occur; and (7) where and when derivatives and their related gains or losses are reported in the statements of financial position, cash flows, and results of operations.

As for disclosures of quantitative and qualitative information, the SEC rule[85] is limited to required disclosures of market risk; other risks, like credit risks, are not covered. With respect to quantitative information, the Commission allows registrants to choose among three alternatives: tabular presentation, sensitivity analysis, or value at risk.

Tabular presentation includes information about fair values of instruments, expected principal or transaction cash flows, weighted average effective rates or prices, and other relevant market risk information. The tabular information would be presented for different risk exposure categories, e.g. interest rate risk, and within the foreign currency exchange rate risk category by functional currency (the currency of the primary economic environment of the registrant).

The Commission rule further provides that, at a minimum, instruments should be distinguished by the following characteristics: "(i)

---

[83] SEC, *Disclosure of Accounting Policies for Derivative Financial Instruments and Derivative Commodity Instruments and Disclosure of Qualitative and Quantitative Information About Market Risk Inherent in Derivative Financial Instruments, Other Financial Instruments, and Derivative Commodity Instruments,* 62 Federal Register 6044 (1997).
[84] 17 C.F.R. §210.4-08.
[85] 17 C.F.R. §229.305.

[f]ixed rate or variable rate assets or liabilities; (ii) long or short forwards or futures; (iii) written or purchased put or call options; (iv) receive fixed or receive variable interest rate swaps; (v) the currency in which the instruments' cash flows are denominated."[86]

Sensitivity Analysis permits registrants "to express the potential loss in future earnings, fair values, or cash flows of market risk sensitive instruments resulting from one or more selected hypothetical changes in interest rates, foreign currency exchange rates ..." and other similar market price changes.[87]

Value at Risk (VaR) analysis expresses the potential loss in fair values, earnings, or cash flows of market risk sensitive instruments over a selected period of time with a selected likelihood of occurrence from changes in interest rates, foreign currency exchange rates, and other relevant market rates or prices. Registrants are required to report either: "(i) the average, high and low amounts, or the distribution of value at risk amounts for the reporting period; (ii) the average, high and low amounts, or the distribution of actual changes in fair values, earnings, or cash flows from market risk sensitive instruments occurring during the reporting period; or (iii) the percentage or number of times the actual changes in fair values, earnings, or cash flows from market risk sensitive instruments that exceeded the reported value at risk amounts during the reporting period."[88]

The rules also require disclosure of the model assumptions and parameters underlying the registrant's value at risk model. At a minimum, this would include how loss was defined by the model, a general description of the modeling technique, e.g. historical or Monte Carlo simulation, how options are dealt with, the types of instruments covered, and relevant model parameters, such as holding period and confidence interval.

With respect to qualitative information, the SEC rule is less specific. It acknowledges that SFAS 119 already requires that certain qualitative disclosures be made.

Securities industry representatives have questioned whether the rules requiring particular types of disclosure will inhibit the development of new ways to manage and measure risk; the SEC has dismissed these objections given the flexibility provided as to what type of method of disclosure to use and how to apply the particular method selected. A more genuine issue is the value obtained by such disclosures given the difficulties of comparing information as between different financial statements.

Finally, the Commission has provided that registrants supplying forward-looking information pursuant to its rule, outside of the financial

---

[86] Instructions to Paragraph 305(a).
[87] 62 Federal Register 6049.
[88] *ibid.*

statement, would be protected from liability by a safe harbor made available by the Private Securities Litigation Reform Act of 1995.[89]

A study in 2001 concluded that the SEC's required risk disclosures may have drawbacks. It found that derivative users may have more complex evaluations of risk than perhaps the SEC anticipated, that the flexibility permitted in presenting risk may lead investors to form inconsistent risk perceptions for the same underlying economic situation and that since certain quantitative disclosure is not required, inappropriate risk assessments can occur.[90]

c.   THE BASEL COMMITTEE-IOSCO GUIDELINES

In February 1999, the Basel Committee and IOSCO issued a joint report on disclosure.[91] This was followed up on by a subsequent paper, "Recommendations for Public Disclosure of Trading and Derivatives Activities of Banks and Securities Firms" (October 1999). The recommendations generally cover similar ground as the SEC rules, but in much less detail. There are two major differences, however. The Recommendations are not binding, and are addressed to a wider set of risks, credit and liquidity risk as well as market risk.

3.   MARKET REPORTING

The BIS, through the Working Group of the Euro-currency Standing Committee of the Central Banks of the Group of Ten countries, put forward a discussion paper on "Public Disclosure of Market and Credit Risks by Financial Intermediaries" (September 1994). The paper is known as the Fisher Report, after the Chairman of the group, Peter R. Fisher, then Executive Vice President of the Federal Reserve Bank of New York. The Report seems concerned with the need for disclosure to market participants in order that participants may correctly assess their risks of dealing with each other.

The Report recommends that all financial intermediaries should move in the direction of publicly disclosing periodic quantitative information that expresses, in summary form, the estimates relied upon by the firm's management of:

- the market risks in the relevant portfolio or portfolios, as well as the firm's actual performance in managing the market risks in these portfolios;

---

[89] Pub. L. No. 104-67, 109 Stat. 737 (1995).
[90] L. Hodder, L. Koonce, and M. McNally, "SEC Market Risk Disclosures: Implications for Judgment and Decision Making," 15 Accounting Horizons (2001), p. 49.
[91] "Recommendations for Public Disclosure of Trading and Derivative Activities," Consultative paper issued jointly by the Basel Committee on Banking Supervision and the Technical Committee of the International Organization of Securities Commissions.

- the counterparty credit risks arising from its trading and risk management activities, including current and potential future credit exposure as well as counterparty credit worthiness, in a form which permits evaluation of the firm's performance in managing credit risk.

The Report envisions disclosure of value-at-risk analysis of derivatives portfolios for market risks. The Report suggests that what might be disclosed, as an example, would be the high, low, and average value-at-risk for holding periods of one day, and two weeks, that occurred during the reporting period. The Report, however, does not suggest mandating any particular method of calculating market risk.

As for credit risks, basic information would consist of current credit exposure (net replacement values when close-out netting arrangements are in place, otherwise gross replacement values), broken down by credit quality class, and/or counterparty type. It might also include further breakdowns by maturity, estimates of future credit exposure, and measures of losses over the reporting period. Again, no particular form of disclosure is envisioned.

A study shows that VaR disclosures by banks are actually useful in the sense that banks which disclose they have more risky portfolios have more volatility in trading revenues.[92]

Notes and Questions

1.   Should there be a difference among disclosures required for purposes of accounting, financial reporting and to market participants?

2.   Which accounting approach would you favor: market-to-market of all instruments, deferred hedging, or accelerated hedging as adopted by FASB?

3.   Should the SEC have promulgated disclosure standards for derivatives? Why doesn't the SEC deal with credit risk?

F.   CAPITAL REQUIREMENTS

A principal way of dealing with the risks of swaps to financial institutions is through capital requirements.

1.   THE BASEL ACCORD: CREDIT RISK

Under the Basel Accord capital rules for credit risk, discussed in Chapter 7, swaps are dealt with as a special type of off-balance sheet asset.

---

[92] P. Jorion, "How Informative Are Value-at-Risk Disclosures," 77 The Accounting Review (2002), p. 91.

This section first discusses the current provisions for swaps and then deals with the revisions to these rules under Basel II.

a.   BASEL I, CURRENT RULES

Swaps must first be converted into asset equivalents and are then risk weighted under the normal Basel risk-weight categories, subject to a maximum risk weight of 50 percent. Thus, a swap with an OECD sovereign would have a 0 percent risk weight, whereas a swap with a private obligor would have a 50 percent risk weight.

The difficulties arise in connection with the conversion of swaps into asset equivalents.[93]

The Basel Accord permits countries to use one of two methods in calculating the asset equivalents of swap contracts, the original exposure or current exposure method. At the Basel conference, Japan strongly pushed to permit countries to use either method. The United States has required banks to use the current exposure method.

Suppose Company A and Company C seek to enter into a fixed-floating rate swap through Intermediary Bank B on the following terms:

Notional principal	$10 million
Maturity	3 years
Floating index	6 months LIBOR (currently 8.5 percent)
Floating reset period	Every 6 months
Fixed rate	T bill rate + 70 basis points
	(current T bill rate = 8 percent)
B's profit (spread)	10 basis points

This transaction can be diagrammed as in Figure 15.3, below:

---

[93] See H. Scott and S. Iwahara, "In Search of a Level Playing Field: The Implementation of the Basel Accord in Japan and the United States," Group of Thirty Occasional Paper 46 (1994), pp. 49-54, from which the following analysis is taken.

Figure 15.3

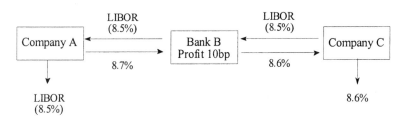

Note that Intermediary Bank B has entered into two independent contracts. Under its contract with Company A, it pays A a floating rate of 8.5 percent and receives a fixed rate of 8.7 percent. Under its contract with Company C, it pays C a fixed rate of 8.6 percent (8.7 - profit of 0.1) and receives a floating rate of 8.5 percent.

Under the current exposure method, the conversion process has two steps. First, a bank marks-to-market the replacement cost of contracts with a positive value (in the money). This reflects the cost the bank would incur if it entered into a new swap on the same terms. Second, the bank calculates the potential future credit exposure on the contract based on its residual maturity. This calculation reflects the potential risk of loss from counterparty default. Contracts with a residual maturity of less than one year are deemed to have no future exposure; contracts with one year and over are deemed to have 0.5 percent risk. Under the 1995 Netting Amendment, the following factors apply to swaps:

Maturity	Interest Rate	Exchange Rate
One year or less	0.0 percent	1.0 percent
Over one year to five years	0.5 percent	5.0 percent
Over five years	1.5 percent	7.5 percent

The asset equivalent amount is the sum of these two calculations: replacement cost plus future exposure.

On the date on which the contracts in Figure 15.3 are entered into, there is no replacement cost—they are entered into at market prices. Since both contracts are for one year and over, the asset equivalent amount of the two contracts is $10,000,000 x .005 x 2, or $100,000. The two contracts would generate risk-weighted assets of $50,000 ($100,000 x .50), and a capital requirement of $4,000 ($50,000 x .08).

Suppose that at the end of one year, interest rates have increased so that Bank B would now have to pay Company D a fixed rate of 8.95 percent to get a six-month LIBOR floating rate, if Company C defaulted.

In this situation, Bank B would have a loss of 0.25 percent of $10,000,000, or $25,000 for each of the two remaining years on the two contracts, the difference between receiving a fixed rate from A of 8.70 percent and paying a fixed rate to D of 8.95 percent. This loss would be discounted to present value using an appropriate discount rate derived from interest rate yield curves for each of the two one-year periods remaining on the contract.

The 50 percent risk weight was justified by the fact that the default rates for swap users are about one half the default rate for all firms.[94] Under the Basel II proposals, however, the 50 percent risk-weight cap would be removed.

Netting

The 1995 Basel Netting Amendment reduces capital requirements by taking netting into account.

The permissibility of bilateral netting under Basel is subject to certain requirements. Supervisors must be assured that a bank has:

(1) a netting contract or agreement with the counterparty which creates a single legal obligation, covering all included transactions, such as that the bank would have either a claim to receive or obligation to pay only the net sum of the positive and negative mark-to-market values of included individual transactions in the event a counterparty fails to perform due to any of the following: default, bankruptcy, liquidation or similar circumstances;

(2) written and reasoned legal opinions that, in the event of a legal challenge, the relevant courts and administrative authorities would find the bank's exposure to be such a net amount under:

— the law of the jurisdiction in which the counterparty is chartered and, if the foreign branch of a counterparty is involved, then also under the law of the jurisdiction in which the branch is located;

— the law that governs the individual transactions; and

— the law that governs any contract or agreement necessary to effect the netting.

(3) The national supervisor, after consultation when necessary with other relevant supervisors, must be satisfied that the netting is enforceable under the laws of each of the relevant jurisdictions; procedures in place to ensure that the legal characteristics of netting arrangements are kept under review in the light of possible changes in relevant law.

Contracts containing walkaway clauses (one-way payments) are not eligible for netting for the purpose of calculating capital requirements pursuant to

---

[94] V. Bhasin, "On the Credit Risk of OTC Derivative Users," Federal Reserve Board Finance and Economics Discussion Series 95-90 (November 1995), p. 26.

this Accord. A walkaway clause is a provision that permits a non-defaulting counterparty to make only limited payments, or no payment at all, to the estate of a defaulter, even if the defaulter is a net creditor.

Basel provides that the potential future credit exposure be multiplied by specified add-on factors. The formula set out below then reduces the add-ons for transactions subject to legally enforceable netting agreements.

$$A_{NET} = 0.5 * A_{GROSS} - 0.5 * NGR * A_{GROSS}$$

where

NGR = level of net replacement cost/level of gross replacement cost for transactions subject to legally enforceable netting agreements

A_{GROSS} = equals the sum of notional principal amounts of all transactions subject to legally enforceable netting agreements times the appropriate add-on factors

Using this formula, banks will always hold capital against potential exposure as the net add-on can never be zero. In this context, the NGR can be seen as somewhat of a proxy for the impact of netting on potential future exposure but not as a precise indicator of future changes in net exposure relative to gross exposure, reflecting the fact that the NGR and potential exposure can be influenced by many idiosyncratic properties of individual portfolios. With the weight at 0.5, the reduction in add-on, assuming an NGR of 0.5, would be 25 percent.

U.S. bank regulators altered the BIS formula in implementing the capital requirements for potential future exposures by giving more weight to the risk reducing potential of netting. The BIS formula only weights the NGR, which reflects the netting, at 50 percent. The U.S. regulators have given it a 60 percent weight, thereby adopting the following formula:[95]

$$A_{NET} = 0.4 * A_{GROSS} - 0.6 * NGR * A_{GROSS}$$

b.   BASEL II

In Basel II terms, the key question for dealing with swaps, is how one calculates EAD, the exposure if a swap contract were to default. This is a more sophisticated way of thinking about the conversion of a swap to a balance sheet item against which risk weights can be applied. This part of the Basel II rules has not yet been finalized. In April 2005, the Basel

---

[95] 60 Federal Register 46170, 46173 (1995).

Committee set forth its proposals.[96] With respect to swaps, three alternatives were proposed: (1) the current exposure method (CEM), the Basel I approach described above; (2) a standardized approach that banks could choose as an alternative to CEM; or (3) an internal model approach, the Effective Expected Positive Exposure Method (EPE), for sophisticated banks. For U.S. banks, the standardized approach would not be available since the U.S. is not adopting the standardized portions of the Basel II proposal. However, the U.S. may decide to refine Basel I to pick up some portions of the standardized approach.

EPE is the time-weighted average of individual exposures estimated for given forecasting horizons (e.g. one year). This method is used to calculate EAD which is then inserted into the general credit risk formula Basel II uses to calculate capital. Once EPE is calculated, through the use of a model, it is multiplied by a factor, normally 1.4 with a floor of 1.2 with supervisory approval (scaling). The standardized approach alters CEM in a few important respects. First, for positions that are deep in the money, EPE is determined almost entirely by current market value whereas positions at the money, exposure is driven only by the potential change in value of the transactions. In addition, replacement cost is to be determined at the level of a portfolio and not individual positions. The standardized approach would also be subject to scaling.

The proposal would also allow cross-product netting, in which swap positions could be netted against positions in other securities financing transactions, subject to supervisory judgments about the adequacy of the legal framework for netting. Industry has been critical of many of these proposals.[97]

2.   BASEL ACCORD: MARKET RISK AMENDMENTS

In 1996, BIS adopted capital requirements for market risk that we have also reviewed in Chapter 7. These requirements covered swaps, as well as debt and equity securities, and permit the models-based approach as an alternative to prescribed BIS methodology. Here, we examine here the prescribed methodology.

a.   DEBT SECURITIES AND INTEREST RATE SWAPS

Interest rate swaps are dealt with in connection with market risk for debt securities. The requirements only apply to debt securities (including interest rate swaps) on a bank's trading book. These are a bank's proprietary positions "which are intentionally held for short-term resale and/or which are

---

[96] Basel Committee on Banking Supervision, Consultative Document, The Application of Basel II to Trading Activities and the Treatment of Double Default (April 2005).

[97] Associations Comment on Application of Basel II to Trading Activities, May 31, 2005.

taken on by the bank with the intention of benefiting in the short-term from actual and/or expected differences between their buying and selling prices, or from other price or interest-rate variations, and positions in financial instruments arising from matched principal brokering and market making, or positions taken in order to hedge other elements of the trading book."[98] The Amendment does, nonetheless, allow banks to exclude from their trading books derivative products such as swaps which are taken on explicitly to hedge positions on the banking book.[99] The market risk capital requirements for swaps are in addition to those for credit risk. This contrasts with debt or equity securities that are only subject to the market risk requirements.[100] Swaps on the banking book continue to be governed by the current credit risk requirements and are not subject to an additional charge for market risk.

The capital requirements for debt securities are, like those for equities, based on a building block approach, in which the specific risk of the instrument (related to the issuer) and the general risk of the market (for example, movement of interest rates) are separately taken into account. However, swaps are treated like government securities, as having no specific market risk.

b.   FOREIGN EXCHANGE POSITIONS AND CURRENCY SWAPS

The approach to capital for foreign exchange positions is less complicated. The bank first calculates its net open currency position in each currency. On a currency swap, the bank would be short on the currency it must deliver and long on the currency it will receive at the end of the swap. Thus, a U.S. bank that had swapped $40 million for ¥5 billion would be long the Dollars and short the Yen.

The amount of the bank's net position in each currency is then converted at current spot rates into the bank's reporting currency, i.e. Dollars for a U.S. bank. The capital charge would be 8 percent of the higher of its long or short positions.

c.   MODELS-BASED APPROACH

The models-based approach specifies certain parameters, relevant to swaps, that must be used in models. Models must use a minimum of 6 interest rates (for different maturities)—the BIS methodology, on the other hand, uses 13. The models must also use exchange rates between the bank's domestic currency and each foreign currency in which the bank has a significant position.

---

[98] Bank for International Settlements, Amendment to The Capital Accord to Incorporate Market Risks, January 1996, §I.2, at 1.
[99] Id., §I.3, at 2.
[100] Id., §I.2, at 4.

3.   CREDIT DERIVATIVES

Under the standardized approach of Basel II, as set forth in June 2004, for qualifying credit derivatives, assets covered by the derivatives are assigned a risk weight that is the risk weight of the seller of protection (unless higher than the risk weight of the underlying obligor), which continues the rule now in place under Basel I.[101] This is termed the substitution approach. As originally proposed, it was to be the weighted average of the obligor's risk weight and the protection seller's risk weight.[102] Under the Foundation IRB approach, banks would assess the risk weight as part of their PD and LGD estimates, subject to the proviso that the derived risk-weight would be no lower than that of a comparable direct exposure to the protection provider.[103]

Industry persuaded the Basel Committee that these proposals did not fully reflect the additional benefit obtained from credit protection—the so-called double default analysis.[104] For financial institutions to suffer loss, there would actually have to be a double default, by the obligor on the asset as well as by the protection provider, and in the case of default an institution might be able to recover from both parties. Under the April 2005 Trading Book proposals, the Basel Committee will now permit banks using the IRB approach to take double default into account.

The Committee proposes to use the following formula:

$$K_{DD} = K_U \cdot (0.15 + 270 \cdot PD_g)$$

K_{DD} is the capital required under the double default method. K_U is the basic capital requirement using the substitution method, taking the capital requirement based on the credit risk formula applied to the protection provider. This capital requirement is then reduced by the formula within the parenthesis derived from empirical studies modified by more conservative assumptions of the Committee. Under the proposal, if both the obligor and the protection provider are of good quality, the proposed formula gives more capital relief than the substitution method but if the quality of both is not good, more capital would be required than under the present approach. In that case banks can use the old substitution method as the double default method is optional.[105]

---

[101] Basel Committee on Banking Supervision, *International Convergence of Capital Measurement and Capital Standards: A Revised Framework* (Basel II), June 2004, ¶ ¶140-141.
[102] Basel Committee on Banking Supervision, *Consultative Document, The New Basel Capital Accord* (January 2001), ¶130.
[103] Basel II, ¶ ¶300-301, 480-482.
[104] An earlier White Paper by the Federal Reserve Board, Treatment of Double-Default and Double-Recovery Effects for Hedged Exposures under Pillar I of the Proposed New Basel Capital Accord, June 2003, had analyzed the deficiencies of the substitution approach.
[105] Global Risk Regulator, Breaking News Service, April 12, 2005.

Currently, the Federal Reserve Board provides specific rules for credit derivatives used by U.S. banks. In August 1996, the Board issued guidance for the treatment of credit derivatives on the banking book.[106] This guidance provides that total rate of return and credit default swaps should be treated as creating synthetic asset positions of the banks creating the credit protection; thus they are treated like loans. For the bank receiving the credit protection, the bank may have an exposure to either the counterparty on the swap, or on the underlying asset, depending on the degree to which the receiving bank has transferred ownership of the underlying asset to the credit protection-selling bank. The guidance allows a bank to use credit derivatives to reduce its exposure from an obligor by entering into an offsetting credit derivative transaction, thus capital required for a loan can be replaced by the capital required by a credit derivative. Thus, banks have the potential to substitute a 20 percent risk-weighting of an OECD bank providing credit protection for the 100 percent risk-weighting on a loan to a private obligor. In June 1997, the Board issued guidance on risk-based capital treatment of credit derivatives held in the trading book.[107] The fundamental idea is that credit derivatives on the trading book are exposed to three different kinds of risk: counterparty credit risk, general market risk, and specific risk, and rules are provided for calculating each type of risk.[108]

Note that if the risk-weight of the seller of protection is lower than the risk-weight of the obligor, a financial institution may have an incentive to transfer the risk to reduce capital requirements. Further note that under the current accord, where the risk-weight of an OECD bank is 20 percent, compared with the risk-weight of other corporates, including insurance companies, of 100 percent, insurance companies selling protection would be somewhat disadvantaged. However, this disadvantage is counterbalanced by the fact that insurance companies are not covered by Basel at all, and are generally subject to lower capital requirements than banks. Thus, insurance companies may be able to use their lower capital requirements to compensate the buyers of protection for the higher risk weights they will receive. Insurance companies will be at a greater advantage under Basel II because the risk-weights of banks and insurance companies will both be determined by ratings.

Notes and Questions

1. What is the better approach for the risk-weight of a credit derivative, looking to the risk of the obligor or the seller of protection?

---

[106] Board of Governors of the Federal Reserve System, *Supervisory Guidance for Credit Derivatives*, SR 96-17 (August 12, 1996).

[107] Board of Governors of the Federal Reserve System, *Application of Market Risk Capital Requirements to Credit Derivatives*, SR 97-18 (June 13, 1997).

[108] L. Darby III, "Recent Regulatory Developments Affecting Credit Derivatives," Derivatives 235 (May/June 1998).

4.   THE SEC BROKER-LITE RULE

As discussed in Chapter 7, the capital requirements for securities firms are generally set by the SEC through their Net Capital Rule. The SEC has, however, adopted special capital rules for broker-dealer affiliates engaged in OTC derivative transactions that have been dubbed the Broker-Dealer Lite (BDL) rules.[109] Many OTC derivative transactions, such as swaps, are generally not considered securities under the securities laws (as discussed below), and thus a corporation solely engaging in such transactions would not be a regulated broker-dealer and, therefore, would not be subject to SEC capital requirements. However, many firms engaged in swap transactions also engage in other OTC derivative transactions that are considered securities, such as OTC options on equity securities or on U.S. government securities, and are thus subject to SEC capital requirements. The combination of the products permits firms to net positions against counterparties with whom the firms have engaged in both types of transactions, those considered securities and those not so considered. The SEC has asserted that U.S. firms subject to such requirements have located their business abroad to escape from U.S. capital requirements (another broker-dealer regulations like margin requirements).

As a response, the SEC has modified its net capital requirements, and other regulations, for such firms (OTC firms). OTC firms have to hold $100 million in tentative net capital and at least $20 million in net capital. OTC firms, unlike fully regulated securities firms, are not required to subtract most unsecured receivables (like accrued net interest payments on swaps) nor are they required to subtract unrealized gains (the amount by which swaps are in the money).

Alternatively, OTC firms can use value-at-risk models to compute capital under which market losses predicted by the model would be subtracted from capital. Modeling is subject to certain parameters like those of Basel, e.g. 99 percent confidence level with an assumed 10-day holding period, including the requirement that the amount of capital determined by the model be multiplied by a factor of 3 to 4 depending on backtesting results, the degree to which the model successfully predicts losses.

Firms using models have to make a two-part deduction from capital for credit risk. First, for each counterparty, an OTC firm must take a charge equal to the net replacement value in the account of the counterparty multiplied by 8 percent and further multiplied by a counterparty factor, ranging from 20 percent to 100 percent, based on the counterparty's credit rating. The SEC's approach to counterparty risk is more nuanced than Basel's. Second, an OTC firm must take an additional charge when it has concentrated risk with one counterparty. When replacement value for one counterparty exceeds 25 percent of the OTC firm's net capital, the deduction

---

[109] SEC Release No. 34-40594 (October 23, 1998).

ranges from 5 percent of the net replacement value in excess of 25 percent of the OTC dealer's tentative net capital for a highly rated counterparty to 50 percent of net replacement value over 25 percent of tentative net capital for lower rated counterparties.

G.   ENFORCEABILITY ISSUES

1.   LIABILITY OF DERIVATIVES DEALERS[110]

Derivatives activity has produced, multimillion-dollar derivative suits in the United States by customers against major securities firms that advised them about derivatives or entered into derivatives transactions with them in the 1990s. *Gibson Greetings v. Bankers Trust Co.*[111] involved a claim for $32 million in compensatory damages and *Proctor & Gamble (P&G) v. Bankers Trust Co.*[112] involved a claim for $195 million. *Gibson* was settled for approximately $14 million (some report $6 million) in 1994. *Proctor & Gamble* was settled in May 1996. The real blockbuster was *Orange County Investment Pool v. Merrill Lynch & Co.*[113] in which Orange County sued for $3 billion in damages. In November 1995, Bankers Trust settled a suit brought by Air Products, a chemical company, for $67 million. In October 1995, the U.S. District Court in *Lehman Brothers Commercial Corp. v Minmetals International Non-Ferrous Metals Trading Co.*[114] permitted a Chinese metal trading company to counterclaim for fraud and lack of suitability in Lehman's breach of contract case involving foreign exchange and swap transactions.[115]

Although there is great variety in the derivative transactions behind the different litigations, many of the transactions were swaps reflecting bets that interest rates would stay constant during 1993 and 1994. The *P&G* and *Gibson* derivatives were complex interest rate swaps where either a rise in short term or long term rates would very quickly put the parties in the red. *Orange County* involved structured notes called inverse floaters that represented a direct bet that interest rates would stay constant or decline.

The complaints in these various litigations are based on a combination of common law and statutory claims that can be broken down into four main categories: ultra vires, fraud, suitability, and contract.

---

[110] This section is taken largely from, H. Scott, "Liability of Derivative Dealers," in *The Future for the Global Securities Market* (F. Oditah ed., 1996).

[111] CV No. C-1-94-620 (S.D. Ohio, filed September 12, 1994).

[112] CV No. C-1-94 735 (S.D. Ohio, filed October 27, 1994).

[113] Ch. 9 Case No. SA 94-22272-JR, Adv. No. SA 94-1045-JR (C.D.B.R. Cal., filed January 12, 1995).

[114] 94 Civ. 8301 (S.D.N.Y. 1995).

[115] 65 BNA Banking Report 724 (1995).

a.   ULTRA VIRES

The basic ultra vires claim is that the customer corporation was prohibited by law from engaging in a particular transaction. For example, Orange County claimed that the transactions it entered into with Merrill Lynch were prohibited by the California Constitution because they required Orange County to become indebted in excess of Orange County's income and revenue for the year. Similarly, in *Lehman Bros. Commercial Corp. v China International United Petroleum and Chemicals Co., Ltd.*[116] (UNIPEC), UNIPEC claimed that its foreign exchange swaps were in violation of Chinese laws prohibiting all persons, except those approved by the State Administration of Exchange Control, from engaging in foreign exchange transactions.

The possibility of ultra vires swap contracts was a risk well known since the English case of *Hazell v Hammersmith*[117] where the House of Lords decided that thousands of interest rate swaps entered into by local authorities with banks were ultra vires and therefore void. The resulting mark-to-market losses to the banks were estimated to be in excess of £500 million.

In U.S. corporate law, the ultra vires defense to contract liability has limited application. Corporate charters are now written in very broad terms and, where they are more limited, courts will allow apparent or inherent authority to trump the lack of actual authority. Courts are particularly reluctant to apply the doctrine when it is only invoked to avoid the losing side of a contractual bet and would not have been invoked if the bet had been profitable. As a matter of economic analysis, these limitations on the doctrine make sense. Generally, it would be cheaper for corporate owners to monitor their agents' compliance with a corporate charter than it would be for third parties contracting with the corporation.

If the Orange County contracts were subjected to this analysis, it might be quite difficult to hold the swap contracts ultra vires. The Treasurer of Orange County quite likely had apparent authority to enter into the contracts even if he did not have actual authority. And clearly the County sought to avoid unprofitable contracts that it might well have profited on. Economically, it would seem a lot cheaper for the state or the county to monitor contractual compliance with the state constitution than it would be for the derivative dealer, particularly where the capacity issue involves novel or difficult issues of interpretation of the enabling statutes or constitution. The problem is not simply solved by obtaining a covenant of capacity from a counterparty. Such a covenant might not be binding absent capacity.

Of course, Orange County is not a private corporation. One could well argue that the validity of the ultra vires defense should be different in the

---

[116] No. 94-CIV-8304 (S.D.N.Y., filed November 15, 1994).
[117] [1992] 2 A.C. 1.

public contracts area because it is seeking to protect the public fisc for the benefit of taxpayers. On the other hand, why should one private firm rather than the public as a whole bear the loss for imprudent actions of public agents?

The Orange County debacle led to a lengthy investigation by the SEC of Merrill Lynch. In August 1998, the SEC charged the firm with negligent conduct for allegedly failing to warn investors of the risks they were taking in buying the county's notes. Simultaneous with the charge, Merrill settled the suit for $2 million. Merrill had previously settled a civil suit with the county for $437 million and had paid $30 million to resolve a criminal investigation by the Orange County district attorney.[118]

b.   FRAUD

The fraud claims arise either out of common law or statutory law related to securities and commodities, the Securities Act of 1933, the Securities Exchange Act of 1934 (together the Securities Laws) or the Commodity Exchange Act. As the common law generally imposes no duty to reveal all material information, plaintiffs have a strong incentive to fit the derivative transaction in question into coverage of the Securities Laws or the Commodity Exchange Act. Coverage under these laws hinges on whether certain derivatives are deemed securities or commodities.

As a result of the *Gibson Greetings* case, the CFTC and the SEC both initiated investigations of Bankers Trust that resulted in consent orders whereby Bankers Trust agreed to pay a $10 million fine.[119] Both the SEC and CFTC concluded that Bankers Trust had committed fraud in the sale of certain derivatives. In fact, the SEC concluded that two of the twelve types of derivative transactions involving swaps were securities, and the CFTC concluded that all twelve derivatives were some type of commodity option or future contract. Subsequent to the SEC order, P&G amended its complaint to include causes of action based on violations of the Securities Laws.

1.   *P&G*: THE U.S. STANDARD

The *P&G* case involved two swaps. In November 1993, the parties entered into a $200 million interest rate swap (the 5/30 swap) with a term of 5 years in which P&G received fixed rate interest at the then current 5-year rate and P&G paid a floating rate at the prevailing commercial paper (CP) rate minus 75 basis points plus an Additional Amount commencing in November 1994. The Additional Amount was to be determined in May 1994 on the basis of treasury rates. The higher those rates, the higher the Additional Amount. Thus, if the Additional Amount was 35 basis points, P&G

---

[118] *The Wall Street Journal*, August 25, 1998.
[119] See *In re BT Securities Corp., Rel Nos. 33-7124, 34-35136, 3-8579*, Fed. Sec. L. Rep. (CCH) [1994-1995 Decisions] ¶85,477 (December 22, 1994).

would pay the CP rate minus 40, rather than the initial rate of CP minus 75. When interest rates dramatically increased in 1994, the Additional Amounts became very significant; under the formula, P&G was required to pay the CP rate *plus* well over 1000 basis points.

The second swap entered into in 1994 was a 162.8 million DM swap with a term of almost five years matching an existing Deutschmark (DM) swap. The DM swap was structured so that P&G would, if certain DM rates remained stable, save 100 basis points on its existing swap. DM rates did not remain stable with the result that P&G was required to pay over 1600 additional basis points.[120]

Various documents produced in discovery in this case became available to the press. They contained various potentially damaging statements by Bankers Trust. In one example, a Bankers Trust salesman responded to an another employee's question as to how the salesman had obtained a derivative customer's confidence: "Funny business, you know? Lure people into that calm and then just totally f*** em."[121]

The federal district court dismissed most of P&G's claims against Bankers Trust. In particular, it found that swaps were not securities under federal or state securities laws. It noted that the transactions in question were different than those that were the subject of the SEC's enforcement action, where the SEC had found the swaps were securities since they could be characterized as options. Moreover, it noted that the SEC's finding had no binding effect on the court. The court also found that Bankers Trust owed no fiduciary duty to P&G. Nonetheless, the court did find that under New York, law Bankers Trust had a duty to disclose "material information to plaintiff both before the parties entered into the swap transactions and in their performance, and also a duty to deal fairly and in good faith during the performance of swap transactions." But P&G had to prove by clear and convincing evidence, and not mere preponderance, that Bankers Trust had failed to meet its disclosure obligations.[122]

The May 1996 settlement, following this decision, reportedly required Bankers Trust to absorb as much as $150 million, or 83 percent of P&G's loss, on the two swaps.[123]

In *Société Nationale d'Exploitation Industrielle des Tabacs et Allumettes v. Salomon Brothers*,[124] the court dismissed plaintiff's claim

---

[120] S. Henderson, "Derivatives Litigation in the United States," in *Swaps and Off-Exchange Derivatives Trading: Law and Regulation* (1996). The two swaps are also described in *Proctor & Gamble Company v Bankers Trust Company et al.*, (1996) US Dist. Lexis 6435 (USD.C. S.D. Ohio, May 8, 1996).

[121] G. Knecht, "P&G Can Add Racketeering to its Claims," *The Wall Street Journal*, October 4, 1995.

[122] *Proctor & Gamble Company v Bankers Trust Company et al.*, (1996) US Dist. Lexis 6435 (USD.C. S.D. Ohio, May 8, 1996) p. 16.

[123] L. Hays, "Bankers Trust Settles Dispute with P&G," *The Wall Street Journal*, May 10, 1996.

against Salomon for breach of fiduciary duty, citing *P&G*. Since the court failed to find that Salomon had agreed to act in a fiduciary capacity, it imposed no fiduciary obligations on Salomon, and the fact that Salomon may have possessed superior knowledge of the transactions did not mean it was a fiduciary. The opinion did not deal with the duties of disclosure of a non-fiduciary.

The CFMA of 2000 contains new provisions of the 1933 and 1934 Acts bearing on the issue of whether swaps are securities. Section 301, which amends the GLB Act, provides that any "swap agreement" (defined to include interest rate, currency, derivative and other similar agreements) subject to individual negotiation between eligible participants is not a security if no material term of the agreement is based "on the price, yield, value, or volatility of any security or any group or index of securities, or any interest therein." Neither non-security based or security-based swap agreements are required to be registered, Section 302. However, security-based swap agreements are subject to the liability provisions of s. 17(a) of the 1933 Act §302(b), and 10(b) of the 1934 Act (and thus Rule 10b-5), under §302(b) and 303(d) of the CFMA.

2.   PRINCIPLES AND PRACTICE

One effort to deal with fraud-type issues has stressed the importance of disclosure. Representatives from various dealer groups, including the International Swaps and Derivatives Association, on August 17, 1995 issued *Principles and Practices for Wholesale Financial Market Transactions* (the Principles). The preparation of the Principles was coordinated by the Federal Reserve Bank of New York. The Principles do not mandate any disclosure. Section 4.2.2 entitled *Reliance on Investment Advice* provides that a "Participant *may* communicate to its counterparty economic or market information relating to Transactions and trade or hedging ideas or suggestions. All such communications (whether written or oral) should be accurate and not intentionally misleading." (emphasis added). Section 4.2.3 entitled "Transaction Information" puts the onus on the investor in obtaining information. It provides that:

> "A Participant should either ask questions and request additional information or seek independent professional advice when it does not have a full understanding of either the risks involved in a Transaction or the fit between a Transaction and its desired risk profile. A counterparty should answer such questions and respond to such requests for additional information in good faith, and the information provided should be accurate and not intentionally misleading. A participant should expect that, if it does not expressly ask

---

[124] Index No. 113154/96 (Supreme Court, February 11, 1998) (on file with author).

questions or request additional information with respect to a transaction, its counterparty will assume that the Participant understands the transaction and has all the information it needs for its decision-making process."

The Principles seem to adopt a common law fraud approach under which disclosure is voluntary and only actionable when inaccurate or intentionally misleading, as contrasted with the Securities Law approach in which disclosure is mandatory, and the failure to disclose material information is actionable. Also, there is some difficulty in making an investor responsible for not asking the right question. How does one know what he doesn't know?

3.   *DHARMALA*: THE ENGLISH STANDARD

A 1995 English decision, *Bankers Trust v. Dharmala*,[125] is the most extensive court decision to date involving dealer liability on swaps. Dharmala was an Indonesian conglomerate engaged in commercial and financial activities. Two swaps were involved. Swap 1, a two-year interest rate swap on $50 million, was entered into on January 19, 1994. It had two parts. Under part one, Dharmala was to pay BT at the rate of 6-month U.S. Dollar LIBOR and was to receive the same plus a 125 basis point margin. In effect, BT paid Dharmala 125 basis points per annum. Under part two, Dharmala paid BT a 5 percent fixed annual rate and received interest at 5 percent multiplied by the fraction N/183. N was defined as the "actual number of days in a six month period commencing on August 15, 1994 ("look period") during which LIBOR was less than 4.125 percent." If the LIBOR rate was never less than 4.125 percent, BT would pay nothing on this part of the swap, and Dharmala would lose 3.75 percent; it would receive 1.25 percent on part one, and pay out 5.00 percent on part two. This would mean a maximum two year loss of $3.75 million ($50 million x .0375 x 2). At the time Swap 1 was entered into, on January 19, 6-month LIBOR was 3.625 percent (the Federal Reserve Board's Fed Funds rate was then 3 percent). On February 4, the Fed Funds rate was raised by 25 basis points pushing LIBOR up to over 3.85 percent. Since it was then anticipated, based on market prices, that LIBOR would rise over 4.125 percent in the look period, Dharmala was seriously out of the money.

On February 16, 1994, the parties cancelled Swap 1 and entered into Swap 2, what BT termed a "Barrier Swap." Swap 2 was also for two years at $50 million but was more complex and riskier. It was a "leveraged" swap since under the formula, a small movement in interest rates against Dharmala imposed on Dharmala a disproportionate increase in liability. As originally agreed, Swap 2 had the two following parts. Under part one, Dharmala received annual interest at the 6-month U.S. Dollar LIBOR rate

---

[125] QBD, 1994 Folio Nos. 2168 and 1396 (1995).

plus 125 basis points. On part two, Dharmala would pay interest at the 6-month U.S. Dollar LIBOR rate less 225 basis points per annum, plus a "Spread." In effect, leaving the Spread aside, Dharmala received 350 basis points (3.5 percent), or $1.75 million, per year.

"Spread" was to be zero if the 6-month LIBOR did not go above a 5.25 percent barrier during a "look" period, the first 12 months of the swap (February 16, 1994 - February 16, 1995). If at any time during that 12 months the rate did pass through the barrier, then "Spread" was to be determined on February 16, 1995, for each of the 2 years of the swap, by taking (6-month LIBOR on February 16, 1995 ÷ 4.50 percent) - 1. If 6-month LIBOR were 6 percent on February 16, the spread would be 0.33 [(.06/.0450)-1], a decimal, not a percentage. Dharmala would have a net obligation to BT of $14.75 million (0.33 x $50 million) – (0.0350 z $50 million). This formula was further complicated by two changes. The nominal amount of $50 million was divided into two tranches of $25 million. On one tranche, the barrier was raised to 5.3125 percent. Also, it was agreed that Dharmala would receive its $1.75 million in advance, discounted to $1.7 million.

Interest rates continued to rise in 1994, so that by May 1994, Swap 2 had a negative value to Dharmala for the remaining terms of $45 million (a BT estimate based on the forward LIBOR rate), and if rates continued to move up, the situation would get worse, and a lawsuit resulted. BT contended that by December 1994 it was owed approximately $65 million. Dharmala sought to rescind the swaps principally on the grounds of BT's misrepresentation and failure to meet its duty of care by explaining the swaps, and the contention that the swaps were unsuitable and also sued for damages.

Some facts about the parties. The chief player for BT was Mr. Hyun, a U.S. citizen born and brought up in New York. He majored in East Asian studies at Yale, graduating in 1985 and joining BT in 1987. During the transactions at issue he was the managing director of BT's Singapore office and had been extremely important in building up a substantial derivatives business. He was described by the court as a "master in the field of derivatives." The chief player for Dharmala was the Indonesian Finance Director, Mr. Thio, aged 38, who attended high school in Singapore and received an MBA from California State University. He was assisted by a Malaysian, Mr. Kong, aged 39, the financial controller, who had an accounting degree from Kent University in England. It appears that Dharmala had limited experience in dealing with swaps before its transactions with BT, although it had entered into a complex Yen-based swap with CS First Boston and had rejected previous BT swap proposals as too risky.

Some facts about the dealings of the parties before they entered into the two swaps. As to Swap 1, Hyun made a presentation but it is unclear whether he presented the formula on which the swap was based and worked out its operation under different scenarios, although it was clear that he indicated the maximum downside was 3.75 percent. The swap was presented in a written proposal as an "attractive interest cost reduction structure that will reduce [Dharmala's] interest exposure on its U.S. Dollar liabilities by 1.25 percent per annum for the next three years" and contained a written economic forecast of interest rates that were low compared with a majority of other economists. BT did not disclose that Swap 1 had a negative market value to Dharmala of $2 million at the time it was entered into.

As for Swap 2, BT represented that it had "a superior risk/return profile" to Swap 1, and contended that it was "unlikely" for interest rates to rise beyond the 5.25 percent barrier. BT's letter proposal was accompanied by a graphed sensitivity analysis showing outcomes at various assumed interest rates but did not extend far enough to show that Dharmala's liability was virtually unlimited if interest rates rose above the barrier. The court found the presentation unbalanced. BT did not disclose that Swap 2 had a negative value to Dharmala of $8 million at the time it was entered into. It is not clear how the court determined this negative value since research has shown that the pricing of these "barrier options" is not precise.[126]

With respect to the misrepresentation issue, the court found that BT had not represented, as claimed by Dharmala, that the swaps were safe and suitable and could be replaced at no cost. The court further found that the economic forecasts, while more optimistic than those made by others, were based on proper research and reasonable. While the court found that BT's presentation on Swap 2 was unbalanced, it concluded that Dharmala was capable of doing its own analysis and did not fully rely on BT's representations. The court further found that it was not up to BT to judge whether the swaps were suitable for Dharmala; Dharmala could make its own judgment on that question. The court also rejected the duty of care claim finding that BT had no duty to disclose the market value of the swaps at their inception. The court gave BT judgment on its claim on Swap 2. It appears that BT settled its case with Dharmala for $12.5 million following the court's decision.

As a point of comparison, in 1999, the Federal Reserve Board charged Guillaume Fonkenell, a trader at Bankers Trust in New York, with a breach of fiduciary duty, violations of safe and sound banking practices, and a scheme to defraud in connection with the Dharmala transaction. Allegedly, Fonkenell was involved in the development of the barrier swap that was marketed to various clients abroad, including Dharmala. The heart of the charge was that Fonkenell had constructed a formula designed to hide the leverage in the second transaction. The spread formula of (6-month LIBOR on February 16, 1995 ÷ 4.50 percent) -1. The Fed contended that "[d]ividing

---

[126] D. Leisen, "Valuation of Barrier Options in a Black-Scholes Setup with Jump Risk," 3 European Finance Review (1999), p. 319.

the formula by 4.50 percent is mathematically equivalent to multiplying the formula by 22.2," and that nowhere in the proposal was this amount of leverage pointed out.[127] The Fed charges were held not to be supported by the facts by an Administrative Law Judge in June 2000, and the Fed dismissed the charges on March 14, 2001.[128]

Notes and Questions

1. How would the *Dharmala* case be decided under U.S. law? Do you think BT made adequate disclosures to Dharmala? Did BT's conduct conform to Principals and Practice?

2. Could there be 10b-5 liability on a swap?

3. In August 2004, the Bank of New York, as trustee of a SPV, filed a suit against Citibank over the sale of investments in a CDO linked to Enron Corporation that could involve as much as $2.5 billion in damages. The suit alleges that Citigroup sold the SPV and ultimately investors positions as sellers of protection for an Enron default to cover Citigroup's own exposure. In the event of default Citigroup was obliged to give investors Enron bonds at a discount from their investments. When Enron defaulted and investors received the bonds, the bonds were subordinated to the claims of other creditors in the Enron bankruptcy, allegedly because Citigroup was involved in aiding and abetting the collapse of Enron by arranging various transactions. The investors claim Citigroup breached its contractual duty to deliver "clean" securities as well as defrauding investors and concealing information.[129]

c.   SUITABILITY

Suitability claims appear in two forms: the pure suitability claim and the disclosure suitability claim. In the pure suitability claim, the plaintiff claims that the defendant violated his duty to recommend and sell only suitable investments. In order to recover, the plaintiff must prove that the investments were unsuitable, the defendant had a duty not to recommend or sell unsuitable investments, the defendant acted with some level of intent, and that the plaintiff reasonably relied on the defendant's recommendation in purchasing the security. Plaintiffs have pointed to four different sources of rules that can create the duty to recommend or sell only suitable investments under U.S. law: the common law of fiduciary duty, Rule 10b-5 of the 1934 Act,

---

[127] *In the Matter of Guillaume Fonkenell, Notices of Charges and of Hearing*, Docket No. 98-032-B-1, 98-032-CMP-1 (May 7, 1999).

[128] For excellent commentary on *Dharmala*, see J. Quitmeyer, "An English Case, *Dharmala*, Looks at the Relationship Between the Dealer and Counterparty," 1 Derivatives (1996); D. Petkovic, "Derivatives and the Banker's Duties of Care," 14 International Banking and Financial Law (1996), p. 93.

[129] H. Sender, "Citigroup is Sued Over Notes Linked to Enron's Credit Status," *The Wall Street Journal*, August 26, 2004.

the New York Stock Exchange's (NYSE) Know Your Customer Rule, and the National Association of Securities Dealers' (NASD) Suitability Rule. As we have seen, the English court rejected the disclosure suitability claim in *Dharmala*.

The central issue in this area is whether a large sophisticated investor should have a suitability claim. While this may seem dubious, the City of San Jose effectively utilized a Rule 10b-5 suitability claim to win a jury verdict against multiple brokerage firms.

A plaintiff's sophistication alone is generally not dispositive of whether a given investment is suitable. An investment bet with a 100-1 payoff would not appear suitable for a sophisticated retiree with limited resources. Courts rather determine suitability based on the investment objectives of the plaintiff. If a defendant recommends a speculative investment to an investor that he knows is pursuing conservative investment goals, one might conclude it was done with fraudulent intent. However, one might argue that sophistication is quite relevant in this context. If the sophisticated retiree accepts the risky bet, perhaps he has changed his investment objectives.

Sophistication is clearly relevant to the issue of reasonable reliance. If the plaintiff knew or could have known that the investment was unsuitable to his investment objectives, there is a strong argument that he should not be allowed to recover.

The disclosure suitability claim is a mixture of a pure suitability claim and a fraud claim. The complaint is that the dealer committed fraud not by recommending or selling an unsuitable security, but by doing so without disclosing that the investment was unsuitable. The sophisticated investor is likely to argue that he reasonably relied on the recommendation given what he was told, but would not have done so if he knew all the facts. The disclosure suitability claim could properly be applied to a sophisticated investor since even a sophisticated investor would be unable to judge the suitability of an investment to his risk preferences without knowing the material risks of the investment. This was the argument in *Dharmala*.

The Principles also deal with the suitability issue. Section 4.2.2. provides:

> "Absent a written agreement or an applicable law, rule or regulation that expressly imposes affirmative obligations to the contrary, a counterparty receiving ... communications should assume that the Participant is acting at arm's length for its own account and that such communications are not recommendations or investment advise on which the counterparty may rely."

Only if an investor informs a dealer that it wishes to rely on its advice, the dealer agrees to do business on that basis and the investor gives the dealer information about his financial situation, will the dealer incur any responsibility for recommending suitable investments.

The drafters explicitly rejected an "alternative approach" that would require a dealer to determine the suitability of an investment recommendation. Their commentary states, "the alternative approach would undermine the finality of agreed Transactions, and create tremendous uncertainty regarding the economic risk position of participants."[130]

In March 1995, six major securities firms, in cooperation with the SEC and CFTC, agreed to adopt a *Framework for Voluntary Oversight* (Voluntary Framework) under which the firms would undertake to have certain management controls, submit quantitative reports covering credit risk exposures, evaluate risk relative to capital, and adopt guidelines for dealing with non-professional counterparties to derivatives contracts. While the Voluntary Framework, like the Principles, generally takes an arm's length approach, it goes significantly further in placing affirmative obligations on dealers. In "Counterparty Relationships," II.C (Nature of Relations), it states:

> "In cases where existing transaction documentation does not expressly address the nature of the relationship between the professional intermediary and its nonprofessional counterparty and the professional intermediary becomes aware that the nonprofessional counterparty believes incorrectly that the professional intermediary has assumed advisory or similar responsibilities towards the nonprofessional counterparty with respect to a prospective OTC derivative transaction, the professional intermediary should take steps to clarify the nature of the relationship."

It goes on to provide in II.E:

> "*Specific Transaction Proposals*. In circumstances where a professional intermediary, at the express request of a nonprofessional counterparty, formulates a specific OTC derivative transaction proposal that is tailored to particular transactional objectives specified by the counterparty, the professional intermediary should formulate the transaction proposal in good faith based on the information and objectives specified by the counterparty and subject to the terms of the parties' contractual arrangement."

And II. F further provides:

> "*Special Situations*. In circumstances where a nonprofessional counterparty has expressly requested assistance in evaluating an OTC derivative transaction in which the payment formula

---

[130] Principles, p. 7.

is particularly complex or which includes a significant leverage component, the professional intermediary should offer to provide additional information, such as scenario, sensitivity or other analyses, to the nonprofessional counterparty or should recommend that the counterparty obtain professional advice."

The Voluntary Framework clearly imposes more obligations on dealers than does the Principles. This partially reflects the different orientation of the regulators involved. The first concern of the SEC in the Voluntary Framework would be to protect investors whereas the first concern of the Federal Reserve Bank of New York in the Principles would be to protect the safety and soundness of banks by limiting their liability. While none of the private rules are binding, they could well be invoked or cited by courts.

d.   CONTRACT

There are two main types of contract claims. The first is that an investor is not bound by his investment agreement. For example, UNIPEC argued that it was not bound by its agreement because it was made by an agent with no authority to bind the corporation, and Gibson argued that a swap with Bankers Trust was not binding because it was made under economic duress in a situation of financial emergency. UNIPEC's argument is a first cousin to the ultra vires argument examined earlier. While UNIPEC does not claim the corporation had no power to enter into the contract, it did claim that the particular agent who entered into the contract had no corporate authority.

The second type of claim is that the contract should embody certain prior oral understandings reached between the parties or, if it does not, that there was no meeting of the minds and thus no contract at all. P&G claimed that it never agreed to the secret and proprietary Bankers Trust early lock-in pricing model as a term of its derivative transactions. UNIPEC claimed that it had an oral agreement with Lehman Brothers to close out all transactions if they reached a net debt position of $5 million (later raised to $8 million). Again, this is just a standard contract claim. Obviously if derivatives dealers breach their contracts they may be held liable. The implications of this claim is that the key characteristics of the instruments may have to be documented and agreed in writing.

e.   SETTLEMENT CALCULATIONS

There have been several English cases dealing with the calculation of the amount of settlement when one party defaults on its swap obligations.[131] In *Peregrine Fixed Income Ltd (in liquidation) v. Robinson Department Store*

---

[131] See S. Henderson, "English Cases Dealing with Settlement Provisions of the ISDA Master Agreement," Butterworths Journal of International Banking and Finance (June 2000).

plc,[132] Peregrine, a Hong Kong financial institution and Robinson, a Thai retailer, had entered into a swap transaction under which Peregrine had no future payments and Robinson had to make 25 annual payments with a present value of $87 million. Peregrine became insolvent and under the ISDA agreement it was necessary to determine the value of the contract to Peregrine.

This was done under the Market Quotation method (which the parties had specified), in which three quotes are obtained to determine what dealers would pay to become Robinson's counterparty. The quotes were $750,000, $9.5 million, and $25.5 million. These quotes were obtained two years after the Peregrine insolvency (it is unstated why Robinson waited so long to get them). They reflected the fact that Robinson had itself become insolvent by that time, so that dealers deeply discounted any obligation that Robinson might have to them. The parties had not specified the alternative Loss Method of calculating the Settlement Amount, under which one includes "any loss of bargain, cost of funding, or, at the election of such party [here Robinson, the party entitled to make the calculation], loss or cost incurred" as a result of termination. The Loss Method also applies if application of the Market Quotation Method "would not (in the reasonable belief of the party making the determination) produce a commercially reasonable result." Although Robinson argued that application of the Market Quotation Method did produce a commercially reasonable method, the Court concluded otherwise and sustained Peregrine's claim for $87 million.[133]

f.   REGULATORY ACTIONS

The SEC and CFTC actions show that derivatives dealers are exposed to federal agency actions, based on the concerns of these agencies with investor protection. Bank dealers are also exposed to actions by bank regulators. A written Agreement between the Federal Reserve Bank of New York and Bankers Trust of December 5, 1994,[134] focuses on Bankers Trust's leveraged derivatives (LDT) business. The Fed's concern is that bank holding companies under its supervision will be damaged by allegations and recoveries based on claims of fraud. Therefore, the remedial measures required by the Agreement require greater disclosure of risks to customers, greater transparency of pricing, and better control over the actions of people involved in marketing and selling derivatives.

For example, the Fed's order requires that BT shall conduct its LDT Business in a manner which seeks to reasonably ensure that each LDT customer has the capability to understand the nature and material terms, conditions, and risks of any LDT entered into with the customer. It further

---

[132] Commercial Court Claim No. 2000-Folio 277 (May 18, 2000).

[133] See A. Gauvin, "Is ISDA Documentation Reliable in Case of Early Termination of the Master Agreement?," 118 The Banking Law Journal (2001), p. 766.

[134] Fed. Banking L. Rep. (CCH) [Current], pp. 90, 332.

provides that BT shall distribute to each customer written term sheets and sensitivity analyses designed to illustrate a broad range of outcomes and distribution of risks at maturity. BT must constantly update its customers as to risks. The Agreement also provides that BT will update its customer as to the value of positions entered into. It is unclear to what extent the practices set forth in the Agreement will be applied to the derivatives business of other banks.

g.   CUSTOMER LIABILITY

Gibson Greetings, Inc., which settled its dispute with Bankers Trust, was charged by the SEC with violations of securities laws' requirements of financial reporting of its losses and potential risks, as well as failures to maintain accurate internal record-keeping and internal controls. These charges were settled in 1996 by the entry of cease and desist orders committing Gibson to avoid such violations in the future.[135]

2.   NETTING AND BANKRUPTCY

The potential problem for a swap party in bankruptcy is that the trustee may not respect the close out netting provisions of the ISDA Master Agreement.

Assume Party A and Party X have three swap contracts between them, and that marking each contract to market, and calculating replacement value, there are two contracts favorable to Party A, and one favorable to Party X. Party X goes bankrupt.

	X	A	
1.	+200,000	-200,000	(A owes X)
2.	+500,000	-500,000	(A owes X)
3.	-800,000	+800,000	(X owes A)

If all the contracts were netted, X would owe A $100,000.

The concern is that the bankruptcy trustee or receiver might not allow the swaps to be netted against each other; the trustee would not honor swaps with a positive value to the counterparty, but would enforce those with a positive value to the bankrupt estate. This is the so-called cherry picking problem.

Thus, the Trustee might enforce contracts 1 and 2 against A, demanding $700,000, and remit A to becoming an unsecured creditor in bankruptcy for the $800,000 owed to A on contract 3. If there were no payments to unsecured creditors in X's bankruptcy, A could lose $700,000. If

---

[135] 65 BNA Banking Report 619 (1995).

the netting was respected, A would only lose $100,000, his net unsecured claim against X.

Under recent (1989, 1990, 1991) amendments to U.S. laws governing bankruptcy of banks and other companies, the Trustee or Receiver of a U.S. firm must respect the netting provisions in swap contracts. And, as complimentary matters, the usual automatic stay in bankruptcy upon the enforcement of rights does not effect the close-out of a netting position. This means that the parties can immediately settle their positions, including the provision of collateral. These rights are not completely uncontroversial even though they are very important to the functioning of the financial markets. They have the effect of giving counterparties to swap contracts super priority, even over other secured creditors that would be bound by the automatic stay.

In 2005, as part of the broad ranging Bankruptcy Reform legislation in the U.S.,[136] a generally broader range of "financial contracts" and type of counterparties ("financial participants") who specify tests for dollar volume of activity in financial markets, e.g. hedge funds as well as financial institutions, were covered by the same provisions. Also, the definition of a "swap agreement," to which the swap provisions apply, now clearly covers a wider range of swaps such as credit default swaps. Indeed, the definition now covers any agreement or transaction that becomes "the subject of recurrent dealings in the swap market". The legislation also prohibits the enforceability of one-way payment or "walkaway" clauses under which a party out of the money on the swap would be excused from paying a bankrupt counterparty.

But this is only U.S. law and the bankrupt counterparty may well be bankrupt under the laws of some foreign jurisdiction. There are opinions from lawyers that swaps netting will hold up in other jurisdictions but most laws are much less certain than the U.S. law.

There has been a deep concern among regulators that the potential lack of valid bilateral netting arrangements could make them more risky, and as a result, until the 1995 Amendments to the Basel Accord, bank capital requirements for future exposure were based on gross rather than net positions.

Problems with netting under the French law were corrected with the enactment of Law No. 96-597, Loi de modernisation des activités financières, in July 1996. As now revised, the netting rules apply to any contract where one of the parties is a provider of investment services (prestataire de services d'investissement). This term is defined as an investment company or bank with authorization to provide investment services. The term "investment company" is defined as any entity (other than a bank) which as its regular

---

[136] Public Law 109-8, 109th Congress, April 20, 2005, Title IX, §§901-911.

and principal business provides investment services.[137] A European Union Netting Directive now makes netting effective across the Community.[138]

Japanese law was quite unclear on the validity of netting. Legislation to uphold netting was introduced in the Diet on March 10, 1998 and took effect in December 1998. In Italy, another country where the validity of netting was unclear, a new law took effect in July 1998.[139]

There is another netting related bankruptcy issue—the extent to which dealers with net positions may, upon the declaration of bankruptcy by a counterparty, net its positions and seize collateral of the debtor to the extent the bankrupt owes the dealer money (on net). As a legal matter, the issue is whether seizure of the debtor's collateral is exempt from the usual automatic stay of creditor collection activity once bankruptcy occurs. Under U.S. bankruptcy laws, such collection actions are permitted. Congress reasoned, in granting this exemption, that this would protect against systemic risk, the bankruptcy of one firm spreading to others. Some have argued that the ability of dealers to terminate their positions outside of the automatic stay could actually cause systemic risk to increase as a result of the bankrupt debtor being deprived of assets and thus being forced to default on contracts. In addition, the liquidation of positions might cause "knock on" effects "because other counterparties and other banks and financial firms held positions similar to LTCM's."[140] I do not find this persuasive. Debtors in bankruptcy cannot use cash or cash equivalent collateral in bankruptcy (absent providing adequate protection of equivalent value), so protecting this collateral under the automatic stay does not increase the debtor's liquidity. Further, it is unclear why foreclosing on such collateral has the asserted knock on effects. It may well be that derivative contracts plunge in value as a result of the default of a major player, but this would happen even if creditors could not foreclose on their collateral. Furthermore, the right of derivatives dealers to foreclose on collateral is now about to be extended to other financial contracts.[141]

While payments on swaps may be protected by bankruptcy netting laws, the same may not be true for fees. Enron is trying to recover about $900 million in transaction fees, allegedly paid in 2001, at a time at which it may

---

[137] S. Mouy & E. Nalbantian, "France Modernizes Collateralization and Netting," International Financial Law Review (September 1996), p. 26.

[138] A. Hudson, "The European Netting Directive," European Financial Services Law (November 1996), p. 309.

[139] 11 Swaps Monitor, No. 11 (April 6, 1998).

[140] F. Edwards and E. Morrison, "Derivatives and the Bankruptcy Code: Why the Special Treatment," Columbia Law School, Center for Law and Economic Studies Working Paper 258 (2004). See also W. Bergman, R. Bliss, C. Johnson, and G. Kaufman, "Netting, Financial Contracts and Banks: The Economic Implications," Market Discipline in Banking: Theory and Evidence, 15 Research in Financial Services: Private and Public Policy 303 (2003).

[141] See Sections 901-911, S. 256, Bankruptcy Abuse and Consumer Protection Act of 2005, 109th Cong. 1st Sess., reported to Senate in February 2005.

have been insolvent. If fees are taken as spreads in the terms of the swaps themselves, as in Figures 15.1 and 15.2 above, it may be difficult to hive them off from netting protections.[142]

CONCLUSIONS

Perhaps the most important conclusion to draw from this Chapter is that financial innovation, however beneficial, can result in formidable regulatory and policy issues for the international financial system.

The first major concern that arose from the development of swaps was their impact on the risk profile of banks. The fact that they were off-balance sheet meant that the risk of these positions was not mitigated through the application of leverage ratios used to measure capital adequacy. On the other hand, the benefit of swaps for hedging credit risk on the balance sheet was ignored as well. While there is now a consensus as to how to account for the credit and market risk of plain vanilla swaps, by marking-to-market, the risks posed by other more "exotic" swaps like credit derivatives, is still under debate. Of particular concern is the use of "fair value" accounting where there is no objective market price of a bank's position. And there is still much disagreement, under new accounting rules, for deciding whether and to what extent a given swap hedges another position.

A second issue is whether the growing level of swap transactions has significantly increased systemic risk. As we shall see in Chapter 16, below, at the heart of the concern in the case of Long Term Capital Management was whether LTCM's huge position in swaps with financial institution counterparties could endanger those institutions, or more generally the financial markets, in the event of LTCM's failure. Although there is no conclusive evidence that was the case, the fear of another more serious LTCM remains.

A third concern, and potentially the most serious, is whether the advent of credit derivatives has increased and redistributed credit risk in an undesirable manner. There is the potential that parties incurring risk may not have a sufficient incentive to control or police risk as a result of having bought protection. Sellers of protection who, as dealers, have hedged their own exposures, may not police the buyers or require the equivalent of deductibles, like normal insurers. Indeed, we do not know to whom the ultimate credit risks have been distributed. All of these issues can have consequences in public (sovereign) credit markets as well as private ones.

As in the case of securities markets, where ATSs compete with exchanges, there is competition in the derivatives markets between the

---

[142] J. Wiggins, "Derivatives Dealers Fight Bid by Enron to Recover $900 Million," *Financial Times*, April 16, 2004.

futures and options exchanges and the OTC market in derivatives. Like their securities exchange brethren, the organized exchanges (and their regulators) have complained of competitive unfairness arising from more regulatory burdens, like trading and margin rules, being put on the organized markets. This has seemed to raise less of a problem in derivatives than in securities markets. Perhaps the reason is that the products on exchanges and OTC are not exactly the same, and because financial institution regulators of OTC positions impose significant regulatory burdens on major players in the OTC markets.

Swaps have also presented challenges to the legal regime. At the outset is the issue of the central role of ISDA that promulgates rules for its members that also greatly affect non-member end-users. While ISDA has struggled to resolve internal dealer differences, as in the case of the appropriate restructuring definition, it is not in the position to accommodate concerns of end-users that may differ from dealers. Secondly, gaps in the contractual arrangements, often involving interpretation of the ISDA agreements, have had to be resolved by the courts. Of particular concern has been the issue of the liability of swap dealers to their customers. While it would seem that many of the dealer counterparties can fend for themselves, through hiring expert advisors if necessary, this is not as clear with respect to others, such as Orange County or even Dharmala. To the extent swap positions become retail, this will become a much more significant problem. Finally, as with payments and the clearing and settlement of securities, there is a need to insure the validity of netting.

CHAPTER SIXTEEN

OFFSHORE MUTUAL FUNDS

Mutual funds are investment vehicles that allow investors to purchase interests representing pro rata shares of the net assets of a pool of securities and other assets. Such funds can be public or private. An open-end fund engages in a continuous offering of its shares and will permit investors to redeem shares at daily net values. A closed-end fund engages in one offering and does not generally permit share redemptions. Investors exit from their investments by selling their shares to other investors in a secondary market.

Mutual funds have emerged as the preferred investment vehicle for most individual investors, since they allow inexpensive diversification of risk under the management of a qualified expert adviser. As of 1999, 41 percent of U.S. households invested in mutual funds; and total mutual fund assets in the U.S. had skyrocketed from about $716 billion at the end of 1986 to over $6 trillion. Investment company assets outside the U.S. increased from under $1 trillion in 1988 to $3.5 trillion in 1999.[1]

There is great potential for growth for foreign investment in mutual funds, as in France and the U.K. As of 1996, only one in ten households in these countries invests in mutual funds, and the ratios are even lower in the rest of the world.

As of 1996, it was estimated that foreign investment advisers managed $141 billion of investment company assets in the United States, or 4.8 percent of total industry assets, while U.S. firms managed $56.6 billion in mutual funds outside the United States, or 3.7 percent of the non-U.S. mutual fund market.[2]

Generally speaking, an offshore mutual fund is a fund organized in a foreign country, as opposed to an onshore fund that is organized in the United States. Offshore funds are often sponsored by well-known financial institutions. Sponsors may receive annual management fees, commissions,

---

[1] Investment Company Institute, *Fact Book 2000*; Investment Company Institute and Securities Industry Association, Equity Ownership in America (1999).
[2] See Response of the Investment Company Institute to IOSCO Cross-Border Marketing Survey, November 14, 1996.

placement fees, and/or an agreed initial fee that may represent a small percentage of the money invested in the fund. The sponsors of the offshore funds appoint professional managers to advise the fund on daily operations. Investment advisers of offshore funds are often located in foreign financial centers and are thereby able to identify investment opportunities and make qualified investment decisions regarding the foreign securities of which a foreign fund is often comprised.

A key part of setting up an offshore fund is the selection of the domicile. Low taxes and the economic and political environment are important factors, as they are for offshore banking centers. The domiciles of choice close to the United States have been the Bahamas, Bermuda, the Cayman Islands, and Curacao.[3]

Offshore mutual funds enable investors to take advantage of the globalization of the economy and further diversify their risk while minimizing the possible disadvantages stemming from unfamiliarity with foreign securities. Meanwhile, the offshore mutual funds provide a stream of capital to foreign corporations. Investors worldwide can also invest in foreign securities through U.S. mutual funds that invest in foreign securities. As we shall see, however, for tax and regulatory reasons U.S. investors tend to invest only in U.S. funds and foreign investors in offshore funds. This is a remarkable pattern given the level of cross-border activity in the primary securities markets between these two areas.

Offshore funds generally take either of two organizational forms: a contract or unit trust form, most often used by German, Japanese or British funds, or a corporate form, used by Mexican and French funds.[4] The common organizational structure taken by U.S. funds is the corporate form. In the contract form, the fund is a creation of its sponsor or manager and is monitored by an independent trustee or government regulator. In the corporate form, the fund is created as a separate entity. The corporate fund is owned and theoretically managed by its shareholders through a board of directors.

A.   UNITED STATES REGULATORY BARRIERS TO OFFSHORE MUTUAL FUNDS

The U.S. mutual funds market is often regarded as the most difficult mutual fund market for an offshore fund to penetrate. Some funds choose not to register in the U.S. because of highly stringent U.S. disclosure

---

[3] See generally, J. Press, "Critical Accounting, Tax and System Issues," in *Hedge Funds* (J. Lederman and R. Klein eds., 1995), p. 199. In Europe, Luxembourg and Dublin have been the leaders.

[4] See D. Silver, "Meeting the Demand for Pooled Investments in a World Market," Investment Company Institute (September 24, 1991), p. 9.

requirements, and corporate form requirements, combined with the expense of U.S. registration. However, the Securities and Exchange Commission (SEC) allows foreigners to freely invest in American mutual funds, and permits foreign mutual funds to freely purchase American securities without having to register.

1.   MUTUAL FUNDS REGISTERED UNDER THE 1940 ACT

a.   REGISTRATION OF FOREIGN FUNDS

The Investment Company Act of 1940 (the 1940 Act)[5] was enacted to address potential abuses in pooled securities funds such as the pyramiding of funds and uncontrolled conflicts of interest. Administered by the SEC, the 1940 Act applies by its terms to all investment companies, including both U.S. and offshore mutual funds. In its inclusive interpretation by the SEC, the 1940 Act defines "investment companies" to include any entity, incorporated or not, which:

- is or holds itself out as being engaged primarily, or proposes to engage primarily, in the business of investing, reinvesting or trading in securities (a subjective test)

- is engaged or proposes to engage in the business of investing, reinvesting, owning, holding or trading in securities and owns or proposes to acquire investment securities having a value exceeding 40 percent of the issuer's total assets (an objective test).

The definition of "security" includes stocks, bonds, notes, certificates of interest or participation in any profit-sharing agreement, certain options, evidences of indebtedness, investment contracts (that is, an arrangement where the person invests money in a common enterprise expecting profits

---

[5] 15 U.S.C. §80a (1988). The 1940 Act provides:
"No investment company organized or otherwise created under the laws of the United States or of a State and having a board of directors, unless registered under section 80a-8 of this title, shall directly or indirectly-

(1)   offer for sale, sell, or deliver after sale, by the use of the mails or any means or instrumentality of interstate commerce, any security or any interest in a security, whether the issuer of such security is such investment company or another person; or offer for sale, sell, or deliver after sale any such security or interest, having reason to believe that such security or interest will be made the subject of a public offering by use of the mails or any means or instrumentality of interstate commerce;

(2)   purchase, redeem, retire, or otherwise acquire or attempt to acquire, by use of the mails or any means or instrumentality of interstate commerce, any security or any interest in a security, whether the issuer of such security is such investment company or another person;

(3)   control any investment company which does any of the acts enumerated in paragraphs (1) and (2) of this subsection;

(4)   engage in any business in interstate commerce; or

(5)   control any company that is engaged in any business in interstate commerce. The provisions of this subsection shall not apply to transactions of an investment company which are merely incidental to its dissolution."

principally from the efforts of a third party), and undivided interests in oil or gas or mineral rights.

Section 7(d) of the 1940 Act[6] prohibits a foreign investment company from using jurisdictional means such as the U.S. mail or any other method of interstate commerce to offer or sell its securities (or shares of its funds, for our purposes) in connection with a public U.S. offering, unless the SEC issues an order permitting the foreign investment company to register under the 1940 Act. Exemptions permitting non-public offers without registration are discussed below.

When §7(d) applies, the foreign fund will be barred from selling shares in the U.S. unless the SEC issues an order permitting the fund to register (with the SEC), and the fund then indeed registers. Section 7(d) authorizes the SEC to issue an order 'permitting' registration only if the SEC finds that it is both legally and practically feasible to enforce the provisions of the 1940 Act against the foreign investment company, and that the issuance of such an order is consistent with public interest and SEC notions of investor protection.

In order to register under the 1940 Act, a foreign investment company will often have to restructure its fund substantially. While the 1940 Act does not explicitly require that mutual funds be organized under a corporate structure, it does impose restrictions that assume such a structure, including the requirements of a board of directors to oversee the fund's operations and contractual obligations, and shareholder voting to elect board members and approve fundamental changes in the nature of the fund and its management. The biggest obstacle for many European and Japanese funds is that they are structured under a more contractual or trust-like model in which the investors' money does not form part of the investment company's own assets, but rather is treated as a collection of separate funds bought by the investment company in the form of securities for the unit holders.

In 1954, to clarify the criteria that a foreign fund would need to satisfy before the SEC would issue a 7(d) order, the SEC adopted Rule 7d-1.[7]

---

[6] 15 U.S.C. §80a-7(d) provides:

"No investment company, unless organized or otherwise created under the laws of the United States or of a State, and no depositor or trustee of or underwriter for such a company not so organized or created, shall make use of the mails or any means or instrumentality of interstate commerce, directly or indirectly, to offer for sale, sell, or deliver after sale, in connection with a public offering, any security of which such company is the issuer. Notwithstanding the provisions of this subsection and of section 80a-8(a) of this title, the Commission is authorized, upon application by an investment company organized or otherwise created under the laws of a foreign country, to issue a conditional or unconditional order permitting such company to register under this subchapter, and to make a public offering of its securities by use of the mails and means or instrumentalities of interstate commerce, if the Commissioner finds that, by reason of special circumstances or arrangements, it is both legally and practically feasible effectively to enforce the provisions of this subchapter against such company and that the issuance of such order is otherwise consistent with the public interest and the protection of investors."

[7] 12 C.F.R. §270.7d-1.

The following are among the Rule 7d-1 requirements: (1) the foreign applicant's charter and by-laws must contain the substantive provisions of the 1940 Act; (2) all parties involved with the management and investment of the funds must file an agreement stating that each will comply with the 1940 Act; (3) at least a majority of the directors and officers of the applicant foreign fund must be U.S. citizens, and of these, a majority must reside in the United States; (4) all of the foreign fund's assets must be maintained in a U.S. bank; and (5) the applicant's principal underwriter and auditor must be U.S. entities.

Following its adoption of Rule 7d-1, the SEC issued a release in 1975 called Guidelines for Filing of Application for Order Permitting Registration of Foreign Investment Companies (the Guidelines or 7d-1 guidelines)[8] to set forth standard conditions for foreign funds seeking 7(d) orders. The Guidelines state that "compliance with the conditions and arrangements in Rule 7d-1 need not necessarily be the only means of satisfying the statutory standards." The SEC emphasized its willingness to consider exemptive applications under §6(c) of the 1940 Act for any offshore fund that could not meet all of the standards of Rule 7d-1, but that proposed alternative methods for protecting investors and for assuring that the provisions of the Act could be adequately enforced against it. The key guidelines provide:

"(1) the foreign applicant's charter and by-laws must contain the substantive provisions of the 1940 Act (investor protection);

(2) all parties involved with the management and investment of the funds must file an agreement stating that each will comply with the 1940 Act (enforcement);

(3) at least a majority of the directors and officers of the applicant foreign fund must be U.S. citizens, and of these, a majority must reside in the United States (enforcement);

(4) all of the foreign fund's assets must be maintained in a U.S. bank (anti-embezzlement); and

(5) the applicant's principal underwriter and auditor must be U.S. entities (enforcement re liability of agents)."

A seminal application under Rule 7d-1 was *Union-Investment Gesellschaft m.b.h., Securities and Exchange Commission, Investment Company Act of 1940.*[9] The major aspects of the application are described below. Some detail is useful for understanding the types of problems foreign funds will encounter under Rule 7d-1. The application was withdrawn after the SEC announced it would hold a hearing on the application.[10] This was widely taken as a sign that the SEC would not have approved the application.

---

[8] 40 Federal Register 45,424 (1975).
[9] Release No. 12863, December 1, 1982.
[10] 48 Federal Register 23342 (1983).

b.   UNION INVESTMENT

Unifonds was one of the three largest mutual funds in West Germany, having over $900 million in assets comprised of cash and a diversified portfolio made up solely of securities of West German issuers that were listed or traded on West German stock exchanges. Under West German law, Unifonds was a "separate estate"; it had no legal personality or existence. It was an unincorporated collection of assets. Union-Investment (UI or Applicant) was one of West Germany's oldest management companies. It advised and administered five separate funds, one of which was Unifonds. Union-Investment was owned by 40 shareholder banks whose liability as owners was limited to the amount of their respective contributions. These banks, not the shareholders of Unifonds, voted on matters concerning Union-Investment, including the election of its Aufsichtsrat (Board of Supervisors).

UI claimed it had difficulties complying with many of the provisions of Rule 7d-1 because of the West German regulatory system and West German business practices, but that the operation of West German law and the conditions and arrangements to which it has consented in its application, together with the application of those provisions of the Act from which it did not request exemption, provided the means for it to meet the standards of s. 7(d).

UI declared that its corporate executives and Unifonds' distributor, custodian, and accountant were not permitted under West German law to be United States citizens or residents. UI also stated that under West German business practice those persons had no personal liability toward fund shareholders. Therefore, such persons and entities would not enter into any agreements to comply with the Act, nor would they consent to the jurisdiction of United States courts and appoint agents for service of process there. However, UI, which was liable to the shareholders of Unifonds under West German law, undertook to comply with those provisions of the Act from which it was not exempted, and consented to jurisdiction of United States courts.

UI further asserted that all of Unifonds' assets must be held in West Germany in Unifonds' custodian bank or, for some of its cash deposits, in Union-Investment's shareholder banks. Under West German law, all sales transactions had to take place through Unifonds' custodian bank in Frankfurt. Thus, in many cases, the United States courts would not have jurisdiction over the persons associated with Union-Investment, Unifonds' assets or the transactions in Unifonds shares.

It would also have been difficult for the Commission or a shareholder to enforce an injunction or bring a criminal action against the European executives of Union-Investment or to attach, liquidate or distribute any of the assets of Union-Investment or Unifonds, all of which were kept in West Germany. UI attempted to compensate for the unavailability of assets in the

United States by arranging for an irrevocable letter of credit in an initial amount of $1 million, and thereafter in an amount equal to five percent of the value of Unifonds shares then outstanding in the United States.

Applicant contended that West Germany had an extensive system of regulation with oversight of the activities of management companies by each fund's respective custodian bank and by the Bundesaufsichtsamt fuer das Kreditwesen (BAK)—the agency in West Germany that regulated investment companies operating there. In addition, Applicant stated that West German law imposed a fiduciary duty upon managers of an investment company to operate the fund on behalf of the fund's shareholders.

In order to facilitate granting its requested order under s. 7(d) of the Act, Union-Investment made certain undertakings and agreed to certain conditions being imposed in such order. Specifically, Union-Investment undertook that the financial statements of Unifonds would meet the requirements of Regulation S-X (except for such differences that were agreed upon by representatives of the Commission's staff and Applicant). While the statements were prepared in accordance with West German generally accepted accounting principles, they were reconciled to U.S. GAAP. Union-Investment also agreed that such financial statements would be audited on a basis that substantially complied with United States generally accepted auditing standards, and that it would engage United States independent public accountants for the purpose of consulting with its independent West German accountants as to such standards.

UI undertook that it would register Unifonds as an investment company under the Act, that it would register Unifonds shares sold to United States investors under the Securities Act of 1933 and would file all appropriate disclosure documents prepared in the prescribed manner, with the exception that Union-Investment would only report the aggregate amount of remuneration paid to its management and the aggregate amount of brokerage fees paid to its shareholder banks. Its application also provided that Union-Investment would be permitted to discuss with the SEC's staff the possible modification or inapplicability of certain items in the disclosure forms.

Pursuant to §6(c) of the Act, Applicant had requested exemptive relief from many provisions of the Act in order to accommodate Unifonds' status as a registered investment company under the Act with West German law and business practices.

For example, Applicant represented that it needed an exemption from the bonding requirements of §17(g) of the Act and Rule 17g-1 thereunder because BAK policy would prohibit it from obtaining a bond to protect United States investors unless it provided bonding protection for all Unifonds' shareholders, which, it contended, would put Applicant at a competitive disadvantage with other West German investment companies.

Applicant stated that owing to the structure of the West German investment company industry and the provisions of West German law, which did not embody the concept of independent directors, it needed an exemption from those provisions of the Act dealing with disinterested directors: Sections 10(a), (b) and (g); 15(c) and 32(a). ... Applicant argued that West German law provided substitute safeguards for these provisions. With respect to §10(a), Applicant represented that West German law imposed a duty on management to act in the interest of Unifonds' shareholders, and provided for independent review of management by Unifonds' custodian bank and by the BAK, both of which could bring suit against UI for management's failure to so act. The BAK could also dismiss a manager who was unfit professionally or who violated laws regulating West German investment companies. Applicant argued that the functions of §10(b) and (g), to prevent conflicts of interest, were fulfilled by provisions of West German law that prohibit members of the Advisory Board and the Board of Supervisors from participating in the daily decisions concerning allocation of brokerage and the investment of assets for Unifonds.

The application also requested exemptive relief so that Applicant could engage in certain affiliated transactions which were typical of West German business practices. Applicant requested exemptions from §10(f) and 17(a), (b) and (e)(2) to be able to continue to use its shareholder banks as depositary banks and as principal underwriters and brokers, and to buy securities from and sell securities to such banks and members of its Advisory Board. Applicant represented that, instead of prohibiting affiliated transactions, West German law prohibited any borrowing of fund assets by anyone except to the extent that cash was deposited in shareholder banks. It also prohibited members of the Board of Supervisors and Board of Managers from buying property from or selling property to a fund. Applicant stated that conflicts of interest were also prevented by a prohibition against participation in daily investment decisions by members of the Board of Supervisors and the Advisory Board, and by limitations on the terms of all transactions, rather than the proscription of affiliated transactions.

Applicant stated that, to the extent its shareholder banks served as depositories for Unifonds' cash, there might be non-compliance with §17(a)(3). It represented, however, that West German law prohibits the participation of the members of the Board of Supervisors in any decision concerning the allocation of cash deposits and required Unifonds' fund manager to make such allocations for the benefit of Unifonds' shareholders.

Applicants also requested an exemption from §17(f) of the Act, claiming that, under West German law, Union-Investment had to keep its assets in West Germany in a West German custodian bank, which played a substantial regulatory role. Applicant further represented that, while Unifonds' custodian bank was not regulated by U.S. laws, it was regulated pursuant to the German Banking Act, and West German law provided protections equivalent to those provided by §17(f) and the rules thereunder applicable to custodians. As stated above, this application was withdrawn in anticipation of SEC denial.

Restrictions on entry by offshore mutual funds is not a policy unique to the United States. Traditionally, the Japanese investment trust markets remained virtually closed to U.S. investment advisers. In early 1995, however, the United States and Japan reached an agreement to open up the Japanese market.[11]

In the 1960-1973 period, the SEC permitted a number of foreign funds from Canada, Australia, Bermuda, the United Kingdom and South Africa to register, although there have been no further registrations (or applications) since that time, most probably because of tax reasons explained later in this Chapter. One matter of interest is the use of an "equivalence" test for foreign regulation as a condition for an exemption. This is different than a mutual recognition standard—which the U.S. does not generally accept.

Notes and Questions

1.   Should the SEC have allowed Union-Investment to register under 7(d)?

2.   Assuming application of U.S. rules effectively precludes foreign funds from registering in the U.S., is that a concern to the United States or to U.S. investors?

3.   Note that Regulation S rules for debt securities apply to mutual fund offerings. See 17 C.F.R. §230.903. How does this affect offshore funds? See Chapter 2. Suppose the foreign fund would attract substantial U.S. investor interest, would it have to wait 40 days after its initial offering to permit a U.S. investor to invest? Is this a problem?

c.   MIRROR FUNDS

The SEC recognizes that it may be too burdensome for a foreign mutual fund company to offer the same level of investor protection as a U.S. mutual fund and that it may be impossible for a foreign investment company to restructure its fund so that it complies with U.S. laws and regulations while complying with the laws and regulations in its home country. As an alternative, the SEC has recommended that foreign fund advisers organize mirror funds in the U.S. and then register these mirror funds to offer shares to U.S. investors.[12] A mirror fund is a separate U.S.-organized company that invests in the same foreign securities as does the foreign fund.

---

[11] "Measures by the Government of the U.S. and the Government of Japan Regarding Financial Services" 34 International Legal Materials (1995), p. 617.
[12] See "Applications of Foreign Investment Companies Filed Pursuant to Section 7(d) of the Investment Company Act of 1940," 49 Federal Register (1984), pp. 55-56.

As of March 1992, 269 foreign investment advisers representing 36 countries had registered in the United States under the Investment Advisers Act of 1940.[13] However, it appears that many foreign funds are reluctant to undertake the establishment of mirror funds due to the high additional costs and losses in economies of scale that would result from operating separately from the foreign investment company.

In addition, a mirror fund is generally unable to make representations about the previous history of success that the overseas foreign investment company may have had prior to the mirror fund's organization. However, the SEC has ruled that during the first year of a U.S. mirror fund's organization, the mirror's prospectus may include information about the recent performance of its non-U.S. mirror.[14]

The SEC has approved in Banque Indosuez Luxembourg (BIL) the use of "cloning" technology in connection with mirror funds.[15] Cloning technology is designed to insure that foreign and domestic funds have identical portfolios.

The decision discusses the problem that the two funds will experience different inflows and outflows of capital on any given day, e.g. U.S. investors redeem shares in the U.S. fund, while foreign investors increase their investment in the offshore fund. This is illustrated in Figure 16.1 below. Absent some solution to this problem, the portfolio of stocks in the U.S. fund would have to contract, while the portfolio of the foreign fund would have to expand. This would make it impossible for the two funds to have the same portfolios; indeed if one fund is larger than the other, they cannot have the same portfolios.

---

[13] *Protecting Investors: A Half-Century of Investment Company Regulation*, SEC Staff Report (Extra Edition) Fed. Sec. L. Rep. (CCH) No. 1504 (May 29, 1992), p. 197, n. 38. Many of these advisers are believed to be advising mirror funds.

[14] Growth Stock Outlook Trust, Inc., SEC No-Action Letter (April 15, 1986).

[15] Banque Indosuez Luxembourg, Securities and Exchange Commission, Response of the Office of Chief Counsel, Division of Investment Management, December 10, 1996.

Figure 16.1
Mirror Funds and Rebalancing

Problem: U.S. investors sell U.S. Fund, while foreign investors increase
investment in Foreign Fund

T_1 Opening Positions

U.S. Fund Portfolio			Foreign Fund Portfolio
($1)	50x	50x	($1)
($1)	50y	50y	($1)
($1)	50z	50z	($1)
($150)			$150

U.S. Fund Portfolio: 50% redemptions

Foreign Fund Portfolio: Purchases
increase by 50%

What does it sell?   What does it buy?

One could keep the same proportions of stock in each fund, but this would require significant adjustments in the portfolios of both funds. In our example, the U.S. fund would have to sell a percentage of each of its stocks and the foreign fund would have to increase the percentage of each of its stocks.

The BIL cloning technology tries to reduce the cost of that operation by having the fund with net sales at the end of the day, the foreign fund in our example, buy a "strip" of the portfolio of the U.S. fund. In effect, the foreign fund gives the U.S. fund cash to meet its redemptions and gets a share of the U.S. fund in return. No underlying securities need be bought or sold.

In addition, the cloning technology permits the "bunching" of trades. This might occur when rebalancing won't work because there is a net inflow/outflow of money. Suppose, for example, new investors increase their investment in both the U.S. and foreign funds and the investment advisor decides to buy IBM; the IBM orders for both funds would be bunched.

d.   MASTER/FEEDER FUNDS

Another possible technique for offering the same or similar funds to both U.S. and foreign investors is the master/feeder fund structure. This is a multi-tiered structure, where feeder funds, with substantially identical investment objectives pool their assets by investing in a single portfolio (master fund), as illustrated in Figure 16.2 below.

Figure 16.2

MASTER FEEDER

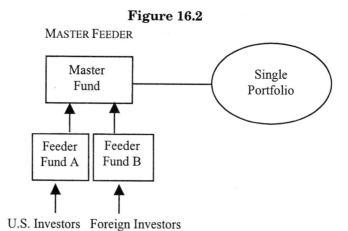

U.S. Investors   Foreign Investors

The Master Feeder achieves an exact duplication between the two funds because each fund owns a share of the Master Fund, and only one portfolio is maintained—by the Master Fund. As a duplication technique this is cheaper and preferable to the mirror/cloning approach. However, the U.S. would require the master/feeder to be registered in the U.S. and comply with all U.S. requirements, which may be more restrictive than those applicable to foreign funds.

Because a master/feeder complex employs a common investment portfolio that must conform with all applicable regulatory requirements, the investment program offered to all investors must comply with the strictest requirement to which any investor is subject. This consequence is sometimes referred to as the "highest common denominator" effect.

For example, a U.S. registered mutual fund is subject to restrictions on its ability to borrow or otherwise leverage its portfolio, and these restrictions have been interpreted by the SEC in a manner that has important implications for the ability of a fund to pursue certain investment strategies. Because of the common investment portfolio, the investment program of all non-U.S. investors would also be subject to this requirement.

The SEC staff has stated that a newly created feeder fund can assume the performance history of its master fund. It is not clear that the SEC staff would take the same position in the context of an international master/feeder complex (e.g. one in which a fund that has compiled a favorable track record in Europe seeks to contribute its assets to a U.S. master fund).[16]

A major obstacle to this structure is that the EU does not permit the master/feeder under UCITS (the directive creating a single market for

---

[16] G. Kenyon, "Globalization of the Mutual Funds Industry–The U.S. Perspective," 29 S&P's Review of Securities and Commodities Regulation (1996), p. 61.

mutual funds). The EU revised UCITS in June 2001,[17] to permit a fund-of-funds structure under which one investment company that sells shares to the public can invest in other funds. This is different than the master/feeder in which two different funds issuing shares to the public (the feeders) invest in one common portfolio (the master). Other jurisdictions also prohibit master/feeders. Even if the EU were to permit master/feeders, they would probably require them to comply with EU requirements. This could raise unresolvable structural conflicts with the U.S. (e.g. U.S. corporate form, EU trust form). The EU reforms also granted mutual funds greater investment powers in money market instruments and derivatives.

Notes and Questions

1.   How would you compare the costs and benefits of using a mirror fund, with cloning technology, to using a master/feeder structure? Which is preferable?

2.   Do the availability of mirror fund and master/feeder funds make it relatively unimportant whether there are regulatory obstacles to foreign funds selling shares to investors in the United States?

e.   CUSTODY OF FOREIGN SECURITIES OF U.S. FUNDS

While this Chapter generally looks at offshore funds, there are also important issues relating to the custody of foreign securities of U.S. funds. Section 17(f) of the Investment Company Act generally permits a U.S. fund to maintain its assets only in custody of a U.S. bank and its foreign branches, a member of a U.S. securities exchange, the fund itself, or a U.S. securities depository, e.g. DTCC. In 1984, the SEC adopted Rule 17f-5 which expanded the foreign custody arrangements available to funds by permitting them to maintain their assets with an "eligible foreign custodian," which included a foreign bank with more than $200 million in equity and a foreign securities depository that operates either the central system for the handling of securities in that country or a transnational system, e.g. Euroclear. The rule, however, imposed detailed obligations on a fund's board of directors with respect to placing assets in a foreign country and the selection of the foreign custodian.

These rules were changed in 1997, effective June 1998.[18] The amendments expanded the class of foreign banks and securities depositories that may serve as custodians of fund assets by eliminating capital requirements that would otherwise block the selection of a suitable custodian without seeking relief from the Commission. The amended rule required

---

[17] Directive 2001/108 (2002), O.J. L41/35; Directive 2001/107 (2002), O.J. L41/20). See D. Rouch and K. Smith, "The UCITS Directive and the Single European Funds Market: A Case Review," Journal of International Banking Law Review 251 (2005).

[18] SEC, "Custody of Investment Company Assets Outside the United States, Final Rule," 62 Federal Register (May 16, 1997), p. 26293.

instead that the selection of a foreign custodian be based on whether the fund's assets will be subject to reasonable care by the custodian, after considering all relevant factors, including the custodian's financial strength, its practices and procedures, and internal controls. The "reasonable care" standard raises a host of questions, probably the most important of which is whether reasonableness should be based on local or U.S. practices.

The amendments also eliminated the requirement that the board consider "prevailing country risks" in choosing a custodian on the grounds that these risks were appropriately considered when investing in a country not when choosing a custodian. Once the decision is made to invest in a country, given that some securities can only be held in custody in the country of the investment, such country risk was unavoidable.

Finally, the amendments permitted fund directors to discharge them responsibility oversight with respect to the custody of fund assets overseas by permitting the board to delegate its duties to select and monitor foreign custodians to others, e.g. a global bank custodian.

In some countries, there is a compulsory depository for local shares. Mutual funds have argued that custodians must make a reasonable care determination for such compulsory depositories as part of their responsibility to assess reasonable care of all depositories. Custodians, on the other hand, have argued that they often do not have sufficient information to do so because the depositories may be government or quasi-government agencies that do not disclose the information needed to make an assessment, and because such a determination is irrelevant since such depositories are compulsory. The custodians argue that the use of compulsory depositories is entailed in the decision of a fund to invest in a particular country. The SEC came down on the side of the funds, but the issue was still controversial.[19] The effective date of the rule was extended to February 1, 1999.

In April 1999, the Commission proposed to further amend Rule 17f-5 and to enact a new Rule 17f-7, as a result of learning that its 1997 rules continued to present problems for the use of foreign securities depositories.[20] Bank custodians refused to accept delegated responsibility to make findings regarding funds' use of most foreign securities depositories. As a result, in May 1998, the Commission suspended the compliance date for many of the 1997 rule changes. Proposed Rule 17f-7 was adopted on April 27, 2000.[21] This Rule eliminates the requirements that certain findings be made by the fund board, its investment adviser or global custodian, and that certain specified terms appear in depository's rules. Instead, the Rule establishes certain standards for foreign securities depositories eligible to be used by funds, and

---

[19] C. Kentouris, "Funds Can Require Custodians to Select Foreign Custodians," *Securities Industry News*, March 9, 1998.
[20] Release No. IC-23815, April 29, 1999.
[21] Release No. IC-24424.

requires the global custodian to furnish a fund with a risk analysis of the foreign depository, through exercising reasonable care. Decisions to maintain assets with a depository are then to be made by the fund and its adviser and not by the custodian.

2.   HEDGE FUNDS

Hedge funds are unregistered mutual funds that engage in a wide variety of speculative activities including derivative and foreign exchange transactions. They are often incorporated outside the U.S. Their sponsors include financial stars like George Soros who some believe can move markets. Based on 2003 estimates, 6,000 to 7,000 hedge funds operate in the United States managing about $600-650 billion in assets. This compared to approximately $5 trillion in public mutual funds in 1999.[22] In 2004, hedge funds had grown to $1.5 trillion.[23] A large part of recent growth have come from fund of hedge funds, discussed below, which are now estimated to constitute 40 percent of invested funds. Returns in 2004, however, were not good—as of September 2004, average returns for the year were 2.75 percent as compared with 11 percent over the past decade.[24]

A key feature of hedge funds is that their advisers can charge unregulated performance based fees to qualified investors, those with a net worth over $1.5 million. This enables hedge funds to attract rocket star advisers who have rivaled investment bankers for fame and wealth. Hedge fund advisers earned $45 billion in 2004, more than their peers in the entire mutual fund industry.[25]

Advisers to publicly registered mutual funds can charge performance based fees but only if the compensation is based on asset value averaged over a specified amount of time and must go down as well as up with the performance of the portfolio.[26] There are a number of registered funds that do pay performance fees. For example, Fidelity and Vanguard use performance fees on a combined 73 funds with $493 billion in assets.[27]

---

[22] Staff Report to the United States Securities and Exchange Commission, *Implications of the Growth of Hedge Funds* (September 2003). (SEC Hedge Fund Report)

[23] T. Buck, "Regulators Step up Hedge Fund Scrutiny Amid Concerns over the Risk of Collapse," *Financial Times*, May 23, 2005.

[24] D. Brewster, "Hedge Funds' Returns Tumble," *Financial Times*, September 16, 2004; P. Skypala, "Hedge Funds of Funds Booming," *Financial Times*, September 26, 2004.

[25] J. Drummon, "Hedge Fund Fees Pull in $45bn, says UBS Study," *Financial Times*, March 23, 2005.

[26] Section 205 of the Investment Advisers Act of 1940. The SEC brought a settled enforcement action against Bridgeway Capital Management in 2004 for its violation of performance based compensation rules for advisers to registered funds, SEC Release 2004-31, September 15, 2004.

[27] K. Damato, "Funds Made Math Mistakes on Fees," *The Wall Street Journal*, April 8, 2005.

a.   THE SECTION 3(C)(1) EXEMPTION

One method hedge funds use to avoid registration is the private fund exemption under §3(c)(1) of the 1940 Act. Originally formulated as part of an SEC No-Action Letter to Touche, Remnant & Co.,[28] §3(c)(1), permits an exemption from §7(d) and the 1940 Act to any issuer of securities, as long as the entity does not offer the shares to the public—there can be no general solicitation—and the shares are beneficially owned by no more than 100 U.S. residents.

For a foreign investment company to comply with the 100 U.S. person beneficial ownership limit of §3(c)(1), before it commences a U.S. offer, it must account for all shareholders of the specific fund. To prevent large groups of investors from investing as one entity for the purpose of circumventing the 100 beneficial owner exemption, the 1940 Act stipulates that for purposes of determination of a fund's number of investors, all investors in an entity formed for the sole purpose of investing in a fund will be counted individually rather than as a single entity.

Due to the restrictive nature of the 100 beneficial owner limit, many foreign investment companies will either refuse to offer their shares in the U.S. under §3(c)(1) or will make it very difficult for U.S. investors to buy shares in their funds. Such actions are taken by foreign investment companies out of fear that one additional U.S. beneficial owner would set them over the limit and cause them to be no longer exempt from the Act. The SEC no-action letter, Investment Funds Institute of Canada, Securities and Exchange Commission, Response of the Office of Chief Counsel, Division of Investment Management, March 4, 1996, considered the question as to whether a foreign fund might violate the 100 beneficial owner limit if some foreign investors, e.g. Canadians, were subsequently to move to the U.S. The SEC opined that it would not.

The SEC reached this conclusion for the following reasons:

"(1) the fund has not publicly offered or sold its securities in the United States;

(2) the fund and its agents or affiliates have not engaged in activities that could reasonably be expected, or are intended, to condition the U.S. market with respect to the fund's securities, such as placing an advertisement in a U.S. publication;

(3) the fund and its agents or affiliates have not engaged in activities that could reasonably be expected, or are intended, to facilitate secondary market trading in the United States with respect to the fund's securities;

---

[28] Touche, Remnant & Co., SEC No-Action Letter, [1984-1985 Transfer Binder] Fed. Sec. L. Rep. (CCH) 77,810, at 79,141 (July 27, 1984).

(4) the fund and its agents or affiliates have not knowingly engaged in a deliberate marketing strategy, adopted directly by the fund's manager or other entity responsible for the business and affairs of the fund, that is calculated to result in the sale of securities to foreign investors who are relocating to the United States;

(5) the 100 U.S. investor limit is exceeded solely because Non-U.S. Holders (i.e. beneficial owners who purchased their securities while residing outside the United States) have relocated to the United States; and

(6) the fund's activities with respect to Non-U.S. Holders are limited to providing the following services: (a) the mailing of securityholder reports, account statements, proxy statements and other materials that are required to be provided by foreign law and the fund's governing documents; (b) the processing of redemption requests and payment of dividends and distributions; (c) the mechanical processing of transfers of ownership; and (d) the issuance of securities pursuant to a dividend reinvestment plan."

b.   THE SECTION 3(c)(7) EXEMPTION

As an alternative to using §3(c)(1), under §3(c)(7) of the Investment Company Act (ICA), added by the National Securities Markets Improvement Act of 1996, funds can offer shares to an unlimited number of "qualified" purchasers, generally those with more than $5 million in investments. Under this alternative, while fund sales are not restricted to 100 U.S. persons, all sales must be made to qualified investors, and the fund must comply with detailed rules to assure that only such investors buy the fund.[29]

Hedge funds usually require high minimum investment amounts and long holding periods which, in addition to the qualified purchaser requirement, tend to limit participation to rich sophisticated investors. There is a concern that such funds may become more available to "retail" investors—albeit still rich ones—if the initial minimum investment requirements imposed by the funds are relaxed. Hedge funds engage in many investment strategies that are forbidden to funds registered with the SEC— they may have concentrated investments, substantial leverage and borrowing, and engage in short-selling.

Some have advocated making hedge funds available to a wider class of investors through relaxing the sophisticated investor requirements. In the last decade some hedge funds have outperformed mutual funds with less volatility therefore making them attractive investments. Why shouldn't such investments be available to all investors? The argument would be that they

---

[29] M. Parry and T. Harman, "The New Qualified Purchaser Fund Rules," 30 Securities & Commodities Regulation (September 24, 1997), p. 195.

are too risky, but even if this is true, should not investors be able to make the risk-reward trade-off for themselves? The SEC has reportedly launched an investigation into whether hedge funds are being marketed to retail investors, and what abuses may have resulted.[30]

Other countries, most notably Singapore and Hong Kong, have made hedge funds available to all investors, subject to much lower minimum investment requirements than imposed by the U.S. But this permission has been accompanied by added disclosure requirements for such funds.

One possible approach in the United States would be to remove the investment restrictions on U.S. registered investment companies that make it impossible for them to sell hedge fund-like investments to the public. U.S. registered funds are greatly restricted in terms of leverage and other features. Section 18(f) of the ICA prohibits the mutual fund from issuing securities to shareholders, requires that all bank borrowings be covered by assets worth 300 percent of the debt, prohibits making investments in illiquid securities (limited to 15 percent of net assets), and limits non-diversification. These are practices that many hedge funds follow. In addition, tax rules only exempt registered funds from tax at the fund level that are diversified. Relaxation of these restrictions would open up hedge funds to all investors, but in the context of the disclosure and other protections of the 1940 Investment Company Act.

Another development is the use of fund-of-funds hedge funds. One fund-of-funds could own several hedge funds. Initial investment in funds-of-funds are much lower than in the hedge funds themselves; some funds only require minimums of $25,000. A fund-of-funds hedge fund that registers under the 1933 and 1940 Acts can be sold to any investor, permitting retail investors to participate indirectly in hedge funds. While some funds-of-funds have so registered, none has apparently been offered to other than investors worth less than $1.5 million—because doing so would subject the fund-of-funds to the prohibition, under §205 of the Investment Advisers Act of 1940, of charging a performance based fee. Hedge fund managers generally charge a fixed fee, plus a performance fee, a practice prohibited for registered funds. Even if the manager of the fund-of-funds did not charge such a fee, it would have to pass on to investors the performance fee of the underlying funds.[31]

Currently, hedge funds are prevented by U.S. laws from advertising, on the theory that only institutional or wealthy investors can invest in the funds. The Managed Funds Association, which represents U.S. hedge funds, has proposed that hedge funds be able to place "tombstone" ads, which would give the basic facts about the fund including that only accredited investors

---

[30] *Financial Times*, March 26, 2003.

[31] See D. Lacey, "Democratizing the Hedge Fund: Considering the Advent of Retail Hedge Funds," International Finance Seminar, Harvard Law School (April 2003), p. 60; see also W. Donaldson, Testimony Concerning Investor Protection Implications of Hedge Funds, Before the U.S. Senate Committee on Banking, Housing and Urban Affairs, April 10, 2003.

can invest. The Investment Company Institute that represents public mutual funds objects, claiming advertising bans are necessary to protect the average investor.[32]

As part of its new policies for the offer of securities over the Internet,[33] the SEC adopted rules for the offer of mutual funds over the Internet which closely parallel the rules for securities. General precautionary measures are required for foreign funds making offers targeted exclusively offshore, while offshore offers by U.S. funds will be required to use more specific precautions like passwords. A foreign fund which is simultaneously making an Internet offshore public offer and a U.S. private offer must include in its general precautionary measures a disclaimer that reflects the existence of the two separate offers and indicates that the Internet offer is not being made in the United States.

Offshore hedge funds that do not sell to U.S. investors in the U.S. are not subject to U.S. regulation, i.e. restrictions on qualifying investors. Hedge funds in many countries have much more lenient requirements. In Germany, for example, hedge funds are open to almost any investor, although such funds are subject to portfolio restrictions, like risk diversification, which many U.S. hedge funds could not meet.[34] The Germans hope to kick start their financial markets by making hedge funds more accessible. However, hedge funds have not attracted substantial investment. Moreover, they became controversial in 2005 when they scuttled Deutsche Börse's bid for the London Stock Exchange (see Chapter 13) and when a small broker specializing in hedge funds was discovered to have cheated investors out of $1.06 billion. The head of the Chancellor Schröder's party called hedge funds "locusts" for picking off vulnerable German businesses, and the government called for a review of how hedge funds were regulated.[35]

c.   THE LONG-TERM CAPITAL MANAGEMENT DEBACLE AND REGULATION OF HEDGE FUNDS

Long-Term Capital Management, LP (LTCM) was an extremely successful hedge fund created in 1994 which by August 1998 had levered around $4.8 billion in capital into more than $125 billion in assets and several times more of off-balance sheet positions. LTCM was a Delaware limited partnership but the fund that it operated, Long-Term Capital Portfolio, L.P. (the Fund), was a Caymans Island partnership that provided a number of different funds.

---

[32] A. Beard, "Hedge Funds Call on SEC to Lift Long-time Advertising Ban," *Financial Times*, April 11, 2001.

[33] SEC Release No. 33-7516, 34-39779, March 23, 1998, see Chapter 2.

[34] A. Pütz and C. Schmies, "Hedge Fund Regulation in Germany," J. of International Banking Law and Regulation 177 (2004).

[35] H. Williamson, R. Milne, and P. Jenkins, "Schröder Calls for Review of Hedge Funds," *Financial Times*, May 14, 2005.

LTCM made very few disclosures to investors about their investment strategies, justifying such silence on proprietary grounds. The lack of disclosure did not seem to matter to the very large and sophisticated investors, as money poured in.

LTCM's balance sheet leverage ratio of 25 to 1 compared with the average leverage ratio of 2 to 1 for all hedge funds. The fund's returns were over 40 percent in both 1995 and 1996, far in excess of the average return of about 17 percent of all hedge funds in these years. LTCM engaged in a huge number of trades on its books, 60,000 as of August 1998. It held positions of over $50 billion in long and short securities, and had futures contracts of over $500 billion, swaps contracts of more than $750 billion, and options and other OTC derivatives of over $150 billion.[36] The fund was run by John Meriwether, a legendary bond trader at Salomon, who had resigned from Salomon after the firm disclosed a series of improper bids at U.S. Treasury note auctions. Meriwether worked closely with a cast of finance stars, including David Mullins Jr., a former Harvard Business Professor and Vice Chairman of the Federal Reserve Board, and two Nobel Prize winners, Robert Merton of the Harvard Business School and Myron Scholes of Black-Scholes model fame. In October 1998, it came to light that LTCM had lost more than 90 percent of its capital and had been bailed out, with an infusion of $3.6 billion in exchange for 90 percent of the equity, by a consortium of 14 Wall Street banks who were both lenders to and counterparties of LTCM, and had huge exposures. For example, Chase acknowledged a $3.2 billion exposure, which amounted to 13 percent of its tangible equity, albeit mostly collateralized.[37]

LTCM engaged primarily in convergence and relative value trades. "For example, recently issued (so-called on-the-run) U.S. Treasury bonds typically traded at slightly lower yields (higher prices) than comparable maturity but older (so-called off-the-run) Treasury bonds. If the spread were sufficiently wide, LTCM might purchase the off-the-run bond, and sell short the lower-yielding on-the-run bond. With attractive financing rates, this position would make money if held to maturity. The position also stood to make significant profits if the yield spread, and hence the value differential narrowed."[38] LTCM would stand to lose, however, if spreads widened. LTCM also lost on equity bets on takeovers, so-called takeover arbitrage. Its problems were compounded because it had taken inadequate or illiquid collateral as security for many of its positions.

---

[36] Report of The President's Working Group on Financial Markets, Hedge Funds, Leverage, and the Lessons of Long-Term Capital Management (April 1999), pp. 11-12. (Hedge Fund Report)

[37] *ibid.* See also "How the Salesmanship and Brainpower Failed at Long-Term Capital," *The Wall Street Journal*, November 16, 1998; "Collateral Damage," *Euromoney* (November 1998).

[38] Harvard Business School, Long-Term Capital Management, L.P. (A), Case N9-200-007 (October 27, 1999). This case contains an excellent analysis of LTCM's various trades.

The bailout of LTCM was engineered by the New York Federal Reserve Bank and the U.S. Treasury.[39] Although no public money was put into the deal, many believe that there was significant "jawboning" by bank regulators to force their regulated banks to bail LTCM out.

McDonough in his congressional testimony gave the following justification for governmental participation:

> "There are several ways that the problems of Long-Term Capital could have been transmitted to cause more widespread financial troubles. Had Long-Term Capital been suddenly put into default, its counterparties would have immediately "closed-out" their positions. If counterparties would have been able to close-out their positions at existing market prices, losses, if any, would have been minimal. However, if many firms had rushed to close-out hundreds of billions of dollars in transactions simultaneously, they would have been unable to liquidate collateral or establish offsetting positions at the previously-existing prices. Markets would have moved sharply and losses would have been exaggerated. Several billion dollars of losses might have been experienced by some of Long-Term Capital's more than 75 counterparties.
>
> These direct effects on Long-Term Capital's counterparties were not our principal concern. While these losses would have been considerable, and would certainly have adversely affected the firms experiencing them, this was not, in itself, a sufficient reason for us to become involved.
>
> Two factors influenced our involvement. First, in the rush of Long-Term Capital's counterparties to close-out their positions, other market participants—investors who had no dealings with Long-Term Capital—would have been affected as well. Second, as losses spread to other market participants and Long-Term Capital's counterparties, this would lead to tremendous uncertainty about how far prices would move. Under these circumstances, there was a likelihood that a number of credit and interest rate markets would experience extreme price moves and possibly cease to function for a period of one or more days and maybe longer. This would have caused a vicious cycle: a loss of investor confidence, leading to a rush out of private credits, leading to a further widening of credit spreads, leading to further liquidations of positions, and so on. Most importantly, this would have led to further increases in the cost of capital to American businesses."

McDonough talks about the fear of a collapse in financial markets; interestingly this issue was downplayed in the President's Working Groups'

---

[39] William J. McDonough, Statement before the Committee on Banking and Financial Services, U.S. House of Representatives, October 1, 1998.

Hedge Fund Report,[40] which talked about potentially sizeable losses for LTCM counterparties—major financial firms—amounting to between $300 and $500 million. There is no assertion that markets would have seized up or that any of these losses would have bankrupted counterparties.

F. Edwards[41] offers the following possible justifications for Fed intervention. First, the financial markets were fragile following the Russian debt default in August. Investors were demanding huge premia for all emerging market securities. A bankruptcy of LTCM could have led to a liquidation of its derivatives portfolio, with potential large losses for its counterparties who were in the money. Since under U.S. bankruptcy law, as well as the laws of other major countries, such liquidations would not be prevented by the automatic stay there would be a rush of creditors to liquidate. "As they all ran for the door, very few could get through before prices collapsed—especially since LTCM's positions constituted a sizeable portion of the total outstandings in some assets."[42] Edwards calls this a "funnel effect." Second, there could be a "knock-on" effect as other financial institutions with positions similar to LTCM suffered losses. Third, there could be a "chain reaction" since losses could result in bankruptcies which could cause further losses and bankruptcies to counterparties, including major banks and securities firms. However, if the chain reaction effect was a serious concern, one could avoid rescuing LTCM and provide liquidity to banks and securities firms experiencing difficulties.

C. Furfine[43] has found that the federal funds markets did not restrict credit to the nine major creditors of LTCM in the period preceding its rescue. The evidence, he argues, suggests that the market never believed that these institutions had a significant probability of default, thus raising significant doubt as to whether there was really a systemic risk problem. Furfine further found that large banking organizations started paying lower interest rates after the resolution of the LTCM crisis. This could be because the market viewed these institutions as safer because they avoided the LTCM problem or because the Fed's action was perceived as an extension of the too-big-to-fail policy. A 2005 study based on 2004 data finds that hedge fund strategies have become more risky, in terms of more leverage and risk concentration and speculates this may increase systemic risk. The study, however, fails to demonstrate any real empirical link between increased risks taken by hedge funds and increased risk to the rest of the financial system from their potential failure.[44]

---

[40] Supra note 36.

[41] "Hedge Funds and the Collapse of Long-Term Capital Management" 13 Journal of Economic Perspectives (1999), p. 189.

[42] Id., at 202.

[43] "The Costs and Benefits of Moral Suasion Evidence from the Rescue of Long-term Capital Management," Federal Reserve Bank of Chicago Working Paper (2002).

[44] N. Chan, M. Getmansky, S. Haas, and A. Lo, "Systemic Risk and Hedge Funds," NBER Working Paper 11200 (March 2005).

Hedge funds generally rebounded in the fourth quarter of 1998, after the LTCM rescue, producing average net returns of nearly 10 percent. Indeed, it is estimated that American hedge funds made average returns in 11.7 percent in 1998 as a whole. LTCM itself was reportedly up 12 percent through April 1999. However, in 2000 many of the largest hedge funds, like those of George Soros, announced their withdrawal from "large-scale and aggressive" hedge fund investing, due to significant losses, 21 percent for the $8.24 billion Quantum Fund and 32 percent for the $1.2 billion Quota Fund, as of April 2000.[45]

Should regulation be enacted forcing hedge funds to make material disclosures to investors? How about to bank investors? The Basel Committee on Banking Supervision has suggested strengthening bank management of risks to highly leveraged institutions (HLIs), in a report entitled *Banks' Interactions with Highly Leveraged Institutions* (January 1999). This was followed by a second report, *Banks' Interactions with Highly Leveraged Institutions: Implementation of the Basel Committee's Sound Practices Paper* (January 2000). Adequate risk management by banks might fully address the issues raised by LTCM. In late November 2004, Tim Geithner, the President of the Federal Reserve Bank of New York, expressed concern that banks were again lowering credit standards to loan to hedge funds.[46]

The Hedge Fund Report stressed that potential losses to counterparties were limited as a result of closeout (right to terminate), netting and collateral provisions. The Report raised the issue as to what would have happened if LTCM had gone bankrupt under Cayman law. Had that been the case, a foreign receiver could have sought to enjoin actions of U.S. creditors to liquidate collateral with potential detrimental consequences to such creditors. The Report recommended an amendment to the Bankruptcy Code to prevent such a possibility in the future.[47] This problem appears to have been resolved by the 2005 amendments to the Bankruptcy Code.[48]

The SEC's 2003 Hedge Fund Report[49] recommended that hedge fund advisers register under the Investment Advisers Act (which has no been required, see below) but rejected any other new regulation. In fact the SEC staff recommended considering lifting the prohibition on general solicitation or advertising of investors for 3(c)(7) funds, those reserved for sophisticated investors.

---

[45] W. Lewis and J. Chaffin, "Soros to Curtail Hedge Fund Activity after Fall in Returns," *Financial Times*, April 29/30, 2000. The Basel Committee on Banking Supervision and IOSCO, *Review of Issues relating to HLIs*, March 2001, found that leverage of hedge funds had been significantly reduced by 2001.

[46] J. Drummond, "Banks Fend Off U.D. Accusations on Hedge Funds," *Financial Times*, November 19, 2004.

[47] Hedge Fund Report, supra note 36, pp. 27-28.

[48] Public Law 109-8, April 20, 2005, §907.

[49] SEC Hedge Fund report, supra note 22.

Some like Mahathir Mohamad, the ex-Prime Minister of Malaysia, have blamed hedge funds, and in particular George Soros, for destabilizing exchange rates and playing a major role in causing the Asian financial crisis. However, this seems highly unlikely given that the major source of capital outflow was attributed to the failure of foreign banks to renew short-term loans to Asian banks, and that hedge funds are small compared to other portfolio investors. Whereas pension funds, mutual funds and insurance companies hold about $25 trillion in assets worldwide, hedge funds control at most about $600 billion by 2003 counts. As a related matter, mutual funds in general and particularly hedge funds have been accused of worsening financial crises by pulling money out of countries at the first sign of distress. A study by E. Borensztein and R. Geloo[50] found that funds do make substantial withdrawals, and tend to do so one month before a crisis. Contrary to some pundits, these funds do not shun all emerging markets when some go bad; the funds withdrawing from Russia in 1998 invested in Latin America even though Latin America was seen by some as suffering from contagion.[51]

A study of offshore funds (funds in tax havens) found that such funds do trade more frequently in Korean securities than onshore funds (those in major markets like the U.S.) but engage less in momentum trading. More importantly, they engage in less herding in a financial crisis than do onshore funds. The authors conclude that it is inappropriate, therefore, to focus on offshore funds as a source of instability.[52] Most studies, however, of instability created by funds, focus on all foreign funds (both onshore and offshore), and particularly hedge funds.

In 2005, there were increased concerns about hedge funds, particularly as it concerned their derivative positions, a matter we looked at in Chapter 15. Various regulators indicated they were keeping a watchful eye on hedge funds, including the SEC and Federal Reserve Board. Regulators urged banks, in particular to review and more tightly manage their exposure to these funds. Following LTCM, an industry group was created to evaluate the effects of the crisis. This group was reactivated in by the New York Federal Reserve Bank in 2004, under the unwieldy title of "Counterparty Risk Management Policy Group II," and the Chairmanship of Gerald Corrigan, a Goldman Sachs Managing Director and former President of the New York Fed, to once again review the issue of hedge fund risks. It is anticipated that it will make recommendations in the summer of 2005.

---

[50] "A Panic Prone Pack? The Behavior of Emerging Market Mutual Funds," IMF Working Paper 00/198, December 2000.

[51] Id., at 11.

[52] W. Kim and S.J. Wei, "Offshore Investment Funds: Monsters in Emerging Markets," 68 J. of Development Economics (2002), pp. 205-224.

Notes and Questions

1. Should the SEC permit indirect retail investment in hedge funds through funds-of-funds? Should the U.S. relax restrictions that prohibit public mutual funds from engaging in hedge fund strategy and management fee practices? Will current restrictions make offshore funds more attractive to U.S. investors?[53]

2. With respect to LTCM, what was the role of the New York Federal Reserve Bank? Was it merely a fact-finder and meeting convener? What justified their involvement?

3. Should regulation be enacted forcing hedge funds to make material disclosures to investors? How about to bank investors? Should regulation limit hedge fund leverage ratios, and if so how? Should hedge funds or their advisors be required to register?

d.   THE INVESTMENT ADVISORS ACT OF 1940 AND REGISTRATION REQUIREMENTS

An offshore mutual fund contemplating selling its shares in the U.S. must also consider the restrictions imposed by the Investment Advisers Act of 1940 (Investment Advisers Act). Under the Investment Advisers Act, regardless of the fund involved, any person, whether a foreign or U.S. citizen, who advises 15 or more U.S. clients, or solicits the advisory business of U.S. citizens, or advises any SEC-registered fund, must register with the SEC. Aside from its registration requirements, the Investment Advisers Act imposes limitations on the methods of investment service provision. Among these restrictions are: limitations on performance fees (for unqualified investors), advertising and affiliate-related transaction limitations, client asset segregation, and the imposition of general fiduciary obligations to clients.

Hedge funds had been exempted from registration because the SEC considered each fund that was advised as a separate client. On December 2, 2004, the SEC adopted a rule by a 3-2 vote requiring any adviser to register who advises 15 or more individuals, looking through the funds to the real investors, effectively mandating the registration of must hedge fund advisers.[54] There was a lot of opposition to this proposal including that of Federal Reserve Board Chairman Alan Greenspan. An adviser with no more than $25 million under management is exempt. The SEC justified its action based on a concern with increasing hedge fund fraud and the increasing "retailization" of hedge fund investments through the fund of funds vehicle previously discussed.

---

[53] See William H. Donaldson, Testimony Concerning Investor Protection Implications of Hedge Funds before the U.S. Senate Committee on Banking, Housing and Urban Affairs, April 10, 2003.

[54] SEC Release IA-2333, 69 Federal Register 72054 (December 10, 2004).

The measure also effectively raises the minimum net worth of an investor in a unregistered hedge fund to $1.5 from $1 million because registered advisers must have only "qualified" clients as opposed to "accredited" clients as required under Regulation D in order to charge performance fees. Advisers to private equity or venture capital funds, which unlike hedge funds do not permit clients to redeem funds for two years, are exempt. Most of the provisions of the new regulation are not effective until February 1, 2006.

To register as an investment adviser with the SEC, an individual must file the registration form (FORM ADV), which requires the listing of owners, prior securities convictions and injunctions, and the distribution of a brochure on business operations for the examination of prospective clients. The Investment Advisers Act also mandates the annual filing of a balance sheet and detailed record-keeping, both personal and fund-related. While the Investment Advisers Act imposes no qualification or examination requirements of its own, very often prospective U.S. advisers must register in each state in which they do business and comply with each of these respective states' own qualification or examination requirements.

The new requirements have special provisions for an offshore adviser, an adviser whose principal office and place of business is outside the U.S. An offshore adviser must only count U.S. citizens in determining whether he has more than 14 clients—so an adviser with foreign clients and less than 15 U.S. clients does not have to register. The SEC has established rules for determining what is a U.S. investor. This is determined by residence, which in the case of a business is the place of the principal office and place of business, and special rules are established for trusts. It remains to be seen whether U.S. residents could establish offshore vehicles to escape being considered U.S. residents.

If an offshore adviser advises only foreign offshore funds, and becomes subject to the registration requirement because of the "look through" rule, the offshore adviser will only be subject to the record keeping and anti-fraud provisions of the Investment Advisers Act. However, the SEC would have the authority to examine such an adviser.[55]

The SEC claimed that the cost of compliance with its new rule would be only $50,000 per year but some put the cost much higher, a particular burden for smaller hedge funds with a few partners and limited staff. [56]

The Shadow Financial Regulatory Committee has questioned the SEC's justification for hedge fund registration.[57] It noted that most of the fraud cases it referred to involved small funds that would not be subject to

---

[55] E. Laurenson, "The Impact of The SEC's New Hedge Fund Registration Rules on Offshore Fund Managers and Investment Advisers," 11 World Securities Law Report 25, January 1, 2005.
[56] C. Kentouris, "The Cost to Comply," *Securities Industry News*, December 6, 2004.
[57] Statement No. 210 on the SEC's Proposal for Regulating Hedge Funds, September 20, 2004.

registration or firms that were already subject to registration.[58] It is also unclear how registration will combat retailization, given the minimal effect of raising the required investor net worth from $1 to $1.5 million. If the SEC is concerned with the fund of funds problem it could require that such funds invest only in registered funds.

In my view, the real objective of the Commission is to get authority to examine and control hedge funds in the event that a major problem arose in the industry—perhaps there is still a concern about the systemic impact of another LTCM. However, it is hard to see what after the fact examination of such funds could do to avoid or deal with such a crisis.

3. TRADING VIOLATIONS

In September 2003, New York Attorney General Eliot Spitzer charged that a fund managed by BankAmerica had allowed Canary Capital Partners, a New Jersey hedge fund, to trade in its fund after the markets had closed at the closing price that day, so-called "late trading." This constituted a violation of Investment Company Act Rule 22c-1a, which mandates that the price of funds must be forward-looking. Thus, funds traded on Day 1, after the 4:00 p.m. closing price has been set, should trade at the 4:00 p.m. closing price on Day 2.

Spitzer has also charged that several other funds, BancOne, Janus and Strong, allowed Canary to jump in and out of their mutual funds to make a fast profit, a practice known as "market timing." Here "timers" would invest on Day 1 at the Day 1 4:00 p.m. net asset value (NAV) before the market close and sell the next day at the Day 2 4:00 p.m. NAV. Market timing is not illegal per se but may violate the Investment Company Act if such practices are stated to be prohibited or discouraged by a fund's prospectus, and such policies are not applied to select investors or the fund's own employees.

Following Spitzer's charges, the SEC and the Putnam Fund agreed to a preliminary settlement of Putnam's improper market timing trading by its own portfolio managers. Putnam's very survival was at stake, as it lost over $21 billion in investments after its practices came to light. On April 8, 2004, the SEC settled with Putnam for $55 million.[59] Massachusetts imposed another $110 million in penalties, including $25 million in restitution, which was later increased by $83.5 million, following an expert report on damages, discussed below. In December 2003, Spitzer charged Invesco with violating its publicly disclosed market timing policies, seeking to recover the $160.8

---

[58] For example, the SEC shut down a Palm Beach hedge fund in March 2005 for a $1 million fraud, and the adviser to that fund had already been registered. The SEC claimed that its speedy action showed the virtues of registration, allowing it immediate access to the funds records—on the other hand the case does not demonstrate the need to require all advisers to register. SEC Release No. 2005-27, March 3, 2005.

[59] SEC Release 2004-49, April 8, 2004.

million management fees allegedly earned by permitting the practice.[60] In March 2004, Bank of America and FleetBoston Financial settled with the SEC and Spitzer for $675 million.[61] It also appears that some of the market timing has been done by hedge funds—it remains to be seen whether these or other timers will be charged with offenses. In addition, as part of the aiding and abetting approach discussed in Chapter 2, banks that financed market timers may also face liability.[62]

How do these practices hurt fund investors? Let us first take "late trading." Suppose that on Day 1 after the U.S. market closes at 4:00 p.m., at a NAV of 10, a significant piece of unanticipated good news occurs, e.g. higher than expected GNP or the arrest of the ten leading terrorists in the world. Suppose further that the fair market NAV of the fund, based on this news, is $12 at 5:00 p.m., when the fund permits a "late trader" to buy in at the 4:00 p.m. $10 NAV price. This permits the late trader to capture part of the $2 gain of the existing shareholders. Of course this gain is hypothetical since the next price at which the existing shareholders (including the late trader) can sell their shares is at the 4:00 p.m. NAV on Day 2. By this time other subsequent negative news could have eliminated the gain. However, the late trader has taken less risk than the other shareholders—he has a shorter time horizon.[63]

How about market timing? Here all investors are on equal footing— they all have the opportunity to time the market. While existing shareholders may be diluted as a result of new shareholders trading on new information, existing shareholders could also increase their purchases. Modeling of the actual extent of dilution is quite complicated.[64] An expert in the Putnam case calculated the damages as $100 million, $75 million more than Putnam agreed to in restitution, but about half of this damage was due not to dilution but the cost to shareholders from the massive withdrawals from Putnam after the scandal was disclosed—the transaction costs incurred to sell the shares to fund the withdrawals.[65]

One factor to consider in assessing the actual amount of loss would be the amount and disposition of fees charged by funds to late traders. If the

---

[60] T. Lauricella and S. Pulliam, "Invesco Charged in Scandal as Strong Out," *The Wall Street Journal*, December 3, 2003.

[61] D. Wells, "BofA and Fleet Boston face $675m Penalties," *Financial Times*, March 16, 2004.

[62] T. Lauricella, "SEC Probes JPMorgan Role in Canary's Improper Trades," *The Wall Street Journal*, December 30, 2004.

[63] A further complicating factor is whether the money received by the late trader is actually invested immediately. To the extent that it is not—which may often be the case—the potential dilution could increase. The inability to invest funds immediately could also cause dilution in cases of market timing, e.g. where funds received at 3:30 pm could not be immediately invested in the types of assets the funds hold.

[64] J. Greene and C. Ciccotello, "Mutual Fund Dilution from Market Timing Trades," Draft (September 27, 2004).

[65] J. Hechinger, "Putnam May Owe $100 million," *The Wall Street Journal,* February 2, 2005.

fees were calibrated to approximate the advantage to late traders, and if the benefit to the management company collecting the fees were passed on to fund shareholders in reduced charges, the potential losses to shareholders would be offset by the value of reduced fees. To what extent either of these possibilities actually occurred is a matter of fact.

In December 2003, the SEC proposed a "hard" trade close rule for investment companies.[66] The proposal provides that an order to purchase or redeem fund shares at the current day's NAV must be received by the time that the fund establishes for calculating NAV. In its proposal, the SEC indicated concern with the fact that some investors in order to avoid the existing prohibition against late trading placed orders before 4:00 p.m. but would only execute them if favorable news occurred after that time. The "hard" trade close rule would prevent the processing of any orders after 4:00 p.m., even if the order had been placed before 4:00 p.m. This could place increased burdens on fund processing, so that funds would have to establish a cut-off time before 4:00 p.m. for the receipt of orders. This in turn would increase the time that shareholders are locked into a fund investment. The problem would be even more severe for holders of 401(k)s who might have to submit orders as early as 9:00 a.m. to allow their employers or providers to meet the new SEC-mandated mutual fund cut-offs. Industry reaction to the "hard" 4:00 p.m. close has been very negative. Reportedly, the SEC is currently evaluating various systems that would ensure all trades are in by 4:00 p.m. even if they are processed later.[67]

The Commission also proposed in March 2004 that mutual funds impose a 2 percent redemption fee on the redemption of shares purchased within the previous 5 days.[68] However, the final rule adopted in 2005 did not require such a fee.[69] The Commission was concerned that such a fee, while it would discourage market timing, would also apply to "harmless" transactions. Instead, redemption fee policies were left to individual funds. The Commission's rule does require funds to enforce such policies. It also required funds to obtain more information from its shareholders, including those holding accounts for other parties, about their use of market timing so that the fund's policies can be better enforced.

In April 2004, the SEC adopted a rule[70] requiring added mutual fund disclosure of market timing practices. The Commission's rule requires a mutual fund to describe in its prospectus the risks, if any, that frequent

[66] SEC, Proposed Rule: Amendment to Rules Governing Pricing of Mutual Funds Shares, Release No. IC-26288 (December 11, 2003).
[67] J. Hintze, "Early Returns Are in on Late Trading Plans," *Securities Industry News*, May 3, 2004.
[68] SEC, Proposed Rule on Mandatory Redemption Fees for Redeemable Fund Securities, Release No. IC-26375A, March 5, 2004.
[69] SEC Final Rule, Mutual Fund Redemption Fees, Release No. IC-26782, March 11, 2005.
[70] SEC, Final Rule, Disclosure Regarding Market Timing and Selective Disclosure of Portfolio Holdings, Release Nos. 33-8408; IC-26418, April 16, 2004.

purchases and redemptions of fund shares may present to other shareholders. It also requires a fund to disclose Board policies with respect to market timing and measures, if any, taken to prevent or permit them.

One other answer to the late trading problem may lie in investing in exchange-trade funds (ETFs), such as those traded on the American Stock Exchange. There were 304 ETFs in 2004 in the U.S. with about $178 billion in assets under management—with $55 billion in ETFs in Europe and Japan.[71] ETFs are index funds that can be traded intraday. Investors can buy or sell shares in the collective performance of an entire stock or bond portfolio as a single security. Since prices are set continually, ETFs avoid the one-day lag in pricing of mutual funds that facilitates late trading. Exchanges are currently considering listing ETFs for actively managed portfolios, where the alleged abuses of mutual funds have occurred.

Another possibility would be so-called fair value pricing of a portfolio, even if some securities in the portfolio are not really being traded. Thus if positive information occurred with respect to securities after the market closed, the securities could be "fair" valued. The SEC has apparently told mutual funds to set fair values for shares when a "significant event" happens after exchanges close, but the definition of a significant event is open to question, as is the methodology of fair valuation.[72]

An alternative proposal comes from the Shadow Financial Regulatory Committee (SFRC) which would require mutual funds to price all transactions at the next day NAV, so called T+1 pricing. Thus, if an investor purchased shares at 9:00 a.m. or 5:00 p.m. on Day 1, the price would be the NAV at 4:00 p.m. on Day 2. This would cut down on the advantages from late trading or market timing. As the SFRC itself points out, however, investors would incur an additional amount of price uncertainty (and risk), and would lose one day of liquidity.

All of these trading violation problems concern U.S. mutual funds, which, as we shall see below, are not, for tax reasons, usually invested in by foreign shareholders. We shall also see that U.S. shareholders, also for tax reasons, do not generally invest in foreign funds. This is important for two reasons in this context. First, foreign investors have not suffered as a result of the alleged abuses. Secondly, the competition from foreign funds for U.S. investors, which might have constrained some of these practices, does not exist. It remains to be seen whether foreign funds engaged in similar late trading and market timing practices as did U.S. funds.

---

[71] D. Fuhr, "Summary of Exchange-Traded Funds Around the World at the End of the First Half of 2004," Fall 2004.

[72] M. McSherry, "Lifting the Lid: Fair Value Pricing not a Cure-all," *Reuters*, November 6, 2003.

4.   OTHER ISSUES

Following the scandals on trading violations, other issues concerning public mutual fund operations have been the focus of attention.

First, there is the use of "soft dollars" which refers to the practice of mutual funds paying brokers higher brokerage commissions than are justified by the cost of executing securities trades in order to obtain other services like research. A U.S. mutual fund can execute trades in most domestic stocks for 0.5 cents a share using electronic agency brokerage systems but choose to do their trades at about 5 cents per share to obtain research and other services from the brokers.[73]

Section 28(e) of the Securities Exchange Act, enacted in 1975 shortly after the SEC banned fixed commission rates, protects an investment adviser from claims of breach of fiduciary duty based on clients paying more than the lowest available commission rates. The SEC estimates the amount of soft fees to be around $1 billion. The primary driver of this practice is that the cost of brokerage commissions is not counted in determining a fund's expense ratio, an important ratio many investors use in determining whether to invest in a fund. Expenses include all direct fees paid, including fees for research and to compensate brokers for marketing or distributing funds. They do not include brokerage fees, however. If research and distribution are paid for through higher brokerage fees, the recorded expenses that would otherwise be incurred for these services are avoided, and the expense ratio is improved. If, for example, one took the Van Eck: International Gold Fund A, its reported expense ratio was 1.965 percent. If, however, one includes brokerage commissions (which includes extra services), that ratio rises to 5.817 percent. There is a much smaller discrepancy for many other funds.[74]

A NASD Task Force has concluded that purchases of research through excess brokerage fees should not be prohibited since otherwise less independent research for buy-side firms would be available. The Task Force did recommend, however, that there be additional disclosure about such arrangements and that the use of soft dollars be restricted to types of services like research that benefit funds rather than advisers, such as the provision of computer services or portfolio accounting services.[75] It appears that an SEC Task Force will reach similar conclusions.[76] A 2004 study finds that funds using soft dollars to obtain research have higher risk-adjusted performance than funds that do not engage in the practice, suggesting that the value of

---

[73] B. Steill, "Get Tough on Soft Commissions," *Financial Times*, December 21, 2004.

[74] J. Heckinger, "Deciphering Funds' Hidden Costs," *The Wall Street Journal*, March 17, 2004.

[75] NASD, Report of the Mutual Fund Task Force, Soft Dollars and Portfolio Transaction Costs, November 11, 2004.

[76] A. Parker, "Soft-Dollar Fees Look Set to Stay," *Financial Times*, February 22, 2005.

excess commissions is being captured by funds rather than advisers.[77] The SEC is separately looking at the practice of brokerage firms rebating cash to advisers on trades paid in soft dollars, and whether advisers have used the cash to pay for research or other services that only benefit the advisers.[78] While there have been no prohibitions on the use of soft dollars through brokerage commissions to pay for research, the use of soft dollars for this purpose has significantly declined, partly as a result of the regulatory cloud overhanging its use.

The SEC has limited the ability of funds to pay for their distribution (as compared with research) through high brokerage commissions. The SEC settled an enforcement action in March 2004 against the Massachusetts Financial Services Company (MFS) for failing to disclose the specifics of its distribution ("shelf space") arrangement with brokerage firms,[79] and has adopted an amendment to Rule 12b-1 and the 1940 Act that prohibits funds from paying for the distribution of their shares with brokerage commissions.[80] The justification for the prohibition is based on asserted conflicts of interest. According to the SEC, more distribution can increase fund sales and lead to higher compensation for fund advisers but not necessarily increased benefits for the shareholders of the funds that pay the brokerage commissions. The SEC also claims that the use of soft dollars for distribution may disadvantage less actively traded funds that pay less brokerage fees.

In addition, the SEC has adopted a rule requiring more simple presentation of disclosures on fund expenses and portfolio holdings.[81] In addition, a 2005 NASD Task Force, has proposed that the SEC require funds to make available to investors a short and easy to understand document that describes how fund shareholders pay for distribution through loads or fees charged to investors.[82] And Spitzer has pressed funds to lower their overall fees. Alliance Capital agreed to cut its management fees by an average of 20

---

[77] S. Horan and D. Johnson, "Does Soft Dollar Brokerage Benefit Portfolio Investors: Agency Problem or Solution," George Mason University School of Law Working Paper 04-50 (March 2004).

[78] S. Pulliam and G. Zuckerman, "SEC Examines Rebates Paid to Large Funds," *The Wall Street Journal*, January 6, 2005.

[79] SEC Release 2004-44, March 31, 2004.

[80] SEC, Final Rule: Prohibition of the Use of Brokerage Commissions to Finance Distribution, Release No. IC-26591, 69 Federal Register 54728, September 9, 2004. See also In the Matter of Putnam Investment, LLC, SEC IC Release No. 2370, March 23, 2005, where the SEC brought a cease and desist order against Putnam for its direction of brokerage for distribution prior to 2004. The SEC was investigating in 2005 an arrangement under which the manager of American Funds directed brokerage to one firm that shared the commissions with another brokerage firm that sold American Funds.

[81] SEC, Final Rule: Shareholder Reports and Quarterly Portfolio Disclosures of Registered Management Investment Companies, Release No. 33-8393, February 27, 2004.

[82] NASD, Report of the Mutual Fund Task Force: Mutual Fund Distribution, April 4, 2005.

percent for the next five years as part of its settlement with Spitzer over improper trading charges.[83]

The third major area of SEC intervention is in the governance of public mutual funds. In 2004, the SEC adopted a rule requiring that most of these funds have independent chairmen and boards with at least 75 percent independent directors.[84] This was adopted on a 3-2 vote and was strongly opposed by many funds, most notably Fidelity. This has led to a suit by the U.S. Chamber of Commerce against the SEC—a first time event—claiming the SEC lacks authority to impose such a rule. The case is pending decision in the U.S. Court of Appeals for the District of Columbia.[85] In late 2004, the Congress passed a spending bill that included SEC funding and a requirement that the SEC analyze whether mutual funds chaired by independent directors perform better, have lower expenses, or have better compliance records than mutual funds chaired by non-independent directors.[86]

B.   TAX CONSIDERATIONS

1.   WHY FOREIGNERS DO NOT INVEST IN U.S. FUNDS

U.S. funds must distribute current realized income to shareholders to avoid being taxed at the fund level. Such distributions are taxable to shareholders. Most foreign funds, most notably those in Luxembourg, are not taxable at the fund level *even if* they make no distribution to shareholders. Since there is substantial benefit in deferring taxes, foreign investors invest in foreign funds that are not required to make distributions.

In addition, any distributions by U.S. funds to foreign investors are subject to 30 percent withholding taxes (reducible to 15 percent by tax treaties), that are not imposed by other jurisdictions.

Finally, the "character" of the income received by the fund's shareholders must be considered. An investor in a fund that makes no distributions would receive any earnings of the fund only in the form of capital gains arising upon redemption of the fund's shares. By contrast, an investor in a fund required to make distributions of its income and realized gain generally will be required to treat the entire amount of these distributions as ordinary income, because the tax laws of the investor's home country will not recognize the capital gain character of a dividend

---

[83] R. Atlas, "In Settlement, Alliance Agrees to Cut Fees," *The New York Times*, December 17, 2003.

[84] SEC, Final Rule, Investment Company Governance, Release No. IC-26520, 69 Federal Register 46378, August 2, 2004.

[85] Chamber of Commerce v. SEC, No. 04-1300 (argument was on April 15, 2005).

[86] Public Law No. 108-447, Title V. December 8, 2004.

distribution from a fund. Most fund investors would prefer to receive capital gains instead of ordinary income, because many countries offer favorable tax treatment to capital gains.

2.   WHY U.S. INVESTORS WILL NOT INVEST IN FOREIGN FUNDS

a.   PFICs

U.S. tax rules provide that U.S. shareholders will pay income tax on the earnings of a passive foreign investment company (PFIC) even if these earnings are not distributed.

A non-U.S. fund will constitute a PFIC if 75 percent or more of its gross income is "passive income" (which includes dividends and interest, and net gains from property which produces such income) or 50 percent or more of its assets produce, or are held for the production of, passive income. The relevant rules apply irrespective of the size of an investor's shareholding or the extent of holdings by U.S. taxpayers in the aggregate, provided the fund is not 50 percent or more owned by U.S. persons (in which case other rules apply).[87]

If a U.S. taxpayer who is an investor in a PFIC elects to treat the PFIC as a "qualified electing fund" (a QEF) and the PFIC complies with prescribed requirements concerning the provision of information,[88] the U.S. taxpayer is taxable currently on its share of the PFIC's undistributed earnings, and subsequent distributions of those earnings are not taxable.

Another possibility is marking-to-market. Under Section 1296 of the Internal Revenue Code, a U.S. person holding an investment in a PFIC may elect to mark the fund shares to market and to pay a tax on any gain of the shares (as measured by net asset value) over the taxpayer's adjusted basis in such shares. This subjects the taxpayer to a tax on a fund's unrealized gains.

If a U.S. taxpayer does not elect to treat a PFIC as a QEF (or if the PFIC does not comply with the information requirements), or employ the mark-to-market alternative, the U.S. taxpayer will be taxable when it receives an "excess distribution" or sells its share in the PFIC. The gain in the case of a sale is not treated as a capital gain and, in the case of both a sale and an excess distribution, an interest charge is imposed (in addition to the regular tax) to reflect the value of deferring the tax. This interest charge

---

[87] *Tax Aspects of the Internationalization of the Investment Fund Industry*, Memorandum of Sullivan & Cromwell, July 1990.

[88] The fund must ordinarily provide an annual information statement which contains information concerning the fund's fiscal year, the shareholder's share of the fund's ordinary earnings and net capital gains, distributions to the shareholder and a statement that the fund will permit the shareholder to inspect the fund's relevant books and records. See Notice 88-125, 1988-2 C.B. 535. It may therefore be the case that, save where a significant proportion of its investors are U.S. residents, an offshore fund may not wish to provide the required statement, thus preventing a U.S. taxpayer's election from taking effect.

may be excessive compared to the actual value of deferral. An "excess distribution" is generally the amount of the distribution received during a taxable year in excess of 125 percent of the average of the distributions during the three preceding years.

As a result of these PFIC rules, taxable U.S. investors are reluctant to invest in offshore mutual funds. Note that these negative tax consequences for offshore investors would not be a consideration for tax-exempt investors like pension funds. However, the U.S. Employee Retirement Income Security Act (ERISA) may impose limitations on use of offshore funds. For example, if an employee benefit plan holds 25 percent or more of the shares of a foreign fund, the fund's assets, in addition to shares of the fund, will be regarded as plan assets for purposes of applying various ERISA reporting, fiduciary and custody requirements.

3.   HEDGE FUNDS AVOID PFIC

Hedge funds are often structured as offshore partnerships in tax havens like the Cayman Islands or Bermuda. This structure permits the investors to escape the consequences of PFIC since PFIC only applies to corporations. This structure cannot be used by normal mutual funds sold to U.S. retail investors since such funds would have to be registered. This would also be the case if a fund-of-funds were sold to the public. Unless registered funds are corporations, they would be subject to onerous regulatory restrictions.[89]

Recently, another offshore vehicle has been used to avoid PFIC. Offshore insurance companies have sold insurance contracts, life insurance and annuities, whose payoff is determined by hedge funds run by the insurance companies. Since insurance companies are exempt from PFIC, the gains to investors escape PFIC treatment. These opportunities can be offered to retail as well as wholesale investors. The IRS has recently issued a notice pointing out that for the PFIC exemption to be available, the insurance company must be primarily engaged in the insurance business. This prevents insurance companies that are primarily hedge funds from taking advantage of the exemption.[90]

Notes and Questions

1. What U.S. tax consequences prevent U.S. investors from investing in offshore mutual funds? What changes, if any, would you make in U.S. tax law to promote such investment?

---

[89] It might be possible for an offshore unregistered mutual fund, organized as a partnership, to sell shares to U.S. investors abroad, without running afoul of PFIC. If the fund made no annual distributions, it would be attractive to both U.S. and foreign investors, and thus avoid the current segmentation in the registered retail market between foreign funds for foreigners and U.S. funds for U.S. investors. Such a fund would have to be sold only abroad.

[90] I.R.S, Notice 2003-34, May 9, 2003.

2. What U.S. tax consequences prevent foreign investors from investing in U.S. mutual funds? What changes, if any, would you make in U.S. tax law to promote such investment?

3. How would you compare globalization in the market for primary securities, with globalization in the mutual funds market? Is there a euromarket for mutual funds?

CONCLUSIONS

There are two major issues confronting the mutual funds markets: market segmentation between U.S. and foreign public funds, and between public and private (hedge) funds.

The segmentation between the market for U.S. and foreign public funds arises from tax. U.S. tax rules require current distributions to shareholders if funds are to avoid tax at the fund level, whereas most foreign jurisdictions do not. Additionally, the U.S. punitively taxes U.S. shareholders that invest in foreign funds that do not make yearly distributions. This has led to the result that U.S. investors invest in U.S. funds (to avoid the punitive tax) and foreign investors invest in foreign funds that defer distributions (to avoid taxes imposed by their own countries on annual distributions by U.S. funds).

This situation can be avoided by changes in either U.S. or foreign tax rules, an unlikely event, or by the use of mutual fund structures, like master/feeders, that permit foreign and U.S. funds to pool assets in a common portfolio. This would require foreign acceptance of the master/feeder structure, as by UCITS. One wonders whether competitive advantages to both U.S. and foreign funds that flow from segmentation account for lack of progress in this area.

The second segmentation concern is between public and private funds. Unlike the case with public funds, the hedge fund market is itself not segmented internationally since the punitive PFIC rules do not apply to U.S. investors in foreign hedge funds. This permits both U.S. and foreign investors to invest in hedge funds that do not make yearly distributions.

There is, however, segmentation between the public and hedge fund market since public funds have significant portfolio and fee restrictions that are not applicable to the private hedge fund market. These differences are under attack since the public has been unable to invest in hedge funds, which have shown impressive returns in recent years. Funds-of-funds are a solution to this problem but it remains to be seen whether the SEC or other regulators will restrict their availability to retail investors, or impose new requirements on them—such as disclosure obligations. A better solution would be to remove most of the restrictions on current public funds.

The market scandals, arising from late trading and market timing, are at root problems traceable to the system of once a day NAV pricing at the 4:00 p.m. close. Efforts to enforce a harder closing price will likely lead to substantial gains for ETFs over mutual funds. Again, we see a recurring problem in financial regulation—the competitive impact on substitutable (but not identical) products of differential regulation.

PART IV

EMERGING MARKETS

Developing countries and the former socialist countries now in transition raise special issues for international finance. Despite huge differences among them, these countries, when contrasted to the more developed markets, offer very different risks and rewards. This is because their basic institutions, such as law, accounting, corporate governance, and even government, are often not well developed. In addition, their economic performance varies much more dramatically over time than that of the developed countries. While this raises the risk for financial firms, savers, and even users of funds, the high potential upside is a tantalizing lure, particularly in China. Since major industrial countries have economic and political stakes in developing and transition countries, the governments of industrial countries intervene in financial markets involving developing countries. This too changes the balance of risk and reward.

This part deals with three types of international finance involving emerging markets. Project finance has been a burgeoning area of activity and legal practice. Chapter 17 examines it in the context of a large power project in the Philippines. Cross-border investment in emerging markets by foreign institutional investors has been one of the most dynamic activities in international finance. Much of this investment is in privatized companies. Chapter 18 deals with that subject by focusing on the Mexican Telmex offer and the impact of the Peso crisis that followed it. Emerging market debt, raised internationally, has funded development but also contributed to the collapse of many economies. Chapter 19 deals with the debt problem that began in the 1960s, the crises this generated in subsequent years, and the efforts to deal with these crises. Chapter 20 covers the subject of banking law reforms in emerging markets, a major initiative of the IMF.

CHAPTER SEVENTEEN

PROJECT FINANCE

A.   INTRODUCTION

This Chapter deals with project finance. Project finance is a form of limited recourse funding. Lenders to the project can only look to specified assets of the borrower for repayment of their loans and payment of interest. The idea is that lenders can evaluate the assets and the projected cash flow (including enhancements like performance bonds) of a discrete project in order to calculate its risk and return. Specifically, if the project fails, the government of the country in which the project is located will generally not stand behind the project's obligations. This type of financing requires lenders and their lawyers to become experts on the economics of the projects they are lending to. Lenders must generally be concerned about the credit risk of their borrowers. But here they must rely on the "project" they are financing for repayment.

Project finance has increased from $17.67 billion in 1994 to $145 billion in 2004, a 5-year compound annual growth rate of 9 percent.[1] In the first nine months of 2004, the value of deals completed was $89.7 billion. Most project finance is in developed countries, although we focus in the Chapter on its use in emerging markets. The power sector accounted for 32 percent of bank project finance lending in 2001. While most project finance is bank lending, project bonds for top-rated credits have increasingly been used in recent years, now constituting about 19 percent of total finances.[2]

These transactions are complicated and can only be understood by looking in depth at a particular transaction; we have chosen the electric power plant Pagbilao project in the Philippines. Work began on this project in April 1993. Consisting of two large coal-fired generators, the plant would be developed for the government's National Power Company (Napocor) by the Hopewell Group of Hong Kong, with Mitsubishi Corporation of Japan as the main builder, for a total cost of $933 million—$535 million for mechanical and electrical work, $167 million for civil construction, $166 million for interest and finance charges, and $65 million for other indirect costs (e.g. lawyers' fees). After construction, scheduled to end no later than April 30,

---

[1] B. Esty and A Sesia Jr., An Overview of Project Finance—2004 Update, Case No. 9-205-065, April 19, 2005, Exhibit 2.
[2] B. Esty and I. Christow, "Recent Trends in Project Finance—A Five Year Perspective," 249 Project Finance International (September 18, 2002), pp. 74-82.

1996 for the first generator and July 31, 1996 for the second, Hopewell would own and operate the plant for 25 years and then transfer ownership to Napocor at no cost. This was a BOOT project: build, own, operate, transfer.

Ben Esty describes the attractions of project finance to independent power producers, such as Hopewell, as follows:[3]

"Project finance is particularly attractive for IPPs because it offers high leverage with limited or no recourse to the sponsor's balance sheet. Sponsors finance IPPs with debt-to-total capitalization ratios ranging from 70-95 percent. Because the ideal assets for project finance require mainly upfront (but little ongoing) investment, the plants generate large amounts of free cash flow. For example, a gas-fired power plant might generate operating margins of 20-50 percent while other projects can generate operating margins of 70-95 percent. By employing high leverage, sponsors ensure that project managers generate and then disgorge free cash flow rather than making negative net present value investments or wasteful expenditures."

The Pagbilao project was significant for several reasons. For the Philippines, it would become the largest coal-fired plant in the country, serving a region including the capital, Manila, that was starved for power. Hopewell was managed by Gordon Wu, a Hong Kong resident and Princeton educated engineer, who takes credit for originating BOOT projects in China in the late 1970s. Pagbilao launched the government's new strategy of relying on the private sector to fund major infrastructure projects. Supplementing the private funds was support from the government-owned export-import banks of Japan and the United States, as well as three multilateral agencies, the Asian Development Bank (ADB), the International Finance Corporation (IFC) (an affiliate of the World Bank), and the Commonwealth Development Corporation (CDC), the public U.K. Agency for promoting privately financed development abroad.

Project finance started to play an increasingly important role in cross-border financial flows in the mid-1980s in many regions of the world. In Asia by the early 1990s, direct investment, of which project finance was a major part, dominated even the booming portfolio investment as a source of cross-border finance. The Philippines was particularly successful in attracting foreign investment to infrastructure projects. Its legal regime for such projects was among the best in Asia.

This Chapter proceeds by explaining the Philippines' need for power, gives background on project finance, and presents the arrangements for the Pagbilao project, emphasizing its financing.

---

[3] B. Esty, "Returns on Project-Financed Investment: Evolution and Managerial Implications," 15 Journal of Applied Corporate Finance (2002), p. 71.

B.   THE PHILIPPINES' NEED FOR POWER

As early as 1987, the government recognized that the country faced a serious shortfall in power. Until then, the Department of Energy regulated electric utilities through concessions. Only Napocor, its wholly-owned company, could generate and transmit power through seven grids for the country. The few private, municipal, and rural utilities were not significant. The country drew over half of its power from thermal plants using imported oil, and most of the rest from coal and hydroelectric sources. Rates were the second highest in Asia because so much of the power was oil-based.[4]

In July 1987, the government authorized the private sector to construct and run power plants. Many projects began to be negotiated, but the process was very slow and the lead-time to actual production was many years. By 1991-92, the Philippines suffered severe power shortages lasting 5 to 12 hours a day. The government tried to end unnecessary consumption. Businesses, institutions, and homes bought electric generators that caused serious health hazards; for example, respiratory diseases in Metro Manila increased 20 percent.

Projections into the near future painted an even more dire picture. If GDP grew at only 4 percent a year, peak demand would be 5,002 megawatts (MW) by the year 2000 and Napocor would need to add 250-300 MW capacity each year. But many existing plants were over 25 years old and scheduled to be phased out soon.

The Philippines faced such an acute crisis due to power shortages that in April 1993 the Congress gave President Ramos emergency powers to deal with it. Without the powers, the law would require bids for each plant, which would be very time consuming. Ramos encouraged private groups to take on new power projects because the red tape surrounding government-run projects would have delayed the initiatives. In 1994, 11 new power plants began to operate, promising up to 1,074 MW. The crisis became less acute, but brownouts and blackouts continued around the Manila area.

Notes and Questions

1.   Evaluate the advantages and disadvantages to the Philippines of relying on the private development of energy.

2.   Is there anything about the long-term supply and demand conditions for power in the Philippines that could concern private developers of these power projects? What could they do to protect themselves?

---

[4] See J. Galang, "Gaining on the Neighbours," *Financial Times Survey*, September 12, 1994, at I.

C.   PROJECT FINANCE IN GENERAL

1.   FOREIGN DIRECT INVESTMENT IN THE PHILIPPINES

Project finance is a form of foreign direct investment (FDI) which gives the foreign investor equity control of a company in the host country. FDI dominated cross-border private investment into much of Asia. It was encouraged by the Philippine government.

The Philippine Constitution safeguarded foreign investments by guaranteeing protection from expropriation without just compensation and allowing remittance of profits, repatriation of investments, and the ability to obtain foreign exchange to repay foreign obligations. Foreign investment, portfolio or direct, equity or debt, had to register with the central bank in order for the investment to be serviced. All foreign exchange transactions had to go through authorized foreign exchange banks.

The Foreign Investment Act of 1991 permitted 100 percent foreign ownership in activities not covered by the Foreign Investment Negative List, which lists specific areas where foreign ownership is limited up to a maximum of 40 percent.

Although the Constitution forbade foreign ownership of land, the government had increased the maximum lease period from 50 to 75 years. Utilities exploiting a natural resource had to be in the hands of citizens.

In July 1987, the Philippine Government issued Executive Order No. 215, which provided for the private sector to build, own, and operate power stations. Soon the policy was embodied in a statute, Republic Act No. 6957, which granted the private sector the right to engage in infrastructure projects through several means: build, own, and transfer (BOT); build, own, operate, and transfer (BOOT); or build and transfer (BT).

2.   PROJECTS AND PROJECT FINANCE

The earliest project finance projects were to extract minerals, which through exports earned foreign exchange. Many later projects earned their income in domestic funds. They often built infrastructure, which included public utilities (like power, water, or telecommunications), public works (roads, dams, canals), and other forms of transport (urban railways, ports, and airports, for example). Infrastructure grew fast over the last decades. For example, in middle income countries, power production per capita grew 55 percent each decade from 1960 to 1990.

Much infrastructure development in the early years took place under the direct control of government agencies. One study found that from 1980-89 the governments of 8 middle income countries devoted almost 60 percent of public investment to infrastructure.[5] The wave of privatization swept through these sectors in the mid-1980s and many countries began looking for ways to develop infrastructure using private firms. The World Bank found that during 1988-92, of the $62 billion in total privatizations in developing countries, almost $20 billion was for infrastructure and $4 billion of this was for power generation. Another $1 billion was for power distribution.

In late 1993, a total of 148 major infrastructure projects were identified worldwide as being underway and another 358 in the pipeline. Of those underway, 77 were in middle-income countries and 16 percent of these were in the power sector (69 percent were in transport). Middle income countries had another 179 infrastructure projects, with value of $77 billion, in the pipeline. Although the study did not report how many of these pipeline projects involved power projects, one can assume the number was significant. Despite the rapid growth of power infrastructure, the need persisted for much more development. For middle-income countries, although power generating capacity (measured by '000 kilowatts/million population) grew from 175 in 1975 to 373 in 1990, it still fell far short of the 2,100 capacity found on average in high income economies.

The power sector differs from some other types of infrastructure in important ways. Providers of power can compete with one another, for example, while other types of infrastructure, such as urban and rural roads, are not amenable to competition.

D.   THE PAGBILAO POWER PROJECT

When the Philippine Government announced in 1987 that it wanted the private sector to develop power plants, the Hopewell Holding Ltd (HHL) group, based in Hong Kong, quickly opened discussions. Hopewell had led major BOT power projects in China and the Philippines. It could offer experience with offtake contracts, turnkey construction, limited recourse financing, fuel supply arrangements, and many of the other elements of the Pagbilao project. Internationally respected, it had a reputation for good work and timely completion. It ranked among the top 20 companies on the Hong Kong Stock Exchange.

1.   THE PLAYERS

In 1993, Hopewell Energy International, Ltd (HEIL), the sponsor, a subsidiary of HHL, and Napocor concluded an Energy Conversion Agreement (ECA). HEIL had two years to arrange the Pagbilao Power Project. The ECA described the parameters of the project, including implementation, fuel supply, basic costs (ultimately fixed at $933 million), payments, energy

---

[5] See World Bank, World Development Report 1994, the main source for this section.

tariffs, and financing. HEIL would build, own, operate, and then transfer the plant as is and at no cost to Napocor after 25 years.

The ECA set target dates:

Commence work	April 30, 1993
Complete Unit 1	April 30, 1996
Complete Unit 2	July 31, 1996
Complete Power Station	July 31, 1996

The arrangements led in late April 1993 to a bundle of contracts (the Agreements).

The Agreements described a complex structure, pictured in Figure 17.1, below. Hopewell Power (Philippines) Corporation (HPPC), a roughly 87 percent subsidiary of HEIL, would be the project company. HEIL promised Napocor it would be jointly and severely liable for all of HPPC's obligations. The contractors building the plant were Mitsubishi Corp. of Japan, the leader, and Slipform Engineering Ltd., a member of the Hopewell Group. Mitsubishi was also a subordinated lender. Napocor would make key contributions during construction. Once the plant was operating, Hopewell Tileman Ltd would manage it, assisted by a specialist firm that would provide technical support. Throughout construction and the first 25 years of operations, HPPC would own the plant and be primarily responsible for it. Napocor agreed to supply the fuel (coal) needed to run the plant and to buy all power it produced according to the agreed tariff. The Philippines and Napocor also supplied the land.

Many contracts documented the arrangement. Loan agreements included the Common Agreement (described later in this Chapter), and separate agreements between HPPC and the Commonwealth Development Corporation (CDC), IFC, ADB, the Japanese Export-Import Bank (JEXIM), the U.S. Export-Import Bank (U.S. EXIM), and the Citibank bank syndicate. CDC, IFC, and ADB also took an equity position. Security documents included a trust (described below), a mortgage trust, an assignment and security, and a pledge, all involving the company, the trustee, and usually the sponsor and one or more lenders. Several completion support agreements were designed to ensure the turnkey project was finished on time. In addition, the Project Documents included the ECA, the turnkey contract, and related agreements.

Figure 17.1

Major Participants in the Pagbilao Project

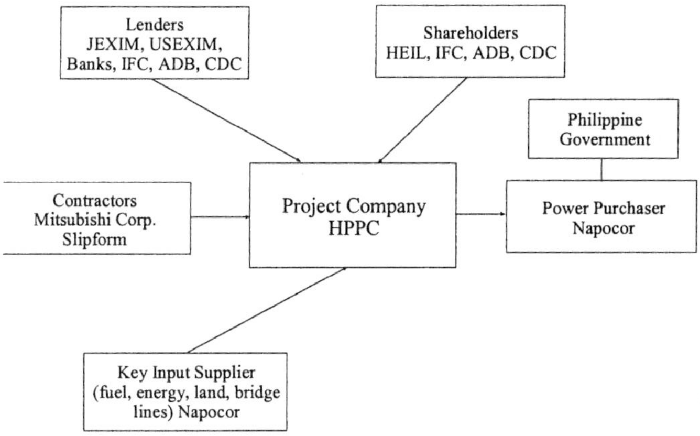

Pagbilao would receive several incentives because it qualified as a "pioneer" under the Philippines Omnibus Investments Code of 1987. These included a six-year income tax holiday from the start of operations, tax-free imports of capital equipment for several years, a tax credit for domestic capital equipment, and the right to employ foreigners. Several lawsuits that tried to block construction on the basis of environmental impact were settled by the government.

Notes and Questions

1. Why would the Philippines Government and Hopewell prefer to work through a locally incorporated subsidiary of Hopewell (HPPC) rather than a formal joint venture?

2. How significant is it that the government and others contract with various units in the Hopewell group, most incorporated abroad, rather than the parent company itself? What would account for this arrangement? What is the function of the Hopewell parent?

2. CONSTRUCTION

The Agreements described the plant, its technology, components, fuel supply, and site. The plant would be built according to international standards. Mitsubishi, selected by bid to be the lead member of the construction consortium, would have overall responsibility. The other member, Slipform Engineering Ltd, the HHL subsidiary, had done similar work on a project in China. It would be responsible for civil construction work. HPPC, as owner, would supervise, aided by its subsidiary Hopewell

Tileman Ltd. The supervisors would review all engineering designs, monitor procurement and quality, ensure construction met contract requirements, monitor progress, testing, and transfer, and assure compliance with governmental approvals and law.

The construction consortium agreed to accept a lump sum price. If the units did not meet guaranteed standards, the consortium would pay liquidated damages, providing a performance bond in support. The consortium would buy insurance for the plant, equipment, and vehicles. HPPC would retain 5 percent of all payments (other than civil and architectural works) until 30 days after it certified the second generator reliable. The consortium warranted against defective equipment and workmanship for two years. Failure to complete the project on time would result in liquidated damages up to an agreed portion of the contract price. Testing of the first generator was to occur six months before it was due to start operating and testing of the second, four months before operations.

HPPC would buy insurance to cover construction risks, including:

1.   Marine Cargo Insurance (including war and strike risks) covering imports of plant, equipment, machinery and materials to the Project site;

2.   Contract Works Insurance covering loss or damage to the Project works during the construction and testing/commissioning periods;

3.   Business Interruption Insurance covering loss, specified standing charges, interest and fees due to delay in start up of the project as a result of damage during transit to site and during construction, testing and commissioning;

4.   Third Party Liability Insurance covering legal liabilities to third parties for injury or damage arising from construction, testing/commissioning and maintenance; and

5.   Other local insurance such as workmen's compensation and motor insurance for the company's personnel and vehicles.

The sponsors, HEIL and HPPC, would be rewarded for early and penalized for late completion. The reward was that HEIL would receive directly 50 percent of the capacity fees and energy fees (described in the following section), after deducting expenses, earned during the period before the target completion dates. The reward was called a Bonus Dividend. As a shareholder, it would also receive its pro rata share of the remaining 50 percent. For delays over 30 days, Napocor could claim for each day, $10,000 the first 60 days and $24,700 beyond that, to a ceiling of $16 million. HEIL had to post a $16 million bond when it signed the ECA, which was reduced 50 percent after the first generator was built. Hopewell was not able to complete the project early, despite having started before financing was completely arranged. Hopewell accused Napocor of failing to do what it had promised.

Napocor agreed to provide at no cost several essential inputs for construction, including the electricity needed for construction, a bridge and power line to the Pagbilao Grande Island, and the land for the site. Napocor retained ownership of the land and paid all real estate taxes and assessments. It agreed to pay all other taxes except for net income tax and construction fees. It would pay for testing and start-up.

The Finance Ministry stated that the obligations of Napocor had the full faith and credit of the Republic, which would make sure that Napocor would be able to discharge them. Any dispute would be resolved using the Australian Commercial Disputes Centre in Sydney, Australia under the rules of UNCITRAL. The government waived sovereign immunity.

Government agencies agreed to give the approvals identified in the Agreements as necessary. For example, the Central Bank needed to approve procedures for foreign exchange transactions. Many other government agencies were involved: the Board of Investment (e.g. to permit 100 percent foreign ownership of HPPC), Securities and Exchange Commission (e.g. that HEIL did not need a license to do business in the country), Department of Finance, Department of Environment and Natural Resources, Napocor, National Economic and Development Authority (as to the project's significance), National Electrification Administration, Energy Regulatory Board, Department of Justice, Regional Development Council for the region, local governments, Insurance Commission, Immigration Commission, local deed registry, and local registry for chattel mortgages.

The parties distinguished between two types of *force majeure*. These were:

Type A Events

Other than as referred to in paragraph B below, any war, declared or not or hostilities, or of belligerence, blockade, revolution, insurrection, riot, public disorder, expropriation, requisition, confiscation or nationalization, export or import restrictions by any governmental authorities, closing of harbors, docks, canals, or other assistances to or adjuncts of the shipping or navigation of or within any place, rationing or allocation, whether imposed by law, decree or regulation by, or by compliance of industry at the insistence of any governmental authority, or fire, unusual flood, earthquake, volcanic activity, storm, typhoons, lightning, tide (other than normal tides), tsunamis, perils of the sea, accidents of navigation or breakdown or injury of vessels, accidents to harbors, docks, canals, or other assistances to or adjuncts of the shipping or navigation, epidemic, quarantine, strikes or combination of workmen, lockouts or other labor disturbances, or any other event, matter or thing, wherever occurring, which shall not be within the reasonable control of the party affected thereby; or

Type B Events

War, declared or not or hostilities occurring in or involving the Republic of the Philippines, or of belligerence, blockade, revolution, insurrection, riot, public disorder, expropriation, requisition, confiscation or nationalization by or occurring in or involving the Republic of the Philippines, export or import restrictions by any governmental, regional or municipal authorities of or within the Republic of the Philippines, closing of harbors, docks, canals, or other assistances to or adjuncts of the shipping or navigation of or within the Republic of the Philippines, rationing or allocation, whether imposed by law, decree or regulation by, or by compliance of industry at the insistence of, any governmental authority of or within the Republic of the Philippines, or any other event, matter or thing, wherever occurring, which shall be within the reasonable control of Napocor or the government of the Republic of the Philippines or any agency or regional or municipal authority thereof.

Napocor promised to buy the project if certain events occurred during construction or operation. These events included agreed changes in circumstances (notably law, regulation, the status of the site, government approvals) that adversely affected Hopewell's rate of return, Type B *force majeure* events, a decision by Napocor to close the plant (permissible only 20 years or more after completion), or Napocor's failure to ensure timely payment. If the buy out occurred before completion, Napocor would pay all Hopewell's actual and incurred costs plus 10 percent. If after completion, it would pay the present value of all remaining capacity fees (except fixed operating fees).

Notes and Questions

1. How do the parties deal with construction risks? How do the incentives and penalties work? How useful is the distinction between Type A and B events in the *force majeure* clause likely to be? Do the parties address other risks? Are there important risks that they ignore? Why?

2. Is this a non-recourse project? What is the function of the government, Napocor, and Hopewell during construction?

3. How much risk did Hopewell take by starting before financing was complete? Why would it do this?

3. OPERATIONS

Once the plants were operational, the parties' obligations and remuneration changed. HPPC remained in charge overall, but it would be assisted by Hopewell Tileman Power Systems Corp, a sister company with operational experience. Also providing technical support would be an international operations and management contractor that specialized in running coal-fired thermal power plants. Though 15 expatriates would be employed in key roles in the work force of 467 people, Hopewell planned to place overall management authority in local hands by the year 2000. It had done so in its earlier projects in the Philippines and in China.

An agreement governed operations and maintenance. Hopewell, as operator, agreed to comply with all relevant laws, control the budget, comply with the ECA and fuel supply arrangements, guarantee performance, and train staff.

a.   CAPACITY AND ENERGY FEES

Payment would take the form of capacity and energy fees. Capacity fees, accounting for over 90 percent of income, were fixed in the contract as flat fees per KW/month. Rates were fixed for four types of capacity: capital costs (accounting for over 80 percent of all capacity fees), fixed operating costs, infrastructure costs, and service (return on investment). The scenarios estimated costs for the first year of operation and increased costs 6 percent each following year. HPPC was entitled to the capacity fees as long as it could demonstrate that it could operate at 85 percent capacity, whether or not Napocor actually needed the power produced.

Energy fees had two parts. One part paid a flat rate per KW hour divided into payments both in U.S. Dollars and Pesos. For the output above the first 75 percent of the generator's capacity, the Dollar payment was 5 percent lower than for the output at or below 75 percent, but the Peso payment did not change. The second part of the energy fee added a bonus for efficient fuel use and deducted a penalty for inefficient use. All fees were indexed to adjust for inflation. The Dollar portion was indexed to Japanese and U.S. export prices and the Peso portion to the official Metro Manila consumer price index. Dollar payments, the bulk, were to be made to Hopewell's account in New York. Peso payments were made to its Manila account. The parties concluded that the return on equity investment would only fall slightly with construction cost overruns of 10 percent or if no energy fees were paid.

b.   INSURANCE

Beginning in the late 1990s, major insurance companies offered a growing array of policies for non-traditional risks in project finance and other single asset endeavors. Traditional insurance includes insurance for finite risk, excess loss, and political risk, as well as financial and performance guarantees. On the non-traditional side is insurance for currency, commodity, operating and credit risks—risks that previously were borne by a company's shareholders or creditors. Rating agencies are increasingly willing to consider non-traditional insurance as mitigating risk in projects they rate, even reducing the spread against investment-grade debt when the project is not investment grade. It seems that only the risk of revenue shortfalls that are in the control of management are necessarily beyond the appropriate scope of insurance, to avoid moral hazard. But the insurance companies are still reluctant to take on risks with a high-Dollar loss per claim, such as the risks of new technologies or a country at war.[6]

Insurance became a serious issue for Pagbilao in 2001, when the project was unable to obtain terrorism insurance in the post-9/11 environment, causing it to go into technical default on $369 million in loans. This problem was later cured in November 2002 when the loan covenants were renegotiated, but power plants in the Philippines became a prime target for terrorist attacks in 2002.

c.   FOREIGN EXCHANGE RISK

To deal specifically with the effect of currency crises on projects like Pagbilao, financial markets introduced the real exchange rate liquidity (Rex) facility. A Rex facility "mitigates the impact of devaluation on local currency revenue streams indexed only to local inflation"[7] According to Dymond and Schoenblum, when the real exchange rate (i.e. the nominal rate adjusted for inflation) moves outside an agreed band and there is a cash-flow shortfall for debt service, the facility provides liquidity to service the debt. The provider's loan is subordinated to senior lenders. The facility requires a floating rate regime, a local currency that is not overvalued, and no significant price controls. The authors identified the Philippines as a country that passed the hurdle.

Notes and Questions

1. What is the function of the capacity and energy fees?

2. Evaluate the assumptions underlying the calculation of the fees. How well do they protect the parties?

3. Does Napocor's role effectively leave the project in private hands?

E.   FINANCING PAGBILAO

1.   THE OVERALL STRUCTURE

Financing for Pagbilao, depicted in Figure 17.2 below, took the form of equity ($235 million) and non-recourse debt ($898 million). HEIL held 86.95 percent of HPPC's shares and IFC, ADB, and CDC held the rest in

---

[6] P. Alderdiece, H. Horwich, and R. Feldman, "Risk Finance for Project Finance: The Expanding Horizon of Credit Enhancement," Journal of Structured and Project Finance (Winter 2001), p. 30.
[7] C. Dymond and J. Schoenblum, "Targeted Risk Capital," Journal of Structured and Project Finance (Summer 2002), p. 32.

equal proportions. HEIL paid for part of its equity stake by capitalizing its preparatory expenditures.

Figure 17.2
Financing for the Pagbilao Project
($ millions)

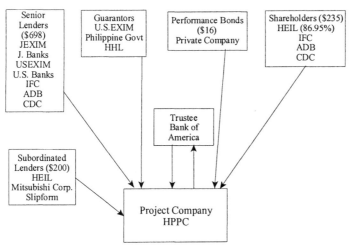

Senior debt of $698 million was provided by JEXIM ($220 million), a consortium of Japanese banks acting with it ($147 million), a construction loan from a Citicorp-led syndicate of banks ($185 million) replaced by a loan from the US EXIM when operations began, and loans from multilaterals ($144 million). All loans matured in ten years (except that from the Citicorp syndicate, the CDC, and one small loan). In addition, the contractors and sponsor (HEIL) agreed to provide $200 million in subordinated loans to HPPC to fund pre-completion cost overruns and funding shortfalls. The amount would be reduced to $100 million after the first generator was completed.

The Japanese lending group included five Japanese and two German banks' Japanese units. Japan contributed this funding because Mitsubishi Corp. was the lead contractor. JEXIM's Dollar loan was made without recourse at a fixed interest rate of 8 percent. JEXIM also acted as agent for the Japanese bank syndicate, whose Dollar loan carried a floating rate of LIBOR (then about 4.5 percent) plus 2.15 percent. The banks syndicate's loan had limited insurance from the Japanese Ministry of International Trade and Industry. The U.S. export credit differed somewhat in amount and structure. This sort of export finance and the U.S. Export-Import Bank are discussed in more detail.

2.   BANK CAPITAL REQUIREMENTS

Private lenders are, of course, concerned about the capital treatment of their loans. Under the Basel I credit risk approach, in effect in 1996, these loans to HPPC were risk-weighted at 100 percent, the risk weight given to all private obligors. These capital requirements have been revised under Basel II.

Banks qualifying for the IRB approach would use their own PD (probability of default) estimates and basically treat project finance loans just like other corporate loans. Other banks must use the risk weights shown in Table 17A below:[8]

Table 17A
Project Finance Risk-Weights

Supervisory Category	Strong	Good	Satisfactory	Weak	Default
External Credit Rating	BBB- or better	BB+ or BB	BB- or B+	B to C-	N.A.
Credit Risk Weight	70%	90%	115%	250%	0%

At national discretion, supervisors may allow banks to assign preferential risk weights of 50 percent to "strong" exposures and 70 percent to "good" exposures, if maturities are less than 2.5 years or the supervisor determines that the banks' underwriting and other risk characteristics are substantially stronger than the norm. Annex 4 to the Basel rules lays out the methodology for determining the appropriate supervisory category.

A study by Standard & Poor's Risk Solutions found that "the average recovery rate of project finance loans in the Lead Banks' portfolios was at or above all other asset classes in the S&P data base." The rates were similar to North American leveraged loans and better than senior debt, secured debt, and senior unsecured debt. The probability of default was that of BBB+ long term unsecured corporate loans. The study said that this was due to credit enhancements and early warning mechanisms available to the banks. They concluded that "since the LGD (loss given default) and expected loss results are lower than corporate finance loans of an equivalent rating, less capital is required."[9] Many regarded the Basel risk-weights as too high.[10] These criticisms undoubtedly contributed to the lowering of risk-weights between

---

[8]   Basel Committee on Banking Supervision, Basel II: International Convergence of Capital Measurement and Capital Standards, A Revised Framework, June 2004, paras. 275-276.

[9] C. Beale, M. Chatain, N. Fox, S. Bell, J. Berner, R. Preminger, and J. Prins, "Credit Attributes of Project Finance," Journal of Structured and Project Finance (Fall 2002), p. 5.

[10] Roundtable, "Banks Need to be Proactive to Avoid the fall-out from the Latest Basel II Proposals," Project Finance (February 2002).

the last draft of the proposal in 2003 and the adoption of the Basel rules in 2004. [11]

The supervisory slotting system will not apply to any U.S. banks given the fact that the United States has only adopted the advanced IRB portion of the Basel II rules (see Chapter 7).

3.   OFFICIAL EXPORT CREDIT: U.S. EXPORT-IMPORT BANK

Projects that need equipment or other inputs from another country can often draw on official export credit. Most industrial countries and many others have quasi-independent government agencies dedicated to financing their countries' exporters. To the extent that exporters competing from different countries cannot distinguish their goods according to quality, price is critical and the cost of credit is an important factor in cost.

The U.S. Export-Import Bank, founded in 1934, is a statutory corporation directed by a president and board appointed by the U.S. President. The view in the mid-1930s was that exports could help the U.S. economy climb out of its depression. Congress has to renew the charter every four years. U.S. EXIM is financed by Congressional appropriations. Its purpose is to supplement private capital rather than compete with it.

U.S. EXIM's portfolio of services has broadened over the last few decades. It initially made loans to a buyer/borrower equal to 95 percent of the value of the U.S. exports being purchased. In the 1970s, its practices changed in response to competitive pressure from other countries. Many exporting countries used their export-import banks as competitive tools, offering loans at below-market interest rates and subsidizing them to do so. Often they gave mixed credits, combining export credits and foreign aid to lower the price of credit even further. Borrowers in developing countries began to play the export-import banks off against one another, bargaining the rates down. U.S. EXIM responded by diversifying its services, offering a variety of loans for different purposes, and by adding guarantees and insurance to its portfolio. Guarantees required only 25 percent of the capital U.S. EXIM had to allocate to loans, allowing it to leverage its resources.

Project finance had become increasingly important to U.S. EXIM. In June 1994, it established a Project Finance Division. During its first year, the division approved eight projects generating over $2 billion in U.S. exports. Its general policies included requirements that projects have long-term contracts extending beyond the maturity of the U.S. EXIM funding, that project costs and pricing should be market-based, and that revenues should be largely in hard currency to reduce currency risk.

---

[11] For an excellent case on the project finance capital requirements, see B. Esty and A. Sesia Jr., Basel II: Assessing the Default and Loss Characteristics of Project Finance Loans N9-204-094, Harvard Business School, January 27, 2004 (B) and January 26, 2004 (A).

Working through the Organization for Economic Cooperation and Development (OECD), U.S. EXIM sought a consensus to limit export credit pricing to market rates and eliminate financing that mixed export credits and aid. Eventually, OECD members agreed to an Arrangement setting minimal standards. The IMF summarized the *Arrangement on Guidelines for Officially Supported Export Credits*, prepared by the Export Credit Group of the OECD.[12] The most important elements were:

1. a cash payment at least 15 percent of the export contract's value;

2. repayment at regular intervals, with a 5 year limit for richer importing countries and a 10 year limit for poorer ones;

3. "minimum interest rates linked to market rates;"

4. "minimum levels of concessionality for 'tied-aid' financing."

U.S. EXIM's fiscal year 1996 program budget was $894 million, which it estimated supported exports of almost $15 billion. This was only 2 percent of total U.S. exports, in contrast to support from the Japanese Export-Import Bank amounting to 32 percent of Japanese exports and from the French agency of 18 percent. At year-end 2002, U.S. EXIM had $15.3 billion in assets, and had received a $587.9 billion appropriation, less than in 1996 when world economic activity was more robust. In 2002, it made $10.1 billion in loans, $600 million of which was for project finance, mainly in power and gas in Mexico and Turkey. U.S. EXIM estimates that from 1997-2002, it supported $6.6 billion in U.S. exports.[13]

In the early 1990s, export credits were an important source of external debt for all developing and transitional countries. The credits were particularly important for the 20 largest recipients, of which the Philippines was one. Its debt to official export credit agencies doubled from $4 billion in 1987 to $8.1 billion in 1992.

A major problem for export credit banks was that many borrowing countries lagged when it came to repaying. Arrears and unrecovered claims were high in Brazil ($12 billion, about 55 percent of its total), Nigeria ($14 billion, 78 percent of total), Russia and the former USSR ($14 billion, 29 percent) and Iran ($4 billion, 24 percent). Even the Philippines appeared on this list in 1992, owing arrears of $2 billion, or 25 percent of the total. It corrected this problem when it rescheduled its official external debt in December 1995 through a formal inter-governmental mechanism known as the Paris Club.

---

[12] See M. Kuhn, B. Horvath, and C. Jarvis, *Officially Supported Export Credits* (March 1995), p. 6.

[13] Annual Report 2002.

Notes and Questions

1. How risky would the Philippines appear to a commercial lender? An export credit agency? How significant is the Philippines inclusion in the Top 20? How significant is its arrears and the resolution of the problem? What do you make of the fact that the Philippines was in arrears when the Pagbilao project was financed? Should U.S. EXIM and JEXIM have participated in the financing?

2. What is the function of export-credit banks? Some export credit agencies saw their role as an insurer, while others saw it as export promotion. How would these different perceptions have affected their activities? How would they explain the need for and components of the OECD Arrangement? How would importing countries view the Arrangement? Why would the U.S. government want to promote such an arrangement when governments of other major industrial countries did not?

a.   DIRECT LOANS

U.S. EXIM made direct loans to buyers, but the amount of the loan varied with the degree of foreign content in the U.S. exports. With 10-15 percent foreign content, the U.S. EXIM loan would be for up to 85 percent of the contract price. The buyer had to pay 15 percent in cash. If the goods had 15-50 percent foreign content, U.S. EXIM financed only the portion with the U.S. content and it would not finance exports with more than 50 percent foreign content. The bank disbursed funds directly to the U.S. exporter. U.S. EXIM charges fees based on its assessment of the credit-worthiness of the borrower or guarantor, the country risk, and the maturity of the loan. U.S. EXIM's policy was not to lend for a project during the construction period when there was a risk that construction might not be completed. Instead, it offered only a political risk guarantee to banks lending to support the exports during construction. After construction, U.S. EXIM would provide credit.

This was what happened with Pagbilao. The Citibank syndicate loaned HPPC funds to finance its purchase of the U.S. equipment for the project, but their loan only lasted through the construction phase. U.S. EXIM ensured that its criteria (such as U.S. content) were met. When Pagbilao became operational, U.S. EXIM's own direct loan to HPPC replaced the Citibank syndicate: U.S. EXIM charged fees for all its services, and New York law governed the various contracts.

b.   POLITICAL RISK GUARANTEE

U.S. EXIM provided a political risk guarantee to the Citibank syndicate for its $185 million loan. The guarantee covered payments of principal and interest as they became due, regardless of whether they were accelerated, but did not cover penalties. U.S. EXIM received a commitment fee and a fee of about 2 percent of the disbursed loans. Political risk included Transfer Risk, Expropriation Risk, and Political Violence.

1.   Transfer Risk

Transfer risk was non-payment that occurred solely because the borrower could not lawfully obtain Dollars in a market in the Philippines or transfer the Dollars to the lenders. The barriers could include any law, order, decree, or regulation by an authority within the de facto control of the Philippine government. The borrower could not have any lawful market through which it could make the payment. The barrier could not have been caused by the action of the borrower, the lenders, or Citibank as agent. It could not be the result of a rule in a country other than the Philippines. The lenders could not have known at the time of the loan that the borrower would face this barrier. U.S. EXIM would pay compensation in dollars if all these conditions were met.

2.   Expropriation Risk

Expropriation occurred by the act of a government agency that had de facto control over the part of the Philippines where HPPC operated. That agency must have caused the default, violating international law by:

1. preventing the Borrower from paying when payment is due;
2. depriving the Borrower of control or disposal of its property or its ability to operate the project;
3. canceling previously issued authorizations to import the item being exported after shipment; or
4. substantially causing the default or depriving the Agent, Lenders, or Trustee of fundamental creditors' rights, such as rights to levy against security or commercial guarantees.

This also included U.S. government restrictions on export of the goods (but no other acts of the U.S. government). The default must have persisted for 90 days. Expropriation did not include acts resulting from (according to the agreement):

"(a) any law, decree, regulation or administrative action of the Government of the Philippines which:

(i) is not by its express terms for the purpose of nationalization, confiscation or expropriation (including by not limited to intervention, condemnation or other taking),

(ii) is reasonably related to constitutionally sanctioned governmental objectives,

(iii) is not arbitrary,

(iv) is based upon a reasonable classification of entities to which it applies, and

(v) does not violate generally accepted principles of international law; or

(b) an action in accordance with any agreement voluntarily made by the Borrower, Agent, Guaranteed Lenders or Trustee [defined later in this Chapter]; or

(c) a provocation or instigation by the Agent, Guaranteed Lenders or Trustee, including corrupt practice which is unlawful at the time under the laws of the United States or the Philippines, provided that (i) actions taken in compliance with a specific request of the Government of the United States or (ii) any reasonable measure taken in good faith by the Agent, Guaranteed Lenders or Trustee, by way of a judicial, administrative or arbitral proceeding respecting any action in which the Government of the Philippines is involved shall be deemed not to be provocations or instigations under this Section 6.02 (c); or

(d) the insolvency of, or creditor's proceedings against, the Borrower under applicable law; or

(e) bona fide exchange control actions by the Government of the Philippines (or its instrumentalities or state enterprises); or

(f) any action which (i) is lawful under the laws of the Philippines of the type described in [this agreement], and (ii) is taken by the Government of the Philippines in any capacity or through the exercise of any powers as shareholder, director or manager of the Project; provided, however, the shares in question have not been acquired through an act or series of acts that, under the criteria set forth in Article VI, constitute Expropriation; or

(g) Any abrogation, impairment, repudiation or breach by the Government of the Philippines (or its instrumentalities or state enterprises) of any undertaking, agreement or contract relating to the Project or Items, provided that the foregoing exclusion shall not preclude a claim otherwise eligible under this Article VI; or

(h) Any action or actions by the Government of the Philippines (or its instrumentalities or state enterprises) that terminate or restrict the use of or maintenance of the Retention Account [defined later in this Chapter] or any offshore accounts of the Borrower, provided that the foregoing exclusion shall not preclude a claim otherwise eligible under this Article VI or Article V related to the Retention Account or any account of the Borrower (or the Proceeds thereof), which, in either case, has been transferred to the Philippines from offshore; ..."

3.   POLITICAL VIOLENCE

Political violence that directly caused default in a payment due on the loan obligated U.S. EXIM to pay compensation. Political violence referred to any violent act intended to achieve a political end. Examples included war, hostile acts of armed forces, civil war, revolution, insurrection, civil strife, terrorism, or sabotage.

c.   THE OVERALL ROLE OF THE EXIMS AND MULTILATERALS

The EXIMs and the multilaterals were the dominant source of funds: 82 percent of the senior loans, plus some equity. To some extent, this represents a subsidy. If the price was right, commercial lenders could have taken a larger share.

However, even if their share of credit had been much smaller, these official institutions would still have had a vital role ensuring the borrower (and its home government) performed. The Philippines has a continuing interest in staying on the right side of the EXIMs, World Bank, and Asian Development Bank, in order to get more money from them. Most of the time private banks like to co-partner with EXIMs and multilaterals to enhance the probability of performance. However, it is possible that the official lenders would not want to enforce claims against a borrower in default for political or developmental reasons, in circumstances in which the private lenders would want to. This could be a particular problem in Pagbilao. The official lenders made over 80 percent of the loans and, since 75 percent of the senior lenders are needed for a suit against a defaulting party, the official lenders would have to approve the suit.

4.   IMPORTANT ARRANGEMENTS AMONG THE PARTIES

The following subsections describe the Common Agreement between the Senior Lenders and HPPC over key terms and the Trust Agreement governing payments by HPPC to the Senior Lenders.

a.   THE COMMON AGREEMENT

HPPC and each of the Senior Lenders entered an agreement, governed by New York law, setting out terms that would apply to all the agreements. The Common Agreement defined terms, set forth principles of construction, gave the financing plan, and then detailed the conditions precedent to initial and all disbursements, the representations and warranties, affirmative and negative covenants, and events of default.

Some elements may be summarized: the debt/equity ratio could not exceed 75/25. The independent engineer could not have disapproved any payments to the contractors. HPPC must consult with any lender about any adverse report of the engineer. All necessary government approvals must remain in full force. HPPC must have no subsidiaries or equity interests in any other person. HPPC must maintain records and make regular reports as stipulated.

The following material from the agreement illustrates some of the most important provisions:

"Representations and Warranties

Submission to Law and Jurisdiction. As of the Initial Borrowing Date, the choice of governing law for each of the respective Project Documents will be recognized in the courts of the Republic, and those courts will recognize and give effect to any judgment in respect of any Project Document obtained against the Company or HEIL in the courts the jurisdictions of which the Company has submitted.

Single-Purpose Company. The company has not traded or incurred any liabilities other than in connection with its participation in the transactions contemplated by the Project Documents.

Status of the Senior Loans. The Obligations constitute direct, unconditional, and general obligations of the Company and rank not less than pari passu as to priority of payment with all other Indebtedness of the company ... or where such Indebtedness is secured by a Permitted Lien. Except as permitted by ... the Agreement, the Company has not secured or agreed to secure any such Indebtedness by any Lien upon any of its present or future revenues or assets or capital stock.

Negative Covenants

6.03 *Dividends: Restricted Payments.* (a) The Company will not declare or pay any dividends, or return any capital, to its stockholders or authorize or make any other distribution, payment or delivery of property or cash to its stockholders as such, or redeem, retire, purchase or otherwise acquire, directly or indirectly, for consideration, any shares of any class of its capital stock now or hereafter outstanding (or any options or warrants issued by the Company with respect to its capital stock), or set aside any funds for any of the foregoing purposes, unless:

(i) such dividend or other action is permitted by applicable law;

(ii) no Default or Event of Default is then in existence (or would be in existence after giving effect to such dividend or other action);

(iii) such dividend or other action is permitted under the Trust and Retention Agreement; and

(iv) either such dividend is a Bonus Dividend or in the case of a cash dividend or distribution, such dividend or distribution is made only after the Project Completion Date and if, after giving effect to such dividend or distribution, (a) the Long-term Debt to Equity Ratio would not exceed 65:35 and (b) the Senior Debt Annual Cover Ratio would be no less than 1.4:1

(b) *Payments of principal and interest on the Sponsor Subordinated Loans* permitted by the Trust and Retention Agreement shall not be deemed restricted by Section ... (a) above.

6.09 *Other Transactions.* The Company will not enter into any partnership, profit-sharing, or royalty agreement or other similar arrangement whereby the Company's income or profits are, or might be, shared with any other Person, or enter into any management contract or similar arrangement whereby its business or operations are managed by any other Person, other than the Project Management Agreement and the Operation and Maintenance Agreement.

6.11 *No Other Business.* The Company will not carry on any business other than in connection with the completion and operation of the Project and will take no action whether by acquisition or otherwise which would constitute or result in any material alteration to the nature of that business.

Events of Default

7.06 *Project Events.* (a) (i) Any of the Operating and Maintenance Agreement, the Project Management Agreement and the Technical Support Agreements shall be assigned or otherwise transferred, materially amended or prematurely terminated (other than by reason of any default on the part of the Lenders or the Trustee) by any other party thereto other than with the written consent of the Required Lenders and no alternative arrangement satisfactory to the Required Lenders has been effected within 30 days thereof or (ii) any of the Project Documents (other than the Operating and Maintenance Agreement, the Project Management Agreement and the Technical Support Agreements) shall be assigned or otherwise transferred, materially amended or prematurely terminated by any party thereto other than with the written consent of the Required Lenders; or

(b) the Company shall cease to have the right to possess and use the Site; or

(c) any event shall have occurred which entitles the Company or NAPOCOR to give a notice under ... the Energy Conversion Agreement; or

(d) the Company shall abandon the Project or otherwise cease to pursue the operation of the Project in accordance with standard industry practice, or shall (except as permitted by [this agreement]) sell or otherwise dispose of any of its interest in the Project; or

(e) the Company shall fail to maintain any of the insurance policies described in ... [this agreement]; or

(f) the Project Completion Date shall not have occurred by February 6, 1997; ...

7.07 *Material Adverse Change.* One or more events, conditions or circumstances (including without limitation Force Majeure as defined in Articles 14.1 (a) and 14.1 (b) of the Energy Conversion Agreement) [discussed earlier] shall exist or shall have occurred which, in the reasonable judgment of the Required Lenders, would adversely affect the ability of the Company or HHL or either of the Turnkey Contractors) in a material respect to meet as required their respective obligations hereunder or under any of the Loan Documents, the Energy Conversion Agreement or the Shareholders Agreement; ...

7.09 *Ownership of the Borrower.* (a) HHL shall cease to maintain Control (as defined below) of the Company or shall sell, transfer, assign or otherwise dispose of (each a "Transfer"), or create or permit to exist any Lien on or in respect of any shares of capital stock of HEIL if, after giving effect to such Transferor Lien, HHL owns directly or indirectly, or possesses voting power in respect of, capital stock of HEIL representing less than fifty-one (51 percent) of total voting power of HEIL (for purposes of this Section 7.09, "Control" means the possession, directly or indirectly, of the power to direct or cause the direction of the management and policies of a Person, whether through ownership of voting securities, by contract, or otherwise); or

(b) HEIL shall cease to maintain Control of the Company [HPPC] or shall Transfer or create or permit to exist any Lien on or in respect of any shares of capital stock of the Company if, after giving effect to such Transfer or Lien, HEIL owns of record or beneficially, or possesses voting power in respect of, capital stock of the Company representing less than sixty-seven (67 percent) of total voting power of the Company; or

(c) the Company or HEIL shall, without the prior consent of the Required Lenders, issue or have outstanding any securities convertible into or exchangeable for its capital stock or issue or grant or have outstanding any rights to subscribe for or to purchase, or any options or warrants for the purchase of, or any agreements, arrangements or understandings providing for the issuance (contingent or otherwise) of, or any calls, commitments or claims of any character relating to, its capital stock, other than as provided in the Financial Plan, the Shareholders Agreement, and the Board of Investments Approval; ..."

The definition of "Required Lenders" is those senior lenders which hold 75 percent or more of the loans committed (before drawdown) or outstanding (if drawn) and are 75 percent of the number of lenders. For this calculation, JEXIM spoke for the Japanese banks and Citibank spoke for its syndicate members.

Other events of default included:

1.   failure to pay any senior loan principal on time or interest within 7 days after the date it was due;

2.   default, beyond the grace period, on debt exceeding $1 million by HEIL, Hopewell Tileman Power, Slipform, or Hopewell Tileman Ltd, or exceeding $10 million by HHL;

3.   a bankruptcy decree against HPPC, HEIL, Hopewell Tileman Power, Hopewell Tileman Ltd., Slipform, or Mitsubishi;

4.   judgments not fully insured against HPPC or HEIL of more than $10 million) or, before the project completion date, against HHL ($10 million), Slipform ($5 million), or Mitsubishi ($20 million).

When an event of default occurred, each lender had the right to notify HPPC that its loan was immediately due and payable. If a bankruptcy decree is entered or if Napocor buys the plant, all loans immediately become due and payable without notice and any obligation to lend more ends.

b.   RISKS FOR SENIOR LENDERS

1.   COMPLETION AND OPERATIONAL RISK

Senior Lenders faced both completion and operational risks. With respect to completion risks, collateral is the most common way senior lenders secure their debt, and Pagbilao had land and plant as possible collateral. But neither provides the kind of protection it would give in most developed countries. The Philippine Constitution prohibited foreigners from owning land, and the plant is only useful if it produces power. Further, claims on both would have to be enforced through inefficient and possibly corrupt Philippine courts. In lieu of collateral, Senior Lenders received commitments from the contractors and HEIL to finance cost overruns up to $200 million. While not providing 100 percent protection, the loan commitment amounted to over 25 percent of the value of the Mitsubishi and Hopewell contracts ($535 million and $167 million). In the case of late completion, Senior

Lenders could draw on the $16 million performance bond from Hopewell and the contractors (Mitsubishi, Hopewell) would pay penalties.

As for operational risks, which could be a decrease in demand for power or a devaluation of the peso, the Senior Lenders were basically protected by capacity fees, and Napocor's agreement to pay dollars to HPPC to allow HPPC to service its dollar debt. The capacity fee makes Napocor liable to pay more than enough to service the senior debt as long as HPPC can produce at 85 percent capacity.

2. POLITICAL RISK

In addition to the risks discussed above, there was political risk. What if a government decided not to allow Napocor and HPPC to service the senior loans? This would constitute Force Majeure under clause B: "rationing or allocation ... imposed by ... decree ... or any other event ... within the reasonable control of ... the government." Napocor would then be required to buy the project for the present value of remaining capacity fees (except fixed operating costs).

This would not give the senior lenders much real protection, however, since any New York decision for the lenders would have to be enforced in the Philippines. In addition, the multilaterals and EXIMs could oppose a suit. Note that if this had occurred during construction, the U.S. bank syndicate could have claimed against the U.S. EXIM political risk insurance (for transfer risk).

Notes and Questions

1. Overall, evaluate the protection given by the Common Agreement to the various parties. Who are the major beneficiaries? What are their principal forms of protection?

2. What accounts for the limitations on HPPC's activities?

3. Who stands to lose most if the events of default occur? Are the events under their control?

4. How effectively has HHL separated itself from the risks of the project?

c. THE TRUST AGREEMENT

HPPC, HEIL, HHL, the contractors in their capacity as subordinated lenders, Mitsubishi Hong Kong as a subordinated lender, and Bank of America as trustee, entered into a trust and retention agreement subject to New York law governing payment on the project. The same parties, other than the lenders and trustee, made an Assignment and Security Agreement creating for the Trustee and the benefit of the lenders, and Mitsubishi Hong Kong security for the obligations. The agreement set priorities among claimants to income streams and security, and procedures for acting if a default occurred.

HPPC and HEIL instructed other parties that owed the project money to pay the Trustee. The Trustee set up a "Retention Account" in its New York office to hold the funds. Most forms of income for the project would be paid into the trust. Most would be dollar accounts, but the Trustee would keep Peso receipts as pesos unless otherwise instructed. Subaccounts would hold different types of proceeds: funds from HPPC's sale of energy to Napocor, insurance payments, liquidated damages paid by the sponsor or contractors for late delivery, funds from the subordinated loans (completion support), and funds from reserves and a security letter of credit. The funds were held for the benefit of the senior lenders then, subordinated to them, Mitsubishi Hong Kong and finally HPPC as residual beneficiary. Only the Trustee controlled the Retention Account. The basic idea of the Trust Arrangement was to get funds out of the Philippines, and avoid Philippines courts in the event of dispute over the funds.

The Trust Agreement set priorities for accounts from which withdrawals from the Retention Account would be made if no event of default had occurred. The Trustee would rely on quarterly reports submitted by HPPC and the lenders to determine the amounts due. When an "extraordinary casualty" occurred, the Trustee could release up to $7.5 million to HPPC in any one fiscal year. The Trustee would also pay any bonus due to HPPC, on the instructions of the Required Lenders. By written notice in advance, the Required Lenders could prevent the Trustee from paying HPPC, HHL, HEIL, or Slipform if they asserted a breach of contract.

HPPC was obliged to have a leading international bank issue a "security letter of credit" (LC) immediately after the first scheduled repayment of the senior loans. The one-year LC would be payable to the Trustee. The amount of the LC would be 33 percent of the amount left due after subtracting $46 million from the funds remaining in the Retention Account after all uses had been satisfied. The Required Lenders could instruct the Trustee to draw on the Security LC according to circumstances specified in the Common Agreement. If a new LC was not received within 30 days of the expiration of the old one, the proceeds from the old one could be deposited in the Security Subaccount. The Trustee could pay senior debt service and principal from this subaccount if the proceeds, reserve, and completion support sub-account lacked funds. Any remaining amounts would meet operating and maintenance costs if funds were not available.

The Trust Agreement also gave the Trustee authority over liquidated damage payments owed by the sponsors or contractors to Napocor.

When a lender alleged default, the rules changed. Any lender could do so in writing. The Trustee's powers depended on whether a large majority of lenders agreed with the allegations. If the Required Lenders did not act after the allegation, the Trustee would not take any enforcement action for six months. The Required Lenders (including the alleging lenders) could determine that the event was cured, in which case the Trustee would take no action. They could waive defaults on covenants, but not on payments of the senior loans or the Mitsubishi loan. If the Required Lenders instructed the Trustee not to enforce the security, no action could be taken for a two-year period from the first notice. After that, the Trustee had to enforce for the benefit of all lenders, by declaring all obligations due and taking any necessary court action.

Overall, project finance today is structured to limit the Senior Creditors' risks substantially, so much so that the government remains obligated to pay even if there is falling demand for the output. Much of the revenue stream is moved off shore and becomes subject to N.Y. law. But ultimately the project's success and the enforcement of the creditors' claims in the event of default must be in the host country. This risk cannot be entirely avoided by the foreign lenders.

A study of all projects in which the Dutch group ING was involved from 1995 to 1997 examined those in which an event entitled lenders to cancel their loans. The two major causes were commercial developments specified in the contracts and the debt service coverage ratio. The study also found two factors that correlated negatively with default: technology with a successful track record and the sponsor's experience with similar projects.[14]

Notes and Questions

1.   In many Asian countries, the civil law tradition was not clear about whether BOT and other types of projects were subject to private law, treating the state as another private party, or to laws governing the state. In the latter case, the bureaucracy could play an important role. This is one more reason to apply the law of a major financial center rather than the host.

2.   Given the role of Napocor and the Philippines government, is this project really non-recourse?

3.   How does the Trust Agreement protect senior lenders? Where do they stand in the order of priorities? Why? How flexible are the provisions?

4.   How well do the various agreements protect senior lenders from political risk? Consider also the role of Eximbank and the multilateral lenders.

5.   Overall, how well does the structure of the Pagbilao project resolve the problems with foreign direct investment encountered by investors and host countries in the past?

---

[14] R. Klompjan and M. Wouters, "Default Risk in Project Finance," Journal of Structured and Project Finance (Fall 2002), p. 10.

F.   SUBSEQUENT DEVELOPMENTS

1.   THE ASIAN CRISIS IMPACT ON PROJECT FINANCE

The Pagbilao project went into operation in 1996, and shortly thereafter, U.S. Southern, an Atlanta-based company, took over Gordon Wu's Consolidated Electric Power Asia, including Hopewell, the indirect owner of HEIL and HPPC, after Hopewell experienced severe financial difficulties. Hopewell was hardly unique among construction firms. The 1997 currency crisis in Asia, discussed in Chapter 19, slowed the growth of projects and project finance throughout that region. The fundamental problem was that energy demand fell. Napocor was at risk because the capacity fees it paid were based on a showing that HPPC could operate at 85 percent of capacity, whether or not the demand for energy justified that amount of output.

Napocor's losses could only be recovered by higher fees to consumers or government subsidies, each of which raised severe political issues. Investors thus faced possible renegotiation of their agreements.

2.   PRIVATIZATION OF NAPOCOR

The IMF, World Bank, and ADB had made privatization of power a key to their release of further loans to the Philippines. Subsidies for Napocor were a major cause of the government's large fiscal deficit.

The Philippine Electric Power Industry Reform Act (EPIRA) was passed in June 2001. The government was to restructure the industry, privatize Napocor's assets and liabilities, open generation and distribution to competition, and transfer transmission to a National Transmission Corporation. The government would assume up to Pesos 200 billion ($4 billion) of Napocor's debts and Napocor would assess consumers for the remainder. During the transition, a new Power Sector Assets and Liabilities Management Corp. (PSALM) would take on Napocor's assets for sale.

The government has had a difficult time finding buyers. By March 2002, Napocor's debt had reached Pesos 310 billion ($6.1 billion), of which 57 percent was owed to multilateral and bilateral creditors, 15 percent to bondholders, and the remaining 28 percent to banks.

3.   RENEGOTIATION

Under s. 68 of EPIRA, a committee was set up to review all contracts with independent power producers, like Pagbilao, which were "grossly disadvantageous or onerous to the government." The Committee identified Pagbilao as one of those projects. This resulted in a restructuring of the

Napocor relationship with Pagbilao, saving an estimated $277 to $387 million over 25 years, a rather minor adjustment.[15]

After Enron, lending to power and energy projects slowed as creditors wondered how many other projects were mismanaged or manipulated. "Investors, lenders, and ratings agencies ... began to perceive independent power producers (IPPs) and traders as riskier ... [and] suspected earnings manipulation." They noted, however, that "'traditional' project finance is cash-flow-based, asset-based finance that has little in common with Enron's heavily criticized off-balance-sheet partnerships."[16]

4.   ENVIRONMENTAL PROBLEMS

In recent years, coal-fired plants like Pagbilao have been the subject of intense environmental concerns. This has been an ongoing issue in the legislature, with some calling for the shutting down of the plant. This would leave Napocor with its continuing obligations to HPPC and nothing in return. The result would be substantially higher power charges, which are already quite high.

In July 2002, Mirant, a spin-off of Southern, and the indirect owner of the Pagbilao project, declared bankruptcy, but the Mirant subsidiary that owns Pagbilao remained unaffected.

CONCLUSIONS

This is the first Chapter that examines financial issues for emerging markets. The advent of project finance reflects a constant theme throughout the book—how markets are able to devise creative solutions to the needs of the users and suppliers of funds. Key to the success of the tool has been a pricing and flow of funds structure that minimizes country risk for both the lender and supplier of funds, but at the same time provides long-term financing for needed infrastructure projects.

Two major policy issues arise in this area. First, is the use of developed country subsidies through the provision of credit and guarantee/insurance arrangements. As in other areas of support from the developed to developing countries, there is a concern that government guarantees create moral hazard for both the countries and the private sector.

The second issue is whether these arrangements are truly in the interest of the countries involved. To the extent that these projects depend on long-term pricing arrangements, that are not tied to consumer demand, e.g.

---

[15] *Megawatt Daily*, October 30, 2002.
[16] H. Davis, "How Enron Has Affected Project Finance," Journal of Structured and Project Finance (Spring 2002), pp. 19-20.

the capacity fees of Pagbilao, they may impose significant burdens on countries which may ultimately result in renegotiation.

CHAPTER EIGHTEEN

PRIVATIZATION AND INSTITUTIONAL INVESTORS

A. INTRODUCTION

The growth of stock markets in many developing countries has outstripped that in industrial countries since the mid-1980s. Fuelling this growth was an almost insatiable appetite for emerging market securities on the part of investors worldwide, often for newly privatized companies. This Chapter examines this phenomenon by looking at the case study of the privatization of a telecommunications company in Mexico.

In 1989, the new president of Mexico, Carlos Salinas de Gortari, announced that the government would divest itself of its controlling interest in Telefonos de Mexico, S.A. de C.V. (Telmex), the third largest company in Mexico, ranked by assets. A Harvard-trained economist, he took office in a close and bitter election in which he had promised to reform the country's economy.

This Chapter starts with background about privatization worldwide. It describes the circumstances in Mexico before 1990 that prompted the government's action. The two options considered were to divest by a public sale followed by a listing on the Mexican stock exchange or to sell the government's full share in a block to foreign investors.

The actual privatization had two stages. The first, in 1990, transferred voting control (but not all of the government's capital) to a private consortium of Mexican and foreign investors. The second stage, in 1991, sold much of the government's remaining stake on equity markets in Mexico, the U.S., Japan, and Europe. Institutional investors, such as pension funds, were major buyers.

B.   PRIVATIZATION IN THE 1980S AND 1990S

Government control of business seemed to be a permanent feature of the landscape in almost every country well into the 1970s. When Margaret Thatcher became U.K. Prime Minister in 1979, she set out to reverse this trend in her country and soon officials were devising ways the government could divest itself of productive firms. Momentum picked up as other industrial and developing countries saw benefits for themselves in the early and mid-1980s. Then communist countries across Eastern Europe and Asia shifted toward market economies and the prospect of the largest asset transfer in the history of the world became dazzling.

During the 1990s, the amounts raised from privatization rose dramatically, from $29.9 billion in 1990 to $153.8 billion in 1997, then retreated to only $114.5 billion in 1998 as the Asian crisis took its toll. About 75 percent of these funds was raised in OECD countries.

1.   WHAT IS PRIVATIZATION?[1]

Privatization is the process of transferring operations and assets from the public to the private sector.

Privatization is fundamentally a political as well as a commercial process. It changes the distribution of power within a society, as it diminishes control of the economy by the state and government-appointed managers.

2.   TYPES OF PRIVATIZATION

Privatization techniques include the following:

Small business auctions are a normal procedure for privatizing small businesses. Given the size of the enterprises, elaborate bid evaluations and valuations are not appropriate and will only serve to delay the process.

Auctions are generally not appropriate for larger enterprises because the bids will not be as readily comparable: the quality of the new ownership group becomes important—what technology will it bring, is it well-financed, what investments will it commit to making, where will it market the product, will it close the business to limit competition, etc.?[2]

Larger enterprises are often sold by soliciting investors to submit bids outlining the terms under which they would purchase shares of the enterprise. The seller must value the enterprise and analyze the strengths and weaknesses of the bidding groups, and then negotiate with the highest ranked bidder.

---

[1] This section relies heavily on J. Waddell, Testimony before the Small Business Committee of the U.S. House of Congress (April 14, 1994).

[2] *ibid.*

Initial Public Offerings (IPOs) are the sale of shares directly to the public. Most of the privatizations conducted in the United Kingdom during the 1980s were done through this method. These sales involve unsophisticated investors and are subject to tight control by securities regulators. IPOs have the virtue of increasing share ownership in society.

IPOs do not bring new capital to the enterprise and do not bring in new managerial talent or resources. Thus, they are often only used if the performance of existing management is satisfactory. In addition, IPOs are very time-consuming and expensive to conduct, and generally require the existence of a securities market.

Another form of privatization is the joint venture. An investor approaches the government and offers to contribute something of value to an enterprise, such as capital, management, or technology, and in return receives a share of the ownership of the newly constituted business. Joint ventures are often attractive because the government does not relinquish all control of the enterprise.

A significant disadvantage to joint ventures is that the government remains involved in management and its liability for poor performance is retained.

One of the significant innovations in privatization techniques was the development of mass privatization programs in former communist countries. Shares are distributed for nothing to the public, or in exchange for specially created privatization vouchers.

Mass privatization programs diffuse ownership across broad groups and create powerful management not subject to effective shareholder control.

As we saw in Chapter 17, on Project Finance, governments have turned to the private sector to finance, build, and operate needed infrastructure facilities. In return, the government gives certain assurances to the investor and pays fees for the services provided.

State-owned enterprises with limited prospects are sometimes liquidated and their assets auctioned to the private sector. Liquidation ends the government's commitment to support an enterprise and lays the groundwork for private sector investment.

C.   TELMEX AS A STATE–OWNED ENTERPRISE

A group of Mexican investors acquired Telmex in 1953, but from the 1950s onward the government was closely involved in the Company's strategic and financial planning. In 1972, the government acquired the majority of the Company's capital stock, and in 1976, a new concession was granted to serve as a general framework for the Company's activities.

As of December 31, 1990, the Mexican telephone system comprised 5.4 million lines in service, or 6.6 lines in service per 100 inhabitants, and 10.3 million telephone sets. It was the 18th-largest national telephone system in the world based on the number of lines in service at year-end 1988. It ranked 83rd in phone line per capita. The average waiting period for a new line was three years.

The business of the Company and the rates it charged for telephone services were subject to comprehensive regulation by the Communications Ministry under the Communications Law, the Telecommunications Regulations, and the Concession.

Of the consolidated revenues of the Company in 1990, approximately 29.1 percent was attributable to international long-distance service, 35.5 percent to domestic long-distance service, and 31.6 percent to local service. Rates, through 1989, were below cost for local service and far above cost for international service, 90 percent of which was with the United States and Canada.

The Company had been managed with little emphasis on operating efficiency. An audit after the sale found $300 million of equipment scattered in 105 Telmex warehouses throughout the country. Telmex has nearly twice as many employees per line as the average Bell company. Accordingly, productivity was always substandard. Repair crews traditionally sold their services to the highest bidder.

In 1990, Telmex had assets of $9.6 billion, total long-term debt of $2.7 billion, and total stockholders' equity of $5.3 billion. Its operating income was $1.05 billion. Its workforce of 65,200 was one of the largest in Mexico aside from the government.

The Telmex capital structure was two classes of stock, AA and A shares. They had identical rights except for voting. Class AA shares had 51 percent of voting rights and capital. Class A has 49 percent of voting rights and capital. AA shares could only be owned by Mexican citizens because Mexican law, described shortly below, required that Telmex be controlled by Mexicans. The A shares could be owned by anyone.

The government owned all of the AA stock, representing 51 percent of the capital, and had voting control. The government also owned 4.9 percent of the A shares. In total it had 55.9 percent of the capital. The A shares were traded on the Mexican Stock Exchange. Mexico's government-owned banks took positions in A Shares and Nacional Financiera (Nafin), one of those banks accounted for on average 10 percent of all A share trades on the Mexican exchange.

About 60 percent of the A shares were held as American Depositary Shares (ADSs) quoted on NASDAQ. Prices of the A shares moved in tandem on the Mexican stock exchange and NASDAQ.

D.   INVESTMENT IN MEXICO

1.   THE MEXICAN STOCK EXCHANGE

The Mexican Stock Exchange, located in Mexico City, was the only stock exchange in Mexico. Founded in 1907, it was organized as a corporation whose shares were held by the brokerage firms, which were exclusively authorized to trade on the floor of the Exchange.

In 1990, the 10 most actively traded equity issues represented 66.6 percent of the total volume of equity issues traded on the Exchange. A Shares of Telmex were the most actively traded equity issue in 1990, accounting for 17.6 percent of total shares traded on the Exchange.

The government had started developing its capital markets in the mid–1970s. Mexico adopted a Securities Market Law in 1975. Institutional development followed the law. The country opened a central depository institution for shares in 1978, a Stock Market Law Academy in 1979, a Mexican Brokerage Houses Association, a Mexican Capital Markets' Institute, and a Contingency Fund in 1980.

The National Securities Commission (CNV), which reported to the Ministry of Finance and Public Credit, regulated the stock market.

Mexico's exchange was among the largest in emerging markets and it equaled the combined volume of the four other leading Latin American exchanges.

2.   FOREIGN INVESTMENT

For over 50 years, Mexico had rules limiting or prohibiting the ability of foreigners to control Mexican business. About the time of the Second World War, foreign control of the country's oil industry was ended by fiat. Soon after, foreigners were prohibited from owning banks in Mexico. Mexicans wanted to assure the country's independence from economic as well as political domination.

Mexico's foreign investment law was designed to protect the country from foreign control.

Ownership by non-Mexicans of shares of Mexican enterprises in certain economic sectors, including telephone services, was regulated by the 1973 Law to Promote Mexican Investment and Regulate Foreign Investment (the Foreign Investment Law) and the 1989 Regulations thereunder (the Foreign Investment Regulations). The National Commission on Foreign Investment (the Foreign Investment Commission) was responsible for administration of the Foreign Investment Law and Regulations. In order to comply with restrictions on the percentage of their capital stock that could be owned by non-Mexican investors, Mexican companies typically limited particular classes of their stock to Mexican ownership.

Non-Mexicans could not own more than 49 percent of the capital stock of a Mexican corporation in the telephone business. No foreign state could own shares directly or indirectly in it.

A Mexican company with foreign owners of its shares had to register those owners, including a depositary for ADSs, with the National Registry of Foreign Investment. No unregistered foreign owner could vote its shares or receive dividends on those shares.

Notes and Questions

1.   Many countries have had rules to limit foreign investment. Many of these countries have been removing or reducing those limits through formal changes in the laws. Mexico has been reluctant to do so. What might account for Mexico's concern about foreign domination of its economy?

2.   How does this law affect the ability of the Mexican government to sell its shares in Telmex? Is it a serious obstacle?

E.   THE TRANSFER OF CONTROL OVER TELMEX TO THE CONSORTIUM

1.   THE REASON FOR PRIVATIZING TELMEX

Salinas' objectives in privatizing Telmex were to reduce the government's role in the economy and to finance the government. The government's budget deficit in 1990 amounted to $7.7 billion, 3 percent; modest compared to many countries. The sale of Telmex would bring the government over $3 billion over two calendar years (1990 and 1991).

The privatization combined two approaches. It was a sale to a strategic investor. The winning consortium, as described below, consisted of two foreign telephone companies and a local group of investors. Their shareholding gave them a stake in the profits and a strong interest in making Telmex perform well.

It also resembled a joint venture since the government retained a 26 percent stake. But the government relinquished any direct control when it sold all its voting shares.

2.   THE WINNING BIDDERS

The government decided to sell its AA shares to a private group. Three groups bid. The winner was Southwestern Bell, with France Telecom and Grupo Carso as partners, which paid $1.8 billion for the shares. Of this, the Mexican partner, Grupo Carso, provided 51 percent.

Grupo Carso led by Mexican industrialist Carlos Slim was an entrepreneurial organization with a solid track record in running diverse enterprises. Grupo Carso had experience in basic industry, finance, retailing, and real estate, all of which had application in making Telmex a world class provider of telecom services.

Southwestern Bell was one of the most highly regarded U.S. telecommunications companies with a reputation for particular excellence in cellular communications, telephone directories, general marketing, and customer service skills. Furthermore, 2000 miles of common border made for significant interest in Telmex.

France Telecom had substantial experience in rapid modernization, having built up the French network from 4 million access lines in 1971 to approximately 28 million lines by 1980, a compound annual growth rate of almost 11 percent sustained over two decades. This achievement was particularly relevant given the government's requirement that access lines growth in Mexico be no less that 12 percent a year for 5 years, more than double Telmex's historical growth level.

The foreign phone companies brought experience Telmex needed. Bell's customer service skills would help Telmex expand and strengthen its customer base. Bell's cellular phone technology could substitute for a shortage of phone lines. France Telecom had rapidly modernized France's phone system. Grupo Carso had experience in related industries like real estate, but not telecommunications.

3.   THE NEW CAPITAL STRUCTURE

The government transferred to the consortium all of the AA stock in Telmex and with it 51 percent of the votes. Table 18A, below, shows the resulting shift in ownership.

Table 18A

Owner groups	Share of Capital (percentage)	
	Before sale to Consortium	After sale to Consortium
Government	55.9	26.0
Government subject to consortium option		5.1
Consortium		20.4
Employees of Telmex		4.4
Public	44.1	44.1

At the time of the sale to the consortium, Telmex's capital stock was increased 1.5 times by the addition of a new type of share, the L share. The L shares were issued as a stock dividend to existing shareholders. The L share effectively had no voting power. The L shareholders could only elect 2 of the board's 19 directors, so they were treated as having no vote. The AA and A shares, after the issue of the L shares, accounted for 40 percent of Telmex's total capital stock and 100 percent of its voting stock.

Table 18B, below, compares changes in the distribution of shares by voting rights and by class.

Table 18B

	Distribution by class of stock (percentage)				
	of voting rights		of capital stock		
	AA	A	AA	A	L
Before the L share dividend	51	49	51.0	49.0	
After the L share dividend (12/20/91)	51	49	20.4	19.6	60.0

The consortium had 20.4 percent of all shares and 51 percent of voting rights through its ownership of the AA shares. These shares were put into a trust. Among members of the consortium, beneficial ownership in the trust was distributed to Grupo Carso, 28 percent itself and 23 percent through 50 other Mexican investors for a total of 51 percent, and control, and 24.5 percent to each of the two foreign members.

Did this structure reflect the spirit of the Mexican foreign investment laws? Mexicans still had voting control. The foreign strategic investors were willing to accept only 49 percent beneficial ownership of the AA shares in the trust. The A holders still had 49 percent of the voting shares, which they had before. The L holders accepted no voting rights.

But the "controlling" Mexicans were in business with the 49 percent foreign partners, who had the expertise to manage Telmex and on whose expertise the Mexican AA investors depended to exercise their control. It is quite possible that effective control of the voting power of the trust was in the hands of the two foreign companies.

It is difficult to legislate control. IBM's experience in India in the 1970s is a poignant example. Indian law changed to forbid IBM from having a 100 percent subsidiary. IBM sold its entire stake to a local investor, which became the service company for IBM equipment and IBM imports. IBM thus had no shares in the new India company. However, the service company depended on IBM so completely that IBM retained effective control. Control can be exercised even without shares; it rests with the party that has the leverage.

4.   THE MODIFIED CONCESSION

Mexican laws were modified to embody the government's new policies. Some new rules set standards that Telmex would have to meet. Others provided incentives to the new owners to meet these standards.

The Communications Law, adopted in 1940, and the Telecommunications Regulations, adopted in October 1990, provided the general legal framework for the regulation of telecommunications services in Mexico. Under the Communications Law and the Telecommunications Regulations, a provider of public telecommunications services, such as Telmex, had to operate under a concession granted by the Communications Ministry.

Substantial changes in the regulatory regime applicable to Telmex occurred in 1990, including the amendment of the Concession, the adoption of the Telecommunications Regulations, and the elimination of excise taxes on telephone services.

Rates

Through 1990, the Company's rates were established separately for each category of service by the Communications Ministry, upon application by the Company. Under the 1990 amendment to the Concession, beginning in 1991 the Company's rates for basic telephone services, including installation, monthly rent, measured local service, and long-distance service, were subject to a ceiling on the price of a "basket" of such services. Within this aggregate "price cap," the Company was free to determine the structure of its own rates. Approval of the Communications Ministry was not required for rates to take effect, although the Company was required to publish its rates and register them with the Ministry. The Communications Ministry also has the power, subject to the basis set forth in the Concession for determining rates, to modify rates when required in the public interest.

The price cap varied directly with the National Consumer Price Index (NCPI), permitting the Company to raise nominal rates to keep pace with inflation. The Concession also provided that, beginning on January 1, 1997, the price cap would be adjusted downward periodically to pass on the benefits of increased productivity to the Company's customers. Beginning on January 1, 1999, and every four years thereafter, the Communications Ministry would set the amount of the periodic adjustment of the price cap, following administrative proceedings, to permit the Company to maintain an internal rate of return equal to the Company's weighted average cost of capital.

A principal goal of the government in establishing the price cap system was to permit the Company to increase local service rates to meet its costs and to reduce long-distance rates in anticipation of possible competition beginning in August 1996. The Company was required under the Concession and the Telecommunications Regulations to eliminate cross subsidies between different categories of services, subject to specified exemptions such as rural telephone services.

The Company could set its prices free of rate regulation for "value-added" services extending beyond basic telephone services. These services included the Integrated Digital Network, private circuits, directory services, and new services based on digital technology such as call waiting, speed calling, and automatic re-dialing. The Company was required to register the rates it charged for value-added services, and the Communications Ministry had power under the Telecommunications Regulations to begin regulating rates for such services if it determined that there was no effective competition and that the Company was abusing monopoly power in pricing such services. Rates for cellular mobile telephone services were regulated under separate concessions.

Taxation of Telephone Services

Through 1989, the government imposed a high level of taxation of telephone use. In 1989, for example, telephone charges were subject to an excise tax that ranged from 22 percent on international long-distance calls to 72 percent on local commercial service charges, and to a value added tax of 15 percent calculated on the aggregate of the charges plus the excise tax. Beginning on January 1, 1990, excise taxes no longer applied to telephone charges. Also beginning on January 1, 1990, the Company was subject to a tax on revenues from telephone services.

Expansion and Modernization Requirements

As amended in 1990, the Concession required the Company to expand, improve, and modernize its telephone network. In particular, the Company had to: (i) during the period between August 10, 1990 and December 31, 1994, expand the number of lines in service by an average minimum annual rate of 12 percent; (ii) expand its services to rural areas, and in particular provide each town in Mexico with more than 500 inhabitants (as determined by the 1990 Census) with at least one public telephone booth or agency for providing long-distance services by December 31, 1994; (iii) expand the number of public telephone booths from a current density of 0.8 booths per 1,000 inhabitants to 2 booths per 1,000 inhabitants by the end of 1994 and 5 booths per 1,000 inhabitants by the end of 1998; and (iv) reduce the maximum waiting time for installation of telephone service (in cities with automatic exchanges) to six months by 1995 and to one month by 2000.

The amended Concession also set forth extensive goals for the quality of the Company's services, including reductions in line failures, reductions in repair time, reductions in the time required to obtain a dial tone, improvements in the percentage of calls completed on the first attempt, and reductions in installation time.

Competition

The Telecommunications Regulations and the 1990 amendment to the Concession contained various provisions designed to introduce competition in the provision of communications services. In general, the Communications Ministry was authorized to grant concessions to other parties for the provision of any of the services provided by the Company under the Concession, except that, as long as the Company was in compliance with the Concession, no competing provider of domestic or international long-distance services could operate before August 1996. After August 1996, the Communications Ministry could grant concessions to other long-distance carriers. The Company was required to permit any other concessionaire to connect to its network and, after December 31, 1996, it had to permit other long-distance telephone networks to be connected in a manner that enabled customers to choose the network by which their calls were carried. The Company was also required to permit users of its telephone network to resell excess capacity, except that until August 1996 it was not required to permit the resale of any excess capacity for use in providing long-distance services. Concessions were not required to operate certain private local telecommunications networks or to provide value-added services, although other authorizations could be required.

Termination of the Concession

The Concession further provided that it would remain in force until 2026, and that it could be renewed by the Company for an additional 15 years subject to additional requirements the Communications Ministry may impose.

The Concession provided that upon its expiration, the government was entitled to purchase the telecommunications assets of the Company at a price determined on the basis of an appraisal by a public official, and the Telecommunications Regulations provided that upon expiration of the Concession, the government had a right of first refusal to acquire the telecommunications assets of the Company. The Communications Law, however, provided that upon expiration of the Concession, the telecommunications assets of Telmex would revert to the government free of charge. There was substantial doubt as to whether the provisions of the Concession and the Telecommunications Regulations would prevail.

The Communications Law and the Concession included various provisions under which the Concession could be terminated before its scheduled expiration date.

The Communications Law provided that in the event of early termination of the Concession for specified causes, including violation of the prohibition on ownership of the Company's shares by foreign states, the Company would forfeit all of its telecommunications assets to the government. In the event of early termination of the Concession for any other cause, the Communications Law provided that a portion of the Company's telecommunications assets would revert to the government free of charge, and that the Company could be required to dismantle the remaining portion.

Protection of the Consortium Against Future Competition

A major way for Telmex to protect against adverse government regulation or more competition was by getting its investment back quickly.

The consortium paid $1.8 billion. To recoup this in four years, before its monopoly was eroded, it would need to receive roughly $450 million each year in dividends. Given its 20.4 percent interest, this meant that total equity would have to earn five times $450 million or $2.25 billion each year. This was a 25 percent return on assets of $9.6 billion in 1990 and a 42 percent return on equity (dividends were tax free to non-residents of Mexico). In fact, Goldman Sachs estimated in 1991 that Telmex would earn a 37 percent return on equity. So consortium investors might have concluded in 1990 that they could repay their investment before the monopoly ended.

Notes and Questions

1.   Compare the old and new capital structures. What accounts for the added complexity? Does the new capital structure reflect the spirit of the foreign investment laws?

2.   How does the modified concession protect Mexico now that the government no longer controls Telmex? Compare the performance requirements with the incentives given to the restructured company. How complete is this privatization?

3.   Why would the consortium want to enter this transaction? What incentives are given to them?

4.   Suppose the consortium manages Telmex successfully and the company is very profitable. Should the consortium be concerned about anything? Evaluate the rules governing the termination of the Concession from the perspective of members of the winning group.

F.   THE OFFER OF TELMEX SHARES IN WORLD MARKETS

In May 1991, the government sold another 14 percent of its Telmex shares in a $2.17 billion global public offering. The offering consisted of 100 million L shares offered in Mexico, to be listed on the Mexican Exchange, and 70 million American Depositary Shares (ADSs), each representing 20 L shares, to be listed on the NYSE. A shares could be converted on a one-for-one basis into L shares.

1.   THE EVOLUTION OF THE TELMEX CAPITAL STRUCTURE

After the May privatization, the government's ownership of all shares had fallen from almost 56 percent before the sale to the consortium to just under 10 percent. Table 18C, below, shows the capital charges.

Table 18C

Owner groups	Before sale to winning consortium (%)	After sale to winning consortium (%)	After May 1991 offering (%)
Government	55.9	26.0	9.5
Government subject to option of controlling shareholders		5.1	5.1
Consortium		20.4	20.4
Employees of Telmex		4.4	5.8
Public	44.1	44.1	59.2

The offering shifted voting rights and the distribution of the stock among the three categories of shares as shown in Table 18D:

Table 18D

	Distribution by class of stock (percentage)				
	of voting rights		of capital stock		
	AA	A	AA	A	L
Before the L share dividend	51	49	51	49	60.0
At the L share dividend (12/20/91)	51	49	20.4	19.6	
After the May 1991 public offering	64	36	20.4	11.5	68.1

2.   THE AMERICAN DEPOSITARY RECEIPTS

The ADSs on the L shares would be listed on the New York Stock Exchange. Morgan Guaranty Trust Company was to serve as the depositary for the L Shares. The depositary would issue American Depositary Receipts evidencing American Depositary Shares. The Banco Nacional de Mexico, as custodian, would hold the L shares. Any L shareholder could place the shares with the custodian and receive ADSs from the depositary. Any ADS holder could surrender the ADSs to the depositary and receive L shares. Cash payments of dividends on L shares would be converted promptly by the depositary into U.S. Dollars and distributed to ADS holders. Mexico would impose no taxes on any distribution or on capital gains.

The government did not offer its L shares on the Mexican Exchange because it could not raise the $3 billion there. The exchange had grown substantially, but in 1990 its total capitalization was the equivalent of only $33 billion. A $3 billion offering would have swamped it. Further, Mexico needed dollars to build up its reserves—it had an $80 billion foreign debt.

In the first two months after the May offering, about 70 percent of all A ADR holders converted into L shares in ADR form, one-for-one. However, only 1.2 percent of A shareholders in Mexico opted to convert into L shares; these investors wanted to be in pesos. L shares were priced in Dollars. Also A shares had a vote, even if only a minority.

Notes and Questions

1.   Why would an A shareholder, after the May 1991 closing, want to exchange its shares for L shares? Why would investors trading ADSs in Telmex A shares on NASDAQ want to switch to L shares? What do they gain and what do they lose? Why would investors trading Telmex A shares in Mexico not want to switch to L shares?

2.   What accounts for the complex nature of this offer? Is the offer and its structure consistent with the spirit of the Mexican foreign investment law?

3.   What is likely to be the relation between the L shares traded on the Mexican Stock Exchange and the L ADSs traded on the New York Stock Exchange? Would you expect pricing in one market to lead the other? If so, what are the implications for the country whose exchange follows the other?

G.   DEMAND FOR THE TELMEX OFFER

The market for the Telmex offer was institutional investors in the U.S., Europe, and Japan. Less than a decade earlier, pension funds, insurance companies, and mutual funds showed little interest in foreign equities, particularly in developing countries. Regulations that limited their freedom to invest were sometimes said to be the reason: a U.S. insurance company might be allowed to invest no more than 5 percent of its assets in foreign securities. A German pension fund would be required to invest a large part of its assets in government debt, ostensibly because these carried no or low risk, and also limited to investing only 30 percent of its funds in equity. But these rules were not so binding, since few funds pushed against the regulatory ceilings. German pension funds, for example, invested barely 3 percent of their funds in equity.

H.   THE DECEMBER 1994 PESO CRISIS

On December 20, 1994, the Mexican government devalued the Peso 15 percent against the Dollar to 25 cents/Peso and two days later let the Peso float. It fell almost 50 percent in four weeks. Foreign investors in Telmex ADSs and other Mexican securities reeled. Mutual funds specializing in Mexican paper saw their price fall 5 percent on December 21 alone and plummet after that. Chapter 19 describes the crisis and its aftermath for emerging market debt.

1.   TELMEX AND THE CRISIS

In 1993, several years into transition, Telmex had $3 billion profits on $8 billion in sales, foreign investors who had invested $18 billion, 18 percent of the Mexican Stock Exchange's capitalization, and 23 percent of its trading volume. Telmex benefited from the wealth and power of its principal Mexican owner, Carlos Slim, who was the richest man in the country. On the other hand, Telmex had a bad reputation for service and only 8.8 phones existed for each 100 people.

The crisis hit Telmex on and off the exchanges. Its L ADS's high on the NYSE in 1994 was $76, but by early March 1995 it traded at $25. The Peso price of the L shares on the Mexican exchange moved down the same percentage in Dollar terms. Telmex announced a loss during the first quarter of 1995 of P390 million ($67 million) because of foreign exchange losses of P4.3 billion. Telmex sharply cut its capital expenditures to reduce costs. This worried investors, who expected that Telmex would be hurt by new legislation to increase competition in both local and long-distance markets in 1997.[3]

There are several reasons why the Peso's decline hurt Telmex's prospects:

a.   To the extent Telmex bought capital equipment from the U.S., essential to upgrade service, the cost substantially increased.

b.   Calls out of the country would diminish to the extent that the customers' costs were in foreign currencies (e.g. payments to American long distance company).

c.   It would reduce Telmex's revenues as customers' spending capacity fell.

d.   Telmex's Peso cost of borrowing Dollars abroad increased. If the government austerity program included tighter monetary policy, the cost of borrowing in Pesos would also rise.

The Peso value of Telmex's dollar earnings from long distance did increase, but that advantage still left P4.3 billion in FX losses. The fact that Telmex's huge profits offset all but P390 million of this loss was not completely reassuring for the long run because Telmex might soon face competition.

The Mexican government seemed to be proceeding with its plan to open the country's phone market to competition. In July 1994, it issued rules permitting unlimited competition and forcing Telmex to give competitors access to its exchanges. Only the fees due from new entrants remained to be set. Foreign firms were positioning themselves. AT&T entered a joint venture in November 1994 with a major industrial conglomerate, Grupo Alfa, in which Carlos Slim held a 15 percent share. Other companies, like MCI and Motorola, entered similar ventures with Mexican firms. Telmex's original

---

[3] See D. Dombey, "Telmex Blames Heavy Forex Loss for Fall into Red," *Financial Times*, April 29, 1995.

partners were seen as inexperienced with the complex billing software that Telmex needed to keep a high market share, so Telmex allied with Sprint.

The Mexican Government sought ways to offset the likely damage of this expected competition to Telmex, which depended on long-distance revenues to show a profit. A revised fee schedule in 1995 gave Telmex a subsidy to offset the losses on its domestic services since the profits from long distance service would not subsidize domestic services as much as in the past. Another source of help was an agreement between Mexico and the U.S. Government that as long as Telmex had at least 75 percent of the northbound phone traffic it would be entitled to handle 75 percent of the southbound traffic regardless of which foreign carrier originated the call.[4]

The recession in 1995 hurt Telmex, so that its net sales fell 6 percent below the 1994 level. Nevertheless, the company was able to securitize $280 million of telephone receivables in international markets in early 1996. The Mexican government set up a regulatory commission for telecommunications, anticipating the end of Telmex's monopoly. And Carlos Slim spun his company's interest in Telmex off into a separate firm, apparently to protect his company from loss if Telmex should suffer. But by 1996, his company was buying Telmex stock.

The prospect of a competitive telecommunications industry in 1997 was daunting. Telmex began to connect its exchanges to competitors' long-distance lines in January 1997, having already lowered its long-distance prices in anticipation. Two rivals launched an advertising blitz to announce the new regime. They were linked, respectively, to MCI and AT&T and expected to invest $1 billion each by 2000. A 20 percent per annum growth was forecast in the long-distance market and Telmex's rivals hoped to win a 40 percent market share by 2000. But in June 1997, 70 percent of Mexican customers in 26 cities opted, by choice or inertia, to stay with Telmex as their long distance carrier, leaving its rivals a small share of the market. The rivals, however, argued that government policy continued to support Telmex to their disadvantage. Anticipating this challenge, Telmex had invested $11 billion since it was privatized. It cut costs and diversified. Mexico City's phone system was much improved. A Telmex subsidiary dominated the limited cellular phone market.

2.   TELMEX AND THE WTO

Telmex prospered and grew in international markets. It retained 90 percent of the domestic market in mid-2002. It had become cash-rich while most of the telecommunications industry around the world languished. Telmex shares rose in value, buoying the Mexican Exchange. It was looking for opportunities. It expanded in or entered all Latin American countries

---

[4] T. Bardacke, "Tough Times for Telmex as Mexico Prepares to Open Market," *Financial Times*, November 17, 1994.

except Argentina. In late 1997, Telmex won FCC preliminary approval to enter the U.S. market with Sprint, targeting Hispanic communities in the Southwest. When AT&T and MCI froze payments due to Telmex and challenged Telmex's entry into the U.S. market, Telmex threatened to seek redress from the World Trade Organization. In May 2003, the Federal Communication Commission allowed Telmex to operate in the U.S.

Telmex shared its good fortune with local consumers. In 2002, local rates were still not up to market prices and Telmex was expected to continue to subsidize them for at least two more years from the connection fees paid by its competitors.

Not everyone was pleased. Mexico's antitrust commission fined Telmex in October 2001 for offering long distance rates to its own subscribers at rates below those it charged competitors who had to use the Telmex network. In November 2002, the commission decided that Telmex also violated the anti-trust law by refusing competitors' requests for hardware needed to provide long distance service, delayed servicing competitors' phone lines, and delayed processing payments to them.[5]

Telmex leveraged its political and economic power to impose onerous conditions on long-distance competitors, because they had to use Telmex to reach almost all of their Mexican customers. In an action urged by the U.S. competitors, the FTC fined Telmex's U.S. subsidiary $100,000 for unfair practices and high interconnection costs. Then in July 2000, the US trade representative, Charlene Barshevsky, started a process to bring Mexico before the WTO. She was responding to complaints from U.S. companies like AT&T and WorldCom that Telmex was keeping them out of phone markets in Mexico, with the help of the country's regulators. The U.S. said that "Telmex overcharges to connect local calls to the long-distance networks, applies unfair fees for incoming international long-distance phone calls, and denies competitors the high-traffic lines they need for Internet service."[6] Then Mexican regulators, trying to avoid the WTO, ordered Telmex to cut its interconnection rates 63 percent and the U.S. put its action on hold. In April 2001, the U.S. gave Mexico until June 1 to remove the barriers still in place, or the WTO arbitration would proceed.

The U.S. finally acted on its threat, starting a WTO action in October 2002. It alleged that Mexico permitted Telmex to charge three times cost for calls it carried into Mexico, to cross-subsidize, avoid implementing commitments, and remain a monopolist. In April 2004, the Dispute Resolution Panel at WTO ruled that Mexico's interconnection charges were too high when the Panel was established in February 2002, 13.5 cents per

---

[5] Intelecon Research & Consultancy Ltd., *Mexico's Antitrust Commission Rules Against Telmex*, January 16, 2003.
[6] A. DePalma, "U.S. Seeks W.T.O. Talks On Mexican Phone Market," *The New York Times*, July 29, 2000.

minute. Rates had fallen, however, to 9.2 cents by the time of the ruling, but still more than double the charges the U.S. believed were justified on the basis of costs. In June 2004, when the panel's report was adopted by the Dispute Settlement Body, the U.S. and Mexico announced an accord to resolve the dispute. Mexico will scrap legislation giving Telmex exclusive authority to negotiate rates with U. S. carriers as to call from the U.S. completed by a Mexican operator and Mexico will allow the resale of international services from Mexico to other countries.[7]

CONCLUSIONS

This Chapter examines two key phenomena in emerging markets, privatization through foreign investment and the use of foreign stock exchanges to trade in privatized company shares.

The major issue raised by the Telmex case was the decision of Mexico to guarantee a monopoly to foreign investors for a significant period of time so as to maximize its revenues from the privatization. As recent history has shown, once a privately owned monopoly is entrenched it may be difficult to get rid of it even after it is no longer legally or contractually entitled to the monopoly position.

The use of foreign stock exchanges seems even more important to emerging markets than to developed market firms. Since foreign markets generally are more efficient, provide more liquidity, and represent bonding opportunities, they are very attractive to large emerging market issuers. Unlike the case for developed market issuers, where most trading in dual listed shares either remains or moves back to the home market, the foreign venue becomes the market of choice for emerging market issuers.

---

[7] WT/DS 204/R, April 2, 2004; F. Williams, "Mexico and U.S. in Accord on Telecoms Access," *Financial Times*, June 2, 2004.

CHAPTER NINETEEN

EMERGING MARKET DEBT

A. INTRODUCTION

On international markets, borrowers from developing countries have a spotty record of debt service extending back over 150 years.

In the 19th century, Europeans bought bonds issued by "railroads and mines in Spain, Austria, Turkey, and Russia, banks in Egypt, Mexico, Haiti, and the Balkans, nickel in Caledonia, guano in Peru, the canal at Panama."[1] Bonds financed the construction of U.S. railroads. Waves of default on these bonds swept the world during economic depression and war: 1873, 1893, 1914-18, 1929, and 1939-45.

Borrowers from many countries defaulted. One borrower was the khedive, or ruler, of Egypt from 1863 to 1879, Pasha Ismail. Egyptian cotton rode an export boom during the U.S. Civil War, when prices soared worldwide. The Khedive issued bonds in the U.K. and France to finance "grandiose schemes, including irrigation projects, schools, palaces, the construction of the Suez Canal and the extensions of Egyptian rule in the Sudan. Much of the money was wasted."[2] Then came the depression of 1873, and the Pasha could not repay the debt on schedule.

The 19th century solution to default was straightforward. The British government, supported by France, led the effort to help the Pasha service his debt. In 1876, they set up a bondholders commission to help the Pasha manage his finance. After an armed uprising in 1879, Britain sent troops. Its consul general took de facto control of Egypt's government. Ismail's son replaced the father as pasha. The parties agreed to reschedule the debt over a 30-year period and Britain agreed to retain control of Egypt's government pending full payment. British capital and skills integrated Egypt into the British Empire as a valuable agricultural producer and a market for British goods. This was an outcome Pasha Ismail had probably not looked for when he started to borrow.[3] It was echoed so widely then that former U.S. President Ulysses S. Grant warned the emperor of Japan, during a visit there, not to let his country borrow in international markets if it wanted to retain its independence.

---

[1] H. Feis, *Europe, The World's Banker: 1870–1914* (1936), p. 64.

[2] *Columbia Encyclopaedia* (3rd Ed., 1963), p. 1052.

[3] See R. Mabro and S. Radwan, *The Industrialization of Egypt, 1839-1973: Policies and Performance* (1976), p. 19.

A century later, creditor governments seemed no less interested in protecting their lenders but were more circumspect when enforcing the claims.

Since the 1960s, many different types of credit flowed to borrowers in emerging markets, which include developing, or less developed, countries (LDCs) and those in transition from communism. The debt includes loans from other governments (called official bilateral debt) and multilateral agencies such as the World Bank, and banks, as well as international bonds, notes, and short-term credit instruments.

The crises are more frequent now than before 1914 and the techniques to resolve them have become more complex. Generally, the external debt crisis combines with a foreign exchange crisis to cripple the borrowing country. One study found 85 percent of all defaults linked to a currency crisis.[4] The impact of debt and exchange crises on output is bad, but the combination is not worse than the separate impact of each component, according to M. Hutchison, and I. Neuberger.[5]

The frequency of debt crises raises the question of why they happen so much. Are international capital markets deficient? Why do the same countries appear on the default list repeatedly? One convincing view is that governments find it easy to borrow but do not like to repay. They are debt intolerant because of weak domestic institutions and political systems, essentially problems of governance. Lenders know this, so they lend short term and in strong currencies that raise the cost of debt service. These countries almost never reduce their debt burden by growing out of it.[6]

This Chapter is organized into two parts. Part One in Section B describes the overall features of emerging market debt, together with an examination of the major crises between 1982 and the present. Part Two in Section C deals with the general lessons to draw from these crises, and possible methods to alleviate their frequency and impact.

B.   THE DEBT PROBLEM

1.   OVERALL CHARACTERISTICS

Table 19A, below, records the outstanding external long-term (over one-year) debt of 157 low and middle income developing countries from 1970.

---

[4] C. Reinhart, "Default, Currency Crises, and Sovereign Credit Ratings," NBER Working Paper 8738 (January 2002).

[5] "How Bad Are Twins? Output Costs of Currency and Banking Crises" Federal Reserve Bank of San Francisco Pacific Basin Working Paper (January 2002).

[6] C. Reinhart, K. Rogoff, and M. Savastano, "Debt Intolerance," NBER Working Paper 9908 (August 2003) and R. Litan, M. Pomerleano, and V. Sundararajan, "Strengthening Financial Sector Governance in Emerging Markets" Brookings Conference Report (July 2002).

The countries include South Korea and Mexico, as well as many poorer economies. This table reveals the following trends: (1) significant growth—debt with over one year maturity increased from $46.2 billion to $1.5 trillion; (2) shift from bank to bond debt—1970 bank debt was $3.6 billion as compared to bond debt of $1.8 billion, whereas in 2000, bond debt was $368.4 billion as compared to bank debt of $157.8 billion; and (3) the growth of IMF debt outstanding from $800 million in 1970 to $108.7 billion in 2003. Short-term debt has also increased, from 21 percent of long-term debt in 1970 to 33 percent in 2003. Interestingly, short-term debt has decreased little since the 1997 Asian Crisis when it was about 34.5 percent.

There is a very active market in emerging market debt. The Emerging Market Trade Association (EMTA) estimates that trading in emerging market debt was $4.65 billion in 2004, a 17 percent increase over 2003.[7] Despite all the debt difficulties described in this chapter, 2004 saw 21.9 percent of all sovereign ratings improve, the highest upgrade rate since 1975.[8]

Table 19A
Long-term Debt Outstanding of All Developing Countries:[9]
($ billions, end of year)

Creditors	1970	1980	1990	1997	2000	2003
A. Public and publicly guaranteed long term debt[1] *of which*:	45.4	341.7	1041.2	1314.9	1376.5	1427.5
Commercial banks	3.6	122.7	250.4	195.7	157.8	154.1
Bonds	1.8	12.8	104.3	288.7	368.4	416.3
Other private creditors[2]	7.0	56.4	135.6	99.2	69.7	51.7
Bilateral official creditors	25.8	103.8	347.7	448.6	448.0	430.7
Multilateral creditors (not IMF)	7.3	46.2	203.2	282.8	332.7	374.7
B. Use of IMF credit	0.8	11.6	34.7	59.7	58.5	108.7
C. Subtotal (A + B)	46.2	353.3	1075.9	1374.6	1435.0	1536.2
D. Short-term debt (all types of creditors and borrowers)	9.5	143.7	250.7	453.0	381.8	473.0
E. Private non-guaranteed long-term debt	15.2	68.3	60.1	354.7	546.7	532.8
F. Total (A + B + D + E)	70.9	565.3	1386.7	2182.3	2363.5	2542.0
Note: Commercial banks, bonds, and other private creditors as percent of line C	26%	54%	46%	42%	42%	41%

1. Long term debt is debt with an original maturity of more than 1 year.
2. Other private creditors are manufacturers, exporters, and other suppliers of goods, and bank credits covered by a guarantee of an export credit agency

[7] EMTA, Survey, February 28, 2005.
[8] P. Munter, "Sovereign Ratings Improving Fast," *Financial Times*, September 29, 2004.
[9] World Bank *Global Development Finance* (2004) Statistical tables.

The debt load of emerging markets despite increasing in absolute terms has actually decreased overall in the last decade. In 1996 as compared to 2005, external debt to exports was 151.6 compared to 86.2, and external debt to GDP was 37.8 compared to 31.8. Further in 1995 external government debt was 37.2 percent of GDP as compared with 36 percent in 2002.[10] While major defaults are still a significant problem, overall default rates are falling. Overall, there are 25 current defaults, 11 in sub-Saharan Africa, 8 in Latin America, 4 in Asia-Pacific, and 1 each in Central Europe and the Middle East and North Africa. The issuer default rate on foreign currency debt is 12.4 percent compared to a peak of nearly 31 percent in 1990.[11]

2.   DEBT CRISES 1982-1990

a.   SYNDICATED BANK LOANS TO DEVELOPING COUNTRIES: THE 1982 DEBT CRISIS AND THE FORCED RESCHEDULINGS OF THE 1980S

1.   LENDING BY BANKS TO BORROWERS FROM DEVELOPING COUNTRIES TO 1982

Until the early 1970s, the major cross-border flow of funds to emerging markets was from official sources (government or multilateral), supplemented by foreign direct investment and credit to support exports to the borrowers. A mere seven years later, the share of bank loans doubled to 39 percent of total flows, $48 billion.[12]

Much of the new bank lending allowed borrowing countries to finance huge deficits in the balance of trade caused by the first oil shock, the sudden quadrupling in the oil price in 1973. Since the oil exporting countries deposited much of their huge trade surpluses in international banks, people said the banks were recycling the oil money. The U.S. Treasury estimated that in 1974 the oil producers placed $22.5 billion of their $71 billion current account surplus in Eurocurrency markets.[13]

The banks loaned the money in various ways, but their major instrument was the medium-term floating-rate syndicated Eurocurrency loan or Eurocredit. Chapter 11 describes this financial market, the institutions in it, and the major provisions of a Eurocredit contract.

When OPEC doubled the price of oil in 1979, creating the second oil shock, the major non-oil producing developing companies (NODCs) borrowers were in Latin America. Their current account deficits almost tripled from

---

[10] IMF, World Economic Outlook, September 2004.

[11] Standard & Poor's, Sovereign Defaults Set to Fall Again in 2005, September 28, 2004.

[12] Organization for Economic Cooperation and Development, *Development Cooperation Review 1970 and 1977.*

[13] Office of International Banking and Portfolio Investment, U.S. Treasury Department, *Estimates of the Disposition of OPEC Investable Surplus, 1974-1979* (June 13, 1980); P. Wellons, *World Money and Credit: The Crisis and Its Causes* (1983), p. 43.

$4.5 billion in 1973 to $11.3 in 1978, and their borrowing grew. While the banks were much less willing to lend, they were afraid that if they stopped completely the borrowers would not be able to service the outstanding debt. So they continued to lend, but increasingly short term and at a slower rate.

Banks more eagerly increased their lending to oil-producing countries, such as Mexico. From December 1978 to December 1981, banks increased their loans to Mexico by 138 percent from $23.3 billion. By comparison, they increased their lending to other Latin American countries by only 84 percent.[14]

2.   THE MEXICAN CRISIS OF 1982

a.   THE CRISIS

Mexico failed to service its debt in August 1982, declaring a moratorium on $80 billion owed to 1400 banks. Shortly thereafter the Peso lost over 80 percent of its value as against the Dollar. Mexico sought help from its stunned creditors, and set off a crisis lasting 10 years for some countries. Almost immediately, other developing countries with large debts to banks also failed to pay. According to W. Cline,[15] four major factors from 1974 to 1982 led to the crisis. First, the increase in the real cost of oil (the nominal cost increase in excess of U.S. inflation) was $260 billion. Second, the U.S. central bank dramatically increased U.S. interest rates to counter a persistent inflation. Dollar LIBOR, on which so much Euro credit was based, rose from a low of 5 percent in 1976 to almost 17 percent in 1981, adding $41 billion to the borrowers' debt service costs. Third, the NODCs' exports earned less than in the past, creating a loss of $79 billion. The combined effect of the second and third factors was that the ratio of their real debt servicing costs to their exports, a common measure of the relative burden of a country's debt, rose from 6 percent in 1975 to over 20 percent in 1982. The fourth factor was the world recession in 1981-82 that reduced the NODCs' exports by $21 billion. In total, these four factors explain $401 billion of the $482 billion increase in the NODCs' debt from 1973 to 1982.

Between August 1982 and October 1983, 28 countries including Mexico rescheduled their debt. Sixteen were Latin American. They owed banks $239 billion, but the debt was concentrated in four countries—Mexico, Brazil, Venezuela, and Argentina—that owed $176 billion or 79 percent of the total. These four countries owed the nine largest U.S. banks $39 billion, which was 130 percent of their capital. All NODCs owed these 9 banks 221 percent of their capital.[16]

---

[14] P. Wellons, *Passing the Buck: Governments and Third World Debt* (1987), p. 239. (Wellons 1987)

[15] *International Debt: Systemic Risk and Policy Response* (1984), p. 5.

[16] Wellons 1987, supra note 14, p. 225; W. Cline, *International Debt: Systemic Risk and Policy Response* (1984), p. 22. (Cline 1984)

These countries failed to service their debt as it became due, which most people would describe as default, but they were not technically in default according to the terms of the loan agreements. That was because most syndicated loans provided that a majority of the participating banks had to decide that the loan was in default and instruct their agent bank to take action against the borrower. Almost all participating banks decided not to declare their borrowers in default. Had default been declared, many banks, including the biggest ones in the U.S., would have had to recognize the loss. U.S. accounting rules required a bank to record a loss when the loan was in default but permitted it not to recognize a loss when the loan was rescheduled, or when payments were missed. This was true even when the real value of the loan was much lower than its face value or the prospect of total repayment at market rates was impossible. The banks with the most exposure lacked the reserves or capital to absorb such a huge loss. Their strategy had to be to buy time, building their provisions and capital until they could afford to write off the losses. Their vulnerability and importance in their home financial systems raised the spectre of economic crisis if they collapsed. This prompted their home governments to look for ways to help them buy time.

b.   RESPONDING TO THE CRISIS

Within days of Mexico's declared debt moratorium, a Federal Reserve Board engineered rescue package was announced. The U.S. Commodity Credit Corporation loaned $1 billion to Mexico, the Bank for International Settlements provided a $1 billion dollar for peso swap, a U.S. oil reserve fund advanced $1 billion against future purchases of oil from Mexico, and the Fed loaned almost $1 billion short term, pending funds from the IMF. Because of the moratorium, which lasted for a year, none of these funds serviced the banks' loans.

Working closely with the U.S. government, in November 1982 the IMF provided a $3.7 billion stand-by loan, to be drawn over three years, on the condition that in 1983 the banks make new loans to Mexico of $5 billion. The IMF stand-by was also conditional on fiscal and monetary austerity in Mexico.

London Club

The rescheduling of bank loans took place under the auspices of the London Club. The London Club is a forum housed in London—the center of the Eurocurrency market—to help private banks reschedule their loans to developing country governments. The London Club has no secretariat. It does not follow rigorous formal procedures, but it has a common practice. For each debtor government, the creditor banks appoint a Bank Advisory Committee of the 12-15 banks with the largest stakes, led by the bank that has the most exposure. The committee negotiates an agreement in principle with the debtor government. All lending banks must then approve and sign it.

Prodded by the U.S., other governments, and the IMF, the banks rescheduled $19.5 in largely short term loans originally due by December 1984, at higher spreads and for a rescheduling fee of 0.5 percent.

The exercise to inject new funds and reschedule both official and bank loans took place under the guidance of Paul Volcker, the Fed Chairman, the U.S. Treasury, and the IMF. They rallied other countries' regulators and made sure the banks followed the plan. They pressured the banks with formal and informal tools. Banks that balked at lending new money or that threatened to sue in the hope of being repaid immediately received a Federal Reserve Bank warning to reconsider or risk unstated, but possibly dire, sanctions.

Soon each debtor major country had signed a multi-year rescheduling agreement (MYRA) for loans coming due over the next five years or so and received from the banks longer term funds and new money. The banks did not lend voluntarily.

Paris Club

The negotiations to reschedule the banks' loans took place along side other negotiations about rescheduling official credit. The Paris Club, whose core members are the governments of industrial countries, managed the rescheduling of most official debt. The Paris Club was established in 1956 to help reschedule Argentine debt. Since 1979, the French Treasury has housed the Paris Club and provided a modest staff. The Paris Club sometimes acts as a partial mediator between creditor and debtor governments, advised by the IMF and the World Bank. In the Paris Club discussions, the lenders and borrower agree to general terms for rescheduling, then each creditor government negotiates its own new agreement bilaterally with the debtor government.

Over time, conventions evolved to guide the Paris Club. Comparability of terms requires private creditors to accept a rescheduling of their loans to the borrower that is no less onerous than that adopted by the Paris Club. Certain debt must be fully paid on time and is not rescheduled: loans from multilateral agencies like the World Bank; interbank deposits (after they were included in some of the early reschedulings, the Bank of England won an exemption to protect the interbank market); and trade credits such as letters of credit (although they were included in restructurings of the debt of Brazil, Philippines, and Morocco).[17]

The initial reschedulings in 1982 were followed by others. In 1986, again using Mexico as an example, the banks rescheduled payments due over

---

[17] See M. Rahnama-Moghadam, D. Dilts, and H. Samavati, "The Clubs of London & Paris: International Dispute Resolution in Financial Markets" 53 Dispute Resolution Journal (November 1998), p. 71-72; K. Clark, "Sovereign Debt Restructurings: Parity of Treatment Between Equivalent Creditors in Relation to Comparable Debts," 20 Int'l Law (1986); and IMF *Official Financing for Developing Countries* (April 1994 and February 1998).

three years and made $12.8 billion in new loans, while the multilateral extended over $30 billion in new money.

The debt crises in the 1980s raised several concerns. First was the overall growth of public compared to private lending. This sheltered borrowing countries from market forces, increasing debtor moral hazard. Second, there was an increase in creditor moral hazard, since public money helped the banks avoid the full consequences of their imprudent lending. Third, the crises triggered real systemic risk concerns since major banks could have gone bankrupt and the crises were apparently contagious among Latin American countries. Fourth, although not a subject examined here, there was real doubt about the efficacy of the economic reform conditions imposed by the multilaterals, principally the IMF. Fifth, the problem did not go away. Repeated schedulings resulted in longer term and greater debt obligations.

Notes and Questions

1. Why not just let the private debtors work out solutions themselves? Many banks, particularly those with smaller stakes, argued that they were coerced into lending new money and rescheduling the loans. After all, the IMF and the Fed linked new official lending to the banks' rescheduling. What would the banks have done if official funds were not involved?

2. The strategy was to reschedule existing loans and supply new money. This suggests that the problem is one of liquidity and so one needs only to stretch out repayment and provide temporary liquidity. Later events proved this wrong.

3. How new were the "new" funds supplied by banks? Why not reduce the debt rather than reschedule it?

4. When a government intervenes in financial markets to rescue one or more banks faced with loss, the danger of moral hazard exists. Banks may anticipate the intervention and lend without adequately pricing for risk because they can count on the government's intervention. How would this response to the crisis affect moral hazard for banks' international lending in the future?

5. What is the argument for favoring some creditors over others? Why separate official and private creditors (Paris and London clubs)?

b.   DEBT SERVICE REDUCTION AND SECURITIZATION: THE BAKER PLAN AND
      THE GROWTH OF THE SECONDARY MARKETS

1.   THE BAKER PLAN

The Baker Plan, named for the U.S. Treasury Secretary, James Baker, was announced in 1986. It set targets for new loans to help 17 countries with the greatest debt, most in Latin America, restructure their economies. Over three years, banks would lend $20 billion in new money, long term and at rates similar to those of the MYRAs. The point of the plan was to require new funds as a supplement to the reschedulings that were already underway.

The failure of the Baker Plan was acknowledged by 1988. Both the official creditors and the banks supplied much less new money than the plan required. Banks actually only loaned $12.8 billion of the promised $20 billion to the 10 countries that adopted acceptable economic policies.

Toward the end of the 1980s, banks were starting to position themselves to recognize losses. During the Baker Plan period, banks took different routes to reduce their problem debts, setting the stage for the Brady Plan, discussed below. European banks were willing to capitalize interest due from the borrowers. U.S. banks began to build provisions for the bad debt so that they could write it off. In 1987, Citicorp, for example, set aside $3 billion in provisions, while the Bank of Boston raised its provisions for bad loans over 50 percent. By 1987, the large U.S. banks had increased their capital and slowed the growth of lending to developing countries, reducing their vulnerability.[18]

2.   THE GROWTH OF SECONDARY MARKET TRADING

Also during the end of the 1980s a small secondary market developed in sovereign debt, setting the stage for Brady Bonds. Most Eurocredit agreements gave each participating bank notes showing the principal and the procedure to calculate interest owed on each payment date. Many of the agreements provided that these notes were negotiable.

A secondary market in negotiable notes began to develop. One estimate put trading at $600 million face value in 1983 and $15 billion by 1987. Companies, such as IBM and Volkswagen, swapped the sovereign debt they acquired for equity in local companies, a way to invest at a discount in the countries.[19] Discounts on the face value varied. In early 1986, Chilean debt traded at 65-69 percent and Argentine debt at 62-66 percent of face value.

---

[18] Cline 1984, supra note 16, pp. 214-15.
[19] R. Buckley, *Emerging Markets Debt: An Analysis of the Secondary Market* (1999), pp. 70, 130. (Buckley 1999)

Documentation of trades evolved during the 1980s from individually negotiated agreements to standard formats followed by the major traders. Thus by the late 1980s, "the assignment agreements of the eight largest traders contained clauses on virtually identical matters cast in substantially similar wording."[20]

"The usual layout was three to four pages of standard text followed by schedules into which were inserted the details of the credit being assigned, the consideration for the assignment [cash or other loans], and details of payment offices and addresses for notices. The schedules would also contain any non-standard clauses required for this particular transaction. Typical standard terms addressed the following matters: assignment and assumption; allocation of payments under the credit; representation and warranties; and a host of miscellaneous 'boilerplate' type provisions."[21]

In 1987, Argentina offered to let the regional banks convert their outstanding loans at a discount to par into "exit bonds" offered by the Argentine government, with interest rates below market. Exit bond holders would not have to supply new money. But the discount was so big that no bank responded. The proposal, however, set the stage for the Brady plan.

c.   THE BRADY PLAN

The Bush Administration, having just taken office in 1989, launched a new approach to the LDC debt problem. The idea was to bring permanent relief using market-based debt and debt-service reduction and forgiveness to countries adopting strong economic reform programs.[22] A study in 2005 looked at the effect on countries of writing down their debts.[23] It found that stock markets in countries adopting Brady plans appreciated by an average of 60% in real dollar terms—a $42 billion increase in shareholder value, while there was no significant market increase for a control group that did not adopt a Brady plan. The market capitalization of U.S. commercial banks with developing country loan exposure also roles—by $13 billion. The authors suggest that this demonstrates how both the borrower and lenders can benefit by debt relief. More certainty about debt service helps lenders and less burden helps borrowers. This is in some sense obvious because it explains why there are reorganizations in the corporate world. The real issue is how much relief. The authors suggest that these results may not apply to the poorest countries (see the discussion of relief for highly indebted poor countries (HIPCs), below, because their problem may be lack of political and economic institutions rather than excessive debt.

---

[20] Id., p. 240.
[21] Id., p. 41.
[22] J. Clark, "Debt Reduction and Market Reentry Under the Brady Plan" Federal Reserve Bank of New York Quarterly Review (Winter 1993-94), p. 38.
[23] S. Arslanalp and P. Henry, "Is Debt Relief Efficient?," LX Journal of Finance 1017 (2006).

The government of the debtor country issued so-called Brady Bonds (named after the Secretary of the Treasury) in exchange for outstanding debt in arrears to banks, at a negotiated discount related to the market price of the notes traded in the secondary market. A crucial part of the scheme was the security for the new debt—U.S. zero coupon bonds. An example of how this worked are the Brady Bonds issued by Mexico in March 1990.

The banks could exchange their loans for newly issued 30-year discount dollar bonds with principal and 12-18 months interest secured by 30-year zero-coupon U.S. Treasury bonds. The banks had two options with respect to the bonds. They could have their loans converted into "par bonds"—bonds with the same face value as the loans—which paid interest at the discounted fixed rate of 6.25 percent, very substantially below the market rate. Or, the banks could exchange their loans for discounted bonds, reflecting the current market price, e.g. a discount of 35 percent, but receive a market rate of interest, LIBOR plus 13/16 percent. Or, the banks could abstain from the swap options and lend new funds, in the amount of 25 percent of their outstanding medium and long-term exposure.

The flows are illustrated in Figure 19.1, below. Mexico borrowed funds, $84 million, from a fund set up by the IMF, the World Bank, and Japan, paying interest at the IMF borrowing rate plus a small spread. Mexico then purchased $650 million in zero coupons for $104 million, a very cheap price. These Treasury bonds were then put in escrow to secure the $650 million Mexican Brady Bonds swapped for $1 billion in outstanding bank loans. The subsidies from the multilateral fund and favorable pricing of the bonds were crucial to the success of the scheme.

Figure 19.1

Mexican Brady Discount Bond Example: Subsidized Collateral

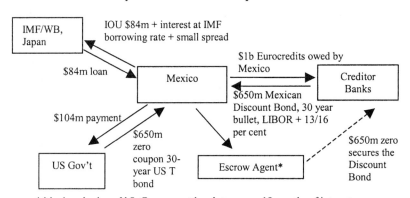

* Mexico also buys U.S. Government bonds to secure 18 months of interest

The prospects of the Brady proposal were greatly enhanced by a letter of July 14, 1989 from the SEC to David Mulford, Under Secretary of the

Treasury, which "clarified" the application to the Mexican Brady restructuring of Financial Accounting Standards No. 15, Accounting by Debtors and Creditors for Troubled Debt Restructurings (FAS 15). The relevant part of FAS 15 provided that if, in full settlement of a debt, a creditor receives assets of which the fair value is less than the recorded value of the debt, then the creditor must record the shortfall as a loss.

David Mulford, doubtless, shaped the letter which stated that a loss need not be recognized if "the total future undiscounted cash receipts specified by the new terms of the loan, including receipts designated as both principal and interest, equal or exceed the book value of the loan." Upon this criterion, the banks could accept Mexico's Brady Bonds in exchange for their loans without having to recognize a loss notwithstanding that shortly after issue the par bonds were trading at 42 percent of face value and the discount bonds at 63 percent. By ensuring that Brady Bonds could be accepted by banks without provisions or write-downs, the SEC made the Mexican restructuring far more palatable for U.S. banks; at the cost of ignoring reality.

A great deal of arm-twisting by regulators was required to secure the participation of all banks. Banks elected to convert 41 percent of total indebtedness into discounted principal bonds, 49 percent into discounted interest (par) bonds, and to advance new money for the remaining 10 percent. Of the three options, new money was to prove by far the most lucrative.

The Brady restructuring failed to help Mexico in one important respect. Mexico's net annual transfer to the banks before the restructuring was $3.24 billion. After the restructuring it was $3.59 billion. This is because before Brady, most of the interest payments were funded by new money. But the Brady process served an important function in breaking the upward spiral of total indebtedness and in reducing the demands on the scarce time of government ministers and civil servants that arose from the periodic restructurings of the 1980s. More than one-half the debt stock was securitized through Bradys.

Many people assumed that the use of bonds would reduce the frequency of restructurings. One reason was that, unlike syndicated loans, bonds had no clause for sharing. Sharing clauses limit direct action against the issuer by forcing a lender who sues and collects from a debtor to share the proceeds with the others participating in the loan. Bond holders could sue and expect to recover amounts owed to them. They would not be forced to cooperate with other lenders in restructuring agreements. Practical reasons keep sharing clauses out of bond agreements, according to A. Yianni.[24] Bond instruments and their holders are diverse. Their sheer number would make it very difficult to identify and reach those entitled to share the proceeds.

---

[24] "Resolution of Sovereign Financial Crises—Evolution of the Private Sector Restructuring Process," Bank of England Financial Stability Review (June 1999), p. 78.

Later Brady Bonds differed from Mexico's, leading to multiple forms of the instrument. Venezuela, for example, offered five options: collateralized par bonds or discount bonds; new money bonds, equal to 20 percent of the bank's loans; seventeen year temporary interest reduction bonds in exchange for loans; or the banks could sell its loans to the country's government at the going rate in the secondary market, 45 percent of face value.

By 1994, many of the countries saw their economies recover and gradually became eligible to return to financial markets. Bank claims (loans still outstanding) on the Brady Bonds[25] traded on the secondary market. The market value of these claims rose from 34 percent of the face value in 1990 to 70 percent in late 1994 (before the Mexico crisis discussed in the next section). Private capital began to flow into these countries again. After net outflows from 1983 to 1988, net inflows to Latin American countries rose from about $3 billion in 1990 to over $50 billion in 1993.[26]

The secondary market for Brady Bonds grew through 1997, then trading slowed. The range of investors in emerging market debt broadened with the advent of Brady Bonds. High yield investors moved from U.S. junk bonds to this emerging market debt. Then institutional investors entered: pension funds and insurance companies from the U.S. and non-banks from Europe. Table 19B, below, shows the growth of trading in Brady Bonds and other emerging market debt, from 1993, when reliable data began to be collected.

Table 19B Emerging Market Instruments: Trading Volume[27] (US$ billions)						
Instruments	1993	1994	1995	1996	1997	1998
Brady Bonds	1,021	1,684	1,580	2,690	2,403	1,541
Non-Brady Eurobonds	177	159	211	568	1,335	1,021
Loans	274	244	175	249	305	213
Local Markets Instruments	n/a	524	593	1,274	1,506	1,176
Derivatives (Options, etc.)	57	142	179	471	367	223
Total	1,979	2,766	2,739	5,297	5,916	4,174

---

[25] The original 15 major participating countries were Argentina, Bolivia, Brazil, Chile, Colombia, Ecuador, Ivory Coast, Mexico, Morocco, Nigeria, Peru, the Philippines, Uruguay, Venezuela, and the former Yugoslavia.

[26] See IMF, *Official Financing for Developing Countries* (April 1994), pp. 10, 15.

[27] Emerging Market Traders Association, 1998 Annual Report, pp. 12-13.

Market practices became increasingly standard as traders adopted similar norms. They founded the Emerging Market Traders Association (EMTA) in 1990. It designed standard comprehensive terms for loan assignments. It introduced an automated trade confirmation and matching system in 1995. Not only did it largely eliminate error between execution and trade, but it also made pricing transparent. EMTA began to distribute volume and price data almost in real time.

Brady Bonds adopted New York covenants for modifying the bonds, requiring the consent of each bond holder to any proposal to modify the payment terms of the bond. English covenants allow a super-majority holding 75 percent of the value of the bonds to modify payment terms.

Brady Bonds are now on their way out, disappearing through subsequent debt swaps or early repayments. Mexico retired its last $1.28 billion in Brady Bonds in June 2003.

Notes and Questions

1. Was the Brady Plan an improvement over the 1980s reschedulings?

2. Was the debt reduction significant enough? Was debt reduction preferable to default?

3. Was the Brady Plan correct in allowing the banks to choose among the options? What if all had opted for debt reduction options? What if all opted for new money? How attractive would par and discount exchanges be to the countries?

d.   BRADY BOND HOLDOUTS: ELLIOTT ASSOCIATES

Vulture funds threatened Brady Bond restructurings. They bought defaulted loans from banks at a discount, then held out for payment at full value. Four months after the government of Peru announced its Brady Bond package in 1995, Elliott Associates, LP paid two banks $11.4 million for loans guaranteed by the government of Peru in 1983 with a face value of $20.7 million. Elliott rejected the Brady offers, then sued Peru and the borrower in New York courts for full payment and won a judgment of $55.7 million in 2000. Peru was not protected by sovereign immunity. Under U.S. law, there is a commercial activity exception to sovereign immunity, and under *Republic of Argentina v. Weltover*,[28] issuing bonds is regarded as a commercial activity.[29] Chase Bank was the agent for the Brady Bonds. Elliott obtained an

---

[28] (1992) 504 U.S. 607. Such rulings are now routine. In *EM Ltd. V. The Republic of Argentina,* the Second Circuit affirmed a $740 million judgment against Argentina due to its 2001 bond default, 382 F.3d 291 (2004).

[29] M. Gulati and K. Klee, "Sovereign Piracy," 56 Business Lawyer (2001), p. 635. (Gulati and Klee)

injunction restraining Chase Bank from using any funds it received from Peru to service the Brady Bond debt.[30]

Rather than transfer more funds to Chase in New York, Peru tried to service the debt through Euroclear in Belgium. In the first instance Belgian court, Elliott lost its ex parte request for an order restraining Euroclear from "either accepting money from Peru or paying it to the other creditors."[31] On an ex parte appeal, the Court of Appeals reversed, restraining JPMorgan as operator of Euroclear from either accepting the money or paying it to creditors. Peru then settled.[32]

Elliott successfully argued that the *pari passu* clause in the 1983 loan agreement required the debtor to pay all creditors, including Elliott, pro rata. An expert opinion from Professor Andreas Lowenfeld, of New York University Law School, argued that the *pari passu* clause "entitles each Lender to share equally and rateably with any other holder of External Indebtedness" (this included investors in Brady Bonds).[33]

Gulati and Klee argue[34] that the clause only ensures the borrower cannot create "a class of creditors whose claims will rank senior in priority to the lending claims of the current creditors." They claim it had nothing to do with pro-rata sharing of debt payments.

Notes and Questions

1. Which interpretation of the *pari passu* clause do you agree with, that of *Elliott* or Gulati and Klee? Has Elliott Associates discovered an effective way to attach substantial assets of defaulting sovereign debtors?

2. Apart from payments on Brady Bonds, what other sovereign assets could a holdout creditor seize? Recognize that Central Bank assets are generally protected under sovereign immunity laws.

3.   DEBT CRISIS MANAGEMENT IN THE 1990S: BAILOUTS, RESTRUCTURINGS, AND DEFAULTS

We now turn to the debt crises of the 1990s following the Brady plan. The 1990s differed substantially from the 1980s in many respects. First,

---

[30] *Elliott Associates v Banco de la Nacion and the Republic of Peru* (2nd Cir. 1999). 194 F.3d 363.

[31] Gulati and Klee, supra note 29, p. 636.

[32] Court of Appeals of Belgium, LP Elliott Associates, Petitioner, General Docket No. 2000/QR/92, September 26, 2000.

[33] Typical language of the clause is: "The bonds and the coupons are direct, unconditional and unsecured obligations of the issuer and rank and will rank at least pari passu, without any preference among themselves, with all other outstanding, unsecured and unsubstantiated obligations of the issuer, present and future." P. Wood, "Pari Passu Clauses—What Do They Mean?," Butterworths Journal of International Banking and Financial Law (November 2001), pp. 371-74. (Wood, like Gulati and Klee, believes the clause only refers to creditor rankings in insolvency.)

[34] Gulati and Klee, supra note 29, p. 639.

there were many different types of crises, not just an inability to service too much debt. Many of the 1990s crises were triggered, if not caused, by rapid foreign exchange rate depreciations. Indeed, some crises seemed resolvable by increasing liquidity through additions to government reserves, and stopping the depreciation. Other crises seemed less about liquidity and more about too much debt and fundamental economic problems.

Second, the crises involved defaults or potential defaults on bonds as well as loans. Given the number and diversity of bond holders—and the lack of developed country regulatory levers to deal with them (as compared to banks), resolutions of the crises were much more difficult.

Third, there was much less of a threat of systemic risk to the banking system. Bank exposure as a percentage of capital in the 1990s was substantially less than it was in the 1980s. There was still a country contagion issue, however, particularly in the 1997 Asian crisis.

Fourth, there were very few actual debt moratoria—the usual pattern in the 1980s. Argentina in 2000, was a notable exception.

Fifth, the role of the IMF, both as a provider of funds—often without any preceding agreements of private creditors to restructure or to provide new money, as in the 1980s—and manager of debt crises grew enormously. The rather straightforward conditionality programs for fiscal and monetary policy austerity of the 1980s were transformed into detailed structural conditions ranging from privatization to law reform.

Sixth, the nature of the debt in crisis became more complicated. As we shall see, a large part of the South Korean crisis was private bank debt guaranteed by the government. And a large part of the Mexican, Russian, and Turkish crises was domestic currency debt owed to foreigners.

a.   MEXICO'S DECEMBER 1994 PESO CRISIS

1.   THE CRISIS

During 1994, rather than devalue, the Mexican government had spent close to $20 billion to defend the peso as the country's reserves dwindled to $6 billion. On December 20, 1994, the Mexican government devalued the Peso 15 percent against the Dollar to 1 Peso for 25 cents and 2 days later let the Peso float. It fell almost 50 percent in 4 weeks.

When the crisis occurred, about 75 percent of the government's debt was in the form of Tesobonos, short term peso denominated securities indexed to the Dollar, usually maturing in 91 days. Non-residents owned almost 80 percent of all outstanding Tesobonos by December 1994.[35] Tesobonos, worth the equivalent of $28 billion, were due through 1995. Of this, over $4 billion was due in January and early February. The rapid

---

[35] IMF, November 1995, p. 48.

depreciation of the peso made the dollar-indexed debt enormously expensive, 65 percent more expensive than before the crisis.

2.   THE RESCUE PACKAGE

The Clinton administration rallied to Mexico's aid in January 1995. The U.S. government concluded that the peso's free fall would hurt Mexico, the U.S., and other developing countries. The U.S. took the major role in the rescue. This was not surprising given Mexico's presence on the U.S. border, and the prospect of accelerated illegal immigration. Led by the new Treasury Secretary and former investment banker Robert Rubin, the U.S. Government arranged a $9 billion credit line at the Federal Reserve on which the Mexicans could draw to maintain Peso convertibility and stop its fall. The Bank for International Settlements (BIS) assembled a $5 billion loan from several central banks that would serve as a bridge until the IMF could advance funds. By late January, the IMF offered a $7.8 billion loan. Canada stood ready to lend just over $1 billion. Several private banks offered to arrange a $3 billion syndicated loan. And the Clinton administration asked Congress to enable it to guarantee up to $40 billion in bonds the Mexican government would issue at the U.S. Treasury bond rate. Mexico would put future oil revenues in escrow as a guarantee. Mexico drew some of the Fed credit line, but nothing else during January. None of the public support was conditional on private reschedulings or new money, as had been the case in the 1980s.

The new Republican majority in the U.S. Congress was unwilling to approve the guarantee facility quickly. Many members balked at what they saw as bailing out not Mexico but foreign investors who should have known better. They complained that U.S. securities firms had enriched themselves, having earned $133 million a year underwriting Mexican securities from 1992 to 1994 and $305 million underwriting Latin American securities. These firms should not be helped by bailing out the customers who had invested in Tesobonos.[36]

On January 31, President Clinton announced a second package by executive order (avoiding Congress) to replace the first. The U.S. Exchange Stabilization Fund, which was set up to stabilize the Dollar and held $25 billion in Yen and DM, would exchange into dollars up to $20 billion, then swap the Dollars for Pesos with Mexico for 3 to 5 years. Mexico would pay a fee for the swap and set aside oil revenues as security. In fact, the U.S. only advanced $12.5 billion, $10.5 billion as medium-term swaps and $2 billion as short-term swaps. The IMF provided a stand-by credit of $17.8 billion, conditional on some important macroeconomic policy changes. This was three times more than it had ever loaned before, and seven times the quota it was

---

[36] R. Smith, R. McGough, and T. Vogel, Jr, "U.S. Securities Firms and Mutual Funds Have Big Bucks Riding on Mexico Rescue," *The Wall Street Journal*, February 1, 1995.

allowed to lend to Mexico. BIS central banks stood ready to loan another $10 billion which was never drawn on.

Critics of President Clinton's emergency package disputed its legality. In an article titled "Adventures in the Zone of Twilight: Separation of Powers and National Economic Security in the Mexican Bailout,"[37] R. Covey argued that Clinton's use of the Emergency Stabilization Fund (ESF) was improper. The President lacked statutory or constitutional authority without a formal appropriation by Congress. Neither the ESF statute, its legislative history, or past usage permitted the funds to be used to help Mexico. Nor did the President have independent constitutional authority to use the money.

By mid-April 1995, Mexico was announcing a turn-around. Shortly after the ESF was drawn on, the free fall of the Peso ended. The currency stabilized around 15 Pesos to the Dollar, and Mexico serviced and repaid all of its loans on time and at the contracted rate. By 1996 Mexico had returned to private international debt markets, issuing a $750 million global bond. Its GDP grew at a 3.5 percent rate. As of January 2005, it had no loans outstanding from the IMF.

The lesson drawn from the Mexican crisis was that a foreign exchange crisis can be stopped by the massive provision of liquidity, and a debt crisis can thereby be avoided.

Mexico's crisis was selectively contagious. Financial flows into other Latin American countries quickly fell and outflows rose as capital fled. Argentina, Brazil, and other countries asked the IMF for emergency help. But investors differentiated among Latin American countries to some extent. The stock market in Chile stayed close to its end-1994 values. Investors saw Chile as having a consistently better managed economy. Asian countries were also hit, particularly in their stock markets. But most recovered within several months.

As world economic conditions worsened in late 2002, the IMF reviewed Mexico's economic and financial performance and concluded that Mexico "would be able to weather a replay of past capital account crises arising from contagion, and that there exists the institutional capacity to maintain prudent economic management and react in an appropriate manner to adverse shocks."[38]

Notes and Questions

1.   Why should the U.S. rescue Mexico? Was the rescue package appropriate?

2.   How did the resolution of the 1994/95 Mexican crisis differ from the resolution of the 1982 Mexican crisis? Were the crises different?

---

[37] 105 Yale Law Journal 1311 (1996).
[38] IMF Staff Report, *Mexico*, October 2002.

3. Why was a Brady Bond approach not used in the 1994/95 Mexican crisis?

b.   THE ASIAN FINANCIAL CRISIS OF 1997: FOREIGN BANKS' FOREIGN CURRENCY LOANS TO LOCAL BANKS AND OTHER COMPANIES

In mid-1997, the exchange rates for many countries in East and Southeast Asia collapsed, throwing them into a calamitous financial crisis. Each of the countries managed its foreign exchange rate, generally tying its currency to the Dollar or a basket dominated by the Dollar. Foreign exchange markets bet that the countries could not maintain their current rates. Starting in mid-1997 with Thailand, the problem spread within six months to Malaysia, the Philippines, Indonesia, and South Korea.

1.   THE CRISIS

There is much debate about the cause of the crisis. One view emphasizes the dominant role of poor domestic economic policy and the weakness of the domestic financial institutions. Another view explains the collapse as a panic of external investors and bad policy by the IMF and other institutions that stepped in to help the countries respond. S. Radelet and J. Sachs[39] acknowledge significant domestic weaknesses but argue that these problems were known for many years. For Sachs and Radelet, the rapid reversal of private capital flows from incoming to outgoing defined the crisis for the five countries. Net external inflows of funds grew from $47.4 billion in 1994 to $92.8 billion in 1996. The suppliers were about 60 percent private commercial banks, with equity investors and non-banks providing almost 40 percent. Official funding was negligible and the countries' reserves grew. Private flows reversed in 1997. Net, $12.1 billion flowed out of the countries. Of this, 75 percent represented the fall in dollar lending by commercial banks, mostly short-term, e.g. 67 percent in South Korea, or twice the size of exchange reserves. The ability to rapidly contract short-term lending by these banks made the Asian countries susceptible to a sudden contraction of exchange reserves.

Foreign banks loaned mainly to banks in South Korea, to non-bank commercial borrowers in Indonesia, and more to non-banks than banks elsewhere, according to Radelet and Sachs. They argue that, except for South Korea, the foreign banks were unlikely to have loaned in reliance on an implicit guarantee from the host government.

The imbalance leading to the crisis, say Radelet and Sachs, was that the short-term debt exceeded most countries' reserves. A rational response by a lender concerned about possible delinquency would simply be to lend only short term and refuse to roll over its loan when due, forcing repayment and

---

[39] In *The Onset of the East Asian Financial Crisis,* Harvard Institute for International Development, March 30, 1998.

allowing this lender to escape before reserves ran out. The problem was most severe in South Korea. In mid-1997, 67 percent of South Korea's debt to foreign banks was short term. This $67.5 billion was over twice the size of South Korea's reserves. The ratio of short-term debt to reserves was 1.7 for Indonesia and 1.5 for Thailand. It was 0.8 for Philippines and only 0.6 for Malaysia.

Yet another view is that the Asian crisis was the result of asset bubbles in each country. In this view, the crises in South Korea and Southeast Asia were caused by the same factors that led to the financial and economic crisis in Japan (described in Chapter 6).

2.   RESCUE PACKAGES: THE SOUTH KOREA EXAMPLE

South Korea negotiated a 3-year $57 billion assistance package on December 4, 1997. The IMF provided a stand-by arrangement of $21 billion, the World Bank and Asian Development Bank (ADB) provided $14 billion in loans, and G7 countries contributed an additional $22 billion, but only if the multilaterals' funds proved inadequate. South Korea was able to draw $8 billion immediately, but the remaining installments were to be advanced over 2 or more years as South Korea complied with the structural reforms the IMF required for its economy.

The IMF $8 billion was not conditional on the banks stretching out their existing loans or committing new funds. This was later attacked by many as a bailout and a major cause of moral hazard. M. Goldstein[40] argues that the criticism of the bailout is overstated. He contends that "the rescue packages go primarily for purposes other than to prevent rescheduling of debt to private creditors; namely they go to cushion the (inevitable) recession in the crisis countries, to help to rebuild international reserves, and to help recapitalize the banking system." Goldstein supplies no data to substantiate this point, and the IMF has not released data to show what it anticipated its funds would be spent on. The point about building reserves has a robbing Peter to pay Paul quality if existing reserves are used to pay foreign creditors and IMF money is used to replace them. The December package assumed that it would allow South Korea to service its external debt as payment came due, in part because foreign lenders would now be willing to roll over their short-term credit. But foreign banks decided that the package would not solve South Korea's problems and withdrew their funds. This threatened to sabotage South Korea's recovery.

A fundamental question was why South Korea did not declare a moratorium as Latin American countries had done in the 1980s, and block repatriation of short-term funds. The answer seems largely to be that South Korea, which had recently joined the ranks of the OECD, did not want to be considered in the same class as the "deadbeat" countries of Latin America—

---

[40] *The Asian Financial Crisis: Causes, Cures, and Systemic Implications* (June 1998), p. 38.

its concern with its reputation was paramount. In late December, the IMF agreed to accelerate its funds and the G7 made their $22 billion available, provided the banks restructured $28 billion in loans. The banks acquiesced in late January and the restructuring agreement was completed at the end of March 1998. The restructuring required the banks to exchange existing loans for one to three year loans backed by South Korean government guarantees. Interest rates were at 2.25-2.75 percent over LIBOR. South Korea could repay at six-month intervals without prepayment penalties. South Korea used most of the funds to pay off its external short-term debt and to increase its reserves. The assistance package might have been, but was not, used to recapitalize South Korean banks, clean up the domestic financial system, or stimulate the economy.

For its help, the IMF required from South Korea a contractionary fiscal policy, tight domestic credit, the closure of the many unviable banks and financial institutions to limit losses, enforcement of capital adequacy standards and recognition of huge loan and FX losses, full repayment of foreign debt backed by funds mobilized by the IMF, and restructuring of domestic industry to increase competition. Equity investors in South Korea suffered substantial losses and bonds were trading at 400 basis points off U.S. treasuries as compared with 60 off before the crisis. The country went through very painful change and the impact of the crisis was felt for years. In 2000, for example, large conglomerates threatened or declared bankruptcy. Domestic banks continued to require substantial government funding.[41]

South Korea recovered with strong growth and had international reserves of $100 billion by 2001. Indeed, the government repaid the last tranche of the IMF loan in August 2001. By 2002, international rating agencies signaled success of the major restructuring that had taken place. Moody's raised the ratings of 7 South Korean banks, noting that they had cleaned out their bad loans and consolidated. Their spreads over U.S. Treasuries declined from about 800 basis points in early 2002 to only 250 by mid-2002.[42] As of January 31, 2005, South Korea had no loans outstanding from the IMF.

While fear that a default could trigger failures of foreign banks was a real concern in the Latin America debt crisis of the 1980s, it was not in Asia. For example, U.S. banks had loaned $10 billion, barely 6 percent of the capital of the top 10 U.S. banks. Japanese bank loans of $24 billion represented about 9 percent of the capital of Japanese banks. This was small even assuming an extremely improbable default on all debt.

---

[41] C. Lee, "Creditors Agree Funds for Daewoo," *Financial Times*, November 30, 2000; S. Len, "South Korea to Spend $44 Billion More to Support Banks," *The New York Times*, September 23, 2000.

[42] L. Lucas, "Korean Banks Earn Ratings Upgrades," *Financial Times*, June 21, 2002.

Notes and Questions

1. Should Korea have defaulted? After all, most borrowers were in the private sector, not governmental. Korea's major borrowers were private banks controlled de facto by the government. In other countries, such as Indonesia, the borrowers were private companies.

2. Treasury Secretary Rubin argued that Korean default on foreign bank debt might trigger capital flight and reduce access to new private capital. Is this argument convincing in the case of Korea?

3. If a Korean default risked contagion, causing lenders to pull out of other countries, should the default be averted?

4. If Korea defaulted, would that create moral hazard by signaling other debtors that they could take on more unsupportable debt in the future? Some people argue that defaults would dry up future funding. How compelling is this? How compelling is the counter argument that the very possibility of the bailout makes the debtor country more reckless in borrowing?

5. If Korea were about to default, would significant national security concerns of the lending countries, such as the country's relations with North Korea, justify preventing the default?

6. Prime Minister Mahathir Mohamad, of Malaysia, explained the crisis in his country as largely due to foreign speculators, such as George Soros and the hedge funds that had played an important role in the 1992-93 currency crises in Europe. But for them, he said, the Asian crisis would not have occurred. Bailey, Farrell, and Lund came to the opposite conclusion. Their analysis of the financial flows in and out of the five crisis countries showed that bank lending shifted from large net inflows (75 percent of all foreign investment) before the crisis to large net outflows after. Portfolio investors (including hedge funds) shifted from much smaller net inflows before the crisis to continued net inflows of half the volume after. Bailey et al. at 103 attribute the banks' behavior to the nature of their contracts:

> Bank loans are mostly illiquid, fixed-price assets—they cannot be quickly converted into cash, and once priced, their interest rate does not go up and down to reflect new information about a borrower (except in the case of a breach of contract or a default). Because the "price" of a loan—the interest rate—does not automatically adjust to changing market conditions, banks adjust the quantity of lending instead. A bank can avoid a default by simply declining to roll over its loan if it sees a borrower in trouble.

The authors note that hedge funds are small players, accounting for only 4 percent of the assets of the big institutional investors worldwide. They acknowledge that hedge funds did bet against currencies like the Thai baht just before the crisis, but quote one trader in Thailand who asked "Who wasn't betting against the baht?"[43] Do you agree with the explanation of the banks' behavior given by Bailey et al.?

c.   RUSSIAN CRISIS OF 1998: DEFAULT ON RESCHEDULED SECURITIES AND BONDS[44]

In 1999, Russia defaulted on instruments it had issued as part of an earlier rescheduling of Soviet debt, as well as other subsequently issued bonds. The financial turmoil that hit Russia in 1998 affected many forms of outstanding government debt, some in Rubles held by foreigners and some in foreign currency. Russia chose to treat different types of debt differently.

a.   THE CRISIS: PLAYERS AND INSTRUMENTS

As of July 1998, before its default, Russia had a total external debt of about $160 billion. Part of this debt, about $100 billion, was inherited from the Soviet Union, pre 1-1-1992 debt, and the other part, about $60 billion, was contracted by the Russian Federation, post 1-1-1992.

The $100 billion in Soviet era debt consisted of $40 billion in Paris Club debt, $29 billion in restructured London Club debt, $7.5 billion in MinFins, series 3-5 (Dollar bonds issued under Russian law), and $22 billion in official non-Paris Club and commercial debt. The $29 billion in restructured London Club debt consisted of two securities, $22 billion in PRINs, principal bonds, and $7 billion in IANs, interest arrears notes, listed in Luxembourg, that were effectively also bonds.

The $60 billion in Russian Federation debt consisted of about $19.3 billion owed to the IMF, $14 billion on nine Eurobonds, $1.3 billion in MinFin, series 6-7, and the remainder to the World Bank ($6.3 billion) and other official creditors.[45] In addition, it owed $15 billion to foreigners on domestic Ruble bonds (at July 1998 exchange rates) held by foreigners. These domestic Ruble bonds consisted of two different instruments, GKOs, short-term zero coupon bonds, and OFZs, mid-term variable coupon bonds. These totaled about $72 billion (RUR 435 billion converted at July 1998 exchange rates), so foreigners held about 22 percent. Russian banks were mandated to hold GKOs and had 35 percent of their assets in them.

After the Asian crisis hit, investors began to withdraw from Russia, taking out about $5 billion in November 1997. Political uncertainty and weak financial indicators prompted further outflow. Yields on government debt rose to offset the outflows and government debt service costs rose. The rising

---

[43] M. Baily, D. Farrell, and S. Lund, "The Color of Hot Money," 79 Foreign Affairs (March/April 2000), p. 99.

[44] This section on Russia has greatly benefited from A. Nadmitov, "Russian Debt Restructuring: Overview, Structure of Debt, Lessons of Default, Seizure Problems, and the IMF SDRM Proposal," International Finance Seminar, Harvard Law School, May 2004. (Nadmitov)

[45] Central Bank of Russia data for January 1, 1999 as reported in Nadmitov, supra note 44.

domestic rates hurt the Ruble; rather than attract new capital inflows, they signaled the weakness of the economy. Reserves fell from $24 billion in mid-1997 to $18 billion in January 1998 and $15 billion in June 1998.

On August 17, 1998, the government and central bank ended support for the Ruble and suspended trading in GKOs and OFZs. They decreed that GKOs maturing between August 17, 1998 and December 31, 1999 would become new securities with characteristics not then defined. They placed a 90-day moratorium on repaying hard currency loans from non-residents, paying margin calls, and paying forward currency contracts. The government prohibited foreign investment in Ruble assets due in one year or less.

The economy spiraled down over the next weeks. The Ruble collapsed against the dollar. The stock market collapsed. Banks stopped lending, as the value of their holdings of GKOs evaporated. Close to illiquid, they froze accounts and stopped making transfers and interbank payments.

b.   THE RESPONSE

Russia's strategy was to basically to default on and then restructure its Soviet era debt and Russian domestic debt (including GKOs and OFZs owned by foreigners). It continued to honor all Dollar-denominated Russian external debt. It negotiated with the London Club to restructure the commercial debt, and write off some. It asked the Paris Club to restructure and write-off the debt to official creditors. Buchheit stated: "[N]egotiations lasted into 2000. In part, all parties were buying time. Russia earned foreign exchange by exporting oil. The price of oil was rising substantially in 1999 and into 2000. Russia reported a $30 billion trade surplus for 1999 and the best economic growth in the 1990s. This reassured creditors that Russia could service rescheduled debt and strengthened Russia's hand."[46]

Restructuring GKOs. The government converted the frozen GKOs in March 1999 and reorganized the market in June. It extended the notes' maturity from below 12 months to an average of about 30 months and reduced the face value of those outstanding by 33 percent in nominal terms and 67 percent allowing for inflation. The market, however, was illiquid and secondary market yields were 60 percent in late 1999.[47] All but 20 percent of the payments received had to be deposited in restricted Ruble accounts. Non-residents who owned the accounts could repatriate the funds only after depositing them in a non-interest bearing account for a year. Alternatively, they could bid in foreign currency for their funds. By some calculations, foreign investors would receive only 5 cents on the Dollar. Russian institutional investors would receive a bit more. Non-residents who did not agree to the novation would not be able to repatriate them for five years.

---

[46] L. Buchheit, *Sovereign Debtors and their Bondholders* (Unitar 2000), pp. 13–14.
[47] IMF, *World Economic Outlook* (October 1999), p. 63; IMF, *The GKO OFZ Novation, Russian Federation: Recent Economic Developments* (September 1999).

The Restructured Soviet London Club debt. Russia and the London Club reached agreement on this debt in August 2000. London Club debt was exchanged for Eurobonds issued by the Russian Federation, with an effective reduction of $13.5 billion. These new Eurobonds contained a cross-default and cross-acceleration clause linked to the previously issued Russian Eurobonds—thus a default on the 2000 bonds would constitute a default on and acceleration of all Russian Eurobonds.

The Soviet Paris Club debt. The $40 billion due to other governments, incurred by the Soviet Union, had been restructured in 1996 by the Paris Club. About half was owed to the German government. In late 1998, Russia defaulted on $685 million it owed the German and French governments. The Paris Club, on August 1, 1999, restructured $8 billion in arrears and debt falling due from 1999-2000. Russia's request to write off some of this debt was declined. As of March 2004, Russia owed about $42 billion to Paris Club creditors. Russia did not default on Paris Club debt incurred by Russia. In May 2005, it appeared that Russia and the Paris Club had reached agreement as to the repayment of the debt. Creditor countries had been insisting on a premium payment over par to reflect the below-market interest rates on the loans, but relented and accepted the Russian proposal for repayment at par. $15 billion of the debt was to be repaid ahead of schedule from June to August of 2005.

Russian Debt to Multilateral Institutions. As indicated, $19 billion was owed to the IMF and $4.7 billion of that came due in 1999. IMF debt cannot be rescheduled, according to the terms of the loans. Russia also was due to pay the World Bank $800 million in 1999. Russia met these payments on schedule. From late 1999, however, the IMF was unwilling to disburse additional funds to Russia. The country had promised to make many structural changes, such as enacting a new bankruptcy law. But it had failed to accomplish many of these conditions on schedule. Not everyone accepted this as the reason for the delay. Some saw it as pressure to end the war in Chechnya.[48] As of April 2004, Russian debt to the IMF was about $5 billion and to the World Bank, $6.5 billion. On January 31, 2005, Russia repaid all of its then outstanding debt of $3.33 billion to the IMF ahead of schedule.

MinFins. Russian defaulted on only one MinFin, series 3 ($1.2 billion), even though the series 4 and 5 MinFins ($6.2 billion) were also Soviet era debt. Later Russian MinFins, series 6-7, were completely honored.

Other debt. Russia made the payments due in 1999 on the $16 billion in outstanding Eurobonds. While the official reason was that it constituted post-Soviet era debt, some believe that this was because, "default on such obligations would trigger cross-defaults accelerating the entire indebtedness, and would also effectively exclude Russia from world capital

---

[48] B. Aris, "Living With a Lie," Euromoney (January 2000), p. 75.

markets for the foreseeable future."[49] Of the $32 billion in outstanding trade credit, $2.5 billion was due in 1999. Russia also serviced this debt.

Foreign creditors renegotiated individually with debt owed to them by Russian banks. The leverage of creditors was limited because they could not force the banks into bankruptcy because no law existed for bank insolvency. A major concern to foreign creditors was the banks' forward currency contracts. Recent court cases in Russia held that the agreements were illegal as gambling and could not be enforced. By the end of 1999, most had been renegotiated and a lower amount paid.

Only a few years later, Russian issuers discovered that bond markets welcomed them again. The country's oil wealth made it ever more attractive as the oil price rose. A new Eurobond issue is reportedly planned for 2005. Total external debt was, however, largely unchanged from 1998, totaling $154 billion.

Four main features characterize the Russian approach. First, it defaulted on much of its external debt. This had not occurred in a major borrower country since the 1980s. Perhaps Russia was confident that its superpower status and earnings prospects permitted this. Second, Russia selectively defaulted and restructured some debt but not other. While this was largely based on the Soviet-Russian distinction, Russia failed to default on $6.2 billion in Soviet MinFins. Third, Russia received no IMF assistance, refusing IMF conditions. Fourth, domestic Ruble debt owed to foreigners was a significant part of the problem. Indeed Russia was the first country to default on local currency debt rather than just printing money. Overall, Russia reduced its debt and then was able to repay it.

Notes and Questions

1.   Should Russia be permitted to treat some debt differently from other debt?

2.   Suppose foreign investors in GKOs and OFZs looked to the courts to enforce their contractual rights. How effective would this remedy be?

3.   The Russian crisis spilled over into other transition countries, particularly those with close economic ties to Russia, such as former members of the Soviet Union. Their currencies fell 30 percent to 80 percent against the dollar as their exports to Russia dropped. Output declined. The financial sectors of these countries weakened significantly and confidence in them ebbed further. Capital flowed out.[50]

---

[49] See B. Horrigan, "Debt Recovery by Foreign Investors in Post-Crisis Russia," European Business Journal (1999), p. 88.

[50] IMF, *World Economic Outlook* (October 1999), p. 66-70.

c.   ECUADOR: SOVEREIGN DEFAULT ON BRADY BONDS AND EUROBONDS

Ecuador's 1999 debt crisis was significant in two respects: its default on Brady Bonds and Eurobonds—Russia had fully serviced its Eurobonds—and its use of a bond exchange with exit amendments to restructure its bond indebtedness.

1.   THE AUGUST 1999 CRISIS

Hit by El Nino, falling prices for key export commodities, and a weak domestic banking sector, the government of Ecuador defaulted on some of its Brady Bonds in August 1999, and on its Eurobonds in October.

Ecuador's external debt, at the end of 1998, consisted of $5.8 billion in Brady bonds, $3.6 billion in bank loans, $2.8 billion in debt to multilateral agencies, $1.1 billion of official bilateral loans, a Eurobond of $0.7 billion, and trade credits of $0.6 billion.[51]

2.   THE RESPONSE

Ecuador had considered defaulting only on some of its Brady Bonds, but rejected this as an unequal treatment of creditors. Ironically, however, it continued to service its other debt, including its bank loans. The IMF's response was measured. Initially, it was not willing to provide Ecuador with emergency funds that would allow the country to service the debt. Lenders saw this as a response by the IMF to its critics during the Asian financial crisis, and a signal that the IMF would not bail out foreign lenders. Eventually, in April 2000, just as Ecuador prepared to offer the exchange described below, the IMF negotiated a $286 million stand-by. It allowed Ecuador to draw this in four tranches up to December 2001. In March 2003, the IMF approved a new $205 million stand-by.

Bond Exchange

On July 27, 2000, the government of Ecuador offered to exchange U.S. Dollar Global Bonds due in 2030 for the Brady Bonds and the Eurobonds.

The relative value of the different existing bonds was determined by the gross payment streams due on the bonds. The shortest-dated instruments, such as the Eurobonds, were exchanged for 2030 bonds at par, while the longer dated Brady bondholders received 2030 bonds discounted at 42 percent and 60 percent. The 2030 Bonds would pay interest of 4 percent in the first year, stepping up 1 percent a year to 10 percent in 2006 and thereafter, below market rates. Their holders would also receive cash payments for overdue interest.

---

[51] P. Graf, "Ecuador's External Debt Problem," BIS International Banking and Financial Market Developments (November 1999), p. 6.

Bondholders could elect to receive 2012 Bonds in lieu of 2030 Bonds, but had to accept a discount 35 percent greater than on the 2030 Bonds. They would receive 12 percent interest, however. Ecuador would only issue 2012 Bonds with a total face value of $1.25 billion, and would give priority to these bonds to holders of shorter-dated Eurobonds and Brady Bonds. Almost 97 percent of the bondholders accepted the offer and Ecuador reduced the aggregate value of its bond obligations by almost 40 percent.[52] In 1999, Ecuador's external debt had been 82.8 percent of GDP, by 2002 it was only 46.9 percent, and it was expected to fall to 42.2 percent in 2003.[53]

Ecuador accepted several important limits. Principal reinstatement was one. If the government defaulted on servicing the 2030 Bonds in the first 10 years, it would automatically issue more of the Bonds. The additional Bonds would reinstate the principal on the old bonds that the bondholders had relinquished. Mandatory debt management guidelines required Ecuador to retire an agreed portion of the outstanding 2030 Bonds starting 11 years after issue and 2012 Bonds starting 6 years after issue. The purpose was to avoid relying on Ecuador's ability to make a bullet payment at the end, while recognizing that the parties could not set a repayment schedule with any confidence in 2001.

Exit Amendments

Ecuador's Brady Bonds had New York-style covenants that required unanimous consent of bondholders to any alteration of payment terms. Under the terms of the bond, however, a majority of creditors could modify non-payment terms. Ecuador used so-called exit amendments to alter the non-payment terms of its old bonds in order to discourage old bond holders from holding out and refusing to participate in the exchange. This was done by having old bondholders, who did participate in the exchange, alter the terms of the old bonds before exchanging them.

For example, exit amendments removed the cross-default, cross-acceleration, and negative pledge clauses in the old bonds. The amendments also removed covenants to make annual reports, include the old bonds in later conversions, keep the bonds listed, and prevent the government from buying old bonds while they were in default.

Notes and Questions

1.   Is the repurchase of bonds by the issuer an appropriate way for a government to deal with a debt crisis?

---

[52] L. Buchheit, "How Ecuador Escaped the Brady Bond Trap," International Financial Law Review (December 2000), p. 17; Republic of Ecuador, *Offer to Exchange*, Offering Circular, July 27, 2000.

[53] IMF Public Information Notice No. 03/47, *IMF Concludes 2003 Article IV Consultations with Ecuador*, April 7, 2003.

2. Are exit amendments an appropriate way to encourage bond holders to participate in a restructuring? Suppose many more governments than Ecuador use them to prod reluctant investors to exchange their bonds. How would that affect the evolution of the international bond market?

4.   TURKEY: SOVEREIGN DEFAULT ON DOMESTIC BONDS

While the crises dealt with above involved IMF help in servicing government foreign currency debt, the focus of the Turkish crisis was IMF aid in dealing with government domestic currency debt.

The crisis began in November 2000 when the medium-sized Demir Bank failed, triggering a lack of confidence in the Turkish economy. Foreign investors pulled funds out of government Lira securities, converting Lira receipts to foreign currency. In a few days, Turkey's reserves fell 20 percent.

In December, to help stem the outflow, the IMF supplemented the outstanding stand-by credit of $3.7 billion it had granted in December 1999 by $7.3 billion, adding many conditions to restructure the economy, but this did not alleviate the pressure on the Lira, and Turkey was forced to abandon its crawling peg against the Dollar, a regime previously encouraged by Stanley Fischer, the then second highest ranking IMF official (see Chapter 8 for the criticisms of crawling peg regimes.)

The immediate problem facing Turkey was the large government short-term debt in Lira. Much of this debt—the equivalent of about $20 billion—was due within the next six months. The government had planned, as in the past, simply to roll it over at current rates. But if the outflow of foreign currency continued, it would reduce the supply of funds in domestic markets, which would in turn push interest rates up even more and raise the servicing costs to unacceptably high levels for the government. The government lacked funds in its budget to meet existing debt service, let alone an increase. It could not simply print more Lira to service the domestic debt. That would hurt the economy. Inflation was already over 100 percent. Even higher inflation would worsen the exchange rate.

On the horizon was a threat to Turkey's financial system like that in the crisis in South Korea, a danger of which the IMF was keenly aware. Private Turkish banks were the main investors in the government's short term Lira paper. They had financed their purchases of government debt by borrowing funds denominated in foreign currency, mainly Deutschmark, from foreign banks. If the government were to default on its short term Lira debt, this would make it impossible for Turkish banks to service their foreign currency debt.

The IMF responded in mid-May 2001, by expanding its stand-by credit to $19 billion. The idea was to restore confidence in the Lira, an approach that had worked in Mexico but not in Asia. The IMF would immediately provide $3.8 billion, and disburse another $9 billion by the end of the year if Turkey complied with conditions, including putting a lid on the growth of money, making structural changes in its banking sector, and combating corruption.[54] Foreign banks with loans to Turkish banks had already been pressed by their home governments to roll over the loans. The foreign banks' supervisors, working with the IMF, put in place a system to monitor performance. In addition, the World Bank added another $1.8 billion for specified projects to the $5 billion in loans that it was already providing.[55] This failed to work.

The IMF agreed in February 2002 to increase its potential funding from $19 billion to $31 billion. Of the $12 billion in new money, half would be used to repay $6 billion coming due to the IMF in 2002, in effect lengthening the maturity by 4 years. This new money was seen as "further evidence of the willingness of the fund's largest member states to act generously with countries that are seen as strategically important to the war against terrorism and are also pursuing aggressive economic reform programmes." The U.S. had "strongly supported" the new money "to prevent destabilization in a key regional ally."[56] As of April 2004, Turkey's IMF stand-by stood at $19.7 billion and discussions were underway in early 2005 about the continuance of the stand-by. In 2003-04, Turkey borrowed $2.94 billion from the IMF but repaid $8.4 billion. In May 2005, Turkey and the IMF agreed that a new $10 billion three year stand-by to replace the $19.7 billion stand-by. The funds were conditional on Turkish reforms to social security, the banking sector and tax administration.

In 2003, the economy improved, growing about 6 percent and inflation dropped to below 20 percent, but the debt burden remained high. Recapitalization of the banking sector had been substantially completed and corporate debt restructuring was underway. Turkey continued to press for admission to the EU. In 2004-2005 continued improvements were made. GNP growth continued strong, inflation was down to 6.8 percent and the net debt of the public sector was down to $60 billion from a high of $90 billion in 2001.

Turkey's crisis demonstrated the close connection between domestic and foreign debt. The link was largely through banks that used foreign liabilities to fund purchases of domestic currency government debt. Turkey also demonstrated the continued importance of foreign policy issues in dealing with debt crises. Turkey's key role as a U.S. ally in the Islamic world bolstered its case for official and multilateral support. Of course, these considerations could work both ways, as when the U.S. financially penalized

---

[54] *Letter of Intent to IMF from the Prime Minister of Turkey*, May 3, 2001, p. 9.

[55] IMF Survey, *IMF Executive Board Approves $8 billion Augmentation of Stand-By Credit for Turkey*, May 21, 2001; S. Fidler, "Turkish Crisis Set to Test U.S. Aversion to Bail-Outs," *Financial Times*, March 2, 2001; L. Boulton and S. Fidler, "Turkey Wins Backing for $19bn Loans," *Financial Times*, May 16, 2001; D. Frantz, "Turkish Bailout is Joined to a Political Overhaul," *The New York Times*, May 18, 2001.

[56] E. Aiden, "Turkish Reforms Bring $16bn IMF Loan," *Financial Times*, February 5, 2002.

Turkey for its failure to permit the opening of a U.S. northern front in Iraq. Finally, Turkey was a throwback to older debt crises, like Mexico and South Korea, where massive public funds were made available before foreign banks had agreed to restructuring or new money.

5.   ARGENTINA: A MAJOR SUSTAINED DEFAULT

Argentina captured the title for the largest sovereign default when it defaulted on its $141 billion external debt in late December 2001.

a.   THE CRISIS

The genesis of the Argentine debt crisis traces back a decade. In 1991, the government adopted a Currency Board, fixing the Peso equal to one U.S. Dollar under the guidance of then Economy Minister Domingo Cavallo. With tight money, the initial effect was to end very high inflation and economic growth was a healthy 4 percent per year from 1994 to 1998. External debt, however, doubled in the same period.

In April 2001, the third year of recession, the government recalled Cavallo as Economy Minister. He instituted an austerity program that promised a zero fiscal deficit and a weakening of the Peso/Dollar link. Gradually these policies, coupled with low commodity prices and the devalued currency of competing countries, produced bankruptcies, unemployment, runs on banks, riots, and capital flight conservatively estimated at $13 billion.

In June 2001, the government swapped about $30 billion in short-term external bonds for new bonds with longer maturities. The interest on the new bonds was a higher-than-market long-term rate as a sweetener but the government still saved $16 billion in interest over the next four years.

In late October and November, the government asked investors to swap up to $95 billion of bonds due in the next decade for ones paying much lower interest and postponing full payment for three years. The swap would let the government pay $4 billion less in interest each year. Foreign rating agencies said that the swap was a form of default and rated bonds eligible for the swap as being in default. In the event, some local investors–including banks–accepted the offer. For foreign investors, Argentina hoped to make a global offer for all bonds sometime between January and March 2002, but events outdistanced it.

The government limited bank depositors to withdrawals from peso accounts to 2,000 Pesos a month, and froze withdrawals from Dollar accounts. It imposed controls on transfers of funds out of Argentina. It reduced the interest payments on $45 billion of government bonds held by local investors. It made local banks roll over $360 million of Treasury bills to avoid a formal default on public debt.

In late December, the government defaulted on its debt, which included more than 90 different financial instruments, and the next month it ended the 1:1 Peso:Dollar rate and the Currency Board. Millions of retail investors held this debt, many of whom were Italians and Japanese.

b.   THE PRE-COLLAPSE ROLE OF THE IMF

During the two years leading up to the crisis, the IMF repeatedly loaned Argentina funds. U.S. government officials were involved in each IMF decision. The IMF allowed Argentina a three year stand-by loan of $7 billion in March 2000, raised it to $14 billion in January 2001, and raised it once again to $22 billion on September 7, 2001. The September arrangement let Argentina draw about $6 billion immediately, another $6 billion in 2002, and $1.3 billion in 2003, and also allowed Argentina to draw immediately $3 billion of the later funds if it improved the structure of government debt. In January 2002, the IMF extended by one year repayment of a $933 million loan due that month.[57]

Each agreement included specific targets for economic reform. For example, in March 2000, Argentina agreed to reduce the deficit of the central and provincial governments substantially, but in January 2001, the IMF agreed to accept only a small reduction in the short run. Then in September 2001, the IMF required Argentina to eliminate the federal deficit immediately. Argentina had passed a zero deficit law that required increasing taxes and cutting spending, including wages and pensions. The government failed, however, to achieve the zero deficit quickly. Many provincial governors refused to take part. So in December, the IMF delayed releasing $1.26 billion to Argentina from the September 2001 package. The World Bank and Inter-American Development Bank froze another $1.1 billion. It was soon thereafter, in December 2001, that Argentina defaulted.

Critics of the IMF said that it should have led a bailout like that for Mexico, infusing $50 billion that would jump start the economy. The Bush administration, far from allowing this, had prevented the IMF in December 2001 from advancing the stand-by funds, once again trying to get tough on the expansion of official and multilateral debt and its contribution to creditor moral hazard.

c.   ARGENTINA AFTER DEFAULT

In the months after the crisis, the new Duhalde government, the fifth since mid-December, instituted capital controls. In late March, it limited daily investment by individuals to $1,000 and by companies, to $10,000. It halved the daily operating time of exchanges to 3.5 hours. It limited the amount of Dollars banks and business could hold. It limited the ability of

---

[57] J. Fuerbringer, with R. Stevenson, "No Bailout Is Planned For Argentina," *The New York Times*, July 14, 2001.

investors and brokers to buy stock in the U.S., where they traded in Dollars at a premium over the Peso market. It tried to shield the banking sector, which was severely hurt by controls, devaluation, and loss of confidence, but most banks were insolvent, and laid off a large portion of their staff.[58]

Major foreign banks, which dominated much of Argentina's banking system, wrote down huge amounts or withdrew. Provisions were set up for problem loans by Citibank ($2.1 billion), HSBC ($1.5 billion), and FleetBoston ($1.4 billion). Two Spanish banks wrote off their entire investments in Argentina ($2.9 billion total). The Bank of Nova Scotia of Canada and Credit Agricole ($278 million) did the same and refused to inject further funds.

One debt holder, Allan Applestein, sued to collect on his $245,000 of Argentine bonds. The big institutional creditors formed the Argentine Bondholders Committee. It opposed the suit and proposed that the government consult them regularly before proposing repayment methods, treat all creditors equally, and renounce efforts to coerce them by, for example, exercising or requiring exit clauses.[59]

At first, the central bank continued to service its debt to multilateral agencies, but this changed in November 2002. The central bank paid the World Bank $680 million interest in May 2002, then in November paid the World Bank only $79 million of the $805 million installment due. The government explained that it could not service such a large amount until it had IMF help. It then also fell into arrears to the Inter-American Development Bank.[60] This was the first significant default on multilateral debt.

The IMF continued its tough stance toward Argentina through 2002, demanding fiscal reforms and refusing to disburse more funds until this was done.

The government began to relax some of its crisis policies in late 2002. In December, it ended the freeze on peso current accounts, and in late March 2003, promised to end many remaining curbs over the next four months. More controls fell in January 2003. Transfers abroad to pay interest, dividends, and profits no longer required prior government authorization, nor did sales of foreign exchange to non-residents.

---

[58] M. Mulligan, "Argentine Rescue Plan 'Back to Square One,'" *Financial Times*, May 14, 2002; L. Rohter, "Peso Down Steeply, Argentines Strengthen Currency Curbs," *The New York Times*, March 26, 2002.

[59] B. Boccara, *Analysis: Argentina*, Standard & Poor's, January 11, 2002; T. Catan and S. Silver, Telecom "Argentina Defaults on $3.3bn of Debt Repayments," *Financial Times*, April 3, 2002; Argentina Bondholders' Committee, *Principles for the Restructuring of Argentina International Bonds* (May 3, 2002); D. Gopinath, "The Debt-Crisis Crisis," *Institutional Investor* (August 2002), p. 37.

[60] L. Rohter, "Argentina Defaults on Big Payment to World Bank," *The New York Times*, November 15, 2002; P. Hudson and C. Daniel, "IMF Plays Down Argentine Default," *Financial Times*, November 16-17, 2002.

The IMF announced an interim Stand-By Arrangement in mid-January 2003 to help Argentina through the April presidential election. The IMF rolled over obligations to it and provided liquidity to pay arrears due the World Bank and IDB, and service debt coming due from January to August. The World Bank and IDB would increase their lending to Argentina. The net result was an increase of $1.3 billion in the international financial institutions' exposure to Argentina. The IMF stand-by was seen as a major change in its approach to Argentina, one that might undermine its credibility worldwide. Horst Köhler and Anne Krueger, the top two officials of the IMF, had each taken publicly uncompromising positions earlier. Argentina had not met the criteria for new IMF assistance. Now the IMF was helping anyway. Pressure from France, Spain, and Italy, as well as the U.S., caused the about face. It looked as though Argentina had won a game of "chicken."[61]

When the country's new president, Nestor Kirchner, won the election by default in April 2003, the country's economy seemed to have turned around. IMF and World Bank lending were to resume, GNP was expected to grow 4 percent in 2003, inflation was single digit, and the Peso had risen 20 percent against the Dollar in 4 months, forcing the central bank to intervene. In September 2003, Argentina put forward a bold—and to creditors a shocking—debt restructuring proposal, proposing to reduce debt obligations by 75 percent and not to pay back about $18 billion in past due interest on defaulted debt. In October, it released more details. Argentina proposed to swap defaulted bonds for three new securities which would have maturities of up to 42 years and interest rates of as little as 0.5 percent. Prices on outstanding bonds fell to 29.30 cents on the dollar, reflecting the new reality.

In March 2004, after lengthy negotiations, the IMF agreed to rollover a $3.1 billion payment then due from Argentina. President Kirchner had refused to make the payment then due unless the IMF agreed to disburse new funds roughly in the same amount. Moreover, Kirchner refused to agree to more than a 3 percent primary surplus target—funds available to service external debt—even though his economy was recovering, and Brazil and Turkey have respective targets of 4.25 and 6 percent. The rollover was conditioned on Argentina negotiating with its creditors to achieve a high participation rate in any proposed debt restructuring. Reportedly, some members of the G7, other than the U.S., opposed the rollover.

Consider that of the total $106.2 billion in IMF credit outstanding as of January 31, 2004, roughly 16 percent, or $15.8 billion, was owed by Argentina.[62] On March 16, 2004, in what was dubbed as the Copacabana Act,

---

[61] IMF Country Report No. 03/101, *Argentina: Request for Stand-By Arrangement* (April 2003); A. Beattie, "Argentine 'Blackmail': As the IMF Prepares a $6bn Debt Roll-Over, Doubts About the Fund's Credibility Resurface," *Financial Times*, January 21, 2003.

[62] As of January 1, 2004, IMF credit outstanding, apart from Argentina, was Brazil $28.2 billion, Turkey $23.8 billion, and other $38.3 billion. "Argentina and the IMF: Which is the Victim?," The Economist, March 6, 2004.

President Kirchner and President Lula of Brazil declared their intention to jointly negotiate with the IMF on debt restructuring. If both these countries defaulted on their IMF debt, the IMF would be bankrupt. This puts tremendous pressure on the IMF to avoid such a default by rolling over its debt. While the IMF did not increase its exposure to Argentina in 2004, the Inter-American Development Bank approved a $5 billion package of loans to Argentina in November 2004, so overall the multilaterals continued to lend despite Argentina's intransigence.

In June 2004, Argentina announced its intention to make an exchange offer for $102 billion of its defaulted debt, $82 billion in principal and $20 billion in past due interest. This promised to be the largest bond restructuring ever, comparing with the next largest Russian restructuring of about $30 billion. Prior to June, Argentina had been considering an offer worth about 10 cents on the Dollar. The terms of the offer announced in June raised this to about 25 cents on the Dollar by agreeing to include unpaid interest accruals since the date of default, amounting to about $22.5 billion as of June. The Argentine benchmark global bond that matured in 2008 was trading at about 30.55 cents on the Dollar. Further details of the offer became clear in November. 152 different bonds with a face value of $81.8 billion, held by more than 500,000 bondholders worldwide, would be exchanged for nine new bonds issued under four different legal systems and currencies, with a face value of $41.8 billion with lower interest rates and longer maturities.

The final details became clear in the registration statement Argentina filed with the SEC on December 27, 2004, that was supplemented on January 10, 2005. Investors were given a choice of three different types of bonds: (1) a par bond due 2038, paying an interest rate beginning at 1.33 percent and rising to 5.25 percent; (2) a discount bond, with a haircut of 66 percent from the value of old bonds, due 2033, with interest from 3.97 percent to 8.28 percent over the period; and (3) a quasi-par bond maturing in 2045, with a haircut of 30 percent, paying 3.31 percent, and capitalizing interest accruals prior to 2014. Par bonds were capped at $10-$15 billion depending on the rate of acceptance. Retail investors apparently preferred these bonds and a certain amount of these bonds were reserved for them. In addition, Argentina provided a GDP "kicker" under which interest rates would increase in the event that Argentine GDP over the maturity of the bonds exceeded certain baseline projections. The bonds were to rank pari passu with all other bonds. They were rated B- by S&P, one notch above C, the rating for a country expected to default within a year.

There was widespread creditor dissatisfaction with the terms of the offer, particularly given the improvement in the Argentine economy. Its real GDP grew by 7 percent in 2004 and inflation was below 5 percent. Furthermore, Argentina generated revenue from a tax on exports designed to capture "windfalls" from the devaluation. Creditors argued that it could afford to pay much more than 25 percent of its debt. As a point of comparison, in 20 sovereign debt restructurings since 1990 the average haircut was just 36 percent as compared with the 70-75 percent overall haircut on the Argentine exchange offer.[63] One representative of creditors, the Argentine Bond Restructuring Agency (ABRA), which represented German and Austrian creditors, indicated that it would not accept the offer because of an asserted loophole in the most-favored creditor clause under which any bondholders accepting the exchange were assured future payments if holdouts were to later get a better deal. The Argentine legislator quickly passed a bill that prevented the government making a subsequent better offer to holdouts, but it was observed that such deals might still be made by state-controlled entities and that Argentina could always change the law. Abra eventually accepted the exchange.

Certain dissatisfied creditors tried to stop the exchange to no avail. In H.W. Urban GMBH v. Sylvia Seijas, 02 CV 5699 (SDNY, November 16, 2004), a class action of foreign bondholders against Argentina, Judge Griesa refused to enjoin the exchange on the ground that Argentina did not enter into good faith negotiations with its creditors. The Judge ruled that creditors should be given the choice of whether or not to go along with the exchange or pursue damage claims. Some creditor/traders seemed to do quite well having bought the debt when it was trading below the value of the Argentine offer which in February was valued around 32 cents on the Dollar. This compares with the Russian restructuring of 2000, where Russia paid from 35-43 percent of face value, depending on the type of bond in question.[64]

The exchange was deemed a success by Argentina in March 2005, when bondholders with 76 percent of the old bonds accepted the exchange by tendering their new bonds. Argentina announced it would issue $35.2 billion in new debt, consisting of $15 billion in par bonds, $8.3 billion in quasi-par bonds and $11.9 billion in discount bonds. While 76 percent seemed high, it actually compares with a 90 percent rate that would normally be required for the IMF to regard the transaction as successful. Recent acceptance rates have been much higher: Ecuador 2000-97 percent; Pakistan 1999-95 percent; Russia 1998 to 2000-98 percent; Ukraine 1998-2000-95 percent; and Uruguay 2003-93 percent.[65] The 76 percent rate was also below the effective rate that would have been required to bar holdouts under the new bonds' own collective action clauses which require a 75 percent vote excluding controlled entities like state-owned banks. The 76 percent rate included all comers. Some believe the foreign creditor acceptance rate was below 50 percent. Finance Minister Lavagna said that the exchange enabled Argentina to reduce almost $103 billion in defaulted debt, $81.8 billion in bonds and more than $20 billion in past-due interest, to $35 billion, saving the country $67

---

[63] M. Moffett, Argentina Squeezes Bondholders," *The Wall Street Journal*, January 11, 2005.

[64] "Shooting the Messenger," The Economist, September 23, 2004.

[65] A. Porzecanski, "Form Rogue Creditors to Rogue Debtors: Implications of Argentina's Default," 6 Chicago Journal of International Law 312 (2005) (Rogue Debtors)

billion. He further indicated that the debt servicing costs would drop to 15 percent of reserves as compared to 70 percent three years earlier.[66]

On March 21, 2005, holdout creditors on Argentine bonds owed $361 million (principal plus interest), for which they paid $114 million in the secondary market, sought an attachment of $7 billion of the old bonds that had been tendered to Argentina in the debt exchange—the $7 billion figure assumed that the old bonds that had not been tendered were worth 5 percent of their face value.

Under the Foreign Sovereign Immunities Act, attachments can only be granted with respect to the debtor's property within the United States.[67] The argument of the creditors was that once these old bonds had been tendered, Argentina had a property right in the bonds—they had a right to receive the bonds once the exchange was completed. The property was in the United States, as the bonds were held in what amounted to an escrow account of the Bank of New York at the Depository Trust Co, (see Chapter 10 on clearing and settlement). So the attachment would first be of Argentina's right to the bonds and then of the bond themselves. While it was unclear whether these $7 billion in bonds could actually fetch anything in the secondary market, the effect of the attachment would be to increase Argentina's outstanding debt by $7 billion. This would conflict with the very purpose of entering into the bond exchange.

Judge Griesa, who continued to hear litigation on the Argentine bonds, granted on March 21, 2005, a preliminary ex parte attachment order—Argentina was not present, as in many attachment applications where notice to the debtor of a hearing might result in removal of assets from the court's jurisdiction.[68] On March 29, Judge Griesa had a full hearing with both parties. Argentina's principal argument was that the attachment would frustrate the bond exchange, as they would not go through with the exchange if the tendered old bonds were to be attached. Argentina also argued that the bonds were not their property, nor did they have any right to the bonds, until they gave the old bondholders new bonds, which they had not yet done.

The court vacated the attachment, but stayed his order pending the resolution of an appeal to the Second Circuit.[69] The court appeared to accept the argument that Argentina had a property right in the bonds. The court believed, however, that part of Argentina's rights to the bonds included its right to cancel the bonds which the attaching creditors would obviously not do, and the failure of Argentina to achieve cancellation, would lead them to pull out of the exchange entirely, which they would have a right to do under the circumstances. The Second Circuit heard the appeal and affirmed the

---

[66] A. Thomson, "Creditors Back Argentina Debt Terms," *Financial Times*, March 3, 2005.

[67] 28 U.S.C. §1610 (a),(d).

[68] *NML Capital Ltd. et. al. v. The Republic of Argentina*, 03 Civ. 8845 (TPG), March 21, 2005.

[69] *NML Capital Ltd. et. al. v. The Republic of Argentina*, 03 Civ. 8845 (TPG), Hearing Transcript, pp. 36-41, March 29, 2005.

District Court's denial of the attachment order on May 13, 2005 in a summary order. The court stated that the District Court had provided a sufficient and dispositive reason for vacating the attachment, quoting the lower court: "If these attachments [and restraints] are still in effect, we throw into doubt, to say the least, the conclusion of the exchange offer." The Second Circuit noted that the grant of attachment orders was largely a matter of discretion of the District Court and it had not abused its discretion.

It was left to conjecture as to why the courts should care whether the exchange was or was not completed—arguably the U.S. courts should just enforce creditor rights without regard to the impact on Argentina. Perhaps the courts were worried about the impact on other creditors who had tendered and wanted the exchange to go through (however coercive it had been). On the other hand, the other creditors may have benefited—if Argentina pulled out of the exchange, it might have to improve a subsequent offer to get sufficient participation. Later in this Chapter we discuss improving creditor rights. One candidate for improvement would be to facilitate by legislation the ability of creditors to attach assets of all kind.

One other unsuccessful attack on the exchange bears mentioning. In *Capital Ventures International v. Argentina*, 05 CV 4085 (2005), holdout creditors sought to attach the collateral held for the Brady bonds, U.S. Treasury zero coupon bonds held in a collateral account at the New York Federal Reserve Bank, that were part of the debt exchange (see discussion above of Brady Bonds). The collateral arrangements provided that if the Brady Bonds were redeemed prior to maturity, Argentina would be entitled to the return of the collateral. Interestingly, the Brady bondholders were not entitled to the collateral upon default on the bonds, because under the terms of the arrangement the collateral would only be available upon the maturity of the bonds. It would appear that under the terms of the bond exchange, the Brady bondholders were to receive the normal package of new bonds *plus* whatever collateral Argentina was to receive back from the collateral account. The Brady collateral was worth about 50 percent of the face value of the Brady bonds—so Brady bondholders received a package of compensation worth about 83.7 percent of the face value of their bonds (50 percent in cash from the sale of the U.S. treasuries and 33.7 percent in new bonds).

It is unclear why the Brady bondholders were to be treated so much better than the other bondholders. They were not entitled to the collateral. Perhaps, Argentina realized that if the collateral, or its proceeds, was not returned to the tendering bondholders, it would be available for attaching creditors. Judge Griesa denied this attachment motion on April 25, 2005, while the other attachment case was pending in the Second Circuit. He ruled that since the collateral was owed to the tendering Brady bondholders under the terms of the exchange, the collateral could not be attached by the holdout creditors.[70] What remains unclear from the litigation is why the Court should respect the terms of the exchange itself—the collateral seemed to be the property of Argentina under the terms of the collateral arrangements. The fact that they decided to give it to the Brady bondholders arguably was irrelevant. Even if the Brady bondholders were entitled to receive this collateral under the collateral agreement, it is even more puzzling why Argentina would top up this collateral with a package of new bonds.

One quite interesting aspect of the Argentine litigation was the failure of the United States to make an appearance or file a statement of interest on the side of Argentina, which they had done in earlier litigation with Argentina over the meaning of the in pari passu clause.[71] The U.S. was not there to support the idea that the bond exchange was good and that it would be wrong of the court to grant the attachment. This may reflect a change in U.S. thinking on Argentina, as reflected in the urging of the G-7 and the International Monetary Fund that Argentina should come to some resolution of the substantial amount of old bonds outstanding after the exchange was completed. [72]

On June 3, 2005, Argentina announced the bond exchange had been completed. At its conclusion the exchange was valued at 34 cents on the dollar in the "when issued" market. Argentina now has to reach some resolution of its debt situation with the IMF.

Notes and Questions

1. What are the future implications of the Argentine default?

2. Should the IMF have rolled over the $3.1 billion due in 2004?

3. Why would Argentina care if there were more old bonds outstanding after the bond exchange?

6.   BRAZIL: MEXICO 1984 REDUX?

Brazil found itself in difficulties in 2002. It had a large public debt, about $290 billion, and the prospect of left wing political leadership, in the form of the popular candidate Lula da Silva. This put significant pressure on the Real-Dollar exchange rate.

---

[70] See Hearing Transcript, April 25, 2005.

[71] In 2003, Argentina sought a declaratory judgment in the Southern District of New York that creditors should not be permitted to use the broad interpretation of in pari passu to enforce judgments against Argentina, *EM Ltd. v. Argentina*, 03-CV-2507. The U.S. and the Federal Reserve Bank of New York respectively filed a statement of interest and an amicus brief supporting the position of Argentina. The court ruled on January 15, 2004, that the issue was not yet ripe for decision, Hearing Transcript, in the matter of *Allan Applestein, Trustee FBO D.C.A. Grantor Trust v. The Republic of Argentina*, pp. 6-10.

[72] T. Dawson, Transcript of Press Briefing, April 8, 2005.

In June, Brazil indicated it would draw on a $10 billion IMF stand-by credit and received approval from the IMF to free up another $5 billion in reserves by lowering its reserve floor from $20 billion to $15 billion. Around the same time, U.S. Treasury Secretary Paul O'Neill stated that he was against throwing money at Brazil because of political uncertainty, and that money lent to Brazil and Argentina could end up in Swiss bank accounts. By the end of July the Real was down 30 percent.

In August, the IMF approved a $30 billion loan, $6 billion to be disbursed immediately, with the balance coming in 2003 after the elections. O'Neill now said Brazil was different from Argentina because it had the right economic policies in place. No restructurings were done by private creditors, indeed some analysts urged creditors to use the reserve infusion to get out. Following the rescue package, the Real depreciated another 4.1 percent. In December, Brazil drew another $3.1 billion of the IMF credit.

Lula da Silva took power in January 2003 and his new Finance Minister said that the former commitments to control inflation would be honored. Whether or not the situation has stabilized is as yet unclear. Brazil might be another "liquidity" crisis like Mexico, perhaps the strongest type of case for continued IMF support.

In 2004, Brazil's GDP grew by 4 percent and inflation declined. In fact, Brazil issued new international debt in September 2004 by way of an 8-year bond of EUR750 million that was rated B+ by Fitch. In November, the IMF agreed to renew its expiring loan program, in the amount of $14 billion ($8 billion left over from the old agreement and $6 billion in new money). In addition, there was a postponement of $5.5 billion repayments due in 2005 and 2006. As of January 31, 2005, Brazil's IMF stand-by was $41.95 billion, of which $26.36 billion had been drawn. However, no drawings had been made since September 2003. In addition it had a loan outstanding of $24.75 billion.

C.   REFORM OF THE DEBT RESOLUTION PROCESS[73]

The Asian financial crisis triggered an outpouring of proposals for reforming the international financial system aimed primarily at preventing international financial crises and dealing better with them when they do occur. These proposals are referred to as the new International Financial Architecture (IFA).[74] This Section focuses on the areas of IFA relating to the debt problem: the role of the IMF, the use of collective action clauses, and the possible need for an international bankruptcy system for sovereigns. It does

---

[73] This section relies heavily on H. Scott, "A Bankruptcy Procedure for Sovereign Debtors," 37 International Lawyer 103 (2003).

[74] An excellent review of them is found in B. Eichengreen, *Toward a New International Financial Architecture* (1999).

not deal with the issue of exchange rate systems. As seen in Chapter 8, many economists have criticized pegged rates and have advocated moving more towards floating rates or currency boards.[75]

Any set of possible reforms must be evaluated against the problems they are intended to solve.

1.   THE SOVEREIGN DEBT PROBLEM: LESSONS FROM THE LAST THREE DECADES

In reviewing the experience with handling debt crises over the last 30 years, certain key concerns emerge: (1) the large expenditure of developed country public funds and the increase of emerging market sovereign debt levels; (2) the transformation of the IMF into the lender of last resort, for government guaranteed and domestic currency debt, as well as foreign currency debt; (3) the increase in creditor moral hazard; (4) the ineffectiveness of IMF conditionality; (5) sovereign debtors' discrimination among different kinds of debt; and (6) the problem of holdout creditors.

a.   LARGE EXPENDITURES OF DEVELOPED COUNTRY PUBLIC FUNDS AND INCREASING EMERGING MARKET DEBT

One clear feature of these crises is that they have required large expenditures of money by the IMF and other official lenders. IMF debt outstanding as of April 2003 was $91 billion.[76] On top of this, as of 1999, other multilateral and official creditors had extended over $877 billion in funds. While much of this is structural development lending, some substantial part is related to financial crises.

The debt burden of major debtors is significant. Argentina, Brazil, and Mexico had $8.4 billion in long-term debt in 1970, as compared with $267 billion in 1999. Debt in these three countries rose from 23.4 percent of GNP in 1970 to 62.3 percent by 1999. Both creditors and debtors would be better off with a significant reduction in debt levels.

Not all of this debt is current; 4 percent is in arrears. Official country debt has been continually been rescheduled through the Paris Club process. Argentina just recently defaulted on World Bank debt, and would have defaulted on the IMF but for permitted rollovers. And neither the IMF nor the United States has received anything close to a market rate on its loans. Indeed, it appears that average official and multilateral interest rates to

---

[75] See e.g. Council of Foreign Relations, *Independent Task Force Report on Safeguarding Prosperity in a Global Financial System: The Future International Financial Architecture* (2000), pp. 13-15. (CFR Report)
[76] IMF Financial Statement, 1st Quarter 2003.

developing countries are less than LIBOR or rates paid by AAA-rated U.S. corporates.[77]

b. IMF AS LENDER OF LAST RESORT

This period has seen the emergence of the IMF as an international lender of last resort (LLR). While the IMF cannot be a classical LLR, because it cannot print its own currency, it does command very sizeable resources due to support from G7 countries. The IMF (as supplemented by other multilaterals and sovereigns) has extended loans when the market would not do so itself. In South Korea and Turkey, it extended loans exceeding 2000 percent of these countries' quotas. While one can argue that all of these crises represented liquidity rather than insolvency situations, since governments could have commanded the resources to repay debts on time through tax and borrowing powers (albeit with a huge cost), they are unlike classic domestic liquidity crises, where a temporary extension of funds remedies irrational or speculative attacks on debtor banks. The only case where this was plausibly true was Mexico in 1994, and perhaps Brazil in 2000. In all the rest, fundamental problems in the economy and financial systems caused these crises. Vast amounts of aid did not restore the health of banks or values of currencies. And even in Mexico, it is clear that fundamental problems in the system existed before and after the 1994 crisis.

The type of debt that has been bailed out by IMF assistance has been extended in the 1990s beyond foreign currency debt to foreign lenders in two significant ways. First, it now includes sovereign guaranteed debt. This was the clear message of the South Korean crisis, where the government needed reserves in order to provide them to private banks (recently privatized) to serve the banks' foreign short-term debt. These funds were not made available because of a formal government guarantee of bank debt. The government decided, like many other governments have, that it did not want its banks to fail due to the damage this would do to the financial system and economy. Moreover, there were no established procedures in South Korea at the time for dealing with bank bankruptcies. Extension of IMF assistance to cover guarantees naturally makes the use of guarantees more likely and increases their value to beneficiaries.

A second extension has been the use of IMF assistance to cover domestic currency debt. This has been seen most dramatically in the Turkish crisis. While Turkey could have printed money to service its domestic currency debt, this would have been inflationary, and have created political instability if accompanied by contractionary fiscal policies. Also, inflationary policies would have reduced the value of government bonds imposing significant losses on already shaky Turkish banks.

---

[77] P. Benczur, "The Composition of Sovereign Debt: A Description," Central European University Department of Economics Working Paper 7/2003 (June 2003).

c.   INCREASE IN CREDITOR AND DEBTOR MORAL HAZARD

A third important feature of these crises, as they have progressed, is that they increase moral hazard, thereby decreasing market discipline on sovereign borrowing. If private creditors will be bailed out, they are more likely to make bad loans. The moral hazard effect may be reflected in the general statistics concerning sovereign lending over the 1982-2000 period. Bank debt, on which there were significant defaults and reschedulings in the 1980s, followed by reductions as part of the Brady Bond process, dropped precipitously in the 1990s, and was replaced by bond debt on which there had been no defaults.

If the market disciplined sovereign borrowing, the number and intensity of crises and the concomitant need of public funds would decrease. The moral hazard problem has become worse over time. In the 1980s, no public funds were extended during a crisis until banks had agreed to reschedule their debt and lend new funds. Although, banks were insulated from default, and thus the necessity to write-off loans under existing accounting rules, they did experience severe consequences. And when the Brady Plan was adopted, the banks actually did have significant write-offs of their loans as part of the debt exchange.

In contrast, in the 1994 Mexican case, the U.S. and IMF extended over $38 billion of funds to Mexico, used to service external debt, without any negative consequences for existing creditors. While this has been justified on the grounds that the official support staved off a crisis, the result was that public funds were used to pay off private debt, thus increasing moral hazard. In South Korea in 1997, the IMF gave the government $8 billion before obtaining any rollover commitments from foreign banks. This was justified on the grounds of the intensity of the crisis and the need to act swiftly, but again foreign creditors were bailed out without agreeing to rescheduling or write-offs. There is a real question whether bank creditors ever experienced negative consequences from their bad lending decisions given that the lengthening of loan maturities as part of a later rescheduling was accompanied by up to 275 basis point spreads over LIBOR and South Korean government guarantees. And again in Turkey, the IMF in December 2000 extended $3.8 billion to the government without any rescheduling or rollover commitments from private creditors. And the same proved true in Brazil in 2002.

Some have argued that creditor moral hazard is not a major problem. Some studies posit that if moral hazard were a problem, spreads on government bonds generally should decrease after the IMF provides support on the theory that such support shows that default on outstanding bonds is more unlikely. Some studies have shown such decreases but others have not.[78] Bond spread analysis is flawed, however. First, it lumps together the debt of all countries. The real question is whether demonstrations of bailouts decrease creditors' risks in any significant countries. Indeed, one study shows that the Russian default failed to reduce creditor moral hazard in those countries that have stronger political connections to the IMF.[79] Second, new bailouts may not serve to increase the estimated probability of future bailouts but rather to confirm previous estimated probability levels. In such case, spreads should not be significantly affected. Finally, a variety of other more important factors could be affecting bond spreads, such as changes in rates of interest and inflation. A different approach is taken in A. Haldane and J. Scheibe, "IMF Lending and Creditor Moral Hazard," Bank of England Working Paper 216 (2004). They examined the response of the market valuation of U.K. banks to IMF loan packages, and find a significant positive response. The returns are larger, the larger the IMF package and the larger the banks' emerging market portfolio.

Others have argued that in many countries creditors have paid a price. Debt was rescheduled in Asia, restructured on terms that reduced net present value in Ecuador, Pakistan and the Ukraine, and defaulted on in Russia and Argentina. However, the issue is not whether creditors have paid a price for making bad loans, but whether the price has been commensurate to the risk. The IMF and official support have sheltered creditors from paying the full price of the risks they have assumed. The result has been that they have been more willing to make loans than they would otherwise have been, and that debtor countries have incurred more debt or engaged in less prudent fiscal and monetary policies than they otherwise would have had they known no official support would be forthcoming. In short, there has been a huge deficit in market discipline.

Bailouts also increase debtor moral hazard—the prospect of a bailout makes countries more ready to borrow than they otherwise would be. It appears that debtor moral hazard due to bailouts depends on the importance of the country. The more significant, the more likely the bailout and the greater moral hazard.[80]

---

[78] S. Kamin, "Identifying the Role of Moral Hazard in International Financial Markets," 7 J. of International Finance 25 (2004) (no increase in spreads); but see O. Jeanne & J. Zettelmeyer, "International Bailouts, Moral Hazard, and Conditionality," CESife Working Paper 563 (2001), p. 3 (increase in spreads in Russia and Pakistan where the IMF did not intervene). A Dreher, "Does the IMF Cause Moral Hazard? A Critical Review of the Evidence," Draft (December 2004), reviews all the studies and concludes there is considerable evidence of moral hazard in bond markets.

[79] J. Lee and K. Shin, "IMF Bailouts and Moral Hazards," Draft (December 2004).

[80] P. Gai and A. Taylor, "International Financial Rescues and Debtor-Country Moral Hazard," 7 J. of International Finance 391 (2004).

d.   IMF CONDITIONALITY DOES NOT WORK

One possible justification for official assistance, particularly from the IMF, is that it provides the leverage to achieve reforms, both macro and micro, in debtor countries. As the argument goes, the IMF would not be able to achieve reform without providing funds, and debtor governments would not be politically able to implement reforms without the justification of the need for funds. Put another way, if the IMF did not lend, the government would be unable to implement reforms. There are two major weaknesses in this argument. First, there is little evidence that IMF conditions, usually requiring contractionary fiscal and monetary policies, have worked. After all, Latin America has experienced repeated debt crises in the last two decades despite numerous IMF conditionality programs. Furthermore, as Morris Goldstein has argued, IMF conditionality has been extended substantially beyond traditional macro policy to a variety of micro issues, like bankruptcy law reform and corporate governance, with little proof of success in reducing debt crises. These policies may be generally good for countries but are better pursued in the context of international standard setting rather than linked to financial support.

While conditionality may not work, there is a separate issue as to whether IMF lending in and of itself is beneficial to a country. One study finds that both macroeconomic aggregates and capital flows improve following the adoption of an IMF program. Programs are broadly defined to include programs that do not involve bailouts. IMF programs have the most impact on countries with bad internal conditions (ratio of: current account default to GDP between 3 and 6 percent; reserves to imports between 1.25 and 3 percent; short-term debt to reserves between 2 and 4 percent; external debt to GDP between .4 and .6 percent). The theory underlying these findings is that IMF intervention may signal a good housekeeping seal of approval, increase monitoring of economic policies, and spur catalytic lending— provisions of credit by the IMF may lead to rollover of private credit.[81]

e.   DEBTOR DISCRIMINATION AMONG PRIVATE CREDITORS

The problem of sovereign debtors discriminating among private creditors is a rather recent one, related mainly to the rise in bond debt. There were very few problems of this kind related to bank lending. Bank lending to sovereigns is invariably syndicated; many banks loan to the sovereign within the structure of one loan document. That document provides that default as against one lender is default as against all lenders (cross-default clause) and that a payment to one lender must be shared pro-rata with all lenders (pro-rata sharing clause). While these clauses effectively constrain discrimination

---

[81] M. Bordo, A Mody, and N. Oomes, "Keeping Capital Flowing: The Role of the IMF," NBER Working Paper 10834 (October 2004).

among members of a syndicate, there is still the potential problem of discrimination among different syndicated loan agreements.

This is partially addressed by cross-default clauses which permit lenders in Syndicate A, subject to certain voting procedures for their group, to accelerate their loans and declare default if the sovereign defaults on any other loan agreement, e.g. Syndicate B. The fear would be that the sovereign was going to make some payments to Syndicate B (even following default on B), or perhaps even to Syndicate C, without paying Syndicate A. The threat of cross-default would, in theory, prevent such discrimination from occurring. But using the acceleration and cross-default power might make the A creditors worse off, as the result might be that the sovereign would be unable to pay A anything. A might be better off being discriminated against and getting partial payments or making a deal to get at least more than B. In fact, such discrimination on bank loans is constrained not by legal clauses but by three institutional factors.

First, many large banks will be members in all of the syndicates, thus greatly decreasing their potential gains as beneficiaries of discrimination. The fact that they are repeat players decreases their incentives to extract the maximum advantage from one "game" of debt default. Second, sovereign defaults on bank loans have been handled through Bank Advisory Committees under the control of large banks who pressure small banks to go along with an equal treatment regime. Third, this pressure is "enforced" by central banks who threaten to impose sanctions, e.g. restricted discount window access or more supervisory scrutiny, if small banks do not go along.

The problem with bonds is that the institutional mechanisms to avoid discrimination are missing. The holders of these claims are more numerous than bank lenders, there are no major players to hold everyone together, and there is no enforcement counterpart for bondholders of central bank "suasion" over banks. So, there is a much greater potential for the sovereign discriminating among claimants under different bond issues, and more generally between bondholders and bank creditors.

f.   INCREASED DIFFICULTY IN RESTRUCTURING BOND DEBT–THE ISSUE OF HOLDOUT CREDITORS AND THE PROSPECT OF FOREIGN ASSET SEIZURES

A key problem in restructuring is the holdout creditor, often a vulture fund investor who seeks to profit by not going along with restructuring. After restructurings have been agreed, these creditors seek full collection of their debts in foreign courts. As we have seen, bond debt obligations are not normally protected in foreign courts by sovereign immunity as the issuance of such debt is regarded as a commercial activity, and commercial activities are outside the protection of sovereign immunity.[82] Sovereigns normally waive sovereign immunity (Russia is a notable exception) in international debt

---

[82] See *The Republic of Argentina v. Weltover* 504 US 607 (1992).

instruments, so their assets in the U.S., with some exceptions, e.g. those of the central bank, would be subject to attachment 28 U.S.C. 1610(a)(1).

Pursuit of court remedies by holdout creditors will only be effective in the most part if there are assets, outside of the jurisdiction of the debtor country, for creditors to obtain in satisfaction of court judgments.[83] The extent of such assets has been subject to much debate, given that most sovereign assets are within their borders and effectively immune from seizure. However, there may be significant assets available for attachment abroad. Cross-border foreign payments, whether on restructured bonds, other debt, or even for the importation or export of goods and services, may be fair game for attachment by creditors.[84] There may also be other significant assets abroad, like foreign bank and security custody accounts. Countries hold foreign bank accounts to make and receive payments and as a store of value. They also have foreign securities in custody abroad, often in connection with central bank reserve holdings. Argentina reportedly transferred a substantial portion of its deposits out of New York in anticipation of its default.

Finally, there is the issue as to whether assets of state-owned enterprises are subject to seizure. In principle, such assets might be thought to be generally immune from seizure in that they are owned by different entities than the sovereign. In corporate bankruptcies, assets of an affiliate are not generally available to creditors of a sister. Thus, if Holding Company (HC) fully owns shares of Companies A and B, and A fails, creditors of A cannot generally seize the assets of B. There is a limited exception to this rule under the doctrine of collapsible corporations which provides that if B is generally run as part of A, the assets of B might be collapsible into A in the event of A's bankruptcy. In effect, A's bankruptcy would trigger the consolidated bankruptcy of both A and B, with the consolidated assets of both companies subject to both companies' creditors.

On the other hand, if HC were to go bankrupt, HC's creditors could seize the assets of HC, including its equity in A and B, and then liquidate the assets of A and B in satisfaction of their own debts, after satisfying the creditors of A and B. The latter situation is more analogous to the sovereign debt situation. Default by a sovereign would expose its equity holdings in state-owned entities to seizure, and thus could result in the liquidation or reorganization of such entities, a prospect that sovereigns would regard with

---

[83] Of course, one should not automatically assume that local courts would protect local assets from seizure where a foreign judgment was being enforced. This would depend on whether the laws of the debtor's country shielded the sovereign from such enforcement actions and whether local courts would, in fact, respect such laws in the face of sovereign pressure.

[84] Export receipts or import payments in connection with trade by the sovereign could be attachable, and the sovereign could lose access to short-term trade financing. See W. Bratton and G. Mitu Gulati, "Sovereign Debt Restructuring and the Best Interests of Creditors," (2003) Georgetown Law and Economics Research Paper 387880, p. 16.

great trepidation.[85] However, if one obtained a judgment of this kind from a U.S. court, that court would not have jurisdiction, under the U.S. Foreign Sovereign Immunities Act, to garnish the sovereign's stock in the state-owned enterprise, if the stock were located outside the U.S.[86]

The chances of holdout creditors collecting on their debts is a real one. This explains why sovereigns, like Peru in the *Elliot* case, have generally paid off the holdouts. The problem going forward is that payoffs to holdouts make it less likely that creditors will agree to restructurings in the first place. Why should they accept a greater discount on restructured debt than do holdouts on the original debt?

Some have argued that the holdout problem can be minimized through the exit amendment process, where old bonds are poisoned by tendering creditors. In the Ecuador restructuring, creditors tendering old bonds agreed to amendments to the old bonds that were designed to make them unattractive. But vultures do not care that the bonds are unattractive—they acquire them to enforce their payment terms, which cannot be altered except by unanimity, when they contain New York style covenants. Further, it is quite unclear whether courts would sustain such exit amendments if it regarded them as an abuse of minority bondholders. The only way to make sure that holdouts are avoided is through legal compulsion. The need to avoid holdouts on private debt is a main reason for the creation of bankruptcy laws.

In *Greylock Global Opportunity Master Fund Ltd. V. Province of Mendoza*,[87] plaintiff creditor argued that an exit consent amendment in an exchange offer made by an Argentine province violated the unanimity requirement for changes in payment terms and the right to initiate suits. The amendment provided that the previous complete waiver of sovereign immunity would now be qualified so as not to apply to any payments made by the province to the new bondholders. The Court held that this was not a change in payment terms or the right to initiate suits. The bondholder could still sue, albeit one type of asset would not longer be available for attachment.[88]

Notes and Questions

1.   In light of Argentina, should we strengthen the rights of creditors to seize assets of defaulting sovereigns? If so, how could we best do that?

---

[85] See *First National Citibank v. Banco Para El Commercio Exterior De Cuba* 462 US 611 (1983).
[86] See *Fidelity Partners, Inc. v. Philippines Export and Foreign Loan Guarantee Corp.*, 921 F. Supp. 1113, 1118-19 (SDNY 1996).
[87] 2005 U.S. Dist. LEXIS 1742 (SDNY, February 8, 2005).
[88] In the Uruguay 2003 bond exchange, adopting new CACs, a similar exit amendment was used to change the sovereign immunity clause in the old tendered bonds. The purpose was to protect these payments from holdout creditors, L. Buchheit and J. Pam, "Uruguay's Innovations," Journal of International Banking Law Review 28 (2004).

2.   KEY AREAS OF REFORM

We turn now to seven specific areas of reform: (1) the role of the IMF; (2) the use of collective action clauses; (3) the use of bankruptcy-type procedures—the sovereign debt restructuring mechanism (SDRM); (4) cancellation of debt for the poorest countries; (5) the strengthening of creditor rights; (6) the adoption of general principles; and (7) facilitating prioritized debt and debt linked to indices.

a.   THE ROLE OF THE IMF

1.   THE MELTZER COMMISSION AND THE COUNCIL ON FOREIGN RELATIONS REPORT

(a)   THE MELTZER COMMISSION

In November 1998, the U.S. Congress established the International Financial Institutions Advisory Commission, dubbed the Meltzer Commission for its Chairman, Allan Meltzer. The Commission's mission was to consider the future roles of international financial institutions including most prominently the IMF. The Meltzer Commission recommended that the IMF be restructured as a smaller institution with three responsibilities: collect financial and economic data, provide advice without conditions relating to economic policy and "to act as a quasi-lender of last resort to solvent emerging economies by providing short-term liquidity assistance to countries in need under a mechanism designed to avoid the abuse of liquidity assistance to sponsor bail outs and under a system that would not retard the development of those institutions within the recipient country that would attract capital from commercial sources. ..."

The Meltzer Commission would end IMF long-term lending tied to policy conditions. The Commission further proposed that liquidity lending only be to countries meeting minimum prudential standards, that it not be tied to policy reforms, that it should be limited to illiquid not insolvent borrowers, and that it should not be used to salvage insolvent domestic financial institutions or to protect foreign lenders from losses. The Commission further proposed that the loans should be for a maximum of 120 days with one permissible rollover, should carry a penalty interest rate, and should require that the IMF be given priority in payment over all other lenders. At the same time, the Commission recommended that the IMF, the World Bank and the regional development banks write-off in their entirety all claims against heavily indebted poor countries.

The Meltzer Commission's recommendations were criticized by then U.S. Treasury Secretary Lawrence Summers for putting a straitjacket on the IMF's response to crisis. While he agreed with the emphasis of moving from long-term to short-term lending, he disagreed with the pre-qualification conditions imposed on short-term lending.[89] Stanley Fischer, the Deputy Managing Director of the IMF, disagreed with the short-term lending approach and has emphasized the role of the IMF in promoting economic reform. Others, including Joseph Stiglitz former chief economist and vice president of the World Bank, have rejoined that IMF macroeconomic policy of budget cutting and tighter monetary policies was often mistaken.[90] To this point Stiglitz said that the IMF staff frequently "consists of third-rank students from first-rate universities."[91]

(b)   THE COUNCIL ON FOREIGN RELATIONS REPORT (CFR)

The CFR Report takes a more moderate approach to IMF reform.[92] It proposed that international bonds be required to contain collective action clauses because this would facilitate rescheduling of bonds and reduce moral hazard. This proposal is discussed later in the Chapter. The CFR Report was critical of the size of IMF rescue packages.

The CFR proposed to address moral hazard by having the IMF make known that it will provide emergency financial assistance only when there is a good prospect of the recipient's country achieving "balance of payments viability" in the medium term. Further, in "extreme cases" in which the "existing debt profile is clearly unsustainable," the IMF would expect, as a condition for its support, that debtors engage in good faith discussion with their private creditors to achieve a more sustainable debt and debt-servicing profile, and that no category of debt would be presumed exempt from such discussions. In such cases, the IMF would recognize a temporary payments standstill, say for 30-60 days, during which time "the IMF would encourage debtors to seek an agreement that is non-discriminatory between foreign and domestic holders of debt and to provide creditor banks with timely and reliable information on interbank exposures to the country. Likewise, the Fund would encourage creditor banks to maintain interbank lines and to refrain from legal challenges during the period of the standstill."[93] This was a precursor of the sovereign bankruptcy procedures proposed by the IMF in 2001, discussed later in this Chapter.

On the other hand the CFR was willing to entertain larger rescue packages in the "rare situations" of widespread cross-border contagion of financial crises where failure to intervene would threaten the world's economy. This would be done by creating a new "contagion facility" that would replace the existing Supplemental Reserve Facility (SRF) and the Contingency Credit Line (CCL).

---

[89] 74 BNA Banking Report 592 (March 27, 2000).
[90] "What I Learned at the World Economic Crisis," The New Republic, April 17 & 24, 2000. (New Republic)
[91] Id., p. 7.
[92] Id., pp. 12-13, 15-16.
[93] New Republic, supra note 90, p. 64.

2.   THE CLINTON ADMINISTRATION REFORMS: SRF, CCL, AND LENDING
       INTO ARREARS

The SRF was introduced in 1997 to supplement the normal Fund
borrowing arrangements to provide financial assistance for exceptional
balance of payments difficulties "owing to a large short-term financing need
resulting from a sudden and disruptive loss of market confidence such as
occurred in the Mexican and Asian financial crises of 1995 and 1997."[94]

In April 1999, the IMF's Executive Board agreed to provide the CCL
only to member countries with strong economic policies as a precautionary
line of defense against future balance of payments problems that might arise
from international financial contagion. Countries apply in advance for pre-
qualification. The CCL provides commitments to short-term financing to
overcome balance of payments difficulties "that can arise from a sudden and
disruptive loss of market confidence due to contagion, that is, circumstances
that are largely beyond the member's control and stem primarily from
adverse developments in international capital markets consequent upon
developments in other countries."[95]

In September 2000, the IMF adopted changes to its CCL program
after noting that no country has used its program. The IMF lowered the
intensity of monitoring arrangements used to assure the strong economic
policies requirement, made the availability of resources in a crisis more
automatic, and changed the rate of charge. The initial surcharge was reduced
from 300 to 150 basis points, with rates rising over time to 350 basis points.[96]

Some contended that CCLs, which are a pre-crisis financing
commitment, are preferable to post-crisis "spot" financing because they
reduce moral hazard by putting limits—known in advance to both debtors
and creditors—on the amount of borrowing.[97] But this assumes CCLs and
post-crisis financing are mutually exclusive, which they need not to be, and
are not required to be by the IMF. In any event, as of late 2001, no country
had applied for pre-qualification. Doing so might be regarded as a signal that
a country expects its currency to be attacked.[98] In November 2003, the IMF
dropped the program entirely.

Before the Asian crisis, the IMF had a formal policy of not lending
into arrears—it would not lend money to a country that had defaulted and
was thus in arrears. Of course, what was actually a "default" was open to
interpretation. This made IMF assistance conditional on the absence of

---

[94] IMF, *How We Lend* (March 27, 2000). Repayments are to be made within 2½ years.

[95] IMF, *IMF Tightens Defences Against Financial Contagion by Establishing Contingent Credit Lines,* April 25, 1999.

[96] IMF, *IMF Board Agrees on Changes to Fund Financial Facilities,* September 18, 2000.

[97] S. Plant and A. Melnick, "International Institutional Lending Arrangements to Sovereign Borrowers," 22 Journal of International Money and Finance (2003), p. 459.

[98] M. Feldstein, "Economic and Financial Crises in Emerging Market Economies: Overview of Prevention and Management," NBER Working Paper 8837 (March 2002).

default. That policy was changed when the Board of the Fund decided that it would lend into arrears on a case-by-case basis.[99]

3.   OTHER PROPOSALS FOR RESTRAINTS ON IMF LENDING

The question remains as to how credible limits can be placed on IMF funding. The joint proposal of the Bank of Canada and the Bank of England offers one approach.[100] Using the U.S. FDICIA legislation as a model, the proposal would require extraordinary procedures to be adopted before the IMF lent funds. The idea is that the necessity to engage in such procedures would deter lending. Exceptional lending would only be provided upon a recommendation in a report of the IMF staff followed by a super-majority vote of the Executive Board.

In March 2003, The IMF Board reached agreement on specific criteria that must be met before the IMF engages in large-scale lending: "(1) balance of payments pressures on capital account, (2) high probability of debt sustainability, (3) good prospects of regaining access to private markets so that IMF financing provides a bridge, and (4) good economic policies in place. In addition the IMF Board adopted the requirement that, in cases of exceptional access, a new exceptional access report has to be prepared and published by the IMF management. The aim of the exceptional access report is to provide accountability in the same way that monetary policy reports or inflation reports provide some accountability at central banks."[101] These are very soft constraints, however. It is difficult to see how some of these criteria were satisfied in connection with the $3.1 billion rollover of IMF debt to Argentina. This was weakly justified by the idea that Argentina was already in "[e]xceptional access territory and the goal is to exit from these exceptional access territories over time."[102]

Another element of the limit approach is to make clear that the presumption is that the "IMF rather than the official creditor government is responsible for providing large scale loan financing. This provides an overall budget constraint and literally an overall limit on loan assistance, recognizing that IMF resources are limited."[103] One could argue that the presumption is wrong. Instead, it should be presumed that only creditor governments and not the IMF should extend credit—this might, as a political matter, lead to less not more lending.

---

[99] IMF, *A Guide to Progress in Strengthening the Architecture of the International Financial System,* April 28, 1999.
[100] A. Haldane and M. Kruger, "The Resolution of International Financial Crises: Private Finance and Public Funds," Bank of Canada Working Paper 2001-20 (November 2001).
[101] J. Taylor, Under Secretary of the Treasury, Remarks to the IMF Conference in honor of Guillermo Calvo, April 16, 2004.
[102] Id., p. 6.
[103] Id., p. 5.

Notes and Questions

1. What justifications are there for the IMF lending money to countries before there is a reduction in or at least a rescheduling of debt on concessionary terms? Is moral hazard a serious concern given that in most cases creditors or investors have lost money?

2. Can the lending activities of the IMF be rationalized as part of the need for an international lender of last resort? C. Goodhart and H. Huang argue that it is the fragility of the world's banking system and the limited ability of a domestic central bank to provide international liquidity that causes currency crisis, which further triggers a banking crisis.[104] While the international banking market can supply liquidity this comes at the cost of international financial contagion. The international lender of last resort (ILLR) could supply the liquidity without the risk of contagion. But the IMF does not have the unlimited resources, the hallmark of domestic central banks. Could the IMF role in lending to Korea during the Asian crisis or to Mexico in the 1994 Peso Crisis, or to Russia in 1998, be justified as fulfilling its role as lender of last resort? Are all crises liquidity crises?

Anna Schwartz has proposed abolishing the IMF entirely, *Time to Terminate the ESF and the IMF* (August 26, 1998). Schwartz observes that it is no longer serving its original purpose, to defend fixed-exchange rates, and has tried to become an ILLR. She argues that, it cannot serve this function because it cannot create high-powered money, bank reserves, and that its official resources are limited. In her view, the power to make loans to foreign governments should belong to Congress and not to an international organization. Further, she contends that the IMF is not lending to solvent borrowers, as is required for an ILLR as evidenced in the Korean crisis where it bailed out insolvent Korean banks.

3. Should we be concerned that the default of the IMF's three major creditors, Argentina, Brazil and Turkey, could bankrupt the IMF itself?

b.   THE MODIFICATION OF BOND CLAUSES

One important issue in the reform debate is whether bond clauses should be modified to facilitate rescheduling. As we have seen, an increasing part of cross-border debt is held in the form of bonds rather than loans and dealing with bondholders in the case of a financial crises is much more difficult than dealing with lenders. The primary focus of current international reform efforts to deal with sovereign debt problems is to encourage or perhaps even coerce emerging market countries to adopt collective action clauses (CACs) in their bonds, as set forth below.

---

[104] "A Simple Model of an International Lender of Last Resort," IMF Working Paper/00/75 (April 2000).

1.   HOW CACS WORK

The major focus of the call for CACs has been on clauses that permit a super-majority of creditors to change the financial and other terms of sovereign bonds in a restructuring. Sovereign bonds issued under U.S. law, approximately 69 percent of the $154 billion outstanding, require unanimity to change terms. This is in contrast to sovereign bonds issued under U.K. law, which permits majority action clauses in so-called British style covenants. These covenants typically allow a two-thirds majority of creditor to change any bond terms. In effect, British requirements are actually lower since the percentage usually applies to bondholders represented at a meeting rather than all bonds outstanding.

Bonds issued under U.S. law do appear to permit a majority of creditors to change non-payment terms, like the waiver of sovereign immunity or listing permissions, through Ecuador Type exit amendments. But they prohibit majority action on payment terms. Restrictions on changing bond terms spring from a concern that a majority of creditors can abuse a minority. This fear was reflected in the enactment in 1939 of the Trust Indenture Act (TIA) restricting the use of majority action clauses in corporate issues.

Although the TIA applies only to corporate and not sovereign bonds, contracting practice for sovereign bonds has followed the statutory requirements for corporate bonds. While one might attribute this to path dependence, there are two competing explanations. First, creditors may generally prefer such restrictions. Indeed foreign investors have expressed concerns that domestic investors holding sovereign bonds, which in some cases might constitute a significant percentage and even a majority, might be pressured by their sovereigns to abuse the foreign creditors. This can be made harder by restricting majority action. Second, there is a possibility that U.S. courts would use common law doctrines like abuse of fiduciary duty to nullify majority actions that were seen as abusive to a minority. It is not clear that U.S. courts will even sustain exit amendments changing the non-financial terms of bonds. If these considerations are important, then CACs could only be used with confidence if federal or New York statutory law (U.S. bonds are invariably issued under New York law) legitimated CACs. Current CAC proposals do not contemplate such enactment. While this problem could be circumvented by issuing bonds under U.K. law, U.S. creditors may generally feel more comfortable in having their disputes governed by New York law and New York courts.

While the G7 and creditor groups both favored use of CACs, the G7, including the U.S., has favored a lower majority percentage, 75 percent, than private creditor groups which have favored a 90 percent requirement.[105] This difference reflects different objectives and concerns. Private creditors are concerned that too low a percentage would give sovereigns more leverage, through their control of domestic creditors as discussed above. Further, too low a percentage would make it generally easier for the sovereign to make a deal. Requiring a higher percentage can give creditors more leverage to get better terms. Here is an example of a creditor negotiation line: 75 percent of us are willing to agree to a 35 percent discount but you are never going to get the other 25 percent to agree to this—they would rather wait for an IMF bailout or take you to court. We can only get a deal with less of a discount, say 25 percent.[106]

The other important CAC currently used in sovereign bonds deals with acceleration. Most sovereign bonds, whether issued under U.S. or U.K. law permit and require a vote of 25 percent of creditors to accelerate payments, i.e. full payment of interest and principal. This is important because acceleration of claims increases the potential cost of default for debtors. Absent a vote of 25 percent of creditors, a creditor seeking to recover on a default could only ask for payment of past due interest payments. The 25 percent requirement would seem to impose some break on vulture creditors, but, in practice, some bond syndicates are quite small, e.g. less than $100 million, and when bonds trade down to 20 cents on the Dollar, it does not take much money to obtain a 25 percent position. Also, vultures prefer to exercise their rights after the more passive creditors have been taken out in an exchange offer, leaving it relatively easy for the remaining bond holders to get a 25 percent position. One might think that such an obstacle could be strengthened by creating an even higher percentage requirement. But this would probably not be in the interest of many creditors who would fear too high a percentage would decrease their leverage in negotiations. Another example of a creditor negotiation line: your offer of a 35 percent discount is unacceptable to at least 25 percent of the creditors. Unless you improve the offer, they will accelerate and sue.

The important point about collective action clauses is that there is a tension for creditors in considering appropriate percentages. Debtors would always want a relatively low majority action percentage and a high

---

[105] The Group of Ten Working Group on Contractual Clauses, September 26, 2002. The Working Group consulted widely with lawyers representing both debtors and creditors and then prepared model clauses. They proposed a 75 percent requirement for changing payment terms. This group also proposed requiring a 25 percent majority vote before the initiation of litigation, the prohibition entirely on individual actions, and a pro-rata sharing clause, all to restrict holdout creditor litigation.

[106] J. Fisch and C. Gentile, "Vultures or Vanguards? The Role of Litigation in Sovereign Debt Restructuring," 53 Emory L. J. 1043 (2004) argue that holdout creditors serve as a check on opportunistic defaults and unreasonable restructuring terms.

acceleration percentage, both to limit holdouts and preserve their negotiation leverage. Creditors would share the debtors' percentage preferences with respect to holdouts but would want a relatively high majority action percentage and low acceleration percentage to maximize their leverage. To the extent the G7 is advocating CACs to make debt restructuring easier, it may have a more debtor-oriented view of the appropriate percentages. Indeed the very fact that the G7 seeks to change current practice suggests a leaning toward the debtor side.

There are two other kinds of CACs, not presently in sovereign bonds, that have been suggested by John Taylor, the Under Secretary of the U.S. Treasury. The first is a clause that would subject the initiation of litigation to a majority vote or delegate it to a representative. This clause would pose a more substantial obstacle to holdout creditors than the 25 percent acceleration requirement. It could also be used to impose a standstill at the outset of negotiations. The second is a sharing clause that would require creditors recovering assets in satisfaction of claims to share the proceeds pro-rata with other creditors. Such clauses are common in syndicated loans but not bonds. Again, it is far from clear that creditors would want such clauses since they have an interest in maximizing leverage through threats of litigation. An initiation clause would make the commencement of litigation more difficult and a sharing clause would make litigation less profitable. Moreover, there would be the problem of foreign creditors sharing with domestic ones.

2.   ARE CACS THE SOLUTION?

We turn to the question as to whether majority action clauses on payment restructuring (the main clauses at issue) offer a plausible solution to the sovereign debt problem. This is highly doubtful.

First, creditors and debtors may not want them. As already discussed, creditors may only want them with very high percentage requirements, making them less useful in facilitating debt restructuring. Further, although debtor countries might prefer the clauses in the abstract, they recognize that the increased leverage they would obtain would come at a price of a higher cost of credit. While empirical studies, looking at the comparative costs of bonds issued under U.S. and British style covenants, are inconclusive, there seems to be more of a consensus that there would be substantial first mover costs. Countries adopting CACs for the first time might rightfully be concerned that they were signaling an increased probability of default with a consequence of higher debt costs.

Mexico did adopt a 75 percent CAC (of all bonds outstanding) in a $1 billion bond offering in February 2003, albeit at what some believe was a cost of 25 basis points, and announced its intention to use such clauses in the future. On the other hand, the yield on the new bonds, due in 2015, was consistent with the yield on other previously issued bonds with similar maturities that did not contain CACs.[107] Some saw this as a favor to the U.S. Treasury that applauded Mexico's action.

Brazil followed by issuing $1 billion of bonds with CACs in April 2003, using an 85 percent requirement. Many other countries in 2003 adopted CACs under New York law, but there were substantial dissenters, e.g. China, Chile, the Philippines, and Peru (Peru did some with and some without).[108] If indeed, there was no cost of issuing bonds with CACs, this may be because they would have no effect—the market might believe they would never be used. If such clauses were to affect future restructurings, they should have some price effect. If restructurings were to be more expensive for creditors, they should increase in price; if less expensive, they should decrease.

One reason the bonds may have been more attractive to creditors is that they also weakened the possibility of using exit consents by expanding the list of "reserved matters"—those subject to the CAC procedures. Reserved matters include governing law, description of events of default, *pari passu* ranking, and submission to jurisdiction of New York courts.[109] Second, there would be a substantial transition issue since 69 percent of bonds outstanding (as of 2002) do not presently have such clauses and have an average maturity of five years. It is estimated it would take 10 years to replace these non-CAC bonds. This process could be accelerated with bond swaps, but this could impose significant "sweetener" costs to create an incentive to exchange and would risk opposition from holdout creditors due to the inability to use exit amendments to alter payment terms.

Third, there is the issue, already discussed, as to whether courts applying U.S. law, particularly U.S. courts, would uphold majority action where there was a case that a minority, with different interests, was being abused. This could only be guarded against by new statutory enactments that would be difficult to obtain. But there are two more major problems.

As Anne Kreuger, the First Deputy Managing Director of the IMF, has repeatedly observed, the CAC solution will not work across different credit instruments. Even if the same CAC were inserted in all sovereign bonds, other major debt that would be simultaneously subject to restructuring negotiations, like syndicated bank debt or trade credit, would not have such clauses. In addition, a major issue in the Asian crisis, as well as elsewhere, was the government guarantee of private interbank debt to foreign banks. Such guaranteed debt would also have to be restructured and would not have collection action clauses. Indeed, it is a heroic assumption to

[107] See M. Gugiatti and A. Richards, "Do Collective Action Clauses Influence Bond Yield? New Evidence From Emerging Markets," Reserve Bank of Australia Research Discussion Paper 2003–02 (March 2003).
[108] E. Koch, "Collective Action Clauses—The Way Forward," Draft (February 24, 2004), Table 3.
[109] S. Galvis and A. Saad, "Collective Action Clauses: Recent Proposals and Challenges Ahead," Working Draft (February 20, 2004).

think that all bonds would have the same CACs, some might have a 75 percent requirement, others 90 percent.

This raises a very fundamental point. The very existence of corporate bankruptcy laws responds to the collective action problem of providing for such a process through private contract. It simply cannot be done because different creditors, not in privity, interact with debtors over time and provide different terms in their contractual documentation for the resolution of disputes. A common set of procedures can only be provided by statutory or common (judge-made) law; contract will not work. Although legal scholars like Alan Schwartz have argued that the state should permit parties to contract for the corporate bankruptcy system they prefer, such contracting takes place against a default system of law. The same goes for private ordering through workouts—it is shaped by the shadow of law. Such a shadow is entirely missing in the Taylor CAC proposal and thus will not work.

Studies of bond defaults in the 1930s reveal that a structure for representing bondholders did exist, i.e. the U.K. Corporation of Foreign Bondholders (CFBH) and the U.S. Foreign Bondholders Protective Council (FBPC).[110] But it is unclear whether these committees were dealing with bonds with different CACs. Indeed, it appears that there were co-ordination problems between CFBH and FBPC, in part, because of the different terms of interest rates and collateral between the two kinds of bonds. There were also co-ordination problems between bondholders and commercial lenders. Attempts to recreate this historical framework today in the form of a so-called "New York Club" might be useful,[111] but the claim that this would make a substantial contribution to coping with the aggregation problem in unfounded.

In May 2003, Uruguay announced completion of the swap of $5.1 billion of old bonds for new ones with longer maturities. The interest rate on the new bonds is lower than current market yields and the maturity is stretched out. The new bonds have CACs that contain two interesting features.[112]

First, 75 percent of bondholders, measured by principal amount, must approve any change in payment terms. However, bonds "owned or controlled directly or indirectly" by the government of Uruguay or any public sector entity are excluded from the calculation of the required percentage. This substantially increases the effective majority required above the nominal 75 percent; it could easily push it to 90 percent. This is a very *weak* form of majority action compared to U.K. covenants of 75 percent, with no creditor

---

[110] B. Eichengreen and R. Portes, "After the Deluge: Default, Negotiation, and Readjustment during the Interwar Years," in *The International Debt Crisis in Historical Perspective* (B. Eichengreen and P. Lindert, eds., 1989), pp. 12-47.

[111] R. Portes, "Resolution of Sovereign Debt Crises," OECD Financial Paper (May 2003).

[112] Argentina issued bonds with similar CACs as part of its March 2005 exchange offer.

exclusions. "Control" is defined as "the power, directly or indirectly, through the ownership of voting securities or other ownership interests or otherwise, to direct the management of or elect or appoint a majority of the board of directions or other persons" exercising similar functions.[113]

Second, Uruguay has provided a method for facilitating majority action across different bonds. The new bonds provide that the payment terms of multiple bonds in a "series" (ones issued under the indenture) can be changed with a vote of 85 percent of the aggregate principal amount of outstanding bonds (again subject to the exclusions of state controlled entities discussed above), and 66.6 percent of each issue. If an issue falls short of 66.6 percent, it is not included in the aggregate deal. It is unclear, however, what would happen if a subsequent issue contained a provision rejecting the attempt at "series control" of the earlier issue. But it does seem clear that "series control" can simply be avoided by starting a new series. A recent paper by Eichengreen, Kletzer, and Mody[114] concludes that the market is more concerned about aggregation with respect to poor credits, and that because investors may not anticipate the relapse of good credits into repayment difficulties, aggregation across issues may also become a problem for other issues. The paper also points out that the severity of the aggregation problem across bonds depends on the number of different bonds outstanding—pointing out that the Ukraine had five and Ecuador had six different issues of bonds outstanding at the time of their respective defaults, while Argentina had 80.[115] Further, the attempt at aggregation across bonds cannot deal with the need for aggregation across different types of debt.

Following the Uruguay issue, Brazil issued $7 billion in bonds with 85 percent CACs, with no aggregation across bonds, again without apparently any impact on yield curves. Brazil apparently used a higher percentage to assure market acceptance.[116]

Finally, CACs will do very little to facilitate restructurings as long as IMF or official lending is available. Creditors and debtors will wait for a bailout rather than restructuring. Both benefit by subsidized credit, at least in the short term.

Notes and Questions

1. How effective can CACs be in solving the sovereign debt problem?

---

[113] Other new bonds with CACs, like those of Mexico and Brazil, provide similar exclusions.

[114] "Crisis Resolution: Next Steps," Federal Reserve Bank of San Francisco Pacific Basin Working Paper (June 2003).

[115] Id., p. 19.

[116] F. Salomon, "Brazil Goes off on a CAC Tangent," Euromoney (June 2003).

c.   AN INTERNATIONAL BANKRUPTCY SYSTEM FOR SOVEREIGNS

There has been much debate about the idea of adopting some form of an international bankruptcy system. A main feature of such a system is the automatic stay, which prevents creditors from bringing actions to collect their debts, or to foreclose on assets. Those favoring bailouts have justified them on the basis of the difficulty in preventing creditors from engaging in a race to grab the debtor country's assets.[117] This has led those opposing bailouts to favor the bankruptcy process on the theory the protection of debtor assets will make bailouts less necessary. However, it is far from clear that seizure of assets is a significant problem, as we discussed.

Most advocates of an international bankruptcy process believe that it would help reduce bailouts and therefore moral hazard. For example, Jeffrey Sachs has argued that a system facilitating debtor defaults through an orderly bankruptcy process would be an alternative to the current IMF lending process, that is if debtors could have orderly defaults IMF lending would not be necessary.[118]

The debate over the need for sovereign bankruptcy procedures greatly accelerated in late November 2001 after a speech by Anne Krueger, the new First Deputy Managing Director of the International Monetary Fund (the number two position).[119] This was later refined some four months later.[120] The major change in the interim was to lessen the role of the IMF in the process and to increase the control of creditors.

Until Paul O'Neill was replaced by John Snow as U.S. Treasury Secretary in early 2003, the U.S. had taken the position, along with the G7, of advocating adoption of CACs in the short-term while encouraging further work on SDRM as a longer-term solution. In April 2003, however, the U.S. Treasury announced its opposition to SDRM, after intense lobbying by creditors. The IMF subsequently stated on April 11, 2003, that it would cease pursuing SDRM but that it would continue to explore solutions to various problems, some of which gave rise to SDRM proposal: co-ordination between official bilateral and private creditors, how to solve the problem of co-ordinating creditor action across multiple debt instruments, and enhancing transparency and disclosure.[121] Despite the formal hiatus in SDRM development, informal design efforts continue. This is desirable given the

---

[117] Stanley Fischer, "Mechanism Must be Found to Avoid Moral Hazard in Crises," IMF Deputy Says" (October 20, 1997) 69 Banking Report, p. 623.

[118] "Do We Need an International Lender of Last Resort," Frank D. Graham Lecture, Princeton University (April 20, 1995).

[119] "International Financial Architecture for 2002: A New Approach to Sovereign Debt Restructuring," November 26, 2001.

[120] "New Approaches to Sovereign Debt Restructuring: An Update on our Thinking," April 1, 2002.

[121] IMF, *Report of the Managing Director to the International Monetary and Financial Committee on the IMF's Policy Agenda,* April 11, 2003.

serious questions about the efficacy of the CACs being incorporated in some new bond issues.

1.   AN ANALYSIS OF THE IMF'S SOVEREIGN DEBT RESTRUCTURING MECHANISM (SDRM)

The IMF proposal envisions that at the debtor's request a super-majority of creditors could impose a standstill on payments and a stay on creditor litigation for a fixed duration of time that was potentially renewable. A number of Executive Directors of the IMF believed that such stay/standstill should be automatic upon the sovereign triggering SDRM. And at one time the IMF contemplated that it could itself impose the standstill and stay, upon a finding that such an SDRM was justified, while creditors themselves met to decide this issue for themselves.

The proposal also contemplates that a super-majority of creditors supplying new financing during the SDRM could subordinate existing claims, modeled on debtor-in-possession (DIP) financing in corporate bankruptcy.

Certain creditors would not be subject to the SDRM. Multilaterals like the IMF and the World Bank would not be included. Whether Paris Club creditors would be included is unclear. In the last version of the proposal, domestic debt would have been excluded. Excluded creditors would continue to be paid outside SDRM although their debt could be restructured in parallel proceedings.

A restructuring plan, like under CACs, could be approved by a super-majority of creditors in each class. The final IMF plan contemplated a 75 percent requirement (by value), the percentage required under U.K. CACs rather than the 66.6 percent requirement required under U.S. chapter 11, and did not require approval by a majority of creditors as does chapter 11. The approval of the plan, however, would have to be informed by the IMF's view as to whether the remaining debt level was sustainable. Future IMF funding would be conditional on such a finding. The SDRM could be terminated, without a plan, upon the vote of 40 percent of the outstanding principal of verified claims, after the completion of a process in which claims were registered and verified.

An independent tribunal, perhaps a quasi-judicial organ, would adjudicate issues like lack of equitable treatment or valuation of claims.

Neither IMF lending nor lending by other multilaterals or countries was restricted under SDRM. Indeed, Kreuger stated: "Under an SDRM, the nature of the financing decisions that the IMF would need to make before, during and after a debt restructuring would not change."

The SDRM would be adopted by an amendment to the IMF Articles of Agreement which requires 3/5ths of the votes of members having 85 percent of the votes. This means that the U.S., which has over 15 percent of the votes, would have to agree.

2.   THE CHAPTER 11 MODEL

The U.S. bankruptcy model has provided the intellectual origins of the SDRM, but there is a significant issue as to whether even a modified chapter 11 model is appropriate for sovereign debt.

The whole SDRM process is fundamentally different from chapter 11. Chapter 11 converts debt to equity. Typically prior equity is ousted and the value of the firm as a going concern is distributed in the form of new equity claims to creditors in accord with their priority–the absolute priority rule–and their debt claims are reduced. Creditors must receive at least as much in a chapter 11 reorganization as they would in a chapter 7 liquidation. A single creditor can torpedo a plan by showing that he is worse off in chapter 11 than in chapter 7.

In sovereign restructurings, there is no conversion of debt to equity, for obvious reasons. The exercise is different. Debt is restructured only by changing its amount or terms. Further, there is no chapter 7 liquidation value for judging whether creditors are fairly compensated. These fundamental differences make chapter 11 an inappropriate model. Whereas the U.S. has a chapter 9 for municipal bankruptcies, where similar problems exist, chapter 9 has been rarely used and most commentators think it does not really work.

The lack of benchmarking for a proposed SDRM plan is perhaps the approach's biggest weakness.[122] One possible solution would be to develop an agreed methodology for determining how much a sovereign could pay. The new literature on "debt intolerance" may be useful in this regard. It attempts to understand how much debt sovereigns can tolerate before defaulting, e.g. perhaps by developing a more refined ratio than GNP/external debt. This may be useful in judging whether a proposed plan is fair going forward, after default. "Debt intolerance" seems to be rather country specific, depending not only on debt ratios but also the history of prior defaults.[123]

It is interesting to compare the two procedures in terms of their protections for creditors. Absent the liquidation alternative, creditors in SDRM have much less leverage than they do under chapter 11. They cannot threaten to liquidate an uncooperative debtor. Further, under SDRM they would have little confidence that the debtor would manage itself in the future to fulfill its new restructured obligations. Under chapter 11, creditors control the selection and continued operations of new management. Finally, in chapter 11, there is no discrimination against or in favor of certain creditors. All creditors are subject to a common set of procedures and a court makes sure there is equitable treatment for all. Under the proposed SDRM,

---

[122] H. Scott, "How Would a New Bankruptcy Regime Help," Brookings Paper on Economic Activity, Vol I (2002); pp. 334-340.

[123] C. Reinhart, K. Rogoff, and M. Savastano, "Debt Intolerance," NBER Working Paper 9908 (August 2003).

multilateral creditors are entirely excluded, and Paris Club creditors may be excluded. And domestic creditors be excluded as well. These exclusions make the solution less comprehensive and create serious issues of fairness.

In some respects, however, creditors are given more rights under SDRM than they would have under chapter 11. The sovereign debtor must obtain approval from the creditors to invoke the SDRM. Under chapter 11, the debtor merely files. The choice of the debtor to invoke the protections of bankruptcy is not subject to creditor approval, nor does it even depend on a showing of insolvency. It is true that under the chapter 9 procedure for municipal insolvencies, and under some non-U.S. bankruptcy regimes, filing is subject to a showing of insolvency, but it is never subject to creditor approval as under the proposed SDRM.

In addition, the SDRM proposal does not contemplate a cramdown procedure. SDRM rather simply provides that a super-majority of creditors can approve a restructuring plan. Under chapter 11, junior classes of creditors or equity holders can be forced by the court to accept a plan, if senior classes are fully compensated and one impaired class approves the plan, again assuming no creditor gets less than in liquidation. Perhaps, SDRM is silent on a cramdown because it contemplates that there will only be one class of unsecured creditors and that there is thus no need for a cramdown. If so, then it is significant that SDRM leaves the acceptability of the plan entirely to a vote of creditors. Under chapter 9, where it is likely that all creditors are unsecured, a court can disallow a plan, even if voted for by the creditors, if it is not in the "best interests of the creditors."

In fact, there could well be senior sovereign creditors, given that Brady bondholders are secured by U.S. zero coupon bonds and that some forms of trade debt involve security. Furthermore, multilateral debt is currently treated as senior to all other debt even though it is not secured. If it were to be included in SDRM with its current priority, it would constitute another class of senior debt. SDRM does not contemplate that senior classes could bind more junior ones to a plan through a cramdown. While this may be better for the junior creditors, it may be worse for the more senior ones. The latest version of SDRM excluded all claims that "benefit from a statutory, judicial or contractual privilege, to the extent of the value of the privilege. ..." While this would seem to exclude secured debt from SDRM, it might have been better to just recognize its priority. This would allow it to be enforced as part of the SDRM rather than compelling separate and costly foreclosure procedures.

3.   THE LACK OF A SDRM CONSTITUENCY

The adoption of SDRM was problematic from the outset because of political opposition. Emerging market sovereigns and their private creditors generally opposed SDRM because they believed it would raise the price of credit due to the increased ease of restructuring and the corresponding decrease in bailouts. This would increase the debt service cost for sovereigns and lead to lower levels of borrowing. While this may be good for sovereigns in the longer term, they would prefer not to take the medicine and continue to enjoy subsidized borrowing rates due to bailout expectations. Creditors are on the same page. They do not like a reform that will lead to less demand for their funds and higher risks for funds they do provide. While they will presumably be compensated for this risk through higher rates, there is some level of risk that they may find unacceptable at any price. And they may take an unanticipated hit on outstanding debt.

The main beneficiaries of the SDRM proposal are the taxpayers of the debtor and creditor countries. But it is unclear that their interests will ever prevail. Debtor governments may only focus on their short-term debt servicing costs rather than the burden on their taxpayers. Creditor governments may be unwilling to limit bailouts due to political objectives, e.g. the case of Turkey, or for fear of financial contagion, the case of the Asian crisis, whatever the cost to their taxpayers.

4.   SDRM DESIGN PROBLEMS

SDRM also has substantial design problems. SDRM significantly increases the power of the IMF. Under the proposal, the IMF continues its lending, plus is heavily involved in the SDRM mechanism. It may approve the initial invocation of the procedure, makes a judgment of debt sustainability as part of the approval of the plan, and may be the tribunal for adjudicating disputes. Giving the IMF a major role in SDRM is problematic. As a major "priority" lender, it has an obvious interest in seeing that its own debt is repaid which may color its decisions on many issues. For example, it may prefer to reduce the level of private debt service to insure its own debt can be repaid.

Also, the IMF is an organization which often does the bidding of the governments of the major creditors. This may dispose it to pursue solutions that have a political payoff but may be financially unattractive to debtors and/or creditors. In short, the IMF is not impartial. Allowing the IMF to operate the SDRM mechanism would be like putting a class of secured creditors, rather than a court, in charge of a corporate reorganization.

It is rather clear, however, that some central authority would be necessary, even if it is not the IMF. Indeed, one study has argued that the IMF plays a crucial role in current debt restructurings by serving, in effect, as a referee, to avoid unjustified preferences among creditors and to arbitrate a fair settlement.[124]

Another concern arises from doubt whether SDRM can be fair or effective. The issue of fairness arises from the exclusion of significant

---

[124] P. Gai and N. Vause, "Sovereign Debt Workouts with the IMF as Delegated Monitor—A Common Agency Approach," Bank of England Working Paper 187 (2003).

creditors. The issue of effectiveness relates to the lack of a cramdown power and questions about whether the procedure will ever be used, given the possibility of IMF or official creditor bailouts. This is the same problem that plagues the effective use of CACs. Even if one were to assume that no bailout would be forthcoming, there is the issue of what benefit the SDRM would provide to a sovereign that it could not achieve acting on its own outside of SDRM, as did Russia in the 1998 crisis. The SDRM's major benefit is the stay on asset seizures and the binding of holdout creditors once a plan has been approved. A sovereign might believe that the threat of asset seizures and holdout creditor suits was low, and prefer to fashion its own set of procedures to scale down its debt.

Finally, there is the problem that the very existence of SDRM could cause faster withdrawals of credit once there was a whiff of bankruptcy in the air. This is a real concern and could only be met by the fashioning of voidable preference rules that would permit recovering funds withdrawn from some period prior to the commencement of SDRM.

While SDRM has been put aside for the time being, my view is that CACs are not a real solution and work on SDRM should proceed. Some believe that SDRM should become more "heavy" than "lite" because the real problem is forcing a solution between creditors and the debtor not co-ordination among creditors.[125]

Notes and Questions

1. Would you favor some form of an SDRM? If so, what features would it contain?

d.   HIPC

The IMF and the World Bank have put forward a special initiative for heavily indebted poor countries (HIPC). These are countries that have an unsustainable debt burden. Countries who have adopted a Poverty Reduction Strategy Paper and have made progress in implementing the strategy can qualify. These are economic policies that the IMF approves. Qualifying countries will receive sufficient funds to reduce their debt to sustainable levels once satisfactory assurances have been received by other creditors. Bilateral and commercial creditors are generally expected to reschedule obligations coming due, with a 90 percent reduction in net present value. The total cost of the initiative for multilaterals and other official creditors, for

---

[125] A. Haldane, A. Penalver, V. Saporta, and H. Shin, "Analytics of Sovereign Debt Restructuring," Bank of England Working Paper 202 (September 2003). The conclusion that CACs can solve inter-creditor coordination problems does not reflect a look at the aggregation problem across different bonds or forms of credit. Indeed the authors state that differences among creditors lower the chances of an agreement, p. 22.

providing assistance to 37 countries, is estimated at about $55 billion in net present value terms.[126]

It is far from clear whether countries that obtain HIPC debt relief will avoid incurring unsustainable levels of debt in the future without concessionary grants and loans. This is due to their inability to make necessary fiscal adjustments without severe social welfare costs.[127] If a country's government is totally corrupt, reduction of debt burden merely allows those in power to issue more debt for bad purposes. If one is dealing with a reasonable government, with additional needs for social funding, additional lending by the public sector, not debt reduction may make sense. Reducing debt will not help fund new projects. If a country needs funds for commercially viable projects, some debt reduction may make sense—but leaving enough public debt so private lenders lend responsibly. All in all, there is no one size fits all solution for HIPCs.[128]

To date, the HIPC Initiative has resulted in commitments of $32 billion (net present value terms) in debt reduction for 27 countries, 23 of them in Africa, representing about two-thirds of these countries' outstanding stock of external debt. It is estimated that the total debt stock of HIPC countries remains at about $90 billion.[129]

The U.K. has been pressing for the cancellation of all official HIPC debt. This would occur through the Word Bank and IMF writing off their debts. The issue is how such write-offs would be financed. The IMF could use part of its gold reserve to fund its $9 billion in loans. The World Bank presents a trickier matter. If the World Bank merely wrote off its loans, it might endanger its credit rating, and thus raise its cost of bonds—the World Bank funds its activities through the issuance of bonds. The U.K. has proposed that rich nations cover the World Bank's losses, but the U.S. has favored a write-off without reimbursements.[130]

The G7 Finance Ministers indicated a willingness in February 2005 to provide 100 percent relief, which was reiterated in a meeting between President Bush and Prime Minister Blair in early June 2005. This agreement between the two leaders was followed by an announcement on June 11, 2005, at the G8 meeting of Finance Ministers, that the multilateral debt of 18 countries, mostly from sub-Saharan Africa, amounting to $40 billion, would be cancelled immediately. The eligibility of 20 other countries was subject to meeting good governance and anti-corruption requirements.[131]

---

[126] IMF, *Debt Relief under the Heavily Indebted Poor Countries Initiative, A Factsheet,* September 2004.

[127] S. Edwards, "Debt Relief and Fiscal Sustainability," NBER Working Paper 8939 (May 2002).

[128] R. Rajan, "Debt Relief and Growth," 42 Finance and Development (June 2005).

[129] C. Swann, "G8 Fails to Cancel Debt of Poorest Countries," *Financial Times,* June 11, 2004.

[130] M. Phillips, "Poorest Nations May Get Debt Relief," *The Wall Street Journal*, February 2, 2005.

[131] Associated Press, June 12, 2005.

e.   STRENGTHENING CREDITOR RIGHTS

The sustained default of Argentina has focused new attention on the rights of creditors, particularly where debtors act in what is perceived to be an unreasonable fashion.

As this Chapter has already detailed, all creditors generally have the right to recover their debts from defaulting sovereigns. The problem is how to attach assets of the sovereign when the sovereign refuses to pay. This is also an issue with respect to private debtors–getting a judgment for the debt is only the first step. One must then enforce the judgment by actually collecting the money. In the case of private debtors, creditors are generally free to attach any assets of the debtor, and if necessary can always put the debtor into bankruptcy. In the case of sovereign debtors, bankruptcy is an unavailable remedy (even under SDRM only the debtor can invoke the procedure). Furthermore, the existence of sovereign assets outside the debtor's country is limited and Sovereign Immunity Acts of creditor countries provide that sovereign assets of various kinds are immune from creditor process.

At the outset, there is a policy question of whether it is in the interest of creditor countries to strengthen creditor rights. While creditor countries should have an interest in providing rights to their own creditors, there are some countervailing concerns.

First, creditor countries may be concerned that an increase in the rights of creditors may undermine the debt rescheduling process. The fact that some creditors can sue and recover may make all creditors less willing to negotiate a deal. Thus, in the case of Argentina there was a concern that allowing creditors successfully to enforce their rights before a deal will make a deal less likely. Creditors will resort to the courts instead of negotiating– which may leave creditors as a whole worse off. Not all creditors, particularly those with fewer resources, may have effective access to the courts. In addition, there is a concern that allowing creditors to successfully enforce their rights after a deal has been made (the holdout creditors) may equally undermine the willingness of both sides to enter into a deal in the first place. On the other hand, limiting creditor rights may expose creditors to unfair deals, as seems to be the case with Argentina. It may be the pressure and threat of successful lawsuits that may bring a debtor country to the table in a reasonable matter.

Second, creditor countries are concerned that access of creditors to certain assets, such as diplomatic property or central bank reserves, could interfere in the ability of the sovereign country to conduct its normal business abroad or, in the case of central bank reserves, to manage its monetary or exchange rate policy. Under the Foreign Sovereign Immunities Act in the U.S., property of a foreign central bank "held for its own account" is immune from attachment.[132] It is likely that central bank reserves may be the most significant external assets held abroad by many emerging market countries. It remains to be determined how important such reserves are to countries, particularly those that have or should be abandoning fixed exchange rate systems. Furthermore, there is the distinct possibility that central bank reserves can be used to shelter assets of the government or private influential parties. This might be prevented. In *Birch Shipping Co. v. United Republic of Tanzania*, the court held that Tanzania could not shelter commercial assets from execution by commingling them in an immune embassy account.[133] And in *Weston Compagnie de Finance et D'Investissement, S.A. v. La Republica del Ecuador*, the court indicated that funds in a central bank account used to finance commercial transactions of private parties would not be immune since these were not funds "held for its account."

The possibility that central bank accounts in the United States might be attachable in some cases, has led sovereigns to hold these accounts elsewhere, or to remove fund from U.S. accounts once litigation is brought. The preferred place to hold such funds is at the Bank for International Settlements (BIS). Article 10 of the Constituent Charter of the BIS provides: "The Bank, its property and assets and all deposits entrusted to it shall be immune in time of peace and in time of war from any measure such as expropriation, requisition, seizure, confiscation, prohibition or restrictions of gold or currency export or import, and any other similar measures."[134] So the major countries of the world through these agreements have given all countries' central banks a complete safe haven for all of their liquid assets, whatever the purpose for which they are held. Creditor rights could be enhanced by eliminating or narrowing such protections, at least for countries that have defaulted on their sovereign debt. Developed countries might be reluctant to do this for fear that they themselves might default some time in the future. At the least, a mechanism should be provided by which the developed countries that control the BIS could withdraw the protections for countries under certain circumstances, e.g. prolonged debt default without attempt to engage in good faith negotiations with creditors.

---

[132] 28 U.S.C. §1611(b)(1). This immunity can be waived but only with respect to post-judgment attachment (attachments in aid of execution). See *Weston Compagnie de Finance et D'Investissement, S.A. v. La Republica del* Ecuador, 823 F. Supp. 1066 (S.D.N.Y. 1993). This allows the debtor to withdraw assets from the U.S. once litigation is brought. Another useful addition to creditor rights would be to allow waiver of pre-judgment attachments.

[133] 507 F. Supp. 311 (D.D.C. 1980).

[134] 104 League of Nations Treaty Series 441 (including Constituent Charter and Statutes); Compendium of Swiss laws (Recueil systématique); 0.192.122.971 (including Constituent Charter). In addition, there is a so-called "Headquarters Agreement" between the BIS and the Swiss government entered into on February 10, 1987, which provides in Article 4.4 that all deposits entrusted to the Bank are "immune from any measure of execution (including seizure, attachment, freeze or any other measure of execution, enforcement or sequestration, and in particular of attachment within the meaning of Swiss law."

Two specific areas of creditor rights deserve some additional discussion, the use of the *pari passu* clause and the ability to seize assets of state-owned enterprises (SOEs). As concerns *pari passu,* we have already discussed the use of this clause in the *Elliott* case in Peru. Holdout creditors were able to attach payments to Brady bondholders in satisfaction of Peru's obligations on outstanding syndicated loans.[135] In principle, this right could be made clear in law and extended to other dollar payments made by the sovereign, as for imports or payments to other trade creditors. Litigation continues about the meaning and scope of the clause, in New York and in Belgium.

Developed country governments persist in weakening and not strengthening creditor rights. Thus, the United States has intervened in litigation in New York against Argentina to oppose the view of the plaintiff creditors on the meaning of the *pari passu* clause.[136] In so doing, the U.S. has taken the view that an expansive view of creditor rights would impede progress between creditors and Argentina, the policy issue discussed above. Further, Belgium has amended its law to explicitly provide that no funds to be credited to a Euroclear account can be attached.[137] The international system is moving in the wrong direction if stronger creditor rights would lead to fewer defaults.

A second area of interest is the possible seizure of the assets of SOEs in satisfaction of debts owed by sovereigns. While the doctrine of separateness would protect SOEs from being liable for the debts of their owners, assuming separateness was respected in the management of a SOE, creditors of the sovereign would still be entitled to become the owners of the SOE, since the sovereign's stock in the SOE is an asset of the sovereign.

---

[135] For the view of the narrow meaning of the *pari passu* clause as propounded by counsel (Cleary, Gottlieb) for emerging market countries, based on a review of history, see L. Buchheit and J. Pam, "The Hunt for *Pari Passu,*" Butterworths International Financial Law Review 20 (February 2004) and 47 (March 2004). For a view that the clause has a wider meaning based on its plain meaning, see Declaration of Professor Lowenfeld and Declaration of Professor Scott (this author) submitted to the Brussels Court of Appeal in 2004 in the case of *LNC Investments v. Nicaragua,* Cause No. 2004/1831. The clause in that case, typical of most clauses, provided that the debt in question (syndicated loans) would rank "at least *pari passu* in priority of payment and in rank of security with all other External Indebtedness. ..." The Court did not reach the meaning of the clause in its decision denying the plaintiff relief. The basis of the Court's decision related to its view that the lower court order permitting an attachment of incoming funds was an unwarranted interference with the Euroclear Bank processing the funds. Decision of March 19, 2004.

[136] Statement of Interest of the United States, *Macrotecnic International Corp. v. Republic of Argentina,* 02 CV 5932 (TPG), January 12, 2004.

[137] The new law modifies the Belgian Act of April 28, 1999, which was the Belgian implementation of the EU's Settlement Finality Directive. The amended law provides (with changes in italics): "No cash settlement account with a settlement system operator or agent, *nor any transfer of money to be credited to such cash settlement account, via a Belgian or foreign credit institution,* may in any manner whatsoever be attached, put under trusteeship or blocked by a participant (other than the settlement system operator or agent), a counterparty or a third party."

Under the Foreign Sovereign Immunities Act (FSIA), as interpreted, a U.S. court cannot attach or garnish sovereign assets located outside the United States.[138] This is not true in the case of private debtors.[139] FSIA could be changed to provide that U.S. courts could attach or garnish stock even though the stock was outside the U.S. If the sovereign or the garnishee failed to deliver the stock, the Court could assign ownership of SOE assets, at least those in the United States, to the private creditors. One would then have to work out the priority issue as between the creditors of the sovereign and the SOE.[140]

In the future, attention should be focused on removing protections for debtor assets. It is often claimed that debtors have no significant foreign currency assets abroad, but this is in part true because of the legal protections afforded assets abroad. If payment flows or central bank reserves (which are protected by being deposited at the Bank for International Settlements) were available for seizure, at least in the case of rogue debtors, more pressure would exist for countries to pay their debts. A recent case in point is *Af-Cap v. Republic of Congo*,[141] where the Court allowed a creditor of the Congo to attach tax and royalty obligations payable to the Congo by a third party, but only because this property had been used in the past for a commercial purpose (the revenues were used to pay other creditors) since otherwise it would be protected by the FSIA. These kind of restrictions on creditors could be removed.

The international system could seek to put sovereign debt on a contractual par with non-sovereign debt by providing creditors of sovereigns with the same remedies enjoyed by creditors in the private sector. It is true that complete parity would require a collective action vehicle to deal with default, which is largely unattainable. Even if there were a SDRM, creditors of sovereigns would never have the liquidation value benchmark for reorganizations that they enjoy in the case of corporate bankruptcies. But this is no excuse for giving creditors less rights in general.

---

[138] *Philippine Export and Foreign Loan Guarantee Corp v. Chuidian,* 267 Cal. Rept. 457 (Cal Ct. App. 1990); *Fidelity Partners, Inc. V. Philippine Export & Loan Guarantee Corp.,* 921 F. Supp. 1113 (S.D.N.Y. 1996). The idea in these cases is that while the Act specifically permits waiver of sovereign immunity for assets in the United States, its failure to provide for a waiver of sovereign immunity for assets outside the United States means such assets are protected by an unwaivable sovereign immunity.

[139] J. Loeb, "Strengthening Bond Creditors' Remedies Under the Foreign Sovereign Immunities Act," Paper for the Seminar on International Finance, Harvard Law School (May 2004).

[140] SOEs' own assets are protected under the FSIA, 28 U.S.C. §1603(a), because an SOE may be considered an "agency" of a foreign state if it is either an "organ" of a foreign state or a majority of its shares are owned by a foreign state. There is a split in the circuits as to whether such immunity applies to indirectly owned SOEs, e.g. lower tiered subsidiaries. See *Filler v. Hanvit* 378 F.3rd 213 (2nd Cir. 2004).

[141] 383 F.3d 361 (5th Cir. 2004).

f.   KEY PRINCIPLES

In November 2004, sovereign issuers, the Institute of International Finance, and the International Primary Markets Association announced "Key Principles for Stable Capital Flows and Fair Debt Restructuring."[142] The principles focus on four areas: transparency and timely flow of information; close debtor-creditor dialogue and cooperation to avoid restructuring; good faith actions (including negotiations); and fair treatment, including lack of discrimination. The principles were endorsed by the G-20.[143] The principles are so general that one may question their usefulness.

g.   PRIORITIES AND INDICES

Two more suggestions for reform received attention in 2004: the need for creditor priorities and indexation of payoffs on sovereign debt to economic indices.

Priorities

With respect to priorities, some have argued that the lack of explicit priorities on sovereign debt has led to the threat of dilution—meaning that the sovereign is able to issue more debt than it would otherwise be able to do with priorities. If earlier debt had priority, subsequent debt that leads to overborrowing would be less likely to occur.[144] Another point in this literature is that there is a Gresham's law for sovereign debt. Because there is no de jure priority system, creditors attempt to obtain de facto priority through broader waivers of sovereign immunity or higher thresholds for collective action that may make needed restructurings of their debt more difficult This problem has led some to suggest a first in time priority rule.[145]

There are a number of problems with this line of argument. First, the possibility that later creditors can get priority over earlier ones is a commonplace in corporate financing where later secured creditors can dilute the value of earlier unsecured debt. It is not clear why this is more of a problem with sovereign than corporate debt. In the corporate world the earlier unsecured creditors can compensate for this risk by charging higher rates of interest. It is not clear why this is a more undesirable outcome in sovereign than corporate debt. Sovereign creditors could also, like corporate creditors, put covenants in their loan agreements preventing the debtor from making additional borrowings without the consent of the earlier creditors. This would not technically be a negative pledge clause since that clause classically prevents subsequent secured borrowing. But both clauses are

---

[142] http://www.iif.com/data/public/Principles.pdf

[143] Statement of U.S. Secretary of the Treasury Snow, Conclusions of Meeting of G-20 Finance Ministers, November 21, 2004.

[144] P. Bolton and O. Jeanne, "Structuring and Restructuring Sovereign Debt: The Role of Seniority," NBER Working Paper 11071 (January 2005). (Seniority)

[145] IMF, Research Department, "Sovereign Debt Structure for Crisis Prevention," July 2, 2004 (Debt Structure)

enforceable against third parties. The negative pledge clause would be enforced by attaching the collateral of the subsequent creditor who knowingly took the collateral in violation of the clause.[146] The restrictive covenant would be enforced through an action for damages against the subsequent lender who interfered with the earlier lender's contract rights. Tortious interference claims would not require cooperation of the sovereign borrower as they could be brought against foreign creditors in foreign courts.

Furthermore, an "absolute" first in time statutory rule is not self-executing—how would it be more easily enforced than a tortuous interference claim? The answer is it couldn't be without a new sovereign bankruptcy framework which we have seen is not likely to be adopted, and is only triggered with the consent of the sovereign.

There is no first-in time statutory priority in the corporate world— why is it more necessary in the sovereign context? Perhaps, the argument is that such a system would insure that later creditors would have to charge the debtor more in interest or impose restrictive terms, and that this is desirable because it will deter later lending and thus overborrowing. In the sovereign world, the costs of such overborrowing are often externalized to foreign governments through bailouts, which is not the case in corporate debt. While this is true, the problem is that not all second in time borrowing is bad or creates overborrowing. Yet this statutory rule will always make it more expensive. Furthermore, the basic problem is the bailouts and not the deficiencies of contract.

Second, if later debt dilution were a problem at all, it would be especially a problem for first in time creditors without priority. That is these first in time creditors should have adequate incentives to protect themselves against dilution. They do not need a statute. As already indicated, they could use restrictive covenants. However, if such covenants were thought to be insufficient protection, such creditors could issue secured debt. There is no contractual obstacle to this. As with the Brady bonds, collateral could be placed with a trusted third party in the country of the creditors. Also, some governments have secured their debt with proceeds from receivables, like royalties from oil exploration or remittances for exports.[147] Indeed, more use could be made of secured debt arrangements if unwaivable sovereign immunity protections against assets, like central bank reserves, were removed. It is true that secured debt is used less for sovereigns than for corporates—according to a 1995 study secured debt constitutes 53 percent of corporate debt as compared with 6.2 percent of sovereign debt,[148] but this

---

[146] See T. Mitchell, "The Negative Pledge Clause and the Classification of Financing Devices: A Question of Perspective," 60 American Bankruptcy Law Journal 263 (1986).

[147] Seniority, supra note 144, states that only 6.2 percent of the face amount of sovereign debt is secured. It is unclear how this compares to corporate debt or whether Brady bonds have been included.

[148] Seniority, supra note 144.

comparison excludes Brady bonds, the primary example of sovereign secured debt. And even if the comparison were accurate, what does it prove? Only that we need to make it easier to collateralize sovereign debt, not that we necessarily need a sovereign bankruptcy procedure.

One can also observe that priorities exist with respect to sovereign debt that do not exist with non-sovereign debt. Multilaterals like the IMF and World Bank enjoy priority in practice over other creditors Also, under the Paris Club rules repayment to private creditors cannot be on better terms than repayments to official creditors, perhaps a quasi priority. However, Roubini and Setser[149] point out that sovereigns often default on Paris Club debt treating it as junior, because the Paris Club would rarely, if ever, take any offensive action, e.g. attachments, against other sovereigns.

Earlier in the Chapter, I proposed that IMF lending might be constrained by giving it junior rather than senior priority. Roubini and Setser[150] would like to strengthen the role of the IMF as lender of last resort to deal with liquidity crises—in their view this requires IMF priority. Apart from the obvious problem of distinguishing liquidity and insolvency crises, it is not clear why a lender of last resort needs priority (as opposed to central bank lenders of last resort that need collateral). Collateral requirements actually constrain central bank lending, while uncollateralized priority promotes IMF lending.

Indexation

With respect to indexation, the idea is to index payments on debt to either GNP or some commodity index such as oil prices. The purpose of this approach would be to link debt servicing burdens more directly to the capacity of a country to pay.[151] Such arrangements have been used to a limited extent in the past—indeed Argentina put a GNP "kicker" into its debt exchange under which higher rates of interest would be paid on its new debt if Argentine GNP exceeded some specified baseline. The problem with GNP is that its measurement would be in control of the sovereign debtor. This could not be controlled for by delegating GNP measurement for this purpose to a third party because the third party would still have to rely on data supplied by the sovereign. Measurement of the value of commodity indices would not be a problem, but for many countries there would be no link between such commodities and their debt service capability. Even countries that are commodity exporters can experience debt crises because of over borrowing.

In the cases of priorities or indexing, there are no substantial legal obstacles to contracting with respect to these matters in sovereign bonds. The likely reason they are not used more is that the contracting parties do not find them useful.

---

[149] N. Roubini and B. Setser, "Bailouts or Bail-Ins," 257-259 (2004)
[150] Id., at 253-254.
[151] Debt Structure, supra note 145.

CONCLUSIONS

This Chapter's review of the 1990s shows how varied the debt crises have been in terms of whether they: were caused by fundamentals (Asian crisis) or temporary lack of liquidity (Mexico); were banking-centered (South Korea) or more general (Indonesia); involved domestic debt (Turkey) or foreign debt (South Korea) or a combination (Russia); were foreign exchange based (Mexico) or not (Asia); and involved politically key countries (Turkey and Mexico), or not (Argentina, Thailand). In some cases the IMF approach worked (Mexico, Brazil) and in some it did not (Asia). This century commenced with the case of Argentina, a sustained default.

Overall, certain problems emerged. The IMF incurred increasingly large expenditures in lending to sovereigns, often seeming to assume the role of an international lender of last resort. The sovereigns themselves incurred ever larger levels of debt. As a result, creditors were bailed out thus increasing creditor moral hazard, and debtors were allowed to restructure or default, thus increasing debtor moral hazard. The entire process was disorderly and fraught with discrimination against particular creditors.

One key question was whether the threat from unpaid creditors, whether seeking redress before a restructuring, or holding out once a restructuring plan was agreed, was significant. This primarily depends on the availability of seizure of foreign assets. As was learned, a major potential source of such assets could be cross-border hard currency payments by or to a sovereign, as in *Elliott*.

Current efforts at reform are focusing on the adoption of collective action clauses in bonds. The very marginal price effects of such covenants, if any, raises a significant question of whether the clauses are having any significant impact on making default more manageable. Further, the clauses cannot solve the collective action problems in dealing with non-bond creditors, or even with bond creditors with no or different CACs. This reform could well be a palliative of little consequence.

The SDRM proposal is waiting in the wings. Even in its "lite" form it gives too much power to the IMF. Further, it needs to be more inclusive, covering all sovereign debt, domestic or foreign, official/multilateral or private.

The most basic reform, however, is the need to limit IMF bailouts. If IMF money continues to be freely forthcoming, neither CACs nor SDRM will be used to reduce debt to manageable levels.

The Argentine case may well point toward a new real default option. A huge scale reduction in debt with large losses for creditors has occurred. It may result in a real test of the ability of holdout creditors to discipline the sovereign by asset seizures. It may also result in a new attitude of creditors that can no longer depend on IMF bailouts or "reasonable" restructuring measures by sovereigns. The length and disorderliness of the process may suggest the need of some form of a SDRM and the need to strengthen creditor rights.

CHAPTER TWENTY

BANKING SYSTEM REFORMS

A. AN INTERNATIONAL BANKING STANDARD

The G7 countries (Canada, France, Germany, Italy, Japan, the United Kingdom, and the United States) at the Lyons summit in 1996, largely in response to the Mexican crisis of 1994, directed finance ministries and central banks to come up with proposals for emerging market banking supervision in time for the June 1997 Denver summit. This led to or stimulated various efforts to develop some form of international banking standards.

1. DOMESTIC STANDARDS

Morris Goldstein[1] has championed the approach of developing and enforcing an international banking standard (IBS). He bases the need for such a standard on the fact that since 1980, domestic banking crises have been a common feature of the world's financial system. At least 14 countries had banking crises so serious that total losses or costs ranged from 10 percent to 55 percent of GDP. These countries were:

Latin America	Industrial	Africa	Other
Argentina	Spain	Benin	Israel
Chile	Japan	Ivory Coast	Bulgaria
Venezuela		Mauritania	Hungary
Mexico		Senegal	
		Tanzania	

Other countries had very serious banking crises that did not result in quite such large costs: Finland, Norway, and Sweden. The cost of resolving banking crises in developing and transition countries since 1980 has been estimated to be about $250 billion, which equaled an average of four years of development assistance from all sources during the same period. The major

---

[1] M. Goldstein, *The Case for an International Banking Standard* (Institute for International Economics, 1997). (Goldstein)

concern is that such crises may have spillover effects on other countries; indeed this concern with international transmission of systemic risk underlies much of U.S. regulation of foreign banks.

It is questionable whether there is generally the same global concern about banking crises in developing countries. This is largely because banks from many developing countries have few linkages with developed countries, i.e. they do not operate in other countries and do not do much cross-border business. It is also questionable whether "country" banking crises are the major problem. After all, BCCI, which triggered many of the U.S. regulatory reforms, had nothing to do with a country crisis—it was a failure of a poorly regulated multinational bank.

While much of the support behind international banking standards is premised on contagion, the case for the actual existence of contagion is not strong. One major problem is determining whether a simultaneous financial crisis in two countries is a result of transmission between the two countries, e.g. banking crisis in Ecuador spreads to Argentina, or whether both crises are a result of an external common cause, e.g. a rise in U.S. interest rates.[2] Further, there is great difficulty in showing that a crisis that is transmitted between two countries is a result of general interdependence, e.g. through trade flows, or is caused by a banking crisis in one of the countries. If contagion is generally caused by exchange rates or trade disruption, the international focus on banking regulation may be unjustified.

Goldstein uses the existence of these crises to argue that the world needs an International Banking Standard (IBS) to prevent these crises. His IBS would include the following four policies, among others:

Public disclosure. Banks would be required to furnish timely and accurate information on their financial condition to investors. A balance sheet, income statement, large off-balance sheet exposures, and major concentrations of credit and market risk should be consolidated globally in accordance with international accounting standards and certified by an independent external auditor. Serious penalties would apply for false or misleading data. Banks would disclose their ratings, or lack of them, from international credit rating agencies.

Bank capital. The IBS would require adherence to the Basel risk-weighted capital standards that are examined at length in Chapter 7. To qualify as strong, banks in a relatively volatile operating environment would apply a 'safety factor' if their recent history of loan defaults, restructured

---

[2] T. Mozer, "What is International Financial Contagion?," 6 International Finance (2003), pp. 157-178. See also M. Pericoli and M. Sbraccia, "A Primer on Financial Contagion," 17 J. of Economic Surveys (2003), pp. 571-608. See also C. Van Rijckeghem and B. Weder, "Spillovers through Banking Centers: A Panel Data Analysis of Bank Flows," 22 J. of International Money and Finance (2003), pp. 487-509, suggesting that contraction of international bank lending in several countries due to a crisis in one can be a mechanism of contagion.

loans, and/or government assistance to troubled banks was significantly higher than the OECD average over, say, the past five years. The safety factor could require a 1.5 capital multiple, so that a 12 percent risk-weight would apply instead of the ordinary 8 percent.

Safety net. The safety net for banks would consist of the following features, mimicking features of U.S. banking regulation:

> "(1) government deposit insurance ... for small depositors; (2) deposit insurance premiums paid by banks are risk weighted ...; (3) banks become subject to progressively harsher regulatory sanctions (e.g. eliminating dividends, restricting asset growth, and changing management) as their capital falls below multiple capital-zone trip wires; (4) ... well capitalized banks receive 'carrots' in the form of wider bank powers and lighter regulatory oversight; (5) regulators' discretion is sharply curtailed (with respect to initiating 'prompt corrective actions') and resolving a critically undercapitalized bank at least cost to the insurance fund ...; (6) ... the insurance fund is generally prohibited from protecting uninsured depositors or creditors at a failed bank if this would increase the loss to the deposit insurance fund; and (7) provision is made for a discretionary, systemic-risk override to protect all depositors in exceptional circumstances ... but [its] activation requires explicit, unanimous approval by the most senior economic officials and subjects any bailout to increased accountability. ..."[3]

Consolidated supervision and cooperation among host- and home-country supervisors. The IBS would require participants to implement the 1992 Basel rules:

> "(1) all international banks be supervised on a globally consolidated basis by a capable home-country supervisor; (2) home-country supervisors be able to gather information from their cross-border banking establishments; (3) before a cross-border banking establishment is created, it receive prior consent from both the host- and home-country authorities; and (4) host countries have recourse to certain defensive actions (e.g. prohibit the establishment of banking offices) if they determine that conditions (1)-(3) are not being satisfied."[4]

Goldstein's proposal raises the question of whether one standard set of rules could be applied to all banks in all countries. As we have already seen in our examination of the Basel Accord, the future of regulation may be more "models"-based, where regulators pass on models used by banks to control risks, rather than mandating specific rules. The same could be said for countries. There may be several valid ways for countries to supervise banks,

---

[3] Goldstein, supra note 1, pp. 46-47.
[4] Goldstein, supra note 1, p. 50.

not just one incorporated in an IBS. This suggests that, at most, international regulators should pass on country approaches rather than mandate one approach.

Goldstein would have the IMF and World Bank enforce his standards. But neither of these organizations is particularly expert in banking regulation, and would be called upon to enforce rules that other experts, like BIS, had formulated. Could BIS enforce these rules? It seems unlikely.

Notes and Questions

1.   Why, if at all, should the banking crises described by Goldstein be of international concern, that is to countries other than those in which a particular crisis occurred?

2.   In what areas of international financial regulation have we already developed international financial standards? You will have to briefly review the prior chapters to answer that question. Have these standards been mainly developed in banking or securities regulation? Have they been successful?

3.   Do you agree with Goldstein about the need for an International Banking Standard to deal with banking crises? Should we have binding international standards that are enforced? If so, how and by whom could such standards be enforced? Do the IMF and World Bank have the expertise to assess whether countries are complying with principles formulated by the Basel Committee?

2.   CROSS-BORDER STANDARDS

In October 1996, the Basel Committee on Banking Supervision and the Offshore Group of Banking Supervisors issued a report entitled *The Supervision of Cross-Border Banking* which addressed various proposals for overcoming problems in supervising the cross-border operations of international banks. These problems were of two kinds. First, home country supervisors had difficulty in obtaining necessary information about foreign operations as a result of secrecy laws and impediments to on-site inspections by home country supervisors. Second, host and home country supervisors had no common standard to assess the adequacy of each other's supervision, and supervisory gaps continued to exist as a result of "booking offices in the form of so-called 'shell branches,' parallel-owned banks, i.e. 'sister' institutions in under-regulated financial centers."[5] The Report encouraged the Offshore Group (a forum for supervisory cooperation of supervisors in certain offshore financial centers) and other regional groups to adopt common standards, and offered its own checklist of principles in that regard. However, the Basel Committee stated that it did "not wish its Secretariat to become directly

---

[5] Goldstein, supra note 1, p. 2.

involved in an exercise of this nature [monitoring compliance with standards] because of the moral hazard involved in appearing to give a 'seal of approval.'"[6]

The moral hazard may be that monitoring by the Basel Committee, by issuing the seal of approval, would take local regulators off the hook of doing their own day-to-day jobs. This is doubtful. It would be well understood that Basel approval was a necessary but not sufficient condition for adequate regulation. The real problem is political; a small group of elite OECD central bankers do not think they will be able to pass judgment on developing countries'—or for that matter each other's—banking systems.

If there is no current body to enforce the standards, the temptation would be to create a new one, but that would be extremely difficult to do. An alternative would be to assign responsibility to particular countries involved with transactions, i.e. the home or host country.[7]

B.   THE INTERNATIONAL FINANCIAL ARCHITECTURE APPROACH

The G7 countries have formulated their own approach to financial institution reform, mainly focusing on banks, as part of the International Financial Architecture. The general idea is to establish workable guidelines for supervision and regulation of banks that should be observed by all countries.

1.   BIS CORE PRINCIPLES

In April 1997, the BIS Committee on Banking Supervision issued a Consultative Paper on *Core Principles for Effective Banking Supervision*. It formulated 25 "Core Principles" for Effective Banking Supervision under the headings of Licensing and Structure, Prudential Regulations and Requirements, Methods of Ongoing Bank Supervision, Information Requirements, Formal Powers of Supervisors and Cross-Border Banking. These principles were later issued in final form in September 1997. They are quite general. The first Principle, a precondition for effective supervision in all areas, conveys the generality of the approach. It provides:

> "An effective system of banking supervision will have clear responsibilities and objectives for each agency involved in the supervision of banks. Each such agency should possess operational independence and adequate resources. A suitable legal framework for

---

[6] Goldstein, supra note 1, p. 18.

[7] This was the approach of the Basel Concordats, and is also the direction largely taken in S. Key and H. Scott, *International Trade in Banking Services: A Conceptual Framework* (Group of Thirty, 1991).

banking supervision is also necessary, including provisions relating to the authorization of banking establishments and their ongoing supervision; powers to address compliance with laws as well as safety and soundness concerns; and legal protection for supervisors. Arrangements for sharing information between supervisors and protecting the confidentiality of such information should be in place."

The G10 deputies (deputy finance ministers and senior central bank officials), together with representatives of emerging market economies, known as the Working Party on Financial Stability in Emerging Market Economies, issued another report, also in April 1997, *Financial Stability in Emerging Market Economies*. This goes beyond the topics dealt with in the BIS *Core Principles*, and deals with such issues as accounting standards, payment systems, and competition. Its strategy for achieving stability has four major components: (1) development of an international consensus on the key elements of a sound financial and regulatory system by representatives of the G10 and emerging economies (this would be the *Core Principles*); (2) formulation of sound principles and practices by international groupings of national authorities with relevant expertise and experience such as the Basel Committee, the IAIS (the accounting standards organization) and IOSCO; (3) use of market discipline and market access channels to provide incentives for the adoption of sound supervisory systems, better corporate governance and other key elements of a robust financial system; and (4) promotion by multilateral institutions such as the IMF, the World Bank and the regional development banks of the adoption and implementation of sound principles and practice. One might call these "soft" principles since they would not be binding on particular countries nor enforced by any international body. These objectives were further elaborated in the Working Group Report on Strengthening Financial Systems of the G22 countries of October 1998 (Working Group Report of 1998). One important addition to the prior statements on banking supervision was the stress on developing improvements in the techniques of asset valuation and loan loss provisioning as related to accounting standards.

In 1999, the Basel Committee issued a key paper further elaborating standards for banking regulation. *Core Principles Methodology* (October 1999) sets forth a methodology for testing whether countries are in compliance with the Core Principles. The Committee recognized that effective banking supervision required a set of preconditions to be in place: (1) sound and sustainable macroeconomic policies; (2) a well-developed public infrastructure, i.e. effective courts, accountants and auditors; (3) effective market discipline, e.g. financial transparency and effective corporate governance; (4) procedures for the efficient resolution of problems in banks; and (5) mechanisms for providing an appropriate level of systemic protection (or public safety net).

Is it likely that countries will be able to comply with the Core Principles? It can be argued that the Core Principles mimic supervisory standards in developed countries (particularly the United States), assume a well-trained body of supervisors and sophisticated bankers, and thus are inappropriate for many countries. Further, there is little proof that use of such standards will make financial crises less likely. Indeed, such strict standards, which give government officials tremendous power, seem to be more likely to increase corruption in many countries. It may be far better to design mechanisms which give more sway to private sector control of excesses, e.g. disclosure, mandatory issuance of subordinated debt, and the facilitation of the entry of foreign banks. These were the findings of a survey of regulatory and supervisory policies in 107 countries.[8]

Legal institutions clearly play a big role in a well-functioning financial system. Law and finance theory shows that in countries where legal systems enforce and support private contractual rights, and protect investors and savers, finance is more valuable and financial markets flourish.[9] This is true even in Asia, where law was widely regarded as unimportant.[10] How countries are governed is also crucial. Many have contended that bad governance is at the root of slow growth in Africa. A broad and careful index of governance constructed by World Bank economists is used to show that weak governance is a major factor in poor income countries.[11] But not everyone agrees. Sachs and others have argued that causation runs in the other direction, low incomes lead to poor governance.[12]

Notes and Questions

1.   What do you think of the Core Principles approach? Does it work?

2.   Why might the presence of foreign banks be important to the development of financial markets?

2.   IMF FINANCIAL SECTOR ASSESSMENT PROGRAM (FSAP)

While the Basel Committee has taken the lead in promulgating standards, the IMF and World Bank have undertaken the lead since 1999 in assessing whether the Basel Core Principles are being complied with. These

---

[8] J. Barth, G. Caprio Jr., and R. Levine, "Bank Regulation and Supervision: What Works Best?," NBER Working Paper 9323 (November 2002). See also D. Gros, "Who Needs Foreign Banks," CESifo Working Paper 998 (July 2003).

[9] S. Djankov, E. Glaeser, R. La Porta, F. Lopez-de-Silanes, and A. Shleifer, "The New Comparative Economics," 31 J. of Comparative Economics 595 (2003); T. Beck and R. Levine, "Legal Institutions and Financial Development," NBER Working Paper 10126 (December 2003).

[10] Asian Development Bank, *The Role of Law and Legal Institutions in Asian Economic Development, 1960-1995* (1999).

[11] D. Kaufmann, A. Kraay, and M. Mastruzzi, "Governance Matters IV: Governance Indicators for 1996-2004," The World Bank (May 2005).

[12] J. Sachs, J. McArthur, G. Schmidt-Traub, M. Kruk, C. Bahadur, M. Faye, and G. McCord, "Ending Africa's Poverty Trap," Brookings Papers on Economic Activity (2004).

are called Core Principles Assessments (CPA). Most of the countries surveyed at that time were developing countries, but Canada was also included (probably on the "what's good for the goose is good for the gander" principle). The average time spent in a country making the assessment was about three weeks. The surveys found a wide range of compliance with particular Core Principles. This assessment has also led to some feedback to the Basel Committee on the standards themselves. It is up to countries as to whether to publish the assessments. Performance on standards is taken into account by the Fund in making lending and other decisions regarding country assistance.[13]

The IMF also conducts a financial sector adjustment program (FSAP) which assesses compliance with a wider set of standards than just the Basel Core Principles. It covers the IMF's Code of Good Practices on Transparency in Monetary and Financial Policies, the Basel Committee on Payment and Settlement Systems' Core Principles for Systematically Important Payment Systems, IOSCO's Objectives and Principles of Securities Regulation, and the International Association of Insurance Supervisors' Insurance Core Principles. The Codes now cover a total of 12 core areas. FSAPs had been completed for 52 countries in 2003. The IMF has developed 45 measures of the financial soundness of a financial system to facilitate quantitative evaluations[14] but has yet to compile an overall assessment of country compliance. Voluntary assessments of member countries' observance of standards and codes are made by member countries in the form of Reports on the Observance of Standards and Codes, or ROSCs. As of October 2003, over 432 ROSCs had been prepared for 94 countries.

The IMF also grants access to and conditionality of its lending facilities to enforce international standards. For example, in its Letter of Intent of June 19, 2002, in connection with the IMF provision of a $17 billion standby, Turkey committed to adhere to various core banking principles.

3.   MARKET DISCIPLINE

While the focus of international banking reforms has been on the adoption of best practice regulation, there has been more consideration of late of strengthening market discipline. The conventional wisdom is that little reliance can be placed on market forces where liquidity, transparency, and other underlying characteristics of markets are lacking. However, there are certain offsetting factors: (1) less complex banking systems; (2) growing

---

[13] See IMF, *Experience with Basel Core Principle Assessments,* April 12, 2000; IMF, *Financial Sector Assessment Program (FSAP) A Review: Lessons from the Pilot and Issues Going Forward,* November 27, 2000. By December 2001, CPs had been surveyed in 36 countries, 22 of which have been published. IMF, *Quarterly Report on the Assessment of Standards and Codes—December 2001,* February 6, 2002.

[14] See G. Slack, "Availability of Financial Soundness Indicators," IMF Working Paper WP/03/58 (March 2003).

presence of internationalization through the presence of foreign banks and the international trading of the debt and equity securities of local banks; and (3) the smaller size of the business and financial community. On the other hand, the dominance of publicly owned banks in these markets weakens market discipline.[15]

There are also other problems in relying on market discipline. There are thin securities markets. Stock traded/GDP in 2001 was 17.6 percent in emerging markets compared to 128.1 percent in high-income, non-OECD countries. There are also more widespread "too big to fail" policies. The percentage of cases where banks were repeatedly recapitalized was 28 percent in emerging markets compared to 11 percent in developed countries, and the coverage of deposit insurance was 2.4 times GDP capita in emerging markets as compared to 1.8 times in high income OECD countries. There is also less accounting disclosure and poorer corporate governance.[16]

4.   FINANCIAL STABILITY FORUM (FSF)

The FSF was created in 1999, in part to coordinate efforts of various international regulatory bodies. It brings together three representatives, finance ministers, central bankers and financial regulators, from each G7 country. In addition, the IMF and World Bank have two members each, as does the Basel Committee on Banking Supervision, IOSCO and the International Association of Insurance Supervisors. Finally, the Bank for International Settlements itself, OECD, the Basel Committee on Payment and Settlement, and the Basel Committee on Global Financial Systems each have one seat, for a grand total of 35. The Chair is Roger Ferguson Jr., Vice Chairman of the Federal Reserve Board. The FSF has a small secretariat and no formal enforcement power. Nor does it have any direct representation from emerging market countries. The objective of the forum is to coordinate the policy actions of its members.[17]

Given its small secretariat, at least for now, it is unlikely that the FSF could take any operational role. It appears that the IMF is assuming this responsibility. The FSF, in its *Report of the Follow-Up Group on Incentives to Foster Implementation Standards* (August 31, 2000) has identified what it considers 12 key international standards. In addition to those subject to FSAPs, as discussed above, they include: IMF standards on fiscal policy transparency and data dissemination, the World Bank's Principles and Guidelines on Effective Insolvency Systems, the OECD's Principles of

---

[15] G. Caprio and P. Honohan, "Can the Unsophisticated Market Provide Discipline?," paper prepared for the BIS-Chicago Fed Conference on Market Discipline (October 2003).

[16] E. Levy-Yeyati, M. Peria, and S. Schmukler, "Market Discipline: The Evidence across Countries and Industries," presentation at BIS-Chicago Fed Conference, October 30-November 1, 2003.

[17] A summary of its ever-widening range of activities is set forth in FSF, *Ongoing and Recent Work Relevant to Sound Financial Systems* (March 14, 2002).

Corporate Governance, IASC's International Accounting Standards, the International Federation of Auditors Committee's (IFAC), International Standards on Auditing, and the Financial Action Task Force's Recommendations on Money Laundering. FSF issued its *Final Report of the Follow-Up Group* on September 6/7, 2001. While it found increasing worldwide awareness and understanding of the standards, implementation of the standards lagged behind.

Two interesting ideas appear in this Report. First, the FSF states that FSF members should encourage voluntary disclosure in prospectuses for international sovereign bond issues on observance of relevant standards, and also encourage the use of such information by banks in assessing lending risks. Also, FSF suggests that its members should give greater weight to a foreign jurisdiction's observance of relevant standards in making market access decisions and in the supervision and regulation of subsidiaries or branches of institutions from that jurisdiction or of domestic institutions dealing with counterparties in that jurisdiction.

The IFAC does generally contemplate more transparency about IMF programs in order to facilitate countries being subject to market discipline although the IMF has stated that the benefits of transparency must be balanced against the IMF's role as confidential policy advisor and the need to have candor in communications to the IMF from the countries.

Notes and Questions

1. Should FSF be expanded into a role as an international financial regulator with standard-setting and enforcement power?

5.   JOINT FORUM

Another important contribution to regulatory coordination is represented by the Joint Forum, composed of the Basel Committee on Banking Supervision, IOSCO, and the International Association of Insurance Supervisors, housed at BIS. It has initiated important work comparing principles of regulation across the banking, securities, and insurance industries.[18] This work is also highly relevant to the regulation of financial conglomerates, firms that engage in all of these activities.[19]

C.   CAPITAL CONTROLS

Capital controls come in many forms. They can restrict inward or outward capital flows or both. They can control capital flows by outright

---

[18] Joint Forum, *Core Principles* (November 2001).
[19] See Joint Forum on Financial Conglomerates, *Supervision of Financial Conglomerates* (February 1999).

prohibitions, explicit quantitative limits or an approval procedure. Capital controls can also be indirect, taking the form of dual or multiple-exchange rate systems, explicit taxation, indirect taxation in the form of non-interest bearing compulsory reserve/deposit requirements or other price or quantity restrictions.

In dual exchange rate systems, different exchange rates apply to different kinds of transactions. They have typically been used where authorities did not want to maintain exchange rates by generally imposing higher interest rates. Foreign exchange rates for trade and inward investment are generally exempted, thus allowing local currencies to depreciate against the Dollar for such transactions and imposing higher costs for those exchanging local currency in connection with such transactions, e.g. importers.[20]

Many arguments have been used to justify capital controls. For example, second-best arguments identify situations in which capital controls may compensate for market imperfections such as information asymmetry. In addition, policy implementation arguments are invoked, primarily to permit monetary policy autonomy, usually aimed at lower interest rates while preventing the currency from depreciating. Also, capital controls may be justified as protecting monetary and financial stability, as where short-term interbank inflows reflect inadequate risk assessment by local or foreign banks. And capital controls can also be imposed to support policies of financial repression to provide cheap government financing.[21]

S. Radelet and J. Sachs[22] have proposed to impose inward capital controls to limit countries' short-term borrowings. Joseph Stiglitz, the former chief economist at the World Bank, also favors such an approach. Much of the steam behind new calls for inward capital controls comes from the exposure of Korea and Thailand to sharp outflows of short-term capital in the Asian crisis, where there were no significant inward controls, and the ability of Chile to use inward controls to limit the inflow of short-term capital.

1.   CHILEAN EXPERIENCE

Chile imposed capital controls in June 1991 when a surge of capital inflows threatened a significant appreciation of the currency with the result that the central bank faced a problem in managing money supply. Originally, all portfolio inflows were subject to a 20 percent reserve deposit that earned no interest. For maturities of less than a year, the deposit applied for the duration of the credit, while for longer maturities, the reserve requirement

---

[20] IMF, *Country Experiences with the Use and Liberalization of Capital Controls* (September 1999).

[21] Id., at 3.

[22] "The East Asian Financial Crisis: Diagnosis, Remedies, Prospects," Brookings Papers on Economic Activity 1:1998.

was only for one year. Certain transactions were exempted, like trade flow, foreign currency deposits in commercial banks, and foreign direct investment. The controls were initially readily avoided by misdescribing the purpose of the inflow so as to qualify for an exemption. The Chilean authorities responded in July 1992 by raising the reserve requirement to 30 percent and extending coverage to trade credit and loans related to direct foreign investment. In 1995, the controls were further extended to investments by Chilean residents in Chilean stocks traded on the New York Stock Exchange and to international bond issues.[23]

The purpose of the Chilean controls was not to reduce short-term inflows in order to reduce the possibility of sudden outflows, the objective of Radelet and Sachs. The purpose was more traditional, to reduce upward pressure on the Chilean Peso, which would interfere with the Chilean export promotion policy, and preserve monetary policy autonomy. Since the mid 1980s, the Chilean Central Bank had pursued a disinflation policy by targeting real interest rates.

Were the Chilean controls successful in achieving their objectives? It appears that the controls clearly affected the maturities of inflows but the aggregate inflows were not affected. The controls also appeared to generate a small and temporary increase in interest rates giving the Central Bank some aid in controlling inflation. And the controls resulted in a small, 2.5 percent, depreciation in the peso. On the other hand, there was an increase in the cost of domestic capital, particularly for small firms that could not evade the controls.[24] The IMF Report concludes that there "is no discernible evidence that the [reserve requirements] had an effect on the exchange rate path or total capital inflows."[25] These studies fail to comment on another cost of controls—possible corruption associated with avoiding controls.

2.   MALAYSIAN EXPERIENCE

E. Kaplan and D. Rodrik examined the September 1998 Malaysian capital controls in *Did the Malaysian Capital Controls Work?*.[26] In 1997, in order to stem the decline of the Ringgit (MR) in the wake of the Asian financial crisis in Thailand and Korea, Malaysian authorities followed orthodox policies, raising interest rates and cutting spending, without effect. Consumption and investment demand decreased as a result of capital flows. Malaysia was intent on reflating the economy through lowering interest

---

[23] IMF, *Country Experiences with the Use and Liberalization of Capital Controls* (September 1999), p. 5; S. Edwards, "How Effective are Capital Controls?," NBER Working Paper 7413 (November 1999).

[24] J. De Gregorio, S. Edwards, and R. Valdes, "Controls on Capital Inflows: Do They Work?," NBER Working Paper 7645 (April 2000).

[25] IMF, *Country Experiences with the Use and Liberalization of Capital Controls* (September 1999), Part II, p. 6.

[26] NBER Working Paper 8142 (February 2001).

rates, but any attempt to do so was undercut by growing speculation against the Ringgit in offshore markets, mainly Singapore. Institutions borrowed Ringgit at double or triple the prevailing interest rates in Malaysia to purchase Dollars and bet in favor of the Ringgit's collapse. It is against this background that capital controls were imposed in September 1998 along with a new fixed rate of exchange of MR against the Dollar of 3.80, about 10 percent higher than the rate at which the MR was trading against the Dollar immediately preceding the adoption of controls.

Kaplan and Rodrik find that the capital controls worked. Malaysia was able to lower interest rates and make the fixed-exchange rate regime work without creating a black market. The authors leave open the issue of whether the controls intensified cronyism and had negative implications for political governance. One important point the authors make is that the imposition of capital controls avoided the necessity of going to the IMF for assistance. In this respect, capital controls may perform a similar function to the adoption of an international system for automatic stays or payment standstills, discussed in Chapter 19.

The IMF had consistently tried to prohibit countries from imposing capital controls on the ground that they distort international capital flows and are ultimately unenforceable.[27] After the Asian crisis, it began to reconsider this position stating that while "there remain differences of view on the merits of capital controls, it is generally agreed that controls cannot substitute for sound macroeconomic policies, although they may provide a breathing space for corrective action."[28] A 2003 IMF report[29] concludes that the case for the benefit to countries from financial integration is increasingly unclear. The Report concludes that it is difficult to establish a robust causal relationship between the degree of financial integration and output growth performance, and that there is little evidence that integration stabilizes fluctuations in consumption growth. Nonetheless, it does not recommend broad adoption of capital controls, stating that the desirability of such controls can only be addressed in the context of country-specific and institutional features.

A 2005 multi-country study by Edwards analyzes the relationship between restrictions to capital mobility and external crises. He finds no systematic evidence suggesting that countries with higher capital mobility

---

[27] See Stanley Fischer, "Capital-Account Liberalization and the Role of the IMF," in *Should the IMF Pursue Capital-Account Convertibility?*, Princeton Essays in International Finance No. 207 (1998).

[28] *Report of the Acting Management Director to the International Monetary and Financial Committee on Progress in Reforming the IMF and Strengthening the Architecture of the International Financial System* (April 12, 2000), p. 14.

[29] E. Prasad, K. Rogoff, S-J Wei, and A. Kose, "Effects of Financial Globalization on Developing Countries," IMF Occasional Paper 220 (2003); see also by same authors, "Financial Globalization, Growth and Volatility in Developing Countries," CEPR Working Paper 4772 (December 2004).

tend to have a higher incidence of crises or face a higher probability of having a crisis, than countries with lower capital mobility. His results also suggest, however, that countries with higher capital mobility may ex-post, after the crisis, face a higher cost in terms of growth decline.[30] A previous study found that countries with liberalized capital accounts experience a lower likelihood of currency crises, even controlling for strength of economies.[31] Recent microeconomic studies that look at how capital controls really work conclude that capital controls have significant economic costs and lead to a misallocation of resources.[32]

The Monetary and Financial Committee (formerly called the Interim Committee) of the IMF has favored another approach—raising the cost of short-term cross-border capital flow to the borrowers. The specific proposals are to "[m]ake capital requirements [for banks] a function of the type of funding; have the monetary authority charge banks for the existence of sovereign guarantees; and on the lending side, assign higher risk weighting to interbank lines under the Basel Capital Accord."[33] Federal Reserve Board Chairman Greenspan has suggested that banks might be required to post reserve requirements for loans from foreign banks.

CONCLUSIONS

The Asian financial crisis has triggered a new demand for international solutions to the problems of globalization in an increasingly interdependent world. These solutions, broadly conceived, result in increased power for international institutions, whether they be the IMF, the Basel Committee or newly created institutions like the Financial Stability Forum. These institutions are increasingly being relied upon to formulate and enforce international standards. Their growing importance parallels that of the WTO in trade.

It is not yet clear how the work of the various fora, e.g. BIS, IOSCO, IMF, World Bank, will be coordinated. One possibility is the Financial Stability Forum (FSF), created in 1999. The objective of the forum is to coordinate the policy actions of its members. Given its small secretariat, at least for now, it is unlikely that the FSF could take any operational role. It appears that the IMF is assuming this responsibility. The WTO has an established international framework but without expertise or authority in the

---

[30] S. Edwards, "Capital Controls, Sudden Stops, and Current Account Reversals," NBER Working Paper 11170 (March 2005).

[31] R. Glick, X. Gao, and M. Hutchison, "Currency Crises, Capital Account Liberalization, and Selection Bias," Draft (June 2004).

[32] K. Forbes, "The Microeconomic Evidence on Capital Controls: No Free Lunch," MIT Sloan School of Management Working Paper 4523-05 (February 2005).

[33] IMF, *A Guide to Progress in Strengthening the Architecture of the International Financial System*, April 28, 1999, p. 9.

financial area, as reflected in the prudential carve-out. Financial officials do not want to entrust trade officials with this responsibility.

There could be substantial costs if this development towards international regulation proceeds unchecked. It could result in the transfer of significant power to undemocratically controlled institutions. The American voters and their elected officials may be unable to control these institutions in the way they have done in the past since it appears that the world is moving to a bipolar (with EU) and probably a tripolar financial system (with the eventual economic recovery of Japan) in which the U.S. will increasingly have to share economic power. One key point in favor of FSF is that it is more directly within the control of the major economic powers than is IMF; however, it lacks in resources. Perhaps the point is that any international institution with the necessary resources to deal with emerging market problems, like the IMF, will have a bureaucracy with its own agenda.

A single set of mandated international rules will be more inflexible and less adaptable than multiple rules of sovereigns which compete with each other to attract financial institution activity. It is highly unlikely that the same rules fit all. Further, the advisability of mandated rules, in general, is contradicted by our recent experience with financial innovation (derivatives)—that regulators often do not know what to do. Indeed, this is behind the development of models-based regulation and the self-regulation approach of the Group of Thirty.[34]

One general alternative to international rules is for countries to cooperate on the issue of which country should regulate what, but leave the content of the regulation to the regulating country.[35] This builds on the 1975 and 1983 Basel Concordats discussed in Chapter 3. It is probably desirable for a few core principles, such as non-discrimination and national treatment, to be adopted at the international level. Such rules are currently embodied in the GATS Treaty and various statements of OECD. But this is a far cry from having such organizations concretely apply such rules to financial matters. In our view, much of the impetus for international rules is premised on the spillover effect of financial crises, but this has proven to be quite limited—the Asian crisis did not spillover into the West. More importantly, it is premised on IMF bailouts: developed countries are trying to limit the cost of bailouts by improving the financial systems of emerging market countries. From this point of view, the most urgent reforms are those facilitating orderly sovereign defaults, a matter discussed at length in Chapter 19.

---

[34] See D. Llewellyn, "The Institutional Structure of Regulatory Agencies," in *How Countries Supervise Their Banks, Insurers and Securities Markets*, (N. Courtis ed., 1999) for an excellent checklist of the pros and cons of centralized international regulation.

[35] See H. Scott and S. Key, "International Trade in Banking Services: A Conceptual Framework," Group of Thirty Occasional Paper 35 (1991); E. Kapstein, *Governing the Global Economy, International Finance and the State* (1994).

The call for international rules sometimes ignores the tendency for firms to locate their activities in jurisdictions with the optimal amount of regulation—and, as we have seen, this may not be the jurisdiction with the least amount of regulation. As long as there are jurisdictional holes in the international order, regulation havens that do not subscribe to international rules, there may be significant limits on enforcing international rules and this problem may be intensified by the Internet and the development of electronic money.

However, as discussed in Chapter 11, on the Eurodollar market, institutions are only able to locate operations abroad to escape regulation because host countries are not willing to reach out unilaterally or in concert to stop these offshore activities. They have adequate tools to do so, through cutting off market access to firms located offshore, e.g. the U.S. could say Bahamian corporations cannot do business in the United States, cutting off use of their payment systems, e.g. the U.S. could say Bahamian corporations could not have accounts at U.S. banks, or use such accounts to transfer funds, or penalizing citizens doing business with such companies, e.g. the U.S. could say any U.S. underwriter of securities of a Bahamian corporation, whether they were sold in the U.S. or abroad, would pay a fine. But some of these tools are very costly to U.S. financial institutions and to the primacy of the U.S. Dollar as a reserve currency.

PART V

FIGHTING TERRORISM

This concluding Part of the book focuses on only one subject, the fighting of terrorism through attacking its financing. These efforts have been spurred on by 9/11. The Chapter details how the United States and the world have built on anti-money laundering efforts to fight terrorism through controls in the financial system.

CHAPTER TWENTY-ONE

CONTROLLING THE FINANCING OF TERRORISM, TERRORISM INSURANCE, AND FINANCIAL TERRORISM

The events of September 11, 2001 shook the world. One of the important parts of the U.S. and worldwide response was to try to cut off funding to terrorists and to track terrorists through their use of the financial system. This Chapter focuses on how the U.S. and other countries have built on past efforts to stop money laundering to fight terrorism and how asset freezes operate. In addition, it looks at the issues involved with countries, in particular the United States, backing up the private sector in providing insurance against terrorism.

A. MONEY LAUNDERING AND ANTI-TERRORISM

1. NATURE OF THE PROBLEM

Before September 11, 2001, the U.S. had in place, along with many other countries, rules designed to stop money laundering. This is the process in which criminal activities like drug trafficking generate large cash receipts which are deposited in the banking system of major countries, where the drugs are sold, and then moved to offshore banking centers or into legitimate businesses. The point of anti-money laundering laws was twofold. First, to make it harder to deposit such cash without attracting attention from authorities and second, to record information about such deposits, or wire transfers generally, which could later be used to investigate criminal activities.

The financing of terrorism differs from money laundering in some important respects. First, the source of funding is different. Although some funding may come from illegal activities in the form of cash, much of the funding does not. It can come from rich individuals like Osama bin Laden or from terrorist states such as pre-war Iraq. These parties will already hold funded bank accounts, albeit under cloaked identities; their funding will often not start with cash deposits.

Second, the amount of individual funds transfers and the total amount of funds to support terrorism appear to be less than is generated by criminal activities such as drug trafficking. The transfer of funds to the terrorists involved in 9/11 through wire transfers were quite small. It appears that the financing for subsequent terrorist financing was also quite small: an estimated $50,000 for the October 2002 Bali bombings, less than $50,000 for the Istanbul bombings of November 2003, and about $10,000 for the Madrid train bombings of March 2004.[1] Although we have no estimates of the amount of funds used for terrorism, it is likely to be considerable less than the estimates of total funds laundered, $600 billion to $2 trillion per year.

Third, the origin of terrorist funding will often be external to the major economic powers, given who the terrorists are, and funds will then be moved to operatives inside the major economic powers. Criminal proceeds, however, are usually generated in the major markets and then moved offshore.

Dennis M. Lormel[2] testified that the 19 hijackers involved in 9/11 opened 24 domestic bank accounts at 4 different banks. The following financial profile was developed from the hijackers' domestic accounts.

Account profile

1. Accounts were opened with cash/cash equivalents in the average amount of $3,000 to $5,000.
2. Identification used to open the accounts were visas issued through Saudi Arabia or the UAE.
3. Accounts were opened within 30 days after entry into the U.S.
4. All accounts were normal current accounts with debit cards.
5. None of the hijackers had a social security number.
6. They tended to open their accounts in groups of three or four individuals.
7. Some of the accounts were joint accounts with others.
8. Addresses used usually were not permanent (i.e. mail boxes, etc.) and changed frequently.
9. Hijackers would often use the same address/telephone numbers on the accounts.

---

[1] S. Fidler, "Al-Qaeda Outsmarts Sanctions, Says UN," *Financial Times*, August 28, 2004.
[2] Statement for the Record, House Committee on Financial Services, Subcommittee on Oversight and Investigations, Washington, D.C., February 12, 2002.

10. No savings accounts or safe deposit boxes were opened.
11. Hijackers would open their accounts at branches of large well-known banks.
12. The majority of hijackers (12) opened accounts at the same bank.

Transaction profile

1. Some accounts would directly receive/send wire transfers of small amounts to foreign countries such as the UAE, Saudi Arabia, Germany.
2. Hijackers would make numerous attempts of cash withdrawals that often would exceed the limit of the debit card.
3. High percentage of withdrawals were from debit cards vs. low percentage of checks written.
4. Numerous balance inquiries were made.
5. Hijackers would often travel domestically.
6. There was a tendency to use Western Union to wire money.
7. One deposit would be made and then the money would trickle out a little at a time.
8. Account transactions did not reflect normal living expenses for rent, utilities, auto payments, insurance, etc.
9. There was no normal consistency with timing of deposits/disbursements.
10. Funding for normal day to day expenditures was not evident from transactions.
11. Overall transactions are below reporting requirements.
12. Funding of the accounts dominated by cash and overseas wire transfers.
13. ATM transactions occur where more than one hijacker was present (uninterrupted series of transactions involving several hijackers at the same ATM).
14. Use of debit cards by hijackers who did not own affected accounts.

International Activity

1. Three of the hijackers supplemented their financing by opening foreign current accounts and credit card accounts at banks located in the UAE.
2. While in the U.S., two of the hijackers had deposits made on their behalf by unknown individuals.
3. Hijackers on all four flights purchased traveler's checks overseas and brought them to the U.S. These traveler's checks were partially deposited into their U.S. checking accounts.
4. Three of the hijackers (pilots/leaders) continued to maintain bank accounts in Germany after moving to the U.S.

5. Two of the hijackers (pilots/leaders) had credit cards issued by German banks and maintained those after moving to the U.S.

6. It is suspected that other unknown foreign accounts exist that were opened by the hijackers to further supplement the financing of the September 11, 2001 attacks.

7. One of the hijackers (pilot/leader) received substantial funding through wire transfers into his German bank in 1998 and 1999 from one individual.

8. In 1999, this same hijacker opened an account in the UAE, giving power of attorney over the account to this same individual who had been wiring money to his German account.

9. More than $100,000 was wired from the UAE account of the hijacker to the German account of the hijacker in a 15-month period.

It is unclear what one does with the profiles. Are they really useful in identifying terrorists? If banks were to run the account profile against their existing accounts, it is highly doubtful whether terrorists, as opposed to Arab students, would be identified, and the cost of making such checks would be high. This raises a general problem about cost-benefit calculations with regard to anti-terrorist policies. Suppose there was a very low probability that a terrorist would be identified, say less than 0.5 percent, but that a terrorist act in the future might involve a nuclear bomb. Should governments require the banks to make the assessment? Certainly, one would want to use the cheapest way of making the identification, e.g. it might be cheaper to check the visas of all Arab students. There is an additional issue as to who should pay for these measures. Should the costs be imposed on the banks, and therefore the banks' customers, or should they be deferred by taxpayers more generally?

A further problem with terrorism financing is that it is often done outside the formal financial system. One of the methods used is Hawala which is prevalent in Arab countries as well as in southern Africa and southern Asia. Hawala operates through a network of agents who maintain running balances with each other that are periodically settled. It very much resembles the system used for cross-border payments in Europe before the invention of the modern banking system. Let us take an example. Suppose Somali A is in Minneapolis (where there are 50,000 Somalis) and wants to send money to Somali B in Somalia. She takes cash to a local Hawala agent who issues her a receipt. The local agent telephones or faxes another agent in Somalia who gives out cash to the beneficiary, Somali B. Over time, there will be movement in both directions. As a result, each agent will have a net position, one positive and the other negative. The two agents will settle in person by cash, commodities or through conventional payment systems. The system, which was set up to provide a cheap payment system to poor people without bank accounts, is now being used to make payments to terrorists.[3] The U.S. has encouraged other countries to regulate these informal systems, and some countries like the United Arab Emirates and Pakistan have done so. The U.S. has also required money service transmission businesses, including Hawalas, to register and be subject to regulation in the U.S.[4] In addition, banks have been encouraged to bring the informal sector into the banking system by reducing their costs.

One result of the crackdown on informal networks was to make banks reluctant to open accounts for any money service businesses. Federal regulators have urged the banks to use their normal procedures in determining whether to take such accounts. The U.S. obviously wants to encourage such services to use the banking system where they can more easily be monitored and controlled.[5]

2.   THE UNITED STATES RESPONSE

The United States has responded to the terrorist threat by modifying its money laundering rules. On October 26, 2001, President Bush signed into law the Uniting and Strengthening America by Providing Appropriate Tools to Intercept and Obstruct Terrorism Act of 2001 (PATRIOT Act). Title III of this Act is the International Money Laundering Abatement and Anti-Terrorist Financing Act of 2001, which both amends existing anti-money laundering law and imposes new requirements.

a.   U.S. ANTI-MONEY LAUNDERING LAW: THE BASICS[6]

This section describes the key features of the basic anti-money laundering law together with PATRIOT Act amendments.

The core of U.S. anti-money laundering law is the Bank Secrecy Act of 1970 (BSA), which has been frequently amended. The BSA authorizes the Secretary of the Treasury to regulate record keeping and reporting requirements for banks and other financial institutions, and to require financial institutions and some other private businesses and citizens to report certain kinds of financial transactions. In addition, banks are required

---

[3] For an excellent overview of how money laundering and terrorist funding works, and some of the differences, see Financial Action Task Force on Money Laundering, *Report on Money Laundering Typologies 2001-2002* (February 1, 2002). See also FinCEN and INTERPOL/FOPAC, *The Hawala Alternative Remittance System and Its Role in Money Laundering* (2004).

[4] Testimony of Assistant Secretary Terrorist Financing and Financial Crimes, U.S. Department of the Treasury, before the House Financial Services Committee, Subcommittee on Oversight and Investigations, February 16, 2005.

[5] Board of Governors of the Federal Reserve System, Federal Deposit Insurance Corporation, Federal Crimes Enforcement Network, National Credit Union Administration, Office of the Comptroller of the Currency, Office of Thrift Supervision, Joint Statement on Providing Banking Services to Money Services Businesses, March 30, 2005.

[6] This section relies heavily on Wilmer, Cutler and Pickering, *Anti-Money Laundering Guidance for Financial Institutions,* January 30, 2001

by their regulators to "know your customer" (KYC). FinCEN was the agency created by Treasury to deal with money laundering issues. However, in March 2004, the Treasury established a new office, the Office of Terrorism and Financial Intelligence, which will oversee FinCEN and the Office of Foreign Assets Control, which has responsibility for implementing asset freezes.

1.   SUSPICIOUS ACTIVITY REPORTING

Every bank operating in the United States must where warranted file a suspicious activity report (SAR). After December 31, 2001, money services and other types of financial businesses have also been required to do so. Between July and December 2003, 495 SARs were filed with a box checked for terrorist financing. A total of about 1.5 million SARs had been filed as of 2003, with about 500,000 filed in 2003.[7] As of June 2004, 319,942 filings had been made, indicating that SARs filings are rapidly increasing.[8] According to the Treasury Department's Office of the Inspector General, many of these reports are incomplete, leaving out critical information.[9] FinCEN believe partial reports are better than no reports but the Inspector General questions this assumption, observing that incomplete filings would simply be ignored.

Some have referred to the amount of SARs filings as a glut, contending that the more filings that are made the less useful they may be. The terrorist activity reports, however, are a small subset of the total SARs filings. While 319, 942 total filings were made in the first half of 2004, as indicated above, only 1046 of these reports related to terrorist financing.[10] Thus, it appears the glut only affects crime, where immediate follow-up is less urgent than for terrorism.

Regardless of the amount involved, a bank must file a SAR when the bank believes it was an actual or potential victim of a criminal violation or has a substantial basis for believing that its own people were so involved. Banks must also file SARs, depending on the size of aggregate transactions, where a suspect of a crime can be detected ($5000 or more), where a crime is suspected but no suspect has been identified ($25,000 or more), or when the bank suspects that a transaction involves funds derived from illegal activities, is designed to evade regulations, or has no apparent purpose ($5000 or more). FinCEN has provided substantial guidance about what may be suspicious together with examples of the kind of narratives required in reports.[11]

---

[7] The SAR Activity Review, *By The Numbers*, May 2004.
[8] The SAR Activity Review, *By The Numbers*, December 2004.
[9] H.Bergman, "SAR Report–Over Half Incomplete, Get Ignored," *American Banker*, April 4, 2005.
[10] The SAR Activity Review, *Trends, Tips and Issues*, April 2005.
[11] FinCEN, *Guidance on Preparing a Complete and Sufficient Suspicious Activity Narrative* (November 2003); see also Bank Secrecy Act Advisory Group, 6 The SAR Activity Review (November 2003).

In May 2004, the Riggs National Bank of Washington, D.C. agreed to pay a fined of $25 million to the Office of the Comptroller of the Currency for its failure to reports suspicious activities in the nature of funds transfers by foreign government officials, in particular those of former Chilean dictator General Augusto Pinochet. These transfers seemed to be possibly connected with money laundering rather than terrorism. This was followed by a Justice Department civil prosecution of a Birmingham, Alabama based bank, AmSouth, resulted in a $50 million fine, $40 million assessed by the Justice Department and $10 million assessed by the Federal Reserve Board (its bank regulator) and FinCEN. In AmSouth's case, the unreported transactions involved a fraudulent Ponzi scheme by two of its customers. There was also discussion of possible criminal action but that did not materialize. In 2005, Riggs pled guilty to a criminal charge of failing to file timely SARs and paid a $16 million fine. Issues of possible liability for individuals remain.

These cases raised three primary concerns. First, it might result in banks swamping federal authorities with SARs to protect themselves from hindsight accusations that they should have been suspicious when they were not. This was of particular concern to government officials fighting terrorism who believed the Justice Department's concerns with a specific money laundering problem might result in rendering SARs useless in the fight against terrorism. Indeed, SARs reports were already rapidly increasing even before the actions in mid-2004 against the banks. Secondly, banks may refuse to take accounts of customers who have transactions in the Middle East. Reportedly, AmSouth closed accounts of customers of Middle Eastern descent after it settled its civil and criminal actions.[12] Secondly, the threat of criminal prosecution of a bank raised the specter of a possible bank failure. It is probable that any bank under criminal prosecution would find itself in a liquidity crunch as other banks refused to extend it credit. The criminal plea in the Riggs case did not test the solvency issue since before the plea Riggs had agreed to be taken over by another bank, PNC Financial Corporation of Pittsburgh. There have been various stories about the criminal prosecutions of other major banks. The banking agencies are now attempting to develop more specific guidelines for the filing of SARs that might protect the banking system from the exposure of criminal prosecutions. It is difficult to see how guidance is going to be able to be more precise than it has been in the past.

Actions to remedy the failure to file SARs have not been restricted to U.S. banks. In February 2005, the New York branch of Arab Bank PLC, a Jordanian bank, entered into a consent order with the Office of the Comptroller of the Currency to improve the monitoring of its funds transfers, and agreed to close its branch in New York.[13] This followed reports that the

---

[12] D. Paletta, "Laundering's New Bind – Terminating the Account," *American Banker*, December 30, 2004.
[13] G. Simpson, "Arab Bank's Link to Terrorism Poses Dilemma for U.S. Policy," *The Wall Street Journal*, April 20, 2005.

OCC was investigating the use of the branch as a conduit for funds for Hamas. The involvement of Arab Bank posed a dilemma for U.S. policy makers as it is a pillar of the Mideast economy, and is sometimes a valuable ally of Israel and the U.S.

2.   CURRENCY TRANSACTION REPORTING

Every financial institution, including banks and securities firms, must file a report for each non-exempted "deposit, withdrawal, exchange of currency or other payment or transfer, by, through, or to the financial institution which involves a transaction in currency of more than $10,000" in one business day.[14] Multiple transactions of less than $10,000 by the same person must be aggregated. Transactions with certain persons who generate large currency transactions in the normal course of business, such as other banks, large corporations listed on an exchange, and government agencies, are exempt from reporting. Pursuant to the PATRIOT Act amendments, the U.S. Treasury has adopted an Interim Rule, extending this requirement to nonfinancial businesses.[15]

3.   WIRE (FUNDS) TRANSFER REQUIREMENTS

Under the so-called "Travel" rule, for any transmittal of funds of $3000 or more, involving more than one financial institution, each financial institution must forward certain information to the next financial institution. This facilitates the tracing of laundering transactions between U.S. and foreign financial institutions. Certain transmittals are exempt, for example, where both the transmitter and the recipient are a U.S. bank. All transmittal orders must include: the transmitter's name, address and account number; the identity of the transmitter's financial institution, the amount, the execution date and the recipient's financial institution. Certain recipient information must also be included if the bank receives it, i.e. name, address, account number and any specific identifier. In addition, financial institutions must keep records of wire transfers of $3000 and over.

4.   KNOW YOUR CUSTOMER (KYC)

In December 1998, the Federal Reserve Board and other U.S. banking regulators promulgated proposed KYC regulations.[16] The basic idea was that banks must know their customers and their businesses to decide whether they are engaged in suspicious or illegal activities. The KYC regulation would have required, among other things, that banks determine the sources of funds and the normal and expected transactions of their customers. The proposal was withdrawn due to thousands of comments complaining of

---

[14] 31 C.F.R. §103.22(b).
[15] 66 Federal Register 67680 (December 31, 2001).
[16] 63 Federal Register 67,516 (December 7, 1998).

invasion of privacy. Banks were also opposed due to the significant new costs that would be imposed. The regulatory agencies did, however, adopt examination guidelines, referred to as "enhanced due diligence," requiring many of the KYC practices. In addition to the procedures described above, additional regulatory guidance exists for so-called high-risk banking products, private banking and correspondent banking. "High-risk" in this context refers to banking transactions that have a high-risk of involving money laundering.

Section 326 of the PATRIOT Act requires financial institutions to adopt KYC policies. It requires that financial institutions implement reasonable procedures to: (1) verify the identity of any person opening an account; (2) maintain records of the information used to verify the person's identity; and (3) determine whether the person appears on any list of known or suspected terrorists or terrorist organizations.

After almost one year since it was proposed, a rule implementing the PATRIOT Act's KYC provisions was adopted by the Treasury through the Financial Crimes Enforcement Network (FinCEN) and the federal banking agencies.[17] The new rule provides that financial institutions establish a compliance program for obtaining identifying information from customers opening new accounts. The institutions must implement procedures for collecting standard information such as a customer's name, address, date of birth and a taxpayer identification number, such as a social security number for U.S. persons and similar numbers for foreigners. The financial institution must also have procedures to verify the identity of customers within a reasonable time after the account is opened. This can be done by examining documents such as a driver's license or passport. This rule becomes effective on October 1, 2003. The final rule relaxed many of the initial proposals out of concern with the burden on financial institutions, and adopted different versions of the rule for different kinds of institutions, e.g. banks or mutual funds.

The KYC rule under the PATRIOT Act did not engender any significant opposition from individuals concerned with privacy. This is for two reasons. First, 9/11 dramatically changed the degree to which people were willing to trade incursions on privacy for increases in safety. Second, the terrorism version of KYC does not require financial institutions to inquire into the business activities of their customers, an inquiry related to detecting money laundering. It rather requires checking to make sure people are supplying their correct identities. This permits more accurate ex-post investigations of people engaged in terrorism and may detect the location and funds of terrorists in advance when the depositor turns out to be on a terrorist list.

---

[17] 68 Federal Register 25090 (May 9, 2003).

5.   INFORMATION SHARING

Section 314(a) of the PATRIOT Act provides that financial institutions may be compelled to share information with law enforcement officials about their clients. Banks have long been subject to subpoena powers but this makes it easier for the government to obtain information.[18] Treasury uses §314(a) to send "blast faxes" to financial institutions to locate quickly the accounts and transactions of those suspected of money laundering or the financing of terrorism.

6.   PRIVATE BANKING

Private banking involves the provision of banking services to high net worth individuals, including money management and financial advice. Such services often involve setting up offshore facilities and banking arrangements. Banking regulators give guidance on how to handle these activities so as to minimize the possibility of money laundering.[19] For example, private banking often involves the creation of Personal Investment Companies (PICs), offshore legal entities to hold client assets and to keep confidential the name of the beneficial owner. Banks are advised to use extra caution in dealing with the beneficial owners, and following heightened KYC type policies. On October 30, 2000, a group of large international financial institutions released a set of anti-money laundering guidelines for private banking known as the Wolfsberg Principles. They include the principle that numbered or alternate name accounts will only be accepted if the bank has established the identity of the client and the beneficial owner.

b.   KEY ADDITIONS OF THE PATRIOT ACT: CORRESPONDENT OR SHELL
       BANKING AND SPECIAL MEASURES

1.   CORRESPONDENT ACCOUNTS

Terrorists and money launderers can make use of the correspondent banking system to cover their tracks. While a U.S. bank is in the position to take measures to assure that its foreign respondent banks (foreign banks holding accounts with it) have taken similar measures with respect to its customers as are required by U.S. law of the U.S. bank with respect to its customers, it has no way of knowing whether sub-respondents of the foreign bank (foreign banks which bank with its foreign bank respondent) have done so. Let us take an example. Assume Terrorist B has an account in the Bank of Somalia. Bank of Somalia in turn holds an account with BNP-Paribas, a large French bank, and BNP holds an account with Citibank, NY. Terrorist B sends funds to Terrorist A, who holds an account at Citibank. Citibank can try to assure that its bank respondents like BNP take precautions against

---

[18] See 67 Federal Register 60579 (September 26, 2002).
[19] See e.g. *Federal Guidance on Private Banking Activities*, SR-97-19, June 30, 1997.

terrorists opening accounts and keep records to permit tracking of transactions after-the-fact. But Citibank cannot know whether Bank of Somalia does so, and may not even know that Bank of Somalia is a respondent of BNP.

The PATRIOT Act tries to address the problem of correspondent accounts in a variety of ways. First, §312 adds a new §5318(i) to the BSA, imposing a general due diligence obligation on U.S. banks that have correspondent accounts. Institutions must establish procedures and controls that are reasonably designed to detect and report instances of money laundering through those accounts. Second, a higher level of due diligence may be imposed on banks maintaining correspondent accounts for three categories of foreign banks: (1) foreign banks operating outside the United States under an "offshore banking license," which is a license to conduct banking activities which prohibits the licensed entity from conducting banking activities with local citizens or in local currencies; (2) banks operating under a license in a foreign country that has been designated as noncooperative with international anti-money laundering principles by an intergovernmental group of which the U.S. is a member (like the Financial Action Task Force (FATF), discussed below); and (3) foreign banks operating under a license issued by a foreign country that has been designated by the Secretary as warranting special measures.

Additional due diligence requires U.S. banks to ascertain the ownership of the foreign bank, conduct enhanced scrutiny of the correspondent account to guard against money laundering, report any suspicious transactions and determine whether the foreign bank provides correspondent accounts to other foreign banks and if so, which ones. Also, they are required to determine what these second-tier foreign banks do to prevent money laundering or terrorist financing. It is far from clear how U.S. banks will obtain such information from their respondent or sub-respondent. It is also unclear how far up the correspondent chain such procedure is to be used. Suppose in our earlier example, the Bank of Somalia banks with a Lichtenstein bank which in turn banks with BNP. Citibank would have to ask BNP (assuming contra-factually that BNP was a bank within one of the three categories listed above) who its respondents were. Assuming BNP would or could disclose such information, Citibank would have to get due diligence information from the Lichtenstein bank, but it is unclear it would have to do so from the Bank of Somalia.

In addition, new §5318(k) of the BSA requires any covered financial institution that provides a correspondent account to a foreign bank to maintain records of the foreign bank's owners and agent in the United States designated to accept service of legal process for records regarding the correspondent account and permits the Secretary and the Attorney General to subpoena those records. If a foreign bank fails to comply, a financial institution must terminate the account upon notice from the Secretary or Attorney General.

Even stronger requirements apply to "shell banks." Section 313 of the PATRIOT Act prohibits covered financial institutions from establishing or maintaining a correspondent account for a shell bank and requires them to take reasonable steps to assure that correspondent accounts of foreign banks are not being used indirectly by shell banks, e.g. where a shell bank banks with BNP which banks with Citibank. A shell bank is a foreign bank that *does not* have a "physical presence" in any country. A foreign bank *does* have a physical presence if it maintains a place of business at a fixed physical address in the foreign bank's licensing jurisdiction at which the bank has one or more full-time employees, maintains operating records, and is subject to inspection by the foreign bank's licensing banking authority. Shell banks affiliated with U.S. banks are generally exempt. Treasury has issued Interim Rules[20] and proposed rules[21] implementing the subpoena power and shell bank requirements. Both rules provide safe harbors if U.S. banks obtain specified model certifications from their foreign bank customers. Senate Banking Chairman Paul Sarbanes has criticized the certification approach to the extent it substitutes certification for due diligence.[22]

The U.S. ability to coordinate its efforts in fighting the financing of terrorism has been enhanced by the creation within the U.S. Treasury of the Executive Office for Terrorist Financing and Financial Crimes. FinCEN, the Financial Crimes Enforcement Network, reports to it. The new office will be responsible for money laundering as well as terrorism.

2.   SPECIAL MEASURES

Section 311 of the PATRIOT Act authorizes the Treasury to designate certain jurisdictions, institutions or types of transactions as posing particular threats for anti-money laundering or anti-terrorism investigations, and to require financial institutions to take additional steps to monitor those transactions, including heightened reporting or record keeping, all of which can be done through Executive Order. Factors to be taken into account with respect to jurisdictions include:

1. evidence of terrorist activity in that jurisdiction.
2. bank secrecy provisions, and similar benefits for non-residents.
3. quality of bank supervision.
4. imbalances between the volume of financial transactions and real economy.
5. designations of the jurisdiction as an 'offshore haven' by international experts.

---

[20] 66 Federal Register 59342 (November 27, 2001).
[21] 66 Federal Register 67460 (December 28, 2001).
[22] 78 BNA Banking Report 192 (February 4, 2002).

    6.   prevalence of corruption in that country.

For foreign institutions and types of transactions, the criteria are similar, and similarly broad:

    1.   whether the institution or transaction is commonly used to facilitate money laundering.

    2.   whether that type of transaction has any legitimate purpose.

    3.   whether the proposed regulatory action will "continue ... to guard against international money laundering."[23]

The Secretary may require a domestic financial institution or domestic financial agency to maintain records and file reports concerning the aggregate amount of transactions in any of the above cases, or with regard to particular transactions, require the following information: (1) the identity and address of the transaction participants (including the originator of a funds transfer); (2) the legal capacity in which a participant is acting; (3) the beneficial owner of the funds; and (4) a description of the transaction. The Secretary may also require domestic financial institutions or agencies to ascertain the beneficial ownership of an account that is opened or maintained by a foreign person in the United States.

In May 2004, Treasury imposed Section 311 measures against Burma and two Burmese financial institutions. These measures prohibit certain U.S. financial institutions, including banks, from establishing or maintaining correspondent accounts for any Burmese bank, including the two specifically identified. U.S. financial institutions are also required to ensure that no foreign bank accounts from other countries are being used to service Burmese bank transactions.[24] On May 11, 2004, the Commercial Bank of Syria (CBS, Syria's commercial bank) was designated as a financial institution of "primary money laundering concern," permitting special measures to be taken against the bank. At the same time the Treasury issued a proposed regulation to cut off CBS from U.S. correspondent accounts. [25]

It is not clear how a U.S. financial institution could actually determine whether a foreign bank, like the Commercial Bank of Syria (CBS) was accessing another foreign bank's correspondent account with a U.S. bank. In the proposed Treasury regulation, Treasury would require that a U.S. financial institution notify correspondents that they may not provide CBS with access to its correspondent account. No certification from correspondent account holders is required. In addition, a U.S. financial institution would have to take "reasonable steps" to identify indirect use, which would include applying "an appropriate screening mechanism to be

---

[23] 31 U.S.C., §5318A(c)(2)(B).

[24] Board of Governors of the Federal Reserve System, Imposition of Special Measures Against Burma, Myanmar, Mayflower Bank, and Asian Wealth Bank, SR004-6, May 3, 2004.

[25] U.S. Department of Treasury, Notice of Proposed Rulemaking, Amendments to 31 C.F.R. §103.188(b), 69 Federal Register 28098, 28102 (May 18, 2004).

able to identify a funds transfer order that on its face listed CBS as the originator's or beneficiary's financial institution, or otherwise referenced CBS." As of May 2005, this regulation has not been adopted indicating that the U.S. is trying to use the threat of a cut-off to influence Syrian policy toward terrorists.

The heightened use of special measures has, also led to cut-offs of foreign banks from correspondent accounts. The New York branch of the major Dutch bank ABN Amro has severed relationships with hundreds of foreign banks in Russia, Eastern Europe and the Carribean as part of its settlement of probes of its dealings with these banks. The effect has been to leave these foreign banks with no access to the U.S. dollar payment system which can have an economic impact on their local economies.

c.   GOING TO THE SOURCE: SAUDI ARABIA

Individuals in Saudi Arabia have long been thought of as an important source of funds for al-Qaeda's operations. U.S. policy makers were initially very circumspect about pressuring its "ally" to crack down on such funding. This situation changed on May 12, 2003 when al-Qaeda bombed housing compounds in Riyadh used by U.S. foreign residents. This was followed by other terrorist incidents in the Kingdom in 2003 and 2004. This changed the Saudi attitude toward al-Qaeda and made the U.S. more willing to confront Saudi Arabia openly on the issue. As a result Saudi Arabia has significantly revamped its own internal anti-terrorist financing system and collaborated with the United States in making joint designations of terrorist entities. It also used force in hunting down terrorist financiers. This has apparently had a significant impact on al-Qaeda's financing.[26]

3.   INTERNATIONAL INITIATIVES

a.   FINANCIAL ACTION TASK FORCE (FATF)

Work on identifying jurisdictions that pose money-laundering threats has been carried on by the FATF, an organization of 31 countries including the United States.[27] The FATF was founded by the G7 nations in 1989 to foster money laundering controls worldwide.

In 1990, FATF issued *Forty Recommendations on Money Laundering* that has been repeatedly endorsed by major countries. The Recommendations call for the criminalization of money laundering, international cooperation in money laundering cases, and a wide range of money laundering control duties for financial institutions, including customer identification, mandatory

---

[26] Council on Foreign Relations, *Update on the Global Campaign Against Terrorist Financing* (June 15, 2004).
[27] FATF, *Review to Identify Non-Cooperative Countries or Territories: Increasing The Worldwide Effectiveness of Anti-Money Laundering Measures* (June 22, 2000).

suspicious activity reporting, and due diligence. In May 2002, FATF issued a Consultation Paper, *Review of the FATF Forty Recommendations*, seeking comment on proposed changes in the *Forty Recommendations*. The measures would generally put more obligations on financial institutions to adopt KYC polices and enhance suspicious transaction reporting. It also discusses the application of the standards to a broad range of financial institutions and would impose obligations on some non-financial businesses and professions (including lawyers). In line with the PATRIOT Act, it would impose heightened obligations with respect to correspondent banking. It would also impose special requirements on dealings with political leaders and electronic and other non face-to-face transactions. In addition, the paper discusses problems of identifying the beneficial owners of "corporate vehicles" and trusts, and the use of bearer shares.

In March 2001, the Basel Committee on Banking Supervision weighed in on money laundering. The Committee stated its focus was on the integrity and safety and soundness of banks rather the crime prevention agenda of FATF. Nevertheless, their recommendations cover some of the same territory, e.g. KYC programs.[28]

FATF has also formulated certain principles to determine when a *jurisdiction* was not taking adequate measures to combat money laundering: (1) loopholes in financial regulation; (2) lack of regulatory mechanisms to identify beneficial owners of accounts; (3) obstacles to international cooperation, such as laws prohibiting information exchange; and (4) inadequate resources devoted to prevent and detect money laundering. These requirements were further elaborated in February 2000 by setting forth twenty five criteria that would be used to make these determinations.[29] As of April 2003, nine jurisdictions were identified as non-cooperating countries and territories (NCCTs), including Egypt, Indonesia and the Philippines. In 2001, Russia and Israel were also on the list but have been subsequently removed.

The FATF's direct involvement in anti-terrorism stems from October 2001 when it issued *Eight Special Recommendations on Terrorist Financing*. The recommendations provide that countries should:

> "1. ratify and implement all applicable UN instruments.
> 2. criminalize the financing of terrorism and associated money laundering.
> 3. freeze and confiscate terrorist assets.
> 4. report suspicious transactions related to terrorism.
> 5. cooperate with other states' investigations relating to the financing of terrorism.

---

[28] Basel Committee on Banking Supervision Consultative Document, *Customer Due Diligence for Banks* (January 2001).
[29] FATF, *Report on Non-Cooperative Countries and Territories* (2000).

6. eliminate or regulate alternative remittance systems.

7. require more complete record-keeping regarding wire transfers.

8. review laws relating to non-profits that may be exploited for terrorist purposes."

FATF has developed sanctions to enforce its standards, by subjecting financial institution transactions from offending countries with FATF member countries to increased scrutiny, prohibiting the establishment in member countries of banks from offending countries, and warning non-financial sector businesses that transactions with entities from offending countries might run the risk of being regarded as money laundering. These sanctions were applied to the Ukraine in December 2002 and then rescinded in February 2003 after the Ukraine improved its system.

In October 2003, FATF adopted guidance for government officials freezing terrorist assets. Drafted as an interpretive note to the third special recommendation, it devises a mechanism for simultaneous government action.[30]

b.   THE INTERNATIONAL MONETARY FUND

Chapter 20 described the efforts of the IMF in monitoring and assessing the implementation of international standards through the Financial Sector Assessment Program. The IMF Directors generally agreed in November 2001 that the FATF *Forty Recommendations* on money laundering should become part of that process, following the development of an appropriate methodology and assessment procedure.[31]

c.   THE UNITED NATIONS

On September 28, 2001, the Security Council of the United Nations adopted Resolution 1373 under Chapter VII of the UN Charter, which authorizes the Security Council "to maintain or restore international peace and security," through measures binding on all members. This resolution requires countries to criminalize terrorist funding, freeze terrorist assets, prohibit terrorists from obtaining financial services, and cooperate with criminal investigations of other countries. This was followed up four months later with Resolution 1390 that essentially establishes an international embargo on financial, military, political or any other form of aid to Osama bin Laden, Al Qaeda or the Taliban. The UN resolutions require action by the Security Council which, given the current Middle East problems, is likely to disagree on the meaning of terrorism, a term left undefined by the resolutions.

---

[30] 81 BNA Banking Report, October 6, 2003, p. 511.

[31] International Monetary Fund, *Intensified Fund Involvement in Anti-Money Laundering Work and Combating the Funding of Terrorism,* November 5, 2001. This report contemplates that the Fund would have a similar role with respect to FATF's anti-terrorist funding recommendations.

Prior to September 11, the United Nations General Assembly approved the International Convention for the Suppression of Financing of Terrorism, signed by 132 states, but only ratified by 24 (not including the United States). The Convention largely overlaps with the UN resolutions.

d.   THE EUROPEAN UNION DIRECTIVE

On December 4, 2001, the European Union adopted a Directive on prevention of the use of the financial system for the purpose of money laundering.[32]

The most interesting part of the new Directive is that its anti-money laundering prohibitions are imposed not only on financial institutions but on a wide array of other persons, including auditors, external accountants, tax advisers, notaries, real estate agents, dealers in high value goods, and attorneys. The Directive exempts independent members of professions like attorneys from reporting requirements where the information is obtained in connection with representation of a client unless the attorney is herself involved in the money laundering. Moreover, it permits attorneys to make their reports to the bar rather than to governmental agencies. In June 2004, the Commission of the European Union proposed to update the EU's policies to conform to the recommendations of FATF and to specifically cover terrorist financing.[33] This would bring Europe's approach quite close to that of the United States.

There have been differences between the European Union and the United States as to how to fight terrorism, both generally as well as through the financial system—indeed there has been disagreement as to who are terrorists. The EU and the U.S. have moved closer to each other however, as reflected in a June 2004 Declaration on Combating Terrorism.[34]

4.   ADDITIONAL MEASURES

What additional measures might be considered beyond those set forth above? First, FATF could promulgate a NCCT country list with respect to anti-terrorist funding measures and then establish international sanctions for violations. It is relatively clear that the U.S. cannot rely exclusively on unilateral measures, particularly where terrorist financing circumvents the U.S. banking system entirely. While such circumvention would be difficult for terrorist activities that occur in the United States, it could easily be done where American interests were attacked abroad. And even when the U.S. banking system is involved, the tiering nature of correspondent accounts

[32] Directive 2001/97/EEC, O.J. L344/6, December 28, 2001. This amended a prior Directive on money laundering, Directive 91/308/EEC, O.J. L166/77, June 28, 1991.
[33] Commission of the European Communities, Proposal for a Directive of the European Parliament and the Council on the Prevention of the Use of the Financial System for the Purpose of Money Laundering, including Terrorist Financing, COM(2004) 448 final, June 30, 2004.
[34] Declaration of June 26, 2004 at the U.S.-E.U. Summit Dromoland Castle, Shannon, Ireland.

necessitates cooperation of other countries in enforcing their own anti-terrorist measures. FATF would seem preferable to the United Nations as the agency to formulate international standards, given its composition and expertise. The IMF could monitor and assess country compliance.

However, there is the issue of what the sanctions would be. As of yet, the international financial system has not established sanctions for the violation of banking standards generally; they are still precatory and resemble guidelines more than binding rules. This is unacceptable when it comes to terrorism. However, given the disagreement on what actually constitutes terrorism, it may be difficult to get international agreement on sanctions. Such disagreement has already manifested itself in the freezing of terrorist assets. For example, Germany and France, the latter with a significant local Arab population and strong international Arab ties, have ordered their banks to block accounts of just 140 of the 192 people and entities on the U.S. list, leaving untouched organizations like Hamas, the Palestinian group that has taken responsibility for many suicide bombings in Israel.[35] It is conceivable, however, that there will be less disagreement over matters pertaining to regulation of the financial system than there is over the freezing of particular accounts.

A second possibility might be the establishment of national registries of bank accounts which are accessible to other countries, or perhaps even to other countries' financial institutions under certain conditions. Germany is planning to implement such a system. The German register will list the name, date and place of birth of all account holders, as well as the date when the account was opened, the name of the bank and the account number. This plan has been criticized by some as impinging on bank secrecy.[36] Indeed, even a recent recommendation of the U.S. Senate's Permanent Subcommittee on Investigations[37] that banks closing accounts due to suspicious activities be required to notify other banks, to whom they are sending the funds in the closed accounts, of the reason for the transfer, has met with opposition. Some think it is a good idea but would make the warnings voluntary.[38]

Linked national registries could greatly aid in the detection or tracking of terrorism. For example, suppose a foreigner in the United States,

---

[35] M. Phillips and I. Johnson, "U.S.-European Divisions Hinder Drive to Block Terrorists' Assets," *The Wall Street Journal*, April 11, 2002.

[36] H. Simonian, "Germany Plans Central Bank Account Register," *Financial Times*, October 6/7, 2001. The proposal for an international deposit registry was developed in Philippe Scharf, "Money Laundering, Terrorist Financing and the Global Financial System: Structure, Evolution and Proposals to Ameliorate and Protect the System," LL.M. Paper, Harvard Law School, May 2002 (on file with the author).

[37] United States Senate, Permanent Subcommittee on Investigations, Committee on Homeland Security and Governmental Affairs, *Money Laundering and Foreign Corruption: Enforcement and Effectiveness of the Patriot Act* (March 16, 2005).

[38] R. Blackwell, "Debate Over Mandatory Bank-to-Bank Warnings," *American Banker*, March 21, 2005.

who was a Pakistani student from Germany, deposited substantial funds in a U.S. bank, and that bank filed a SAR. The FBI could check with German authorities as to whether the individual had funds in a German bank account. If not, further enforcement measures could be taken. Further, suppose that this same student committed an act of terrorism in the U.S. Law enforcement agencies would be able to determine in which countries the individual had accounts. This assumes that terrorists would only be able to open accounts under their real identities, perhaps a heroic assumption. Difficult issues would be encountered in establishing which law enforcement agencies, and perhaps in limited circumstances which financial institutions, would be granted access to these databases, and under what conditions such access would be granted.

A third possibility, apparently being considered by a working group within the Treasury, would give the government access to logs of international wire transfers in and out of U.S. banks. Authority for such a measure was granted in the intelligence reform bill passed by Congress in December 2004.[39] This would allow the government to monitor all transfers of funds in dollars, and conceivably on a real time basis, as the legislation authorizes the Treasury to request the "report...of certain cross-border electronic transmittal of funds. ..." There are reportedly a half-billion international wire transfers a year—Fincen would have to create a profile of those that were possibly linked to terrorists.[40]

A third possibility would be to try to eliminate informal payment mechanisms like Hawala, which bypass the official banking system. Such elimination would obviously be quite difficult. However, one could try to increase the costs of such system by steering legitimate transactions into the formal system through reducing the costs of holding accounts and through educational initiatives. With fewer legitimate transactions, the costs of maintaining such networks for illegitimate transactions would increase. Saudi Arabian, in cooperation with the United States, has adopted such measures in 2003-2004.[41]

Two further possibilities are much more radical, contemplating fundamental changes in the current international banking system. The U.S. could prohibit second tier correspondent banking in the United States. Thus no foreign bank could access the U.S. payment system without holding an account directly in the United States. U.S. banks would be required to obtain assurances from all foreign banks whose accounts it held that that bank was not accessing its U.S. account on behalf of any other foreign bank. Thus, if a Bank in Somalia wanted to access the U.S. payment system it would have to

---

[39] Public Law 108-458, December 17, 2004, §6302.

[40] E. Lichtblau, "U.S. Seeks Access to Bank Records to Deter Terror," *The New York Times*, April 10, 2005.

[41] Testimony of Juan C. Zarate before the U.S. House International Relations Subcommittee on the Middle East and Central Asia, March 24, 2004.

hold an account with a U.S. bank. If the Treasury believed that such a bank, or Somalia itself, was not adequately complying with anti-terrorist funding policies, such an account could be prohibited. The Secretary has this power today under the PATRIOT Act, but it is unlikely that the Bank of Somalia would ever hold a direct correspondent account in the U.S. It is free under the existing regime to access the U.S. indirectly.

This proposal founders largely on the cost it would impose on international banking. It is more efficient for many small foreign banks to hold accounts with foreign correspondents rather than to establish direct access to the U.S. banking system. The same pattern obtains within the U.S. where a small country bank in Pennsylvania that receives wire transfers for its customers from a California bank will do so through an account at a Philadelphia bank rather than opening an account with the California bank. Further, foreign banks currently serving as correspondent banks for smaller foreign banks would vigorously oppose such a measure because of the loss of business. Of course, such added costs should properly be weighed against the terrorist savings.

One could envision another radical change. Cash could be banned entirely in favor of electronic banking systems that permitted the tracking of transactions. A step along this road would be to ban cash transactions (not just require reporting) of over relatively small amounts. Without cash, terrorists could arguably be more easily tracked. These kind of more radical solutions will only be seriously considered if the cost of terrorism increases dramatically.

Notes and Questions

1. Do you think the difference between money laundering and terrorist funding requires different policies in combating them?

2. How effective do you think current U.S. policies on anti-terrorist funding will be in significantly reducing such funding?

3. Should we favor the development of internationally linked central registries of bank accounts? Would it be more effective than current policies? What costs would it impose on the system? Would you favor any other more radical changes?

B.   FREEZING TERRORIST ASSETS

An important weapon in the war on terrorist finances is the freezing of accounts. This section begins with an account of Libyan Arab Foreign Bank v. Manufacturers Hanover Trust Co. (*LAFB*).[42]

---

[42] [1998] 1 Lloyd's Law Reports 259, QBD.

1.   THE LAFB LITIGATION

In *Libyan Arab Foreign Bank v. Bankers Trust Co. (LAFB)*, an English court held that the United States freeze of Libyan assets in American banks could not block a Libyan bank's $131 million Eurodollar call account at Bankers Trust Company's London branch. The same issues had been previously raised but not resolved in litigation involving the 1979 United States freeze of Iranian assets. Various lawsuits in France, England, West Germany, and Turkey, involving $5.6 billion in foreign deposits held at American banks, were dropped when the hostages were released. The Libyan asset freeze, imposed in January 1986 as a response to state-sponsored terrorism, was in effect until September 2004 when the U.S. and Libya normalized their relations. No appeal was taken from the Commercial Court's decision since the United States, in November 1987, issued a license permitting Bankers Trust to pay Libyan Arab Foreign Bank its funds.

The LAFB v. Bankers Trust case follows:

Mr. Justice STAUGHTON

The plaintiffs are a Libyan corporation, wholly owned by the Central Bank of Libya. They carry on what is described as an offshore banking business, in the sense that they do not engage in domestic banking within Libya. I shall call them "the Libyan Bank." The defendants are a New York corporation with their head office there. They no doubt have a number of branches in various parts of the world; but I am concerned with one in particular, their branch in London. I shall refer to them as "Bankers Trust," and when it is necessary to refer to particular offices as "Bankers Trust London" or "Bankers Trust New York."

In January 1986 the Libyan Bank had an account with Bankers Trust London, denominated in United States Dollars. That was a call account, which meant that no cheque book was provided, interest was payable on the balance standing to the credit of the account at rates which varied from time to time, and some minimal period of notice might be required before instructions relating to the account had to be complied with. The suggestion in this case is that instructions would have to be given before noon if they were to be carried out that day. In English practice it would, I think be described as a species of deposit account. The amount standing to the credit of that account at the close of business on 8 January 1986 was U.S. $131,506,389.93. There may be a small element of subsequent adjustment in that figure. But the point is not material.

The Libyan Bank also had an account with Bankers Trust New York, again denominated in United States dollars. This was a demand account. No interest was paid on the balance, and no significant period of notice was required before instructions had to be complied with. But there was not, so far as I am aware, a cheque book. In England it would have been a current account. The amount standing to the credit of that account at the close of business on 8 January 1986 was U.S. $251,129,084.53.

Relations between Libya and the United States in January 1986 were not good. At 8.06 p.m. New York time on 7 January the President of the United States of America issued an executive order, which had the force of law with immediate effect. It provided, so far as material:

"Section 1. The following are prohibited, except to the extent provided in regulations which may hereafter be issued pursuant to this Order: ... (f) The grant or extension of credits or loans by any United States person to the Government of Libya, its instrumentalities and controlled entities."

That order did not in itself have any great effect on the events with which this case is concerned. But there followed it at 4.10 p.m. New York time on 8 January a second order, reading as follows:

"I, Ronald Reagan, President of the United States, hereby order blocked all property and interests in property of the Government of Libya, its agencies, instrumentalities and controlled entities and the Central Bank of Libya that are in the United States that hereafter come within the United States or that are or hereafter come within the possession or control of U.S. persons including overseas branches of U.S. persons. The Secretary of the Treasury, in consultation with the Secretary of State, is authorized to employ all powers granted to me by the International Emergency Economic Powers Act 50 U.S.C. 1701 et seq. to carry out the provisions of this Order. This Order is effective immediately and shall be transmitted to the Congress and published in the Federal Register.

Ronald Reagan

The White House
8 January 1986

It is not in dispute that Bankers Trust are a United States person; or that Bankers Trust London are an overseas branch of a United States person; or that the Libyan Bank are an agency, instrumentality or controlled entity of the Government of Libya. Consequently by the law of and prevailing in the State of New York (which I shall refer to as New York law for the sake of brevity) it was illegal at and after 4.10 p.m. on 8 January 1986 for Bankers Trust to make any payment or transfer of funds to or to the order of the Libyan Bank in New York, either by way of debit to the Libyan Bank's account or as the grant of credit or a loan. Similarly it was illegal, by the law of New York or of any other American state, for Bankers Trust to make any such payment or transfer of funds in London or anywhere else.

The United Kingdom Parliament did not enact any similar legislation. No doubt there were reasons of high policy for that forbearance; but with them I am not concerned. It is sufficient to say that nothing in English domestic law prohibited such a transaction. So the main issues in this case are concerned with the rules of conflict of laws, which determine when and to what extent the law of New York is given effect in our courts, and with the contractual obligations of banks. In a word, Bankers Trust say that they cannot, or at any rate are not obliged to, transfer a sum as large as U.S. $100m. or more without using the payment machinery that is available in New York; consequently they have a defence to the Libyan Bank's claim, because performance of this contract would have required them to commit an illegal act in New York. Alternatively they say that their contract with the Libyan Bank is governed by the law of New York, so that performance is for the time being illegal by the proper law of the contract.

The Libyan Bank's claims

These are as follows (using a slightly different system of numbering from that adopted in the pleadings and in argument):

(1) The first claim is for the balance of U.S. $131,506,389.93 standing to the credit of the London account at the close of business on 8 January 1986. It is said that this sum is due to the Libyan Bank, and can be claimed on a cause of action in debt. Alternatively it is said that Bankers Trust ought to have responded to demands for U.S. $131m. that were made by the Libyan Bank in various different ways after 8 January, and are liable in damages.

(2) If they are right on the first claim, the Libyan Bank further say that one or other of three sums ought to have been transferred from the New York account to the London account on 7 and 8 January, thus increasing the amount which they are entitled to recover. These are: (i) U.S. $165,200,000 on 7 January, *or* (ii) U.S. $6,700,000 on 8 January, *or* (iii) U.S. $161,400,000 on 8 January. Indeed it is said that the sum of U.S. $6,700,000 was in fact transferred to London on 8 January, with the consequence that the Libyan Bank are in any event entitled to recover that additional amount.

(3) Largely but not entirely as an alternative to the second claim, the Libyan Bank say that they gave a number of payment instructions to Bankers Trust New York for execution on 8 January, those instructions could and should have been executed before 4.10 p.m. on that day, but were not. Consequently the Libyan Bank claim damages in the sum of U.S. $226,147,213.88.

. . .

History of the banking relationship

This can be considered in three stages. The first stage was from 1972 to 15 December 1980.

The Libyan Bank came into existence in June 1972. A correspondent relationship was established between the Libyan Bank and Bankers Trust. Initially an account was opened for that purpose with the Paris branch of Bankers Trust. But in April 1973 that account was closed, and an account opened with the London branch. It was described as a 7-day notice account. However, any requirement that notice of that length should be given before debits were allowed on the London account was not enforced. In this period the Libyan Bank did not wish to have any account with Bankers Trust New York.

.   .   .

In 1980 [a new] proposal was more actively pursued. At first it was suggested by Bankers Trust that the current account should be in London. But by the time of a meeting in New York on 7 July it was again proposed that there should be a demand account there. Following that meeting Bankers Trust wrote from London to the Libyan Bank with details of the proposed managed account system:

> "We will establish a 'peg' (or target) balance for the demand account of U.S. $750,000. That amount is intended to compensate Bankers Trust Co. for the services which we expect to provide, and is subject to periodic renegotiation as appropriate, for example when our costs increase, when interest rates decline significantly or when our level of servicing is materially changed. Each morning our account management team will review the demand account's closing book balance from the previous business day. If that balance is in excess of the 'peg,' they will transfer in multiples of U.S. $100,000 the excess amount to your call account in London with value the previous business day.
>
> "Similarly, if the demand account balance is below the U.S. $750,000 peg, they will transfer funds back from your call account with value the previous business day.... As you can appreciate, our account management team must closely follow the balance in your call account. Given time zone differences with London, all entries to your call account must be passed by that team in New York, and all your instructions to effect payments or foreign exchange settlements must be directed to our money transfer department in New York."

The figure of U.S. $750,000 as the peg balance was later agreed at U.S. $500,000.

There was some discussion of political risk at the New York meeting. I am confident that political risk was at any rate in the minds of both parties, seeing that the freeze on Iranian assets had occurred only eight months previously. Mr. Abduljawad, then deputy chairman, is recorded as saying: "Placing at call is not an effort to avoid political risk, which he believes to be unavoidable." Whilst I accept that record as accurate, I also accept Mr. Abduljawad's oral evidence that "political risk is always being taken into consideration." Mr. Van Voorhees, who was among those attending the meeting on behalf of Bankers Trust, accepted that the Iranian crisis was at the back of everyone's mind in 1980.

. . .

It was, as I find, a term of that arrangement that all the Libyan Bank's transactions should pass through New York.   Although not mentioned in the correspondence by which agreement was ultimately reached, this had plainly been a requirement of Bankers Trust throughout the later stages of the negotiations, and I conclude that it was tacitly accepted by the Libyan Bank. It was virtually an essential feature of the system: Bankers Trust New York would know about and rely on the credit balance in London in deciding what payments could be made from New York; they might be exposed to risk if the balance in London could be reduced without their knowledge. It was argued that such a term is not to be found in the pleadings of Bankers Trust; but in my judgment it is, in paragraph 3(4)(v) of the re-re-amended points of defence. There remains an important question whether the managed account arrangement was irrevocable, or whether it could be determined. I shall consider that later.

The second stage [of the arrangement] ran from December 1980 to November 1985. Before very long Bankers Trust took the view that the remuneration which they received from the relationship, in the form of an interest-free balance of between U.S. $500,000 and U.S. $599,999 in New York, was insufficient reward for their services. On 15 March 1983 they proposed an increase in the peg balance to $1.5m. Negotiations continued for a time but without success. By 15 March 1984 Bankers Trust had formed the view that the Libyan Bank would not agree to an increase in the peg balance; so, on 3 April 1984, they decided unilaterally on a different method of increasing the profitability of the relationship for Bankers Trust; and it was put into effect on 17 April.

The new method required a consideration of the balance on the New York account at 2 p.m. each day. If it exceeded the peg balance of U.S. $500,000 the excess was transferred in multiples of U.S. $100,000 to the London account with value that day. Consideration was also given on the following morning to the balance at the close of the previous day. If it was less than the peg balance, a transfer of the appropriate amount was made from London to New York on the next day, with value the previous business day; if it was more than the peg balance there was, it seems, a transfer to London with value the same day. The effect of the change was that the Libyan Bank lost one day's interest whenever (i) credits received after 2 p.m. exceeded payments made after 2 p.m., and

(ii) the closing balance for the day would under the existing arrangements have required a transfer (or a further transfer if one had been made at 2 p.m.) to be made with value that day. If a weekend intervened, three days interest might be lost. I am not altogether sure that I have stated the effect of the change correctly; but precision as to the details is not essential.

. . .

7 and 8 January 1986

At 2 p.m. on 7 January the balance to the credit of the New York account was U.S. $165,728,000. (For present purposes I use figures rounded down to the nearest U.S. $1,000, save where greater accuracy is desirable.) Subject to two points which I shall consider later; a transfer of $165.2m. should then have been made to London. Mr. Fabien Arnell, an account manager of Bankers Trust New York says somewhat laconically in his statement.

> "On 7 January 1986 I instructed the managed account clerk not to make a 2 p.m. investment. I cannot now recall the precise reason why I gave that instruction."

During the rest of that day there were substantial transfers out of the New York account, with the result that it would have been overdrawn to the extent of $157,925,000 if the 2 p.m. transfer had been made. There would then have had to be a recall of U.S. $158,500,000 from London on 8 January, with value the previous business day, to restore the peg balance. As no 2 p.m. transfer had been made, the closing balance was in fact U.S. $7,275,000 in credit.

On the morning of 8 January there was an amount of $6,700,000 available to transfer to London. The same amount would have been left as a net credit to the London account if $165.2m. had been transferred at 2 p.m. on 7 January and $158.5m. recalled on 8 January with value the previous day. An instruction for the transfer of U.S. $6,700,000 was prepared. But in the event the computer which kept the accounts in New York was not ordered to effect this transfer, nor was the London branch informed of it.

At 2 p.m. on 8 January the balance to the credit of the New York account was U.S. $161,997,000. After deducting the peg balance of U.S. $500,000 there was a sum of U.S. $161,400,000 available to transfer to London. No transfer was made. Those figures assume, as was the fact, that U.S. $6,700,000 had not been transferred to London in respect of the excess opening balance on that day.

Bankers Trust New York had received payment instructions totalling U.S. $347,147,213.03 for execution on 8 January. All of them had been received by 8.44 a.m. New York time. None of them were executed, for reasons which I shall later explain. (In case it is thought that not even the combined London and New York accounts could have sustained such payments, I should mention that substantial credits were received in New York during 8 January for the account of the Libyan Bank. If all the payment instructions had been implemented, there would still at the end of the day have been a net balance due to the Libyan Bank on the total of the two accounts).

In the hope of rendering those figures somewhat more intelligible, I set out a summary of the actual state of the New York account on 7 and 8 January 1986, with notes:

	U.S.	
Balance at 2 p.m. 7 January	$165,728,000	(1)
Post 2 p.m. operations	(158,453,000)	
Opening balance 8 January	7,275,000	(2)
Receipts before 2 p.m.	154,722,000	
Balance at 2 p.m. 8 January	161,997,000	(3)
Receipts after 2 p.m.	89,132,000	(4)
Closing balance 8 January	251,129,000	

Notes:
(1) $165.2m. available for transfer to London
(2) $6.7m. available for transfer
(3) $161.4m. available for transfer
(4)   This figure contains some minor adjustments of no consequence.

Next I turn to the Civil Evidence Act statement of Mr. Brittain, the chairman of Bankers Trust. Late in the afternoon of 7 January he received a telephone call from Mr. Corrigan, the president of the Federal Reserve Bank of New York. Mr. Corrigan asked that Bankers Trust should pay particular attention on the next day to movement of funds on the various Libyan accounts held by Bankers Trust, and report anything unusual to him.

Late in the morning of the next day Mr. Brittain informed the New York Fed. (as it is sometimes called) that "it looked like the Libyans were taking their money out of the various accounts." (So far as the Libyan Bank were concerned, it will be remembered that they had already given instructions for payments totalling over U.S. $347m. on that day.) Later Mr. Brittain learnt that sufficient funds were coming in to cover the payment instructions; he telephoned Mr. Corrigan and told him that the earlier report had been a false alarm. Mr. Corrigan asked Mr. Brittain not to make any payments out of the accounts for the time being, and said that he would revert later.

That assurance was repeated several times during the early afternoon. Mr. Brittain's statement continues:

"Finally I telephoned Mr. Corrigan at about 3:30 p.m. and told him that we now had sufficient funds to cover the payments out of the various Libyan accounts and were going to make them. Mr.

> Corrigan's response to this was, 'You'd better call Baker' (by which he meant the Secretary of the United States Treasury, Mr. James A. Baker III). I said that I would release the payments and then speak to Mr. Baker. Mr. Corrigan's reply to this was. 'You'd better call Baker first'."

Mr. Brittain was delayed for some 20 minutes talking to Mr. Baker and to an assistant secretary of the Treasury on the telephone. Then at approximately 4.10 to 4.16 p.m. Mr. Baker said: "The President has signed the order, you can't make the transfers."

Mr. Brittain adds in his statement that this was the first occasion on which he became aware that an order freezing the assets was contemplated. In a note made a few weeks after 8 January he adds: "That is how naive I was." I am afraid that I can but agree with Mr. Brittain's description of himself. It seems to me that a reasonable banker on the afternoon of 8 January would have realised, in the light of the first executive order made on the previous day, the requests of Mr. Corrigan, and particularly his saying "You'd better call Baker first," that a ban on payments was a distinct possibility.

There is other evidence as to Mr. Brittain's telephone conversations. First, Mr. Blenk was in Mr. Brittain's office and heard what was said by him. There was not, it seems, any reference by name to Libyan Arab Foreign Bank, but merely to "the Libyans," which meant some six Libyan entities (including the Libyan Bank) which had accounts with Bankers Trust. Secondly, Mr. Sandberg, a senior vice-president of the Federal Reserve Bank of New York, heard Mr. Corrigan's end of the conversations. He accepted in evidence that the New York Fed. probably knew which Libyan banks held accounts with Bankers Trust.

(1) The U.S. $131 million claim

(a) Conflict of laws—the connecting factor

There is no dispute as to the general principles involved. Performance of a contract is excused if (i) it has become illegal by the proper law of the contract, or (ii) it necessarily involves doing an act which is unlawful by the law of the place where the act has to be done. I need cite no authority for that proposition (least of all my own decision in Euro-Diam Ltd. v. Bathurst [1987] 2 W.L.R. 1368, 1385) since it is well established and was not challenged. Equally it was not suggested that New York law is relevant because it is the national law of Bankers Trust, or because payment in London would expose Bankers Trust to sanctions under the United States legislation, save that Mr. Sumption for Bankers Trust desires to keep the point open in case this dispute reaches the House of Lords.

There may, however, be a difficulty in ascertaining when performance of the contract "necessarily involves" doing an illegal act in another country. In *Toprak Mahsullerr Ofisi v. Finagrain Compagnie Commerciale Agricole et Financière S.A.* [1979] 2 Lloyd's Rep. 98,

Turkish buyers of wheat undertook to open a letter of credit "with and confirmed by a first class United States or West European bank." The buyers were unable to obtain exchange control permission from the Turkish Ministry of Finance to open a letter of credit, and maintained that it was impossible for them to open a letter of credit without exporting money from Turkey. It was held that this was no answer to a claim for damages for nonperformance of the contract. Lord Denning M.R. said, at p. 114:

> "In this particular case the place of performance was not Turkey. Illegality by the law of Turkey is no answer whatever to this claim. The letter of credit had to be a confirmed letter of credit, confirmed by a first-class West European or U.S. bank. The sellers were not concerned with the machinery by which the Turkish state enterprise provided that letter of credit at all. The place of performance was not Turkey.

> "This case is really governed by the later case of Kleinwort, Sons & Co. v. Ungarische Baumwolle Industrie Aktiengesellschaft [1939] 2 K.B. 678 where bills of exchange were to be given and cover was to be provided in London, but at the same time there was a letter saying, 'We have to get permission from Hungary.' It was said that because of the illegality by Hungarian law in obtaining it, that would be an answer to the case. But Branson J. and the Court of Appeal held that the proper law of the contract was English law; and, since the contract was to be performed in England, it was enforceable in the English courts even though its performance might involve a breach by the defendants of the law of Hungary.

> "That case has been quoted in all the authorities as now settling the law.... The only way that Mr. Johnson (for the Turkish state enterprise) could seek to escape from that principle was by saying—' ... Although there was no term, express or implied, in the contract that anything had to be done in Turkey as a term of the contract, nevertheless it was contemplated by both parties. It was contemplated by both parties that the Turkish buyers would have to go through the whole sequence in Turkey of getting exchange control permission, and all other like things: and, if the contemplated method of performance became illegal, that would be an answer. Equally, if it became impossible, that would be a frustration.'

> "I am afraid that those arguments do not carry the day. It seems to me in this contract, where the letter of credit had to be a confirmed letter of credit—confirmed by a West European or U.S. bank—the sellers are not in the least concerned as to the method by which the Turkish buyers are to provide that letter of credit. Any troubles or difficulties in Turkey are extraneous to the matter and do not afford any defence to an English contract ... "

From that case I conclude that it is immaterial whether one party has to equip himself for performance by an illegal act in another country. What matters is whether performance itself necessarily involves such an act. The Turkish buyers might have had money anywhere in the world which they could use to open a letter of credit with a United States or West European bank. In fact it would seem that they only had money in Turkey, or at any rate needed to comply with Turkish exchange control regulations if they were to use any money they may have had outside Turkey. But that was no defence, as money or a permit was only needed to equip themselves for performance, and not for performance itself.

. . .

Some difficulty may still be encountered in the application of that principle. For example, if payment in dollar bills in London was required by the contract, it would very probably have been necessary for Bankers Trust to obtain such a large quantity from the Federal Reserve Bank of New York, and ship it to England. That, Mr. Sumption accepts, would not have been an act which performance necessarily involved; it would merely have been an act by Bankers Trust to equip themselves for performance as in the Toprak case. By contrast, if the contract required Bankers Trust to hand over a banker's draft to the Libyan Bank in London, Mr. Sumption argues that an illegal act in New York would necessarily be involved, since it is very likely that the obligation represented by the draft would ultimately be honoured in New York. I must return to this problem later.

(b) The proper law of the contract

As a general rule the contract between a bank and its customer is governed by the law of the place where the account is kept, in the absence of agreement to the contrary. Again there was no challenge to that as a general rule; the fact that no appellate decision was cited to support it may mean that it is generally accepted. However, since the point is of some importance, I list those authorities that were cited. They are X A.G. v. A Bank [1983] 2 All E.R. 464; Mackinnon v. Donaldson, Lufkin & Jenrette Securities Corporation [1986] Ch. 482, 494; Dicey & Morris, The Conflict of Laws, 11th ed. (1987), p. 1292, n. 51; Rabel, The Conflict of Laws, 2nd ed., p. 17; American Law Institute, Restatement of the Law, Conflict of Laws 2d, vol. 4 (1979), para. 622, and the Memorandum of Law in the Wells Fargo case which I have referred to, and the Lexis report of judgment in that action.

That rule accords with the principle, to be found in the judgment of Atkin L.J. in N. Joachimson v. Swiss Bank Corporation [1921] 3 K.B. 110, 127, and other authorities, that a bank's promise to repay is to repay at the branch of the bank where the account is kept.

In the age of the computer it may not be strictly accurate to speak of the branch where the account is kept. Banks no longer have books in which they write entries; they have terminals by which they give instructions; and the computer itself with its magnetic tape, floppy disc or some other device may be physically located elsewhere. Nevertheless it should not be difficult to decide where an account is kept for this purpose, and it is not in the present case. The actual entries on the London account were, as I understand it, made in London, albeit on instructions from New York after December 1980. At all events I have no doubt that the London account was at all material times "kept" in London.

· · ·

In my judgment, the true view is that after December 1980 there was one contract, governed in part by the law of England and in part by the law of New York.

· · ·

I hold that the rights and obligations of the parties in respect of the London account were governed by English law.

· · ·

(d) Means of transfer

The credit balance of the Libyan Bank with Bankers Trust constituted a personal right, a chose in action. At bottom there are only two means by which the fruits of that right could have been made available to the Libyan Bank. The first is by delivery of cash, whether dollar bills or any other currency, to or to the order of the Libyan Bank. The second is the procuring of an account transfer. (I leave out of account the delivery of chattels, such as gold, silver or works of art, since nobody has suggested that Bankers Trust were obliged to adopt that method. The same applies to other kinds of property, such as land.)

An account transfer means the process by which some other person or institution comes to owe money to the Libyan Bank or their nominee, and the obligation of Bankers Trust is extinguished or reduced pro tanto. "Transfer" may be a somewhat misleading word, since the original obligation is not assigned (notwithstanding dicta in one American case which speak of assignment); a new obligation by a new debtor is created.

· · ·

(e) Particular forms of transfer

I set out below those which have been canvassed in this case, and discuss the extent to which they involve activity in the United States.

(i) In-house transfer at Bankers Trust London

This is quite simple, as has been explained. It involves no action in the United States. But it cannot take place unless the Libyan Bank are able to nominate some beneficiary who also has an account with Bankers Trust London.

(ii) Correspondent bank transfer

Again, this is relatively simple and involves no action in the United States. But for it to be effective in this case a bank must be found outside the United States where two conditions are satisfied: the first is that Bankers Trust have a credit balance there of U.S. $131m. or more; the second, that an account is also held there for the Libyan Bank or for some beneficiary whom they nominate.

(iii) C.H.I.P.S. or Fedwire

These are two methods of complex account transfer which are used for a high proportion of large dollar transactions. They can only be completed in the United States.

[a description of other less relevant forms of transfer is omitted]

. . .

(ix) Cash—dollar bills

I am told that the largest notes in circulation are now for U.S. $100, those for U.S. $500 having been withdrawn. Hence there would be formidable counting and security operations involved in paying U.S. $131m. by dollar bills. Bankers Trust would not have anything like that amount in their vault in London. Nor, on balance, do I consider that they would be likely to be able to obtain such an amount in Europe. It could be obtained from a Federal Reserve Bank and sent to London by aeroplane, although several different shipments would be made to reduce the risk. The operation would take some time—up to seven days.

Banks would seek to charge for this service, as insurance and other costs would be involved, and they would suffer a loss of interest from the time when cash was withdrawn from the Federal Reserve Bank to the time when it was handed over the counter and the customer's account debited—assuming that the customer had an interest-bearing account. I cannot myself see any basis on which a bank would be entitled to charge, although there might be a right to suspend payment of interest. If a bank chooses, as all banks do for their own purposes, not to maintain a sum equal to all its liabilities in the form of cash in its vaults, it must bear the expense involved in obtaining cash when a demand is made which it is obliged to meet. If a customer demanded U.S. $1,000 or U.S. $10,000 in cash, I do not see how a charge could be made. When the sum is very much larger it is an important question—which I shall consider later—whether the bank is obliged to meet a demand for cash at all. If it is so obliged, there is not, in my opinion, any right to charge for fulfilling its obligation.

As I have already mentioned, it is accepted that there would be no breach of New York law by Bankers Trust in obtaining such an amount of cash in New York and despatching it to their London office.

(x) Cash—sterling

There would be no difficulty for Bankers Trust in obtaining sterling notes from the Bank of England equivalent in value to U.S. $131m., although, once again, there would be counting and security problems. Bankers Trust would have to reimburse the Bank of England, or the correspondent through whom it obtained the notes, and this would probably be done by a transfer of dollars in New York. But, again, it was not argued that such a transfer would infringe New York law.

(f) Termination of the managed account arrangement

Those means of transfer are all irrelevant so long as the managed account arrangement subsists; for I have found it to be a term of that arrangement that all the Libyan Bank's transactions should pass through New York. Apart from some minor teething problems at the start in 1980, that term was observed. The only entries on the London call account were credits from, or debits to, the New York demand account. It was the New York account that was used to make payments to, or receive credits from, others with whom the Libyan Bank had business relations. If the arrangement still exists, the London account can only be used to transfer a credit to New York, which would be of no benefit whatever to the Libyan Bank.

In my judgment, the Libyan Bank was entitled unilaterally to determine the managed account arrangement on reasonable notice, which did not need to be more than 24 hours (Saturdays, Sundays and non-banking days excepted). The important feature of the arrangement from the point of view of Bankers Trust was that their operators could make payments in New York, on occasion giving rise to an overdraft in New York, safe in the knowledge that there was a credit balance in London which they could call upon and which would not disappear. If it were determined, Bankers Trust New York would be entitled to refuse to make payments which would put the account there into overdraft. For the Libyan Bank an important feature was that they obtained both the speed and efficiency with which current account payments could be made in New York, and the advantage of an account in London bearing interest at Eurodollar rates. If the arrangement were determined and the Libyan Bank began once again to use the London account as if it were a current account, Bankers Trust would be entitled (again on notice) to reduce the rate of interest payable on that account, or to decline to pay interest altogether.

. . .

What, then, was the position after determination? The New York account remained, as it always had been, a demand account. Subject to New York law, Bankers Trust were obliged to make transfers in accordance with the Libyan Bank's instructions to the extent of the credit balance, but they were not obliged to allow an overdraft—even a daylight overdraft, as it is called when payments in the course of a day exceed the credit balance but the situation is restored by further credits before the day ends. The London account remained an interest-bearing account from which Bankers Trust were obliged to make transfers on the instructions of the Libyan Bank, provided that no infringement of United States law in the United States was involved. If Bankers Trust became dissatisfied with the frequency of such transfers, they were, as I have said, entitled on notice to reduce the rate of interest or bring the account to an end. And if I had not held that the rights and obligations of the parties in respect of the London account were governed by English law at all times, I would have been inclined to hold that they were once more governed by English law when the managed account arrangement was determined, although there is clearly some difficulty in recognising a unilateral right to change the system of law governing part of the relations between the parties.

(g) Implied term and usage

It is said in paragraph 4(2) of the re-re-amended points of defence that there was an implied term that transfer of funds from the London account, whether or not effected through the New York account

> "would be effected by instructing a transfer to be made by the defendants' New York Head Office through a United States clearing system to the credit of an account with a bank or a branch of a bank in the United States nominated or procured to be nominated by or on behalf of the plaintiffs for that purpose."

In other words, of the various forms of transfer which I have mentioned, only C.H.I.P.S. or Fedwire were permitted. That term is said to be implied (i) from the usage of the international market in Eurodollars, and (ii) from the course of dealing between the parties since 1980.

. . .

The high point of Bankers Trust's case on this issue lies in the expert report of Dr. Stigum from which I quote some brief extracts:

> "The usages and practices that apply to wholesale Eurodollar accounts are moreover, well understood by *all* wholesale participants in the Eurodollar market ... Cash transactions are a feature of only an insignificant portion of total Eurodollar deposits, namely those held by small retail accounts. At the

wholesale level, the Eurodollar market is understood by *all* participants to be a *strictly non-cash* market.... *All* wholesale Eurodollar transactions (these occurring not just in London, but in other centres around the world as well) must, unless they involve a movement of funds from one account at a given bank to another account at that same bank, be cleared in the United States. The reason for this custom and usage is that the ultimate effect of the clearing of a wholesale, Eurodollar transaction is to remove dollars from the reserve account of one bank at the Fed. to the reserve account of another bank at the Fed."

Even as it stands, that passage does not support the implied term pleaded, that transfers would be made "through a United States clearing system." However, it is fair to say that in the particulars of usage there were added by amendment to the points of defence the words "save where book transfers fail to be made between accounts at the same branch"—which would allow, as Dr. Stigum apparently does, both an in-house transfer and a correspondent bank transfer.

Dr. Stigum is an economist and not a banker. I did not find her oral evidence impressive. On the other hand, Mr. Osbourne, who was until 1985 an assistant general manager of Barclays Bank, did seem to me an impressive witness, whose evidence was very sound on most points. His views were inconsistent with the usage alleged, at any risk in the case of an account such as that of the Libyan Bank with Bankers Trust London.

Furthermore, the supposed usage was inconsistent with the course of dealing between the parties, to which I now turn. It is, of course, true that from December 1980 to January 1986 all transactions by the Libyan Bank were carried out in New York. That is not in itself proof of a course of dealing, since, as I have found, there was an express term to that effect—until the managed account arrangement was brought to an end. What happened between 1973 and December 1980? Fortunately the parties agreed to treat one month as a suitable sample. That was December 1979, in which there were 497 transactions. They have been analysed as follows:

"Entries generated internally by Bankers Trust London,
that is to say, mostly intra-branch transfers   15
London clearable bank drafts, London dollar clearing
eligible bank drafts   8
London dollar clearing bankers payments   1
Intra-branch transfers between Bankers Trust London
and accounts at Bankers Trust New York   68
Intra branch transfers between Bankers Trust London
and accounts at Bankers Trust Paris   3
Payments through Fedwire   13
Payments through C.H.I.P.S.   389."

There was still a slight dispute as to how the London/Paris transfers were effected but that is not material.

The vast majority of those transactions (402) were, as the suggested implied term required, through a United States clearing system. If one adds the in-house transfers of one kind or another in Bankers Trust, as Dr. Stigum's custom permits, the total reaches 488. But there were 9 transactions in that month alone (London bank drafts and a London banker's payment) which were not permitted, either by the implied terms which Bankers Trust allege or by Dr. Stigum's custom and usage, although they may very well have been for relatively small amounts.

I find difficulty in seeing how course of dealing by itself could support a negative implied term of the kind alleged. The phrase is often used to elucidate a contract or to add a term to it. But if course of dealing is to eliminate some right which the contract would otherwise confer, I would require evidence to show, not merely that the right had never been exercised, but also that the parties recognised that as between themselves no such right existed. In other words, there must be evidence establishing as between the parties what would be a usage if it applied to the market as a whole. But whether that be so or not, I find no implied term such as Bankers Trust allege to be established either by usage, or by course of dealing, or by both.

. . .

(h) Obligations in respect of the London account

Having considered and rejected the two methods by which Bankers Trust seek to limit their obligations in respect of the London account—that is, an express term from the managed account arrangement still subsisting, or an implied term—I have to determine what those obligations were. What sort of demands were the Libyan Bank entitled to make and Bankers Trust bound to comply with? As I said, earlier, it is necessary to distinguish between services which a bank is obliged to provide if asked, and services which many bankers do provide but are not obliged to.

. . .

I now turn again to the forms of transfer discussed in subsection (e) of this judgment, in order to consider in relation to each whether it was a form of transfer which the Libyan Bank were entitled to demand, whether it has in fact been demanded, and whether it would necessarily involve any action in New York.

. . .

(ix) Cash—dollar bills

Of course it is highly unlikely that anyone would want to receive a sum as large as $131m in dollar bills, at all events unless they were engaged in laundering the proceeds of crime. Mr. Osbourne said in his report:

> As to the demand for payment in cash, I regard this simply as the assertion of a customer's inalienable right. In practice, of course, where such a large sum is demanded in this manner, fulfilment of the theoretical right is unlikely, in my experience, to be achieved. A sensible banker will seek to persuade his customer to accept payment in some more convenient form, and I have yet to encounter an incident of this nature where an acceptable compromise was not reached, even where the sum was demanded in sterling.

I would substitute "fundamental" for "inalienable"; but in all other respects that passage accords with what, in my judgment, is the law. One can compare operations in futures in the commodity markets; everybody knows that contracts will be settled by the payment of differences, and not by the delivery of copper, wheat or sugar as the case may be; but an obligation to deliver and accept the appropriate commodity, in the absence of settlement by some other means, remains the legal basis of these transactions. So in my view every obligation in monetary terms is to be fulfilled, either by the delivery of cash, or by some other operation which the creditor demands and which the debtor is either obliged to, or is content to, perform. There may be a term agreed that the customer is not entitled to demand cash; but I have rejected the argument that there was any subsisting express term, or any implied term, to that effect. Mr. Sumption argued that an obligation to pay on demand leaves very little time for performance, and that U.S. $131m. could not be expected to be obtainable in that interval. The answer is that either a somewhat longer period must be allowed to obtain so large a sum, or that Bankers Trust would be in breach because, like any other banker they choose, for their own purposes, not to have it readily available in London.

Demand was in fact made for cash in this case, and it was not complied with. It has not been argued that the delivery of such a sum in cash in London would involve any illegal action in New York. Accordingly I would hold Bankers Trust liable on that ground.

(x) Cash-sterling

Dicey & Morris, The Conflict of Laws, 11th ed. state in Rule 210, at p. 1453:

> "If a sum of money expressed in a foreign currency is payable in England, it may be paid either in units of the money of account or in sterling at the rate of exchange at which units of the foreign

legal tender can, on the day when the money is paid, be bought in London...."

See also *Chitty on Contracts,* 25th ed., para. 2105.

"Where a debtor owes a creditor a debt expressed in foreign currency ... the general rule is that the debtor may choose whether to pay in the foreign currency in question or in sterling."

.   .   .

Given that a foreign currency debtor is entitled to choose between discharging his obligations in foreign currency or sterling, I consider that he should not be entitled to choose the route which is blocked and then claim that his obligation is discharged or suspended. I prefer the view that he must perform in one way or the other; so long as both routes are available he may choose; but if one is blocked, his obligation is to perform in the other.

.   .   .

(2) The claim that a further sum should have been transferred from New York

This arises in three different ways on the facts. First it is said that U.S. $165.2m. should have been transferred to London at 2 p.m. on 7 January 1986.

Bankers Trust have two answers to this claim. First they say that instructions had been received and were pending for further payments to be made on 7 January after 2 p.m., which exceeded the amount then standing to the credit of the New York account (and, for that matter, the London account as well). It was only because further receipts also occurred after 2 p.m. that the New York account ended the day with a credit balance of U.S. $7.275m., and the London account remained untouched.

Secondly, Bankers Trust say that, if they were obliged to make a transfer to London on 7 January, they could lawfully have postponed it until after 8:06 p.m. New York time, when the first Presidential order came into force. Thereafter, they say, the transfer would have been illegal because it would have left the New York account overdrawn and would have constituted the grant of credit or a loan to the Libyan Bank.

In my judgment both those arguments fail. The telex of 27 November 1986, from which I have already quoted, contained this passage:

Each day, at 2 p.m., the balance position of your account is determined and any credits received up to that time, less payments and less the peg balance, are immediately invested.

It is said that "payments" there are not confined to payments actually made, and include payments for which instructions were pending. In view of the precision with which the time of 2 p.m. is stated, and the word "immediately," I do not consider that to be right. Mr. Sumption argued that "immediately" is coloured (one might say contradicted) by the illustration given in the telex; but I do not agree. The argument that Bankers Trust were entitled to delay the transfer until after 8:06 p.m. also fails, for the same reason, and it is unnecessary to decide whether it would have been a breach of the first Presidential order to allow an overdraft in New York which was less than the credit balance in London. They would certainly have been entitled in any event not to make payments which exceeded the net credit balance of the two accounts. But after credits which were received during the afternoon there was no need to do that.

Mr. Sumption also argued that the passage in the telex set out above was merely an illustration of how the arrangement would work, and not part of the revised terms of the managed account arrangement. That argument I also reject.

Some attention was paid to the course of dealing on these points. Mr. Blackburn's evidence showed that there was no consistency in the treatment of unprocessed payments, sometimes they were taken into account in deciding whether a 2 p.m. transfer should be made, and at other times they were ignored. As to the actual timing of the transfer, it was always booked in New York on the same day, and in London on the following day with one day's back value. The important feature to my mind is that, so long as there was no legislative interference, it did not make any difference to the parties whether the actual transfer was made at 2 p.m. or at any time up to midnight. Banking hours in London had already ended. Nor did it necessarily make a difference whether unprocessed payments were taken into account; if they were not, and a debit balance in New York resulted at the end of the day, Bankers Trust would recall an appropriate amount next morning from London, with one day's back value. It was only when the Presidential orders came to be made that timing became important. Bankers Trust were, as I hold, in breach of contract in failing to transfer U.S. $165.2m. to London at 2 p.m. on 7 January.

If they had done so, they would have been entitled to recall U.S. $158.5m. from London next morning, so that the net loss to the London account was only U.S. $6.7m. Mr. Cresswell argues that, in practice, Bankers Trust only recalled sums from the London account late in the day, and therefore after 4:10 p.m. when the second Presidential order came into effect; a transfer from London would thereafter have been illegal. In point of fact that may well be correct. But I have no doubt at all that, if there had been a large overdraft on the New York account on the morning of 8 January 1986, Bankers Trust would on that particular day have recalled the appropriate sum from London with the utmost despatch.

No transfer to London having in fact been made on 7 January, and no recall the next morning, U.S. $6.7m. should then have been transferred, as the amount by which the New York balance exceeded the peg of U.S. $500,000. The only issue of potential importance here is whether the transfer was actually made. Although preparations were made for effecting the transfer, I am satisfied that it was countermanded and did not take effect. There is no need for me to decide precisely when the transfer ought to have been made, since that is subsumed in the next point.

The Libyan Bank's third complaint under this head is that, no transfers between New York and London having in fact been made at 2 p.m. on 7 January or in the morning of 8 January, the balance in New York at 2 p.m. on 8 January was U.S. $161,997,000. It is said that a sum of U.S. $161.4m. should then have been transferred to London. In answer to that Bankers Trust rely on points that are the same as, or similar to, those raised in respect of 2 p.m. on 7 January: they say that they were entitled to take pending payment instructions into account; and that they were entitled to delay payment until after 4:10 p.m. when the second Presidential order had been made, which certainly prohibited such a transfer. I reject both arguments for the reasons already given, based on the telex of 27 November 1985. It is true that if the pending payment instructions were to be executed in the afternoon, there were grounds for apprehension that the New York account would become overdrawn, which might be a breach of the first Presidential order, and even that the total of both accounts would be overdrawn, which would plainly be a breach of that order. The solution for Bankers Trust was not to execute those pending instructions unless and until further credits were received in New York. Some were in fact received—the New York account ended the day in credit to the extent of U.S. $251,129,000. Payment instructions for that day totalled U.S. $347,147,213.03, and none of them were in fact executed. So on any view the New York account would have been overdrawn if all had been executed, and that much more overdrawn if in addition U.S. $161.4m. had been transferred to London at 2 p.m. But the net total of the two accounts would still have been a credit balance. If Bankers Trust took the view that an overdraft on the New York account would itself be a breach of the Presidential order, and if they were right, the solution as I have said was to execute the pending instructions only as and when credits received permitted them to do so.

Accordingly I hold that (i) Bankers Trust were in breach of contract in failing to transfer U.S. $165.2m. to London at 2 p.m. on 7 January; (ii) if they had done that, they could and would have recalled U.S. $158.5m. from London in the morning of 8 January; but, (iii) on the assumption that both those steps had been taken, there would have been a further breach in failing to transfer U.S. $154.7m. to London at 2 p.m. on 8 January. (I trust that the calculation of this last figure is not too obscure. The 2 p.m. transfer on 8 January should have been U.S.

$161.4m. if *neither* of the previous transfers had been made—as in fact they were not. If they had both been made, the figure would have been reduced to U.S. $154.7m.)

The balance resulting from those three figures is a net loss to the London account of U.S. $161.4m. I hold that this must be added to the Libyan Bank's first claim, as an additional sum for which that claim would have succeeded but for breaches of contract by Bankers Trust. It is said that this loss is not recoverable, because it arose from a new intervening act and is too remote. In the circumstances as they were on 7 and 8 January I have no hesitation in rejecting that argument.

. . .

Conclusion

The Libyan Bank are entitled to recover U.S. $131m. on claim (1) and U.S. $161m. (the amount of their demand) on claim (2). Claims (3) and (4) fail. Claim (5) would have failed if it had been material. On claim (6) the Libyan Bank must have judgment for damages to be assessed.

Postscript

In August of this year there were 20 working days. Fourteen of them were entirely consumed in the preparation of this judgment. In those circumstances it is a shade disappointing to read in the press and elsewhere that High Court judges do no work at all in August or September and have excessively long holidays.

Judgment for plaintiffs.

Notes and Questions

1. The basic features of the managed account relationship are set out below:

New York	London
Operational Accounts	Investment Account
(for payments)	(Call account at LIBOR+)

Peg Arrangement

a. N.Y. balances in excess of $500k peg transferred daily at 2:00 p.m. N.Y. time to London account for same day value.

b. If at 2:00 p.m. N.Y. time, N.Y. balance below $500k peg, transfer from London account to N.Y. account, value previous day.

Transfer Mechanics (e.g. to London)

a. BTNY credits BTL branch on its books, with notice to BTL of amount.

b. BTL credits LAFB on its books.

What was the point of this arrangement for LAFB and for BT?

2. Let us look at some freeze basics. Let's start with the first freeze order of January 7, 1986. At 8:06 p.m. N.Y. time, President Reagan signed an Executive Order prohibiting "U.S. persons," which included foreign branches but not foreign subsidiaries of U.S. banks, from extending credit to certain Libyan entities. This prohibited BTNY or BTL from extending credit to LAFB.

At 2:00 p.m. that day, the N.Y. account had a balance of $165.7 million. Under the peg arrangement $165.2 mm (165.7– .5) should have been transferred to London account but was not. Why wasn't this transfer made?

The second freeze order came at 4:10 p.m. on January 8, 1986. At 8:44 a.m., BTNY had on hand $347.1 million in payment instructions. Why were none of these payments ever made? At 2:00 p.m., the N.Y. account had a balance of $161.997, but there was no transfer to the London account. Why not? How naive was Mr. Brittain?

When the freeze was imposed, there was $251.1mm in the N.Y. account and $131.5mm in the London account.

3. The second freeze order (1) prohibited transfers or cash withdrawals from Libyan accounts; (2) applied only to foreign branches of U.S. banks, not subsidiaries; (3) applied only to Dollar accounts; and (4) prohibited any transaction whose purpose or effect was to evade the freeze. Why didn't the U.S. impose the freeze order on foreign subsidiaries of U.S. bank holding companies or foreign currency accounts of foreign branches of U.S. banks?

4. There were various actors affected by the freeze: (1) the United States; (2) the United Kingdom; (3) U.S. banks (including BT); and (4) foreign banks. How did they view the benefits and costs of the freeze? Did they want it to be effective?

5. BT contended that there was an established usage that all dollar payments had to be made through the United States (New York). Why was this an important argument in the lawsuit? Was there such a usage? Are there ways to transfer Dollars abroad without going through the United States?

6. As a result of the court's decision, BT was required to pay LAFB approximately $300 million in Dollar cash or Sterling. How could BTL actually pay this judgment? Could the bank actually get the Dollar cash? If it couldn't get Dollars, why didn't BTL have a valid impossibility defense to its contractual obligation?

7. Do you think a London bank should be required to pay off Dollar accounts in Sterling if it can't do so with Dollars?

8. Could BT pay this judgment in Sterling without being subject to criminal penalties in the United States? Couldn't the United States (through

a U.S. court) enjoin BT from making the Sterling payment? If the United States did this, what legal remedies might LAFB pursue in the United Kingdom?

9. Judgment was given in Dollars, but the statutory judgment interest rate was 15 percent (near the market interest rate on sterling but considerably in excess of the 7 percent Dollar interest rate). What impact might this have had in persuading the Treasury to issue a license to BT— which Treasury, in fact, did—to enable BT to pay the judgment? Ironically, BT made the payment under the license through a CHIPS transfer.

2.   THE INEFFECTIVENESS OF UNILATERAL FREEZES

The *LAFB* case demonstrates that a freeze order must be multilateral to be effective. In that case it was the failure of the U.K. to adopt its own freeze order that made the U.S. freeze order ineffective. The U.S. claimed in *LAFB* that it should be able to exercise jurisdiction over Eurodollar accounts because all transfers of Dollars occur in the U.S. through the U.S. payment system, but the court found that not to be the case. For example, Dollar transfers between the accounts of two customers at the same foreign bank or foreign branch of a U.S. bank involve no movement of funds in the U.S.; nor do various correspondent bank transfers.[43]

Even if the U.S. could in fact stop Dollar transfers in the United States, the same would not be true for accounts in other currencies like the Euro, at non-U.S. banks, over which the U.S. has no power whatsoever. The U.S. needs the support of other countries to make freeze orders effective. Freezes following the Libyan freeze, like the one imposed on Iraq after Gulf War I, have been multilateral.

3.   TERRORIST ASSET FREEZES POST-9/11

Pursuant to Executive Order 13224, under the International Emergency Economic Powers Act, the U.S. has reportedly seized assets of $200 million from over 361 individuals and entities. With respect to terrorists, the major problem is knowing what accounts to freeze. This is an intelligence matter. It is much harder to identify terrorist accounts than to identify Libyan or Iraqi entity accounts since anyone may be a terrorist. The banks cannot tell you who the terrorists are (for the most part); they can just freeze accounts.

Islamic charities have been a key target of freeze orders. Five U.S. charities and 35 international charities have been identified, and Saudi charities have been principal offenders. Domestically a little over $8 million, and internationally about $20 million in terrorist-related charitable funds

---

[43] H. Scott, "Where Are the Dollars?—Offshore Funds Transfers" 3 Banking and Finance Law Review (1989), p. 243.

have been frozen. For example, Enaam Arnaout, the head of Benevolence International, a Chicago based Saudi charity, has been charged with supporting Al-Qaeda. He pled guilty in 2003 to the lesser offence of diverting funds raised for humanitarian purposes to Muslim fighters in Chechnya and Bosnia. There are some important individual rights questions involved in the freezing of terrorist assets. The PATRIOT legislation permits freezing assets of anyone associated with terrorists; association could be complicit or innocent. The U.S. has also used the I.R.S. that examines the tax-exempt status of charities to help law enforcement officials in policing terrorist use of charities. The U.S. has also spread its knowledge as to how charities can be misused to other countries.

Multilateral blocking of terrorist assets is achieved through a UN process, the so-called UN 1267 Committee. There are significant problems of implementing international freezes, in terms of different standards of proof of terrorism connections, the application of such orders to the legitimate work of charities that may have diverted some funds to terrorists, and basic disagreements over what is, in fact, terrorism, e.g. is Hamas a terrorist organization? These same problems plague even more limited bilateral or G7 coordinated assets freezes.

Unlike state frozen assets which may in the future be unfrozen and returned to the state, or made available to creditors or those whose assets have been expropriated by states, e.g. the case of Cuba or North Vietnam, it is not clear what should be done with frozen terrorist assets. A related question is which country, in a multilateral freeze, decides this.

A dispute arose in 2003 between the U.S. and the U.K. over the disposition of Iraqi assets that have been subject to freeze since the first Gulf War. There are reportedly $600 million in such assets frozen outside the U.S., with a significant amount in the U.K. The U.S. apparently demanded that all frozen assets, in the form of bank accounts, be turned over to the U.S. It is unclear whether such demand extended to just the U.K. branches of U.S. banks, or to U.S. subsidiaries of U.S. banking organizations, or to all banks.

4.   IRAQ

The U.S. and its allies continue to freeze Iraqi assets of Saddam Hussein and his confederates. These funds are transferred to the Development Fund for Iraq (DFI), to finance Iraq's recovery. About $2.6 billion in frozen assets have been transferred to DFI.

C.   REINSURANCE CRISIS

It has been estimated by the IMF that the U.S. cost of the 9/11 attack was $40 billion.[44] It is further estimated that $35 billion in these losses were covered by reinsurance, obligations of reinsurance companies to pay off on underlying insurance contracts. Actually, in the case of the World Trade Center's destruction, many reinsurance companies were primary insurers. Many of these reinsurers declared substantial losses in 2001 (over and above reserves). For example, Swiss Re declared a $118 million loss, its first in 135 years. Premium rates on renewals went up substantially for policies on which there was a terrorist risk. By mid-December, according to the Institute of Actuaries, rates for aviation insurance went up on average by 600-800 percent, while property and casualty rates generally rose by 50 percent and in some cases by 100 percent. In a bid to replenish losses and to take advantage of the new rates, the insurance industry, as of August 2002 had raised over $27 billion in new capital with over $12 billion in the pipeline.[45]

It is unclear to what extent projects are not proceeding due to the added risk of terrorism, either because of the added expense or the unavailability of insurance or reinsurance. The lack of affordable terrorist insurance does seem to have impacted the New York property market.[46] Outside New York, there did not appear to be any systematic evidence of a serious problem.[47] Nonetheless, there was much concern that the lack of available terrorist insurance would have negative impact on the national economy and on New York, in particular.

Terrorism is a type of extreme event, one that has a low probability of occurring but very large damages. There are other such events, like natural disasters, for which insurance or catastrophic bonds (bonds in which investors lose principal and/or interest in the event of a catastrophe) covers the risk. But as Kunreuther et al. have shown, terrorism is quite different than a natural catastrophe, see Table 21A below, in ways that make insurance or other forms of risk spreading more difficult.[48]

---

[44] J. Brown, R. Kroszner, and B. Jenn, "Federal Terrorism Risk Insurance" NBER Working Paper 9271 (October 2002).

[45] M. Sisk, "The Reinsurance Rush," U.S. Banker (August 2002), p. 36.

[46] P. Taylor, "Insurance Question Clouds NY Property Market," *Financial Times*, November 20, 2001.

[47] M. Miller, "No Terror Insurance, But Lenders Still Lending," *American Banker*, January 7, 2002.

[48] H. Kunreuther, E. Michel-Kerjan, and B. Porter, "Assessing, Managing, and Financing Extreme Events: Dealing with Terrorism" NBER Working Paper 10179 (December 2003), p. 7.

	Natural Hazards **Potential catastrophic** **losses**	**Terrorism Risks** **Potential catastrophic losses**
Historical Data	**Some historical data:** Record of several extreme events already occurred.	**No historical data:** 9/11 events were the first terrorist attacks worldwide with such a huge concentration of victims and insured damages.
Risk of Occurrence	**Risk reasonably well-specified:** Well-developed models for estimating risks based on historical data and experts' estimates.	**Considerable ambiguity of risk:** Terrorists can purposefully adapt their strategy (target, weapons, time) depending on their information on vulnerabilities; dynamic uncertainty.
Geographic Risk	**Specific areas at risk:** Some geographical areas are well known for being at risk (e.g., California for earthquakes or Florida for hurricanes).	**All areas at risk:** Some cities may be considered riskier than others (e.g., New York City, Washington), but terrorists may attack anywhere, any time.
Information	**Information sharing:** New scientific knowledge on natural hazards can be shared with all the stakeholders.	**Asymmetry of information:** Governments keep secret new information on terrorism for obvious national security reasons.
Event Type	**Natural event:** To date no one can influence the occurrence of an extreme natural event (e.g., an earthquake).	**Resulting event:** Governments can influence terrorism (e.g., foreign policy; international cooperation; national security measures).
Preparedness and Prevention	Insureds can invest in well-known mitigation measures.	Weapons and configurations are numerous. Negative externalities of self-protection effort; substitution effect in terrorist activity. Insureds may have difficulty in choosing measures to reduce consequences of an attack; Federal agencies may be in a better position to develop more efficient global mitigation programs.
Catastrophe Modeling	Developed in late 1980's and early 1990's.	The first models were developed in 2002.

Table 21A

Natural Hazards versus Terrorism Risks

On November 26, 2002, the Terrorism Risk Insurance Act (TRIA) became effective. It establishes a federal program that ends on December 31, 2005, of shared public and private compensation for insured commercial property and casualty losses resulting from terrorism. Under the program, the government reinsures 90 percent of losses from terrorism subject to substantial deductibles and a cap of $100 billion. The deductibles in program year 1 (calendar year 2003) are 7 percent of direct earned premiums for commercial property and casualty insurance in calendar year 2002, rising to

15 percent by the fifth year of the program. The Treasury can recoup government payments up to $10 billion in the first year, rising to $15 billion in the fifth year, through up to a 3 percent surcharge to policyholders. TRIA requires that insurers make available terrorist insurance to all policyholders (even existing ones) on similar terms and conditions to other coverage but leaves to insurers the price of such insurance. It is as yet unclear what the impact of the new program is, although it seems that only those insureds who are forced to obtain insurance by their mortgagees or other contractual obligations, are willing to pay the high prices for the coverage.[49] In general, demand has been low. A national survey of the Council of Insurance Agents and Brokers (CIAB) found that 72 percent of the brokers indicated their commercial customers are not purchasing terrorism insurance. In Manhattan, premiums are 100 percent or more of those for standard commercial policies.[50]

Federal intervention into the private market could be justified by short-term capital needs of the insurance industry, the difficulties in pricing such insurance given the lack of actuarial experience, and the political reality that without such insurance the government would have to compensate many victims for their losses since many insurers would not offer terrorism coverage and many insureds would not purchase such coverage due to its expense. There is concern, however, that such intervention would interfere with market adjustments to terrorism, e.g. fewer tall trophy buildings, fewer buildings in New York City.

A 2004 study assessed the economic impact of TRIA by studying the stock price reaction of firms in the industry most affected by the Act— banking, construction, insurance, real estate investment trusts, transportation, and public utilities. The study found that TRIA was at best value neutral for the property-casualty insurance sector. In the months following 9/11, insurers eliminated terrorism coverage from most large commercial insurance policies; TRIA nullified these exclusions. Moreover, U.S. insurers required to provide terrorism insurance cannot, in most cases, privately reinsure to cover their potential losses, which are not completely covered by the federal program. Effects on other industries were also ambiguous. The study voices concern that TRIA may have impeded the emergence of more efficient private market mechanisms for financing terrorism losses.[51]

TRIA was only a three-year program, 2003-2005. The Treasury indicated in December 2003 that it had no intention to seek an extension. As December 31, 2005 approaches, it is unclear whether TRIA will be extended.

[49] BestWire, April 10, 2003.
[50] CIAB, Commercial Market Index Survey, News Release, July 22, 2003.
[51] J. Brown, J. Cummins, C. Lewis, and R. Wei, "An Empirical Analysis of the Economic Impact of Federal Terrorism Reinsurance" 51 J. of Monetary Economics 861 (2004).

Notes and Questions

1. Should the U.S. government have provided reinsurance for terrorism? If so, was TRIA the right approach?

D.   ATTACKING THE FINANCIAL SYSTEM

Increasing attention is being given to the possibility that terrorists might try to disrupt countries' financial systems. Indeed, in the case of 9/11 much damage was done to the financial system through the damage done to the communication and computer systems on which the financial system relies. As a result, post 9/11 much has been done by regulators to require backup systems at remote sites. In addition, the Federal Reserve made clear that it would inject whatever needed liquidity to avoid the possibilities that financial institutions would be unable to settle their positions due to delays in payments or securities clearings.[52] It appears that while considerable cost can be imposed on the infrastructure of the financial system through physical damage, the system will be able to continue to function, short of a more catastrophic even like a nuclear bomb.

A different concern is terrorist attack on the banking system itself, a scenario in which terrorist hackers mount a cyber attack on the banking system, either trying to steal funds or poison the functioning of the system through the introduction of a computer virus. Of course, this threat may be from a broader source than terrorists, e.g. common criminals or hackers who just enjoy doing damage through hacking. This threat was underscored by the reported March 2005 attempt to steal £220 million from the London offices of Sumitomo, the Japanese banking group.[53] One would assume that efforts to secure the system from these kind of attacks have been increased.

E.   COSTS AND BENEFITS

A 2004 book by Peter Reuter and Ted Truman, *Chasing Dirty Money: The Fight Against Money Laundering*, has attempted to assess the costs and benefits of the anti-money laundering efforts, look at both crime and terrorism.[54] The authors begin by putting a price on the amount of money laundering. They cite estimates ranging from $2 trillion for crime (5 percent of world GDP in 2004 dollars), put forward by the IMF Managing Director in 1998) to $10 billion, the amount of international trafficking in drugs. They observe that the amount of terrorist financing is a pittance, which conforms

---

[52] See J. Lacker, "Payment System Disruptions and the Federal Reserve Following September 11, 2001," 51 J. of Monetary Economics 935 (2004).

[53] P. Larsen, "High-Tech Gang in City Theft Attempt," *Financial Times*, March 17, 2005.

[54] Institute for International Economics 2004. A short version of their conclusions is P. Reuter and E. Truman, "Anti-Money Laundering Overkill?," 19 The International Economy 56 (2005).

with the views of other analysts. They put the cost of the regime at $7 billion. This number is largely drawn out of a hat, but clearly the costs are quite high.

In terms of benefits, the authors believe that if the anti-drug financing efforts increased the cost of money laundering from 5 to 10 percent it would only increase the retail price of drugs by 1.25 percent. They conclude that the accomplishments of AML accomplishments are very difficult to detect. With respect to terrorism, they focus on the amount of fund frozen, $300 million in assets form 2001-2004. Assuming, that these efforts resulted in seizing 33 percent of the universe of terrorist funds, they calculate that over $20 million per month would still go to the terrorists. The authors obviously believe that the high costs are not worth the benefits.

If the phrase voodoo economics did not exist, it would have to be invented to describe this "analysis." The measure of costs is silly. The cost of crime is not measured by the cost of illegal drugs, but rather by the cost of crime generally—this is probably what the IMF had in mind in using the $2 trillion figure. As for the cost of terrorism, again this is not measured by the amount of money spent to commit terrorist acts but rather by the cost of such acts. The IMF, as discussed above, estimated the cost of 9-11 alone at around $70 billion. Both the costs of crime and terrorism would be projected into the future and then discounted to present value. Of course, anti-money laundering or terrorist financing measures will not by themselves prevent the costs; the issue is how less probable the events would be as a result of these efforts. Let's assume that the present value of both crime and terrorism was $5 trillion, probably quite low compared to the real costs—given the possibility of chemical or nuclear terrorism. If the anti-financing efforts decreased these potential costs by only 1 percent, it would be worth a cost of $500 billion a year, much less than the $7 billion we currently spend.

CONCLUSIONS

This is arguably the most important issue in international finance facing the world today. A failure to stop terrorism will be far more consequential than the failure to deal with the economic problems that are the principal focus of this book.

Combating terrorism financing is a formidable task. It is difficult to identify terrorists from profiles of bank users. In addition, there is the problem of the use of informal non-banking systems to make payments. Nonetheless, once terrorists are identified—a big if—the monitoring of their activities through the banking system may be greatly facilitated by the surveillance of their payments.

International cooperation is essential not only in freezes—where a significant degree of co-ordination has been achieved—but also in controlling terrorist payments. FATF may have to play a larger role in the future in not only promulgating but enforcing standards. FATF can name and shame countries, but it has to date not monitored actual bank behavior.

The U.S. has tried to project its own controls abroad by forcing its own banks to monitor the compliance of foreign banks with U.S. requirements, e.g. KYC policies, but it is arguable as to whether U.S. banks in general can actually know, with enough specificity, what is actually going on in foreign banks (with extensive branch networks throughout the world).

A more radical redesign of the international banking system, with more centralization of hard currency payments, could result from new major terrorist events.

GLOSSARY*

ABS. See Asset-based securities.

ACE. A European trade confirmation and matching service.

ADR. See American Depositary Receipts.

Allotments. A method of distributing previously unissued shares in a limited company in exchange for a contribution of capital. The company accepts the application by dispatching a letter of allotment to the applicant stating how many shares have been allotted.

American Depositary Receipts (ADR). Receipt for the shares of a foreign-based corporation held by a U.S. bank entitling the shareholder to all dividends and capital gains. Instead of buying shares of foreign-based companies in overseas markets, Americans can buy shares in the U.S. in the form of an ADR.

American Shares. Also called **American Depository Shares.** See American Depositary Receipts.

Amortization. The process of treating as an expense the annual amount deemed to waste away from a fixed asset. This accounting procedure gradually reduces the cost value of a limited life or intangible asset through periodic charges to income.

Arbitrage. Profiting from differences in price when the same security, currency, or commodity is traded on two or more markets. For example, an arbitrageur simultaneously buys one contract of gold in the New York market and sells one contract of gold in the Chicago market, locking in a profit because at that moment the price on the two markets is different. Index arbitrage exploits price differences between stock index futures and underlying stocks.

Article 65. A section of Japan's Securities and Exchange Law, often referred to as the Japanese Glass-Steagall because of its resemblance to the U.S. Glass-Steagall Act.

Asset-backed securities (ABS). Bonds or notes backed by loan paper or accounts receivable originated by banks, credit card companies, or other providers of credit.

Asset freeze. Government action that prevents the owner of assets from using or selling them.

Bank Law of 1981. Law regulating Japanese banks and branches of foreign banks located in Japan.

---

*Sources: H. Bonham, *The Complete Investment and Finance Dictionary* (2001); P. Moles and N. Terry, *The Handbook of International Financial Terms* (1997); G. Bannock and W. Manser, *The Penguin International Dictionary of Finance* (2nd ed. 1995); *The New Palgrave Dictionary of Money and Finance* (P. Newman, M. Milgate and J. Eatwell eds., 1994); *A Dictionary of Finance* (Oxford Paperback Reference 1993); *Barron's Dictionary of Finance and Investment Terms* (3rd ed. 1991).

Bankers acceptance. Corporate note which bank agrees to pay.

Base. The rate of interest used as a basis by banks for the rates they charge their customers. In practice most customers will pay a premium over base rate to take account of the bank's risk involved in lending, competitive market pressures, and to regulate the supply of credit.

Basis point. A standard unit of measure for bond yields which equals 1/100 of 1 percent; 1 percent equals 100 basis points.

Basel Committee on Banking Supervision. An international banking regulatory group established in 1974 and consisting of representatives from the G-10 countries, Switzerland and Luxembourg.

Basel Concordat. This agreement, made in Switzerland in 1975 and revised in 1983, regulates international banking. Parent countries (those in which a bank is incorporated or has its main business activities) are primarily responsible for overseeing solvency; parent and host countries (those in which a bank's foreign branches are located) share responsibility for monitoring liquidity.

Benchmark. Point in an index or rate that is important, and that can be used to compare with other figures.

Beneficial owner. Person who enjoys the benefits of ownership even though title is in another name. When shares of a mutual fund are held by a custodian bank or when securities are held by a broker in street name, the real owner is the beneficial owner, even though, for safety or convenience, the bank or broker holds title.

Benelux countries. An association of countries in western Europe, consisting of Belgium, the Netherlands, and Luxembourg.

BHC (Bank Holding Company). Company that owns or controls one or more banks or other bank holding companies, as defined in the U.S. Bank Holding Company Act of 1956. Such companies must register with the Board of Governors of the Federal Reserve System and hence are called registered bank holding companies.

BHCA (Bank Holding Company Act). See BHC.

BIF (Bank Insurance Fund). Federal Deposit Insurance Corporation (FDIC) unit providing deposit insurance for banks other than thrifts.

"Big bang". Major change in operation of the London Stock Exchange (LSE) on 26 October 1986. Changes included the abolition of LSE rules mandating a single-capacity (restricting firms to acting only as broker, dealer or jobber etc.), the abolition of fixed commission rates charged by stockbrokers to their clients, the closure of the trading floor of the stock exchange in favor of off-the-floor telephone dealing, and a major expansion in dealing with international securities. Also refers generally to radical financial reform, as in Japan in 1997.

Bill discount market. The part of the U.K. money market consisting of banks, discount houses, and bill brokers. By borrowing money at short notice from commercial banks or discount houses, bill brokers are able to discount bills of exchange, especially Treasury bills, and make a profit.

BIS (Bank for International Settlements). An international bank originally established in 1930 as a financial institution to coordinate the payment of war reparations between European central banks. It was hoped that the BIS, with headquarters in Basel, would develop into a European central bank but many of its functions were taken over by the International Monetary Fund (IMF) after World War II. Since then the BIS has fulfilled several roles including acting as a trustee and agent for various international groups, such as the OECD, European Monetary Agreement, etc. The frequent meetings of the BIS directors have been a useful means of cooperation between central banks, especially in combating short-term speculative monetary movements. Since 1986 the BIS has acted as a clearing house for interbank transactions in the form of European Currency Units (ECU). The BIS also promulgates international capital adequacy standards.

Blue sky laws. State laws in the U.S. regulating securities.

BoE. Bank of England.

Bonds. Any interest-bearing or discounted government or corporate security that obligates the issuer to pay the bondholder a specified sum of money, usually at specific intervals, and to repay the principal amount of the loan at maturity. Bondholders have an IOU from the issuer, but no corporate ownership privileges, as stockholders do.

> **convertible.** These bonds give their owners the privilege of exchanging them for other specified assets, usually other securities of the issuing company, at some future date and under prescribed conditions.
>
> **corporate.** Bonds whose issuer is a corporation.
>
> **domestic.** Bonds issued within a country by local issuers.
>
> **floating rate.** Bonds with a variable interest rate usually linked to a specified benchmark such as the LIBOR.
>
> **foreign.** Bonds issued in a country other than that of the issuer.
>
> **global.** Bonds launched simultaneously in the major markets with a single worldwide price.
>
> **government.** Bonds whose issuer is a government.
>
> **high grade.** Bond rated triple-A or double-A by Moody's or Standard & Poor's rating service.
>
> **high yield.** Bond with a high yield.
>
> **international.** See Eurobonds.
>
> **Samurai.** Bonds offered by a non-resident issuer in Japan and denominated in Japanese Yen.
>
> **Shogun.** Bonds offered by a non-resident issuer in Japan and denominated in U.S. Dollars.
>
> **straight.** Fixed-rate bonds--the usual kind.

Book entry securities. Securities that are not represented by a certificate but by book entries on the books of a custodian bank.

Bookrunner. Lead underwriter of securities or loans.

Bourse. The French term for stock exchange

Brady bond exchanges. An initiative by the first Bush Administration using market-based debt and debt-service reduction and forgiveness to bring permanent relief to countries adopting strong economic reform programs.

Breaking the syndicate. Terminating the investment banking group formed to underwrite a securities issue. More specifically, terminating the agreement among underwriters, thus leaving the members free to sell remaining holdings without price restrictions. The agreement among underwriters usually terminates the syndicate 30 days after the selling group, but the syndicate can be broken earlier by agreement of the participants.

Bretton Woods. A conference (official title: the United Nations Monetary and Financial Conference) held at Bretton Woods, New Hampshire, U.S., in July 1944, called to consider the postwar organization of international monetary relations and resulting in the establishment of the International Bank for Reconstruction and Development (World Bank) and the International Monetary Fund (IMF).

Bubbles. An inflated price of a security or asset that far exceeds the true value of that security or asset. When the bubble "bursts" the price of that security or asset falls precipitously until it reaches a more realistic level. For example, in the early 1600's Dutch tulip prices rose until they tulips were worth more than gold. Eventually the bubble burst, bringing prices down to more realistic levels.

Build, operate, transfer (BOT) and **build, own, operate, transfer (BOOT)** refer to forms of project finance in which host government gives the project company a concession to construct the project, mange its operations and, after an agreed period, transfer the project to the government or one of its agencies. BOOT refers to circumstances in which the project company owns the project's assets until transfer occurs.

Bulge. Quick, temporary price rise that applies to an entire commodities or stock market, or to an individual commodity or stock.

Bulge-bracket firms. Large securities firms.

CAD (Capital Adequacy Directive). A set of capital adequacy rules issued in 1993, affecting banks located in the EU.

Call account. Short-term bank account paying interest and on which funds can be withdrawn on call.

Call option. Right to buy a specified number of shares at a specified price by a fixed date. See option.

Cap. See collar.

Capitalization. The total value at market prices of a company's or market's securities.

CBOT (Chicago Board of Trade). A Chicago-based commodity and futures exchange.

CDS. Certificates of deposit.

CEDEL (Centrale de Livraison de Valeurs Mobilières). One of the two settlement systems for trading in Eurobonds and other international securities, established in Luxembourg in 1970. See also Euroclear.

Central bank swaps. In international monetary relations, the opening by one central bank of a line of credit in its own currency against the opening of an equivalent line of credit in another currency by the relevant central bank.

Certificate of deposit. Debt instrument issued by a bank that usually pays interest. Institutional CDS are issued in denominations of $100,000 or more, and individual CDS start as low as $100. Maturities range from a few weeks to several years. Interest rates are set by competitive forces in the marketplace.

CFTC (Commodities Futures Trading Commission). Established by Congress in 1974 to regulate futures securities.

Cherry picking. Selectively repudiating only disadvantageous financial contracts.

CHIPS (Clearing House Interbank Payment System). Electronic clearing house for funds transfer.

Chokoku funds. Japanese bond trusts similar to U.S. money market mutual funds.

Clearing. The offsetting of liabilities or purchases and sales between two parties. See clearing house.

Clearing house. Any institution that settles mutual indebtedness between a number of participants, such as CHIPS.

Closed-End Mutual Fund. A mutual fund which engages in one offering and does not generally permit share redemptions. Investors exit from their investments by selling their shares to other investors in a secondary market.

CME (Chicago Mercantile Exchange). A Chicago-based securities and commodities exchange.

CNS (Continuous Net Settlement). Method of securities clearing and settlement that uses a clearinghouse, such as the National Securities Clearing Corporation, and a depository, such as Depository Trust Company, to match transactions to securities available in the firm's position, resulting in one net receive or deliver position at the end of the day.

Collar. Two interest-rate options combined to protect an investor against wide fluctuations in interest rates. One, the cap, covers the investor if the interest rate rises against him or her; the other, the floor, covers the investor if the rate of interest falls too far.

Collateralized mortgage obligations (CMOs). Mortgage-backed bonds.

Commercial paper (CP). Short-term corporate debt usually maturing in 90 days or less.

Concessional finance. Funding, generally in the form of a loan supplied by official lenders, advanced at terms below the market rate for the borrower. Usually the interest rate is low and the maturity extended beyond what private lenders would provide.

Conservator. See receiver.

Convertible securities. Shares or bonds that are exchangeable for a set number in another form at a prestated price.

Counterparty. A person who is a party to a contract.

CRA. U.S. Community Reinvestment Act of 1977 requiring banks to serve their communities.

Cross-acceleration. A loan provision that allows creditors to accelerate the servicing and repayment of the loan when another loan meets the requirements of acceleration.

Cross-border trading. Trading by investors located in foreign countries who use a domestic exchange to perform their trades.

Cross-default. A loan provision that allows creditors to declare the loan in default when another loan meets the requirements of default.

Cross-exchange trading. Trading stocks on stock exchanges located in a market other than the issuer's home market.

Deliverable. A security deliverable on a certain date.

Depositary receipts. See American Depositary Receipts.

International, Continental, and European depositary receipts. The equivalent to ADRs, held in foreign countries.

Derivatives. Financial instruments whose value is based on that of another security or its underlying asset. Derivatives include futures, options, swaps, and warrants.

Devaluation. A decrease in the value of a currency relative to the currencies of other countries or to a fixed standard such as gold.

DKV. German securities clearing system.

Dollar LIBOR. The rate of interest on LIBOR deposits or loans denominated in dollars. See LIBOR.

Dragon bond market. The emerging bond markets in the Pacific basin, including Indonesia, Malaysia, the Philippines, and Thailand.

DTB (Deutsche Terminborse). German stock exchange.

DTC (Depository Trust Company). Central securities depository in U.S. where stock and bond certificates are exchanged.

DVP (Delivery versus Payment). Securities industry procedure, common with institutional accounts, whereby delivery of securities sold is made to the buying customer's bank in exchange for simultaneous payment.

EC (European Community). Now known as EU or European Union.

ECB (European Central Bank). Though this bank currently exists only on paper, its creation is planned in the treaty for EMU.

ECP (Euro-commercial paper). Commercial paper issued in a eurocurrency, the market for which is centered in London.

ECU (European Currency Unit). A currency medium and unit of account created in 1979 to act as the reserve asset and accounting unit of the European Monetary System. The value of the ECU is calculated as a weighted average of a basket of specified amounts of European Union currencies.

EMI (European Monetary Institute). Institute to help coordinate monetary policy among the European central banks and prepare the arrangements for the ESCB.

EMS (European Monetary System). A European system of exchange-rate stabilization involving the countries of the European Union.

EMTN. Euro-commercial paper with a maturity term of several years.

EMU (Economic and Monetary Union). The planned merger of the currencies of the member states of the European Union.

EOC (Euroclear Operations Center).

ERM (Exchange Rate Mechanism). Exchange-rate system of the European Union.

ESCB (European System of Central Banks). A proposed European central banking system intended to take effect as part of EMU.

EU. European Union.

EUCLID. The telecommunications system of Euroclear.

Eurobond. Bonds that are a) underwritten by an international syndicate, b) offered simultaneously to investors in a number of countries, c) outside the jurisdiction of any single country, and d) in unregistered form.

  Eurodollar. Eurobonds offered in U.S. currency.

  Euroyen. Eurobonds offered in Japanese currency.

Eurocheque. A standardized cheque accepted in 39 countries. It can be made out in any desired amount, often in local currency, and must be used with an EC Card, a combination debit/ATM card used in the EU.

Euroclear. One of the two clearing and settlement systems for Eurobonds and other international securities, operated by the Brussels branch of the Morgan Guaranty Trust Co. of New York. The other is CEDEL.

Eurocurrency market. Market for supplying and borrowing eurocurrencies.

Euroloan. A loan made in a eurocurrency.

Euromarket. A market centered in London that emerged in the 1950s for financing international trade. Its main business is in Eurobonds, Euro-commercial paper, Euronotes, and Eurocurrencies.

Euronote. A form of Euro-commercial paper consisting of short-term negotiable bearer notes. They may be in any currency but are usually in dollars or ECUs. The euronote facility is a form of note issuance facility set up by a syndicate of banks, which underwrites the notes.

Exchange-traded. Traded in a stock exchange rather than over the counter.

Exchange offers. Offers to exchange one set of securities for another.

Exchange rate volatility. The fluctuations in the rate of exchange between currencies.

Export credit agency. An institution to provide financing for a county's exports, usually established, controlled, and funded by the government of the country.

FASB. Financial Accounting Standards Board, accounting standards setting organization in the U.S.

FBSA. U.S. Foreign Bank Supervision Act of 1991.

FBSEA. U.S. Foreign Bank Supervision Enhancement Act of 1991.

FDI (foreign direct investments). Investment in the capital of foreign businesses.

FDIC (Federal Deposit Insurance Corporation). U.S. federal agency established in 1933 that guarantees (within limits) funds on deposit in member banks and thrift institutions and performs other bank regulatory functions. In 1989, Congress passed savings and loan association bailout legislation that reorganized FDIC into two insurance units: the Bank Insurance Fund (BIF) continues the traditional FDIC functions with respect to banking institutions; the Savings Association Insurance Fund (SAIF) insures thrift institution deposits, replacing the Federal Savings and Loan Insurance Corporation (FSLIC), which ceased to exist.

Federal Reserve Bank (FRB). One of the 12 U.S. banks that, with their branches, make up the Federal Reserve System. These banks are located in Boston, New York, Philadelphia, Cleveland, Richmond, Atlanta, Chicago, St. Louis, Minneapolis, Kansas City, Dallas, and San Francisco. The role of each Federal Reserve Bank is to monitor the commercial and savings banks in its region to ensure that they follow Federal Reserve Board regulations and to provide those banks with access to emergency funds from the discount window. The reserve banks act as depositories for member banks in their regions, providing money transfer and other services.

Federal Reserve Board. Governing board of the U.S. Federal Reserve System. Its seven members are appointed by the President of the United States, subject to Senate confirmation, and serve 14-year terms.

Fedwire. A high-speed electronic link in the USA between the 12 Federal Reserve Banks and the Treasury, used to move large sums of money for themselves and their customers.

FIBV. Federation Internationale des Bourses de Valeurs (International Federation of Stock Exchanges). A private foundation that exchanges information on international stock markets.

Financial intermediaries. A bank, building society, finance house, insurance company, investment trust, etc., that holds funds borrowed from lenders in order to make loans to borrowers.

Financial leverage. Debt in relation to equity in a firm's capital structure.

Financial Reform Act of 1992. Amends Japan's Securities and Exchange Law, its Banking Law, and other statutes.

Firewall restrictions. Restrictions on dealings between a bank and its affiliates to protect bank solvency.

FIRICA. U.S. Financial Institutions Regulatory and Interest Control Act of 1978.

FIRREA. U.S. Financial Institutions Reform, Recovery, and Enforcement Act of 1989. Legislation to resolve the crisis affecting savings and loan associations.

Fixed-price offering. Method of pricing underwritten securities by which the price remains fixed as long as the syndicate remains in effect. In contrast, Eurobonds, which are also sold through underwriting syndicates, are often offered on a basis that permits discrimination among customers; i.e. the underwriting spread may be adjusted to suit the particular buyer.

Floating exchange rate. Movement of a currency's exchange rate in response to changes in the market forces of supply and demand; also known as flexible exchange rate. The opposite of the floating exchange rate is the fixed exchange rate system. See also par value of currency.

Floor. See collar.

Foreign Exchange and Foreign Trade Control Law (FECL). Japanese law governing foreign-exchange and other international matters.

Forward markets. Markets where there is a contract to buy or sell a currency at a fixed price in the future, without a corresponding offsetting transaction.

Fourth market. Direct trading of large blocks of securities between institutional investors to save brokerage commissions. The fourth market is aided by computers, notably by a computerized subscriber service called Instinet, an acronym for Institutional Networks Corporation.

FRB. See Federal Reserve Bank, Federal Reserve Board.

Friction costs. Costs associated with transactions, such as fees, risks.

FRN (floating rate note). Debt instrument with a variable interest rate. Interest adjustments are made periodically, often every six months, and are tied to a money-market index such as Treasury bill rates. Also known as a floater.

Futures. An agreement to buy or sell a fixed quantity of a particular commodity, currency, or security for delivery at a fixed date in the future at a fixed price. Unlike an option, a futures contract involves a definite purchase or sale and not an option to buy or sell; it therefore may entail a potentially unlimited loss.

G-7 (Group of Seven). Group formed by the seven leading industrial nations (U.S., Japan, Germany, France, U.K., Italy, and Canada) in order to foster economic and political coordination.

G-10 (Group of Ten). The ten industrial nations that agreed in 1962 to lend money to the International Monetary Fund (IMF). They are Belgium, Canada, France, Italy, Japan, Netherlands, Sweden, Germany, U.K., and U.S.

GAAP. Generally accepted accounting principles.

GATT (General Agreement on Tariffs and Trade). A trade treaty that has been in operation since 1948.

GDP (gross domestic product). The monetary value of all the goods and services produced by an economy over a specified period.

GDR (global depositary receipt). Also called **GDS (global depositary shares).** See ADR.

Gensaki. The Japanese money market for the resale and repurchase of medium- and long-term government securities.

Glass-Steagall. U.S. legislation of 1933 separating banking and securities businesses.

Globex. International after-hours screen trading system developed in 1992 dealing in currency futures and options.

Gold standard. A former monetary system in which a country's currency unit was fixed in terms of a specific quantity of gold bullion.

Grey market. A market in shares that have not been issued but are due to be issued in a short time.

Group of Thirty. A 'think tank' composed of 30 high-level individuals drawn from central banks, commercial bank management, the economics profession and finance ministries in both developed and developing countries.

Haircuts. Securities industry term referring to the formulas used in the valuation of securities below current market prices for the purpose of calculating a broker-dealer's net capital. The haircut varies according to the class of a security, its market risk, and the time to maturity.

Hedge fund. Form of private mutual fund which engages in a range of speculative activities ("hedge" is quite a misnomer).

Hedging. Strategy used to offset investment risk. A perfect hedge is one eliminating the possibility of future gain or loss.

Herstatt risk. The risk of loss in a foreign exchange transaction, where one side of the bargain is completed, but the other is not. Named after the Herstatt Bank of Germany which failed in 1974.

IBA. U.S. International Banking Act of 1978.

IBBEA. U.S. Interstate Banking and Branching Efficiency Act of 1994.

ICA. U.S. Investment Company Act of 1940 regulating mutual funds.

IDTCA. U.S. Interest and Dividend Tax Compliance Act of 1983.

IFS (international finance subsidiary). Subsidiary created and used to escape tax provisions in the international bond market; revisions in the tax code have made its use largely unnecessary.

ILLR. International lender-of-last-resort. See lender-of-last-resort.

IMF (International Monetary Fund). A specialized agency of the United Nations established in 1945 to promote international monetary cooperation and expand international trade, stabilize exchange rates, and help countries experiencing short-term balance of payments difficulties to maintain their exchange rates.

Impact day. The day on which the terms of a new issue of shares are made public.

Index. Statistical composite that measures changes in the economy or in financial markets, often expressed in percentage changes from a base year or from the previous month.

Indexes also measure the ups and downs of stock, bond, and commodities markets, reflecting market prices and the number of shares outstanding for the companies in the index. Some well-known indexes are the New York Stock Exchange Index, the American Stock Exchange Index, Standard & Poor's Index, and the Value Line Index. Subindexes for industry groups such as beverages, railroads, or computers are also tracked. Stock market indexes form the basis for trading in index options.

Index fund. Mutual fund whose portfolio matches that of a broad-based index such as Standard & Poor's Index and whose performance therefore mirrors the market as a whole.

Interbank lending. The money market in which banks borrow or lend money among themselves.

Interest rate parity. Relationship between changes of exchange-rates and interest rates between countries.

Intermediated credit. Credit arranged by a broker, bank, or agent.

International Primary Marketing Association (IPMA). A London-based membership group for Euro-issuers.

Investment Adviser's Act of 1940. U.S. legislation that requires all investment advisers to register with the Securities and Exchange Commission. The Act is designed to protect the public from fraud or misrepresentation by investment advisers.

Investment grade securities. Those with a rating ranging from AAA to BBB.

IOSCO (International Organization of Securities Commissioners). International regulatory body for securities.

IPO (initial public offering). Corporation's first offering of stock to the public.

ISDA. International Swaps and Derivatives Association.

Issue price. The price at which a new issue of shares is sold to the public. Once the issue has been made the securities will have a market price, which may be above (at a premium on) or below (at a discount on) the issue price.

Issuer. Legal entity that has the power to issue and distribute a security.

JSDA. Japanese Securities Dealers Association.

Junior security. Security with lower priority claim on assets and income than a senior security.

Keiretsu. A Japanese company group formed by interlocking shareholdings. Keiretsu normally contain a bank. They differ from Zaibatsu in that the bank is not the group holding company, post-war legislation having reduced a bank's permitted shareholding in a company to 5 percent.

LBO (leveraged buy-out). Takeover of a company, using borrowed funds. Most often, the target company's assets serve as security for the loans taken out by the acquiring firm, which repays the loans out of cash flow of the acquired company. Management may use this technique to retain control by converting a company from public to private.

LDC. Less developed country.

LDC (London Dollar Clearing Scheme). A net settlement system for clearing dollar transactions outside the U.S.

Legal tender. Money that must be accepted in discharge of a debt.

Lender-of-last resort. An institution, normally a central bank, that stands ready to lend to the commercial banking system when the later is in overall shortage of funds. This power is often used by central banks to avert bank failures.

Letter of credit. A non-negotiable order from a bank to a bank abroad, authorizing payment to a named person of a particular sum of money or up to a limit of a certain sum.

LIBOR (London Interbank Offered Rate). The rate of interest offered on loans to first-class banks in the London interbank market for a specified period (usually three or six months). The rate may apply to sterling or Eurodollars. The corresponding rate for deposits is the interbank market bid rate (IBMBR), the interbank bid rate (IBBR) or the London interbank bid rate (LIBID). Some other financial centers have interbank bid and offer rates, e.g. the Paris interbank offered rate (PIBOR) and the Tokyo interbank offered rate (TIBOR).

LIFFE (London International Financial Futures Exchange). A London financial futures market to provide facilities within the European time zone for dealing in options and futures contracts, including those in government bonds, stock-and-share indexes, foreign currencies, and interest rates.

Limit orders. Order to buy or sell a security at a specific price or better. The broker will execute the trade only within the price restriction.

Liquidity. Ability of assets to be converted into cash without significant loss.

Locked-in. Unable to take advantage of preferential tax treatment on the sale of an asset because the required holding period has not elapsed.

Long position. A position held by a dealer in securities, commodities, currencies, etc., in which holdings exceed sales, because the dealer expects prices to rise enabling a profit to be made by selling at the higher levels. Compare short position.

Managed account. Investment account consisting of money that one or more clients entrust to a manager, who decides when and where to invest it.

Mandate. A written authority given by one person (the mandator) to another (the mandatory) giving the mandatory the power to act on behalf of the mandator. Issuers of securities give mandates to their underwriters.

Margin account. Brokerage account allowing customers to buy securities with money borrowed from the broker.

initial margin. Collateral deposited with a broker, when opening a trading account, to cover possible losses.

maintenance margin. Collateral kept with a broker to cover possible trading losses.

Mark-to-market. The daily valuation of securities at market prices.

Market makers. A dealer who maintains firm bid and offer prices in a given security by standing ready to buy or sell the security at publicly quoted prices.

Market order. Order to buy or sell a security at the best available price.

Master feeder fund. A multi-tiered structure for mutual funds, whereby separate feeder funds with substantially identical investment objectives pool their assets by investing in a single portfolio (master fund).

MATIF (Marché à Terme Internationale de France). French futures exchange.

MBS. See mortgage-backed security.

Medium-term note. An unsecured note issued in a Eurocurrency with a maturity of about three to six years.

Mezzanine debt. A term signifying an intermediate stage in a financing operation.

Mirror fund. A mutual fund that invests in the same securities as another mutual fund, e.g. a U.S.-organized fund that invests in the same securities in which the foreign fund invests.

MJDS (Multi-jurisdictional Disclosure System). SEC disclosure system streamlining offerings made jointly in the U.S. and Canada.

MOF. Japan's Ministry of Finance.

Mortgage backed security (MBS). Security backed by mortgages.

Multilateral agency or **multilateral organization.** An institution established by treaty. Governments are members and supply the capital. A secretariat carries out its mandate. Examples include the Asian Development Bank or the International Finance Corporation.

Multiple (price-earnings ratio). Price of a stock divided by its earnings per share.

Mutual fund. A system of group investment which allow investors to purchase interests representing pro rata shares of the net assets of a pool of securities and other assets.

Mutual recognition. EU approach to regulation; it requires each country to recognize the validity of other member countries' laws, regulations, and administrative practices and is intended to preclude the use of national rules to restrict access to financial markets.

NASD (National Association of Securities Dealers). A self-regulatory organization of securities dealers that set up and now regulates NASDAQ and the OTC market.

NASDAQ (NASD Automated Quotation System). Owned and operated by NASD, a computerized system that provides price quotations for securities.

NASDAQ National Market System (NMS). A system providing information on the quoted price of stocks, the latest price paid, the high and low for the day and the current volume. NMS brokers are required to report this information through the system within 90 seconds of the trade.

National Securities Clearing Corporation. Securities clearing organization formed in 1977. It clears securities traded on the NYSE and NASDAQ.

NCD (negotiable certificates of deposit). Large-Dollar amount, short-term certificates of deposit that can be negotiated to third parties. Such certificates are issued by large banks and bought mainly by corporations and institutional investors.

Negative pledge. Negative covenant or promise that states the borrower will not pledge any of its assets.

Netting. The process of setting off matching sales and purchases against each other.

Net debit cap. Limits on the maximum net debit position of clearinghouse participants; intended to reduce the risk of settlement defaults.

NIF (note issuance facility). A means of enabling short-term borrowers in the eurocurrency markets to issue euronotes with maturities of less than one year when the need arises, rather than having to arrange a separate issue of euronotes each time they need to borrow.

Non-recourse finance. An investment whose servicing and repayment depends only on the profitability of the underlying project and not on any other source.

Notional principal. The notional amount of an obligation used as a basis of calculation, as with interest rate swaps.

Novation. The replacement of one legal agreement by a new obligation, with the agreement of all the parties.

NYSE (New York Stock Exchange). The leading U.S. stock exchange and largest in the world in terms of market capitalization.

OCC (Office of the Comptroller of the Currency). Office of the U.S. Department of Treasury responsible for regulating national banks.

OCC (Options Clearing Corporation). A New-York based clearinghouse that clears option contracts.

OECD (Organization for Economic Cooperation and Development). Organization formed in 1961 and based in Paris to promote cooperation among industrialized member countries on economic and social policies.

Off- balance sheet exposures. Potential exposures to loss not reflected on a balance sheet, e.g. bank issued letters of credit.

Offering circulars. See Prospectus.

Offering period. Period during which a public offering is made.

Open-end Mutual Fund. An mutual fund which engages in a continuous offering of its shares and permits investors to redeem shares at current net values.

Open-outcry system. Quoting prices, making offers, bids, and acceptances, and concluding transactions by word of mouth in a commodity market or financial futures exchange, usually in a trading pit.

Operational risk. Risk that loss will result from the breakdown of a systems operational component such as hardware, software, or communications.

Options. A contract giving its beneficiary the right to buy or sell a financial instrument or a commodity at a specified price within a specified period.

   naked. Option for which the buyer or seller has no underlying security position. .

Order-driven. Denoting a market in which prices are determined by the publication of orders to buy or sell shares, with the objective of attracting a counterparty.

OSE. Osaka Stock Exchange.

OTC (over the counter). Market in which securities transactions are conducted through a telephone and computer network connecting dealers in stocks and bonds, rather than through an exchange.

Overdraft. A loan made to a customer by allowing an account to go into debit, usually up to a specified limit (the overdraft limit). Interest is charged on the daily debit balance.

Parastatal. An organization founded and owned by a government but a legally separate person.

Pass through. Security, representing pooled debt obligations repackaged as shares, that passes income from debtors through the intermediary to investors. The most common type of pass-through is a mortgage-backed certificate, usually government-guaranteed.

Pathfinder prospectus. An outline prospectus concerning the flotation of a new company in the U.K.; it includes enough details to test the market reaction to the new company but not its main financial details or the price of its shares. Pathfinder prospectuses are known in the U.S. as red herrings.

Peg. To fix something to another standard; for example, to fix an exchange rate to the price of another country's currency or to the price of gold.

Perpetual. Bond that has no maturity date, is not redeemable, and pays a steady stream of interest indefinitely; also called annuity bond. The only notable perpetual bonds in existence are the consols first issued by the British Treasury to pay off smaller issues used to finance the Napoleonic Wars (1814).

   perpetual FRN. A floating rate note having no maturity, i.e. not to be repaid; used chiefly as an investment instrument.

Phillips Curve. The proposition that, other things equal, the rate at which the nominal wage level changes is a decreasing function of the level of the unemployment rate.

Pink Sheets. U.S. National Quotation Bureau publications listing the bid and offer prices of the securities available in the over-the-counter markets.

POP Directive (publication of prospectus). An EU direction requiring information disclosure in the form of a prospectus, before a securities offering.

PORTAL. U.S. system operated by the NASD for qualified investors to trade in unregistered securities.

Praecipium. Fee given to the lead manager of an underwriting.

Preferred stock. Stock that pays dividends at a specified rate and that has preference over common stock in the payment of dividends and the liquidation of assets. Most preferred stock is cumulative; if dividends are passed (not paid for any reason), they accumulate and must be paid before common dividends. A passed dividend on noncumulative preferred stock is generally gone forever.

Premium. An amount in excess of the issue price of a share or other security. When dealings open for a new issue of shares, for instance, it may be said that the market price will be at a premium over the issue price.

Price dumping. Discounting on an issue price in order to sell the issue, usually one initially priced too high. Fixed-price reofferings are intended to eliminate this practice.

Primary offering. Any sale of a new issue of a stock or bonds. Not the same as an initial public offering (IPO), which refers only to a company's first public sale of stock.

Prime. Interest rate banks charge to their most creditworthy customers.

Private placements. Sale of unregistered stocks, bonds, or other investments directly to an institutional investor like an insurance company.

Privatization. The process of selling a publicly owned company to the private sector.

Professionals' exemption. General practice under many foreign regulatory regimes of allowing the sale of securities to large institutions and market professionals with few regulations.

Proprietary trading systems. Screen-based automated trading systems typically owned by broker-dealers.

Prospectus. Formal written offer to sell securities that sets forth the plan for a proposed business enterprise or the facts concerning an existing one that an investor needs to make an informed decision.

Public float. The proportion of a corporation's stocks held by the public rather than by insiders.

Public offering. Offering to the investment public, after registration requirements have been complied with, of new securities, usually by an investment banker or a syndicate made up of several investment bankers, at a public offering price agreed upon between the issuer and the investment bankers.

Public style covenants. Fewer and less restrictive than the covenants found in many private placements, these covenants are used in loan agreements to specify the criteria with which the bond issuer in a public offering has to comply.

Purchasing power parity. Parity between two currencies at a rate of exchange that will give each currency exactly the same purchasing power in its own economy.

Put option. Gives the option holder the right to sell an asset—at a set time, for a set price.

QIB. Under SEC Rule 144A, a qualified institutional buyer.

Quote-driven. Denoting an electronic stock-exchange system in which prices are determined by the quotations made by market makers or dealers. The London Stock Exchange and NASDAQ System use quote-driven arrangements. Compare order driven.

RAP. Regulatory accounting principles, which may differ from generally acceptable accounting principles (GAAP) or tax accounting principles.

Rating system. Evaluation of securities investment and credit risk, performed by private services such as Fitch's, Moody's, and Standard & Poor's. Ratings range from AAA (best) to D.

Receiver. Also called a conservator. Court-appointed person who takes possession of, but not title to, the assets and affairs of a business or estate that is in bankruptcy.

Redemption. The repayment at maturity of a bond or other document certifying a loan, by the borrower to the lender.

Regulation D. Refers to both SEC rule exempting certain securities offerings from registration and Federal Reserve Board (FRB) Regulation specifying reserve requirements for banks.

Regulation K. FRB regulation of international banking.

Regulation O. FRB regulation on loans to bank insiders.

Regulation S. SEC regulation governing applicability of U.S. securities laws to foreign offers of securities.

Regulation Q. FRB regulation that used to set ceilings on rates of interest paid by banks on their deposits.

REIT (Real Estate Investment Trust). A company that manages a portfolio of real estate investments.

Repatriate. The return of capital from a foreign investment to investment in the country from which it originally came.

Replacement cost risk. Risk of loss resulting from a credit default.

Repurchase agreement (repo). A transaction whereby funds are borrowed through the sale of short-term securities, usually governments, on the condition that the instruments are repurchased at a given date.

Risk-weighted assets. The assets, shown on the balance sheet of a bank, that have had a risk weighting applied to them.

Rollovers. The extension or reissuing of an instrument of debt upon its date of maturity.

RTGS (real-time gross settlement system). Payment system like Fedwire in which each transaction is finally settled as it occurs, without netting.

RUF (revolving underwriting facility). See NIF.

Saitori. Members of the Tokyo Stock Exchange who act as intermediaries between brokers. They cannot deal on their own account or for non-members of the exchange; they may only be allowed to deal in a limited number of stocks.

SEAQ (Stock Exchange Automated Quotation System). System of quoting stocks on London Stock Exchange.

Second Banking Directive. An EU directive governing the provision of banking in the EU.

SEC (Securities and Exchange Commission). U.S. agency for the regulation of the markets in securities set up in 1934.

Secondary market. Exchanges and over-the-counter markets where securities are bought and sold subsequent to original issuance in the primary market.

Secretariat. Within an international organization, the administrative office that supports the governing body.

Selling concession. Discount at which securities in a new issue offering (or a secondary distribution) are allocated to the members of a selling group by the underwriters. Since the selling group cannot sell to the public at a price higher than the public offering price, its compensation comes out of the difference between the price paid to the issuer by the underwriters and the public offering price, called the spread. The selling group's portion, called the concession, is normally one half or more of the gross spread, expressed as a discount off the public offering price.

SESC. Securities and Exchange Surveillance Commission, Japan.

Shelf registration. SEC Rule 415 adopted in the 1980s, which allows a corporation to comply with registration requirements up to two years prior to a public offering of securities. With the registration "on the shelf," the corporation, by simply updating regularly filed annual, quarterly, and related reports to the SEC, can go to the market as conditions become favorable with a minimum of administrative preparation.

Short position. For commodities, contract in which a trader has agreed to sell a commodity at a future date for a specific price; for stocks, shares that an individual has sold short (by delivery of borrowed certificates) and has not covered as of a particular date.

SIMEX (Singapore International Mercantile Exchange).

Sovereign lending. A loan made by a bank to a foreign government.

Spot markets. Markets in which goods or currencies are sold for cash and delivered immediately.

Spread. The difference between the buying and selling price made by a dealer.

SPV (Special Purpose Vehicle). An entity used to issue securities in the securitization process.

Stabilization. Intervention in new issues market by an underwriter to keep the market price from falling below a given price during the offering period.

Stagflation. Term coined by economists in the 1970s to describe the previously unprecedented combination of slow economic growth and high unemployment (stagnation) with rising prices (inflation).

Stick position. The amount of an allotment unsold at the close of an offering period.

Straddle. A strategy used by dealers in traded options or futures. In the traded option market it involves simultaneously purchasing a put and call option; it is most profitable when the price of the underlying security is very volatile.

Strike price. Also called exercise price, this is the price at which the stock or commodity underlying a call or put option can be purchased (call) or sold (put) over the specified period.

Subordinated debt. A debt that can only be claimed by an unsecured creditor, in the event of a liquidation, after the claims of secured creditors have been met.

Subscription. Agreement of intent to buy newly issued securities.

Swap. Exchange of obligations as with interest rates and currency swaps.

> **basis swap.** Interest rate swap in which the same type of interest rate obligations are swapped (floating for floating or fixed for fixed) but the basis of the two rates are different, e.g. floating LIBOR for floating PIBOR.

> **commodity swap.** Exchange of two commodities to be reexchanged at future date.

> **currency swap.** An interest rate swap consisting of the exchange of two streams of interest in different currencies, as well as the principal amounts.

> **interest rate swap.** A transaction under which two streams of interest rate payments are exchanged, usually floating for fixed.

> **matched swap.** Swap which is hedged by another swap.

Swaption. An offer to enter into a swap contract.

SWIFT (Society for Worldwide International Financial Telecommunications). A credit-transfer system between banks.

Syndicated loan. A very large loan made to one borrower by a group of banks.

Tanshi. A market maker in the Japanese money market.

Tax haven. A country or independent area that has a low rate of tax and therefore offers advantages to individuals or companies that can arrange their affairs so that their tax liability falls at least partly in the low-tax haven.

TEFRA. U.S. Tax Equity and Fiscal Responsibility Act of 1982.

Third market trading. Nonexchange-member broker/dealers and institutional investors trading over-the-counter in exchange-listed securities.

TIFFE. Tokyo International Financial Futures Exchange.

Tokyo Dollar Clearing. Japanese system for clearing dollar payments among banks.

Tombstone. Advertisement placed in newspapers by investment bankers in a public offering of securities.

Trade comparison. The process of confirming and matching the terms of a securities transaction.

Tranche. A predetermined part of a financial transaction (from the French, meaning 'slice').

Transfers. In banking, the movement of money from one bank account to another.

> **correspondent.** A transfer involving two or more banks.
>
> **in-house.** A transfer between accounts at the same bank.

Transparency rules. Rules designed to the extent that to which transaction prices and volumes in a securities market are visible to all market operators.

Treasury bills. Short-term securities with maturities of one year or less, issued at or at a discount from face value.

Trust Indenture Act of 1939. U.S. law requiring all corporate bonds and other debt securities to be issued under an indenture agreement approved by the SEC and providing for the appointment of a qualified trustee free of conflict of interest with the issuer.

Unit Trust Fund. United Kingdom mutual fund which is regulated by a trust deed, the trustees being separate from management.

Universal banking system. System in which banks can engage in businesses other than banking, e.g. securities.

VAR (Value-at-Risk). The potential profit and losses on one's investments over a defined period of time.

Warrants. Type of security, often issued together with a bond or preferred stock, that entitles the holder to buy a proportionate amount of common stock at a specified price, usually higher than the market price at the time of issuance, for a period of years or to perpetuity.

Wind down. Set in order the affairs of a failed institution.

Withholding taxes. Tax deducted at source from dividends or other income paid to non-residents of a country.

Yankee securities. Dollar-denominated securities issued in the U.S. by foreign issuers.

Yield. The income from a security as a proportion of its current market price.

Zaibatsu. A large interlocking grouping of Japanese companies, similar to a U.S. trust or a German Konzern; dominated by a bank, holding controlling interests in the other members of the group. The zaibatsu have been largely outmoded by legislation since the Second World War, their place being taken by the keiretsu.

Zero coupon rate. Refers to the effective rate of interest from bonds that do not provide interest payments, but rather are sold at a discount from their par value.

INDEX

†